# GOVT5

California Student Edition

Edward Sidlow | Beth Henschen | Larry N. Gerston | Terry Christensen

CENGAGE
Learning·

Australia • Brazil • Japan • Korea • Mexico • Singapore • Spain • United Kingdom • United States

**GOVT5: California Student Edition**

GOVT5, Fifth Edition
Edward I. Sidlow, Beth Henschen

© 2014, 2012 Cengage Learning. All rights reserved.

California Politics & Government: A Practical Approach, Eleventh Edition
Larry N. Gerston | Terry Christensen

© 2012, 2009, 2007 Cengage Learning. All rights reserved.

Senior Project Development Manager:
  Linda deStefano

Market Development Manager:
  Heather Kramer

Senior Production/Manufacturing Manager:
  Donna M. Brown

Production Editorial Manager:
  Kim Fry

Sr. Rights Acquisition Account Manager:
  Todd Osborne

For product information and technology assistance, contact us at
**Cengage Learning Customer & Sales Support, 1-800-354-9706**

For permission to use material from this text or product,
submit all requests online at **cengage.com/permissions**
Further permissions questions can be emailed to
**permissionrequest@cengage.com**

This book contains select works from existing Cengage Learning resources and was produced by Cengage Learning Custom Solutions for collegiate use. As such, those adopting and/or contributing to this work are responsible for editorial content accuracy, continuity and completeness.

**Compilation © 2013 Cengage Learning**
ISBN-13: 978-1-285-90819-9

ISBN-10: 1-285-90819-8

**Cengage Learning**
5191 Natorp Boulevard
Mason, Ohio 45040
USA

Cengage Learning is a leading provider of customized learning solutions with office locations around the globe, including Singapore, the United Kingdom, Australia, Mexico, Brazil, and Japan. Locate your local office at:
**international.cengage.com/region.**
Cengage Learning products are represented in Canada by Nelson Education, Ltd.
For your lifelong learning solutions, visit **www.cengage.com/custom.**
Visit our corporate website at **www.cengage.com.**

Printed in the United States of America

# GOVT BRIEF CONTENTS

# GOVT ⟩ CONTENTS

## CHAPTER 3
### Federalism 48

### PART II  Our Liberties and Rights 72

## CHAPTER 4
### Civil Liberties 72

## CHAPTER 5
### Civil Rights 97

---

**PART III The Politics of Democracy 124**

CHAPTER 6
**Interest Groups 124**

CHAPTER 7
**Political Parties 147**

## CHAPTER 8
## Public Opinion and Voting 170

## CHAPTER 9
## Campaigns and Elections 194

## CHAPTER 10
### Politics and the Media 219

## PART IV  Institutions 242

## CHAPTER 11
### Congress 242

## PART V  Public Policy 342

## CHAPTER 15
### Domestic Policy 342

## CHAPTER 16
### Foreign Policy 365

# APPENDICES

Democratic president Barack Obama was reelected in 2012 after a long, hard-fought political battle. Contrary to early predictions, the Democrats also added seats in the U.S. Senate. They were only able to pick up a handful of new members in the U.S. House. Throughout the 2012 elections, the Republican Party, under presidential candidate Mitt Romney, argued for a dramatic new course for America based on more limited government. Liberal voices predicted disaster should the Republicans prevail. Many conservatives argued that the Democrats were leading the nation to catastrophe.

Political conflict and divergence of opinion have always characterized our political traditions and way of governing. Nonetheless, our democracy endures, and the U.S. Constitution continues to serve as a model for new democracies around the world. The fifth edition of *GOVT* looks at government and politics in this country as a series of conflicts that have led to compromises.

This text was written with today's generation of students in mind. As such, it does the following:

- Provides the historical context for today's most significant political controversies.

- Presents different perspectives on key issues currently being debated.

- Helps students test their beliefs and assumptions and determine their positions on major political issues.

- Assists students in the process of acquiring informed political values and opinions.

- Fully explains major problems facing the American political system.

- Looks at the global connections between the American political system and the systems of other countries.

## A Groundbreaking Format and Portable Study Tools

*GOVT5*'s daring format has been specially designed to engage students with concise, current chapters; clear learning goals; and dynamic visual appeal. Our "debate-the-issues" approach effectively involves readers in discussing and debating concepts of American government. Streamlined and complete with portable study resources, this text does more than ever before to accommodate the way students actually use their textbooks, prepare for class, and study for exams in multiple formats:

- *Ready to study?*—An end-of-chapter quiz lets students review what they have read. Answers to the questions are located on the *Chapter in Review* cards at the back of the student edition of this book.

- *Chapter in Review* tear-out cards—Located at the end of the book, these cards provide summaries of key concepts correlated with the Learning Outcomes, key terms and definitions, and Study Tools quiz answers for each chapter.

- CourseMate **Go Online to** *CourseMate*—Accessible at www.cengagebrain.com, CourseMate provides these additional review materials:

  - Practice Quizzes.
  - Key Term Flashcards and Crossword Puzzles.
  - Audio Summaries.
  - Simulations and Animated Learning Modules.
  - Interactive Timelines.
  - Videos.
  - American Government NewsWatch.

The site is available at no additional cost with each new student text.

## Features That Teach

As exciting as the innovative *GOVT5* format may be, we have not lost sight of the essential goals and challenges of teaching American government. Any government text must present the basics of the political process and institutions, and it must excite and draw the student into the *subject*.

Additionally, we present many of today's controversial political issues in special features. Each of the more than one hundred features contained in the text covers a topic of high interest to students. *GOVT5* includes the following types of features:

- *SkillPrep: A Study Skills Module*—A new introductory section outlines tips for studying, writing papers and essays, delivering a speech, and taking tests.

- *Learning Outcomes*—Every chapter-opening page includes a list of four or more **Learning Outcomes** that lets students know what concepts will be covered in the chapter. Each Learning Outcome is repeated under the major heading for the section in which that topic is presented. This allows students to quickly locate the section in the chapter where a particular topic is discussed.

- *America at Odds*—Each chapter-opening debate asks students to critically evaluate both sides of a current controversy in U.S. politics.

- Chapter-ending *America at Odds* feature—Summarizes some of the most important debates raised by the chapter text. The questions can be used as a springboard for in-class discussion.

- *Take Action* tips—Located immediately after each chapter-ending **America at Odds** feature, **Take Action** offers tips on what students can do to make a difference in an area of interest to them.

- *Elections 2012*—We place the 2012 presidential and congressional election results in the context of each chapter's subject matter and analyze how the results will affect political processes.

- *Join the Debate*—Expanding on the debate theme, each of these features gives students an opportunity to review opposing opinions and form their own.

- *The Rest of the World*—This feature discusses how countries other than the United States deal with the topic at hand.

- *Our Challenging Times*—Students gain insight into issues raised by the current economic downturn and other major issues facing the nation.

- *Perception versus Reality*—These features tackle commonly held beliefs about our government system and gives students the "real story."

- *For Critical Thinking* question—At the end of every major section, we present a critical-thinking question to encourage students to think further about the material.

- *Social Media in Politics*—This small marginal feature lets students know how they can find resources using Facebook, Twitter, and other social media tools.

# New to This Edition

The entire book—including figures, tables, photos, Web sites, and data—has been updated.

- Chapter 1 includes new features on unemployment, online piracy, and the 2012 elections. The elections are cited in the text as well.

- In Chapter 2, a new feature discusses the constitutionality of the Affordable Care Act (Obamacare).

- Chapter 3 contains a new section on federal grants and state budgets. The impact of recent Supreme Court decisions on the federal system is discussed. The issue of federal lands is now described in the text and in a feature.

- In Chapter 4, a new feature debates stand-your-ground firearms laws. The doctrine of "clear and present danger," the "bad tendency rule," and the "imminent lawless action test" are now clearly defined.

- We have updated the discussion of same-sex marriage and affirmative action in Chapter 5. A new feature covers the Arizona immigration law controversy. A new graphic shows poverty rates by race. An *Elections 2012* feature focuses on women and minority group members.

- Interest groups discussed in Chapter 6 include the Tea Party movement and Occupy Wall Street. We also discuss religious groups and their impact on spending for the poor. Discussions of lobbying and campaign finance reflect recent developments.

- In addition to the election results and an *Elections 2012* feature, Chapter 7 discusses changes in popular support for the major parties. A feature deals with the fiscal crisis anticipated during the 2012 "lame-duck" session of Congress.

- In Chapter 8, the issue of the employer's paying for contraception is cited as an example of how questions can be "framed." A new feature examines how foreign countries view one another.

- In Chapter 9, the Republican presidential primaries are covered in full. The entire section on campaign finance has been completely rewritten in response to current developments. A new feature debates whether *Citizens United v. FEC* should be reversed.

- In Chapter 10, we discuss how the presidential candidates attempted to present themselves through the media. A feature asks whether politicians are successfully "gaming the press." We describe difficulties that online sites of traditional media face in obtaining advertising revenue.

- New features in Chapter 11 explain why members of Congress introduce legislation that can never pass and how they bend the rules that ostensibly ban earmarks.

- A new feature in Chapter 12 asks whether the president really can fix the economy. We also note that in today's polarized climate, a presidential appeal to the public can prove counterproductive.

- In Chapter 13, the history of the growth in governmental employment is now more detailed. The discussion of governmental pay levels has been thoroughly revised.

- In Chapter 14, the section on the Roberts Court has been completely revised. The descriptions of "strict construction" and "original intent" have also been completely rewritten to improve student comprehension.

- In Chapter 15, a new chart shows the growth in health-care spending. The section on energy and the environment has been completely rewritten to cover new developments such as fracking.

- In Chapter 16, we have updated the discussions of Egypt, the Eurozone, Iran, Libya, North Korea, and Syria.

# Supplements for the Instructor

## CourseMate

**Political Science CourseMate for Sidlow & Henschen's GOVT5**
Book with Printed Access Card ISBN-13: 9781133956099
Printed Access Card ISBN-13: 9781285057521
Instant Access Code ISBN-13: 9781285057491
Cengage Learning's Political Science CourseMate brings course concepts to life with interactive learning, study tools, and exam preparation tools that support the printed textbook. Use **Engagement Tracker** to assess student preparation and engagement in the course, and watch student comprehension soar as your class works with the textbook-specific Web site. An **interactive eBook** allows students to take notes, highlight, search, and interact with embedded media. Other resources include video activities, animated learning modules, simulations, case studies, interactive quizzes, and timelines. Students can purchase instant access via CengageBrain.com or via a printed access card available in your bookstore.

The **American Government NewsWatch** is a real-time news and information resource, updated daily, that includes interactive maps, videos, podcasts, and hundreds of articles from leading journals, magazines, and newspapers from the United States and the world.

Also included is the **KnowNow! American Government Blog,** which highlights three current-event stories per week and consists of a succinct analysis of each story, multimedia, and discussion-starter questions. Access your course via www.cengage.com/login.

**PowerLecture DVD with ExamView® and JoinIn® for Sidlow & Henschen's GOVT5**
ISBN-13: 9781133956075
An all-in-one multimedia resource for class preparation, presentation, and testing, this DVD includes Microsoft® PowerPoint® slides, a test bank in both Microsoft® Word and ExamView® formats, online polling and JoinIn™ clicker questions, an Instructor's Manual, and a Resource Integration Guide.

The **book-specific PowerPoint® slides** of lecture outlines, as well as photos, figures, and tables from the text, make it easy for you to assemble lectures for your course. The **media-enhanced PowerPoint® slides** help bring your lecture to life with audio and video clips, animated learning modules illustrating key concepts, tables, statistical charts, graphs, and photos from the book as well as outside sources.

The **test bank,** offered in Microsoft Word® and ExamView® formats, includes sixty-plus multiple-choice questions with answers and page references, along with ten essay questions for each chapter. ExamView® features a user-friendly testing environment that allows you to publish not only traditional paper and computer-based tests, but also Web-deliverable exams. JoinIn™ offers "clicker" questions covering key concepts, enabling instructors to incorporate student response systems into their classroom lectures.

The **Instructor's Manual** includes learning outcomes, chapter outlines, summaries, discussion questions, lecture launchers, suggestions for class activities and projects, tips on integrating media into your class, and suggested readings and Web resources. The **Resource Integration Guide** provides a chapter-by-chapter outline of all available resources to supplement and optimize learning. Contact your Cengage representative to receive a copy upon adoption.

**The Wadsworth News DVD for American Government 2014**
ISBN-13: 9781285053455
This collection of two- to five-minute video clips on relevant political issues serves as a great lecture or discussion launcher.

**Instructor Companion Web Site for Sidlow & Henschen's GOVT5**
ISBN-13: 9781285057514
This password-protected Web site for instructors features all of the free student assets plus an instructor's manual, book-specific PowerPoint® presentations, JoinIn™ "clicker" questions, Resource Integration Guide, and a test bank. Access your resources by logging into your account at www.cengage.com/login.

## CourseReader

**CourseReader: American Government, 0-30 Selections**
Printed Access Card ISBN-13: 9781111479954
Instant Access Code ISBN-13: 9781111479978
**CourseReader: Presidential Election Milestones, 2012, 0-30 Selections**
Printed Access Card ISBN-13: 9781285172347
Instant Access Code ISBN-13: 9781285172361
CourseReader: American Government and CourseReader: Presidential Election Milestones, 2012 allow you to create your reader, your way, in just minutes. These affordable, fully customizable online readers provide access to thousands of permissions-cleared readings, articles, primary sources, and audio and video selections from the regularly updated Gale research library database. This easy-to-use solution allows you to search for and select exactly the materials you want for your courses.

Each selection opens with a descriptive introduction to provide context, and concludes with critical-thinking and multiple-choice questions to reinforce key points. CourseReader is loaded with convenient tools like highlighting, printing, note-taking, and downloadable MP3 audio files for each reading.

CourseReader is the perfect complement to any Political Science course. It can be bundled with your current textbook, sold alone, or integrated into your learning management system. CourseReader 0-30 allows access to up to thirty selections in the reader. For a demo, please visit www.cengage.com/coursereader, or contact your Cengage sales representative for details.

To access CourseReader materials go to www.cengage.com/sso, click on "Create a New Faculty Account," and fill out the registration page. Once you are in your new SSO account, search for "CourseReader" from your dashboard, and select "CourseReader: American Government" or "CourseReader: Presidential Election Milestones, 2012." Then select "CourseReader 0-30: American Government Instant Access Code" or

"CourseReader 0-30: Presidential Election Milestones, 2012," and click "Add to my bookshelf." To access the live CourseReader, click on the product title under "Additional resources" on the right side of your dashboard.

**Election 2012: An American Government Supplement**
Printed Access Card ISBN-13: 9781285090931
Instant Access Code ISBN-13: 9781285420080
Written by John Clark and Brian Schaffner, this booklet addresses the 2012 congressional and presidential races, with real-time analysis and references. Access your course via www.cengage.com/login.

**Custom Enrichment Module: Latino-American Politics Supplement**
ISBN-13: 9781285184296
This revised and updated thirty-two-page supplement uses real examples to detail politics related to Latino Americans and can be added to your text via our custom publishing solutions.

## Supplements for Students

**Free Student Companion Web Site**
The text's free companion website, accessible at **www.cengagebrain.com**, contains a wealth of study aids and resources for students. Students will find open access to learning objectives, tutorial quizzes, chapter glossaries, flashcards, and crossword puzzles, all correlated by chapter. At the CengageBrain.com home page, search for the ISBN of your title (from the back cover of your book) using the search box at the top of the page. This will take you to the product page where these resources can be found.

## CourseMate

**Political Science CourseMate for Sidlow & Henschen's GOVT5**
Cengage Learning's Political Science CourseMate brings course concepts to life with interactive learning, study tools, and exam preparation tools that support the printed textbook. The more you study, the better the results. Make the most of your study time by accessing everything you need to succeed in one place. Read your textbook, take notes, watch videos, read case studies, take practice quizzes, and more—online with CourseMate. CourseMate also gives you access to the American Government **NewsWatch**

Web site, a real-time news and information resource updated daily, and **KnowNow!**—the go-to blog about current events in American government.

If you've purchased a new copy of *GOVT5*, refer to the access card at the front of the book for CourseMate log-in instructions. Purchase instant access via CengageBrain or via a printed access card available in your bookstore if your copy of *GOVT* does not include an access card. Visit www.cengagebrain.com for more information. CourseMate should be purchased only when assigned by your instructor as part of your course.

# Acknowledgments

A number of political scientists have reviewed *GOVT*, and we are indebted to them for their thoughtful suggestions on how to create a text that best suits the needs of today's students and faculty.

**Dilshod Achilov**
East Tennessee State University

**Kristian Alexander**
University of Utah

**Joshua D. Ambrosius**
West Virginia State University

**Anita Anderson**
University of Alabama

**Kimberly Arvanigian**
California State University, Fresno

**Yan Bai**
Grand Rapids Community College

**Janet Barton**
Mineral Area College

**Kelly Bauer**
George Washington University

**R. Matthew Beverlin**
Rockhurst University

**Catherine Bottrell**
Tarrant County College

**J. St. Lawrence Brown**
Spokane Community College

**Monique Bruner**
Rose State College

**Stephanie Burkhalter**
Humboldt State University

**Michael Ceriello**
Clark College

**Andrew Civettini**
Knox College

**Mark Daniels**
Slippery Rock University

**Paul Davis**
Truckee Meadows Community College

**Frank DeCaria**
West Virginia Northern Community College

**Robert De Luna**
St. Philip's College

**David Edwards**
University of Texas at Austin

**Mark Ellickson**
Missouri State University

**Henry Esparza**
University of Texas at San Antonio and Northeast Lakeview College

**Traci Fahimi**
Irvine Valley College

**Michaela Fazecas**
University of Central Florida

**Shawn Fonville**
Western Texas College

**Barry D. Friedman**
North Georgia College & State University

**Michael Gattis**
Gulf Coast Community College

**Jack Goodyear**
Dallas Baptist University

**Arie Halachmi**
Tennessee State University

**Kerstin Hamann**
University of Central Florida

**Jack Hames**
Butte College

**Jeff Harmon**
University of Texas at San Antonio

**David M. Head**
John Tyler Community College

**Jeneen Hobby**
Cleveland State University

**Steve Hoggard**
Chowan University

**Kristen Huyck**
Mt. San Jacinto Community College, Mira Costa Community College, and Anthem Online College

**Jose Luis Irizarry**
St. Francis College

**Lilias Jarding**
Oglala Lakota College

**Wendy Johnston**
SUNY Adirondack Community College

**Jean Gabriel Jolivet**
Southwestern College

**Michael Kanner**
University of Colorado

**David R. Katz III**
Mohawk Valley Community College

**Christine Kelleher**
University of Michigan

**Sean Kelly**
California State University–Channel Islands

**William E. Kelly**
Auburn University

**John Kerr**
University of Arkansas

Magen Knuth
Madison Area Technical College

Jeffrey Kraus
Wagner College

Kevin Lasher
Francis Marion University

Julie Lester
Macon State University

William Lester
Jacksonville State University

Teresa Levesque
Damar College

William D. Madlock
University of Memphis

Khalil Marrar
DePaul University and The
University of Chicago

Michael McConachie
Collin College–Central Park
Campus

Matthew McNiece
Howard Payne University

David J. Meyer
Regent University

Gay Michele
El Centro College

Amy Miller
Western Kentucky University

Eric Miller
Blinn College–Bryan

Kathleen Murnan
Ozarks Technical Community
College

Leah A. Murray
Weber State University

Jalal Nejad
Northwest Vista College

James Newman
Idaho State University

Rusty Nichols
Southwestern College

Joseph L. Overton
Kapiolani Community College

James Pawlik
Baldwin-Wallace College

Lisa Perez-Nichols
Austin Community College

James Peterson
Valdosta State University

David Pollak
Lakes Region Community College

Daniel Ponder
Drury University

Brett Ramsey
Austin Peay State University

Jason Roberts
Quincy College

Rob Robinson
University of
Alabama–Birmingham

John Roche
Palomar College

Cy Rosenblatt
University of Mississippi

Robert Sahr
Oregon State University

Brett Sharp
University of Central Oklahoma

John Shively
Longview Community College

Susan Siemens
Ozarks Technical Community
College

Frank Signorile
Campbell University

Chris Sixta-Rinehart
Francis Marion University

Brian William Smith
St. Edward's University

Robert Sullivan
Dallas Baptist University

Gabriel Ume
Palo Alto College

Nate Vanden Brook
Oklahoma City Community
College

John Vento
Antelope Valley College

Stephanie M. Walls
Bowling Green State
University—Firelands

Gerald Watkins
West Kentucky Community and
Technical College

Stephen Wiener
University of California–Santa
Barbara

Donald C. Williams
Western New England College

Bruce M. Wilson
University of Central Florida

Robert S. Wood
University of North Dakota

I Wu
Towson University

Bradford Young
Ocean County College

Mary Young
Southwestern Michigan College

Maryann Zihala
Ozarks Technical
Community College

Our styles of teaching and mentoring students were shaped in important ways by our experiences with the graduate faculty at The Ohio State University. We especially thank Lawrence Baum and Herbert Asher for lessons well taught. Will McLauchlan, Marvin Overby and Barry Pyle—colleagues we have had the pleasure of working with during the course of our careers—continue, by their actions, to remind us that the learning environment extends well beyond the classroom. The students we have had the privilege of working with at many fine universities have also taught us a great deal. Of course, we owe an immeasurable debt to our daughter, Sarah, and to our extended families, whose divergent views on political issues reflect an America at odds.

We thank Suzanne Jeans, Senior Publisher for all of her encouragement and support throughout our work on this project. We were also fortunate to have the editorial advice of Anita Devine, Acquisitions Editor, and Carolyn Merrill, Executive Editor. We are grateful for the assistance of Rebecca Green, our Development Editor, who supervised all aspects of the text and carefully read the page proofs. We thank Patrick Roach, Assistant Editor, for his coordination of the supplements and related items; Laura Hildebrand for her work on the CourseMate; and Eireann Aspell for her editorial assistance. We thank Gregory Scott for his tremendous help in researching the project and for his copyediting and proofreading assistance. We also thank Roxie Lee for her extraordinary project management and other assistance that ensured a timely and accurate text. The copyediting services of Jeanne Yost and the proofreading by Judy Kiviat and Beverly Peavler will not go unnoticed. We are also grateful to Sue Jasin of K&M Consulting.

We are especially indebted to the staff at Parkwood Composition. Their ability to generate the pages for this text quickly and accurately made it possible for us to meet our ambitious schedule. Ann Borman and Ann Hoffman, our cheerful Content Project Managers at Cengage Learning, made sure that all the pieces came together accurately, attractively, and on time. We appreciate the enthusiasm of Lydia LeStar and Kyle Zimmerman, our hardworking marketing managers. We would also like to acknowledge Linda May, art director, for her part in producing the most attractive and user-friendly American government text on the market today.

If you or your students have ideas or suggestions, we would like to hear from you. You can e-mail our marketing manager, Kyle, at kyle.zimmerman@cengage.com, or send us information through Wadsworth, a part of Cengage Learning. Our Web site is www.cengage.com/political science.

E.I.S.
B.M.H.

4LTR Press solutions are designed for today's learners through the continuous feedback of students like you. Tell us what you think about **GOVT5** and help us improve the learning experience for future students.

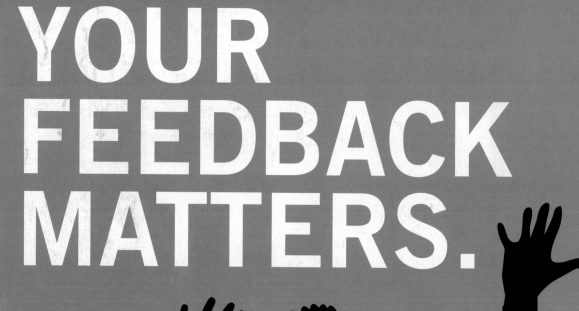

# YOUR FEEDBACK MATTERS.

Complete the Speak Up survey in CourseMate at www.cengagebrain.com

 **Follow us at www.facebook.com/4ltrpress**

# SKILL PREP

## A STUDY SKILLS MODULE

### WHAT'S INSIDE

After reading through and practicing the material in this study skills module, you will be better prepared to . . .

- **Make good choices**
  (LifePrep, p. SP–3)
- **Manage your time**
  (TimePrep, p. SP–5)
- **Be engaged in your studies**
  (StudyPrep, p. SP–7)
- **Study for quizzes and exams**
  (TestPrep, p. SP–11)
- **Read your textbook for learning**
  (ReadPrep, p. SP–13)
- **Write your papers**
  (WritePrep, p. SP–15)
- **Deliver a speech**
  (SpeechPrep, p. SP–20)

René Mansi/iStockphoto.com

# Welcome!

With this course and this textbook, you've begun what we hope will be a fun, stimulating, and thought-provoking journey into the world of American government and politics. In this course, you will learn all about the foundation of the American system, civil rights and liberties, public opinion, interest groups, political parties, campaigns, elections, the media, our governing institutions, and public policy. Knowledge of these basics will help you think critically about political issues and become an active citizen.

To help you get the most out of this course, and this textbook, we have developed this study skills module. You may be a recent high school graduate, or a working professional continuing your education, or an adult making your way back to the classroom after a few years. Whatever type of student you are, you want RESULTS when you study. You want to be able to understand the issues and ideas presented in the textbook, to be able to talk about them intelligently during class discussions, and to be able to remember them as you prepare for exams and papers.

This kind of knowledge doesn't just come from natural talent. Instead, it comes from the use of good study skills. This module is designed to help you develop the skills and habits you'll need to get the results that you want from this course. With tips on lifestyle decisions, how to manage your time more effectively, how to be more engaged when you study, how to get the most out of your textbook, how to prepare for quizzes and exams, how to write papers, and how to prepare and deliver a speech, this guide will help you become the best learner you can be!

It takes several things to succeed in a class—hard work, concentration, and commitment to your studies. In order to work hard, concentrate, and demonstrate commitment, you need energy. When you are full of energy, time seems to pass quickly, and it is easier to get things done. When you don't have energy, time feels as if it is standing still, and even your favorite activities can feel like a burden. To have the energy you need to be a great learner, it is important to make good lifestyle choices. You need to get enough sleep, eat well, take care of yourself, and maintain good relationships. An important part of being a successful student is to pay attention to what goes on in your life so that you have all the ingredients you need to maintain your focus and energy.

Here are some suggestions that you can use to keep up your energy and develop other aspects of your life so that you can succeed in everything you do.

- Too often, we become so busy with other aspects of our lives that we neglect our health. It is crucial that you eat a balanced diet, exercise regularly, and get enough sleep. If you don't take care of your physical well-being, other areas of your life will inevitably suffer.

- Hearing is not the same thing as listening. Many people are not good listeners. We often hear what we want to hear as we filter information through our own experiences and interests. When talking with friends, instructors, or family members, focus carefully on what they say—it may reveal something unexpected.

**Most people who succeed have a plan.**

- Be very careful about what you post on the Internet. A good rule of thumb is "Don't post anything that you wouldn't want the world to know." Many employers search the Internet for information concerning potential employees, and one embarrassing photo or tweet can have long-term damaging consequences.

- Most people who succeed have a plan—what they want to accomplish and when. Do you have a life plan? If not, you can start by making a list of your lifetime goals, even though they may change later on. You can also create a career plan that includes a list of skills you will need to succeed. Then, choose classes and extracurricular activities that will help you develop these skills.

- When we start doing something new, whether in school or in other areas of life, we usually aren't very good at it. We need feedback from those who are good in that area—such as instructors—to improve and succeed. Therefore, you should welcome feedback, and if it isn't given, you should ask for it.

- Many studies have shown that exercise benefits the mind as well as the body. Students at all levels who participate in organized sports or who regularly engage in their own training programs often do better on standardized math and reading tests than those students who do not. Regular exercise in whatever form should become a part of your daily routine. Not only will you feel great, you'll become a better learner. In other words, exercise should become a habit.

- Do you want to become a better writer? Your college or university probably has a writing center with resources to help you with your writing assignments. If not, you should be able to find a tutor who will help you figure out what you are trying to communicate and how to put it effectively on paper.

- Filing systems are an easy way to keep track of your money. First, label file folders for different categories of income, such as paycheck stubs, bank statements, and miscellaneous. Then, do the same for expenses, such as clothes, food, and entertainment. If you find you need another category, just set up a new folder.

- Do you want to become a better public speaker? Consider using your campus's audiovisual resources to develop this difficult but rewarding skill. Record yourself speaking and then critique your performance. Join a school organization such as a debate or drama club to gain confidence in front of a live audience.

- If you feel that you are overly dependent on family or friends, nurture skills that lead to independence. For example, learn how to cook for yourself. Get a job that does not interfere (too much) with your schoolwork. Save money and pay your own bills. Rent your own living space. Most important, have confidence in yourself.

- More often than not, in school and life, things do not go as planned. When this happens, you need to be flexible. Do not focus on your disappointment. Instead, try to accept the situation as it is, and deal with it by looking at the future rather than dwelling on the past.

- Be thankful for the people who care about you. Your family and good friends are a precious resource.

When you have problems, don't try to solve them by yourself. Talk to the people in your life who want you to succeed and be happy, and listen to their advice.

- Critical thinking is a crucial skill, and, as with any other skill, one gets better at it with practice. So, don't jump to conclusions. Whether you are considering a friend's argument, a test question, a major purchase, or a personal problem, carefully weigh the evidence, balance strengths and weaknesses, and make a reasoned decision.

- Rather than constantly seeking approval from others, try to seek approval from the person who matters the most—yourself. If you have good values, then your conscience will tell you when you are doing the right thing. Don't let worries about what others think run, or ruin, your life.

**If you don't take care of your physical well-being, other areas of your life will inevitably suffer.**

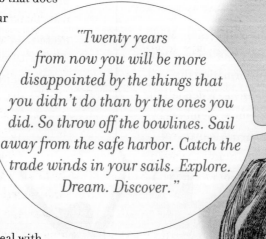

"Twenty years from now you will be more disappointed by the things that you didn't do than by the ones you did. So throw off the bowlines. Sail away from the safe harbor. Catch the trade winds in your sails. Explore. Dream. Discover."

**Mark Twain**
(American author, 1835–1910)

# TIME PREP

Taking a college-level course involves a lot of work. You have to go to class, read the text-book, pay attention to lectures, take notes, complete homework assignments, write papers, and take exams. On top of that, there are other things in the other areas of your life that call for your time and attention. You have to take care of where you live, run daily errands, take care of family, spend time with friends, work a full- or part-time job, and find time to unwind. With all that you're involved in, knowing how to manage your time is critical if you want to succeed as a learner.

The key to managing your time is to know how much time you have and to use it well. At the beginning of every term, you should evaluate how you use your time. How much time is spent working? How much caring for your home and family? On entertainment? How much time do you spend studying? Keep a record of what you do hour by hour for a full week. Once you see where all your time goes, you can decide which activities you might modify in order to have "more" time.

*To manage your time well, you need to know where it is going.*

Here are some other helpful tips on how to make the most of your time.

- Plan your study schedule in advance. At the beginning of each week, allocate time for each subject that you need to study. If it helps, put your schedule down on paper or use one of the many "calendar" computer programs for efficient daily planning.
- Don't be late for classes, meetings with professors, and other appointments. If you find that you have trouble being on time, adjust your planning to arrive fifteen minutes early to all engagements. That way, even if you are "late," in most cases you will still be on time.
- To reduce the time spent looking for information on the Internet, start with a clear idea of your

research task. Use a trusted search engine and focus only on that subject. Do not allow yourself to be sidetracked by other activities such as checking e-mail or social networking.

- Set aside a little time each day to assess whether you are going to meet the deadlines for all of your classes—quizzes, papers, and exams. It is critical to ensure that deadlines don't "sneak up" on you. A great way to do this is to use a calendar program or app, which can help you keep track of target dates and even give you friendly reminders.
- Nothing wastes more time—or is more aggravating—than having to redo schoolwork that was somehow lost on your computer. Back up all of your important files periodically. You can copy them onto an external hard drive, a DVD, or a USB flash drive.

## Concentrate on doing one thing at a time.

- Concentrate on doing one thing at a time. Multitasking is often a trap that leads you to do several things quickly but poorly. When you are studying, don't carry on a text conversation with a friend or have one eye on the Internet at the same time.
- Set deadlines for yourself, not only with schoolwork but also with responsibilities in other areas of your life. If you tell yourself, "I will have this task done by Monday at noon and that other task finished before dinner on Wednesday," you will find it much easier to balance the many demands on your time.
- Regularly checking e-mail and text messages not only interrupts the task at hand, but also is an easy excuse for procrastination. Set aside specific times of the day to check and answer e-mail, and, when necessary, make sure that your cell phone is off or out of reach.
- Sometimes, a task is so large that it seems impossible, making it more tempting to put off. When given a large assignment, break it into a

series of small assignments. Then, make a list of the assignments, and as you finish each one, give yourself the satisfaction of crossing it off.

- Many of us have a particular time of day when we are most alert—early morning, afternoon, or night. Plan to do schoolwork during that time, when you will be most efficient, and set aside other times of the day for activities that do not require such serious concentration.

- Because we like to be helpful, we may have a hard time saying "no" when others ask for favors that take up our time. Sometimes, though, unless the person is experiencing a real emergency, you have to put your schoolwork or job first. If you are worried that the person will be offended, explain why and trust that she or he will understand how important your schoolwork or job is.

- Slow down. You may think that you are getting more work done by rushing, but haste inevitably leads to poor decisions, mistakes, and errors of judgment, all of which waste time. Work well, not quickly, and you will wind up saving time.

- If you can, outsource. Give someone else some of your responsibilities. If you can afford to, hire someone to clean your house. Send your dirty clothes to a laundry. If money is tight, split chores with friends or housemates so that you can

better manage your work-life responsibilities.

- In marketing, *to bundle* means to combine several products in one. In time management, it means combining two activities to free up some time. For example, if you need to exercise and want to socialize, bundle the two activities by going on a jog with your friends. Take along some schoolwork when you head to the laundromat—you can get a lot done while you're waiting for the spin cycle. Or you can record class lectures (ask the professor for permission) so that you can review class material while you're out running errands.

- Develop a habit of setting time limits for tasks, both in and out of school. You will find that with a time limit in mind, you will waste less time and work more efficiently.

- Even the best time management and organization can be waylaid by forgetfulness. Most e-mail systems have free calendar features that allow you to send e-mail reminders to yourself concerning assignments, tests, and other important dates.

- A Chinese adage goes, "The longest journey starts with a single step." If you are having trouble getting started on a project or assignment, identify the first task that needs to be done. Then do it! This helps avoid time-wasting procrastination.

*Bundling, or combining two activities, will help you save time.*

# STUDY PREP

What does it take to be a successful student? Like many people, you may think that success depends on how naturally smart you are, that some people are just better at school than others. But in reality, successful students aren't born, they're made. What this means is that even if you don't consider yourself naturally "book smart," you can do well in this course by developing study skills that will help you understand, remember, and apply key concepts.

There are five things you can do to develop good study habits:

> be engaged
> ask questions
> take notes
> make an outline
> mark your text

## BE ENGAGED

If you've ever heard elevator music, you know what easy listening is like—it stays in the background. You know it's there, but you're not really paying attention to it, and you probably won't remember it after a few minutes. That is *not* what you should be doing in class. You have to be engaged. Being *engaged* means listening to discover (and remember) something. In other words, listening is more than just hearing. Not only do you have to hear what the professor is saying in class, you have to pay attention to it. And as you listen with attention, you will hear what your instructor believes is important. One way to make sure that you are listening attentively is to take notes. Doing so will help you focus on the professor's words and will help you identify the most important parts of the lecture.

## ASK QUESTIONS

If you are really engaged in your American government course, you will ask a question or two whenever you do not understand something. You can also ask a question to get your instructor to share her or his opinion on a subject. However you do it, true engagement requires you to be a participant in your class. The more you participate, the more you will learn (and the more your instructor will know who you are!).

## TAKE NOTES

Note-taking has a value in and of itself, just as outlining does. The physical act of writing makes you a more efficient learner. In addition, your notes provide a guide to what your instructor thinks is important. That means you will have a better idea of what to study before the next exam if you have a set of notes that you took during class.

## MAKE AN OUTLINE

As you read through each chapter of your textbook, you might want to make an outline—a simple method for organizing information. You can create an outline as part of your reading or at the end of your reading. Or you can make an outline when you reread a section before moving on to the next. The act of physically writing an outline for a chapter will help you retain the material in this text and master it, thereby obtaining a higher grade in class. Even if you make an outline that is no more than the headings in this text, you will be studying more efficiently than you would be otherwise.

To make an effective outline, you have to be selective. Outlines that contain all the information in the text are not very useful. Your objectives in outlining are, first, to identify the main concepts and, then, to add the details that support those main concepts.

Your outline should consist of several levels written in a standard format. The most important concepts are assigned Roman numerals; the second most important, capital letters; the third most important, numbers; and the fourth most important, lowercase letters. Here is a quick example:

I. Why Is Government Necessary?

   A. The Need for Security

      1. Order: a state of peace and security

      2. The example of Afghanistan

   B. Protecting Citizens' Freedoms

      1. To protect the liberties of the people: the greatest freedom of the individual that is equal to the freedom of other individuals in the society

   C. Authority and Legitimacy

      1. Authority: The right and power of a government to enforce its decisions and compel obedience

      2. Legitimacy: Popular acceptance of the right and power of government authority

         a. Iraq as an example of authority without legitimacy

## MARK YOUR TEXT

Now that you own your own textbook for this course, you can greatly improve your learning by marking your text. By doing so, you will identify the most important concepts of each chapter, and at the same time, you'll be making a handy study guide for reviewing material at a later time.

### WAYS OF MARKING
The most common form of marking is to underline important points. The sec-

ond most commonly used method is to use a felt-tipped highlighter, or marker, in yellow or some other transparent color. Marking also includes circling, numbering, using arrows, jotting brief notes, or any other method that allows you to remember things when you go back to skim the pages in your textbook prior to an exam.

### IMPORTANT

winterling/iStockphoto.com

### WHY MARKING IS IMPORTANT
Marking is important for the same reason that outlining is—it helps you to organize the information in the text. It allows you to become an active participant in the mastery of the material. Researchers have shown that the physical act of marking, just like the physical acts of note-taking during class and outlining, helps you better retain the material. The better the material is organized in your mind, the more you'll remember. There are two types of readers—passive and active. The active reader outlines or marks. Active readers typically do better on exams. Perhaps one of the reasons that active readers retain more than passive readers is that the physical act of outlining and/or marking requires greater concentration. It is through greater concentration that more is remembered.

### TWO POINTS TO REMEMBER WHEN MARKING

Read one section at a time before you do any extensive marking. You can't mark a section until you know what is important, and you can't know what is important until you read the whole section.

Don't overmark. Just as an outline cannot contain everything that is in a text (and notes can't include everything), marking can't cover the whole book. Don't fool yourself into thinking that you have done a good job just because each page is filled up with arrows, asterisks, circles, and underlines. If you do mark the whole book, when you go back to review the material, your markings will not help you remember what was important.

Take a look at the two paragraphs below:

In our democratic republic, citizens play an important role by voting. Although voting is extremely important, it is only one of the ways that citizens can exercise their political influence. Americans can also join a political organization or interest group, stage a protest, or donate funds to a political campaign or cause. There are countless ways to become involved. Informed participation begins with knowledge, however, and this text aims to provide you with a strong foundation in American government and politics. We hope that this book helps introduce you to a lifetime of political awareness and activity.

In our democratic republic, citizens play an important role by voting. Although voting is extremely important, it is only one of the ways that citizens can exercise their political influence. Americans can also join a political organization or interest group, stage a protest, or donate funds to a political campaign or cause. There are countless ways to become involved. Informed participation begins with knowledge, however, and this text aims to provide you with a strong foundation in American government and politics. We hope that this book helps introduce you to a lifetime of political awareness and activity.

The second paragraph, with all of the different markings, is hard to read and understand because there is so much going on. There are arrows and circles and underlines all over the place, and it is difficult to identify the most important parts of the paragraph. The first paragraph, by contrast, has highlights only on a few important words, making it much easier to identify quickly the important elements of the paragraph. The key to marking is *selective* activity. Mark each page in a way that allows you to see the most important points at a glance. You can follow up your marking by writing out more in your subject outline.

With these skills in hand, you will be well on your way to becoming a great student. Here are a few more hints that will help you develop effective study skills.

- Read textbook chapters actively! Underline the most important topics. Put a check mark next to material that you do not understand. After you have completed the entire chapter, take a break. Then, work on better comprehension of the check-marked material.

- As a rule, do schoolwork as soon as possible when you get home after class. The longer you wait, the more likely you will be distracted by television, video games, phone calls from friends, or social networking.

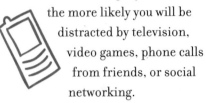

We study **best** when we are **free from distractions**.

- Many students are tempted to take class notes on a laptop computer. This is a bad idea for two reasons. First, it is hard to copy diagrams or take other "artistic" notes on a computer. Second, it is easy to get distracted by checking e-mail or surfing the Web.

- We study best when we are free from distractions such as the Internet, cell phones, and our friends. That's why your school library is often the best place to work. Set aside several hours a week of "library time" to study in peace and quiet.

- Reward yourself for studying! From time to time, allow yourself a short break for surfing the Internet, going for a jog, taking a nap, or doing something else that you enjoy. These interludes will refresh your mind and enable you to study longer and more efficiently.

WWW

- When you are given a writing assignment, make sure you allow yourself enough time to revise and polish your final draft. Good writing takes time—you may need to revise a paper several times before it's ready to be handed in.

- A neat study space is important. Staying neat forces you to stay organized. When your desk is covered with piles of papers, notes, and textbooks, things are being lost even though you may not realize it. The only work items that should be on your desk are those that you are working on that day.

Paul Ijsendoorn/iStockphoto.com

- Often, studying involves pure memorization. To help with this task, create flash (or note) cards. On one side of the card, write the question or term. On the other side, write the answer or definition. Then, use the cards to test yourself on the material.

- Mnemonic (pronounced ne-mon-ik) devices are tricks that increase our ability to memorize. A well-known mnemonic device is the phrase ROY G BIV, which helps people remember the colors of the rainbow—Red, Orange, Yellow, Green, Blue, Indigo, Violet. Of course, you don't have to use mnemonics that other people made. You can create your own for whatever you need to memorize. The more fun you have coming up with mnemonics for yourself, the more useful they will be.

- Take notes twice. First, take notes in class. Then, when you get back home, rewrite your notes. The rewrite will act as a study session by forcing you to think about the material. It will also, invariably, lead to questions that are crucial to the study process.

- Notice that each major section heading in this textbook has been written in the form of a question. By turning headings or subheadings in all of your textbooks into questions—and then answering them—you will increase your understanding of the material.

- Multitasking while studying is generally a bad idea. You may think that you can review your notes and watch television at the same time, but your ability to study will almost certainly suffer. It's OK to give yourself TV breaks from schoolwork, but avoid combining the two.

= BAD IDEA!

Paul Ijsendoorn/iStockphoto.com

Troels Graugaard/iStockphoto.com

# TEST PREP

You have worked hard throughout the term, reading the book, paying close attention in class, and taking good notes. Now it's test time, when all that hard work pays off. To do well on an exam, of course, it is important that you learn the concepts in each chapter as thoroughly as possible, but there are additional strategies for taking exams. You should know which reading materials and lectures will be covered. You should also know in advance what type of exam you are going to take—essay or objective or both. (Objective exams usually include true/false, fill-in-the-blank, matching, and multiple-choice questions.) Finally, you should know how much time will be allowed for the exam. By taking these steps, you will reduce any anxiety you feel as you begin the exam, and you'll be better prepared to work through the entire exam.

## FOLLOW DIRECTIONS

Students are often in a hurry to start an exam, so they take little time to read the instructions. The instructions can be critical, however. In a multiple-choice exam, for example, if there is no indication that there is a penalty for guessing, then you should never leave a question unanswered. Even if only a few minutes are left at the end of an exam, you should guess on the questions that you remain uncertain about.

Additionally, you need to know the weight given to each section of an exam. In a typical multiple-choice exam, all questions have equal weight. In other types of exams, particularly those with essay questions, different parts of the exam carry different weights. You should use these weights to apportion your time accordingly. If the essay portion of an exam accounts for 20 percent of the total points on the exam, you should not spend 60 percent of your time on the essay.

Finally, you need to make sure you are marking the answers correctly. Some exams require a No. 2 pencil to fill in the dots on a machine-graded answer sheet. Other exams require underlining or circling. In short, you have to read and follow the instructions carefully.

## OBJECTIVE EXAMS

An objective exam consists of multiple-choice, true/false, fill-in-the-blank, or matching questions that have only one correct answer. Students usually commit one of two errors when they read objective/exam questions: (1) they read things into the questions that do not exist, or (2) they skip over words or phrases. Most test questions include key words such as:

● all     ● never     ● always     ● only

If you miss any of these key words, you may answer the question wrong even if you know the information. Consider the following example:

> True or False?
> The First Amendment to the U.S. Constitution prohibits all restrictions on free speech.

In this instance, you may be tempted to answer "True," but the correct answer is "False," because the First Amendment applies only to governmental restrictions on free speech. In addition, certain types of speech, such as obscenity, are not protected by the First Amendment.

Whenever the answer to an objective question is not obvious, start with the process of elimination. Throw out the answers that are clearly incorrect. Typically, the easiest way to eliminate incorrect answers is to look for those that are meaningless, illogical, or inconsistent. Often, test authors put in choices that make perfect sense and are indeed true, but they are not the answer to the question under study.

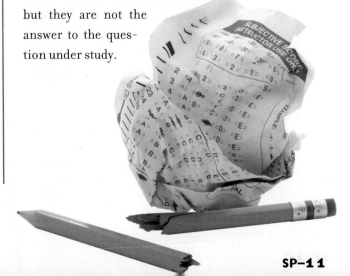

If you follow the above tips, you will be well on your way to becoming an efficient, results-oriented student. Here are a few more that will help you get there.

- Instructors usually lecture on subjects they think are important, so those same subjects are also likely to be on the exam. Therefore, be sure to take extensive notes in class. Then, review your notes thoroughly as part of your exam preparation.

- At times, you will find yourself studying for several exams at once. When this happens, make a list of each study topic and the amount of time needed to prepare for that topic. Then, create a study schedule to reduce stress and give yourself the best chance for success.

- When preparing for an exam, you might want to get together a small group (two or three other students) for a study session. Discussing a topic out loud can improve your understanding of that topic and will help you remember the key points that often come up on exams.

- If the test requires you to read a passage and then answer questions about that passage, read the questions first. This way, you will know what to look for as you read.

- When you first receive your exam, look it over quickly to make sure that you have all the pages. If you are uncertain, ask your professor or exam proctor. This initial scan may uncover other problems as well, such as illegible print or unclear instructions.

- Grades aren't a matter of life and death, and worrying too much about a single exam can have a negative effect on your performance. Keep exams in perspective. If you do poorly on one test, it's not the end of the world. Rather, it should motivate you to do better on the next one.

- Review your lecture notes immediately after each class, when the material is still fresh in your mind. Then, review each subject once a week, giving yourself an hour to go back over what you have learned. Reviews make tests easier because you will feel comfortable with the material.

- Some professors make old exams available, either by

# Grades aren't a matter of life and death, and worrying about them can have a negative effect on your performance.

posting them online or by putting them on file in the library. Old tests can give you an idea of the kinds of questions the professor likes to ask. You can also use them to take practice exams.

- With essay questions, look for key words such as "compare," "contrast," and "explain." These will guide your answer. If you have time, make a quick outline. Most important, get to the point without wasting your time (or your professor's) with statements such as "There are many possible reasons for . . . ."

- Cramming just before the exam is a dangerous proposition. Cramming tires the brain unnecessarily and adds to stress, which can severely hamper your testing performance. If you've studied wisely, have confidence that the information will be available to you when you need it.

- When you finish a test early, your first instinct may be to hand it in and get out of the classroom as quickly as possible. It is always a good idea, however, to review your answers. You may find a mistake or an area where some extra writing will improve your grade.

- Be prepared. Make a list of everything you will need for the exam, such as a pen or pencil, watch, and calculator. Arrive at the exam early to avoid having to rush, which will only add to your stress. Good preparation helps you focus on the task at hand.

- Be sure to eat before taking a test. Having food in your stomach will give you the energy you need to concentrate. Don't go overboard, however. Too much food or heavy foods will make you sleepy during the exam.

# Cramming
*just before the exam is* **a dangerous** *proposition.*

# READPREP

This textbook is the foundation for your introduction to American government. It contains key concepts and terms that are important to your understanding of what American government is all about. This knowledge will be important not only for you to succeed in this course, but for your future as you pursue a career in politics and government, or learn to be a good citizen. For this reason, it is essential that you develop good reading skills so that you get the most out of this textbook.

Of course, all students know how to read, but reading for a college-level course goes beyond being able to recognize words on a page. As a student, you must read to learn. You have to be able to read a chapter with the goal of understanding its key points and how it relates to other chapters. In other words, you have to be able to read your textbook and be able to explain what it is all about. To do this, you need to develop good reading habits and reading skills.

## READING FOR LEARNING REQUIRES FOCUS

Reading (and learning from) a textbook is not like reading a newspaper or a magazine or even a novel. The point of reading for learning isn't to get through the material as fast as you can or to skip parts to get to the stuff you're interested in. A textbook is a source of information about a subject, and the goal of reading a textbook is to learn as much of that information as you can. This kind of reading requires attention. When you read to learn, you have to make an effort to focus on the book and tune out other distractions so that you can understand and remember the information it presents.

## READING FOR LEARNING TAKES TIME

When reading your textbook, you need to go slow. The most important part of reading for learning is not how many pages you get through or how fast you get through them. Instead, the goal is to learn the key concepts of American government that are presented in each chapter. To do that, you need to read slowly, carefully, and with great attention.

Andrzej Tokarski/iStockphoto.com

## READING FOR LEARNING TAKES REPETITION

Even the most well-read scholar will tell you that it's difficult to learn from a textbook just by reading through it once. To read for learning, you have to read your textbook a number of times. This doesn't mean, though, that you just sit and read the same section three or four times. Instead, you should follow a preview-read-review process. Here's a good guide to follow:

THE FIRST TIME The first time you read a section of the book, you should preview it. During the preview, pay attention to how the chapter is formatted. Look over the title of the chapter, the section headings, and highlighted or bolded words. This will give you a good preview of the important ideas in the chapter. You should also pay close attention to any graphs, pictures, illustrations, or figures that are used in the chapter, since these provide a visual illustration of important concepts. You should also pay special attention to the first and last sentence of each paragraph. First sentences usually introduce the main point of the paragraph, while last sentences usually sum up what was presented in each paragraph.

The goal of previewing the section is to answer the question "What is the main idea?" Of course, you may not be able to come up with a detailed answer yet, but that's not the point of previewing. Instead, the point is to develop some general ideas about what the section is about so that when you do read it in full, you can have a guide for what to look for.

THE SECOND TIME After the preview, you'll want to read through the passage in detail. During this phase, it is important to read with a few of questions in mind: What is the main point of this paragraph? What does

the author want me to learn from this? How does this relate to what I read before? Keeping these questions in mind will help you to be an attentive reader who is actively focusing on the main ideas of the passage.

It is helpful to take notes while reading in detail. There are several different methods of doing this—you can write notes in the margin, highlight important words and phrases, or write an outline. Whatever method you prefer, taking notes will help you read actively, identify important concepts, and remember them. Then when it comes time to review for the exam, the notes you've made will make your studying more efficient. Instead of reading through the entire chapter again, you can focus your studying energy on the areas that you've identified as most important.

After you have completed a detailed read of the chapter, take a break so that you can rest your mind (and your eyes). Then you should write up a summary or paraphrase of what you just read. You don't need to produce a detailed, lengthy summary of the whole chapter. Instead, try to produce a brief paraphrase that covers the most important ideas of the chapter. This paraphrase will help you remember the main points of the chapter, check the accuracy of your reading, and provide a good guide for later review.

THE THIRD TIME (AND BEYOND) After you've finished a detailed reading of the chapter, you should take the time to review the chapter (at least once, but maybe even two, three, or more times). During this step, you should review each paragraph and the notes you made, asking this question: "What was this paragraph about?" At this point, you'll want to answer the question in some detail—that is, you should develop a fairly good idea of the important points of what you read before.

A reading group is a great way to review the chapter. After completing the reading individually, group members should meet and take turns sharing what they

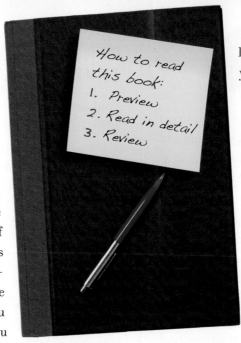

learned from their reading. Sharing what you learned from reading and explaining it to others will reinforce and clarify what you already know. It also provides an opportunity to learn from others. Getting a different perspective on a passage will increase your knowledge, since different people will find different things important during a reading.

Whether you're reading your textbook for the first time or reviewing it for the final exam, here are some tips that will help you be an attentive and attuned reader.

clu/iStockphoto.com

### *Set aside time and space.*

To read effectively, you need to be focused and attentive, and that won't happen if your phone is ringing every two minutes, if the TV is on in the background, if you're updating Twitter, or if you're surrounded by friends or family. Similarly, you won't be able to focus on your book if you're trying to read in a room that is too hot or too cold, or sitting in an uncomfortable chair. So when you read, find a quiet, comfortable place that is free from distractions where you can focus on one thing—learning from the book.

### *Take frequent breaks.*

Reading your textbook shouldn't be a test of endurance. Rest your eyes and your mind by taking a short break every twenty to thirty minutes. The concentration you need to read attentively requires lots of energy, and you won't have enough energy if you don't take frequent breaks.

brave-carp/iStockphoto.com

### *Keep reading.*

Effective reading is like playing sports or a musical instrument—practice makes perfect. The more time that you spend reading, the better you will be at learning from your textbook. Your vocabulary will grow, and you'll have an easier time learning and remembering information you find in textbooks.

# WRITE PREP

A key part of succeeding as a student is learning how to write well. Whether writing papers, presentations, essays, or even e-mails to your instructor, you have to be able to put your thoughts into words and do so with force, clarity, and precision. In this section, we outline a three-phase process that you can use to write almost anything.

1. Getting ready to write
2. Writing a first draft
3. Revising your draft

## PHASE 1: GETTING READY TO WRITE

First, make a list. Divide the ultimate goal—a finished paper—into smaller steps that you can tackle right away. Estimate how long it will take to complete each step. Start with the date your paper is due and work backward to the present: For example, if the due date is December 1, and you have about three months to write the paper, give yourself a cushion and schedule November 20 as your targeted completion date. Plan what you want to get done by November 1, and then list what you want to get done by October 1.

PICK a TOPIC  To generate ideas for a topic, any of the following approaches work well:

- **Brainstorm with a group.** There is no need to create in isolation. You can harness the energy and the natural creative power of a group to assist you.
- **Speak it.** To get ideas flowing, start talking. Admit your confusion or lack of clear ideas. Then just speak. By putting your thoughts into words, you'll start thinking more clearly.
- **Use free writing.** Free writing, a technique championed by writing teacher Peter Elbow, is also very effective when trying to come up with a topic. There's only one rule in free writing: Write without stopping. Set a time limit—say, ten minutes—and keep your fingers dancing across

the keyboard the whole time. Ignore the urge to stop and rewrite. There is no need to worry about spelling, punctuation, or grammar during this process.

REFINE YOUR IDEA  After you've come up with some initial ideas, it's time to refine them:

- **Select a topic and working title.** Using your instructor's guidelines for the paper or speech, write down a list of topics that interest you. Write down all of the ideas you think of in two minutes. Then choose one topic. The most common pitfall is selecting a topic that is too broad. "Political Campaigns" is probably not a useful topic for your paper. Instead, consider "The Financing of Political Campaigns."
- **Write a thesis statement.** Clarify what you want to say by summarizing it in one concise sentence. This sentence, called a *thesis statement*, refines your working title. A thesis is the main point of the paper; it is a declaration of some sort. You might write a thesis statement such as "Recent decisions by the Supreme Court have dramatically changed the way that political campaigns are funded."

SET GOALS  Effective writing flows from a purpose. Think about how you'd like your reader or listener to respond after considering your ideas.

- If you want someone to think differently, make your writing clear and logical. Support your assertions with evidence.
- If your purpose is to move the reader into action, explain exactly what steps to take and offer solid benefits for doing so.

To clarify your purpose, state it in one sentence—for example, "The purpose of this paper is to discuss and analyze the various explanations for the increasing partisanship in Congress."

BEGIN RESEARCH At the initial stage, the objective of your research is not to uncover specific facts about your topic. That comes later. First, you want to gain an overview of the subject. Say that you want to persuade the reader to vote against a voter ID requirement in your state. You must first learn enough about voter ID laws to summarize for your reader the problems such laws may cause for some voters and whether the laws actually deter voting fraud.

MAKE AN OUTLINE An outline is a kind of map. When you follow a map, you avoid getting lost. Likewise, an outline keeps you from wandering off topic. To create your outline, follow these steps:

1. Review your thesis statement and identify the three to five main points you need to address in your paper to support or prove your thesis.
2. Next, look closely at those three to five major points or categories and think about what minor points or subcategories you want to cover in your paper. Your major points are your big ideas. Your minor points are the details you need to fill in under each of those ideas.
3. Ask for feedback. Have your instructor or a classmate review your outline and offer suggestions for improvement. Did you choose the right categories and subcategories? Do you need more detail anywhere? Does the flow from idea to idea make sense?

DO IN-DEPTH RESEARCH Three-by-five-inch index cards are an old-fashioned but invaluable tool for in-depth research. Simply write down one idea or piece of information per card. This makes it easy to organize—and reorganize—your ideas and information. Organizing research cards as you create them saves time. Use rubber bands to keep source cards (cards that include the bibliographical information for a source)

separate from information cards (cards that include nuggets of information from a source) and to maintain general categories.

When creating your cards, be sure to:

- Copy all of the information correctly.
- Always include the source and page number on information cards.
- Be neat and organized. Write legibly, using the same format for all of your cards.

In addition to source cards and information cards, generate idea cards. If you have a thought while you are researching, write it down on a card. Label these cards clearly as containing your own ideas.

## PHASE 2: WRITING A FIRST DRAFT

To create your draft, gather your index cards and confirm that they are arranged to follow your outline. Then write about the ideas in your notes. It's that simple. Look at your cards and start writing. Write in paragraphs, with one idea per paragraph. As you complete this task, keep the following suggestions in mind:

- **Remember that the first draft is not for keeps.** You can worry about quality later. Your goal at this point is simply to generate lots of words and lots of ideas.
- **Write freely.** Many writers prefer to get their first draft down quickly and would advise you to keep writing, much as in free writing. Of course, you may pause to glance at your cards and outline. The idea is to avoid stopping to edit your work.
- **Be yourself.** Let go of the urge to sound "official" or "scholarly" and avoid using unnecessary big words or phrases. Instead, write in a natural voice.

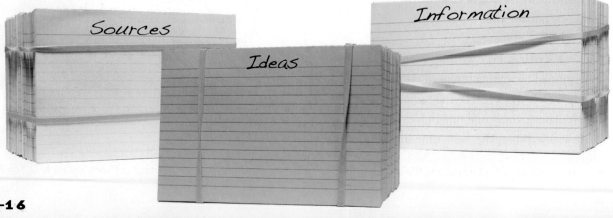

stuartbur/iStockphoto.com

Address your thoughts not to the teacher but to an intelligent student or someone you care about. Visualize this person, and choose the three or four most important things you'd say to her about the topic.

- **Make writing a habit.** Don't wait for inspiration to strike. Make a habit of writing at a certain time each day.
- **Get physical.** While working on the first draft, take breaks. Go for a walk. Speak or sing your ideas out loud. From time to time, practice relaxation techniques and breathe deeply.
- **Hide your draft in your drawer for a while.** Schedule time for rewrites before you begin, and schedule at least one day between revisions so that you can let the material sit. The brain needs that much time to disengage itself from the project.

## PHASE 3: REVISING YOUR DRAFT

During this phase, keep in mind the saying "Write in haste; revise at leisure." When you are working on your first draft, the goal is to produce ideas and write them down. During the revision phase, however, you need to slow down and take a close look at your work. One guideline is to allow 50 percent of writing time for planning, researching, and writing the first draft. Then use the remaining 50 percent for revising.

There are a number of especially good ways to revise your paper:

### 1. Read it out loud.

The combination of voice and ears forces us to pay attention to the details. Is the thesis statement clear and supported by enough evidence? Does the introduction tell your reader what's coming? Do you end with a strong conclusion that expands on what's in your introduction rather than just restating it?

### 2. Have a friend look over your paper.

This is never a substitute for your own review, but a friend can often see mistakes you miss. Remember, when other people criticize or review your work, they are not attacking you. They're just commenting on your paper. With a little

Izabela Habur/iStockphoto.com

practice, you will learn to welcome feedback because it is one of the fastest ways to approach the revision process.

### 3. Cut.

Look for excess baggage. Avoid at all costs and at all times the really, really terrible mistake of using way too many unnecessary words, a mistake that some student writers often make when they sit down to write papers for the various courses in which they participate at the fine institutions of higher learning that they are fortunate enough to attend. (Example: The previous sentence could be edited to "Avoid unnecessary words.") Also, look for places where two (or more sentences) could be rewritten as one. Resist the temptation to think that by cutting text you are losing something. You are actually gaining a clearer, more polished product. For maximum efficiency, make the larger cuts first—sections, chapters, pages. Then go for the smaller cuts—paragraphs, sentences, phrases, words.

### 4. Paste.

In deleting both larger and smaller passages in your first draft, you've probably removed some of the original transitions and connecting ideas. The next task is to rearrange what's left of your paper or speech so that it flows logically. Look for consistency within paragraphs and for transitions from paragraph to paragraph and section to section.

5. **Fix.**

Now it's time to look at individual words and phrases. Define any terms that the reader might not know, putting them in plain English whenever you can. In general, focus on nouns and verbs. Using too many adjectives and adverbs weakens your message and adds unnecessary bulk to your writing. Write about the details, and be specific. Also, check your writing to ensure that you are:

- Using the active voice. Write *"The research team began the project"* rather than (passively) *"A project was initiated."*

- Writing concisely. Instead of *"After making a timely arrival and perspicaciously observing the unfolding events, I emerged totally and gloriously victorious,"* be concise with *"I came, I saw, I conquered."*

- Communicating clearly. Instead of *"The speaker made effective use of the television medium, asking in no uncertain terms that we change our belief systems,"* you can write specifically, *"The senatorial candidate stared straight into the television camera and said, 'Take a good look at what my opponent is doing! Do you really want six more years of this?'"*

6. **Prepare.**

In a sense, any paper is a sales effort. If you hand in a paper that is wearing wrinkled jeans, its hair tangled and unwashed and its shoes untied, your instructor is less likely to buy it. To avoid this situation, format your paper following accepted standards for margin widths, endnotes, title pages, and other details. Ask your instructor for specific instructions on how to cite the sources used in writing your paper. You can find useful guidelines in the *MLA Handbook for Writers of Research Papers*, a book from the Modern Language Association. If you cut and paste material from a Web page directly into your paper, be sure to place that material in quotation marks and cite the source. Before referencing an e-mail message, verify the sender's identity. Remember that

anyone sending e-mail can pretend to be someone else. Use quality paper for the final version of your paper. For an even more professional appearance, bind your paper with a plastic or paper cover.

7. **Proof.**

As you ease down the home stretch, read your revised paper one more time. This time, go for the big picture and look for the following:

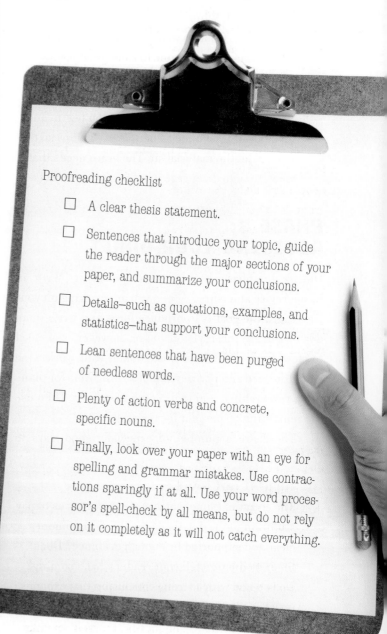

Feng Yu/iStockphoto.com

Proofreading checklist

☐ A clear thesis statement.

☐ Sentences that introduce your topic, guide the reader through the major sections of your paper, and summarize your conclusions.

☐ Details—such as quotations, examples, and statistics—that support your conclusions.

☐ Lean sentences that have been purged of needless words.

☐ Plenty of action verbs and concrete, specific nouns.

☐ Finally, look over your paper with an eye for spelling and grammar mistakes. Use contractions sparingly if at all. Use your word processor's spell-check by all means, but do not rely on it completely as it will not catch everything.

When you are through proofreading, take a minute to savor the result. You've just witnessed something of a miracle—the mind attaining clarity and resolution. That's the *aha!* in writing.

# ACADEMIC INTEGRITY: AVOIDING PLAGIARISM

Using another person's words, images, or other original creations without giving proper credit is called *plagiarism*. Plagiarism amounts to taking someone else's work and presenting it as your own—the equivalent of cheating on a test. The consequences of plagiarism can range from a failing grade to expulsion from school. Plagiarism can be unintentional. Some students don't understand the research process. Sometimes, they leave writing until the last minute and don't take the time to organize their sources of information. Also, some people are raised in cultures where identity is based on group membership rather than individual achievement. These students may find it hard to understand how creative work can be owned by an individual.

To avoid plagiarism, ask an instructor where you can find your school's written policy on this issue. Don't assume that you can resubmit a paper you wrote for another class for a current class. Many schools will regard this as plagiarism even though you wrote the paper. The basic guidelines for preventing plagiarism are to cite a source for each phrase, sequence of ideas, or visual image created by another person. While ideas cannot be copyrighted, the specific way that an idea is *expressed* can be. You also need to list a source for any idea that is closely identified with a particular person. The goal is to clearly distinguish your own work from the work of others. There are several ways to ensure that you do this consistently:

- **Identify direct quotes.** If you use a direct quote from another writer or speaker, put that person's words in quotation marks. If you do research online, you might find yourself copying sentences or paragraphs from a Web page and pasting them directly into your notes. This is the same as taking direct quotes from your source. To avoid plagiarism, identify such passages in an obvious way.

- **Paraphrase carefully.** Paraphrasing means restating the original passage in your own words, usually making it shorter and simpler. Students who copy a passage word for word and then just rearrange or delete a few phrases are running a serious risk of plagiarism. Remember to cite a source for paraphrases, just as you do for direct quotes. When you use the same sequence of ideas as one of your sources—even if you have not paraphrased or directly quoted—cite that source.

- **Note details about each source**. For books, details about each source include the author, title, publisher, publication date, location of publisher, and page number. For articles from print sources, record the article title and the name of the magazine or journal as well. If you found the article in an academic or technical journal, also record the volume and number of the publication. A librarian can help identify these details. If your source is a Web page, record as many identifying details as you can find—author, title, sponsoring organization, URL, publication date, and revision date. In addition, list the date that you accessed the page. Be careful when using Web resources, as not all Web sites are considered legitimate sources. Wikipedia, for instance, is not regarded as a legitimate source, but the National Institute of Justice's Web site is.

- **Cite your sources as endnotes or footnotes to your paper.** Ask your instructor for examples of the format to use. You do not need to credit wording that is wholly your own. Nor do you need to credit general ideas, such as the suggestion that people use a to-do list to plan their time. When you use your own words to describe such an idea, there's no need to credit a source. But if you borrow someone else's words or images to explain the idea, do give credit.

# SPEECH PREP

In addition to reading and writing, your success as a student will depend on how well you can communicate what you have learned. Most often, you'll do so in the form of speeches. Many people are intimidated by the idea of public speaking, but it really is just like any other skill—the more often you do it, the more you practice, the better you will get. Developing a speech is similar to writing a paper. Begin by writing out your topic, purpose, and thesis statement. Then carefully analyze your audience by using the strategies listed below.

**If your topic is new to listeners . . .**

- Explain why your topic matters to them.
- Relate the topic to something that they already know and care about.
- Define any terms that they might not know.

**If listeners already know about your topic . . .**

- Acknowledge this fact at the beginning of your speech.
- Find a narrow aspect of the topic that may be new to listeners.

- Offer a new perspective on the topic, or connect it to an unfamiliar topic.

**If listeners disagree with your thesis . . .**

- Tactfully admit your differences of opinion.
- Reinforce points on which you and your audience agree.
- Build credibility by explaining your qualifications to speak on your topic.
- Quote experts who agree with your thesis—people whom your audience is likely to admire.
- Explain to your listeners that their current viewpoint has costs for them and that a slight adjustment in their thinking will bring significant benefits.

**If listeners might be uninterested in your topic . . .**

- Explain how listening to your speech can help them gain something that matters deeply to them.
- Explain ways to apply your ideas in daily life.

Remember that audiences generally have one question in mind: *So what?* They want to know that your presentation relates to their needs and desires. To convince people that you have something worthwhile to say, think of your main topic or point. Then see if you can complete this sentence: I'm telling you this because . . . .

Jacob Wackerhausen/iStockphoto.com / JazzIRT/iStockphoto.com

# ORGANIZE YOUR PRESENTATIONS

Consider the length of your presentation. Plan on delivering about one hundred words per minute. Aim for a lean presentation—enough words to make your point but not so many as to make your audience restless. Leave your listeners wanting more. When you speak, be brief and then be seated. Speeches are usually organized in three main parts: the introduction, the main body, and the conclusion.

## 1. The introduction.

Rambling speeches with no clear point or organization put audiences to sleep. Solve this problem by making sure your introduction conveys the point of your presentation. The following introduction, for example, reveals the thesis and exactly what's coming. It reveals that the speech will have three distinct parts, each in logical order:

*Illegal immigration is a serious problem in many states. I intend to describe the degree of illegal immigration around the country, the challenges it presents, and how various states are addressing the issue.*

Some members of an audience will begin to drift during any speech, but most people pay attention for at least the first few seconds.

Highlight your main points in the beginning sentences of your speech. People might tell you to open your introduction with a joke, but humor is tricky. You run the risk of falling flat or offending somebody. Save jokes until you have plenty of experience with public speaking and know your audiences well. Also avoid long, flowery introductions in which you tell people how much you like them and how thrilled you are to address them. If you lay it on too thick,

your audience won't believe you. Draft your introduction, and then come back to it after you have written the rest of your speech. In the process of creating the main body and conclusion, your thoughts about the purpose and main points of your speech might change.

## 2. The main body.

The main body of your speech accounts for 70 to 90 percent of your speech. In the main body, you develop your ideas in much the same way that you develop a written paper. Transitions are especially important in speeches. Give your audience a signal when you change points. Do so by using meaningful pauses, verbal emphasis, and transitional phrases: "On the other hand, until the public realizes what is happening to children in these countries . . ." or "The second reason that the national debt is . . ." In long speeches, recap from time to time. Also preview what's to come. Hold your audience's attention by using facts, descriptions, expert opinions, and statistics.

## 3. The conclusion.

At the end of the speech, summarize your points and draw your conclusion. You started with a bang—now finish with drama. The first and last parts of a speech are the most important. Make it clear to your audience when you have reached the end. Avoid endings such as "This is the end of my speech." A simple standby is "So, in conclusion, I want to reiterate three points: First . . . ." When you are finished, stop speaking. Although this sounds quite obvious, a good speech is often ruined by a speaker who doesn't know when, or how, to wrap things up.

**Speeches** are usually organized in three main parts: the **introduction**, the **main body**, and the **conclusion**.

## SUPPORT YOUR SPEECH WITH NOTES AND VISUALS

To create speaking notes, you can type out your speech in full and transfer key words or main points to a few three-by-five-inch index cards. Number the cards so that if you drop them, you can quickly put them in order again. As you finish the information on each card, move it to the back of the pile. Write information clearly and in letters large enough to be seen from a distance. The disadvantage of the index card system is that it involves card shuffling—so some speakers prefer to use standard outlined notes.

You can also create supporting visuals. Presentations often include visuals such as PowerPoint slides or handwritten flip charts. These visuals can reinforce your main points and help your audience understand how your presentation is organized. Use visuals to *complement* rather than *replace* speech. If you use too many visuals or visuals that are too complex, your audience might focus on them and forget about you. To avoid this fate, follow these tips:

## OVERCOME FEAR OF PUBLIC SPEAKING

You may not be able to eliminate fear of public speaking entirely, but you can take steps to reduce and manage it.

PREPARE THOROUGHLY Research your topic thoroughly. Knowing your topic inside and out can create a baseline of confidence. To make a strong start, memorize the first four sentences that you plan to deliver, and practice them many times. Delivering them flawlessly when you're in front of an audience can build your confidence for the rest of your speech.

ACCEPT YOUR PHYSICAL SENSATIONS You have probably experienced the physical sensations that are commonly associated with stage fright: dry mouth, a pounding heart, sweaty hands, muscle jitters, shortness of breath, and a shaky voice. One immediate way to deal with such sensations is to simply notice them. Tell yourself, "Yes, my hands are clammy. Yes, my stomach is upset. Also, my face feels numb." Trying to deny or

- Use fewer visuals rather than more. For a fifteen-minute presentation, a total of five to ten slides is usually enough.

- Limit the amount of text on each visual. Stick to key words presented in short sentences or phrases and in bulleted or numbered lists.

- Use a consistent set of plain fonts. Make them large enough for all audience members to see.

- Stick with a simple, coherent color scheme. Use light-colored text on a dark background or dark text on a light background.

ignore such facts can increase your fear. In contrast, when you fully accept sensations, they start to lose power.

FOCUS ON CONTENT, NOT DELIVERY If you view public speaking simply as an extension of a one-to-one conversation, the goal is not to perform but to communicate your ideas to an audience in the same ways that you would explain them to a friend. This can reduce your fear of public speaking. Instead of thinking about yourself, focus on your message. Your audience is more interested in what you have to say than in how you say it. Forget about giving a "speech." Just give people valuable ideas and information that they can use.

## PRACTICE YOUR PRESENTATION

The key to successful public speaking is practice.

☐ **Use your "speaker's voice."** When you practice, do so in a loud voice. Your voice sounds different when you talk loudly, and this fact can be unnerving. Get used to it early on.

☐ **Practice in the room in which you will deliver your speech.**

☐ **Get familiar with the setting.** If you can't practice your speech in the actual room in which it will be given, at least visit the site ahead of time. Also make sure that the materials you will need for your speech, including any audiovisual equipment, will be available when you want them.

☐ **Make a recording.** Many schools have video recording equipment available for student use. Use it while you practice. Then view the finished recording to evaluate your presentation. Pay special attention to your body language—how you stand, your eye contact, how you use your hands.

☐ **Listen for repeated words and phrases.** Examples include *you know, kind of,* and *really,* plus any instances of *uh, umm,* and *ah.* To get rid of them, tell yourself that you intend to notice every time they pop up in your daily speech.

☐ **Keep practicing.** Avoid speaking word for word, as if you were reading a script. When you know your material well, you can deliver

it in a natural way. Practice your presentation until you could deliver it in your sleep. Then run through it a few more times.

## DELIVER YOUR PRESENTATION

Before you begin, get the audience's attention. If people are still filing into the room or adjusting their seats, they're not ready to listen. Wait for people to settle into their seats before you begin.

For a great speech, keep these tips in mind:

DRESS FOR THE OCCASION The clothing you choose to wear on the day of your speech delivers a message that's as loud as your words. Consider how your audience will be dressed, and then choose a wardrobe based on the impression you want to make.

PROJECT YOUR VOICE When you speak, talk loudly enough to be heard. Avoid leaning over your notes or the podium.

MAINTAIN EYE CONTACT When you look at people, they become less frightening. Remember, too, that it is easier for people in the audience to listen to someone when that person is looking at them. Find a few friendly faces around the room, and imagine that you are talking to each of these people individually.

**NOTICE YOUR NONVERBAL COMMUNICATION, YOUR BODY LANGUAGE** Be aware of what your body is telling your audience. Contrived or staged gestures will look dishonest. Hands in pockets, twisting your hair, chewing gum, or leaning against a wall will all make you appear less polished than you want to be.

**WATCH THE TIME** You can increase the impact of your words by keeping track of the time during your speech. It's better to end early than to run late.

**PAUSE WHEN APPROPRIATE** Beginners sometimes feel that they have to fill every moment with the sound of their voice. Release that expectation. Give your listeners a chance to make notes and absorb what you say.

**HAVE FUN** Chances are that if you lighten up and enjoy your presentation, so will your listeners.

## REFLECT ON YOUR PRESENTATION

Review and reflect on your performance. Did you finish on time? Did you cover all of the points you intended to cover? Was the audience attentive? Did you handle any nervousness effectively? Welcome evaluation from others. Most of us find it difficult to hear criticism about our speaking. Be aware of resisting such criticism, and then let go of your resistance. Listening to feedback will increase your skill.

Paul Ijsendoorn/iStockphoto.com

## TALKING ABOUT PRACTICE

When practicing your speech, you'll need to do more than just read through it silently. While it's good to use practice sessions to memorize the contents of your speech, they are also important times to work on how you use your voice and body as you speak. To make your practice time efficient and beneficial, follow the two-step process shown below and repeat it two or three (or more times) until you're ready to deliver a masterful speech.

### 1. Practice

- If possible, practice your speech in the location where you will be actually giving it. If this is not possible, make your practice setting as similar to the actual setting as possible.
- Record your practice so that you can analyze it later.
- Working from your outline or notes, go through the entire speech without stopping. If you make mistakes, try to fix them as you go along.

### 2. Review

Watch the recording of your first practice and ask yourself:

- Did I leave out important ideas?
- Did I focus too much on one point and not enough on others?
- Did I talk too fast or too slow?
- Did I speak clearly?
- Was my body language distracting or helpful?
- Did I maintain good eye contact?

After watching the recording, write down three or four specific changes that you will make to improve your speech.

# America in the Twenty-First Century

WENDY SUE LAMM/CONTRASTO/REDUX

The **Learning Outcomes** labeled 1 through 4 are designed to help improve your understanding of the chapter. After reading this chapter, you should be able to:

**1–1** Explain what is meant by the terms *politics* and *government*.

**1–2** Identify the various types of government systems.

**1–3** Summarize some of the basic principles of American democracy and basic American political values.

**1–4** Define common American ideological positions, such as "conservatism" and "liberalism."

**Remember to visit page 21 for additional Study Tools**

# AMERICA AT ODDS

## Has Our Government Grown Too Large?

JEFF MALET PHOTOGRAPHY/NEWSCOM

For much of America's history, there was little discussion about whether our government had grown too large. The government, after all, wasn't that big. Since the Great Depression of the 1930s, however, the government has grown by leaps and bounds.

Americans are at odds over the proper size of government. Indeed, the size of government lies at the very heart of the differences between Republicans and Democrats. Republicans, who gained a majority in the U.S. House of Representatives in the 2010 elections, called for trillions of dollars in federal budget cuts over the next decade. Democrats, however, believe that cuts of this size may endanger important programs such as Medicare and Medicaid. Many Americans believed that the outcome of the 2012 elections would help determine the size of our government for many years to come.

## Big Government Must Shrink

Many of those who believe that big government must shrink admit that government programs can help many people in need of, for example, medical care or better education. The problem is that once government programs are in place, they expand. The result is an "assisted society." Opponents of big government believe that too many people spend too much time seeking government assistance rather than taking care of their problems by themselves or with the help of family and friends.

Conservatives argue that government spending must be cut to avoid higher taxes. So far, increases in federal government spending have meant larger budget deficits rather than increased taxes. The government has simply borrowed what it needs. Conservative economists believe that this new government borrowing means there are fewer funds available for private individuals and businesses to borrow. Moreover, they say, the higher taxes that will eventually be needed to pay back the sums the government has borrowed will reduce people's incentives to work and to invest, now and in the future. Ultimately, that means less economic growth.

## We Need What the Government Does

Liberal economists dismiss the conservative worry that government spending will "crowd out" private spending. Liberals admit that could happen during a boom, but they also contend that when millions of people are unemployed, government spending puts people back to work.

More generally, liberals argue that we need the programs that a big government can provide. Medicare, Medicaid, Social Security, and national defense together make up well over half of all federal spending. The first three programs assist people who cannot get by just with the help of family or friends. Most of the smaller programs, such as education and veterans' benefits, serve equally important purposes.

Liberals agree that we should do whatever we can to limit wasteful spending and get more "bang" for the taxpayer's buck. But when the only alternatives are higher taxes or eliminating crucial services, then we will simply have to pay for the benefits we need. We can do this. As a share of our economy, taxes today are lower than they have been in any year since the 1950s.

## Where do you stand?

1. Is big government necessary in times of crisis, such as after the terrorist attacks of 9/11 and during the Great Recession that began in December 2007? Explain your answer.
2. Would you favor a law that reduced the budget of every federal, state, and local agency by, say, 15 percent? What would be the consequences?

## Explore this issue online

- The issue of big government divides liberals and conservatives. You can find examples of conservative views by typing that term into a search engine such as Google. Entering "liberal," however, brings up more sites hostile to liberalism than ones that actually represent the philosophy. Instead, try using terms such as "progressive blogs" or "progressive politics."

# Introduction

Regardless of how Americans feel about government, one thing is certain: they can't live without it. James Madison (1751–1836) once said, "If men were angels, no government would be necessary." Today, his statement still holds true. People are not perfect. People need an organized form of government and a set of rules by which to live.

Note, though, that even if people were perfect, they would still need to establish rules to guide their behavior. They would somehow have to agree on how to divide up a society's resources, such as its land, among themselves and how to balance individual needs and wants against those of society generally. These perfect people would also have to decide *how* to make these decisions. They would need to create a process for making rules and a form of government to enforce those rules. It is thus not difficult to understand why government is one of humanity's oldest and most universal **institutions.** No society has existed without some form of government. The need for authority and organization will never disappear.

As you will read in this chapter, a number of different systems of government exist in the world today. In the United States, we have a democracy in which decisions about pressing issues ultimately are made by the people's representatives in government. Because people rarely have identical thoughts and feelings about issues, it is not surprising that in any democracy citizens are often at odds over many political and social issues, including the very size of government, as discussed in the chapter-opening feature. Throughout this book, you will read about contemporary issues that have brought various groups of Americans into conflict with one another.

Differences in opinion are part and parcel of a democratic government. Ultimately, these differences are resolved, one way or another, through the American political process and our government institutions.

## 1–1 What Are Politics and Government?

**Learning Outcome 1–1**
Explain what is meant by the terms *politics* and *government.*

> **"THE ULTIMATE RULERS**
> of our democracy are . . .
> the voters of this country."
> ~ FRANKLIN D. ROOSEVELT ~
> THIRTY-SECOND PRESIDENT
> OF THE UNITED STATES
> 1933–1945

game played in Washington, D.C., in state capitols, and in city halls, particularly during election time. To others, politics involves all of the tactics and maneuvers carried out by the president and Congress. Most formal definitions of politics, however, begin with the assumption that **social conflict**—disagreements among people in a society over what the society's priorities should be—is inevitable. Conflicts will naturally arise over how the society should use its scarce resources and who should receive various benefits, such as status, health care, and higher education. Resolving such conflicts is the essence of **politics.** Political scientist Harold Lasswell perhaps said it best when he defined politics as the process of determining "who gets what, when, and how" in a society.[1]

There are also many different notions about the meaning of government. From the perspective of political science, though, **government** can best be defined as the individuals and institutions that make society's rules and also possess the *power* and *authority* to enforce those rules. Although this definition of government sounds remote and abstract, what the government does is very real indeed. As one scholar put it, "Make no mistake. What Congress does directly and powerfully affects our daily lives."[2] The same can be said for decisions made by state legislators and local government officials, as well as for decisions rendered by the courts—the judicial branch of government.

Of course, a key question remains: How do specific individuals obtain the power and authority to govern? As you will read shortly, the answer to this question varies from one type of political system to another.

To understand what government is, you need to understand what it actually does for people and society. Generally, in any country government serves at least three essential purposes: (1) it resolves

Politics means many things to many people. To some, politics is an expensive and extravagant

**institution** An ongoing organization that performs certain functions for society.

**social conflict** Disagreements among people in a society over what the society's priorities should be.

**politics** The process of resolving conflicts over how society should use its scarce resources and who should receive various benefits, such as public health care and public higher education.

**government** The individuals and institutions that make society's rules and also possess the power and authority to enforce those rules.

conflicts, (2) it provides public services, and (3) it defends the nation and its culture against attacks by other nations.

## 1–1a Resolving Conflicts

Even though people have lived together in groups since the beginning of time, none of these groups has been free of social conflict. As mentioned, disputes over how to distribute a society's resources inevitably arise because valued resources, such as property, are limited, while people's wants are unlimited. To resolve such disputes, people need ways to determine who wins and who loses, and how to get the losers to accept those decisions. Who has the legitimate power—the authority—to make such decisions? This is where governments step in.

Governments decide how conflicts will be resolved so that public order can be maintained. Governments have **power**—the ability to influence the behavior of others. Power is getting someone to do something that he or she would not otherwise do. Power may involve the use of force (often called coercion), persuasion, or rewards. Governments typically also have **authority,** which they can exercise only if their power is legitimate. As used here, the term *authority* means the ability to use power that is collectively recognized and accepted by society as legally and morally correct.

> ## "The thing about democracy,
> beloveds, is that it is not neat, orderly or quiet. It requires a certain relish for confusion."
>
> ~ MOLLY IVINS ~
> AMERICAN JOURNALIST
> 1944–2007

Power and authority are central to a government's ability to resolve conflicts by making and enforcing laws, placing limits on what people can do, and developing court systems to make final decisions.

For example, the judicial branch of government—specifically, the United States Supreme Court—resolved the highly controversial question of whether the Second Amendment to the Constitution grants individuals the right to bear arms. In 2008 and 2010, the Court affirmed that such a right does exist. Because of the Court's stature and authority as a government body, there was little resistance to its decision, even from gun control advocates.

## 1–1b Providing Public Services

Another important purpose of government is to provide **public services**—essential services that many individuals cannot provide for themselves. Governments undertake projects that individuals usually would not or could not carry out on their own, such as building and maintaining roads, establishing welfare programs, operating public schools, and preserving national parks. Governments also provide such services as law enforcement, fire protection, and

**power** The ability to influence the behavior of others, usually through the use of force, persuasion, or rewards.

**authority** The ability to legitimately exercise power, such as the power to make and enforce laws.

**public services** Essential services that individuals cannot provide for themselves, such as building and maintaining roads, establishing welfare programs, operating public schools, and preserving national parks.

Conflicts exist among groups in any nation. Here, one group wants government to more heavily tax another group. Ultimately, Congress and the president attempt to resolve such conflicts.

public health and safety programs. As Abraham Lincoln once stated:

> The legitimate object of government is to do for a community of people, whatever they need to have done, but cannot do, *at all*, or cannot, *so well* do, for themselves—in their separate, individual capacities. In all that the people can individually do as well for themselves, government ought not to interfere.[3]

### Services for All and Services for Some

Some public services are provided equally to all citizens of the United States. For example, government services such as national defense and domestic law enforcement allow all citizens, at least in theory, to feel that their lives and property are safe. Laws governing clean air and safe drinking water benefit all Americans. Other services are provided only to citizens who are in need at a particular time, even though they are paid for by all citizens through taxes. Examples of such services include health and welfare benefits, as well as public housing. Laws such as the Americans with Disabilities Act explicitly protect the rights of people with disabilities, although all Americans pay for such protections whether they have disabilities or not.

### Managing the Economy

One of the most crucial public services that the government is expected to provide is protection from hardship caused by economic recessions or depressions. From 2008 on, this governmental objective became more important than almost any other, due to the severity of the recession that began in December 2007. One of the most damaging consequences of the recession has been high rates of unemployment, which have continued into the present. These rates were posted even though the recession officially ended in June 2009 when economic growth resumed. We examine the unemployment problem in the *Our Challenging Times* feature on the following page.

## 1–1c  Defending the Nation and Its Culture

Historically, matters of national security and defense have been given high priority by governments and have demanded considerable time, effort, and expense. The U.S. government provides for the common defense and national security with its Army, Navy, Marines, Air Force, and Coast Guard. The departments of State, Defense, and Homeland Security, plus the Central

"In all that the people can individually do as well for themselves, **government ought not to interfere.**"

~ ABRAHAM LINCOLN ~
SIXTEENTH PRESIDENT
OF THE UNITED STATES
1861–1865

Intelligence Agency, National Security Agency, and other agencies, also contribute to this defense network.

As part of an ongoing policy of national security, many departments and agencies in the federal government are constantly dealing with other nations. The Constitution gives our national government exclusive power over relations with foreign nations. No individual state can negotiate a treaty with a foreign nation.

Of course, in defending the nation against attacks by other nations, a government helps to preserve the nation's culture, as well as its integrity as an independent unit. Failure to defend successfully against foreign attacks may have significant consequences for a nation's culture. For example, consider what happened in Tibet in the 1950s. When that country was taken over by the People's Republic of China, the conquering Chinese set out on a systematic program, the effective result of which was large-scale cultural destruction.

Since the terrorist attacks on the World Trade Center and the Pentagon in 2001, defending the homeland against future terrorist attacks has become a priority of our government.

## 1–1d  Why Politics Matters to You

As the last few pages have shown, the government performs a wide range of functions that are of extreme importance. From the time we are born until the day we die, we constantly interact with various levels of government. Most (although not all) students attend government-run schools. All of us travel on government-owned streets and highways. Many of us serve in the military—a completely government-controlled environment. A few of us get into trouble and meet up with the government's law enforcement system.

All of us pay substantial sums in taxes. Every citizen after reaching the age of sixty-five can expect the government to help with medical and living expenses. When the new health-care reform legislation—Obamacare—finally takes full effect, the government will ensure that the medical needs of all citizens are met, regardless of age or income.

In a representative democracy such as ours, it is politics that controls what the government decides to do. As discussed in this chapter's opening

## The Problem of Unemployment

In 2009, our usual 5 to 6 percent unemployment rate shot to 9 percent. Further, the U.S. rate was still above 8 percent in 2012, five years after the Great Recession first struck. If you also count discouraged workers who had stopped looking for jobs, the rate was about 15 percent. The United States has not seen so much long-term unemployment since the Great Depression of the 1930s.

### THE POLITICAL IMPACT OF HIGH UNEMPLOYMENT

For incumbent politicians, especially a president running for reelection, unemployment can mean the difference between winning and losing. Voters do judge incumbent presidents based on the unemployment situation. It's not the rate of unemployment itself that matters, however. Presidents have won reelection when unemployment was high and when it was low. What voters really care about is whether the state of the economy is improving—or growing worse. During 2012, the economy did grow somewhat, but the number of new jobs created each month was small. Considering previous election results, these circumstances seemed to predict a very close presidential elections in November.

### FEWER ADULTS ARE IN THE LABOR FORCE

Many economists look beyond the unemployment rate and the number of jobs created each month to another, underlying statistic. This figure is the percentage of adults who have jobs, regardless of whether they are looking for work or any other factor. From 2000 to 2007, that figure averaged about 62 to 64 percent. Since 2010, however, it has been stuck at about 53 percent. The few jobs that have been created in recent years are just enough to compensate for population growth. The number of people who say they want a job has also fallen—some people have given up and just "dropped out."

### YOUTH UNEMPLOYMENT REMAINS SERIOUS

Young people who are entering the workforce have been especially hard hit by our stagnating economy. About half of the population aged eighteen to nineteen is looking for work. (Most of the rest are in school or the military and not yet seeking employment.) In mid-2012, these young people had an unemployment rate of 23 percent. African American teenagers faced even bleaker circumstances. For black youth aged eighteen to nineteen, the unemployment rate was 40 percent. Studies have shown that youthful unemployment can cripple a person's income prospects for the rest of his or her life. These are indeed challenging times.

**YOU BE THE JUDGE** Is it right to blame an incumbent president for high unemployment? Why or why not?

*America at Odds* feature, the primary question is: How big should the government be? This leads to other questions, including the following: What combination of taxes and government services is best? Should industries such as agriculture and alternative energy be subsidized? When should our leaders use military force against foreign nations or rebellions in foreign countries? How the nation answers these and many other questions will have a major impact on your life—and participation in politics is the only way you can influence what happens.

**FOR CRITICAL THINKING**

Young Americans have the lowest voter-turnout rate of any group in the country. Some believe that if voting were made easier, young Americans would turn out in greater numbers. Others believe that America's youth stay away from the polls because they are not interested in politics. *What is your position on this issue?*

## 1-2 Different Systems of Government

Through the centuries, the functions of government just discussed have been performed by many different types of structures. A government's structure is influenced by a number of factors, such as a country's history, customs, values, geography, resources, and human experiences and needs. No two nations have exactly the same form of government. Over time, however, political analysts have developed ways to classify different systems of government. One of the most meaningful ways is according to *who* governs. Who has the power to make the rules and laws that all must obey?

### 1-2a Undemocratic Systems

Before the development of democratic systems, the power of the government was typically in the hands of an authoritarian individual or group. When such power is exercised by an individual, the system is called **autocracy.** Autocrats can gain power by traditional or nontraditional means.

**Monarchy** One form of autocracy, known as a **monarchy,** is government by a king, queen, emperor, empress, tsar, or tsarina. In a monarchy, the monarch, who usually acquires power through inheritance, is the highest authority in the government.

Historically, many monarchies were *absolute monarchies,* in which the ruler held complete and unlimited power. Until the eighteenth century, the theory of "divine right" was widely accepted in Europe. This **divine right theory,** variations of which had existed since ancient times, held that God gave those of royal birth the unlimited right to govern other men and women. In other words, those of royal birth had a "divine right" to rule, and only God could judge them. Thus, all citizens were bound to obey their monarchs, no matter how unfair or unjust they seemed to be. Challenging this power was regarded not only as treason against the government but also as a sin against God.

Most modern monarchies, however, are *constitutional monarchies,* in which the monarch shares governmental power with elected lawmakers. Over time, the monarch's power has come to be limited, or checked, by other government leaders and perhaps by a constitution or a bill of rights. Most constitutional monarchs today serve merely as ceremonial leaders of their nations, as in Spain, Sweden, and the United Kingdom (Britain).

**Dictatorship** Undemocratic systems that are not supported by tradition are called **dictatorships.** Often, a dictator is a single individual, although dictatorial power can be exercised by a group, such as the Communist Party of China. Dictators are not accountable to anyone else.

A dictatorship can also be *totalitarian,* which means that a leader or group of leaders seeks to control almost all aspects of social and economic life. The needs of the nation come before the needs of individuals, and all citizens must work for the common goals established by the government.

Examples of this form of government include Adolf Hitler's Nazi regime in Germany from 1933 to 1945 and Joseph Stalin's dictatorship in the Soviet Union (Russia) from 1929 to 1953. A more contemporary example of a totalitarian dictator is the new leader of North Korea, Kim Jong Un.

### 1-2b Democratic Systems

The most familiar form of government to Americans is **democracy,** in which the supreme political authority rests with the people. The word *democracy* comes from the Greek *demos,* meaning "the people," and *kratia,* meaning "rule." The main idea of democracy is that government exists only by the consent of the people and reflects the will of the majority.

### The Athenian Model of Direct Democracy

Democracy as a form of government began long ago. In its earliest

During the spring of 2011, revolutions in favor of democratic reforms spread across north Africa. In 2012, these Moroccans reminded the world that "there's no going back" to dictatorship.

because it demanded a high degree of citizen participation, others point out that most residents in the Athenian city-state (women, foreigners, and slaves) were not considered citizens and thus were not allowed to participate in government.

Clearly, direct democracy is possible only in small communities in which citizens can meet in a chosen place and decide key issues and policies. Nowhere in the world does pure direct democracy exist today. Some New England towns, though, and a few of the smaller political subunits, or cantons, of Switzerland still use a modified form of direct democracy.

form, democracy was simpler than the system we know today. What we now call **direct democracy** exists when the people participate directly in government decision making. In its purest form, direct democracy was practiced in Athens and several other ancient Greek city-states about 2,500 years ago. Every Athenian citizen participated in the governing assembly and voted on all major issues. Although some consider the Athenian form of direct democracy ideal

**Representative Democracy** Although the founders of the United States were aware of the Athenian model and agreed that government should be based on the consent of the governed, they believed that direct democracy would deteriorate into mob rule. They thought that large groups of people meeting together would ignore the rights and opinions of people in the minority and would make decisions without careful thought. They believed that representative assemblies were superior because they would enable public decisions to be made in a calmer and more deliberate manner.

In a **representative democracy,** the will of the majority is expressed through smaller groups of individuals elected by the people to act as their representatives. These representatives are responsible to the people for their conduct and can be voted out of office. Our founders preferred to use the term **republic,** which means essentially a representative democracy—with one qualification.

A republic, by definition, has no king or queen. Rather, the people are sovereign. In

**direct democracy** A system of government in which political decisions are made by the people themselves rather than by elected representatives. This form of government was practiced in some parts of ancient Greece.

**representative democracy** A form of democracy in which the will of the majority is expressed through groups of individuals elected by the people to act as their representatives.

**republic** Essentially, a representative democracy in which there is no king or queen and the people are sovereign.

"People often say that, in a democracy, decisions are made by a majority of the people. Of course, that is not true.

# DECISIONS ARE MADE BY A MAJORITY OF . . . THE PEOPLE WHO VOTE—

a very different thing."

~ WALTER H. JUDD ~
U.S. REPRESENTATIVE FROM MINNESOTA
1943–1963

These voters are listening to a debate at a town hall meeting in Plainfield, Vermont. Some New England towns use such meetings to engage in a form of direct democracy. Why doesn't the United States as a nation have direct democracy?

AP PHOTO/TOBY TALBOT

contrast, a representative democracy may be headed by a monarch. For example, as Britain evolved into a representative democracy, it retained its monarch as the head of state (but with no real power).

**Types of Representative Democracy**  In the modern world, there are basically two forms of representative democracy: presidential and parliamentary. In a *presidential democracy,* the lawmaking and law-enforcing branches of government are separate but equal. For example, in the United States, Congress is charged with the power to make laws, and the president is charged with the power to carry them out.

In a *parliamentary democracy,* the lawmaking and law-enforcing branches of government are united. In Britain, for example, the prime minister and the cabinet are members of the legislature, called Parliament, and are responsible to that body. Parliament thus both enacts the laws and carries them out.

## 1–2c Other Forms of Government

*Monarchy, dictatorship,* and *democracy* are three of the most common terms for describing systems of government, but there are others. For example, the term *aristocracy,* which in Greek means "rule by the best," describes a government run by members of old, noble families. Aristocracies have rarely had complete power, but have usually shared power with other forces, such as a monarch. *Plutocracy,* a somewhat similar form, means "government by the wealthy." The term typically refers to systems in which the rich have a disproportionate influence.

A difficult form of government for Americans to understand is *theocracy*—a term derived from the Greek words meaning "rule by the deity" or "rule by God." In a theocracy, there is no separation of church and state. Rather, the government rules according to religious precepts. In most Muslim countries, government and the Islamic religion are intertwined to a degree that is quite startling to both Europeans and Americans. In Iran, for example, the Holy Koran (or Qur'an), not the national constitution, serves as the basis for the law. The Koran consists of sacred writings that Muslims believe were revealed to the prophet Muhammad by God. In Iran, the Council of Guardians, an unelected group of religious leaders, ensures that laws and lawmakers conform to their interpretation of the teachings of Islam.

**FOR CRITICAL THINKING** Chinese Communist leader Mao Zedong (1893–1976) once said, "Political power grows out of the barrel of a gun." *Are there governments in today's world that tend to confirm Mao's point? Are there forms of government that disprove his statement?*

## 1–3  American Democracy

This country, with all its institutions, belongs to the people who inhabit it. Whenever they shall grow weary of the existing government, they can exercise their constitutional right to amend it, or their revolutionary right to dismember or overthrow it.[4]

With these words, Abraham Lincoln underscored the most fundamental concept of American government: that the people, not the government, are ultimately in control.

## 1-3a
## The British Legacy

In writing the U.S. Constitution, the framers incorporated two basic principles of government that had evolved in England: *limited government* and *representative government*. In a sense, then, the beginnings of our form of government are linked to events that occurred centuries earlier in England. They are also linked to the writings of European philosophers, particularly the English political philosopher John Locke. From these writings, the founders of our nation derived ideas to justify their rebellion against Britain and their establishment of a "government by the people."

**Limited Government**   At one time, the English monarch claimed to have almost unrestricted powers. This changed in 1215, when King John was forced by his nobles to accept the Magna Carta, or the Great Charter. This monumental document provided for a trial by a jury of one's peers (equals). It prohibited the taking of a free man's life, liberty, or property except through due process of law. The Magna Carta also forced the king to obtain the nobles' approval of any taxes he imposed on them. Government thus became a contract between the king and his subjects.

The importance of the Magna Carta to England cannot be overemphasized, because it clearly established the principle of **limited government**—a government on which strict limits are placed, usually by a constitution. This form of government is characterized by institutional checks to ensure that it serves public rather than private interests. Hence, the Magna Carta signaled the end of the monarch's absolute power. Although many of the rights provided under the original Magna Carta applied only to the nobility, the document formed the basis of the future constitutional government for England and eventually the United States.

**The English Bill of Rights**   In 1689, the English Parliament passed the English Bill of Rights, which further extended the concept of limited government. This document included several important ideas:

- The king or queen could not interfere with parliamentary elections.

- The king or queen had to have Parliament's approval to levy (collect) taxes or to maintain an army.

- The king or queen had to rule with the consent of the people's representatives in Parliament.

The English colonists in North America were also English citizens, and nearly all of the major concepts in the English Bill of Rights became part of the American system of government.

**Representative Government**   In a representative government, the people, by whatever means, elect individuals to make governmental decisions for all of the citizens. Usually, these representatives of the people are elected to their offices for specific periods of time. In England, this group of representatives is called a **parliament**. The English form of government provided a model for Americans to follow. Each of the American colonies established its own legislature.

**Political Philosophy: Social Contracts and Natural Rights**   Our democracy resulted from what can be viewed as a type of **social contract** among early Americans to create and abide by a set of governing rules. Social-contract theory was developed in the seventeenth and eighteenth centuries by philosophers such as John Locke (1632–1704). According to this theory, individuals voluntarily agree with one another, in a "social contract," to give up some of their freedoms to obtain the benefits of orderly government. The government is given adequate power to secure the mutual protection and welfare of all individuals.

CORBIS YELLOW/RF

---

**limited government**
A form of government based on the principle that the powers of government should be clearly limited either through a written document or through wide public understanding. It is characterized by institutional checks to ensure that government serves public rather than private interests.

**parliament** The name of the national legislative body in countries governed by a parliamentary system, such as Britain and Canada.

**social contract** A voluntary agreement among individuals to create a government and to give that government adequate power to secure the mutual protection and welfare of all individuals.

Locke also argued that people are born with **natural rights** to life, liberty, and property. He theorized that the purpose of government was to protect those rights. If it did not, it would lose its legitimacy and need not be obeyed. As you will read in Chapter 2, when the American colonists rebelled against British rule, such concepts as natural rights and a government based on a social contract became important theoretical tools in justifying the rebellion.

## 1–3b Principles of American Democracy

We can say that American democracy is based on five fundamental principles:

- *Equality in voting.* Citizens need equal opportunities to express their preferences about policies or leaders.

- *Individual freedom.* All individuals must have the greatest amount of freedom possible without interfering with the rights of others.

- *Equal protection of the law.* The law must entitle all persons to equal protection.

- *Majority rule and minority rights.* The majority should rule, while guaranteeing the rights of minorities.

- *Voluntary consent to be governed.* The people who make up a democracy must collectively agree to be governed by the rules laid down by their representatives.

These principles frame many of the political issues that you will read about in this book. They also frequently lie at the heart of America's political conflicts. Does the principle of minority rights mean that minorities should receive preferential treatment in hiring and firing decisions to make up for past mistreatment? Does the principle of individual freedom mean that individuals can express whatever they want on the Internet, including hateful, racist comments? Such conflicts over individual rights and freedoms and over society's priorities are natural and inevitable. Resolving these conflicts is what politics is all about. The key point is that Americans are frequently able to reach acceptable compromises because of their common political heritage.

## 1–3c American Political Values

Historically, as the nations of the world emerged, the boundaries of each nation normally coincided with the boundaries of a population that shared a common ethnic heritage, language, and culture.

From its beginnings as a nation, however, America has been defined less by the culture shared by its diverse population than by a set of ideas, or its political culture. A **political culture** can be defined as a patterned set of ideas, values, and ways of thinking about government and politics.

Our political culture is passed from one generation to another through families, schools, and the media. This culture is powerful enough to win over most new immigrants. Indeed, some immigrants come to America precisely because they are attracted by American values.

The ideals and standards that constitute American political culture are embodied in the Declaration of Independence, one of the founding documents of this nation, which will be discussed further in Chapter 2 and presented in its entirety in Appendix A. The political values outlined in the Declaration of Independence include natural rights (to life, liberty, and the pursuit of happiness), equality under the law, government by the consent of the governed, and limited government powers. In some ways, the Declaration of Independence defines Americans' sense of right and wrong. It presents a challenge to anyone who might wish to overthrow our democratic processes or deny our citizens their natural rights.

The rights to liberty, equality, and property are fundamental political values shared by most Americans. These values provide a basic framework for American political discourse and debate because they are shared, yet Americans often interpret their meanings quite differently. The result of these differences can be sharp conflict in the political arena.

**Liberty** The term *liberty* refers to a state of being free from external controls or restrictions. In the United States, the Constitution sets forth our *civil liberties* (see Chapter 4), including the freedom to practice whatever religion we choose and to be free from any state-imposed religion. Our liberties also include the freedom to speak freely on any topic and issue. Because people cannot govern themselves unless they are free to voice their opinions, freedom of speech is a basic requirement in a true democracy.

**natural rights** Rights that are not bestowed by governments but are inherent within every man, woman, and child by virtue of the fact that he or she is a human being.

**political culture** The set of ideas, values, and attitudes about government and the political process held by a community or a nation.

Clearly, though, if we are to live together with others, there have to be some restrictions on individual liberties. If people were allowed to do whatever they wished, without regard for the rights or liberties of others, pandemonium would result. Hence, a more accurate definition of **liberty** would be as follows: *liberty is the freedom of individuals to believe, act, and express themselves as they choose so long as doing so does not infringe on the rights of other individuals in the society.*

While almost all Americans believe strongly in liberty, differing ideas of what, in practice, liberty should mean have led to some of our most heated political disputes. Should women have the liberty to obtain abortions? Should employers be free to set the wages and working conditions of their employees? Should individuals be allowed to smoke marijuana? Over the years, Americans have been at odds over these and many other issues that concern liberty.

### Equality

The goal of **equality** has always been a central part of American political culture. The Declaration of Independence confirmed the importance of equality to early Americans by stating, "We hold these Truths to be self-evident, that all Men are created equal." Because of the goal of equality, the Constitution prohibited the government from granting titles of nobility. Article I, Section 9, of the Constitution states, "No Title of Nobility shall be granted by the United States." (The Constitution did not prohibit slavery, however—see Chapter 2.)

But what, exactly, does equality mean? Does it mean simply political equality—the right to vote and run for political office? Does it mean that individuals should have equal opportunities to develop their talents and skills? What about those who are poor, suffer from disabilities, or are otherwise at a competitive disadvantage? Should it be the government's responsibility to ensure that such individuals also have equal opportunities? Although most Americans believe that all persons should have the opportunity to fulfill their potential, few contend that it is the government's responsibility to totally eliminate the economic and social differences that lead to unequal opportunities.

Indeed, some contend that efforts to achieve equality, in the sense of equal treatment for all, are fundamentally incompatible with the value of liberty.

### Property

As noted earlier, the English philosopher John Locke asserted that people are born with natural rights and that among these rights are life, liberty, and *property.* The Declaration of Independence makes a similar assertion: people are born with certain "unalienable" rights, including the right to life, liberty, and the pursuit of happiness. For Americans, property and the *pursuit of happiness* are closely related. Americans place a great value on land ownership, on material possessions, and on their businesses. Property gives its owners political power and the liberty to do what they want—within limits.

Private property in America is not limited to personal possessions such as automobiles and houses. Property also consists of assets that can be used to create and sell goods and services, such as factories, farms, and shops. Private ownership of wealth-producing property is at the heart of our capitalist economic system. **Capitalism** enjoys such widespread support in the United States that we can reasonably call it one of the nation's fundamental political values. In addition to the private ownership of productive property, capitalism is based on *free markets*—markets in which people can freely buy and sell goods, services, and financial investments without undue constraint by the government. Freedom to make binding

What function does "flag waving" have?

KIDSTOCK/BLEND IMAGES/CORBIS

**liberty** The freedom of individuals to believe, act, and express themselves as they choose so long as doing so does not infringe on the rights of other individuals in the society.

**equality** A concept that holds, at a minimum, that all people are entitled to equal protection under the law.

**capitalism** An economic system based on the private ownership of wealth-producing property, free markets, and freedom of contract. The privately owned corporation is the preeminent capitalist institution.

contracts is another element of the capitalist system. The preeminent capitalist institution is the privately owned corporation.

Although capitalism is supported by almost all Americans, there is no equivalent agreement on the relationship between capitalism and the government. Is it best for the government to leave businesses alone in almost all circumstances—or would this lead to excessive inequality and unethical business practices that injure consumers? As with the values of liberty and equality, Americans are divided over what the right to property should mean. We examine a conflict that pits property rights against the value of liberty in this chapter's *Join the Debate* feature below.

## 1–3d Political Values and a Divided Electorate

Differences among Americans in interpreting our collectively held values underlie the division between the Republican and Democratic parties. Recent election results suggest that the voters are split right down the middle. Elections have often been close. In 2000, for example, Republican George W. Bush narrowly won the presidency in a contested election. Since then, support for the parties has swung back and forth without giving either one a long-term advantage.

Public rejection of the war in Iraq was enough to give the Democrats control of Congress in the 2004 elections. The economic crisis of 2008 then handed Democrat Barack Obama the presidency and gave

## JOIN THE DEBATE

### Should We Crack Down on Online Piracy?

Consider songs and movies that are downloaded from the Internet without paying a fee to the copyright owner. This action is so common among young people that it often does not occur to them that what they are doing is illegal. Industry representatives claim that downloaders pay for only 5 percent of the online music they obtain. One result: revenues from music album sales are less than 50 percent of what they were in 1999. Within a few years, sales of DVDs and Blu-ray discs could undergo a similar collapse. Written material is not exempt from this process. Millions of people are now reading pirated copies of books on their iPads and similar devices.

#### It's Time to Crack Down Hard

We need to protect intellectual property. Musicians, actors, filmmakers, authors, and the companies that support them are no longer being rewarded for the hard work they put into creating and marketing music, films, and literature. It is time that major online sites such as Google, Facebook, and YouTube start using their resources to enforce copyright protection. All they need is the will to do the right thing.

Members of Congress had the right idea when they supported the Stop Online Piracy Act (SOPA) in 2012. That legislation has been abandoned under pressure from major online firms, but it should be resurrected. If something is not done about online piracy now, we will end up with many fewer individuals who can afford to devote their lives to creating the best music, movies, and books.

#### Don't Exaggerate the Problem

Those supposed billions of dollars lost by content providers are a gross exaggeration. Such estimates are based on the notion that every pirated song or movie would have been purchased at full price if there were no piracy. In fact, most copiers would simply do without that song or movie.

Free entertainment is not new. You can hear advertiser-supported music on the radio or watch advertiser-supported movies on TV. You can read library books for free. Before downloading became easy, people would often lend their books, CDs, and DVDs to others. True, we should shut down criminal enterprises that profit from distributing stolen copies of creative works. But ordinary people should have the liberty to borrow and lend freely. Copyright protection has already gone too far. Should the song "Happy Birthday," which is over one hundred years old, really still be under copyright? (It is.)

**FOR CRITICAL ANALYSIS** Apple has a successful business selling music legally, and Netflix makes a legitimate profit by renting out movies. In an era of rampant piracy, why are people willing to deal with these companies?

the Democrats large margins in the U.S. House and Senate. Within a year, many voters turned away from the Democrats, believing that they had failed to curb unemployment and were letting the government grow too fast. In 2010, Republicans took control of the House, gained six senators and six governors, and won control of many state legislatures.

In 2011, however, spurred on by the uncompromising conservatives of the Tea Party movement, House Republicans proposed major changes to the government's Medicare and Medicaid programs. The alterations would make the programs much less generous. (Medicare is a federal health insurance program for the elderly, and Medicaid provides health-care funding for the poor, including the elderly poor.) Meanwhile, several new Republican governors made large spending cuts and campaigned against public employee unions. During the Republican presidential primary campaigns in late 2011 and early 2012, candidates vied with each other to see who could be the most conservative.

Some moderate voters appeared to be troubled by the extent of Republican conservatism, and the Republicans seem to have lost the edge that they enjoyed in the 2010 elections. Yet the Democrats were not out of the woods, either. The 2012 elections promised to be close.

## 1–3e Political Values in a Multicultural Society

From the earliest English and European settlers to the many cultural groups that today call America their home, American society has always been multicultural. Until recently, most Americans viewed the United States as the world's melting pot. They accepted that American society included numerous ethnic and cultural groups, but they expected that the members of these groups would abandon their cultural distinctions and assimilate the language and customs of earlier Americans. One of the outgrowths of the civil rights movement of the 1960s, however, was an emphasis on *multiculturalism,* the belief that the many cultures that make up American society should remain distinct and be protected—and even encouraged—by our laws.

Despite the growth in multiculturalism, Americans of all backgrounds remain committed to the values described in the last few sections of this text. Inevitably, however, different groups will interpret these values in varying ways, thus adding to our political divisions. African Americans, for example, given their collective history, will often have a different sense of what equality means than do Americans whose ancestors came from Europe.

The ethnic makeup of the United States has changed dramatically in the last two decades and will continue to change (see Figure 1–1 below). Already, non-Hispanic whites are a minority in California. For

### FIGURE 1–1

# Distribution of the U.S.
## Population by Race and Hispanic Origin, 2010 to 2050

By 2050, minorities will constitute a majority of the U.S. population.

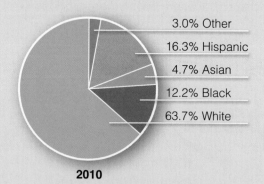

3.0% Other
16.3% Hispanic
4.7% Asian
12.2% Black
63.7% White

**2010**

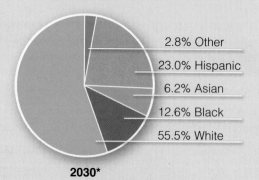

2.8% Other
23.0% Hispanic
6.2% Asian
12.6% Black
55.5% White

**2030***

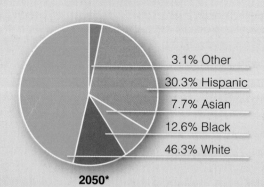

3.1% Other
30.3% Hispanic
7.7% Asian
12.6% Black
46.3% White

**2050***

*Data for 2030 and 2050 are projections.

Figures do not necessarily sum to 100%, because of rounding. Hispanics may be of any race. The chart categories "White," "Black," "Asian," and "Other" are limited to non-Hispanics.
"Other" consists of the following non-Hispanic groups: "American Indian," "Alaska Native," "Native Hawaiian," "Other Pacific Islander," and "Two or More Races."
Sources: U.S. Bureau of the Census and authors' calculations.

the nation as a whole, non-Hispanic whites will be in the minority before the year 2050. Some Americans fear that rising numbers of immigrants will threaten traditional American political values and culture. Others are confident that newcomers will adopt American values.

**FOR CRITICAL THINKING**

Describe some ways in which the values of equality and property can come into conflict with each other. *Many people see liberty and property as highly compatible values, but can you think of ways (other than the example given in the* Join the Debate *feature) in which these values, too, might come into conflict?*

## 1–4 American Political Ideology

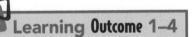

### Learning Outcome 1–4

Define common American ideological positions, such as "conservatism" and "liberalism."

In a general sense, **ideology** refers to a system of political ideas. These ideas typically are rooted in religious or philosophical beliefs about human nature, society, and government. Often, assumptions as to what the government's role should be in promoting basic values, such as liberty and equality, help shape a person's ideology.

When it comes to ideology, Americans are often placed in two broad political camps: conservatives and liberals. The term *conservative* originally referred to persons who wished to conserve—keep—traditional social and political habits and institutions. The term *liberal* referred to those who wanted to be free from tradition, and to establish new policies and practices. In today's American political arena, however, these simple definitions of *liberalism* and *conservatism* are incomplete. Both terms mean much more.

### 1–4a Conservatism

Modern American **conservatism** does indeed value traditions—specifically, American ones. For much of U.S. history, business enterprise was largely free from government control or regulation. That freedom began to break down during the administration of Franklin D. Roosevelt (1933–1945). Roosevelt's New Deal programs, launched in an attempt to counter the effects of the Great Depression, involved the government in the American economy to an extent previously unknown. Roosevelt gave conservatives a common cause: opposition to the New Deal and to big government. The tradition that conservatives sought to maintain was a version of capitalism that was free of government regulation or control.

**The Conservative Movement** The emergence of the **conservative movement** in the 1950s and 1960s was essential to the development of modern conservatism. Previously, economic conservatives were often seen as individuals who feared that government activity might personally cost them wealth or power. The conservative movement, in contrast, was clearly

**ideology** Generally, a system of political ideas that are rooted in religious or philosophical beliefs concerning human nature, society, and government.

**conservatism** A set of political beliefs that include a limited role for the national government in helping individuals and in the economic affairs of the nation, and support for traditional values and lifestyles.

**conservative movement** A strongly ideological movement that arose in the 1950s and 1960s and continues to shape conservative beliefs.

Republican Mitt Romney is shown campaigning for president in 2012. Is he a conservative?

MATT SULLIVAN/REUTERS

ideological. It provided a complete way of viewing the world, and it attracted millions of followers who were not necessarily motivated by narrow economic self-interest. The conservative movement emerged as a major force in 1964, when Arizona senator Barry Goldwater won the Republican presidential nomination on a relatively radical platform. Goldwater was soundly defeated by Democrat Lyndon B. Johnson (1963–1969). In 1980, however, Republican Ronald Reagan became the first "movement conservative" to win the White House.

### Conservatism Today

A key element in conservative thinking is the belief that the distribution of social and economic benefits that would exist if the government took little or no action is usually optimum. Conservatives believe that individuals and families should take responsibility for their own economic circumstances, and if that means that some people have less, so be it. Conservatives also place a high value on the principle of order, on family values, and on patriotism. Conservatism has always included those who want society and the government to reflect traditional religious values, and Christian conservatives remain an important part of the conservative coalition today.

### 1–4b Liberalism

While modern American **liberalism** can trace its roots to the New Deal programs of Franklin D. Roosevelt, the ideology did not take its fully modern form until the 1960s, during the Johnson administration. Johnson went well beyond the programs of Roosevelt with new economic initiatives, such as Medicare and Medicaid. These programs—and the recent healthcare reforms—reflect the strong liberal belief that the social and economic outcomes that exist in the absence of government action are frequently unfair. Conservatives commonly accuse liberals of valuing "big government" for its own sake. Liberals reject

**liberalism** A set of political beliefs that include the advocacy of active government, including government intervention to improve the welfare of individuals and to protect civil rights.

President Barack Obama is shown campaigning for reelection in 2012. How would you classify his political views?

that characterization and argue that big government is simply a necessary tool for promoting the common welfare.

### The Civil Rights Revolution

In the 1960s, liberals in the Democratic Party were able to commit their party firmly to the cause of African American equality, permanently overriding those Democratic conservatives who still supported legal segregation of the races. In a matching development, conservatives in the Republican Party began to appeal to traditionalist whites who were upset by the African American civil rights movement. As the party of Lincoln, the Republicans had once been the natural political home of African Americans. This was no longer true. Support for minority rights of all kinds became an integral part of liberal ideology, while conservatism came to include skepticism toward minority claims.

### Other Liberal Values

The Vietnam War (1965–1975) also influenced liberal thinking. Although American participation in the conflict was initiated by President Johnson, liberals swung against the war more strongly than

**SOCIAL MEDIA**
**In Politics**

You can follow top conservative and liberal opinion pieces on Facebook and Twitter. In either system, search on "national review" for conservative commentary. For a liberal take on the issues, try "think progress" on either Facebook or Twitter.

other Americans. Liberalism therefore came to include a relatively negative view of American military initiatives abroad. (That distrust has declined in recent years, however.)

Liberals strongly favor the separation of church and state. They generally think that the government should avoid laws that endorse or impose traditional religious values. These beliefs sharply contrast with those of religious conservatives. In this area, at least, liberals do not stand for big government, but rather the reverse.

**Liberals and Progressives** Not all political labels are equally popular, and the term *liberal* has taken a particular beating in the political wars of the last several decades. One result is that most politicians who might have called themselves liberals in the past have labeled their philosophy **progressivism** instead. The term *progressive* dates back to the first years of the twentieth century, when it referred to a reform movement that was active in both major political parties. Later, the progressive label fell into disuse, until it was resurrected in recent years.

### 1–4c The Traditional Political Spectrum

Traditionally, liberalism and conservatism have been regarded as falling within a political spectrum that ranges from the left to the right. As Figure 1–2 below illustrates, modern conservatives typically identify themselves politically as Republicans. Similarly, liberals—or progressives—identify with the Democratic Party. The identification of the parties with specific ideologies is clear today but was not always so noticeable in the past. Conservative Democrats and liberal Republicans were once common, but they are now rare.

COURTESY WWW.SANDERS.SENATE.GOV

U.S. Senator Bernie Sanders of Vermont describes himself as a "democratic socialist."

People whose views fall in the middle of the traditional political spectrum are generally called **moderates.** By definition, moderates do not classify themselves as either liberal or conservative. Moderates may vote for either Republicans or Democrats, although in public opinion polls Democrats are about twice as likely as Republicans to identify themselves

**progressivism** An alternative, more popular term for the set of political beliefs also known as liberalism.

**moderates** Persons whose views fall in the middle of the political spectrum.

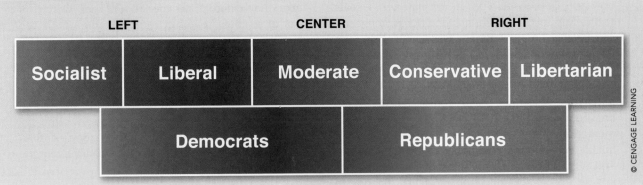

**FIGURE 1–2** **The Traditional Political Spectrum**

| LEFT | | CENTER | | RIGHT |
| --- | --- | --- | --- | --- |
| Socialist | Liberal | Moderate | Conservative | Libertarian |
| | Democrats | | Republicans | |

© CENGAGE LEARNING

as moderates. Still, a large number of moderates do not support either major political party and often describe themselves as *independent* (see Chapter 7).

## 1–4d Beyond Conservatism and Liberalism

Many Americans do not adhere firmly to a particular political ideology. Some are not interested in political issues. Others may have opinions that do not neatly fit under the liberal or conservative label. For example, conservatives typically support restrictions on the availability of abortion. They also may favor banning the procedure altogether. Liberals usually favor the right to have an abortion. Many liberals believe that the government ought to guarantee that everyone can find a job. Conservatives generally reject this idea. Millions of Americans, however, support restrictions on abortion while supporting government jobs programs. Many other citizens would oppose both of these positions. Conservatism and liberalism, in other words, are not the only ideological possibilities.

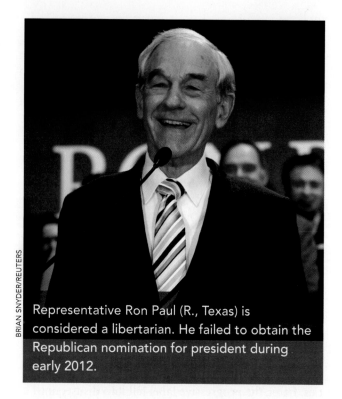

BRIAN SNYDER/REUTERS

Representative Ron Paul (R., Texas) is considered a libertarian. He failed to obtain the Republican nomination for president during early 2012.

**Socialism** To the left of liberalism on the traditional ideological spectrum lies **socialism**. This ideology has few adherents in the United States, although a

## ELECTIONS 2012

### Let the Voters Decide

Election year 2012 was moderately good for the Democrats—better, in fact, than political experts had predicted. Democratic president Barack Obama was reelected with a provisional popular vote margin of 2.7 percent. Many observers had predicted that the Democrats would lose control of the U.S. Senate. They gained two seats. In the U.S. House, however, Democrats won an estimated 201 seats to the Republican's 234. In other words, the partisan balance in government was unchanged. The Democrats continued to hold the presidency and the Senate, while the Republicans had the House.

As Senator Lindsey Graham (R., S.C.) famously remarked, "Elections have consequences." One consequence of the 2012 elections was full implementation of the Affordable Care Act, the 2010 health-care reforms commonly called Obamacare. The most important provisions of Obamacare do not go into effect until January 2014. Changes to

the nation's tax system were probably inevitable. Obama had campaigned for higher tax rates on annual incomes above $250,000, and there was a good chance that he would get his way.

The most important result of the elections, however, was that the Republicans failed to elect their presidential candidate, Mitt Romney, and failed to take the Senate. Had the Republicans won control of all branches of government, they promised a dramatic more limited-government program. Tax rates would be cut. Obamacare would be repealed. Domestic social programs would be cut back to an unprecedented degree. There were some changes that many Americans were willing to support in 2012—voters in three states endorsed same-sex marriage. A radical overhaul of the nation's entitlement programs, however, was not a change that the majority was willing to accept.

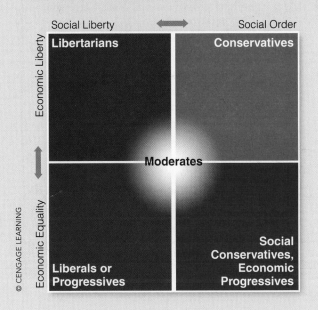

## FIGURE 1-3

# A Two-Dimensional
## Political Classification

Social Liberty ⟷ Social Order

Economic Liberty

**Libertarians**          **Conservatives**

**Moderates**

Economic Equality

**Liberals or Progressives**          **Social Conservatives, Economic Progressives**

© CENGAGE LEARNING

small handful of Democrats and independents accept the label. In much of the world, however, the main left-of-center party describes itself as socialist. Socialists have a stronger commitment to egalitarianism than do U.S. liberals and a greater tolerance for strong government. Indeed, in the first half of the twentieth century, most socialists advocated government ownership of major businesses. Few European or American socialists endorse such proposals today, however.

Western socialists strongly support democracy, but early in the twentieth century an ultra-left breakaway from the socialist movement—the *Communists*—established a series of brutal dictatorships, initially in Russia (the Soviet Union). Communists remain in power in China and a few other nations. Despite Communist rule, in recent years capitalist businesses have thrived in China.

**Libertarianism** Even as socialism is weak in America compared with the rest of the world, the right-of-center ideology of **libertarianism** is unusually strong. Libertarians oppose almost all government regulation of the economy and government redistribution of income.

Many ardent conservatives, such as the members of the **Tea Party movement,** share these beliefs. What distinguishes true libertarians from Tea Party supporters, however, is that libertarians also oppose government involvement in issues of private morality. In this belief, they often have more in common with liberals than they do with conservatives. For most people, however, economic issues remain the more important ones, and a majority of libertarians ally with conservatives politically and support the Republicans.

### Economic Progressives, Social Conservatives

Many other voters are liberal on economic issues even as they favor conservative positions on social matters. These people favor government intervention to promote both economic "fairness" *and* moral values. Low-income people frequently are economic progressives and social conservatives. A large number of African Americans and Hispanics fall into this camp. While it is widespread within the electorate, this "anti-libertarian" point of view has no agreed-upon name.

In sum, millions of Americans do not fit neatly into the traditional liberal-conservative spectrum. We illustrate an alternative, two-dimensional political classification in Figure 1–3 above.

**libertarianism** The belief that government should do as little as possible, not only in the economic sphere, but also in regulating morality and personal behavior.

**Tea Party movement** A grassroots conservative movement that arose in 2009 after Barack Obama became president. The movement opposes big government and current levels of taxation, and also rejects political compromise.

**FOR CRITICAL THINKING**

Suppose you are a representative in Congress and ran for office on a platform that clearly articulated your strong beliefs. *Should you be willing to compromise with others in the hopes of obtaining at least some of what you favor—or is it better to stand on principle, even if you lose?*

# AMERICA AT
# ODDS Key Conflicts in America in the Twenty-First Century

As you learned in this chapter, Americans are united by a common political culture. At the same time, however, Americans are at odds over how much weight should be given to various fundamental principles. We can summarize these most basic disputes as follows:

- How large should our government be? Should it offer a wide range of services, along with the resulting taxes—or should it provide relatively few services and collect less in taxes?

- Should businesses be strictly regulated to ensure the common good—or should regulation be minimized to promote economic freedom and growth?

- More generally, should we place a greater value on economic liberty and property rights—or on economic egalitarianism and improving the condition of those who are less well-off?

- How active should the government be in promoting moral behavior by Americans? Should the government support traditional values—or place a high value on social liberty?

- Are progressive or liberal policies best for the nation—or does conservatism provide better answers? Alternatively, is libertarianism the solution—or social conservatism combined with progressive economic policies?

## TAKE ACTION

Our democratic republic is now more than two hundred years old, and it is easy to assume that it will last forever. It is also easy to forget that the reason we still enjoy the rights and benefits our system provides is that whenever they have been threatened in the past, people spoke out and took action to remove the threat. In the remaining chapters of this book, this *Take Action* section will give examples of how you can take action to make a difference. To function as a free person in our complex society, it is important to know the basic facts about government and politics that are covered in this text.

### Majoring in Political Science

Political science, however, goes well beyond the basics that every citizen ought to know. It is an important field of study in its own right. Students who major in political science find employment in almost every kind of job imaginable. Naturally, some take employment with government at the federal, state, or local level. Political science is also the most popular major for students who seek to attend law school.

### Other Possible Jobs

A political science major also can prepare a student for many other jobs. Almost every chapter of this book suggests a possible career. Public opinion?

Along with statistics, political science is a valuable background for poll takers. The media? Political science makes a good start if you want to go on to study journalism in preparation for a career. Political science can prepare you for jobs in campaign consulting, public relations, or business. Of course, political scientists also teach their subject at the high school and college levels. Regardless of what career they choose, one thing unites all political science majors—they like politics and find it fascinating.

LORI SHEPLER/REUTERS

California college students protest state budget cuts to higher education in 2012.

# STUDY TOOLS

## Ready to study?

- Review what you've read with the quiz below. Check your answers on the Chapter in Review card at the back of the book. For any questions you miss, read the corresponding Learning Outcome section again to prepare for class and your exam.
- Rip out and study the Chapter in Review card.

## . . . Or you can go online to CourseMate

at www.cengagebrain.com for these additional review materials:

- Practice Quizzes
- Key Term Flashcards or Crossword Puzzles.
- Audio Summaries
- Simulations, Animated Learning Modules, and Interactive Timelines
- Videos
- American Government NewsWatch

---

## Fill-In

1. _____ can best be defined as the individuals and institutions that make society's rules and also possess the power and authority to enforce those rules.

2. Generally, in any country government serves at least three essential purposes: _____.

3. In an _____, the power and authority of the government are in the hands of a single person.

4. In a _____, the will of the majority is expressed through groups of individuals elected by the people to act as their representatives.

5. The philosopher John Locke argued that people are born with natural rights to _____.

6. American democracy is based on five fundamental principles: _____.

7. When it comes to ideology, Americans are often placed in two broad political camps: _____.

8. People whose views fall in the middle of the traditional political spectrum are generally called _____.

9. _____ oppose almost all government regulation of the economy and government redistribution of income, while also opposing government involvement in issues of private morality.

---

## Multiple Choice

10. Political scientist Harold Lasswell defined _____ as the process of determining "who gets what, when, and how" in a society.
    a. government   b. power   c. politics

11. The system of government in the United States is best described as a _____ democracy.
    a. parliamentary   b. presidential   c. direct

12. In an _____, there is no separation of church and state. Rather, the government rules according to religious precepts.
    a. plutocracy   b. aristocracy   c. theocracy

13. Which of the following best describes a social contract?
    a. The set of ideas, values, and attitudes about government and the political process held by a community or a nation.

    b. A voluntary agreement among individuals to create a government and to give that government adequate power to secure the mutual protection and welfare of all individuals.

    c. An economic system based on the private ownership of wealth-producing property, free markets, and freedom of contract.

14. Because of the political value of _____, Article I, Section 9, of the U.S. Constitution prohibits the government from granting titles of nobility.
    a. equality   b. liberty   c. multiculturalism

15. American liberalism took its fully modern form in the
    a. 1960s, during the administration of Lyndon Johnson.
    b. 1990s, during the administration of Bill Clinton.
    c. 2000s, during the administration of Barack Obama.

# 2

# The Constitution

The **Learning Outcomes** labeled 1 through 5 are designed to help improve your understanding of the chapter. After reading this chapter, you should be able to:

**2–1** Point out some of the influences on the American political tradition in the colonial years.

**2–2** Explain why the American colonies rebelled against Britain.

**2–3** Describe the structure of government established by the Articles of Confederation and some of the strengths and weaknesses of the Articles.

**2–4** List some of the major compromises made by the delegates at the Constitutional Convention, and discuss the Federalist and Anti-Federalist positions on ratifying the Constitution.

**2–5** Summarize the Constitution's major principles of government, and describe how the Constitution can be amended.

**Remember to visit page 47 for additional Study Tools**

© TED SPIEGEL/CORBIS

# AMERICA AT ODDS
## Is It Constitutional to Ban Same-Sex Marriage?

Until recently, the idea of marriage by same-sex couples never even occurred to most people. During the last few decades, however, gay marriage has become a newsworthy topic. Such marriages are now legal in several states. Many others, however, have adopted laws or constitutional amendments banning the practice.

Consider California. In May 2008, the California Supreme Court ruled that the state constitution required the recognition of same-sex marriages. To overturn this ruling, opponents of gay marriage placed an amendment to the state constitution on the ballot. This was Proposition 8, which passed in November 2008. Supporters of same-sex marriage then sued to reverse Proposition 8 in a federal district court. In 2010, Judge Vaughn R. Walker ruled that Proposition 8 violated the U.S. Constitution. In 2012, a federal appeals court affirmed Walker's ruling but limited its scope to California. The United States Supreme Court may ultimately resolve this conflict. Americans are at odds over how the courts should rule.

## The Constitution Never Implied Same-Sex Marriage

Supporters of laws that ban same-sex marriage observe that the founders never imagined the practice. More to the point, the leaders who drafted the Fourteenth Amendment to the Constitution after the Civil War never contemplated it. The equal protection clause states: ". . . nor shall any State . . . deny to any person within its jurisdiction the equal protection of the laws." Southern state governments had passed laws that severely limited the rights of African Americans. The equal protection clause was meant to overturn such laws. It was not meant to protect gay men or lesbians—gay sexual relations were illegal in all states at that time, with harsh penalties.

Opponents of same-sex marriage argue that we must interpret the Constitution based on the *original intent* of the authors. If we let modern-day preferences affect how we interpret the Constitution, the document will soon have no value at all. Judges will be able to reinterpret it to mean anything.

## The Constitution Protects Equal Rights for All

Supporters of same-sex marriage point out that no level of government may enforce a law that violates the Fourteenth Amendment's equal protection clause unless the law is "rationally related" to a "legitimate" government interest. Satisfying popular prejudices—even prejudices with strong historical roots—is not a legitimate interest. Federal district court judge Walker found no legitimate interest that justified the banning of same-sex marriage.

The original intent of the Constitution's authors cannot be the only standard for judgment. The founders themselves rejected this principle. Over the course of two hundred years, our nation has experienced huge changes in technology and social values. No constitution could survive such transformations unless judges were permitted to reinterpret it based on modern circumstances. Today, a slim majority of U.S. citizens supports same-sex marriage in public opinion polls. The courts need to take this fact into account.

## Where do you stand?

1. Opinions about same-sex marriage vary dramatically from state to state. If the Supreme Court were to find that same-sex marriage is constitutionally protected, how might the people in more conservative states react?
2. Should marriage rights be a public concern at all, or should marriage be an entirely private matter? Explain your thinking.

## Explore this issue online

- Using a search engine, enter the phrase "same-sex marriage." You will be directed to news stories on court cases and state legislation, as well as debates on the topic.
- For information on ways in which the Constitution can be interpreted, try searching on "constitution original intent."

# Introduction

Whether lesbians and gay men have a constitutional right to marry their partners is just one of many debates concerning the government established by the U.S. Constitution. The Constitution, which was written more than two hundred years ago, continues to be the supreme law of the land. Time and again, its provisions have been adapted to the changing needs and conditions of society. The challenge before today's citizens and political leaders is to find a way to apply those provisions to a society and an economy that could not possibly have been anticipated by the founders. Will the Constitution survive this challenge? Most Americans assume that it will—and with good reason: no other written constitution in the world today is as old as the U.S. Constitution.

To understand the principles of government set forth in the Constitution, you have to go back to the beginnings of our nation's history.

# 2–1 The Beginnings of American Government

When the framers of the Constitution met in Philadelphia in 1787, they brought with them some valuable political assets. One asset was their English political heritage (see Chapter 1). Another was the hands-on political experience they had acquired during the colonial era. Their political knowledge and experience enabled them to establish a constitution that could meet not only the needs of their own time but also the needs of generations to come.

The American colonies were settled by individuals from many nations, including France, Germany, Ireland, the Netherlands, Spain, and Sweden. The majority of the colonists, though, came from England and Scotland. The British colonies in North America were established by private individuals and private trading companies and were under the rule of the British Crown. The colonies, which were located along the Atlantic seaboard of today's United States, eventually numbered thirteen.

Although American politics owes much to the English political tradition, the colonists

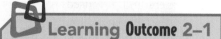

**Learning Outcome 2–1**

Point out some of the influences on the American political tradition in the colonial years.

MPI/GETTY IMAGES

Jamestown was the first permanent English settlement in North America. The Virginia Company of London established it as a trading post in 1607.

actually derived most of their understanding of social compacts, the rights of the people, limited government, and representative government from their own experiences. Years before Parliament adopted the English Bill of Rights or John Locke wrote his *Two Treatises on Government* (1690), the American colonists were putting the ideas expressed in those documents into practice.

## 2–1a The First English Settlements

The first permanent English settlement in North America was Jamestown, in what is now Virginia.[1] Jamestown was established in 1607 as a trading post of the Virginia Company of London.[2]

The first New England colony was founded by the Plymouth Company in 1620 at Plymouth, Massachusetts. Most of the settlers at Plymouth were Pilgrims, a group of English Protestants who came to the New World on the ship *Mayflower*. Even before the Pilgrims went ashore, they drew up the **Mayflower Compact,** in which they set up a government and promised to obey its laws.

The reason for the compact was that the group was outside the territory assigned to the Virginia Company, which had arranged for them to settle in what is now New York, not Massachusetts. Fearing that some of the passengers might decide that they were no longer subject to any rules of civil order, the leaders on board the *Mayflower* agreed that some form of governmental authority was necessary.

The Mayflower Compact, which was essentially a social contract, has historical significance because it was the first of a series of similar contracts among the colonists to establish fundamental rules of government.[3]

The Massachusetts Bay Colony was established as another trading outpost in New England in 1630. In 1639, some of the Pilgrims at Plymouth, who felt that they were being persecuted by the Massachusetts Bay Colony, left Plymouth and settled in what is now Connecticut. They developed America's first written constitution, which was called the Fundamental Orders of Connecticut. This document called for the laws to be made by an assembly of elected representatives from each town. The document also provided for the popular election of a governor and judges.

Other colonies, in turn, established fundamental governing rules. The Massachusetts Body of Liberties protected individual rights. The Pennsylvania Frame of Government, passed in 1682, and the Pennsylvania Charter of Privileges of 1701 established principles that were later expressed in the U.S. Constitution and

FIGURE 2–1

# The Thirteen Colonies
## before the American Revolution

The western boundary of the colonies was set by the Proclamation Line of 1763, which banned European settlement in western territories that were reserved for Native Americans.

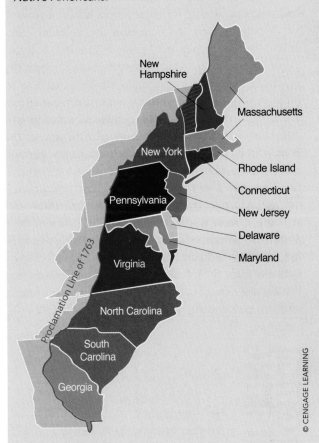

© CENGAGE LEARNING

Bill of Rights (the first ten amendments to the Constitution). By 1732, all thirteen colonies had been established, each with its own political documents and constitution (see Figure 2–1 above).

## 2–1b Colonial Legislatures

As mentioned, the British colonies in America were all under the rule of the British monarchy. Britain,

**Mayflower Compact** A document drawn up by Pilgrim leaders in 1620 on the ship *Mayflower*. The document stated that laws were to be made for the general good of the people.

**Bill of Rights** The first ten amendments to the U.S. Constitution. They list the freedoms—such as the freedoms of speech, press, and religion—that a citizen enjoys and that cannot be infringed on by the government.

however, was thousands of miles away—it took two months to sail across the Atlantic. Thus, to a significant extent, colonial legislatures carried on the "nuts and bolts" of colonial government. These legislatures, or *representative assemblies,* consisted of representatives elected by the colonists. The earliest colonial legislature was the Virginia House of Burgesses, established in 1619. By the time of the American Revolution, all of the colonies had representative assemblies, many of which had been in existence for more than a hundred years.

Through their participation in colonial governments, the colonists gained crucial political experience. Colonial leaders became familiar with the practical problems of governing. They learned how to build coalitions among groups with diverse interests and how to make compromises. Indeed, according to Yale University professor Jon Butler, by the time of the American Revolution in 1776, Americans had formed a complex, sophisticated political system.

They had also created a wholly new type of society characterized by, among other things, ethnic and religious diversity.[4] The colonists benefited from their political experiences. They were quickly able to establish their own constitutions and state systems of government after they declared their independence from Britain in 1776. Eventually, they were able to set up a national government as well.

**FOR CRITICAL THINKING**

When first founded, each of the colonies had very few people. *How might that have made it easier to draw up founding documents?*

## 2-2 The Rebellion of the Colonists

Scholars of the American Revolution point out that by and large, the American colonists did not want to become independent of Britain. For the majority of the colonists, Britain was the homeland, and ties of loyalty to the British monarch were strong. Why, then, did the colonists revolt against Britain and declare their independence? What happened to sever the political, economic, and emotional bonds that tied

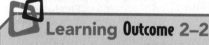

**Learning Outcome 2-2**

Explain why the American colonies rebelled against Britain.

the colonists to Britain? The answers to these questions lie in a series of events in the mid-1700s that culminated in a change in British policy toward the colonies. Table 2–1 below shows the chronology of the major political events in early U.S. history.

One of these events was the Seven Years' War (1756–1763) between Britain and France, which Americans often refer to as the French and Indian War. The British victory in the Seven Years' War permanently altered the relationship between Britain and its American colonies. After successfully ousting the French from North America, the British expanded their authority over the colonies. To pay its war debts and to finance the defense of its expanded North American empire, Britain needed revenues. The British government decided to obtain some of these revenues by imposing taxes on the American

**TABLE 2-1**

### Significant Events in Early U.S. Political History

| Year | Event |
| --- | --- |
| 1607 | Jamestown established; Virginia Company lands settlers. |
| 1620 | Mayflower Compact signed. |
| 1630 | Massachusetts Bay Colony set up. |
| 1639 | Fundamental Orders of Connecticut adopted. |
| 1641 | Massachusetts Body of Liberties adopted. |
| 1682 | Pennsylvania Frame of Government passed. |
| 1701 | Pennsylvania Charter of Privileges written. |
| 1732 | Last of thirteen colonies established (Georgia). |
| 1756 | French and Indian War declared. |
| 1765 | Stamp Act; Stamp Act Congress meets. |
| 1773 | Boston Tea Party. |
| 1774 | First Continental Congress meets. |
| 1775 | Second Continental Congress; Revolutionary War begins. |
| 1776 | Declaration of Independence signed. |
| 1777 | Articles of Confederation drafted. |
| 1781 | Last state signs Articles of Confederation. |
| 1783 | "Critical period" in U.S. history begins; weak national government until 1789. |
| 1786 | Shays' Rebellion. |
| 1787 | Constitutional Convention held. |
| 1788 | Constitution ratified. |
| 1791 | Bill of Rights ratified. |

colonists and exercising more direct control over colonial trade.

At the same time, Americans were beginning to distrust the expanding British presence in the colonies. Having fought alongside British forces, Americans thought that they deserved more credit for the victory. The British, however, attributed the victory solely to their own effort.

Furthermore, the colonists began to develop a sense of identity separate from the British. Americans were shocked at the behavior of some of the British soldiers and the cruel punishments meted out to enforce discipline among the British troops. The British, in turn, had little good to say about the colonists alongside whom they had fought. They considered them brutish, uncivilized, and undisciplined. It was during this time that the colonists began to use the word *American* to describe themselves.

## 2–2a "Taxation without Representation"

In 1764, the British Parliament passed the Sugar Act, which imposed a tax on all sugar imported into the American colonies. Some colonists, particularly in Massachusetts, vigorously opposed this tax and proposed a boycott of certain British imports. This boycott developed into a "nonimportation" movement that soon spread to other colonies.

**The Stamp Act of 1765**  The following year, in 1765, Parliament passed the Stamp Act, which imposed the first direct tax on the colonists. Under the act, all legal documents and newspapers, as well as certain other items, including playing cards and dice, had to use specially embossed (stamped) paper that was purchased from the government.

The Stamp Act generated even stronger resentment among the colonists than the Sugar Act. James Otis, Jr., a Massachusetts attorney, declared that there could be "no taxation without representation." The American colonists were not represented in the British Parliament. They viewed Parliament's attempts to tax them as contrary to the principle of representative government. The British saw the matter differently. From the British perspective, it was only fair that the colonists pay taxes to help support the costs incurred by the British government in defending its American territories and maintaining the troops that were permanently stationed in the colonies following the Seven Years' War.

> "Every generation needs a
> # NEW REVOLUTION."
> ~ THOMAS JEFFERSON ~
> THIRD PRESIDENT OF THE UNITED STATES
> 1801–1809

In October 1765, nine of the thirteen colonies sent delegates to the Stamp Act Congress in New York City. The delegates prepared a declaration of rights and grievances, which they sent to King George III. This action marked the first time that a majority of the colonies had joined together to oppose British rule. The British Parliament repealed the Stamp Act.

**Further Taxes and the Coercive Acts**  Soon, however, Parliament passed new laws designed to bind the colonies more tightly to the central government in London. Laws that imposed taxes on glass, paint, lead, and many other items were passed in 1767. The colonists protested by boycotting all British goods. In 1773, anger over taxation reached a powerful climax at the Boston Tea Party, in which colonists dressed as Mohawk Indians dumped almost 350 chests of British tea into Boston Harbor as a gesture of tax protest.[5]

TIME LIFE PICTURES/MANSELL/GETTY IMAGES

During the Boston Tea Party in 1773, the colonists dumped chests of British tea into Boston Harbor as a gesture of tax protest.

The British Parliament was quick to respond to the Tea Party. In 1774, Parliament passed the Coercive Acts (sometimes called the "Intolerable Acts"), which closed Boston Harbor and placed the government of Massachusetts under direct British control.

## 2–2b The Continental Congresses

In response to the "Intolerable Acts," New York, Pennsylvania, and Rhode Island proposed a colonial congress. The Massachusetts House of Representatives requested that all colonies select delegates to send to Philadelphia for such a congress.

**The First Continental Congress** The **First Continental Congress** met on September 5, 1774, at Carpenter's Hall in Philadelphia. Of the thirteen colonies, only Georgia did not participate. The congress decided that the colonies should send a petition to King George III to explain their grievances, which they did. The congress also called for a continued boycott of British goods and required each colony to establish an army.

To enforce the boycott and other acts of resistance against Britain, the delegates to the First Continental Congress urged that "a committee be chosen in every county, city and town . . . whose business it shall be attentively to observe the conduct of all persons." The committees of "safety" or "observation," as they were called, organized militias, held special courts, and suppressed the opinions of those who remained loyal to the British Crown. Committee members spied on neighbors' activities and reported to the press the names of those who violated the boycott against Britain. The names were then printed in the local papers, and the transgressors were harassed and ridiculed in their communities.

**The Second Continental Congress** Almost immediately after receiving the petition from the First Continental Congress, the British

> # "The Constitution . . .is an instrument for the people to restrain the government—lest it come to dominate our lives and interests."
>
> ~ PATRICK HENRY ~
> AMERICAN STATESMAN AND
> OPPONENT OF THE CONSTITUTION
> 1736–1799

government condemned the actions of the congress as open acts of rebellion. Britain responded with even stricter and more repressive measures. On April 19, 1775, British soldiers (Redcoats) fought against colonial citizen soldiers (Minutemen) in the towns of Lexington and Concord in Massachusetts, the first battles of the American Revolution.

Less than a month later, delegates from all thirteen colonies gathered in Pennsylvania for the **Second Continental Congress,** which immediately assumed the powers of a central government. The Second Continental Congress declared that the militiamen who had gathered around Boston were now a full army. It also named George Washington, a delegate to the congress who had some military experience, as its commander in chief.

The delegates to the Second Continental Congress still intended to reach a peaceful settlement with the British Parliament. One declaration stated specifically that "we [the congress] have not raised armies with ambitious designs of separating from Britain, and establishing independent States." The continued attempts to effect a reconciliation with Britain, even after the outbreak of fighting, underscore the colonists' reluctance to sever their relationship with the home country.

## 2–2c Breaking the Ties: Independence

Public debate about the problems with Britain continued to rage, but the stage had been set for declaring independence. One of the most rousing arguments in favor of independence was presented by Thomas Paine, a former English schoolmaster and corset maker, who wrote a pamphlet called *Common Sense*.

In that pamphlet, which was published in Philadelphia in January 1776, Paine addressed the crisis using "simple fact, plain argument, and common sense." He mocked King George III and attacked every argument that favored loyalty to the king. He called the king a "royal brute" and a "hardened, sullen-tempered Pharaoh [Egyptian king in ancient times]."[6]

Paine's writing went beyond a personal attack on the king. He contended that America could survive economically on its own and no longer needed its British connection. He wanted the developing

**First Continental Congress** A gathering of delegates from twelve of the thirteen colonies, held in 1774 to protest the Coercive Acts.

**Second Continental Congress** The congress of the colonies that met in 1775 to assume the powers of a central government and to establish an army.

colonies to become a model republic in a world in which other nations were oppressed by strong central governments.

None of Paine's arguments was new. In fact, most of them were commonly heard in tavern debates throughout the land. Instead, it was the wit and eloquence of Paine's words that made *Common Sense* so effective:

> A government of our own is our natural right: and when a man seriously reflects on the precariousness of human affairs, he will become convinced, that it is infinitely wiser and safer, to form a constitution of our own in a cool and deliberate manner, while we have it in our power, than to trust such an interesting event to time and chance.[7]

Many historians regard Paine's *Common Sense* as the single most important publication of the American Revolution. The pamphlet became a best seller. More than one hundred thousand copies were sold within a few months after its publication.[8] It put independence squarely on the agenda. Above all, *Common Sense* helped sever the remaining ties of loyalty to the British monarch, thus removing the final psychological barrier to independence. Indeed, later John Adams would ask,

> What do we mean by the Revolution? The War? That was no part of the Revolution. It was only an effect and consequence of it. The Revolution was in the minds of the people, and this was effected, from 1760 to 1775, in the course of fifteen years before a drop of blood was drawn at Lexington.[9]

## Independence from Britain—The First Step

By June 1776, the Second Continental Congress had voted for free trade at all American ports with all countries except Britain. The congress had also suggested that all colonies establish state governments separate from Britain. The colonists realized that a formal separation from Britain was necessary if the new nation was to obtain supplies for its armies and commitments of military aid from foreign governments. On June 7, 1776, the first formal step toward independence was taken when Richard Henry Lee of Virginia placed the following resolution before the congress:

> RESOLVED, That these United Colonies are, and of right ought to be, free and independent States, that they are absolved from allegiance to the British Crown, and that all political connection between them and the state of Great Britain is, and ought to be, totally dissolved.

The congress postponed consideration of Lee's resolution until a formal statement of independence could be drafted. On June 11, a "Committee of Five" was appointed to draft a declaration that would present to the world the colonies' case for independence.

## The Significance of the Declaration of Independence

Adopted on July 4, 1776, the Declaration of Independence is one of the world's most famous documents. Like Paine, Thomas Jefferson, who wrote most of the document, elevated the dispute between Britain and the American colonies to a universal level. Jefferson opened the second paragraph of the declaration with the following words, which have since been memorized by countless American schoolchildren and admired the world over:

> We hold these Truths to be self-evident, that all Men are created equal, that they are endowed by their Creator with certain unalienable Rights, that among these are Life, Liberty, and the Pursuit of Happiness—That to secure these Rights, Governments are instituted among Men, deriving their just Powers from the Consent of the Governed, that whenever any Form of Government becomes destructive of these Ends, it is the Right of the People to alter or to abolish it, and to institute new Government.

The committee chosen to draft a declaration of independence is shown at work in this nineteenth-century engraving. They are, from the left, Benjamin Franklin, Thomas Jefferson, John Adams, Philip Livingston, and Roger Sherman.

LIBRARY OF CONGRESS

The concepts expressed in the Declaration of Independence clearly reflect Jefferson's familiarity with European political philosophy, particularly the works of John Locke.[10] Locke's philosophy, though it did not cause the American Revolution, provided philosophical underpinnings by which the revolution could be justified.

### From Colonies to States

Even before the Declaration of Independence, some of the colonies had transformed themselves into sovereign states with their own permanent governments. In May 1776, the Second Continental Congress had directed each of the colonies to form "such government as shall . . . best be conducive to the happiness and safety of their constituents [those represented by the government]."

Before long, all thirteen colonies had created constitutions. Eleven of the colonies had completely new constitutions. The other two, Rhode Island and Connecticut, made minor modifications to old royal charters. Seven of the new constitutions contained bills of rights that defined the personal liberties of all state citizens. All constitutions called for limited governments.

### Republicanism

Many citizens were fearful of a strong central government because of their recent experiences under the British Crown. They opposed any form of government that resembled monarchy in any way. Consequently, wherever such antiroyalist sentiment was strong, the legislature—composed of elected representatives—became all-powerful. In Pennsylvania and Georgia, for example, **unicameral** (one-chamber) **legislatures** were unchecked by any executive authority. Indeed, this antiroyalist— or *republican*—sentiment was so strong that the executive branch was extremely weak in all thirteen states.

The republican spirit was strong enough to seriously interfere with the ability of the new nation to win the Revolutionary War—for example, by failing to adequately supply General Washington's army. Republicans of the Revolutionary Era (not to be confused with supporters of the later Republican Party) were suspicious not only of executive authority in their own states but also of national authority as represented by the Continental Congress. This anti-authoritarian, localist impulse contrasted with the *nationalist* sentiments of many of the nation's founders, especially such leaders as George Washington and Alexander Hamilton. Nationalists favored an effective central authority. Of course, many founders, such as Thomas Jefferson, harbored both republican and nationalist impulses.

Who were the republicans? As with all political movements of the time, the republicans were led by men of "property and standing." Leaders who were strongly republican, however, tended to be less prominent than their nationalist or moderate counterparts. Small farmers may have been the one group that was disproportionately republican. Small farmers, however, were a majority of the voters in every state.

**unicameral legislature** A legislature with only one chamber.

**confederation** A league of independent states that are united only for the purpose of achieving common goals.

**Articles of Confederation** The nation's first national constitution, which established a national form of government following the American Revolution. The Articles provided for a confederal form of government in which the central government had few powers.

**FOR CRITICAL THINKING** The American colonists did not have the right to elect members of the British Parliament. *How might American history have been different if the British had permitted such representation?*

## 2–3 The Confederation of States

Republican sentiments influenced the thinking of the delegates to the Second Continental Congress, who formed a committee to draft a plan of confederation. A **confederation** is a voluntary association of *independent* states (see Chapter 3). The member states agree to let the central government undertake a limited number of activities, such as forming an army, but do not allow the central government to place many restrictions on the states' own actions. The member states typically can still govern most state affairs as they see fit.

On November 15, 1777, the Second Continental Congress agreed on a draft of the plan, which was finally signed by all thirteen colonies on March 1, 1781. The **Articles of Confederation,** the result of this

**Learning Outcome 2–3**

Describe the structure of government established by the Articles of Confederation and some of the strengths and weaknesses of the Articles.

plan, served as this nation's first national constitution and represented an important step in the creation of our governmental system.[11]

The Articles of Confederation established the Congress of the Confederation as the central governing body. This congress was a unicameral assembly of representatives, or ambassadors, as they were called, from the various states. Although each state could send from two to seven representatives to the congress, each state, no matter what its size, had only one vote. The issue of sovereignty was an important part of the Articles of Confederation:

> Each State retains its sovereignty, freedom, and independence, and every power, jurisdiction, and right, which is not by this Confederation expressly delegated to the United States in Congress assembled.

The structure of government under the Articles of Confederation is shown in Figure 2–2 below.

## 2–3a Powers of the Government of the Confederation

Congress had several powers under the Articles of Confederation, and these enabled the new nation to achieve a number of accomplishments (see Figure 2–3 on the following page). The Northwest Ordinance settled states' claims to many of the western lands and established a basic pattern for the government of new territories. Also, the 1783 peace treaty negotiated with Britain granted to the United States all of the territory from the Atlantic Ocean to the Mississippi River and from the Great Lakes and Canada to what is now northern Florida.

In spite of these accomplishments, the central government created by the Articles of Confederation was quite weak. The Congress of the Confederation had no power to raise revenues for the militia or to force the states to meet military quotas. Essentially, this meant that the new government did not have the power to enforce its laws. Even passing laws was difficult because the Articles of Confederation provided that nine states had to approve any law before it was enacted. Figure 2–4 on page 33 lists these and other powers that the central government lacked under the Articles of Confederation.

Nonetheless, the Articles of Confederation proved to be a good "first draft" for the Constitution, and at least half of the text of the Articles would later appear in the Constitution. The Articles were an unplanned experiment that tested some of the principles of government that had been set forth earlier in the Declaration of Independence. Some argue that without the experience of government under the Articles of Confederation, it would have been difficult, if not impossible, to arrive at the compromises that were necessary to create the Constitution several years later.

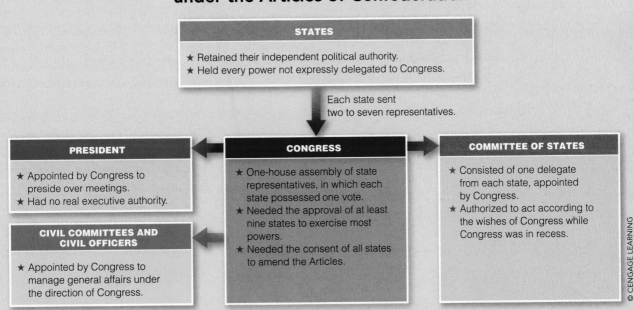

**FIGURE 2–2**

# American Government
## under the Articles of Confederation

**STATES**
- ★ Retained their independent political authority.
- ★ Held every power not expressly delegated to Congress.

*Each state sent two to seven representatives.*

**PRESIDENT**
- ★ Appointed by Congress to preside over meetings.
- ★ Had no real executive authority.

**CIVIL COMMITTEES AND CIVIL OFFICERS**
- ★ Appointed by Congress to manage general affairs under the direction of Congress.

**CONGRESS**
- ★ One-house assembly of state representatives, in which each state possessed one vote.
- ★ Needed the approval of at least nine states to exercise most powers.
- ★ Needed the consent of all states to amend the Articles.

**COMMITTEE OF STATES**
- ★ Consisted of one delegate from each state, appointed by Congress.
- ★ Authorized to act according to the wishes of Congress while Congress was in recess.

© CENGAGE LEARNING

FIGURE 2-3

# Powers of the Central Government
## under the Articles of Confederation

Although the Articles of Confederation were later scrapped, they did allow the early government of the United States to achieve several important goals, including winning the Revolutionary War.

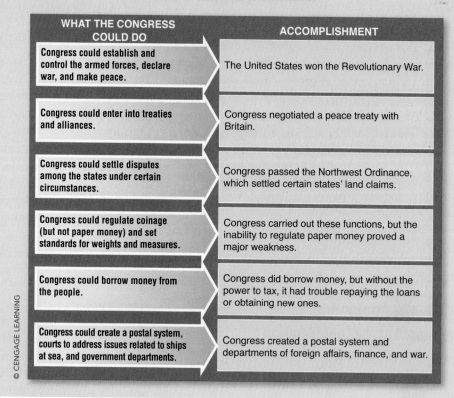

| WHAT THE CONGRESS COULD DO | ACCOMPLISHMENT |
| --- | --- |
| Congress could establish and control the armed forces, declare war, and make peace. | The United States won the Revolutionary War. |
| Congress could enter into treaties and alliances. | Congress negotiated a peace treaty with Britain. |
| Congress could settle disputes among the states under certain circumstances. | Congress passed the Northwest Ordinance, which settled certain states' land claims. |
| Congress could regulate coinage (but not paper money) and set standards for weights and measures. | Congress carried out these functions, but the inability to regulate paper money proved a major weakness. |
| Congress could borrow money from the people. | Congress did borrow money, but without the power to tax, it had trouble repaying the loans or obtaining new ones. |
| Congress could create a postal system, courts to address issues related to ships at sea, and government departments. | Congress created a postal system and departments of foreign affairs, finance, and war. |

© CENGAGE LEARNING

## 2–3b A Time of Crisis—The 1780s

The Revolutionary War ended on October 18, 1781. The Treaty of Paris, which confirmed the colonies' independence from Britain, was signed in 1783. Peace with the British may have been won, but peace within the new nation was hard to find. The states bickered among themselves and refused to support the new central government in almost every way. As George Washington stated, "We are one nation today and thirteen tomorrow. Who will treat [with] us on such terms?"

Indeed, the national government, such as it was, did not have the ability to prevent the various states from entering into agreements with foreign powers, despite the danger that such agreements could completely disrupt the confederation, pitting state against state. When Congress proved reluctant to admit Vermont into the Union, Britain began negotiations with influential Vermonters with the aim of annexing the district to Canada.

**Shays' Rebellion** A rebellion of angry farmers in western Massachusetts in 1786, led by former Revolutionary War captain Daniel Shays. This rebellion and other similar uprisings in the New England states emphasized the need for a true national government.

Likewise, the Spanish governor of Louisiana energetically sought to detach Tennessee and the lands south of it from the United States. Several prominent individuals—including Daniel Boone—accepted Spanish gold.

The states also increasingly taxed each other's imports and at times even prevented trade altogether. By 1784, the new nation was suffering from a serious economic depression. States started printing their own money at dizzying rates, which led to inflation. Banks were calling in old loans and refusing to issue new ones. Individuals who could not pay their debts were often thrown into prison.

**Shays' Rebellion**   The tempers of indebted farmers in western Massachusetts reached the boiling point in August 1786. Former Revolutionary War captain Daniel Shays, along with approximately two thousand armed farmers, seized county courthouses and disrupted the debtors' trials. Shays and his men then launched an attack on the national government's arsenal in Springfield. **Shays' Rebellion** continued to grow in intensity and lasted into the winter, when it was finally stopped by the Massachusetts volunteer army, which was paid by Boston merchants.[12]

FIGURE 2-4

# Lack of Central Government Powers
## under the Articles of Confederation

The government's lack of certain powers under the Articles of Confederation taught the framers of the Constitution several important lessons, which helped them create a more effective government under that new document.

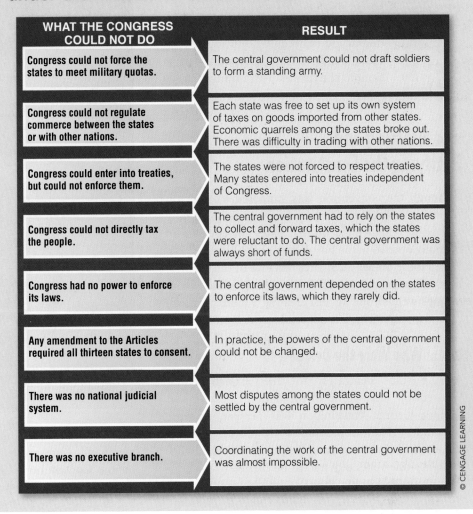

| WHAT THE CONGRESS COULD NOT DO | RESULT |
|---|---|
| Congress could not force the states to meet military quotas. | The central government could not draft soldiers to form a standing army. |
| Congress could not regulate commerce between the states or with other nations. | Each state was free to set up its own system of taxes on goods imported from other states. Economic quarrels among the states broke out. There was difficulty in trading with other nations. |
| Congress could enter into treaties, but could not enforce them. | The states were not forced to respect treaties. Many states entered into treaties independent of Congress. |
| Congress could not directly tax the people. | The central government had to rely on the states to collect and forward taxes, which the states were reluctant to do. The central government was always short of funds. |
| Congress had no power to enforce its laws. | The central government depended on the states to enforce its laws, which they rarely did. |
| Any amendment to the Articles required all thirteen states to consent. | In practice, the powers of the central government could not be changed. |
| There was no national judicial system. | Most disputes among the states could not be settled by the central government. |
| There was no executive branch. | Coordinating the work of the central government was almost impossible. |

© CENGAGE LEARNING

Similar disruptions occurred throughout most of the New England states and in some other areas as well. The upheavals, and particularly Shays' Rebellion, were an important catalyst for change. The revolts frightened American political and business leaders and caused more and more Americans to realize that a *true* national government had to be created.

**The Annapolis Meeting** The Virginia legislature called for a meeting of representatives from all of the states at Annapolis, Maryland, on September 11, 1786, to consider extending national authority to issues of commerce. Five of the thirteen states sent delegates, two of whom were Alexander Hamilton of New York and James Madison of Virginia. Both of these men favored a strong central government.[13] They persuaded the other delegates to issue a report calling on the states to hold a convention in Philadelphia in May of the following year.

The Congress of the Confederation at first was reluctant to give its approval to the Philadelphia convention. By mid-February 1787, however, seven of the states had named delegates to the Philadelphia meeting. Finally, on February 21, the Congress called on the states to send delegates to Philadelphia "for the sole and express purpose of revising the Articles of Confederation." That Philadelphia meeting became the **Constitutional Convention.**

**Constitutional Convention** The convention (meeting) of delegates from the states that was held in Philadelphia in 1787 for the purpose of amending the Articles of Confederation. In fact, the delegates wrote a new constitution (the U.S. Constitution) that established a federal form of government to replace the governmental system that had been created by the Articles of Confederation.

*Given that all Americans would have benefited from an army capable of keeping the peace and defending the country, why would the states have been so reluctant to fund the national government?*

## 2–4 Drafting and Ratifying the Constitution

Although the convention was supposed to start on May 14, 1787, few of the delegates had actually arrived in Philadelphia on that date. The convention formally opened in the East Room of the Pennsylvania State House on May 25, after fifty-five of the seventy-four delegates had arrived.[14] Only Rhode Island, where feelings were strong against creating a more powerful central government, did not send any delegates.

### 2–4a Who Were the Delegates?

Among the delegates to the Constitutional Convention were some of the nation's best-known leaders. George Washington was present, as were Alexander Hamilton, James Madison, George Mason, Robert Morris, and Benjamin Franklin (who, at eighty-one years old, had to be carried to the convention on a portable chair).

Some notable leaders were absent, including Thomas Jefferson and John Adams, who were serving as ambassadors in Europe, and Patrick Henry, who did not attend because he "smelt a rat." (Henry was one of Virginia's most strongly republican leaders.)

For the most part, the delegates were from the best-educated and wealthiest classes. Thirty-three delegates were lawyers, nearly half of the delegates were college graduates, three were physicians, seven were former chief executives of their respective states, six owned large plantations, at least nineteen owned slaves, eight were important business owners, and twenty-one had fought in the Revolutionary War.

In other words, the delegates to the convention con-

### Learning Outcome 2–4

List some of the major compromises made by the delegates at the Constitutional Convention, and discuss the Federalist and Anti-Federalist positions on ratifying the Constitution.

Alexander Hamilton was among the key delegates at the Constitutional Convention that convened on May 25, 1787.

stituted an elite assembly. No ordinary farmers or merchants were present. Indeed, in his classic work on the Constitution, Charles Beard maintained that the Constitution was produced primarily by wealthy bondholders who had made loans to the government under the Articles and wanted a strong central government that could prevent state governments from repudiating debts.[15] Later historians, however, rejected Beard's thesis, concluding that bondholders played no special role in writing the Constitution.

### 2–4b The Virginia Plan

James Madison had spent months reviewing European political theory before he went to the Philadelphia convention. His Virginia delegation arrived before anybody else, and he immediately put its members to work. On the first day of the convention, Governor Edmund Randolph of Virginia was able to present fifteen resolutions outlining what was to become known as the *Virginia Plan.* This was a masterful political stroke on the part of the Virginia delegation. Its proposals immediately set the agenda for the remainder of the convention.

The fifteen resolutions contained in the Virginia Plan proposed an entirely new national government under a constitution. The plan, which favored large states such as Virginia, called for the following:

- A **bicameral** (two-chamber) **legislature.** The lower chamber was to be chosen by the people. The smaller, upper chamber was to be chosen by the elected members of the lower chamber. The number of representatives would be in proportion to each state's population (the larger states would have more representatives). The legislature could void any state laws.

- A national executive branch, elected by the legislature.

- A national court system, created by the legislature.

The smaller states immediately complained because they would have fewer representatives in the legislature. After two weeks of debate, they offered their own plan—the *New Jersey Plan.*

## 2–4c The New Jersey Plan

William Paterson of New Jersey presented an alternative plan favorable to the smaller states. He argued that because each state had an equal vote under the Articles of Confederation, the convention had no power to change this arrangement. The New Jersey Plan proposed the following:

- Congress would be able to regulate trade and impose taxes.

- Each state would have only one vote.

- Acts of Congress would be the supreme law of the land.

- An executive office of more than one person would be elected by Congress.

- The executive office would appoint a national supreme court.

## 2–4d The Compromises

Most delegates were unwilling to consider the New Jersey Plan. When the Virginia Plan was brought up again, however, delegates from the smaller states threatened to leave, and the convention was in danger of dissolving. On July 16, Roger Sherman of Connecticut broke the deadlock by proposing a compromise plan. Compromises on other disputed issues followed.

**The Great Compromise** Roger Sherman's plan, which has become known as the **Great Compromise** (or the Connecticut Compromise), called for a legislature with two chambers:

- A lower chamber (the House of Representatives), in which the number of representatives from each

> "The Constitution only gives people the right to **PURSUE HAPPINESS.** You have to catch it yourself."
>
> ANONYMOUS—ATTRIBUTED TO
> ~ BENJAMIN FRANKLIN ~
> AMERICAN STATESMAN
> 1706–1790

state would be determined by the number of people in that state.

- An upper chamber (the Senate), which would have two members from each state. The members would be elected by the state legislatures.

The Great Compromise gave something to both sides: the large states would have more representatives in the House of Representatives than the small states, yet each state would be granted equality in the Senate—because each state, regardless of size, would have two senators. The Great Compromise thus resolved the small-state/large-state controversy.

**The Three-Fifths Compromise** A second compromise had to do with how many representatives each state would have in the House of Representatives. Although slavery was legal in parts of the North, most slaves and slave owners lived in the South. Indeed, in the southern states, slaves constituted about 40 percent of the population. Counting the slaves as part of the population would thus greatly increase the number of southern representatives in the House. The delegates from the southern states wanted the slaves to be counted as persons, but the delegates from the northern states disagreed.

Eventually, the **three-fifths compromise** settled

**bicameral legislature** A legislature made up of two chambers, or parts. The United States has a bicameral legislature composed of the House of Representatives and the Senate.

**Great Compromise** A plan for a bicameral legislature in which one chamber would be based on population and the other chamber would represent each state equally. The plan, also known as the Connecticut Compromise, resolved the small-state/large-state controversy.

**three-fifths compromise** A compromise reached during the Constitutional Convention by which three-fifths of all slaves were to be counted for purposes of representation in the House of Representatives.

The delegates to the Constitutional Convention discuss the fine points of the new Constitution in 1787.

this deadlock: each slave would count as three-fifths of a person in determining representation in Congress. (The three-fifths compromise was eventually overturned in 1868 by the Fourteenth Amendment.)

**Slave Importation** The three-fifths compromise did not satisfy everyone at the Constitutional Convention. Many delegates wanted slavery to be banned completely in the United States. The delegates compromised on this question by agreeing that Congress could prohibit the importation of slaves into the country beginning in 1808. The issue of slavery itself, however, was never really addressed by the delegates to the Constitutional Convention. As a result, the South won twenty years of unrestricted slave trade and a requirement that escaped slaves who had fled to the northern states be returned to their owners. Domestic slave trading was untouched.

**Banning Export Taxes** The South's economic health depended in large part on its exports of agricultural products. The South feared that the northern majority in Congress might pass taxes on these exports. This fear led to yet another compromise: the South agreed to let Congress have the power to regulate **interstate commerce** as well as commerce with other nations. In exchange, the Constitution guaranteed that no export taxes would be imposed on products exported by the states. Today, the United States is one of the few countries that does not tax its exports.

## 2–4e Defining the Executive and the Judiciary

The Great Compromise was reached by mid-July. Still to be determined was the makeup of the executive branch and the judiciary. One of the weaknesses of the Confederation had been the lack of an independent executive authority. The Constitution remedied this problem by creating an independent executive—the president—and by making the president the commander in chief of the army and navy and of the state militias when called into national service. The president was also given extensive appointment powers, although Senate approval was required for major appointments.

Another problem under the Confederation was the lack of a judiciary that was independent of the

**interstate commerce**
Trade that involves more than one state.

state courts. The Constitution established the United States Supreme Court and authorized Congress to establish other "inferior" federal courts.

To protect against possible wrongdoing, the Constitution also provided a way to remove federal officials from office—through the impeachment process. The Constitution provides that a federal official who commits "Treason, Bribery, or other high Crimes and Misdemeanors" may be *impeached* (accused of, or charged with, wrongdoing) by the House of Representatives and tried by the Senate. If found guilty of the charges by a two-thirds vote in the Senate, the official can be removed from office and prevented from ever assuming another federal government post.

## 2–4f The Final Draft Is Approved

A five-man Committee of Detail handled the executive and judicial issues, plus other remaining work. In August, it presented a rough draft to the convention. In September, a committee was named to "revise the stile [style] of, and arrange the Articles which had been agreed to" by the convention. The Committee of Style was headed by Gouverneur Morris of Pennsylvania.[16] On September 17, 1787, the final draft of the Constitution was approved by thirty-nine of the remaining forty-two delegates (some delegates had left early).

As we look back on the drafting of the Constitution, an obvious question emerges: Why didn't the founders ban slavery outright? Certainly, as already mentioned, many of the delegates thought that slavery was morally wrong and that the Constitution should ban it entirely. Many Americans have since regarded the framers' failure to deal with the slavery issue as a betrayal of the Declaration of Independence, which proclaimed that "all Men are created equal." Others have pointed out how contradictory it was that the framers of the Constitution complained about being "enslaved" by the British yet ignored the problem of slavery in this country.

A common argument supporting the framers' action (or lack of it) with respect to slavery is that they had no alternative but to ignore the issue. If they had taken a stand on slavery, the Constitution certainly would not have been ratified. Indeed, if the anti-slavery delegates had insisted on banning slavery, the delegates from the southern states might have walked out of the convention—and there would have been no Constitution to ratify. For another look at this issue, however, see this chapter's *Perception versus Reality* feature on the following page.

## 2–4g The Debate over Ratification

The ratification of the Constitution set off a national debate of unprecedented proportions. The battle was fought chiefly by two opposing groups—the **Federalists** (those who favored a strong central government and the new Constitution) and the **Anti-Federalists** (those who opposed a strong central government and the new Constitution).

In the debate over ratification, the Federalists had several advantages. They assumed a positive name, leaving their opposition with a negative label. (Instead, the Anti-Federalists could well have called themselves republicans and their opponents nationalists.) The Federalists also had attended the Constitutional Convention and thus were familiar with the arguments both in favor of and against various constitutional provisions.

The Anti-Federalists, in contrast, had no actual knowledge of those discussions because they had not attended the convention. The Federalists also had time, funding, and prestige on their side. Their impressive list of political thinkers and writers included Alexander Hamilton, John Jay, and James Madison. The Federalists could communicate with one another more readily because many of them were bankers, lawyers, and merchants who lived in urban areas, where communication was easier. Accordingly, the Federalists organized a quick and effective ratification campaign to elect themselves as delegates to each state's ratifying convention.

### The Federalists Argue for Ratification

Alexander Hamilton, a leading Federalist, began to answer the Constitution's critics in New York by writing newspaper columns under the pseudonym "Caesar." The Caesar letters appeared to have little effect, so Hamilton switched his pseudonym to "Publius" and enlisted John Jay and James Madison to help him write the papers. In a period of less than a year, these three men wrote a series of eighty-five essays in defense of the Constitution. These essays, which were printed not only in New York newspapers but also in other papers throughout

**Federalists** A political group, led by Alexander Hamilton and John Adams, that supported the adoption of the Constitution and the creation of a federal form of government.

**Anti-Federalists** A political group that opposed the adoption of the Constitution because of the document's centralist tendencies and because it did not include a bill of rights.

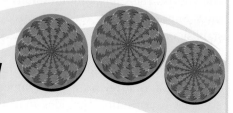

# Perception versus Reality
## The Slavery Issue

In the Declaration of Independence, Thomas Jefferson, a Virginia slave owner, pronounced that "all Men are created equal." Jefferson considered slavery a "hideous blot" on America. George Washington, also a southern slave owner, regarded the institution of slavery as "repugnant." Patrick Henry, another southerner, also publicly deplored slavery. Given such views among the leading figures of the era, why didn't the founders stay true to the Declaration of Independence and free the slaves?

### THE PERCEPTION

Most Americans assume that southern economic interests and racism alone led the founders to abandon the principles of equality expressed in the Declaration of Independence. African slaves were the backbone of American agriculture, particularly for tobacco, the most profitable export. Without their slaves, southern plantation owners would not have been able to earn such high profits. Presumably, southerners would not have ratified the Constitution unless it protected the institution of slavery.

### THE REALITY

The third chief justice of the United States Supreme Court, Oliver Ellsworth, declared that "as population increases, poor laborers will be so plenty as to render slaves useless. Slavery in time will not be a speck in our country."[17] He was wrong, of course. But according to historian Gordon S. Wood, Ellsworth's sentiments mirrored those of most prominent leaders in the United States in the years leading up to the creation of our Constitution. Indeed, great thinkers of the time firmly believed that the liberal principles of the Revolution would destroy the institution of slavery.

At the time of the Constitutional Convention, slavery was disappearing in the northern states (it would be eliminated there by 1804). Many founders thought the same thing would happen in the southern states. After all, there were more antislavery societies in the South than in the North. The founders also thought that the ending of the international slave trade in 1808 would eventually end slavery in the United States. Consequently, the issue of slavery was taken off the table when the Constitution was created simply because the founders had a mistaken belief about the longevity of the institution. They could not have predicted at the time that growing cotton would give slavery a new lease on life.[18]

**BLOG ON** Slavery and the Constitution is just one of many subjects that you can read about in the Legal History Blog, which you can find by entering "legal history blog" into a search engine. If you enter "slavery" into the box at the top left of the screen, you will see the postings on this topic.

the states, are known collectively as the *Federalist Papers.*

Generally, the papers attempted to allay the fears expressed by the Constitution's critics. One fear was that the rights of those in the minority would not be protected. Many critics also feared that a republican form of government would not work in a nation the size of the United States. Various groups, or **factions,** would struggle for power, and

**faction** A group of persons forming a cohesive minority.

chaos would result. Madison responded to the latter argument in *Federalist Paper* No. 10 (see Appendix F), which is considered a classic in political theory. Among other things, Madison argued that the nation's size was actually an advantage in controlling factions: in a large nation, there would be so many diverse interests and factions that no one faction would be able to gain control of the government.[19]

**The Anti-Federalists' Response** Perhaps the greatest advantage of the Anti-Federalists was that they stood for the status quo. Usually, it is more difficult to institute changes than it is to keep what is already known and understood. Among the Anti-Federalists were such patriots as Patrick Henry and Samuel Adams. Patrick Henry said of the proposed Constitution, "I look upon that paper as the most fatal plan that could possibly be conceived to enslave a free people."

In response to the *Federalist Papers,* the Anti-Federalists published their own essays, using such pseudonyms as "Montezuma" and "Philadelphiensis." They also wrote brilliantly, attacking nearly every clause of the new document. Many Anti-Federalists contended that the Constitution had been written by aristocrats and would lead the nation to aristocratic **tyranny** (the exercise of absolute, unlimited power). Other Anti-Federalists feared that the Constitution would lead to an overly powerful central government that would limit personal freedom.[20]

The Anti-Federalists argued vigorously that the Constitution needed a bill of rights. They warned that without a bill of rights, a strong national government might take away the political rights won during the American Revolution. They demanded that the new Constitution clearly guarantee personal freedoms. The Federalists generally did not think that a bill of rights was all that important. Nevertheless, to gain the necessary support, the Federalists finally promised to add a bill of rights to the Constitution as the first order of business under the new government. This promise turned the tide in favor of the Constitution.

## 2–4h Ratification

The contest for ratification was close in several states, but the Federalists finally won in all of the state conventions. In 1787, Delaware, Pennsylvania, and New Jersey voted to ratify the Constitution, followed by Georgia and Connecticut early in the following year. Even though the Anti-Federalists were perhaps the majority in Massachusetts, a successful political campaign by the Federalists led to ratification by that state on February 6, 1788.

Following Maryland and South Carolina, New Hampshire became the ninth state to ratify the Constitution on June 21,

**tyranny** The arbitrary or unrestrained exercise of power by an oppressive individual or government.

> ## "The liberties of a people
> never were nor ever will be secure when the transactions of their rulers may be concealed from them."
>
> ~ PATRICK HENRY ~
> AMERICAN STATESMAN AND ANTI-FEDERALIST
> 1736–1799

1788, thus formally putting the Constitution into effect. New York and Virginia had not yet ratified, however, and without them the Constitution would have no true power. That worry was dispelled in the summer of 1788, when both Virginia and New York ratified the new Constitution. North Carolina waited until November 21 of the following year to ratify the Constitution, and Rhode Island did not ratify until May 29, 1790.

## FOR CRITICAL THINKING

Suppose that Rhode Island had refused to ratify the Constitution and join the Union. *Would American history have been seriously altered by such an event?*

# 2–5 The Constitution's Major Principles of Government

The framers of the Constitution were fearful of the powerful British monarchy, against which they had so recently rebelled. At the same time, they wanted a central government strong enough to prevent the kinds of crises that had occurred under the weak central authority of the Articles of Confederation. The principles of government expressed in the Constitution reflect both of these concerns.

## 2–5a Limited Government and Popular Sovereignty

The Constitution incorporated the principle of limited government, which means that government can do only what the people allow it to do through the

**Learning Outcome 2–5**

Summarize the Constitution's major principles of government, and describe how the Constitution can be amended.

exercise of a duly developed system of laws. This principle can be found in many parts of the Constitution. For example, while Articles I, II, and III indicate exactly what the national government *can* do, the first nine amendments to the Constitution list the ways in which the government *cannot* limit certain individual freedoms.

## Popular Sovereignty

Implicitly, the principle of limited government rests on the concept of popular sovereignty. Remember the phrases that frame the Preamble to the Constitution: "We the People of the United States . . . do ordain and establish this Constitution for the United States of America." In other words, it is the people who form the government and decide on the powers that the government can exercise. If the government exercises powers beyond those granted to it by the Constitution, it is acting illegally.

## The Rule of Law

The idea that no one, including government officers, is above the law is often called the **rule of law.** Ultimately, the viability of a democracy rests on the willingness of the people and their leaders to adhere to the rule of law. A nation's written constitution may guarantee numerous rights and liberties for its citizens. Yet, unless the government of that nation enforces those rights and liberties, the law does not rule the nation. Rather, the government decides what the rules will be.

**rule of law** A basic principle of government that requires those who govern to act in accordance with established law.

**federal system** A form of government that provides for a division of powers between a central government and several regional governments. In the United States, the division of powers between the national government and the states is established by the Constitution.

**commerce clause** The clause in Article I, Section 8, of the Constitution that gives Congress the power to regulate interstate commerce (commerce involving more than one state).

"The truth is that all men having power **ought to be mistrusted.**"

~ JAMES MADISON ~
FOURTH PRESIDENT
OF THE UNITED STATES
1809–1817

## 2–5b The Principle of Federalism

The Constitution also incorporated the principle of *federalism,* or a **federal system** of government in which the central (national) government shares sovereign powers with the various state governments. Federalism was the solution to the debate over whether the national government or the states should have ultimate sovereignty.

## National Powers

The Constitution gave the national government significant powers—powers that it had not had under the Articles of Confederation. For example, the Constitution expressly states that the president is the nation's chief executive as well as the commander in chief of the armed forces. The Constitution also declares that the Constitution and the laws created by the national government are supreme—that is, they take precedence over conflicting state laws. Other powers given to the national government include the power to coin money, to levy and collect taxes, and to regulate interstate commerce, a power granted by the **commerce clause.** Finally, the national government was authorized to undertake all laws that are "necessary and proper" for carrying out its expressly delegated powers.

One of the main reasons for convening the Constitutional Convention was interference with interstate commerce by various states—hence, the commerce clause. Indeed, granting the national government power over interstate commerce was the official justification for summoning the convention in the first place. The scope of federal authority under the commerce clause, however, has been the subject of an important constitutional dispute ever since. This controversy is a major topic discussed in Chapter 3. For a modern-day dispute over the commerce clause, see this chapter's *Join the Debate* feature on the facing page.

## State Powers

Because the states feared too much centralized control, the Constitution also allowed for many states' rights. These rights include the power to

James Madison (1751–1836). Madison's contributions at the Constitutional Convention in 1787 earned him the title "Master Builder of the Constitution." As a member of Congress from Virginia, he advocated the Bill of Rights. He was secretary of state under Thomas Jefferson (1801–1809) and became our fourth president in 1809.

© LIBRARY OF CONGRESS

## Was the Supreme Court Right in Upholding Obamacare?

In June 2012, the United States Supreme Court upheld most of the Affordable Care Act, the health-care reform legislation nicknamed Obamacare.

President Barack Obama signed the act into law in 2010. Immediately, twenty state attorneys general joined together to sue the federal government. The basis of the suit was that the *individual mandate* in the new law was unconstitutional. Beginning in 2014, the mandate requires individuals who do not obtain some form of health-care insurance to pay a penalty as part of their federal income taxes.

The Obama administration argued that the penalty imposed by the individual mandate was not really a tax. Ironically, Supreme Court Chief Justice John G. Roberts, Jr., ruled that while the penalty could not be defended under the Constitution's commerce clause, it was still constitutional precisely because it was a tax.

### The Supreme Court Wandered into Troubled Waters

Justice Anthony M. Kennedy, usually the tiebreaker in Supreme Court votes, joined three conservative members of the Court and wrote a stinging dissent from Chief Justice Roberts's decision. Kennedy argued that the entire act should have been ruled unconstitutional and that the Supreme Court majority was engaged in "vast judicial overreaching." While it is true that state governments have the right to require, for example, drivers to buy automobile insurance to travel on public roads, nothing in the Constitution gives the federal government the right to impose similar requirements.

The commerce clause of the Constitution cannot be used to require citizens to buy any service or good, and that includes health-care insurance. Roberts himself agreed with that, although the four liberals on the Court did not. But if it is unconstitutional for the government to do something, *any* method of accomplishing the unconstitutional goal is also unconstitutional, including taxes. By refusing to accept that point, Roberts's decision was completely muddled.

### Let's Move On— Health-Care Reform Is Alive and Well

The Supreme Court did the right thing, according to defenders of the Affordable Care Act. States' rights arguments are nonsense. The supremacy of national law was confirmed in 1819 in the Supreme Court case *McCulloch v. Maryland,* and the reach of the commerce clause was settled in 1824 in *Gibbons v. Ogden.* It is the four liberals on the Court who interpreted the commerce clause in accordance with these precedents.

As for the issue at hand, the very nature of insurance is that it spreads the costs of disastrous events widely enough so that no one is ruined by the disaster. For this to work, everyone must pay premiums. Otherwise, people could wait until they were already sick to buy insurance. If people did that, no insurance company could possibly have enough money to pay its claims.

The penalty on those who do not buy insurance is indeed a tax, as Chief Justice Roberts ruled. The federal courts have always held that Congress can place incentives in the tax code. You pay more in income taxes if you don't get married, if you don't have children, or if you don't buy a house with a mortgage. How is the individual mandate any different from these incentives?

**FOR CRITICAL ANALYSIS** Apparently, Chief Justice Roberts changed his mind on this case very late in the game. What might have influenced the chief justice's opinion?

regulate commerce within state borders and generally the authority to exercise any powers that are not delegated by the Constitution to the central government.

## 2–5c Separation of Powers

As James Madison once said, after you have given the government the ability to control its citizens, you have to "oblige it to control itself." To force the government to "control itself" and to prevent the rise of tyranny, Madison devised a scheme, the **Madisonian Model,** in which the

**Madisonian Model**
The model of government devised by James Madison, in which the powers of the government are separated into three branches: legislative, executive, and judicial.

powers of the national government were separated into different branches: legislative, executive, and judicial.[21] The legislative branch (Congress) passes laws, the executive branch (the president) administers and enforces the laws, and the judicial branch (the courts) interprets the laws. By separating the powers of government, the framers ensured that no one branch would have enough power to dominate the others. This principle of **separation of powers** is laid out in Articles I, II, and III of the Constitution.

## 2–5d Checks and Balances

A system of **checks and balances** was also devised to ensure that no one group or branch of government can exercise exclusive control. Even though each branch of government is independent of the others, it can also check the actions of the others. Look at Figure 2–5 on the facing page, and you can see how this is done. As the figure shows, the president checks Congress by holding a **veto power,** which is the ability to return bills to Congress for reconsideration. Congress, in turn, controls taxes and spending, and the Senate must approve presidential appointments. The judicial branch of government can also check the other branches of government through *judicial review*—the power to rule congressional or presidential actions unconstitutional.[22] In turn, the president and the Senate exercise some control over the judiciary through the president's power to appoint federal judges and the Senate's role in confirming presidential appointments.

### Controlling Federal Office Holders

Among the other checks and balances built into the American system of

**separation of powers**
The principle of dividing governmental powers among the legislative, the executive, and the judicial branches of government.

**checks and balances** A major principle of American government in which each of the three branches is given the means to check (to restrain or balance) the actions of the others.

**veto power** A constitutional power that enables the chief executive (president or governor) to reject legislation and return it to the legislature with reasons for the rejection. This prevents or at least delays the bill from becoming law.

government are staggered terms of office. Members of the House of Representatives serve for two years, members of the Senate for six, and the president for four. Federal court judges are appointed for life but may be impeached and removed from office by Congress for misconduct. Staggered terms and changing government personnel make it difficult for individuals within the government to form controlling factions. The American system of government also includes numerous other checks and balances, many of which you will read about in later chapters of this book.

## 2–5e Limited versus Effective Government

Such American constitutional principles as the separation of powers and a system of checks and balances are not universal among representative democracies. Compared with the United States, many countries place less emphasis on limited government and a higher value on "effective government." The *parliamentary system* is a constitutional form that reflects such values, and we describe it in this chapter's *The Rest of the World* feature on page 44.

## 2–5f The Bill of Rights

To secure the ratification of the Constitution in several important states, the Federalists had to provide assurances that amendments would be passed to protect individual liberties against violations by the national government. At the state ratifying conventions, delegates set forth specific rights that should be protected. James Madison considered these recommendations as he labored to draft what became the Bill of Rights.

After sorting through more than two hundred state recommendations, Madison came up with sixteen amendments. Congress tightened the language somewhat and eliminated four of the amendments. Of the remaining twelve, two—one dealing with the apportionment of representatives and the other with the compensation of the members of Congress—were not ratified by the states during the ratification process.[23] By 1791, all of the states had ratified the ten amendments that now constitute our Bill of Rights. We discuss the Bill of Rights in depth in Chapter 4.

## 2–5g Amending the Constitution

Since the Constitution was written, more than eleven thousand amendments have been introduced in Congress. Nonetheless, in the years since the ratification of the Bill of Rights, the first ten amendments

FIGURE 2-5

# Checks and Balances
## among the Branches of Government

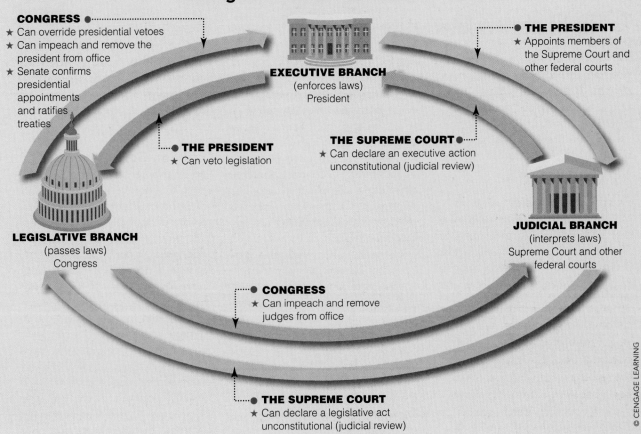

**CONGRESS** ●
★ Can override presidential vetoes
★ Can impeach and remove the president from office
★ Senate confirms presidential appointments and ratifies treaties

**EXECUTIVE BRANCH**
(enforces laws)
President

● **THE PRESIDENT**
★ Appoints members of the Supreme Court and other federal courts

● **THE PRESIDENT**
★ Can veto legislation

**THE SUPREME COURT** ●
★ Can declare an executive action unconstitutional (judicial review)

**LEGISLATIVE BRANCH**
(passes laws)
Congress

**JUDICIAL BRANCH**
(interprets laws)
Supreme Court and other federal courts

● **CONGRESS**
★ Can impeach and remove judges from office

● **THE SUPREME COURT**
★ Can declare a legislative act unconstitutional (judicial review)

© CENGAGE LEARNING

to the Constitution, only seventeen proposed amendments have actually survived the amendment process and become a part of our Constitution. It is often contended that members of Congress use the amendment process simply as a political ploy. By introducing an amendment, a member of Congress can show her or his position on an issue, knowing that the odds *against* the amendment's being adopted are high.

One of the reasons there are so few amendments is that the framers, in Article V, made the formal amendment process difficult (although it was easier than it had been under the Articles of Confederation). There are two ways to propose an amendment and two ways to ratify one. As a result, there are four possible ways for an amendment to be added to the Constitution.

## Methods of Proposing an Amendment
The two methods of proposing an amendment are as follows:

1. A two-thirds vote in the Senate and in the House of Representatives is required. All of the twenty-seven existing amendments have been proposed in this way.
2. If two-thirds of the state legislatures request that Congress call a national amendment convention, then Congress must call one. The convention may propose amendments to the states for ratification. There has yet to be a successful amendment proposal using this method.

The notion of a national amendment convention is exciting to many people. Many national political and judicial leaders, however, are uneasy about the prospect of convening a body that conceivably could do what the Constitutional Convention did—create a new form of government.

In two separate instances, the call for a national amendment convention almost became reality.

## THE REST OF THE WORLD

# The Parliamentary Alternative

An alternative to our form of government is the *parliamentary system*. Britain—the United Kingdom—has a typical parliamentary system. In contrast to the American system, the British one is based on the *fusion* of powers rather than the *separation* of powers.

### First, a Few Basics

Members of Parliament (MPs) are elected just as we elect members of Congress. Here the similarity ends. British voters do not directly choose a chief executive, as we do when we vote for president. Rather, the chief executive is chosen by the lower house of Parliament—the House of Commons, analogous to our House of Representatives. (There is an upper house, the House of Lords, but it has little power.)

Each political party selects a leader well before the general elections. The leader then chooses other MPs who, if the party wins, will take cabinet posts, such as minister of defense or minister of justice. If one party wins a majority of the seats in the House of Commons, it can name its leader as the *prime minister*—the chief executive of the nation.

### The Fusion of Powers

MPs who join the cabinet keep their seats in Parliament. The prime minister is both the chief executive of the nation and the leader of his or her party in the legislature. The legislature and the executive are fused, not separated. In contrast, the U.S. Constitution explicitly requires members of Congress who join the president's administration to resign from Congress.

Americans often view the parliamentary system as undemocratic because voters cannot choose the chief executive. Citizens of parliamentary countries do not see the system in quite that way, however. Voters know who the party leaders are in advance of the elections. When they vote, they are choosing a party and its leader. The identity of their own local MP usually has little impact on how they cast their ballot.

What the parliamentary system really does is prevent voters from choosing a chief executive from one party and a legislative representative from another. In America after the 2010 elections, for example, Democratic president

Barack Obama faced a House of Representatives controlled by the Republicans. That kind of divided government is impossible under the parliamentary system.

### Coalition Governments

The parliamentary system does foster a different kind of divided government. It encourages the formation of multiple major parties, thus providing voters with more options than is common in America. But what if no party wins a majority in the lower house of Parliament? Two options are possible. The largest party can form a *minority government* with the acquiescence of other parties. Alternatively, two, three, or more parties can agree to form a *coalition government*.

Many countries that use the parliamentary system are normally governed by coalitions, but until 2010 Britain had not had one for decades. Following the elections in that year, the Conservative Party formed a coalition with the Liberal Democratic Party.

 **FOR CRITICAL ANALYSIS** Why is it so hard to form effective third parties in the United States?

---

Between 1963 and 1969, thirty-three state legislatures (out of the necessary thirty-four) attempted to call a convention to amend the Constitution to overturn the Supreme Court's "one person, one vote" decisions (see Chapter 11). Since 1975, thirty-two states have asked for a national convention to propose an amendment requiring that the federal government balance its budget. Generally, the major national convention campaigns have reflected dissatisfaction on the part of conservative and rural groups

with the national government's social and economic policies.

**Methods of Ratifying an Amendment**   There are two methods of ratifying a proposed amendment:

1. Three-fourths of the state legislatures can vote in favor of the proposed amendment. This method is considered the "traditional" ratification method and has been used twenty-six times.

2. The states can call special conventions to ratify the proposed amendment. If three-fourths of the states approve, the amendment is ratified. This method has been used only once—to ratify the Twenty-first Amendment.[24]

You can see the four methods for proposing and ratifying amendments in Figure 2–6 below. As you can imagine, to meet the requirements for proposal and ratification, any amendment must have wide popular support throughout the country.

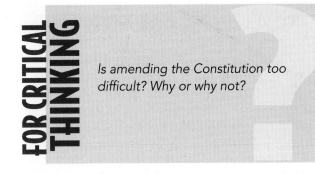

**FOR CRITICAL THINKING**

*Is amending the Constitution too difficult? Why or why not?*

**FIGURE 2-6**

# The Process of Amending the Constitution

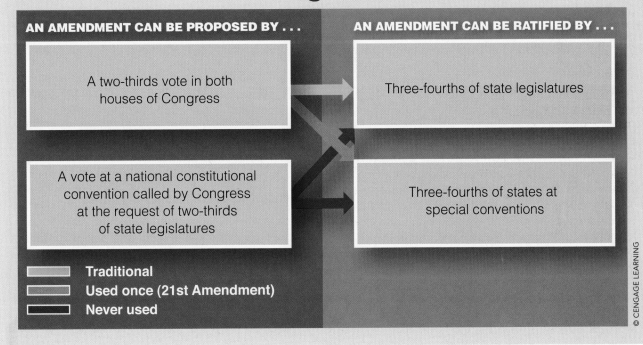

**AN AMENDMENT CAN BE PROPOSED BY . . .**

A two-thirds vote in both houses of Congress

A vote at a national constitutional convention called by Congress at the request of two-thirds of state legislatures

**AN AMENDMENT CAN BE RATIFIED BY . . .**

Three-fourths of state legislatures

Three-fourths of states at special conventions

◼ Traditional
◼ Used once (21st Amendment)
◼ Never used

© CENGAGE LEARNING

# AMERICA AT
# ODDS The Constitution

Americans engaged in intense disputes about the ratification of the Constitution, as you have learned in this chapter. The most important of these disputes was over the relative power of the states and the national government. This dispute is central to the topic of federalism, which we will take up in Chapter 3. Proposed constitutional amendments have also been the source of many controversies throughout U.S. history. These controversies include the following:

- The Equal Rights Amendment of 1972 stated, "Equality of rights under the law shall not be denied or abridged by the United States or by any state on account of sex." The amendment failed to win approval from enough states. Should it be revived—or are equal rights for women unacceptable because women could not then be exempted from a military draft?

- Members of the Tea Party movement have advocated the repeal of the Seventeenth Amendment, which transferred the election of U.S. senators from state legislatures to the people of the respective states. The argument is that giving the choice of senators back to state legislatures would strengthen the relative power of the states. Is this a good argument—or is popular election of senators the superior system?

- Conservatives have campaigned for a constitutional amendment to ban same-sex marriage. Would such a measure be desirable—or repugnant as the first attempt to write a limit on freedoms into the Constitution?

- What about an amendment to ban the destruction of the American flag as an act of protest? Is such a ban important to the dignity of our fallen soldiers—or would it be an unacceptable limit on free speech?

# TAKE ACTION

The founders envisioned that the Constitution, to remain relevant, would need to be changed over time. You can take action over the Constitution by supporting a proposed constitutional amendment. Currently, two organized efforts seek constitutional amendments—the Tea Party movement and a campaign to limit corporate campaign contributions.

## Tea Party Amendments

Members of the Tea Party movement could be described as obsessed with the Constitution. Some carry copies of the document with them at all times. Perhaps the best summary of Tea Party ideas is expressed in the "Contract *from* America," which you can find by entering "contract from america" into a search engine. The contract endorses "individual liberty, limited government, and economic freedom." The document also calls for amending the Constitution to require a balanced budget and impose a two-thirds-majority requirement for tax increases. If these ideas appeal to you, the Tea Party Patriots Web site provides a long list of local groups (search on "tea party patriots").

## Amendments to Curb Money in Politics

If you are more concerned about the dangers of big business than big government, several groups support a constitutional amendment to overturn the Supreme Court's 2010 decision *Citizens United v. the Federal Election Commission*. In this ruling, the Court found that corporations (and presumably labor unions) have the same free speech rights as individual persons. The Court therefore overturned decades of legislation governing campaign finance. Many progressives fear that the result will be a tsunami of political corporate cash. Public-interest groups opposed to the ruling have organized Free Speech for People (search on "free speech for people"). Other active groups are Move to Amend (search on "move to amend") and People for the American Way (search on "pfaw take action").

# STUDY TOOLS

## Ready to study?

- Review what you've read with the quiz below. Check your answers on the Chapter in Review card at the back of the book. For any questions you miss, read the corresponding Learning Outcome section again to prepare for class and your exam.
- Rip out and study the Chapter in Review card.

## . . . Or you can go online to CourseMate

at www.cengagebrain.com for these additional review materials:

- Practice Quizzes
- Key Term Flashcards or Crossword Puzzles
- Audio Summaries
- Simulations, Animated Learning Modules, and Interactive Timelines
- Videos
- American Government NewsWatch

## Fill-In

1. Even before the Pilgrims went ashore, they drew up the _____, in which they set up a government and promised to obey its laws.

2. After the Seven Years' War, the British government decided to obtain revenues to pay its war debts and to finance the defense of its North American empire by _____.

3. The British Parliament imposed several taxes on the colonists, including the _____.

4. The Articles of Confederation established the _____ as the central governing body.

5. _____, a rebellion of angry farmers in western Massachusetts in 1786, along with similar uprisings throughout most of the New England states, emphasized the need for a true national government.

6. At the Constitutional Convention in 1787, the delegates forged the Great Compromise, which established a bicameral legislature composed of the _____.

7. The Constitution provides that a federal official who commits "_____" may be impeached by the House of Representatives and tried by the Senate.

8. During the debate over ratification, the Anti-Federalists argued that the Constitution needed a _____ because a strong national government might take away the political rights won during the American Revolution.

9. The principle of dividing governmental powers among the legislative, the executive, and the judicial branches of government is known as the _____.

10. Among the checks and balances built into the American system of government are the _____.

## Multiple Choice

11. The majority of American colonists came from
    a. Germany and Spain.
    b. France and Ireland.
    c. England and Scotland.

12. Before the mid-1700s, the majority of American colonists were
    a. secretly planning to declare their independence from Britain.
    b. loyal to the British monarch and viewed Britain as their homeland.
    c. loyal to France.

13. Under the Articles of Confederation, the new nation
    a. could not declare war.
    b. could enter into treaties and alliances.
    c. regulated interstate commerce.

14. The three-fifths compromise reached at the Constitutional Convention had to do with
    a. how slaves would be counted in determining representation in Congress.
    b. the imposition of export taxes.
    c. the regulation of commerce.

15. All of the existing amendments to the Constitution have been proposed
    a. by a two-thirds vote in the Senate and in the House of Representatives.
    b. by a vote in three-fourths of the state legislatures.
    c. at national constitutional conventions.

# 3

# Federalism

## Learning Outcomes

The **Learning Outcomes** labeled 1 through 5 are designed to help improve your understanding of the chapter. After reading this chapter, you should be able to:

**3–1** Explain what federalism means, how federalism differs from other systems of government, and why it exists in the United States.

**3–2** Indicate how the Constitution divides governing powers in our federal system.

**3–3** Summarize the evolution of federal–state relationships in the United States over time.

**3–4** Describe developments in federalism in recent years.

**3–5** Explain what is meant by the term *fiscal federalism*.

Remember to visit page 71 for additional **Study Tools**

# AMERICA AT
# ODDS
## Should the States Lower the Drinking Age?

Our political system is a federal one in which power is shared between the states and the national government. The Tenth Amendment to the U.S. Constitution reserves all powers not delegated to the national government to the states and to the people. Nonetheless, the central—federal—government has been able to exercise power over matters that traditionally have been under the control of state governments, such as the minimum age for drinking alcoholic beverages. The federal government has been able to do so by its ability to give or withhold federal grants. In the 1980s, for example, the national government wanted the states to raise the minimum drinking age to twenty-one years. States that refused to do so were threatened with the loss of federal highway construction funds. The threat worked—it was not long before all of the states had changed their minimum drinking age laws.

## It's Time to End This Charade—College Students Still Drink

Underage drinking did not disappear when the minimum drinking age requirement was raised to twenty-one years. Indeed, the problem got worse. Millions of young people today are, in effect, criminals, because they are breaking the law by drinking. The minimum drinking age of twenty-one years has not reduced drunk driving among teenagers, because it is largely unenforceable. Additionally, it has bred contempt for the law in general among teenagers. That is why a group of 135 U.S. college presidents and chancellors endorsed the Amethyst Initiative, a movement calling for the reconsideration of U.S. drinking age laws. Prohibition did not work in the 1920s, and prohibiting those under twenty-one from drinking will not work in the twenty-first century. Almost no other country has such a high minimum drinking age. It is time to lower the drinking age everywhere in the United States. Responsible drinking can be taught through role modeling by parents and through educational programs.

## Keep the Age-Twenty-One Requirement Because It's Working

Mothers Against Drunk Driving (MADD) leads the opposition to lowering the drinking age. That group contends that the current drinking age laws have saved more than twenty thousand lives. The National Transportation Safety Board, the American Medical Association, and the Insurance Institute for Highway Safety all agree. After all, young persons' brains are not fully developed, so they are more susceptible to alcohol. The drinking age limit of twenty-one helps to protect young people from being pressured to drink. Teenagers who drink are a danger not only to themselves but also to others—particularly when driving. Young people away at college must deal with enough new responsibilities. They don't need drinking as yet another problem. Fatalities involving eighteen- to twenty-year-old drivers have decreased since the laws establishing the minimum drinking age of twenty-one were enacted. These laws are working as planned, so we should keep them.

## Where do you stand?

In the Supreme Court ruling that upheld the health-care law known as Obamacare, Chief Justice John Roberts also held that the national government cannot pressure the states to expand Medicaid by threatening to take away all of their Medicaid funds. Roberts argued that cutting the states off completely would do too much damage to their budgets. Is there any chance that the Court might extend this logic and overturn the law that forces states to adopt a twenty-one-year-old drinking age? Why or why not?

## Explore this issue online

- Professor David J. Hanson, of the State University of New York at Potsdam, maintains a Web site that explores alcohol-related issues, including the minimum drinking age controversy. You can find it by searching on his name—"david j hanson."
- You can find the Mothers Against Drunk Driving site by entering "madd" into your search engine. For a related organization, Students Against Destructive Decisions, enter "sadd."

# Introduction

The controversy over the drinking age is just one example of how different levels of government in our federal system can be at odds with one another. Let's face it—those who work for the national government based in Washington, D.C., would like the states to cooperate fully with the national government in the implementation of national policies. At the same time, those who work in state government don't like to be told what to do by the national government, especially when the implementation of a national policy is costly for the states. Finally, those who work in local governments would like to run their affairs with the least amount of interference from both their state governments and the national government.

Such conflicts arise because our government is based on the principle of **federalism**, which means that government powers are shared by the national government and the states. When the founders of this nation opted for federalism, they created a practical and flexible form of government capable of enduring for centuries. At the same time, however, they planted the seeds for future conflict between the states and the national government over how government powers should be shared. As you will read in this chapter—and throughout this book—many of today's most pressing issues have to do with which level of government should exercise certain powers. Sometimes two levels of government collaborate. For example, California and the federal government jointly manage Redwood National Park.

The relationship between the national government and the governments at the state and local levels has never been free of conflict. Indeed, even before the Constitution was adopted, the Federalists and Anti-Federalists engaged in a heated debate over the issue of national versus state powers. As you learned in Chapter 2, the Federalists won the day by convincing Americans to adopt the Constitution. The Anti-Federalists' concern for states' rights, however, has surfaced again and again in the course of our history.

## 3–1 Federalism and Its Alternatives

**federalism** A system of shared sovereignty between two levels of government—one national and one subnational—occupying the same geographic region.

There are various ways of ordering relations between central governments and local units. Federalism is one of these ways. Learning about federalism and how it differs from other forms of government is important to understanding the American political system.

## LearningOutcome 3–1

Explain what federalism means, how federalism differs from other systems of government, and why it exists in the United States.

## 3–1a What Is Federalism?

Nowhere in the Constitution does the word *federalism* appear. This is understandable, given that the concept of federalism was an invention of the founders. Since the Federalists and the Anti-Federalists argued more than two hundred years ago about what form of government we should have, hundreds of definitions of federalism have been offered. Basically, as mentioned in Chapter 2, government powers in a *federal system* are divided between a central government and regional, or subdivisional, governments.

**Defining *Federalism*** Although the definition given here seems straightforward, its application certainly is not. After all, almost all nations—even the most repressive totalitarian regimes—have some kind of subnational governmental units. Thus, the existence of national and subnational governmental units by itself does not make a system federal. *For a system to be truly federal, the powers of both the national units and the subnational units must be specified and limited.*

Under true federalism, individuals are governed by two separate governmental authorities (national and state authorities) whose expressly designated powers cannot be altered without changing the fundamental nature of the system—for example, by amending a written constitution. Table 3–1 on the facing page lists some of the countries that the Central Intelligence Agency has classified as having a federal system of government.[1]

**U.S. Federalism in Practice** Federalism in theory is one thing—federalism in practice is another. As you will read shortly, the Constitution sets forth specific powers that can be exercised by the national government and provides that the national government has the implied power to undertake actions necessary to carry out its expressly designated powers. All other powers are "reserved" to the states. The broad language of the Constitution, though, has left much

TABLE 3–1

## Countries That Have a Federal System Today

| Country | Population (in Millions) |
|---|---|
| Argentina | 42.2 |
| Australia | 22.0 |
| Austria | 8.2 |
| Brazil | 205.7 |
| Canada | 34.3 |
| Ethiopia | 93.8 |
| Germany | 81.3 |
| India | 1,205.1 |
| Malaysia | 29.2 |
| Mexico | 115.0 |
| Nigeria | 170.1 |
| Pakistan | 190.3 |
| Switzerland | 7.7 |
| United States | 313.8 |

Source: Central Intelligence Agency, *The World Fact Book*. The current edition is online and can be located by searching on "cia-factbook." Population figures are for 2011.

room for debate over the specific nature and scope of certain powers, such as the national government's implied powers and the powers reserved to the states. Thus, the actual workings of our federal form of government have depended, to a great extent, on the historical application of the broad principles outlined in the Constitution.

To further complicate matters, the term *federal government*, as it is used today, refers to the national, or central, government. When individuals talk of the federal government, they mean the national government based in Washington, D.C. They are *not* referring to the federal *system* of government, which is made up of both the national government and the state governments.

### 3–1b Alternatives to Federalism

Perhaps an easier way to define federalism is to discuss what it is *not*. Most of the nations in the world today have a **unitary system** of government. In such a system, the constitution vests all powers in the national government. If the national government so chooses, it can delegate certain activities to subnational units. The reverse is also true: the national government can take away, at will, powers delegated to subnational

governmental units. In a unitary system, any subnational government is a "creature of the national government." The governments of Britain, France, Israel, Japan, and the Philippines are examples of unitary systems.

In the United States, because the Constitution does not mention local governments (cities and counties), we say that city and county governmental units are "creatures of state government." That means that state governments can—and do—both give powers to and take powers from local governments.

The Articles of Confederation created a confederal system (see Chapter 2). In a **confederal system,** the national government exists and operates only at the direction of the subnational governments. Few true confederal systems are in existence today, although some people contend that the European Union—a group of twenty-seven European nations that has established many common institutions—qualifies as such a system.

### 3–1c Federalism—An Optimal Choice for the United States?

The Articles of Confederation failed because they did not allow for a sufficiently strong central government. The framers of the Constitution, however, were fearful of tyranny and a too-powerful central government. The outcome had to be a compromise—a federal system.

The appeal of federalism was that it retained state powers and local traditions while establishing a strong national government capable of handling common problems, such as national defense. A federal form of government also furthered the goal of creating a division of powers (to be discussed shortly). There are other reasons why the founders opted for a federal system, and a federal structure of government continues to offer many advantages (as well as some disadvantages) for U.S. citizens.

**Advantages of Federalism: Size**  One of the reasons a federal form of government is well suited to the United States is our country's large size. Even in the days when the United States consisted of only thirteen states, its geographic area was larger than that of

**unitary system** A centralized governmental system in which local or subdivisional governments exercise only those powers given to them by the central government.

**confederal system** A league of independent sovereign states, joined together by a central government that has only limited powers over them.

FIGURE 3-1

# Governmental Units
## in the United States Today

The most common type of governmental unit in the United States is the special district, which is generally concerned with a specific issue such as solid waste disposal, mass transportation, or fire protection.

Often, the jurisdiction of special districts crosses the boundaries of other governmental units, such as cities or counties. Special districts also tend to have fewer restrictions than other local governments as to how much debt they can incur and so are created to finance large building projects.

**THE NUMBER OF GOVERNMENTS IN THE UNITED STATES TODAY**

| Government | Number |
|---|---|
| Federal government | 1 |
| State governments and District of Columbia | 51 |
| Local governments | |
| Counties | 3,034 |
| Municipalities (mainly cities or towns) | 19,492 |
| Townships (less extensive powers) | 16,519 |
| Special districts (water, sewer, and so on) | 37,381 |
| School districts | 13,051 |
| Subtotal local governments | 89,477 |
| **Total** | **89,529** |

Source: U.S. Census Bureau

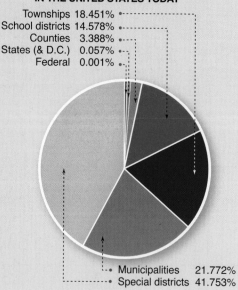

**PERCENTAGE OF ALL GOVERNMENTS IN THE UNITED STATES TODAY**

Townships 18.451%
School districts 14.578%
Counties 3.388%
States (& D.C.) 0.057%
Federal 0.001%

Municipalities 21.772%
Special districts 41.753%

England or France. In those days, travel was slow and communication was difficult, so people in outlying areas were isolated. The news of any particular political decision could take several weeks to reach everyone. Therefore, even if the framers of the Constitution had wanted a more centralized system (which most of them did not), such a system would have been unworkable.

Look at Figure 3–1 above. As you can see, to a great extent the practical business of governing this country takes place in state and local governmental units. Federalism, by providing a multitude of arenas for decision making, keeps government closer to the people and helps make democracy possible.

### Advantages of Federalism: Experimentation

The existence of numerous government subunits in the United States also makes it possible to experiment with innovative policies and programs at the state or local level. Many observers, including Supreme Court justice Louis Brandeis (1856–1941), have emphasized that in a federal system, state governments can act as "laboratories" for public-policy experimentation. For example, many states have adopted minimum-wage laws that establish a higher minimum wage than the one set by national legislation. State governments have a wide variety of policies on how or whether state employees can form labor unions. Following the 2010

elections, several state governments tightened the rules. Do state employees have too many rights and privileges? We examine that question in this chapter's *Join the Debate* feature on the facing page.

Depending on the outcome of a specific experiment, other states may (or may not) implement similar programs. State innovations can also serve as models for federal programs. For instance, California was a pioneer in air-pollution control. Many of that state's regulations were later adapted by other states and eventually by the federal government.

### Advantages of Federalism: Subcultures

We have always been a nation of different political subcultures. The Pilgrims who founded New England were different from the settlers who established the agricultural society of the South. Both of these groups were different from those who populated the Middle Atlantic states. The groups that founded New England had a religious focus, while those who populated the Middle Atlantic states were more business oriented. Those who settled in the South were more individualistic than the other groups. That is, they were less inclined to act as a collective and more inclined to act independently of each other.

A federal system of government allows the political and cultural interests of regional groups to be reflected in the laws governing those groups.

## Have State and Local Employees Become Too Powerful?

From 2010 through 2012, most state governments experienced serious budget problems. Many governors argued that a key source of these problems was high pay for state and local employees, and that generous pension plans especially threatened to force huge tax rate increases. These pension plans represent promises that state and local governments have made to employees to support them during their retirement years. You might wonder how this could have happened. Doesn't the federal government oversee these pension plans? Wouldn't it force the states to budget more carefully? Because of our federal system, the answers to these two questions are no and no. The Supreme Court has repeatedly affirmed that state governments have the responsibility for making rules for their own employees. The question remains: Have state and local employees become too powerful?

### Cut Them Down to Their Proper Size

If you count all their benefits, including those great pensions, the average public-sector employee makes at least a third more than a private-sector worker. Moreover, if you work for a state or local government, you often have much better job security than you would if you worked in the private sector. One way to cut these employee groups down to size is to remove their ability to bargain through unions. While such a position may seem anti-union, it is really just pro-taxpayer. Those states with the largest deficits—California, Illinois, and New Jersey—also have the strongest public-sector unions.

Public unions usually collect their revenues through mandatory dues. They use some of these funds as campaign cash to help elect politicians. Those politicians, when elected, are supposed to represent taxpayers when they negotiate with those same unions. But they don't.

### Leave the Public Sector Alone

All of the attacks on "too powerful" public employees are really just attacks on unions in general. Indeed, when Wisconsin's Republican governor Scott Walker attempted to limit the rights of public-sector unions, President Barack Obama called that action "an assault on unions." Moreover, the claims about high public-sector pay are false. Sure, public-sector pay is higher, but for a reason—54 percent of public-sector employees have college degrees compared to 35 percent in the private sector. Many studies show that when educational attainment is considered, state and local employees are underpaid compared to their private-sector counterparts. No one balks at corporation presidents earning gigantic retirement packages, but a guaranteed pension for a public worker is considered lavish. Rather than worrying that public-sector pensions are too generous, we ought to be concerned that private-sector pensions for ordinary workers aren't generous enough.

**FOR CRITICAL ANALYSIS** Why did the Great Recession bring the public employee debate into the spotlight?

As we noted earlier, nations other than the United States have benefited from the principle of federalism. One of them is Canada. Because federalism permits the expression of varying regional cultures, Canadian federalism naturally differs from the American version, as you will discover in this chapter's *The Rest of the World* feature on the following page.

**Some Drawbacks to Federalism** Federalism offers many advantages, but it also has some drawbacks. Consider that although federalism in many ways promotes greater self-rule, or democracy, some scholars point out that local self-rule may not always be in society's best interests. These observers argue that the smaller the political unit, the higher the probability that it will be dominated by a single political group, which may or may not be concerned with the welfare of many of the local unit's citizens. For example, entrenched segregationist politicians in southern states denied African Americans their civil rights and voting rights for decades, as we discuss further in Chapter 5.

Powerful state and local interests can block progress and impede national plans. State and local interests often diverge from those of the national government. For example, several of the states have recently been at odds with the national government

## Canadian versus American Federalism

Canada has a federal system similar in some ways to that of the United States—but also with some big differences. When the 1867 Constitution Act created modern Canada, the United States had just concluded the Civil War. Canada's founders blamed that war on the weakness of the U.S. central government. Therefore, the Canadian Constitution gave far more power to the central government than did the U.S. Constitution.

### The Powers of Lower-Level Governments

Our lower levels of government are called states, whereas in Canada they are called provinces. Right there, the powers of the central government are emphasized. The word *state* implies sovereignty. A *province*, however, is never sovereign and is typically set up for the convenience of the central government.

In the United States, the powers of the national government are limited to those listed in the Constitution. In the Canadian Constitution, it is the powers of the provinces that are limited by a list. The Tenth Amendment to the U.S. Constitution reserves residual powers to the states or to the people. In Canada, residual powers rest with the national government. Under the 1867 Canadian Constitution, the central government could veto any provincial legislation. No such clause appears in the U.S. Constitution.

### Changes over Time

By land area, Canada is the second-largest country in the world. Physically, the country seems designed for a federal system of government.

Over time, the powers of the U.S. federal government grew at the expense of the states. The opposite happened in Canada. By the end of the nineteenth century, the Canadian government in practice had abandoned the power to veto provincial legislation. The Great Depression of the 1930s strengthened the national government in the United States. In Canada, it strengthened the provinces.

### Two Languages

Another striking difference between Canada and the United States is that Canada has two national languages. A majority of Canadians speak English, but most of the population of Québec speaks French. The Parti Québécois (PQ), which wants Québec to be a separate country, has gained power in that province twice. Both times, it held referenda on whether Québec should demand "sovereignty-association," a euphemism for independence. In 1995, the PQ almost obtained a majority vote for its position. The PQ has returned to power in 2012 but may not have enough votes to hold another referendum. Nevertheless, the possibility exists that Canada could actually break apart.

**FOR CRITICAL ANALYSIS** The Canadian Constitution is based on the principles of "peace, order, and good government." Contrast that phrase with the words in the Declaration of Independence— "life, liberty, and the pursuit of happiness." How do the statements differ?

over how to address possible global warming. Finding acceptable solutions to such conflicts has not always been easy. Indeed, as will be discussed shortly, in the 1860s, war—not politics—decided the outcome of a struggle over states' rights.

Federalism has other drawbacks as well. One of them is the lack of uniformity of state laws, which can complicate business transactions that cross state borders. Another problem is the difficulty of coordinating government policies at the national, state, and local levels. Additionally, the simultaneous regulation of business by all levels of government creates red tape that imposes substantial costs on the business community.

In a federal system, there is always the danger that national power will be expanded at the expense of the states. President Ronald Reagan (1981–1989) once said, "The Founding Fathers saw the federalist system as constructed something like a masonry wall. The States are the bricks, the national government is the mortar. . . . Unfortunately, over the years, many people have increasingly come to believe that Washington is the whole wall."[2]

**FOR CRITICAL THINKING** The national government imposed a uniform highway speed limit on the entire country from 1974 until its repeal in 1995. *Why should we leave speed limits to the states—or why should they be a federal responsibility?*

# 3-2 The Constitutional Division of Powers

The founders created a federal form of government by dividing sovereign powers into powers that could be exercised by the national government and powers that were reserved to the states. Although there is no systematic explanation of this **division of powers** between the national and state governments, the original Constitution, along with its amendments, provides statements on what the national and state governments can (and cannot) do.

## 3-2a The Powers of the National Government

The Constitution delegates certain powers to the national government. It also prohibits the national government from exercising certain powers.

**Powers Delegated to the National Government** The national government possesses three types of powers: expressed powers, implied powers, and inherent powers. Article I, Section 8, of the Constitution expressly enumerates twenty-seven powers that Congress may exercise. Two of these **expressed powers,** or *enumerated powers,* are the power to coin money and the power to regulate interstate commerce. Constitutional amendments have provided for other expressed powers. For example, the Sixteenth Amendment, added in 1913, gives Congress the power to impose a federal income tax.

One power expressly granted to the national government is the right to regulate commerce not only among the states, but also "with the Indian Tribes." As a result, relations between Native American tribal governments and the rest of the country have always been a national responsibility. A further consequence is that state governments face significant limits on their authority over Indian reservations within their borders.

**IMPLIED POWERS.** The constitutional basis for the **implied powers** of the national government is found in Article I, Section 8, Clause 18, often called the **necessary and proper clause.** This clause states that Congress has the power to make "all Laws which shall be necessary and proper for carrying into Execution the foregoing [expressed] Powers, and all other Powers vested by this Constitution in the Government of the United States, or in any Department or Officer thereof." The necessary and proper clause is often referred to as the *elastic clause,* because it gives elasticity to our constitutional system.

**INHERENT POWERS.** The national government also enjoys certain **inherent powers**—powers that governments must have simply to ensure the nation's integrity and survival as a political unit. For example, any national government must have the inherent ability to make treaties, regulate immigration, acquire territory, wage war, and make peace. While some inherent powers are also enumerated in the Constitution, such as the powers to wage war and make treaties, others are not. For example, the Constitution does not speak of regulating immigration or acquiring new territory. Although the national government's inherent powers are few, they are important.

> ## "THE GREAT DIFFICULTY LIES IN THIS:
> you must first enable the government to control the governed; and in the next place, oblige it to control itself."
>
> ~ JAMES MADISON ~
> FOURTH PRESIDENT OF THE UNITED STATES
> 1809–1817

**division of powers** A basic principle of federalism established by the U.S. Constitution, by which powers are divided between the national and state governments.

**expressed powers** Constitutional or statutory powers that are expressly provided for by the U.S. Constitution; also called *enumerated powers.*

**implied powers** The powers of the federal government that are implied by the expressed powers in the Constitution, particularly in Article I, Section 8.

**necessary and proper clause** Article I, Section 8, Clause 18, of the Constitution, which gives Congress the power to make all laws "necessary and proper" for the federal government to carry out its responsibilities; also called the *elastic clause.*

**inherent powers** The powers of the national government that, although not always expressly granted by the Constitution, are necessary to ensure the nation's integrity and survival as a political unit. Inherent powers include the power to make treaties and the power to wage war or make peace.

AP PHOTO/DOUGLAS C. PIZAC

President Clinton declared Utah's 1.9 million-acre Grand Staircase-Escalante area a national monument in 1996. Utah's governor and its congressional delegation objected. Why?

**FEDERAL LANDS.** One inherent power is older than the Constitution itself—the power to own land. The United States collectively owned various western lands under the Articles of Confederation. The Northwest Territory, which included the modern states of Illinois, Indiana, Michigan, Ohio, Wisconsin, and part of Minnesota, joined United States lands together with lands given up by New York and Virginia. The Northwest Territory was organized during the ratification of the Constitution—indeed, establishing the territory as the collective property of the entire Union was necessary to secure support for ratification in several states, including Maryland.

**police powers** The powers of a government body that enable it to create laws for the protection of the health, safety, welfare, and morals of the people. In the United States, most police powers are reserved to the states.

The United States then sold land to new settlers—land sales were a major source of national government income throughout much of the 1800s. To this day, the national government owns most of the acres in many far western states, a fact that annoys many Westerners. We discuss that issue in this chapter's *Our Challenging Times* feature on the facing page.

**Powers Prohibited to the National Government**   The Constitution expressly prohibits the national government from undertaking certain actions, such as imposing taxes on exports, and from passing laws restraining certain liberties, such as the freedom of speech or religion. Most of these prohibited powers are listed in Article I, Section 9, and in the first eight amendments to the Constitution. Additionally, the national government is implicitly prohibited from exercising certain powers. For example, most authorities believe that the federal government does not have the power to create a national public school system, because such power is not included among those that are expressed and implied.

### 3–2b The Powers of the States

The Tenth Amendment to the Constitution states that powers that are not delegated to the national government by the Constitution nor prohibited to the states "are reserved to the States respectively, or to the people."

**Police Powers**   The Tenth Amendment thus gives numerous powers to the states, including the power to regulate commerce within their borders and the power to maintain a state militia. In principle, each state has the ability to regulate its internal affairs and to enact whatever laws are necessary to protect the health, safety, welfare, and morals of its people. These powers of the states are called **police powers**. The establishment of public schools and the regulation of marriage and divorce have traditionally been considered to be entirely within the purview of state and local governments.

Because the Tenth Amendment does not specify what powers are reserved to the states, these powers have been defined differently at different times in our history. In periods of widespread support for increased regulation by the national government, the Tenth Amendment tends to recede into the background.

When the tide of support turns, the Tenth Amendment is resurrected to justify arguments supporting increased states' rights (see, for example, the discussion of the new federalism later in this chapter). Because the United States Supreme Court is the ultimate arbiter

# OUR **CHALLENGING** TIMES

## Does the Federal Government Own Too Much Land?

If you live in the states east of the Rocky Mountains, most of the land around you is privately owned. If you live in the Mountain States or the far west, the national government owns much of the land. In California, half of the total land area is federal. In Utah, the figure is 68 percent. In Nevada it's 88 percent. In more typical states such as Missouri or Georgia, the figure is about 9 percent. In the state of New York, it's 0.4 percent.

### DID CONGRESS RENEGE ON ITS PROMISES?

Some Westerners claim that the federal government reneged on congressional promises. They argue that the national government's control of tens of millions of acres in the West in the 1800s was supposed to be temporary. These advocates point out that the founding documents of most states contain language that presumes federal lands will be transferred to the state or to private parties. That obviously didn't happen in the West.

In 2012, Utah adopted legislation under which the state would attempt to reclaim most federal lands. The Arizona legislature passed a similar measure in 2012, but the governor vetoed it. The proponents of these bills point out that national policies have created two different halves of one nation—the public-lands states and the private-property states. Some

question whether the federal government should own so much land in a supposedly capitalist society.

### THE PROS AND CONS OF TRANSFERRING THE LAND

Proponents of the transfer of federal lands to the states contend that such measures would stimulate economic growth. Most of the federal lands have experienced almost no economic development. In contrast, consider Texas and North Dakota, where almost all land is private. Both states are currently experiencing an oil and natural gas boom. Such development is easy to undertake on private land but not on federally owned land. Several western states, notably California, face crushing debt loads. These debts could be reduced if they were allowed to sell public land, lease it, or at least build state government concessions on it.

Opponents of these bills contend that state governments would be poor stewards of the lands in question. For most environmentalists, the undeveloped nature of much federal real estate is a benefit, not a problem. Recreational activities would be impossible if these lands were privatized. Other opponents point out that the demands contained in the Utah bill are flatly unconstitutional. Lawsuits based on the legislation would be a waste of time and dollars. Transfer supporters, however, note that the United States Supreme Court has taken an increasingly favorable view of states' rights in recent years, so transfer legislation may have a chance in the courts.

**YOU BE THE JUDGE** If the federal government were to transfer most of its lands to the states, what kinds of real estate should nonetheless remain under federal ownership and control?

of the Constitution, the outcome of disputes over the extent of state powers often rests with the Court.

**Powers Prohibited to the States** Article I, Section 10, denies certain powers to state governments, such as the power to tax goods that are transported across state lines. States are also prohibited from entering into treaties with other countries. In addition, the Thirteenth, Fourteenth, Fifteenth, Nineteenth,

Twenty-fourth, and Twenty-sixth Amendments prohibit certain state actions. (The complete text of these amendments is included in Appendix B.)

### 3–2c Interstate Relations

The Constitution also contains provisions relating to interstate relations. The states have constant commercial and social interactions among themselves, and these interactions often do not directly involve the national government. The relationships among the states in our federal system of government are sometimes referred to as *horizontal federalism.*

The Constitution outlines a number of rules for interstate relations. For example, the Constitution's full faith and credit clause requires each state to honor every other state's public acts, records, and judicial proceedings. The issue of gay marriage, however, has made this constitutional mandate difficult to follow. If a gay couple legally married in Massachusetts moves to a state that bans same-sex marriage, which state's law takes priority? The federal government attempted to answer that question through the 1996 Defense of Marriage Act (DOMA), which provided that no state is *required* to treat a relationship between persons of the same sex as a marriage, even if the relationship is considered a marriage in another state.

A second part of the law barred the national government from recognizing same-sex marriages in states that legalize them. In July 2010, however, a U.S. district court judge threw out this part of DOMA and ruled that the federal government was required to provide marriage-based benefits to Massachusetts residents who are joined in same-sex marriages. This ruling has been appealed, and ultimately, the United States Supreme Court will have to decide this issue.

Horizontal federalism also includes agreements, known as *interstate compacts,* among two or more states to regulate the use or protection of certain resources, such as water or oil and gas. California and Nevada, for example, have formed an interstate compact to regulate the use and protection of Lake Tahoe, which lies on the border between those states.

## 3–2d Concurrent Powers

**Concurrent powers** can be exercised by both the state governments and the federal government. Generally, a state's concurrent powers apply only within the geographic area of the state and do not include functions that the Constitution delegates exclusively to the national government, such as the coinage of money and the negotiation of treaties. An example of a concurrent power is the power to tax. Both the states and the national government have the power to impose income taxes—and a variety of other taxes. States, however, are prohibited from imposing tariffs (taxes on imported goods), and, as noted, the federal government may not tax articles exported by any state. Figure 3–2, on the facing page, summarizes the powers granted and denied by the Constitution and lists other concurrent powers.

## 3–2e The Supremacy Clause

The Constitution makes it clear that the federal government holds ultimate power. Article VI, Clause 2, known as the **supremacy clause,** states that the U.S.

**concurrent powers**
Powers held by both the federal and the state governments in a federal system.

**supremacy clause**
Article VI, Clause 2, of the Constitution, which makes the Constitution and federal laws superior to all conflicting state and local laws.

DAVID BUTOW/REDUX

Few issues today are as controversial as state-legalized gay marriages. A federal judge in California ruled that Proposition 8, which nullified such marriages, was unconstitutional.

FIGURE 3-2

# The Constitutional Division of Powers

The Constitution grants certain powers to the national government and certain powers to the state governments, while denying them other powers. Some powers, called *concurrent powers*, can be exercised at either the national or the state level, but generally the states can exercise these powers only within their own borders.

## Powers Granted by the Constitution

**NATIONAL**
- To coin money
- To conduct foreign relations
- To regulate interstate commerce
- To declare war
- To raise and support the military
- To establish post offices
- To admit new states
- Powers implied by the necessary and proper clause

**CONCURRENT**
- To levy and collect taxes
- To borrow money
- To make and enforce laws
- To establish courts
- To provide for the general welfare
- To charter banks and corporations

**STATE**
- To regulate intrastate commerce
- To conduct elections
- To provide for public health, safety, welfare, and morals
- To establish local governments
- To ratify amendments to the federal Constitution
- To establish a state militia

## Powers Denied by the Constitution

**NATIONAL**
- To tax articles exported from any state
- To violate the Bill of Rights
- To change state boundaries without consent of the states in question

**CONCURRENT**
- To grant titles of nobility
- To permit slavery
- To deny citizens the right to vote

**STATE**
- To tax imports or exports
- To coin money
- To enter into treaties
- To impair obligations of contracts
- To abridge the privileges or immunities of citizens or deny due process and equal protection of the laws

© CENGAGE LEARNING

Constitution and the laws of the federal government "shall be the supreme Law of the Land." In other words, states cannot use their reserved or concurrent powers to counter national policies. Whenever state or local officers, such as judges or sheriffs, take office, they become bound by an oath to support the U.S. Constitution. National government power always takes precedence over any conflicting state action.[3]

## FOR CRITICAL THINKING

The national government also exercises police powers, such as environmental regulation. *Name some other federal activities that might fall into this category.*

## 3-3 The Struggle for Supremacy

Much of the political and legal history of the United States has involved conflicts between the supremacy of the national government and the desire of the states to preserve their sovereignty. The most extreme example of this conflict was the Civil War in the 1860s. Through the years, because of the Civil War and several important Supreme Court decisions, the national government has increased its power.

### 3-3a Early United States Supreme Court Decisions

Two Supreme Court cases, both

**LearningOutcome 3-3**

Summarize the evolution of federal–state relationships in the United States over time.

John Marshall, chief justice of the U.S. Supreme Court (1801–1835).

STOCK MONTAGE/GETTY IMAGES

of which were decided in the early 1800s, played a key role in establishing the constitutional foundations for the supremacy of the national government. Both decisions were issued while John Marshall was chief justice of the Supreme Court. In his thirty-four years as chief justice (1801–1835), Marshall did much to establish the prestige and the independence of the Court. In *Marbury v. Madison*,[4] he clearly enunciated the principle of *judicial review*, which has since become an important part of the checks and balances in the American system of government. Under his leadership, the Supreme Court also established, through the following cases, the superiority of federal authority under the Constitution.

### McCulloch v. Maryland (1819)

The issue in *McCulloch v. Maryland*,[5] a case decided in 1819, involved both the necessary and proper clause and the supremacy clause. When the state of Maryland imposed a tax on the Baltimore branch of the Second Bank of the United States, the branch's chief cashier, James McCulloch, declined to pay the tax. The state court ruled that McCulloch had to pay it, and the national government appealed to the United States Supreme Court. The case involved much more than a question of taxes. At issue was whether Congress had the authority under the Constitution's necessary and proper clause to charter and contribute capital to the Second Bank of the United States. A second constitutional issue was also involved: If the bank was constitutional, could a state tax it? In other words, was a state action that conflicted with a national government action invalid under the supremacy clause?

Chief Justice Marshall pointed out that no provision in the Constitution grants the national government the *expressed* power to form a national bank. Nevertheless, if establishing such a bank helps the national government exercise its expressed powers, then the authority to do so could be implied. Marshall also said that the necessary and proper clause included "all means that are appropriate" to carry out "the legitimate ends" of the Constitution.

Having established this doctrine of implied powers, Marshall then answered the other important constitutional question before the Court and established the doctrine of *national supremacy*. Marshall declared that no state could use its taxing power to tax an arm of the national government. If it could, the Constitution's declaration that the Constitution "shall be the supreme Law of the Land" would be empty rhetoric without meaning. From that day on, Marshall's decision became the basis for strengthening the national government's power.

### Gibbons v. Ogden (1824)

As Chapter 2 explained, Article I, Section 8, gives Congress the power to regulate commerce "among the several States." But the framers of the Constitution did not define the word *commerce*. At issue in *Gibbons v. Ogden*[6] was how the *commerce clause* should be defined and whether the national government had the exclusive power to regulate commerce involving more than one state.

The New York legislature had given Robert Livingston and Robert Fulton the exclusive right to operate steamboats in New York waters, and Livingston and Fulton licensed Aaron Ogden to operate a ferry between New York and New Jersey. Thomas Gibbons, who had a license from the U.S. government to operate boats in interstate waters, decided to compete with Ogden, but

"We here highly resolve that . . . **This Nation . . . shall have a new birth of freedom;** and that government of the people, by the people, for the people, shall not perish from the earth."

~ ABRAHAM LINCOLN ~
GETTYSBURG ADDRESS
1863

he did so without New York's permission. Ogden sued Gibbons in the New York state courts and won. Gibbons appealed.

Chief Justice Marshall defined *commerce* as including all business dealings, including steamboat travel. Marshall also stated that the power to regulate interstate commerce was an *exclusive* national power and had no limitations other than those specifically found in the Constitution. Since this 1824 decision, the national government has used the commerce clause repeatedly to justify its regulation of almost all areas of economic activity.

## 3-3b The Civil War— The Ultimate Supremacy Battle

The great issue that provoked the Civil War (1861–1865) was the future of slavery. Because people in different sections of the country had radically different beliefs about slavery, the slavery issue took the form of a dispute over states' rights versus national supremacy. The war brought to a bloody climax the ideological debate that had been outlined by the Federalist and Anti-Federalist factions even before the Constitution was ratified.

### Nullification and Secession   As just discussed, the Supreme Court headed by John Marshall interpreted the commerce clause in such a way as to increase the power of the national government at the expense of state powers. By the late 1820s, however, a shift back to states' rights had begun, and the question of the regulation of commerce became one of the major issues in federal–state relations. When the national government, in 1828 and 1832, passed laws imposing tariffs (taxes) on goods imported into the United States, southern states objected, believing that such taxes were against their interests.

One southern state, South Carolina, attempted to *nullify* the tariffs, or to make them void. South Carolina claimed that in conflicts between state governments and the national government, the states should have the ultimate authority to determine the welfare of their citizens. President Andrew Jackson was prepared to use force to uphold national law, but Congress reduced the tariffs. The crisis passed.

**SOCIAL MEDIA In Politics**

Searching on "civil war" in Facebook brings up the Civil War page of the *New York Times*. This page has a wealth of historical information plus popular discussions about these crucial events.

Additionally, some Southerners believed that democratic decisions could be made only when all the segments of society affected by those decisions were in agreement. Without such agreement, a decision should not be binding on those whose interests it violates. This view was used to justify the **secession**—withdrawal—of the southern states from the Union in 1860 and 1861.

### States' Rights and Slavery   The defense of slavery and the promotion of states' rights were both important elements in the South's decision to secede, and the two concepts were commingled in the minds of Southerners of that era. Which of these two was the more important remains a matter of controversy even today. Modern defenders of states' rights and those who distrust governmental authority often present southern secession as entirely a matter of states' rights. Liberals and those who champion the rights of African Americans see slavery as the sole cause of the crisis.

When the South was defeated in the war, the idea that a state has a right to secede from the Union was defeated also. Although the Civil War occurred because of the South's desire for increased states' rights, the result was just the opposite—an increase in the political power of the national government.

## 3-3c Dual Federalism— From the Civil War to the 1930s

Scholars have devised various models to describe the relationship between the states and the national government at different times in our history. These models are useful in describing the evolution of federalism after the Civil War.

The model of **dual federalism** assumes that the states and the national government are more or less equals, with each level of government having separate and distinct functions and responsibilities. The states exercise sovereign powers over certain matters, and the national government exercises sovereign powers over others.

For much of our nation's history, this model of federalism prevailed. After the expansion of national authority during the Civil War, the courts again tended to support the states' rights to

**secession** The act of formally withdrawing from membership in an alliance; the withdrawal of a state from the federal Union.

**dual federalism** A system of government in which the federal and the state governments maintain diverse but sovereign powers.

exercise police powers and tended to strictly limit the powers of the federal government under the commerce clause. In 1918, for example, the Supreme Court ruled unconstitutional a 1916 federal law excluding from interstate commerce the products created through the use of child labor. The law was held unconstitutional because it attempted to regulate a local problem.[7]

The era of dual federalism came to an end in the 1930s, when the United States was in the depths of the greatest economic depression it had ever experienced.

## 3–3d Cooperative Federalism and the Growth of the National Government

The model of **cooperative federalism,** as the term implies, involves cooperation by all branches of government. This model views the national and state governments as complementary parts of a single governmental mechanism, the purpose of which is to solve the problems facing the entire United States. For example, federal law enforcement agencies, such as the Federal Bureau of Investigation, lend technical expertise to solve local crimes, and local officials cooperate with federal agencies.

Cooperative federalism grew out of the desire to solve the pressing national problems caused by the Great Depression, which began in 1929. In an attempt to bring the United States out of the Depression, President Franklin D. Roosevelt (1933–1945) launched his **New Deal,** which involved many government-spending and public-assistance programs. Roosevelt's New Deal legislation not only ushered in an era of cooperative federalism, which has more or less continued until the present day, but also marked the real beginning of an era of national supremacy.

Before the period of cooperative federalism could be truly established, it was necessary to obtain the concurrence of the United States Supreme Court. As mentioned, in the early part of the twentieth century, the Court held a very restrictive view of what the federal government could do under the commerce clause. In the 1930s, the Court ruled again and again that various economic measures were unconstitutional.

In 1937, Roosevelt threatened to "pack" the Court with up to six new members who presumably would be more favorable to federal action. This move was widely considered to be an assault on the Constitution, and Congress refused to support it. Later that year, however, Roosevelt had the opportunity—for the first time since taking office—to appoint a new member of the Supreme Court. Hugo Black, the new justice, tipped the balance on the Court. After 1937, the Court ceased its attempts to limit the scope of the commerce clause.

**Cooperative Federalism and the Welfare State** The 1960s and 1970s saw an even greater expansion of the national government's role in domestic policy. The Great Society legislation of President Lyndon Johnson's administration (1963–1969) created Medicaid, Medicare, the Job Corps, Operation Head Start, and other programs. The Civil Rights Act of 1964 prohibited discrimination in public accommodations, employment, and other areas on the basis of race, color, national origin, religion, or gender. In the 1970s, national laws protecting consumers, employees, and the environment imposed further regulations on

**cooperative federalism** A model of federalism in which the states and the federal government cooperate in solving problems.

**New Deal** The policies ushered in by the Roosevelt administration in 1933 in an attempt to bring the United States out of the Great Depression. The New Deal included many government-spending and public-assistance programs, in addition to thousands of regulations governing economic activity.

NATIONAL ARCHIVES/MCT/LANDOV

President Franklin Roosevelt supported many new federal programs during the Great Depression.

Head Start is a program initiated by the federal government but administered by local nonprofit organizations. Why doesn't the federal government operate this program directly?

GARY CAMERON/REUTERS

the economy. Today, few activities are beyond the reach of the regulatory arm of the national government.

Nonetheless, the massive social programs undertaken in the 1960s and 1970s also precipitated greater involvement by state and local governments. The national government simply could not implement those programs alone. For example, Head Start, a program that provides preschool services to children of low-income families, is administered by local nonprofit organizations and school systems, although it is funded by federal grants. The model in which every level of government is involved in implementing a policy is sometimes referred to as **picket-fence federalism.**

In this model, the policy area is the vertical picket on the fence, while the levels of government are the horizontal support boards. America's welfare system has relied on this model of federalism, although, as you will read, from time to time there have been attempts to give more power to state and local governments.

### United States Supreme Court Decisions and Cooperative Federalism

The two United States Supreme Court decisions discussed earlier, *McCulloch v. Maryland* and *Gibbons v. Ogden*, became the constitutional cornerstone of the regulatory powers that the national government enjoys today. From 1937 on, the Supreme Court consistently upheld Congress's power to regulate domestic policy under the commerce clause. Even activities that occur entirely within a state were rarely considered to be outside the regulatory power of the national government. For example, in 1942 the Supreme Court held that wheat production by an individual farmer intended wholly for consumption on his own farm was subject to federal regulation because the home consumption of wheat reduced the demand for wheat and thus could have an effect on interstate commerce.[8]

In 1980, the Supreme Court acknowledged that the commerce clause had "long been interpreted to extend beyond activities actually in interstate commerce to reach other activities that, while wholly local in nature, nevertheless substantially affect interstate commerce."[9] Today, Congress can regulate almost any kind of economic activity, no matter where it occurs. In recent years, though, the Supreme Court has, for the first time since the 1930s, occasionally curbed Congress's regulatory powers under the commerce clause. You will read more about this development shortly.

John Marshall's validation of the supremacy clause of the Constitution has also had significant consequences for federalism. One important effect of the supremacy clause today is that the clause allows for federal **preemption** of certain areas in which the national government and the states have concurrent powers. When Congress chooses to act exclusively in an area in which the states and the national government have concurrent powers, Congress is said to have *preempted* the area. In such cases, the courts have held that a valid federal law or regulation takes precedence over a conflicting state or local law or regulation covering the same general activity.

**picket-fence federalism** A model of federalism in which specific policies and programs are administered by all levels of government—national, state, and local.

**preemption** A doctrine rooted in the supremacy clause of the Constitution that provides that national laws or regulations governing a certain area take precedence over conflicting state laws or regulations governing that same area.

FOR CRITICAL THINKING

The national government has used the commerce clause to prevent state governments from loosening the laws that regulate marijuana. *Is this good policy? Why or why not?*

## 3–4 Federalism Today

By the 1970s, some Americans had begun to question whether the national government had acquired too many powers. Had the national government gotten too big? Had it become, in fact, a threat to the power of the states and the liberties of the people? Should steps be taken to reduce the regulatory power and scope of the national government? Since that time, the model of federalism has evolved in ways that reflect these and other concerns.

### 3–4a The New Federalism— More Power to the States

Starting in the 1970s, several administrations attempted to revitalize the doctrine of dual federalism, which they renamed the "new federalism." The **new federalism** involved a shift from *nation-centered* federalism to *state-centered* federalism. One of the major goals of the new federalism was to return to the states certain powers that had been exercised by the national government since the 1930s. The term **devolution**— the transfer of powers to political subunits—is often used to describe this process. Although a product of conservative thought and initiated by Republicans, the devolutionary goals of the new federalism were also espoused by the Clinton administration (1993–2001). An example of the new federalism is the welfare reform legislation passed by Congress in 1996, which gave the states more authority over welfare programs.

### 3–4b The Supreme Court and the New Federalism

During and since the 1990s, the Supreme Court has played a significant role in furthering the cause of states' rights. In a landmark 1995 decision, *United States v. Lopez*,[10] the Supreme Court held, for the first time in sixty years, that Congress had exceeded its constitutional authority under the commerce clause. The Court concluded that the Gun-Free School Zones Act of 1990, which banned the possession of guns within one thousand feet of any school, was unconstitutional because it attempted to regulate an area that had "nothing to do with commerce." In a significant 1997 decision, the Court struck down portions of the Brady Handgun Violence Prevention Act of 1993, which obligated state and local law enforcement officers to do background checks on prospective handgun buyers until a national instant-check system could be implemented. The Court stated that Congress lacked the power to "dragoon" state employees into federal service through an unfunded **federal mandate** of this kind.[11]

Since then, the Court has continued to limit the national government's regulatory powers. In 2000, for example, the Court invalidated a key provision of the federal Violence Against Women Act of 1994, which allowed women to sue in federal court when they were victims of gender-motivated violence, such as rape. The Court upheld a federal appellate court's ruling that the commerce clause did not justify national regulation of noneconomic, criminal conduct.[12]

Other recent Supreme Court decisions have had the effect of enhancing the power of the states. For example, in one case, *Massachusetts v. Environmental Protection Agency*,[13] Massachusetts and several other states sued the Environmental Protection Agency (EPA) for failing to regulate greenhouse-gas emissions. The states asserted that the agency was required to do so by the Clean Air Act of 1990. The EPA argued that it lacked the authority under the Clean Air Act to regulate greenhouse-gas emissions alleged to promote global warming. The Court ruled for the states, holding that the EPA did have the authority to regulate such emissions and should take steps to do so.

### 3–4c The Shifting Boundary between Federal and State Authority

Clearly, the boundary between federal and state authority has been shifting. Notably, issues relating to the federal structure of our government, which at one time were not at the forefront of the political arena, have in recent years been the subject of heated debate among Americans and their leaders. The federal government and the states seem to be in a constant

**new federalism** A plan to limit the federal government's role in regulating state governments and to give the states increased power in deciding how they should spend government revenues.

**devolution** The surrender or transfer of powers to local authorities by a central government.

**federal mandate** A requirement in federal legislation that forces states and municipalities to comply with certain rules. If the federal government does not provide funds to the states to cover the costs of compliance, the mandate is referred to as an *unfunded* mandate.

These members of the Colorado National Guard help in the aftermath of a major fire. Every state has its own National Guard, yet the president can take control of these units in certain circumstances.

greater role in education and educational funding than ever before.

Many Republicans also supported a constitutional amendment that would ban same-sex marriages nationwide. Liberals, recognizing that it was possible to win support for same-sex marriages only in a limited number of states, took a states' rights position on this issue. Finally, consider that the Bush administration made repeated attempts to block California's medical-marijuana initiative and Oregon's physician-assisted suicide law.

tug-of-war over federal regulations, federal programs, and federal demands on the states.

### The Politics of Federalism
The Republican Party is often viewed as the champion of states' rights. Certainly, the party has claimed such a role. For example, when the Republicans took control of both chambers of Congress in 1995, they promised devolution—which, as already noted, refers to a shifting of power from the national level to the individual states. Smaller central government and a state-centered federalism have long been regarded as the twin pillars of Republican ideology. In contrast, Democrats usually have sought greater centralization of power in Washington, D.C.

Since the Clinton administration, however, there have been times when the party tables seem to have turned. As mentioned earlier, it was under Clinton that welfare reform legislation giving more responsibility to the states—a goal that had been endorsed by the Republicans for some time—became a reality. Conversely, the No Child Left Behind Act of 2001, passed at the request of Republican president George W. Bush, gave the federal government a much

> ## "GIVING MONEY AND POWER TO GOVERNMENT
>
> is like giving whiskey and car keys to teenage boys."
>
> ~ P. J. O'ROURKE ~
> AMERICAN HUMORIST
> 1947–PRESENT

### Federalism and the Economic Crisis
Unlike the federal government, state governments are supposed to balance their budgets. This requirement is written into the constitution of every state except Vermont. Such requirements do not prevent the states from borrowing, but typically when a state borrows, it must follow a strict series of rules laid down in its constitution. Frequently, a vote of the people is required before a state or local government can go into debt by issuing bonds. In contrast, when the federal government runs a budget deficit, the borrowing that results takes place almost automatically—the U.S. Treasury continually issues new Treasury securities.

**STATE SPENDING IN A RECESSION.** A practical result is that when a major recession occurs, the states are faced with severe budget problems. Because state citizens are earning and spending less, state income and sales taxes fall. At the same time, people who have lost their jobs require more state services. The costs of welfare, unemployment compensation, and Medicaid (health care for low-income persons) all rise. During a recession, state governments may be forced either to

Immigration reform is not the only hot-button issue that creates conflicts in Arizona. Because of continuing budget problems, the Arizona state government has tried to alter the way the public employee unions are allowed to operate.

reduce spending and lay off staff—or to raise taxes. Either choice helps make the recession worse. State-spending patterns tend to make economic booms more energetic and busts more painful—in a word, they are *procyclical*.

**FEDERAL SPENDING IN A RECESSION.** The federal government has no difficulty in spending more on welfare, unemployment compensation, and Medicaid during a recession. Even though revenue raised through the federal income tax may fall, the federal government often cuts tax rates in a recession to spur the economy. It makes up the difference by going further into debt, an option not always available to the states. The federal government even has the power to reduce its debt by issuing new money. In a recession, the actions of the federal government are normally *anticyclical*.

One method of dealing with the procyclical nature of state spending is to increase federal grants to the states during a recession. Such grants were included in the February 2009 stimulus legislation championed by President Obama. By the middle of 2010, however, the grants had largely dried up. From 2010 through 2012, the states laid off a substantial number of employees.

**The Supreme Court: Immigration**  In June 2012, the United States Supreme Court issued two rulings that dealt with the relative power of the national government and the states. In the first of these, *Arizona v. United States,* the Supreme Court confirmed national authority over immigration by striking down three provisions of a tough Arizona immigration law. The rejected provisions would have (1) subjected illegal immigrants to criminal penalties for activities such as seeking work, (2) made it a state crime for immigrants to fail to register with the federal government, and (3) allowed police to arrest people without warrants if they had reason to believe that the individuals were deportable.

The Court stated that "Arizona may have understandable frustrations with the problems caused by illegal immigration . . . but the State may not pursue policies that undermine federal law." The Court did allow Arizona to check the immigration status of individuals arrested for reasons other than immigration status. But it reserved the right to rule against Arizona on that issue, too, if the state were shown to practice racial discrimination in its arrests.[14]

**The Supreme Court: Health-Care Reform**
The second of the Court's major rulings on federalism in 2012 concerned the constitutionality of the Affordable Care Act, popularly known as Obamacare. We discussed this decision in the *Join the Debate* feature in Chapter 2.

In this case, *National Federation of Independent Business v. Sebelius,* the Court upheld most of the law. Two of Chief Justice John Roberts's arguments, however, seemed to set new limits on the powers of the national government. Roberts contended that the federal government could not, under the commerce clause of the Constitution, *require* individuals to purchase something—in this case, health-care insurance. Roberts did allow the government to encourage such behavior through the tax code, however. Roberts also ruled that the national government cannot force the states to expand Medicaid by threatening to take away all of their Medicaid funds if they do not. Roberts argued that cutting the states off completely would do too much damage to their budgets.[15]

Both of these arguments—on purchasing insurance and on forcing the states to expand Medicaid—were novel, at least in the opinion of most constitutional scholars. Many observers also doubt, however, that these two arguments will have much impact in the future. It is not likely that Congress would want to require individuals to purchase a service in contexts other than health-care insurance. Also, the ruling against the government on Medicaid was based on the enormous size of the penalty. If Congress in the future wanted to pressure the states to expand Medicaid, it presumably could do so by threatening to withhold, say, 10 percent of a state's Medicaid funds instead of all of them.

While the effects of the decision on Obamacare were modest, the case did demonstrate that the Court was more willing to challenge the national government on its use of the commerce clause than at any time since 1937. Indeed, four of the nine justices advocated positions on the commerce clause that, in terms of recent legal understanding, were almost revolutionary.

**FOR CRITICAL THINKING**

*Do you think that the relative power of the state and national governments will be more of an issue in future years, or do you think the dispute will become less important? Explain your reasoning.*

## 3–5 The Fiscal Side of Federalism

**LearningOutcome 3–5**

Explain what is meant by the term *fiscal federalism*.

Since the advent of cooperative federalism in the 1930s, the national government and the states have worked hand in hand to implement programs mandated by the national government. Whenever Congress passes a law that preempts a certain area, the states are, of course, obligated to comply with the requirements of that law. As already noted, a requirement that a state provide a service or undertake some activity to meet standards specified by a federal law is called a *federal mandate*. Many federal mandates concern civil rights or environmental protection. Recent federal mandates require the states to provide persons with disabilities with access to public buildings, sidewalks, and other areas, to establish minimum water-purity and air-purity standards, and to extend Medicaid coverage to all poor children.

To help the states pay for some of the costs associated with implementing national policies, the national government gives back some of the tax dollars it collects to the states—in the form of grants. As you will see, the states have come to depend on grants as an important source of revenue. When taxes are collected by one level of government (typically the national government) and spent by another level (typically state or local governments), we call the process **fiscal federalism.**

### 3–5a Federal Grants

Even before the Constitution was adopted, the national government granted lands to the states to finance education. Using the proceeds from the sale of these lands, the states were able to establish elementary schools and, later, *land-grant colleges.* Cash grants started in 1808, when Congress gave funds to the states to pay for the state militias. Federal grants were also made available for other purposes, such as building roads and railroads.

Only in the twentieth century, though, did federal grants become an important source of funds to the states. The major growth began in the 1960s, when the dollar amount of grants quadrupled to help pay for the Great Society programs of the Johnson administration. Grants became available for education, pollution control, conservation, recreation, highway construction and maintenance, and other purposes.

There are two basic types of federal grants: categorical grants and block grants. A **categorical grant** is targeted for a specific purpose as defined by federal law—the federal government defines hundreds of categories of state and local spending. Categorical grants give the national government control over how states use the funds by imposing certain conditions. For

**fiscal federalism** The allocation of taxes collected by one level of government (typically the national government) to another level (typically state or local governments).

**categorical grant** A federal grant targeted for a specific purpose as defined by federal law.

example, a categorical grant may require that the funds must be used for the purpose of repairing interstate highways and that the projects cannot pay below the local prevailing wage. Depending on the project, the government might require that an environmental impact statement be prepared.

In contrast, a **block grant** is given for a broad area, such as criminal justice or mental-health programs. The term *block grant* was coined in 1966 to describe a series of programs initiated by President Lyndon B. Johnson, although a number of federal grants issued earlier in our history shared some of the characteristics of modern block grants. Block grants now constitute a growing percentage of all federal aid programs.

A block grant gives the states more discretion over how the funds will be spent. Nonetheless, the federal government can exercise control over state decision making through these grants by using *cross-cutting requirements,* or requirements that apply to all federal grants. Title VI of the 1964 Civil Rights Act, for example, bars discrimination in the use of all federal funds, regardless of their source.

## 3–5b Federal Grants and State Budgets

Currently, about 15 percent of state and local revenue comes from the national government. In fiscal year 2013, the federal government transferred about $580 billion to state and local governments—more than half a trillion dollars. By far, the largest transfer was for Medicaid, the health-care program for the poor. It totaled $294 billion. The federal government provided the states with about $103 billion for education. Highway grants ran more than $40 billion.

When the media discuss state and local budgets, they typically refer just to the general fund budgets, which are largely supported by state and local taxes. But, in fact, state and local taxes support only about half of state and local spending. Federal funds aren't listed in general fund budgets. Further, almost a quarter of state and local spending goes to fee-for-service operations, in which governments charge for the services they provide. This spending applies to functions such as water supply, sewers, and other public utilities; fees charged by government-owned hospitals and airports; college tuition; and much else. Typically, these operations are also excluded from general fund budgets.

> "**Taxes,** after all, are the dues that we pay for the privileges of membership in an **organized society."**
>
> ~ FRANKLIN D. ROOSEVELT ~
> THIRTY-SECOND PRESIDENT
> OF THE UNITED STATES
> 1933–1945

## 3–5c Using Federal Grants to Control the States

Grants of funds to the states from the national government are one way that the Tenth Amendment to the U.S. Constitution can be bridged. Remember that the Tenth Amendment reserves all powers not delegated to the national government to the states and to the people. You might well wonder, then, how the federal government has been able to exercise control over matters that traditionally have been under the control of state governments, such as the minimum drinking age. The answer involves the giving or withholding of federal grant dollars.

For example, as noted in the *America at Odds* feature at the beginning of this chapter, the national government forced the states to raise the minimum drinking age to twenty-one by threatening to withhold federal highway funds from states that did not comply. Obamacare also raised questions about forcing the states to expand Medicaid, as discussed earlier in this chapter. The education reforms embodied in the No Child Left Behind (NCLB) Act rely on federal funding for their implementation as well. The states receive block grants for educational purposes and, in return, must meet federally imposed standards for testing and accountability. A common complaint, however, is that the existing NCLB Act is an underfunded federal mandate. Critics argue that the national government does not provide sufficient funds to implement it.

## 3–5d The Cost of Federal Mandates

As mentioned earlier, when the national government passes a law preempting an area in which the states and the national government have concurrent powers, the states must comply with that law in accordance with the supremacy clause of the Constitution. Thus, when such laws require the states to implement certain programs, the states must comply—but compliance with federal mandates can be costly. The cost of compliance has been estimated by some at $29 billion annually, and others believe the true figure to be much

**block grant** A federal grant given to a state for a broad area, such as criminal justice or mental-health programs.

higher. Although Congress passed legislation in 1995 to curb the use of unfunded federal mandates, that legislation was more rhetoric than reality.

### 3–5e Competitive Federalism

The debate over federalism is sometimes reduced to a debate over taxes. Which level of government will raise taxes to pay for government programs, and which will cut services to avoid raising taxes?

**The Right to Move** How states answer that question gives citizens an option: they can move to a state with fewer services and lower taxes, or to a state with more services but higher taxes. Political scientist Thomas R. Dye calls this model of federalism **competitive federalism.** State and local governments compete for businesses and citizens. If the state of Ohio offers tax advantages for locating a factory there, for example, a business may be more likely to build its factory in Ohio, thereby providing more jobs for Ohio residents.

If Ohio has very strict environmental regulations, however, that same business may choose not to build there, no matter how beneficial the tax advantages, because complying with the regulations would be costly. Although Ohio citizens lose the opportunity for more jobs, they may enjoy better air and water quality than citizens of the state where the new factory is ultimately built.

**Advantages and Disadvantages of Competition** Some observers consider such competition an advantage: Americans have several variables to consider when they choose a state in which to live. Others consider it a disadvantage: a state that offers more social services or lower taxes may experience an increase in population as people "vote with their feet" to take advantage of that state's laws. The resulting population increases can overwhelm the state's resources and force it to cut social services or raise taxes. Regulations that make it easier to build new housing may also draw in new residents. Recent studies suggest that much of the difference in population growth rates among states in recent decades may be due to differences in the cost of housing.

It appears likely, then, that the debate over how our federal system functions, as well as the battle for control between the states and the federal government, will continue. The Supreme Court, which has played umpire in this battle, will also likely continue to issue rulings that influence the balance of power.

> **competitive federalism** A model of federalism, devised by Thomas R. Dye, in which state and local governments compete for businesses and citizens, who in effect "vote with their feet" by moving to jurisdictions that offer a competitive advantage.

**FOR CRITICAL THINKING**

*What kinds of factors might cause you to consider moving to a different state? Are any of these factors under the control of state governments?*

This Hyundai manufacturing plant is located in Montgomery, Alabama. City and state government officials had to offer tax and other incentives to Hyundai Motors to entice the company to build the plant. Alabama was competing with other states.

MARK ELIAS/BLOOMBERG/GETTY IMAGES

# AMERICA AT
# ODDS Federalism

The topic of federalism raises one of the most enduring disputes in American history—the relative power of the national government versus that of the governments of the states. As you read in the last two chapters, Americans have been at odds over the strength of the central government since well before the American Revolution. The issue of centralization versus decentralization has taken a number of specific forms:

- Is it right for the national government to use its financial strength to pressure states into taking actions such as raising the drinking age by threatening to withhold subsidies—or are such pressures an abuse of the federal system?

- Should the national government intervene in the issue of legalizing or banning same-sex marriages—or leave such matters strictly to the states?

- Should the commerce clause be interpreted broadly, granting the federal government much power to regulate the economy—or should it be interpreted as narrowly as possible to keep the government from interfering with the rights of business owners?

- Should the federal government have a role in setting national policies for public education—or should that be left entirely to the states?

- Should the federal government establish a national system for funding health care—or should that, too, be left to the states or to the private sector?

# TAKE ACTION

Many people believe that it's possible to have a real impact on the problems we face—the economy, poverty, health care, or the environment—only at the national level. You can do a lot to address these issues at the state and local levels, however. Consider that an individual or a small group can have much more influence on a state government than on the national one, and can make an even bigger impact on a local government.

As the slogan goes, "Think globally, act locally." Your local government controls construction and land-use issues, oversees the police or sheriff's department, and can pass all kinds of local ordinances. Will banning the sale of Styrofoam cups lead to a tidier environment—or is it a ridiculous infringement on personal freedoms? There are hundreds of such issues that you and your friends could take up.

Acting locally does not have to mean political engagement, however. You can also volunteer your services for a cause that concerns you, such as improving the environment or helping the poor or the elderly. Volunteer activities can be very gratifying, and you could make a big difference in the lives that you touch. Try using VolunteerMatch to find volunteer opportunities in your community. Just enter your ZIP code on its Web site (search on "volunteermarch"). Other organizations that work to meet critical needs include AmeriCorps ("americorps") and the Corporation for National and Community Service ("nationalservice").

# STUDY TOOLS

## Ready to study?

- Review what you've read with the quiz below. Check your answers on the Chapter in Review card at the back of the book. For any questions you miss, read the corresponding Learning Outcome section again to prepare for class and your exam.
- Rip out and study the Chapter in Review card.

## . . . Or you can go online to CourseMate

at www.cengagebrain.com for these additional review materials:

- Practice Quizzes
- Key Term Flashcards or Crossword Puzzles
- Audio Summaries
- Simulations, Animated Learning Modules, and Interactive Timelines
- Videos
- American Government NewsWatch

## Fill-In

1. The advantages of a federal system of government in the United States include _____.

2. The constitutional basis for the implied powers of the national government is the _____ clause.

3. The Constitution's ___°_____ clause requires each state to honor every other state's public acts, records, and judicial proceedings.

4. In *McCulloch v. Maryland*, a case decided in 1819, the United States Supreme Court established the doctrines of _____.

5. Cooperative federalism grew out of the need to solve the pressing problems caused by _____.

6. The relationship of national, state, and local levels of government in implementing massive social programs in the 1960s and 1970s is often referred to as _____ federalism.

7. A _____ is a requirement in federal legislation that forces states and municipalities to comply with certain rules.

8. The national government forced the states to raise the minimum drinking age to twenty-one by _____.

## Multiple Choice

9. In a unitary system,
   a. subdivisional governments exercise only those powers given to them by the central government.
   b. sovereign states are joined together by a central government that has only limited powers over them.
   c. there are no local or subdivisional governments.

10. There are ___ governmental units in the United States today.
    a. 51   b. nearly 3000   c. almost 90,000

11. Article I, Section 8, of the U.S. Constitution enumerates twenty-seven powers that Congress may exercise. Two of these _____ powers are the power to coin money and the power to regulate interstate commerce.
    a. concurrent   b. expressed   c. inherent

12. The relationships among the states in our federal system of government are sometimes referred to as _____ federalism.
    a. picket-fence   b. cooperative   c. horizontal

13. The era of _____ federalism came to an end in the 1930s.
    a. dual   b. new   c. competitive

14. The welfare reform legislation passed by Congress in 1996 is an example of _____ federalism.
    a. dual   b. cooperative   c. new

15. Block grants
    a. are targeted for specific purposes as defined by federal law.
    b. are federal grants given to a state for broad areas, such as criminal justice or mental-health programs.
    c. give the states less discretion than categorical grants over how funds will be spent.

# Civil Liberties

TRAVIS LONG/RALEIGH NEWS & OBSERVER/MCT/NEWSCOM

## Should States Repeal Their Stand-Your-Ground Laws?

Traditionally, the legal doctrine that covers the justifiable use of deadly force for self-defense was straightforward. Until recently, most states allowed people to use deadly force only when they had a reasonable belief that death or bodily harm would otherwise result. Also, when in public, if a threatened person could retreat, she or he was required to do so instead of using force. (There is no obligation to retreat when you are in your own home or business, however.)

In Florida, all that has changed. In 2005, Florida became the first state to pass a stand-your-ground law. Since then, more than twenty other states have passed similar laws. A typical stand-your-ground statute allows the use of deadly force to prevent the commission of a "forcible felony," including not only murder, but also such crimes as robbery, carjacking, and sexual battery. In other words, in most stand-your-ground states, a resident has the right to shoot an intruder in his or her home—or someone else's home—even if there is no physical threat to the gun owner's safety.

These statutes also allow persons to use deadly force to repeal an attack when they are in public without imposing any duty to retreat. In other words, armed citizens are allowed to "stand their ground" and shoot. Today, however, following a 2012 incident in which a neighborhood-watch volunteer in Florida killed an African American youth, stand-your-ground laws are under attack.

DAVID MANNING/REUTERS

### A Person's Home Is His or Her Castle

Certain types of stand-your-ground laws have a long history. These laws are called "castle" laws, based on the legal precept from eighteenth-century common law that "a man's house is his castle" and no one may enter it without invitation. Thus, the reasoning goes, anyone attempting to enter illegally should suffer the consequences.

In Florida, supporters of the current law cite a more than 20 percent decrease in violent crime during the first five years the law was in effect. Criminals now know that they can be shot and even killed if they illegally enter houses or commit other felonies. Indeed, states that have passed stand-your-ground laws have seen an increase in justifiable homicides. According to Florida state representative Dennis Baxley, a co-sponsor of the original law, that means that these laws are working. "The perpetrators suffered instead of the persons they were victimizing."

### Stand-Your-Ground Laws Mean Vigilante Justice

Opponents of stand-your-ground laws argue that they lead to too many "justifiable" homicides. In Florida, the annual number has surged from an average of twelve to more than forty. Even in cases of home burglary, it is not proper to kill intruders who are attempting to flee. Shooting a perpetrator who poses no threat of bodily harm is vigilante justice. The criminal justice system—not an armed homeowner—should determine the penalty for a felony.

Furthermore, prosecutors in stand-your-ground states now find it more difficult to secure murder convictions because so many defendants claim self-defense. In many such cases, the shooters themselves may have been engaging in illegal activities. Unless that can be proved, however, a killer may go free. Finally, those who cite falling crime rates in states with stand-your-ground laws fail to observe that crime rates are also falling in other states.

### Where do you stand?

1. Under what circumstances, if any, do you believe that you would be justified in shooting a burglar in your home?
2. Depending on the jurisdiction and the crime, police as well as private citizens may be barred from shooting fleeing suspects. Under what conditions is such a rule appropriate?

### Explore this issue online

- Using an Internet search engine to look up "justifiable homicide" yields many articles relevant to stand-your-ground laws. For a broader approach to the topic, search on "self defense."

# Introduction

The debate over stand-your-ground laws, discussed in the chapter-opening *America at Odds* feature, is but one of many controversies concerning our civil liberties. **Civil liberties** are legal and constitutional rights that protect citizens from government actions. For example, the First Amendment to the U.S. Constitution prohibits Congress from making any law that abridges (restricts) the right to free speech. The First Amendment also guarantees freedom of religion, freedom of the press, and freedom to assemble (to gather together for a common purpose, such as to protest against a government policy or action). These and other freedoms and guarantees set forth in the Constitution and the Bill of Rights are essentially *limits* on government action.

Perhaps the best way to understand what civil liberties are and why they are important to Americans is to look at what might happen if we did not have them. If you were a student in China, for example, you would have to exercise some care in what you said and did. That country prohibits a variety of kinds of speech, notably any criticism of the leading role of the Communist Party. If you criticized the government in e-mail messages to your friends or on your Web site, you could end up in court on charges that you had violated the law—and perhaps even go to prison.

Note that some Americans confuse *civil liberties* (discussed in this chapter) with *civil rights* (discussed in the next chapter) and use the terms interchangeably. Scholars, however, make a distinction between the two. They point out that whereas civil liberties are limitations on government action, setting forth what the government *cannot* do, civil rights specify what the government *must* do—for example, to ensure equal protection under the law for all Americans.

**civil liberties** Individual rights protected by the Constitution against the powers of the government.

**writ of *habeas corpus*** An order that requires an official to bring a specified prisoner into court and explain to the judge why the person is being held in jail.

**bill of attainder** A legislative act that inflicts punishment on particular persons or groups without granting them the right to a trial.

***ex post facto* law** A criminal law that punishes individuals for committing an act that was legal when the act was committed.

# 4-1 The Constitutional Basis for Our Civil Liberties

The founders believed that the constitutions of the individual states contained ample provisions to protect citizens from government actions. Therefore, the founders did not include many references to individual civil liberties in the original version of the Constitution. Many of our liberties were added by the Bill of Rights, ratified in 1791. Nonetheless, the original Constitution did include some safeguards to protect citizens against an overly powerful government.

**LearningOutcome 4-1**

Define the term *civil liberties*, explain how civil liberties differ from civil rights, and state the constitutional basis for our civil liberties.

## 4-1a Safeguards in the Original Constitution

Article I, Section 9, of the Constitution provides that the writ of *habeas corpus* (a Latin phrase that roughly means "produce the body") will be available to all citizens except in times of rebellion or national invasion. A **writ of *habeas corpus*** is an order requiring that an official bring a specified prisoner into court and show the judge why the prisoner is being held in jail. If the court finds that the imprisonment is unlawful, it orders the prisoner to be released. If our country did not have such a constitutional provision, political leaders could jail their opponents without giving them the opportunity to plead their cases before a judge. Without this opportunity, many opponents might conveniently be left to rot away in prison.

The Constitution also prohibits Congress and the state legislatures from passing bills of attainder. A **bill of attainder** is a legislative act that directly punishes a specifically named individual (or a group or class of individuals) without a trial. For example, no legislature can pass a law that punishes a named Hollywood celebrity for unpatriotic statements.

Finally, the Constitution also prohibits Congress from passing *ex post facto laws*. The Latin term *ex post facto* roughly means "after the fact." An ***ex post facto* law** punishes individuals for committing an act that was legal when it was committed.

## 4-1b The Bill of Rights

As you read in Chapter 2, one of the contentious issues in the debate over ratification of the Constitution was the lack of protections for citizens from government actions. Although many state constitutions provided such protections, the Anti-Federalists wanted more. The promise of the addition of a bill of rights to the Constitution ensured its ratification.

The Bill of Rights was ratified by the states and became part of the Constitution on December 15, 1791. Look at the text of the Bill of Rights in Table 4–1 on the following page. As you can see, the first eight amendments grant the people specific rights and liberties. The remaining two amendments reserve certain rights and powers to the people and to the states.

Basically, in a democracy, government policy tends to reflect the view of the majority. A key function of the Bill of Rights, therefore, is to protect the rights of those in the minority against the will of the majority. When there is disagreement over how to interpret the Bill of Rights, the courts step in. The United States Supreme Court, as our nation's highest court, has the final say as to how the Constitution, including the Bill of Rights, should be interpreted. The civil liberties that you will read about in this chapter have all been shaped over time by Supreme Court decisions. For example, it is the Supreme Court that determines where freedom of speech ends and the right of society to be protected from certain forms of speech begins.

## 4-1c The Incorporation Issue

For many years, the courts assumed that the Bill of Rights limited only the actions of the national government, not the actions of state or local governments. In other words, if a state or local law was contrary to a basic freedom, such as the freedom of speech or the right to due process of law, the federal Bill of Rights did not come into play. The founders believed that the states, being closer to the people, would be less likely to violate their own citizens' liberties. Moreover, state constitutions, most of which contain bills of rights,

**The First Amendment** to the Constitution mandates separation of church and state. Nonetheless, references to God are common in public life, as the phrase "In God We Trust" on this coin demonstrates.

protect citizens against state government actions. The United States Supreme Court upheld this view when it decided, in *Barron v. Baltimore* (1833), that the Bill of Rights did not apply to state laws.[1]

Eventually, however, the Supreme Court began to take a different view. Because the Fourteenth Amendment played a key role in this development, we look next at the provisions of that amendment.

### The Right to Due Process

In 1868, three years after the end of the Civil War, the Fourteenth Amendment was added to the Constitution. The **due process clause** of this amendment requires that state governments protect their citizens' rights. (A similar requirement, binding on the federal government, was provided by the Fifth Amendment.) The due process clause reads, in part, as follows:

No State shall . . . deprive any person of life, liberty, or property, without due process of law.

The right to **due process of law** is simply the right to be treated fairly under the legal system. That system and its officers must follow "rules of fair play" in making decisions, in determining guilt or innocence, and in punishing those who have been found guilty.

**PROCEDURAL DUE PROCESS.** *Procedural* due process requires that any governmental decision to take life, liberty, or property be made equitably. For example, the government must use "fair procedures" in determining whether a person will be subjected to punishment or have some burden imposed on him or her. Fair procedure has been interpreted as requiring that the person have at least an opportunity to object to a proposed

**due process clause** The constitutional guarantee, set out in the Fifth and Fourteenth Amendments, that the government will not illegally or arbitrarily deprive a person of life, liberty, or property.

**due process of law** The requirement that the government use fair, reasonable, and standard procedures whenever it takes any legal action against an individual; required by the Fifth and Fourteenth Amendments.

## TABLE 4–1

# The Bill of Rights

### Amendment I.
### Religion, Speech, Press, Assembly, and Petition

Congress shall make no law respecting an establishment of religion, or prohibiting the free exercise thereof; or abridging the freedom of speech, or of the press; or the right of the people peaceably to assemble, and to petition the Government for a redress of grievances.

*Congress may not create an official church or enact laws limiting the freedom of religion, speech, the press, assembly, and petition. These guarantees, like the others in the Bill of Rights (the first ten amendments), are not absolute—each may be exercised only with regard to the rights of other persons.*

### Amendment II.
### Militia and the Right to Bear Arms

A well regulated Militia, being necessary to the security of a free State, the right of the people to keep and bear Arms, shall not be infringed.

*Each state has the right to maintain a volunteer armed force. Although individuals have the right to bear arms, states and the federal government may regulate the possession and use of firearms by individuals.*

### Amendment III.
### The Quartering of Soldiers

No Soldier shall, in time of peace be quartered in any house, without the consent of the Owner, nor in time of war, but in a manner to be prescribed by law.

*Before the Revolutionary War, it had been common British practice to quarter soldiers in colonists' homes. Military troops do not have the power to take over private houses during peacetime.*

### Amendment IV.
### Searches and Seizures

The right of the people to be secure in their persons, houses, papers, and effects, against unreasonable searches and seizures, shall not be violated, and no Warrants shall issue, but upon probable cause, supported by Oath or affirmation, and particularly describing the place to be searched, and the persons or things to be seized.

*Here, the word warrant refers to a document issued by a magistrate or judge indicating the name, address, and possible offense committed. Anyone asking for the warrant, such as a police officer, must be able to convince the magistrate or judge that an offense probably has been committed.*

### Amendment V.
### Grand Juries, Self-Incrimination, Double Jeopardy, Due Process, and Eminent Domain

No person shall be held to answer for a capital, or otherwise infamous crime, unless on a presentment or indictment of a Grand Jury, except in cases arising in the land or naval forces, or in the Militia, when in actual service in time of War or public danger; nor shall any person be subject for the same offense to be twice put in jeopardy of life or limb; nor shall be compelled in any criminal case to be a witness against himself, nor be deprived of life, liberty, or property, without due process of law; nor shall private property be taken for public use, without just compensation.

*There are two types of juries. A grand jury considers physical evidence and the testimony of witnesses and decides whether there is sufficient reason to bring a case to trial. A petit jury hears the case at trial and decides it. "For the same offense to be twice put in jeopardy of life or limb" means to be tried twice for the same crime. A person*

may not be tried for the same crime twice or forced to give evidence against herself or himself. No person's right to life, liberty, or property may be taken away except by lawful means, called the due process of law. Private property taken for public purposes must be paid for by the government.

### Amendment VI.
### Criminal Court Procedures

In all criminal prosecutions, the accused shall enjoy the right to a speedy and public trial, by an impartial jury of the State and district wherein the crime shall have been committed, which district shall have been previously ascertained by law, and to be informed of the nature and cause of the accusation; to be confronted with the witnesses against him; to have compulsory process for obtaining witnesses in his favor, and to have the Assistance of Counsel for his defence.

*Any person accused of a crime has the right to a fair and public trial by a jury in the state in which the crime took place. The charges against that person must be made clear. Any accused person has the right to a lawyer to defend him or her and to question those who testify against him or her, as well as the right to call people to speak in his or her favor at trial.*

### Amendment VII.
### Trial by Jury in Civil Cases

In Suits at common law, where the value in controversy shall exceed twenty dollars, the right of trial by jury shall be preserved, and no fact tried by a jury, shall be otherwise re-examined in any Court of the United States, than according to the rules of the common law.

*A jury trial may be requested by either party in a dispute in any case involving more than $20. If both parties agree to a trial by a judge without a jury, the right to a jury trial may be put aside.*

### Amendment VIII.
### Bail, Cruel and Unusual Punishment

Excessive bail shall not be required, nor excessive fines imposed, nor cruel and unusual punishments inflicted.

*Bail is that amount of money that a person accused of a crime may be required to deposit with the court as a guarantee that she or he will appear in court when requested. The amount of bail required or the fine imposed as punishment for a crime must be reasonable compared with the seriousness of the crime involved. Any punishment judged to be too harsh or too severe for a crime shall be prohibited.*

### Amendment IX.
### The Rights Retained by the People

The enumeration in the Constitution, of certain rights, shall not be construed to deny or disparage others retained by the people.

*Many civil rights that are not explicitly enumerated in the Constitution are still held by the people.*

### Amendment X.
### Reserved Powers of the States

The powers not delegated to the United States by the Constitution, nor prohibited by it to the States, are reserved to the States respectively, or to the people.

*Those powers not delegated by the Constitution to the federal government or expressly denied to the states belong to the states and to the people. This clause in essence allows the states to pass laws under their "police powers."*

action before an impartial, neutral decision maker (who need not be a judge).

**SUBSTANTIVE DUE PROCESS.** *Substantive* due process focuses on the content, or substance, of legislation. If a law or other governmental action limits a *fundamental right*, it will be held to violate substantive due process, unless it promotes a *compelling* or *overriding state interest.* All First Amendment rights plus the rights to interstate travel, privacy, and voting are considered fundamental. Compelling state interests could include, for example, the public's safety.

## Other Liberties Incorporated
The Fourteenth Amendment also states that no state "shall make or enforce any law which shall abridge the privileges or immunities of citizens of the United States." For some time, the Supreme Court considered the "privileges and immunities" referred to in the amendment to be those conferred by state laws or constitutions, not the federal Bill of Rights.

Starting in 1925, however, the Supreme Court gradually began using the due process clause to say that states could not abridge a civil liberty that the national government could not abridge. In other words, the Court *incorporated* the protections guaranteed by the national Bill of Rights into the liberties protected under the Fourteenth Amendment. As you can see in Table 4–2 below, the Supreme Court was particularly active during the 1960s in broadening its interpretation of the due process clause to ensure that states and localities could not infringe on civil liberties protected by the Bill of Rights.

Today, the liberties still not incorporated include the right to refuse to quarter soldiers and the right to a grand jury hearing. The right to bear arms described in the Second Amendment was incorporated only in 2010.

**FOR CRITICAL THINKING**

Congress often passes laws that are so narrowly defined that only one individual or corporation is covered by the legislation. *Should such laws be considered bills of attainder and thus unconstitutional? Why or why not?*

## TABLE 4–2

### Incorporating the Bill of Rights into the Fourteenth Amendment

| Year | Issue | Amendment Involved | Court Case |
|------|-------|--------------------|------------|
| 1925 | Freedom of speech | I | *Gitlow v. New York*, 268 U.S. 652. |
| 1931 | Freedom of the press | I | *Near v. Minnesota*, 283 U.S. 697. |
| 1932 | Right to a lawyer in capital punishment cases | VI | *Powell v. Alabama*, 287 U.S. 45. |
| 1937 | Freedom of assembly and right to petition | I | *De Jonge v. Oregon*, 299 U.S. 353. |
| 1940 | Freedom of religion | I | *Cantwell v. Connecticut*, 310 U.S. 296. |
| 1947 | Separation of church and state | I | *Everson v. Board of Education*, 330 U.S. 1. |
| 1948 | Right to a public trial | VI | *In re Oliver*, 333 U.S. 257. |
| 1949 | No unreasonable searches and seizures | IV | *Wolf v. Colorado*, 338 U.S. 25. |
| 1961 | Exclusionary rule | IV | *Mapp v. Ohio*, 367 U.S. 643. |
| 1962 | No cruel and unusual punishments | VIII | *Robinson v. California*, 370 U.S. 660. |
| 1963 | Right to a lawyer in all criminal felony cases | VI | *Gideon v. Wainwright*, 372 U.S. 335. |
| 1964 | No compulsory self-incrimination | V | *Malloy v. Hogan*, 378 U.S. 1. |
| 1965 | Right to privacy | Various | *Griswold v. Connecticut*, 381 U.S. 479. |
| 1966 | Right to an impartial jury | VI | *Parker v. Gladden*, 385 U.S. 363. |
| 1967 | Right to a speedy trial | VI | *Klopfer v. North Carolina*, 386 U.S. 213. |
| 1969 | No double jeopardy | V | *Benton v. Maryland*, 395 U.S. 784. |
| 2010 | Right to bear arms | II | *McDonald v. Chicago*, 130 S.Ct. 3020. |

# 4–2 Protections under the First Amendment

## LearningOutcome 4–2

List and describe the freedoms guaranteed by the First Amendment and explain how the courts have interpreted and applied these freedoms.

As mentioned earlier, the First Amendment sets forth some of our most important civil liberties. Specifically, the First Amendment guarantees the freedoms of religion, speech, the press, and assembly, as well as the right to petition the government. In the pages that follow, we look closely at the first three of these freedoms and discuss how, over time, Supreme Court decisions have defined their meaning and determined their limits.

## 4–2a Freedom of Religion

The First Amendment prohibits Congress from passing laws "respecting an establishment of religion, or prohibiting the free exercise thereof." The first part of this amendment is known as the **establishment clause.** The second part is called the **free exercise clause.**

**Laws on Religion in the Colonies**   That freedom of religion was the first freedom mentioned in the Bill of Rights is not surprising. After all, many colonists came to America to escape religious persecution. Nonetheless, these same colonists showed little tolerance for religious freedom within the communities they established. For example, in 1610 the Jamestown colony enacted a law requiring attendance at religious services on Sunday "both in the morning and the afternoon." Repeat offenders were subjected to particularly harsh punishments. For those who twice violated the law, for example, the punishment was a public whipping. For third-time offenders, the punishment was death. In all, nine of the thirteen colonies had established official religions by the time of the American Revolution.

**STATE POWERS.**   These examples of religious laws provide a context that is helpful in understanding why, in 1802, President Thomas Jefferson, a great proponent of religious freedom and tolerance, wanted the establishment clause to be "a wall of separation between church and state." The context also helps to explain why even state leaders who supported state religions might have favored the establishment clause—to keep the national government from interfering in such state matters. After all, the First

**establishment clause**
The section of the First Amendment that prohibits Congress from passing laws "respecting an establishment of religion." Issues concerning the establishment clause often center on prayer in public schools, the teaching of fundamentalist theories of creation, and government aid to parochial schools.

**free exercise clause**
The provision of the First Amendment stating that the government cannot pass laws "prohibiting the free exercise" of religion. Free exercise issues often concern religious practices that conflict with established laws.

AP PHOTO/AMY SMOTHERMAN BURGESS/KNOXVILLE NEWS SENTINEL

Most Americans are religious. Therefore, they often are in favor of some form of prayer in public schools. To what extent does the Constitution allow prayers in school?

Amendment says only that *Congress* can make no law respecting an establishment of religion. It says nothing about whether the *states* could make such laws.

**THE INTERNATIONAL CONTEXT.** Today, although freedom of religion is protected in many nations other than the United States, there are also a large number of countries in which followers of various religions are subject to discrimination and even severe persecution. We look at some examples in this chapter's *The Rest of the World* feature below.

**The Establishment Clause** The establishment clause forbids the government from establishing an official religion. This makes the United States different from countries that are ruled by religious governments, such as the Islamic government of Iran. It also makes us different from nations that have in the past strongly discouraged the practice of any religion at all, such as the People's Republic of China.

What does this separation of church and state mean in practice? For one thing, religion and government, though constitutionally separated in the United

# THE REST OF THE WORLD

## Religious Persecution Abroad

While Americans take religious liberty for granted, the citizens of some nations are not so fortunate. These include Burma (Myanmar), China, Cuba, North Korea, Saudi Arabia, and Sudan, just to name a few. Governments are not the only violators of religious freedom, however.

In India, Muslims, Christians, and Sikhs have suffered from mob violence. Recently, Pakistan's minister for minority affairs—a long-time champion of religious freedom for all people—was assassinated. Egypt's Coptic Christians have experienced numerous attacks both before and after the so-called Arab Spring, including a 2011 New Year's Day church bombing in Alexandria that left twenty-three dead. All too often, crimes such as these go unpunished.

### Iran: A Case Study
Religious intolerance in Iran has been widespread for decades. Victims have included Christians, Jews, and members of minority Muslim groups. The treatment of followers of the

Bahá'í religion, who number about three hundred thousand, has been particularly harsh. Iranian authorities view the Bahá'í as "heretics" rather than as members of a minority faith. In the last forty years, Iran's Islamist government has killed at least two hundred Bahá'í leaders.

More than ten thousand members of this religion have been dismissed from university and government jobs. Bahá'í believers are officially prohibited from establishing independent religious associations or places of worship. Bahá'í cemeteries are regularly desecrated and defaced. In 2010, seven Bahá'í leaders were convicted of "propaganda activities against the Islamic order," "cooperation with Israel," "corruption on earth," and other charges. They received twenty-year prison sentences.

### No Place for Christians in Iraq?
Under the dictatorship of Saddam Hussein, the Sunni Muslim denomination dominated the government

of Iraq, even though Sunnis make up only about a fifth of the population. Shi'a Muslims, who are in the majority, were repressed. After Hussein was ousted, the Shi'ites dominated the Sunnis. No matter who is in charge, though, Iraq's Christians are at risk.

Since 2004, Christians have been tortured, beheaded, kidnapped, raped, and evicted from their homes. Their churches have been repeatedly bombed. In October 2010, during Sunday mass in a Baghdad church, almost one hundred worshipers were killed or wounded by an al Qaeda affiliate. Iraq's human rights minister has said that the goal of the perpetrators was "to empty Iraq of Christians."

Not surprisingly, there has been a mass exodus of Christians from Iraq in recent years—more than half of the original population of about seven hundred thousand have left. Several smaller religious minorities have lost up to 80 percent of their members to emigration.

**FOR CRITICAL** **ANALYSIS**   Is there anything the United States can do to reduce religious persecution abroad?

States, have never been enemies or strangers. The establishment clause does not prohibit government from supporting religion in *general*. Religion remains a part of public life.

Most government officials take an oath of office in the name of God, and our coins and paper currency carry the motto "In God We Trust." Clergy of different religions serve in each branch of the armed forces. Public meetings and even sessions of Congress open with prayers. Indeed, the establishment clause often masks the fact that Americans are, by and large, religious and prefer that their political leaders be people of faith.

**THE WALL OF SEPARATION.** The "wall of separation" that Thomas Jefferson referred to, however, does exist and has been upheld by the Supreme Court on many occasions. An important ruling by the Supreme Court on the establishment clause came in 1947 in *Everson v. Board of Education*.[2] The case involved a New Jersey law that allowed the state to pay for bus transportation of students who attended parochial schools (schools run by churches or other religious groups). The Court stated as follows: "No tax in any amount, large or small, can be levied to support any religious activities or institutions."

The Court upheld the New Jersey law, however, because it did not aid the church *directly* but provided for the safety and benefit of the students. The ruling both affirmed the importance of separating church and state and set the precedent that not *all* forms of state and federal aid to church-related schools are forbidden under the Constitution.

A full discussion of the various church–state issues that have arisen in American politics would fill volumes. Here, we examine three of these issues: prayer in the schools, the teaching of evolution versus creationism or intelligent design, and government aid to parochial schools.

**PRAYER IN THE SCHOOLS.** On occasion, some public schools have promoted a general sense of religion without proclaiming allegiance to any particular church or sect. Whether the states have a right to allow this was the main question presented in 1962 in *Engel v. Vitale*,[3] also known as the "Regents' Prayer case." The State Board of Regents in New York had composed a nondenominational prayer (a prayer not associated with any particular church) and urged school districts to use it in classrooms at the start of each day. The prayer read as follows:

Almighty God, we acknowledge our dependence upon Thee, and we beg Thy blessings upon us, our parents, our teachers, and our Country.

Some parents objected to the prayer, contending that it violated the establishment clause. The Supreme Court agreed and ruled that the Regents' Prayer was unconstitutional. Speaking for the majority, Justice Hugo Black wrote that the First Amendment must at least mean "that in this country it is no part of the business of government to compose official prayers for any group of the American people to recite as a part of a religious program carried on by government."

**PRAYER IN THE SCHOOLS—THE DEBATE CONTINUES.** Since the *Engel v. Vitale* ruling, the Supreme Court has continued to shore up the wall of separation between church and state in a number of decisions. Generally, the Court has had to walk a fine line between the wishes of those who believe that religion should have a more prominent place in our public institutions and those who do not. For example, in a 1980 case, *Stone v. Graham*,[4] the Supreme Court ruled that a Kentucky law requiring that the Ten Commandments be posted in all public schools violated the establishment clause. Many groups around the country opposed this ruling.

**MOMENTS OF SILENCE.** Another controversial issue is whether "moments of silence" in the schools

The high school student on the left sought, with the help of her attorney on the right, to have a prayer banner removed from her school's hallway. A federal court agreed with her in 2012.

are constitutional. In 1985, the Supreme Court ruled that an Alabama law authorizing a daily one-minute period of silence for meditation and voluntary prayer was unconstitutional. Because the law specifically endorsed prayer, it appeared to support religion.[5]

Since then, the lower courts have generally held that a school may require a moment of silence, but only if it serves a clearly secular purpose (such as to meditate on the day's activities).[6] Yet another issue concerns prayers said before public school sporting events, such as football games. In 2000, the Supreme Court held that student-led pregame prayer using the school's public-address system was unconstitutional.[7]

In sum, the Supreme Court has ruled that public schools, which are agencies of government, cannot sponsor religious activities. It has *not,* however, held that individuals cannot pray, when and as they choose, in schools or in any other place. Nor has it held that the schools are barred from teaching *about* religion, as opposed to engaging in religious practices.

**EVOLUTION VERSUS CREATIONISM.** Certain religious groups have long opposed the teaching of evolution in public schools. These groups contend that evolutionary theory, a theory with overwhelming scientific support, directly counters their religious belief that human beings did not evolve but were created fully formed, as described in the biblical story of the creation. In fact, surveys have repeatedly shown that a majority of Americans believe that humans were directly created by God rather than having evolved

When an Oklahoma school attempted to bar a young Muslim girl from wearing a head scarf to school, the federal government intervened. Why would the U.S. government protect the right to wear religious symbols in public schools? What civil liberties ensured by the U.S. Constitution might protect the right to wear religious dress in public schools?

from other species. The Supreme Court, however, has held that state laws forbidding the teaching of evolution in the schools are unconstitutional.

For example, in *Epperson v. Arkansas,*[8] a case decided in 1968, the Supreme Court held that an Arkansas law prohibiting the teaching of evolution violated the establishment clause because it imposed religious beliefs on students. In 1987, the Supreme Court also held unconstitutional a Louisiana law requiring that the biblical story of the creation be taught along with evolution. The Court deemed the law unconstitutional in part because it had as its primary purpose the promotion of a particular religious belief.[9]

Nevertheless, some state and local groups continue their efforts against the teaching of evolution. In 2008, Louisiana adopted the Louisiana Science Education Act, which states, "The teaching of some scientific subjects can cause controversy." It encourages Louisiana teachers to "help students understand, analyze, critique, and review in an objective manner the scientific strengths and scientific weaknesses of existing scientific theories." Debate in the state legislature made it clear that the theories in question included evolution and global warming. Critic John Derbyshire commented, "The act will encourage Louisiana local school boards to unconstitutional behavior. That's what it's *meant* to do." The legislation has not yet been challenged in court, however.

**EVOLUTION VERSUS INTELLIGENT DESIGN.** Some activists have advocated the concept of "intelligent design" as an alternative to the teaching of evolution. This concept posits that an intelligent cause, rather than an undirected process such as natural selection, lies behind the creation and development of the universe and living things. Proponents of intelligent design claim that it is a scientific theory and thus that its teaching does not violate the establishment clause in any way. Opponents contend that the "intelligent cause" is simply another term for God.

These arguments were tested in 2004 in Dover, Pennsylvania, when the local school board required ninth-grade biology classes to use a textbook that endorsed intelligent design. In November 2005, the board members who supported the requirement were voted out of office. In December, a federal district court judge ruled that intelligent design was not science, that it was inherently religious, and that the school board's actions were unconstitutional.[10]

**AID TO PAROCHIAL SCHOOLS.** Americans have long been at odds over whether public tax dollars should be used to fund activities in parochial schools—private schools that have religious affiliations. Over the years, the courts have often had to decide whether specific types of aid do or do not violate the establishment clause. Aid to church-related schools in the form of transportation, equipment, or special educational services for disadvantaged students has been held permissible. Other forms of aid, such as funding teachers' salaries and paying for field trips, have been held unconstitutional.

Since 1971, the Supreme Court has held that, to be constitutional, a state's school aid must meet three requirements: (1) the purpose of the financial aid must be clearly secular (not religious), (2) its primary effect must neither advance nor inhibit religion, and (3) it must avoid an "excessive government entanglement with religion." The Court first used this three-part test in *Lemon v. Kurtzman*,[11] and hence it is often referred to as the **Lemon test.** In the 1971 *Lemon* case, the Court denied public aid to private and parochial schools for the salaries even of teachers of secular courses and for textbooks and instructional materials in certain secular subjects. The Court held that the establishment clause is designed to prevent three main evils: "sponsorship, financial support, and active involvement of the sovereign [the government] in religious activity."

**SCHOOL VOUCHER PROGRAMS.** Another contentious issue has to do with the use of **school vouchers**—educational certificates, provided by state governments, that students can use at any school, public or private. In an effort to improve their educational systems, several school districts have been experimenting with voucher systems. Ten states now have limited voucher programs, under which some schoolchildren may attend private elementary or high schools using vouchers paid for by taxpayers' dollars.

In 2002, the United States Supreme Court ruled that a voucher program in Cleveland, Ohio, was constitutional. Under the program, the state provided up to $2,250 to low-income families, who could use the funds to send their children to either public or private schools. The Court concluded that the taxpayer-paid voucher program did not unconstitutionally entangle church and state because the funds went to parents, not to schools. The parents theoretically could use the vouchers to send their children to nonreligious private academies or charter schools, even though 95 percent used the vouchers at religious schools.[12]

Despite the 2002 Supreme Court ruling, several constitutional questions surrounding school vouchers remain unresolved. For example, some state constitutions are more explicit than the federal Constitution in denying the use of public funds for religious education. Even after the Supreme Court ruling in the Ohio case, a Florida court ruled in 2002 that a voucher program in that state violated Florida's constitution.[13]

**The Free Exercise Clause** As mentioned, the second part of the First Amendment's statement on religion consists of the free exercise clause, which forbids the passage of laws "prohibiting the free exercise of religion." This clause protects a person's right to worship or to believe as he or she wishes without government interference. No law or act of government may violate this constitutional right.

**BELIEF AND PRACTICE ARE DISTINCT.** The free exercise clause does not necessarily mean that individuals can act in any way they want on the basis of their religious beliefs. There is an important distinction between belief and practice. The Supreme Court has ruled consistently that the right to hold any *belief* is absolute. The right to *practice* one's beliefs, however, may have some limits. As the Court itself once asked, "Suppose one believed that human sacrifice were a necessary part of religious worship?"

The Supreme Court first dealt with the issue of belief versus practice in 1878 in *Reynolds v. United*

> **The free exercise clause** protects a person's right to worship or to believe as he or she wishes without government interference.

**Lemon test** A three-part test enunciated by the Supreme Court in the 1971 case of *Lemon v. Kurtzman* to determine whether government aid to parochial schools is constitutional. To be constitutional, the aid must (1) be for a clearly secular purpose, (2) neither advance nor inhibit religion in its primary effect, and (3) avoid an "excessive government entanglement with religion." The *Lemon* test has also been used in other types of cases involving the establishment clause.

**school voucher** An educational certificate, provided by a government, that allows a student to use public funds to pay for a private or a public school chosen by the student or his or her parents.

*States.*[14] Reynolds was a Mormon who had two wives. Polygamy, or the practice of having more than one spouse simultaneously, was encouraged by the customs and teachings of his religion at that time. Polygamy was also prohibited by federal law. Reynolds was convicted and appealed the case, arguing that the law violated his constitutional right to freely exercise his religious beliefs. The Court did not agree. It said that to allow Reynolds to practice polygamy would make religious doctrines superior to the law.

**RELIGIOUS PRACTICES AND THE WORKPLACE.** The free exercise of religion in the workplace was bolstered by Title VII of the Civil Rights Act of 1964, which requires employers to accommodate their employees' religious practices unless such accommodation causes an employer to suffer an "undue hardship." Thus, if an employee claims that religious beliefs prevent him or her from working on a particular day of the week, such as Saturday or Sunday, the employer must attempt to accommodate the employee's needs.

Several cases have come before lower federal courts concerning employer dress codes that contradict the religious customs of employees. For example, in 1999 the Third Circuit Court of Appeals ruled in favor of two Muslim police officers in Newark, New Jersey, who claimed that they were required by their faith to wear beards and would not shave them to comply with the police department's grooming policy.[15] Muslims, Rastafarians, and others have refused to change the grooming habits required by their religions and have been successful in court.

Some of the members of fundamentalist Mormon sects engage in polygamy, which is against the law. What can the government do in such situations?

AARON M. SPRECHER/UPI/LANDOV

**INSURANCE FOR BIRTH CONTROL.** A recent free exercise controversy involved the question of whether businesses could be required to supply health-insurance coverage for birth control measures. Such coverage was required in health-insurance plans that met the standards of the Affordable Care Act. Churches and other religious organizations that objected to contraception on principle were exempt from the requirement. In 2012, however, the government ruled that universities, hospitals, and similar organizations had to provide coverage for contraception even if they were affiliated with churches that opposed birth control.

The result was a storm of opposition from organizations such as the Roman Catholic Church, which rejects contraception. These groups argued that they were being forced to support activities to which they were morally opposed. Such a requirement was, in their opinion, a violation of their free exercise rights. This position gained broad support among Republicans in Congress. An alternate view was that the churches were attempting to impose their religious values on employees not directly involved in religious activities. Many employees of Catholic-affiliated universities and hospitals are in fact not Catholic.

President Barack Obama proposed a compromise under which church-affiliated hospitals and schools would not have to pay for the insurance coverage, but employees would still receive the benefit. This plan satisfied many schools and hospitals. It was not acceptable to the Catholic bishops, however, who filed a lawsuit aimed at overturning the requirement.

## 4-2b Freedom of Expression

No one in this country seems to have a problem protecting the free speech of those with whom they agree. The real challenge is protecting unpopular ideas. The protection needed is, in Justice Oliver Wendell Holmes's words, "not free thought for those who agree with us but freedom for the thought that we hate." The First Amendment is designed to protect the freedom to express *all* ideas, including those that may be unpopular.

The First Amendment has been interpreted to protect more than merely spoken words. It also protects **symbolic speech**—speech involving actions and other nonverbal expressions. Some common examples

**symbolic speech** The expression of beliefs, opinions, or ideas through forms other than verbal speech or print; speech involving actions and other nonverbal expressions.

include picketing in a labor dispute or wearing a black armband in protest of a government policy. Even burning the American flag as a gesture of protest has been held to be protected by the First Amendment.

## The Right to Free Speech Is Not Absolute

Although Americans have the right to free speech, not *all* speech is protected under the First Amendment. Our constitutional rights and liberties are not absolute. Rather, they are what the Supreme Court—the ultimate interpreter of the Constitution—says they are. Although the Court has zealously safeguarded the right to free speech, at times it has imposed limits on speech in the interests of protecting other rights of Americans. These rights include security against harm to one's person or reputation, the need for public order, and the need to preserve the government.

Generally, throughout our history, the Supreme Court has attempted to balance our rights to free speech against other needs of society, as just mentioned. As Justice Holmes once said, even "the most stringent protection of free speech would not protect a man in falsely shouting fire in a theatre and causing a panic."[16] We look next at some of the ways that the Court has limited the right to free speech.

## Early Restrictions on Expression

At times in our nation's history, various individuals have opposed our form of government. The government, however, has drawn a fine line between legitimate criticism and the expression of ideas that may seriously harm society. Clearly, the government may pass laws against violent acts. But what about **seditious speech,** which urges resistance to lawful authority or advocates overthrowing the government?

As early as 1798, Congress took steps to curb seditious speech when it passed the Alien and Sedition Acts, which made it a crime to utter "any false, scandalous, and malicious" criticism of the government. The acts were considered unconstitutional by many but were never tested in the courts. Several dozen individuals were prosecuted under the acts, and some were actually convicted. In 1801, President Thomas Jefferson pardoned those sentenced under the acts, and Congress soon repealed them.

"FREE SPEECH
is the whole thing,
the whole ball game.
Free speech is life itself."
~ SALMAN RUSHDIE ~
INDIAN-BORN BRITISH WRITER
B. 1947

**CLEAR AND PRESENT DANGER.** During World War I, Congress passed the Espionage Act of 1917 and the Sedition Act of 1918. The 1917 act prohibited attempts to interfere with the operations of the military forces, the war effort, or the process of recruitment. The 1918 act made it a crime to "willfully utter, print, write, or publish any disloyal, profane, scurrilous [insulting], or abusive language" about the government. More than two thousand persons were tried and convicted under this act, which was repealed at the end of World War I. The Supreme Court upheld the constitutionality of the Espionage Act in 1919 when it issued the *clear and present danger test*. Under that test, expression may be restricted if it would cause a dangerous condition, actual or imminent, that Congress has the power to prevent.[17]

**THE BAD TENDENCY RULE.** In 1925, the Court adopted an even more restrictive doctrine, the *bad tendency rule*. Under this rule, speech could be restricted if it might lead to some "evil."[18]

In 1940, Congress passed the Smith Act, which forbade people from advocating the violent overthrow of the U.S. government. In 1951, the Supreme Court upheld the constitutionality of the Smith Act in *Dennis v. United States*,[19] which involved eleven top leaders of the Communist Party who had been convicted of violating the act. The Court found that their activities went beyond the permissible peaceful advocacy of change.

**THE IMMINENT LAWLESS ACTION TEST.** The current standard for evaluating the legality of advocacy speech was established by the Supreme Court in 1969. Under the **imminent lawless action test,** speech can be forbidden only when it is "directed to inciting . . . imminent lawless action."[20] This is a hard standard

**seditious speech**
Speech that urges resistance to lawful authority or that advocates the overthrowing of a government.

**imminent lawless action test** The current Supreme Court doctrine for assessing the constitutionality of subversive speech. To be illegal, speech must be "directed to inciting . . . imminent lawless action."

for prosecutors to meet. As a result, "subversive" speech receives far more protection today than it did in the past.

## Limited Protection for Commercial Speech

Advertising, or **commercial speech,** is also protected by the First Amendment, but not as fully as regular speech. Generally, the Supreme Court has considered a restriction on commercial speech to be valid as long as the restriction "(1) seeks to implement a substantial government interest, (2) directly advances that interest, and (3) goes no further than necessary to accomplish its objective." Problems arise, though, when restrictions on commercial advertising achieve one substantial government interest yet are contrary to the interest in protecting free speech and the right of consumers to be informed. In such cases, the courts have to decide which interest takes priority.

Liquor advertising is a good illustration of this kind of conflict. In one case, Rhode Island argued that its law banning the advertising of liquor prices served the state's goal of discouraging liquor consumption (because the ban discouraged bargain hunting and thus kept liquor prices high). The Supreme Court, however, held that the ban was an unconstitutional restraint on commercial speech. The Court stated that the First Amendment "directs us to be especially skeptical of regulations that seek to keep people in the dark for what the government perceives to be their own good."[21]

## Unprotected Speech

Certain types of speech receive no protection under the First Amendment. Speech has never been protected when the speech itself is part of a crime. An act of fraud, for example, often may be carried out entirely through spoken words. Accused fraudsters who attempted to defend their actions by standing on their First Amendment rights would get nowhere. Other types of unprotected speech include defamation (libel and slander) and obscenity.

**LIBEL AND SLANDER.** No person has the right to libel or slander another. **Libel** is a published report of a falsehood that tends to injure a person's reputation or character. **Slander** is the public utterance (speaking) of a statement that holds a person up for contempt, ridicule, or hatred. To prove libel or slander, certain criteria must be met. The statements made must be untrue, must stem from an intent to do harm, and must result in actual harm.

The Supreme Court has ruled that public figures (public officials and others in the public limelight) cannot collect damages for remarks made against them unless they can prove the remarks were made with "reckless" disregard for accuracy. Generally, it is believed that because public figures have greater access to the media than ordinary persons do, they are in a better position to defend themselves against libelous or slanderous statements.

**OBSCENITY.** Obscene speech is another form of speech that is not protected under the First Amendment. Although the dictionary defines **obscenity** as that which is offensive and indecent, the courts have had difficulty defining the term with any precision. Supreme Court justice Potter Stewart's famous statement, "I know it when I see it," certainly gave little guidance on the issue.

One problem in defining *obscenity* is that what is obscene to one person is not necessarily obscene to another. What one reader considers indecent, another reader might see as "colorful." Another problem is that society's views on obscenity change over time. Major literary works of such great writers as D. H. Lawrence (1885–1930), Mark Twain (1835–1910), and James Joyce (1882–1941), for example, were once considered obscene in most of the United States.

**THE SUPREME COURT'S DEFINITION OF OBSCENITY.** After many unsuccessful attempts to define obscenity, in 1973 the Supreme Court came up with a three-part test in *Miller v. California.*[22] The Court decided that a book, film, or other piece of material is legally obscene if it meets the following criteria:

1. The average person applying contemporary community (present-day) standards finds that the work taken as a whole appeals to the prurient interest—that is, tends to excite unwholesome sexual desire.

**commercial speech** Advertising statements that describe products. Commercial speech receives less protection under the First Amendment than ordinary speech.

**libel** A published report of a falsehood that tends to injure a person's reputation or character.

**slander** The public utterance (speaking) of a statement that holds a person up for contempt, ridicule, or hatred.

**obscenity** Indecency or offensiveness in speech, expression, behavior, or appearance. Whether specific expressions or acts constitute obscenity is normally determined by community standards.

2. The work depicts or describes, in a patently (obviously) offensive way, a form of sexual conduct specifically prohibited by an antiobscenity law.
3. The work taken as a whole lacks serious literary, artistic, political, or scientific value.

The very fact that the Supreme Court has had to set up such a complicated test shows how difficult defining *obscenity* is. The Court went on to state that, in effect, local communities should be allowed to set their own standards for what is obscene. What is obscene to many people in one area of the country might be perfectly acceptable to those in another area.

**OBSCENITY IN CYBERSPACE.** A hugely controversial issue concerning free speech is the question of obscene and pornographic materials in cyberspace. Such materials can be easily accessed by anyone of any age anywhere in the world at countless Web sites. Many people strongly believe that the government should step in to prevent obscenity on the Internet. Others believe, just as strongly, that speech on the Internet should not be regulated.

The issue came to a head in 1996, when Congress passed the Communications Decency Act (CDA). The law made it a crime to transmit "indecent" or "patently offensive" speech or images to minors (those under the age of eighteen) or to make such speech or images available online to minors. In 1997, the Supreme Court held that the law's sections on indecent speech were unconstitutional. According to the Court, those sections of the CDA were too broad in their scope and significantly restrained the constitutionally protected free speech of adults.[23]

**ADDITIONAL ATTEMPTS TO CONTROL ONLINE OBSCENITY.** Congress made a further attempt to regulate Internet speech in 1998 with the Child Online Protection Act. The act imposed criminal penalties on those who distribute material that is "harmful to minors" without using some kind of age-verification system to separate adult and minor Web users.

In 2004, the Supreme Court barred enforcement of the act, ruling that the act likely violated constitutionally protected free speech, and sent the case back to the district court for a trial.[24] The district court found the act unconstitutional, and in 2008 a federal appellate court upheld the district court's ruling.

"The only security of all is in a **free press....** It is necessary, to keep the waters pure."

~ THOMAS JEFFERSON ~
THIRD PRESIDENT OF THE UNITED STATES
1801–1809

Having failed twice in its attempt to regulate online obscenity, Congress decided to try a different approach. In late 2000, it passed the Children's Internet Protection Act (CIPA). This act requires schools and libraries to use Internet filtering software to protect children from pornography or risk losing federal funds for technology upgrades. The CIPA was also challenged on constitutional grounds, but in 2003 the Supreme Court held that the act did not violate the First Amendment. The Court concluded that because libraries can disable the filters for any patrons who ask, the system is reasonably flexible and does not burden free speech to an unconstitutional extent.[25]

**Free Speech for Students?** America's schools and college campuses experience an ongoing tension between the guarantee of free speech and the desire to restrain speech that is offensive to others. Typically, cases involving free speech in the schools raise the following question: Where should the line between unacceptable speech and merely offensive speech be drawn? Schools at all levels—elementary schools, high schools, and colleges and universities—have grappled with this issue.

**ELEMENTARY AND HIGH SCHOOLS.** Generally, the courts allow elementary schools wide latitude to define what students may and may not say to other students. At the high school level, the Supreme Court has allowed some restraints to be placed on the freedom of expression. For example, as you will read shortly in the discussion of freedom of the press, the Court does allow school officials to exercise some censorship over high school publications. And, in a controversial 2007 case, the Court upheld a school principal's decision to suspend a high school student who unfurled a banner reading "Bong Hits 4 Jesus" at an event off the school premises. School officials maintained that the banner appeared to advocate illegal drug use in violation of school policy. Many legal commentators and scholars strongly criticized this decision.[26]

**UNIVERSITY SPEECH CODES.** A difficult question that many universities face today is whether the right to free speech includes the right to make hateful remarks about others based on their race, gender, or sexual orientation. Some claim that allowing people with extremist views to voice their opinions can lead to violence. In response to this question, several universities have gone so far as to institute speech codes to minimize the disturbances that hate speech might cause. Although these speech codes have often been ruled unconstitutional on the ground that they restrict freedom of speech,[27] such codes continue to exist on many college campuses.

For example, the policy on acceptable e-mail usage at Claremont McKenna College provides that "the College's system must not be used to create or transmit material that is derogatory, defamatory, obscene or offensive. Such material includes, but is not limited to, slurs, epithets or anything that might be construed as harassment or disparagement based on race, color, national origin, sex, sexual orientation, age, disability, or religious or political beliefs." Presumably, under a policy such as this, it would be a violation to say "Democrats are idiots" or "Republicans are insane."

**CYBERBULLYING.** The courts have regularly upheld the right of schools to ban bullying even when bullying consists entirely of spoken or written words. Such bans are justified as a protection of a school's basic educational mission. Bullying can disrupt the educational process by making it difficult or impossible for the victim to carry on in school. Matters are less clear at the college level, or even when a perpetrator is an adult who is not under the authority of the school system.

Recently, several cyberbullies have been charged with crimes. One example is the case of a Rutgers student who committed suicide after his roommate secretly taped a sexual encounter he had with another man and then posted it online. The roommate was convicted of multiple computer-related crimes but is appealing his convictions.

Another example is a woman who pretended online to be a boy so as to harass one of her daughter's classmates. After the young victim was told that "the world would be a better place without you," she committed suicide. The woman's computer crime conviction was overturned on appeal. Both of these cases raise troubling questions about the extent to which verbal harassment is protected by the First Amendment.

## 4–2c Freedom of the Press

The framers of the Constitution believed that the press should be free to publish a wide range of opinions and information, and generally the free speech rights just discussed also apply to the press. The courts have placed certain restrictions on freedom of the press, however. Over the years, the Supreme Court has developed various guidelines and doctrines to use in deciding whether freedom of speech and the press can be restrained.

### The Preferred-Position Doctrine

One major guideline, called the *preferred-position doctrine*, states that certain freedoms are so essential to a democracy that they hold a preferred position. According to this doctrine, any law that limits these freedoms should be presumed unconstitutional unless the government can show that the law is absolutely necessary. The idea behind this doctrine is that freedom of speech and the press should rarely, if ever, be

MICHAEL S. GORDON/THE REPUBLICAN/LANDOV

Cyberbullying has become a serious problem for some young people. Why is there a tension between laws controlling cyberbullying and the First Amendment?

diminished, because spoken and printed words are the prime tools of the democratic process.

**Prior Restraint** Stopping an activity before it actually happens is known as *prior restraint*. With respect to freedom of the press, prior restraint involves *censorship,* which occurs when an official removes objectionable materials from an item before it is published or broadcast. An example of censorship and prior restraint would be a court's ruling that two paragraphs in an upcoming article in the local newspaper had to be removed before the article could be published. The Supreme Court has generally ruled against prior restraint, arguing that the government cannot curb ideas before they are expressed.

In certain circumstances, however, the Court has allowed prior restraint. For example, in a 1988 case, *Hazelwood School District v. Kuhlmeier,*[28] a high school principal deleted two pages from the school newspaper just before it was printed. The pages contained stories on students' experiences with pregnancy and discussed the impact of divorce on students at the school. The Supreme Court, noting that students in school do not have exactly the same rights as adults in other settings, ruled that high school administrators can censor school publications. The Court said that school newspapers are part of the school curriculum, not a public forum. Therefore, administrators have the right to censor speech that promotes conduct inconsistent with the "shared values of a civilized social order."

**FOR CRITICAL THINKING** The establishment of religious chaplains in the armed forces has been justified on the basis that otherwise, service members on active duty would have no access to religious services and counseling. *Do you agree with this argument? Why or why not?*

## 4–3 The Right to Privacy

Supreme Court justice Louis Brandeis stated in 1928 that the right to privacy is "the most comprehensive of rights and the right most valued by civilized men."[29] The majority of the justices on the Supreme Court at that time did not agree. In 1965, however, in the landmark case of *Griswold v. Connecticut,*[30] the justices on the Supreme Court held that a right to privacy is implied by

other constitutional rights guaranteed in the First, Third, Fourth, Fifth, and Ninth Amendments. For example, consider the words

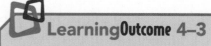

of the Ninth Amendment: "The enumeration in the Constitution, of certain rights, shall not be construed to deny or disparage others retained by the people." In other words, just because the Constitution, including its amendments, does not specifically mention the right to privacy does not mean that this right is denied to the people.

Although Congress and the courts have acknowledged a constitutional right to privacy, the nature and scope of this right are not always clear. For example, Americans continue to debate whether the right to privacy includes the right to have an abortion or the right of terminally ill persons to commit physician-assisted suicide. Since the terrorist attacks of September 11, 2001, another pressing privacy issue has been how to monitor potential terrorists to prevent another attack without violating the privacy rights of all Americans.

### 4–3a Congressional Actions

During the last several decades, Congress has also passed laws ensuring the privacy rights of individuals. For example, in 1966 Congress passed the Freedom of Information Act, which, among other things, allows any person to request copies of any information about her or him contained in government files. In 1974, Congress passed the Privacy Act, which restricts government disclosure of data to third parties.

In 1994, Congress passed the Driver's Privacy Protection Act, which prevents states from disclosing or selling a driver's personal information without the driver's consent.[31] In late 2000, the federal Department of Health and Human Services issued a regulation ensuring the privacy of a person's medical information. Health-care providers and insurance companies are restricted from sharing confidential information about their patients. In 2011, however, the Supreme Court struck down a Vermont law that prevented pharmacies from selling the prescription records of physicians to drug companies.[32]

### 4–3b The Abortion Controversy

One of the most divisive and emotionally charged issues debated today is whether the right to privacy means that women can choose to have abortions.

**Abortion and Privacy** In 1973, in the landmark case of *Roe v. Wade,*[33] the Supreme Court, using the *Griswold* case as a precedent, held that the "right of privacy . . . is broad enough to encompass a woman's decision whether or not to terminate her pregnancy." The right is not absolute throughout pregnancy, however. The Court also said that any state could impose certain regulations to safeguard the health of the mother after the first three months of pregnancy and, in the final stages of pregnancy, could act to protect potential life.

Since the *Roe v. Wade* decision, the Supreme Court has adopted a more conservative approach and has upheld restrictive state laws requiring counseling, waiting periods, notification of parents, and other actions prior to abortions.[34] Yet the Court has never overturned the *Roe* decision. In fact, in 1997 and again in 2000, the Supreme Court upheld laws requiring "buffer zones" around abortion clinics to protect those entering the clinics from unwanted counseling or harassment by antiabortion groups.[35]

In 2000, the Supreme Court invalidated a Nebraska statute banning "partial-birth" abortions, a procedure used during the second trimester of pregnancy.[36] Undeterred by the fate of the Nebraska law, President George W. Bush signed the Partial Birth Abortion Ban Act in 2003. In a close (five-to-four) and controversial 2007 decision, the Supreme Court upheld the constitutionality of the 2003 act.[37]

Many were surprised at the Court's decision on partial-birth abortion, given that the federal act banning this practice was quite similar to the Nebraska law that had been struck down by the Court in 2000, just seven years earlier. The Court became more conservative in 2006, however, when President George W.

Both sides of the abortion issue continue to spar in the public arena.

Bush appointed Justice Samuel Alito to replace Sandra Day O'Connor. Dissenting from the majority opinion in the case, Justice Ruth Bader Ginsburg said that the ruling was an "alarming" departure from three decades of Supreme Court decisions on abortion.

## 4–3c Do We Have the "Right to Die"?

Whether it is called euthanasia (mercy killing), assisted suicide, or a dignified way to leave this world, it all comes down to one basic question: Do terminally ill persons have, as part of their civil liberties, a right to die and to be assisted in the process by physicians or others? Phrased another way, are state laws banning physician-assisted suicide in such circumstances unconstitutional?

In 1997, the issue came before the Supreme Court, which characterized the question as follows: Does the liberty protected by the Constitution include a right to commit suicide, which itself includes a right to assistance in doing so? The Court's clear and categorical answer to this question was no. To hold otherwise, said the Court, would be "to reverse centuries of legal doctrine and practice, and strike down the considered policy choice of almost every state."[38]

Although the Court upheld the states' rights to ban such a practice, the Court did not hold that state laws *permitting* assisted suicide were unconstitutional. In 1997, Oregon became the first state to implement such a law. In 2008, Washington and Montana became the second and third states, respectively, to allow the practice. Oregon's law was upheld by the Supreme Court in 2006.[39]

## 4–3d Personal Privacy and National Security

Since the terrorist attacks of September 11, 2001, a common debate in the news media and on Capitol Hill has concerned how the United States can address the urgent need to strengthen national security while still protecting civil liberties, particularly the right to privacy. For example, the Homeland Security Act passed in late 2002 included language explicitly prohibiting a controversial program called Operation TIPS (Terrorism Information and Prevention System).

Operation TIPS was proposed to create a national reporting program for "citizen volunteers" who regularly work in neighborhoods and communities, such as postal carriers and meter readers, to report suspicious activity to the government. The public backlash against the program was quick and resolute—neighbors would not spy on neighbors.

**The USA Patriot Act**   Other laws and programs that infringe on Americans' privacy rights were also created in the wake of 9/11 in the interests of protecting the nation's security. For example, the USA Patriot Act of 2001 gave the government broad latitude to investigate people who are only vaguely associated with terrorists.

Under this law, the government can access personal information on American citizens to an extent heretofore never allowed by law. The Federal Bureau of Investigation (FBI) was also authorized to use "National Security Letters" to demand personal information about individuals from private companies (such as banks and phone companies). In one of the most controversial programs, the National Security Agency (NSA) was authorized to monitor certain domestic phone calls without first obtaining a warrant. When Americans learned of the NSA's actions in 2005, the ensuing public furor forced the Bush administration to agree to henceforth obtain warrants for such monitoring activities.

**The Civil Liberties Debate**   Some Americans, including many civil libertarians, are so concerned about the erosion of privacy rights that they wonder why the public outcry has not been even more vehement. They point out that trading off even a few civil liberties, including our privacy rights, for national security is senseless. After all, these liberties are at the heart of what this country stands for. When we abandon any of our civil liberties, we weaken our country rather than defend it.

Essentially, say some members of this group, the federal government has achieved what the terrorists were unable to accomplish—the destruction of our freedoms. Other Americans believe that we have little to worry about. Those who have nothing to hide should not be concerned about government surveillance or other privacy intrusions undertaken by the government to make our nation more secure against terrorist attacks.

While running for president in 2008, Barack Obama strongly defended civil liberties in issues involving terrorism. Has President Obama lived up to his promises? We examine that question in this chapter's *Perception versus Reality* feature on the facing page.

**FOR CRITICAL THINKING**

*Could the government's current policies on screening airline passengers be considered a violation of privacy rights? Why or why not?*

## 4–4 The Rights of the Accused

The United States has one of the highest murder rates in the industrialized world. It is therefore not surprising that many Americans have extremely strong opinions about the rights of persons accused of criminal offenses. Indeed, some Americans complain that criminal defendants have too many rights.

Why do criminal suspects have rights? The answer is that all persons are entitled to the protections afforded by the Bill of Rights. If criminal suspects were deprived of their basic constitutional liberties, all people would suffer the consequences, because there is nothing to stop the government from accusing anyone of being a criminal. In a criminal case, a state official (such as the district attorney, or D.A.) prosecutes the defendant, and the state has immense resources that it can bring to bear against the accused person. By protecting the rights of accused persons, the Constitution helps to prevent the arbitrary use of power by the government.

FBI director Robert Mueller often faces questioning during congressional hearings on national security.

AP PHOTO/CLIFF OWEN

**LearningOutcome 4–4**

Summarize how the Constitution and the Bill of Rights protect the rights of accused persons.

# Perception versus Reality

## Obama's Antiterrorism Policies

During the administration of President George W. Bush, civil libertarians denounced the antiterrorism policies of Bush and his vice president, Dick Cheney. Senator Barack Obama (D., Ill.) was among those who condemned the president's policies. Campaigning for the presidency in 2008, Obama promised to defend civil liberties and end the use of enhanced interrogation techniques that some called torture. He promised to restore *habeas corpus* rights (described on page 74) and close the prison at Guantánamo Bay Naval Station, where suspected terrorists were held outside the reach of U.S. law.

Obama also promised to protect whistle-blowers who expose government corruption and to run a more open administration.

### THE PERCEPTION

In 2009, former vice president Cheney criticized Obama for abandoning the Bush administration's aggressive approach to terrorism. According to Cheney, Obama's new policies made the country "less safe." In fact, civil liberties have been much less of a public issue under Obama than under Bush.

### THE REALITY

At most, the excessive antiterrorism policies of the Bush administration—championed by Cheney—

lasted for three years after 9/11. During Bush's second term, officials tried to close Guantánamo and begged foreign governments to take some of its prisoners. The most famous "enhanced" interrogation method—waterboarding—was halted well before Obama took office.

As of 2013, the Guantánamo prison remains in business, although the Supreme Court has recognized the *habeas corpus* rights of detainees there. The Obama administration, however, has been able to maintain the Bush policy of holding prisoners outside the reach of American law by sending them to Bagram Air Base in Afghanistan. Unlike the Guantánamo base, Bagram is not on American soil, and the courts have never granted *habeas corpus* rights to its detainees. The Obama administration has also continued the Bush-era policy of shielding itself from lawsuits by claiming they would reveal classified information.

Indeed, on some issues, the Obama administration has broken new ground. Rather than protecting the jobs of whistleblowers, the government has arrested several of them and charged them with crimes. The number of whistleblowers arrested under Bush? Zero.

In another departure, it was revealed in 2010 that Obama had approved the killing of Anwar al-Awlaki, an al Qaeda cleric living in the nation of Yemen. Al-Awlaki was born in the United States, which may make Obama the first president in U.S. history to openly order the assassination of an American citizen. In 2011, Cheney reversed his earlier position and praised Obama's antiterror efforts.

**BLOG ON** The number of national security blogs is vast, and we can mention only a few. Entering "national security blog" into a search engine yields expert posts at the *National Journal*. It also brings up the national security page of the Heritage Foundation, a conservative group. Entering "gitmo blog" gives you the Guantánamo Blog, which defends the rights of Guantánamo detainees.

## 4–4a The Rights of Criminal Defendants

The basic rights, or constitutional safeguards, provided for criminal defendants are set forth in the Bill of Rights. These safeguards include the following:

- The Fourth Amendment protection from unreasonable searches and seizures.

- The Fourth Amendment requirement that no warrant for a search or an arrest be issued without probable cause—cause for believing that there is a substantial likelihood that a person has committed or is about to commit a crime.

- The Fifth Amendment requirement that no one be deprived of "life, liberty, or property, without due process of law." As discussed earlier in this chapter, this requirement is also included in the Fourteenth Amendment, which protects persons against actions by state governments.

- The Fifth Amendment prohibition against **double jeopardy**—being tried twice for the same criminal offense.

- The Fifth Amendment provision that no person can be required to be a witness against (incriminate) himself or herself. This is often referred to as the constitutional protection against **self-incrimination.** It is the basis for a criminal suspect's "right to remain silent" in criminal proceedings.

- The Sixth Amendment guarantees of a speedy trial, a trial by jury, a public trial, and the right to confront witnesses.

AP PHOTO/CODY DUTY/HOUSTON CHRONICLE

This supporter of striking union members is being taken into custody. Does she automatically have the right to counsel?

- The Sixth Amendment guarantee of the right to counsel at various stages in some criminal proceedings. The right to counsel was strengthened in 1963 in *Gideon v. Wainwright*.[40] The Supreme Court held that if a person is accused of a felony and cannot afford an attorney, an attorney must be made available to the accused person at the government's expense.

- The Eighth Amendment prohibitions against excessive bail and fines and against cruel and unusual pun-

ishments. Should the death penalty be considered a cruel and unusual punishment? We discuss that question in this chapter's *Join the Debate* feature on the facing page.

## 4–4b The Exclusionary Rule

Any evidence obtained in violation of the constitutional rights spelled out in the Fourth Amendment normally is not admissible at trial. This rule, which has been applied in the federal courts since at least 1914, is known as the **exclusionary rule.** The rule was extended to state court proceedings in 1961.[41] The reasoning behind the exclusionary rule is that it forces law enforcement personnel to gather evidence properly. If they do not, they will be unable to introduce the evidence at trial to convince the jury that the defendant is guilty.

## 4–4c The *Miranda* Warnings

In the 1950s and 1960s, one of the questions facing the courts was not whether suspects had constitutional rights—that was not in doubt—but how and when those rights could be exercised. For example, could the right to remain silent (under the Fifth Amendment's prohibition against self-incrimination) be exercised during pretrial interrogation proceedings or only during the trial? Were confessions obtained

## JOIN THE DEBATE

## Is the Death Penalty a Cruel and Unusual Punishment?

The Eighth Amendment to the U.S. Constitution explicitly states that the government cannot inflict "cruel and unusual punishments." It is also true that criminals have been executed since the earliest days of the republic.

Even before there were prisons in America, we had the death penalty, also called "capital punishment." In 1608, a man named George Kendall was executed by a firing squad in Virginia on charges of spying for Spain. Since Kendall's time, more than eighteen thousand Americans have been executed as punishment for their crimes. In addition to murder, a variety of other crimes have been punished by death in this country. In the 1700s, citizens were executed for robbery, forgery, and illegally cutting down trees.

No state executes people for such crimes today. In our modern world, though, is the death penalty itself cruel and unusual, and therefore a violation of the Eighth Amendment?

### An Eye for an Eye Makes the Whole World Blind

Some argue that the death penalty is inappropriate even for someone who has committed murder. Violence and death may always be with us, but the law should not encourage violent sentiments. Already in 1764, the Italian jurist Cesare Beccaria asserted that

"the death penalty cannot be useful, because of the example of barbarity it gives men."

As United States Supreme Court justice Arthur J. Goldberg once wrote, "The deliberate institutionalized taking of human life by the state is the greatest conceivable degradation of the dignity of a human personality." Face it—capital punishment is barbaric whether it is carried out by a firing squad, an electric chair, a gas chamber, lethal injection, or hanging. Nations other than the United States that permit capital punishment are not ones that we would seek to emulate: they include China, Iran, North Korea, and Saudi Arabia. Almost all of our allies have abolished the practice.

### There Is Nothing Cruel and Unusual about Executing a Murderer

Strangely enough, some who are against capital punishment have argued that life in prison without parole is even crueler than death. Prisoners are confined in an environment of violence where they are treated like animals, and the suffering goes on for decades. If you think about it, this is an argument that the death sentence can be merciful.

In any event, capital punishment is not cruel and unusual as meant by the Eighth Amendment. Indeed, the current method of execution used in most states—lethal injection—appears quite civilized compared with methods of execution used in England back in the 1700s, which included drawing and quartering and burning at the stake. Practices such as these are what the founders sought to ban.

**FOR CRITICAL ANALYSIS** Can there be a humane method of extinguishing someone's life? Why or why not?

---

from suspects admissible in court if the suspects had not been advised of their right to remain silent and other constitutional rights? To clarify these issues, in 1966 the Supreme Court issued a landmark decision in *Miranda v. Arizona.*[42] In that case, the Court enunciated the ***Miranda* warnings** that are now familiar to virtually all Americans:

> Prior to any questioning, the person must be warned that he has a right to remain silent, that any statement he does make may be used against him, and that he has a right to the presence of an attorney, either retained or appointed.

### 4–4d The Erosion of *Miranda*

As part of a continuing attempt to balance the rights of accused persons against the rights of society, the Supreme Court has made a number of exceptions to the *Miranda* ruling. In 1986, for example, the Court held that

***Miranda* warnings**
A series of statements informing criminal suspects, on their arrest, of their constitutional rights, such as the right to remain silent and the right to counsel; required by the Supreme Court's 1966 decision in *Miranda v. Arizona.*

a confession need not be excluded even though the police failed to inform a suspect in custody that his attorney had tried to reach him by telephone.[43] In an important 1991 decision, the Court stated that a suspect's conviction will not be automatically overturned if the suspect was coerced into making a confession. If the other evidence admitted at trial was strong enough to justify the conviction without the confession, then the fact that the confession was obtained illegally can be, in effect, ignored.[44]

### Requesting One's Rights

In yet another case related to *Miranda,* in 1994 the Supreme Court ruled that a suspect must unequivocally and assertively state his right to counsel in order to stop police questioning. Saying "Maybe I should talk to a lawyer" during an interrogation after being taken into custody is not enough. The Court held that police officers are not required to decipher the suspect's intentions in such situations.[45]

In a parallel ruling in 2010, the Court found that suspects must explicitly invoke the right to remain silent if they wish to avail themselves of that right.[46] In 2011, however, the Court ruled that because children are more susceptible to pressure than adults, police officers must take extra care in ensuring the *Miranda* rights of child suspects.[47]

### Recording Confessions

*Miranda* may eventually become obsolete regardless of any decisions made in the courts. A relatively new trend in law enforcement has been for agencies to digitally record interrogations and confessions. Thomas P. Sullivan, a former U.S. attorney in Chicago, and his staff interviewed personnel in more than 230 law enforcement agencies in thirty-eight states that record interviews of suspects who are in custody. Sullivan found that nearly all police officers said the procedure saved time and money, created valuable evidence to use in court, and made it more difficult for defense attorneys to claim that their clients had been illegally coerced.[48]

Some scholars have suggested that recording all custodial interrogations would satisfy the Fifth Amendment's prohibition against coercion and in the process render the *Miranda* warnings unnecessary.

**FOR CRITICAL THINKING**

*Regardless of whether executions can be carried out humanely, should the death penalty be abolished? Explain your reasoning.*

Eventually, all arrests and all interrogations will be digitally filmed and stored. If so, would *Miranda* rights still be an issue? Why or why not?

CASECRACKER.CARDINALPEAK.COM

# ODDS Civil Liberties

Civil liberties represent a contentious topic, and Americans are at odds over many of its issues. Almost all Americans claim to believe in individual rights, but how should this freedom be defined? Often, one right appears to interfere with another. Some of the resulting disputes include the following:

- Should the First Amendment's establishment clause be interpreted strictly, so that no one's rights are infringed on by government sponsorship of religion—or should it be interpreted loosely, to recognize that the United States is a very religious country?

- What kinds of religious practices should be allowed under the free exercise clause? In particular, should religious groups that limit or ban participation by gay men and lesbians receive the same government benefits as any other group—or may they be penalized for discrimination?

- Should advertising receive the same free speech rights as any other kind of speech—or should advertisers be held accountable for making false claims?

- Has the government gone too far in restricting liberties in an attempt to combat terrorism—or are the restrictions trivial compared with the benefits?

- Consider the most intense controversy of all: Should women have a privacy right to terminate a pregnancy for any reason—or should abortion be a crime?

## TAKE ACTION

If you are ever concerned that your civil liberties are being threatened by a government action, you can exercise one of your liberties—the right to petition the government—to object to the action. Yet, often those who want to take such action feel that they are alone in their struggles until they begin discussing their views with others. Brenda Koehler, a writing student attending college in Kutztown, Pennsylvania, relates how one of her friends, whom we will call "Charyn," took action in response to the USA Patriot Act of 2001. Concerned about the extent to which this act infringed on Americans' civil liberties, Charyn began e-mailing her friends and others about the issue. Eventually, a petition against the enforcement of the act in her town was circulated, and the city council agreed to consider the petition. Charyn did not expect anything to come from the review and assumed that the council would dismiss the petition without even reading the three-hundred-page Patriot Act. On the day of the hearing, the council chambers were packed with town citizens who shared Charyn's and her friends' concerns. The council adjourned the meeting for a week so that it could review the act, and when it met the next week, the resolution to oppose enforcing the act was adopted. Although one person's efforts are not always so successful, there will certainly be no successes at all if no one takes action.[49]

## MIRANDA WARNING

1. **YOU HAVE THE RIGHT TO REMAIN SILENT.**

2. ANYTHING YOU SAY CAN AND WILL BE USED AGAINST YOU IN A COURT OF LAW.

3. YOU HAVE THE RIGHT TO TALK TO A LAWYER AND HAVE HIM PRESENT WITH YOU WHILE YOU ARE BEING QUESTIONED.

4. IF YOU CANNOT AFFORD TO HIRE A LAWYER, ONE WILL BE APPOINTED TO REPRESENT YOU BEFORE ANY QUESTIONING IF YOU WISH.

5. YOU CAN DECIDE AT ANY TIME TO EXERCISE THESE RIGHTS AND NOT ANSWER ANY QUESTIONS OR MAKE ANY STATEMENTS.

### WAIVER

DO YOU UNDERSTAND EACH OF THESE RIGHTS I HAVE EXPLAINED TO YOU? HAVING THESE RIGHTS IN MIND, DO YOU WISH TO TALK TO US NOW?

COURTESY OF WWW.USA.GOV

# STUDY TOOLS

## Ready to study?

- Review what you've read with the quiz below. Check your answers on the Chapter in Review card at the back of the book. For any questions you miss, read the corresponding Learning Outcome section again to prepare for class and your exam.
- Rip out and study the Chapter in Review card.

## . . . Or you can go online to CourseMate

at **www.cengagebrain.com** for these additional review materials:

- Practice Quizzes
- Key Term Flashcards or Crossword Puzzles
- Audio Summaries
- Simulations, Animated Learning Modules, and Interactive Timelines
- Videos
- American Government NewsWatch

## Fill-In

1. The _____ clause of the Fourteenth Amendment to the U.S. Constitution guarantees that state governments will not arbitrarily deprive any person of life, liberty, or property.

2. The *Lemon* test enunciated by the Supreme Court in 1971 to determine whether government aid to parochial schools is constitutional states that the aid must _____.

3. The current Supreme Court standard for assessing the constitutionality of _____ is the imminent lawless action test.

4. _____ is a published report of a falsehood that tends to injure a person's reputation or character.

5. The Supreme Court's _____ doctrine states that certain freedoms are so essential to a democracy that any law that limits these freedoms should be presumed to be unconstitutional unless the government can show that the law is absolutely necessary.

6. Under the USA Patriot Act of 2001, the FBI is authorized to use _____ to demand personal information about individuals from private companies, such as banks and phone companies.

7. In _____, the Supreme Court held that the "right of privacy . . . is broad enough to encompass a woman's decision whether or not to terminate her pregnancy."

8. The _____ Amendment includes protection from unreasonable searches and seizures.

9. The Eighth Amendment prohibits _____.

## Multiple Choice

10. A(n) _____ is an order requiring that an official bring a specified prisoner into court and explain to the judge why the prisoner is being held in jail.
    a. *ex post facto* law
    b. writ of *habeas corpus*
    c. bill of attainder

11. Thomas Jefferson wanted the establishment clause of the First Amendment to be a
    a. "bridge connecting government and religion."
    b. "barrier between government and the freedom of speech."
    c. "wall of separation between church and state."

12. The Supreme Court has ruled that public schools
    a. cannot sponsor religious activities.
    b. are allowed to determine for themselves the number of religious exercises they will sponsor in any given year.
    c. are barred from teaching about religion.

13. The Supreme Court, in *Griswold v. Connecticut* (1965), held that a right to privacy is implied by other constitutional rights guaranteed in the
    a. Magna Carta.
    b. First, Third, Fourth, Fifth, and Ninth Amendments to the Constitution.
    c. Declaration of Independence.

14 The Fifth Amendment
    a. includes a protection against self-incrimination.
    b. guarantees a speedy trial and a trial by jury.
    c. guarantees the right to counsel at various stages in some criminal proceedings.

15. _____ require(s) that illegally obtained evidence not be admissible in court.
    a. Double jeopardy
    b. The exclusionary rule
    c. Probable cause

# Civil Rights

The **Learning Outcomes** labeled 1 through 5 are designed to help improve your understanding of the chapter. After reading this chapter, you should be able to:

**5–1** Explain the constitutional basis for our civil rights and for laws prohibiting discrimination.

**5–2** Discuss the reasons for the civil rights movement and the changes it caused in American politics and government.

**5–3** Describe the political and economic achievements of women in this country over time and identify some obstacles to equality that women continue to face.

**5–4** Summarize the struggles for equality that other groups in America have experienced.

**5–5** Explain what affirmative action is and why it has been so controversial.

**Remember to visit page 123 for additional Study Tools**

Learning Outcomes

# AMERICA AT
# ODDS
## Should Each State Have Its Own Immigration Laws?

AP PHOTO/ROSS D. FRANKLIN

Around 11 million unauthorized immigrants live in the United States. Some people believe that the federal government is not doing enough to protect our national borders. As a result, some states have passed their own laws to deal with immigration. The Constitution grants the national government the right to establish uniform laws concerning *naturalization*—the granting of citizenship to immigrants. The Constitution, however, makes no explicit mention of laws about immigration. Should the power to control immigration be limited to the federal government? Or can the federal and state governments share this power. That is, should it be concurrent? Today, half a dozen states have adopted their own stringent laws to restrict illegal immigration.

Arizona's law, which is one of the strictest, has been reviewed by the United States Supreme Court. The Court ruled that no state could make it a crime for immigrants to seek work or to fail to carry federal papers. Importantly, though, Arizona's "show me your papers" provision was not struck down—police can ask for proof of legal status from persons stopped for other reasons. The Court did indicate that if enforcement of this provision encourages discriminatory behavior in Arizona, the Court could find it unconstitutional at a later date.[1]

States' rights advocates believe the Court should have let the Arizona law stand. Others disagree. Americans, therefore, are at odds over whether the states can have their own immigration laws.

## The States Have Rights—Let Them Keep Them

In public opinion polls, large majorities of respondents agree that we should crack down on illegal immigration. Certainly, each state has the right to pass its own laws to satisfy its own needs. Federal enforcement of our existing national immigration laws has failed. States should be able to encourage state and local police officers to stop suspected illegal immigrants and demand that they show their papers. States should be allowed to ban these people from employment. In short, the recent Supreme Court decision on the Arizona law should be reversed. If a future Court takes a more positive view of states' rights, such a reversal could happen. After all, nothing in the Constitution explicitly prohibits the states from having their own immigration enforcement policies. Illegal immigrants should not be allowed to compete for employment with immigrants who are here legally—or with American citizens.

## One Nation—One Immigration Policy

The states' rights argument has been used before to deny civil rights to African Americans and Latino U.S. citizens. The argument in favor of individual state immigration laws is just an excuse for discrimination today. States will use their immigration laws to harass individuals who look Hispanic. Such "racial profiling" is un-American. Individuals should not be stopped and asked for their papers simply because of the way they look. You can be sure that no fair-skinned illegal immigrants from Ireland, for example, will ever be stopped and asked for their papers under state immigration laws. Arizona-style immigration laws create distrust of the police and undermine law enforcement. Undocumented workers come to the United States because jobs are available that U.S. citizens will not fill. Instead of cracking down on illegal immigrants, we should find ways for them to earn legal status.

## Where do you stand?

1. Who benefits and who loses from strict state immigration laws?
2. Can vigorous enforcement of immigration laws interfere with a police department's ability to combat what we normally think of as crime? Why or why not?

## Explore this issue online

- Go to the Oyez Project of the Illinois Institute of Technology by entering "oyez" into your favorite Internet search engine. Then you can search for videos, recordings, and articles on the Supreme Court decision in *Arizona v. United States*.

# Introduction

As noted in Chapter 4, people sometimes confuse civil rights with civil liberties. Generally, though, the term **civil rights** refers to the rights of all Americans to equal treatment under the law, as provided by the Fourteenth Amendment. One of the functions of our government is to ensure—through legislation or other means—that this constitutional mandate is upheld.

Although the democratic ideal is for all people to have equal rights and equal treatment under the law, and although the Constitution guarantees those rights today, this ideal has often remained just that—an ideal. It is people who put ideals into practice, and as James Madison (1751–1836) often pointed out, people are not angels. As you will read in this chapter, the struggle of various groups in American society to obtain equal treatment has been a long one, and it continues. Latinos make up one such group, and we discussed an issue that concerns them in this chapter's opening *America at Odds* feature.

In a sense, the history of civil rights in the United States is a history of discrimination against various groups. Discrimination against women, African Americans, and Native Americans dates back to the early years of this nation, when the framers of the Constitution did not grant these groups rights that were granted to others (that is, to white, property-owning males). During our subsequent history, as people from around the globe immigrated to this country at various times and for various reasons, each of these immigrant groups faced discrimination in one form or another. More recently, other groups, including persons with disabilities and gay men and lesbians, have struggled for equal treatment under the law.

Central to any discussion of civil rights is the interpretation of the equal protection clause of the Fourteenth Amendment to the Constitution. For that reason, we look first at that clause and at how the courts, particularly the United States Supreme Court, have interpreted it and applied it to civil rights issues.

## 5–1 The Equal Protection Clause

You learned about the due process clause of the Fourteenth Amendment in Chapter 4 on pages 75

All Americans are entitled to **EQUAL TREATMENT UNDER THE LAW,** as provided by the Fourteenth Amendment.

and 77. Equal in importance to the due process clause is the **equal protection clause** in Section 1 of that amendment, which reads as follows: "No State shall . . . deny to any person within its jurisdiction the equal protection of the laws." Section 5 of the amendment provides a legal basis for federal civil rights legislation: "The Congress shall have power to enforce, by appropriate legislation, the provisions of this article."

The equal protection clause has been interpreted by the courts, and especially the Supreme Court, to mean that states must treat all persons in an equal manner and may not discriminate *unreasonably* against a particular group or class of individuals. The task of distinguishing between reasonable discrimination and unreasonable discrimination is difficult. Generally, in deciding this question, the Supreme Court balances the constitutional rights of individuals to equal protection against government interests in protecting the safety and welfare of citizens. Over time, the Court has developed various tests, or standards, for determining whether the equal protection clause has been violated.

### 5–1a Strict Scrutiny

If a law or action prevents some group of persons from exercising a **fundamental right** (such as one of our First Amendment rights), the law or action will be subject to the "strict-scrutiny" standard. Under

**civil rights** The rights of all Americans to equal treatment under the law, as provided by the Fourteenth Amendment to the Constitution.

**equal protection clause** Section 1 of the Fourteenth Amendment, which states that no state shall "deny to any person within its jurisdiction the equal protection of the laws."

**fundamental right** A basic right of all Americans, such as First Amendment rights. Any law or action that prevents some group of persons from exercising a fundamental right is subject to the "strict-scrutiny" standard, under which the law or action must be necessary to promote a compelling state interest and must be narrowly tailored to meet that interest.

this standard, the law or action must be necessary to promote a *compelling state interest* and must be narrowly tailored to meet that interest. A law based on a **suspect classification,** such as race, is also subject to strict scrutiny by the courts, meaning that the law must be justified by a compelling state interest.

## 5–1b Intermediate Scrutiny

Because the Supreme Court had difficulty deciding how to judge cases in which men and women were treated differently, another test was developed—the "intermediate scrutiny" standard. Under this standard, also known as "exacting scrutiny," laws based on gender classifications are permissible if they are "substantially related to the achievement of an important governmental objective."

For example, a law punishing males but not females for statutory rape has been ruled valid by the courts. The reasoning is that there is an important governmental interest in preventing teenage pregnancy in those circumstances and almost all of the harmful and identifiable consequences of teenage pregnancies fall on young females.[2] A law prohibiting the sale of beer to males under twenty-one years of age and to females under eighteen years would not be valid, however.[3]

AP PHOTO/ANDY ALONSO

Women broke the state government–supported gender barrier at Virginia Military Institute in 1996.

**suspect classification**
A classification, such as race, that provides the basis for a discriminatory law. Any law based on a suspect classification is subject to strict scrutiny by the courts, meaning that the law must be justified by a compelling state interest.

**rational basis test** A test (also known as the "ordinary scrutiny" standard) used by the Supreme Court to decide whether a discriminatory law violates the equal protection clause of the Constitution. It is used only when there is no classification—such as race or gender—that would require a higher level of scrutiny. Few laws evaluated under this test are found invalid.

### Declaring Gender-based Laws Unconstitutional

Generally, since the 1970s, the Supreme Court has scrutinized gender classifications closely and has declared many gender-based laws unconstitutional. In 1979, the Court held that a state law allowing wives to obtain alimony judgments against husbands but preventing husbands from receiving alimony from wives violated the equal protection clause.[4] In 1982, the Court declared that Mississippi's policy of excluding males from the School of Nursing at Mississippi University for Women was unconstitutional.[5]

**The Virginia Military Institute Case** In a controversial 1996 case, *United States v. Virginia,*[6] the Court held that Virginia Military Institute, a state-financed institution, violated the equal protection clause by refusing to accept female applicants. The Court said that the state of Virginia had failed to provide sufficient justification for its gender-based classification.

## 5–1c The Rational Basis Test (Ordinary Scrutiny)

A third test used to decide whether a discriminatory law violates the equal protection clause is the **rational basis test.** This test is employed only when there is no classification—such as race or gender—that would require a higher level of scrutiny. When applying this test to a law that classifies or treats people or groups differently, the courts ask whether the discrimination is rational. In other words, is it a reasonable way to achieve a legitimate government objective? Few laws tested under the rational basis test—or the "ordinary scrutiny" standard, as it is also called—are found invalid, because few laws are truly unreasonable.

A municipal ordinance that prohibits certain vendors from selling their wares in a particular area of the city, for example, will be upheld if the city can meet this rational basis test. The rational basis for the ordinance might be the city's legitimate government interest in reducing traffic congestion in that particular area.

**FOR CRITICAL THINKING**

When evaluating cases of discrimination against gay men or lesbians, some judges have employed the rational basis test, while others have applied intermediate scrutiny. *Which standard do you consider appropriate, and why?*

# 5–2 African Americans

## LearningOutcome 5–2

Discuss the reasons for the civil rights movement and the changes it caused in American politics and government.

The equal protection clause was originally intended to protect the newly freed slaves after the Civil War (1861–1865). In the early years after the war, the U.S. government made an effort to protect the rights of blacks living in the former states of the Confederacy. The Thirteenth Amendment (which granted freedom to the slaves), the Fourteenth Amendment (which guaranteed equal protection under the law), and the Fifteenth Amendment (which stated that voting rights could not be abridged on account of race) were part of that effort.

By the late 1880s, however, southern legislatures had begun to pass a series of segregation laws—laws that separated the white community from the black community. Such laws were commonly called "Jim Crow" laws (from a song that was popular in minstrel shows that caricatured African Americans). Some of the most common Jim Crow laws called for racial segregation in the use of public facilities, such as schools, railroads,

and, later, buses. These laws were also applied to housing, restaurants, hotels, and many other facilities.

## 5–2a Separate but Equal

In 1892, a group of Louisiana citizens decided to challenge a state law that required railroads to provide separate railway cars for African Americans. A man named Homer Plessy, who was seven-eighths European and one-eighth African, boarded a train in New Orleans and sat in the railway car reserved for whites. When Plessy refused to move at the request of the conductor, he was arrested for breaking the law.

Four years later, in 1896, the Supreme Court provided a constitutional basis for segregation laws. In *Plessy v. Ferguson*,[7] the Court held that the law did not violate the equal protection clause if *separate* facilities for blacks were *equal* to those for whites.

The lone dissenter, Justice John Marshall Harlan, disagreed: "Our Constitution is colorblind, and neither knows nor tolerates classes among citizens." The majority opinion, however, established the **separate-but-equal doctrine**, which was used to justify segregation in many areas of American

**separate-but-equal doctrine** A Supreme Court doctrine holding that the equal protection clause of the Fourteenth Amendment did not forbid racial segregation as long as the facilities for blacks were equal to those for whites. The doctrine was overturned in the *Brown v. Board of Education of Topeka* decision of 1954.

The separate-but-equal doctrine was applied to segregated schools for decades. These demonstrators did not agree with the law in the early 1950s.

© BETTMANN/CORBIS

life for nearly sixty years. Separate facilities for African Americans, when they were provided at all, were in practice almost never truly equal.

In the late 1930s and the 1940s, the United States Supreme Court gradually moved away from this doctrine. The major breakthrough, however, did not come until 1954, in a case involving an African American girl who lived in Topeka, Kansas.

## 5–2b The *Brown* Decisions and School Integration

In the 1950s, Topeka's schools, like those in many cities, were segregated. Mr. and Mrs. Oliver Brown wanted their daughter, Linda Carol Brown, to attend a white school a few blocks from their home instead of an all-black school that was twenty-one blocks away. With the help of lawyers from the National Association for the Advancement of Colored People (NAACP), Linda's parents sued the board of education to allow their daughter to attend the nearby school.

In *Brown v. Board of Education of Topeka*,[8] the Supreme Court reversed *Plessy v. Ferguson*. The Court unanimously held that segregation by race in public education was unconstitutional. Chief Justice Earl Warren wrote as follows:

> Does segregation of children in public schools solely on the basis of race, even though the physical facilities and other "tangible" factors may be equal, deprive the children of the minority group of equal educational opportunities? We believe that it does. . . . [Segregation generates in children] a feeling of inferiority as to their status in the community that may affect their hearts and minds in a way unlikely ever to be undone. . . . We conclude that in the field of public education the doctrine of "separate but equal" has no place. Separate educational facilities are inherently unequal.

In 1955, in *Brown v. Board of Education*[9] (sometimes called *Brown II)*, the Supreme Court ordered desegregation to begin "with all deliberate speed," an ambiguous

**de jure segregation**
Racial segregation that occurs because of laws or decisions by government agencies.

**de facto segregation**
Racial segregation that occurs not as a result of deliberate intentions but because of social and economic conditions and residential patterns.

**busing** The transportation of public school students by bus to schools physically outside their neighborhoods to eliminate school segregation based on residential patterns.

phrase that could be (and was) interpreted in a variety of ways.

**Reactions to School Integration** The Supreme Court ruling did not go unchallenged. Bureaucratic loopholes were used to delay desegregation. Another reaction was "white flight." As white parents sent their children to newly established private schools, some formerly white-only public schools became 100 percent black. In Arkansas, Governor Orval Faubus used the state's National Guard to block the integration of Central High School in Little Rock in 1957. A federal court demanded that the troops be withdrawn. Only after President Dwight D. Eisenhower federalized the Arkansas National Guard and sent in additional troops did Central High finally become integrated.

By 1970, *de jure* segregation—segregation that is established by law—had been abolished by school systems. But that meant only that no public school could legally identify itself as being reserved for all whites or all blacks. It did not mean the end of *de facto* segregation—segregation that is not imposed by law but is produced by circumstances, such as the existence of neighborhoods or communities populated primarily by African Americans. Attempts to overcome de facto segregation have included redrawing school district lines, reassigning pupils, and establishing busing.

**Busing** In respect to civil rights, **busing** is the transporting of students by bus to schools physically outside their neighborhoods in an effort to achieve racially desegregated schools. The Supreme Court first endorsed busing in 1971 in a case involving the school system in Charlotte, North Carolina.[10] Following this decision, the Court upheld busing in several northern cities.[11] Proponents believed that busing improved the educational and career opportunities of minority children and also enhanced the ability of children from different ethnic groups to get along with one another.

Nevertheless, busing was unpopular with many groups from its inception. By the mid-1970s, the courts had begun to retreat from their former support for busing. In 1974, the Supreme Court rejected the idea of busing children across school district lines.[12] In 1986, the Court refused to review a lower court decision that ended a desegregation plan in Norfolk, Virginia.[13] Today, busing orders to end *de facto* segregation are not upheld by the courts. Indeed, *de facto* segregation in America's schools is still widespread.

The Reverend Dr. Martin Luther King, Jr., civil rights leader (1929–1968).

FLIP SCHULKE/BLACKSTAR PHOTOS/NEWSCOM

## 5-2c The Civil Rights Movement

In 1955, one year after the first *Brown* decision, an African American woman named Rosa Parks, a long-time activist in the NAACP, boarded a public bus in Montgomery, Alabama. When it became crowded, she refused to move to the "colored section" at the rear of the bus. She was arrested and fined for violating local segregation laws. Her arrest spurred the local African American community to organize a year-long boycott of the entire Montgomery bus system.

The protest was led by a twenty-seven-year-old Baptist minister, the Reverend Dr. Martin Luther King, Jr. During the protest period, he was jailed and his house was bombed. Yet, despite white hostility and what appeared to be overwhelming odds against them, the protesters were triumphant in the end.

In 1956, a federal court prohibited the segregation of buses in Montgomery, and the era of the **civil rights movement**—the movement by minorities and concerned whites to end racial segregation—had begun. The movement was led by a number of groups and individuals, including Martin Luther King and his Southern Christian Leadership Conference (SCLC). Other groups, such as the Congress of Racial Equality

(CORE), the NAACP, and the Student Nonviolent Coordinating Committee (SNCC), also sought to secure equal rights for African Americans.

**Nonviolence as a Tactic**   Civil rights protesters in the 1960s began to apply the tactic of nonviolent **civil disobedience**—the deliberate and public refusal to obey laws considered unjust—in civil rights actions throughout the South. For example, in 1960, in Greensboro, North Carolina, four African American students sat at the "whites only" lunch counter at Woolworth's and ordered food. The waitress refused to serve them, and the store closed early, but more students returned the next day to sit at the counter, with supporters picketing outside. **Sit-ins** spread to other lunch counters across the South.

**SUCCESSES.** In some instances, students participating in sit-ins were heckled or even dragged from Woolworth's by angry whites. But the protesters never reacted with violence. They simply returned to their seats at the counter, day after day. Within months of the first sit-in, lunch counter managers began to reverse their policies of segregation.

**THE NATIONAL REACTION.** Civil rights activists were trained in the tools of nonviolence—how to use nonthreatening body language, how to go limp when dragged or assaulted, and how to protect themselves from clubs and police dogs. As the civil rights movement gained momentum, the media images of nonviolent protesters being assaulted by police, sprayed with fire hoses, and attacked by dogs shocked and angered Americans across the country. This public backlash led to nationwide demands for reform. The March on Washington for Jobs and Freedom, led by Martin Luther King in 1963, aimed in part to demonstrate the widespread public support for legislation to ban discrimination in all aspects of public life.

> **civil rights movement**
> The movement in the 1950s and 1960s, by minorities and concerned whites, to end racial segregation.
>
> **civil disobedience** The deliberate and public act of refusing to obey laws thought to be unjust.
>
> **sit-in** A tactic of nonviolent civil disobedience. Demonstrators enter a business, college building, or other public place and remain seated until they are forcibly removed or until their demands are met. The tactic was used successfully in the civil rights movement and in other protest movements in the United States.

### Civil Rights Legislation in the 1960s

As the civil rights movement demonstrated its strength, Congress began to pass civil rights laws. While the Fourteenth Amendment prevented the *government* from discriminating against individuals or groups, the private sector—businesses, restaurants, and the like—could still freely refuse to employ and serve nonwhites. Therefore, Congress sought to address this issue.

The Civil Rights Act of 1964 was the first and most comprehensive civil rights law. It forbade discrimination on the basis of race, color, religion, gender, and national origin. The major provisions of the act were as follows:

- It outlawed discrimination in public places of accommodation, such as hotels, restaurants, snack bars, movie theaters, and public transportation.

- It provided that federal funds could be withheld from any federal or state government project or facility that practiced any form of discrimination.

- It banned discrimination in employment.

- It outlawed arbitrary discrimination in voter registration.

- It authorized the federal government to sue to desegregate public schools and facilities.

Other significant laws passed by Congress during the 1960s included the Voting Rights Act of 1965, which made it illegal to interfere with anyone's right to vote in any election held in this country (see Chapter 8 for a discussion of the historical restrictions on voting that African Americans faced), and the Civil Rights Act of 1968, which prohibited discrimination in housing.

### The Black Power Movement

Not all African Americans embraced nonviolence. Several outspoken leaders in the mid-1960s were outraged at the slow pace of change in the social and economic status of blacks. Malcolm X, a speaker and organizer for the Nation of Islam (also called the Black Muslims), rejected the goals of integration and racial equality espoused by the civil rights movement.

> # "INJUSTICE
> anywhere is a threat to justice everywhere."
> ~ MARTIN LUTHER KING, JR. ~
> U.S. CIVIL RIGHTS LEADER
> 1929–1968

He called instead for black separatism and "black pride." Although he later moderated some of his views, his rhetorical style and powerful message influenced many African American young people.

By the late 1960s, with the assassinations of Malcolm X in 1965 and Martin Luther King in 1968, the era of mass acts of civil disobedience in the name of civil rights had come to an end.

## 5–2d Political Participation

As you will read in Chapter 8, in many jurisdictions African Americans were prevented from voting for years after the Civil War, despite the Fifteenth Amendment (1870). These discriminatory practices persisted in the twentieth century. In the early 1960s, only 22 percent of African Americans of voting age in the South were registered to vote, compared with 63 percent of voting-age whites. In Mississippi, the most extreme example, only 6 percent of voting-age African Americans were registered to vote. Such disparities led to the enactment of the Voting Rights Act of 1965, which ended discriminatory voter-registration tests and gave federal voter registrars the power to prevent racial discrimination in voting.

Black Muslim leader Malcolm X speaks to an audience at a Harlem rally in 1963. His talk, in which he restated the Black Muslim theme of complete separation of whites and African Americans, outdrew a nearby rally sponsored by a civil rights group by ten to one.

Today, the percentages of voting-age blacks and whites registered to vote are nearly equal. As a result of this dramatic change, political participation by African Americans has increased, as has the number of African American elected officials.

More than nine thousand African Americans now serve in elective office in the United States. At least one congressional seat in each southern state is held by an African American, as are more than 15 percent of the state legislative seats in the South. A number of African Americans have achieved high government office, including Colin Powell, who served as President George W. Bush's first secretary of state, and Condoleezza Rice, his second secretary of state.

Of course, in 2008 Barack Obama, a U.S. senator from Illinois, became the first African American president of the United States. Obama's election reflects a significant change in public opinion. Fifty years ago, only 38 percent of Americans said that they would be willing to vote for an African American as president. Today, this number has risen to more than 90 percent. Nonetheless, only two African Americans have been elected to a state governorship, and only a handful of African Americans have been elected to the U.S. Senate since 1900.

## 5–2e Continuing Challenges

Although African Americans no longer face *de jure* segregation, they continue to struggle for income and educational parity with whites. Recent census data show that average incomes in black households are only 59 percent of those in non-Hispanic white households. The poverty rate for blacks is roughly three times that for whites. The loss of jobs caused by the Great Recession tended to make matters worse for African Americans and other minority group members.

**Problems with Education**  The education gap between blacks and whites also persists despite continuing efforts by educators—and by government, through programs such as the federal No Child Left Behind Act—to reduce it. Recent studies show that, on average, African American students in high school read and do math at the level of whites in junior high school. Also, while black adults have narrowed the gap with white adults in earning high school diplomas, the disparity has widened for college degrees.

These problems tend to feed on one another. Schools in poorer neighborhoods generally have fewer educational resources available, resulting in lower achievement levels for their students. Thus, some educational experts suggest that it all comes down to

money. In fact, many parents of minority students in struggling school districts are less concerned about integration than they are about funds for their children's schools. A number of these parents have initiated lawsuits against their state governments, demanding that the states give poor districts more resources.

**Class versus Race in Educational Outcomes**
Researchers have known for decades that when students enrolled at a particular school come almost entirely from impoverished families, regardless of race, the performance of the students at that school is seriously depressed. When low-income students attend schools where the majority of the students are middle class, again regardless of race, their performance improves dramatically—without dragging down the performance of the middle-class students. Because of this research and recent United States Supreme Court rulings that have struck down some racial integration plans, several school systems have adopted policies that integrate students on the basis of socioeconomic class, not race.[14]

## FOR CRITICAL THINKING

*Why might low-income students do better in their studies, on average, when most of their classmates are middle class instead of poor?*

## 5–3 Women

In 1848, Lucretia Mott and Elizabeth Cady Stanton organized the first "woman's rights" convention in Seneca Falls, New York. The three hundred people who attended approved a Declaration of Sentiments: "We hold these truths to be self-evident: that all men *and women* are created equal." In the following years, other women's groups held conventions in various cities in the Midwest and the East. With the outbreak of the Civil War, though, women's rights advocates devoted their energies to the war effort.

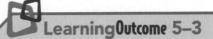

**Learning Outcome 5–3**

Describe the political and economic achievements of women in this country over time and identify some obstacles to equality that women continue to face.

## 5–3a The Struggle for Voting Rights

The movement for political rights gained momentum again in 1869, when Susan B. Anthony and Elizabeth Cady Stanton formed the National Woman Suffrage Association. **Suffrage**—the right to vote—became their goal. Members of this association saw suffrage as only one step on the road toward greater social and political rights for women. Lucy Stone and other women, who founded the American Woman Suffrage Association, however, thought that the right to vote should be the only goal.

By 1890, the two organizations had joined forces, and the resulting National American Woman Suffrage Association had indeed only one goal—enfranchisement (being given the right to vote). When little progress was made, small, radical splinter groups took to the streets. Parades, hunger strikes, arrests, and jailings soon followed.

World War I (1914–1918) marked a turning point in the battle for women's rights. The war offered many opportunities for women. Thousands of women served as volunteers, and about a million women joined the workforce, holding jobs vacated by men who entered military service.

After the war, President Woodrow Wilson wrote to Carrie Chapman Catt, one of the leaders of the women's movement: "It is high time that [that] part of our debt should be acknowledged." Two years later, in 1920, seventy-two years after the Seneca Falls convention, the Nineteenth Amendment to the Constitution was ratified: "The right of citizens of the United States to vote shall not be denied or abridged by the United States or by any State on account of sex."

## 5–3b The Feminist Movement

After winning the right to vote, women engaged in little independent political

> "The right of citizens of the United States to vote **shall not be denied or abridged . . . on account of sex.**"
>
> ~ THE NINETEENTH AMENDMENT TO THE UNITED STATES CONSTITUTION ~
> 1920

**SOCIAL MEDIA In Politics**

For discussions about what feminism means to many women, visit the "who needs feminism" page on Facebook.

**suffrage** The right to vote; the franchise.

**feminism** The doctrine advocating full political, economic, and social equality for women.

activity for many years. In the 1960s, however, a new women's movement arose—the feminist movement. Women who faced discrimination in employment and other circumstances were inspired in part by the civil rights movement and the campaign against the war in Vietnam.

The National Organization for Women (NOW), founded in 1966, was the most important new women's organization. But the feminist movement also consisted of thousands of small, independent "women's liberation" and "consciousness-raising" groups established on campuses and in neighborhoods throughout the nation. **Feminism,** the goal of the movement, meant full political, economic, and social equality for women.

**Gender Discrimination** During the 1970s, NOW and other organizations sought to win passage of the Equal Rights Amendment (ERA) to the Constitution, which would have written equality into the heart of the nation's laws. The amendment did not win support from enough state legislatures, however, and it failed. Campaigns to change state and national laws affecting women were much more successful. Congress and the various state legislatures enacted a range of measures to provide equal rights for women. The women's movement also enjoyed considerable success in legal action. Courts at all levels accepted the argument that *gender discrimination* violated the Fourteenth Amendment's equal protection clause.

**Abortion** In addition to banning gender discrimination, the feminist movement took up a number of other issues important to women. Some campaigns, such as the one to curb domestic violence, have been widely supported. Others have resulted in heated debate. Perhaps the most controversial issue of all has been the right to have an abortion, which we discussed in Chapter 4 on pages 88 and 89. But even though abortion is legal, how available is the procedure in practice? We examine that question in this chapter's *Perception versus Reality* feature on the facing page.

## 5–3c Women in American Politics Today

More than ten thousand members have served in the U.S. House of Representatives. Only 1 percent of them have been women, and women continue to face

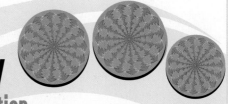

# Perception versus Reality

## The Availability of Abortion

Before 1973, abortion was illegal in much of the United States. In that year, the United States Supreme Court issued its decision in *Roe v. Wade*. The outcome of this landmark case seemed to settle the abortion issue once and for all. Women had the right to terminate their pregnancies.

### THE PERCEPTION

The highest court in the land made it clear—women could have an abortion if they so decided and no state laws could prevent this, at least during the first trimester of pregnancy. During the second trimester, only state laws that limited access to abortion to protect the health of pregnant women were constitutional. It follows that since 1973, abortion must be freely available throughout the land.

### THE REALITY

The pro-life and pro-choice sides of the abortion debate seem to agree on one thing. In practice, *Roe v. Wade* is no longer the law of the land. In 2011, legislators in twenty-four states passed a record ninety-two laws restricting abortions. By mid-2012,

235 bills had been introduced around the country to limit abortions, and a dozen had passed.

Half a dozen states now prohibit abortion more than twenty weeks into a pregnancy. Virginia requires women seeking an abortion to have an abdominal ultrasound, and other states are considering this measure as well. In Mississippi, where in 2010 the voters rejected an antiabortion ballot proposal, the legislature in 2012 hit upon a new way to shut down the state's only abortion clinic. Physicians at the clinic would be required to have admission privileges at a local hospital. Legislators could then rely on the hospitals to refuse such privileges. In July, a federal judge blocked implementation of the law.

Most of these new laws violate *Roe v. Wade* and subsequent Supreme Court rulings. Supporters of abortion rights, however, have been reluctant to challenge these laws because they are afraid that the Supreme Court might narrow abortion rights further. After all, in 2007 the Supreme Court ruled that a federal ban on so-called partial-birth abortions was constitutional, reversing an earlier precedent. In any event, state attempts to make abortion difficult or impossible are on the rise. Already, for all practical purposes, women cannot get an abortion in several small-population Great Plains and Rocky Mountain states.

**BLOG ON**
On the Slate Web site, pro-choice writer Dahlia Lithwick has written a call to alarm on the state of *Roe v. Wade*. If you enter "lithwick roe wade" into a search engine, you'll find both that article and a host of responses, a majority of them written by pro-life advocates.

---

a "men's club" atmosphere in Congress. In 2002, however, a woman, Nancy Pelosi (D., Calif.), was elected minority leader of the House of Representatives. She was the first woman to hold this post. Pelosi again made history when, after the Democratic victories in the 2006 elections, she was elected Speaker of the House of Representatives, the first woman ever to lead the House. After the Republicans took control of the House in 2011, Pelosi again became minority leader.

**Federal Offices** Women have been underrepresented when receiving presidential appointments to

federal offices. Franklin D. Roosevelt (1933–1945) appointed the first woman to a cabinet post—Frances Perkins, who was secretary of labor from 1933 to 1945. Several women have held cabinet posts in more recent administrations, however. All of the last three presidents have appointed women to the most senior cabinet post—secretary of state. Bill Clinton (1993–2001) appointed Madeleine Albright to this position, George W. Bush (2001–2009) picked Condoleezza Rice for the post in his second term, and most recently, Barack Obama chose New York senator Hillary Clinton to be secretary of state.

REUTERS/MOLLY RILEY

Former First Lady Hillary Clinton went on to become a U.S. senator from New York and then secretary of state under President Obama.

In addition, Ronald Reagan (1981–1989) appointed the first woman to sit on the Supreme Court, Sandra Day O'Connor. Bill Clinton appointed Ruth Bader Ginsburg to the Supreme Court. Barack Obama selected Sonia Sotomayor for the Court in 2009 and Elena Kagan in 2010.

**State Politics**   Women have made greater progress at the state level, and the percentage of women in state legislatures has been rising steadily. Women now constitute nearly one-fourth of state legislators. Notably, in 1998, women won races for each of the top five offices in Arizona, the first such occurrence in U.S. history. Generally, women have been more successful politically in the western states than elsewhere. In Washington, more than one-third of the state's legislative seats are now held by women. At the other end of the spectrum are states such as Alabama. In that state, fewer than 10 percent of the lawmakers are women.

**glass ceiling** An invisible but real discriminatory barrier that prevents women and minorities from rising to top positions of power or responsibility.

**sexual harassment** Unwanted physical contact, verbal conduct, or abuse of a sexual nature that interferes with a recipient's job performance, creates a hostile environment, or carries with it an implicit or explicit threat of adverse employment consequences.

## 5–3d Women in the Workplace

An ongoing challenge for American women is to obtain equal pay and equal opportunity in the workplace. In spite of federal legislation and programs to promote equal treatment of women in the workplace, women continue to face various forms of discrimination.

**Wage Discrimination**   In 1963, Congress passed the Equal Pay Act. The act requires employers to pay an equal wage for substantially equal work—males cannot be paid more than females who perform essentially the same job. The following year, Congress passed the Civil Rights Act of 1964, Title VII of which prohibits employment discrimination on the basis of race, color, national origin, gender, and religion. Women, however, continue to face wage discrimination.

It is estimated that for every dollar earned by men, women earn about 80 cents. Although the wage gap has narrowed significantly since 1963, when the Equal Pay Act was enacted (at that time, women earned 58 cents for every dollar earned by men), it still remains. This is particularly true for women in management positions and older women. Female managers now earn, on average, only 70 percent of what male managers earn. And women between the ages of forty-five and fifty-four make, on average, only 73 percent of what men in that age group earn. Notably, when a large number of women are in a particular occupation, the wages that are paid in that occupation tend to be relatively low.

**The Glass Ceiling**   Even though an increasing number of women now hold business and professional jobs once held only by men, relatively few of these women are able to rise to the top of the career ladder in their firms due to the lingering bias against women in the workplace. This bias has been described as the **glass ceiling**—an invisible but real discriminatory barrier that prevents women and minorities from rising to top positions of power or responsibility. Today, less than one-sixth of the top executive positions in the largest American corporations are held by women.

**Sexual Harassment**   Title VII's prohibition of gender discrimination has also been extended to prohibit sexual harassment. **Sexual harassment** occurs when job opportunities, promotions, salary increases, or even the ability to retain a job depends on whether an employee complies with demands for sexual favors. A special form of sexual harassment, called *hostile environment harassment,* occurs when an employee is subjected to sexual conduct or comments in the workplace that interfere with the employee's job performance or that create an intimidating, hostile, or offensive environment.

The Supreme Court has upheld the right of persons to be free from sexual harassment on the job on a number of occasions. In 1998, the Court made it clear that sexual harassment includes harassment by members of the same sex.[15] In the same year, the Court held that employers are liable for the harassment of employees by supervisors unless the employers can show that (1) they exercised reasonable care in preventing such problems (by implementing anti-harassment policies and procedures, for example), and (2) the employees failed to take advantage of any corrective opportunities provided by the employers.[16]

The Civil Rights Act of 1991 greatly expanded the remedies available for victims of sexual harassment. Under the act, victims can seek damages as well as back pay, job reinstatement, and other compensation.

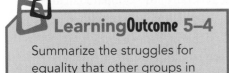

**FOR CRITICAL THINKING**

In recent years, a greater percentage of young women have received college diplomas than have young men. *In the future, how might this development change the social and economic roles of women and men?*

## 5–4 Securing Rights for Other Groups

**LearningOutcome 5–4**

Summarize the struggles for equality that other groups in America have experienced.

In addition to African Americans and women, a number of other groups in U.S. society have faced discriminatory treatment. One lingering result of past discrimination can be that a group suffers from below-average incomes and relatively high rates of poverty. Figure 5–1 on the right shows the percentage of persons with incomes below the poverty line for five major racial or ethnic groups. The chart provides statistics for children as well as the overall population. Note that in all groups, children are much more likely than adults to live in poverty. This reality makes poverty that much more damaging.

In this chapter, we look at three groups that have had to struggle for equal treatment—Latinos, Asian Americans, and Native Americans (or American Indians). Then we examine the struggles of several other groups of Americans—persons with disabilities and gay men and lesbians.

### 5–4a Latinos

Latinos, or Hispanics, constitute the largest ethnic minority in the United States. Whereas African Americans represent 12.2 percent of the U.S. population, Latinos now constitute 16.3 percent. Each year, the Hispanic population grows by nearly 1 million people, one-third of whom are newly arrived legal immigrants. By 2050, Latinos are expected to constitute about 30 percent of the U.S. population.

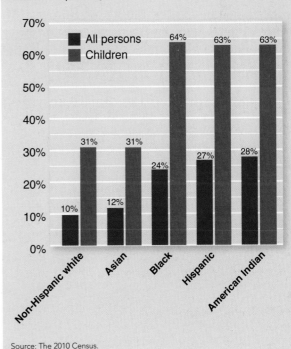

**FIGURE 5–1**

# Persons in Poverty in the
## United States by Race and Hispanic Origin, 2010

Blacks, Hispanics, and American Indians are more likely than whites or Asians to have incomes below the poverty line. Children are substantially more likely than adults to live in families with incomes below the poverty line.

Source: The 2010 Census.

According to the U.S. Census Bureau definition, Hispanics can be of any race. Note that while *Hispanic* is official U.S. government terminology, a majority of this group prefers the term *Latino*—or *Latina* in the feminine case. In fact, though, most Latinos prefer to identify with their country of origin rather than be categorized as either Hispanics or Latinos.

As you can see in Figure 5–2 below, the largest Hispanic group consists of Mexican Americans, who constitute about 65 percent of the Latino population living in the United States. About 9 percent of Latinos are Puerto Ricans, and 3.7 percent are Cuban Americans. Most of the remaining Hispanics are from Central and South American countries.

Economically, Latino households are often members of this country's working poor. As Figure 5–1 shows, many have incomes below the government's official poverty line. Latino leaders tend to attribute the low income levels to language problems, lack of job training, and continuing immigration. Immigration disguises statistical progress because language problems and lack of job training are usually more notable among new immigrants than among those who have lived in the United States for many years.

**Party Identification**   In their party identification, Latinos tend to follow some fairly well-established patterns. Traditionally, Mexican Americans and Puerto Ricans identify with the Democratic Party, which has favored more government assistance and support programs for disadvantaged groups.

Cubans, in contrast, tend to identify with the Republican Party. This is largely because of a different history. Cuban émigrés fled from Cuba during and after the Communist revolution led by Fidel Castro. The strong anti-Communist sentiments of the Cubans propelled them toward the more conservative party—the Republicans. Today, relations with Communist Cuba continue to be a key political issue for Cuban Americans.

Immigration reform has been an important issue for many Latinos. Even legal immigrants often have friends or relatives who are in the country illegally. In recent years, however, the Republican Party has taken a stand against any reform that would let unauthorized immigrants regularize their status. This stand has pushed many Latinos toward the Democrats.

In earlier years, a number of Republicans favored immigration reform. These included President George W. Bush, who also made serious efforts to court Hispanic communities. As a result, Bush was relatively popular among Latinos, although he was unable to win a majority of the Hispanic vote. Barack Obama, in contrast, received strong support from Latino voters. Latinos continued to vote Democratic by substantial margins in 2012.

**Political Participation**   Generally, Latinos in the United States have had a comparatively low level of political participation. This is understandable, given that more than one-third of Hispanics are below voting age, and also that more than one-fourth are not citizens and thus cannot vote. Although voter turnout among Latinos is generally low compared with the population at large, the Latino voting rate is rising as more immigrants become citizens and as more Hispanics reach voting age. Indeed, when comparing citizens of equal incomes and educational backgrounds, Latino citizens' participation rate is higher than average.

Latinos increasingly hold political office, particularly in states with large Hispanic populations. Today, more than 5 percent of the state legislators in Arizona, California, Colorado, Florida, New Mexico, and Texas are of Hispanic ancestry. Cuban Americans have been notably successful in gaining local political power, particularly in Dade County, Florida.

George W. Bush appointed a number of Latinos to federal offices, including cabinet positions. Barack Obama appointed Senator Ken Salazar (D., Colo.)

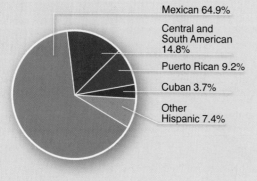

**FIGURE 5-2**

# Hispanics Living in the
## United States by Place of Origin

As you can see in this chart, most Latinos (just under two-thirds) are from Mexico.

Mexican 64.9%

Central and South American 14.8%

Puerto Rican 9.2%

Cuban 3.7%

Other Hispanic 7.4%

Source: The 2010 Census.

to head the Interior Department and Representative Hilda Solis (D., Calif.) as secretary of labor. Latinos are also increasing their presence in Congress, albeit slowly. As of 2013, 31 Latinos serve in either the U.S. House of Representatives or the Senate.

## 5–4b Asian Americans

Asian Americans have also suffered, at times severely, from discriminatory treatment. The Chinese Exclusion Act of 1882 prevented people from China and Japan from coming to the United States to prospect for gold or to work on the railroads or in factories in the West. After 1900, immigration continued to be restricted—only limited numbers of Chinese or Japanese individuals were allowed to enter the United States. Those who were allowed into the country faced racial prejudice from Americans who had little respect for their customs and culture. In 1906, after the San Francisco earthquake, Japanese American students were segregated into special schools so that white children could use their buildings.

**Internment of Japanese Americans**  The Japanese bombing of Pearl Harbor in 1941, which launched the entry of the United States into World War II (1939–1945), intensified Americans' fear of the Japanese. Actions taken under an executive order issued by President Franklin D. Roosevelt in 1942 subjected many Japanese Americans to curfews, excluded them from certain "military areas," and evacuated most of the West Coast Japanese American population to internment camps (also called "relocation centers").[17] In 1988, Congress provided funds to compensate former camp inhabitants—$1.25 billion for approximately 60,000 people.

Some Asians argue that they face discrimination in college admissions.

**A "Model Minority"?**  Today, Asian Americans lead other minority groups in median income and median education. Indeed, Asians who have immigrated to the United States since 1965 (including immigrants from India) represent the most highly skilled immigrant groups in American history. Nearly 40 percent of Asian Americans over the age of twenty-five have college degrees.

The image of Asian Americans as a "model minority" has created certain problems for its members, however. Some argue that leading private colleges and universities have discriminated against Asian Americans in admissions because so many of them apply. We discuss that issue in this chapter's *Join the Debate* feature on the following page.

More than a million Indochinese war refugees, most from Vietnam, have immigrated to the United States since the 1970s. Many came with relatives and were sponsored by American families or organizations. Thus, they had support systems to help them get started. Some immigrants from other parts of Indochina, however, have experienced difficulties because they come from cultures that have had very little contact with the practices of developed industrial societies.

## 5–4c Native Americans

When we consider population figures since 1492, we see that the Native Americans experienced one catastrophe after another. We cannot know exactly how many people lived in America when Columbus arrived. Current research estimates the population of what is now the continental United States to have been anywhere from 3 million to 8 million. The Europeans brought with them diseases to which these Native Americans had no immunity. As a result, after a series of terrifying epidemics, the population of the continental United States was reduced to perhaps eight hundred thousand people by 1600. Death rates elsewhere in the New World were comparable. When the Pilgrims arrived at Plymouth, the Massachusetts coast was lined with abandoned village sites.[18]

In subsequent centuries, the Native American population continued to decline, bottoming out at about half a million in 1925. These were centuries in which the European American and African American populations experienced explosive growth. By 2010, the Native American population had recovered to almost 3 million, or more than 5 million if we count individuals who are only part Indian.

In 1789, Congress designated the Native American tribes as foreign nations so that the government could

VIEWSTOCK/STOCK CONNECTION USA/NEWSCOM

## Are Admissions at Top Schools Unfair to Asian Americans?

There are more than 15 million Asian Americans. They are a diverse group. Outside the United States, people from China, India, Japan, and Korea have little in common. Only in America are they lumped together—and in this country, people from East Asia and South Asia do have a few things in common. Their average family income is higher than that of whites. They are also well educated. By one estimate, Asian Americans make up as many as 30 percent of the top college candidates as determined by SAT scores. In the Ivy League, however, Asian admissions have consistently run below 20 percent. In other words, many excellent Asian American students are being turned away.

### College Admission Isn't Just about Grades and Test Scores

While it may appear to high-scoring Asian Americans who don't get into their college of choice that they have suffered from discrimination, it is not necessarily true. Universities routinely manage admissions to obtain the freshman classes they wish to have. They try to include the right number of football and basketball players, for example, as well as minorities. Only if you believe that high test scores should be the sole basis for admission can you argue that university admission preferences constitute discrimination.

The goal of a diverse freshman class is to expose all students to a mix of races, ethnicities, and viewpoints. A freshman class that is, say, 40 percent Asian American does not look like America.

### Discrimination Is Discrimination—Period

Lately, Ivy League–level private universities have established techniques to limit the number of Asian American students admitted to their institutions. These same techniques were used before World War II (and sometimes even after) to limit the number of Jewish students. The basic scheme, then and now, is to award lots of extra points for being "well-rounded" and then to define *well-rounded* as everything that young Asian Americans aren't (or that the young Jews weren't).

There is no need to set Asian Americans in competition with other minorities in admissions. More than 20 percent of the spaces at top private universities are currently set aside for legacy students, children of the rich and famous, and athletes. (Legacy students are the children of alumni or alumnae.) If the number of these unjustified preferences were merely cut in half, there would be enough room for qualified Asian youths.

**FOR CRITICAL ANALYSIS** Why do some universities reserve spots for the children of their graduates?

---

sign land and boundary treaties with them. As members of foreign nations, Native Americans had no civil rights under U.S. laws. This situation continued until 1924, when the citizenship rights spelled out in the Fourteenth Amendment to the Constitution were finally extended to American Indians.

## Early Policies toward Native Americans

The Northwest Ordinance, passed by Congress under the Articles of Confederation in 1787, stated that "the utmost good faith shall always be observed towards the Indians; their lands and property shall never be taken from them without their consent . . . ." Over the next hundred years, these principles were violated more often than they were observed.

In 1830, Congress instructed the Bureau of Indian Affairs (BIA), which Congress had established in 1824 as part of the War Department, to remove all tribes to reservations west of the Mississippi River in order to free land east of the Mississippi for white settlement. The resettlement was a catastrophe for Indians in the eastern states.

In the late 1880s, the U.S. government changed its policy. The goal became the "assimilation" of Native Americans into American society. Each family was given a parcel of land within the reservation to farm. The remaining acreage was sold to whites, thus reducing the number of acres in reservation status from 140 million to about 47 million. Tribes that would not cooperate with this plan lost their reservations altogether.

## Women and Minority Group Members in the 2012 Elections

As of 2012, America continued to become increasingly diverse. Congress now contained four Buddhists, two Muslims, and a Hindu. Gains by major minority groups were more modest. About 18 percent of the U.S. House consisted of minority group members, only a slight increase. Women experienced greater gains. Twenty members of the U.S. Senate were now women, and about 18 percent of the House was female as well. The House now contained six openly gay, lesbian, or bisexual members, and Tammy Baldwin (D., Wisc.) became the first openly gay or lesbian member of the Senate.

Minority group members may have exercised their greatest influence as voters. Turnout was up. In Ohio, a key state in the 2012 elections, the African American share of the vote increased from 11 percent in 2008 to 15 percent in 2012. Nationwide, Latinos were 10 percent of the electorate, up from 9 percent in 2008 and 8 percent in 2004. One factor contributing to high turnout among Democratic voters was Obama's extraordinarily effective get-out-the-vote drive. Another was the anger felt by many minority group members over alleged efforts to suppress the minority vote. These included tough voter ID laws and purportedly heavy-handed poll-watching campaigns in minority precincts. Any attempt at voter suppression appears to have backfired.

Women as a whole voted 55 percent for Obama. Among unmarried women, the figure was 67 percent. Especially notable were the Democratic Senate victories in Indiana and Missouri. In both states, Tea Party backed Republican candidates made unfortunate statements when trying to justify banning abortion even in cases of rape. The resulting loss of support cost the Republicans two seats that they otherwise would have won.

---

The BIA also set up Native American boarding schools for children to remove them from their parents' influence. In these schools, American Indian children were taught to speak English, to practice Christianity, and to dress like white Americans.

### Native American Activism

Native Americans have always found it difficult to obtain political power. In part, this is because the tribes are small and scattered, making organized political movements difficult. Today, American Indians remain fragmented politically because large numbers of their population live off the reservations.

Nonetheless, beginning in the 1960s, some Native Americans formed organizations to strike back at the U.S. government and to reclaim their heritage, including their lands. For example, in 1973, supporters of the American Indian Movement took over Wounded Knee, South Dakota, where about 150 Sioux Indians had been killed by the U.S. Army in 1890.[19] The occupation was undertaken to protest the government's policy toward Native Americans.

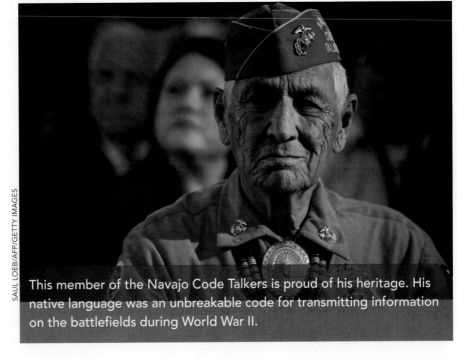

SAUL LOEB/AFP/GETTY IMAGES

This member of the Navajo Code Talkers is proud of his heritage. His native language was an unbreakable code for transmitting information on the battlefields during World War II.

**Compensation for Injustices of the Past** As more Americans became aware of the sufferings of Native Americans, Congress began to compensate them for past injustices. In 1990, Congress passed the Native American Languages Act, which declared that Native American languages are unique and serve an important role in maintaining Indian culture and continuity. Courts, too, have shown a greater willingness to recognize Native American treaty rights. For example, in 1985, the Supreme Court ruled that three tribes of Oneida Indians could claim damages for the use of tribal land that had been unlawfully transferred in 1795.[20]

The Indian Gaming Regulatory Act of 1988 allows Native Americans to have gambling operations on their reservations. Although the profits from casinos have helped to improve the economic and social status of many Native Americans, poverty and unemployment remain widespread on the reservations. We discuss Native American tribal governments and Indian gambling operations in the *Our Challenging Times* feature on the facing page.

## 5–4d Obtaining Rights for Persons with Disabilities

Discrimination based on disability crosses the boundaries of race, ethnicity, gender, and religion. Persons with disabilities, especially those with physical deformities or severe mental impairments, face social bias. Although attitudes toward persons with disabilities have changed considerably in the last several decades, such persons continue to suffer from discrimination.

Persons with disabilities first became a political force in the 1970s, and in 1973 Congress passed the initial legislation protecting this group—the Rehabilitation Act. This act prohibited discrimination against persons with disabilities in programs receiving federal aid. The Individuals with Disabilities Education Act (formerly called the Education for All Handicapped Children Act of 1975) requires public schools to provide children with disabilities with free, appropriate, and individualized education in the least restrictive environment appropriate to their needs.

Further legislation in 1978 led to regulations for ramps, elevators, and the like in all federal buildings. The Americans with Disabilities Act (ADA) of 1990, however, is by far the most significant legislation protecting the rights of this group of Americans.

**The Americans with Disabilities Act** The ADA requires that all public buildings and public

ALEX WONG/GETTY IMAGES

Representative Jim Langevin (D., R.I.) attends a hearing of the Energy and Power Subcommittee of the House Energy and Commerce Committee.

services be accessible to persons with disabilities. The act also mandates that employers "reasonably accommodate" the needs of workers or job applicants with disabilities who are otherwise qualified for particular jobs unless to do so would cause the employer to suffer an "undue hardship."

The ADA defines persons with disabilities as persons who have physical or mental impairments that "substantially limit" their everyday activities. Health conditions that have been considered disabilities under federal law include blindness, a history of alcoholism, heart disease, cancer, muscular dystrophy, cerebral palsy, paraplegia, diabetes, and acquired immune deficiency syndrome (AIDS). The ADA, however, does not require employers to hire or retain workers who, because of their disabilities, pose a "direct threat to the health or safety" of their co-workers.

**Limiting the Scope of the ADA** From 1999 to 2002, the Supreme Court handed down a series

# OUR CHALLENGING TIMES

## Tribal Governments and Casinos

In our federal system, we have a national government in Washington, D.C. States and localities have their own governments. We also have American Indian tribal governments—a unique, third type of institution. Indian affairs are a national, not a state, responsibility. The tribes exercise power over their territories and over their members. State governments do have some powers over reservation lands, but only when Congress grants these powers to the states.

Since the establishment of Indian reservations in the latter part of the 1800s, severe poverty has been the norm for most American Indians. Tribal governments have long faced challenging times, regardless of the condition of the rest of the nation.

### CASINOS TO THE RESCUE

Beginning in the 1980s, a few inspired tribal leaders began promoting economic development through bingo gambling on their reservations. Normally, states control gambling, but Indian territories are separate government entities, as noted earlier. In 1987, the Supreme Court ruled that if a state allowed some forms of gambling, it could not prevent Indian gambling operations. In 1988, Congress passed the Indian Gaming Regulatory Act to regulate tribal gambling.

The floodgates opened. About 360 tribal gambling establishments currently exist, many of which are similar to casinos you will find in Las Vegas. Not all Indian tribes have been successful in this process, however. Out of about 550 federally recognized tribes, only about 240 operate gambling establishments. Just 22 tribes collect more than half of the revenues. Widespread poverty on reservations continues to be a reality.

### A "RECESSION-PROOF" INDUSTRY?

Until 2008, Native American casinos saw revenues rise each year. From 2002 to 2007, revenues rose by an average of just over 10 percent per year. When the Great Recession hit, however, the growth stopped. Gambling had always been considered a "recession-proof" industry, but Indian gambling revenues have been essentially constant from 2008 on. A number of casinos have responded by cutting staff levels and by installing more slot machines, which require little labor.

Most Native American reservations are located far from major cities. High gasoline prices in recent years have dissuaded some gambling visitors. Tribes that have enjoyed the most economic success have generally done so by investing gambling profits in other employment-intensive enterprises.

**YOU BE THE JUDGE** Many states operate lotteries. Casinos and other legal gambling opportunities exist throughout the country. Should gambling be allowed everywhere and in any form—or would this create serious problems? Explain your answer.

of rulings that substantially limited the scope of the ADA. The Court found that any limitation that could be remedied by medication or by corrective devices such as eyeglasses did not qualify as a protected disability. According to the Court, even carpal tunnel syndrome was not a disability.[21] In 2008, however, the ADA Amendments Act overturned most of these limits. Carpal tunnel syndrome and other ailments may again qualify as disabilities. (The need for eyeglasses was not, however, covered by the new law.)

In 2001, the Supreme Court reviewed a case raising the question of whether suits under the ADA could be brought against state employers. The Court concluded that states are immune from lawsuits brought to enforce rights under this federal law.[22]

## 5-4e Gay Men and Lesbians

Until the late 1960s and early 1970s, gay men and lesbians tended to keep quiet about their sexual orientation because exposure usually meant facing harsh consequences. This attitude began to change after a 1969 incident in the Greenwich Village neighborhood of New York City, however. When the police raided the Stonewall Inn—a bar popular with gay men and lesbians—on June 27 of that year, the bar's patrons responded by throwing beer cans and bottles at the police. The riot continued for two days. The Stonewall Inn uprising launched the "gay power" movement. By the end of the year, gay men and lesbians had formed fifty organizations, including the Gay Activist Alliance and the Gay Liberation Front.

### A Changing Legal Landscape

The number of gay and lesbian organizations has grown from fifty in 1969 to several thousand today. These groups have exerted significant political pressure on legislatures, the media, schools, and churches. In the decades following Stonewall, more than half of the forty-nine states that had sodomy laws—laws prohibiting homosexual conduct and certain other forms of sexual

> ## "THE LIBERTY PROTECTED BY THE CONSTITUTION
>
> allows homosexual persons the right to choose to enter upon relationships in the confines of their homes and their own private lives and still retain their **DIGNITY AS FREE PERSONS."**
>
> ~ UNITED STATES SUPREME COURT ~
> *LAWRENCE V. TEXAS,*
> 2003

activity—repealed them. In seven other states, the courts invalidated such laws. Then, in 2003, the United States Supreme Court issued a ruling that effectively invalidated all remaining sodomy laws in the country.

**GAINING LEGAL STATUS.** In *Lawrence v. Texas,*[23] the Court ruled that sodomy laws violated the Fourteenth Amendment's due process clause. According to the Court, "The liberty protected by the Constitution allows homosexual persons the right to choose to enter upon relationships in the confines of their homes and their own private lives and still retain their dignity as free persons."

**ANTIDISCRIMINATION LAWS.** Today, twenty-one states and more than 170 cities and counties in the United States have laws prohibiting discrimination against homosexuals in at least some contexts. The laws may prohibit discrimination in housing, education, banking, employment, or public accommodations. In a landmark case in 1996, *Romer v. Evans,*[24] the Supreme Court held that a Colorado constitutional amendment that would have invalidated all state and local laws protecting homosexuals from discrimination violated the equal protection clause of the U.S. Constitution. The Court stated that the amendment would have denied to homosexuals in Colorado—but to no other Colorado residents—"the right to seek specific protection from the law."

### Changing Attitudes

Laws and court decisions protecting the rights of gay men and lesbians reflect social attitudes that are much changed from the 1960s. Liberal political leaders have been supporting gay rights for at least two decades. Even some conservative politicians have softened their stance

STEVEN GREAVES/CORBIS

TOGETHER 34 YEARS

Gay rights have changed dramatically in the last fifty years in the United States.

on the issue. For example, during his 2000 presidential campaign, George W. Bush met with representatives of gay groups to discuss issues important to them. Bush promised that he would not disqualify anyone from serving in his administration on the basis of sexual orientation.

According to a Gallup poll taken in 2012, public support for gay and lesbian rights has continued to rise. The survey showed that 63 percent of respondents believed that gay or lesbian relations between consenting adults should be legal, up from 43 percent in 1978. In a separate poll, an even larger share of those interviewed—70 percent—believed that openly gay or lesbian persons should be allowed to serve in the military.

Support for same-sex marriage, which was endorsed by only 27 percent of Americans in 1996, has risen ever since. In a striking development, three polling organizations reported in mid-2011 that for the first time ever, an absolute majority of those questioned supported same-sex marriage. Support in these polls ranged from 51 to 53 percent.

### Same-Sex Marriage

Today, same-sex marriage is legal in nine states—Connecticut, Iowa, New Hampshire, New York, Maine, Maryland, Massachusetts, Vermont, and Washington—and in the District of Columbia. It was temporarily legal in California during part of 2008, between a state supreme court ruling in May that legalized the practice and a constitutional amendment passed by the voters in November that banned it again. California continues to recognize those same-sex couples who married between May and November 2008 as lawfully wedded. Three

states endorsed same-sex marriage in the 2012 elections—Maine, Maryland, and Washington. These votes marked the first time that voters endorsed such marriages. Previously, state legislatures or the courts had legalized them. Also, Rhode Island does not perform same-sex marriages but recognizes those performed elsewhere.

**SAME-SEX MARRIAGE IN THE COURTS.** As noted previously, two major court cases dealing with same-sex marriage appear to be headed to the United States Supreme Court, which may rule on them in the term ending in 2013. In the Chapter 2 *America at Odds* feature on page 23, we described a case in which a federal court overturned California's vote to ban same-sex marriage. If opponents of the ban are successful, same-sex marriage would become legal again, at least in California.[25]

We discussed a second case in Chapter 3 on page 58. In this instance, a federal district court in Massachusetts ruled that the federal government could not refuse to recognize same-sex marriages authorized by the states. If gay marriage supporters win this case, same-sex couples in Massachusetts and other states will receive a variety of federal benefits that are based on marriage.[26]

**CIVIL UNIONS AND DOMESTIC PARTNERSHIPS.** A number of states have civil union or domestic partnership laws that grant most of the benefits of

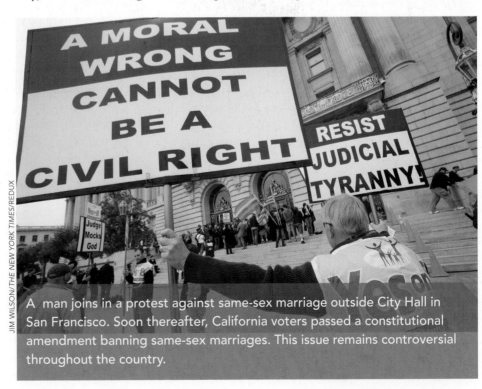

A man joins in a protest against same-sex marriage outside City Hall in San Francisco. Soon thereafter, California voters passed a constitutional amendment banning same-sex marriages. This issue remains controversial throughout the country.

**affirmative action**
A policy that gives special consideration, in jobs and college admissions, to members of groups that have been discriminated against in the past.

marriage to registered same-sex couples. These include California, Illinois, Hawaii, Nevada, New Jersey, Oregon, Rhode Island, and Washington. More limited benefits are provided in Colorado, Maine, Maryland, and Wisconsin. Either through a constitutional amendment or through legislation, same-sex marriage is explicitly banned in most states without domestic partnership laws—and even in some of the states just mentioned.

### Gays and Lesbians in the Military

For gay men and lesbians who wish to join the military, one of the battles they faced was the "don't ask, don't tell" policy. This policy, which banned openly gay men and lesbians from the military, was implemented in 1993 by President Bill Clinton when it became clear that more liberal alternatives would not be accepted. During his presidential campaign, Barack Obama pledged to abolish the policy. Later, gay and lesbian rights activists accused him of "putting the issue on a back burner."

The courts forced the issue, however. In September 2010, a U.S. district court ruled that "don't ask, don't tell" was unconstitutional.[27] A U.S. appeals court stayed (suspended) the ruling, but the possibility that "don't ask, don't tell" might be thrown out by the courts forced Congress to take action. In the "lame duck" session between the November 2010 elections and the swearing-in of new members in January 2011, Congress repealed the policy on a gradual basis. Full repeal was implemented later in 2011. As a result, gay men and lesbians may now serve openly in the nation's armed forces.

**FOR CRITICAL THINKING**

The number of Latinos in the United States continues to grow. *What impact do you think this will have on American culture and politics?*

## 5–5 Beyond Equal Protection— Affirmative Action

One provision of the Civil Rights Act of 1964 called for prohibiting discrimination in employment. Soon after the act was passed, the federal government began to legislate programs promoting *equal employment opportunity.*

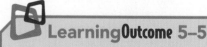

**Learning Outcome 5–5**

Explain what affirmative action is and why it has been so controversial.

Such programs require that employers' hiring and promotion practices guarantee the same opportunities to all individuals. Experience soon showed that minorities often had fewer opportunities to obtain education and relevant work experience than did whites. Because of this, minorities were still excluded from many jobs. Even though discriminatory practices were made illegal, the change in the law did not make up for the results of years of discrimination. Consequently, under President Lyndon B. Johnson (1963–1969), a new policy was developed.

Called **affirmative action,** this policy requires employers to take positive steps to remedy *past* discrimination. Affirmative action programs involve giving special consideration, in jobs and college admissions, to members of groups that have been discriminated against in the past.

Until recently, all public and private employers who received federal funds were required to adopt and implement these programs. Thus, the policy of affirmative action has been applied to all agencies of the federal, state, and local governments and to all private employers who sell goods to or perform services for any agency of the federal government. In short, it has covered nearly all of the nation's major employers and many of its smaller ones.

### 5–5a Affirmative Action Tested

The Supreme Court first addressed the issue of affirmative action in 1978 in *Regents of the University of California v. Bakke.*[28] Allan Bakke, a white male, had been denied admission to the University of California's medical school at Davis. The school had set aside sixteen of the one hundred seats in each year's entering class for applicants who wished to be considered as members of designated minority groups. Many of the

In 1996, California voters passed Proposition 209. This initiative prohibited affirmative action in all state government institutions, including universities.

a *compelling* government interest. In effect, the *Adarand* decision narrowed the application of affirmative action programs.

An affirmative action program can no longer make use of quotas or preferences and cannot be maintained simply to remedy past discrimination by society in general. It must be narrowly tailored to remedy actual discrimination that has occurred, and once the program has succeeded, it must be changed or dropped.

### 5–5c The Diversity Issue

Following the *Adarand* decision, several lower courts faced cases raising the question of whether affirmative action programs designed to achieve diversity on college campuses were constitutional.

students admitted through this special program had lower test scores than Bakke.

Bakke sued the university, claiming that he was a victim of **reverse discrimination**—discrimination against whites. Bakke argued that the use of a **quota system,** in which a specific number of seats were reserved for minority applicants only, violated the equal protection clause.

The Supreme Court was strongly divided on the issue. Some justices believed that Bakke had been denied equal protection and should be admitted. A majority on the Court concluded that although both the Constitution and the Civil Rights Act of 1964 allow race to be used as a factor in making admissions decisions, race cannot be the *sole* factor. Because the university's quota system was based solely on race, it was unconstitutional.

### 5–5b Strict Scrutiny Applied

In 1995, the Supreme Court issued a landmark decision in *Adarand Constructors, Inc. v. Peña.*[29] The Court held that any federal, state, or local affirmative action program that uses racial classifications as the basis for making decisions is subject to "strict scrutiny" by the courts. As discussed earlier in this chapter, this means that, to be constitutional, a discriminatory law or action must be narrowly tailored to meet

**The *Hopwood* Case** In a 1996 case, *Hopwood v. State of Texas,*[30] two white law school applicants sued the University of Texas School of Law in Austin, claiming that they had been denied admission because of the school's affirmative action program. The program allowed admissions officials to take racial and other factors into consideration when determining which students would be admitted.

A federal appellate court held that the program violated the equal protection clause because it discriminated in favor of minority applicants. In its decision, the court directly challenged the *Bakke* decision by stating that the use of race even as a means of achieving diversity on college campuses "undercuts the Fourteenth Amendment." In other words, race could never be a factor, even if it was not the sole factor, in such decisions.

**The University of Michigan Cases** In 2003, the United States Supreme Court reviewed two cases involving issues similar to that in the *Hopwood* case. Both cases involved admissions programs at the University of Michigan. In *Gratz v. Bollinger,*[31] two white

**reverse discrimination** Discrimination against those who have no minority status.

**quota system** A policy under which a specific number of jobs, promotions, or other types of placements, such as university admissions, are given to members of selected groups.

applicants who were denied undergraduate admission to the university alleged reverse discrimination.

**UNDERGRADUATE ADMISSIONS.** The University of Michigan's policy gave each applicant a score based on a number of factors, including grade point average, standardized test scores, and personal achievements. The system *automatically* awarded every "underrepresented" minority (African American, Hispanic, and Native American) applicant twenty points—one-fifth of the points needed to guarantee admission. The Court held that this policy violated the equal protection clause.

**LAW SCHOOL ADMISSIONS.** In contrast, in *Grutter v. Bollinger*,[32] the Court held that the University of Michigan Law School's admissions policy was constitutional. In that case, the Court concluded that "[u]niversities can, however, consider race or ethnicity more flexibly as a 'plus' factor in the context of individualized consideration of each and every applicant."

The significant difference between the two admissions policies, in the Court's view, was that the law school's approach did not apply a mechanical formula giving "diversity bonuses" based on race or ethnicity. In short, the Court concluded that diversity on college campuses was a legitimate goal and that limited affirmative action programs could be used to attain this goal.

## 5–5d The Supreme Court Revisits the Issue

The Michigan cases were decided in 2003. By 2007, when another case involving affirmative action came before the Court, the Court had a new chief justice, John G. Roberts, Jr., and a new associate justice, Samuel Alito, Jr. Both men were appointed by President George W. Bush, and the conservative views of both justices moved the Court to the right. Justice Alito replaced Sandra Day O'Connor, who had often been the "swing" vote on the Court, sometimes voting with the more liberal justices and sometimes joining the conservative bloc. Hers was the deciding vote in the five-to-four decision upholding the University of Michigan Law School's affirmative action program.

### The Seattle and Louisville School Cases

Some claim that the more conservative composition of today's Court strongly influenced the outcome in a case that came before the Court in 2007: *Parents Involved in Community Schools v. Seattle School District No. 1*.[33] The case concerned the policies of two school districts—one in Louisville, Kentucky, and one in Seattle, Washington. Both schools were trying to achieve a more diversified student body by giving preference to minority students if space in the schools was limited and a choice among applicants had to be made.

These students are applauding a classmate who won a college scholarship in a competition. Depending on where they apply, some of these students may benefit from affirmative action policies.

Parents of white children who were turned away from schools in these districts because of these policies sued the school districts, claiming that the policies violated the equal protection clause. Ultimately, the case reached the Supreme Court, and the Court, in a five-to-four vote, held in favor of the parents, ruling that the policies violated the equal protection clause. The Court's decision did not overrule the 2003 case involving the University of Michigan Law School, however, for the Court did not deny that race could be used as a factor in university admissions policies. Nonetheless, some claim that the decision represents a significant change on the Court with respect to affirmative action policies.

**Current Changes**   Further changes in the Court's positions are possible. In the term ending in 2013, the Court will decide *Fisher v. University of Texas*. In this case, the courts have been asked to explicitly overturn *Grutter v. Bollinger*, the Michigan case that provided limited protection to affirmative action plans. If the Court reverses *Grutter*, affirmative action at public universities in the United States will probably cease.[34]

## 5–5e State Actions

Beginning in the mid-1990s, some states have taken actions to ban affirmative action programs or replace them with alternative policies. For example, in 1996, by a ballot initiative, California amended its state constitution to prohibit any "preferential treatment to any individual or group on the basis of race, sex, color, ethnicity, or national origin in the operation of public employment, public education, or public contracting."

**Further Actions**   Two years later, voters in the state of Washington approved a ballot measure ending all state-sponsored affirmative action. Florida has also ended affirmative action. In 2006, a ballot initiative in Michigan—just three years after the Supreme Court decisions discussed above—banned affirmative action in that state. In the 2008 elections, Nebraska also banned affirmative action, but voters in Colorado

rejected such a measure. Arizona banned affirmative action in 2010, and Oklahoma did so as well in 2012.

In July 2011, however, a federal appeals court overturned the affirmative action ban in Michigan. This case may ultimately be decided by the Supreme Court.[35]

**"Race-Blind" Admissions**   In the meantime, many public universities are trying to find "race-blind" ways to attract more minority students to their campuses. For example, Texas has established a program under which the top students at every high school in the state are guaranteed admission to the University of Texas, Austin. Originally, the guarantee applied to students who were in the top 10 percent of their graduating class. In 2009, the guarantee was limited to students in the top 8 percent of their class. Beginning in 2005, the university reinstated an affirmative action plan, but it was limited to students who were not admitted as part of the top-student guarantee.

**CONSEQUENCES OF THE TEXAS PLAN.**   The guarantee ensures that the top students at minority-dominated inner-city schools can attend the state's leading public university. It also assures admission to the best white students from rural, often poor, communities. Previously, these students could not have hoped to attend the University of Texas. The losers are students from upscale metropolitan neighborhoods or suburbs who have high test scores but are not the top students at their schools. One result is that more students with high test scores enroll in less famous schools, such as Texas Tech University and the University of Texas, Dallas—to the benefit of these schools' reputations.

**FOR CRITICAL THINKING**

*Is the Texas plan to admit the top students from each high school to the University of Texas fair? Why or why not?*

# AMERICA AT
# ODDS Civil Rights

During the first part of the twentieth century, discrimination against African Americans and members of other minority groups was a social norm in the United States. Indeed, much of the nation's white population believed that the ability to discriminate was a constitutionally protected right. Today, the "right to discriminate" has very few defenders. America's laws—and its culture—now hold that discrimination on the basis of race, gender, religion, national origin, and many other characteristics is flatly unacceptable.

Even if civil rights are now broadly supported and protected by law, however, questions remain as to how far these protections should extend. Americans are at odds over a number of civil rights issues, including the following:

- If unauthorized immigrants have certain rights as *persons* under the Fourteenth Amendment to the Constitution, should these rights be construed broadly—or as narrowly as possible?

- Should same-sex marriages by lesbians and gay men be recognized—or prohibited?

- Should we allow lesbians and gay men to serve openly in the nation's armed forces—or was it a mistake to abandon the "don't ask, don't tell" policy?

- Is affirmative action still a necessary policy—or should it be abandoned?

- When colleges and universities consider admissions, is it legitimate to promote racial, ethnic, gender, or socioeconomic diversity—or are such considerations just new forms of discrimination?

# TAKE ACTION

Despite the progress that has been made toward attaining equal treatment for all groups of Americans, much remains to be done. Countless activist groups continue to pursue the goal of equality for all Americans. If you wish to contribute your time and effort toward this goal, there are hundreds of ways to go about it.

- You can learn about the Equal Employment Opportunity Commission and the laws it enforces by entering "eeoc" into your favorite search engine.

- The Leadership Conference on Civil and Human Rights encourages people to contact Congress on matters of interest. You can find its site using the search term "civil rights coalition."

## Minority Groups

- Searching on "martin luther king" will yield much information on this famous leader. To see the collection at Stanford University's King Institute, enter "king stanford."

- You can locate the Web sites of various civil rights groups by entering the abbreviations of their names. For example, use "naacp" to find the National Association for the Advancement of Colored People, the oldest body representing African Americans.

- For material on Hispanic Americans, enter "lulac" to locate the League of United Latin American Citizens.

- An additional source of information on Latino issues is the National Council of La Raza (enter "la raza").

- If you are interested in the rights of immigrants, a good place to start is the Justice for Immigrants Web site (search on "justice for immigrants"). Justice for Immigrants was organized by twenty major Roman Catholic organizations.

## Women

- The most important group participating in the modern feminist movement is the National Organization for Women. Surprisingly, it is the first entry to appear when you type "now" into most search engines. (Naturally, searching on such a common word brings up a variety of other topics as well.)

- Entering "feminist" provides you with a number of definitions and groups. Check out the Feminist Majority Foundation, which is located several entries down from the top.

## Other Groups

- For information on the Americans with Disabilities Act, including the text of the act, enter "askjan ada."

- You can find the Gay and Lesbian Alliance against Defamation by typing in "glaad."

# STUDY TOOLS

## Ready to study?

- Review what you've read with the quiz below. Check your answers on the Chapter in Review card at the back of the book. For any questions you miss, read the corresponding Learning Outcome section again to prepare for class and your exam.
- Rip out and study the Chapter in Review card.

## ... Or you can go online to CourseMate

at www.cengagebrain.com for these additional review materials:

- Practice Quizzes
- Key Term Flashcards or Crossword Puzzles
- Audio Summaries
- Simulations, Animated Learning Modules, and Interactive Timelines
- Videos
- American Government NewsWatch

## Fill-In

1. A law based on a suspect classification, such as race, is subject to _____ scrutiny by the courts.

2. In *Plessy v. Ferguson* (1896), the Supreme Court established the _____ doctrine, which was used to justify segregation in many areas of life for nearly sixty years.

3. The Civil Rights Act of 1964 forbade discrimination on the basis of _____.

4. The feminist movement that began in the 1960s sought _____ for women.

5. It is estimated that for every dollar earned by men, women earn about _____.

6. _____ constitute the largest ethnic minority in the United States.

7. Actions taken under an executive order issued by President Franklin D. Roosevelt in 1942 subjected many _____ Americans to curfews and evacuated many of those on the West Coast to "relocation centers."

8. Affirmative action is best defined as a policy _____.

9. In *Adarand Constructors, Inc. v. Peña* (1995), the Supreme Court held that any federal, state, or local affirmative action program that uses racial classifications as the basis for making decisions is subject to _____ scrutiny by the courts.

## Multiple Choice

10. The equal protection clause of the ____ Amendment reads: "No State shall . . . deny to any person within its jurisdiction the equal protection of the laws."
    a. Fifth
    b. Fourteenth
    c. Nineteenth

11. "Jim Crow" laws
    a. separated the white community from the black community.
    b. were justified by the Supreme Court's decision in *Brown v. Board of Education of Topeka* (1954).
    c. required an end to segregation.

12. In *Brown II* (1955), the Supreme Court ordered desegregation to begin
    a. "immediately."
    b. "with caution and care."
    c. "with all deliberate speed."

13. _____ appointed the first woman to serve as a justice of the United States Supreme Court.
    a. Ronald Reagan
    b. George W. Bush
    c. Barack Obama

14. In 1789, Congress designated the Native American tribes as _____ so that the government could sign land and boundary treaties with them.
    a. enemies
    b. sovereign states composed of American citizens
    c. foreign nations

15. In *Gratz v. Bollinger* (2003), the Supreme Court held that the undergraduate admissions policy at the University of Michigan violated the equal protection clause because it
    a. automatically awarded every "underrepresented" minority applicant one-fifth of the points needed to guarantee admission.
    b. failed to take into account an applicant's race or ethnicity.
    c. failed to take into account an applicant's gender.

# 6

# Interest Groups

AP PHOTO/JOSEPH KACZMAREK

## LearningOutcomes

The **Learning Outcomes** labeled 1 through 4 are designed to help improve your understanding of the chapter. After reading this chapter, you should be able to:

**6–1** Explain what an interest group is, why interest groups form, and how interest groups function in American politics.

**6–2** Identify the various types of interest groups.

**6–3** Discuss how the activities of interest groups help to shape government policymaking.

**6–4** Describe how interest groups are regulated by government.

Remember to visit page 146 for additional **Study Tools**

# AMERICA AT
# ODDS
## Are Farmers Getting a Deal That's Too Good?

JOHN MOORE/GETTY IMAGES

**M**any people, including those who live in large cities, have a romantic view of farming and farmers. This view is one of many reasons why interest groups representing farmers are so successful in winning support from the federal government. Over the last five years, about 2 million farmers received subsidies. These funds included $1.2 billion per year in disaster assistance, $2.6 billion for conservation programs, $5.4 billion in subsidies for crop insurance, and $6.4 billion in commodity subsidies. These last payments are among the most controversial. Some are paid out when crop prices are low. But growers of corn, cotton, rice, soybeans, and wheat get a special, additional deal: they receive more than $4 billion per year in *direct payments*, based solely on a history of planting particular crops.

The farm program is authorized by five-year farm bills, and the next one became due in 2012. In 2012, however, Congress was searching for ways to cut spending. Farm subsidies, previously almost untouchable, were suddenly up for debate. Should they be cut? Are farmers getting too good a deal?

## Agriculture Works—Don't Mess with Success

**F**arming is one of the riskiest businesses around. Farmers are ten times as likely to be killed on the job as the average worker. The weather is a constant worry. Every year, thousands of farmers lose their crops to floods or drought—as in 2012. Further, unlike many businesses, farmers can't set their own prices for what they sell. If you manufacture dishwashers, you expect that you can set a price for them that will cover your costs. Not so in agriculture. Prices are set by world commodity markets, where prices can swing wildly from month to month.

Despite the dangers, agriculture is a success story. Farm exports are booming as poor countries become richer and their people demand better diets—and the United Nations predicts that farmers will need to produce 70 percent more food by 2050 to keep up with population increases. Farm programs are an important safety net that helps keep our farmers in business. At less than half a percent of the federal budget, these programs are also a bargain.

## Wealthy Farmers Don't Need These Subsidies

**E**verybody loves small farmers, but most of the subsidies don't go to these farmers. Large commercial farms amass 62 percent of all federal payments. The average family income for these farmers exceeds $200,000 per year. Their subsidies average about $30,000 per year, as opposed to $7,000 for farms that are small (but still provide a full-time occupation for their owners). Why are we giving so much federal aid to people who are that well off?

There's no doubt that farming is risky. That's why the great majority of farmers carry crop insurance, which—as noted above—is subsidized. Insuring 50 percent of your crop is free. You can insure the rest at reduced rates. How can you lose? Some may claim that we still need disaster assistance and conservation programs. Insurance subsidies have a certain appeal, although they can encourage farmers to plant on marginal acres. But at the very least we can get rid of the direct payments. American food consumers and taxpayers have paid too much for too long.

## Where do you stand?

1. What effect might farm programs have on rural residents who are not farmers?
2. How easy do you think it is for farmers to buy health insurance—and what effect might that have on their incomes?

## Explore this issue online

- You can find the site of the Environmental Working Group (EWG), a critic of farm subsidies, by entering "ewg database" into a search engine. The EWG database contains a complete record of farm program recipients and what they were paid.
- To find arguments in support of the farm programs, search on "farm policy facts."

# Introduction

The groups supporting and opposing farm programs provide but one example of how Americans form groups to pursue or protect their interests. All of us have interests that we would like to have represented in government: labor unionists would like it to be easier to organize unions, young people want good educational opportunities, and environmentalists want cleaner air and water.

The old saying that there is strength in numbers is certainly true in American politics. Special interests significantly influence American government and politics. Indeed, some Americans think that this influence is so great that it jeopardizes representative democracy. Others maintain that interest groups are a natural consequence of democracy. After all, throughout our nation's history, people have organized into groups to protect special interests. Because of the important role played by interest groups in the American system of government, we examine such groups in this chapter. We look at what they are, why they are formed, and how they influence policymaking.

> "Politics is about **people,** not politicians."
>
> ~ SCOTT SIMMS ~
> CANADIAN POLITICIAN
> B. 1969

staffers reviewing testimony with representatives from women's groups. Later that morning, you might visit the Supreme Court and watch a civil rights lawyer arguing on behalf of a client in a discrimination suit. Lunch in a popular Washington restaurant might find you listening in on a conversation between an agricultural lobbyist and a congressional representative.

That afternoon you might visit an executive department, such as the Department of Labor, and watch bureaucrats working out rules and regulations with representatives from a business interest group. Then you might stroll past the headquarters of the National Rifle Association (NRA), AARP (formerly the American Association of Retired Persons), or the National Wildlife Federation.

## 6-1a The Constitutional Right to Petition the Government

The right to form interest groups and to lobby the government is protected by the Bill of Rights. The First Amendment guarantees the right of the people "to petition the Government for a redress of grievances." This important right sometimes gets lost among the other, more well-known First Amendment guarantees, such as the freedoms of religion, speech, and the press. Nonetheless, the right to petition the government is as important and fundamental to our democracy as the other First Amendment rights.

The right to petition the government allows citizens and groups of citizens to lobby members of Congress and other government officials, to sue the government, and to submit petitions to the government. Whenever someone writes to her or his congressional representative for help with a problem, such as not receiving a Social Security payment, that person is petitioning the government.

## 6-1b Why Interest Groups Form

The United States is a vast country of many regions, scores of ethnic groups, and a huge variety of businesses and occupations. The number of potential interests that can be represented is therefore very large. Beyond the sheer size of the country, however, there are a number of specific reasons why the United States has as many interest groups as it does.

It is worth remembering that not all groups are interest groups. A group becomes an interest group

# 6-1 Interest Groups and American Government

An **interest group** is an organized group of people sharing common objectives who actively attempt to influence government policymakers through direct and indirect methods. Whatever their goals—more or fewer social services, higher or lower prices—interest groups pursue these goals on every level and in every branch of government.

On any given day in Washington, D.C., you can see national interest groups in action. If you eat breakfast in the Senate dining room, you might see congressional committee

**interest group** An organized group of individuals sharing common objectives who actively attempt to influence policymakers.

when it seeks to affect the policies or practices of the government. Many groups do not meet such a standard. A social group, for example, may be formed to entertain or educate its members, with no broader purpose. Churches, organized to facilitate worship and community, frequently have no political aims. (Indeed, certain political activities, such as campaigning for or against candidates for office, could cost a church its tax-exempt status.)

A group founded with little or no desire to influence the government can become an interest group, however, if its members decide that the government's policies are important to them. Alternatively, lobbying the government may initially be only one of several activities pursued by a group and then grow to become the group's primary purpose.

The National Rifle Association (NRA) provides an example of this process. From its establishment in 1871 until the 1930s, the group took little part in politics. As late as the 1970s, a large share of the NRA's members joined for reasons that had nothing to do with politics. Many joined solely to participate in firearms training programs or to win marksman certifications. The NRA continues to provide such services today, but it is now so heavily politicized that anyone likely to take out a membership is certain to broadly agree with the NRA's political positions.

## More Government, More Interest Groups

Interest groups may form—and existing groups may become more politically active—when the government expands its scope of activities. More government, in other words, means more interest groups. Prior to the 1970s, for example, the various levels of government were not nearly as active in attempting to regulate the use of firearms as they were thereafter.

This change provides one explanation of why the NRA is much more politically active today than it was years ago. Consider another example—AARP, formerly the American Association of Retired Persons. AARP is a major lobbying force that seeks to preserve or enhance Social Security and Medicare benefits for citizens sixty-five years of age and older. Before the creation of Social Security in the 1930s, however, the federal government did not provide income support to the elderly, and there would have been little reason for an organization such as AARP to exist.

## Defending the Group's Interests
Interest groups also may come into existence in response to a perceived threat to a group's interests. In the example of the NRA, the threat was an increase in the frequency of attempts to regulate or even ban firearms. This increase threatened the interests of gun owners. As another example, the National Right to Life Committee formed in response to *Roe v. Wade*, the United States Supreme Court's decision that legalized abortion. Interest groups can also form in reaction to the creation of other interest groups, thus pitting two groups against each other. Political scientist David B. Truman coined the term *disturbance theory* for his description of this kind of defensive formation of interest groups.[1]

## The Importance of Leaders
Political scientist Robert H. Salisbury provided another analysis of the organization of interest groups that he dubbed *entrepreneurial theory*. This line of thought focuses on the importance of the leaders who establish the organization. The desire of such individuals to guarantee a viable organization is important to the group's survival.[2] AARP is an example of a group with a committed founder—Dr. Ethel Percy Andrus, a retired high school principal. Andrus organized the group in 1958 to let older Americans purchase health-care insurance collectively. As with the NRA, AARP did not develop into a lobbying powerhouse until years after it was founded.

## Incentives to Join a Group
The French political observer and traveler Alexis de Tocqueville wrote in 1835 that Americans have a tendency to form "associations" and have perfected "the art of pursuing in common the object of their common desires. . . . In no other country of the world, has the principle of association been more successfully used or applied to a greater multitude of objectives than in America."[3] Of course, Tocqueville could not foresee the thousands of associations that now exist in this country. Surveys show that more than 85 percent of Americans

| TABLE 6–1 | |
| --- | --- |
| **Percentage of Americans Belonging to Various Groups** | |
| Social clubs | 17% |
| Neighborhood groups | 18 |
| Hobby, garden, and computer clubs | 19 |
| PTA and school groups | 21 |
| Professional and trade associations | 27 |
| Health, sport, and country clubs | 30 |
| Religious groups | 61 |

Source: AARP.

belong to at least one group. Table 6–1 on page 127 shows the percentage of Americans who belong to various types of groups today.

Political scientists have identified various reasons why people join interest groups. Often, people have one or more incentives to join such organizations. If a group stands for something that you believe is very important, you can gain considerable satisfaction in taking action from within that group. Such satisfaction is referred to as a **purposive incentive.** Some people enjoy the camaraderie and sense of belonging that come from associating with other people who share their interests and goals. That enjoyment can be called a **solidary incentive.**

Finally, some groups offer their members material incentives for joining, such as discounts on products, subscriptions, or group insurance programs. Each of these could be characterized as a **material incentive.** But sometimes none of these incentives is enough to persuade people to join a group.

> # "THE HEALTH OF A DEMOCRATIC SOCIETY
> may be measured by the quality of functions performed by private citizens."
> ~ ALEXIS DE TOCQUEVILLE ~
> FRENCH HISTORIAN AND POLITICAL SCIENTIST
> 1805–1859

People cannot be excluded from enjoying a public good, such as national defense, just because they did not pay for it. As a result, public goods are often provided by the government, which can force people to pay for the public good through taxation.

The existence of persons who benefit but do not contribute is called the **free rider problem.** Much of what we know about the free rider problem comes from Mancur Olson's classic work of political science, *The Logic of Collective Action.*[4]

**INTEREST GROUPS AND PUBLIC GOODS.** Lobbying, collective bargaining by labor unions, and other forms of representation can also be public goods. If an interest group is successful in lobbying for laws that will improve air quality, for example, everyone who breathes that air will benefit, whether they paid for the lobbying effort or not.

Alexis de Tocqueville (1805–1859) was a well-known French political historian. He lived during a time of political upheaval in France and took a keen interest in the new democracy in America. He toured the United States and Canada as a young man and collected his observations in *Democracy in America,* which was published in 1835.

THE GRANGER COLLECTION

## The Free Rider Problem

The world in which we live is one of scarce resources that can be used to create *private goods* and *public goods.* Most of the goods and services that you use are private goods. If you consume them, no one else can consume them at the same time. If you eat a sandwich, no one else can have it.

With the other class of goods, called public goods, however, your use of a good does not diminish its use by someone else. National defense is a good example. If this country is protected through its national defense system, your protection from enemy invasion does not reduce any other person's protection.

**purposive incentive**
A reason to join an interest group—satisfaction resulting from working for a cause in which one believes.

**solidary incentive**
A reason to join an interest group—pleasure in associating with like-minded individuals.

**material incentive**
A reason to join an interest group—practical benefits such as discounts, subscriptions, or group insurance.

**free rider problem**
The difficulty that exists when individuals can enjoy the outcome of an interest group's efforts without having to contribute, such as by becoming members of the group.

**ADDRESSING THE PROBLEM.** In some instances, the free rider problem can be overcome. For example, social pressure may persuade some people to join or donate to a group for fear of being ostracized. For this and other reasons, it is much easier for a relatively small number of people to organize around an interest that they share.

The government can also step in to ensure that the burden of lobbying for the public good is shared by all. When the government classifies interest groups as nonprofit organizations, it confers on them tax-exempt status. The groups' operating costs are reduced because they do not have to pay taxes, and the impact of the government's lost revenue is absorbed by all taxpayers.

## 6–1c How Interest Groups Function in American Politics

Despite the bad press that interest groups tend to get in the United States, they do serve several purposes in American politics:

- Interest groups help bridge the gap between citizens and government and enable citizens to explain their views on policies to public officials.

- Interest groups help raise public awareness and inspire action on various issues.

- Interest groups often provide public officials with specialized and detailed information that might be difficult to obtain otherwise. This information may be useful in making policy choices.

- Interest groups serve as another check on public officials to make sure that they are carrying out their duties responsibly.

**Access to Government** In a sense, the American system of government invites the participation of interest groups by offering many points of access for groups wishing to influence policy. Consider the possibilities at just the federal level.

An interest group can lobby members of Congress to act in the interests of the group. If the Senate passes a bill opposed by the group, the group's lobbying efforts can shift to the House of Representatives. If the House passes the bill, the group can try to influence the new law's application by lobbying the executive agency that is responsible for implementing the law. The group might even challenge the law in court, directly (by filing a lawsuit) or indirectly (by filing a brief as an *amicus curiae,*[5] or "friend of the court").

Interest groups can seek a variety of different benefits when lobbying the government. A frequent goal is favorable treatment under federal or state regulations. Groups may also seek outright subsidies that benefit their members. An increasingly popular objective is special treatment in the tax code. Tax breaks for a special interest can be easier to obtain than subsidies because the breaks don't look like government spending. We take a closer look at that issue in this chapter's *Join the Debate* feature on the following page.

**Pluralist Theory** The **pluralist theory** of American democracy focuses on the participation of groups in a decentralized government structure that offers many points of access to policymakers. According to the pluralist theory, politics is a contest among various interest groups. These groups vie with one another—at all levels of government—to gain benefits for their members. Pluralists maintain that the influence of interest groups on government is not undemocratic because individual interests are indirectly represented in the policymaking process through these groups.

Although not every American belongs to an interest group, inevitably some group will represent each individual's interests. Thus, each interest is satisfied to some extent through the compromises made in settling conflicts among competing interest groups.

Pluralists also contend that because of the extensive number of interest groups vying for political benefits, no one group can dominate the political process. Additionally, because most people have more than one interest, conflicts among groups do not divide the nation into hostile camps. Not all scholars agree that this is how interest groups function, however.

## 6–1d How Do Interest Groups Differ from Political Parties?

Although interest groups and political parties are both groups of people joined together for political purposes, they differ in several important ways. As you will read in Chapter 7, a political party is a group of individuals who organize to win elections, operate the government, and determine policy. Interest groups, in contrast, do not seek to win elections or operate the government, although they do seek to influence policy. Interest groups differ from political parties in the following ways:

> **pluralist theory** A theory that views politics as a contest among various interest groups—at all levels of government—to gain benefits for their members.

## Should We Close Tax Loopholes?

When you hear the words "tax loophole," you might think of tax breaks for the rich—perhaps the people who fly in corporate jets. (In fact, there is a tax loophole for corporate jets.) A tax loophole is a legal method to reduce taxes owed. Tax loopholes are also called *tax expenditures* in federal government bookkeeping circles. If your parents obtain a tax credit for your tuition, that is a tax loophole—a tax expenditure. People who own houses can usually reduce their federal income taxes by a percentage of whatever they paid in local property taxes. That's also a tax loophole.

The above two examples, though, are peanuts. The first one adds up to only $12 billion a year and the second to about $25 billion. The total amount of tax expenditures, though, is closer to $1 trillion per year. The three largest are tax exclusions for employer contributions to health insurance, exclusions for pension contributions, and the deduction for mortgage interest.

### Eliminate—or at Least Reduce—All Tax Loopholes

In 2012, a substantial number of politicians campaigned on a platform of closing tax loopholes. They pointed out that the federal government has been running red ink to the tune of over $1 trillion a year for the past four years. That's a sum roughly equivalent to the size of all tax expenditures. Some sacred cows will have to be slaughtered, such as the tax deduction for mortgage interest. As with all tax loopholes, this deduction is worth much more to the rich, who are in higher marginal income tax rate brackets (and have bigger houses). Moreover, reducing the incentive to families to buy homes that they cannot afford could prevent another housing bubble.

There is a basic fairness issue for all tax loopholes: Is it right to choose a particular expenditure, such as interest on a home mortgage, and declare that it is so vital to society that it must be subsidized? Why privilege such personal spending over everything else?

### Not So Fast— Those Tax Loopholes Can Be Useful

Some tax experts say "not so fast" when it comes to abolishing tax expenditures. Blogger Matt Yglesias, for example, points out that we have tax loopholes because the government wants to attain real policy objectives. The employer-provided health-insurance tax break, for example, supports the health-insurance plans of most adults in the United States. The break makes it possible for large employers to turn their workforces into risk-sharing pools.

The tax break for charitable deductions is essential to funding higher education and research, including medical research. The tax breaks for certain private pension plans serve an important goal—they allow people to individually provide for themselves in old age, rather than relying completely on Social Security. Providing tax loopholes might not be the most efficient way to attain policy goals. But we need to think up other ways to accomplish these goals before we stop funding them through tax breaks.

**FOR CRITICAL ANALYSIS** How much should we worry about people who are negatively affected when a tax loophole is eliminated?

- Interest groups are often policy *specialists*, whereas political parties are policy *generalists*. Political parties are broad-based organizations that must attract the support of many opposing groups and consider a large number of issues. Interest groups, in contrast, may have only a handful of key policies to push. An environmental group, obviously, will not be as concerned about the economic status of Hispanics as it is about polluters. A manufacturing group is more involved with pushing for fewer regulations than it is with inner-city poverty.

- Interest groups are usually more tightly organized than political parties. They are often financed through contributions or dues-paying memberships. Organizers of interest groups communicate with members and potential members through conferences, mailings, newsletters, and electronic formats such as e-mail, Facebook, and Twitter.

- A political party's main sphere of influence is the electoral system. Parties run candidates for political office. Interest groups may try to influence the outcome of elections, but unlike parties, they do not compete for public office. Although a candidate for office may be sympathetic to—or even be a member of—a certain group, he or she does not run for election as a candidate of that group.

**FOR CRITICAL THINKING**

Identify some public goods other than national defense. *Are any of these public goods associated with a significant free rider problem? Why or why not?*

## 6–2 Different Types of Interest Groups

**Learning Outcome 6–2**

Identify the various types of interest groups.

American democracy embraces almost every conceivable type of interest group, and the number is increasing rapidly. No one has ever compiled a *Who's Who* of interest groups, but you can get an idea of the number and variety by looking through the annually published *Encyclopedia of Associations*.

Some interest groups have large memberships. AARP, for example, has about 40 million members. Others, such as the Colorado Auctioneers Association, have barely a hundred members. Some, such as the U.S. Chamber of Commerce, are household names and have been in existence for many years, while others crop up overnight. Some are highly structured and are run by full-time professionals, while others are loosely structured and informal.

The most common interest groups are those that promote private interests. These groups seek public policies that benefit the economic interests of their members and work against policies that threaten those interests. Other groups, sometimes called **public-interest groups,** are formed with the broader goal of working for the "public good." The American Civil Liberties Union and Common Cause are examples. Let there be no mistake, though, about the name *public interest.*

There is no such thing as a clear public interest in a nation of more than 315 million diverse people. The two so-called public-interest groups just mentioned do not represent all American people but only a relatively small part of the American population. In reality, all lobbying groups, organizations, and other political entities always represent special interests.

### 6–2a Business Interest Groups

Business has long been well organized for effective action. Hundreds of business groups are now operating in Washington, D.C., in the fifty state capitals, and at the local level across the country. Table 6–2 on the following page lists some top business interests and their campaign contributions through mid-2012. Two umbrella organizations that include small and large corporations and businesses are the U.S. Chamber of Commerce and

**public-interest group**
An interest group formed for the purpose of working for the "public good." Examples of public-interest groups are the American Civil Liberties Union and Common Cause.

MIKE MAPLE/THE COMMERCIAL APPEAL/LANDOV

The National Association of Realtors is a business interest group. It favors continued favorable tax treatment for mortgage interest payments. Why?

**TABLE 6–2**

## Top Business Campaign Donors, 1989–2012

| Firm or Group | Total, 1989 to Mid-2012 |
| --- | --- |
| 1. AT&T, Inc. | $49,162,460 |
| 2. National Association of Realtors | $44,024,138 |
| 3. Goldman Sachs (bank) | $39,330,264 |
| 4. Citigroup, Inc. (bank) | $29,863,045 |
| 5. National Auto Dealers Assn. | $27,970,008 |
| 6. United Parcel Service | $26,855,383 |
| 7. Altria Group (cigarettes) | $26,091,582 |
| 8. American Bankers Assn. | $25,964,669 |
| 9. National Beer Wholesalers Assn. | $25,413,295 |
| 10. JPMorgan Chase & Co. (bank) | $24,898,338 |

the National Association of Manufacturers (NAM). In addition to representing about 3 million individual businesses, the Chamber has more than three thousand local, state, and regional affiliates. It has become a major voice for millions of small businesses.

### Trade Organizations

The hundreds of **trade organizations** are far less visible than the Chamber of Commerce and the NAM, but they are also important in seeking policies that assist their members. Trade organizations usually support policies that benefit specific industries. For example, people in the oil industry work for policies that favor the development of oil as an energy resource.

Other business groups work for policies that favor the development of coal, solar power, and nuclear power. Trucking companies work for policies that would lower their taxes. Railroad companies would, of course, not want other forms of transportation to receive special tax breaks, because that would hurt their business.

**trade organization**
An association formed by members of a particular industry, such as the oil industry or the trucking industry, to develop common standards and goals for the industry. Trade organizations, as interest groups, lobby government for legislation or regulations that specifically benefit their groups.

### How Business Interest Groups Support Both Parties

Traditionally, business interest groups have been viewed as staunch supporters of the Republican Party. This is because Republicans are more likely to promote a "hands-off" government policy toward business.

Over the last decade, however, donations from corporations to the Democratic National Committee have more than doubled. Why would business groups make contributions to the Democratic National Committee? One reason is that in some fields, business leaders are more likely to be Democrats than in the past. Financial industry leaders were once almost entirely Republican, but today many of them support the Democrats. Information technology, a new industry, contains both Republicans and Democrats.

An additional reason why many business interests support both parties is to ensure that they will benefit regardless of who wins the elections. Fred McChesney, a professor of law and business, offers still another reason why business interests might want to contribute to both parties: campaign contributions are often made not to gain political favors but rather to avoid political disfavor. He argues that just as government officials can take away wealth from citizens (in the form of taxes, for example), politicians can implicitly extort from private enterprises payments *not* to damage their business.[6]

**SOCIAL MEDIA**
**In Politics**

Most important interest groups are heavily involved with social media. The U.S. Chamber of Commerce, for example, has an active Facebook page. Search on "chamber of commerce." On Twitter, follow the Chamber at "uschamber."

## 6–2b Labor Interest Groups

Interest groups representing labor have been some of the most influential groups in our country's history. They date back to at least 1886, when the American Federation of Labor (AFL) was formed. The largest and most powerful labor interest group today is the AFL-CIO (the American Federation of Labor–Congress of Industrial Organizations), a confederation of fifty-six unions representing 9 million organized workers and 3.2 million community affiliates.

Unions not affiliated with the AFL-CIO also represent millions of members. The Change to Win federation consists of seven unions and 5.5 million workers. Dozens of other unions are independent. Examples include the National Education Association, the United Electrical Workers (UE), and the Major League Baseball Players Association. We list some top labor and professional groups in Table 6–3 on the facing page.

### Union Goals

Like labor unions everywhere, American unions press for policies to improve

## TABLE 6-3

### Top Labor and Professional Campaign Donors, 1989–2012

| Union or Group | Total, 1989 to Mid-2012 |
|---|---|
| 1. American Fed. of State, County & Municipal Employees | $60,633,873 |
| 2. National Education Assn. | $42,066,188 |
| 3. Service Employees Int'l. Union | $39,714,097 |
| 4. American Assn. for Justice (trial lawyers) | $36,432,428 |
| 5. Int'l. Brotherhood of Electrical Workers | $35,728,225 |
| 6. American Federation of Teachers | $34,118,316 |
| 7. Teamsters Union | $33,478,028 |
| 8. Laborers Union | $33,246,240 |
| 9. Carpenters & Joiners Union | $31,994,910 |
| 10. Communications Workers of America | $31,633,527 |

working conditions and ensure better pay for their members. Unions may compete for new members. In many states, for example, the National Education Association and the AFL-CIO's American Federation of Teachers compete fiercely for members.

**The Decline of Unions**  Although unions were highly influential in the 1930s, 1940s, and 1950s, their strength and political power have waned in the last several decades, as you can see in Figure 6–1 on the right. Today, members of organized labor make up only 11.8 percent of the **labor force**—defined as all of the people over the age of sixteen who are working or actively looking for jobs.

REASONS FOR LABOR'S DECLINE.  There are several reasons why the power of organized labor has declined in the United States. One is the continuing fall in the proportion of the nation's workforce employed in such blue-collar activities as manufacturing and transportation. These sectors have always been among the most heavily unionized.

Another important factor in labor's decline, however, is the general political environment. Forming and maintaining unions is more difficult in the United States than in most other industrial nations. Among the world's wealthy democracies, the United States is one of the most politically conservative, at least on economic issues. Economic conservatives

are traditionally hostile to labor unions. Further, many business owners in the United States do not accept unions as legitimate institutions and will do anything legal within their power to ensure that their own businesses remain ununionized.

DIFFERING STATE LAWS. The impact of the political environment on labor's organizing ability can be easily seen by comparing rates of unionization in various states. These rates are especially low in conservative southern states. Georgia and North Carolina are both major manufacturing states, but unions represent only 4.6 percent of the workforce in Georgia and only 5 percent in North Carolina.

Compare these figures with rates in more liberal states, such as California and New York: unions represent 19.5 percent of the workforce in California and 26.6 percent in New York. One factor that depresses unionization rates in many states is the existence of so-called **right-to-work laws.**

**labor force** All of the people over the age of sixteen who are working or actively looking for jobs.

**right-to-work laws** Laws that ban unions from collecting dues or other fees from workers whom they represent but who have not actually joined the union.

### SOCIAL MEDIA In Politics

To see an example of a labor union Facebook page, check out the National Education Association by searching on its name. To see it on Twitter, enter "neatoday."

## FIGURE 6-1

# Union Membership, 1952 to Present

This figure shows the percentage of the workforce who have been members of unions from 1952 to the present. As you can see, union membership has declined significantly over the past several decades.

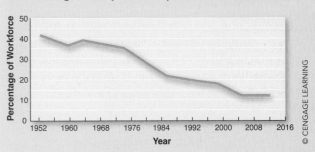

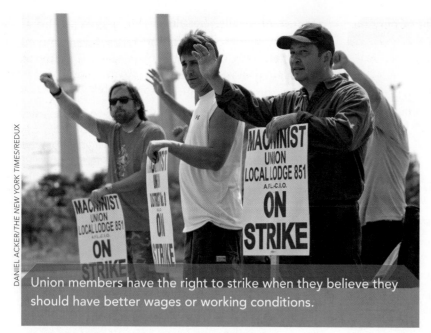

DANIEL ACKER/THE NEW YORK TIMES/REDUX

Union members have the right to strike when they believe they should have better wages or working conditions.

These laws ban unions from collecting dues or other fees from workers whom they represent but who have not actually joined the union. Such laws create a significant free rider problem for unions. Twenty-three states have right-to-work laws.

**Public-Sector Unions**  While labor groups have generally experienced a decline in lobbying power, public employee unions have grown in both numbers and political clout in recent years. Public employees enjoy some of the nation's best health-care and retirement benefits because of the efforts of their labor groups.

## 6–2c Professional Interest Groups

Most professions that require advanced education or specialized training have organizations to protect and promote their interests. These groups are concerned mainly with the standards of their professions, but they also work to influence government policy. Major professional groups include the American Medical Association (AMA), representing physicians; the American Bar Association, representing lawyers; and the American Association for Justice, representing trial lawyers. In addition, there are dozens of less well-known and less politically active professional groups, such as the National Association of Social Workers and the American Political Science Association.

Competing interests sometimes divide professional interest groups from one another. For example, consider the issue of torts (injuries under the law). Advocates of

tort reform contend that it is too easy for lawyers to sue physicians, insurance companies, and other businesses, and that generous settlements drive up the cost of health care and other goods. The AMA generally favors tort reform. The American Association for Justice, naturally, opposes it.

## 6–2d Agricultural Interest Groups

Many groups work for general agricultural interests at all levels of government. Three broad-based agricultural groups represent millions of American farmers, from peanut farmers to dairy producers to tobacco growers. They are the American Farm Bureau Federation (Farm Bureau), the National Grange, and the National Farmers Union.

The Farm Bureau, representing more than 5.5 million families (a majority of whom are not actually farm families), is the largest and generally the most effective of the three. Founded in 1919, the Farm Bureau achieved one of its greatest early successes when it helped to obtain government guarantees of "fair" prices during the Great Depression of the 1930s.[7] Producers of various specific farm commodities, such as dairy products, soybeans, grain, fruit, corn, cotton, beef, and sugar beets, have formed their own organizations.

Interest groups representing farmers have been spectacularly successful in winning subsidies from the federal government, as we explained in the chapter-opening *America at Odds* feature. Subsidies are not the only way in which the federal government can benefit growers of a particular crop. The government can also restrict imports of a specific commodity, such as sugar. The restrictions raise the price of sugar, which benefits sugar beet growers at the expense of consumers.

## 6–2e Consumer Interest Groups

Groups organized for the protection of consumer rights were very active in the 1960s and 1970s. Some are still active today. One well-known group is Consumers Union, a nonprofit organization started in 1936. In addition to publishing *Consumer Reports* magazine, Consumers Union has been influential in pushing for the removal of phosphates from detergents, lead from gasoline, and pesticides from food. Consumers Union strongly criticizes government agencies when they appear to act against consumer interests. Other major groups include Consumer Action, the Consumer Federation of America, and Public Citizen.

Consumer groups have been organized in every city. They deal with such problems as poor housing, discrimination against minorities and women, discrimination in the granting of credit, and business inaction on consumer complaints.

## 6–2f Identity Interest Groups

Americans who share the same race, ethnicity, gender, or other characteristic often have important common interests. African Americans, for example, have a powerful interest in combating the racism and racial discrimination that have marked American history from the beginning. Slaves, of course, were not able to form interest groups. For many years after the abolition of slavery, organizing African American interest groups remained impossibly dangerous. Such groups did not come into existence until the twentieth century.

The National Association for the Advancement of Colored People was founded in 1909, and the National Urban League was created in 1910. During the civil rights movement of the 1950s and 1960s, African Americans organized a number of new groups, some of which lasted (the Southern Christian Leadership Conference, founded in 1957) and some of which did not (the Student Nonviolent Coordinating Committee, organized in 1960).

The campaigns for dignity and equality of Native Americans, Latinos, women, lesbians and gay men, Americans with disabilities, and many other groups have all resulted in important interest groups. You learned about many of these organizations in Chapter 5. One identity-based group not discussed in that chapter is older Americans. Senior citizens are numerous, are politically active, and have a great deal at stake in debates over certain programs, such as Social Security and Medicare. As a result, groups representing them, such as AARP, can be a potent political force.

## 6–2g Ideological Interest Groups

Some interest groups are organized to promote not an economic interest or a collective identity but a shared political perspective or ideology. Examples include MoveOn, an Internet-oriented liberal group, and the Club for Growth, a conservative antitax organization.

**The Tea Party Movement** The highly decentralized Tea Party movement, which sprang into life in 2009, has been described as an ideological interest group. The activities of the Tea Party movement, however, raise the question of whether it really is an interest group at all. The point is that interest groups, while they are often very concerned about who wins an election and may endorse candidates, do not themselves attempt to gain control of the machinery of government. Most Tea Party leaders claim that the movement is nonpartisan and that it contains not only Republicans but independents, libertarians, and even some Democrats.

Still, some Tea Party groups have attempted to gain control of local Republican Party organizations. It may be only a matter of terminology, but political scientists refer to groups that compete for control of a political party as *factions,* not interest groups.

**Environmental Groups** Environmental groups have supported pollution controls, wilderness protection, and clean-air legislation. They have opposed strip mining, nuclear power plants, logging activities, chemical waste dumps, and many other potential environmental hazards.

AP PHOTO/ROGER ALFORD

Some interest groups are formed for ideological reasons. These college students are part of the Liberty for All association. Its goal is to help elect conservative candidates to Congress.

**direct technique** Any method used by an interest group to interact with government officials directly to further the group's goals.

**lobbying** All of the attempts by organizations or by individuals to influence the passage, defeat, or contents of legislation or to influence the administrative decisions of government.

In the past, environmental groups have been characterized as single-interest groups, not ideological organizations. Issues such as global warming, however, have led many modern environmental groups to advocate sweeping changes to the entire economy. Groups with such broad agendas could be considered a type of ideological interest group. Environmental interest groups range from traditional organizations, such as the National Wildlife Federation with 4 million members, to more radical groups, such as Greenpeace USA with a membership of 250,000.

**Religious Groups** Religious organizations are another type of group that could be included in the ideological category. Many religious groups work on behalf of conservative social causes. Others take a strong interest in the well-being of those suffering from poverty. How much representation do the poor receive in the political system? We look at that question in the *Perception versus Reality* feature on the facing page. We also list some top ideological and miscellaneous interest groups in Table 6–4 below.

## 6–2h Single-Issue Interest Groups

Numerous interest groups focus on a single issue. For example, Mothers Against Drunk Driving (MADD) lobbies for stiffer penalties for drunk driving. Formed in 1980, MADD now boasts more than 3 million members and supporters. The abortion debate has created various single-issue groups, such as the Right

to Life organization (which opposes abortion) and NARAL Pro-Choice America (founded as the National Association for the Repeal of Abortion Laws in 1969, when abortion was widely illegal). Other examples of single-issue groups are the NRA and the American Israel Public Affairs Committee (a pro-Israel group).

## 6–2i Government Interest Groups

Efforts by state and local governments to lobby the federal government have escalated in recent years. When states experience budget shortfalls, these governments often lobby in Washington, D.C., for additional federal funds. The federal government has sometimes lobbied in individual states, too. Until 2009, for example, the U.S. Attorney General's office lobbied against medical marijuana use in states that were considering ballot measures on the issue.

*Are you a member of any interest groups? If so, why? If not, which existing groups might best serve your interests? Again, why?*

## 6–3 How Interest Groups Shape Policy

Interest groups operate at all levels of government and use a variety of strategies to steer policies in ways beneficial to their interests. Sometimes, they attempt to influence policymakers directly, but at other times they try to exert indirect influence on policymakers by shaping public opinion. The extent and nature of the groups' activities depend on their goals and their resources.

**Learning**Outcome **6–3**

Discuss how the activities of interest groups help to shape government policymaking.

## 6–3a Direct Techniques

Lobbying and providing election support are two important **direct techniques** used by interest groups to influence government policy.

**Lobbying** Today, **lobbying** refers to all of the attempts by organizations or by individuals to

| TABLE 6–4 | | |
| --- | --- | --- |
| **Top Ideological and Miscellaneous Campaign Donors, 1989–2012** | | |
| Group | | Total, 1989 to Mid-2012 |
| 1. ActBlue (Democratic) | | $60,633,873 |
| 2. EMILY's List (Democratic) | | $25,852,913 |
| 3. National Rifle Assn. | | $18,923,422 |
| 4. Club for Growth (conservative) | | $14,761,124 |
| 5. Human Rights Campaign | | $11,070,292 |

© CENGAGE LEARNING

# Perception versus Reality

## The Unrepresented Poor

America has not eliminated poverty. Indeed, every year we read stories about poor Americans and about Americans who have fallen into poverty. Given that the poor are in no position to lobby for themselves, it seems obvious that rich individuals and major corporations, because they do lots of lobbying, must get all the benefits from government.

### THE PERCEPTION

Because the poor have no access to the halls of government, they are underrepresented. Low-income persons simply do not have the time, funds, or spare energy to compete with moneyed interests, at either the state or the national level.

### THE REALITY

While it may be true that lobbyists are often successful in getting "special deals" for the rich and for big corporations, the tax burden on wealthy individuals remains heavy. The richest 10 percent of Americans pay about half of all federal income and payroll taxes. (Payroll taxes are Social Security and Medicare taxes.) The top 1 percent of Americans pay about one-quarter of these taxes. Low-income taxpayers are largely exempt from the income tax. They pay only payroll taxes, and in many cases, they can get rebates on these. Even without being able to lobby for themselves, low-income families and individuals receive beneficial tax treatment.

Now consider spending. Ron Haskins of the Brookings Institution estimates that all federal low-income programs together cost more than $800 billion a year. One of the most important of these programs is food stamps (now called Supplemental Nutrition Assistance Program, or SNAP). Just since 2007, when the Great Recession struck, the number of food stamp recipients has risen from 26 million to 45 million. The average monthly value of the benefit is close to $300. Other programs for the poor include Medicaid and the refundable portions of the Earned-Income Tax Credit and the Additional Child Tax Credit.

The reality is that for decades, many liberal groups have lobbied on behalf of those suffering from poverty. Mainstream religious groups have done the same—including Catholic organizations, Lutherans, the National Council of Churches, the Friends (Quakers), and many others. Liberal and religious interests have done for the poor what the poor cannot do for themselves. The result: If there were no federal tax and spending programs aimed at low-income persons, as many as 25 percent of U.S. families would have incomes below the official poverty line. If you take into account all benefits that low-income families obtain, that number drops to about 10 percent.

## BLOG ON

- For a vast collection of data on social services provided by the federal government, see the *Green Book* of the Ways and Means Committee of the U.S. House of Representatives. Enter "green book ways and means" into an Internet search engine.
- For another source of information, see the Web site of the University of Kentucky Center for Poverty Research. Search on "kentucky poverty."

influence the passage, defeat, or contents of legislation or to influence the administrative decisions of government. (The term *lobbying* arose because, traditionally, individuals and groups interested in influencing government policy would gather in the foyer, or lobby, of the legislature to corner legislators and express their concerns.) A **lobbyist** is an individual who handles a particular interest group's lobbying efforts. Most of the larger interest groups have lobbyists in Washington, D.C. These lobbyists often include former members of Congress

**lobbyist** An individual who handles a particular interest group's lobbying efforts.

Tosca, a restaurant on F Street, is a hot spot for power lunchers from the Washington, D.C., political establishment.

example, pharmaceutical companies may lobby the Food and Drug Administration to speed up the process of approving new prescription drugs. Lobbying can also be directed at changing international policies. For instance, after political changes had opened up Eastern Europe to business in the late 1980s and early 1990s, intense lobbying by Western business groups helped persuade the United States and other industrial powers to reduce controls on the sale of high-technology products, such as personal computers, to Eastern European countries.

**Providing Election Support**  Interest groups often become directly involved in the election process. Many group members join and work with political parties to influence party platforms and the nomination of candidates. Interest groups provide campaign support for legislators who favor their policies and sometimes encourage their own members to try to win posts in party organizations.

Most important, interest groups urge their members to vote for candidates who support the views of the group. They can also threaten legislators with the withdrawal of votes. No candidate can expect to have support from all interest groups, but if the candidate is to win, she or he must have support from many of the strongest ones.

**POLITICAL ACTION COMMITTEES (PACs).**  Since the 1970s, federal laws governing campaign financing have allowed corporations, labor unions, and special interest groups to raise funds and make campaign contributions through **political action committees (PACs).** Both the number of PACs and the amount of money PACs spend on elections have grown astronomically in recent years. There were about 1,000 PACs in 1976. Today, there are more than 4,500 PACs. In 1973, total spending by PACs amounted to $19 million. In the 2007–2008 presidential election cycle, total spending by PACs exceeded $400 million. Even though presidential candidates were not on the ballot in 2009–2010, PAC spending easily matched that figure. When all the data are in, PAC spending in 2011–2012 will have set a new record.

Even with the growth in PACs, they provided a smaller share of campaign spending in the years after 1988, principally because of the development of other funding sources, such as "soft money" and issue ads. (We discuss these sources in the following section.)

**SUPER PACs.**  In 2010, the United States Supreme Court upended the world of campaign finance in

or former employees of executive bureaucracies who are experienced in the methods of political influence and who "know people."

**STATE-LEVEL LOBBYING.**  Many lobbyists also work at state and local levels. In fact, lobbying at the state level has increased in recent years as states have begun to play a more significant role in policymaking. Table 6–5 on the facing page summarizes some of the basic methods by which lobbyists directly influence legislators and government officials.

**TYPES OF LOBBYING.** Lobbying can be directed at the legislative branch of government, at administrative agencies, and even at the courts. For

**political action committee (PAC)** A committee that is established by a corporation, labor union, or special interest group to raise funds and make campaign contributions on the establishing organization's behalf.

## TABLE 6-5

### Direct Lobbying Techniques

| Technique | Description |
|---|---|
| **Making Personal Contacts with Key Legislators** | A lobbyist's personal contacts with key legislators or other government officials—in their offices, in the halls of Congress, or on social occasions such as dinners, boating expeditions, and the like—comprise one of the most effective direct lobbying techniques. |
| **Providing Expertise and Research Results for Legislators** | Lobbyists often have knowledge and expertise that are useful in drafting legislation, and this expertise can be a major strength for an interest group. Harried members of Congress cannot possibly be experts on everything they vote on and therefore eagerly seek information to help them make up their minds. |
| **Offering "Expert" Testimony before Congressional Committees** | Lobbyists often provide "expert" testimony before congressional committees for or against proposed legislation. Each expert offers as much evidence as possible to support her or his position. |
| **Providing Legal Advice to Legislators** | Many lobbyists assist legislators in drafting legislation or prospective regulations. Lobbyists are a source of ideas and sometimes offer legal advice on specific details. |
| **Following Up on Legislation** | Because executive agencies responsible for carrying out legislation can often change the scope of the new law, lobbyists may also try to influence the bureaucrats who implement the policy. |

© CENGAGE LEARNING

*Citizens United v. Federal Election Commission.*[8] The Court ruled that PACs could accept unlimited contributions from individuals, unions, and corporations for the purpose of making independent expenditures. These are election expenses that are not coordinated with any candidate's campaign. This ruling led, in short order, to the creation of super PACs, which channeled vast new sums into election spending. Many super PACs were funded by wealthy individuals, and many of them concentrated on negative ads. (We will discuss election finances in greater detail in Chapter 9.)

Although campaign contributions do not guarantee that officials will vote the way the groups wish, contributions usually do ensure that the groups will have the ear of the public officials they have helped to elect.

## 6-3b Indirect Techniques

Interest groups also try to influence public policy indirectly through third parties or the general public. The effects of such **indirect techniques** may appear to be spontaneous, but indirect techniques are generally as well planned as the direct lobbying techniques just discussed. Indirect techniques can be particularly effective because public officials are often more impressed by contacts from voters than from lobbyists.

**Shaping Public Opinion** Public opinion weighs significantly in the policymaking process, so interest groups cultivate their public images carefully. If public opinion favors a certain group's interests, then public officials will be more ready to listen and more willing to pass legislation favoring that group. To cultivate public opinion, an interest group's efforts may include online campaigns, television publicity, newspaper and magazine advertisements, mass mailings, and the use of public relations techniques to improve the group's image.

For example, environmental groups often run television ads to dramatize threats to the environment. Oil companies may respond to criticism about increased gasoline prices with advertising that shows how hard they are working to develop new sources of energy. The goal of all these activities is to influence public opinion.

**Rating Systems** Some interest groups also try to influence legislators through **rating systems.** A group selects legislative issues that it believes are important to its goals and rates legislators according to the percentage of times they vote favorably on that legislation. For example, a score of 90 percent on the Americans for Democratic

**indirect technique** Any method used by interest groups to influence government officials through third parties, such as voters.

**rating system** A system by which a particular interest group evaluates (rates) the performance of legislators based on how often the legislators have voted with the group's position on particular issues.

Pulitzer Prize–winning journalist José Antonio Vargas—himself an unauthorized immigrant— often speaks out on immigration reform.

Action (ADA) rating scale means that the legislator supported that liberal group's position to a high degree.

Other groups tag members of Congress who support (or fail to support) their interests to a significant extent with telling labels. For instance, the Communications Workers of America refers to policymakers who take a position consistent with its views as "Heroes" and those who take the opposite position as "Zeroes." Needless to say, such tactics can be an effective form of indirect lobbying, particularly with legislators who do not want to earn a low ADA score or be placed on the "Zeroes" list.

### Issue Ads and "527s"

One of the most powerful indirect techniques used by interest groups is the "issue ad"—a television or radio ad taking a position on a particular issue. The Supreme Court has made it clear that the First Amendment's guarantee of free speech protects interest groups' rights to set forth their positions on issues when they fund such activities through **independent expenditures** that are not coordinated with a candidate's campaign or a political party. Nevertheless, issue advocacy is controversial because the funds spent to air issue ads have had a clear effect on the outcome of elections.

Both parties have benefited from such interest group spending. As you will read in Chapter 9, the Bipartisan Campaign

**independent expenditure** An expenditure for activities that are independent from (not coordinated with) those of a political candidate or a political party.

Reform Act of 2002 banned unlimited donations to campaigns and political parties, called *soft money*. In subsequent years, interest groups that had previously given soft money to parties set up new groups called "527s" (after the provision of the tax code that covers them). The 527s engaged in such practices as voter registration, but they also began making large expenditures on issue ads—which were legal so long as the 527s did not coordinate their activities with candidates' campaigns.

In the run-up to the 2008 presidential elections, clever campaign finance lawyers hit upon a new type of group, the 501(c)4 organization, also named after a section of the tax code. Groups such as the Sierra Club and Citizens Against Government Waste have set up special 501(c)4 organizations.

Lawyers argued that a 501(c)4 group could spend some of its funds on direct campaign contributions as long as most of the group's spending was on issue advocacy. Further, a 501(c)4 group could conceal the identity of its contributors. Federal agencies and the courts have not yet determined the legality of these claims. We will discuss this issue in greater depth in Chapter 9.

### Mobilizing Constituents

Interest groups sometimes urge members and other constituents to contact government officials—by letter, e-mail, Facebook, Twitter, or telephone—to show their support for or opposition to a certain policy. Such efforts are known as *grassroots organizing*. Large interest groups can generate hundreds of thousands of letters, e-mail messages, tweets, and phone calls. Interest groups often provide form letters or postcards for constituents to fill out and mail. The NRA has successfully used this tactic to fight strict federal gun control legislation by delivering half a million letters to Congress within a few weeks.

Policymakers recognize that such communications are initiated by interest groups, however, and are impressed only when the volume of letters or e-mail communications is very large. Campaigns that masquerade as grassroots mobilizations, but are not, have been given the apt label *Astroturf lobbying*.

### Going to Court

The legal system offers another avenue for interest groups to influence the political process. In the 1950s and 1960s, civil rights groups paved the way for interest group litigation with major victories in cases concerning equal housing, school desegregation, and employment discrimination. Environmental groups, such as the Sierra Club, have also successfully used litigation to press their concerns. For example, an environmental group might challenge in court an activity that threatens to pollute the environment or that will destroy the natural habitat of an endangered species. The legal challenge forces those engaging in the activity to defend their actions and may delay the project. In fact, much of the success of environmental groups has been linked to their use of lawsuits.

Interest groups can also influence the outcome of litigation without being a party to a lawsuit. Frequently, an interest group files an *amicus curiae* brief. The brief states the group's legal argument in support of its desired outcome in a case. For example, in the case *Metro-Goldwyn-Mayer Studios, Inc. v. Grokster, Ltd.,*[9] involving the legality of file-sharing software used to trade copyrighted material, hundreds of *amicus* briefs were filed by various groups on behalf of the petitioners. Groups filing *amicus* briefs for the case, which was heard by the Supreme Court in 2005, included the National Basketball Association, the National Football League, the National Association of Broadcasters, the Association of American Publishers, and numerous state governments. Often, interest groups cite statistics and research that support their position on a certain issue, and this research can have considerable influence on the judges deciding the case.

## Demonstrations

Some interest groups stage protests to make a statement in a dramatic way. The Boston Tea Party of 1773, in which American colonists dressed as Native Americans and threw tea into Boston Harbor to protest British taxes, is testimony to how long this tactic has been around. Over the years, many groups have organized protest marches and rallies to support or oppose legalized abortion, gay and lesbian rights, the treatment of Native Americans, restrictions on the use of federally owned lands in the West, and the activities of global organizations such as the World Trade Organization.

In some nations, it is dangerous to set up permanent interest groups in an attempt to change government policy. Rather, demonstrations may be the most effective means of protest in these countries. Often, demonstrations can be organized without advance notice to the authorities. We look at how Chinese activists are using demonstrations to oppose pollution in *The Rest of the World* feature on the following page.

**THE OCCUPY TOGETHER MOVEMENT.** In 2011 and 2012, a major series of demonstrations swept across the United States. The first of these, Occupy Wall Street, began in September 2011 when activists set up a tent encampment to "occupy" Wall Street. (The camp actually was set up in a nearby park.) Major demands were that the government should take steps to reduce economic inequality and to increase employment, especially for young people. The principal slogan was "We are the 99 percent," as opposed to the richest 1 percent. Several hundred encampments subsequently sprang up across the nation and around the world.

The movement is credited with placing the issue of inequality squarely on the political agenda. By 2012, however, the protests were dying down. Few of the protesters had official permission to camp overnight at their various sites, and one by one, the camps were taken down by police orders.

**VIOLENT DEMONSTRATIONS.** Not all demonstration techniques are peaceful. Some environmental groups, for example, have used such dangerous tactics as spiking trees and setting traps on logging roads to puncture truck tires. Pro-life groups have bombed abortion clinics, and members of the Animal Liberation Front have broken into laboratories and freed animals being used for experimentation. Some evidence exists that violent demonstrations can be counterproductive—that is, that they can hurt the demonstrators' cause by angering the public. Historians continue to debate whether violent demonstrations against the Vietnam War (1964–1975) helped or hurt the antiwar cause.

> "Never doubt that a small group of thoughtful, committed citizens can **CHANGE THE WORLD;** indeed, it's the only thing that ever has."
>
> ~ MARGARET MEAD ~
> AMERICAN ANTHROPOLOGIST
> 1902–1978

**FOR CRITICAL THINKING**

*Why might some lawmakers pay more attention to contacts by ordinary people than contacts by lobbyists?*

# China's Growing Environmental Movement

China is known for having some of the world's dirtiest air, most dangerous mines, and weakest environmental standards. Nonetheless, Chinese people are making their voices heard on environmental issues.

## Stopping a Copper Smelter Before It's Too Late

The Chinese government has planned to revitalize an area in Sichuan province that was devastated by an earthquake in 2008. To that end, it decided to build one of the world's largest copper smelting complexes. Local people had a different idea. In 2012, tens of thousands of local residents defied police to protest. The demonstrations made national headlines and were the subject of blogs throughout that country. The government backed down (at least for now). As retired environmental protection official Zhao Zhangyuan said, "The standards for environmental protection are higher and higher, from the public and also from the government."

## Protests against Energy Projects

When word spread that a huge coal-fired power plant was to be built in Haimen, near Hong Kong, almost 30,000 people marched to block the construction. Solar energy companies have been targeted as well. One plant near Shanghai was forced to close after demonstrations around the plant objected to the chemicals used.

## It's the Internet

The reason that so many protests against environmentally harmful activities have been successful is the Internet. China has more "Internauts" than any other country. "Micro-blogging" and other systems are used to get the word out. Chinese government officials have been taking note of public opinion. Consequently, they have raised the environmental requirements for many new projects, even when they are government projects.

**FOR CRITICAL ANALYSIS** Why might it take longer for environmental activism to become effective in China than in this country?

# 6-4 Today's Lobbying Establishment

## LearningOutcome 6-4

Describe how interest groups are regulated by government.

Without a doubt, interest groups and their lobbyists have become a permanent feature in the landscape of American government. The major interest groups all have headquarters in Washington, D.C., close to the center of government.

Professional lobbyists and staff members of various interest groups move freely between their groups' headquarters and congressional offices and committee rooms. Interest group representatives are routinely consulted when Congress drafts new legislation. As already mentioned, interest group representatives are frequently asked to testify before congressional committees or subcommittees on the effect or potential effect of particular legislation or regulations. In sum, interest groups have become an integral part of the American government system.

As interest groups have become a permanent feature of American government, lobbying has developed into a profession. A professional lobbyist—one who has mastered the techniques of lobbying discussed earlier in this chapter—is a valuable ally to any interest group seeking to influence government. Professional lobbyists can and often do represent a number of different interest groups over the course of their careers.

In recent years, it has become increasingly common for those who leave positions with the federal government to become lobbyists or consultants for the private-interest groups they helped to regulate. In spite of legislation and regulations designed to reduce this "revolving door" syndrome, it is still functioning quite well.

## 6-4a Why Do Interest Groups Get Bad Press?

Despite their importance to democratic government, interest groups, like political parties, are often criticized by both the public and the press. Our image of interest groups and their special interests is not very favorable. You may have run across political cartoons depicting lobbyists standing in the hallways of Congress with briefcases stuffed with money.

These cartoons are not entirely factual, but they are not entirely fictitious either. President Richard Nixon (1969–1974) was revealed to have responded to the campaign contributions of milk producers by authorizing a windfall increase in milk subsidies.

As another example, in the early 1990s it was learned that a number of senators who received generous contributions from a particular savings and loan association subsequently supported a "hands-off" policy by savings and loan regulators. The savings and loan association in question later got into financial trouble, costing the taxpayers billions of dollars. (One of the senators criticized for having exercised poor judgment during the savings and loan scandal was John McCain, the 2008 Republican presidential candidate. It may have been this painful experience that inspired McCain to become an ardent advocate of campaign-finance reform.)

"MY GREATEST ASSET IS I'M SO RICH, I CAN'T BE BOUGHT BY ANY INTEREST GROUP."

© 2009 HARLEY SCHWADRON

## 6–4b The Regulation of Interest Groups

In an attempt to control lobbying, Congress passed the Federal Regulation of Lobbying Act in 1946. The major provisions of the act are as follows:

- Any person or organization that receives money to influence legislation must register with the clerk of the House and the secretary of the Senate.

- Any groups or persons registering must identify their employer, salary, amount and purpose of expenses, and duration of employment.

- Every registered lobbyist must make quarterly reports on his or her activities.

- Anyone violating this act can be fined up to $10,000 and be imprisoned for up to five years.

The act did not succeed in regulating lobbying to any great degree for several reasons. First, the Supreme Court restricted the application of the law to only those lobbyists who sought to influence federal legislation directly.[10] Any lobbyist seeking to influence legislation indirectly through public opinion did not fall within the scope of the law. Second, only persons or organizations whose principal purpose was to influence legislation were required to register. Many groups avoided registration by claiming that their principal function was

something else. Third, the act did not cover those whose lobbying was directed at agencies in the executive branch or lobbyists who testified before congressional committees. Fourth, the public was almost totally unaware of the information in the quarterly reports filed by lobbyists. Not until 1995 did Congress finally address those loopholes by enacting new legislation.

## 6–4c The Lobbying Disclosure Act of 1995

In 1995, Congress passed new expanded lobbying legislation—the Lobbying Disclosure Act—that reformed the 1946 act in the following ways:

- Strict definitions now apply to determine who must register with the clerk of the House and the secretary of the Senate as a lobbyist. A lobbyist is anyone who either spends at least 20 percent of his or her time lobbying members of Congress, their staffs, or executive-branch officials, or is paid more than $5,000 in a six-month period for such work. Any organization that spends more than $20,000 in a six-month period conducting such lobbying activity must also register. These amounts have since been altered to $2,500 and $10,000 per quarter, respectively.

- Lobbyists must report their clients, the issues on which they lobbied, and the agency or chamber of Congress they contacted, although they do not need to disclose the names of those they contacted.

Tax-exempt organizations, such as religious groups, were exempted from these provisions, as were organizations that engage in grassroots lobbying, such

Many believe that lobbying negatively affects democracy. Why?

REUTERS/JONATHAN ERNST

as a media campaign that asks people to write or call their congressional representative. Nonetheless, the number of registered lobbyists nearly doubled in the first few years after the new legislation.

## 6–4d Recent Reform Efforts

In 2005, a number of lobbying scandals in Washington, D.C., came to light. As a result, following the midterm elections of 2006, the new Democratic majority in the Senate and House of Representatives undertook a lobbying reform effort. This involved changes to the rules that the two chambers impose on their own members.

*Bundled* campaign contributions, in which a lobbyist arranges for contributions from a variety of sources, would have to be reported. Expenditures on the sometimes lavish parties to benefit candidates would have to be reported as well. (Of course, partygoers were expected to pay for their food and drink with a check written out to the candidate.) The new rules covered PACs as well as registered lobbyists, which led one lobbyist to observe sourly that this wasn't lobbying reform but campaign-finance reform.

President George W. Bush signed the Honest Leadership and Open Government Act in 2007. The new law increased lobbying disclosure requirements

> **"An honest politician**
> is one who, when he is bought, will stay bought."
>
> ~ SIMON CAMERON ~
> U.S. FINANCIER AND POLITICIAN
> 1799–1889

and placed further restrictions on the receipt of gifts and travel by members of Congress paid for by lobbyists and the organizations they represent. The act also included provisions requiring the disclosure of lawmakers' requests for earmarks in legislation. (We discuss earmarks in more depth in Chapter 11.)

## 6–4e Lobbyists and the Obama Administration

During his first campaign for the presidency, Barack Obama pledged that "lobbyists won't find a job in my White House." Given how many talented individuals with experience in government have served as lobbyists, that pledge turned out to be unenforceable.

Senior administration officials soon included dozens of persons who had served as lobbyists within the past five years. Interest groups represented by these former lobbyists included the Campaign for Tobacco-Free Kids, the mortgage giant Fannie Mae, the investment bank Goldman Sachs, Mothers Against Drunk Driving, the National Council of La Raza, the defense industry giant Raytheon, and the Service Employees International Union.

Other restrictions imposed by the new administration included a rule that the White House would log and publicize all meetings with lobbyists. As a result, White House staff members began meeting with lobbyists in other government buildings not subject to the publicity rules. Many old hands in Washington considered Obama's policies toward lobbyists absurd.

**FOR CRITICAL THINKING**

As noted at the beginning of this chapter, the right to lobby is protected by the Constitution. *If that weren't so, would it be a good idea to ban lobbying? Why or why not?*

# AMERICA AT
# ODDS Interest Groups

Interest groups are one of the most controversial features of our democratic system. The right to lobby may be protected by the First Amendment, but many people consider lobbying by interest groups to be a source of corruption within the political system. Of course, people can readily see the problems with lobbying when it is done for a cause that they oppose. On the other hand, it is easy to support political action for something you believe in, regardless of what others might think of it. Some of the controversies surrounding interest group lobbying include the following:

• Should labor unions be allowed to organize workplaces by obtaining signed cards—or are secret-ballot elections an essential safeguard?

• Are farm subsidies a valid protection for an important industry—or just another giveaway to the politically powerful?

• Does lobbying always harm legislation—or can lobbying improve it?

• Free riders benefit from a particular activity without paying their share of its costs. Is free riding inherently unfair—or is it only a problem when it is so pervasive that it makes the activity in question (for example, lobbying by consumer groups) unaffordable?

• Are there too many lobbyists—or is the real problem that there aren't enough lobbyists for ordinary people?

# TAKE ACTION

An obvious way to get involved in politics is to join an interest group whose goals you endorse—perhaps one of the organizations on your campus. You can find lists of interest groups operating at the local, state, and national levels by simply going to an online search engine, such as Google, and keying in the words "interest groups." Alternatively, you can go directly to one of the Web pages that list interest groups. You can find such lists simply by searching on "lists of interest groups."

Almost all interest groups have Web sites, and you'll want to check them out. A very large number of groups have Facebook pages as well—just type the name of the organization into your Facebook search box.

If you have a particular interest or goal that you would like to promote, consider forming your own group, as some Iowa students did when they formed

a group called Students Toward Environmental Protection. In the photo below, students from Grinnell College in Iowa are seen staging a protest rally at the state capitol. The students wanted Iowa's lawmakers to issue tougher regulations governing factory farms and to expand the state's bottle deposit requirements.

AP PHOTO/CHARLIE NEIBERGALL

# STUDY TOOLS

## Fill-In

1. The right to form interest groups and to lobby the government is protected by the _____ Amendment to the U.S. Constitution.

2. _____ theory describes the defensive formation of interest groups.

3. Today, members of organized labor make up only _____ percent of the labor force.

4. _____ laws ban unions from collecting dues or other fees from workers whom they represent but who have not actually joined the union.

5. *Lobbying* refers to _____.

6. Interest groups can influence the outcome of litigation without being a party to a lawsuit by filing _____.

7. It has become increasingly common for those who leave positions with the federal government to become lobbyists or consultants for the private-interest groups they helped to regulate. This is called the _____ syndrome.

## Multiple Choice

8. There are various reasons why people join interest groups. Some people find that they gain considerable satisfaction from taking action from within that group. Such satisfaction is referred to as a _____ incentive.
   a. free rider  b. purposive  c. material

9. Interest groups
   a. are often policy generalists.
   b. compete for public office.
   c. help bridge the gap between citizens and government.

10. The American Association for Justice represents the interests of
   a. trial lawyers.
   b. children.
   c. senior citizens.

11. MoveOn and the Club for Growth are _____ interest groups.
   a. business  b. consumer  c. ideological

12. _____ is a direct technique used by interest groups to influence public policy.
   a. The use of rating systems
   b. Providing election support
   c. Staging demonstrations

13. The Supreme Court has made it clear that the First Amendment's guarantee of free speech
   a. protects interest groups' rights to set forth their positions on issues when they fund such activities through independent expenditures that are not coordinated with a candidate's campaign or a political party.
   b. protects issue advocacy as long as that advocacy is coordinated with a candidate's campaign or a political party.
   c. does not include protection for interest groups to set forth their positions on issues.

14. Lobbying campaigns that masquerade as grassroots mobilizations (but are not) have been labeled _____ lobbying.
   a. *Bluegrass*  b. *Turfgrass*  c. *Astroturf*

15. During his first campaign for the presidency, Barack Obama
   a. declared that "lobbyists make the best White House staffers."
   b. promised to repeal the Honest Leadership and Open Government Act of 2007.
   c. pledged that "lobbyists won't find a job in my White House."

# Political Parties

XINHUA/EYEVINE/REDUX

The **Learning Outcomes** labeled 1 through 5 are designed to help improve your understanding of the chapter. After reading this chapter, you should be able to:

**7–1** Summarize the origins and development of the two-party system in the United States.

**7–2** Describe the current status of the two major parties.

**7–3** Explain how political parties function in our democratic system.

**7–4** Discuss the structure of American political parties.

**7–5** Describe the different types of third parties and how they function in the American political system.

**Remember to visit page 169 for additional Study Tools**

# ODDS
## Is the Republican Party Too Conservative?

AP PHOTO/MIKE CARLSON

In 2008, with the economy in crisis, the Republicans lost seats in Congress and the presidency as well. Not surprisingly, these results touched off a debate within the party. In 2009, a few Republicans argued that their party should moderate its conservatism to attract independent voters. A much larger number of Republicans, however, often supported by Tea Party activists, claimed that Republican politicians were not conservative enough. In 2010, Tea Party candidates won primaries across the country, and the Republican representatives and governors who took office in 2011 were among the most conservative ever. Most of the Republican candidates who ran in 2012 were equally conservative. But were they too conservative?

## Uncompromising Conservatism Is the Only Way Forward

Uncompromising conservatives believe that the Republicans must steer to the political right. Even though only 24 percent of voters call themselves Republicans, 40 percent say that they are conservatives. Support is rising for such conservative positions as the right to bear arms and opposition to abortion.

Conservative activists argue that their values are not only popular but also "correct" in a very deep sense. Values such as religious belief, strong families, and individual self-reliance are the foundation of our civilization. Liberalism erodes these values and paves the road to cultural collapse.

In 2011 and 2012, Republicans claimed that success in the 2010 elections meant that they had a mandate from the voters, and the Democrats did not. Therefore, conservative policies should prevail, even if the Senate and presidency were still in the hands of the Democrats. To accomplish that end, it was essential that House Republicans be as uncompromising as possible.

Americans are starting to rebel against big government and a culture of immorality. If the Republicans don't stand firm for true conservatism, these Americans won't have anyone to vote for.

## Radical Conservatism Spells Disaster in the Long Run

A minority of Republicans argue that the party's improved electoral prospects in 2010 were largely due to Democratic mistakes. The resulting Republican advantage may be only temporary. The face of America is changing. Support for gay rights has risen dramatically. The number of Hispanic voters rises year by year, and by 2050, non-Hispanic whites will be a minority of the U.S. population. Despite these changes, some conservatives seem intent on ensuring that the Republicans are seen as the "nasty party"—the party that hates people.

Republicans require young voters, but tirades against gays are poison to that constituency. If the vast majority of Latinos come to reject the Republicans because of the party's anti-immigrant rhetoric, eventually the Republicans will even fail to carry Texas. If voters conclude that Republicans see large numbers of their fellow Americans as "the enemy," the party will lose future elections, no matter how well it did in 2010 and 2012.

A complete refusal to compromise is also not a winning formula. Many Americans, especially the independents who decide elections, strongly favor cooperation between the parties. If either party refuses to compromise, in time the voters are likely to take notice.

## Where do you stand?

1. Pastor Rick Warren, author of *The Purpose Driven Life,* accepts that homosexuality is a sin, but he also emphasizes his belief in God's love for all people. Why might some members of the religious right reject Warren's formula?

2. American-style cultural conservatism is not popular in much of Europe. Many of these nations are also facing declines in their populations. Some conservatives would argue that these facts are connected. Is this argument reasonable? Why or why not?

## Explore this issue online

- Web sites that advocate a more moderate Republican Party include David Frum's column in The Daily Beast, which you can locate by searching on "Frum beast." For full-throttle conservatism, try Rush Limbaugh's site by typing "limbaugh" into your favorite search engine.

# Introduction

Political ideology can spark heated debates among Americans, as you read in the chapter-opening *America at Odds* feature. A **political party** can be defined as a group of individuals who organize to win elections, operate the government, and determine policy.

Political parties serve as major vehicles for citizen participation in our political system. It is hard to imagine democracy without political parties. Political parties provide a way for the public to choose who will serve in government and which policies will be carried out. Even citizens who do not identify with any political party or who choose not to participate in elections are affected by the activities of parties and their influence on government.

Political parties were an unforeseen development in American political history. The founders defined many other important institutions, such as the presidency and Congress, and described their functions in the Constitution. Political parties, however,

"Both of our political parties . . . agree conscientiously in the same object: **the public good;** but they differ essentially in what they deem the means of promoting that good."

~ THOMAS JEFFERSON ~
IN A LETTER TO ABIGAIL ADAMS, 1804

are not even mentioned in the Constitution. In fact, the founders decried factions and parties. Thomas Jefferson probably best expressed the founders' antiparty sentiments when he declared, "If I could not go to heaven but with a party, I would not go there at all."[1]

If the founders did not want political parties, though, who was supposed to organize political campaigns and mobilize supporters of political candidates? Clearly, there was a practical need for some kind of organizing group to form a link between citizens and their government. Even our early national leaders, for all their antiparty feelings, soon realized this. Several of them were active in establishing or organizing the first political parties.

## 7–1 A Short History of American Political Parties

Throughout the course of our history, several parties have formed, and some have disappeared. Even today, although we have only two major political parties, several other parties have been organized, as will be discussed later in this chapter.

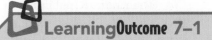

**Learning Outcome 7–1**

Summarize the origins and development of the two-party system in the United States.

### 7–1a The First Political Parties

The founders rejected the idea of political parties because they believed, as George Washington said in his Farewell Address, that the "spirit of party . . . agitates the community with ill-founded jealousies and false alarms, kindles the animosity of one part against another, foments occasionally riot and insurrection."[2] At some point in the future, the founders feared, a party leader might even seize power as

John Adams (1735–1826) was the Federalists' candidate to succeed George Washington. Adams defeated Thomas Jefferson in 1796, but lost to him in 1800.

**political party** A group of individuals who organize to win elections, operate the government, and determine policy.

**realignment** A process in which the popular support for and relative strength of the parties shift and the parties are reestablished with different coalitions of supporters.

a dictator. Nonetheless, two major political factions—the Federalists and the Anti-Federalists—were formed even before the Constitution was ratified. Remember from Chapter 2 that the Federalists pushed for the ratification of the Constitution because they wanted a stronger national government than the one that had existed under the Articles of Confederation. The Anti-Federalists argued against ratification. They supported states' rights and feared a too-powerful central government.

These two national factions continued, in somewhat altered form, after the Constitution was ratified. Alexander Hamilton, the first secretary of the Treasury, became the leader of the Federalist Party, which Vice President John Adams also joined. The Federalists supported a strong central government that would encourage the development of commerce and manufacturing. The Federalists generally thought that a republic should be ruled by its wealthiest and best-educated citizens.

Opponents of the Federalists and Hamilton's policies referred to themselves as Republicans. Today, they are often referred to as Jeffersonian Republicans, or Democratic Republicans (a name never used at the time), to distinguish this group from the later-established Republican Party. The Jeffersonian Republicans favored a more limited role for government. They believed that the nation's welfare would be best served if the states had more power than the central government. In their view, Congress should dominate the government, and government policies should serve farming interests rather than promote commerce and manufacturing.

## 7–1b From 1796 to 1860

The nation's first two parties clashed openly in the elections of 1796, in which John Adams, the Federalists' candidate to succeed George Washington as president, defeated Thomas Jefferson. Over the next four years, Jefferson and James Madison worked to extend the influence of the Jeffersonian Republican Party. In the presidential elections of 1800 and 1804, Jefferson won the presidency, and his party also won control of Congress.

**Triumph of the Jeffersonians**   The transition of political power from the Federalists to the Jeffersonian Republicans is the first example in American history of what political scientists have called a **realignment.** In a realignment, a substantial number of voters change their political allegiance, which usually also changes the balance of power between the two major parties. In fact, the Federalists never returned to power and thus became the first (but not the last) American party to go out of existence. (See the time line of American political parties in Figure 7–1 on the facing page.)

Thomas Jefferson (1743–1826) became our third president and served two terms. The Jeffersonian Republicans (not to be confused with the later Republican Party of Abraham Lincoln) dominated American politics for more than two decades.

LIBRARY OF CONGRESS

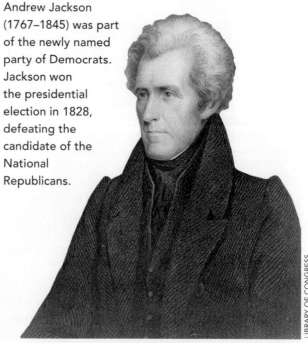

Andrew Jackson (1767–1845) was part of the newly named party of Democrats. Jackson won the presidential election in 1828, defeating the candidate of the National Republicans.

LIBRARY OF CONGRESS

FIGURE 7-1

# A Time Line of U.S. Political Parties

Many of these parties—including the Constitutional Union Party, Henry Wallace's Progressive Party, and the States' Rights Democrats—were important during only one presidential election.

## Evolution of the Major American Political Parties and Splinter Groups

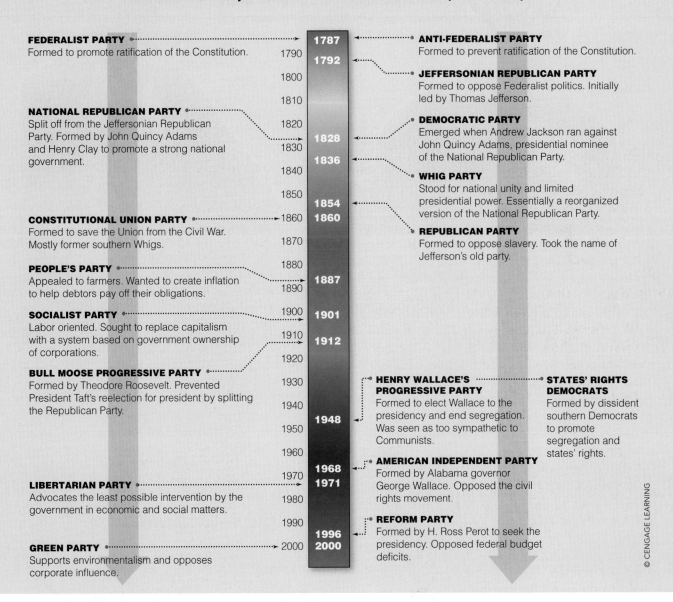

**FEDERALIST PARTY**
Formed to promote ratification of the Constitution.

**1787**
1790
**1792**

**ANTI-FEDERALIST PARTY**
Formed to prevent ratification of the Constitution.

1800

**JEFFERSONIAN REPUBLICAN PARTY**
Formed to oppose Federalist politics. Initially led by Thomas Jefferson.

1810

**NATIONAL REPUBLICAN PARTY**
Split off from the Jeffersonian Republican Party. Formed by John Quincy Adams and Henry Clay to promote a strong national government.

1820
**1828**
1830
**1836**

**DEMOCRATIC PARTY**
Emerged when Andrew Jackson ran against John Quincy Adams, presidential nominee of the National Republican Party.

1840

1850

**WHIG PARTY**
Stood for national unity and limited presidential power. Essentially a reorganized version of the National Republican Party.

**1854**
1860
**1860**

**CONSTITUTIONAL UNION PARTY**
Formed to save the Union from the Civil War. Mostly former southern Whigs.

1870

**REPUBLICAN PARTY**
Formed to oppose slavery. Took the name of Jefferson's old party.

1880

**PEOPLE'S PARTY**
Appealed to farmers. Wanted to create inflation to help debtors pay off their obligations.

**1887**
1890

1900

**SOCIALIST PARTY**
Labor oriented. Sought to replace capitalism with a system based on government ownership of corporations.

**1901**
1910
**1912**

1920

**BULL MOOSE PROGRESSIVE PARTY**
Formed by Theodore Roosevelt. Prevented President Taft's reelection for president by splitting the Republican Party.

1930

1940

**HENRY WALLACE'S PROGRESSIVE PARTY**
Formed to elect Wallace to the presidency and end segregation. Was seen as too sympathetic to Communists.

**STATES' RIGHTS DEMOCRATS**
Formed by dissident southern Democrats to promote segregation and states' rights.

**1948**
1950

1960

**AMERICAN INDEPENDENT PARTY**
Formed by Alabama governor George Wallace. Opposed the civil rights movement.

1970
**1968**
**1971**

**LIBERTARIAN PARTY**
Advocates the least possible intervention by the government in economic and social matters.

1980

1990

**REFORM PARTY**
Formed by H. Ross Perot to seek the presidency. Opposed federal budget deficits.

2000
**1996**
**2000**

**GREEN PARTY**
Supports environmentalism and opposes corporate influence.

© CENGAGE LEARNING

The Jeffersonian Republicans dominated American politics for the next twenty years. Jefferson was succeeded in the White House by two other members of the party—James Madison and James Monroe. In the mid-1820s, however, the Jeffersonian Republicans split into two groups. This was the second realignment in American history. Supporters of Andrew Jackson, who was elected president in 1828, called themselves Democrats. The Democrats appealed to small farmers and the growing class of urbanized workers. The other group, the National Republicans (later the Whig Party), was led by John Quincy Adams, Henry Clay, and the great orator Daniel Webster. It had the support of bankers, business owners, and many southern planters.

**The Impending Crisis** As the Whigs and Democrats competed for the White House throughout

From the election of Abraham Lincoln (shown here) in 1860 until the election of Franklin Delano Roosevelt in 1932, the Republican Party was the more successful party in presidential politics.

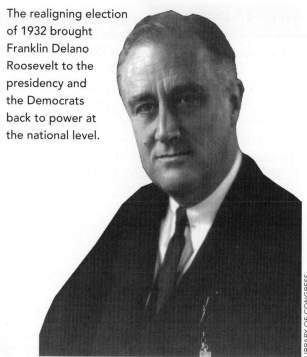

The realigning election of 1932 brought Franklin Delano Roosevelt to the presidency and the Democrats back to power at the national level.

the 1840s and 1850s, the two-party system as we know it today emerged. Both parties were large, with well-known leaders and supporters across the nation. Both had grassroots organizations of party workers committed to winning as many political offices (at all levels of government) for the party as possible. Both the Whigs and the Democrats tried to avoid the issue of slavery.

By the mid-1850s, the Whig coalition had fallen apart, and most northern Whigs were absorbed into the new Republican Party, which opposed the extension of slavery into new territories. Campaigning on this platform in 1860, the Republicans succeeded in electing Abraham Lincoln—the first president elected under the banner of the new Republican Party.

## 7–1c From the Civil War to the Great Depression

When the former Confederate states rejoined the Union after the Civil War, the Republicans and Democrats were roughly even in strength, although the Republicans were more successful in presidential contests. In the 1890s, however, the Republicans gained a decisive advantage. In that decade, the Democrats allied themselves with the Populist movement, which consisted largely of indebted farmers in the West and South. The Populists—the People's

Party—advocated inflation as a way of lessening their debts. Urban workers in the Midwest and East strongly opposed this program, which would erode the value of their paychecks. After the election of 1896, the Republicans established themselves in the minds of many Americans as the party that knew how to manage the nation's economy.

As a result of a Republican split, the Democrats under Woodrow Wilson won power from 1912 to 1920. Otherwise, the Republicans remained dominant in national politics until the onset of the Great Depression.

## 7–1d After the Great Depression

The Great Depression of the 1930s destroyed the belief that the Republicans could better manage the economy and contributed to another realignment in the two-party system. In a realignment, the minority (opposition) party may emerge as the majority party, and this is certainly what happened in 1932. (Realignment can also reestablish the majority party in power with a different coalition of supporters or leave the two parties closely balanced.)

The election of 1932 brought Franklin D. Roosevelt to the presidency and the Democrats back to power at the national level. The elections of 1860 and 1896 are also considered to represent realignments.

**A Civil Rights Plank** Roosevelt's programs to fight the Depression were called the *New Deal*. Those who joined the Democrats during Roosevelt's New Deal included a substantial share of African Americans—Roosevelt's relief programs were open to people of all races. (Until the 1930s, African Americans had been overwhelmingly Republican.) In 1948, for the first time ever, the Democrats adopted a civil rights plank as part of the party platform at their national convention. A number of southern Democrats revolted and ran a separate States' Rights ticket for president.

In 1964, the Democrats, under incumbent president Lyndon Johnson, won a landslide victory, and liberals held a majority in Congress. In the political environment that produced this election result, a coalition of northern Democrats and Republicans crafted the major civil rights legislation that you read about in Chapter 5. The subsequent years were turbulent, with riots and marches in several major cities and student protests against the Vietnam War (1965–1975).

**A "Rolling Realignment"** Conservative Democrats did not like the direction in which their party seemed to be taking them. Under President Richard Nixon, the Republican Party was receptive to these conservative Democrats, and over a period of years, most of them became Republican voters. This was a major alteration in the political landscape, although it was not exclusively associated with a single election. Republican president Ronald Reagan helped cement the new Republican coalition.

The Democrats continued to hold majorities in the House and Senate until 1994, but partisan labels were somewhat misleading. During the 1970s and 1980s, a large bloc of Democrats in Congress, mostly from the South, sided with the Republicans on almost all issues. In time, these conservative Democrats were replaced by conservative Republicans.

The result of this "rolling realignment" was that the two major parties were fairly evenly matched. The elections of 2000 were a striking demonstration of how closely the electorate was now divided. Republican George W. Bush won the presidency in that year by carrying Florida with a margin of 538 votes. Democrat Al Gore actually received about half a million more popular votes than Bush. Following the elections, the Senate was made up of 50 Republicans and 50 Democrats. The Republicans controlled the House by a razor-thin margin of seven seats.

## 7–2 America's Political Parties Today

Historically, political parties drew together like-minded individuals. Today, too, individuals with similar characteristics tend to align themselves more often with one or the other major party. Such factors as race, age, income, education, marital status, and geography all influence party identification. For example, upper-income voters traditionally have been more likely to support the Republican Party. But is this still true today? We examine that question in this chapter's *Perception versus Reality* feature on the following page.

**Learning Outcome 7–2**

Describe the current status of the two major parties.

### 7–2a Red States versus Blue States

Geography is one of the many factors that can determine party identification. Examine the national electoral map shown in Figure 7–2 on page 155. In 2012, Republican Mitt Romney did well in the South, in the Great Plains, and in parts of the Midwest and Mountain West. Democrat Barack Obama did well in the Northeast, in parts of the Midwest, and on the West Coast. Beginning with the presidential elections of 2000, the press has made much of the supposed cultural differences between the "blue" states that vote for the Democratic candidate and the "red" states that vote for the Republican.[3] In reality, though, many states could better be described as "purple"—that is, a mixture of red and blue. These states could give their electoral votes to either party.

For another way to consider the influence of geography, see the map of Ohio in Figure 7–3 on page 156. Most of Ohio is red, and a quick glance might lead you to believe that Romney carried the state. In fact, Obama carried Ohio by a margin of 1.9 percentage

# Perception versus Reality

## Wealthy People Are Republicans

Many people in the United States, as in most other countries, see the wealthy as conservative (on the political right). Likewise, the poor are seen as liberal (on the political left). In America, that means the wealthiest citizens should be Republicans and the poor should be Democrats. It's assumed that rich people oppose programs to help the poor, and so by definition they cannot be Democrats.

### THE PERCEPTION

The political left—Democrats and others—is united in favor of policies that help the poor. Democrats also dislike the rich and want to increase taxes on the wealthiest taxpayers. Consequently, the wealthy vote against Democrats because Democrats will raise their taxes. The rich therefore speak with one voice—a Republican voice.

### THE REALITY

Consider the results of exit polling after the 2012 elections, in which Democrat Barack Obama won the presidency. As you move up the income ladder, you indeed see fewer votes for Obama. Families making from $100,000 to $200,000 per year were more Republican than those making $50,000 to $100,000. Moving up to the $200,000 to $250,000 category, however, support for Obama jumps from 44 percent

to 47 percent. It falls again above $250,000—but this last group consists precisely of those people whose taxes Obama proposed to raise. In any event, we all know that many rich and famous Hollywood stars lean well toward the left. In addition, many executives in high-tech companies are Democrats. Some are quite liberal indeed.

The fact is, there are conservatives *and* liberals among the rich—particularly, among the very rich. Class warfare is not on the American agenda. The cosmopolitan cultural attitudes of the wealthy cause many of them to favor liberal politics. Even when Democrats, including President Obama, talk about raising tax rates for the rich, many of these people believe that such policies are "fair." For example, at a Facebook forum with President Obama, Facebook founder Mark Zuckerberg said that he was "cool" with paying more in taxes.

Note, though, that many of the super-rich are not particularly affected by higher income tax rates. People like Zuckerberg receive most of their income as capital gains—notably as an increase in the value of their stocks. Capital gains have been taxed at a relatively low 15 percent rate. Most of Romney's income was taxed at this low rate, a fact that became a campaign issue in 2012. Obama advocated raising the rate to 20 percent, but that is still much lower than the top rate on salary income. It is certainly easier for the super-rich to support Democrats who want to raise income tax rates if they know that for the most part they are not going to pay those additional taxes.

**BLOG ON** You can check out recent exit polls for yourself. You'll see how income, education, race, religion, ideology, and many other variables affect people's votes. For the 2010 exit polls, search on "exit polls 2010." For the 2012 polls, try "exit polls 2012."

points. Ohio looks red because Romney carried almost all of the rural parts of the state. The Obama counties had larger populations. This pattern was seen all over the country: the more urban the county, the more likely it was to vote Democratic.

## 7–2b Shifting Political Fortunes

As noted earlier, by 2000 the two major parties were very closely matched in terms of support. Public opinion polls reported that voters continued to view the parties with roughly equal favor.

## FIGURE 7-2

# The 2012 Presidential
## Election Results

This map shows the 2012 presidential election results by state. While Barack Obama won the election, Mitt Romney picked up two states that Obama carried in 2008.

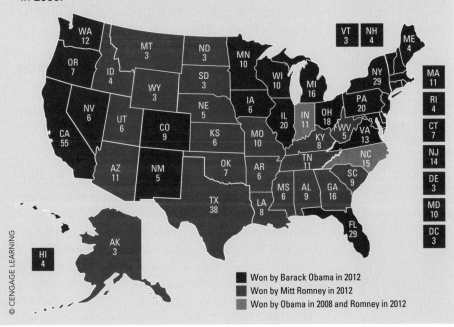

■ Won by Barack Obama in 2012
■ Won by Mitt Romney in 2012
■ Won by Obama in 2008 and Romney in 2012

---

health-care reform package. Millions of voters concluded that the government was growing too big, too fast. In November 2010, the voters handed an additional sixty-three seats in the U.S. House to the Republicans, granting that party control of the chamber. (The Democrats still controlled the Senate.)

By late 2011, however, commentators were beginning to wonder whether the strong conservatism of the newly elected Republicans in Congress and around the country might be alienating some independent voters. The result was to deprive the Republicans of the edge they enjoyed in the 2010 elections.

## The Triumph of Partisanship
A key characteristic of recent politics has been the extreme partisanship of party activists and members of Congress. As noted earlier, in the 1960s party coalitions contained a variety of factions with differing politics. Many Democrats in Congress were conservatives from the South. Likewise, the Republican Party contained a large liberal faction based in the Northeast. The rolling realignment after the elections of 1968 resulted in parties that were much more homogeneous.

Political scientists have calculated that by the time of the 111th Congress (2009–2011), the most conservative Democrat in the House was to the left of the most moderate Republican. The effect was even more pronounced in the 112th Congress (2011–2013). Many relatively conservative Democrats lost their seats in the 2010 elections, and the newly elected Republicans were, on average, more conservative than ever. This type of political sorting continued in the 2012 congressional elections.

**MAKING THE OTHER PARTY LOOK WEAK.** Ideological uniformity has made it easier for the parties to maintain discipline in Congress. Personal friendships

---

**Trouble for the Republicans** During 2005, however, the partisan deadlock began to break up. The grinding, seemingly endless war in Iraq began to cut into support for the Republicans. By 2006, that party had lost about 5 percentage points in popularity relative to the Democrats, as measured by Gallup. Even before the start of the Great Recession, therefore, the Republicans were in trouble. In 2006, the Democrats regained control of the House and Senate. In 2008, in the shadow of a global financial crisis, Americans elected Barack Obama as president.

**Trouble for the Democrats** Within one year of Obama's inauguration, the Democratic advantage had vanished. Both parties were now distinctly less popular than they had been five years earlier.

Continued high rates of unemployment were a major reason that the Democrats lost support. Also, the sharp increase in government activity during Obama's first two years in office appeared to bother many voters. A large economic stimulus package was followed by the bailout of Chrysler and General Motors. In March 2010, Congress passed a major

FIGURE 7-3

# The 2012 Presidential
## Election Results in Ohio

This map displays the Ohio counties carried by Barack Obama (blue) and Mitt Romney (red) in the 2012 presidential elections. The cities shown on the map are the ten most populous municipalities in Ohio. Obama did well in urban and suburban counties, but poorly in nonmetropolitan regions. (Note that one nonmetropolitan county that Obama carried contains a major university.)

© CENGAGE LEARNING

across party lines, once common in Congress, have become rare. The belief has grown that compromise with the other party is a form of betrayal. According to this view, the minority party should not attempt to improve legislation proposed by the majority, but it should oppose majority-party measures in an attempt to make the majority appear ineffective. The Republican Party was able to employ such tactics as early as the 1990s. Democrats soon began to match these capabilities.

**dealignment** Among voters, a growing detachment from both major political parties.

**THE IMPACT OF THE TEA PARTY MOVEMENT.** Political polarization, already great, grew even

more severe after the 2010 elections. Many of the new Republican members of Congress were pledged to the Tea Party philosophy of no-compromise conservatism. These members were fully prepared to revolt if the Republican leadership presented them with legislation that Democrats could support.

Given that the Democrats still controlled the Senate and the presidency, political deadlock seemed inevitable. We take a closer look at that issue in this chapter's *Our Challenging Times* feature on page 158.

## 7-2c Realignment, Dealignment, and Tipping

Despite the narrowness of the Republican margin after 2000, Republican strategists dreamed of a new realignment that would force the Democrats into the minority. These hopes were not fulfilled. After 2006, many Democrats anticipated a realignment that would benefit the Democrats. These dreams were shattered as well. For a major realignment to take place, a large number of voters must conclude that their party is no longer capable of representing their interests and ideals, and that another party can do better. It is hard to identify large groups of voters who could be swayed to support a different party today.

**Dealignment** One political development that may rule out realignment is the growth in the number of independent voters. By 2012, fully 38 percent of the electorate claimed to be independent. True, many of these voters admitted to leaning toward the Republicans or the Democrats. Still, anyone claiming to be an independent has a weakened attachment to the parties.

Some political scientists argue that with so many independent voters, the concept of realignment becomes irrelevant. Realignment has been replaced by **dealignment.** In such an environment, politics would be unusually volatile, because the large body of unattached independents could easily swing from one party to another. The dramatic changes in fortune experienced by the two major parties in recent years provides some evidence to support the dealignment theory. By 2012, as deadlock gripped the political system, both parties experienced record-high unfavorable scores in public opinion polls.

**Tipping** Realignment is not the only process that can alter the political landscape. What if the various types of voters maintain their political identifications—but one type of voter becomes substantially more numerous? This can happen due to migration between states or between nations, or even by changes

## The Parties in the 2012 Elections

Right up until the time when the results came in on Election Day, top Republicans were sure that 2012 would be a Republican year. This is not what happened. Following the election, Republicans asked themselves what they could do to improve their results in the future. One problem was obvious. Latinos, who cast 40 percent of their votes for Republican president George W. Bush in 2004, gave only 27 percent of their votes to Romney. Asian Americans gave Romney only 26 percent. Both of these groups represent a rapidly growing share of the electorate. After the 2012 vote, some Republicans called on their party to consider measures to grant unauthorized immigrants some type of recognized status. The hope was that such an initiative would repair relations between the Republican Party and Latinos. President Ronald Reagan once said, "Latinos are Republicans—they just don't know it yet." He was referring to the conservatism of many Hispanics on social issues and to their entrepreneurial spirit. There was a problem with such an analysis, however. Most Latino—and Asian—Americans support generous levels of social spending. The new immigrant groups tend to agree with the Democrats on the key economic issues. Anti-immigrant Republicans argued that their party should instead redouble its attempt to appeal to the white working class. Many pundits, however, strongly doubted that such an effort would be sufficient to return the Republicans to the White House.

in education levels and occupations. The result could tip a state from one party to another. Many Democratic strategists believe that such *tipping* will benefit their party greatly in the future.

**FOR CRITICAL THINKING**

Demographers expect that minority group members will be a majority of the U.S. population by 2050. *How might this affect the two major parties?*

## 7-3 What Do Political Parties Do?

### LearningOutcome 7-3

Explain how political parties function in our democratic system.

As noted earlier, the Constitution does not mention political parties. Historically, though, political parties have played a vital role in our democratic system. Their main function has been to link the people's policy preferences to actual government policies. Political parties also perform many other functions.

### 7-3a Selecting Candidates

One of the most important functions of the two political parties is to recruit and nominate candidates for political office. This function simplifies voting choices for the electorate. Political parties take the large number of people who want to run for office and narrow the field. They accomplish this by the use of the **primary,** which is a preliminary election to choose a party's final candidate. This candidate then runs against the opposing party's candidate in the general election.

Voter turnout for primaries is lower than it is for general elections. The voters who do go to the polls are often strong supporters of their party. Indeed, in many states, independents cannot participate in primary elections, even if they lean toward one or the other of the two major parties. As a result, the Republican primary electorate is very conservative, and Democratic primary voters are quite liberal. Candidates often find that they must run to the political right or left during the primaries. Frequently, they then move to the center during the general election campaign. Chapter 9 provides much more detail on primary and general elections.

**primary** A preliminary election held for the purpose of choosing a party's final candidate.

# OUR CHALLENGING TIMES

## Polarized Politics and the Threat of Taxmageddon

Armageddon is the great biblical battle between good and evil during the "end times." By 2012, politicians and pundits alike were alarmed over the prospect of a catastrophic political scenario that came to be called "Taxmageddon." The disaster would take place if Republicans and Democrats in Congress could not come to an agreement on taxes and spending in the "lame duck" period between the November elections and the end of 2012.

### THE PROBLEM OF FEDERAL BUDGET DEFICITS

During most of modern U.S. history, the federal government has spent more in every year than it has collected in taxes and other revenues. Rarely, though, have deficits been as large as they have been recently. For the last four years, the budget deficit has averaged well over $1 trillion per year. So Congress and the president would like to reduce that annual deficit. If Congress did absolutely nothing, the federal budget deficit would drop dramatically on January 1, 2013.

### THE CONSEQUENCES OF DOING NOTHING

The details of Taxmageddon are simple. In recent years, Congress passed a variety of laws that expired at the end of 2012 or went into effect at the beginning of 2013. Tax-rate cuts adopted when George W. Bush was president were to end. The "marriage penalty" for joint filers would return. The Social Security payroll tax would increase. Medicare taxes were to increase on upper-income individuals. The list was quite long, and it included significant cuts to military and domestic spending. In the months leading up to the elections, Congress did nothing about the approaching crisis because of polarized politics.

So why do anything? Why not let the deficit fall? Indeed, in the long run, everyone wants the deficit to be reduced. In the short run, however, pulling vast sums out of the economy through huge tax increases seemed certain to push the nation back into a full-blown recession. Republicans and Democrats held very different economic theories, but they agreed on this point.

### THE INSURMOUNTABLE DIVIDE

Partisan politics can be summarized in two sentences: Republicans do not want tax-rate increases. Most Democrats do not want to cut spending on Social Security, Medicare, or Medicaid. Both parties know, even if they will not admit it, that it is impossible to maintain these major programs, called *entitlement programs*, in their current form without eventually increasing taxes or reducing benefits. These three programs make up 41 percent of the federal budget. To keep them, plus other federal programs, Democrats would raise taxes, particularly on the rich. Republicans say that if tax rates are increased, in the long run we will end up with a slow-growth economy.

There seems to be no middle ground in our new world of polarized politics.

**YOU BE THE JUDGE** What would be the consequences of reducing government spending on entitlements as opposed to the consequences of raising tax rates?

## 7–3b Informing the Public

Political parties help educate the public about important political issues. In recent years, these issues have included environmental policies, health-care reform, our tax system, education, Social Security, and ways to stimulate the economy. Each party presents its view of these issues through television announcements, newspaper articles or ads, Web site materials, campaign speeches, rallies, debates, and leaflets. These activities help citizens learn about the issues, form opinions, and consider proposed solutions.

## 7–3c Coordinating Policymaking

In our complex government, parties are essential for coordinating policy among the various branches of the government. The political party is usually the major institution through which the executive and legislative branches cooperate with each other. Each president, cabinet head, and member of Congress is normally a member of the Democratic Party or the Republican Party. The president works through party leaders in Congress to promote the administration's legislative program.

Ideally, the parties work together to fashion compromises—legislation that is acceptable to both parties and that serves the national interest. Yet in recent years, as we noted earlier, there has been little bipartisanship in Congress. (For a more detailed discussion of the role played by political parties in Congress, see Chapter 11.) Parties also act as the glue of our federal structure by connecting the various levels of government—state and national—with a common bond.

## 7–3d Checking the Power of the Governing Party

The party with fewer members in the legislature is the **minority party.** The party with more members is the **majority party.** The party that does not control Congress or a state legislature, or the presidency or a state governorship, also plays a vital function in American politics. The "out" party does what it can to influence the "in" party and its policies, and to check the actions of the party in power.

For example, depending on how evenly Congress is divided, the out party, or minority party, may be able to attract to its side some of the members of the majority party to pass or defeat certain legislation. The minority party will also work to inform voters of the shortcomings of

> ## "DEMOCRACY IS
> the recurrent suspicion that more than half of the people are right more than half of the time."
>
> ~ E. B. WHITE ~
> AMERICAN WRITER
> 1900–1965

of interests and opinions who join together to support the party's platform, or parts of it.

The Democratic Party, for example, includes a number of groups with different views on such issues as health care, immigration, and global warming. The role of party leaders in this situation is to adopt a view broad enough on these issues that the various groups will not be alienated. In this way, different groups can hold

the majority party's agenda and to plan strategies for winning the next election.

## 7–3e Balancing Competing Interests

Political parties are often described as vast umbrellas under which Americans with diverse interests can gather. Political parties are essentially **coalitions**—alliances of individuals and groups with a variety

**minority party** The political party that has fewer members in the legislature than the opposing party.

**majority party** The political party that has more members in the legislature than the opposing party.

**coalition** An alliance of individuals or groups with a variety of interests and opinions who join together to support all or part of a political party's platform.

These delegates to the 2012 Republican National Convention applaud Mitt Romney's acceptance speech.

AP PHOTO/DAVID GOLDMAN

their individual views and still come together under the umbrella of the Democratic Party.

Leaders of both the Democratic Party and the Republican Party modify contending views and arrange compromises among different groups. In so doing, the parties help to unify, rather than divide, their members.

### 7–3f Running Campaigns

Through their national, state, and local organizations, parties coordinate campaigns. Political parties take care of a large number of small and routine tasks that are essential to the smooth functioning of the electoral process. For example, they work at getting party members registered and at conducting drives to recruit new voters. Sometimes, party volunteers staff the polling places.

## FOR CRITICAL THINKING

Presidents often have political goals that are different from those of senators and representatives from the president's own party. *What might such goals be?*

## 7–4 How American Political Parties Are Structured

### LearningOutcome 7–4

Discuss the structure of American political parties.

Each of the two major American political parties consists of three components: the party in the electorate, the party organization, and the party in government.

1.  The party in the **electorate** is the largest component, consisting of all of those people who describe themselves as Democrats or Republicans. Members of the party in the electorate never need to work on a campaign or attend a party meeting. In most states, they may register as Democrats or Republicans, but registration can be changed at will.

2.  Each major party has a nationwide organization with national, state, and local offices. As will be discussed later in this section, the party organizations include several levels of people who maintain the party's strength between elections, make its rules, raise money, organize conventions, help with elections, and recruit candidates.

3.  The party in government consists of all of the party's candidates who have won elections and now hold public office. Even though members of Congress, state legislators, presidents, and all other officeholders almost always run for office as either Democrats or Republicans, members of any one party do not always agree with one another on government policy. The party in government helps to organize the government's agenda by coaxing and convincing its own party members to vote for its policies. If the party is to translate its promises into public policies, the job must be done by the party in government.

### 7–4a The Party in the Electorate

Let's look more closely at the largest component of each party—the party in the electorate. What does it mean to belong to a political party? In many European countries, being a party member means that you actually join a political party. You get a membership card to carry in your wallet, you pay dues, and you vote to select your local and national party leaders. In the United States, becoming a member of a political party is far less involved.

In most states, voters may declare a party preference when they register to vote. This declaration allows them to participate in party primaries. Some states do not register party preferences, however. In short, to be a member of a political party, an American citizen has only to think of herself or himself as a Democrat or a Republican (or a member of a third party, such as the Green Party or the Libertarian Party). Members of parties do not have to work for the party or attend party meetings. Nor must they support the party platform.

**Identifiers and Activists** Generally, the party in the electorate consists of **party identifiers** (those

**electorate** All of the citizens eligible to vote in a given election.

**party identifier** A person who identifies himself or herself as being a supporter of a particular political party.

who identify themselves as being members of a particular party) and **party activists**—party members who choose to work for the party and even become candidates for office. Political parties need year-round support from the latter group to survive. During election campaigns in particular, candidates depend on active party members and volunteers to mail literature, answer phones, conduct door-to-door canvasses, organize speeches and appearances, and, of course, donate money.

Between elections, parties also need active members to plan the upcoming elections, organize fundraisers, and stay in touch with party leaders in other communities to keep the party strong. The major functions of American political parties are carried out by the party activists.

## Why People Join Political Parties

In a few countries, such as the People's Republic of China, people belong to a political party because they are required to do so to get ahead in life, regardless of whether they agree with the party's ideas and candidates. In the United States, though, people generally belong to a political party because they agree with many of its main ideas and support some of its candidates. Their reasons for choosing one party over another may include solidarity, material, or purposive incentives.

**SOLIDARITY INCENTIVES.** Some people join a particular party to express their **solidarity,** or mutual agreement, with the views of friends, loved ones, and other like-minded people. People also join parties because they enjoy the excitement of engaging in politics with like-minded others.

**MATERIAL INCENTIVES.** Many believe that by joining a party, they will benefit materially through better employment or personal career advancement. The traditional institution of **patronage**—rewarding the party faithful with government jobs or contracts—lives on, even though it has been limited to prevent abuses.[4] Back in the nineteenth century, when almost all government employees got their jobs through patronage, people spoke of it as the "spoils system," as in "the spoils of war."

**PURPOSIVE INCENTIVES.** Finally, some join political parties because they wish to actively promote a set of ideals and principles that they feel are important to American politics and society. As a rule, people join political parties because of their overall agreement with what a particular party stands for.

Thus, when interviewed, people may make the following remarks when asked why they support the Democratic Party: "It seems that the economy is better when the Democrats are in control." "The Democrats are for the working people." People might say about the Republican Party: "The Republicans favor a smaller government than the Democrats do." "The Republicans deal better with national defense issues."

## 7–4b The Party Organization

In theory, each of the major American political parties has a standard, pyramid-shaped organization. This theoretical structure is much like that of a large company, in which

**party activist** A party member who helps to organize and oversee party functions and planning during and between campaigns, and may even become a candidate for office.

**solidarity** Mutual agreement among the members of a particular group.

**patronage** A system of rewarding the party faithful and workers with government jobs or contracts.

Delegates cheer from the floor during the 2012 Democratic National Convention in Charlotte, North Carolina.

BONNIE JO MOUNT/THE WASHINGTON POST/GETTY IMAGES

the bosses are at the top and the employees are at various lower levels.

Actually, neither major party is a closely knit or highly organized structure. Both parties are fragmented and *decentralized,* which means there is no central power with a direct chain of command. If there were, the national chairperson of the party, along with the national committee, could simply dictate how the organization would be run, just as if it were Apple or Google. In reality, state party organizations are all very different and are only loosely tied to the party's national structure. Local party organizations are often quite independent from the state organization.

There is no single individual or group who directs all party members. Instead, a number of personalities, frequently at odds with one another, form loosely identifiable leadership groups.

### State Organizations

The powers and duties of state party organizations

> "Under democracy one party always devotes its chief energies to trying to prove that the other party is **unfit to rule**—and both commonly succeed."
>
> ~ H. L. MENCKEN ~
> AMERICAN JOURNALIST
> 1880–1956

differ from state to state. In general, the state party organization is built around a central committee and a chairperson. The committee works to raise funds, recruit new party members, maintain a strong party organization, and help members running for state offices.

The state chairperson is usually a powerful party member chosen by the committee. In some instances, however, the chairperson is selected by the governor or a senator from that state.

### Local Organizations
Local party organizations differ greatly, but generally there is a party unit for each district in which elective offices are to be filled. These districts include congressional and legislative districts, counties, cities and towns, wards, and precincts.

A **ward** is a political division or district within a city. A **precinct** can be either a political district within a city, such as a block or a neighborhood, or a rural portion of a county. Polling places are located within the precincts. The local, grassroots foundations of politics are formed within voting precincts.

### The National Party Organization
On the national level, the party's presidential candidate is

**ward** A local unit of a political party's organization, consisting of a division or district within a city.

**precinct** A political district within a city, such as a block or a neighborhood, or a rural portion of a county; the smallest voting district at the local level.

WILLIAM B. PLOWMAN/NBC/NBC NEWSWIRE VIA AP IMAGES

Representative Debbie Wasserman Schultz (D., Fla.) is chair of the Democratic National Committee, and Reince Priebus is chair of the Republican National Committee.

considered to be the leader of the party. Well-known members of Congress may also be viewed as national party leaders. In addition to the party leaders, the structure of each party includes four major elements: the national convention, the national committee, the national chairperson, and the congressional campaign committees.

### THE NATIONAL CONVENTION.

Much of the public attention that the party receives comes at the **national convention,** which is held every four years during the summer before the presidential elections. The news media always cover these conventions, and as a result, they have become quite extravagant. Lobbyists, big business, and interest groups provide millions of dollars to put on these events. Such organizations have an interest in government subsidies, tax breaks, and regulatory favors.

The conventions inspire and mobilize party members throughout the nation. They provide the voters with an opportunity to see and hear the candidates directly, rather than through a media filter or characterizations provided by supporters and opponents. Candidates' speeches draw huge audiences. For example, in 2012 more than 30 million people watched the acceptance speeches of Barack Obama and Mitt Romney.

The national conventions are attended by delegates chosen by the states in various ways, which we describe in Chapter 9. The delegates' most important job is to nominate the party's presidential and vice-presidential candidates, who together make up the **party ticket.** The delegates also write the **party platform,** which sets forth the party's positions on national issues. Essentially, through its platform, the party promises to initiate certain policies if it wins the presidency. Despite the widespread perception that candidates can and do ignore these promises once they are in office, in fact, many of the promises become law.

### THE NATIONAL COMMITTEE.

Each state elects a number of delegates to the **national party committee.** The Republican National Committee and

the Democratic National Committee direct the business of their respective parties during the four years between national conventions. The committees' most important duties, however, are to organize the next national convention and to plan how to obtain a party victory in the next presidential election.

### THE NATIONAL CHAIRPERSON.

Each party's national committee elects a **national party chairperson** to serve as administrative head of the national party. The main duty of the national chairperson is to direct the work of the national committee from party headquarters in Washington, D.C. The chairperson is involved in raising funds, providing for publicity, promoting party unity, encouraging the development of state and local organizations, recruiting new voters, and other activities.

In presidential election years, the chairperson's attention is focused on the national convention and the presidential campaign.

### THE CONGRESSIONAL CAMPAIGN COMMITTEES.

Each party has a campaign committee, made up of senators and representatives, in each chamber of Congress. Members are chosen by their colleagues and serve for two-year terms. The committees work to help elect party members to Congress.

## 7–4c The Party in Government: Developing Issues

When a political party wins the presidency or control of one or more chambers of Congress, it has the opportunity to carry out the party platform it developed at its national convention. The

---

**national convention** The meeting held by each major party every four years to nominate presidential and vice-presidential candidates, write a party platform, and conduct other party business.

**party ticket** A list of a political party's candidates for various offices. In national elections, the party ticket consists of the presidential and vice-presidential candidates.

**party platform** The document drawn up by each party at its national convention that outlines the policies and positions of the party.

**national party committee** The political party leaders who direct party business during the four years between the national party conventions, organize the next national convention, and plan how to obtain a party victory in the next presidential election.

**national party chairperson** An individual who serves as a political party's administrative head at the national level and directs the work of the party's national committee.

platform represents the official party position on various issues, although, neither all party members nor all candidates running on the party's ticket are likely to share these positions exactly.

FOR CRITICAL THINKING

The parties often hope they can win additional votes in a state by holding their national convention in that state. *Do you think this strategy is likely to be effective? Why or why not?*

## 7–5 The Dominance of Our Two-Party System

### LearningOutcome 7–5

Describe the different types of third parties and how they function in the American political system.

In the United States, we have a **two-party system**. This means that the two major parties—the Democrats and the Republicans—dominate national politics. Why has the two-party system become so firmly entrenched in the United States? According to some scholars, the first major political division between the Federalists and the Anti-Federalists established a precedent that continued over time and ultimately resulted in the domination of the two-party system.

As noted earlier, a third or more of the voters identify themselves as independents (although they may lean toward one party or the other). For these individuals, both of the major parties evidently fail to address issues that are important to them or represent their views. Nonetheless, the two-party system continues to thrive. A number of factors help to explain this phenomenon.

### 7–5a The Self-Perpetuation of the Two-Party System

One of the major reasons for the perpetuation of the two-party system is simply that there is no alternative. Minor parties, called **third parties,**[5] have found it extremely difficult to compete with the major parties for votes. There are many reasons for this, including election laws and institutional barriers.

### Election Laws Favoring Two Parties

American election laws tend to favor the major parties. In many states, for example, the established major parties need relatively few signatures to place their candidates on the ballot, whereas a third party must get many more signatures. The number of signatures required is often based on the total party vote in the last election, which penalizes a new party that is competing for the first time.

The rules governing campaign financing also favor the major parties. As you will read in Chapter 9, both major parties receive federal funds for presidential campaigns and for their national conventions. Third parties, in contrast, receive federal funds only if they garner 5 percent of the vote, and they receive the funds only *after* the election.

### Institutional Barriers to a Multiparty System

The structure of many of our institutions prevents third parties from enjoying electoral success. One of the major institutional barriers is the election, by the people, of governors and (through the electoral college) the president. Voting for governors and members of the electoral college takes place on a statewide, winner-take-all basis. (Maine and Nebraska are exceptions—they can, under certain circumstances, split their electoral votes.)

Third-party candidates find it hard to win when they must campaign statewide instead of appealing to voters in a smaller district that might be more receptive to their political positions.

**THE PARLIAMENTARY ALTERNATIVE.** The popular election of executive officers contrasts with the parliamentary system described in *The Rest of the World* feature in Chapter 2. In that system, parliament—not the voters—chooses the nation's executive officers. Third-party voters therefore have a greater chance of affecting the outcome by electing a few members of parliament.

**SINGLE-MEMBER DISTRICTS.** Another institutional barrier to a multiparty system is the single-member district. Today, all federal and most state legislative districts are single-member districts—that is, voters elect one member from their district to the House of

**two-party system**
A political system in which two strong and established parties compete for political offices.

**third party** In the United States, any party other than one of the two major parties (Republican and Democratic).

 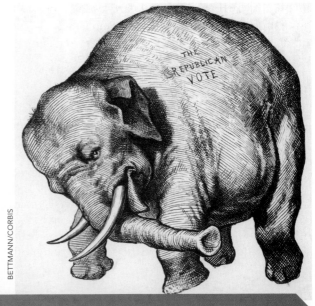

BETTMANN/CORBIS
BETTMANN/CORBIS

Most colleges and universities have mascots that represent their athletic teams. So, too, do the two major political parties. On the left, you see the donkey that became the Democratic Party mascot. On the right, you see the elephant that became the Republican Party mascot.[6]

Representatives and to their state legislature.[7] In most European countries, by contrast, districts are drawn as multimember districts and are represented by multiple elected officials from different parties, according to the proportion of the vote their party received.

While third parties are rarely successful in the United States, the two major parties do not compete in all elections. Some state offices and many local offices are filled by *nonpartisan elections,* in which party identification never appears on the ballot. Are there benefits to the nonpartisan system? We examine that question in this chapter's *Join the Debate* feature on the following page.

## 7–5b Third Parties in American Politics

Despite difficulties, throughout American history third parties have competed for influence in the nation's two-party system. Indeed, as mentioned earlier, third parties have been represented in most of our national elections. These parties are as varied as the causes they represent, but all have one thing in common: their members and leaders want to challenge the major parties because they believe that certain needs and values are not being properly addressed.

"I am not a member of any organized political party.

# I AM A DEMOCRAT."

~ WILL ROGERS ~
AMERICAN HUMORIST
1879–1935

Some third parties have tried to appeal to the entire nation. Others have focused on particular regions, states, or local areas. Most third parties have been short lived. A few, however, such as the Socialist Party (founded in 1901 and disbanded in 1972), lasted for a long time. The number and variety of third parties make them difficult to classify, but most fall into one of the general categories discussed in the following subsections.

### Issue-Oriented Parties

An issue-oriented third party is formed to promote a particular cause or timely issue. For example, the Free Soil Party was organized in 1848 to oppose the expansion of slavery into the western territories. The Prohibition Party was formed in 1869 to advocate banning the manufacture and use of alcoholic beverages.

Most issue-oriented parties fade into history as the issue that brought them into existence fades from public attention, is taken up by a major party, or is resolved. Some issue-oriented parties endure, however, when they expand their focus beyond a single area of concern. For example, the Green Party was founded in 1972 to raise awareness of environmental issues, but it is no longer a single-issue party. Today, the Green

## Are Nonpartisan Elections a Good Idea?

It's hard to miss the partisan battles in Washington, D.C. To a lesser extent, nasty fights also occur in state legislatures and even city councils. As you've learned, the framers of the U.S. Constitution never mentioned political parties. They thought that the nation would be better off without them. Dream on. We will never eliminate partisan elections at the federal level. But what about the state and, particularly, the local levels? Would the states be better off with nonpartisan elections?

### Take the Nastiness Out of Elections—Go Nonpartisan

Advocates of nonpartisan elections believe that the two major political parties are the reason that many states are "ungovernable." Political deadlock would be eliminated if state senators and representatives were voted into office without a party label. Currently, ideological activists—Republicans and Democrats— largely determine the identity of state legislative candidates.

Where does that leave independents and moderates? The answer is: underrepresented. More than two-thirds of American cities have embraced nonpartisan voting. After all, local issues are very different from national ones, and knowing that a candidate

is a Republican or a Democrat tells you little about that candidate's policy positions on local issues. It's time to extend nonpartisan elections to state legislatures as well. Nebraska, for one, has such a legislature already.

### Nonpartisan Elections Lead to Less-Informed Voters

While enticing in theory, nonpartisan elections do not result in better government. In some nonpartisan systems, candidates are still affiliated with political parties. Even so, without party labels on the ballot, citizens find it more difficult to cast an informed vote. Ordinary citizens cannot take the time to analyze in any detail the political positions of legislative candidates. Take the example of nonpartisan state elections in Minnesota before 1973. There, prominent local figures were able to win elections even when their politics were unrepresentative of their districts. After partisan labels were introduced in 1973, the state legislature was transformed.

According to law professor David Schleicher, nonpartisan balloting at the city level also leaves voters poorly informed and reduces turnout in elections. True, party labels provide less information in municipal contests than in national elections. They provide at least *some* information, however, and without them, citizens often know nothing at all. As a result, Schleicher says, voters tend to rely on racial or ethnic clues in candidates' names.

**FOR CRITICAL ANALYSIS** If you were independently wealthy and could finance an expensive campaign, would you prefer partisan or nonpartisan elections? Why?

---

Party campaigns against alleged corporate greed and the major parties' ostensible indifference to a number of issues, including poverty, the excesses of globalism, and the failure of the war on drugs.

**Ideological Parties** As discussed in Chapter 1, a *political ideology* is a system of political ideas rooted in beliefs about human nature, society, and government. An ideological party supports a particular political doctrine or a set of beliefs. For

> "Let us not seek the Republican answer or the Democratic answer, but the **right answer.**"
>
> ~ JOHN FITZGERALD KENNEDY ~
> THIRTY-FIFTH PRESIDENT
> OF THE UNITED STATES
> 1961–1963

example, a party such as the (still-existing) Socialist Labor Party may believe that our free enterprise system should be replaced by one in which workers control all of the factories in the economy. The party's members may believe that competition should be replaced by cooperation and social responsibility so as to achieve an equitable distribution of income.

In contrast, an ideological party such as the Libertarian Party may oppose almost all forms of government interference with personal liberties and private enterprise.

## Splinter or Personality Parties

A splinter party develops out of a split within a major party. This split may be part of an attempt to elect a specific person. For example, when Theodore Roosevelt did not receive the Republican Party's nomination for president in 1912, he created the Bull Moose Party (also called the Progressive Party) to promote his candidacy. From the Democrats have come Henry Wallace's Progressive Party and the States' Rights (Dixiecrat) Party, both formed in 1948. In 1968, the American Independent Party was formed to support George Wallace's campaign for president.

Most splinter parties have been formed around a leader with a strong personality, which is why they are sometimes called *personality parties*. When that person steps aside, the party usually collapses. An example of a personality party is the Reform Party, which was formed in 1996 mainly to provide a campaign vehicle for H. Ross Perot.

## 7-5c The Effects of Third Parties

Although most Americans do not support third parties or vote for their candidates, third parties have influenced American politics in several ways, some of which we examine here.

## Third Parties Bring Issues to the Public's Attention

Third parties have brought many political issues to the public's attention. They have exposed and focused on unpopular or highly debated issues that major parties have preferred to ignore. Third parties are in a position to take bold stands on issues that major parties avoid, because third parties are not trying to be all things to all people. Progressive social reforms such as the minimum wage, women's right to vote, railroad and banking legislation, and old-age pensions were first proposed by third parties. The Free Soilers of the 1850s, for example, were the first true antislavery party, and the Populists and Progressives put many social reforms on the political agenda.

Some people have argued that third parties are often the unsung heroes of American politics, bringing new issues to the forefront of public debate. In the past, some of the ideas proposed by third parties were never accepted, while others were taken up by the major parties as those ideas became increasingly popular.

## Third Parties Can Affect the Vote

Third parties can also influence election outcomes. On occasion, they have taken victory from one major party and given it to another, thus playing the "spoiler" role.

For example, in 1912, when the Progressive Party split from the Republican Party, the result was three major contenders for the presidency: Woodrow Wilson, the Democratic candidate; William Howard Taft, the regular Republican candidate; and Theodore Roosevelt, the Progressive candidate. The presence of the Progressive Party "spoiled" the Republicans' chances for victory and gave the election to Wilson, the Democrat. Without Roosevelt's third party, Taft might have won. Similarly, some commentators contended that Green Party candidate Ralph Nader "spoiled" the chances of Democratic candidate Al Gore in the 2000 elections, because many of those who voted for Nader would have voted Democratic had Nader not been on the ballot.

## Third Parties Provide a Voice for Dissatisfied Americans

Third parties also provide a voice for voters who are frustrated with and alienated from the Republican and Democratic parties. Americans who are unhappy with the two major political parties can still participate in American politics through third parties that reflect their opinions on political issues. For example, many new Minnesota voters turned out during the 1998 elections to vote for Jesse Ventura, a Reform Party candidate for governor in that state. Ventura won.

Theodore Roosevelt and his Progressive (Bull Moose) Party changed the outcome of the 1912 election.

BETTMANN/CORBIS

Ultimately, third parties in national elections find it difficult to break through in an electoral system that perpetuates their failure. Because third parties normally do not win elections, Americans tend not to vote for them or to contribute to their campaigns, so they continue not to win. As long as Americans hold on to the perception that third parties can never win big in an election, the current two-party system is likely to persist.

# AMERICA AT ODDS Political Parties

By their very nature, arguments about the parties are some of the most divisive conflicts in politics. We can list only a sampling of the disputes:

- Is the Republican Party, by excessive conservatism, driving off voters that it needs—or can it win by upholding basic conservative values? For that matter, are the Democrats too liberal—or not liberal enough?

- Is it better when the two chambers of Congress and the presidency are held by the same party, thus guaranteeing effective government—or is it better when Congress and the presidency are held by different parties, so that the two parties can check each other?

- Is the increasing importance of political independents a positive development—or is it a sign that citizens are becoming dangerously detached from our political system?

- Are political parties desirable and inevitable—or should elections be nonpartisan whenever possible?

- Is it better to support a third party when you are in greater agreement with its positions than with those of either major party—or should you avoid wasting your vote and always support the major party that is closer to your politics?

- Finally, looking forward, do the Republicans or the Democrats offer the best solutions for our problems?

# TAKE ACTION

Getting involved in political parties is as simple as going to the polls and casting your vote for the candidate of one of the major parties—or of a third party. If you want to go a step further, you can attend a speech given by a political candidate or even volunteer to assist a political party or a specific candidate's campaign activities.

You can also consider another alternative—becoming a delegate to a party convention. National conventions aren't the only ones that the parties hold. There are state conventions, and most local party units conduct regular conventions as well. Depending on the state, parties may hold conventions by U.S. House district, by county, or by state legislative district. In many states, the lowest-level conventions are open to anyone who shows up.

Voting rights at a convention, however, may be restricted to those who are elected as precinct delegates in a party primary. In much of the country, precinct delegate slots go unfilled. If this is true in your area, you can become a precinct delegate with a simple write-in campaign. You merely need to write in your own name and persuade a small handful of friends or neighbors to write you in as well. Whether you attend a convention as a voting delegate or as a guest, you'll have a firsthand look at how politics operates. You'll hear debates on resolutions. You might participate in electing delegates to higher-level conventions—perhaps even the national convention if it is a presidential election year. Few exercises are more educational.

# STUDY TOOLS

## Ready to study?

- Review what you've read with the quiz below. Check your answers on the Chapter in Review card at the back of the book. For any questions you miss, read the corresponding Learning Outcome section again to prepare for class and your exam.
- Rip out and study the Chapter in Review card.

## . . . Or you can go online to CourseMate

at **www.cengagebrain.com** for these additional review materials:

- Practice Quizzes
- Key Term Flashcards or Crossword Puzzles
- Audio Summaries
- Simulations, Animated Learning Modules, and Interactive Timelines
- Videos
- American Government NewsWatch

## Fill-In

1. The nation's first two political parties, the _____, clashed openly in the elections of 1796.

2. In 1860, Abraham Lincoln was the first president elected under the banner of the new _____ Party.

3. Dealignment among voters refers to _____.

4. Political parties link the people's policy preferences to actual government policies. Parties also perform many other functions, including _____.

5. A _____ is a preliminary election held for the purpose of choosing a party's final candidate.

6. The Republican and Democratic candidates for president and vice president are nominated at each party's _____.

7. A party platform is _____.

8. Third parties have influenced American politics in several ways, including _____.

## Multiple Choice

9. _____ refers to a process in which a substantial number of voters change their political allegiance, which usually also changes the balance of power between the two major parties.
   a. Realignment   b. Dealignment   c. Tipping

10. After the election of 1896, the _____ established themselves in the minds of many Americans as the party that knew how to manage the nation's economy, and they remained dominant in national politics until the onset of the Great Depression.
    a. Democrats   b. Republicans   c. Whigs

11. Beginning with the presidential elections of 2000, the press has made much of the supposed cultural differences between the
    a. "red" states that vote for the Democratic candidate and the "blue" states that vote for the Republican candidate.
    b. "red" states that vote for the Republican candidate and the "blue" states that vote for the Democratic candidate.
    c. "scarlet" states that vote for the Republican candidate and the "gray" states that vote for the Democratic candidate.

12. After the 2010 elections, many of the new Republican members of Congress were pledged to the Tea Party philosophy of
    a. moving the Republican Party toward more liberal positions.

    b. breaking political deadlock in Washington to solve national problems.
    c. no-compromise conservatism.

13. Which of the following statements best describes the way in which political parties perform the function of balancing competing interests?
    a. The political party is usually the major institution through which the executive and legislative branches cooperate with each other.
    b. Political parties are essentially coalitions—alliances of individuals and groups with a variety of concerns and opinions who join together to support the party's platform or parts of it.
    c. Political parties take the large number of people who want to run for office and narrow the field.

14. To be a member of a political party in the United States, a citizen
    a. must join the party and pay membership dues.
    b. must support the party platform.
    c. has only to think of himself or herself as a Democrat or a Republican (or a member of a third party).

15. An issue-oriented third party
    a. supports a particular political doctrine or a set of beliefs.
    b. is formed to promote a particular cause.
    c. is also referred to as a splinter party.

# 8

# Public Opinion and Voting

**Learning Outcomes**

The **Learning Outcomes** labeled 1 through 4 are designed to help improve your understanding of the chapter. After reading this chapter, you should be able to:

**8–1** Explain how public opinion polls are conducted, problems with polls, and how they are used in the political process.

**8–2** Describe the political socialization process.

**8–3** Discuss the different factors that affect voter choices.

**8–4** Indicate some of the factors that affect voter turnout, and discuss what has been done to improve voter turnout and voting procedures.

**Remember to visit page 193 for additional Study Tools**

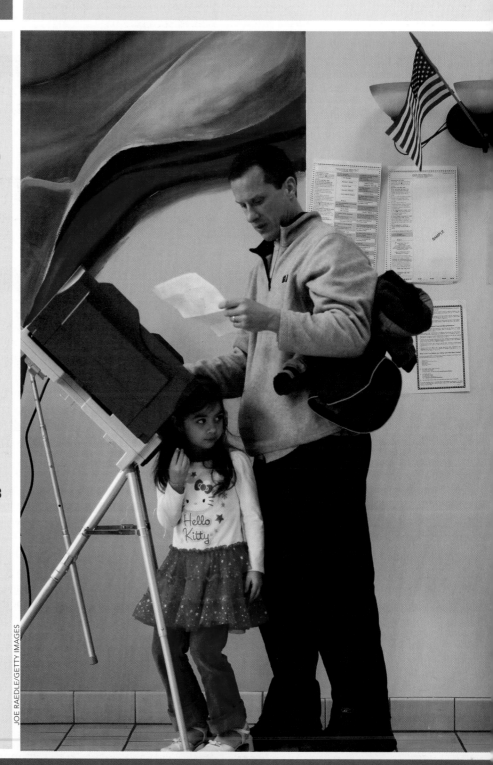

JOE RAEDLE/GETTY IMAGES

# AMERICA AT ODDS
## Should Felons Be Allowed to Vote?

As governor of Florida, Charlie Crist supported allowing felons to vote.

AP PHOTO/ALAN DIAZ

Suppose that you commit a crime that is punishable by a prison term. You serve your time and are released. You are now a felon—someone who has been convicted of a serious crime. You may believe that you have "repaid your debt to society" by going to prison, but that does not mean that all of your rights are restored after you have served your sentence. In many states, felons—ex-convicts, or ex-cons—do not have the right to vote. Many people will agree that those who are actually serving time in prison should not be able to vote. But what about those who have rejoined society?

Because America puts a larger share of its people behind bars than any other nation, the number of ex-cons is staggering. At least 13 percent of the nation's African American male population is disenfranchised. The United States takes a much harder line on this issue than most countries. Many of our allies, in fact, allow most people to vote while they are still in prison. Among our European allies, only Belgium permanently disenfranchises felons. Should such people have the right to vote?

## No One Should Be Denied the Right to Vote

Felony disenfranchisement affects almost 6 million persons in the United States. That means that 6 million Americans cannot express their political beliefs by voting. One negative result of this exclusion is racial discrimination. The percentage of African Americans who are felons is much greater than their share of the total population. The result: compared with whites, a disproportionate number of blacks are excluded from the democratic process because of state laws that prevent felons from voting.

Regardless of race, those who are convicted of felonies are disproportionately poor. By excluding many poor persons and minority group members from the voting rolls, we bias the vote. Some question how we can call ourselves a fully democratic country if we disenfranchise so many people. Those who want felons to regain the right to vote contend that our current situation is patently unfair.

## When You Break the Rules, You Lose Some Rights

No one questions the right of society to incarcerate those convicted of serious crimes. No one questions the need for punishment when individuals violate our accepted rules of behavior. Therefore, why should anyone question each state's right to prevent convicts and former convicts from exercising all of the rights enjoyed by law-abiding citizens? Felons are not the kind of people we want to choose our leaders.

Some opponents of felon enfranchisement also contend that proponents are making a mountain out of a molehill. When Florida passed a law allowing former convicts to register to vote, the results were not encouraging. Only about 10,000 out of a potential 120,000 former convicts actually registered. Those in favor of allowing felons to vote are misplacing their efforts. They should instead attempt to reduce incentives for Americans to commit crimes.

## Where do you stand?

1. Would you be in favor of allowing individuals currently in prison to be able to register to vote? Why or why not?
2. If the millions of former convicts in America could register to vote, would it make any difference? Why or why not?

## Explore this issue online

- You can find stories on felon disenfranchisement by entering the title of the story into a search engine such as Google. Type in "voting behind bars" for an article that raises the question of whether disenfranchisement is constitutional. Enter "states restore voting rights for ex-convicts" for details about the Florida experience.

# Introduction

For a democracy to be effective, members of the public must form opinions and openly express them to their elected officials. Only when the opinions of Americans are communicated effectively to elected representatives can those opinions form the basis of government action.

So public opinion is a vital component of our political system in America. But public opinion surveys are also used to examine a wide variety of attitudes and beliefs that are only indirectly related to politics. For example, a survey might seek to determine the extent of various religious beliefs in the United States so as to learn whether they have changed over time. We examine some popular attitudes in other countries in this chapter's *The Rest of the World* feature on the facing page.

public arena, such as taxes, health care, Social Security, clean-air legislation, and unemployment. When you hear a news report or read a magazine article stating that "a significant number of Americans" feel a certain way about an issue, you are probably hearing that a particular opinion is held by a large enough number of people to make government officials listen.

If public opinion is to affect public policy, then public officials must be made aware of it. They must know which issues are of current concern to Americans and how strongly people feel about those issues. They must also know when public opinion changes. Public officials commonly learn about public opinion through election results, personal contacts, interest groups, and media reports. The best way to measure public opinion between elections, however, appears to be through the use of public opinion polls.

> "A government can be no better than the
> # PUBLIC OPINION
> that sustains it."
>
> ~ FRANKLIN DELANO ROOSEVELT ~
> THIRTY-SECOND PRESIDENT
> OF THE UNITED STATES
> 1933–1945

**public opinion** The views of the citizenry about politics, public issues, and public policies; a complex collection of opinions held by many people on issues in the public arena.

**public opinion poll** A survey of the public's opinion on a particular topic at a particular moment.

**sample** In the context of opinion polling, a group of people selected to represent the population being studied.

**straw poll** A nonscientific poll in which there is no way to ensure that the opinions expressed are representative of the larger population.

**biased sample** A poll sample that does not accurately represent the population.

## 8–1 Measuring Public Opinion

What exactly is *public opinion*? How can public opinion be measured accurately? How do we form our opinions on political issues? Finally, what factors affect voter participation? Perhaps the most important way that Americans participate in their democracy is through voting—expressing their opinions in the polling places. Who may vote is therefore an important issue, as explained in this chapter's opening *America at Odds* feature.

We define **public opinion** as the sum total of a complex collection of opinions held by many people on issues in the

### 8–1a Public Opinion Polls

A **public opinion poll** is a survey of the public's opinion on a particular topic at a particular moment. The results of opinion polls are most often cast in terms of percentages: 62 percent feel this way, 31 percent do not, and 7 percent have no opinion.

Of course, a poll cannot survey the entire U.S. population. Therefore, public opinion pollsters have devised scientific polling techniques for measuring public opinion through the use of **samples**—groups of people who are typical of the general population.

### 8–1b Early Polling Efforts

Since the 1800s, magazines and newspapers have often spiced up their articles by conducting **straw polls** of readers' opinions. Straw polls simply ask a large number of people the same question. The problem with straw polls is that the opinions expressed usually represent an atypical subgroup of the population, or a **biased sample.** A survey of those who read

# THE REST OF THE WORLD

## How Foreign Countries View Each Other

As Americans, we are of course usually concerned about how the rest of the world views the United States rather than how foreign countries view each other. But let's take a look at the interesting question of how the rest of the world views countries other than our own.

### The Most Positively Viewed Nations

The world in general used to have a more positive opinion of the nations of Europe than it did of any other group of countries. According to a global poll undertaken for the British Broadcasting Corporation (BBC), however, Japan is the most positively viewed major nation today. In fact, Asian countries are viewed positively by much of the world. Many now view China in particular in a positive light.

Clearly, the economic turmoil in the European Union (EU) has influenced how other countries view that region. Just a few short years ago, polling data showed that more than 55 percent of the world saw the EU as a positive influence. Today that number is 48 percent. In contrast, China's positive-influence rating has risen to 50 percent. (The United States' rating has been stable at about 47 percent.)

### Economic Conditions Matter

Unquestionably, economic conditions in different nations are influencing people's views of foreign countries. China is now considered to be a source of prosperity. People see Europe as exporting serious trouble, however. A collapse of the euro currency could destabilize economies throughout the world. (Germany, though, with the strongest European economy, continues to collect positive reviews.)

According to the Pew Research Center's Global Attitudes Project, the economic mood is extremely downbeat throughout the world. There are exceptions: residents of Brazil, China, and Turkey are upbeat about their own national economic conditions. These countries even show an unusually high degree of enthusiasm for the free-market economic system. Europeans, Japanese, and Americans are much more pessimistic. As examples, only 2 percent of Greeks and 6 percent of Spanish and Italians believe that their national economic situations are good.

**FOR CRITICAL ANALYSIS** Why do you think that the people of China and Brazil are so optimistic?

---

*People* will most likely produce different results than a survey of those who read *Sports Illustrated*.

The most famous of all straw-polling errors was committed by the *Literary Digest* in 1936 when it tried to predict the outcome of that year's presidential elections. The *Digest* forecast that Republican Alfred Landon would easily defeat Democratic incumbent Franklin D. Roosevelt. Instead, Roosevelt won by a landslide. The editors of the *Digest* had sent mail-in cards to names in telephone directories, to its own subscribers, and to automobile owners—a staggering 2,376,000 people. In the Depression year of 1936, however, people who owned a car or a telephone or who subscribed to the *Digest* were not representative of most Americans. The vast majority of Americans could not afford such luxuries. The sample turned out to be unrepresentative and consequently inaccurate.

Several newcomers to the public opinion poll industry, however, did predict Roosevelt's victory.

Two of these organizations are still at the forefront of the polling industry today: the Gallup Organization, started by George Gallup, and Roper Associates, founded by Elmo Roper and now known as the Roper Center.

### 8–1c Polling Today

Today, polling is used extensively by political candidates and policymakers. Politicians and the news media generally place a great deal of faith in the accuracy of poll results. Polls can be quite accurate when they are conducted properly. In the

**SOCIAL MEDIA**
**In Politics**

For a storm of tweets on public opinion polling, join statistical expert Nate Silver on Twitter by following "fivethirtyeight."

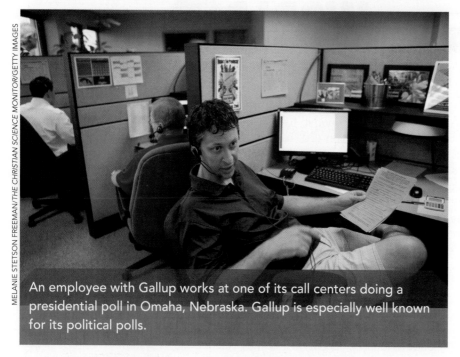

An employee with Gallup works at one of its call centers doing a presidential poll in Omaha, Nebraska. Gallup is especially well known for its political polls.

twenty presidential elections in which Gallup has participated, its polls conducted in late October correctly predicted the winner in sixteen of the twenty races.[1] Even polls taken several months in advance have been able to predict the eventual winner.

### Types of Polls
In the earliest days of scientific polling, interviewers typically went door to door locating respondents. Such in-person surveys were essential in the mid-twentieth century, when a surprisingly large number of homes did not have a telephone.

In time, however, the number of homes without phones dwindled, and polling organizations determined that they were able to obtain satisfactory samples of voters through telephone interviews alone. In recent years, poll takers have even replaced human interviewers with prerecorded messages that solicit responses. Such methods allow companies to conduct very large numbers of polls at little cost. Questions have arisen as to whether automated polling is as accurate as polling that uses live interviewers, however.

Further complications for telephone poll takers are the increase in the use of cell phones—which not all pollsters bother to call. Today, many cell phone users no longer even have a landline number. An

**random sample** In the context of opinion polling, a sample in which each person within the entire population being polled has an equal chance of being chosen.

additional problem is the public's growing use of Skype and other Internet-based telephone systems. Poll takers have not yet determined a way to integrate such users into their polls. Finally, a growing number of people simply refuse to participate in telephone surveys.

Technological advances have opened up a new possibility—the Internet survey. The Harris Poll now specializes in this type of research. As when telephone interviews were introduced, serious questions exist today as to whether the samples obtained by Harris and other Internet polling firms can be representative. Internet usage has become extremely widespread, but it is still not universal.

### Sampling
Today, the most reputable polls sample between 1,500 and 2,000 people. How can interviewing such a small group possibly indicate what millions of voters think? To be successful, a sample must consist of people who are typical of the population. If the sample is not properly chosen, then the results of the poll may not reflect the beliefs of the general population.

The most important principle in sampling is randomness. A **random sample** means that each person within the entire population being polled has an equal chance of being chosen. For example, if a poll is trying to measure how women feel about an issue, the sample should include respondents from all groups within the female population in proportion to their percentage in the entire population. A properly drawn random sample would include appropriate numbers of women in terms of age, race and ethnicity, geography, income, and religious affiliation.

### What Polls Really Tell Us
As noted earlier, poll results are almost always publicized using exact numbers. A typical result would be that 80 percent of those polled are partly or completely dissatisfied with the actions of the U.S. Congress, 12 percent are partly or completely satisfied, and 8 percent have no opinion. Figures such as these, though, can provide a misleading picture of what the poll is actually saying. Public opinion polls are fundamentally *statistical*. The true result

of a poll is not a single figure, but a range of probabilities. In the example just given, the figure 80 percent is merely the midpoint of all the possible results.

A professional polling firm might state of a given poll that it has "95 percent confidence that the maximum margin of sampling error is plus or minus 4 percentage points." (**Sampling error** is the difference between what the poll shows and what the results would have been if *everyone* in the relevant population had been interviewed.) To claim "95 percent confidence" means that there is one chance in twenty that this poll is off by four points or more. The 95 percent figure is an industry standard. That means that out of the thousands of polls released every year, 5 percent yield results that are outside their own margin of error.

It follows that there is not much point in paying attention to small, short-lived changes in polling results. Consider a polling firm's report that President Barack Obama's popularity rating was, in five consecutive weeks, 45 percent, 43 percent, 44 percent, 47 percent, and 45 percent. Do these figures mean that Obama was less popular in week two and more popular in week four? Almost certainly not. The fluctuation in the figures is most likely due to random error—it is statistical "noise."

"A popular government without popular information, or the means of acquiring it, is but

**A PROLOGUE TO A FARCE OR A TRAGEDY,**

or perhaps both."

~ JAMES MADISON ~
FOURTH PRESIDENT OF THE UNITED STATES
1809–1817

## Statistical Modeling and House Effects

Sampling error is not the only source of inaccuracy in public opinion polling. Another source of error follows from the fact that it is almost impossible to obtain a body of respondents that truly reflects the population at large. Many people refuse to be interviewed. Some kinds of people—including poor people and students—are hard to reach.

It happens that women answer the telephone more frequently than do men. Polling firms respond to these difficulties by *weighting* the responses of various groups. If the survey did not locate enough evangelical Christians, for example, the responses of the evangelicals who were contacted will be weighted more heavily. Thus, a pollster might double the numerical value of the answers provided by the evangelicals before adding the results back into the total sample. A pollster would do this if, in the initial sample, the number

of evangelicals interviewed was half what it should have been. If the model that the pollster uses to weight the responses is flawed, however, the poll results will be off as well.

**WEIGHTING DIFFICULTIES.** Weighting for purely demographic variables is a small part of the modeling problem. Errors are much more common when pollsters attempt to adjust for the number of Republicans, Democrats, and independents in their samples. Perhaps the greatest difficulty is determining who is likely to turn out and vote. In the months leading up to the 2012 elections, each major polling firm had its own model for weighting groups of respondents and determining who was a likely voter. Most of these models were trade secrets. One result of the differing models was a substantial variation in predicted results.

**HOUSE EFFECTS.** Based on their differing models, some polling firms consistently published results more favorable to one or the other of the two major parties than the results released by other pollsters. When a pollster's results appear to consistently favor one of the parties, polling experts refer to the phenomenon as a *house effect*. Not surprisingly, firms that exhibited house effects in 2012 frequently had ties to the political party favored by their results. The connection was not exact, however.

Some partisan firms did not exhibit a house effect, and some pollsters who were well known for nonpartisanship did have one. Also, a firm with a house effect is not always wrong. It may be noticing something that most of its competitors have missed. Figure 8–1 on the following page shows an example of variation in predictions by polling firms.

## Bias in Framing Questions

To obtain accurate results, poll takers also want to ensure that there is no bias in their polling questions. How a question is phrased can significantly affect how people answer it.

**sampling error** In the context of opinion polling, the difference between what the sample results show and what the true results would have been had everybody in the relevant population been interviewed.

FIGURE 8–1

# Final Poll Results for the
## 2010 California Governor's Race

The figure shows the predicted margin of victory for Democrat Jerry Brown over Republican Meg Whitman, listed by polling firm. Note that Wilson Research predicted that Whitman would win. Both Wilson and Public Policy Polling had explicit partisan identifications. In the end, Brown won a larger share of the votes than most pollsters had predicted.

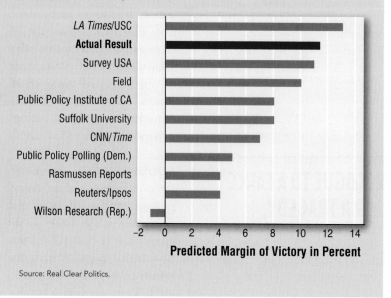

**Predicted Margin of Victory in Percent**

Source: Real Clear Politics.

Polls, in other words, came up with differing results based on whether respondents were encouraged to think about women's health or to consider religious liberties. (In the end, the administration announced a compromise that was acceptable to most church-affiliated schools and hospitals—but not the Catholic bishops, who filed a lawsuit.)

**YES AND NO QUESTIONS.** Polling questions also sometimes reduce complex issues to questions that simply call for "yes" or "no" answers. For example, a survey question might ask respondents whether they favor giving aid to foreign countries. A respondent's opinion on the issue might vary depending on the recipient country or the purpose of the aid. The poll would nonetheless force the respondent to give a "yes" or "no" answer that does not fully reflect his or her opinion.

**INADEQUATE INFORMATION.** Respondents sometimes answer "I don't know" or "I don't have enough information to answer," even when the poll does not offer such options. Interestingly, a study of how polling is conducted on the complex issue of school vouchers (school vouchers were discussed in Chapter 4) found that about 4 percent volunteered the answer "I don't know" when asked if they favored or opposed vouchers. When respondents were offered the option of answering "I haven't heard or read enough to answer," however, the proportion choosing that answer jumped to about 30 percent.[2]

In addition to potential bias in framing questions, poll takers must also be concerned about other issues that affect the reliability of their polls. For example, respondents interviewed may be influenced by the interviewer's personality or tone of voice. They may give the answer that they think will please the interviewer.

**AN EXAMPLE: THE BIRTH CONTROL CONTROVERSY.** Consider a dispute that arose in 2012. The Affordable Care Act—Obamacare—included a provision stating that qualifying employer-provided health-insurance plans should cover contraception, or birth control services. Churches opposed to contraception were exempt. The Obama administration, however, ruled that hospitals and colleges with religious affiliations were not exempt. The Catholic Church and several other bodies objected vehemently to this ruling. Republicans in Congress backed the churches.

What did the public think about the issue? Public opinion depended overwhelmingly on how the question was phrased. One poll asked whether the insurance plans of religiously affiliated institutions should be required to cover contraception. Respondents supported coverage 61 percent to 31 percent. A later poll by the same organization included the language "opt out based on religious and moral objections." This time, those interviewed agreed 57 percent to 36 percent that the institutions ought to be able to opt out.

**Timing of Polls** Opinion polls of voter preferences cannot reflect rapid shifts in public opinion unless they are taken frequently. One example of this problem was the polls taken during the presidential elections of 1980. The candidates in that year were incumbent Democratic president Jimmy Carter and Republican Ronald Reagan. Almost to the end of the campaign, polls showed Carter in the lead. Only the most capable analysts took note of the very large number of undecided voters. In the last week before the elections, these voters broke sharply for Reagan. Few polls were conducted late enough to detect this development.

**Exit Polls**  The reliability of polls was also called into question by the use of exit polls in the 2000 presidential elections. The Voter News Service (VNS)—a consortium that no longer exists—conducted polls of people exiting polling places on Election Day. These exit polls were used by the news networks to predict the winner of the Florida race—and they were wrong, not just once, but twice. First, they claimed that the Florida vote had gone to Al Gore. Then, a few hours later, they said it had gone to George W. Bush. Finally, they said the Florida race was too close to call.

In 2008, the television networks were careful about making predictions based on exit polls. It was clear early that Obama was winning, but the networks wanted viewers to keep watching, so they maintained

> "I have experienced many instances of being obliged to **change opinions,** even on important subjects, which I once thought right but found to be otherwise."
>
> ~ BENJAMIN FRANKLIN ~
> AMERICAN STATESMAN
> 1706–1790

the suspense. How well did pollsters do in predicting the outcome of the various races in the 2012 elections? We answer that question in this chapter's *Elections 2012* feature below.

**Misuse of Polls**  Today, a frequently heard complaint is that, instead of measuring public opinion, polls can end up creating it. For example, to gain popularity, a candidate might claim that all the polls show that he or she is ahead in the race. People who want to support the winner may back this candidate despite their true feelings. This is often called the "bandwagon" effect. Presidential approval ratings lend themselves to the bandwagon effect.

The media also sometimes misuse polls. Many journalists take the easy route during campaigns and base their political coverage almost exclusively on poll findings. Media companies often report only the polls conducted by their affiliated pollsters, announcing the results as the absolute truth regardless of whether the results are typical or are at serious variance with polls taken by other organizations.

## ELECTIONS 2012

## The Accuracy of the Polls in 2012

As a whole, public opinion polls did an excellent job of predicting the 2012 election results. Poll averages did show a slight lean to the Republicans, but this tendency was primarily due to the Republican bias of a handful of pollsters. These, however, included some of the biggest names in the field. Gallup, for example, seriously overestimated turnout among Republican voters and underestimated turnout among Democrats. As early voting began, it became clear that these turnout forecasts were way off. In its last poll, Gallup corrected its results by 5 points, but it still had Romney as the winner.

Rasmussen, the top Republican poll taker, treated party identification as a fixed attribute, like race or gender. When it found fewer Republicans than expected, it weighted the Republican responses more heavily.

Unfortunately, many Tea Party supporters were now identifying as independents. This switch did not change their voting preferences. Rasmussen in effect counted these respondents twice, once as Republicans and again as independents. The result was a 3-percentage point bias toward the Republicans.

Many conservative bloggers believed Gallup and Rasmussen rather than the mainstream poll takers who showed Obama ahead. Some even accused pollsters of deliberately skewing the results to encourage Democratic voters and discourage Republicans. Others contended that data-driven predictions were less worthy than the "gut feelings" of experts. Nate Silver, the *New York Times* statistics guru, was the target of many of these attacks. In the end, however, the results proved that Silver and the other polling experts were correct.

Indeed, given the diversity of results among different polling organizations, savvy political analysts look at as many different polls as they can. Experts often average the results of polls that ask a particular question. Some of them even weight these polls based on how reliable they believe each firm to be.

A useful checklist for evaluating the quality of opinion polls is presented in Table 8–1 on the right. For additional information that is useful in evaluating polls, see this chapter's *Perception versus Reality* feature on the facing page.

**The Problem of Push Polls** One tactic in political campaigns is to use **push polls,** which ask "fake" polling questions that are actually designed to "push" voters toward one candidate or another. The National Council on Public Polls describes push polls as outright political manipulation—the spreading of rumors and lies by one candidate about another. Push pollsters usually do not give their name or identify the poll's sponsor. The interviews last less than a minute, whereas legitimate pollsters typically interview a respondent for five to thirty minutes.

**AN EXAMPLE: JOHN McCAIN.** Republican presidential candidate John McCain was the target of a famous push poll in the 2000 Republican presidential primary in South Carolina. White voters were asked, "Would you be more likely or less likely to vote for John McCain for president if you knew he had fathered an illegitimate black child?" In fact, McCain and his wife had adopted a girl with a cleft palate from an orphanage in Bangladesh.

**PUSH POLLS AND LEGITIMATE POLLS.** Some researchers argue that identifying a push poll is not always straightforward, however. Political analyst Charlie Cook points out that "there are legitimate polls that can ask push questions, which test potential arguments against a rival to ascertain how effective those arguments might be in future advertising. . . . These are not only legitimate tools of survey research, but any political pollster who did not use them would be doing her or his clients a real disservice."[3]

Distinguishing between push polls and push questions, then, can be

**push poll** A campaign tactic used to feed false or misleading information to potential voters, under the guise of taking an opinion poll, with the intent to "push" voters away from one candidate and toward another.

---

### TABLE 8–1

## Checklist for Evaluating Public Opinion Polls

Because public opinion polls are so widely used by the media and policymakers, and their reliability is so often called into question, several organizations have issued guidelines for evaluating polls. Below is a list of questions that you can ask to evaluate the quality and reliability of a poll.

1. Who conducted the poll, and who sponsored or paid for it?

2. How many people were interviewed for the survey, and what part of the population did they represent?

3. How were these people chosen, and how random was the sample?

4. How were respondents contacted and interviewed? Were they questioned by a live person or by a recorded script? Were cell phone users contacted?

5. What is the margin of error for the poll?

6. Were any of the questions worded in a way that might influence the answers?

7. When was the poll conducted?

8. What other polls were conducted on this topic, and do they report similar findings?

challenging—which is usually the intent of the push pollsters. A candidate does not want to be accused of conducting push polls, because the public considers them a "dirty trick" and may turn against the candidate who uses them.

## FOR CRITICAL THINKING

Suggest some poll questions that most respondents would probably answer in the same way. Think of some others that would divide those who are being interviewed into two distinct camps.

## 8–2 How Do People Form Political Opinions?

When asked, most Americans are willing to express an opinion on political issues. Not one

**Learning Outcome 8–2**

Describe the political socialization process.

# Perception versus Reality

## The Reliability of Public Opinion Polls

Today, more than ever before, Americans are bombarded with the results of public opinion polls. If you can think of a political candidate, topic, issue, or concept, chances are that one or more public polling organizations can tell you what "Americans really think" about that candidate or topic. Polling organizations increasingly use automated telephone interviews and the Internet to conduct their polls. Because these polls are much cheaper to conduct than polls that use live interviewers, it is not surprising that more poll results are available every day.

### THE PERCEPTION

Americans who hear or read about the results of public opinion polls naturally assume that polling organizations undertook those polls in a scientific way and presented accurate results. Those who know a little bit about polling also assume that the small numbers of people polled represented a random sample.

### THE REALITY

Many "polls" are not based on a random sample, contrary to popular belief. Consider a poll published by the *Military Times* in 2008, which found that 58 percent of respondents opposed military service by openly gay individuals. Further, 10 percent claimed that they would not reenlist if the ban on openly gay service members was lifted. The press gave this survey widespread coverage without questioning its methodology. One pundit claimed, on the basis of the poll, that gay persons in the military would "destroy" the institution. In fact, the poll was not based on a random sample but on a self-selected pool of *Military Times* readers, who tended to be older and more conservative than the military as a whole.

On occasion, pollsters have been accused of issuing fraudulent reports. In 2009, polling experts accused a Georgia-based company of making up results without conducting any actual surveys. This claim was never tested in court, but immediately after the accusation was made, the firm ceased issuing polls and vanished from sight. In 2010, a polling firm was sued by its largest customer—the Daily Kos, a leading progressive blog. Kos accused the company of manufacturing its results. The case was settled out of court in 2011, with the firm paying a penalty to Kos.

Polling expert Nate Silver has released calculations of pollster-introduced error (PIE) based on general election polls dating back to 1998. PIE is the average amount of error that a pollster introduces above and beyond ordinary sampling error. Among those releasing more than fifty polls, the lowest error rates were posted by SurveyUSA (1.19), Mason-Dixon (1.57), and Gallup (1.66). The worst results were as high as 4.17.

**BLOG ON** For additional assessments of poll takers, including their performance in the 2012 elections, search on "rating polling firms nate silver."

of us, however, was born with such opinions. Most people acquire their political attitudes, opinions, beliefs, and knowledge through a complex learning process called **political socialization.** This process begins in childhood and continues throughout life.

Most political socialization is informal, and it usually begins during early childhood, when the dominant influence on a child is the family. Although parents normally do not sit down and say to their children, "Let us explain to you the virtues of becoming a Republican," their children nevertheless come to know the parents' feelings, beliefs, and attitudes. The

**political socialization**
The learning process through which most people acquire their political attitudes, opinions, beliefs, and knowledge.

strong early influence of the family later gives way to the multiple influences of school, church, peers, television, co-workers, and other groups. People and institutions that influence the political views of others are called **agents of political socialization.**

## 8–2a The Importance of Family

As just suggested, most parents or caregivers do not deliberately set out to form their children's political ideas and beliefs. They are usually more concerned with the moral, religious, and ethical values of their offspring. Yet a child first sees the political world through the eyes of his or her family, which is perhaps the most important force in political socialization. Children do not "learn" political attitudes the same way they learn to master in-line skating. Rather, they learn by hearing their parents' everyday conversations and stories about politicians and issues and by observing their parents' actions and reactions.

The family's influence is strongest when children can clearly perceive their parents' attitudes, and most can. In one study, more high school students could identify their parents' political party affiliation than their parents' other attitudes or beliefs. The political party of the parents often becomes the political party of the children, particularly if both parents support the same party.

## 8–2b Schools and Churches

Education also strongly influences an individual's political attitudes. From their earliest days in school, children learn about the American political system. They say the Pledge of Allegiance and sing patriotic songs. They celebrate national holidays, such as Presidents' Day and Veterans' Day, and learn about the history and

HILL STREET STUDIOS/BLEND IMAGES/CORBIS

Family support for going to college often matters.

symbols associated with them. In the upper grades, young people acquire more knowledge about government and democratic procedures through civics classes and participation in student government and various clubs. They also learn citizenship skills through school rules and regulations. Generally, those with more education have more knowledge about politics and policy than those with less education. The level of education also influences a person's political values, as will be discussed later in this chapter.

A majority of Americans hold strong religious beliefs, and these attitudes can also contribute significantly to political socialization. For example, if a family's church emphasizes that society has a collective obligation to care for the poor, the children in that family may be influenced in a liberal direction. If the church instead depicts the government as irreligious and morally threatening, children will receive a conservative message.

## 8–2c The Media

The **media**—newspapers, magazines, television, radio, and the Internet—also have an impact on political socialization. The most influential of these media is television, which continues to be a leading source of political information for older voters. As explained later in this chapter, older citizens turn out to vote significantly more often than younger ones.

Some contend that the media's role in shaping public opinion has increased to the point that the media are as influential as the family, particularly

**agents of political socialization** People and institutions that influence the political views of others.

**media** Newspapers, magazines, television, radio, the Internet, and any other printed or electronic means of communication.

among high school students. For example, in her analysis of the media's role in American politics, media scholar Doris A. Graber points out that high school students, when asked where they obtain the information on which they base their attitudes, mention the Internet and social media far more than they mention their families, friends, and teachers.[4]

Other studies have shown that the media's influence on people's opinions may not be as great as some have thought. Generally, people go online, watch television, or read articles with preconceived ideas about the issues. These preconceived ideas act as a kind of perceptual screen that blocks out information that is not consistent with those ideas. Generally, the media tend to wield the most influence over the views of persons who have not yet formed opinions about various issues or candidates. (See Chapter 10 for a more detailed discussion of the media's role in American politics.)

## 8–2d Opinion Leaders

Every state or community has well-known citizens who are able to influence the opinions of their fellow citizens. These people may be public officials, religious leaders, teachers, or celebrities. They are the people to whom others listen and from whom others draw ideas and convictions about various issues of public concern. These opinion leaders play a significant role in the formation of public opinion.

Opinion leaders often include politicians or former politicians. For example, President Barack Obama asked former U.S. presidents George W. Bush (2001–2009) and Bill Clinton (1993–2001) to lead a nationwide fund-raising drive following the January 2010 earthquake in Haiti, which destroyed much of that country.

Sometimes, however, opinion leaders can fall from grace when they express views radically different from what most Americans believe. One example is former president Jimmy Carter (1977–1981), who lost much popularity after he published a book that harshly criticized Israel's actions toward the Palestinians.[5] (Most Americans of both parties are strongly pro-Israel.)

## 8–2e Major Life Events

Often, the political attitudes of an entire generation of Americans are influenced by a major event. For example, the Great Depression (1929–1939), the most severe economic depression in modern U.S. history, persuaded many Americans who lived through it

that the federal government should step in when the economy is in decline. A substantial number of voters came to believe that the New Deal programs and policies of President Franklin Roosevelt showed that the Democratic Party was concerned about the fate of ordinary people, and so they became supporters of that party.

The generation that lived through World War II (1939–1945) tends to believe that American intervention in foreign affairs is good. In contrast, the generation that came of age during the Vietnam War (1965–1975) is more skeptical of American interventionism. A national tragedy, such as the terrorist attacks of September 11, 2001, is also likely to influence the political attitudes of a generation, though in what way is difficult to predict. The recent Great Recession and the financial crisis that struck in September 2008 will surely affect popular attitudes in years to come.

## 8–2f Peer Groups

Once children enter school, the views of friends begin to influence their attitudes and beliefs. From junior high school on, the **peer group**—friends, classmates, co-workers, club members, or religious group members—becomes a significant factor in the political socialization process.

Most of this socialization occurs when the peer group is involved with political activities or other causes. For example, your political beliefs might be influenced by a peer group with which you are working on a common cause, such as cleaning up a local river bank or campaigning for a favorite candidate. Your political beliefs probably would not be as strongly influenced by peers with whom you snowboard regularly or attend concerts.

## 8–2g Economic Status and Occupation

A person's economic status may influence her or his political views. For example, poorer people are more likely to favor government assistance programs. On an issue such as abortion, lower-income people are more likely to be conservative—that is, to be against abortion—than are higher-income groups (of course, there are many exceptions).

**peer group** Associates, often close in age to one another; may include friends, classmates, co-workers, club members, or religious group members. Peer group influence is a significant factor in the political socialization process.

Where a person works also affects her or his opinions. Co-workers who spend a great deal of time working together tend to influence one another. For example, labor union members working together for a company may have similar political opinions, at least on issues of government involvement in the economy. Individuals working for a nonprofit agency that depends on government funds will tend to support government spending in that area. Business managers are more likely to favor tax laws helpful to businesses than are factory workers.

**FOR CRITICAL THINKING**

*Thinking about your own life, what sources of political socialization were most important to you? How did they influence your beliefs?*

## 8–3 Why People Vote as They Do

**LearningOutcome 8–3**

Discuss the different factors that influence voter choices.

What prompts some citizens to vote Republican and others to vote Democratic? What persuades voters to choose certain kinds of candidates? Researchers have collected more information on voting than on any other form of political participation in the United States. These data shed some light on why people decide to vote for particular candidates.

### 8–3a Party Identification

Many voters have a standing allegiance to a political party, or a party identification, although the proportion of the population that does so has fallen in recent decades. For established voters, party identification is one of the most important and lasting predictors of how a person will vote. Party identification is an emotional attachment to a party that is influenced by family, age, peer groups, and other factors that play a role in the political socialization process discussed earlier.

A large number of voters call themselves independents. Despite this label, many independents actually support one or the other of the two major parties quite regularly.

### 8–3b Perception of the Candidates

Voters often base their decisions on the perceived character of the candidates rather than on their qualifications or policy positions. Such perceptions were important in 2010. Following the elections, many political analysts concluded that the Republican Party had forfeited two to three U.S. Senate races by nominating Tea Party–supported candidates that were regarded by many voters as "too extreme." This perception was, to a large extent, based not on the political positions taken by the candidates, but on personality traits.

In Delaware, for example, it appeared that moderate Republican Mike Castle, a former governor, was sure to win the Senate seat previously held by Vice President Joe Biden. Castle, however, was defeated in the Republican primary by Tea Party favorite Christine O'Donnell. Even before the primary, O'Donnell's former campaign manager accused the candidate of diverting campaign funds to personal use. The state Republican Party chair stated that O'Donnell was either "unhinged" or a "liar." A low point was the revelation that as a young woman, O'Donnell had dabbled in witchcraft. In November, Democratic candidate Chris Coons scored a 17-percentage-point victory.

### 8–3c Policy Choices

When people vote for candidates who share their positions on particular issues, they are engaging in policy voting. If a candidate for senator in your state opposes gun control laws, for example, and you decide to vote for him or her for that reason, you have engaged in policy voting.

Historically, economic issues have had the strongest influence on voters' choices. When the economy is doing well, it is very difficult for a challenger, particularly at the presidential level, to defeat the incumbent. In contrast, when the country is experiencing inflation, rising unemployment, or high interest rates, the incumbent will likely be at a disadvantage. The main issue in the elections of 2008, 2010, and 2012 was the financial crisis facing Americans.

Some of the most heated debates in American political campaigns have involved social issues, such as abortion, gay and lesbian rights, the death penalty, and religion in the schools. Often, presidential candidates prefer to avoid emphasizing their stand on these types of issues, because voters who have strong opinions about such issues are likely to be offended if a candidate does not share their views.

## 8-3d Socioeconomic Factors

Some factors that influence how people vote can be described as socioeconomic. These factors include educational attainment, occupation and income, age, gender, religion and ethnicity, and geographic location. Some of these factors have to do with the circumstances into which individuals are born. Others have to do with personal choices. Figure 8–2 on the following page shows how various groups voted in the 2012 presidential elections.

**Educational Attainment** As a general rule, people with more education are more likely to vote Republican, although, in recent years, voters with postgraduate degrees have tended to vote Democratic. Educational attainment, of course, can be linked to income level. Recent studies show that among students from families with income in the bottom fifth of the population, only 12 percent earn a bachelor's degree by the age of twenty-four. In the top fifth, the figure is 73 percent.

**Occupation and Income** Businesspersons tend to vote Republican and have done so for many years. This is understandable, given the pro-business stand traditionally adopted by that party. Recently, professionals (such as attorneys, professors, and physicians) have been more likely to vote Democratic than in earlier years. It appears that institutional and social changes have made it less likely that professionals will see themselves as small businesspersons or identify with business interests.

Manual laborers, factory workers, and especially union members are more likely to vote for the Democrats, who have a history of pro-labor positions.

In the past, the higher the income, the more likely it was that a person would vote Republican. Conversely, a much larger percentage of low-income individuals voted Democratic. But this pattern is also breaking down. (For more on this topic, see the *Perception versus Reality* feature on page 154 in Chapter 7.)

"In politics, an organized minority is

# A POLITICAL MAJORITY."

~ REV. JESSE JACKSON ~
CIVIL RIGHTS ACTIVIST
1941–PRESENT

**Age** The conventional wisdom is that the young are liberal and the old are conservative. Certainly, younger voters were unusually supportive of Barack Obama in the 2008 and 2012 elections. Yet in years past, age differences in support for the parties have often been quite small.

One age-related effect is that people's attitudes are shaped by the events that unfolded as they grew up. Many voters who came of age during Franklin Roosevelt's New Deal held on to a preference for the Democrats. Voters who were young when Ronald Reagan was president have had a tendency to prefer the Republicans. Younger voters are noticeably more liberal on one set of issues, however—those dealing with the rights of minorities, women, and gay males and lesbians.

**Gender** Until about thirty years ago, there seemed to be no fixed pattern of voter preferences by gender in presidential elections. Women and men tended to vote for the various candidates in roughly equal numbers. Some political analysts believe that a **gender gap** became a major determinant of voter decision making in the 1980 presidential elections, however. In that year, Ronald Reagan outdrew Jimmy Carter by 16 percentage points among male voters, whereas women gave about an equal number of votes to each candidate. In the years since, the gender gap has been a continuing phenomenon. For example, Barack Obama carried the female vote by 55 to 44 percentage points, while losing the male vote by a 45 to 52 percent margin.

The modern feminist movement and the recognition that women have suffered from various types of discrimination doubtless have something to do with the gender gap. It also appears, however, that compared with men, women on average have a stronger commitment to the liberal value of the common welfare and a weaker belief in the conservative value of self-reliance.

**Religion and Ethnic Background** A century ago, at least in the northern states, white Catholic voters were likely to be Democrats, and white Protestant voters were

**gender gap** The difference between the percentage of votes cast for a particular candidate by women and the percentage of votes cast for the same candidate by men.

FIGURE 8-2

# Voting by Groups
## in the 2012 Presidential Elections

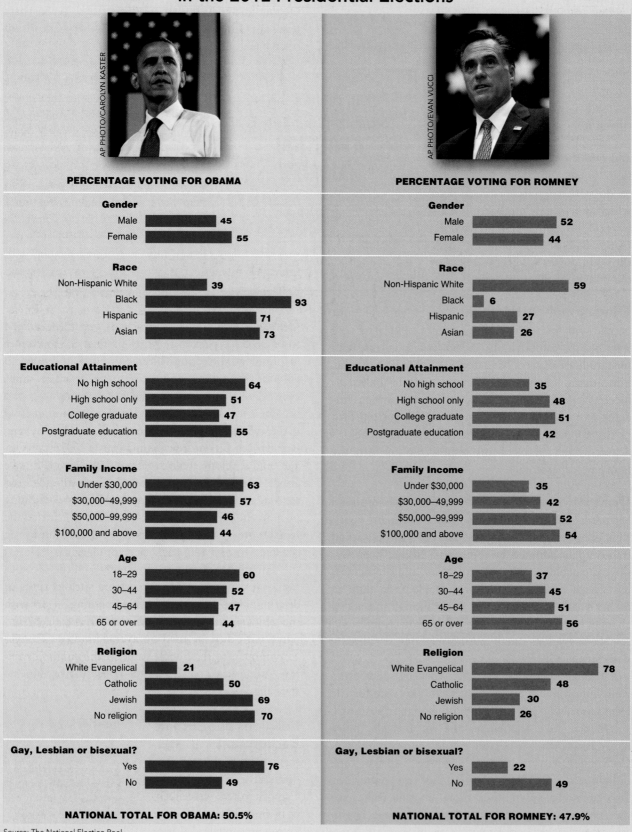

**PERCENTAGE VOTING FOR OBAMA**

**Gender**
| | |
|---|---|
| Male | 45 |
| Female | 55 |

**Race**
| | |
|---|---|
| Non-Hispanic White | 39 |
| Black | 93 |
| Hispanic | 71 |
| Asian | 73 |

**Educational Attainment**
| | |
|---|---|
| No high school | 64 |
| High school only | 51 |
| College graduate | 47 |
| Postgraduate education | 55 |

**Family Income**
| | |
|---|---|
| Under $30,000 | 63 |
| $30,000–49,999 | 57 |
| $50,000–99,999 | 46 |
| $100,000 and above | 44 |

**Age**
| | |
|---|---|
| 18–29 | 60 |
| 30–44 | 52 |
| 45–64 | 47 |
| 65 or over | 44 |

**Religion**
| | |
|---|---|
| White Evangelical | 21 |
| Catholic | 50 |
| Jewish | 69 |
| No religion | 70 |

**Gay, Lesbian or bisexual?**
| | |
|---|---|
| Yes | 76 |
| No | 49 |

**NATIONAL TOTAL FOR OBAMA: 50.5%**

**PERCENTAGE VOTING FOR ROMNEY**

**Gender**
| | |
|---|---|
| Male | 52 |
| Female | 44 |

**Race**
| | |
|---|---|
| Non-Hispanic White | 59 |
| Black | 6 |
| Hispanic | 27 |
| Asian | 26 |

**Educational Attainment**
| | |
|---|---|
| No high school | 35 |
| High school only | 48 |
| College graduate | 51 |
| Postgraduate education | 42 |

**Family Income**
| | |
|---|---|
| Under $30,000 | 35 |
| $30,000–49,999 | 42 |
| $50,000–99,999 | 52 |
| $100,000 and above | 54 |

**Age**
| | |
|---|---|
| 18–29 | 37 |
| 30–44 | 45 |
| 45–64 | 51 |
| 65 or over | 56 |

**Religion**
| | |
|---|---|
| White Evangelical | 78 |
| Catholic | 48 |
| Jewish | 30 |
| No religion | 26 |

**Gay, Lesbian or bisexual?**
| | |
|---|---|
| Yes | 22 |
| No | 49 |

**NATIONAL TOTAL FOR ROMNEY: 47.9%**

Source: The National Election Pool.

Barack Obama supporters hold signs during a "Women's Rally for the Change We Need" in Coral Gables, Florida. Was there a gender gap in the 2012 voting?

tend to favor the Democrats, although Vietnamese Americans are strongly Republican.

**MUSLIM AMERICANS.** Muslim Americans are an interesting example of changing preferences. In 2000, a majority of Muslims of Middle Eastern background voted Republican because of Islamic cultural conservatism. Today, Muslims are the most Democratic religious group in the nation. Anti-Muslim campaigns by certain conservative groups appear to be a major cause of this transformation.

**Geographic Region** In today's presidential contests, states in the South, the Great Plains, and parts of the Rocky Mountains are strongly Republican. The Northeast, the West Coast, and Illinois are firmly Democratic. Many of the swing states that decide elections are located in the Midwest, although several Rocky Mountain states swing between the parties as well.

This pattern is an almost complete reversal of the one that existed a century ago. In those years, most white southerners were Democrats, and people spoke of the **Solid South**—solidly Democratic, that is. The Solid South lasted for a century after the Civil War and in large part was the result of southern resentment of the Republicans for their role in the "War between the States" and their support of African Americans in the postwar era. At the end of the nineteenth century, the Republicans were strong in the Northeast and much of the Midwest, while the Democrats were able to find support outside the South in the Great Plains and the Far West.

The ideologies of the two parties have likewise undergone something of a reversal. One hundred years ago, the Democrats were seen as *less* likely than the Republicans to support government intervention in the economy. The Democrats were also the party that opposed civil rights. Today, the Democrats are often regarded as the party that supports "big government" and affirmative action programs.

probably Republicans. There are a few places around the country where this pattern continues to hold, but for the most part, white Catholics are now almost as likely as their Protestant neighbors to support the Republicans.

**REGULAR CHURCH ATTENDANCE.** In recent years, a different religious variable has become important in determining voting behavior. Regardless of their denomination, white Christian voters who attend church regularly have favored the Republicans by substantial margins. White voters who attend church rarely or who find religion less important in their lives are more likely to vote Democratic.

Although some churches do promote liberal ways of thinking, the number of churches that promote conservative values is much larger. Jewish voters are strongly Democratic, regardless of whether they attend services.

**AFRICAN AMERICANS.** Most African Americans are Protestants, but African Americans are one of the most solidly Democratic constituencies in the United States. This is a complete reversal of the circumstances that existed a century ago. As noted in Chapter 7, for many years after the Civil War, those African Americans who could vote were overwhelmingly Republican. Not until President Franklin Roosevelt's New Deal did black voters begin to turn to the Democrats.

Latino voters have supported the Democrats by margins of about two to one, with some exceptions: Cuban Americans are strongly Republican. Asian Americans

> **Solid South** A term used to describe the tendency of the southern states to vote Democratic after the Civil War.

### 8-3e Ideology

Ideology is another indicator of voting behavior. A significant percentage of Americans today identify themselves as conservatives. Recent polls indicate that 40 percent of Americans consider themselves to be conservatives, 21 percent consider themselves liberals, and 35 percent identify themselves as moderates.

For many Americans, where they fall in the political spectrum is a strong indicator of how they will vote: liberals and some moderates vote for Democrats, and conservatives vote for Republicans. The large numbers of Americans who fall in the political center do not adhere strictly to an ideology. In most elections, the candidates compete aggressively for these voters because they know their "base"—on the political left or right—is secure.

**The Vital Center** In 1949, historian Arthur Schlesinger, Jr., described the position between the political extremes as the **vital center.** The center is vital because without it, necessary compromises may be difficult, if not impossible, to achieve. One problem with activating the vital center is that voter apathy and low voter turnout are found most commonly among those in the center. The most motivated voters are the "ideologically zealous."[6]

**Ideology in Recent Elections** In 2008, Barack Obama swept the liberal vote, won a majority among moderates, and even captured 20 percent of the vote of self-identified conservatives. In the 2010 midterm elections, Democrats continued to win the liberal vote, but their support among moderates and conservatives fell by several points. What really contributed to the Republican wave in that year, however, was turnout.

> ## "WHENEVER A FELLOW TELLS ME HE IS BIPARTISAN, I know he is going to vote against me."
>
> ~ HARRY TRUMAN ~
> THIRTY-THIRD PRESIDENT
> OF THE UNITED STATES
> 1945–1953

As noted earlier in this text, the result was a large number of new Republican members of Congress, many elected with Tea Party support, who were pledged to resist all compromise. Also, many moderate Democratic candidates were defeated in 2010. The subsequent severe polarization in Congress and in American politics generally made it hard for the vital center to play a role. Its absence was mourned by many in the press and in the public at large.

**IDEOLOGY AND THE 2012 ELECTIONS.** Observers have remarked that Americans often voice conservative, small-government principles even as they defend the specific benefits that government provides. In 2011 and 2012, House Republicans endorsed long-term budget plans that would dramatically scale back federal support for Medicaid and privatize Medicare for anyone currently under the age of fifty-five. These plans and other Republican steps alarmed independent voters. Fears about what the Republicans might do to entitlement programs now counterbalanced concerns about Democratic affection for "big government." The result was an election that promised to be very close, especially given that the state of the economy predicted a close election as well.

## FOR CRITICAL THINKING

*For what reasons might Cuban Americans and Vietnamese Americans be more conservative than members of other minority groups?*

**vital center** The center of the political spectrum; those who hold moderate political views. The center is vital because without it, it may be difficult, if not impossible, to reach the compromises that are necessary to a political system's continuity.

**THE CONSERVATIVE TRIUMPH.** The only ideological category to display a large increase in turnout compared with earlier midterm elections was "conservative Republican." Even moderate Republicans did not vote significantly more than in the past.

## 8-4 Voting and Voter Turnout

Voting is arguably the most important way in which citizens participate in the political process. Because we do not live in a direct democracy,

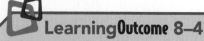

### LearningOutcome 8-4

Indicate some of the factors that affect voter turnout, and discuss what has been done to improve voter turnout and voting procedures.

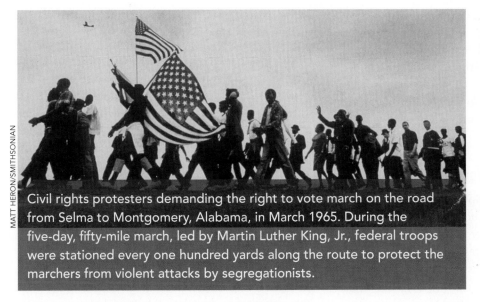

Civil rights protesters demanding the right to vote march on the road from Selma to Montgomery, Alabama, in March 1965. During the five-day, fifty-mile march, led by Martin Luther King, Jr., federal troops were stationed every one hundred yards along the route to protect the marchers from violent attacks by segregationists.

## 8-4a Factors Affecting Voter Turnout

If voting is so important, then why do so many Americans fail to exercise their right to vote? Why is *voter turnout*— the percentage of those who actually turn out to vote from among those eligible to vote— relatively low? As you will read shortly, in the past, legal restrictions based on income, gender, race, and other factors kept a number of people from voting. In the last decades of the twentieth century, these restrictions were almost completely eliminated, and yet voter turnout in presidential elections still hovered around 55 percent, as shown in Figure 8–3 below. In the last three presidential elections, however, turnout reached or exceeded 60 percent—a welcome, if modest, improvement.

According to a Pew Research Center survey, one of the reasons for low voter turnout is that many

Americans use the vote to elect politicians to represent their interests, values, and opinions in government. In many states, public-policy decisions—for example, access to medical marijuana—are also decided by voters through referendums and initiatives. Our right to vote also helps keep elected officials accountable because they must face reelection.

## FIGURE 8-3 — Voter Turnout since 1968

The figures in this chart show voter turnout as a percentage of the population that is eligible to vote.

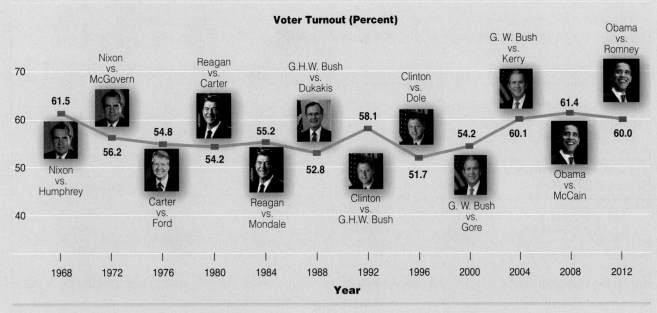

Sources: *Statistical Abstract of the United States*, various issues; the Committee for the Study of the American Electorate; and authors' updates.

nonvoters (close to 40 percent) do not feel that they have a duty to vote. The survey also found that nearly 70 percent of nonvoters said that they did not vote because they lacked information about the candidates.[7] Finally, some people believe that their vote will not make any difference, so they do not bother to become informed about the candidates and issues or go to the polls.

## 8–4b The Legal Right to Vote

In the United States today, citizens who are at least eighteen years of age and who are not felons have the right to vote. This was not always true, however. Recall from Chapter 5 that restrictions on *suffrage,* the legal right to vote, have existed since the founding of our nation. Expanding the right to vote has been an important part of the gradual democratization of the American electoral process. Table 8–2 below summarizes the major amendments, Supreme Court decisions, and laws that extended the right to vote to various American groups.

**Historical Restrictions on Voting**   Those who drafted the Constitution left the power to set suffrage qualifications to the individual states. Most states limited suffrage to adult white males who owned property, but these restrictions were challenged early on in the history of the republic. By 1828, laws restricting the right to vote to Christians were abolished in all states, and property ownership and tax-payment requirements gradually began to disappear as well. By 1850, all white males were allowed to vote. Restrictions based on race and gender continued, however.

The Fifteenth Amendment, ratified in 1870, guaranteed suffrage to African American males. Yet, for many decades, African Americans were effectively denied the ability to exercise their voting rights. Using methods ranging from mob violence to

### TABLE 8–2

### Extension of the Right to Vote

| Year | Action | Impact |
| --- | --- | --- |
| 1870 | Fifteenth Amendment | Discrimination based on race outlawed. |
| 1920 | Nineteenth Amendment | Discrimination based on gender outlawed. |
| 1924 | Congressional act | All Native Americans given citizenship. |
| 1944 | *Smith v. Allwright* | Supreme Court prohibits white primary. |
| 1957 | Civil Rights Act of 1957 | Justice Department can sue to protect voting rights in various states. |
| 1960 | Civil Rights Act of 1960 | Courts authorized to appoint referees to assist voter-registration procedures. |
| 1961 | Twenty-third Amendment | Residents of District of Columbia given right to vote for president and vice president. |
| 1964 | Twenty-fourth Amendment | Poll tax in national elections outlawed. |
| 1965 | Voting Rights Act of 1965 | Literacy tests prohibited; federal voter registrars authorized in seven southern states. |
| 1970 | Voting Rights Act Amendments of 1970 | Voting age for federal elections reduced to eighteen years; maximum thirty-day residency required for presidential elections; state literacy tests abolished. |
| 1971 | Twenty-sixth Amendment | Minimum voting age reduced to eighteen for all elections. |
| 1975 | Voting Rights Act Amendments of 1975 | Federal voter registrars authorized in ten more states; bilingual ballots to be used in certain circumstances. |
| 1982 | Voting Rights Act Amendments of 1982 | Extended provisions of Voting Rights Act Amendments of 1970 and 1975; private parties allowed to sue for violations. |
| 2006 | Voting Rights Act extension | Extended Voting Rights Act for another twenty-five years. |

© CENGAGE LEARNING

economic restrictions, groups of white southerners kept black Americans from voting.

Some states required citizens to pass **literacy tests** and to answer complicated questions about government and history before they could register to vote. Registrars made sure that African Americans would always fail such tests. The **poll tax**, a fee of several dollars, was another device used to discourage African Americans from voting. At the time, this tax was a sizable burden, not only for most blacks but also for poor whites.

Another restriction was the **grandfather clause,** which had the effect of restricting voting rights to those whose ancestors had voted before the 1860s. This technique was prohibited by the United States Supreme Court in 1915.[8]

Still another voting barrier was the **white primary**—African Americans were prohibited from voting in Democratic primary elections. The Supreme Court initially upheld this practice on the grounds that the political parties were private entities, not public, and thus could do as they wished. Eventually, in 1944, the Court banned the use of white primaries.[9]

**Voting Rights Today**   Today, these devices for restricting voting rights are explicitly outlawed by constitutional amendments and by the Voting Rights Act of 1965, as discussed in Chapter 5. Furthermore, the Nineteenth Amendment gave women the right to vote in 1920. In 1971, the Twenty-sixth Amendment reduced the minimum voting age to eighteen.

Some restrictions on voting rights still exist. Every state except North Dakota requires voters to register with the appropriate state or local officials before voting. Residency requirements are also usually imposed for voting. Since 1970, however, no state can impose a residency requirement of more than thirty days. Twenty-five states require that length of time, while the other twenty-five states require fewer or no days.

Another voting requirement is citizenship. Noncitizens may not vote in any public election held anywhere in the United States. (Until the early twentieth century, several states allowed noncitizens to cast ballots.) Most states also do not permit prison inmates, mentally ill people, felons, or election-law violators to vote. (See the feature on page 171.)

## 8–4c Attempts to Improve Voter Turnout

Attempts to improve voter turnout typically have a partisan dimension. This is because the kinds of people who find it difficult to register to vote tend to be disproportionately Democratic in their sympathies.

Many, for example, are African Americans, a reliably Democratic voting bloc. As a result, Republicans are generally wary of efforts to make registration easier.

For example, most Republicans opposed the passage of the National Voter Registration Act (the "Motor Voter Law") of 1993, which simplified the voter-registration process. The act requires states to provide all eligible citizens with the opportunity to register to vote when they apply for or renew a driver's license. The law also requires that states allow mail-in registration. Forms are available at public assistance agencies. The law, which took effect in 1995, has facilitated millions of registrations.

In 1998, Oregon voters approved a ballot initiative requiring that all elections in that state, including presidential elections, be conducted exclusively by mail. In the 2012 presidential elections, 65 percent of Oregonians eligible to vote cast ballots, a figure that is somewhat higher than the national average but not exceptionally so.

Some argue that if mail-in voting were allowed nationwide, voter turnout would increase. Others believe that voting by mail has a number of disadvantages, including greater possibilities for voter fraud. We examine whether voter fraud is a serious issue in the *Join the Debate* feature on the following page.

## 8–4d Attempts to Improve Voting Procedures

Because of serious problems in achieving accurate vote counts in recent elections, particularly in the 2000 presidential elections, steps have been taken to attempt to ensure more accuracy in the voting process. In 2002, Congress passed the Help America Vote Act, which, among other things, provided funds to the states to help them purchase new electronic voting equipment.

**literacy test** A test given to voters to ensure that they could read and write and thus evaluate political information. This technique was used in many southern states to restrict African American participation in elections.

**poll tax** A fee of several dollars that had to be paid before a person could vote. This device was used in some southern states to discourage African Americans and low-income whites from voting.

**grandfather clause** A clause in a state law that had the effect of restricting the franchise (voting rights) to those whose ancestors had voted before the 1860s. It was one of the techniques used in the South to prevent African Americans from exercising their right to vote.

**white primary** A primary election in which African Americans were prohibited from voting. The practice was banned by the Supreme Court in 1944.

## JOIN THE DEBATE

## Voter Fraud—A Real Problem or Much Ado about Nothing?

Cries of voter fraud came from the Democrats in 2000. The Democrats believed that votes were handled improperly in Florida and that this kept Democratic presidential candidate Al Gore from carrying the state and winning the presidency. In 2008, accusations of voter fraud became a major campaign issue when Republican John McCain claimed that a group called Acorn was "on the verge of maybe perpetrating one of the greatest frauds in voter history." Acorn, since dissolved, was a nonprofit group that advocated for the poor.

### Voter Fraud Is a Real Problem

Many Americans believe that voter fraud is a significant problem. For example, when Acorn mounted a voter-registration drive in 2008, some of its employees handed in registration forms that bore the names of cartoon characters and out-of-state major-league athletes. The Election Assistance Commission issued a report indicating that the extent of voter fraud is still open to debate. Lapses in enforcing voting and registration rules continue to occur. Thousands upon thousands of ineligible voters are allowed to vote. Many felons—who are not allowed to vote in most states—end up voting anyway. The only effective method of reducing voter fraud is to require photo IDs at polling places, as is done in such states as Indiana.

### Voter Fraud Is a Myth

Political analyst Harold Meyerson of the *Los Angeles Times* wrote, "Voter fraud is a myth—not an urban or a real myth, as such, but a Republican one." Voter fraud is not a serious problem today. Rather, the Republicans have raised the specter of voter fraud in order to pass laws, such as those requiring photo IDs, that make it harder for disadvantaged persons (mostly Democrats) to vote.

Strictly speaking, the Acorn problem was not voter fraud, but registration fraud. Voter fraud would occur only if someone using the name Mickey Mouse actually turned up at the polls and tried to vote. Acorn fired the offending employees and argued that state laws required it to hand in even obviously bogus registration forms, which it had marked as suspect.

**FOR CRITICAL ANALYSIS** Why might people who find it harder to register and vote tend to support the Democratic Party?

A young voter receives instructions on the new voting procedures as he confirms his voter registration with a signature.

AP PHOTO/MANUEL BALCE CENETA

Concerns about the possibility of fraudulent manipulation of electronic voting machines then replaced the worries over inaccurate vote counts caused by the previous equipment.

**Problems in 2006** In the 2006 elections, about half of the states that were using new electronic voting systems reported problems. Some systems "flipped" votes from the selected candidate to the opposing candidate. In one Florida district, about eighteen thousand votes apparently were unrecorded by electronic equipment, and this may have changed

A retired Army veteran makes his way to the voting booth in Columbia, South Carolina, as a line of voters snakes through the cafeteria behind him.

AP PHOTO/BRETT FLASHNICK

the outcome of a congressional race. Many experts have demanded that electronic systems create a "paper trail," so that machine errors can be tracked and fixed.

### Voting Systems in Recent Elections

Because of problems with electronic systems, fewer polling places used them in 2008 and 2010. Indeed, more than half of all votes cast in these years used old-fashioned paper ballots. As a result, vote counting was slow.

In 2012, the development of voter-verified paper audit trail (VVPAT) printers led to the reintroduction of electronic machines in many states. Often, a limited number of such machines were installed to serve voters with disabilities. Two-thirds of all votes nationwide, however, were still cast using paper ballots. In seventeen states, some or all of the votes were cast through electronic devices that lacked a paper audit trail. A full quarter of all votes were cast using these questionable systems.[10]

One feature of the elections was the large number of states that allowed early voting at polling places that opened weeks before Election Day. A benefit of early voting was that it allowed election workers time to ensure that all systems were working properly by Election Day.

### 8–4e Who Actually Votes

Just because an individual is eligible to vote does not necessarily mean that the person will go to the polls on Election Day and vote. Why do some eligible voters go to the polls while others do not? Although nobody can answer this question with absolute conviction, certain factors appear to affect voter turnout.

### Educational Attainment

Among the factors affecting voter turnout, education appears to be the most important. The more education a person has, the more likely it is that she or he will be a regular voter. People who graduated from high school vote more regularly than those who dropped out, and college graduates vote more often than high school graduates.

### Income Level and Age

Differences in income also lead to differences in voter turnout. Wealthy people tend to be over-represented among regular voters. Generally, older voters turn out to vote more regularly than younger voters do, although participation tends to decline among the very elderly. Participation likely increases with age because older people tend to be more settled, are already registered, and have had more experience with voting.

### Minority Status

Racial and ethnic minorities traditionally have been underrepresented among the ranks of voters. In several recent elections, however, participation by these groups, particularly African Americans and Hispanics, has increased. In part because the number of Latino citizens has grown rapidly, the increase in the Hispanic vote has been even larger than the increase in the black vote.

### Immigration and Voter Turnout

The United States has experienced high rates of immigration in recent decades, and that has had an effect on voter-turnout figures. In the past, voter turnout was often expressed as a percentage of the **voting-age population,** the number of people residing in the United States who are at least eighteen years old. Due to legal and illegal immigration, however, there are many people of voting age who are not eligible to vote because they are not citizens. Millions more cannot vote because they are felons. Additionally, the voting-age population excludes Americans abroad, who are eligible to cast absentee ballots.

**voting-age population**
The number of people residing in the United States who are at least eighteen years old.

Today, political scientists calculate the **vote-eligible population,** the number of people who are actually entitled to vote in American elections. They have found that there may be 20 million fewer eligible voters than the voting-age population suggests. Therefore, voter turnout is actually greater than the percentages sometimes cited.

Some experts have argued that the relatively low levels of voter turnout often reported for the years between 1972 and 2000 were largely due to immigration.[11] Beginning in 2004, voter turnout has improved by any calculation method.

## AMERICA AT ODDS Public Opinion and Voting

Public opinion polls reveal that Americans are in broad agreement on many issues, such as the basic political structure of our nation. Nevertheless, polls also report that Americans are at odds with one another on many other issues. After all, the questions posed by poll takers are typically divisive ones. Issues surrounding who votes and why can also be contentious. Some examples include the following:

- Is the disenfranchisement of felons a form of racial discrimination—or a rational part of the punishment process?

- Given that historical events shape popular attitudes toward the parties, when all is said and done, will the impact of the Great Recession benefit one of the major parties—or will the effects of the recession prove trivial?

- Should legislators follow public opinion as faithfully as they can—or, as the Democrats did on health-care reform, should lawmakers do what they think is best for the country regardless of the polls?

- We discussed push polls on page 178. Should push polls be banned—or would that violate First Amendment guarantees of free speech?

- Should voters be more concerned with the policy positions of the presidential candidates—or are the presidential candidates' personalities and personal characteristics of equal or greater concern?

## TAKE ACTION

"Citizens at the polls are the most powerful agents of change." Thus say political analysts Thomas Mann and Norman Ornstein.[12] But if citizens are not informed about the political issues of the day or the candidates' qualifications, there is little sense in going to the polls.

Indeed, as mentioned in this chapter, one of the reasons for the relatively low voter turnout in this country is a sense on the part of some citizens that they lack information. As also noted, peer groups are important in the political socialization process. But just as you might be influenced by your peers, you can also influence them.

If you would like to take action to increase interest in our political life, one thing you might do is host a political salon. This would be a gathering, either in your home or at some other place, that would focus on learning about political issues and opinions. You could invite friends, other students, co-workers, or other persons who might be interested in attending the salon, which could be held weekly, monthly, or at some other interval.

At the first meeting, you could set the "rules" for the salon. What topics do you want to discuss? How much time do you want to devote to each topic? What reading or research, if any, should be undertaken before the meetings? Depending on the views and energies of those who attend the salon, you might also devise an activist agenda to increase voter turnout. For example, you could plan a get-out-the-vote drive for the next election.

# STUDY TOOLS

## Ready to study?

- Review what you've read with the quiz below. Check your answers on the Chapter in Review card at the back of the book. For any questions you miss, read the corresponding Learning Outcome section again to prepare for class and your exam.
- Rip out and study the Chapter in Review card.

## . . . Or you can go online to CourseMate

at www.cengagebrain.com for these additional review materials:

- Practice Quizzes
- Key Term Flashcards or Crossword Puzzles
- Audio Summaries
- Simulations, Animated Learning Modules, and Interactive Timelines
- Videos
- American Government NewsWatch

---

## Fill-In

1. A random sample means that _____.

2. When a pollster's results appear to consistently favor a particular political party, polling experts refer to the phenomenon as a _____.

3. A _____ is a campaign tactic used to feed false or misleading information to potential voters, under the guise of conducting an opinion poll.

4. Agents of political socialization include _____.

5. For established voters, _____ is one of the most important and lasting predictors of how a person will vote.

6. When people vote for candidates who share their positions on particular issues, they are engaging in _____.

7. Socioeconomic factors that influence how people vote include _____.

8. Methods used to keep African Americans from voting even after the Fifteenth Amendment to the U.S. Constitution was ratified included _____.

---

## Multiple Choice

9. A *Literary Digest* poll incorrectly predicted that Alfred Landon would win the presidential election in 1936 because the
   a. pollsters used an unrepresentative sample.
   b. pollsters used a random sample.
   c. sample size was too small.

10. Most political socialization is informal, and it usually begins
    a. in college.
    b. in high school.
    c. during early childhood.

11. The family is an important agent of political socialization because
    a. most families deliberately set out to form their children's political ideas and beliefs.
    b. a child first sees the political world through the eyes of his or her family.
    c. parents are responsible for registering their children to vote.

12. Historically, ____ issues have had the strongest influence on voters' choices.
    a. foreign policy
    b. social
    c. economic

13. The term *gender gap*
    a. refers to the difference between the percentage of votes cast for a particular candidate by women and the percentage of votes cast for the same candidate by men.
    b. describes the difference in voter turnout between men and women.
    c. describes the differences in the campaign styles of male and female candidates.

14. In 1971, the Twenty-sixth Amendment reduced the minimum voting age to
    a. sixteen.
    b. eighteen.
    c. twenty-one.

15. Among the factors affecting voter turnout, ____ appears to be the most important.
    a. educational attainment
    b. race
    c. income level

# GOVT

# 9

# Campaigns and Elections

## LearningOutcomes

The **Learning Outcomes** labeled 1 through 5 are designed to help improve your understanding of the chapter. After reading this chapter, you should be able to:

**9–1** Explain how elections are held and how the electoral college functions in presidential elections.

**9–2** Discuss how candidates are nominated.

**9–3** Indicate what is involved in launching a political campaign today, and describe the structure and functions of a campaign organization.

**9–4** Describe how the Internet has transformed political campaigns.

**9–5** Summarize the current laws that regulate campaign financing and the role of money in modern political campaigns.

**Remember to visit page 218 for additional Study Tools**

194

# AMERICA AT
# ODDS
## Should We Elect the President by Popular Vote?

WIN MCNAMEE/GETTY IMAGES

When Americans go to the polls every four years to cast their ballots for president, many are unaware that they are not, in fact, voting directly for the candidates. Rather, they are voting for electors—individuals chosen in each state by political parties to cast the state's electoral votes for the candidate who wins that state's popular vote. The system by which electors cast their votes for president is known as the *electoral college*.

Each state is assigned electoral votes based on the number of its members in the U.S. Senate and House of Representatives. Each state has the same number of senators in the Senate (two), and the number of representatives a state has in the House is determined by the size of its population. There are currently 538 electoral votes.[1]

To win in the electoral college, a presidential candidate must win 270 of these votes. Most states have a "winner-take-all" system in which the candidate who receives more of the popular votes than any other candidate receives all of that state's electoral votes, even if the margin of victory is very slight. A candidate who wins the popular vote nationally may yet lose in the electoral college. Many Americans believe that we should let the popular vote, not the electoral college, decide who becomes president.[2] Others are not so sure.

## Let the People Elect Our President

In 2000, Democratic candidate Al Gore won the popular vote yet narrowly lost to Republican George W. Bush in the electoral college. Many Americans questioned the legitimacy of Bush's election. If the 2012 presidential elections had been closer than they were, Democrat Barack Obama could easily have been elected with fewer popular votes than Republican Mitt Romney—or vice versa.

The electoral college was designed to ensure that the interests of smaller states are not overshadowed by those of their more populous neighbors. Yet the college gives the smaller states a disproportionate amount of clout. Consider, for example, that one electoral vote in California now corresponds to roughly 685,000 people, while an electoral vote in more sparsely settled Wyoming represents only about 190,000. Clearly, the votes of Americans are not weighted equally, and this voting inequality is contrary to the "one person, one vote" principle of our democracy.

## The Electoral College Protects the Small States and Ensures Stability

Supporters of the electoral college argue that it helps to protect the small states from being overwhelmed by the large states. The electoral college also helps to maintain a relatively stable and coherent party system. If the president were elected by popular vote, we might have multiple parties vying for the nation's highest office—as occurs in such nations as France, Germany, and Italy.

The current system helps to discourage single-issue or regional candidates—candidates who are not focused on the interests of the nation as a whole. To prevail in the electoral college, a candidate must build a national coalition. Finally, the electoral college vote has diverged from the popular vote in only three elections during our nation's history—in 1876, 1888, and 2000. These exceptions do not justify abolishing the system. There is a relevant saying, "If it ain't broke, don't fix it." Let's apply it to the electoral college debate.

## Where do you stand?

1. Do you believe that a candidate elected by the popular vote would be more representative of the entire nation than a candidate elected by the electoral college? Why or why not?

2. Suppose that states awarded their electoral votes according to the share of the popular vote each candidate received. How would this affect presidential elections?

## Explore this issue online

- To see proposals to elect the president by popular vote, enter "fair vote inequalities" into your favorite search engine.
- To find articles defending the electoral college, search on "case for electoral college."

# Introduction

During elections, candidates vie to become representatives of the people in both national and state offices. The population of the United States is now more than 315 million. Clearly, all citizens who are eligible to vote cannot gather in one place to make laws and run the government. We have to choose representatives to govern the nation and to act on behalf of our interests. We accomplish this through popular elections.

Campaigning for election has become an arduous task for every politician. As you will see in this chapter, American campaigns are long and expensive undertakings. The rules that govern our elections can be complicated, as we discussed in the chapter-opening *America at Odds* feature. Yet America's campaigns are an important part of our political process, because it is through campaigns that citizens learn about the candidates and decide how they will cast their votes.

## 9-1 How We Elect Candidates

The ultimate goal of a political campaign and the associated fund-raising efforts is, of course, winning the election. The most familiar kind of election is the **general election,** which is a regularly scheduled election held in even-numbered years on the Tuesday after the first Monday in November. During general elections, the voters decide who will be the U.S. president, vice president, and senators and representatives in Congress. The president and vice president are elected every four years, senators every six years, and representatives every two years.

General elections are also held to choose state and local government officials, often at the same time as those for national offices. A **special election** is held at the state or local level when the voters must decide an issue before the next general election or when vacancies occur by reason of death or resignation.

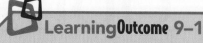
### LearningOutcome 9-1

Explain how elections are held and how the electoral college functions in presidential elections.

### 9-1a Conducting Elections and Counting the Votes

Since 1888, all states in the United States have used the **Australian ballot**—a secret ballot that is prepared, distributed, and counted by government officials at public expense. As its name implies, this ballot was first developed in Australia in 1856. An Australian innovation that we do not use in this country is compulsory voting, which we describe in this chapter's *The Rest of the World* feature on the facing page.

Recall from Chapter 8 that local units of government, such as cities, are divided into smaller voting districts, or precincts. Within each precinct, voters cast their ballots at a designated polling place.

An election board supervises the polling place and the voting process in each precinct. The board sets hours for the polls to be open according to the laws of the state and sees that ballots or voting machines are available.

In most states, the board provides the list of registered voters and makes certain that only qualified voters cast ballots in each precinct. When the polls close, staff members count the votes and report the results, usually to the county clerk or the board of elections.

Representatives from each party, called **poll watchers,** are allowed at each polling place to make sure the election is run fairly and that fraud doesn't occur.

### 9-1b Presidential Elections and the Electoral College

When citizens vote for president and vice president, they are not voting directly for the candidates. Instead, they are voting for **electors** who will cast their ballots in the **electoral college.** The electors are selected

---

**general election** A regularly scheduled election to choose the U.S. president, vice president, and senators and representatives in Congress. General elections are held in even-numbered years on the Tuesday after the first Monday in November.

**special election** An election that is held at the state or local level when the voters must decide an issue before the next general election or when vacancies occur by reason of death or resignation.

**Australian ballot** A secret ballot that is prepared, distributed, and counted by government officials at public expense; used by all states in the United States since 1888.

**poll watcher** A representative from one of the political parties who is allowed to monitor a polling place to make sure that the election is run fairly and that fraud doesn't occur.

**elector** A member of the electoral college.

**electoral college** The group of electors who are selected by the voters in each state to elect officially the president and vice president. The number of electors in each state is equal to the number of that state's representatives in both chambers of Congress.

during each presidential election year by the states' political parties, subject to the laws of the state. Each state has as many electoral votes as it has U.S. senators and representatives (see Figure 9–1 on the next page). In addition, there are three electors from the District of Columbia, even though it is not a state.

**The Winner-Take-All System** The electoral college system is primarily a **winner-take-all system,** in which the candidate who receives the largest popular vote in a state is credited with all that state's electoral votes. The only exceptions are Maine and Nebraska.[3]

In December, after the general election, electors (either Republicans or Democrats, depending on which candidate has won the state's popular vote) meet in their state capitals to cast their votes for president and vice president. When the Constitution was drafted, the framers intended that the electors would use their own discretion in deciding who would make the best president. Beginning as early as 1796, however, electors have usually voted for the candidates to whom they are pledged. The electoral college ballots are then sent to the U.S. Senate, which counts and certifies them before a joint session of Congress held early in January. The candidates who receive a majority of the electoral votes are officially declared president and vice president.

**What It Takes to Win** To be elected, a candidate must receive

> **winner-take-all system**
> A system in which the candidate who receives the most votes wins. In contrast, proportional systems allocate votes to multiple winners.

# THE REST OF THE WORLD

## Compulsory Voting Improves Voter Turnout

No matter what the election is, no matter what the issues are, and no matter who is running, voter turnout in the United States is low compared with that in many other countries. Obviously, the United States would have higher voter participation if we had a compulsory voting law. Australia is a good example of how such a system works.

### Compulsory Voting in Australia
In Australia, citizens over the age of eighteen must register to vote, and they must show up at the polls on Election Day. Otherwise, they are subject to fines. This law has been in effect since 1924.

Australia does make voting easier than it is in America, however. Elections are always held on Saturday, not Tuesday. Voters can vote from anywhere in the country.

### The Effects of Australia's Law
Before 1924, in a typical year Australia saw a turnout of registered voters that was about on a par with that of the United States—an average of 47 percent. Currently, voter turnout is roughly 95 percent. Candidates in Australia do not have to engage in "get out the vote" activities. In other words, campaigns can focus on issues rather than on encouraging voters to go to the polls. In the United States, much effort goes into getting citizens to register and then getting them to go to the polls.

One odd result of compulsory voting is known as the "donkey vote." Citizens who do not care about the elections may simply vote for the first name on a list of candidates. Before 1984, when lists were typically in alphabetical order, candidates could obtain a detectable advantage if their last name began with the letter A. Since that year, however, names have been listed in random order.

### Compulsory Voting in Other Countries
Australia is not alone in enforcing compulsory voting. The following nations also do so:

| | |
|---|---|
| Argentina | Nauru |
| Brazil | Peru |
| Chile | Singapore |
| Congo (Kinshasa) | Turkey |
| Ecuador | Uruguay |
| Luxembourg | |

Thirteen other countries have compulsory voting laws but do not attempt to enforce them.

 **FOR CRITICAL ANALYSIS** Some critics of compulsory voting claim that it is undemocratic. Why do you think they would make this argument?

FIGURE 9-1

# State Electoral Votes in 2012

The size of each state reflects the number of electoral votes that state has, following the changes required by the 2010 census. The colors show which party the state voted for in the 2012 presidential elections: red for Republican, blue for Democratic. A candidate must win 270 electoral votes to be elected president.

© CENGAGE LEARNING

more than half of the 538 electoral votes available. Thus, a candidate needs 270 votes to win. If no presidential candidate gets an electoral college majority (which has happened twice—in 1800 and 1824), the House of Representatives votes on the candidates, with each state delegation casting only a single vote. If no candidate for vice president gets a majority of electoral votes, the vice president is chosen by the Senate, with each senator casting one vote.

Even when a presidential candidate wins by a large margin in the electoral college and in the popular vote—a *landslide election*—it does not follow that the candidate has won the support of the majority of those eligible to vote. We explore this paradox in this chapter's *Perception versus Reality* feature on the facing page.

## FOR CRITICAL THINKING

*Should the District of Columbia be admitted as a state—and therefore elect members to the U.S. House and Senate in addition to participating in the electoral college?*

WILLIAM WEST/AFP/GETTY IMAGES

People line up to vote in the Australian national election outside a polling station in the Melbourne suburb of Essendon in 2010.

## 9-2 How We Nominate Candidates

The first step on the long road to winning an election is the nomination process. Nominations narrow the field of possible candidates and limit each political party's choice to one person. For many local government posts, which are often nonpartisan, self-nomination is the

# Perception versus Reality

## Presidents and the "Popular Vote"

Some presidential contests are very close, such as the 2000 race between Al Gore and George W. Bush. Others are less so, such as the one between Lyndon B. Johnson and Barry Goldwater in 1964. When a presidential candidate wins the race by a wide margin, as Johnson did, the result is called a *landslide victory* for the winning candidate.

### THE PERCEPTION

The traditional perception has been that, in general, our presidents are elected by a majority of eligible American voters. A president who has been swept into office by a landslide victory may thus claim to have received a "mandate from the people" to govern the nation. Moreover, a president may assert that his or her "landslide" victory proves that a policy or program endorsed in campaign speeches is backed by popular support.

### THE REALITY

In reality, the "popular vote" is not all that popular, in the sense of representing the wishes of a majority of American citizens who are eligible to vote. In fact, the president of the United States has never received the votes of a majority of all eligible adults. Lyndon Johnson, in 1964, came the closest of any president in history, and even he won the votes of less than 40 percent of those who were eligible to cast a ballot.

The hotly contested presidential elections of 2000 and 2004 were divisive, leaving the millions of Americans who had voted for the losing candidates unhappy with the results. Indeed, in winning the election of 2000, Bush received the votes of a mere 26.0 percent of those with the right to vote.

Nonetheless, Bush assumed that his reelection in 2004 was a signal from the American people to push his controversial domestic ideas, such as Social Security reform, as well as an endorsement of his foreign policy and the war on terrorism. Barack Obama likewise claimed a personal mandate based on his strong performance in 2008, and he parlayed it into a sweeping program of domestic initiatives. Yet Obama had won the support of only 32.9 percent of eligible voters.

It is useful to keep these figures in mind whenever a president claims to have received a mandate from the people. The truth is, no president has ever been elected with sufficient popular backing to make this a serious claim.

**BLOG ON** Dave Leip's Atlas of U.S. Presidential Elections provides detailed figures on presidential election results. Find the Atlas by searching on "leip."

## LearningOutcome 9–2

Discuss how candidates are nominated.

most common way to become a candidate. A self-proclaimed candidate usually files a petition to be listed on the ballot. Each state has laws that specify how many signatures a candidate must obtain to show that he or she has some public support. An alternative is to be a *write-in candidate*—voters write the candidate's name on the ballot on Election Day.

Candidates for major offices are rarely nominated in these ways, however. As you read in Chapter 7, most candidates for high office are nominated by a political party and receive considerable support from party activists throughout their campaigns.

## 9–2a Party Control over Nominations

The methods used by political parties to nominate candidates have changed during the course of American history. Broadly speaking, the process has grown more open over the years, with the involvement of ever-greater numbers of local leaders and ordinary citizens. Today, any voter can participate in choosing party candidates. This was not true as recently as

1968, however, and was certainly not possible during the first years of the republic.

## The Caucus System

George Washington was essentially unopposed in the first U.S. presidential elections in 1789—no other candidate was seriously considered in any state. By the end of Washington's eight years in office, however, political divisions among the nation's leaders had solidified into political parties, the Federalists and the Jeffersonian Republicans (see Chapter 7). These early parties were organized by gatherings of important persons, who often met in secret. The meetings came to be called **caucuses.**[4]

Beginning in 1800, members of Congress who belonged to the two parties held caucuses to nominate candidates for president and vice president. The Republican caucus chose Thomas Jefferson in 1800, as expected, and the Federalist caucus nominated the incumbent president, John Adams. By 1816, the Federalist Party had ceased to exist, and the Jeffersonian Republican congressional caucus was in complete control of selecting the president of the United States.

## The Death of "King Caucus"

The congressional caucus system collapsed in 1824.[5] It was widely seen as undemocratic—opponents derided it as "King Caucus." A much-diminished caucus nominated a presidential candidate who then came in third in the electoral vote. The other three major candidates were essentially self-nominated.[6] The four candidates split the electoral vote so completely that the House of Representatives had to decide the contest. It picked John Quincy Adams, even though Andrew Jackson had won more popular and electoral votes.

**caucus** A meeting held to choose political candidates or delegates.

**nominating convention** An official meeting of a political party to choose its candidates. Nominating conventions at the state and local levels also select delegates to represent the citizens of their geographic areas at a higher-level party convention.

**delegate** A person selected to represent the people of one geographic area at a party convention.

> **"A POLITICIAN SHOULD HAVE THREE HATS:** one for throwing into the ring, one for talking through, and one for pulling rabbits out of if elected."
>
> ~ CARL SANDBURG ~
> AMERICAN POET AND HISTORIAN
> 1878–1967

## 9–2b The Nominating Convention

In the run-up to the 1828 elections, two new parties grew up around the major candidates. Adams's supporters called themselves the National Republicans (later known as the Whigs). Jackson's supporters organized as the Democratic Party, which won the election.

In 1832, both parties settled on a new method of choosing candidates for president and vice president—the national nominating convention. A number of state parties had already adopted the convention system for choosing state-level candidates. New Jersey held conventions as early as 1800.

**Nominating Conventions** A **nominating convention** is an official meeting of a political party to choose its candidates. Those who attend the convention are called **delegates,** and they are chosen to represent the people of a particular geographic area. Conventions can take place at multiple levels. A county convention might choose delegates to attend a state convention. The state convention, in turn, might select delegates to the national convention. By 1840, the convention system was the most common method of nominating political party candidates at the state and national levels.

**Limits of the Convention System** While the convention system drew in a much broader range of leaders than had the caucus, it was not a particularly democratic institution. Convention delegates were rarely chosen by a vote of the party's local members. Typically, they were appointed by local party officials, who were usually, with good reason, called bosses. These local leaders often gained their positions in ways that were far from democratic. Not until 1972 did ordinary voters in all states gain the right to select delegates to the national presidential nominating conventions.

## 9–2c Primary Elections and the Loss of Party Control

The corruption that so often accompanied the convention system led reformers to call for a new way to choose candidates—the **primary election,** in which voters go to the polls to decide among candidates who seek the nomination of their party. Candidates who win a primary election then go on to compete against the candidates from other parties in the general election.

The first primary election may have been held in 1842 by Democrats in Crawford County, Pennsylvania. The technique was not widely used, however, until the end of the nineteenth century and the beginning of the twentieth. These were years in which reform was a popular cause.

BARRY CHIN/THE BOSTON GLOBE VIA GETTY IMAGES

Massachusetts Senate candidates Scott Brown (Republican) and Elizabeth Warren (Democrat) greet each other before their first debate in 2012.

**Direct and Indirect Primaries** The rules for conducting primary elections are highly variable, and a number of different types of primaries exist. One major distinction is between a direct primary and an indirect primary. In a **direct primary,** voters cast their ballots directly for candidates. In an *indirect primary,* voters choose delegates, who in turn choose the candidates. The delegates may be pledged to a particular candidate but sometimes run as *unpledged delegates.*

The major parties use indirect primaries to elect delegates to the national nominating conventions that choose candidates for president and vice president. The elections that nominate candidates for Congress and for state or local offices are almost always direct primaries.

**The Role of the States** Primary elections are normally conducted by state governments. States set the dates and conduct the elections. They provide polling places, election officials, and registration lists, and they then count the votes. By sponsoring the primaries, state governments have obtained considerable influence over the rules by which the primaries are conducted. The power of the states is limited, however, by the parties' First Amendment right to freedom of association, a right that has been repeatedly confirmed by the United States Supreme Court.[7]

On occasion, parties that object to the rules imposed by state governments have opted out of the state-sponsored primary system altogether.[8] Note that third parties typically do not participate in state-sponsored primaries, but hold nominating conventions instead. The major parties rarely opt out of state elections, however, because the financial—and political—costs of going it alone are high. (When primary elections are used to choose candidates for local *nonpartisan* positions, state control is uncontested.)

**Primary Voters** Voter turnout for primaries is lower than it is in general elections. The voters who do go to the polls are often strong supporters of their party. Indeed, as you will learn shortly, independents cannot participate in primary elections in some states, even if they lean toward one or the other of the two major parties. As a result, the Republican primary electorate is very conservative, and Democratic primary voters are quite liberal. Candidates often find that they must run to the political right or left during the primaries. Frequently, they then move to the center during the general election campaign.

**primary election** An election in which voters choose the candidates of their party, who will then run in the general election.

**direct primary** An election held within each of the two major parties—Democratic and Republican—to choose the party's candidates for the general election. Voters choose the candidate directly, rather than through delegates.

## Insurgent Candidates

Primary elections were designed to take nominations out of the hands of the party bosses. Indeed, the most important result of the primary system has been to reduce dramatically the power of elected and party officials over the nominating process. Ever since primary elections were established, the insurgent candidate who runs against the party "establishment" has been a common phenomenon. Running against the "powers that be" is often a very effective campaign strategy, and many insurgents have won victories at the local, state, and national levels.

Occasionally, an insurgent's platform is strikingly different from that of the party as a whole. Yet even when an insurgent's politics are abhorrent to the rest of the party—for example, an insurgent might make an outright appeal to racism—the party has no way of denying the insurgent the right to the party label in the general election.

## Open and Closed Primaries

Primaries can be classified as closed or open.

**CLOSED PRIMARIES.** In a **closed primary,** only party members can vote to choose that party's candidates, and they may vote only in the primary of their own party. Thus, only registered Democrats can vote in the Democratic primary to select candidates of the Democratic Party. Only registered Republicans can vote for the Republican candidates. A person usually establishes party membership when she or he registers to vote. Some states have a *semiclosed* primary, which allows voters to register with a party or change their party affiliations on Election Day.

Regular party workers favor the closed primary because it promotes party loyalty. Independent voters usually oppose it because it forces them to select a party if they wish to participate in the nominating process.

**closed primary**
A primary in which only party members can vote to choose that party's candidates.

**open primary** A primary in which voters can vote for a party's candidates regardless of whether they belong to the party.

**OPEN PRIMARIES.** In an **open primary,** voters can vote for a party's candidates regardless of whether they belong to the party. In most open primaries, all voters receive both a Republican ballot and a Democratic ballot. Voters then choose either the Democratic or the Republican ballot in the privacy of the voting booth. In a *semiopen* primary, voters request the ballot for the party of their choice.

**MIXED FORMS.** The fifty states have developed dozens of variations on the open and closed primary plans. In some states, primaries are closed only to persons registered to another party, and independents can vote in either primary. In several states, an independent who votes in a party primary is automatically enrolled in that party. In other states, the voter remains an independent. The two major parties often have different rules. For example, in two states the Democrats allow independents to vote in the primaries, but the Republicans do not.

## Blanket and "Top Two" Primaries

Until 2000, California and a few other states employed a *blanket primary,* in which voters could choose the candidates of more than one party. A voter might participate in choosing the Republican candidate for governor, for example, and at the same time vote to pick the Democratic candidate for the U.S. Senate. In that year, however, the Supreme Court ruled that the blanket primary violated the parties' right to freedom of association.[9] Similar primary systems in Washington and Alaska were struck down in later cases.

Louisiana has for many years had a unique system in which all candidates participate in the same primary, regardless of party. The two candidates receiving the most votes then proceed on to the general election. In 2008, Louisiana abandoned this system for the U.S. House and Senate, but kept it for state and local offices.

Even as Louisiana was backing away from this system, however, other states began picking it up. Washington adopted the Louisiana system in 2004, and in 2008 the Supreme Court ruled that it was constitutional.[10] In June 2010, California voters adopted a system known as the *"top two" primary* that was patterned on the one in Washington.

Political parties continue to have the right to designate preferred candidates, using conventions or other means, but such endorsements do not appear on the ballot. An insurgent Republican and a "regular" Republican, for example, would both be labeled simply "Republican." The California system went into effect in 2011, and given California's size and importance, its top two primary was closely watched.

## 9–2d Nominating Presidential Candidates

In some respects, being nominated for president is more difficult than being elected. The nominating process narrows a very large number of hopefuls down to a single candidate from each party. Choosing a presidential candidate is unlike nominating candidates for any other office. One reason for this is that the nomination process combines several different methods.

**Presidential Primaries** Most of the states hold presidential primaries, beginning early in the election year. For a candidate, a good showing in the early primaries results in plenty of media attention as television networks and newspaper reporters play up the results. Subsequent primaries tend to eliminate candidates unlikely to be successful.

The presidential primaries do not necessarily follow the same rules the states use for nominating candidates for the U.S. Congress or for state and local offices. Often, the presidential primaries are not held on the same date as the other primaries. States frequently hold the presidential primaries early in hope of exercising greater influence on the outcome.

**Caucuses** The caucus system is an alternative to primary elections. Strictly speaking, the caucus system is a convention system. The caucuses are party conventions held at the local level that elect delegates to conventions at the county or congressional district level. These midlevel conventions then choose the delegates to the state convention, which finally elects the delegates to the national party convention.

Unlike the caucuses of two centuries ago, modern caucuses are open to all party members. It is not hard to join a party. At the famous Iowa caucuses, you become a party member simply by attending a local caucus.

While some states, such as Iowa and Minnesota, rely on the caucus/convention system to nominate candidates for state and local positions, the system is more frequently used only to choose delegates to the Democratic and Republican national conventions. Most states with presidential caucuses use primaries to nominate state and local candidates. Twelve states choose national convention delegates through caucuses. Four states use caucuses to allocate some of the national convention delegates and use primaries to allocate the others.

**Primaries—The Rush to Be First** Traditionally, states have held their presidential primaries at various times over the first six months of a presidential election year. In an effort to make their primaries

AP PHOTO/MATT ROURKE

Republican presidential candidates: former Pennsylvania senator Rick Santorum, former Massachusetts governor Mitt Romney, former House Speaker Newt Gingrich, and Representative Ron Paul, (R., Tex.) take the stage before the start of one of numerous Republican presidential candidate debates during 2011 and 2012.

prominent in the media and influential in the political process, however, many states have moved the date of their primary to earlier in the year—a practice known as *front-loading*. In 1988, a group of southern states created a "Super Tuesday" by holding their primaries on the same day in early March. Then, other states moved their primaries to an earlier date, too.

The practice of front-loading primaries has gained momentum over the last decade. The states with later primary dates found that most nominations were decided early in the season, leaving their voters "out of the action." As more states moved up their primary dates, the early primaries became even more important, and other states, to compete, also moved up their primaries.

This rush to be first was particularly notable in the year or so preceding the 2008 presidential primaries. By 2007, about half the states had moved their primaries to earlier dates. Many of these states opted for February 5—or "Super-Super Tuesday," as some called it—as the date for their primaries.

> "THERE IS NO EXCITEMENT
> anywhere in the world . . .
> to match the excitement of
> an American presidential
> campaign."
> ~ THEODORE H. WHITE ~
> AMERICAN JOURNALIST AND HISTORIAN
> 1915–1986

### The Impact of Front-Loading
Many Americans worried that with a shortened primary season, long-shot candidates would no longer be able to propel themselves into serious contention by doing well in small early-voting states, such as New Hampshire and Iowa. Traditionally, a candidate who had a successful showing in the New Hampshire primary had time to obtain enough financial backing to continue in the race. The fear was that an accelerated schedule of presidential primaries would favor the richest candidates.

**FRONT-LOADING IN 2008.** In practice, front-loading did not have this effect in 2008. On the Republican side, the early primaries might have benefited a front-runner—but there was no Republican front-runner in January 2008. By February 5, however, Arizona senator John McCain had developed a clear lead. The Republican primaries were mostly conducted on a winner-take-all basis, a rule that allowed McCain to wrap up the nomination on March 4.

The Democrats, however, allocated delegates on a proportional basis, so that each candidate received delegates based on his or her share of the vote. That rule made an early decision impossible, and Barack

Obama did not obtain a majority of the Democratic delegates until June 3. As a result, many of the most important Democratic primaries took place late in the season. States that had moved their primaries to February 5 discovered that they were lost in the crowd of early contests. Front-loading, in other words, had become counterproductive.

**FRONT-LOADING IN 2012.** In 2012, the Democrats were expected to renominate President Obama without opposition, and so the Republican primaries were the only ones that mattered. In an attempt to reduce front-loading, the Republican National Committee ruled that only four traditionally early states, including Iowa and New Hampshire, could choose delegates before March 6. States choosing delegates through the rest of March would have to allocate them proportionally. From April 1 on, delegates could be selected on a winner-take-all basis. In the end, Arizona, Florida, and Michigan violated the rules by choosing delegates before March 6. As a result, these states had their delegations to the national convention cut in half. Six states that held *nonbinding* contests before March 6—contests that selected no delegates—were not penalized.

### The 2012 Republican Primaries
Two characteristics of the 2011–2012 Republican primary cycle stood out. One was the importance of a series of debates among the presidential candidates, held from May 2011 through February 2012. The second was the long-running attempt by Republican conservatives to find an alternative to former Massachusetts governor Mitt Romney, the eventual winner.

**THE REPUBLICAN PRESIDENTIAL DEBATES.** In previous years, the parties had often scheduled debates among the presidential candidates. During 2011, however, the Republican debates assumed an importance never before seen. In some ways, the thirteen debates held in 2011 *were* the Republican presidential campaigns of that year. Millions of Republicans and others tuned in to view them. As a result, campaign finance was temporarily of little importance, a striking development. Candidates were able to present themselves to the public regardless of the size of their treasuries. The only other event of significance in 2011 was the Iowa straw poll in August, won by Minnesota congresswoman Michele Bachmann.

**ANYBODY BUT ROMNEY.** Throughout 2011 and early 2012, ultraconservative Republicans backed a series of candidates in an attempt to challenge Romney, the presumed front-runner. During the 2011–2012 campaigns, Romney's position on the issues was as conservative as that of any other candidate. Romney, however, had a history that was not particularly conservative. The state-level health-care insurance reforms he sponsored as governor of Massachusetts were particularly notable. This legislation bore a striking resemblance to Obamacare.

Michele Bachmann was the first candidate backed by conservatives who distrusted Romney, but her campaign faded early. In August, Texas governor Rick Perry entered the race. His strong résumé and genial manner quickly propelled him into first place in the public opinion polls. Perry proved to be a disaster as a debater, however, and his support soon collapsed. Conservatives then pinned their hopes on Georgia businessman Herman Cain, an African American with no obvious background to prepare him to be president. Cain was an excellent speaker, and by October he led the polls. In November, Cain's campaign was destroyed when several women alleged that he had harassed them sexually.

By the time the primaries actually took place in 2012, the two conservative champions were former House Speaker Newt Gingrich of Georgia and former Pennsylvania senator Rick Santorum. Romney, however, was finally able to take advantage of his immense financial war chest. Romney defeated Gingrich in the Florida primary with the help of a barrage of negative advertisements. For his part, Santorum was unable to assemble the campaign necessary to compete with Romney on a level basis. Romney effectively secured the nomination in April, and his two chief rivals endorsed him in May. How effective was Romney's general election campaign? We answer that question in this chapter's *Elections 2012* feature below.

### National Party Conventions

Born in the 1830s, the American national political convention is unique in Western democracies. Elsewhere,

## The Campaigns in 2012

Political campaigns can be divided into the air game and the ground game. The air game is advertising. The ground game is the get-out-the-vote drive. Candidate campaigns and outside super PACs spent hundreds of millions of dollars on negative advertising. Such advertising had its successes. Obama's portrayal of Romney as a heartless plutocrat may have been vital to Obama's reelection. But when political advertising exceeds a certain saturation level, voters tune out. In a modern ground game, campaigns collect as much data as they can to identify the people who they want to vote. The data are used to make human contact more efficient, by directing volunteers toward the voters who they most need to reach. Obama had

years to perfect his ground game, and it showed. Romney's ground game, in contrast, was a comedy of errors. His volunteers were forever calling the wrong voters. The team developed a major digital voter turnout and poll monitoring program to allocate resources on Election Day, called Orca. It crashed. A staffer reported: "Orca is lying on the beach with a harpoon in it." Even if Orca had worked perfectly, Election Day was far too late to be allocating resources. That Obama's get-out-the-vote-drive was effective does not mean that voter turnout was up overall in 2012. In fact, it was down. Millions of voters seem to have stayed home because they could not support either the "plutocrat" or the "socialist from Kenya."

**Credentials Committee**
A committee of each national political party that evaluates the claims of national party convention delegates to be the legitimate representatives of their states.

**political consultant**
A professional political adviser who, for a fee, works on an area of a candidate's campaign. Political consultants include campaign managers, pollsters, media advisers, and "get out the vote" organizers.

candidates for prime minister or chancellor are chosen within the confines of party councils. That is actually closer to the way the framers of the Constitution wanted it done.

At one time, the conventions were indeed often giant free-for-alls. It wasn't always clear who the winning presidential and vice-presidential candidates would be until the delegates voted.

As more states opted to hold presidential primaries, however, the drama of national conventions diminished. Today, the conventions have been described as massive pep rallies. Nonetheless, each convention's task remains a serious one. In late summer, two thousand to three thousand delegates gather at each convention to represent the wishes of the voters and political leaders of their home states.

On the first day of the convention, delegates hear the reports of the **Credentials Committee**, which inspects each prospective delegate's claim to be seated as a legitimate representative of her or his state. When the eligibility of delegates is in question, the committee decides who will be seated. A carefully chosen keynote speaker whips up enthusiasm among the delegates. Later, the convention deals with committee reports and debates on the party platform. Finally, it turns to nominations and voting.

Balloting takes place with an alphabetical roll call in which states and territories announce their votes. The vice-presidential nomination takes place later. Acceptance speeches by the presidential and vice-presidential candidates are timed to take place during prime-time television. We provided more details on the national party conventions in Chapter 7 on page 163.

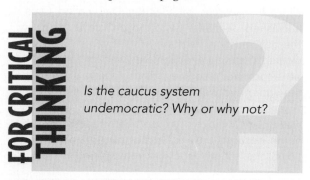

**FOR CRITICAL THINKING**

*Is the caucus system undemocratic? Why or why not?*

## 9–3 The Modern Political Campaign

Once nominated, candidates focus on their campaigns. The term *campaign* originated in the military context. Generals mounted campaigns, using their scarce resources (soldiers and materials) to achieve military objectives. Using the term in a political context is apt. In a political campaign, candidates also use scarce resources (time and funds) in an attempt to defeat their adversaries in the battle for votes.

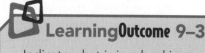

**LearningOutcome 9–3**

Indicate what is involved in launching a political campaign today, and describe the structure and functions of a campaign organization.

### 9–3a Responsibilities of the Campaign Staff

To run a successful campaign, the candidate's campaign staff must be able to raise funds for the effort, get media coverage, produce and pay for political ads, schedule the candidate's time effectively with constituent groups and potential supporters, convey the candidate's position on the issues, conduct research on the opposing candidate, and persuade the voters to go to the polls.

When party identification was firmer and TV campaigning was still in its infancy, a strong party organization on the local, state, or national level could furnish most of the services and expertise that the candidate needed. Less effort was spent on advertising each candidate's position and character, because the party label communicated that information to many of the voters.

Today, party organizations are no longer as important as they once were. Instead of relying so extensively on political parties, candidates now turn to professionals to manage their campaigns.

### 9–3b The Professional Campaign Organization

With the rise of candidate-centered campaigns in the past several decades, the role of the political party in managing campaigns has declined. Professional **political consultants** now manage nearly all aspects of a presidential candidate's campaign. Most candidates for governor, the House, and the Senate also rely on consultants. Political consultants generally specialize in a particular area of the campaign, such as researching the opposition, conducting polls, developing the candidate's advertising, or organizing "get out the vote" efforts.

Nonetheless, most candidates have a campaign manager who coordinates and plans the **campaign strategy.** Figure 9–2 below shows a typical presidential campaign organization. The political party continues to play an important role in recruiting volunteers and getting out the vote.

A major development in contemporary American politics is the focus on reaching voters through effective use of the media, particularly television. At least half of the budget for a major political campaign is consumed by television advertising. Media consultants are therefore pivotal members of the campaign staff. The nature of political advertising is discussed in more detail in Chapter 10.

**campaign strategy**
The comprehensive plan developed by a candidate and his or her advisers for winning an election. The strategy includes the candidate's position on issues, slogan, advertising plan, press events, and personal appearances, as well as other aspects of the campaign.

FIGURE 9-2

# A Typical Presidential
## Campaign Organization

Most aspects of a candidate's campaign are managed by professional political consultants, as this figure illustrates.

**CANDIDATE**

**Campaign Manager**
Develops overall campaign strategy, manages finances, oversees staff

**Campaign Staff**
Undertakes the various tasks associated with campaigning

| MEDIA CONSULTANTS | FUND-RAISERS | SPEECHWRITERS | PRESS SECRETARY | POLICY EXPERTS |
|---|---|---|---|---|
| Help to shape candidate's image, manage campaign advertising | Raise money to subsidize campaign | Prepare speeches for candidate's public appearances | Maintains press contacts, is responsible for disseminating campaign news | Provide input on foreign and domestic policy issues |
| **LAWYERS AND ACCOUNTANTS** | **PRIVATE POLLSTER** | **RESEARCHERS** | **TRAVEL PLANNER** | **WEB CONSULTANT** |
| Monitor legal and financial aspects of campaign | Gathers up-to-the-minute data on public opinion | Investigate opponents' records and personal history | Arranges for candidate's transportation and accommodations | Oversees candidate's Internet presence |

**State Chairpersons**
Monitor state and local campaigns

**Local Committees**
Direct efforts of local volunteers

**Volunteers**
Publicize candidates at local level through personal visits, phone calls, direct mailings, and online activities

© CENGAGE LEARNING

### 9-3c Opposition Research

Major campaigns, such as those for governor, senator, and U.S. president, typically make use of **opposition research.** A staff member—or even an entire team—spends time discovering as much negative information about opposing candidates as possible. Journalists often rely on opposition researchers for their stories.

One campaign adviser described the 2011–2012 political season as a "golden age of opposition research." In many ways, it was. A notable characteristic of opposition research in this period, though, was that candidate campaigns played a relatively modest role. Much of the research was undertaken by political activists operating independently of the campaigns.

**Republican Versus Republican** Republican candidates for president in 2012 had little reason to fund opposition research on President Obama. This research had already been done in the 2008 elections, and there was little prospect of finding anything new. It was necessary only to repeat themes that had been developed earlier, such as Obama's alleged radicalism. Republican candidates for president were much more vulnerable to opposition research because these politicians were not as well known to the voters as Obama was. Because the Republican presidential primary campaigns were long and hard-fought, some of the damage done to the various candidates was done by other Republicans.

**The Cain Takedown** One of the most effective examples of opposition research was the revelation by Politico, an online blog, that two women had charged Herman Cain with sexual harassment when he was head of the National Restaurant Association, an interest group. Two other women later made similar charges. From the timing, it was clear that the accusations were an attempt to force Cain out of the race. Cain insinuated that one or another of his Republican rivals was behind the charges, but no evidence of such a connection ever surfaced.

**Attempts to Define Mitt Romney** Opposition research aimed at Mitt Romney, in contrast, was clearly tied to the Obama campaign. Obama supporters focused on Romney's time as CEO of Bain Capital, a financial firm. Democrats accused Romney of sabotaging profitable companies and of shipping jobs overseas.

> **opposition research**
> The attempt to learn damaging information about an opponent in a political campaign.

They also publicized Romney's failure to release any income tax returns for years before 2010, and the relatively low 14 percent tax on his income that he paid on the returns he did release. Clearly, the intent of these allegations was to define Romney as a cold-hearted businessman with little concern for the problems of ordinary Americans.

**FOR CRITICAL THINKING**

Some people have accused political consultants of "managing the candidate" too well, making the candidate appear stilted and unnatural. *How could a candidate prevent that from happening?*

## 9-4 The Internet Campaign

Over the years, political leaders have benefited from understanding and using new communications technologies. In the 1930s, command of a new medium—radio—gave President Franklin D. Roosevelt an edge. In 1960, Democratic presidential candidate John F. Kennedy gained an advantage over Republican Richard Nixon because Kennedy had a better understanding of the visual requirements of television.

**Learning Outcome 9-4**

Describe how the Internet has transformed political campaigns.

Today, the ability to make effective use of social media and the Internet is essential to a candidate. In the 2008 presidential elections, Barack Obama gained an edge on his rivals in part because of his superior use of the new technologies. His team relied on the Internet for fund-raising, targeting potential supporters, and creating local political organizations. Obama's success in 2008 meant that other candidates in subsequent years had a strong interest in improving their use of the Web.

### 9-4a Fund-Raising on the Internet

Internet fund-raising grew out of an earlier technique: the direct-mail campaign. In direct mailings, campaigns send solicitations to large numbers of likely prospects, typically seeking contributions. Developing good lists of prospects is central to an effective direct-mail operation. Postage, printing, and the rental of address lists push the marginal cost of each additional letter well above a dollar. Response rates are low—a 1 percent response rate is a tremendous success. In many direct-mail campaigns, most of the funds raised are used up by the costs of the campaign itself. From the 1970s on, conservative organizations became especially adept at managing direct-mail campaigns. For a time, this expertise gave conservative causes and candidates an advantage over liberals.

To understand the old system is to recognize the superiority of the new one. The marginal cost of each additional e-mail message is essentially zero. Lists of prospects need not be prepared as carefully, because e-mail sent to unlikely prospects does not waste resources. E-mail fund-raising did face one problem when it was new—many people were not yet online. Today, that issue is no longer so important.

The new technology brought with it a change in the groups that benefited the most. Conservatives were no longer the most effective fund-raisers. Instead, liberal and libertarian organizations enjoyed some of the greatest successes.

**Obama Online** Barack Obama took Internet fund-raising to a new level during his 2008 presidential bid. One of the defining characteristics of his fund-raising was its decentralization. The Obama campaign attempted to recruit as many supporters as possible to act as fund-raisers who would solicit contributions from their friends and neighbors. As a result, Obama was spared much of the personal fund-raising effort that consumes the time of most national politicians. By November 2008, 2.5 million people had donated to Obama's campaign. In the end, Obama raised more than $500 million online in 2007 and 2008—two-thirds of his overall fund-raising.

Obama's online operation in 2011–2012 made a major contribution to his $1.25 billion fund-raising total. Even more so than in his first race, the sums came largely from smaller donors. Many of the wealthy individuals who had contributed to Obama earlier were now alienated by the president's policies and his rhetorical attacks on the rich.

**Republicans Online** Already in 2008, one Republican candidate was able to use the Internet

with great success—Texas representative Ron Paul, who espoused a libertarian philosophy that was highly appealing to many high-tech enthusiasts. Paul pioneered the online *moneybomb* technique, described by the San José *Mercury News* as "a one-day fund-raising frenzy." A moneybomb organized by Paul supporters in December 2007 raised $6.3 million, a new record for one-day fund-raising. (In September 2008, however, a $10 million Obama moneybomb bested Paul's totals.) Despite Paul's fund-raising prowess, his libertarian politics were sufficiently far from the conservative Republican mainstream that he was able to win only a handful of national convention delegates.

By the 2010 midterm elections, Republicans were widely perceived to have caught up to Democrats in their use of the Web. Their candidates were now more likely to raise funds through targeted e-mail appeals than by waiting for supporters to drop by the campaign Web page.

In 2012, Mitt Romney was less reliant on the Internet than many other recent candidates. In part, this was because much of his campaign finance came in large chunks from wealthy individuals—the reverse of Obama's experience. Romney's campaign fund-raising roughly matched Obama's—about $1.25 billion in total.

> **"IN CONSTANT PURSUIT OF MONEY** to finance campaigns, the political system is simply unable to function. Its deliberative powers are paralyzed."
>
> ~ JOHN RAWLS ~
> AMERICAN EDUCATOR
> 1921–2000

## 9–4b Targeting Supporters

In 2004, President George W. Bush's chief political adviser, Karl Rove, pioneered a new campaign technique known as *microtargeting*. The process involves collecting as much information as possible about voters in a gigantic database and then filtering out various groups for special attention.

Through microtargeting, for example, the Bush campaign could identify Republican prospects living in heavily Democratic neighborhoods—potential supporters whom the campaign might have neglected because the neighborhood as a whole seemed so unpromising. In 2004, the Democrats had nothing to match Rove's efforts. By 2008, however, microtargeting was employed by all major candidates.

## 9–4c Support for Local Organizing

Perhaps the most effective use of the Internet has been as an organizing tool. One of the earliest Internet

At the end of each election, the winning presidential candidate appears with his family for a victory celebration. Here, Barack Obama continued the tradition at Grant Park in Chicago on November 4, 2008.

young people who either cannot or do not vote. Indeed, surveys in 2012 showed that those least likely to vote supported Obama by a two-to-one margin. The question for the Obama campaign, therefore, was whether it could turn politically disengaged social media participants into actual voters.

**Local Support Groups**   By gathering information on large numbers of potential supporters, the Obama campaign in 2007–2008 was able to create local support groups in towns and counties across the country. For example, the campaign assembled a group of forty volunteers in Avery County, North Carolina, a locality in the Blue Ridge Mountains traditionally carried by Republican presidential candidates at rates of more than three to one. The volunteers were often surprised to discover that neighbors they had known for years were fellow Democrats.

Obama's national Internet fund-raising success meant that he could field hundreds of paid organizers in North Carolina, some of whom supported local groups of volunteers such as this one. In the end, McCain easily carried Avery County, but Obama carried the state.[11]

techniques was to use the site Meetup.com to organize real-world meetings. In this way, campaigns were able to gather supporters without relying on the existing party and activist infrastructure.

**Obama's Campaign**   As with fund-raising, Barack Obama took Web-based organizing to a new level. In part, his campaign used existing sites such as Facebook. By June 2008, Obama had 953,000 Facebook backers to John McCain's 142,000. On YouTube, Obama's videos were viewed 50 million times, compared with 4 million for McCain's. Obama's own Web site was especially important to the campaign. My.BarackObama.com eventually racked up more than a million members.

In 2012, Obama had seven times as many Facebook supporters as Romney (28 million versus 4 million). This was a substantial advantage, but not necessarily as significant as you might think. The problem is that the Facebook demographic is heavily weighted toward

## FOR CRITICAL THINKING

Some candidates are more successful than others in using the Internet. *Do such candidates have any traits in common? If so, what might these be?*

## 9–5 What It Costs to Win

The modern political campaign is an expensive undertaking. Candidates must spend huge sums for professional campaign managers and consultants, television and radio ads, the printing

### Learning Outcome 9–5

Summarize the current laws that regulate campaign financing and the role of money in modern political campaigns.

of campaign literature, travel, office rent, equipment, and other necessities.

To get an idea of the cost of waging a campaign for Congress today, consider that in the 2010 mid-term election cycle, the average House incumbent raised about $1.7 million. The average House challenger raised close to $700,000. In the Senate, a typical incumbent took in more than $13 million. The average challenger spent almost $5 million. Of course, some contests were much more expensive than the average. Barbara Boxer, the incumbent running for reelection to the Senate from California, raised more than $26 million, while her challenger, Carly Fiorina, spent over $16 million.

## 9–5a Presidential Spending

Presidential campaigns are even more costly. As noted, in the 2011–2012 presidential election cycle, spending by the two major candidates approached $2.5 billion. Despite restrictions on how the major political parties could raise funds, each had accumulated about $600 million by September 2012.

Furthermore, in today's campaign-finance environment, the sums spent by the candidates themselves and by the parties are only part of the story. Independent expenditures by outside groups, nominally unconnected with the candidate campaigns, have become as important as the spending by the candidates themselves. Total presidential campaign spending, including by candidates who lost in the primaries and through independent expenditures, reached $4.5 billion in the 2011–2012 cycle.

The groups responsible for much of this spending, known as *super PACs*, are a new development. They became prominent only in the 2011–2012 campaign cycle. Super PACs resulted from recent court decisions, especially the Supreme Court's ruling in *Citizens United v. Federal Election Commission,* discussed later in this section. First, however, let us examine the development of our campaign-finance system.

## 9–5b The Federal Election Campaign Act

The high cost of campaigns gives rise to the fear that campaign contributors and special interest groups will try to buy favored treatment from those who are elected to office. In an attempt to prevent these abuses, the government has tried to regulate campaign financing.

Legislation to regulate campaign finance was passed in 1925 and 1939, but these early efforts were almost completely ineffective. The first reform that actually had teeth was the Federal Election Campaign Act (FECA) of 1971.[12] The act was amended in 1974. As amended, the new law did the following:

- Restricted the amount that could be spent on mass media advertising, including television.

- Limited how much individuals and groups could contribute to candidates.

- Limited the amount that candidates and their families could contribute to their own campaigns.

- Prevented corporations and labor unions from participating directly in political campaigns, but allowed them to set up political action committees (discussed shortly).

- Required disclosure of all contributions and expenditures of more than $100.

- Created the Federal Election Commission (FEC) to administer and enforce the act's provisions.

Finally, the act provided public financing for presidential primaries and general elections, funded by a checkoff on federal income tax returns. Presidential candidates who raised money on their own could get

Volunteers check in to help Republican presidential candidate Texas congressman Ron Paul at the Iowa Straw Poll.

additional funds for primary campaigns. For the general election, presidential candidates received federal funding for almost all of their expenses if they were willing to accept campaign-spending limits.

From 1976 through 2000, presidential campaigns were largely funded by the public purse. Beginning in 2004, however, leading Democratic and Republican presidential candidates were refusing public funding for the primaries. In 2008, Barack Obama became the first major-party candidate in decades to refuse federal funding for the general election as well. By 2012, the public financing of presidential campaigns was effectively over.

### Freeing Up Self-Financing
In 1976, the United States Supreme Court declared unconstitutional the provision in the 1971 act that limited the amount each individual could spend on his or her own campaign. The Court held that a "candidate, no less than any other person, has a First Amendment right to engage in the discussion of public issues and vigorously and tirelessly to advocate his own election."[13]

### The Rise of PACs
The FECA allowed corporations, labor unions, and special interest groups to set up national *political action committees (PACs)* to raise money for candidates. PACs can contribute up to $5,000 per candidate in each election, but there is no limit on the total amount of PAC contributions during an election cycle.

As discussed in Chapter 6, the number of PACs grew significantly from the 1970s, as did their campaign contributions. In the 2004 election cycle, about 36 percent of campaign funds spent on House races came from PACs.[14] Since 2004, however, other methods of raising campaign funds have reduced the relative importance of traditional PACs.

BOBBY YIP/REUTERS

Casino billionaire Sheldon Adelson and his wife each donated $5 million to Newt Gingrich's super PAC.

corporations soon developed such practices. One way to skirt the rules was to contribute to the political parties instead of the candidates. A second was to make independent expenditures not coordinated with a candidate's campaign or a political party.

### Soft Money
The FECA and its amendments did not prohibit individuals or corporations from contributing to political parties. Contributors could make donations to the parties to cover the costs of registering voters, printing flyers, advertising, developing campaigns to "get out the vote," and holding fund-raising events. Contributions to political parties were called **soft money**.

By 2000, the parties raised nearly $463 million through soft money contributions. Soft dollars became the main source of campaign money in the presidential race until after the 2002 elections, when they were banned, as you will read shortly.

### Independent Expenditures
The campaign-financing laws did not prohibit corporations, labor unions, and special interest groups from making **independent expenditures** in an election campaign. Independent expenditures, as the term implies, are

**soft money** Campaign contributions not regulated by federal law, such as some contributions that are made to political parties instead of to particular candidates.

**independent expenditure** An expenditure for activities that are independent from (not coordinated with) those of a political candidate or a political party.

## 9–5c Skirting the Campaign-Financing Rules

The FECA was designed to regulate funds given to the campaign organizations of candidates for office. There are ways, however, to influence the political process without giving money directly to a candidate's campaign. Individuals and expenditures for activities that are independent of (not coordinated with) those of a candidate or a political party.

Decisions by the courts have distinguished two types of independent expenditures. In the first type, an interest group or other contributor wages an "issue campaign" without going so far as to say "Vote for Candidate X." An issue campaign might, however, go so far as to publish voter guides informing voters of candidates' positions. The courts have repeatedly upheld the right of groups to advocate their positions in this way.

Alternatively, a group might explicitly campaign for particular candidates. The Supreme Court has held that an issue-oriented group has a First Amendment right to advocate the election of its preferred candidates as long as it acts independently of the various campaigns. In 1996, the Court held that these guidelines apply to expenditures by political parties as well.[15]

## 9–5d The Bipartisan Campaign Reform Act of 2002

The growth of soft money and of independent expenditures led to a demand for further campaign-finance reform. In 2002 Congress passed, and the president signed, the Bipartisan Campaign Reform Act. The measure is also known as the McCain-Feingold Act after its chief sponsors, Senators John McCain (R., Ariz.) and Russell Feingold (D., Wisc.).

The new law banned soft money at the national level. It also regulated campaign ads paid for by interest groups and prohibited any such issue-advocacy commercials within thirty days of a primary election or sixty days of a general election.

The 2002 act set the amount that an individual could contribute to a federal candidate at $2,000 and the amount that an individual could give to all federal candidates at $95,000 over a two-year election cycle. (Under the law, some individual contribution limits are indexed for inflation and thus may change slightly with every election cycle.) Individuals could still contribute to state and local parties, so long as the contributions did not exceed $10,000 per year per individual. The new law went into effect the day after the 2002 general elections.

> ## "A PROMISING YOUNG MAN
> should go into politics so that he can go on promising for the rest of his life."
>
> ~ ROBERT BYRNE ~
> AMERICAN AUTHOR
> B. 1930

**The Supreme Court Upholds McCain-Feingold** Several groups immediately filed lawsuits challenging the constitutionality of the new law. Supporters of the restrictions on campaign ads by special interest groups argued that the large amounts of funds spent on these ads create an appearance of corruption in the political process. In contrast, an attorney for the National Rifle Association (NRA) argued that because the NRA represents "millions of Americans speaking in unison . . . [it] is not a *corruption* of the democratic political process; it *is* the democratic political process."[16] In December 2003, the Supreme Court upheld nearly all of the clauses of the act in *McConnell v. Federal Election Commission.*[17]

**The Supreme Court Changes Its Mind** Beginning in 2007, however, the Supreme Court began to chip away at the limits on independent expenditures contained in McCain-Feingold. In that year, in *Federal Election Commission v. Wisconsin Right to Life, Inc.,* the Court invalidated a major part of the 2002 law and overruled a portion of its own 2003 decision upholding the act. In the four years since the earlier ruling, Chief Justice John Roberts, Jr., and Associate Justice Samuel Alito, Jr., had been appointed, and both were conservatives.

In a five-to-four decision, the Court held that issue ads could not be prohibited in the time period preceding elections (thirty days before primary elections and sixty days before general elections) *unless* they were "susceptible of no reasonable interpretation other than as an appeal to vote for or against a specific candidate."[18] The Court concluded that restricting *all* television ads paid for by corporate or labor union treasuries in the weeks before an election amounted to censorship of political speech.

**Citizens United v. Federal Election Commission (FEC)** A January 2010 Supreme Court ruling helped establish our current wide-open campaign-finance system. This decision, *Citizens United v. FEC,* was initially seen as fostering a vast new wave of corporate spending on elections. The actual results were somewhat different.

In the *Wisconsin Right to Life* case described earlier, the Court ruled out bans on issue ads placed by

In this artist's rendering, U.S. Solicitor General Elena Kagan, right, argues her first case before the Supreme Court, *Citizens United v. Federal Election Commission*, in Washington, D.C.

AP PHOTO/DANA VERKOUTERAN

corporations and other organizations in the run-up to an election. In *Citizens United v. FEC*, the Court extended this protection to ads that attack or praise specific candidates, including ads that suggest voting for particular candidates.[19] Two months later, in *Speechnow v. FEC*, a federal court of appeals held that it was not possible to limit contributions to independent-expenditure groups based on the size or source of the contribution.[20] As a result of these two decisions, *Citizens United* and *Speechnow*, there is now no limit on the ability of corporations, unions, nonprofit groups, or individuals to fund advertising, provided that they do not contribute directly to a candidate's campaign.

While Republican leaders applauded the *Citizens United* ruling as a victory for free speech, most Democratic leaders were appalled. They feared that the ruling would result in a massive tilting of the political landscape toward corporate wealth. We discuss that controversy in this chapter's *Join the Debate* feature on the facing page.

## 9–5e The Current Campaign-Finance Environment

Because *Citizens United* was issued less than a year before the 2010 elections, its impact in that year was modest. By 2012, however, the new rules had entirely shaped the campaign-finance environment. Individuals and PACs still faced limits on what they could contribute

directly to candidate's campaigns and to the parties. Despite these limits, the campaigns and parties were still able to raise huge sums. Meanwhile, independent organizations stood out as the wildcard in American politics. We list the largest independent committees as of August 2012 in Table 9–1 on page 216.

**Super PACs** A new type of organization came into existence to take advantage of the new rules. Known officially as "independent-expenditure only committees," the new bodies were soon dubbed super PACs. Their supposed independence from campaigns, however, turned out to be a convenient fiction. By 2011, every major presidential candidate had one or more affiliated super PACs, usually run by former members of the candidate's own campaign. Newt Gingrich, Ron Paul, Rick Perry, Mitt Romney, Rick Santorum—and Barack Obama—each had an associated super PAC. A division of labor soon developed. Super PACs would run negative ads to damage a candidate's opponents, while candidate committees accentuated the positive about the candidate.

When *Citizens United* was handed down, a flood of corporate cash was expected to enter the political system. The ruling did result in more corporate (and union) spending but far less than anticipated. Apparently, many companies were reluctant to take stands that might alienate a large number of customers. What caught everyone by surprise was the huge volume of finance poured into super PACs by individuals, notably individuals of great wealth.

For example, Charles and David Koch, two brothers with a long-standing commitment to conservative politics, set up their own independent committee, which soon became one of the largest. In January, Sheldon Adelson, a casino billionaire, contributed $5 million to Newt Gingrich's super PAC, and shortly thereafter Adelson's wife kicked in another $5 million. The Adelsons are credited with keeping Gingrich's campaign alive for an extra month. In June, Adelson donated $10 million to Mitt Romney's super PAC. While conservative donors

## Should *Citizens United* Be Overturned?

Federal restrictions on campaign financing have existed for decades. The latest of these was imposed by the Bipartisan Campaign Reform Act, also known as McCain-Feingold. A major portion of the act addressed issue-advocacy ads. Ads could not be paid for by a corporation or by a labor union using general corporate or union funds.

The Supreme Court struck down this part of the legislation in its controversial *Citizens United v. Federal Election Commission* decision in 2010. Those in favor of allowing unions and corporations to express their views about candidates hailed *Citizens United* as a free speech victory. Those who worry about corporate funds buying access to politicians would like the *Citizens United* decision to be overturned, either by a constitutional amendment or by a Supreme Court with new members. Who's right?

### Political Speech Must Always Be Free

"If the First Amendment has any force, it prohibits Congress from fining or jailing citizens, or associations of citizens, for simply engaging in political speech." So concludes the *Citizens United* opinion. Supporters of *Citizens United* say, "It can't be any simpler, can it?" The Constitution prohibits laws that hinder free speech, even if that speech involves highly negative criticism of political candidates. If unions or corporations want to spend money on criticizing one candidate in order to elect the other, so be it. Besides, given the widespread access of everyone to the "new" media—social networks, blogs, podcasts, Internet radio and TV—it doesn't matter how much corporations and unions spend on campaigns. All Americans have access to alternative ways to find out "the truth."

### Big Money Leads to Big Corruption

The *Citizens United* decision paved the way for the creation of super PACs. Corporations, unions, and super-rich individuals can now give money to these massive political action committees without limit. Today, so much money has been donated to super PACs that we are inundated with their ads. And, as everyone knows, these ads are almost uniformly negative. The individuals and corporations behind such advertising are well known to the candidates. When a winning candidate knows that a donor spent big money helping the candidate win, that winner knows something is expected in return. In fact, big spending on campaigns is likely to be a tacit bribe. Normally, we call this corruption. Opponents of the decision say, "Overturn *Citizens United* now."

**FOR CRITICAL ANALYSIS** Is it bad that we don't always know who is financing a political advertising campaign? Why or why not?

---

gained much attention, some billionaires also backed Democrats. As far back as 2004, for example, financier George Soros gave almost $24 million to independent groups dedicated to defeating Republican president George W. Bush.

### 527 and 501c Committees

Super PACs were not the only type of independent committee in existence. One alternate form was the *527 committee*, named after the provision of the tax code that covers it. Spending by 527s rose rapidly after 2002, and in the 2004 election cycle, the committees spent about $612 million to "advocate positions," as they were not allowed to "expressly advocate" voting for specific candidates. By 2008, 527 committees began to decline in importance, and by 2012 they were replaced almost completely by super PACS, which were allowed to campaign for and against candidates.

One reason for the decline of the 527 in 2008 was the creation of a new kind of body, the *501(c)4 organization*, known as the *501c*. Like the 527, this type of committee was named after a provision in the tax code. According to some lawyers, a 501c could make limited contributions directly to campaigns and—perhaps more importantly—could conceal the identities of its donors. So far, the FEC has refused to rule on the legality of this technique. Table 9–1 on the next page indicates which major independent committees are super PACs and which are 501c organizations. Some groups have organized both types.

TABLE 9–1

## The Twenty Top Groups Making Independent Expenditures during the 2011–2012 Cycle

This table lists independent expenditures only. Some groups, such as the party committees, have designated only a small part of their total fundraising as independent expenditures.

| Committee | Affiliation | Raised by October 2012 | Type | Disclosure of Contributors |
|---|---|---|---|---|
| American Crossroads & Crossroads GPS | Republican | $129,099,398 | Super PAC, 501c | partial |
| Restore Our Future | Mitt Romney | $117,405,715 | Super PAC | full |
| National Republican Congressional Committee | Republican | $57,052,468 | Party committee | full |
| Priorities USA Action | Barack Obama | $56,816,026 | Super PAC | partial |
| Democratic Congressional Campaign Committee | Democratic | $46,351,273 | Party committee | full |
| Democratic Senatorial Campaign Committee | Democratic | $42,272,748 | Party committee | full |
| Americans for Prosperity | Koch brothers (conservative) | $30,800,720 | 501c | none |
| Republican National Committee | Republican | $29,196,231 | Party committee | full |
| U.S. Chamber of Commerce | business | $28,873,817 | 501c | none |
| Service Employees International Union | labor | $28,069,574 | Super PAC, 527S | full |
| Majority PAC | Senate Democrats | $27,114,691 | Super PAC | full |
| National Republican Senatorial Committee | Republican | $21,537,108 | Party committee | full |
| House Majority PAC | Democratic | $21,377,797 | Super PAC | full |
| Winning Our Future | Newt Gingrich | $17,002,762 | Super PAC | full |
| Club for Growth | anti-tax | $15,781,250 | Super PAC, 501c | partial |
| American Federation of State, County & Municipal Employees | labor | $12,002,066 | 501c | full |
| Freedom Works | Dick Armey (conservative) | $11,858,959 | Super PAC | partial |
| Americans for Job Security | conservative | $11,387,275 | 501c | no |
| Americans for Tax Reform | anti-tax | $11,225,018 | 501c | no |
| American Future Fund | conservative | $10,113,905 | 501c | no |

Source: Center for Responsive Politics.

The creation of a committee that could hide its contributors created a new campaign-finance issue. Republicans argued that donors needed the right to remain anonymous so that they would not have to fear retribution. Democrats contended that anonymous contributions were simply a further corruption of the political process. Attempts to end such anonymity through legislation failed.

**FOR CRITICAL THINKING**

*Under what circumstances would you consider political contributions to be free speech— and under what circumstances would you see them as thinly veiled bribes to public officials?*

# AMERICA AT ODDS Campaigns and Elections

Some observers believe that if the founders could see how presidential campaigns are conducted today, they would be shocked at how candidates "pander to the masses." Whether they would be shocked at the costliness of modern campaigns is not as clear. After all, the founders themselves were an elitist, wealthy group, as are many of today's successful candidates for high political office. In any event, Americans today are certainly stunned by how much it takes to win an election. Some of the specific controversies that divide Americans concerning campaigns are the following:

- Is the electoral college a dangerous anachronism—or a force for stability within our political system?

- Should all voters be free to participate in any party primary—or does such a step make it too difficult for the parties to present a coherent group of candidates and policies?

- Should states retain their treasured right to set the dates of their presidential primaries—or should the national parties assume responsibility for establishing a rational primary schedule?

- Are campaign contributions a constitutionally protected form of free speech—or are they too often a source of corruption within the political system?

- Should all politically active groups be required to furnish the identities of their major contributors—or should we allow contributors to remain anonymous because they might suffer reprisals due to their contributions?

## TAKE ACTION

The most obvious way you can take action in political campaigns or elections is to join the campaign of a candidate you support. Any campaign has an insatiable desire for volunteers. Consider that by volunteering, you are, in effect, making a substantial political contribution that does not have to be reported to anyone. Volunteers can assemble mailings, answer the telephone, or make calls to encourage voters to support their candidate. Even if you have little free time or are not comfortable talking to strangers, most campaigns will be able to find a way in which you can participate.

An alternative is to work for a public-interest group. Many groups have worked toward reforming the way campaign funds are raised and spent in politics today. One nonprofit, nonpartisan grassroots organization that lobbies for campaign-finance reform is Common Cause. In the photo to the right, a participant in Colorado Common Cause's effort to reform campaign financing displays a mock-up of a TV remote control with a large mute button at a news conference. The group was asking voters to "mute" attack ads directed against a Colorado initiative to amend the state constitution to limit campaign financing and set contribution limits.

AP PHOTO/ED ANDRIESKI

# STUDY TOOLS

## Ready to study?

- Review what you've read with the quiz below. Check your answers on the Chapter in Review card at the back of the book. For any questions you miss, read the corresponding Learning Outcome section again to prepare for class and your exam.
- Rip out and study the Chapter in Review card.

## ... Or you can go online to CourseMate

at www.cengagebrain.com for these additional review materials:

- Practice Quizzes
- Key Term Flashcards or Crossword Puzzles
- Audio Summaries
- Simulations, Animated Learning Modules, and Interactive Timelines
- Videos
- American Government NewsWatch

## Fill-In

1. The electoral college system is primarily a winner-take-all system, in which the candidate _____.

2. A candidate must win at least _____ electoral votes, cast by the electors, to become president through the electoral college system.

3. In a _____ primary, voters cast their ballots directly for candidates.

4. In the context of presidential primaries, the practice known as front-loading refers to _____.

5. The attempt to learn damaging information about an opponent in a political campaign is called _____ research.

6. A campaign technique known as microtargeting involves _____.

7. The Federal Election Campaign Act of 1971 and its amendments provided public financing for presidential primaries and general elections, funded by a checkoff on _____

8. As a result of the Supreme Court's decision in *Citizens United v. Federal Election Commission* (2010), a new type of organization came into existence. Known officially as "independent-expenditure only committees," the new bodies were soon dubbed _____.

## Multiple Choice

9. The total number of electoral votes available is
   a. 538.   b. 535.   c. 435.

10. If no presidential candidate receives the required number of electoral votes,
    a. a runoff election is held in January.
    b. the House of Representatives votes on the candidates, with each state delegation casting only a single vote.
    c. the Senate votes on the candidates, with each senator casting one vote.

11. In a(n) ____ primary, only party members can vote to choose that party's candidates, and they may vote only in the primary of their own party.
    a. closed   b. open   c. indirect

12. In late summer of a presidential election year, ____ gather at their party's national convention to adopt the party platform and to nominate the party's presidential and vice-presidential candidates.
    a. poll watchers   b. delegates   c. electors

13. With the rise of candidate-centered campaigns in the past several decades, the role of the political party in managing campaigns has
    a. increased.
    b. stayed about the same.
    c. declined.

14. In the 2008 presidential elections, Barack Obama gained an edge on his rivals in part because of his superior use of
    a. radio.
    b. television.
    c. social media and the Internet.

15. The Federal Election Campaign Act allows corporations, labor unions, and interest groups to set up PACs to raise money for candidates. PACs can contribute up to ____ per candidate in each election, but there is no limit on the total amount of PAC contributions during an election cycle.
    a. $2,000   b. $5,000   c. $95,000

# Politics and the Media

BRIAN CAHN/ZUMA PRESS/CORBIS

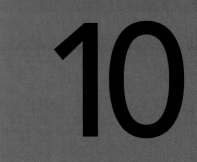

**Learning Outcomes**

The **Learning Outcomes** labeled 1 through 5 are designed to help improve your understanding of the chapter. After reading this chapter, you should be able to:

**10–1** Explain the role of the media in a democracy.

**10–2** Summarize how television influences the conduct of political campaigns.

**10–3** Explain why talk radio has been described as the Wild West of the media.

**10–4** Describe types of media bias and explain how such bias affects the political process.

**10–5** Indicate the extent to which the Internet is reshaping news and political campaigns.

**Remember to visit page 241 for additional Study Tools**

# ODDS

## Are Politicians Successfully "Gaming" the Press?

AP PHOTO/JOSH REYNOLDS

The First Amendment to the Constitution upholds the important role of a free press. The news media have been placed in a specially protected position in our country to serve as a watchdog against abuses by government and by politicians. Some Americans believe that the press has lost its ability to act in this way. Politicians have discovered that they can get away with saying anything that sounds plausible, even if it is an outright falsehood. (Comedian Stephen Colbert coined the word *truthiness* to describe statements that merely feel true.) Others argue that the press is doing more to expose falsehoods than ever before.

## Politicians Now Believe They Can Lie with Impunity

The 2012 presidential campaigns offer many examples of candidates getting away with falsehoods. Republican Mitt Romney claimed in an ad that Obama had a "plan to gut welfare reform by dropping work requirements. Under Obama's plan, you wouldn't have to work and wouldn't have to train for a job. They just send you your welfare check . . . ." In fact, the administration had granted several states, some with Republican governors, the flexibility to alter certain welfare program rules if they could show that the changes would *increase* the number of welfare recipients moving into employment. The Romney campaign refused to pull the ad, which insiders claimed was highly effective. "We're not going to let our campaign be dictated by fact-checkers," said Romney staffer Neil Newhouse (shown in the photo above).

For its part, Obama's super PAC ran an ad implying that Romney and Bain Capital were to blame for a woman's death when they closed the plant where her husband worked. In fact, Bain's responsibility for the closure was dubious, Romney was no longer running Bain at the time the plant closed, and the woman's loss of health-care insurance was not due to the closure.

## But Fact-Checkers Are on the Job

Those who defend the press observe that politicians have been abusing the facts for centuries, but journalistic fact-checkers have never been more active than they are today. Multiple fact-checking operations are now in business, many of them new. They include the Pulitzer Prize–winning PolitiFact, a project of the *Tampa Bay Times*. FactCheck is a project of a public-policy center at the University of Pennsylvania. Major newspapers, such as the *Washington Post,* now have their own in-house fact-checkers.

These operations make it much easier for journalists to crack down on political lies and misrepresentations. Reporters have always been reluctant to take responsibility for characterizing statements as false, whether they are made by politicians or anyone else. Findings by fact-checkers, however, are themselves newsworthy, and journalists can report on them as they would any other story. Fact-checkers do face one problem: voters may not care whether a particular statement is true or not. If people ignore what the press reveals, however, that is not the fault of the media. The press has still done its job.

## Where do you stand?

1. Psychologists have discovered that publicly debunking a false story can actually cause more people to believe it. Why might that happen?
2. Some news outlets, such as Fox News and MSNBC, adopt partisan viewpoints. Does this interfere with their ability to serve as watchdogs—or can it be advantageous? Explain.

## Explore this issue online

- To locate Web sites of important fact-checkers, enter "PolitiFact" or "factcheck" into your favorite search engine.
- To obtain a list of organizations that monitor the media for bias, search on "dmoz watchdogs." (DMOZ is an alternate name for the Open Directory Project.)

# Introduction

The debate over how effective politicians are at misleading journalists, described in the chapter-opening *America at Odds* feature, is just one aspect of an important topic: the role of the media in American politics. Strictly defined, the term *media* means communication channels. It is the plural form of *medium*, as in a medium, or means, of communication. In this strict sense, any method used by people to communicate—including the telephone—is a communication medium.

In this chapter, though, we look at the **mass media**—channels through which people can communicate to large audiences. These channels include the **print media** (newspapers and magazines) and the **electronic media** (radio, television, and the Internet).

# 10–1 The Role of the Media in a Democracy

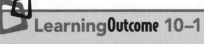

**LearningOutcome 10–1**

Explain the role of the media in a democracy.

What the media say and do has an impact on what Americans think about political issues. But just as clearly, the media also *reflect* what Americans think about politics. Some scholars argue that the media are the fourth "check" in our political system—checking and balancing the power of the president, the Congress, and the courts. The power of the media today is enormous, but how the media use their power is an issue about which Americans are often at odds.

## 10–1a Media Characteristics

The media are a dominant presence in our lives largely because they provide entertainment. Americans today enjoy more leisure than at any time in history, and we fill it up with e-books, movies, Web surfing, texting, and television—a huge amount of television. But the media play a vital role in our political lives as well, particularly during campaigns and elections. Politicians and political candidates have learned—often the hard way—that positive media exposure and news coverage are essential to winning votes.

As you read in Chapter 4, one of the most important civil liberties protected in the Bill of Rights is freedom of the press. Like free speech, a free press is considered a vital tool of the democratic process. If people are to cast informed votes, they must have access to a forum in which they can discuss public affairs fully and assess the conduct and competency of their officials. The media provide this forum.

In contrast, government censorship of the press is common in many nations around the globe. One example is China, where the Web is heavily censored, even though China now has more Internet users than any other country on earth.

## 10–1b The New Media and the Old

From the founding of the nation through the early years of the twentieth century, all media were print media—newspapers, magazines, and books. Beginning in the twentieth century, however, new media forms were introduced. Radio and motion pictures were the first new media, and they became important in the first half of the twentieth century.

Following World War II (1939–1945), broadcast television became the dominant form of communication. Cable television networks arrived in the 1970s. The Internet, including e-mail and the World Wide Web, came into widespread use by the general public in the 1990s.

**The Decline of the Old Media** Film and radio did not displace print media in the early twentieth century. Rather, television had a much greater effect. Beginning about 1950, the number of adults reading a daily paper began to decline, although circulation remained steady due to population growth.

**mass media**
Communication channels, such as newspapers and radio and television broadcasts, through which people can communicate to large audiences.

**print media**
Communication channels that consist of printed materials, such as newspapers and magazines.

**electronic media**
Communication channels that involve electronic transmissions, such as radio, television, and the Internet.

Later, the Internet proved to be much more devastating to newspapers than was television. Newspaper circulation fell modestly in the 1990s. In 2006, however, circulation began to collapse, declining more than 5 percent each year. We take a closer look at the problems of the newspaper industry in this chapter's *Our Challenging Times* feature on the facing page.

**Youth and the New Media**  Today, millions of Americans have developed unprecedented habits of media consumption. Leaders of the revolution include the wealthy and "early adopters" of new technology. Above all, the new consumers include the young. As one might expect, the upcoming generation of media users rarely read newspapers. But even television is now of lesser importance.

True, young people still watch a variety of television programs. Many of them, however, primarily view such shows online, as streaming video. Even e-mail has been abandoned by many of today's youth. Instead, messages are transmitted via Facebook, Twitter, Tumblr, Google+, and the smartphone. For such persons, old-media personalities such as television news anchors and radio talk-show hosts are completely obsolete.

**New Media versus Old Voters**  Yet radio, television, and print media remain important to American politics and government. Older Americans largely rely on these more traditional media outlets, and older voters outnumber the young. As of the 2010 census, approximately 100 million Americans were age fifty or older. The number of U.S. residents age eighteen through twenty-nine was about half that figure. Older voters are also much more likely to turn out to vote than younger ones. Finally, some of the most enthusiastic adopters of new media are not yet eighteen and cannot vote even if they want to.

To give an example, many young people may find radio host Rush Limbaugh—with his audience largely composed of middle-aged white men—to be irrelevant to their lives. Limbaugh is not irrelevant to American politics, however. His millions of listeners vote, and they can influence the outcome of Republican presidential primaries.

Considering the electorate as a whole, television remains the dominant medium in terms of political influence. Much of this chapter, therefore, deals with the impact of television.

## 10–1c The Media and the First Amendment

As noted earlier, freedom of the press is essential if the media are to play their role in supporting the democratic process. The concept of freedom of the press has been applied to print media since the adoption of the Bill of Rights. Such freedoms were not, however, immediately extended to other types of media as they came into existence.

Film was one of the first types of new media to be considered under the First Amendment, and in 1915 the United States Supreme Court ruled that "as a matter of common sense," freedom of the press did not apply to the movies.[1] Radio received no protection upon its development, and neither did television.

The Court did not extend First Amendment protections to the cinema until 1952.[2] Although the Court has stated that the First Amendment is relevant to broadcast media such as radio and television, to this day it has not granted these media complete protection.

For example, the Court has never ruled that the *fairness doctrine*, enforced by the Federal Communications Commission (FCC) from 1949

Anderson Cooper is one of the several well-known political commentators who work for CNN.

## The Decline of the Newspaper

The *New York Times*. The *Washington Post*. The *Wall Street Journal*. The *Christian Science Monitor*. These and hundreds of other major and minor newspapers have generated and disseminated the nation's news for more than one hundred years. But recent times have brought great changes to the newspaper industry.

### DWINDLING REVENUES

The Great Recession was hard on newspaper revenues. Some great newspapers have filed for bankruptcy protection. The following newspapers no longer exist: the *Tucson Citizen*, the *Rocky Mountain News*, the *Baltimore Examiner*, the *Cincinnati Post*, and the *Albuquerque Tribune*. Other newspapers have reduced their printing schedules or have gone completely online.

The online revolution has changed the newspaper business—and perhaps will destroy it. The key blow was financial. Classified advertising has always been a major revenue source for newspapers, but in the last decade various Internet sites such as Craigslist have taken over this function.

True, newspapers have gone online, but most have been unable to sell enough advertisements to pay for their online editions. The dean of the U.S. investing community, Warren Buffett, has said that the newspaper business faces "unending losses."

### FREE CONTENT IS EVERYWHERE

Still, Americans have more access to more news than ever before. Online news is available and updated day and night. An enormous number of citizen bloggers will help you find out what is happening anywhere in the world, at any time you want. Even if your hometown newspaper shuts down, "hyperlocal" Web sites are increasingly available to deliver local news. Many of these sites are organized by companies such as EveryBlock, Outside.In, Placeblogger, and Patch.

In the past, most Americans had to put up with whatever point of view their local newspaper provided. That is no longer the case. You can find the news—presented in whatever way you like—on thousands of Internet news sites and millions of blogs. Variety is the spice of life, and we certainly have more variety in news gathering and presentation than ever before.

### BUT WE STILL NEED REAL REPORTERS

Yet people have to be paid to do a good job, no matter what that job is. Journalists have families to feed. Rarely are they independently wealthy amateurs. Where does all that free content on the Web come from? Most of it can ultimately be traced back to journalists working for the print media. This is true of hyperlocal sites as well. Even today, newspapers employ the overwhelming majority of all journalists. How many bloggers bother to attend city council meetings and report what happens? Precious few do. Real reporters are still needed.

**YOU BE THE JUDGE** How much do you think the reputation of a news source really matters?

to 1987, is unconstitutional. Talk radio was essentially impossible until the doctrine was repealed. (You will learn more about the fairness doctrine and talk radio later in this chapter.)

In contrast, the Court extended First Amendment protections to the Internet in 1997, in its first opportunity to rule on the issue.[3] Cable TV received substantial protections in 2000.[4]

## 10–1d The Agenda-Setting Function of the Media

One of the criticisms often levied against the media is that they play too large a role in determining the issues, events, and personalities that are in the public eye. When people take in the day's top news stories, they usually assume that these stories concern the most important issues facing the nation. In actuality, the media decide the relative importance of issues by publicizing some issues and ignoring others, and by giving some stories high priority and others low priority.

By helping to determine what people will talk and think about, the media set the *political agenda*—the issues that politicians will address. In other words, the media are engaged in **agenda setting.** To borrow from Bernard Cohen's classic statement on the media and public opinion, the press (media) may *not* be successful in telling people what to think, but it is "stunningly successful in telling its readers what to think about."[5]

For example, television played a significant role in shaping public opinion about the Vietnam War (1965–1975), which has been called the first "television war." Part of the public opposition to the war in the late 1960s came about as a result of the daily portrayal of the war's horrors on TV news programs. Film footage and narrative accounts of the destruction, death, and suffering in Vietnam brought the war into living rooms across the United States.

### Priming and Framing

Two additional concepts related to agenda setting are *priming* and *framing*. In **priming,** a television show or an Internet blogger publicizes facts or ideas that may influence how the public thinks about a particular issue. As an example of priming, if the public is informed that the general rate of taxation in the United States is lower than it has been at any time since the 1950s, people are likely to be more receptive to the idea of raising tax rates on upper-income individuals.

In contrast, if the media point out that compared with other wealthy nations, the United States collects a much larger share of its tax revenue from the upper classes, then popular responses to proposals to tax our richer citizens may be quite different.

**Framing** an issue involves establishing the context in which it is understood. Frames are stories about how the world works. As an example, consider the different stories that can be told about someone who is experiencing poverty. A TV news show might cover a man whose condition was, to all appearances, due primarily to bad luck. Perhaps he suffered from a life-threatening disease, could not work, lost his job, and then became homeless. This description would set up a particular frame, encouraging viewers to take a positive attitude toward social spending that would provide aid to such an individual.

Another TV report might show a woman who became addicted to alcohol or drugs at an early age, dropped out of high school, and became pregnant without a partner to help support her. Such an account could lead to an entirely different frame, which would lead to a much more skeptical attitude toward spending that benefits the poor.

**Limits of Agenda Setting** The degree to which the media influence public opinion is not always all that clear, however. As you read in Chapter 8, some studies show that people filter the information they receive from the media through their own preconceived ideas about issues. People bring their own frames to political stories, in other words, and these frames can be very powerful.

Scholars who try to analyze the relationship between American politics and the media inevitably confront the chicken-and-egg conundrum: Do the media cause the public to hold certain views, or do the media merely reflect the public's views?

### 10–1e The Medium Does Affect the Message

Of all the media, television still has the greatest impact on most, especially older, Americans. Television reaches almost every home in the United States.

---

**agenda setting** The media's ability to determine which issues are considered to be important by the public and by politicians.

**priming** An agenda-setting technique in which a media outlet promotes specific facts or ideas that may affect the public's thinking on related topics.

**framing** An agenda-setting technique that establishes the context of a media report. Framing can mean fitting events into a familiar story or filtering information through preconceived ideas.

---

"The press may not be successful much of the time in telling people what to think, but it is stunningly successful in telling its readers **what to think about.**"

~ BERNARD C. COHEN ~
AMERICAN POLITICAL SCIENTIST
B. 1926

Even outside their homes, Americans can watch television—in airports, shopping malls, golf clubhouses, and medical offices. People can view television shows on their computers, and they can download TV programs to their smartphones and tablet devices and view the programs whenever and wherever they want.

Today, Americans watch more television than ever, and it is the primary news source for more than 65 percent of the citizenry. As you will read shortly, politicians take maximum advantage of the power and influence of television. But does the television medium alter the presentation of political information in any way? Compare the coverage given to an important political issue by the print media—including the online sites of major newspapers and magazines—with the coverage provided by broadcast and cable TV networks. You will note some striking differences.

For one thing, the print media (particularly leading newspapers such as the *Washington Post*, the *New York Times,* and the *Wall Street Journal*) treat an important issue in much more detail than television does. In addition to news stories based on reporters' research, you will find editorials taking positions on the issue and arguments supporting those positions. Television news, in contrast, is often criticized as being too brief and too superficial.

## Time Constraints

The medium of television necessarily imposes constraints on how political issues are presented. Time is limited. News stories must be reported quickly, in only a few minutes or occasionally in only a **sound bite,** a televised comment lasting for just a few seconds that captures a thought or a perspective and has an immediate impact on the viewers.

## A Visual Medium

Television reporting also relies extensively on visual elements, rather than words, to capture the viewers' attention. Inevitably, the photos or videos selected to depict a particular political event have exaggerated importance to viewers. The visual aspect of television contributes to its power, but it also creates a potential bias. Those watching the news presentation do not know what portions of a video being shown have been deleted, what other photos may have been taken, or whether other records of the event exist. This kind of "selection bias" will be discussed in more detail later in this chapter.

## Television Is Big Business

Today's TV networks compete aggressively with one another to air "breaking news" and to produce interesting news programs. Competition in the television industry understandably has had an effect on how the news is presented. To make profits, or even stay in business, TV stations need viewers. And to attract viewers, the news industry has turned to "infotainment"—programs that inform and entertain at the same time. Slick sets, attractive reporters, and animated graphics that dance across the television screen are now commonplace on most news programs, particularly on the cable news channels.

TV networks also compete with one another for advertising income. Although the media in the United States are among the freest in the world, their programming nonetheless remains vulnerable to the influence of their advertising sponsors.

## Ownership of the Media

Concentrated ownership of media is another issue. Many mainstream media outlets are owned by giant corporations, such as Time Warner, Rupert Murdoch's News Corporation, and even General Electric. An often expressed concern is that these giant corporations will influence news coverage to benefit their interests.

There is little evidence, however, that these corporations significantly influence reporting. Their media outlets do show a generalized support of the capitalist economic system, but capitalism is so widely accepted in this country that the press would probably endorse it under any form of media ownership. It is worth noting that values and opinions that enjoy near-universal support in the United States do not necessarily command the same respect in other countries. We examine a television network that operates in a different cultural environment in this chapter's *The Rest of the World* feature on the next page.

Concentrated ownership may be a more serious problem at the local level than at the national level. If only one or two companies own a city's newspaper and its TV stations, these outlets may not present a diversity of opinion. Further, the owners are unlikely to air information that could be damaging either to their advertisers or to themselves, or even to publicize views that they disagree with politically. For example, TV networks have refused to run antiwar commercials created by religious groups. Still, some media observers are not particularly concerned about concentrated

**sound bite** A televised comment, lasting for only a few seconds, that captures a thought or a perspective and has an immediate impact on the viewers.

## AL JAZEERA

Al Jazeera is the largest and most important television network in the Arab world. About 50 million people watch its Arab-language broadcasts. This network also launched an English-language service in 2006. Al Jazeera is owned and funded by the government of Qatar, a small, oil-rich monarchy, but it claims to be editorially independent.

### Al Jazeera and the Americans

Al Jazeera's relations with the American government have been rocky, to say the least. Before the 9/11 terrorist attacks, the U.S. government praised the network as an independent media outlet.

Thereafter, the George W. Bush administration denounced it for showing and reporting on film clips provided by al Qaeda. Al Jazeera opposed the U.S. invasion of Iraq, as did a majority of the Arab world, and it ran graphic footage of the results of U.S. airstrikes. In 2004, U.S. Defense Secretary Donald Rumsfeld accused

the network of broadcasting "vicious, inaccurate, and inexcusable" reports about the war in Iraq. In Spain, an Al Jazeera reporter was convicted of providing aid to al Qaeda. Al Jazeera offices in Afghanistan and Iraq were actually struck by U.S. missiles.

By 2011, however, the U.S. government was singing a different tune. Al Jazeera's reporting was a major factor in the success of the Arab Spring rebellions in Tunisia, Egypt, and eventually Libya. U.S. Secretary of State Hillary Clinton said of the network, "You may not agree with it, but you feel like you're getting real news around the clock instead of a million commercials." Al Jazeera is regular fare at the Pentagon. Did the U.S. government change—or did Al Jazeera?

### Al Jazeera and the Arabs

Regardless of what the American government has said about Al Jazeera, ordinary Arabs have always thought highly of it. Al Jazeera is seen in most of the Middle East as

a purveyor of fact, rather than a single ideological viewpoint. The network regularly interviews Israeli and American officials, allowing them to argue freely. This practice was seen as shocking when Al Jazeera first initiated it.

Indeed, Arabs are more likely to view Al Jazeera as too partial to the West than as too hard on it. The network has also been accused of failing to cover stories critical of the governments of Oman and next-door Bahrain, and of downplaying events in Saudi Arabia and Iran. Even so, Al Jazeera has at one time or another angered almost every government in the region, ranging from Algeria and Egypt to Israel and Iraq.

Al Jazeera has a reputation for accurate reporting in the Arab world because its reports are seen as truthful *by the citizens of Arab countries.* Arab opinion is key to the network's success—not American opinion or European opinion.

**FOR CRITICAL ANALYSIS** Americans can view the Web site of Al Jazeera English by searching on "jazeera." The only large cities where you can see the network on television, however, are Los Angeles, New York, and Washington, D.C. Why do you think Al Jazeera has such limited distribution?

---

ownership of traditional outlets, because the Internet has generated a massive diversification of media.

**The Murdoch Empire** A possible exception to the claim that major corporations do not influence reporting is the Murdoch media conglomerate. Murdoch's holdings in the United States, which include the Fox television networks, the *Wall Street Journal,* and the *New York Post,* are famous for promoting conservative politics. Fox News, in particular, has a notable influence in Republican circles. Still, Fox News is only one voice among many in America, and no one is required to depend on it for information.

The role of Murdoch's News Corporation has been more troubling in Britain. As of early 2011, the group's newspapers had 37 percent of national circulation in Britain, its radio networks commanded 47 percent of the audience, and it also had a major position in British television. Murdoch newspapers boasted that they had determined the outcome of British elections. Politicians of all parties believed that good relations with News Corporation were essential to their political survival.

In July 2011, however, Murdoch's influence was abruptly curbed by a major scandal. The *Guardian,* an independent newspaper, revealed that the *News of the World*, a Murdoch publication and Britain's largest Sunday paper, had illegally hacked into the cell phones of hundreds of individuals. Private investigators had hacked the phones of the royal family, leading actors and actresses, and even crime victims.

**FOR CRITICAL THINKING**

*How do you typically obtain information about political events? Does it differ from how your parents obtain information? Your grandparents?*

## 10-2 The Candidates and Television

**LearningOutcome 10–2**

Summarize how television influences the conduct of political campaigns.

Given the TV-saturated environment in which we live, it should come as no surprise that candidates spend a great deal of time—and money—obtaining a TV presence through political ads, debates, and general news coverage. Candidates and their campaign managers realize that the time and money are well spent because television has an important impact on the way people see the candidates, understand the issues, and cast their votes.

### 10–2a Political Advertising

Today, televised **political advertising** consumes at least half of the total budget for a major political campaign. In the 2004 election cycle, $1.4 billion was spent for political advertising on broadcast TV. This was almost five times the amount spent in the 1992 election cycle. According to the research firm PQ Media, spending on all forms of political advertising reached $4.5 billion in the 2007–2008 election cycle, including $2.3 billion for broadcast TV in 2008 alone.

For the 2012 election cycle, the Sunlight Foundation has estimated that total spending on political advertisements may have reached $9.8 billion.

**Spending on the Swing States** One characteristic of campaign advertising that was more noticeable in 2012 than ever before was its uneven distribution. By September 2012, residents of the

Pacific states had seen almost no presidential campaign ads. The only visible ads were those run nationwide. Voters in many other parts of the country could report the same.

In highly contested states such as Florida and Ohio, however, the main limitation on television spending appeared to be a shortage of advertising slots available for purchase. By early October, the presidential campaigns had dropped more than $100 million in Florida and more than $90 million in Ohio. In contrast, the campaigns had purchased almost no ads in California and Texas. These states have huge populations, but no amount of advertising would make California vote Republican or Texas Democratic.

**Attack Ads** Political advertising first appeared on television during the 1952 presidential campaign. At that time, there were only about 15 million television sets. Today, there are as many TV sets as people. Initially, political TV commercials were more or less like any other type of advertising. Instead of focusing on the positive qualities of a product, thirty-second or sixty-second ads focused on the positive qualities of a political candidate. Within the decade, however, **negative political advertising** began to appear on TV.

**PERSONAL ATTACKS GO WAY BACK.** Despite the barrage of criticism levied against the candidates' use of negative political ads during recent election cycles, such ads are not new. Indeed, **personal attack ads**—advertising that attacks the character of an opposing candidate—have a long tradition. In 1800, an article in the *Federalist Gazette of the United States* described Thomas Jefferson as having a "weakness of nerves, want of fortitude, and total imbecility of character."

After the terrorist attacks of September 11, 2001, candidates found that ads involving fear of terrorism resonated with

**political advertising**
Advertising undertaken by or on behalf of a political candidate to familiarize voters with the candidate and his or her views on campaign issues; also advertising for or against policy issues.

**negative political advertising** Political advertising undertaken for the purpose of discrediting an opposing candidate in the eyes of the voters. Attack ads are one form of negative political advertising.

**personal attack ad**
A negative political advertisement that attacks the character of an opposing candidate.

*"It's Lamar, Senator, he's going to take our attack ads door to door."*

voters. As a result, candidates routinely accused their opponents of lacking the fortitude to wage war on terrorism.

**PERSONAL ATTACKS IN 2012.** In the 2012 general election, the Obama campaign had much more to gain by "going personal" than the Romney campaign did. Romney's problem was that the voters now had four years of experience with President Obama, and almost all of them had already made up their minds as to what kind of person he was.

Many conservatives regarded the president with outright loathing, and so personal attacks on Obama were useful in mobilizing the faithful. Independents, however, often thought well of Obama as a person, even when they disagreed with his policies or believed him to be a failure on the economic front. Romney's task was to persuade these independents that the Republican team could do better, and trashing Obama personally would not help reach that goal. Romney's speech to the Republican National Convention, therefore, contained very little venom directed at his opponent.

**ATTEMPTS TO DEFINE ROMNEY.** For his part, Obama confronted a candidate who was not as well known to the public as he himself was. The Democrats, therefore, had an opportunity to define Romney in highly negative ways. The Obama campaign and its allies sought to portray Romney as a ruthless, wealthy financier who was out of touch with ordinary

**issue ad** A political advertisement that focuses on a particular issue. Issue ads can be used to support or attack a candidate's position or credibility.

people and who was indifferent to the suffering his policies would cause.

Romney's response was to "go positive" about himself and seek ways to show his genuine concern for other people. There were some favorable attitudes among the voters for Romney to build on. The number-one positive attribute that voters applied to Romney was honesty. This was true even though many Democrats believed that Romney's campaign was more addicted to falsehoods than any other in recent memory.

**Issue Ads** Candidates use negative **issue ads** to focus on flaws in their opponents' positions on various issues, such as health care and the bank-bailout legislation. Candidates also try to undermine their opponents' credibility by pointing to discrepancies between what the opponents say in their campaign speeches and their political records, such as voting records, which are available to the public and thus can easily be verified. As noted in Chapters 6 and 9, issue ads are also used by interest groups to gather support for candidates who endorse the groups' causes.

Issue ads can be even more devastating than personal attacks—as Barry Goldwater learned in 1964 when his opponent in the presidential race, President Lyndon Johnson, aired the "daisy girl" ad. This ad, a new departure in negative advertising, showed a little girl standing quietly in a field of daisies. She held a daisy and pulled off the petals, counting to herself. Suddenly, a deep voice was heard counting: "10, 9, 8, 7, 6, . . . ." When the countdown hit zero, the unmistakable mushroom cloud of an atomic explosion filled the screen. Then President Johnson's voice was heard saying, "These are the stakes: to make a world in which all of God's children can live, or to go into the dark. We must either love each other or we must die." A message on the screen then read: "Vote for President Johnson on November 3." The implication, of course, was that Goldwater would lead the country into a nuclear war.[6]

**Negative Advertising—Is It Good or Bad for Our Democracy?** The debate over the effect of negative advertising on our political system is ongoing. Some observers argue that negative ads can backfire. Extreme ads may create sympathy for the candidate being attacked rather than support for the attacker, particularly when the charges against the candidate being attacked are not credible. Many people fear that attack ads and "dirty tricks" used by

WHEN A
PRESIDENT DOESN'T
TELL THE TRUTH

This is a frame grab from a Romney campaign ad. In contrast, the Republican National Committee had a separate spot using a softer approach to win over disappointed Obama voters.

It is widely believed that Kennedy won the first of the 1960 debates in large part because of Nixon's haggard appearance and poor makeup—many people who heard the debate on the radio thought that Nixon had done well. No presidential debates were held during the general election campaigns of 1964, 1968, or 1972, but the debates have been a part of every election since 1976.

The 1992 debates, which starred Republican George H. W. Bush and Democrat Bill Clinton, also included a third-party candidate, H. Ross Perot. Since 1996, however, the Commission on Presidential Debates, which now organizes the events, has limited the participants to candidates of the two major parties.[9] The commission also organizes debates between the vice-presidential candidates.

both parties during a campaign may alienate citizens from the political process itself and thus lower voter turnout in elections.

Yet candidates and their campaign managers typically assert that they use negative advertising simply because it works. Negative TV ads are more likely than positive ads to grab the viewers' attention and make an impression. Also, according to media expert Shanto Iyengar, "the more negative the ad, the more likely it is to get free media coverage. So there's a big incentive to go to extremes."[7] Others believe that negative advertising is a force for good because it sharpens public debate, thereby enriching the democratic process. This is the position taken by Vanderbilt University political science professor John Geer. He contends that negative ads are likely to focus on substantive political issues instead of candidates' personal characteristics. Thus, negative ads do a better job of informing the voters about important campaign issues than positive ads do.[8]

## 10–2b Television Debates

Televised debates have been a feature of presidential campaigns since 1960, when presidential candidates Republican Richard M. Nixon and Democrat John F. Kennedy squared off in four great TV debates. Television debates provide an opportunity for voters to find out how candidates differ on issues. They also allow candidates to capitalize on the power of television to improve their images or point out the failings of their opponents.

**TV Debates and Election Outcomes**  Many contend that the presidential debates help shape the outcome of the elections. Others doubt that the debates—or the postdebate "spin" applied by campaign operatives and political commentators—have changed many votes. Evidence on this question is mixed.

Gallup polling figures suggest that in 1960 the debates helped Kennedy to victory. In 1980, Republican Ronald Reagan did well in a final debate with Democratic incumbent Jimmy Carter. Reagan impressed many voters with his sunny temperament, which helped dispel fears that he was a right-wing radical. In Gallup's opinion, however, Reagan would have won the election even without the debate.

**The 2012 Presidential Elections**  The 2012 presidential debates, held in October, gave Mitt Romney's campaign a substantial boost. In the months leading up to the debate, the Obama campaign enjoyed some success in defining Romney as a rich man who only cared about the interests of other upper-class Americans. This impression was reinforced by the release of a video in which Romney appeared contemptuous of citizens who were not wealthy enough to pay income taxes.

During the first debate, however, Romney was able to present himself as a caring and moderate candidate.

Obama, in contrast, seemed lethargic and unprepared. Obama turned in much better performances in the second and third debates, but the damage to his campaign was done. In the end, however, Romney's debate performance was not enough to propel him to victory.

## 10–2c News Coverage

Whereas political ads are expensive, coverage by the news media is free. Accordingly, the candidates try to take advantage of the media's interest in campaigns to increase the quantity and quality of news coverage. This is not always easy. Often, the media devote the lion's share of their coverage to polls and other indicators of which candidate is ahead in the race.

In recent years, candidates' campaign managers and political consultants have shown increasing sophistication in creating newsworthy events for journalists and TV camera crews to cover. This effort is commonly referred to as **managed news coverage.** For example, typically one of the jobs of the campaign manager is to create newsworthy events that demonstrate the candidate's strong points so that the media can capture this image of the candidate.[10]

Besides considering how camera angles and lighting affect a candidate's appearance, the political consultant plans political events to accommodate the press. The campaign staff attempts to make what the candidate is doing appear interesting. The staff also knows that journalists and political reporters compete for stories and that these individuals can be manipulated. Hence, they frequently are granted favors, such as exclusive personal interviews with the candidate. Each candidate's press advisers, often called **spin doctors,** also try to convince reporters to give the story or event a **spin,** or interpretation, that is favorable to the candidate.[11]

**managed news coverage** News coverage that is manipulated (managed) by a campaign manager or political consultant to gain media exposure for a political candidate.

**spin doctor** A political candidate's press adviser who tries to convince reporters to give a story or event concerning the candidate a particular "spin" (interpretation, or slant).

**spin** A reporter's slant on, or interpretation of, a particular event or action.

## 10–2d "Popular" Television

Although not normally regarded as a forum for political debate, television programs such as dramas, sitcoms, and late-night comedy shows often use political themes.

AP PHOTO CLIFF OWEN

Stephen Colbert has written and hosted *The Colbert Report* on the Comedy Central channel since 2005.

For example, the popular courtroom drama *Law & Order* regularly broached controversial topics such as the death penalty, the USA Patriot Act, and the rights of the accused. For years, the sitcom *Will and Grace* consistently brought to light issues regarding gay and lesbian rights. The dramatic *West Wing* series gave viewers a glimpse into national politics as it told the story of a fictional presidential administration. Late-night shows and programs such as *The Daily Show with Jon Stewart* and *The Colbert Report* provide a forum for politicians to demonstrate their lighter sides.

**FOR CRITICAL THINKING**

Media experts believe that negative political advertisements often include statements that are flatly untrue. *What, if anything, should the media do when that happens?*

## 10–3 Talk Radio— The Wild West of the Media

**LearningOutcome 10–3**

Explain why talk radio has been described as the Wild West of the media.

Ever since Franklin D. Roosevelt held his first "fireside chats" on radio, politicians have realized the power of that medium. From the beginning, radio has been a favorite outlet for the political right.

During the 1930s, for example, the nation's most successful radio commentator was Father Charles Edward Coughlin, a Roman Catholic priest based at the National Shrine of the Little Flower church in Royal Oak, Michigan. Coughlin's audience numbered more than 40 million listeners—in a nation that had only 123 million inhabitants in 1930. Coughlin started out as a Roosevelt supporter, but he soon moved to the far right, advocating anti-Semitism and expressing sympathy for Adolf Hitler. Coughlin's fascist connections eventually destroyed his popularity.

Modern talk radio took off in the United States during the 1990s. In 1988, there were 200 talk-show radio stations. Today, there are more than 1,200. The growth of talk radio was made possible by the Federal Communications Commission's repeal of the fairness doctrine in 1987.

Introduced in 1949, the *fairness doctrine* required the holders of broadcast licenses to present controversial issues of public importance in a manner that was (in the commission's view) honest, equitable, and balanced. That doctrine would have made it difficult for radio stations to broadcast conservative talk shows exclusively, as many now do.

Nine of the top ten talk-radio shows, as measured by Arbitron ratings, are politically conservative. No liberal commentator ranks higher than twentieth place in the ratings. (Several of the shows ranked higher than twentieth are not political but deal with subjects such as personal finance and paranormal activities.)

"For a politician to complain about the press is like **a ship's captain complaining about the sea.**"

~ ENOCH POWELL ~
BRITISH POLITICIAN
1912–1998

Conservative radio talk-show host Rush Limbaugh.

ALEXIS C. GLENN/UPI/LANDOV

## 10–3a Audiences and Hosts

The Pew Research Center for the People and the Press reports that 17 percent of the public regularly listens to talk radio. This audience is predominantly male, middle-aged, and conservative. Among those who regularly listen to talk radio, 41 percent consider themselves Republicans and 28 percent, Democrats.

Talk radio is sometimes characterized as the Wild West of the media. Talk-show hosts do not attempt to hide their political biases. If anything, they exaggerate them for effect. No journalistic conventions are observed. Leading shows, such as those of Rush Limbaugh, Sean Hannity, Andrew Wilkow, and Michael Savage, espouse a brand of conservatism that is robust, even radical. Opponents are regularly characterized as Nazis, Communists, or both at the same time. Limbaugh, for example, consistently refers to feminists as "feminazis."

Talk-show hosts sometimes appear to care more about the entertainment value of their statements than whether they are, strictly speaking, true. Hosts have often publicized fringe beliefs, such as the contention that President Barack Obama was not really born in the United States. The government of Britain actually banned Michael Savage from entry into that country based on his remarks about Muslims.

## 10–3b  The Wild West Migrates to Television

Commentators at Fox News have always been predominantly conservative, just as liberals are the rule at the smaller MSNBC network. Still, until recently it was widely seen as inappropriate for television personalities to employ the radical style characteristic of such talk-show hosts as Rush Limbaugh. That understanding began to crumble after October 2008, when Fox News hired radio talk-show host Glenn Beck.

In contrast to his large radio audience, Beck's TV audience was smaller than those of his Fox colleagues Bill O'Reilly and Sean Hannity. In short order, however, Beck transformed himself into one of the nation's most politically polarizing figures. Beck's emotional style—he frequently broke into tears—his over-the-top statements, and his apocalyptic views were a new development on television.

Beck gained further attention by using his on-air pulpit as a political organizing tool. Throughout 2009, Beck promoted the Tea Party movement, and in August 2010 he sponsored the Restoring Honor rally at the Lincoln Memorial

> "A nation that is afraid to let its people judge truth and falsehood in an
> ## OPEN MARKET
> is a nation that is afraid of its people."
>
> ~ JOHN FITZGERALD KENNEDY ~
> THIRTY-FIFTH PRESIDENT
> OF THE UNITED STATES
> 1961–1963

in Washington, D.C., which was attended by nearly 200,000 people. Beck's activism appears to be the primary reason that Fox News canceled his show in 2011. The head of Fox News, Roger Ailes, said that Beck's "goals were different from our goals. . . . I need people focused on a daily television show."

## 10–3c  The Impact of Talk Radio

The overwhelming dominance of strong conservative voices on talk radio is justified by supporters as a good way to counter what they perceive as the liberal bias in the mainstream print and TV media. (We discuss the question of bias in the media in the following section.) Supporters say that such shows are simply a response to consumer demand. Those who think that talk radio is good for the country argue that talk shows, taken together, provide a great populist forum. Others are uneasy because they fear that talk shows empower fringe groups, perhaps magnifying their rage.

Those who claim that talk-show hosts go too far ultimately have to deal with the constitutional issue of free speech. While the courts have always given broad support to freedom of expression, broadcast media have been something of an exception, as was explained in Chapter 4. The United States Supreme Court, for example, upheld the fairness doctrine in a 1969 ruling.[12]

Presumably, the doctrine could be reinstated. In 2009, after the Democratic victories in the 2008 elections, a few liberals advocated doing just that. President Obama and the Democratic leadership in Congress, however, quickly put an end to this notion. Americans have come to accept talk radio as part of the political environment, and any attempt to curtail it would be extremely unpopular.

HENRY S. DZIEKAN III/GETTY IMAGES

Andrew Wilko hosts a conservative talk show on the SiriusXM satellite radio network.

## FOR CRITICAL THINKING

*Why, in your opinion, have liberal commentators found it so difficult to develop successful talk-radio shows?*

# 10–4 The Question of Media Bias

**Learning**Outcome 10–4

Describe types of media bias and explain how such bias affects the political process.

The question of media bias is important in any democracy. After all, for our political system to work, citizens must be well informed. And they can be well informed only if the news media, the source of much of their information, do not slant the news. Today, however, relatively few Americans believe that the news media are unbiased in their reporting. Accompanying this perception is a notable decline in the public's confidence in the news media in recent years.

In a 2012 Gallup poll measuring the public's confidence in various institutions, only 25 percent of the respondents stated that they had "a great deal" or "quite a lot" of confidence in newspapers, and 21 percent had the same degree of confidence in television news. Because of these low percentages, some analysts believe that the media are facing a crisis of confidence.

## 10–4a Partisan Bias

For years, conservatives have argued that there is a liberal bias in the media, and liberals have complained that the media reflect a conservative bias. The majority of Americans think that the media reflect a bias in one direction or another. According to a recent poll, 50 percent of the respondents believed that the news media leaned left, whereas only 22 percent thought that the news media had a conservative bias.

**The Attitudes of Journalists** Surveys and analyses of the attitudes and voting habits of reporters have suggested that journalists do indeed hold liberal views. Before the 2008 elections, MSNBC was able to identify 125 journalists who made political contributions to Democrats or liberal causes, according to Federal Election Commission records. Only 16 gave to Republicans. Two gave to both parties. Still, members of the press are likely to view themselves as moderates. In a recent study, the Pew Research Center for the People and the Press found that 64 percent of reporters in both national and local media applied the term *moderate* to themselves. Among journalists working for national outlets, 22 percent described themselves as liberal and only 5 percent as conservative.

In contrast, 14 percent of local reporters called themselves liberals, and 18 percent adopted the conservative label. There is substantial evidence that top journalists working for the nation's most famous newspapers and networks do tend to be liberal. Many journalists themselves perceive the *New York Times* as liberal (although an even larger number view Fox News as conservative).

**The Impact on Reporting** A number of media scholars, including Kathleen Hall Jamieson, suggest that even if many reporters hold liberal views, these views are not reflected in their reporting. Based on an extensive study of media coverage of presidential campaigns, Jamieson, director of the Annenberg Public Policy Center of the University of Pennsylvania, concludes that there is no systematic liberal or Democratic bias in news coverage.[13]

Media analysts Debra Reddin van Tuyll and Hubert P. van Tuyll have similarly concluded that left-leaning reporters do not automatically equate to left-leaning news coverage. They point out that reporters are only the starting point for news stories. Before any story goes to print or is aired on television, it has to go through a progression of editors and perhaps even the publisher. Because employees at the top of the corporate ladder in news organizations are more right leaning than left leaning, the end result of the editorial and oversight process is more balanced coverage.[14]

## 10–4b The Bias against Losers

Kathleen Hall Jamieson believes that media bias does play a significant role in shaping presidential campaigns and elections, but she argues that it is not a partisan bias. Rather, it is a bias against losers. A candidate who falls behind in the race is immediately labeled a "loser," making it even more difficult for the candidate to regain favor in the voters' eyes.[15]

Jamieson says that the media use the winner-loser paradigm to describe events throughout the campaigns. Even a presidential debate is regarded as a "sporting match" that results in a winner and a loser. In the days leading up to the 2012 debates, reporters focused on what each candidate had to do to "win" the debate. When the debate was over, reporters immediately speculated about who had "won" as they waited for post-debate polls to answer that question. According to Jamieson, this approach "squanders the opportunity to reinforce learning." The debates are an important source of political information for the voters, and this fact is eclipsed by the media's win-lose focus.

## 10–4c Selection Bias

As mentioned earlier, television is big business, and maximizing profits from advertising is a major consideration in what television stations choose to air. After all, a station or network that incurs losses will eventually go bankrupt. The expansion of the media universe to include cable channels and the Internet has also increased the competition among news sources. As a result, news directors *select* programming they believe will attract the largest audiences and garner the highest advertising revenues.

Competition for viewers and readers has become even more challenging in the wake of a declining news audience. A recent survey and analysis of reporters' attitudes conducted by the Pew Research Center's Project for Excellence in Journalism found that all media sectors except two are losing popularity. The two exceptions are the ethnic press, such as Latino newspapers and TV programs, and online sources—but even the online sector has stopped growing.[16]

**Selection Bias and the Bottom Line**  The Pew study also indicated that news organizations' struggles to stay afloat are having a notable effect on news coverage. The survey showed that a larger number of reporters than ever before (about 66 percent) agreed that "increased bottom-line pressure is seriously hurting the quality of news coverage." About one-third of the journalists—again, more than in previous surveys—stated that they have felt pressure from either advertisers or corporate owners concerning what to write or broadcast. In other words, these journalists believe that economic pressure—the need for revenues—is making significant inroads on independent editorial decision making.

Generally, the study found that news reporters are not too confident about the future of journalism.

**A Changing News Culture**  A number of studies, including the Pew study just cited, indicate that today's news culture is in the midst of change. News organizations are redefining their purpose and increasingly looking for special niches in which to build their audiences. According to the Pew study, for some markets the niche is *hyperlocalism*—that is, narrowing the focus of news to the local area.

For others, it is personal commentary, revolving around highly politicized TV figures such as Bill O'Reilly and Rachel Maddow. In a sense, news organizations have begun to base their appeal more on *how* they cover the news and less on *what* they cover. Traditional journalism—fact-based reporting instead of opinion and punditry—is becoming a smaller part of this mix.

Another development is the move toward highly specific subject matter that appeals strongly to a limited number of viewers. Magazines have always done this—consider the many magazine titles on topics such as model railroading or home decorating. With the large number of cable channels, *narrowcasting* has

AP PHOTO/JEFF CHRISTENSEN

Today, news organizations look for special niches around which to build their audiences. Bill O'Reilly hosts *The O'Reilly Factor,* a Fox News cable program where O'Reilly covers news stories and provides commentary on them.

WILLIAM B. PLOWMAN/NBC/NBC NEWSWIRE/GETTY IMAGES

Political commentator and journalist Rachel Maddow appears on MSNBC, where she has had a daily show since 2008.

become important on television as well. Networks now appeal to members of particular ethnic groups (BET— Black Entertainment Television), hobbyists (Cooking Channel), or history buffs (Military Channel).

## 10–5 Political News and Campaigns on the Web

**Learning Outcome 10–5**

Indicate the extent to which the Internet is reshaping news and political campaigns.

Cyberspace is getting bigger every day. Almost one-third of the world's inhabitants currently use the Internet, a total of about 2.3 billion people. According to Technorati, a blog search site, bloggers around the world update their blogs with new posts in eighty-one languages at a rate of almost 4 million posts every day. Among U.S. Internet users, 77 percent read blogs, and one blog tracker has identified more than 180 million blogs. In addition, popular networking sites have enormous numbers of personalized pages—Twitter has 500 million accounts, and Facebook has more than one billion.

Not surprisingly, the Internet is now a major source of information for many people. Gone are the days when you and your friends tromped to the library to research a paper. Why should you? You can go online and in a matter of seconds look up practically any subject. Of course, all major newspapers are online, as are transcripts of major television news programs. About two-thirds of Internet users consider the Internet to be an important source of news. Certainly, news abounds on the Web, and having an Internet strategy has become an integral part of political campaigning. Internet strategies have also been important in nations that do not enjoy free elections, as you will learn in this chapter's *Perception versus Reality* feature on the following page.

### 10–5a News Organizations Online

Almost every major news organization, both print and broadcast, delivers news via the Web. Indeed, an online presence is required to compete effectively with other traditional news companies for revenues. Studies of the media, including the study by the Pew Research Center's Project for Excellence in Journalism mentioned earlier, note that the online share of newspaper company revenues has increased over the years. Today, 12 percent of U.S. newspaper revenues come from online sources.

**Characteristics of Newspaper Sites** Web sites for newspapers, such as those of the *Washington Post* and the *New York Times*, have a notable advantage over their printed counterparts. They can add breaking news to their sites, informing readers of events that occurred just minutes ago. Another advantage is that they can link the reader to more extensive reports on particular topics. According to the Pew study, though, many papers shy away from in-text linking, perhaps fearing that if readers leave the news organization's site, they might not return.

Although some newspaper sites simply copy articles from their printed versions, the Web sites for major newspapers, including those for the *Washington Post* and the *New York Times*, offer a different array of coverage and options than their printed counterparts. Indeed, the Pew study noted that the online versions of competing newspapers tend to be much more similar than their printed versions are.

"**THE CITIZEN** can bring our political and governmental institutions back to life, make them responsive and accountable, and keep them honest. **NO ONE ELSE CAN.**"

~ JOHN GARDNER ~
AMERICAN NOVELIST
1933–1982

**Inadequate Revenues** A major problem facing these news organizations is that readers or viewers of online newspapers and news programs are typically the same people who read the printed news editions and view news programs on TV. Web-only readers of

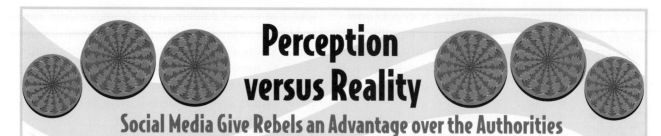

# Perception versus Reality

## Social Media Give Rebels an Advantage over the Authorities

It happened in Iran. It happened in Egypt. It happened in Tunisia. It has happened in China and in other countries with authoritarian regimes. Facebook, Twitter, and other social media have provided the communications necessary to organize demonstrations and other acts of rebellion. In Egypt and elsewhere, such demonstrations have helped bring down the government.

### THE PERCEPTION

Those who rebel against any type of authority can now use social media and cell phones to do more than just "get out the vote." They can generate massive demonstrations against dictatorial governments. Hooligans have also used such media to organize violent "flash mobs" that overwhelm any police presence. Rioters used smartphones to coordinate the vandalism, arson, and massive looting that took place in Britain in the summer of 2011.

### THE REALITY

Authoritarian governments might seem anachronistic, slow moving, and even foolish. But dictatorships are not blind to the uses of advanced technology.

Consider Iran. It was widely believed that incumbent president Mahmoud Ahmadinejad rigged the 2009 elections, guaranteeing his reelection. Rebels, including many young people, took to the streets. Many thought that the corrupt and repressive regime was finished. Far from it. The Green Revolution, as it was called, used Twitter, Facebook, and YouTube to its advantage—at first. But the Iranian government soon began using the same social media to identify activists, determine their connections with each other, and track down support from outside Iran. The government even used what it learned from social media when it put the rebels on trial.

Today, in countries such as Russia and China, government-paid bloggers support the regime. Many citizens who read such blogs do not realize that the government pays these bloggers. Other government supporters are paid to participate in Facebook and Twitter communities. Their "sincere" posts and tweets never fail to support government policies. Facial recognition software is another tool employed by oppressive regimes. Governments can compare the faces of protesters with photos that activists themselves have uploaded on social networks.

In short, social media can help organize a rebellion, but unless the rebellion wins, the advantage in using such media may quickly swing to the authorities.

**BLOG ON** You can find more information on how rebels have used social media by searching on "social media rebellion" and "flash mob." Evgeny Morozov is a major analyst of how authoritarian regimes have used social media. Search on his name to locate his blog and videos of interviews he has given.

a particular newspaper make up a relatively small percentage of those going online for their news. Therefore, investing heavily in online news delivery may not be a solution for news companies seeking to increase readership and revenues.

In fact, the additional revenues that newspapers have gained from their online editions do not come close to making up for the massive losses in advertising revenue suffered by their print editions. In many instances, publications have not sold enough advertising in their online editions even to make up for the additional expense of publishing on the Web.

**"All Your Online Ad Revenue Are Belong to Google"** The problem is not that there is an absolute shortage of online advertising revenue. In fact, by 2012, the advertising industry was spending more on Internet advertising than it spent on all print newspapers and magazines put together—$39.5 billion online versus $33.8 billion. The site eMarketer predicted that by 2016, print ad spending would be down slightly to $32.3 billion while online advertising would be up to $62.0 billion.

The real problem is that *content providers*—such as newspaper sites that hire journalists and create new material—receive a very small share of the online advertising. Most of the revenue goes to *aggregators,* including search engine sites that develop little new content but mostly direct users elsewhere. Google, by far the largest of these aggregators, collects two-fifths of all online ad revenues.

By 2012, the ad revenues of this single company exceeded the revenues of the entire newspaper industry, as shown in Figure 10–1. (Hence, a title of this section—a blogger's reference to a popular online gaming joke.) Of course, if the business of journalism were to collapse, Google would have little to aggregate. As of now, the cybersphere is nowhere close to resolving this issue.

## 10–5b Blogs and the Emergence of Citizen Journalism

As mentioned earlier, the news culture is changing, and at the heart of this change—and of most innovation in news delivery today—is the blogosphere. There has been a virtual explosion of blogs in recent years. To make their Web sites more competitive and appealing, and to counter the influence of blogs run by private citizens and those not in the news business, the mainstream news organizations have themselves been adding blogs to their Web sites.

Blogs are offered by independent journalists, various scholars, political activists, and the citizenry at large. Anyone who wants to can create a blog and post news or information, including videos, to share with others. Many blogs are political in nature, both reporting political developments and discussing politics. Taken as a whole, the collection, analysis, and dissemination of information online by the citizenry is referred to as **citizen journalism.** Other terms that have been used to describe the news blogosphere include *people journalism* and *participatory journalism.* When blogs focus on news and developments in a specific community, the term *community journalism* is often applied.

The increase in news blogs and do-it-yourself journalism on the Web clearly poses a threat to mainstream news sources. Compared with the operational costs faced by a major news organization, the cost of creating and maintaining blogs is trivial. Moreover, the most successful blogs are able to sell advertising, and because of their low costs it does not take much advertising to keep such sites in business. How can major news sources adhere to their traditional standards and still compete with this new world of news generated by citizens?

## 10–5c Podcasting the News

Another nontraditional form of news distribution is **podcasting**—the

**citizen journalism** The collection, analysis, and dissemination of information online by independent journalists, scholars, politicians, and the general citizenry.

**podcasting** The distribution of audio or video files to personal computers or mobile devices such as smartphones.

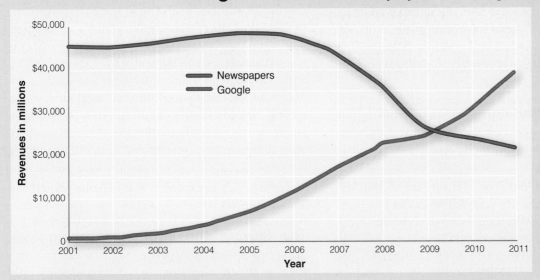

**FIGURE 10–1**

## Advertising Revenues:
### Google versus the Newspaper Industry, 2001–2011

Source: Dan McCarthy, The Media Transformation (blog).

distribution of audio or video files to personal computers or mobile devices such as smartphones.[17] Though still a relatively small portion of the overall news-delivery system, podcasts are becoming increasingly popular. Almost anyone can create a podcast and make it available for downloading onto computers or mobile devices, and like blogging, podcasting is inexpensive. As you will read next, political candidates are using both blogging and podcasting as part of their Internet campaign strategies.

## 10–5d Cyberspace and Political Campaigns

Today's political parties and candidates realize the benefits of using the Internet to conduct online campaigns and raise funds. Voters also are increasingly using the Web to access information about parties and candidates, promote political goals, and obtain political news. Generally, the use of the Internet is an inexpensive way for candidates to contact, recruit, and mobilize supporters, as well as to disseminate information about their positions on issues. In effect, the Internet can replace brochures, letters, and position papers. Individual voters or political party supporters can use the Internet to avoid having to go to special meetings or to a campaign site to do volunteer work or obtain information on a candidate's positions.

That the Internet is now a viable medium for communicating political information and interacting with voters was made clear in the campaigns preceding the 2008, 2010, and 2012 elections. According to a Pew Research Center survey following the 2008 presidential elections, 55 percent of Americans said that they went online for election news—up from 4 percent who did so in the 1996 campaign. Among Internet users, 18 percent posted political comments in a blog or on a social networking site. Fully 45 percent of users watched online videos related to the campaigns. One in three forwarded political content to someone else.

### Online Fund-Raising
The Internet can be an effective—and inexpensive—way to raise campaign funds. Fund-raising on the Internet by presidential candidates became widespread after the Federal Election Commission decided, in June 1999, that the federal government could distribute matching funds for credit-card donations received by candidates via the Internet.

In the 2008 presidential contest, however, the candidates took online fund-raising to an entirely new level, especially in the Democratic primaries. The

Ana Marie Cox founded the left-leaning online magazine wonkette.com, which features satire and political gossip.

fund-raising effort of Hillary Clinton would have been considered outstanding in any previous presidential election cycle. Yet it was eclipsed by the organization put together by Barack Obama.

Obama's online operation was the heart of his fund-raising success. One of its defining characteristics was its decentralization. The Obama campaign attempted to recruit as many supporters as possible to act as fund-raisers who solicited contributions from their friends and neighbors. As a result, Obama personally was spared much of the fund-raising effort that consumes the time of most national politicians.

In the first half of 2007, Obama's campaign raised $58 million, $16.4 million of which was made up of donations of less than $200. The total sum was a record, and the small-donation portion was unusually large. In September 2008, the Obama campaign set another fund-raising record with $150 million, the most ever raised in one month by a presidential campaign. By then, 2.9 million people had donated to Obama's campaign.

### The Rise of the Internet Campaign
An increasingly important part of political campaigning today is the Internet campaign. Candidates typically hire Web managers to manage their Internet campaigns.

The job of the Web manager, or Web strategist, is to create a well-designed, informative, and user-friendly campaign Web site to attract viewers, hold their attention, manage their e-mails, and track their credit-card contributions. The Web manager also hires bloggers to promote the candidate's views, arranges for podcasting of campaign information and updates to supporters, and hires staff to monitor the Web for news about the candidates and to track the online publications of *netroots groups*—online activists who support the candidate but are not controlled by the candidate's organization.

Armed with laptops and handheld video cameras, bloggers record Republican presidential primary candidate Tim Pawlenty as he talks with voters at Brick Street Books and Cafe in Adel, Iowa.

**Controlling the Netroots**   One of the challenges facing candidates today is trying to deliver a consistent campaign message to voters. Netroots groups may publish online promotional ads or other materials that do not represent a candidate's position. Similarly, online groups may attack the candidate's opponent in ways that the candidate does not approve. Yet no candidate wants to alienate these groups, because they can raise significant sums of money and garner votes for the candidate.

**Candidates' 24/7 Exposure**   Just as citizen journalism has altered the news culture, so have citizen videos changed the traditional campaign. For example, a candidate can never know when a comment that she or he makes may be caught on camera by someone with a cell phone or digital camera and published on the Internet for all to see.

A candidate's opponents may post on YouTube or some other Web site a compilation of video clips showing the candidate's inconsistent comments over time on a specific topic, such as abortion or the health-care reform legislation. The effect can be very damaging, because it makes the candidate's "flip-flopping" on the issue apparent.

**Gaffes during the 2012 Campaigns**   Both major-party presidential candidates experienced the dangers of 24/7 exposure during the 2012 campaigns. Republican Mitt Romney became rather well known for *gaffes*—poorly chosen words. The most damaging of these was a video of Romney speaking to wealthy donors: "There are 47 percent of the people who will vote for the president no matter what. . . . who believe that they are victims, who believe the government has a responsibility to care for them, who believe that they are entitled to health care, to food, to housing. . . . These are people who pay no income tax. . . . my job is not to worry about those people. I'll never convince them they should take personal responsibility and care for their lives." This comment powerfully reinforced the Democratic theme of Romney as a rich man out of touch with ordinary citizens. In fact, about half of the 47 percent who pay no income tax vote Republican.

Barack Obama occasionally put his foot in his mouth as well. Speaking to supporters, Obama tried to explain why the wealthy should pay more taxes: "If you were successful . . . somebody helped to create this unbelievable American system that we have that allowed you to thrive. Somebody invested in roads and bridges. If you've got a business—you didn't build that. Somebody else made that happen." In saying "you didn't build that," Obama was referring to infrastructure. A clumsy choice of words, however, made it sound as if he were referring to private businesses themselves. Republicans repeated the shorter version of the quote endlessly.

Sometimes, a gaffe was sufficient to threaten a candidate's entire campaign. In Missouri, Republican Senate candidate Todd Akin stated in an interview that women rarely become pregnant as a result of "legitimate rape." This incorrect statement led national Republicans—including Romney—to call on Akin to withdraw from the race. He refused, and was defeated in the general election.

*To what extent do the media—in particular, the new media—encourage political participation? To what extent might they discourage participation by providing apolitical entertainment?*

# AMERICA AT
# ODDS Politics and the Media

Americans love to hate the media, possibly because we spend so much time watching and reading them. Without a doubt, the media are undergoing a revolution today. With the loss of classified ads to the Internet, newspapers are in serious financial jeopardy. Online news sources, meanwhile, have yet to hit upon a reliable method of generating adequate income. In this changing environment, Americans are at odds over a number of media topics:

• Do the difficulties faced by newspapers threaten the existence of competent journalism—or is this not an important problem?

• Is the media's agenda-setting function a vital contribution to the democratic process—or an improper attempt to manipulate viewers?

• Should protection of the First Amendment be extended to broadcast media without exception—or would such a move threaten the morals of the country and make it impossible for viewers to avoid sexual content?

• Are negative advertisements an inevitable and unremarkable aspect of political campaigns—or should the voters punish politicians who employ them?

• Does talk radio add to the vigor of our political discourse—or is it a corrupting influence that divides the nation?

• Do the mainstream media have a liberal bias—or do they merely publicize facts that do not square with conservative beliefs?

# TAKE ACTION

Today, the media are wide open for citizen involvement. You, too, can report or comment on the news. Millions of people, especially students, are already halfway to becoming bloggers through their Facebook pages. You might consider turning political discussions on Facebook into an actual blog. In addition, Tumblr provides a useful platform for amateur blogs. Such a project is more easily undertaken if several friends share the responsibility for creating the content. That way, one person does not have to carry the entire load. You can set up links to articles or videos of interest at other sites, but an attractive blog isn't just links. It is also a place to view unique content.

A variety of other online projects are possible. You can create videos of events that you believe are newsworthy and post them online. You can podcast video or audio coverage of an event from a Web site that you have created. You, by yourself or with others, can set up a "radio station" to spread your views using the Internet. For example, in the photo shown here, two citizens who supported a proposed Tennessee state tax reform set up their own radio station in Nashville to mock local radio personalities who were opposed to the reform. Lining the street nearby are other supporters of the tax reform.

AP PHOTO/JOHN RUSSELL

**Local talk-radio and news programs abound. They are often irreverent and operated by young people.**

# STUDY TOOLS

## Ready to study?

- Review what you've read with the quiz below. Check your answers on the Chapter in Review card at the back of the book. For any questions you miss, read the corresponding Learning Outcome section again to prepare for class and your exam.
- Rip out and study the Chapter in Review card.

## . . . Or you can go online to CourseMate

at www.cengagebrain.com for these additional review materials:

- Practice Quizzes
- Key Term Flashcards or Crossword Puzzles
- Audio Summaries
- Simulations, Animated Learning Modules, and Interactive Timelines
- Videos
- American Government NewsWatch

## Fill-In

1. _____ is an agenda-setting technique in which a media outlet promotes specific facts or ideas that may affect the public's thinking on related topics.

2. Of all the media, _____ still has the greatest impact on most Americans.

3. A sound bite is _____.

4. _____ is the largest and most important television network in the Arab world.

5. The first televised presidential debate, between _____, took place in 1960.

6. Spin doctors are _____.

7. The talk-radio audience is predominantly _____.

8. Talk radio is sometimes characterized as the Wild West of the media because _____.

9. It has been suggested that the media use the winner-loser framework to describe events throughout the campaigns, contributing to a bias against _____.

10. Citizen journalism refers to _____.

## Multiple Choice

11. In the news business, framing refers to
    a. fitting events into a familiar story or filtering information through preconceived ideas.
    b. news coverage that is managed by a political consultant to gain media exposure for a political candidate.
    c. narrowing the focus of news to the local area.

12. The 1964 "daisy girl" ad is an example of
    a. a personal attack ad.
    b. citizen journalism.
    c. a negative issue ad.

13. Modern talk radio took off in the United States during the
    a. 1930s, after Franklin Roosevelt's first "fireside chat."
    b. 1950s, after political advertising first appeared on television.
    c. 1990s, after the repeal of the fairness doctrine.

14. In a 2012 Gallup poll measuring the public's confidence in various institutions, ____ percent of the respondents stated that they had a "great deal" or "quite a lot" of confidence in television news.
    a. 67
    b. 42
    c. 21

15. ____ refers to the distribution of audio or video files to personal computers or mobile devices such as smartphones.
    a. Blogging
    b. Podcasting
    c. Narrowcasting

# 11

# Congress

## Learning Outcomes

The **Learning Outcomes** labeled 1 through 6 are designed to help improve your understanding of the chapter. After reading this chapter, you should be able to:

**11–1** Explain how seats in the House of Representatives are apportioned among the states.

**11–2** Describe the power of incumbency.

**11–3** Identify the key leadership positions in Congress, describe the committee system, and indicate some important differences between the House of Representatives and the Senate.

**11–4** Summarize the specific steps in the lawmaking process.

**11–5** Identify Congress's oversight functions and explain how Congress fulfills them.

**11–6** Indicate what is involved in the congressional budgeting process.

**Remember to visit page 266 for additional Study Tools**

ALEX WONG/GETTY IMAGES

# AMERICA AT
# ODDS
## Should It Take Sixty Senators to Pass Important Legislation?

MOODBOARD/CORBIS

The number of Senate votes required to force an end to a filibuster is sixty. A filibuster takes place when senators use the chamber's tradition of unlimited debate to block legislation. In years past, filibustering senators would speak for hours—even reading names from the telephone book—to prevent a vote on a proposed bill.

In recent decades, however, Senate rules have permitted filibusters in which actual continuous floor speeches are not required. Senators merely announce that they are filibustering. The threat of a filibuster has created an *ad hoc* rule that important legislation needs the support of sixty senators. (There are exceptions. Budget bills can be handled using a special *reconciliation* rule that does not permit filibusters.)

If one party can elect sixty or more U.S. senators, assuming they all follow the party line, they can force through any legislation they want. The Democrats, in fact, enjoyed a supermajority in the Senate for seven months, from July 7, 2009, until February 4, 2010, when they lost a seat in a special election.

Are sixty votes an appropriate requirement for passing important legislation in the Senate? Should the number be reduced to fifty-five or even to fifty-one—a simple majority of all sitting senators?

## Don't Let the Majority Trample on the Minority

In the course of our history, the filibuster in the U.S. Senate has served us well. Filibusters provide the minority with an effective means of preventing the majority from ramming legislation down the throats of American voters. Rule by a simple majority can be scary. Support for a measure can shift between forty-nine votes and fifty-one votes very quickly. Should such small changes be the basis for passing major legislation?

A simple majority does not signify an adequate degree of consensus. It takes two-thirds of both chambers of Congress to override a veto by the president. That's another supermajority. Changing the Constitution requires a very substantial supermajority—three-quarters of the state legislatures. If these supermajority rules were good enough for the founders, then the principle still is good enough for the Senate.

## Don't Let Obstructionists Determine Legislation

Supermajorities allow a minority to block the preference of the majority. Even James Madison, who worried about the tyranny of the majority over the minority, recognized the opposite possibility. He said that "the fundamental principle of free government" might be reversed by supermajorities. "It would be no longer majority that would rule: the power would be transferred to the minority."

Furthermore, the sixty-vote requirement in the Senate has led to a significant increase in "pork"—that is, special spending provisions inserted into legislation. Senators working on bills find that they must fill them with pork to attract the votes of their colleagues. The Senate should reduce the votes required to end a filibuster to fifty-five or even fifty-one. Let's get on with government by the majority, not the supermajority.

## Where do you stand?

1. Why might it be appropriate to require supermajority voting for important legislation?
2. Under what circumstances do supermajority voting rules prevent democracy from being fully realized?

## Explore this issue online

You can find out more about the filibuster by entering "filibuster" into a search engine. For debates on the merits of the tradition, search on "filibuster pro con."

**apportionment** The distribution of House seats among the states on the basis of their respective populations.

**congressional district** The geographic area that is served by one member in the House of Representatives.

# Introduction

Congress is the lawmaking branch of government. When someone says, "There ought to be a law," at the federal level it is Congress that will make that law. The framers had a strong suspicion of powerful executive authority. Consequently, they made Congress—not the executive branch (the presidency)—the central institution of American government. Yet, as noted in Chapter 2, the founders created a system of checks and balances to ensure that no branch of the federal government, including Congress, could exercise too much power.

Many Americans view Congress as a largely faceless, anonymous legislative body that is quite distant and removed from their everyday lives. Yet the people you elect to Congress represent and advocate for your interests at the very highest level of power.

Furthermore, the laws created by the men and women in the U.S. Congress affect the daily lives of every American in one way or another. Getting to know your congressional representatives and how they are voting in Congress on issues that concern you is an important step toward becoming an informed voter. Even the details of how Congress makes law—such as the Senate rules described in the chapter-opening *America at Odds* feature—should be of interest to the savvy voter.

# 11–1 The Structure and Makeup of Congress

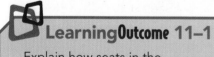

## LearningOutcome 11–1

Explain how seats in the House of Representatives are apportioned among the states.

The framers agreed that the Congress should be the "first branch of the government," as James Madison said, but they did not immediately agree on its organization. Ultimately, they decided on a *bicameral legislature*—a Congress consisting of two chambers. This was part of the Great Compromise, which you read about in Chapter 2.

The framers favored a bicameral legislature so that the two chambers, the House and the Senate, might serve as checks on each other's power and activity. The House was to represent the people. The Senate was to represent the states and would protect the interests of small states by giving them the same number of senators (two per state) as the larger states.

## 11–1a Apportionment of House Seats

The Constitution provides for the **apportionment** (distribution) of House seats among the states on the basis of their respective populations. States with larger populations, such as California, have many more representatives than states with smaller populations, such as Wyoming. California, for example, currently has fifty-three representatives in the House. Wyoming has only one.

Every ten years, House seats are reapportioned based on the outcome of the decennial (ten-year) census conducted by the U.S. Census Bureau. Figure 11–1 on the facing page indicates the states that gained and lost seats based on population changes reported by the 2010 census. This redistribution of seats took effect with the 113th Congress, elected in 2012.

**SOCIAL MEDIA** In Politics

If you are interested in Congress, two sources are worth investigating. Politico is a political news blog, and *Roll Call* is a newspaper covering Congress. Both have Facebook pages, and you can also follow either of them on Twitter.

Each state is guaranteed at least one House seat, no matter what its population. Today, seven states have only one representative.[1] The District of Columbia, American Samoa, Guam, the Northern Mariana Islands, and the U.S. Virgin Islands all send nonvoting delegates to the House. Puerto Rico, a self-governing possession of the United States, is represented by a nonvoting resident commissioner.

## 11–1b Congressional Districts

Whereas senators are elected to represent all of the people in a state, representatives are elected by the voters of a particular area known as a **congressional district.** The Constitution makes no provisions for congressional districts, and in the early 1800s each state was given the right to decide whether to have districts at all.

## FIGURE 11–1

# Election Votes Gained
## and Lost after the 2010 Census

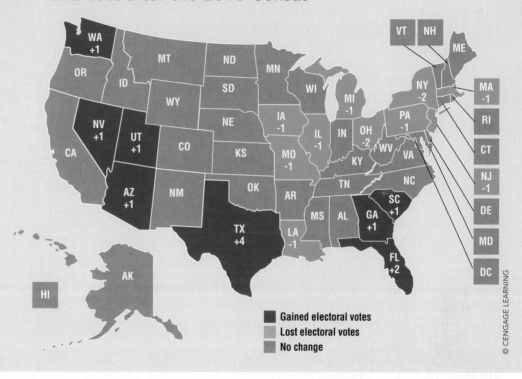

Gained electoral votes
Lost electoral votes
No change

© CENGAGE LEARNING

Most states set up single-member districts, in which voters in each district elected one of the state's representatives. In states that chose not to have districts, representatives were chosen at large, from the state as a whole. In 1842, however, Congress passed an act that required all states to send representatives to Congress from single-member districts, as you read in Chapter 7.

**The Size of the House** For many years, the number of House members increased as the population expanded. In 1929, however, a federal law fixed House membership at 435 members. Thus, today the 435 members of the House are chosen by the voters in 435 separate congressional districts across the country. If a state's population allows it to have only one representative, the entire state is one congressional district. In contrast, states with large populations have many districts. California, for example, because its population entitles it to send fifty-three representatives to the House, has fifty-three congressional districts.

As a result of the rule limiting the size of the House to 435 members, U.S. congressional districts on average now have very substantial populations— about 725,000 people. We compare the size of the U.S. House to the size of parliamentary bodies of other nations in this chapter's *The Rest of the World* feature on the next page.

## The Requirement of Equal Representation

By default, the lines of the congressional districts are drawn by the state legislatures. Alternatively, the task may be handed off to a designated body such as an independent commission. States must meet certain requirements in drawing district boundaries. To ensure equal representation in the House, districts in a given state must contain, as nearly as possible, equal numbers of people. Additionally, each district must have contiguous boundaries and must be "geographically compact," although this last requirement is not enforced very strictly.

If congressional districts are not made up of equal populations, the value of people's votes is not the same. In the past, state legislators often used this fact to their advantage. For example, traditionally, many state legislatures were controlled by rural areas. By drawing districts that were not equal in population, rural leaders attempted to curb the number of representatives from growing urban centers. At one point in the 1960s, in many states the largest district had

# The Size of Congress—How the United States Stacks Up

The U.S. House of Representatives is the "lower" chamber of our Congress. (In international terminology, it is the *lower house*.) The U.S. House consists of 435 members, a number established in 1929. That means, today, the average member of the House represents about 725,000 Americans. In other democracies, members of the lower house represent a far smaller number of people.

Almost all large nations—and even many of the smaller ones—have lower houses that are larger than the U.S. House. Britain's House of Commons has 650 members, each of whom represents about 95,000 inhabitants. The French National Assembly has 577 members, each representing about 113,000 people.

Only one nation in the entire world has a lower house with members who represent more people than House representatives do in America. That nation is India. Each of the 552 members of the House of the People represents about 2.2 million citizens. This makes a certain amount of sense—India has a total population in excess of 1.2 billion.

## Build a Bigger House?

New York University professor of sociology Dalton Connelly argues that as the third most populous nation on earth, the United States should have a larger House of Representatives. The average House member spoke for only 200,000 citizens in 1913. If that ratio were kept today, we would have more than 1,500 representatives. Because districts would be smaller, campaigns would be cheaper. We might have more citizen-legislators and fewer lifetime politicians. We would certainly see our representatives more often. Members of the House would do more of the work of the House, and there would be less reliance on staff members.

**FOR CRITICAL ANALYSIS** To create a larger House of Representatives, Congress itself would have to pass the necessary legislation. Why might current members of Congress be reluctant to do this?

---

twice the population of the smallest district. In effect, this meant that a person's vote in the largest district had only half the value of a person's vote in the smallest district.

For some time, the United States Supreme Court refused to address this problem. In 1962, however, in *Baker v. Carr*,[2] the Court ruled that the Tennessee state legislature's **malapportionment** was an issue that could be heard in the federal courts because it affected the constitutional requirement of equal protection under the law. Two years later, in *Wesberry v. Sanders*,[3] the Supreme Court held that congressional districts must have equal populations. This

principle has come to be known as the **"one person, one vote" rule.** In other words, one person's vote has to count as much as another's vote.

**Gerrymandering** Although in the 1960s the Supreme Court ruled that congressional districts must be equal in population, it continued to be silent on the issue of gerrymandered districts. **Gerrymandering** occurs when a district's boundaries are drawn to maximize the influence of a certain group or political party.

Where a party's voters are scarce, the boundaries of a district can be drawn to include as many of the party's voters as possible. Where the party is strong, the lines are drawn so that the opponent's supporters are spread across two or more districts, thus diluting the opponent's strength. (The term *gerrymandering* was originally used to describe the district lines drawn to favor the party of Governor Elbridge Gerry of Massachusetts prior to the 1812 elections—see Figure 11–2 on the facing page.)

Although there have been constitutional challenges to political gerrymandering,[4] the practice continues. It was certainly evident following the 2010

**malapportionment**
A condition in which the voting power of citizens in one district is greater than the voting power of citizens in another district.

**"one person, one vote" rule** A rule, or principle, requiring that congressional districts have equal populations so that one person's vote counts as much as another's vote.

**gerrymandering** The drawing of a legislative district's boundaries in such a way as to maximize the influence of a certain group or political party.

FIGURE 11-2

# The First "Gerrymander"

Prior to the 1812 elections, the Massachusetts legislature divided up Essex County in a way that favored Governor Elbridge Gerry's party. The result was a district that looked something like a salamander. A newspaper editor of the time referred to it as a "gerrymander," and the name stuck.

Source: *Congressional Quarterly's Guide to Congress*, 3d ed. (Washington, D.C.: Congressional Quarterly Press, 1982), p. 695.

census. Sophisticated computer programs were now able to analyze the partisan leanings of individual neighborhoods and city blocks. District lines were drawn to "pack" the opposing party's voters into the smallest number of districts or "crack" the opposing party's voters into several different districts. Packing and cracking make congressional races less competitive.

In 2003, for example, Texas adopted a controversial redistricting plan that was spearheaded by then House majority leader Tom DeLay (R., Tex.). DeLay and Texas Republicans used pack and crack tactics to redraw districts that had formerly leaned toward Democratic candidates. The plan effectively cost four Democratic representatives their seats in the 2004 elections.[5]

**RACIAL GERRYMANDERING.** Although political gerrymandering has a long history, gerrymandering to empower minority groups is a relatively new phenomenon. In the early 1990s, the U.S. Department of Justice instructed state legislatures to draw district lines to maximize the voting power of minority groups. As a result, several **minority-majority districts** were created.

Many of these districts took on bizarre shapes. For example, North Carolina's newly drawn Twelfth Congressional District was 165 miles long—a narrow strip that, for the most part, followed Interstate 85. The practice of racial gerrymandering has generated heated arguments on both sides of the issue.

Some groups contend that minority-majority districts are necessary to ensure equal representation of minority groups, as mandated by the Voting Rights Act of 1965. They further contend that these districts have been instrumental in increasing the number of African Americans holding political office. Before 1990, redistricting plans in the South often created only white-majority districts.[6]

**LIMITING RACIAL GERRYMANDERING.** Opponents of racial gerrymandering argue that such race-based districting is unconstitutional because it violates the equal protection clause. In a series of cases in the 1990s, the Supreme Court agreed and held that when race is the dominant factor in the drawing of congressional district lines, the districts are unconstitutional and must be redrawn.[7]

In 2001, however, the Supreme Court issued a ruling that seemed to suggest that it would not police racial gerrymandering very closely. North Carolina's Twelfth District, which had been redrawn in 1997, was again challenged in court as unconstitutional, and a lower court agreed. When the case reached the Supreme Court, however, the justices concluded that there was insufficient evidence that race had been the dominant factor in redrawing the district's boundaries.[8]

## 11–1c The Representation Function of Congress

Of the three branches of government, Congress has the closest ties to the American people. Members of Congress represent the interests and wishes of the constituents in their home states. At the same time, they must also consider larger national issues, such as the economy and the environment. Often, legislators find that the interests

**minority-majority district** A district in which minority groups make up a majority of the population.

of their constituents are at odds with the demands of national policy.

For example, limits on emissions of carbon dioxide might help reduce global warming, to the benefit of all Americans and the people of the world generally. Yet members of Congress who come from states where most electricity comes from coal-burning power plants might fear that new laws would hurt the local economy and cause companies to lay off workers. All members of Congress face difficult votes that set representational interests against lawmaking realities. There are several views on how legislators should decide such issues.

**The Trustee View of Representation** Some believe that representatives should act as **trustees** of the broad interests of the entire society, rather than serving only the narrow interests of their constituents. Under the trustee view, a legislator should act according to her or his conscience and perception of national needs. For example, a senator from North Carolina might support laws regulating the tobacco industry, even though the state's economy could be negatively affected.

**The Instructed-Delegate View of Representation** In contrast, others believe that members of Congress should behave as **instructed delegates.** The instructed-delegate view requires representatives to mirror the views of their constituents, regardless of their opinions. Under this view, a senator from Nebraska would strive to obtain subsidies for corn growers, and a representative from the Detroit area would seek to protect the automobile industry.

**The Partisan View of Representation** Because the political parties often take different positions on legislative issues, there are times when members of Congress are very attentive to the wishes of the party leadership. Especially on matters that are controversial, the Democratic members of Congress will be more likely to vote in favor of policies endorsed by a Democratic president, while Republicans will be more likely to oppose them.

**The Politico Style** Typically, members of Congress combine these three approaches in what is often called the "politico" style. Legislators may take a trustee approach on some issues, adhere to the instructed-delegate view on other matters, and follow the party line on still others.

Whichever approach a member takes, a variety of legislative techniques are available. One of these is to sponsor legislation purely for show, with no

## ELECTIONS 2012

### Party
### Control of Congress after the 2012 Elections

In 2012, an additional two U.S. Senate seats were a pleasant surprise for the Democrats. With fifty-five members, however, the Democratic caucus was not large enough to end a filibuster. In the U.S. House, the Democrats picked up only a handful of seats. These results, however, were not quite the sign of Republican strength that they seemed to be at first glance. In 2012, the Republicans won control of state legislatures across the country. These victories occurred just before the states were required to redraw the boundaries of congressional districts following the 2010 census. Republican legislators therefore gerrymandered the districts. To see how effective a gerrymander can be, consider

Pennsylvania. That state went for Barack Obama by 5.3 percentage points. What were the House results? With most of the vote counted, Pennsylvania voters cast 2.72 million votes for Democratic House candidates and 2.65 million votes for Republicans. These votes elected five Democratic representatives and thirteen Republicans. Some states, such as Illinois, had Democratic gerrymanders. The number of states with Republican gerrymanders was greater, however, including Florida, Michigan, North Carolina, Ohio, and Texas. Fortunately for the Democrats, the effects of a gerrymander wear off in time. Still, the Republicans looked set to enjoy the fruits of their 2010 victories for years to come.

expectation that it will pass. We look at examples of such legislation in the *Our Challenging Times* feature on the following page.

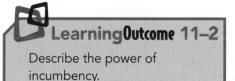

FOR CRITICAL THINKING

Some states have tried to prevent gerrymandering by establishing independent redistricting commissions. *What kinds of individuals should serve on such commissions? Why?*

## 11–2 Congressional Elections

### LearningOutcome 11–2

Describe the power of incumbency.

The U.S. Constitution requires that representatives to Congress be elected every second year by popular vote. Senators are elected every six years, also by popular vote (since the ratification of the Seventeenth Amendment).

Under Article I, Section 4, of the Constitution, state legislatures control the "Times, Places and Manner of holding Elections for Senators and Representatives." Congress, however, "may at any time by Law make or alter such Regulations." As you read in Chapter 9, control over the process of nominating congressional candidates has largely shifted from party conventions to direct primaries, in which the party's supporters select the candidates who will carry that party's endorsement into the general election.

### 11–2a Who Can Be a Member of Congress?

The Constitution sets forth only a few qualifications that those running for Congress must meet. To be a member of the House, a person must have been a citizen of the United States for at least seven years prior to his or her election, must be a legal resident of the state from which he or she is to be elected, and must be at least twenty-five years of age.

To be elected to the Senate, a person must have been a citizen for at least nine years, must be a legal resident of the state from which she or he is to be elected, and must be at least thirty years of age. The Supreme Court has ruled that neither the Congress nor the states can add to these three qualifications.[9]

Once elected to Congress, a senator or representative receives an annual salary from the government—$174,000 for rank-and-file members as of 2012. He or she also enjoys certain perks and privileges. Additionally, if a member of Congress wants to run for reelection in the next congressional elections, that person's chances are greatly enhanced by the power that incumbency brings to a reelection campaign.

### 11–2b The Power of Incumbency

The power of incumbency has long been noted in American politics. Typically, incumbents win so often and by such large margins that some observers have claimed that our electoral system involves something similar to a hereditary entitlement. As you can see in Table 11–1 on page 251, most incumbents in Congress are reelected if they run.

Incumbent politicians enjoy several advantages over their opponents. A key advantage is their fund-raising

MELINA MARA/THE WASHINGTON POST/GETTY IMAGES

Senator Lisa Murkowski (seated, left) speaks to constituents at a meet-and-greet coffee at a private home in Anchorage, Alaska.

# OUR CHALLENGING TIMES

## The Games That Congress Plays

No one doubts that we are experiencing challenging times. The unemployment rate remains historically high. Economic growth isn't strong enough to put everyone back to work. Many state and local governments continue to lay off workers. We could fill a book with the challenges our nation faces. Congress, one would think, should take action.

### BILLS PRESENTED FOR CONSIDERATION

Every year, Democrats and Republicans—and their staff members—spend a great deal of time crafting bills that they will introduce in the House and Senate. The number of such bills has been rising for decades. In the 104th Congress (1995–1996), 6,542 bills were introduced. By the 109th Congress (2005–2006), the number of bills had surpassed 10,000. In the 112th Congress (2011–2012), the number exceeded 11,500. Of these bills, about 10,400 were buried in committee, dead on arrival. For one reason or another, most of the rest would also never see the light of day. The 112th Congress managed to pass fewer bills than any other in the last thirty years.

### BILLS GUARANTEED TO FAIL

With so many bills doomed to failure, members of Congress are encouraged to propose legislation that may sound good to some constituents, but can never possibly pass. Many of these bills appear to be carefully crafted to fail. Consider some examples:

- Representative Dennis Kucinich (D., Ohio) introduced a bill under which taxes on the "windfall profits" of oil and gas companies would be decided by a "reasonable profits board." The chances of such a bill making its way through the pro-business Republican House? Zero.
- Representative David Schweikert (R., Ariz.) introduced a bill to require the approval of a majority of the state legislatures before the national debt ceiling limit could be raised again. The bill went nowhere and is probably unconstitutional to boot.
- Representative Thomas Latham (R., Iowa) thought he had a great idea—withhold congressional salaries if Congress hasn't passed a budget by May 15th of each year. Would Congress vote to withhold its own paychecks? Dream on.
- House Republicans voted to repeal Obamacare even though such a measure would never pass the Senate. This sounds reasonable. The Republicans surely wanted to get everyone's opinion of the Affordable Care Act on the record. But the Republicans voted to repeal Obamacare *thirty-three different times.* Overkill, definitely.

## WHY DO THEY DO IT?

Why would members of Congress waste their time creating bills that they know are destined to fail? One answer is that they can highlight their attempts at "doing something" when they run for reelection. A second reason is just as common: legislators want to force their opponents to vote against a measure that sounds good to many voters.

## YOU BE THE JUDGE
If you were a member of Congress, would you also create bills that were destined to fail? Why or why not?

ability. Most incumbent members of Congress have a much larger network of contacts, donors, and lobbyists than their opponents have. Incumbents raise, on average, twice as much in campaign funds as their challengers. Other advantages that incumbents can put to work to aid their reelection include:

- *Congressional franking privileges*—members of Congress can mail newsletters and other correspondence to their constituents at the taxpayers' expense. (In an era of e-mail and social networking, however, the franking privilege is much less valuable than it used to be.)

TABLE 11–1

## The Power of Incumbency

| | Presidential-Year Elections | | | | | | | | Midterm Elections | | | | | | |
|---|---|---|---|---|---|---|---|---|---|---|---|---|---|---|---|
| **House** | 1984 | 1988 | 1992 | 1996 | 2000 | 2004 | 2008 | 2012 | 1986 | 1990 | 1994 | 1998 | 2002 | 2006 | 2010 |
| Number of incumbent candidates | 411 | 409 | 368 | 384 | 403 | 404 | 404 | 390 | 394 | 406 | 387 | 402 | 393 | 405 | 397 |
| Reelected | 392 | 402 | 325 | 361 | 394 | 397 | 381 | 351 | 385 | 390 | 349 | 395 | 383 | 382 | 338 |
| Percentage of total | 95.4 | 98.3 | 88.3 | 94.0 | 97.8 | 98.3 | 94.3 | 80.7 | 97.7 | 96.0 | 90.2 | 98.3 | 97.5 | 94.3 | 85.1 |
| Defeated | 19 | 7 | 43 | 23 | 9 | 7 | 23 | 39 | 9 | 16 | 38 | 7 | 10 | 23 | 59 |
| **Senate** | | | | | | | | | | | | | | | |
| Number of incumbent candidates | 29 | 27 | 28 | 21 | 29 | 26 | 30 | 23 | 28 | 32 | 26 | 29 | 28 | 29 | 24 |
| Reelected | 26 | 23 | 23 | 19 | 23 | 25 | 26 | 21 | 21 | 31 | 24 | 26 | 24 | 23 | 20 |
| Percentage of total | 89.6 | 85.2 | 82.1 | 90.5 | 79.3 | 96.2 | 86.7 | 90.5 | 75.0 | 96.9 | 92.3 | 89.7 | 85.7 | 79.3 | 83.3 |
| Defeated | 3 | 4 | 5 | 2 | 6 | 1 | 4 | 2 | 7 | 1 | 2 | 3 | 4 | 6 | 4 |

Sources: Norman Ornstein, Thomas E. Mann, and Michael J. Malbin, *Vital Statistics on Congress, 2001–2002* (Washington, D.C.: The AEI Press, 2002); and authors' updates.

- *Professional staffs*—members have large administrative staffs both in Washington, D.C., and in their home districts.

- *Lawmaking power*—members can back legislation that will benefit their states or districts and then campaign on that legislative record in the next election.

- *Access to the media*—because they are elected officials, members have many opportunities to stage events for the press and thereby obtain free publicity.

- *Name recognition*—incumbent members are usually far better known to the voters than challengers are.

Critics argue that the advantages enjoyed by incumbents reduce the competition necessary for a healthy democracy. These incumbency advantages also serve to suppress voter turnout. Voters are less likely to turn out when an incumbent candidate is practically guaranteed reelection.

## 11–2c Congressional Terms

As noted earlier, members of the House of Representatives serve two-year terms, and senators serve six-year terms. This means that every two years we hold congressional elections: the entire House of Representatives and a third of the Senate are up for election. In January of every odd-numbered year, a "new" Congress convenes (of course, two-thirds of the senators are not new, and most House incumbents are reelected, so they are not new to Congress either). Each Congress has been numbered consecutively, dating back to 1789. The Congress that convened in 2013 was the 113th.

**Congressional Sessions** Each congressional term is divided into two regular sessions, or meetings—one for each year. Until about 1940, Congress remained in session for only four or five months, but the complicated rush of legislation and increased demand for services from the public in recent years have forced Congress to remain in session through most of each year.[10] Both chambers, however, schedule short recesses, or breaks, for holidays and vacations. The president may call a *special session* during a recess, but because Congress now meets on nearly a year-round basis, such sessions are rare.

**Term Limits** As you will read in Chapter 12, the president can serve for no more than two terms in office, due to the Twenty-second Amendment. There is no limit on the number of terms a senator or representative can serve, however. For example, Robert Byrd (D., W.V.) served more than fifty-two years in the U.S. Senate, from 1959 until he died in June 2010, at the age of ninety-two. Some observers favor term

AP PHOTO/EVAN VUCCI

COURTESY OF WWW.WIKIPEDIA.ORG

MICHAEL REYNOLDS/EPA/LANDOV

When the Republicans took control of the House after the 2010 elections, former minority leader John Boehner (R., Ohio), left, was elected Speaker of the House, and Eric Cantor (R., Va.), center, was elected House majority leader. Former Speaker Nancy Pelosi (D., Calif.), right, became the new House minority leader.

limits for members of Congress. The Supreme Court, however, has ruled that state-level attempts to impose term limits on members of the U.S. House or Senate are unconstitutional.[11]

## FOR CRITICAL THINKING

*What benefits could a state hope to gain from representation by a long-serving legislator?*

# 11–3 Congressional Leadership, the Committee System, and Bicameralism

The Constitution provides for the presiding officers of both the House and the Senate, and each chamber has added other leadership positions as it has seen fit. Leadership and organization in both chambers are based on membership in the two major political parties. The majority party in each chamber

**Speaker of the House**
The presiding officer in the House of Representatives. The Speaker has traditionally been a longtime member of the majority party and is often the most powerful and influential member of the House.

chooses the major officers of that chamber, controls debate on the floor, selects all committee chairpersons, and has a majority on all committees.

## 11–3a House Leadership

The Constitution states that members of the House are to choose their Speaker and other officers but says nothing more about these positions. Today, important "other officers" include the majority and minority leaders and whips.

**Speaker of the House** Chief among the leaders in the House of Representatives is the **Speaker of the House**. This office is filled by a vote taken at the beginning of each congressional term. The Speaker has traditionally been a longtime member of the majority party who has risen in rank and influence through years of service in the House. The candidate for Speaker is selected by the majority-party caucus. The House as a whole then approves the selection.

As the presiding officer of the House and the leader of the majority party, the Speaker has a great deal of power. In the nineteenth century, the Speaker

Identify the key leadership positions in Congress, describe the committee system, and indicate some important differences between the House of Representatives and the Senate.

had even more power and was known as the "king of the congressional mountain." Speakers known by such names as "Uncle Joe Cannon" and "Czar Reed" ruled the House with almost unchallengeable power. A revolt in 1910 reduced the Speaker's powers and gave some of those powers to various committees. Today, the Speaker still has many important powers, including the following:

- The Speaker has substantial control over what bills are assigned to which committees.

- The Speaker may preside over the sessions of the House, recognizing or ignoring members who wish to speak.

- The Speaker votes in the event of a tie, interprets and applies House rules, rules on points of order (questions about procedures asked by members), puts questions to a vote, and interprets the outcome of most of the votes taken.

- The Speaker plays a major role in making important committee assignments, which all members desire.

- The Speaker schedules bills for action.

The Speaker may choose whether to vote on any measure. If the Speaker chooses to vote, he or she appoints a temporary presiding officer (called a Speaker pro tempore), who then occupies the Speaker's chair. Under the House rules, the only time the Speaker *must* vote is to break a tie. Otherwise, a tie automatically defeats a bill. The Speaker does not often vote, but by choosing to vote in some cases, the Speaker can actually cause a tie and defeat a proposal.

**Majority Leader** The **majority leader** of the House is elected by the caucus of majority-party members to act as spokesperson for the party and to keep the party together. The majority leader's job is to help plan the party's legislative program, organize other party members to support legislation favored by the party, and make sure the chairpersons on the many committees finish work on bills that are important to the party. The House majority leader makes speeches on important bills, stating the majority party's position.

**Minority Leader** The House **minority leader** is the leader of the minority party. Although not as powerful as the majority leader, the minority leader has similar responsibilities. The primary duty of the minority leader is to maintain solidarity within the party. The minority leader persuades influential members of the party to follow its position and organizes fellow party members in criticism of the majority party's policies and programs.

**Whips** The leadership of each party includes assistants to the majority and minority leaders known as **whips.** Whips originated in the British House of Commons, where they were named after the "whipper in," the rider who keeps the hounds together in a fox

In 2006, Democratic senator Harry Reid of Nevada, left, became the Senate majority leader, and Republican senator Mitch McConnell of Kentucky became the Senate minority leader. Both retained their offices following the 2012 elections.

AP PHOTO/CAROLYN KASTER

MCCONNELL.SENATE.GOV/OFFICIAL_PHOTOS.CFM

**majority leader**
The party leader elected by the majority party in the House or in the Senate.

**minority leader**
The party leader elected by the minority party in the House or in the Senate.

**whip** A member of Congress who assists the majority or minority leader in the House or in the Senate in managing the party's legislative program.

hunt. The term is applied to assistant party leaders because of the pressure that they place on party members to uphold the party's positions.

Whips try to determine how each member is going to vote on certain issues and then advise the party leaders on the strength of party support. Whips also try to see that members are present when important votes are to be taken and that they vote with the party leadership. For example, if the Republican Party strongly supports a tax-cut bill, the Republican Party whip might meet with other Republican Party members in the House to try to ensure that they will show up and vote with the party.

## 11–3b Senate Leadership

The Constitution makes the vice president of the United States the president of the Senate. As presiding officer, the vice president may call on members to speak and put questions to a vote. The vice president is not an elected member of the Senate, however, and may not take part in Senate debates. The vice president may cast a vote in the Senate only in the event of a tie.

**President Pro Tempore** Because vice presidents are rarely available—and do not often desire—to preside over the Senate, senators elect another presiding officer, the president pro tempore ("pro tem"), who serves in the absence of the vice president. The president pro tem is elected by the whole Senate and is ordinarily the member of the majority party with the longest continuous term of service in the Senate. In the absence of both the president pro tem and the vice president, a temporary presiding officer is selected from the ranks of the Senate, usually a junior member of the majority party.

**Party Leaders** The real power in the Senate is held by the majority leader, the minority leader, and their whips. The majority leader is the most powerful individual and chief spokesperson of the majority party. The majority leader directs the legislative program and party strategy. The minority leader commands the minority party's opposition to the policies of the majority party and directs the legislative strategy of the minority party.

**standing committee** A permanent committee in Congress that deals with legislation concerning a particular area, such as agriculture or foreign relations.

**subcommittee** A division of a larger committee that deals with a particular part of the committee's policy area. Most standing committees have several subcommittees.

## 11–3c Congressional Committees

Thousands of bills are introduced during every session of Congress, and no single member can possibly be adequately informed on all the issues that arise. The committee system is a way to provide for specialization, or a division of the legislative labor. Members of a committee concentrate on just one area or topic—such as agriculture or transportation—and develop sufficient expertise to draft appropriate legislation when needed.

The flow of legislation through both the House and the Senate is determined largely by the speed with which the members of these committees act on bills and resolutions. The permanent and most powerful committees of Congress are called **standing committees.** Their names are listed in Table 11–2 on the facing page.

**Party Control of Committees** Before any bill can be considered by the entire House or Senate, it must be approved by a majority vote in the standing committee to which it was assigned. As mentioned, standing committees are controlled by the majority party in each chamber. Committee membership is generally divided between the parties according to the number of members in each chamber. In both the House and the Senate, committee *seniority*—the length of continuous service on a particular committee—typically plays a role in determining committee chairpersons.

**Subcommittees** Most House and Senate committees also have **subcommittees** with limited areas of jurisdiction. Today, there are more than two hundred subcommittees.

There are also other types of committees in Congress. Special, or select, committees, which may be either permanent or temporary, are formed to study specific problems or issues.

Joint committees are created by the concurrent action of both chambers of Congress and consist of members from each chamber. Joint committees have dealt with the economy, taxation, and the Library of Congress.

Conference committees, which include members from both the House and the Senate, are formed for the purpose of achieving agreement between the House and the Senate on the exact wording of legislative acts when the two chambers pass legislative proposals in different forms. No bill can be sent to the White House to be signed into law unless it first passes both chambers in identical form.

**TABLE 11–2**

## Standing Committees in the 113th Congress, 2013–2015

| House Committees | Senate Committees |
|---|---|
| Agriculture | Agriculture, Nutrition, and Forestry |
| Appropriations | Appropriations |
| Armed Services | Armed Services |
| Budget | Banking, Housing, and Urban Affairs |
| Education and the Workforce | Budget |
| Energy and Commerce | Commerce, Science, and Transportation |
| Financial Services | Energy and Natural Resources |
| Foreign Affairs | Environment and Public Works |
| Homeland Security | Finance |
| House Administration | Foreign Relations |
| Judiciary | Health, Education, Labor, and Pensions |
| Natural Resources | Homeland Security and Governmental Affairs |
| Oversight and Government Reform | Judiciary |
| Rules | Rules and Administration |
| Science and Technology | Small Business and Entrepreneurship |
| Small Business | Veterans' Affairs |
| Standards of Official Conduct | |
| Transportation and Infrastructure | |
| Veterans' Affairs | |
| Ways and Means | |

© CENGAGE LEARNING

**Rules Committee** A standing committee in the House of Representatives that provides special rules governing how particular bills will be considered and debated by the House. The Rules Committee normally proposes time limits on debate for any bill.

**filibustering** The Senate tradition of unlimited debate undertaken for the purpose of preventing action on a bill.

**cloture** A procedure for ending filibusters in the Senate and bringing the matter under consideration to a vote.

Most of the actual work of legislating is performed by the committees and subcommittees (the "little legislatures"[12]) within Congress. In creating or amending laws, committee members work closely with relevant interest groups and administrative agency personnel. (For more details on the interaction among these groups, see the discussion of "issue networks" and "iron triangles" in Chapter 13.)

## 11–3d The Differences between the House and the Senate

To understand what goes on in the chambers of Congress, we need to look at the effects of bicameralism. Each chamber of Congress has developed certain distinct features. The major differences between the House and the Senate are listed in Table 11–3 on the following page.

**Size Matters**   Obviously, with 435 voting members, the House cannot operate the same way as the Senate, which has only 100 members. With its larger size, the House needs both more rules and more formality—otherwise, no work would ever get done. The most obvious formal rules have to do with debate on the floor.

The Senate normally permits extended debate on all issues that arise before it. In contrast, the House uses an elaborate system: the House **Rules Committee** normally proposes time limits on debate for any bill, which are accepted or modified by the House. Despite its greater size, as a consequence of its stricter time limits on debate, the House is often able to act on legislation more quickly than the Senate.

**In the Senate, Debate Can Just Keep Going and Going**   At one time, both the House and the Senate allowed unlimited debate, but the House ended this practice in 1811. The use of unlimited debate in the Senate to obstruct legislation is called **filibustering** (see the chapter-opening *America at Odds* feature).

Today, under Senate Rule 22, filibusters may be ended by invoking **cloture**—a procedure for closing debate and bringing the matter under consideration to a vote in the Senate. Sixteen senators must sign a

TABLE 11–3

## Major Differences between the House and the Senate

| House* | Senate* |
|---|---|
| Members chosen from local districts | Members chosen from entire state |
| Two-year term | Six-year term |
| Always elected by voters | Originally (until 1913) elected by state legislatures |
| May impeach (accuse, indict) federal officials | May convict federal officials of impeachable offenses |
| Larger (435 voting members) | Smaller (100 members) |
| More formal rules | Fewer rules and restrictions |
| Debate limited | Debate extended |
| Floor action controlled | Unanimous consent rules |
| Less prestige and less individual notice | More prestige and media attention |
| Originates bills for raising revenues | Has power of "advice and consent" on presidential appointments and treaties |
| Local or narrow leadership | National leadership |

© CENGAGE LEARNING

*Some of these differences, such as term of office, are provided for in the Constitution, while others, such as debate rules, are not.

petition requesting cloture, and then, after two days have elapsed, three-fifths of the entire membership must vote for cloture. Normally, that means sixty senators. Once cloture is invoked, each senator may speak on a bill for no more than one hour before a vote is taken. Additionally, a final vote must take place within one hundred hours after cloture has been invoked.

**The Senatorial Hold**  Senators have an additional tool they can use to delay legislation. Individual senators may place a *hold* on a particular bill. A senator simply informs the leader of his or her party of the hold. Party leaders do not announce who has placed a hold, so holds are often anonymous. Recent rule changes designed to curb anonymous holds have been ineffective. Cloture can be used to lift a hold.

Senators often place holds on nominees for executive or judicial positions in an attempt to win concessions from the executive branch. For example, in 2010, Senator Richard Shelby (R., Ala.) placed holds on at least seventy of President Obama's nominations in an attempt to force the administration to support two military spending programs in Alabama.

**The Senate Wins the Prestige Race, Hands Down**  Because of the large number of representatives, few can garner the prestige that a senator enjoys.

Senators have relatively little difficulty in gaining access to the media. Members of the House, who run for reelection every two years, have to survive many reelection campaigns before they can obtain recognition for their activities. Usually, a representative has to become an important committee leader before she or he can enjoy the consistent attention of the national news media.

One consequence of the prestige difference is that it has been very difficult for a member of the House to win a presidential nomination. In contrast, the parties have often nominated senators, and a number of senators have gone on to become president.

FOR CRITICAL THINKING

Vice presidents typically avoid presiding over the Senate, even though that is their chief constitutional responsibility. *Why might they be so reluctant?*

## 11–4 The Legislative Process

Look at Figure 11–3 on the facing page, which shows the basic process through which a bill becomes law at the national level. Not

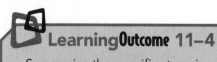

**Learning Outcome 11–4**

Summarize the specific steps in the lawmaking process.

all of the complexities of the process are shown, to be sure. For example, the figure does not indicate the extensive lobbying and media politics that are often involved in the legislative process. There is also no mention of the informal negotiations and "horse trading" that occur to get a bill passed.

**FIGURE 11-3** **How a Bill Becomes a Law**

This illustration shows the most typical way in which proposed legislation is enacted into law. The process is illustrated with two hypothetical bills, House bill No. 100 (HR 100) and Senate bill No. 200 (S 200). Bills must be passed by both chambers in identical form before they can be sent to the president. The path of HR 100 is traced by an orange line, and that of S 200 by a purple line. In practice, most bills begin as similar proposals in both chambers.

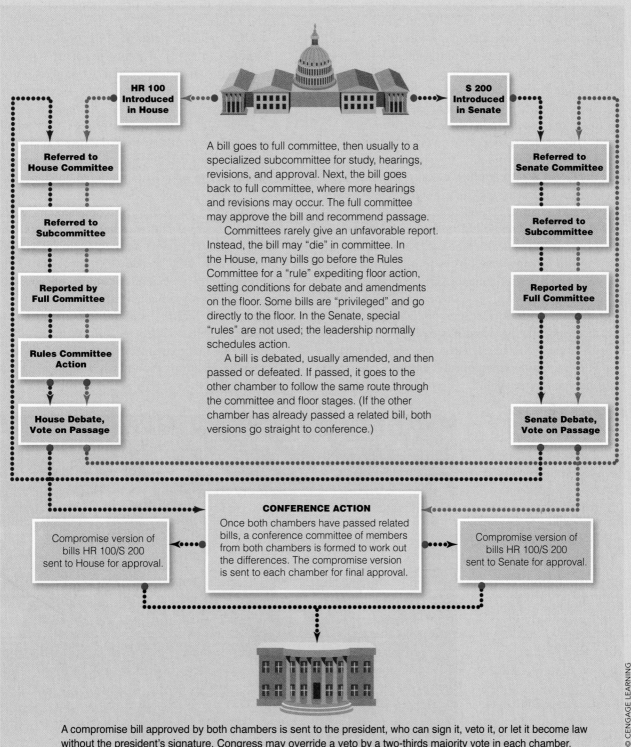

**HR 100 Introduced in House**

**S 200 Introduced in Senate**

**Referred to House Committee**

**Referred to Subcommittee**

**Reported by Full Committee**

**Rules Committee Action**

**House Debate, Vote on Passage**

**Referred to Senate Committee**

**Referred to Subcommittee**

**Reported by Full Committee**

**Senate Debate, Vote on Passage**

A bill goes to full committee, then usually to a specialized subcommittee for study, hearings, revisions, and approval. Next, the bill goes back to full committee, where more hearings and revisions may occur. The full committee may approve the bill and recommend passage.

Committees rarely give an unfavorable report. Instead, the bill may "die" in committee. In the House, many bills go before the Rules Committee for a "rule" expediting floor action, setting conditions for debate and amendments on the floor. Some bills are "privileged" and go directly to the floor. In the Senate, special "rules" are not used; the leadership normally schedules action.

A bill is debated, usually amended, and then passed or defeated. If passed, it goes to the other chamber to follow the same route through the committee and floor stages. (If the other chamber has already passed a related bill, both versions go straight to conference.)

**CONFERENCE ACTION**

Once both chambers have passed related bills, a conference committee of members from both chambers is formed to work out the differences. The compromise version is sent to each chamber for final approval.

Compromise version of bills HR 100/S 200 sent to House for approval.

Compromise version of bills HR 100/S 200 sent to Senate for approval.

A compromise bill approved by both chambers is sent to the president, who can sign it, veto it, or let it become law without the president's signature. Congress may override a veto by a two-thirds majority vote in each chamber.

© CENGAGE LEARNING

The basic steps in the process are as follows:

1. *Introduction of legislation.* Most bills are proposed by the executive branch, although individual members of Congress or their staffs can come up with ideas for new legislation—so, too, can private citizens or lobbying groups. Only a member of Congress can formally introduce legislation, however. In reality, many bills are proposed, developed, and often written by the White House or an executive agency. Then a "friendly" senator or representative introduces the bill in Congress. Such bills are rarely ignored entirely, although they are often amended or defeated.

   To a degree not seen for some decades, the Obama administration during his first term let Congress take the lead on writing important new legislation dealing with issues such as health-care reform and financial regulation. Even under Obama, however, a majority of the legislation considered by Congress has come from the executive branch.

2. *Referral to committees.* As soon as a bill is introduced and assigned a number, it is sent to the appropriate standing committee. In the House, the Speaker assigns the bill to the appropriate committee. In the Senate, the presiding officer assigns the bill to the proper committee. For example, a farm bill in the House would be sent to the Agriculture Committee, and a gun control bill would be sent to the Judiciary Committee.

   A committee chairperson will typically send the bill on to a subcommittee. For example, a Senate bill concerning additional involvement in NATO (the North Atlantic Treaty Organization) in Europe would be sent to the Senate Foreign Relations Subcommittee on European Affairs. Alternatively, the chairperson may decide to put the bill aside and ignore it. Most bills that are pigeonholed in this manner receive no further action.

   If a bill is not pigeonholed, committee staff members go to work researching it. The committee may hold public hearings during which people who support or oppose the bill can express their views. Committees also have the power to order witnesses to testify at public hearings. Witnesses may be executive agency officials, experts on the subject, or representatives of interest groups concerned about the bill.

   The subcommittee must meet to approve the bill as it is, add new amendments, or draft a new bill. This meeting is known as the **markup session.** If members cannot agree on changes, a vote on the changes is taken.

   When a subcommittee completes its work, the bill goes to the full standing committee, which then meets for its own markup session. The committee may hold its own hearings, amend the subcommittee's version, or simply approve the subcommittee's recommendations.

3. *Reports on a bill.* Finally, the committee will report the bill back to the full chamber. It can report the bill favorably, report the bill with amendments, or report a newly written bill. It can

**markup session** A meeting held by a congressional committee or subcommittee to approve, amend, or redraft a bill.

ALEX WONG/GETTY IMAGES

Senator Max Baucus (D., Mont.), on the left, discusses pending legislation with Senator Bill Nelson (D., Fla.) during a Finance Committee hearing.

also report a bill unfavorably, but usually such a bill will have been pigeon-holed earlier instead. Along with the bill, the committee will send to the House or Senate a written report that explains the committee's actions, describes the bill, lists the major changes made by the committee, and gives opinions on the bill.

4. *The Rules Committee and scheduling.* Scheduling is an extremely important part of getting a bill enacted into law. A bill must be put on a calendar. Typically, in the House the Rules Committee plays a major role in the scheduling process. This committee, along with the House leaders, regulates the flow of the bills through the House. The Rules Committee will also specify the amount of time to be spent on debate and whether amendments can be made by a floor vote.

In the Senate, a few leading members control the flow of bills. The Senate brings a bill to the floor by "unanimous consent," a motion by which all members present on the floor set aside the formal Senate rules and consider a bill. In contrast to the procedure in the House, individual senators have the power to disrupt work on legislation—refusing to agree to unanimous consent is the way in which a senatorial hold is enforced.

5. *Floor debate.* Because of its large size, the House imposes severe limits on floor debate. The Speaker recognizes those who may speak and can force any member who does not "stick to the subject" to give up the floor. Normally, the chairperson of the standing committee reporting the bill will take charge of the session during which it is debated. You can often watch such debates on C-SPAN.

Only on rare occasions does a floor debate change anybody's mind. The written record of the floor debate completes the legislative history of the proposed bill in the event that the courts have to interpret it later on. Floor debates also give the full House or Senate the opportunity to consider amendments to the original version of the bill.

6. *Vote.* In both the House and the Senate, the members present generally vote for or against the bill. There are several methods of voting, including

> ## "You've got to work things out in the cloakroom.
> And when you've got them worked out, you can debate a little before you vote."
> ~ LYNDON BAINES JOHNSON ~
> THIRTY-SIXTH PRESIDENT OF THE UNITED STATES
> 1963–1969
> AND MAJORITY LEADER OF THE SENATE
> 1955–1961

voice votes, standing votes, and recorded votes (also called roll-call votes). Since 1973, the House has had electronic voting. The Senate does not have such a system, however.

7. *Conference committee.* To become a law, a bill must be passed in identical form by both chambers. When the two chambers pass differing versions of the same bill, the measure is turned over to a special committee called a **conference committee**—a temporary committee with members from the two chambers, as mentioned earlier.

Most members of the committee are drawn from the standing committees that handled the bill in both chambers. In theory, the conference committee can consider only those points in a bill on which the two chambers disagree. No proposals are supposed to be added. In reality, however, the conference committee sometimes makes important changes in the bill or adds new provisions.

Once the conference committee members agree on the final compromise bill, a **conference report** is submitted to each chamber. The bill must be accepted or rejected by both chambers as it was written by the committee, with no further amendments made. If the bill is approved by both chambers, it is ready for action by the president.

8. *Presidential action.* All bills passed by Congress have to be submitted to the president for approval. The president has ten days to decide whether to sign the bill or veto it. If the president does nothing, the bill goes into effect unless Congress has adjourned before

**conference committee**
A temporary committee that is formed when the two chambers of Congress pass differing versions of the same bill. The conference committee consists of members from the House and the Senate who work out a compromise bill.

**conference report**
A report submitted by a conference committee after it has drafted a single version of a bill.

**pocket veto** A special type of veto power used by the chief executive after the legislature has adjourned. Bills that are not signed die after a specified period of time.

the ten-day period expires. In that case, the bill dies in what is called a **pocket veto.**

9. *Overriding a veto.* If the president decides to veto a bill, Congress can still get the bill enacted into law. With a two-thirds majority vote in both chambers, Congress can override the president's veto.

## 11–5 Investigation and Oversight

Steps 8 and 9 of the legislative process described above illustrate the integral role that the executive and the legislative branches play in making laws. The relationship between Congress and the president is at the core of our system of government, although, to be sure, the judicial branch plays a vital role as well (see Chapter 14).

One of the most important functions of Congress is its oversight (supervision) of the executive branch and its many federal departments and agencies. The executive bureaucracy, which includes the president's cabinet departments, wields tremendous power, as you will read in Chapters 12 and 13. Congress can rein in that power by choosing not to provide the money necessary for the bureaucracy to function. (The budgeting process will be discussed later in this chapter.)

### 11–5a The Investigative Function

Congress also has the authority to investigate the actions of the executive branch, the need for certain legislation, and even the actions of its own members. The numerous congressional committees and subcommittees regularly hold hearings to investigate the actions of the executive branch. Congressional committees receive opinions, reports, and assessments on a broad range of issues.

**LearningOutcome 11–5**
Identify Congress's oversight functions and explain how Congress fulfills them.

AP PHOTO/DOUG MILLS

In 1998, for only the third time in history, the House Judiciary Committee debated impeachment articles to oust a president. Republicans and Democrats bitterly clashed over articles accusing President Bill Clinton of perjury, obstruction of justice, and abuse of power.

A widely held belief is that between 2001 and 2007, when Republicans controlled both chambers of Congress and the presidency, Congress neglected its oversight function out of deference to President Bush. Some believe that Congress also neglected its oversight function from 2009 to 2011, when the Democrats controlled both chambers of Congress and the presidency.

One way in which Congress has "kept itself honest" is by establishing oversight bodies separate from—but responsible to—Congress. One such body is the Congressional Budget Office (CBO), which evaluates the impact of proposed legislation on the federal budget and the budget deficit. The CBO has frequently been in the news in recent years due to its "scoring" of various proposals considered by the House and the Senate. Members of Congress have found themselves tailoring measures to earn a better score from the CBO.

## 11–5b Impeachment Power

Congress has the power to impeach and remove from office the president, vice president, and other "civil officers," such as federal judges. To *impeach* means to accuse a public official of—or charge him or her with—improper conduct in office. The House of Representatives is vested with this power and has exercised it twice against a president.

### Impeaching Presidents

The House voted to impeach Andrew Johnson in 1868 and Bill Clinton in 1998. After a vote to impeach in the full House, the accused official is then tried in the Senate. If convicted by a two-thirds vote, the official is removed from office. Both Johnson and Clinton were acquitted by the Senate. A vote to impeach President Richard Nixon was pending before the full House of Representatives in 1974 when Nixon chose to resign. Nixon is the only president ever to resign from office.

"**LAWS ARE LIKE SAUSAGES.**

It is better if the public does not see how they are made."

~ JOHN GODFREY SAXE ~
AMERICAN POET 1816–1887;
MISATTRIBUTED TO OTTO VON BISMARCK,
CHANCELLOR OF GERMANY
1871–1890

### Impeaching Other Officers

Congress has taken action to remove officials other than the president. For example, the House of Representatives voted to impeach Judge Thomas Porteous in March 2010 on charges of bribery and perjury. In December of that year, the Senate convicted Porteous and disqualified him from ever holding any "office of honor or profit under the United States," as the formal language puts it. Only one United States Supreme Court justice has ever been impeached. The House impeached Samuel Chase in 1804, although he was later acquitted by the Senate.

## 11–5c Senate Confirmation

Article II, Section 2, of the Constitution states that the president may appoint ambassadors, justices of the Supreme Court, and other officers of the United States "with the Advice and Consent of the Senate." The Constitution leaves the precise nature of how the Senate will give this "advice and consent" up to the lawmakers.

In practice, the Senate confirms the president's nominees for the Supreme Court, other federal judgeships, and members of the president's cabinet. Nominees appear first before the appropriate Senate committee—the Judiciary Committee for federal

LARRY DOWNING/REUTERS

Jamie Dimon of JPMorgan Chase answers a question at the U.S. Senate Banking, Housing, and Urban Affairs Committee hearing in Washington, D.C.

judges or the Foreign Relations Committee for the secretary of state, for example. If the individual committee approves the nominee, the full Senate will vote on the nomination.

As you will read further in Chapters 12 and 14, Senate confirmation hearings have been very politicized at times. Judicial appointments often receive the most intense scrutiny by the Senate, because federal judges serve for life.

The president has a somewhat freer hand with cabinet appointments, because the heads of executive departments are expected to be loyal to the president. Nonetheless, Senate confirmation remains an important check on the president's power. We will discuss the relationship between Congress and the president in more detail in Chapter 12.

## FOR CRITICAL THINKING

More and more often in recent years, senators have blocked a president's appointments to make an unrelated point. *Should such an act be considered a legitimate political tactic? Why or why not?*

## 11–6 The Budgeting Process

### LearningOutcome 11–6

Indicate what is involved in the congressional budgeting process.

The Constitution makes it very clear that Congress has the power of the purse. Only Congress can impose taxes, and only Congress can authorize expenditures. To be sure, the president submits a budget, but all final decisions are up to Congress.

The congressional budget is, of course, one of the most important determinants of what policies will or will not be implemented. For example, the president might order executive agencies under presidential control to undertake specific programs, but these orders are meaningless if there is no money to pay for their execution. It is Congress that has the power of the "purse strings," and this power is significant. Congress can nullify a president's ambitious program simply by refusing to allocate the necessary money to executive agencies to implement it.

### 11–6a Authorization and Appropriation

The budgeting process is a two-part procedure. **Authorization** is the first part. It involves the creation of the legal basis for government programs. In this phase, Congress passes authorization bills outlining the rules governing the expenditure of funds. Limits may be placed on how much money can be spent and for what period of time.

**Appropriation** is the second part of the budgeting process. In this phase, Congress determines how many dollars will actually be spent in a given year on a particular government activity. Appropriations must never exceed the authorized amounts, but they can be less.

Many **entitlement programs** operate under open-ended authorizations that, in effect, place no limits on how much can be spent. The government is obligated to provide benefits, such as Social Security benefits, veterans' benefits, and the like, to persons who qualify under entitlement laws. It is usually possible, however, to make a fairly accurate estimate of the cost of any particular entitlement program in any given year.

As the remaining federal programs fall into the category of discretionary spending, they can be altered at will by Congress. National defense is the most important item in the discretionary-spending part of the budget. Discretionary spending also includes earmarks, or "pork," as described in this chapter's *Perception versus Reality* on the facing page.

### 11–6b The Actual Budgeting Process

Look at Figure 11–4 on page 264, which outlines the lengthy budgeting process. The process runs from January, when the president submits a proposed federal budget for the next **fiscal year,** to the start of that

**authorization** A part of the congressional budgeting process—the creation of the legal basis for government programs.

**appropriation** A part of the congressional budgeting process—the determination of how many dollars will be spent in a given year on a particular government activity.

**entitlement program** A government program (such as Social Security) that allows, or entitles, a certain class of people (such as elderly persons) to receive benefits. Entitlement programs operate under open-ended budget authorizations that, in effect, place no limits on how much can be spent.

**fiscal year** A twelve-month period that is established for bookkeeping or accounting purposes. The government's fiscal year runs from October 1 through September 30.

# Perception versus Reality

## Congress Has Banned Pork-Barrel Spending

In recent years, Congress voted to fund a "bridge to nowhere" in Alaska, a program to combat wild hogs in Missouri, and payment of storage fees for Georgia peanut farmers. Such special interest spending is called *pork-barrel* spending—members of Congress "bring home the bacon" this way to benefit local businesses and workers.

Formally, an item of pork is called an *earmark*. The Congressional Research Service defines an earmark as a spending provision that applies to a very limited number of individuals or entities. The Office of Management and Budget defines earmarks as direct allocations of funds that bypass merit-based or competitive allocation processes of the executive branch. Those who defend earmarks often contend that Congress has just as much right to determine who benefits from government spending as the administration does. After all, directing money to particular purposes is a core constitutional function of Congress.

### THE PERCEPTION

In 2010, immediately after the elections that would give them control of the U.S. House, Republicans announced that they would ban earmarks. It follows that pork must be history.

### THE REALITY

The House Republican ban on earmarks certainly made it more difficult for members of Congress to do favors for the folks back home. Still, many members devoted considerable ingenuity to creating end-runs around the rules. A simple method was simply to deny that a particular funding request was an earmark. One senator identified more than one hundred such mislabeled provisions in a single House defense bill.

A common technique was to lobby executive agencies to place specific projects on their approved lists. If the appropriate agency endorsed a project ostensibly on merit-based grounds, then, as if by magic, the project was no longer an earmark. For example, Republicans from Texas and Virginia who opposed a (non-earmarked) high-speed rail project in California were happy to submit letters from the Department of Transportation that endorsed high-speed rail projects—in Texas and Virginia.

One technique for benefiting specific corporations is to lower the tariff (import tax) on goods imported by that firm—and often imported by no one else. You might think that this kind of help would be an unusual procedure. You would be wrong. By mid-2012, members had submitted 1,257 requests for tariff relief. The Republicans had banned these measures along with other types of earmarks, but their resolve appeared to be crumbling. The Republican chair of the House Ways and Means Committee planned to assemble a comprehensive tariff bill in late 2012.

A final point: presidents are fond of inserting special funding requests into their budget proposals at the last minute, regardless of whether executive agencies signed off on these expenditures. The president, in short, is often the biggest "porkmeister" of all.

**BLOG ON** You can visit the Web sites of two groups that oppose pork-barrel spending: Citizens against Government Waste and Taxpayers for Common Sense. Do the recommendations of these groups suggest that they have particular ideological leanings? If so, what are they?

fiscal year on October 1. In actuality, about eighteen months prior to October 1, the executive agencies submit their requests to the Office of Management and Budget (OMB), and the OMB outlines a proposed budget. If the president approves it, the budget is officially submitted to Congress.

The legislative budgeting process begins eight to nine months before the start of the fiscal year. The

FIGURE 11–4

# The Budgeting Process

**Executive Budgeting Process**

| Executive agency requests: about twelve to eighteen months prior to start of fiscal year, or in March to September | → | OMB review and presidential approval: nine to twelve months before start of fiscal year, or in September to December |

↓

**Legislative Budgeting Process**

| Second budget resolution: by October 1 | ← | First budget resolution: in May | ← | Executive branch submittal of budget to Congress: eight to nine months before start of fiscal year, at end of January |

↓

**Execution**

| Start of fiscal year: October 1 | → | Outlays and obligations: October 1 to September 30 | → | Audit of fiscal-year outlays on a selective basis by Government Accountability Office (GAO) |

© CENGAGE LEARNING

---

**first budget resolution** is supposed to be passed in May. It sets overall revenue goals and spending targets and, by definition, the size of the federal budget deficit or surplus.

The **second budget resolution,** which sets "binding" limits on taxes and spending, is supposed to be passed in September, before the beginning of the fiscal year on October 1. When Congress is unable to pass a complete budget by October 1, it usually passes **continuing resolutions,** which enable the executive agencies to keep on doing whatever they were doing the previous year with the same amount of funding. But even continuing resolutions have not always been passed on time.

The budget process involves making predictions about the state of the U.S. economy for years to come. This process is necessarily very imprecise. Since 1996, both Congress and the president have attempted to make ten-year projections for income (from taxes) and spending, but no one can really know what the financial picture of the United States will look like in ten years.

The workforce could grow or shrink, which would drastically alter government revenue from taxes. Any number of emergencies could arise that would require increased government spending—from going to war against terrorists to inoculating federal employees against smallpox.

In any event, when you read about what the administration predicts the budget deficit (or surplus) will be in five or ten years, take such predictions with a grain of salt. While one- or two-year predictions are often close to reality, long-term predictions have never come close to being accurate. Moreover, most times, the longest-term predictions made by administrations will depend on decisions made when *another* administration is in office later on.

**first budget resolution** A budget resolution, which is supposed to be passed in May, that sets overall revenue goals and spending targets for the next fiscal year, beginning on October 1.

**second budget resolution** A budget resolution, which is supposed to be passed in September, that sets "binding" limits on taxes and spending for the next fiscal year.

**continuing resolution** A temporary resolution passed by Congress that enables executive agencies to continue work with the same funding that they had in the previous fiscal year.

**FOR CRITICAL THINKING**

*Why do you think Congress created entitlement programs that operate under open-ended authorizations instead of reauthorizing each of them every year?*

# ODDS Congress

The founders thought that Congress would be the branch of government that was closest to the people. Yet Congress is one of the least popular institutions in America. It seems that anything that Congress does annoys a substantial share of the electorate. Needless to say, Americans are at odds over Congress on a variety of issues:

- Is the Senate's filibuster rule a legitimate safeguard of minority rights—or a disastrous handicap on Congress's ability to address the nation's problems?

- Is political gerrymandering just a normal part of the political game—or does it deprive voters of their rights?

- Does racial gerrymandering allow the voices of minority groups to be heard—or is it an unconstitutional violation of the equal protection clause?

- When voting on legislation, should members of Congress faithfully represent the views of their constituents—or should they stay true to their own beliefs about what is good for the nation?

- Should legislative earmarks, or "pork," be banned as a waste of taxpayers' resources—or is it appropriate for members of Congress to support specific projects in their own districts?

## TAKE ACTION

During each session of Congress, your senators and your representative in the House debate the pros and cons of proposed laws, some of which may affect your daily life or the lives of those you care about. If you want to let your voice be heard, you can do so simply by phoning or e-mailing your senators or your representative. You can learn the names and contact information for the senators and the representative from your area by going to the Web sites of the Senate and the House, which you can locate by searching on "senate" and "congress." Your chances of influencing your members of Congress will be greater if you can convince others, including your friends and family members, to do likewise. Citizens often feel that such efforts are useless. Yet members of Congress do listen to their constituents and often do act in response to their constituents' wishes. Indeed, next to voting, contacting those who represent you in

Congress is probably the most effective way to influence government decision making.

Environmental activists from more than thirty organizations attempt to deliver about 770,000 signatures to Senate leaders urging them not to grant permission to build the Keystone XL pipeline. The signatures were on a disk drive, and the empty boxes were meant to be symbolic.

# STUDY TOOLS

## Fill-In

1. Every _____ years, seats in the House of Representatives are reapportioned based on the outcome of the census.

2. Under the trustee view of representation, a legislator should try to _____.

3. Incumbent members of Congress enjoy several advantages over their challengers in elections, including _____.

4. The Speaker of the House has the power to _____.

5. Filibusters may be ended by invoking _____.

6. A markup session is _____.

7. In the House, the _____ Committee plays a major role in the scheduling process and will also specify the amount of time to be spent on debate.

8. In practice, the Senate's power of "advice and consent" means that the Senate confirms the president's nominees to _____.

9. The budgeting process is a two-part procedure that includes _____.

## Multiple Choice

10. To ensure equal representation in the House, congressional districts in a given state must contain, as nearly as possible, equal numbers of
    a. men and women.
    b. Republicans and Democrats.
    c. people.

11. The U.S. Constitution requires that members of the House of Representatives be elected every
    a. second year by popular vote.
    b. six years by popular vote.
    c. second year by state legislatures.

12. In the Senate, the ____ is typically the most powerful individual and directs the legislative program and party strategy.
    a. vice president
    b. majority leader
    c. president pro tempore

13. As soon as a bill is introduced in either the House or the Senate, it is sent to
    a. the floor of the chamber.
    b. the appropriate standing committee.
    c. a conference committee.

14. The Senate
    a. voted to impeach Richard Nixon.
    b. convicted Bill Clinton of impeachable offenses by a two-thirds vote.
    c. tries officials who have been impeached in the House of Representatives.

15. When Congress is unable to pass a complete budget by the beginning of the fiscal year, it usually passes ____, which enable the executive agencies to keep on doing whatever they were doing the previous year with the same amount of funding.
    a. continuing resolutions
    b. entitlement programs
    c. earmarks

# The Presidency

SAUL LOEB/AFP/GETTY IMAGES

The **Learning Outcomes** labeled 1 through 5 are designed to help improve your understanding of the chapter. After reading this chapter, you should be able to:

**12–1** List the constitutional requirements for becoming president.

**12–2** Explain the roles that a president adopts while in office.

**12–3** Indicate the scope of presidential powers.

**12–4** Describe advantages enjoyed by Congress and by the president in their institutional relationship.

**12–5** Discuss the organization of the executive branch and the role of cabinet members in presidential administrations.

**Remember to visit page 293 for additional** Study Tools

# ODDS

## Is It Too Easy for a President to Send Our Troops into Battle?

LEE A. OSBERRY JR./U.S. AIR FORCE/ GETTY IMAGES

Under the U.S. Constitution, only Congress has the right to declare war. Yet the president's role as commander in chief of the armed forces means that he or she has substantial power to send our soldiers into harm's way, whether Congress has acted or not. In the early twentieth century, presidents ordered troops into Cuba, the Dominican Republic, Haiti, Honduras, Mexico, and Nicaragua. Before the United States entered World War II in 1941, Franklin D. Roosevelt ordered the Navy to "shoot on sight" any German submarine that appeared in the Western Hemisphere security zone.

In 2011, President Barack Obama ordered the U.S. Air Force to bomb the tanks and troops of Libyan dictator Moammar Gadhafi, who was killed in October 2011. The air forces of the United States and other nations spent months aiding the rebels in that country. At no time did Obama ask for a supporting resolution from Congress—he argued instead that bombing Gadhafi's army didn't really amount to "hostilities." Should presidents be allowed such a free hand?

## Obama's War in Libya Violated U.S. Law

The War Powers Resolution, passed by Congress in 1973, states that the president can send our military into action abroad only by authorization of Congress or if there is "a national emergency created by attack upon the United States, its territories or possessions, or its armed forces." It also requires the president to notify Congress within forty-eight hours of deploying troops and limits deployments to sixty days unless Congress approves the action. Under this resolution, Obama was operating outside the law from day one. *Gadhafi did not attack the United States.*

Obama should have asked for congressional support before going into action. In fact, he never asked for support. True, Obama is not the first president to contend that the War Powers Resolution is null and void. Almost all presidents have taken that position. It simply means that most presidents have exceeded their authority. Ours is a nation of "laws, not men." Like everyone else, presidents must obey the law. If they refuse to do so, we are headed for disaster.

## Congress Doesn't Want to Control Foreign Policy

The writers of the Constitution built a powerful tension into the American system when they provided that the president be elected separately from the Congress. Because both the president and Congress are elected, both can claim to represent the people. The resulting struggle for advantage between the executive and legislative branches has lasted throughout our history.

Ultimately, the winner in such a struggle will be the branch that cares the most about the outcome. The 2011 debt ceiling crisis showed that even a single chamber of Congress can exercise enormous leverage on an issue that it truly cares about. But what happened regarding Libya? The House voted to condemn Obama's actions. Then it turned around and refused to vote through a measure to cut off funding. Let's face it—Congress doesn't really want to control U.S. foreign policy. It lacks confidence in its own ability to act effectively and prefers to yield this field to the president. Inevitably, the president will take the lead.

## Where do you stand?

1. What are some of the differences between U.S. military actions in Libya and earlier involvements, such as the wars in Afghanistan and Iraq?
2. Why might Congress lack confidence in its ability to effectively manage U.S. military actions?

## Explore this issue online

- Historian Joyce Appleby believes that institutional conflict between the president and Congress is one of the virtues of the American system. Blogger Matt Yglesias disagrees. You can read their opinions if you search on, respectively, "warring ambitions" and "founding falter."

# Introduction

President Lyndon B. Johnson (1963–1969) stated in his autobiography[1] that "of all the 1,886 nights I was President, there were not many when I got to sleep before 1 or 2 A.M., and there were few mornings when I didn't wake up by 6 or 6:30." President Harry Truman (1945–1953) once observed that no one can really understand what it is like to be president: there is no end to "the chain of responsibility that binds him," and he is "never allowed to forget that he is president." These responsibilities are, for the most part, unremitting. Unlike Congress, the president never adjourns.

At the apex of the political ladder, the presidency is the most powerful and influential political office

"No man will ever bring out of the Presidency the reputation which carries him into it. To myself personally, it brings nothing but increasing **DRUDGERY AND DAILY LOSS OF FRIENDS.**"

~ THOMAS JEFFERSON ~
THIRD PRESIDENT
OF THE UNITED STATES
1801–1809

that any one individual can hold. Presidents can help to shape not only domestic policy but also global developments.

Since the demise of the Soviet Union and its satellite Communist countries in the early 1990s, the president of the United States has been the leader of the most powerful nation on earth. The president heads the greatest military force anywhere. Presidents have more power to reach their political objectives than any other players in the American political system. (We discussed the president's ability to dominate U.S. foreign policy by ordering troops into war in this chapter's opening *America at Odds* feature.) It is not surprising, therefore, that many Americans aspire to attain this office.

## 12–1 Who Can Become President?

The notion that anybody can become president of this country has always been a part of the American mythology. Certainly, the requirements for becoming president set forth in Article II, Section 1, of the Constitution are not difficult to meet:

**Learning Outcome 12–1**

List the constitutional requirements for becoming president.

> No Person except a natural born Citizen, or a Citizen of the United States, at the time of the Adoption of this Constitution, shall be eligible to the Office of President; neither shall any Person be eligible to that Office who shall not have attained to the Age of thirty-five Years, and been fourteen Years a Resident within the United States.

This language does make it impossible for a foreign-born naturalized citizen to become president, even if that person came to this country as an infant. For more on that issue, see this chapter's *Join the Debate* feature on the following page.

### 12–1a Perks of the President

Given the demands of the presidency, why would anyone seek the office? There are some very special perks associated with the presidency. The president enjoys,

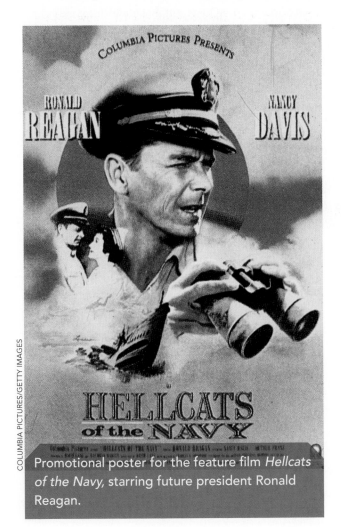

COLUMBIA PICTURES/GETTY IMAGES

Promotional poster for the feature film *Hellcats of the Navy,* starring future president Ronald Reagan.

# JOIN THE DEBATE

## A Foreign-Born President?

As you just read, Article II of the Constitution states that "[n]o Person except a natural born Citizen . . . shall be eligible to the Office of President." This restriction has long been controversial, for it has kept many otherwise qualified Americans from running for president. These persons have included former California governor Arnold Schwarzenegger, who was born in Austria, and former Michigan governor Jennifer M. Granholm, who was born in Canada, both of whom have been U.S. citizens for decades. In all, some 13 million Americans born outside the United States are excluded by this provision. The requirement of native birth has come up most recently because of claims by conspiracy theorists that President Obama was not born in the United States. These individuals claim that Obama's Hawaiian birth certificate was forged, and they are undeterred by the fact that Obama's birth was also announced in Honolulu newspapers.

### An Obsolete Provision

America is a nation of immigrants, so it strikes some as odd that a foreign-born person would be barred from aspiring to the presidency. Naturalized U.S. citizens are allowed to vote, to serve on juries, and to serve in the military. They are also allowed to serve as secretary of state and represent the nation in foreign affairs. Why can't they run for president? Critics of the Constitution's citizenship requirement think that the requirement should be abolished by a constitutional amendment. They point out that the clause was initially included in the Constitution to prevent European princes from attempting to force the young republic back under monarchical rule in the late 1700s. Clearly, the clause is now obsolete and should no longer apply.

### A Requirement Still Valid Today

Other Americans believe that the constitutional ban should remain. They argue that national security could be compromised by a foreign-born president. With the immense power that the president wields, especially in foreign policy, loyalty is of the utmost concern. The current war on terrorism only heightens the need to ensure that the president does not have divided loyalties.

In addition, the Constitution is difficult to amend, requiring support from two-thirds of both chambers of Congress and ratification by three-fourths of the states. The need for an amendment that would allow former Governor Granholm and other immigrants to run for president is hardly as pressing as the need for prior antidiscrimination amendments, such as the ones that abolished slavery and gave women the right to vote, opponents argue.

**FOR CRITICAL ANALYSIS** Do you see a problem with someone born in a foreign country serving as president? Why or why not?

among other things, the use of the White House. The White House has 132 rooms located on 18.3 acres of land in the heart of the nation's capital. At the White House, the president in residence has a staff of more than eighty persons, including chefs, gardeners, maids, butlers, and a personal tailor.

Amenities also include a tennis court, a swimming pool, bowling lanes, and a private movie theater. Additionally, the president has at his or her disposal a fleet of automobiles, helicopters, and jets (including *Air Force One*, which costs about $180,000 an hour to run). For relaxation, the presidential family can go to Camp David, a resort hideaway in the Catoctin Mountains of Maryland. Other perks include free dental and medical care.

## 12–1b Presidential Age and Occupation

Modern presidents have included a haberdasher (Harry Truman), a peanut farmer (Jimmy Carter), and an actor (Ronald Reagan), although all of these men also had significant political experience before assuming the presidency. If you look at Appendix E, though, you will see that the most common previous occupation of U.S. presidents has been the legal profession. Out of forty-four presidents, twenty-seven have been lawyers. Many presidents have also been wealthy.

Although the Constitution states that anyone who is thirty-five years of age or older can become president, the average age at inauguration has been fifty-five. The youngest person elected president was John F. Kennedy

(1961–1963), who assumed the presidency at the age of forty-three (the youngest person to hold the office was Theodore Roosevelt, who was forty-two when he became president after the assassination of William McKinley). The oldest was Ronald Reagan (1981–1989), who was sixty-nine years old when he became president.

## 12–1c Race, Gender, and Religion

For most of American history, all presidential candidates, even those of minor parties, were white, male, and of the Protestant religious tradition. In recent years, however, the pool of talent has expanded. In 1928, Democrat Al Smith became the first Roman Catholic to run for president on a major-party ticket, and in 1960 Democrat John F. Kennedy was elected as the first Catholic president. Among recent unsuccessful Democratic presidential candidates, Michael Dukakis was Greek Orthodox and John Kerry was Roman Catholic.

In 2008, the doors swung wide in the presidential primaries as the Democrats chose between a white woman, Hillary Clinton, and an African American man, Barack Obama. By that time, about 90 percent of Americans told pollsters that they would be willing to support an African American for president, and the same number would support a woman.

In 2012, none of the top three finishers in the Republican primaries was Protestant. Newt Gingrich and Rick Santorum were Catholic. Mitt Romney was a member of the Latter-Day Saints, commonly called the Mormons.

**FOR CRITICAL THINKING**

*Why do some people believe so strongly that Barack Obama must have been born in a foreign country?*

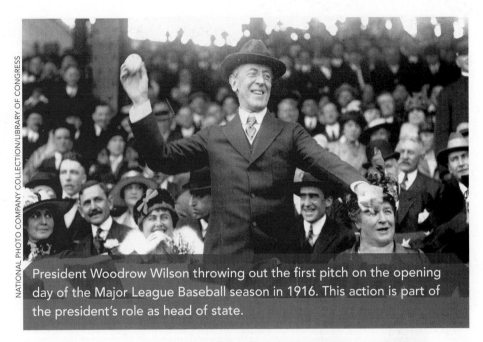

NATIONAL PHOTO COMPANY COLLECTION/LIBRARY OF CONGRESS

President Woodrow Wilson throwing out the first pitch on the opening day of the Major League Baseball season in 1916. This action is part of the president's role as head of state.

## 12–2 The President's Many Roles

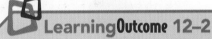
**Learning Outcome 12–2**

Explain the roles that a president adopts while in office.

The president has the authority to exercise a variety of powers. Some of these are explicitly outlined in the Constitution, and some are simply required by the office—such as the power to persuade. In the course of exercising these powers, the president performs a variety of roles. For example, as commander in chief of the armed services, the president can exercise significant military powers.

Which roles a president executes successfully usually depends on what is happening domestically and internationally, as well as on the president's personality. Some presidents, including Bill Clinton (1993–2001) during his first term, have shown much more interest in domestic policy than in foreign policy. Others, such as George H. W. Bush (1989–1993), were more interested in foreign affairs than in domestic ones.

Table 12–1 on the following page summarizes the major roles of the president. An important role is, of course, that of chief executive. Other roles include those of commander in chief, head of state, chief diplomat, chief legislator, and political party leader.

## 12–2a Chief Executive

According to Article II of the Constitution,

> The executive Power shall be vested in a President of the United States of America. . . . [H]e may require the Opinion, in writing, of the principal Officer in

**TABLE 12-1**

## Roles of the President

| | ROLE/DESCRIPTION | EXAMPLES |
|---|---|---|
|  | **Chief executive**<br>Enforces laws and federal court decisions, along with treaties signed by the United States | • Can appoint, with Senate approval, and remove high-ranking officers of the federal government<br>• Can grant reprieves, pardons, and amnesties<br>• Can handle national emergencies during peacetime, such as riots or natural disasters |
|  | **Commander in chief**<br>Leads the nation's armed forces | • Can commit troops for up to ninety days in response to a military threat (War Powers Resolution)<br>• Can make secret agreements with other countries<br>• Can set up military governments in conquered lands<br>• Can end fighting by calling a cease-fire (armistice) |
|  | **Head of state**<br>Performs ceremonial activities as a personal symbol of the nation | • Decorates war heroes<br>• Dedicates parks and post offices<br>• Throws out first pitch of baseball season<br>• Lights national Christmas tree<br>• Receives foreign heads of state |
|  | **Chief diplomat**<br>Directs U.S. foreign policy and is the nation's most important representative in dealing with foreign countries | • Can negotiate and sign treaties with other nations, which go into effect with Senate approval<br>• Can make pacts (executive agreements) with other heads of state, without Senate approval<br>• Can accept the legal existence of another country's government (power of recognition) |
|  | **Chief legislator**<br>Informs Congress about the condition of the country and recommends legislative measures | • Proposes legislative program to Congress in traditional State of the Union address<br>• Suggests budget to Congress and submits annual economic report<br>• Can veto a bill passed by Congress<br>• Can call special sessions of Congress |
|  | **Political party leader**<br>Heads political party | • Chooses a vice president<br>• Makes several thousand top government appointments, often to party faithful (patronage)<br>• Tries to execute the party's platform<br>• Attends party fund-raisers<br>• May help reelect party members running for office as mayors, governors, or members of Congress |

© CENGAGE LEARNING

**chief executive** The head of the executive branch of government; in the United States, the president.

each of the executive Departments, upon any Subject relating to the Duties of their respective Offices . . . and he shall nominate, and by and with the Advice and Consent of the Senate, shall appoint . . . Officers of the United States . . . . [H]e shall take Care that the Laws be faithfully executed.

This constitutional provision makes the president of the United States the nation's **chief executive,** or the head of the executive branch of the federal government.

## The Race for President in 2012

Exit polls in 2012 suggested that many moderate voters considered the Republican platform too conservative. This platform was locked in place during the Republican presidential primary elections, when candidates competed to show who would be the most conservative. Romney, the primary winner, was also bedeviled by a second result of the primaries—he was temporarily short of funding compared to Obama. Ultra-conservative positions and too little money left Romney in a vulnerable position, and Obama's team took full advantage. Its campaign poured most of its carefully husbanded resources into an ad campaign. The goal was to define Romney in the minds of voters before Romney had a chance to define himself. He was portrayed as a vulture capitalist, a wealthy man who loved to fire people. This campaign had some success. It was reinforced by a series of gaffes by Romney. By September, it seemed possible that the presidential elections might not even be close. In early October, however, Romney almost reversed the tide in the first presidential debate. Millions of voters who, in the words of one columnist, expected to see "a cat-stroking James Bond villain," saw instead a candidate who was reasonable, personable, and moderate. The president, in contrast, seemed aloof and detached. Romney's polling scores soared. Obama did better in the next two debates, however. Obama's win in November was no landslide, but it was decisive.

When the framers created the office of the president, they created a uniquely American institution. Nowhere else in the world at that time was there a democratically elected chief executive. The executive branch is also unique among the branches of government because it is headed by a single individual—the president.

## 12–2b Commander in Chief

The Constitution states that the president "shall be Commander in Chief of the Army and Navy of the United States, and of the Militia of the several States, when called into the actual Service of the United States." As **commander in chief** of the nation's armed forces, the president exercises tremendous power.

Under the Constitution, war powers are divided between Congress and the president. Congress was given the power to declare war and the power to raise and maintain the country's armed forces. The president, as commander in chief, was given the power to deploy the armed forces. The president's role as commander in chief has evolved over the last century. We discussed this shared power of the president and Congress in the chapter-opening *America at Odds* feature and will examine it in more detail later in this chapter.

## 12–2c Head of State

Traditionally, a country's monarch has performed the function of **head of state**—the country's representative to the rest of the world. The United States, of course, has no king or queen to act as head of state. Thus, the president of the United States fulfills this role.

The president engages in many symbolic or ceremonial activities, such as throwing out the first pitch to open the baseball season and turning on the lights of the national Christmas tree. The president also decorates war heroes, dedicates parks and post offices, receives visiting heads of state at the White House, and goes on official state visits to other countries.

Some argue that presidents should not perform such ceremonial duties because they take time that the president should be spending on "real work." Most presidents, however, have found the role of head of state to be politically useful. (See this chapter's *The Rest of the World* feature on the following page for more information on how one other country handles this issue.)

## 12–2d Chief Diplomat

A **diplomat** is a person who represents one

**commander in chief** The supreme commander of a nation's military force.

**head of state** The person who serves as the ceremonial head of a country's government and represents that country to the rest of the world.

**diplomat** A person who represents one country in dealing with representatives of another country.

## The Unusual Role of the French President

Earlier in this text, you read about the parliamentary system used by many countries. In that system, the chief executive is chosen by the legislature, not the people. A few countries, however, have a hybrid system that is part parliamentary and part presidential. The best-known example of such a system is in France.

### The Presidential-Parliamentary System

France has a president, currently François Hollande, and a prime minister. Both represent the left-of-center party in France, the Socialists. In France, the president names the prime minister and the members of the cabinet. The prime minister and the cabinet, though, are responsible to the legislature, not the president.

The National Assembly, which is the lower house of Parliament, can force the entire cabinet to resign by passing a motion of no confidence.

In other words, "the government"—the prime minister and the other cabinet members—cannot survive politically unless a majority in the National Assembly supports them, regardless of the president's preferences.

### The Unique French Practice of Cohabitation

For much of the history of the modern French Republic, the legislature's ability to throw out the government was not important, because the president's party had a majority in the National Assembly. French legislators were willing to let the president—the head of the majority party—choose the government. In 1981, the French elected a Socialist president for the first time, and they also gave the Socialists a majority in the National Assembly. In the 1986 elections, however, France voted for a center-right

Assembly majority. The Socialist president, François Mitterrand, still had two years left in his term of office. The French have a quaint term for the resulting situation: "cohabitation." During cohabitation, the prime minister and the rest of the cabinet are from one party and the president is from another.

### Who Does What?

Nowhere in the French constitution is there an explicit statement of the division of powers between the president and the prime minister. The division of duties that exists today has evolved over time. Typically, the president is responsible for foreign policy and the prime minister for domestic policy. This distinction is most carefully observed during periods of cohabitation. When one party is in full control of the government, however, the president tends to take over completely.

**FOR CRITICAL ANALYSIS** Would our government work better if a prime minister served under the president?

country in dealing with representatives of another country. In the United States, the president is the nation's **chief diplomat.** The Constitution did not explicitly reserve this role to the president, but since the beginning of this nation, presidents have assumed the role based on their explicit constitutional powers to recognize foreign governments and, with the advice and consent of the Senate, to appoint ambassadors and make treaties. As chief diplomat, the president directs the foreign policy of the United States and is our nation's most important representative.

**chief diplomat** The role of the president of the United States in recognizing and interacting with foreign governments.

### 12–2e Chief Legislator

Nowhere in the Constitution do the words *chief legislator* appear. The Constitution, however, does require that the president "from time to time give to the Congress Information of the State of the Union, and recommend to their Consideration such Measures as he shall judge necessary and expedient." The president has, in fact, become a major player in shaping the congressional agenda—the set of measures that actually get discussed and acted on.

This was not always the case. In the nineteenth century, some presidents preferred to let Congress lead the way in proposing and implementing policy. Since the administration of Theodore Roosevelt

(1901–1909), however, presidents have taken an activist approach. Presidents are now expected to develop a legislative program and propose a budget to Congress every year.

In the past, this shared power has often put Congress and the president at odds. President Bill Clinton's administration, for example, drew up a health-care reform package in 1993 and presented it to Congress almost on a take-it-or-leave-it basis. Congress left it. To avoid such confrontations, President Obama frequently let Congress determine much of the content of important new legislation, such as the health-care reform bills.

In the example of health-care reform, President Obama's deference to Congress had several negative consequences. These included an unusually large number of earmarks, a protracted and unpopular legislative process, and opportunities for conservatives to mobilize against the reforms. Still, in the end, Obama succeeded where Clinton had failed.

## 12–2f Political Party Leader

The president of the United States is also the *de facto* leader of his or her political party. The Constitution, of course, does not mention this role because, in the eyes of the founders, parties should have no place in the American political system.

As party leader, the president exercises substantial powers. For example, the president chooses the chairperson of the party's national committee. The president can also exert political power within the party by using presidential appointment and removal powers.

Naturally, presidents are beholden to the party members who put them in office, and usually they indulge in the practice of **patronage**—appointing individuals to government or public jobs to reward those who helped them win the presidential contest.

The president may also reward party members with fund-raising assistance. (Campaign financing was discussed in Chapter 9.) The president is, in a sense, "fund-raiser in chief" for his or her party, and recent presidents, including Bill Clinton, George W. Bush, and Barack Obama, have proved themselves to be prodigious fund-raisers.

FOR CRITICAL THINKING

*Does our president have too many roles to fill?*

The four most recent presidents are shown in the Oval Office of the White House. What can a president do after leaving office?

DOUG MILLS/THE NEW YORK TIMES/REDUX

## 12–3 Presidential Powers

The president exercises numerous powers. Some of these powers are set forth in the Constitution. Others, known as *inherent powers*, are

**LearningOutcome 12–3**

Indicate the scope of presidential powers.

**patronage** The practice by which elected officials give government jobs to individuals who helped them gain office.

those that are necessary to carry out the president's constitutional duties. We look next at these powers, as well as at the expansion of presidential powers over time.

## 12–3a The President's Constitutional Powers

As you have read, the constitutional source for the president's authority is found in Article II of the Constitution, which states, "The executive Power shall be vested in a President of the United States of America." The Constitution then sets forth the president's relatively limited constitutional responsibilities.

**The Constitutional Debate** Just how much power should be entrusted to the president was debated at length by the framers of the Constitution. On the one hand, they did not want a king. On the other hand, they believed that a strong executive was necessary if the republic was to survive. The result of their debates was an executive who was granted enough powers in the Constitution to balance those of Congress.

**The Specified Powers** Article II grants the president broad but vaguely described powers. From the very beginning, there were different views as to what exactly the "executive Power" clause enabled the president to do. Nonetheless, Sections 2 and 3 of Article II list the following specific presidential powers. These powers parallel the roles of the president discussed in the previous section:

- To serve as commander in chief of the armed forces and the state militias.

- To appoint, with the Senate's consent, the heads of the executive departments, ambassadors, justices of the Supreme Court, and other top officials.

> **treaty** A formal agreement between the governments of two or more countries.

- To make treaties, with the advice and consent of the Senate.

- To grant reprieves and pardons, except in cases of impeachment.

- To deliver the annual State of the Union address to Congress and to send other messages to Congress from time to time.

- To call either house or both houses of Congress into special sessions.

- To receive ambassadors and other representatives from foreign countries.

- To commission all officers of the United States.

- To ensure that the laws passed by Congress "be faithfully executed."

In addition, Article I, Section 7, gives the president the power to veto legislation. We will now discuss some of these powers in more detail. As you will see, many of the president's powers are balanced by the powers of Congress. We address the complex relationship between the president and Congress later in this chapter.

### Proposal and Ratification of Treaties

A **treaty** is a formal agreement between two or more countries. The president has the sole power to negotiate and sign treaties with other countries. The Senate, however, must approve a treaty by a two-thirds vote of the members present before it becomes effective. If the treaty is approved by the Senate and signed by the president, it becomes law.

Presidents have not always succeeded in winning the Senate's approval for treaties. In 1999, Bill Clinton was unable to persuade the Senate to approve the Comprehensive Test Ban Treaty, which would have prohibited all signers from testing nuclear weapons. Clinton argued that the United States no longer needed to test its nuclear weapons and that the treaty's restrictions on other

AP PHOTO

Lyndon B. Johnson came the closest of any presidential candidate ever to winning a majority of the votes of all citizens eligible to cast a ballot.

President Jimmy Carter (center) met with Egyptian president Anwar Sadat (left) and Israeli prime minister Menachem Begin (right) at the White House for the signing of the Camp David Accords on September 18, 1978. Since then, Egypt and Israel have remained at peace with each other.

countries would enhance our national security. The treaty was defeated largely on a party-line vote, with the Republicans opposed.

In contrast, Barack Obama convinced the Senate to approve the New Strategic Arms Reduction Treaty (New START) with Russia in December 2010. The treaty reduced by half the number of nuclear missiles in both countries and provided for inspections. New START was supported by all of the Democrats and by many Republicans.

### The Power to Grant Reprieves and Pardons

The president's power to grant a pardon serves as a check on judicial power. A *pardon* is a release from punishment or the legal consequences of a crime. It restores a person to the full rights and privileges of citizenship.

In 1925, the United States Supreme Court upheld an expansive interpretation of the president's pardon power in a case involving an individual convicted for contempt of court. The Court held that the power covers all offenses "either before trial, during trial, or after trial, by individuals, or by classes, conditionally or absolutely, and this without modification or regulation by Congress."[2] The president can grant a pardon for any federal offense, except in cases of impeachment.

One of the most controversial pardons was that granted by President Gerald Ford (1974–1977) to former president Richard Nixon (1969–1974) after the

Watergate affair (to be discussed later in the chapter) before any formal charges were brought in court.

Sometimes pardons are granted to a class of individuals as a general amnesty. For example, President Jimmy Carter granted amnesty to tens of thousands of people who had resisted the draft during the Vietnam War by failing to register for the draft or by moving abroad.

### The President's Veto Power

As noted in Chapter 11, the president can **veto** a bill passed by Congress. Congress can override the veto with a two-thirds vote by the members present in each chamber. The result of a veto override is that the bill becomes law against the wishes of the president.

If the president does not send a bill back to Congress after ten congressional working days, the bill becomes law without the president's signature. If the president refuses to sign the bill and Congress adjourns within ten working days after the bill has been submitted to the president, however, the bill is killed for that session of Congress. As mentioned in Chapter 11, this is called a *pocket veto*.

Presidents used the veto power sparingly until the administration of Andrew Johnson (1865–1869). Johnson vetoed twenty-one bills. Franklin D. Roosevelt (1933–1945) vetoed more bills by far than any of his predecessors or successors in the presidency. During his administration, there were 372 regular vetoes, 9 of which were overridden by Congress, and 263 pocket vetoes.

### The Veto in Recent Administrations

President George W. Bush, used his veto power very sparingly. Indeed, during the first six years of his presidency, Bush vetoed only one bill—a proposal to expand the scope of stem-cell research. Bush

> **veto** A Latin word meaning "I forbid"; the refusal by an official, such as the president of the United States or a state governor, to sign a bill into law.

President Bill Clinton used line-item veto powers to eliminate nearly forty projects worth $287 million from a military construction bill in 1997. The line-item veto legislation, passed in 1996, was ruled unconstitutional by the United States Supreme Court in 1998.

Presidents have often argued in favor of a *line-item veto* that would enable them to veto just one (or several) items in a bill. In 1996, Congress passed and President Clinton signed a line-item veto bill. In 1998, though, the Supreme Court concluded that the bill was unconstitutional.[3]

## 12–3b The President's Inherent Powers

In addition to the powers explicitly granted by the Constitution, the president also has *inherent powers*—powers that are necessary to carry out the specific responsibilities of the president as set forth in the Constitution. The presidency is, of course, an institution of government, but it is also an institution that consists, at any one moment in time, of one individual. That means the lines between the presidential office and the person who holds that office often become blurred.

Certain presidential powers that are generally recognized today were simply assumed by strong presidents to be inherent powers of the presidency, and their successors then continued to exercise these powers.

President Woodrow Wilson clearly indicated this interplay between presidential personality and presidential powers in the following observation:

> The President is at liberty, both in law and conscience, to be as big a man as he can. His capacity will set the limit; and if Congress be overborne by him, it will be no fault of the makers of the Constitution—it will be from no lack of constitutional powers on his part, but only because the President has the nation behind him, and Congress has not.[4]

In other words, because the Constitution is vague as to the actual carrying out of presidential powers, presidents are left to define the limits of their authority—subject, of course, to obstacles raised by the other branches of government.

vetoed so few bills largely because the Republican-led Congress during those years strongly supported his agenda. After the Democrats took control of Congress in 2007, Bush vetoed eleven bills. Congress overrode four of the vetoes.

With a Congress led by his own party, President Obama faced circumstances similar to those enjoyed by George W. Bush during the first two years of his presidency. Consequently, in his first two years of office, Obama exercised the veto power only twice. Surprisingly, Obama issued no vetoes during his second two years even though the Republicans were in control of the House. Apparently, no measure that Obama would have opposed was able to make its way through the Democratic-controlled Senate.

**The Line-Item Veto** Many presidents have complained that they cannot control "pork-barrel" legislation—federal expenditures tacked onto bills to "bring home the bacon" to a particular congressional member's district. For example, expenditures on a specific sports stadium might be added to a bill involving crime. The reason is simple: the president would have to veto the entire bill to eliminate the pork—and that might not be feasible politically.

As chief diplomat, George Washington made foreign policy decisions without consulting Congress. This action laid the groundwork for an active presidential role in foreign policy.

By the time Abraham Lincoln gave his Inauguration Day speech, seven southern states had already seceded from the Union. Some scholars believe that Lincoln's skillful and vigorous handling of the Civil War increased the power and prestige of the presidency.

In its attempts to counter the effects of the Great Depression, Franklin D. Roosevelt's administration not only extended the role of the national government in regulating the nation's economic life but also further increased the power of the president.

## 12–3c The Expansion of Presidential Powers

The Constitution defines presidential powers in very general language, and even the founders were uncertain just how the president would perform the various functions. George Washington (1789–1797) set many of the precedents that have defined presidential power. For example, he removed officials from office, interpreting the constitutional power to appoint officials as implying power to remove them as well.[5]

Washington established the practice of meeting regularly with the heads of the three departments that then existed (plus the attorney general) and of turning to them for political advice. He set a precedent for the president to act as chief legislator by submitting proposed legislation to Congress.

**Expansion under Later Presidents**  Abraham Lincoln (1861–1865), confronting the problems of the Civil War during the 1860s, took several important actions while Congress was not in session. He suspended certain constitutional liberties, spent funds that Congress had not appropriated, blockaded southern ports, and banned "treasonable correspondence" from the U.S. mail. Lincoln carried out all of these actions in the name of his power as commander in chief and his constitutional responsibility to "take Care that the Laws be faithfully executed."[6]

Other presidents, including Thomas Jefferson, Andrew Jackson, Woodrow Wilson, Franklin D. Roosevelt, and George W. Bush, also greatly expanded the powers of the president. The power of the president continues to evolve, depending on the person holding the office, the relative power of Congress, and events at home and abroad.

**The President's Expanded Legislative Powers**
Congress has come to expect the president to develop a legislative program. From time to time, the president submits special messages on certain subjects. These messages call on Congress to enact laws that the president thinks are necessary. The president also works closely with members of Congress to persuade them to support particular programs. The president writes, telephones, and meets with various congressional leaders to discuss pending bills. The president also sends aides to lobby on Capitol Hill.

One study of the legislative process found that "no other single actor in the political system has quite the capability of the president to set agendas in given policy areas." As one lobbyist told a researcher, "Obviously, when a president sends up a bill [to Congress], it takes first place in the queue. All other bills take second place." As noted earlier, however, compared with some recent presidents, Barack Obama showed a surprising willingness to let Congress determine the details of important legislation.

## THE POWER TO PERSUADE.

The president's political skills and ability to persuade others play a large role in determining the administration's success. According to Richard Neustadt in his classic work *Presidential Power*, "Presidential power is the power to persuade."[7] For all of the resources at the president's disposal, the president still must rely on the cooperation of others if the administration's goals are to be accomplished. After three years in office, President Harry Truman made this remark about the powers of the president:

> The president may have a great many powers given to him in the Constitution and may have certain powers under certain laws which are given to him by the Congress of the United States; but the principal power that the president has is to bring people in and try to persuade them to do what they ought to do without persuasion. That's what the powers of the president amount to.[8]

Persuasive powers are particularly important when divided government exists. If a president from one political party faces a Congress dominated by the other party, the president must overcome more opposition than usual to get legislation passed.

## GOING PUBLIC.

The president may also use a strategy known as "going public"[9]—that is, using press conferences, public appearances, and televised events to arouse public opinion in favor of certain legislative programs. The public may then pressure legislators to support the administration's programs. A president who has the support of the public can wield significant persuasive power over Congress. Presidents who are voted into office through "landslide" elections have increased bargaining power because of their widespread popularity. Those with less popular support have less bargaining leverage.

The ability of the president to "go public" effectively is dependent on popular attitudes toward the president. It is also dependent on the political climate in Washington, D.C. In periods of severe political polarization—such as the last several years—going

"All the president is, is a glorified public relations man who spends his time flattering, kissing, and kicking people to get them to do what they are supposed to do anyway."

~ HARRY TRUMAN ~
THIRTY-THIRD PRESIDENT
OF THE UNITED STATES
1945–1953

public can actually be counterproductive. Simply by endorsing a proposal that might have had bipartisan support, the president can turn the question into a partisan issue. Without support from at least some members of both parties, the proposal then fails to pass.

## THE POWER TO INFLUENCE THE ECONOMY.

Some of the greatest expansions of presidential power occurred during Franklin Roosevelt's administration. Roosevelt claimed the presidential power to regulate the economy during the Great Depression in the 1930s. Since that time, Americans have expected the president to be actively involved in economic matters and social programs. That expectation becomes especially potent during a major economic downturn, such as the Great Recession that began in December 2007.

Congress annually receives from the president a suggested budget and the *Economic Report of the President*. The budget message proposes what amounts of money the government will need for its programs. The *Economic Report of the President* presents the state of the nation's economy and recommends ways to improve it.

Voters may rate a president based on the state of the economy. Experts have observed that the president's ability to control the level of economic activity is subject to severe limits. From the public's point of view, however, evaluating its leaders based on results makes good sense. If a president is under constant political pressure to improve the economy, he or she is likely to do whatever is possible to reach that goal. How much can a president actually do to affect the economy? We examine that question in the *Perception versus Reality* feature on the following page.

## THE LEGISLATIVE SUCCESS OF VARIOUS PRESIDENTS.

Look at Figure 12–1 on page 282. It shows the success records of presidents in getting their legislation passed. Success is defined as how often the president got his way on roll-call votes on which he took a clear position. As you can see, typically a president's success record was very high when he first took office and then gradually declined. This is sometimes attributed to the president's "honeymoon period," when Congress may

# Perception versus Reality
## Can the President Really Fix the Economy?

The economy has been in bad shape since the end of 2007. As we pointed out in the *Our Challenging Times* feature in Chapter 1, a president running for reelection often won't be reelected if the state of the economy is not improving. There is clearly a public perception that the president can engage in numerous actions to "fix the economy." So, if the economy isn't growing, it's the president's fault.

### THE PERCEPTION

What the president wants, he or she gets. If the president has the right ideas about how to improve the economy, he or she just has to make sure that those ideas become public policy. Therefore, when the economy is not adding jobs and the rate of economic growth is slow or nonexistent, clearly the president is responsible.

### THE REALITY

What presidents say and what happens are not necessarily related. When it comes to the economy, that statement is especially true. Consider *monetary policy*—changing the amount of money in circulation to warm up or cool down the economy. Presidents have almost no control over monetary policy because the independent Federal Reserve System (Fed) carries it out. Presidents can, to be sure, "jawbone" the current head of the Fed—try to exert influence—but that is about the extent of presidential power over monetary policy.

*Fiscal policy*—tax rates, subsidies, decreases and increases in government spending levels—is another policy lever. People often believe that the president can control such variables. The reality is often quite the opposite.

Only Congress can pass laws that change our tax code and that change the amount of taxpayer dollars spent. This is not to say that a president is incapable of influencing tax rates and the level of government spending, but such influence does not usually go very far if one or both chambers of Congress are in the hands of the other party. This is especially true today, given high levels of political polarization. President Ronald Reagan could dramatically lower tax rates when Democrats controlled Congress, but that was another era.

President Obama was able to get a stimulus bill passed in 2009 because the Democrats controlled both chambers of Congress. Since 2010, in contrast, the Republicans have controlled the House. Attempts by the Obama administration to negotiate with the House Republican leadership proved to be extraordinarily difficult. As a result, the president had little influence on taxing and spending decisions.

**BLOG ON**
To learn more about economic policy, try consulting two talented bloggers. A search on "mankiw" will lead you to the blog of Greg Mankiw, currently chair of the Harvard Economics Department and a moderate Republican. Matt Yglesias is a pro-market progressive, and you can find his Slate blog by searching on "yglesias."

be most likely to work with the president to achieve the president's legislative agenda.

The media often put a great deal of emphasis on how successful a president is during the "first hundred days" in office. Ironically, this is also the period when the president is least experienced in the ways of the White House, particularly if the president was a Washington outsider, such as a state governor, before becoming president.

In 2009, President Obama had the most successful legislative year of any president in half a century. Large Democratic majorities in both chambers of Congress were surely important in explaining Obama's ability to obtain the legislation that he sought. Obama was also successful in 2010. After the Democrats lost control of the U.S. House in November 2010, however, Obama's success rate fell considerably.

# FIGURE 12-1 Presidential Success Records

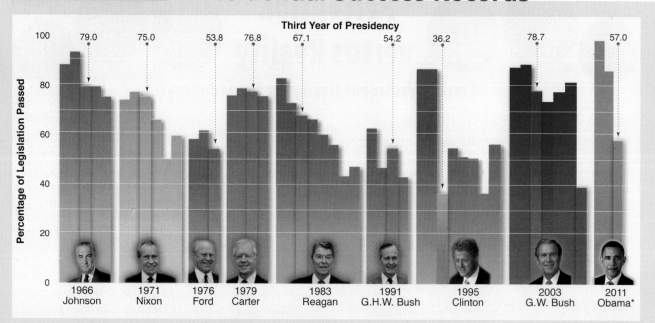

**Third Year of Presidency**

Percentage of Legislation Passed

| | 79.0 | 75.0 | 53.8 | 76.8 | 67.1 | 54.2 | 36.2 | 78.7 | 57.0 |

| 1966 Johnson | 1971 Nixon | 1976 Ford | 1979 Carter | 1983 Reagan | 1991 G.H.W. Bush | 1995 Clinton | 2003 G.W. Bush | 2011 Obama* |

*Obama's first-year success rate (2009) was 96 percent, the highest since the opening days of Franklin Roosevelt's presidency.

Source: *Congressional Quarterly Almanac.*

## The Increasing Use of Executive Orders

As the nation's chief executive, the president is considered to have the inherent power to issue **executive orders,** which are presidential orders to carry out policies described in laws that have been passed by Congress. These orders have the force of law.

Presidents have issued executive orders for a variety of purposes, including to establish procedures for appointing noncareer administrators, to restructure the White House bureaucracy, and to ration consumer goods and administer wage and price controls under emergency conditions. Other goals have included classifying government information as secret, implementing affirmative action policies, and regulating the export of certain items. Presidents issue executive orders frequently, sometimes as many as one hundred a year.

## An Unprecedented Use of Signing Statements

A **signing statement** is a written statement issued by a president at the time he or she signs a bill into law. James Monroe (1817–1825) was the first president to issue such a statement. For many years, signing statements were rare—prior to the presidency of Ronald Reagan, only seventy-five were issued. Most were "rhetorical" in character. They might praise the legislation or the Congress that passed it, or criticize the opposition. On occasion, however, the statements noted constitutional problems with one or more clauses of a bill or provided details as to how the executive branch would interpret legislative language.

Reagan issued a grand total of 249 signing statements. For the first time, each statement was published in the *U.S. Code Congressional and Administrative News,* along with the text of the bill in question. A substantial share of the statements addressed constitutional issues. Reagan staff member Samuel Alito, Jr.—who now sits on the United States Supreme Court—issued a memo in favor of

**SOCIAL MEDIA**
**In Politics**

The Gallup poll has a major social media presence where you can follow news about the president's popularity and many other topics. On Facebook, look for "gallup." On Twitter, follow "gallupnews."

---

**executive order** A presidential order to carry out a policy or policies described in a law passed by Congress.

**signing statement** A written statement, appended to a bill at the time the president signs it into law, indicating how the president interprets that legislation.

using signing statements to "increase the power of the Executive to shape the law."

## Signing Statements under Bush

President George W. Bush took the use of signing statements to an entirely new level. Bush's 161 statements challenged more than 1,100 clauses of federal law—more legal provisions than were challenged by all previous presidents put together. The powers that the statements claimed for the president alarmed some people. One statement rejected Congress's authority to ban torture. Another affirmed that the president could have anyone's mail opened without a warrant.

As a presidential candidate, Barack Obama criticized Bush's use of signing statements and promised to limit his use of them. As president, he reduced the number of signing statements substantially.

## Evolving Presidential Power in Foreign Affairs

The precise extent of the president's power in foreign affairs is constantly evolving. The president is commander in chief and chief diplomat, but only Congress has the power to formally declare war, and the Senate must ratify any treaty that the president has negotiated with other nations. Nevertheless, from the beginning, our country has been led by the president in foreign affairs.

> "If one morning I walked on top of the water across the Potomac River, the headline that afternoon would read:
>
> ## 'PRESIDENT CAN'T SWIM.'"
>
> ~ LYNDON B. JOHNSON ~
> THIRTY-SIXTH PRESIDENT
> OF THE UNITED STATES
> 1963–1969

George Washington laid the groundwork for our long history of the president's active role in foreign policy. For example, when war broke out between Britain and France in 1793, Washington chose to disregard a treaty of alliance with France and to pursue a course of strict neutrality. Since that time, on many occasions presidents have taken military actions and made foreign policy without consulting Congress.

**EXECUTIVE AGREEMENTS.** In foreign affairs, presidential power is enhanced by the ability to make **executive agreements,** which are pacts between the president and other heads of state. Executive agreements do not require Senate approval (even though Congress may refuse to appropriate the necessary money to carry out the agreements), but they have the same legal status as treaties.

Presidents form executive agreements for a wide range of purposes. Some involve routine matters, such as promises of trade or assistance to other countries. Others concern matters of great importance.

In 1940, for example, President Franklin Roosevelt formed an important executive agreement with British prime minister Winston Churchill. The agreement provided that the United States would lend American destroyers to Britain to help protect that nation and its shipping during World War II. In return, the British allowed the United States to use military and naval bases on British territories in the Western Hemisphere.

To prevent presidential abuse of the power to make executive agreements, Congress passed a law in 1972 that requires the president to inform Congress within sixty days of making any executive agreement. The law did not limit the president's power to make executive agreements, however, and they continue to be used far more than treaties in making foreign policy.

**MILITARY ACTIONS.** As you read in the chapter-opening *America at Odds* feature, the U.S. Constitution gives Congress the

President George W. Bush is shown here approving a signing statement attached to a piece of legislation. During his two terms as president, Bush made unprecedented use of signing statements to assert presidential authority.

**executive agreement**
A binding international agreement, or pact, that is made between the president and another head of state and that does not require Senate approval.

power to declare war. Consider however, that although Congress has declared war in only five different conflicts during our nation's history,[10] the United States has engaged in more than two hundred activities involving the armed services.

Without a congressional declaration of war, President Truman sent U.S. armed forces to Korea in 1950, thus involving American troops in the conflict between North and South Korea. The United States also entered the Vietnam War (1965–1975) without a declaration of war. President Nixon did not consult Congress when he made the decision to invade Cambodia in 1970. Neither did President Reagan when he sent troops to Lebanon and Grenada in 1983.

No congressional vote was taken before President George H. W. Bush sent troops into Panama in 1989. Bush did, however, obtain congressional approval to use American troops to force Iraq to withdraw from Kuwait in 1991. Without Congress, President Clinton made the decision to send troops to Haiti in 1994 and to Bosnia in 1995, as well as to bomb Iraq in 1998. In 1999, he also decided on his own authority to send U.S. forces under the command of NATO (North Atlantic Treaty Organization) to bomb Yugoslavia.

**THE WAR POWERS RESOLUTION.** As commander in chief, the president can respond quickly to a military threat without waiting for congressional action. This power to commit troops and to involve the nation in a war upset many members of Congress as the undeclared war in Vietnam dragged on for years into the 1970s. Criticism of the president's role in the Vietnam conflict led to the passage of the War Powers Resolution of 1973.

AP PHOTO/DOUG MILLS

President George H. W. Bush often seemed at ease during his White House press conferences.

"As to the presidency, the two happiest days of my life were those of my entrance upon the office and my surrender of it."

~ MARTIN VAN BUREN ~
EIGHTH PRESIDENT
OF THE UNITED STATES
1837–1841

The law, which was passed over President Nixon's veto, requires the president to notify Congress within forty-eight hours of deploying troops. It also prevents the president from keeping troops abroad for more than sixty days (or ninety days, if more time is needed for a successful withdrawal). If Congress does not authorize a longer period, the troops must be removed.

**THE WAR ON TERRORISM.** President George W. Bush did not obtain a declaration of war from Congress for the war against terrorism that began on September 11, 2001. Instead, Congress passed a joint resolution authorizing the president to use "all necessary and appropriate force against those nations, organizations, or persons he determines planned, authorized, committed, or aided the terrorist attacks that occurred on September 11, 2001."

This resolution was the basis for America's subsequent involvement in Afghanistan. Also, in October 2002, Congress passed a joint resolution authorizing the use of U.S. armed forces against Iraq.

As a consequence of these resolutions, the president was able to invoke certain emergency wartime measures. For example, through executive order the president created military tribunals for trying terrorist suspects. The president also held American citizens as "enemy combatants," denying them access to their attorneys.

**NUCLEAR WEAPONS.** Since 1945, the president, as commander in chief, has been responsible for the most difficult of all military decisions—if and when to use nuclear weapons. In 1945, Harry Truman made the awesome decision to drop atomic bombs on the Japanese cities of Hiroshima and Nagasaki. "The final decision," he said, "on where and when to use the atomic bomb was up to me. Let there be no mistake about it." Today, the president travels at all times with the "football"—the briefcase containing the codes used to launch a nuclear attack.

## 12–4 Congressional and Presidential Relations

### LearningOutcome 12–4
Describe advantages enjoyed by Congress and by the president in their institutional relationship.

Despite the seemingly immense powers at the president's disposal, the president is limited in what he or she can accomplish, or even attempt. In our system of checks and balances, the president must share some powers with the legislative and judicial branches of government. The president's power is checked not only by these institutions but also by the media, public opinion, and the voters. The founders hoped that this system of shared power would lessen the chance of tyranny.

Some scholars believe the relationship between Congress and the president is the most important one in the American system of government. Congress traditionally has had the upper hand in some areas, primarily in passing legislation. In some other areas, though, particularly in foreign affairs, the president can exert tremendous power that Congress has almost no ability to check.

### 12–4a Advantage: Congress

Congress has the advantage over the president in the areas of legislative authorization, the regulation of foreign and interstate commerce, and some budgetary matters. Of course, as you have already read, the president today proposes a legislative agenda and a budget to Congress every year. Nonetheless, only Congress has

the power to pass the legislation and appropriate the money. The most the president can do constitutionally is veto an entire bill if it contains something that she or he does not like. (As noted, however, recent presidents have frequently used signing statements in an attempt to nullify portions of bills that they did not approve.)

Presidential popularity is a source of power for the president in dealings with Congress. Presidents spend a great deal of time courting public opinion, eyeing the "presidential approval ratings," and meeting with the press. Much of this activity is for the purpose of gaining leverage with Congress. The president can put all of his or her persuasive powers to work in achieving a legislative agenda, but Congress still retains the ultimate lawmaking authority.

**Divided Government** When government is divided—with at least one house of Congress controlled by a different party than the White House—the president can have difficulty even getting a legislative agenda to the floor for a vote. President George W. Bush faced such a problem in 2007, when the Democrats gained a majority in Congress. During his first six years

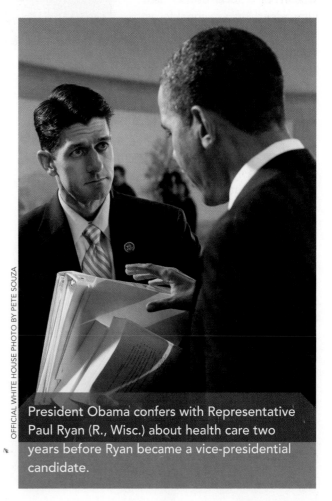

OFFICIAL WHITE HOUSE PHOTO BY PETE SOUZA

President Obama confers with Representative Paul Ryan (R., Wisc.) about health care two years before Ryan became a vice-presidential candidate.

as president, Bush had worked with an extremely cooperative Republican-led Congress.[11] After the Democrats became the majority, however, divided government existed again.

Divided government disappeared during President Obama's first two years in office. Following the elections of 2010 and the Republican takeover of the U.S. House, it returned with a vengeance. Few people in public life could remember a time when partisan hostilities were so intense.

## Different Constituencies

Congress and the president have different constituencies, and this fact influences their relationship. Members of Congress represent a state or a local district, and this gives them a regional focus. As we discussed in Chapter 11, members of Congress like to have legislative successes of their own to bring home to their constituents—military bases that remain operative, public-works projects that create local jobs, or trade rules that benefit a big local employer. Ideally, the president's focus should be on the nation as a whole: national defense, homeland security, the national economy. At times, this can put the president at odds even with members of his or her own party in Congress.

Furthermore, members of Congress and the president face different election cycles (every two years in the House, every six years in the Senate, and every four years for the president), and the president is limited to two terms in office. Consequently, the president and Congress sometimes feel a different sense of urgency about implementing legislation. For example, the president often senses the need to demonstrate legislative success during the first year in office, when the excitement over the elections is still fresh in the minds of politicians and the public.

## 12–4b Advantage: The President

The president has the advantage over Congress in dealing with a national crisis, in setting foreign policy, and

Condoleezza Rice was secretary of state from 2005 to 2009 under President George W. Bush. Before holding that office, she was national security adviser, the first woman to hold that position.

in influencing public opinion. In times of crisis, the presidency is arguably the most crucial institution in government because, when necessary, the president can act quickly, speak with one voice, and represent the nation to the world.

Some scholars have argued that recent presidents have abused the powers of the presidency by taking advantage of crises. Others have argued that there is an unwritten "doctrine of necessity" under which presidential powers can and should be expanded during a crisis. When this has happened in the past, however, Congress has always retaken some control when the crisis was over, in a natural process of institutional give-and-take.

**The War on Terrorism** A problem faced during the George W. Bush administration was that the "war on terrorism" had no obvious end or conclusion. It was not clear when the crisis would be over and the nation could return to normal government relations and procedures. In fact, several of Bush's most controversial initiatives, such as support for "enhanced" interrogation methods, were ended during his second term.

Many supporters of Barack Obama believed that upon election, he would restore civil liberties lost during Bush's war on terrorism. As it turned out, the Obama administration kept most of Bush's policies in place. (You learned about this issue in greater detail in the Chapter 4 *Perception versus Reality* feature on page 91.)

**Executive Privilege** As you read in Chapter 11, Congress has the authority to investigate and oversee the activities of other branches of government. Nonetheless, both Congress and the public have accepted that a certain degree of secrecy by the executive branch is necessary to protect national security. Some presidents have claimed an inherent executive power to withhold information from, or to refuse to appear before, Congress or the courts. This is called executive privilege, and it has been invoked by presidents from the time of George Washington to the present.

### Abuses of Executive Privilege

One of the problems with executive privilege is that it has been used for more purposes than simply to safeguard the national security. President Nixon invoked executive privilege in an attempt to avoid handing over taped White House conversations to Congress during the **Watergate scandal.** President Clinton invoked the privilege in an attempt to keep details of his sexual relationship with White House intern Monica Lewinsky a secret.

After the Democrats took control of Congress in 2007 and began to investigate various actions undertaken by the Bush administration, they were frequently blocked in their attempts to obtain information by the claim of executive privilege. For example, during Congress's investigation of the Justice Department's firing of several U.S. attorneys for allegedly political reasons, the Bush administration raised the claim of executive privilege to prevent several people from testifying or submitting requested documents to Congress.

**FOR CRITICAL THINKING**

*Would we be better off if executive privilege didn't exist, or are there some matters a president must be able to keep private? Discuss.*

## 12–5 The Organization of the Executive Branch

**LearningOutcome 12–5**

Discuss the organization of the executive branch and the role of cabinet members in presidential administrations.

In the early days of this nation, presidents answered their own mail. Only in 1857 did Congress authorize a private secretary for the president, to be paid by the federal government. Even Woodrow Wilson typed most of his correspondence, although by that time several secretaries were assigned to the president. When Franklin Roosevelt became president in 1933, the entire staff consisted of thirty-seven employees. Not until Roosevelt's New Deal and World War II did the presidential staff become a sizable organization.

### 12–5a The President's Cabinet

The Constitution does not specifically mention presidential assistants and advisers. The Constitution states only that the president "may require the Opinion, in writing, of the principal Officer in each of the executive Departments." Since the time of our first president, however, presidents have had an advisory group, or **cabinet,** to turn to for counsel. Originally, the cabinet consisted of only four officials—the secretaries of state, treasury, and war and the attorney general.

Today, the cabinet includes fourteen department secretaries, the attorney general, and a number of other officials. (See Table 12–2 on the following page for the names of the major executive departments represented in the cabinet.) Additional cabinet members vary from one presidency to the next. Typically, the vice president is a member. President Clinton added ten officials to the cabinet, and George W. Bush added five. Barack Obama added the following members, in addition to the vice president:

- The administrator of the Environmental Protection Agency.

- The chair of the Council of Economic Advisers.

- The director of the Office of Management and Budget.

- The United States ambassador to the United Nations.

- The United States trade representative.

- The White House chief of staff.

### Use of the Cabinet

Because the Constitution does not require the president to consult with the

**executive privilege** An inherent executive power claimed by presidents to withhold information from, or to refuse to appear before, Congress or the courts. The president can also accord the privilege to other executive officials.

**Watergate scandal** A scandal involving an illegal break-in at the Democratic National Committee offices in 1972 by members of President Nixon's reelection campaign staff. Before Congress could vote to impeach Nixon for his participation in covering up the break-in, Nixon resigned from the presidency.

**cabinet** An advisory group selected by the president to assist with decision making. Traditionally, the cabinet has consisted of the heads of the executive departments and other officers whom the president may choose to appoint.

cabinet, the use of this body is purely discretionary. Some presidents have relied on the counsel of their cabinets more than others. After a cabinet meeting in which a vote was seven nays against his one aye, President Lincoln supposedly said, "Seven nays and one aye, the ayes have it."[12]

Still other presidents have sought counsel from so-called **kitchen cabinets,** informal groups of unofficial advisers. The term *kitchen cabinet* originated during the presidency of Andrew Jackson, who relied on the counsel of close friends who allegedly met with him in the kitchen of the White House.

In general, presidents usually don't rely heavily on the advice of the formal cabinet. They are aware that department heads are often more responsive to the wishes of their own staffs, to their own political ambitions, or to obtaining resources for their departments than they are to the presidents they serve.

**Obama's "Czars"**   President Obama's response to the need to seek advice was to centralize the advisory function within the White House Office (discussed below) by appointing a large number of in-house "czars." Each of these White House czars had responsibility for a certain policy area.

Critics of the Obama administration believed that the czar system tends to undercut the authority of cabinet members. Congress also loses leverage, because cabinet members must be confirmed by the Senate, whereas czars are responsible only to the president.

**kitchen cabinet** The name given to a president's unofficial advisers. The term was coined during Andrew Jackson's presidency.

**Executive Office of the President (EOP)** A group of staff agencies that assist the president in carrying out major duties. Franklin D. Roosevelt established the EOP in 1939 to cope with the increased responsibilities brought on by the Great Depression.

**White House Office** The personal office of the president. White House Office personnel handle the president's political needs and manage the media, among other duties.

## 12–5b The Executive Office of the President

In 1939, President Franklin Roosevelt set up the **Executive Office of the President (EOP)** to cope with the increased responsibilities brought on by the Great Depression. Since then, the EOP has grown significantly to accommodate the increasingly expansive role played by the national government, including the executive branch, in the nation's economic and social life.

### TABLE 12–2

### The Major Executive Departments

The heads of all of these departments are members of the president's cabinet.

| Department | Year of First Establishment |
|---|---|
| Department of State | 1789 |
| Department of the Treasury | 1789 |
| Department of Defense* | 1789 |
| Department of Justice (headed by the attorney general)† | 1789 |
| Department of the Interior | 1849 |
| Department of Agriculture | 1889 |
| Department of Commerce‡ | 1903 |
| Department of Labor‡ | 1903 |
| Department of Health and Human Services§ | 1953 |
| Department of Housing and Urban Development | 1965 |
| Department of Transportation | 1967 |
| Department of Energy | 1977 |
| Department of Education | 1979 |
| Department of Veterans Affairs | 1989 |
| Department of Homeland Security | 2002 |

*Established in 1947 by merging the Department of War, created in 1789, and the Department of the Navy, created in 1798.
†Formerly the Office of the Attorney General; renamed and reorganized in 1870.
‡Formed in 1913 by splitting the Department of Commerce and Labor, which was created in 1903.
§Formerly the Department of Health, Education, and Welfare; renamed when the Department of Education was spun off in 1979.

© CENGAGE LEARNING

The EOP is made up of the top advisers and assistants who help the president carry out major duties. Over the years, the EOP has changed according to the needs and leadership style of each president. It has become an increasingly influential and important part of the executive branch.

Table 12–3 on the facing page lists various offices within the EOP as of 2012. Note that the organization of the EOP is subject to change. Presidents have frequently added new bodies to its membership and subtracted others. President Obama made a number of changes to the EOP's table of organization during his years in office.

**The White House Office**   Of all of the executive staff agencies, the **White House Office** has the most direct contact with the president. The White

## TABLE 12-3

### The Executive Office of the President as of 2012

**Agency**

Council of Economic Advisers

Council on Environmental Quality

Executive Residence

National Security Staff

Office of Administration

Office of Management and Budget

Office of National Drug Control Policy

Office of Science and Technology Policy

Office of the U.S. Trade Representative

Office of the Vice President

White House Office

Source: www.whitehouse.gov.

House Office is headed by the **chief of staff,** who advises the president on important matters and directs the operations of the presidential staff. A number of other top officials, assistants, and special assistants to the president also aid him or her in such areas as national security, the economy, and political affairs. The **press secretary** meets with reporters and makes public statements for the president. The counsel to the president serves as the White House lawyer and handles the president's legal matters.

The White House staff also includes speechwriters, researchers, the president's physician, and a correspondence secretary. Altogether, the White House Office has more than four hundred employees.

The White House staff has several duties. First, the staff investigates and analyzes problems that require the president's attention. Staff members who are specialists in certain areas, such as diplomatic relations or foreign trade, gather information for the president and suggest solutions. White House staff members also screen the questions, issues, and problems that people present to the president, so matters that can be handled by other officials do not reach the president's desk.

Additionally, the staff provides public relations support. For example, the press staff handles the president's relations with the White House press corps and schedules news conferences. Finally, the White House staff ensures that the president's initiatives are effectively transmitted to the relevant government personnel.

Several staff members are usually assigned to work directly with members of Congress for this purpose.

**chief of staff** The person who directs the operations of the White House Office and advises the president on important matters.

**press secretary** A member of the White House staff who holds news conferences for reporters and makes public statements for the president.

**The First Lady** The White House Office also includes the staff of the president's spouse. First Ladies have at times taken important roles within the White House. For example, Franklin Roosevelt's wife, Eleanor, advocated the rights of women, labor, and African Americans. As First Lady, Hillary Clinton helped develop an unsuccessful plan for a national health-care system. In 2008, she was a leading contender for the Democratic presidential nomination. Had she won the presidency, Bill Clinton would have become the nation's First Gentleman.

President Barack Obama, Vice President Joe Biden, Secretary of State Hillary Clinton, and members of the national security team receive an update on the mission against Osama bin Laden in the Situation Room of the White House on May 1, 2011. Obama later announced that the United States had killed bin Laden in an operation undertaken by U.S. Navy SEALs at a compound in Abbottabad, Pakistan.

PETE SOUZA/THE WHITE HOUSE/GETTY IMAGES

**The Office of Management and Budget**  The **Office of Management and Budget (OMB)** was originally the Bureau of the Budget. Under recent presidents, the OMB has become an important and influential unit of the Executive Office of the President. The main function of the OMB is to assist the president in preparing the proposed annual budget, which the president must submit to Congress in January of each year (see Chapter 11 for details).

The federal budget lists the revenues and expenditures expected for the coming year. It indicates which programs the federal government will pay for and how much they will cost. Thus, the budget is an annual statement of the public policies of the United States translated into dollars and cents. Making changes in the budget is a key way for presidents to influence the direction and policies of the federal government.

The president appoints the director of the OMB with the consent of the Senate. The director oversees the OMB's work and argues the administration's positions before Congress. The director also lobbies members of Congress to support the president's budget or to accept key features of it. Once the budget is approved by Congress, the OMB has the responsibility of putting it into practice. The OMB oversees the execution of the budget, checking on federal agencies to ensure that they use funds efficiently.

Beyond its budget duties, the OMB also reviews new bills prepared by the executive branch. It checks all legislative matters to be certain that they agree with the president's own positions.

**The National Security Council**  The **National Security Council (NSC)** was established in 1947 to manage the defense and foreign policy of the United States. Its members are the president, the vice president, and the secretaries of state and defense. It also includes several informal advisers. The NSC is the president's link to his or her key foreign and military advisers. The president's special assistant for national security affairs heads the NSC staff.

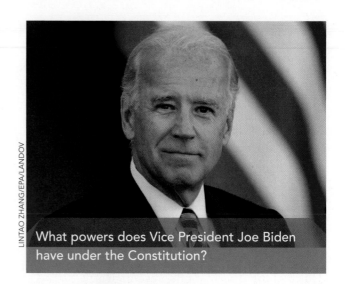

LINTAO ZHANG/EPA/LANDOV

What powers does Vice President Joe Biden have under the Constitution?

## 12–5c The Vice Presidency and Presidential Succession

As a rule, presidential nominees choose running mates who balance the ticket or whose appointment rewards or appeases party factions. For example, to balance the ticket geographically, a presidential candidate from the South may solicit a running mate from the West.

In 2008, Republican candidate John McCain chose as his running mate Alaska governor Sarah Palin. Palin shored up McCain's support among cultural conservatives. President Barack Obama picked Senator Joe Biden, who had thirty-five years of experience in Congress. Obama wished to counter detractors who claimed that he was too inexperienced.

In 2012, Republican presidential candidate Mitt Romney chose Representative Paul Ryan of Wisconsin to join his ticket. Ryan helped Romney appeal to the party's conservative wing. Ryan had gained recognition as chair of the House Budget Committee when he authored a series of proposed budgets that won near-universal Republican support.

**The Role of Vice Presidents**  For much of our history, the vice president has had almost no responsibilities. Still, the vice president is in a position to become the nation's chief executive should the president die, be impeached, or resign the presidential office. Nine vice presidents have become president because of the death or resignation of the president.

In recent years, the responsibilities of the vice president have grown immensely. The vice president has become one of the most—if not *the* most—important of the president's advisers. The first modern vice president to act as a major adviser was Walter Mondale, who served under Jimmy Carter. Later, Bill Clinton relied

**Office of Management and Budget (OMB)**
An agency in the Executive Office of the President that has the primary duty of assisting the president in preparing and supervising the administration of the federal budget.

**National Security Council (NSC)** A council that advises the president on domestic and foreign matters concerning the safety and defense of the nation; established in 1947.

heavily on Vice President Al Gore, who shared many of Clinton's values and beliefs.

Without question, however, the most powerful vice president in American history was Dick Cheney, who served under George W. Bush. A consummate bureaucratic strategist, Cheney was able to place his supporters in important positions throughout the government, giving him access to information and influence. This unprecedented delegation of power, of course, would not have been possible without the president's agreement, and Bush clearly approved of it. Vice President Joe Biden has been one of President Barack Obama's most important advisers, but not at the level of Cheney.

President Gerald Ford (right) confers with Vice President Nelson Rockefeller in the Oval Office of the White House in 1974. For the first time in the history of the United States, neither leader obtained office by winning a general election.

### Presidential Succession

One of the questions left unanswered by the Constitution was what the vice president should do if the president becomes incapable of carrying out necessary duties while in office. The Twenty-fifth Amendment to the Constitution, ratified in 1967, filled this gap.

**THE TWENTY-FIFTH AMENDMENT.** The amendment states that when the president believes that he or she is incapable of performing the duties of the office, he or she must inform Congress in writing of this fact. Then the vice president serves as acting president until the president can resume his or her normal duties.

When the president is unable to communicate, a majority of the cabinet, including the vice president, can declare that fact to Congress. Then the vice president serves as acting president until the president resumes normal duties. If a dispute arises over the return of the president's ability to discharge the normal functions of the presidential office, a two-thirds vote of both chambers of Congress is required if the vice president is to remain acting president. Otherwise, the president resumes these duties.

**VICE-PRESIDENTIAL VACANCIES.** The Twenty-fifth Amendment also addresses the question of how the president should fill a vacant vice presidency. Section 2

of the amendment states, "Whenever there is a vacancy in the office of the Vice President, the President shall nominate a Vice President who shall take office upon confirmation by a majority vote of both Houses of Congress."

In 1973, Gerald Ford became the first appointed vice president of the United States after Spiro Agnew was forced to resign. One year later, President Richard Nixon resigned, and Ford advanced to the office of president. President Ford named Nelson Rockefeller as his vice president. For the first time in U.S. history, neither the president nor the vice president had been elected to his position.

What if both the president and the vice president die, resign, or are disabled? According to the Succession Act of 1947, the Speaker of the House of Representatives will then act as president on her or his resignation as Speaker and as representative. If the Speaker is unavailable, next in line is the president pro tem of the Senate, followed by the permanent members of the president's cabinet in the order of the creation of their departments (see Table 12–2 on page 288).

## FOR CRITICAL THINKING

Members of the Washington political community often harbor a degree of resentment toward those who work in the White House Office. *What might cause these feelings?*

# AMERICA AT
# ODDS The Presidency

The president is the most conspicuous figure in our political system. Everyone has opinions about what the president should do—and in a presidential election year, who the president should be. To an extent not seen in regard to other offices, the public also has a serious interest in the president's personality and character. The president, after all, represents all of us. Americans are at odds over a variety of questions relating to the presidency. These include the following:

- Should the president try, whenever possible, to compromise with other political players, such as the Congress—or should the president generally stand on principle?

- Should the president seek to expand his or her authority so as to deal more effectively with the nation's problems—or should the president try to adhere to a strict constitutional understanding of the powers of the office?

- Is it appropriate for the president to rely primarily on staff members within the White House Office when determining policy—or should the president offer the cabinet a substantial policymaking role?

- Should voters evaluate presidential candidates primarily on the positions they take on the issues—or are the president's character, personality and decision-making style more important considerations?

- Should the president be the "moral leader" of the country in the sense of basing policies on religious values—or should the president avoid any intermingling of religion and policy?

## TAKE ACTION

President James Madison (1809–1817) once said, "The citizens of the United States are responsible for the greatest trust ever confided to a political society." Notice that Madison laid the responsibility for this trust on the "citizens," not the "government." Even though it may seem that one person can do little to affect government policymaking and procedures, this assumption has been proved wrong time and again.

If you would like to influence the way things are done in Washington, D.C., you can do so by helping to elect a president and members of Congress whose views you endorse and who you think would do a good job of running the country. Clearly, you will want to vote in the next elections. Before then, though, you could join others who share your political beliefs and work on behalf of one of the candidates.

You could support a candidate in your home state or join others in "adopting" a candidate from another state who is facing a close race for a congressional seat. You can access that candidate's Web site and offer your services, such as calling voters of the candidate's party and urging them to go to the polls and vote for the candidate. You can also help raise funds for the candidate's campaign and, if you can afford it, even donate some money yourself.

ETHAN MILLER/GETTY IMAGES

CHIP SOMODEVILLA/GETTY IMAGES

# STUDY TOOLS

## Ready to study?

- Review what you've read with the quiz below. Check your answers on the Chapter in Review card at the back of the book. For any questions you miss, read the corresponding Learning Outcome section again to prepare for class and your exam.
- Rip out and study the Chapter in Review card.

## . . . Or you can go online to CourseMate

at www.cengagebrain.com for these additional review materials:

- Practice Quizzes
- Key Term Flashcards or Crossword Puzzles
- Audio Summaries
- Simulations, Animated Learning Modules, and Interactive Timelines
- Videos
- American Government NewsWatch

## Fill-In

1. The most common previous occupation of U.S. presidents has been _____.

2. The president leads the nation's armed forces in his or her role as _____.

3. In his or her role as _____, the president delivers the traditional State of the Union address and has the power to veto bills passed by Congress.

4. The president has the power to issue executive orders, which are _____.

5. The _____ requires the president to notify Congress within forty-eight hours of deploying troops.

6. Executive privilege is _____.

7. Traditionally, the cabinet has consisted of _____.

8. The Executive Office of the President (EOP) is made up of a number of executive staff agencies, including the _____.

## Multiple Choice

9. Which of the following is a constitutional requirement for becoming president of the United States?
   a. Must be at least thirty years old.
   b. Must be of sound moral character.
   c. Must be a natural born citizen of the United States.

10. When the president ____, he is performing his role as head of state.
    a. attends party fund-raisers
    b. makes executive agreements
    c. throws out the first pitch of the baseball season

11. When the president negotiates and signs treaties with other nations, he is performing his role as
    a. chief diplomat.
    b. chief executive.
    c. commander in chief.

12. The presidential strategy known as "going public" refers to
    a. using press conferences, public appearances, and televised events to arouse public opinion in favor of certain legislative programs.
    b. publicly acknowledging mistakes or misconduct.
    c. appearing on talk shows to demonstrate that the president connects with ordinary people.

13. Legislative success for a president is defined as how often the president
    a. got his way on roll-call votes on which he took a clear position.
    b. was able to get his legislative proposals introduced in Congress.
    c. was able to veto legislation.

14. The term *divided government* refers to the
    a. cultural and political differences between the red states and the blue states.
    b. situation when at least one house of Congress is controlled by a different party than the White House.
    c. separation of powers among three branches of government.

15. If a vacancy occurs in the vice presidency,
    a. there is currently no provision for filling the office.
    b. the Speaker of the House, on his or her resignation as Speaker and as representative, acts as vice president.
    c. a vice president is nominated by the president and confirmed by a majority vote in both chambers of Congress.

# 13

# The Bureaucracy

**Remember to visit page 317 for additional Study Tools**

JUSTIN SULLIVAN/GETTY IMAGES

# AMERICA AT
# ODDS How Much Regulation Do We Need?

JUSTIN SULLIVAN/GETTY IMAGES

Many people believe that the financial crisis of 2008 and 2009 was caused by inadequate regulation of financial enterprises. As a result, these businesses took on far too much risk. It's not surprising, therefore, that in July 2010, Congress imposed a large number of new regulations on the financial industry. Compliance will be costly.

In the distant past, there was very little government regulation of health care or other industries. One hundred years ago, drugs were not tested before they were put on the market. Physicians were licensed by the states, but that was about it.

Today, regulation is widespread. Estimates of its costs vary dramatically. According to the Office of Management and Budget (OMB), the annual cost of federal regulations lies between $62 billion and $73 billion, with total benefits of $153 billion to $806 billion. Others argue that the OMB's sums are not comprehensive. One study quoted by conservatives puts total costs at $1.75 trillion per year. Liberals do not find this figure credible. Whatever the true costs are, the question remains: Are current levels of regulation appropriate?

## Unbridled Capitalism Is Dead

The law of the capitalist jungle is what got us into the biggest financial crisis since the Great Depression. Investment banking firms created ever-riskier financial assets, which they sold to unsuspecting individuals and even to local governments as solid, gold-plated investments. In the mortgage industry, unscrupulous salespeople who earned big commissions tricked unsuspecting families into buying homes that were too expensive for their modest means. These problems were largely due to an absence of proper regulation.

Even with something as important as the prescription drugs that we take, the government is not giving us enough protection. Recently, despite its staff members' misgivings, the Food and Drug Administration (FDA) allowed a drug named Avandia to hit the market. That drug turned out to have potential cardiac side effects, and no safety statement on the drug's label warned of them. We need more regulation to protect our lives and our pocketbooks.

## Too Much of Anything Is Bad

While no one proposes that all regulation should be eliminated, many believe that the amount of regulation in effect today is too costly relative to the benefits received. We all want safer products, but the Consumer Product Safety Commission now requires that warning labels appear on even common products. A standard ladder has six hundred words of warning pasted on it, including a warning not to place it in front of a swinging door. What are we, idiots? Every toy has a warning that says, "Small parts may cause a choking risk." Parents don't know this?

Studies indicate that virtually no one reads warning labels anymore because the warnings are either obvious or too long. What happened to personal responsibility in America? The average American is no longer expected to use common sense about any of her or his purchases, activities, or actions. Regulation has its place, but it shouldn't control the entire life of a nation.

## Where do you stand?

1. How much do you think you benefit from regulation in our economy? Give some examples.
2. Are there any circumstances under which warning labels on consumer products could help you? Give some examples.

## Explore this issue online

- Type "approving drugs" into any search engine. The results will include claims that the FDA is not strict enough in regulating medicines, as well as arguments that it is too slow in approving them.

# Introduction

Did you eat breakfast this morning? If you did, **bureaucrats**—individuals who work in the offices of government—had a lot to do with that breakfast. If you had bacon, the meat was inspected by federal agents. If you drank milk, the price was affected by rules and regulations of the Department of Agriculture. If you looked at a cereal box, you saw fine print about fat and vitamins, which was the result of regulations made by several other federal agencies, including the Food and Drug Administration.

If you ate leftover pizza for breakfast, state or local inspectors made sure that the kitchen of the pizza eatery was sanitary and safe. Other bureaucrats ensured that the employees who put together (and perhaps delivered) the pizza were protected against discrimination in the workplace.

Today, the word *bureaucracy* often evokes a negative reaction. For some, it conjures up visions of depersonalized automatons performing chores without any sensitivity toward the needs of those they serve. For others, it is synonymous with government "red tape." A **bureaucracy,** however, is simply a large, complex administrative organization that is structured hierarchically in a pyramid-like fashion.[1] Government bureaucrats carry out the policies of elected government officials.

Members of the bureaucracy—government employees—deliver our mail, clean our streets, teach in our public schools, run our national parks, and attempt to ensure the safety of our food and the prescription drugs that we take. Life as we know it would be quite different without the bureaucrats who keep our governments—federal, state, and local—in operation. Still, Americans disagree over how much regulation is necessary, as discussed in the chapter-opening *America at Odds* feature.

**bureaucrat** An individual who works in a bureaucracy. As generally used, the term refers to a government employee.

**bureaucracy** A large, complex, hierarchically structured administrative organization that carries out specific functions.

## GOVERNMENT BUREAUCRACY:

*"A marvelous labor-saving device which enables ten men to do the work of one."*

~ ATTRIBUTED TO JOHN MAYNARD KEYNES ~
BRITISH ECONOMIST
1883–1946

# 13–1 The Nature and Size of the Bureaucracy

The concept of a bureaucracy is not confined to the federal government. Any large organization has to have a bureaucracy. In each bureaucracy, everybody (except the head of the bureaucracy) reports to at least one other person. In the federal government, the head of the bureaucracy is the president of the United States, and the bureaucracy is part of the executive branch.[2]

**Learning Outcome 13–1**

Describe the size and functions of the U.S. bureaucracy and the major components of federal spending.

## 13–1a The Uses of Bureaucracy

A bureaucratic form of organization allows each person to concentrate on her or his area of knowledge and expertise. In your college or university, for example, you do not expect the basketball coach to solve the problems of the finance department. The reason the federal government bureaucracy exists is that Congress, over time, has delegated certain tasks to specialists.

For example, in 1914 Congress passed the Federal Trade Commission Act, which established the Federal Trade Commission to regulate deceptive and unfair trade practices. Those appointed to the commission were specialists in this area. Similarly, Congress passed the Consumer Product Safety Act in 1972, which established the Consumer Product Safety Commission to investigate the safety of consumer products. The commission is one of many federal administrative agencies.

Another key aspect of any bureaucracy is that the power to act resides in the *position* rather than in the *person*.

In your college or university, the person who is president now has more or less the same authority as any previous president. Additionally, bureaucracies usually entail *standard operating procedures*—directives on what procedures should be followed in specific circumstances. Bureaucracies normally also have a merit system, meaning that people are hired and promoted on the basis of demonstrated skills and achievements.

## 13–1b The Growth of Bureaucracy

The federal government that existed in 1789 was small. It had three departments, each with only a few employees: (1) the Department of State (nine employees), (2) the Department of War (two employees), and (3) the Department of the Treasury (thirty-nine employees). By 1798, nine years later, the federal bureaucracy was still quite small. The secretary of state had seven clerks. His total expenditures on stationery and printing amounted to $500, or about $9,850 in 2013 dollars. The Department of War spent, on average, a grand total of $1.4 million each year, or about $27.6 million in 2013 dollars.

**Growing Government Employment**  Times have changed. Figure 13–1 below shows the number of government employees at the local, state, and national levels from 1952 to 2012 as a percentage of the total U.S. population. Most growth has been at the state and local levels. All in all, the three levels of government employ about 16 percent of the civilian labor force. Today, more Americans are employed by government (at all three levels) than by the entire manufacturing sector of the U.S. economy.

As you examine Figure 13–1, the first thing you will notice is a substantial increase in government employment between 1955 and 1980 relative to the population. During those years, the absolute number of government workers more than doubled. Government employment has been more stable since 1980, when Republican Ronald Reagan was elected president.

**The Impact of President Reagan**  Indeed, during Reagan's first four years in office, government employment fell. Most of this decrease was at the local level. The drop was caused by the double-dip recession of 1980–1982 and by the elimination of revenue sharing. This program had transferred large sums from the federal government to state and especially local governments. The loss of government jobs was made up in Reagan's second term, but the rapid

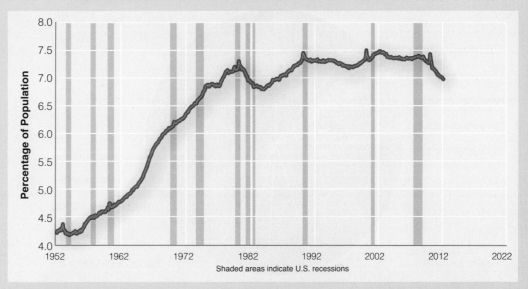

**FIGURE 13–1**

# Government Employees:
## Local, State, and Federal, as a Percentage of the Total U.S. Population (1952–2012)

Shaded areas indicate U.S. recessions

The brief spikes in 1980, 1990, 2000, and 2010 represent temporary federal census workers.

Source: The Federal Reserve Economic Data (FRED) service of the St. Louis Federal Reserve.

rise in government employment relative to population seen before 1980 did not return.

What has happened recently has been a distinct fall in government employment, in absolute as well as relative terms. President Obama's 2009 stimulus program, which transferred large sums to local governments, helped stabilize government employment through 2010. By August 2012, however, almost 700,000 fewer people worked for the various levels of government. Most of those who lost their jobs had worked at the local level.

### 13–1c The Costs of Maintaining the Government

The costs of maintaining the government are high and growing. In 1929, government at all levels accounted for about 11 percent of the nation's gross domestic product (GDP). Today, that figure is about 40 percent. Average citizens pay a significant portion of their income to federal, state, and local governments. They do this by paying income taxes, sales taxes, property taxes, and many other types of taxes and fees.

The government is costly, to be sure, but it also provides numerous services for Americans. Cutting back on the size of government inevitably means a reduction in those services. The trade-off between

government spending and popular services has been central to American politics throughout our history.

### 13–1d Where Does All the Money Go?

It is worth examining where federal spending actually goes. If you ask people on the street, you will get varied responses—from too much spent on wars in Iraq and Afghanistan to too much on welfare or foreign aid. As it turns out, none of those categories makes up a very large percentage of federal government spending. Consider Figure 13–2 below.

**Social Spending** As you can see in Figure 13–2, over half of the federal budget consists of various social programs, shown in shades of blue and green. Some of these programs, such as Social Security, Medicare, and unemployment compensation, are funded by payroll taxes and pay out to all qualifying persons, regardless of income. Together, these three programs make up 37 percent of the federal budget.

Other programs, including Medicaid and food stamps, are available only to low-income individuals. The three "low-income" pie slices make up 18 percent of spending, or almost $700 billion in 2012. Temporary Assistance for Needy Families (TANF)—traditional cash welfare—is hiding in the

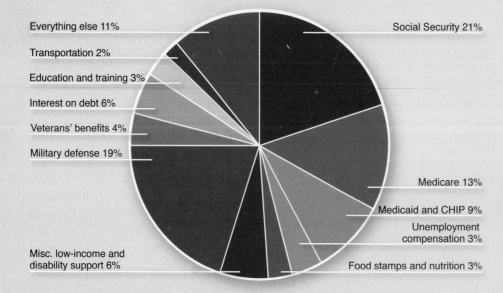

**FIGURE 13–2** — **Major Components of Federal Government Spending**

- Everything else 11%
- Transportation 2%
- Education and training 3%
- Interest on debt 6%
- Veterans' benefits 4%
- Military defense 19%
- Misc. low-income and disability support 6%
- Social Security 21%
- Medicare 13%
- Medicaid and CHIP 9%
- Unemployment compensation 3%
- Food stamps and nutrition 3%

Source: Office of Management and Budget.

"miscellaneous low-income" slice. It accounts for only 0.4 percent of the federal budget—$18 billion. It is completely overshadowed within its pie slice by disability payments, low-income housing programs, and tax refunds.

**Defense** Defense spending is a big number—with veterans' benefits, it amounts to almost a quarter of the whole. The wars in Iraq and Afghanistan have obviously been expensive. One recent estimate of their cost is $170 billion a year, or 4.6 percent of the total. That is serious money, but it's not really "busting the bank."

**Everything Else** At 11 percent of the total, "everything else" includes a vast range of programs. One example is military and economic foreign aid, at 1.5 percent of the total, or $56 billion. That's a substantial sum, but it is less than many people imagine it to be. One item that bears watching is the interest on the national debt, which currently exceeds $200 billion. Federal budget deficits will cause this figure to grow in future years.

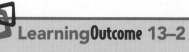

*Does your college or university have a bureaucracy? What does it do?*

# 13–2 How the Federal Bureaucracy Is Organized

**Learning Outcome 13–2**

Discuss the structure and basic components of the federal bureaucracy.

A complete organization chart of the federal government would cover an entire wall. A simplified version is provided in Figure 13–3 on the following page. The executive branch consists of a number of bureaucracies that provide services to Congress, to the federal courts, and to the president directly.

The executive branch of the federal government includes four major types of structures:

- Executive departments.

- Independent executive agencies.

- Independent regulatory agencies.

- Government corporations.

Each type of structure has its own relationship to the president and its own internal workings.

## 13–2a The Executive Departments

You were introduced to the various executive departments in Chapter 12, when you read about how the president works with the cabinet and other close advisers. The fifteen executive departments, which are directly accountable to the president, are the major service organizations of the federal government. They are responsible for performing government functions such as training troops (Department of Defense), printing currency (Department of the Treasury), and enforcing federal laws setting minimum safety and health standards for workers (Department of Labor).

Table 13–1 on page 301 provides an overview of each of the departments within the executive branch. The table lists a few of the many activities undertaken by each department. Because the president appoints the department heads, they are expected to help carry out the president's policy objectives. Often, they attempt to maximize the president's political successes as well. Is this a problem when the cabinet member in question is the U.S. attorney general? We discuss that issue in this chapter's *Join the Debate* feature on page 303.

Each executive department was created by Congress as the perceived need for it arose, and each department manages a specific policy area. In 2002, for example, Congress created the Department of Homeland Security to deal with terrorism and other threats. The head of each department is known as the secretary, except for the Department of Justice, which is headed by the attorney general. Each department head is appointed by the president and confirmed by the Senate.

## 13–2b A Typical Departmental Structure

Each cabinet department consists of the department's top administrators (the secretary of the department, deputy secretary, undersecretaries, and the like), plus a number of agencies. For example, the National Park Service is an agency within the Department of the Interior. The Drug Enforcement Administration is an agency within the Department of Justice.

Although there are organizational differences among the departments, each department

FIGURE 13-3

# The Organization
## of the Federal Government

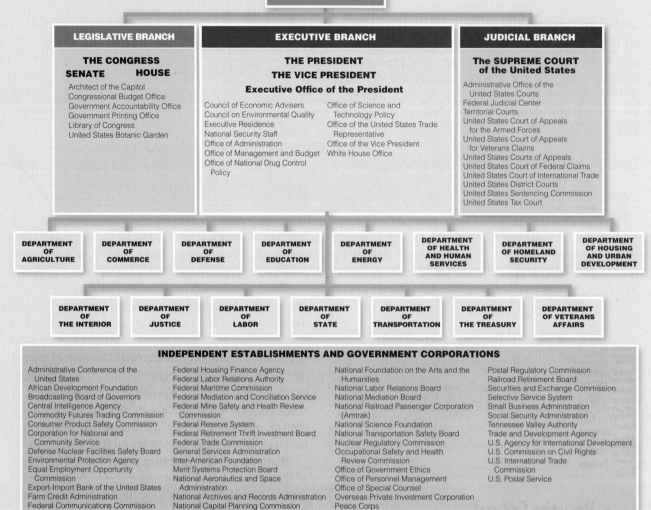

**THE CONSTITUTION**

**LEGISLATIVE BRANCH**

**THE CONGRESS**
**SENATE     HOUSE**

Architect of the Capitol
Congressional Budget Office
Government Accountability Office
Government Printing Office
Library of Congress
United States Botanic Garden

**EXECUTIVE BRANCH**

**THE PRESIDENT**
**THE VICE PRESIDENT**
**Executive Office of the President**

Council of Economic Advisers
Council on Environmental Quality
Executive Residence
National Security Staff
Office of Administration
Office of Management and Budget
Office of National Drug Control
   Policy

Office of Science and
   Technology Policy
Office of the United States Trade
   Representative
Office of the Vice President
White House Office

**JUDICIAL BRANCH**

**The SUPREME COURT**
**of the United States**

Administrative Office of the
   United States Courts
Federal Judicial Center
Territorial Courts
United States Court of Appeals
   for the Armed Forces
United States Court of Appeals
   for Veterans Claims
United States Courts of Appeals
United States Court of Federal Claims
United States Court of International Trade
United States District Courts
United States Sentencing Commission
United States Tax Court

**DEPARTMENT OF AGRICULTURE** · **DEPARTMENT OF COMMERCE** · **DEPARTMENT OF DEFENSE** · **DEPARTMENT OF EDUCATION** · **DEPARTMENT OF ENERGY** · **DEPARTMENT OF HEALTH AND HUMAN SERVICES** · **DEPARTMENT OF HOMELAND SECURITY** · **DEPARTMENT OF HOUSING AND URBAN DEVELOPMENT**

**DEPARTMENT OF THE INTERIOR** · **DEPARTMENT OF JUSTICE** · **DEPARTMENT OF LABOR** · **DEPARTMENT OF STATE** · **DEPARTMENT OF TRANSPORTATION** · **DEPARTMENT OF THE TREASURY** · **DEPARTMENT OF VETERANS AFFAIRS**

**INDEPENDENT ESTABLISHMENTS AND GOVERNMENT CORPORATIONS**

Administrative Conference of the
   United States
African Development Foundation
Broadcasting Board of Governors
Central Intelligence Agency
Commodity Futures Trading Commission
Consumer Product Safety Commission
Corporation for National and
   Community Service
Defense Nuclear Facilities Safety Board
Environmental Protection Agency
Equal Employment Opportunity
   Commission
Export-Import Bank of the United States
Farm Credit Administration
Federal Communications Commission
Federal Deposit Insurance Corporation
Federal Election Commission

Federal Housing Finance Agency
Federal Labor Relations Authority
Federal Maritime Commission
Federal Mediation and Conciliation Service
Federal Mine Safety and Health Review
   Commission
Federal Reserve System
Federal Retirement Thrift Investment Board
Federal Trade Commission
General Services Administration
Inter-American Foundation
Merit Systems Protection Board
National Aeronautics and Space
   Administration
National Archives and Records Administration
National Capital Planning Commission
National Credit Union Administration

National Foundation on the Arts and the
   Humanities
National Labor Relations Board
National Mediation Board
National Railroad Passenger Corporation
   (Amtrak)
National Science Foundation
National Transportation Safety Board
Nuclear Regulatory Commission
Occupational Safety and Health
   Review Commission
Office of Government Ethics
Office of Personnel Management
Office of Special Counsel
Overseas Private Investment Corporation
Peace Corps
Pension Benefit Guaranty Corporation

Postal Regulatory Commission
Railroad Retirement Board
Securities and Exchange Commission
Selective Service System
Small Business Administration
Social Security Administration
Tennessee Valley Authority
Trade and Development Agency
U.S. Agency for International Development
U.S. Commission on Civil Rights
U.S. International Trade
   Commission
U.S. Postal Service

Sources: *United States Government Manual 2012* (National Archives and Records Administration, Office of the Federal Register) and whitehouse.gov.

generally follows a typical bureaucratic structure. The Department of Agriculture provides a model for how an executive department is organized (see Figure 13–4 on the bottom of page 302).

One aspect of the secretary of agriculture's job is to carry out the president's agricultural policies. Another aspect, however, is to promote and protect the department. The secretary spends time ensuring that Congress allocates enough money for the department to work effectively.

The secretary also makes sure that constituents, or the people the department serves—farmers and major

agricultural corporations—are happy. In general, the secretary tries to maintain or improve the status of the department with respect to all of the other departments and units of the federal bureaucracy.

The secretary of agriculture is assisted by a deputy secretary and several assistant secretaries and undersecretaries, all of whom are nominated by the president and put into office with Senate approval. The secretary and assistant secretaries have staffs that help with all sorts of jobs, such as hiring new people and generating positive public relations for the Department of Agriculture.

## 13-2c Independent Executive Agencies

**Independent executive agencies** are federal bureaucratic organizations that have a single function. They are independent in the sense that they are not located within a cabinet department. Rather, independent executive agency heads report directly to the president. A new federal independent executive agency can be created only through cooperation between the president and Congress.

> **independent executive agency**
> A federal agency that is not located within a cabinet department.

---

**TABLE 13-1**

## Executive Departments

| Department (Year of Original Establishment) | Principal Duties | Selected Subagencies |
|---|---|---|
| **State** (1789) | Negotiates treaties; develops our foreign policy; protects citizens abroad. | Bureau of Diplomatic Security; Foreign Service; Bureau of Democracy, Human Rights, and Labor; Bureau of Consular Affairs (passports). |
| **Treasury** (1789) | Pays all federal bills; borrows money; collects federal taxes; mints coins and prints paper currency; supervises national banks. | Internal Revenue Service; U.S. Mint. |
| **Defense** (1789)* | Manages the armed forces (Army, Navy, Air Force, Marines); operates military bases. | National Security Agency; Joint Chiefs of Staff; Departments of the Air Force, Navy, Army; Defense Intelligence Agency; the service academies. |
| **Justice** (1789)† | Furnishes legal advice to the president; enforces federal criminal laws; supervises the federal corrections system (prisons). | Federal Bureau of Investigation; Drug Enforcement Administration; Bureau of Prisons; U.S. Marshals Service. |
| **Interior** (1849) | Supervises federally owned lands and parks; operates federal hydroelectric power facilities; supervises Native American affairs. | U.S. Fish and Wildlife Service; National Park Service; Bureau of Indian Affairs; Bureau of Land Management. |
| **Agriculture** (1889) | Provides assistance to farmers and ranchers; conducts research to improve agriculture; works to protect forests. | Natural Resources Conservation Service; Agricultural Research Service; Food Safety and Inspection Service; Federal Crop Insurance Corporation; Forest Service. |
| **Commerce** (1903)‡ | Grants patents and trademarks; conducts national census; monitors the weather; protects the interests of businesses. | Bureau of the Census; Bureau of Economic Analysis; Minority Business Development Agency; Patent and Trademark Office; National Oceanic and Atmospheric Administration. |
| **Labor** (1903)‡ | Administers federal labor laws; promotes the interests of workers. | Occupational Safety and Health Administration; Bureau of Labor Statistics; Labor-Management Standards Administration; Employment and Training Administration; Wage and Hour Division. |
| **Health and Human Services** (1953)§ | Promotes public health; enforces pure food and drug laws; sponsors health-related research. | Food and Drug Administration; Centers for Disease Control and Prevention; National Institutes of Health; Administration for Children and Families; Centers for Medicare and Medicaid Services. |
| **Housing and Urban Development** (1965) | Deals with the nation's housing needs; develops and rehabilitates urban communities; oversees resale of mortgages. | Government National Mortgage Association; Office of Multifamily Housing Programs; Office of Single Family Housing; Office of Fair Housing and Equal Opportunity. |
| **Transportation** (1967) | Finances improvements in mass transit; develops and administers programs for highways, railroads, and aviation. | Federal Aviation Administration; Federal Highway Administration; National Highway Traffic Safety Administration; Federal Transit Administration. |

© CENGAGE LEARNING

*Continued*

## TABLE 13-1

### Executive Departments—(Continued)

| Department (Year of Original Establishment) | Principal Duties | Selected Subagencies |
|---|---|---|
| **Energy** (1977) | Promotes the conservation of energy and resources; analyzes energy data; conducts research and development. | Office of Civilian Radioactive Waste Management; National Nuclear Security Administration; Energy Information Administration. |
| **Education** (1979) | Coordinates federal programs and policies for education; administers aid to education; promotes educational research. | Office of Special Education and Rehabilitation Services; Office of Elementary and Secondary Education; Office of Postsecondary Education; Office of Vocational and Adult Education. |
| **Veterans Affairs** (1989) | Promotes the welfare of veterans of the U.S. armed forces. | Veterans Health Administration; Veterans Benefits Administration; National Cemetery Administration. |
| **Homeland Security** (2002) | Works to prevent terrorist attacks within the United States, control America's borders, and minimize the damage from potential attacks and natural disasters. | U.S. Customs and Border Protection; U.S. Bureau of Citizenship and Immigration Services; U.S. Coast Guard; Secret Service; Federal Emergency Management Agency. |

© CENGAGE LEARNING

*Established in 1947 by merging the Department of War, created in 1789, and the Department of the Navy, created in 1798.
†Formerly the Office of the Attorney General; renamed and reorganized in 1870.
‡Formed in 1913 by splitting the Department of Commerce and Labor, which was created in 1903.
§Formerly the Department of Health, Education, and Welfare; renamed when the Department of Education was spun off in 1979.

## FIGURE 13-4

# The Organization
## of the Department of Agriculture

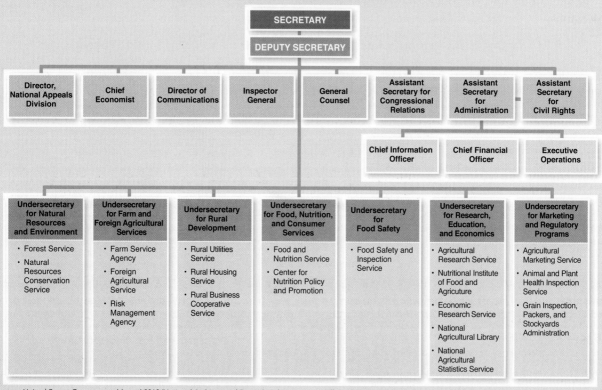

Source: *United States Government Manual 2012* (National Archives and Records Administration, Office of the Federal Register).

## Should the Attorney General Be Independent of the President?

Traditionally, the attorney general has been a close political ally of the president. Ronald Reagan and Jimmy Carter both named reliable cronies to head up the Justice Department. Richard Nixon's attorney general, John Mitchell, was even sentenced to prison for corrupt politicization of his office. George W. Bush's attorney general, Alberto Gonzales, deferred completely to the White House. One result was a politically motivated "midnight massacre," during which eight U.S. attorneys were fired supposedly for purely partisan reasons.

Is it right for the attorney general to be so close to the president? What if it becomes necessary to investigate members of the president's own administration? Shouldn't the nation's chief law enforcement officer be independent and nonpartisan? One way to accomplish this would be to remove the attorney general position from the president's cabinet and appoint that official for a fixed term of years that transcends the term of any one president. That is exactly what we have done with the position of Federal Bureau of Investigation (FBI) director, so why not do it with the position of attorney general?

### Yes, Let's Make the Attorney General Independent

The attorney general should not be the handmaiden of presidential policy. Instead, the attorney general should be able to give the White House frank, independent advice whenever the administration is considering actions that might overreach the bounds of what is permitted by law. Any president needs a personal attorney, but that official should be a member of the White House staff, not the head of the Justice Department.

Presidents appoint FBI directors for a fixed term of ten years, which ensures that directors do not serve under a single president. If the FBI director wants to be reappointed, the director must consider that the president making the reappointment could belong to either political party. In the same way, if the attorney general were removed from the cabinet and appointed to a fixed term, the attorney general would have less political allegiance to any one president.

### We Don't Want a Nonpolitical Attorney General

Those who accept the current situation argue that we don't want a nonpolitical attorney general. We elect a president based on his or her policy proposals. We expect the agenda of the Justice Department to reflect the policies that got the president elected. If the president is an advocate of civil liberties, those who elected the president expect the attorney general to reflect this position. If a president has made a strong commitment to reduce illegal immigration, voters expect the attorney general to follow through on this pledge.

The comparison with an independent FBI director is not valid. The FBI director is in charge of the closest thing we have to a national police force. We obviously do not want that position to be politicized. The attorney general is a different type of creature. The president should be able to name an attorney general whose views reflect the president's.

**FOR CRITICAL ANALYSIS** If a president does not like what the attorney general is doing, does the president have any recourse?

## The Creation of Independent Agencies

Prior to the twentieth century, the federal government did almost all of its work through the executive departments. In the twentieth century, in contrast, presidents began to ask for certain executive agencies to be kept separate, or independent, from existing departments. Today, there are more than two hundred independent executive agencies.

## The Danger of Partisan Politics
Sometimes, agencies are kept independent because of the sensitive nature of their functions. But at other times, Congress creates independent agencies to protect them from **partisan politics**—politics in support of a particular

> **partisan politics** Political actions or decisions that benefit a particular party.

party. The U.S. Commission on Civil Rights, which was created in 1957, is a case in point. Congress wanted to protect the work of the commission from the influences not only of Congress's own political interests but also of the president.

The Central Intelligence Agency (CIA), which was formed in 1947, is another good example. Both Congress and the president know that the intelligence activities of the CIA could be abused if it were not independent. Finally, the General Services Administration (GSA) was created as an independent executive agency in 1949 to provide services and office space for most federal agencies. To serve all parts of the government, it has to be an independent agency.

Among the more than two hundred independent executive agencies, a few stand out in importance either because of the mission they were established to accomplish or because of their large size. We list selected independent executive agencies in Table 13–2 below.

## 13–2d Independent Regulatory Agencies

**Independent regulatory agencies** are responsible for a specific type of public policy. Their function is to create and implement rules that regulate private activity and protect the public interest in a particular sector of the economy. They are sometimes called the "alphabet soup" of government because most such agencies are known in Washington by their initials.

One of the earliest independent regulatory agencies was the Interstate Commerce Commission (ICC), established in 1887. (This agency was abolished in 1995.) After the ICC was formed, other agencies were created to regulate aviation (the Civil Aeronautics Board, or CAB, which was abolished in 1985), communications (the Federal Communications Commission, or FCC), the stock market (the Securities and Exchange Commission, or SEC), and many other areas of business. Table 13–3 on the facing page lists some major independent regulatory agencies.

## 13–2e Government Corporations

Another form of federal bureaucratic organization is the **government corporation,** a business that is owned

**independent regulatory agency**
A federal organization that is responsible for creating and implementing rules that regulate private activity and protect the public interest in a particular sector of the economy.

**government corporation** An agency of the government that is run as a business enterprise. Such agencies engage primarily in commercial activities, produce revenues, and require greater flexibility than most government agencies receive.

---

**TABLE 13–2**

### Selected Independent Executive Agencies

| Name | Date Formed | Principal Duties |
|---|---|---|
| Central Intelligence Agency (CIA) | 1947 | Gathers and analyzes political and military information about foreign countries so that the United States can improve its own political and military status; conducts covert operations outside the United States. |
| General Services Administration (GSA) | 1949 | Purchases and manages property of the federal government; acts as the business arm of the federal government, overseeing federal government spending projects; discovers overcharges in government programs. |
| Small Business Administration (SBA) | 1953 | Promotes the interests of small businesses; provides low-cost loans and management information to small businesses. |
| National Aeronautics and Space Administration (NASA) | 1958 | Is responsible for the U.S. space program, including building, testing, and operating space vehicles. |
| Environmental Protection Agency (EPA) | 1970 | Undertakes programs aimed at reducing air and water pollution; works with state and local agencies to fight environmental hazards. |
| Social Security Administration (SSA)* | 1994 | Manages the government's Social Security programs, including Retirement and Survivors Insurance, Disability Insurance, and Supplemental Security Income. |

© CENGAGE LEARNING

*Separated from the Department of Health and Human Services in 1994; originally established in 1946.

## TABLE 13-3

### Selected Independent Regulatory Agencies

| Name | Date Formed | Principal Duties |
|------|-------------|------------------|
| Federal Reserve System (Fed) | 1913 | Determines policy on interest rates, credit availability, and the money supply. |
| Federal Trade Commission (FTC) | 1914 | Works to prevent businesses from engaging in unfair trade practices and to stop the formation of business monopolies; protects consumers' rights. |
| Securities and Exchange Commission (SEC) | 1934 | Regulates the nation's stock exchanges, where shares of stocks are bought and sold; requires full disclosure of the financial profiles of companies that wish to sell stocks and bonds to the public. |
| Federal Communications Commission (FCC) | 1934 | Regulates interstate and international communications by radio, television, wire, satellite, and cable. |
| National Labor Relations Board (NLRB) | 1935 | Protects employees' rights to join unions and to bargain collectively with employers; attempts to prevent unfair labor practices by both employers and unions. |
| Equal Employment Opportunity Commission (EEOC) | 1964 | Works to eliminate discrimination that is based on religion, gender, race, color, national origin, age, or disability; examines claims of discrimination. |

© CENGAGE LEARNING

by the government. Government corporations are not exactly like corporations in which you buy stock, become a shareholder, and share in the profits by collecting dividends. The U.S. Postal Service (USPS) is a government corporation, but it does not sell shares.

Government corporations are like private corporations in that they provide a service that could be handled by the private sector. They are also like private corporations in that they charge for their services, though sometimes they charge less than private-sector corporations do for similar services. Table 13–4 on the following page lists selected government corporations.

**Facing Losses** When a private business fails to make a profit, its shareholders have a problem. The value of the company may drop, in some instances to zero. If a small business loses money, its owners have the choice of raising more capital or winding up the firm. Likewise, if a government corporation runs at a loss, the taxpayer may be forced to foot the bill.

The U.S. Postal Service is an example of this problem. Mail volume is down 25 percent since 2006, as Americans increasingly rely on the Internet for communications. In 2011, despite attempts to streamline itself and despite large reductions in staff, the USPS faced a shortfall of nearly $10 billion. Losses in 2012 amounted to $14 billion. In August 2012, the service defaulted on a monthly $5.5 billion payment due to the U.S. Treasury to finance retirees' health-care

costs. The USPS also failed to pay a $5.6 billion tab in September.

To solve the problem permanently, the USPS proposed to lay off 120,000 employees, close rural post offices, reduce pension benefits, and even end Saturday delivery. Many of these steps require congressional approval, which was not forthcoming. The alternative would be direct federal subsidies to the service, which has been self-supporting since the early 1980s.

**Bankruptcy** A number of intermediate forms of organization exist that fall between a government corporation and a private one. In some circumstances, the government can take control of a private corporation. When a company goes bankrupt, for example, it is subject to the supervision of a federal judge until it exits from bankruptcy or is liquidated. The government can purchase stock in a private corporation—the government used this technique to funnel funds into major banks during the financial crisis that began in September 2008. The government can also set up a corporation and sell stock to the public.

The Federal Home Loan Mortgage Corporation (Freddie Mac) and the Federal National Mortgage Association (Fannie Mae) are examples of stockholder-owned government-sponsored enterprises. Fannie Mae (founded in 1938) and Freddie Mac (created in 1970) buy, resell, and guarantee home mortgages. In September 2008, the government placed the

TABLE 13-4

## Selected Government Corporations

| Name | Date Formed | Principal Duties |
|---|---|---|
| Tennessee Valley Authority (TVA) | 1933 | Operates a Tennessee River control system and generates power for a seven-state region; promotes the economic development of the Tennessee Valley; controls floods and promotes the navigability of the Tennessee River. |
| Federal Deposit Insurance Corporation (FDIC) | 1933 | Insures individuals' bank deposits up to $250,000* and oversees the business activities of banks. |
| National Railroad Passenger Corporation (Amtrak) | 1970 | Provides a national and intercity rail passenger service network; controls more than 23,000 miles of track with about 505 stations. |
| U.S. Postal Service (formed from the old U.S. Post Office department—the Post Office itself is older than the Constitution) | 1971 | Delivers mail throughout the United States and its territories. Is the largest government corporation. |

© CENGAGE LEARNING

*This limit, previously $100,000, was raised in October 2008 in response to the financial crisis of that year.

**civil service** Nonmilitary government employees.

two businesses into a conservatorship—effectively a bankruptcy overseen by the Federal Housing Finance Agency instead of a federal judge. The government also took an 80 percent share of the stock of each firm. Fannie Mae and Freddie Mac became examples of almost every possible way that the government can intervene in a private company.

## FOR CRITICAL THINKING

Some people have advocated selling off government corporations, such as the U.S. Postal Service, and turning them into truly private enterprises. *Would it be a good idea to "privatize" the U.S. Postal Service? Why or why not?*

## 13-3 How Bureaucrats Get Their Jobs

### LearningOutcome 13-3

Describe how the federal civil service was established and how bureaucrats get their jobs.

As already noted, federal bureaucrats holding top-level positions are appointed by the president and confirmed by the Senate. These bureaucrats include department and agency heads, their deputy and assistant secretaries,

and so on. The list of positions that are filled by appointments is published after each presidential election in a document called *Policy and Supporting Positions*. The volume is more commonly known as the *Plum Book*, because the eight thousand jobs it summarizes are known as "political plums." Normally, these jobs go to those who supported the winning presidential candidate.

### 13-3a The Civil Service

The rank-and-file bureaucrats—the rest of the federal bureaucracy—are part of the **civil service** (nonmilitary employees of the government). They obtain their jobs through the Office of Personnel Management (OPM), an agency established by the Civil Service Reform Act of 1978. The OPM recruits, interviews, and tests potential government workers and determines who should be hired. The OPM makes recommendations to individual agencies as to which persons meet relevant standards (typically, the top three applicants for a position), and the

LAWRENCE MIGDALE/STONE/GETTY

agencies then generally decide which of the recommended individuals they will hire.

The 1978 act also created the Merit Systems Protection Board (MSPB) to oversee promotions, employees' rights, and other employment matters. The MSPB evaluates charges of wrongdoing, hears employee appeals from agency decisions, and can order corrective action against agencies and employees.

## 13-3b Origins of the Merit System

The idea that the civil service should be based on a merit system dates back more than a century. The Civil Service Reform Act of 1883 established the principle of government employment on the basis of merit through open, competitive examinations.

Initially, only about 10 percent of federal employees were covered by the merit system. Today, more than 90 percent of the federal civil service is recruited on the basis of merit. Are public employees paid as well as workers in the private sector? For a discussion of this question, see this chapter's *Perception versus Reality* feature on the following page.

## FOR CRITICAL THINKING

When most private companies hire new employees, they don't use systems similar to those of the civil service. *Why is this so?*

## 13-4 Regulatory Agencies: Are They the Fourth Branch of Government?

### Learning Outcome 13-4

Explain how regulatory agencies make rules and how issue networks affect policymaking in government.

In Chapter 2, we considered the system of checks and balances among the three branches of the U.S. government—executive, legislative, and judicial. Recent history, however, shows that it may be time to regard the regulatory agencies as a fourth branch of the government. Although the U.S. Constitution does not mention regulatory agencies, these agencies can and do make **legislative rules** that are as legally binding as laws passed by Congress. With such powers, this administrative branch has an influence on the nation's businesses that rivals that of the president, Congress, and the courts. Indeed, most Americans do not realize how much of our "law" is created by regulatory agencies.

Regulatory agencies have been on the American political scene since the nineteenth century, but their golden age came during the regulatory explosion of the 1960s and 1970s. Congress itself could not have overseen the actual implementation of all of the laws that it was enacting at that time to control pollution and deal with other social problems. It therefore chose (and still chooses) to delegate to administrative agencies the tasks involved in implementing its laws.

By delegating some of its authority to an administrative agency, Congress may indirectly monitor a particular area in which it has passed legislation without becoming bogged down in the details relating to the enforcement of that legislation—details that are often best left to specialists. In recent years, the government has been hiring increasing numbers of specialists to oversee its regulatory work.

### 13-4a Agency Creation

To create a federal administrative agency, Congress passes **enabling legislation**, which specifies the name, purpose, composition, and powers of the agency being created. The Federal Trade Commission (FTC), for example, was created in 1914 by the Federal Trade Commission Act, as mentioned earlier. The act prohibits unfair and deceptive trade practices. The act also describes the procedures that the agency must follow to charge persons or organizations with violations of the act, and it provides for judicial review of agency orders.

**Rulemaking and Adjudication** Other portions of the act grant the agency powers to "make rules and regulations for the purpose of carrying out the Act," to conduct investigations of business practices, to obtain reports on business practices from interstate corporations, to investigate possible violations of federal antitrust

**legislative rule** An administrative agency rule that carries the same weight as a statute enacted by a legislature.

**enabling legislation** A law enacted by a legislature to establish an administrative agency. Enabling legislation normally specifies the name, purpose, composition, and powers of the agency being created.

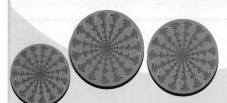

# Perception versus Reality

## Working for the Government at Low Pay

Not all parents jump for joy at the thought of their children going to work for the government. Government work in general in the United States has never been considered the road to riches. Indeed, the common picture of government employment is quite negative.

### THE PERCEPTION

It is often assumed that only individuals working in the private sector can hope to receive large paychecks. Top-level staff members in the executive branch of the federal government make much less than senior executives in the private sector. Although even rank-and-file workers in the public sector receive paid-for medical insurance and a generous retirement program, the perception is that these benefits do not make up for the lower pay they earn.

### THE REALITY

It can be difficult to determine just how the pay of government employees compares to pay in the private sector because this question is so politically loaded. Consider two studies that tried to compare state and local employees with private-sector workers doing similar jobs. A paper by a Boston College team concluded that state and local workers are paid 9.5 percent less than in the private sector, although generous benefits reduce the gap to 4 percent. In contrast, an article by two U.S. Bureau of Labor Statistics (BLS) economists found that, on average, workers in state government have total compensation costs 3 to 10 percent greater than workers in the private sector, while in local government the gap is 10 to 19 percent.[3] Some experts believe that even the BLS study undercounts the value of government pensions.

Move now to the federal government. In 2012, many Republican candidates cited figures from the U.S. Bureau of Economic Analysis that show federal government workers earning an average of $123,049 in wages and benefits, about twice the $61,051 in total compensation for the average private-sector worker. These figures came under criticism for flawed methodology, however.

For one thing, federal workers don't do the same kind of work as employees in the private sector. On average, federal workers are much better educated and more likely to be employed in jobs that are also well paid in the private sector. The Congressional Budget Office, which has a reputation for impartiality, studied federal pay in 2012. It found that the federal government paid 16 percent more than the private sector for comparable jobs. Workers with only a high school education came out best, with 36 percent higher compensation than in the private sector. In contrast, employees with professional degrees actually received 18 percent less.[4]

**BLOG ON** You can find a variety of articles on the issue of government pay by searching on "state local government workers pay" and "federal workers overpaid."

---

**adjudicate** To render a judicial decision. In administrative law, it is the process in which an administrative law judge hears and decides issues that arise when an agency charges a person or firm with violating a law or regulation enforced by the agency.

statutes, to publish findings of its investigations, and to recommend new legislation.

Finally, the act empowers the FTC to hold trial-like hearings and to **adjudicate** (formally resolve) certain kinds of disputes that involve FTC regulations or federal antitrust laws. When adjudication takes place, within the FTC or any other regulatory agency, an administrative law judge (ALJ) conducts the hearing and, after weighing the evidence presented, issues an *order*. Unless it is overturned on appeal, the ALJ's order becomes final.

### The Power of Regulatory Agencies
Enabling legislation makes the regulatory agency a potent organization. For example, the Securities and Exchange Commission (SEC) imposes rules regarding the

disclosures a company must make to those who purchase its new stock. Under its enforcement authority, the SEC also investigates and prosecutes alleged violations of these regulations. Finally, SEC judges decide whether its rules have been violated and, if so, what punishment should be imposed on the offender (although the judgment may be appealed to a federal court).

## 13–4b Rulemaking

A major function of a regulatory agency is **rulemaking**—the formulation of new regulations. The power that an agency has to make rules is conferred on it by Congress in the agency's enabling legislation. For example, the Occupational Safety and Health Administration (OSHA) was authorized by the Occupational Safety and Health Act of 1970 to develop and issue rules governing safety in the workplace. Under this authority, OSHA has issued various safety standards.

### Requirements for Making Rules
For example, OSHA has issued rules to prevent the spread of certain diseases, including acquired immune deficiency syndrome (AIDS). The rules specify various standards—on how contaminated instruments should be handled, for instance—with which health-care workers must comply. Agencies cannot just make a rule whenever they wish, however. Rather, they must follow certain procedural requirements, particularly those set forth in the Administrative Procedure Act of 1946.

Agencies must also make sure that their rules are based on substantial evidence and are not "arbitrary and capricious." Therefore, before proposing a new rule, an agency may engage in extensive investigation to obtain data on the problem to be addressed by the rule. Based on this information, the agency may undertake a cost-benefit analysis of a new rule to determine whether its benefits outweigh its costs.

### Fine Particle Emissions as an Example
As an example of cost-benefit analysis in rulemaking,

Agriculture has been an important sector in our country since its beginning. Each year, the federal government involves itself in agricultural policymaking.

DANIEL ACKER/BLOOMBERG/GETTY IMAGES

consider the Clean Air Fine Particle Implementation Rule, issued by the Environmental Protection Agency (EPA) in 2007. The EPA estimated the costs of the regulation as $7.3 billion per year, with benefits ranging from $19 billion to $167 billion per year. The benefits largely consist of reductions in health-care costs and premature deaths—and, as these figures suggest, such calculations can be highly uncertain.

Rulemaking is not isolated from politics. As you will read shortly, bureaucrats work closely with members of Congress, as well as interest groups, when making rules.

## 13–4c Policymaking

Bureaucrats in federal agencies are expected to exhibit **neutral competency,** which means that they are supposed to apply their technical skills to their jobs without regard to political issues. In principle, they should not be swayed by the thought of personal or political gain. In reality, each independent agency and each executive department is interested in its own survival and expansion. All agencies and departments wish to retain or expand their functions and staffs. To do

**rulemaking** The process undertaken by an administrative agency when formally proposing, evaluating, and adopting a new regulation.

**neutral competency** The application of technical skills to jobs without regard to political issues.

this, they must gain the goodwill of both the White House and Congress.

Although the administrative agencies of the federal government are prohibited from directly lobbying Congress, departments and agencies have developed techniques to help them gain congressional support. Each organization maintains a congressional information office, which specializes in helping members of Congress by supplying any requested information and solving casework problems.

For example, if a member of the House of Representatives receives a complaint from a constituent that his Social Security checks are not arriving on time, that member of Congress may go to the Social Security Administration and ask that something be done. Typically, requests from members of Congress receive immediate attention.

**Iron Triangles** Analysts have determined that one way to understand the bureaucracy's role in policymaking is to examine the **iron triangle,** which is a three-way alliance among legislators (members of Congress), bureaucrats, and interest groups. Presumably, the laws that are passed and the policies that are established benefit the interests of all three corners of the iron triangle, which is shown in Figure 13–5 below. Iron triangles are well established in almost every part of the bureaucracy.

### Agriculture as an Example

As an example, consider agricultural policy. The Department of Agriculture consists of about 100,000 individuals working directly for the federal government and thousands of other individuals who work indirectly for the department as contractors, subcontractors, or

**"BUREAUCRACY DEFENDS THE STATUS QUO**

long past the time when the quo has lost its status."

~ LAURENCE J. PETER ~
AMERICAN EDUCATOR
1919–1990

consultants. Now think about the various interest groups and client groups that are concerned with what the bureaus and agencies in the Agriculture Department can do for them. Some of these groups are the American Farm Bureau Federation, the National Milk Producers Federation, various regional citrus growers associations, and many others. Finally, in Congress two major committees are concerned with agriculture: the House Committee on Agriculture and the Senate Committee on Agriculture, Nutrition, and Forestry.

The bureaucrats, interest groups, and legislators who make up this iron triangle cooperate to create mutually beneficial regulations and legislation. Because of the connections between agricultural interest groups and policymakers within the government, the agricultural industry has benefited greatly over the years from significant farm subsidies.

### Congress's Role
The Department of Agriculture is headed by the secretary of agriculture, who is nominated by the president (and confirmed by the Senate). But that secretary cannot even buy a desk lamp if Congress does not approve the appropriations for the department's budget.

Within Congress, the responsibility for considering the Department of Agriculture's request for funding belongs first to the House and Senate

**iron triangle** A three-way alliance among legislators, bureaucrats, and interest groups to make or preserve policies that benefit their respective interests.

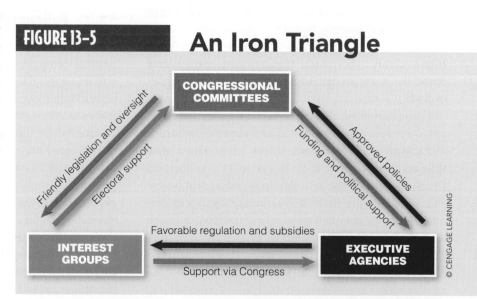

**FIGURE 13–5** **An Iron Triangle**

CONGRESSIONAL COMMITTEES

Friendly legislation and oversight

Electoral support

Approved policies

Funding and political support

INTEREST GROUPS

Favorable regulation and subsidies

Support via Congress

EXECUTIVE AGENCIES

© CENGAGE LEARNING

appropriations committees and then to the agriculture subcommittees of the appropiations committees. The members of those committees, most of whom represent agricultural states, have been around a long time and have their own ideas about what is appropriate for the Agriculture Department's budget. They carefully scrutinize the ideas of the president and the secretary of agriculture.

**The Influence of Interest Groups** The various interest groups—including producers of farm chemicals and farm machinery, agricultural cooperatives, grain dealers, and exporters—have vested interests in what the Department of Agriculture does and in what Congress lets the department do. Those interests are well represented by the lobbyists who crowd the halls of Congress. Many lobbyists have been working for agricultural interest groups for decades. They know the congressional committee members and Agriculture Department staff very well and meet with them routinely.

### 13–4d  Issue Networks

The iron triangle relationship does not apply to all policy domains. When making policy decisions on environmental and welfare issues, for example, many members of Congress and agency officials rely heavily on "experts." Legislators and agency heads tend to depend on their staff members for specialized knowledge of rules, regulations, and legislation.

These experts have frequently served variously as interest group lobbyists and as public-sector staff members during their careers, creating a revolving-door effect. They often have strong opinions and interests regarding the direction of policy and are thus able to exert a great deal of influence on legislators and bureaucratic agencies.

The relationships among these experts, which are less structured than iron triangles, are often referred to as **issue networks**. Like iron triangles, issue networks are made up of people with similar policy concerns. Issue networks are less interdependent and unified than iron triangles, however, and often include more players, such as media outlets.[5] (See Figure 13–6 on the following page.)

A key characteristic of issue networks is that there can be more than one network in a given policy area. To take the example of the environment, one issue network tends to advocate greater environmental regulation, while another network opposes such regulations as undue burdens on businesses and landowners.

**FOR CRITICAL THINKING** Competing interests often form rival issue networks that tend to limit each other's power. *Who—or what—can stop an iron triangle from absorbing ever-greater amounts of government resources?*

## 13–5  Curbing Waste and Improving Efficiency

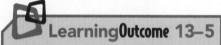

**LearningOutcome 13–5**

Identify some of the ways in which the government has attempted to curb waste and improve efficiency in the bureaucracy.

There is no doubt that our bureaucracy is costly. There is also little doubt that at times it can be wasteful and inefficient. The government has made many attempts to reduce waste, inefficiency, and wrongdoing. For example, federal and state governments have passed laws requiring more openness in government. Other laws encourage employees to report any waste and wrongdoing that they observe.

Over the years, both national administrations and state and local governments have come up with many plans aimed at improving the cost-effectiveness of government. One of these is the idea of selling advertisements. We examine that concept in the *Our Challenging Times* feature on page 313.

### 13–5a  Helping Out the Whistleblowers

The term **whistleblower**, as applied to the federal bureaucracy, has a special meaning: it is someone who blows the whistle, or reports, on gross governmental inefficiency, illegal activities, or other wrongdoing. Whistleblowers often take their complaints to the press. Federal

**issue networks** Groups of individuals or organizations—which consist of legislators and legislative staff members, interest group leaders, bureaucrats, the media, scholars, and other experts—that support particular policy positions on a given issue.

**whistleblower** In the context of government employment, someone who "blows the whistle" (reports to authorities or the press) on gross governmental inefficiency, illegal action, or other wrongdoing.

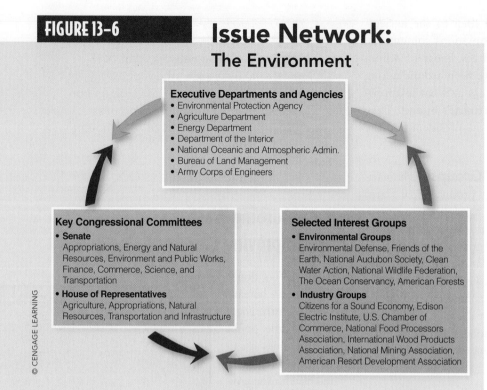

## FIGURE 13-6

## Issue Network:
### The Environment

**Executive Departments and Agencies**
- Environmental Protection Agency
- Agriculture Department
- Energy Department
- Department of the Interior
- National Oceanic and Atmospheric Admin.
- Bureau of Land Management
- Army Corps of Engineers

**Key Congressional Committees**
- **Senate**
  Appropriations, Energy and Natural Resources, Environment and Public Works, Finance, Commerce, Science, and Transportation
- **House of Representatives**
  Agriculture, Appropriations, Natural Resources, Transportation and Infrastructure

**Selected Interest Groups**
- **Environmental Groups**
  Environmental Defense, Friends of the Earth, National Audubon Society, Clean Water Action, National Wildlife Federation, The Ocean Conservancy, American Forests
- **Industry Groups**
  Citizens for a Sound Economy, Edison Electric Institute, U.S. Chamber of Commerce, National Food Processors Association, International Wood Products Association, National Mining Association, American Resort Development Association

© CENGAGE LEARNING

employees may be reluctant to blow the whistle on their superiors for fear of reprisals.

**Laws Protecting Whistleblowers** To encourage federal employees to report government wrongdoing, Congress has passed laws to protect whistleblowers. The Whistle-Blower Protection Act of 1989 authorized the Office of Special Counsel (OSC), an independent agency, to investigate complaints of reprisals against whistleblowers. Many federal agencies also have toll-free hotlines that employees can use to anonymously report bureaucratic waste and inappropriate behavior.

One set of laws encourages reports by making cash rewards to whistleblowers. Under four different programs, if the government saves or retrieves a significant sum as a result of a tip-off, a percentage of the government's gain can be paid to the whistleblower. Under the False Claims Act, a private individual can even pursue a claim in court if the Justice Department fails to proceed.

Many such cases involve tax fraud by corporations and individuals, not government malfeasance. In September 2012, the government paid out the largest such reward ever—$104 million. The money went to a banker who blew the whistle on a Swiss bank that was helping U.S. citizens defraud the IRS.

The whistleblower, however, also had to serve forty months in prison for his part in the fraud.

### Whistleblowers Continue to Face Problems
In spite of these laws, there is little evidence that whistleblowers are adequately protected against retaliation. According to a study conducted by the Government Accountability Office, 41 percent of the whistleblowers who turned to the OSC for protection during a recent three-year period reported that they were no longer employed by the agencies on which they blew the whistle. Indeed, given how difficult it is to fire a federal employee under normal circumstances, it is amazing how quickly most whistleblowers are "shown the door."

Many federal employees who have blown the whistle say that they would not do so again because it was so difficult to get help. Even when they did, the experience was a stressful ordeal. Barack Obama's supporters expected that, as president, he would protect whistleblowers. Many of them were disappointed, however, when the new administration took an unusually harsh line regarding information disclosures. Several individuals responsible for "leaks" were arrested and charged with felonies. For more on that subject, see the *Perception versus Reality* feature in Chapter 4 on page 91.

## 13-5b Improving Efficiency and Getting Results

The Government Performance and Results Act, which went into effect in 1997, has forced the federal government to change the way it does business. Since 1997, virtually every agency (except the intelligence agencies) has had to describe its goals and methods for evaluating how well those goals are met. A goal of an agency could be as broad as lowering the number of highway traffic deaths or as narrow as reducing the number of times an agency's phone rings before it is answered.

# OUR CHALLENGING TIMES

## Should Governments Raise Funds by Selling Ads?

No one is surprised anymore to read yet another article about how a state or city is having a tough time making ends meet. Indeed, a number of municipal governments have even declared bankruptcy. No state has done so, but if some of them were private businesses, they might already be in bankruptcy. So, governments at all levels are desperate for more funds. Why not start raising dollars by selling ads on government Web sites and elsewhere?

### GOVERNMENT PRESENCE ON THE INTERNET IS VAST

The Internet originated as a federally sponsored research network. Not surprisingly, the Internet domain name *gov* is one of the oldest—it was established in 1985, five years before the creation of the World Wide Web. At first, only federal agencies could use the "dot-gov" address. Soon, however, state and local governments were allowed to use it as well.

Some thirty years later, the number of government Web sites has skyrocketed. All of those Web sites have at least some cash potential. That is because every government entity that owns one or more of them could sell ad space, just as many dot-com sites do. These ads could be banner ads, click-on ads, or click-on links to other Web sites. For some of the more popular government Web sites, the revenue could be substantial.

### FIRST, CHANGE THE LAW

The gov domain is administered by the General Services Administration (GSA), a federal agency. Right now, a GSA regulation bans commercial ads on any dot-gov site. If federal, state, or local government agencies were to sell ads on their sites, this regulation would have to go. Several state governments have already called for such a change. Connecticut and Texas are considering legislation that will allow state agencies to sell ad space on their dot-com Web sites.

Selling ad space shouldn't be a problem. It apparently hasn't been a problem for cities that operate bus systems. Today, in almost every city with a transit system, you see ads plastered on the sides of buses and in stations and train cars. In some communities, you can see ads for pizza places on school buses. KFC has actually paid to put its logo on manhole covers and fire hydrants in Indiana, Kentucky, and Tennessee.

The race is on.

## YOU BE THE JUDGE

Proponents of government advertising have argued that governments should sell as many ads as possible before they consider raising taxes. Is there any downside to such a policy?

---

As one example, consider the National Oceanic and Atmospheric Adminstration (NOAA). It improved the effectiveness of its short-term forecasting services, particularly in issuing warnings of tornadoes. The warning time has increased from seven to fifteen minutes. This may not seem significant, but it provides additional critical time for those in the path of a tornado.

President Obama's contribution to the attempt to improve government effectiveness was to create a chief performance officer. This individual reports directly to the president and works with other economic officials in an attempt to increase efficiency and eliminate waste in government.

## 13–5c Another Approach— Pay-for-Performance Plans

For some time, the private sector has used pay-for-performance plans as a means to increase employee productivity and efficiency. About one-third of the major firms in this country use some kind of alternative pay system, such as team-based pay, skill-based pay, profit-sharing plans, or individual bonuses. In contrast, workers for the federal government traditionally have received fixed salaries. Promotions and salary increases are given on the basis of seniority, not output.

The federal government has been experimenting with pay-for-performance systems. For example, the U.S. Postal Service has implemented the Economic Value Added Variable Pay Program, which ties bonuses to performance. As part of a five-year test of a new pay system, three thousand scientists working in Air Force laboratories received salaries based on results.

Many hope that pay-for-performance plans will help counter the entitlement mentality that has allegedly characterized employment within the bureaucracy.

## 13–5d Privatization

Another idea for reforming government bureaucracies is **privatization,** which means turning over certain types of government work to the private sector. Privatization can take place by contracting out (outsourcing) work to the private sector or by *managed competition,* in which the task of providing public services is opened up to competition. In managed competition, both the relevant government agency and private firms can compete for the work.

State and local governments have been experimenting with privatization for some time. Virtually all of the

> ## "The only thing that saves us from the bureaucracy
> is its inefficiency."
>
> ~ EUGENE J. MCCARTHY ~
> U.S. SENATOR FROM MINNESOTA
> 1959–1971

states have privatized at least a few of their services, and some states, including California, Colorado, and Florida, have privatized more than one hundred activities formerly undertaken by government. In Scottsdale, Arizona, the city contracts for fire protection. In Baltimore, Maryland, nine of the city's schools are outsourced to private entities. In other cities, services ranging from janitorial work to management of recreational facilities are handled by the private sector.

## 13–5e Government in the Sunshine

The past four decades saw a trend toward more openness in government. The theory was that because Americans pay for the government, they own it—and they have a right to know what the government is doing with the taxpayers' dollars.

In response to pressure for more government openness and disclosure, Congress passed the Freedom of Information Act in 1966. This act requires federal agencies to disclose any information in agency files, with some exceptions, to any persons requesting it. Since the 1970s, *sunshine laws,* which require

**privatization** The transfer of the task of providing services traditionally provided by government to the private sector.

AP PHOTO/ERIC RISBERG

The Postal Service is struggling with a sharp decline in mail because of the Internet and a tough economy.

government meetings to be open to the public, have been enacted at all levels of American government.

The trend toward greater openness in government came to an abrupt halt on September 11, 2001. In the wake of the terrorist attacks on the World Trade Center and the Pentagon, the government began tightening its grip on information. In the months following the attacks, hundreds of thousands of documents were removed from government Web sites.

No longer can the public access plans of nuclear power plants, descriptions of airline security violations, or maps of pipeline routes. Agencies were instructed to be more cautious about releasing information in their files and were given new guidelines on what should be considered public information.

WWW.FEDERALRESERVE.GOV

Most government agencies have helpful Web sites. Here you see one for the regional Federal Reserve Bank of New York.

## 13–5f Government Online

Increasingly, government agencies have attempted to improve their effectiveness and efficiency by making use of the Internet. One method has been to make information available to the public online. This may appear to run counter to the information restrictions imposed following 9/11, but much government information is not relevant to national security issues.

Under the Obama administration, for example, it is now possible to get annual data on immigration, airline flight delays, and job-related deaths that name employers. The *Federal Register,* a record of government notices, can now be read online.

Local governments have posted such information as real estate records, restaurant health inspection scores, and the geographic location of crimes. Some parts of the government have resisted the trend toward openness, however. Lawyers and other interested parties must often pay to obtain information held by the courts.

**Filing Forms Online**   Another way that government agencies are using the Internet to improve services is to let citizens file forms and apply for services online.

For example, if you change your address, you may be able to request an update sticker for your driver's license by visiting a state Web site. Also, you may be able to apply for unemployment benefits without visiting an unemployment office, and receive payments through a government-issued debit card. The federal government distributes payments for Medicare, tax refunds, and a variety of other programs automatically and electronically.

**E-Fraud**   One danger of automatic payments is the possibility of fraud. This problem is not new. Criminals have long attempted to defraud the government—and the taxpayer—by filing false income tax forms or by making improper claims following natural disasters. The Internet, however, has made it possible for crooks to "game the system" more easily. Claims can be processed without examination by an actual person. Such faulty payment systems demonstrate that bureaucrats still have a role to play, even in the high-tech era.

**FOR CRITICAL THINKING**

In the name of security, some states have gone so far as to bar access to emergency evacuation plans. *Why might these states have done this? What problems could result if citizens lack access to this information?*

# AMERICA AT ODDS The Bureaucracy

Although the story is often told about red tape and wasteful spending generated by our bureaucracy, all in all, the U.S. bureaucracy compares favorably with bureaucracies in other countries. Citizens typically overestimate the amount of "government waste" by very large margins. Still, the U.S. government faces the same problems with its bureaucracy—sluggishness, inefficiency, and even incompetence—that large businesses and organizations throughout the country face. Americans are at odds over a number of issues relating to the bureaucracy, including the following:

- Can new financial regulations eliminate the danger of a catastrophe such as the one we experienced in September 2008—or will clever financiers find ways around any new regulations?

- Do the recent health-care reforms provide vital protection to the citizenry—or are they an example of excessive government meddling in the private sector?

- Are government employees overpaid—or is their pay appropriate, given their responsibilities?

- Is the outsourcing of government services a way to improve efficiency—or does it mostly serve to hide the true cost and scope of government?

- Should our leaders focus on openness and transparency in government—or are such measures dangerous during the war on terrorism?

# TAKE ACTION

Although this chapter's focus is on the federal bureaucracy, realize that all levels of government require bureaucracies to implement their goals. In virtually every community, however, there are needs that government agencies cannot meet. Often, agencies simply lack the funds to hire more personnel or to provide assistance to those in need. To help address these needs, many Americans do volunteer work. If you want to take action in this way, check with your local government offices and find out which agencies or offices have volunteer programs. Volunteer opportunities on the local level can range from helping the homeless and mentoring children in a local school to joining a local environmental clean-up effort. Decide where your interests lie, and consider volunteering your time in a local bureaucracy.

ANDY NEWMAN-FLORIDA KEYS NEWS BUREAU/REUTERS/LANDOV

Staff and volunteers of the Turtle Hospital release a federally protected loggerhead sea turtle back into the ocean.

# STUDY TOOLS

## Ready to study?

- Review what you've read with the quiz below. Check your answers on the Chapter in Review card at the back of the book. For any questions you miss, read the corresponding Learning Outcome section again to prepare for class and your exam.
- Rip out and study the Chapter in Review card.

## ...Or you can go online to CourseMate

at www.cengagebrain.com for these additional review materials:

- Practice Quizzes
- Key Term Flashcards or Crossword Puzzles
- Audio Summaries
- Simulations, Animated Learning Modules, and Interactive Timelines
- Videos
- American Government NewsWatch

## Fill-In

1. All in all, the three levels of government employ about _____ percent of the civilian labor force.

2. The head of each executive department is known as the _____, except for the Department of Justice, which is headed by the attorney general.

3. The _____ Department grants patents and trademarks, conducts the national census, and monitors the weather.

4. Federal bureaucrats holding top-level positions are appointed by the _____ and confirmed by the _____.

5. The Civil Service Reform Act of 1883 established the principle of government employment on the basis of _____.

6. To create a federal administrative agency, Congress passes _____, which specifies the name, purpose, composition, and powers of the agency being created.

7. An iron triangle is _____.

8. A whistleblower is someone who _____.

## Multiple Choice

9. The amount spent on defense, together with veterans' benefits, accounts for about ____ percent of federal spending.
   a. 5
   b. 25
   c. 49

10. The principal duties of the ____ Department include negotiating treaties, developing foreign policy, and protecting citizens abroad.
    a. State
    b. Homeland Security
    c. Defense

11. The independent executive agencies
    a. are businesses owned by the government.
    b. create and implement rules that regulate private activity and protect the public interest in a particular sector of the economy.
    c. are federal bureaucratic organizations that have a single function.

12. The ____ is a government corporation.
    a. General Services Administration
    b. U.S. Postal Service
    c. Securities and Exchange Commission

13. The document called *Policy and Supporting Positions (the Plum Book)* summarizes about ____ jobs that are filled by appointments after each presidential election.
    a. six hundred
    b. one thousand
    c. eight thousand

14. The process undertaken by an administrative agency when formally proposing, evaluating, and adopting a new regulation is called
    a. adjudication.
    b. rulemaking.
    c. neutral competency.

15. "Sunshine laws" require government
    a. meetings to be open to the public.
    b. agencies to outsource work to the private sector.
    c. agencies to let citizens file forms and apply for services online.

# 14

# The Judiciary

Remember to visit page 341 for additional **Study Tools**

TONY AVELAR/THE CHRISTIAN SCIENCE MONITOR/GETTY IMAGES

JEAN KERR MAURER
*JUDGE*

# AMERICA AT
# ODDS

## Are There Prisoners We Must Detain without Trial?

BRENNAN LINSLEY-POOL/GETTY IMAGES

After the September 11, 2001, attacks in the United States, the George W. Bush administration interned hundreds of suspected terrorists at the Guantánamo Bay Naval Base in Cuba. Most of them were foreign fighters captured during the war in Afghanistan, a war initiated just after 9/11. All prisoners were labeled *unlawful enemy combatants* and therefore were afforded neither the legal protections guaranteed to prisoners of war (POWs) under the Geneva Conventions nor the protections required under the conventions for dealing with civilians who commit crimes. Indeed, the Bush administration established the prison at Guantánamo in the belief that the facility would lie outside the reach of American law.

President Barack Obama promised to close the Guantánamo prison, but he failed to do so. Obama furthermore stated that it may be necessary to hold some of the detainees more or less forever without bringing them to trial. There are those who object to this policy, but many who agree with it.

## We Release Terrorists at the Civilized World's Peril

Look back over U.S. history. Federal judges never heard cases brought by Confederate prisoners of war held during the Civil War. During World War II, no civilian courts reviewed the cases of the thousands of German prisoners housed in the United States.

Today, if the president deems that certain terrorist prisoners are too dangerous to be tried and perhaps freed, that is the president's prerogative. After all, under our Constitution, the president has wartime decision-making powers. We also have evidence that at least thirty detainees released from the Guantánamo prison rejoined terrorist organizations and have been responsible for the deaths of innocent people overseas. Who will be responsible for the deaths caused by terrorists if they cannot be convicted and we then let them go?

## Indefinite Detention Is Unconstitutional and Damages Our Image Abroad

It is wrong to hold persons deemed "dangerous" by the government indefinitely. How can we know that the government is correct in its allegations against these people? We have learned that some of the Afghans held at Guantánamo and elsewhere were arrested due to false accusations resulting from long-standing feuds between rival families. U.S. officials were reluctant to release these innocents because it meant admitting that the officials had made a mistake.

The way our government has handled prisoners of war in the past is irrelevant. Traditional POWs were picked up during battle, on the field, in uniform. In contrast, most of the Guantánamo detainees were arrested nowhere near a battlefield. How can we know whether such detainees are truly dangerous if there is no trial?

## Where do you stand?

1. Could Congress fashion a law providing a procedure to determine when an alleged terrorist should never be let out of prison? Could such a law withstand Supreme Court review? Why or why not?
2. Why is it easier to falsely arrest a purported terrorist than a regular military soldier?

## Explore this issue online

- One of the strongest voices in favor of indefinite detention has been John Yoo, who served in President Bush's Justice Department when the detention policies were crafted. You'll find some of Yoo's articles if you enter "john yoo wall street journal" into a search engine.
- Two of the many bloggers who oppose indefinite detentions are Digby and Glenn Greenwald. You can find their work by searching on "digby terrorism" and "greenwald terrorism."

**judiciary** The courts; one of the three branches of government in the United States.

**common law** The body of law developed from judicial decisions in English and U.S. courts, not attributable to a legislature.

**precedent** A court decision that furnishes an example or authority for deciding subsequent cases involving identical or similar facts and legal issues.

**stare decisis** A common law doctrine under which judges normally are obligated to follow the precedents established by prior court decisions. Pronounced *ster*-ay dih-*si*-sis.

# Introduction

As you read in this chapter's opening *America at Odds* feature, the question of whether certain alleged terrorists should be imprisoned indefinitely without trial has elicited a great deal of controversy. Also controversial is the policymaking function of the United States Supreme Court. After all, when the Court renders an opinion on how the Constitution is to be interpreted, it is, necessarily, making policy on a national level.

To understand the nature of this controversy, you first need to understand how the **judiciary** (the courts) functions in this country. We begin by looking at the origins and sources of American law. We then examine the federal court system, at the apex of which is the United States Supreme Court, and consider various issues relating to the courts.

## 14–1 The Origins and Sources of American Law

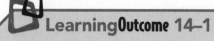

### LearningOutcome 14–1

Summarize the origins of the American legal system and the basic sources of American law.

The American colonists brought with them the legal system that had developed in England over hundreds of years. Thus, to understand how the American legal system operates, we need to go back in time to the early English courts and the traditions they established.

### 14–1a The Common Law Tradition

After the Normans conquered England in 1066, William the Conqueror and his successors began the process of unifying the country under their rule. One of the methods they used was the establishment of the "king's courts," or *curiae regis*. Before the Norman Conquest, disputes had been settled according to the local legal customs and traditions in various regions of the country. The law developed in the king's courts, however, applied to the country as a whole.

What evolved in these courts was the beginning of **common law**—the body of general rules that was applied throughout the entire English realm. Trial by jury is a famous part of the common law tradition. Juries are less common outside the English-speaking world, however.

**The Rule of Precedent** The early English courts developed the common law rules from the principles underlying judges' decisions in actual legal controversies. Judges attempted to be consistent, and whenever possible, they based their decisions on the principles applied in earlier cases.

**LEGAL PRECEDENTS.** Judges not only sought to decide similar cases in a similar way to previous cases, but they also considered new kinds of cases with the awareness that their decisions would make new law. Each interpretation became part of the law on the subject and served as a legal **precedent**—that is, a decision that furnished an example or authority for deciding subsequent cases involving identical or similar legal issues and facts.

**STARE DECISIS.** The practice of deciding new cases with reference to former decisions, or precedents, eventually became a cornerstone of the English and American judicial systems. The practice formed a doctrine called **stare decisis** ("to stand on decided cases").

Under this doctrine, judges are obligated to follow the precedents established in their jurisdictions. For example, if the Supreme Court of Georgia holds that a state law requiring candidates for state office to pass drug tests is unconstitutional, that decision will

> **"It is confidence** in the men and women who administer the judicial system, **that is the true backbone of the rule of law."**
>
> ~ JOHN PAUL STEVENS ~
> ASSOCIATE JUSTICE OF THE
> UNITED STATES SUPREME COURT
> 1975–2010

control the outcome of future cases on that issue brought before the state courts in Georgia.

Similarly, a decision made on a given issue by the United States Supreme Court (the nation's highest court) is binding on all inferior (lower) courts. For example, if the Georgia case on drug testing is appealed to the United States Supreme Court and the Court agrees that the Georgia law is unconstitutional, the high court's ruling will be binding on *all* courts in the United States. In other words, similar drug-testing laws in other states will be invalid and unenforceable.

**Departures from Precedent** Sometimes a court will depart from the rule of precedent if it decides that a precedent is simply incorrect or that technological or social changes have rendered the precedent inapplicable. Cases that overturn precedent often receive a great deal of publicity.

For example, in 1954, in *Brown v. Board of Education of Topeka*,[1] the United States Supreme Court expressly overturned precedent when it concluded that separate educational facilities for African Americans, which had been upheld as constitutional in many earlier cases under the "separate-but-equal" doctrine[2] (see Chapter 5), were inherently unequal and violated the equal protection clause. The Supreme Court's departure from precedent in *Brown* received a tremendous amount of publicity as people began to realize the political and social ramifications of this change in the law.

More recently, the Supreme Court departed from precedent in its 2010 ruling *Citizens United v. Federal Election Commission*.[3] In this decision, the Court determined that the government may not ban political spending by corporations in candidate elections when the spending is undertaken independently of a candidate's campaign. (The ruling implicitly covers unions and nonprofit groups as well.) The Court's verdict overturned two precedents that upheld restrictions on corporate spending: *Austin v. Michigan Chamber of Commerce* (1990)[4] and *McConnell v. Federal Election Commission* (2003).[5]

"IT IS BETTER, so the Fourth Amendment teaches, **THAT THE GUILTY SOMETIMES GO FREE** than that citizens be subject to easy arrest."

~ WILLIAM O. DOUGLAS ~
ASSOCIATE JUSTICE OF THE
UNITED STATES SUPREME COURT
1939–1975

## 14–1b Primary Sources of American Law

In any governmental system, the primary function of the courts is to interpret and apply the law. In the United States, the courts interpret and apply several sources of law when deciding cases. We look here only at the **primary sources of law**—that is, sources that *establish* the law—and the relative priority of these sources when particular laws come into conflict.

**Constitutional Law** The U.S. government and each of the fifty states have separate written constitutions that set forth the general organization, powers, and limits of their respective governments. **Constitutional law** consists of the rights and duties set forth in these constitutions.

The U.S. Constitution is the supreme law of the land. As such, it is the basis of all law in the United States. Any law that violates the Constitution is invalid and unenforceable. Because of the paramount importance of the U.S. Constitution in the American legal system, the complete text of the Constitution is found in Appendix B.

The Tenth Amendment to the U.S. Constitution reserves to the states and to the people all powers not granted to the federal government. Each state in the union has its own constitution. Unless they conflict with the U.S. Constitution or a federal law, state constitutions are supreme within the borders of their respective states.

## SOCIAL MEDIA
### In Politics

Unlike the other branches of government, the judiciary tends to take a dim view of social media because jurors in trials use it to obtain information they are not supposed to have. Still, you can follow one of several services that regularly tweet new rulings by the United States Supreme Court. One of the most informative of these is Supreme Court USA **@iSupremeCourt**.

**primary source of law** A source of law that establishes the law. Primary sources of law include constitutions, statutes, administrative agency rules and regulations, and decisions rendered by the courts.

**constitutional law** Law based on the U.S. Constitution and the constitutions of the various states.

**Statutory Law** Statutes enacted by legislative bodies at any level of government make up another source of law, which is generally referred to as **statutory law.** Federal statutes—laws enacted by the U.S. Congress—apply to all of the states. State statutes—laws enacted by state legislatures—apply only within the state that enacted the law. Any state statute that conflicts with the U.S. Constitution, with federal laws enacted by Congress, or with the state's constitution will be deemed invalid if challenged in court and will not be enforced.

Statutory law also includes the ordinances (such as local zoning or housing-construction laws) passed by cities and counties, none of which can violate the U.S. Constitution, the relevant state constitution, or any existing federal or state laws.

**Administrative Law**

Another important source of American law consists of **administrative law—** the rules, regulations, orders, and decisions of administrative agencies. As you read in Chapter 13, at the federal level Congress creates executive agencies, such as the Food and Drug Administration and the Environmental Protection Agency, to perform specific functions. Typically, when Congress establishes an agency, it authorizes the agency to create rules that have the force of law and to enforce those rules by bringing legal actions against violators.

Rules issued by various government agencies

> **"Our Constitution is colorblind,** and neither knows nor tolerates classes among citizens."
>
> ~ JOHN MARSHALL HARLAN ~
> ASSOCIATE JUSTICE OF THE
> UNITED STATES SUPREME COURT
> 1877–1911

now affect virtually every aspect of our economy. For example, almost all of a business's operations, including the firm's capital structure and financing, its hiring and firing procedures, its relations with employees and unions, and the way it manufactures and markets its products, are subject to government regulation.

Government agencies exist at the state and local levels as well. States commonly create agencies that parallel federal agencies. Just as federal statutes take precedence over conflicting state statutes, federal agency regulations take precedence over conflicting state regulations.

**Case Law** As is evident from the earlier discussion of the common law tradition, another basic source of American law consists of the rules of law announced in court decisions, or **case law.** These rules of law include interpretations of constitutional provisions, of statutes enacted by legislatures, and of regulations issued by administrative agencies.

Thus, even though a legislature passes a law to govern a certain area, how that law is interpreted and applied depends on the courts. The importance of case law, or *judge-made law,* is one of the distinguishing characteristics of the common law tradition.

## 14–1c Civil Law and Criminal Law

All of the sources of law just discussed can be classified in other ways as well. One of the most significant classification systems divides all law into two categories: civil law and criminal law. **Civil law** spells out the duties that individuals in society owe to other persons or to their governments, excluding the duty not to commit crimes.

Typically, in a civil case, a private party sues another private party (although the government can also sue a party for a civil law violation). The object of a civil lawsuit is to make the defendant—the person being sued—comply with a legal duty (such as a contractual promise) or pay money damages for failing to comply with that duty.

**Criminal law,** in contrast, has to do with wrongs committed against the public as a whole. Criminal acts are prohibited by local, state, or federal government statutes. Thus, criminal defendants are prosecuted by public officials, such as a district attorney (D.A.), on

---

**statutory law** The body of law enacted by legislatures (as opposed to constitutional law, administrative law, or case law).

**administrative law** The body of law created by administrative agencies (in the form of rules, regulations, orders, and decisions) in order to carry out their duties and responsibilities.

**case law** The rules of law announced in court decisions. Case law includes the aggregate of reported cases that interpret judicial precedents, statutes, regulations, and constitutional provisions.

**civil law** The branch of law that spells out the duties that individuals in society owe to other persons or to their governments, excluding the duty not to commit crimes.

**criminal law** The branch of law that defines and governs actions that constitute crimes. Generally, criminal law has to do with wrongful actions committed against society for which society demands redress.

behalf of the government, not by their victims or other private parties.

In a criminal case, the government seeks to impose a penalty (usually a fine and/or imprisonment) on a person who has violated a criminal law. For example, when someone robs a convenience store, that person has committed a crime and, if caught and proved guilty, will usually spend time in prison.

## 14–1d Basic Judicial Requirements

A court cannot decide just any issue at any time. Before a court can hear and decide a case, specific requirements must be met. To a certain extent, these requirements act as restraints on the judiciary because they limit the types of cases that courts can hear and decide. Courts also have procedural requirements that judges must follow.

**Jurisdiction** In Latin, *juris* means "law," and *diction* means "to speak." Therefore, **jurisdiction** literally refers to the power "to speak the law." Jurisdiction applies either to the geographic area in which a court has the right and power to decide cases, or to the right and power of a court to decide matters concerning certain persons, types of property, or subjects. Before any court can hear a case, it must have jurisdiction over the person against whom the suit is brought, the property involved in the suit, and the subject matter.

**THE JURISDICTION OF STATE COURTS.** A state trial court usually has jurisdictional authority over the residents of a particular area of the state, such as a county or district. (A **trial court** is, as the term implies, a court in which trials are held and testimony is taken.) A state's highest court (often called the *state supreme court*)[6] has jurisdictional authority over all residents within the state. In some cases, if an individual has committed an offense such as injuring someone in an automobile accident or selling defective goods within the state, the court can exercise jurisdiction even if the individual is a resident of another state.

State courts can also exercise jurisdiction over people who do business within the state. A New York company that distributes its products in California, for example, can be sued by a California resident in a California state court.

**FEDERAL COURT JURISDICTION.** Because the federal government is a government of limited powers, the jurisdiction of the federal courts is limited. Article III, Section 2, of the Constitution states that the federal courts can exercise jurisdiction over all cases "arising under this Constitution, the Laws of the United States, and Treaties made, or which shall be made, under their Authority." Whenever a case involves a claim based, at least in part, on the U.S. Constitution, a treaty, or a federal law, a **federal question** arises. Any lawsuit involving a federal question can originate in a federal court.

> **jurisdiction** The authority of a court to hear and decide a particular case.
>
> **trial court** A court in which trials are held and testimony is taken.
>
> **federal question** A question that pertains to the U.S. Constitution, acts of Congress, or treaties. A federal question provides a basis for federal court jurisdiction.

GETTY IMAGES

A typical civil trial involves a judge, attorneys for both sides, a defendant, and a plaintiff.

Federal courts can also exercise jurisdiction over cases involving **diversity of citizenship.** Such cases may arise when the parties in a lawsuit live in different states or when one of the parties is a foreign government or a foreign citizen. Before a federal court can take jurisdiction in a diversity case, the amount in controversy must be more than $75,000. (Congress raised the limit to $75,000 in 1996. In 1789, the sum was $500.)

In addition to state and federal courts, there are a limited number of international courts. How should the United States react to such institutions? What jurisdiction should they have, if any? We look at one example in *The Rest of the World* feature on page 326.

### Standing to Sue

To bring a lawsuit before a court, a person must have **standing to sue,** or a sufficient "stake" in the matter to justify bringing a suit. Thus, the party bringing the suit must have suffered a harm or been threatened with a harm by the action at issue, and the issue must be justiciable. A **justiciable controversy** is one that is real and substantial, as opposed to hypothetical or academic.

The requirement of standing to sue clearly limits the issues that can be decided by the courts. Furthermore, both state and federal governments can specify by law when an individual or group has standing to sue. For example, the federal government will not allow a taxpayer to sue the Department of Defense for spending tax dollars wastefully.

### Court Procedures

Both the federal and the state courts have established procedural rules that apply in all cases. These procedures are designed to protect the rights and interests of the parties, ensure that the litigation proceeds in a fair and orderly manner, and identify the issues that must be decided by the court—thus saving court time and costs. Different procedural rules apply in criminal and civil cases. Generally, criminal procedural rules attempt to ensure that defendants are not deprived of their constitutional rights.

Parties involved in civil or criminal cases must comply with court procedural rules or risk being held in **contempt of court.** A party who is held in contempt of court can be fined, taken into custody, or both. A court must take care to ensure that the parties—and the court itself—comply with procedural requirements. Procedural errors often serve as grounds for a mistrial or for appealing the court's decision to a higher tribunal.

*Why does national law—even administrative law established by a federal agency—overrule conflicting law that the people of a state have enshrined in their state constitution?*

## 14–2 The Federal Court System

The federal court system is a three-tiered model consisting of U.S. district courts (trial courts), U.S. courts of appeals, and the United States Supreme Court. Figure 14–1 on the facing page shows the organization of the federal court system.

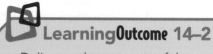

**LearningOutcome 14–2**

Delineate the structure of the federal court system.

Bear in mind that the federal courts constitute only one of the fifty-two court systems in the United States. Each of the fifty states has its own court system, as does the District of Columbia. No two state court systems are exactly the same, but usually each state has different levels, or tiers, of courts, just as the federal system does.

Generally, state courts deal with questions of state law, and the decisions of a state's highest court on matters of state law are normally final. If a federal question is involved, however, a decision of a state supreme court may be appealed to the United States Supreme

**diversity of citizenship** A basis for federal court jurisdiction over a lawsuit that arises when (1) the parties in the lawsuit live in different states or when one of the parties is a foreign government or a foreign citizen, and (2) the amount in controversy is more than $75,000.

**standing to sue** The requirement that an individual must have a sufficient stake in a controversy before he or she can bring a lawsuit. The party bringing the suit must demonstrate that he or she has either been harmed or been threatened with a harm.

**justiciable controversy** A controversy that is not hypothetical or academic but real and substantial; a requirement that must be satisfied before a court will hear a case. *Justiciable* is pronounced jus-*tish*-a-bul.

**contempt of court** A ruling that a person has disobeyed a court order or has shown disrespect to the court or to a judicial proceeding.

FIGURE 14-1

# The Organization
## of the Federal Court System

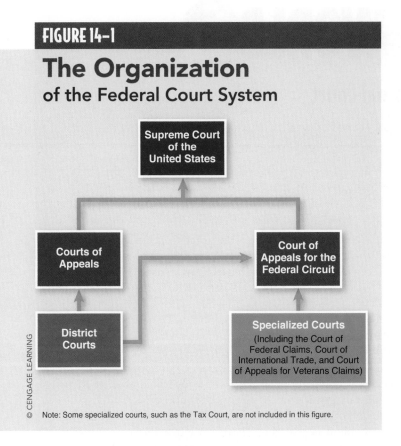

Note: Some specialized courts, such as the Tax Court, are not included in this figure.

© CENGAGE LEARNING

Court. We will discuss the federal court system in the pages that follow.

## 14-2a U.S. District Courts

On the lowest tier of the federal court system are the U.S. district courts, or federal trial courts—the courts in which cases involving federal laws begin. The cases in these courts are decided by a judge or a jury (if it is a jury trial). There is at least one federal district court in every state, and there is one in the District of Columbia.

The number of judicial districts varies over time, primarily owing to population changes and corresponding caseloads. Currently, there are ninety-four judicial districts. Figure 14–2 on page 327 shows their geographic boundaries. The federal system also includes other trial courts, such as the Court of International Trade and others shown in Figure 14–1 above. These courts have limited, or specialized, subject-matter jurisdiction—that is, they can exercise authority only over certain kinds of cases.

## 14-2b U.S. Courts of Appeals

On the middle tier of the federal court system are the U.S. courts of appeals. Courts of appeals, or

**appellate courts,** do not hear evidence or testimony. Rather, an appellate court reviews the transcript of the trial court's proceedings, other records relating to the case, and attorneys' arguments as to why the trial court's decision should or should not stand.

In contrast to a trial court, where normally a single judge presides, an appellate court consists of a panel of three or more judges. The task of the appellate court is to determine whether the trial court erred in applying the law to the facts and issues involved in a particular case.

There are thirteen federal courts of appeals in the United States. The courts of appeals for twelve of the circuits, including the Court of Appeals for the D.C. Circuit, hear appeals from the U.S. district courts located within their respective judicial circuits (see Figure 14–2 on page 327).

Decisions made by federal administrative agencies may be reviewed either by a district court or the court of appeals, depending on the agency. The Court of Appeals for the Federal Circuit has national jurisdiction over certain types of cases, such as those concerning patent law and some claims against the national government.

The decisions of the federal appellate courts may be appealed to the United States Supreme Court. If a decision is not appealed, or if the high court declines to review the case, the appellate court's decision is final.

## 14-2c The United States Supreme Court

The highest level of the three-tiered model of the federal court system is the United States Supreme Court. According to Article III of the U.S. Constitution, there is only one national Supreme Court, but Congress is empowered to create additional ("inferior") courts as it deems necessary. The inferior courts that Congress has created include the second tier in our model—the U.S. courts of appeals—as well as the district courts and any other courts of limited, or specialized, jurisdiction.

**appellate court** A court having appellate jurisdiction. An appellate court normally does not hear evidence or testimony but reviews the transcript of the trial court's proceedings, other records relating to the case, and attorneys' arguments as to why the trial court's decision should or should not stand.

## The Troubled International Criminal Court

In July 2002, the International Criminal Court (ICC) opened for business. Its assignment was to hear cases dealing with genocide, crimes against humanity, and similar international offenses. Its jurisdiction is worldwide. It has a staff of more than seven hundred and an annual budget of over $100 million.

### The United States versus the Court

Even though President Bill Clinton signed the treaty that established the ICC, he had so many doubts about it that he never bothered submitting the treaty to the U.S. Senate. President George W. Bush was more than dubious—he was outright hostile to the new institution, as were other U.S. conservatives. Bush attempted to "unsign" the treaty, a move that many foreign governments considered meaningless.

A principal concern was that U.S. soldiers or diplomats might be brought before the international court by unfriendly parties. The Bush administration exerted considerable pressure on a variety of countries to persuade them to sign agreements that American citizens would always be exempt from the ICC's jurisdiction. The Obama administration dialed back the hostility, but it had no plans to send the treaty to the Senate.

### Much Ado about Very Little

In its first thirteen years of existence, the ICC completed only one trial: it convicted a commander in the Congo civil war of war crimes. Only a handful of other trials are ongoing. The problem is that the ICC has no jurisdiction over nations that have not ratified the treaty. Authoritarian countries that engage in repression of their populations did not ratify the treaty and are

therefore outside the ICC's reach. Moreover, only if domestic legal institutions do not investigate international crimes in good faith can the ICC take over.

Yes, the ICC did charge Libyan dictator Moammar Gadhafi, but rebel forces ended up killing him first. African nations argue that the ICC is biased against Africa because ICC has never charged individuals from any other continent. Some say that the ICC focuses on Africa simply because African governments are weak. Yet one of the goals of the court was to back up weak governments.

In the end, the United States had nothing to worry about. Far from posing a threat to American citizens, the ICC in fact has not been much of a threat to anyone. All the ICC has done is annoy a few nations—but at the cost of many hundreds of millions of dollars.

**FOR CRITICAL ANALYSIS** Why would American conservatives fear that the ICC might go after American citizens?

---

The United States Supreme Court consists of nine justices—a chief justice and eight associate justices—although that number is not mandated by the Constitution. The Supreme Court has original, or trial, jurisdiction only in rare instances (set forth in Article III, Section 2). In other words, only rarely does a case originate at the Supreme Court level. Most of the Court's work is as an appellate court.

The Supreme Court has appellate authority over cases decided by the U.S. courts of appeals, as well as over some cases decided in the state courts when federal questions are at issue.

> **writ of *certiorari*** An order from a higher court asking a lower court for the record of a case. *Certiorari* is pronounced sur-shee-uh-*rah*-ree.

**The Writ of *Certiorari*** To bring a case before the Supreme Court, a party may request that the Court issue a **writ of *certiorari,*** often called "cert.," which is an order that the Supreme Court issues to a lower court requesting the latter to send it the record of the case in question.

Parties can petition the Supreme Court to issue a writ of *certiorari*, but whether the Court will do so is entirely within its discretion. The Court will not issue a writ unless at least four of the nine justices approve. In no instance is the Court required to issue a writ of *certiorari*.[7]

Most petitions for writs of *certiorari* are denied. A denial is not a decision on the merits of a case, however, nor does it indicate that the Court agrees with a lower court's opinion. Furthermore, the denial of

FIGURE 14-2

# U.S. Courts of Appeals
## and U.S. District Courts

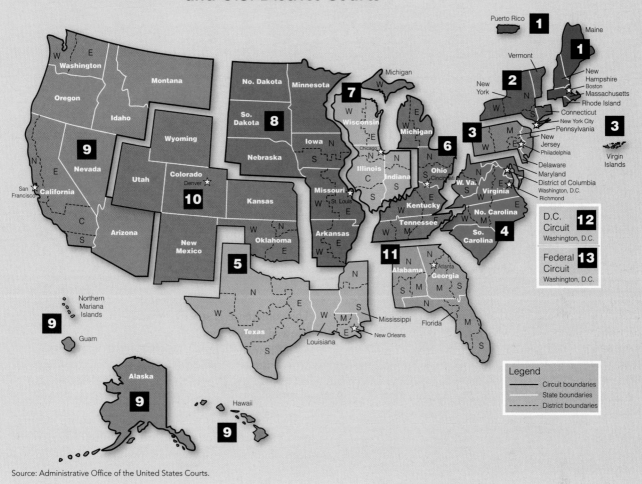

Source: Administrative Office of the United States Courts.

a writ has no value as a precedent. A denial simply means that the decision of the lower court remains the law within that court's jurisdiction.

## Which Cases Reach the Supreme Court?

There is no absolute right to appeal to the United States Supreme Court. Although thousands of cases are filed with the Supreme Court each year, on average the Court hears fewer than one hundred. As Figure 14–3 on the following page shows, the number of cases heard by the Court each year has declined significantly since the 1980s. In large part, this has occurred because the Court has raised its standards for accepting cases in recent years.

Typically, the Court grants petitions for cases that raise important policy issues that need to be addressed. In its 2011–2012 term, for example, the Court heard cases involving such issues as the following:

- Whether the Fourth Amendment banned police departments from surreptitiously attaching GPS devices to vehicles. (The Court ruled that it did.)[8]

- Whether churches had broad liberty to define which of their employees was a minister and therefore exempt from employment discrimination laws. (The Court backed the churches.)[9]

- Whether Arizona had gone too far in a law cracking down on illegal immigrants. (The Court determined that at least in some of the law's provisions, Arizona had gone too far.)[10]

- Whether the provision in the Affordable Care Act (Obamacare) that most U.S. citizens be required to obtain health-care insurance was constitutional. (The Court ruled that it was.)[11]

If the lower courts have rendered conflicting opinions on an important issue, the Supreme Court may review one or more cases involving that issue to define the law on the matter. For example, in 2010

**FIGURE 14-3**

# The Number of
## Supreme Court Opinions

The number of Supreme Court opinions peaked at 151 in the Court's 1982 term, declined more or less steadily through 1995, and then leveled off. During the 2011 term (ending in June 2012), the Court issued 77 opinions.

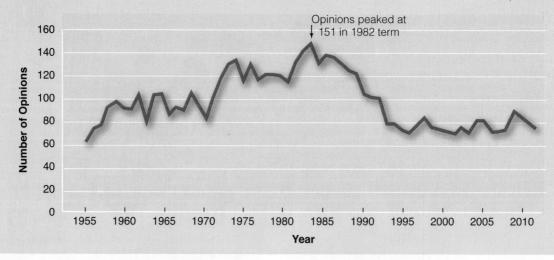

© CENGAGE LEARNING

and 2011 various federal appellate courts issued conflicting opinions as to whether it is constitutional to require citizens to purchase health-care insurance, as provided by the health-care reforms enacted in 2010. The conflicting rulings were eventually resolved by the Court in *National Federation of Independent Business v. Sebelius.* (See the feature *Join the Debate: Was the Supreme Court Right to Uphold Obamacare?* in Chapter 2 on page 41.)

## Supreme Court Opinions

Like other appellate courts, the United States Supreme Court normally does not hear any evidence. The Court's decision in a particular case is based on the written record of the case and the written arguments (legal briefs) that the attorneys submit.

**REACHING AN OPINION.** The attorneys also present **oral arguments**— spoken arguments presented in person rather than on paper—to the Court, after which the justices discuss the case in **conference.**

The conference is strictly private—only the justices are allowed in the room.

When the Court has reached a decision, the chief justice, if in the majority, assigns the task of writing the Court's **opinion** to one of the justices. When the chief justice is not in the majority, the most senior justice voting with the majority assigns the writing of the Court's opinion. The opinion outlines the reasons for the Court's decision, the rules of law that apply, and the judgment.

**CONCURRING AND DISSENTING OPINIONS.** Often, one or more justices who agree with the Court's decision do so for reasons different from those outlined in the majority opinion. These justices may write **concurring opinions,** setting forth their own legal reasoning on

**oral argument** A spoken argument presented to a judge in person by an attorney on behalf of her or his client.

**conference** In regard to the Supreme Court, a private meeting of the justices in which they present their arguments concerning a case under consideration.

**opinion** A written statement by a court expressing the reasons for its decision in a case.

**concurring opinion** A statement written by a judge or justice who agrees (concurs) with the court's decision, but for reasons different from those in the majority opinion.

> ## "AS NIGHTFALL DOESN'T COME AT ONCE, NEITHER DOES OPPRESSION.
>
> In both instances, . . . we must be aware of change in the air, however slight, lest we become unwitting victims of the darkness."
>
> ~ WILLIAM O. DOUGLAS ~
> ASSOCIATE JUSTICE OF THE
> UNITED STATES SUPREME COURT
> 1939–1975

the issue. Frequently, one or more justices disagree with the Court's conclusion. These justices may write **dissenting opinions,** outlining the reasons they feel the majority erred in arriving at its decision.

Although a dissenting opinion does not affect the outcome of the case before the Court, it may be important later. In a subsequent case concerning the same issue, a jurist or attorney may use the legal reasoning in the dissenting opinion as the basis for an argument to reverse the previous decision and establish a new precedent.

**FOR CRITICAL THINKING**

Some people believe that the Supreme Court should accept more cases and thereby resolve more issues. Others contend that such a move would result in less well-thought-out opinions. *Who do you think has the better argument, and why?*

## 14–3 Federal Judicial Appointments

**LearningOutcome 14–3**

Say how federal judges are appointed.

Unlike state court judges, who are often elected, all federal judges are appointed. Article II, Section 2, of the Constitution authorizes the president to appoint the justices of the Supreme Court with the advice and consent of the Senate. Laws enacted by Congress provide that the same procedure is to be used for appointing judges to the lower federal courts as well. Does the practice of appointing judges yield better results than elections—or vice versa? We examine that question in this chapter's *Join the Debate* feature on page 331.

Federal judges receive lifetime appointments (because under Article III of the Constitution they "hold their Offices during good Behaviour"). Federal judges may be removed from office through the impeachment process, but such proceedings are extremely rare and are usually undertaken only if a judge engages in blatantly illegal conduct, such as bribery. In the history of this nation, only fifteen federal judges have been impeached, and only eleven left office due to a conviction or resignation. Normally, federal judges serve until they resign, retire, or die.

Although the Constitution sets no specific qualifications for those who serve on the Supreme Court, those who have done so share one characteristic: all have been attorneys. The backgrounds of the Supreme Court justices have been far from typical of the characteristics of the American public as a whole. Table 14–1 on the following page summarizes the backgrounds of all of the 112 United States Supreme Court justices through 2013.

### 14–3a The Nomination Process

The president receives suggestions and recommendations as to potential nominees for Supreme Court positions from various sources, including the Justice Department, senators, other judges, the candidates themselves, state political leaders, bar associations, and other interest groups. After selecting a nominee, the president submits her or his name to the Senate for approval. The Senate Judiciary Committee then holds hearings and makes its recommendation to the Senate, where it takes a majority vote to confirm the nomination.

**Senatorial Courtesy** When judges are nominated to the district courts (and, to a lesser extent, the U.S. courts of appeals), a senator of the president's political party from the state where there is a vacancy traditionally has been allowed to veto the president's choice. This practice is known as **senatorial courtesy.** At times, senatorial courtesy even permits senators from the opposing party to veto presidential choices. Because of senatorial courtesy, home-state senators of the president's party may be able to influence the choice of the nominee.

**Partisanship** It should come as no surprise that partisanship plays a significant role in the president's selection of nominees to the federal bench, particularly to the Supreme Court, the crown jewel of the federal judiciary. Traditionally, presidents have attempted to strengthen their legacies by appointing federal judges with political and philosophical views similar to their own. In the history of the Supreme Court, fewer than 13 percent of the justices nominated by a president have been from an opposing political party.

> **dissenting opinion**
> A statement written by a judge or justice who disagrees with the majority opinion.
>
> **senatorial courtesy** A practice that allows a senator of the president's party to veto the president's nominee to a federal court judgeship within the senator's state.

## TABLE 14–1

### Backgrounds of United States Supreme Court Justices through 2013

| | Number of Justices (112 = Total) |
|---|---|
| **Occupational Position before Appointment** | |
| Private legal practice | 25 |
| State judgeship | 21 |
| Federal judgeship | 31 |
| U.S. attorney general | 7 |
| Deputy or assistant U.S. attorney general | 2 |
| U.S. solicitor general | 3 |
| U.S. senator | 6 |
| U.S. representative | 2 |
| State governor | 3 |
| Federal executive post | 9 |
| Other | 3 |
| **Religious Affiliation** | |
| Protestant | 83 |
| Roman Catholic | 14 |
| Jewish | 7 |
| Unitarian | 7 |
| No religious affiliation | 1 |
| **Age on Appointment** | |
| Under 40 | 5 |
| 41–50 | 33 |
| 51–60 | 60 |
| 61–70 | 14 |
| **Political Party Affiliation** | |
| Federalist (to 1835) | 13 |
| Jeffersonian Republican (to 1828) | 7 |
| Whig (to 1861) | 1 |
| Democrat | 46 |
| Republican | 44 |
| Independent | 1 |
| **Education** | |
| College graduate | 96 |
| Not a college graduate | 16 |
| **Gender** | |
| Male | 108 |
| Female | 4 |
| **Race** | |
| White (non-Hispanic) | 109 |
| African American | 2 |
| Hispanic | 1 |

Sources: *Congressional Quarterly's Guide to the U.S. Supreme Court* (Washington, D.C.: Congressional Quarterly Press, 1997); and authors' updates.

That said, presidents have often discovered that the justices they appointed took very different positions than expected. President Dwight D. Eisenhower (1953–1961), for example, had no idea when he appointed Chief Justice Earl Warren that Warren would seek to overturn the system of racial segregation. The Court accomplished this goal through rulings such as *Brown v. Board of Education* (see Chapter 5).[12]

**Courts of Appeals**  Appointments to the U.S. courts of appeals can also have a lasting impact. Recall that these courts occupy the level just below the Supreme Court in the federal court system. Also recall that the decisions rendered by these courts—about 60,000 per year—are final unless overturned by the Supreme Court. Given that the Supreme Court renders opinions in fewer than one hundred cases a year, the decisions of the federal appellate courts have a wide-reaching effect on American society.

For example, a decision interpreting the federal Constitution by the U.S. Court of Appeals for the Ninth Circuit, if not overruled by the Supreme Court, establishes a precedent that will be followed in the states of Alaska, Arizona, California, Hawaii, Idaho, Montana, Nevada, Oregon, and Washington.

## 14–3b Confirmation or Rejection by the Senate

The president's nominations are not always confirmed. In fact, almost 20 percent of presidential nominations for the Supreme Court have been either rejected or not acted on by the Senate. The process of nominating and confirming federal judges, especially Supreme Court justices, often involves political debate and controversy. Many bitter battles over Supreme Court appointments have ensued when the Senate and the president have disagreed on political issues.

From 1893 until 1968, the Senate rejected only three Court nominees. From 1968 through 1986, however, two presidential nominees to the highest court were rejected, and two more nominations, both by President Ronald Reagan, failed in 1987. The most significant of these nominees was Robert Bork, who faced hostile questioning about his views on the Constitution during the confirmation hearings. The Bork hearings are often considered to be a turning point after which confirmation hearings became much more contentious.

One of President George H. W. Bush's nominees to the Supreme Court—Clarence Thomas—was also the subject of considerable controversy. The nation

## Should the People Elect Judges?

The founders of the American republic were concerned that too great a degree of popular control over the government could lead to "mob rule," and so they sought to insulate various institutions from direct popular elections. Federal judges, in particular, were to be appointed and serve for life. In contrast, in many states, all judges are popularly elected.

From time to time, judges are defeated at the polls. The most common way to defeat a judge is to accuse that official of being "soft on crime." Some people believe that despite the long prison sentences common in recent years, the judicial system is still too friendly to criminals. Others believe that elections tempt judges to cut corners on civil liberties. Should state judges be named through appointment? Or should the states rely on popular election?

### The People Should Rule

Those who favor electing judges do not believe that judges can be insulated from politics. Governors, who often do the appointing when judges aren't elected, are highly political creatures. They tend to appoint supporters of their own party. If politics is going to play a role in judicial selection, then the people ought to have their say directly. Let the voters decide whether a judge is tough enough on crime or too tough on business. We admit ordinary people into the judicial process through juries, and judges should respond to public opinion as well. Officials who do not have to win a popular election may become remote from the people. Living in upscale neighborhoods, they will never experience what it is like to walk home at night fearing for their safety. Instead, they can end up living in a legal never-never land where abstractions matter more than the real world. It takes elections to give us the kinds of judges that we really want.

### The Courts Must Be Insulated from Popular Pressure

Many opponents of judicial elections believe that they allow too much opportunity for popular panics and prejudices to influence the process. Popular "lock 'em up" attitudes toward criminals do not lead to an optimum strategy for crime reduction. Rather, we need to study what works and what doesn't. In some states, "get tough" policies have led to absurd cases of individuals serving life sentences for trivial offenses. The last thing we need is to place additional pressure on judges by threatening them with removal.

Any move toward greater use of elections would bring with it a further problem—the corrupting influence of campaign contributions. Several states that use judicial elections are famous for their harsh sentences and enthusiasm for the death penalty. Judges in these states are also conspicuously friendly toward the moneyed interests that helped get them elected.

**FOR CRITICAL ANALYSIS** If judges must raise campaign contributions, what kinds of people would be most likely to contribute? Why?

---

watched on television as Anita Hill, a former aide, leveled charges of sexual harassment at Thomas, who nevertheless was confirmed.

### George W. Bush's Appointments
During George W. Bush's second term, Chief Justice William Rehnquist died, and Sandra Day O'Connor, the Court's first woman justice, retired. These events allowed Bush to nominate John G. Roberts, Jr., to replace Rehnquist and Samuel A. Alito, Jr., to replace O'Connor. Both nominations were confirmed by the Senate with relatively little difficulty. The appointment of Alito, in particular, changed the character of the Court, because he was distinctly more conservative than O'Connor.

### Obama's Nominees
In May 2009, as a result of a judicial retirement, President Barack Obama named Sonia Sotomayor to the Court. Sotomayor had served for more than a decade as a judge of the U.S. Court of Appeals for the Second Circuit and was the first Hispanic American ever nominated to the Supreme Court.

A second retirement gave Obama an additional chance to pick a nominee, in May 2010. He chose Elena Kagan, his solicitor general. At her confirmation

Sonia Sotomayor became the first Latina on the Supreme Court when she was confirmed by the Senate in 2009.

hearings, several Republicans seized on an incident that occurred when Kagan was dean of Harvard Law School. In line with Harvard policy, Kagan placed restrictions on military recruiters. The restrictions were in response to the military's "don't ask, don't tell" policy, which prevented lesbians and gay men from serving openly. Still, Kagan was confirmed. It was a sign of the increased political polarization in the Senate that neither Sotomayor nor Kagan received more than a handful of votes from Republican senators.

## FOR CRITICAL THINKING

In recent years, senators have increasingly made use of the filibuster to delay or prevent the approval of judicial nominees. *Is this a legitimate tactic or an example of partisan excess? In either case, why?*

## 14–4 The Courts as Policymakers

**LearningOutcome 14–4**

Explain how the federal courts make policy.

In the United States, judges and justices play a major role in government. Unlike judges in some other countries, U.S.

judges have the power to decide on the constitutionality of laws or actions undertaken by the other branches of government.

Clearly, the function of the courts is to interpret and apply the law, not to make law—that is the function of the legislative branch of government. Yet judges can and do "make law." Indeed, they cannot avoid making law in some cases because the law does not always provide clear answers to questions that come before the courts.

### 14–4a The Issue of Broad Language

The text of the U.S. Constitution is set forth in broad terms. When a court interprets a constitutional provision and applies that interpretation to a specific set of circumstances, the court is essentially "making the law" on that issue. Examples of how the courts, and especially the United States Supreme Court, make law abound.

Consider privacy rights, which we discussed in Chapter 4. Nothing in the Constitution or its amendments specifically states that we have a right to privacy. Yet the Supreme Court, through various decisions, has established such a right by deciding that it is implied by several constitutional amendments. The Court has also held that this right to privacy includes a number of specific rights, such as the right to have an abortion.

Statutory provisions and other legal rules also tend to be expressed in general terms, and the courts must decide how those general provisions and rules apply to specific cases. The Americans with Disabilities Act of 1990 is an example. The act requires employers to reasonably accommodate the needs of employees with disabilities. But the act does not say exactly what employers must do to "reasonably accommodate" such persons. Thus, the courts must decide, on a case-by-case basis, what this phrase means.

Additionally, in some cases there is no relevant law or precedent to follow. In recent years, for example, courts have been struggling with new kinds of legal issues stemming from new communications technologies, including the Internet. Until legislative bodies enact laws governing these issues, it is up to the courts to fashion the law that will apply—and thus make policy.

### 14–4b The Impact of Court Decisions

As already mentioned, how the courts interpret particular laws can have a widespread impact on society. For example, in 1996, in *Hopwood v. Texas*,[13]

Solicitor General Elena Kagan testifies at her Supreme Court confirmation hearings in June 2010.

MARY F. CALVERT/THE NEW YORK TIMES/REDUX

the U.S. Court of Appeals for the Fifth Circuit held that an affirmative action program implemented by the University of Texas School of Law in Austin was unconstitutional. The court's decision in *Hopwood* set a precedent for all federal courts within the Fifth Circuit's jurisdiction (which covers Louisiana, Mississippi, and Texas).

Decisions rendered by the United States Supreme Court, of course, have an even broader impact, because all courts in the nation are obligated to follow precedents set by the high court. For example, in 2003 the Supreme Court issued two rulings on affirmative action programs at the University of Michigan. Unlike the appeals court in the *Hopwood* case, the Supreme Court held that diversity on college campuses is a legitimate goal and that affirmative action programs that take race into consideration as part of an examination of each applicant's background do not necessarily violate the equal protection clause of the Constitution.[14]

This decision rendered any contrary ruling, including the ruling by the court in the *Hopwood* case, invalid. In 2007, however, the Court retreated somewhat from its position in the University of Michigan cases when it declared that Seattle schools could not use race as a determining factor when assigning students to schools.[15]

Thus, when the Supreme Court interprets laws, it establishes national policy. If the Court deems that a law passed by Congress or a state legislature violates the Constitution, for example, that law will be void and unenforceable in any court within the United States.

### 14–4c The Power of Judicial Review

Recall from Chapter 2 that the U.S. Constitution divides government powers among the executive, legislative, and judicial branches. This division of powers is part of our system of checks and balances. Essentially, the founders gave each branch of government the constitutional authority to check the other two branches. The federal judiciary can exercise a check on the actions of either of the other branches through its power of **judicial review.**

The Constitution does not actually mention judicial review. Rather, the Supreme Court claimed the power for itself in *Marbury v. Madison*.[16] In that case, which was decided by the Court in 1803, Chief Justice John Marshall held that a provision of a 1789 law affecting the Supreme Court's jurisdiction violated the Constitution and was thus void. Marshall declared, "It is emphatically the province and duty of the judicial department [the courts] to say what the law is. . . . If two laws conflict with each other, the courts must decide on the operation of each. . . . So if a law be in opposition to the constitution . . . the court must determine which of these conflicting rules governs the case. This is the very essence of judicial duty."

Most constitutional scholars believe that the framers intended that the federal courts should have the power of judicial review. In *Federalist Paper* No. 78, Alexander Hamilton clearly espoused the doctrine. Hamilton stressed the importance of the "complete independence" of federal judges and their

"Everything I did in my life that was worthwhile I caught hell for."

~ EARL WARREN ~
CHIEF JUSTICE OF THE
UNITED STATES SUPREME COURT
1953–1969

**judicial review** The power of the courts to decide on the constitutionality of legislative enactments and of actions taken by the executive branch.

During controversial Supreme Court deliberations, demonstrators often present their views in front of the Court building.

MARK WILSON/GETTY IMAGES

not have precise meanings. Generally, however, an activist judge or justice believes that the courts should actively use their powers to check the legislative and executive branches to ensure that they do not exceed their authority. A restraintist judge or justice, in contrast, generally assumes that the courts should defer to the decisions of the legislative and executive branches. After all, members of Congress and the president are elected by the people, whereas federal court judges are not. In other words, the courts should not thwart the implementation of legislative acts unless those acts are clearly unconstitutional.

special duty to "invalidate all acts contrary to the manifest tenor of the Constitution." Without judicial review by impartial courts, there would be nothing to ensure that the other branches of government stayed within constitutional limits when exercising their powers, and "all the reservations of particular rights or privileges would amount to nothing." Chief Justice Marshall shared Hamilton's views and adopted Hamilton's reasoning in *Marbury v. Madison*.

## 14–4d Judicial Activism versus Judicial Restraint

As already noted, making policy is not the primary function of the federal courts. Yet it is unavoidable that courts do, in fact, influence or even establish policy when they interpret and apply the law. Further, the power of judicial review gives the courts, and particularly the Supreme Court, an important policymaking tool. When the Supreme Court upholds or invalidates a state or federal statute, the consequences for the nation can be profound.

One issue that is often debated is how the federal courts should wield their policymaking power, particularly the power of judicial review. Often, this debate is couched in terms of judicial activism versus judicial restraint.

**Activist versus Restraintist Justices** The terms *judicial activism* and *judicial restraint* do

**Political Ideology and Judicial Activism/ Restraint** One of the Supreme Court's most activist eras occurred during the period from 1953 to 1969 under the leadership of Chief Justice Earl Warren. The Warren Court propelled the civil rights movement forward by holding, among other things, that laws permitting racial segregation violated the equal protection clause (see Chapter 5).

Because of the activism of the Warren Court, the term *judicial activism* has often been linked with liberalism. Indeed, many liberals are in favor of an activist federal judiciary because they believe that the judiciary can "right" the "wrongs" that result from unfair laws or from "antiquated" legislation at the state and local levels. Neither judicial activism nor judicial restraint is necessarily linked to a particular political ideology, however. In fact, many observers claim that today's Supreme Court is often activist on behalf of a conservative agenda.

## FOR CRITICAL THINKING

*If a judge rules that it is unconstitutional for a state to ban same-sex marriage, is this judicial activism? Why or why not?*

# 14–5 Ideology and the Courts

**LearningOutcome 14–5**

Describe the role of ideology and judicial philosophies in judicial decision making.

The policymaking role of the courts gives rise to an important question: To what extent do ideology and personal policy preferences affect judicial decision making? Numerous scholars have attempted to answer this question, especially with respect to Supreme Court justices.

## 14–5a Ideology and Supreme Court Decisions

Few doubt that ideology affects judicial decision making, although, of course, other factors play a role as well. Different courts (such as a trial court and an appellate court) can look at the same case and draw different conclusions as to what law is applicable and how it should be applied. Certainly, there are numerous examples of ideology affecting Supreme Court decisions. As new justices replace old ones and new ideological alignments are formed, the Court's decisions are affected. Yet many scholars argue that there is no real evidence that personal preferences influence Supreme Court decisions to an *unacceptable* extent.

Keep in mind that judicial decision making, particularly at the Supreme Court level, can be very complex. When deciding cases, the Supreme Court often must consider any number of sources of law, including constitutions, statutes, and administrative agency regulations—as well as cases interpreting relevant portions of those sources. At times, the Court may also take demographic data, public opinion, foreign laws, and other factors into account. How much weight is given to each of these sources or factors will vary from justice to justice. After all, reasoning of any kind, including judicial reasoning, does not take place in a vacuum.

It is only natural that a justice's life experiences, personal biases, and intellectual abilities and predispositions will touch on the reasoning process. Nevertheless, it is expected that when reviewing a case, a Supreme Court justice does not start out with a conclusion (such as "I don't like this particular law that Congress passed") and then look for legal sources to support that conclusion.

## 14–5b Ideology and the Supreme Court

In contrast to the liberal Supreme Court under Earl Warren, today's Court is generally conservative. The Court began its rightward shift after President Ronald Reagan (1981–1989) appointed conservative William Rehnquist as chief justice in 1986, and the Court moved farther to the right as other conservative appointments to the bench were made by Reagan and George H. W. Bush (1989–1993).

**The Roberts Court** Many Supreme Court scholars believe that the appointments of John Roberts (as chief justice) and especially Samuel Alito (as associate justice) caused the Court to drift even further to the right.[17] Certainly, the five conservative justices on the bench during the Roberts Court's first five terms voted together and cast the deciding votes in numerous cases. The remaining justices held liberal to moderate views and often formed an opposing bloc.

A notable change in the Court occurred when Alito replaced retiring justice Sandra Day O'Connor. O'Connor had often been the "swing" vote on the Court, sometimes voting with the liberal bloc and at other times siding with the conservatives.

On the Roberts Court, the swing voter is usually Justice Anthony Kennedy, who is generally more conservative in his views than O'Connor was. Although Justice Kennedy dislikes being described as a swing voter, he often decides the outcome of a case. In the 2010–2011 term, for example, Kennedy was in the majority in more than 85 percent of the closely decided cases.

President Obama's naming of Justices Kagan and Sotomayor to the Court did not change its ideological balance. Both women joined the liberal bloc, but the men they replaced had been liberal as well.

Chief Justice John Roberts, Jr.

Justice Samuel Alito, Jr.

**The Supreme Court Today** In recent years, the nature of the Court's conservatism has come into sharper focus. It is a mistake to equate the ideology of the Court's majority with the conservatism, say, of the Republicans in Congress, or the ideology of the conservative movement. To be sure, there are members of the Court who are unmistakably *movement conservatives*. Justices Scalia and Thomas are in this camp.

Yet Justice Kennedy and Chief Justice Roberts—and even Justice Alito—often "march to their own drummer." A leading example was Chief Justice Roberts's ruling on Obamacare, in which he found that incentives to obtain health-care insurance could be written into the tax code. Any conservative hostility that Roberts may have felt toward the health-care reform legislation was clearly constrained by his commitment to judicial restraint. In contrast to this position, the four other conservative justices contended that the Affordable Care Act was unconstitutional as a whole. The four liberal justices believed that the *individual mandate* to obtain insurance followed from the Constitution's commerce clause.

Another area in which Court conservatives have frequently parted from the conservative movement is in their interpretation of the First Amendment's free speech requirements. Often, conservatives have hailed the Court's First Amendment rulings. One example was *Citizens United v. FEC*, which struck down campaign-finance restrictions (see Chapter 9 on page 213). In March 2011, however, the Court determined that

> **"THE CONSTITUTION ITSELF SHOULD BE OUR GUIDE,**
> not our own concept of what is fair, decent, and right."
>
> ~ HUGO L. BLACK ~
> ASSOCIATE JUSTICE OF THE
> UNITED STATES SUPREME COURT
> 1937–1971

members of a radical church had a First Amendment right to demonstrate at the funeral of a U.S. service member.[18] This ruling upset many conservatives and, for that matter, many liberals as well.

## 14–5c Approaches to Legal Interpretation

It would be a mistake to look at the judicial philosophy of today's Supreme Court solely in terms of the political ideologies of liberalism and conservatism. In fact, some Supreme Court scholars have suggested that other factors are as important as, or even more important than, the justices' political philosophies in determining why they decide as they do. These factors include the justices' attitudes toward legal interpretation and their perceptions of the Supreme Court's role in the federal judiciary. Two important judicial philosophies, both of which are often associated with conservative principles, are *strict construction* and *originalism*.

**Strict Construction** The term *strict construction* is widely used in the press and by politicians. Republican presidential candidates routinely promise to appoint justices who will interpret the Constitution strictly and not "legislate from the bench." The opposite of strict construction is *broad construction*. Advocates of strict construction often contend that the government should do nothing that is not specifically mentioned in the Constitution. In 1803, for example, some strict constructionists argued that the national government had no power to double the size of the country by purchasing the Louisiana Territory. Such radical strict constructionism had little support in 1803 and is accepted by few people today.

Despite the wide popularity of strict construction as a concept, members of the Supreme Court generally reject the description. Justice Antonin Scalia, for example, who is normally considered one of the purest examples of a strict constructionist on the Court, prefers to call himself a *textualist* instead. Scalia writes, "I am not a strict constructionist, and no one ought to be . . . . A text should not be construed strictly, and it should not be construed leniently; it should be construed reasonably, to contain all that it fairly means."[19]

What Scalia means by textualism is that when determining the meaning of legislation, he refuses to

Although often considered a conservative when he served on the Rehnquist Court, Justice Anthony Kennedy has typically held the "swing" vote on the closely divided Roberts Court.

AP PHOTO/DAN LOH

Justice Stephen Breyer          Justice Ruth Bader Ginsburg

Justice Clarence Thomas          Justice Antonin Scalia

consider the legislative debates that took place when the measure was passed, the nature of the problem the legislation was meant to address, or anything other than the actual text of the law.

**Original Intent** A second conservative philosophy is called *originalism.* Justice Thomas is a well known advocate of this approach. Originalists believe that to determine the meaning of a particular constitutional phrase, the Court should look to the intentions of the founders. What did the framers of the Constitution themselves intend when they included the phrase in the document? To discern the intent of the founders, justices might look to sources that shed light on the founders' views. These sources could include writings by the founders, newspaper articles from that period, the *Federalist Papers,* and notes taken during the Constitutional Convention.

**Originalism, Textualism, and Modernism** Such analysis, however, is precisely what textualists wish to avoid when it comes to assessing modern-day statute law. Nevertheless, Justice Scalia considers himself an originalist as well as a textualist. In the 2011–2012 term, Scalia was in agreement with Justice Thomas more than 90 percent of the time.

Originalism can be contrasted with what has been called *modernism.* Modernists seek to examine the Constitution in the context of today's society and to consider how modern life affects the words in the document.

***Lawrence v. Texas* as an Example of Originalism versus Modernism** For an example of how originalism and modernism contrast, consider *Lawrence v. Texas,* a 2003 case. The majority

opinion, written by Justice Kennedy, held that laws that criminalize same-sex intimate relations were unconstitutional under the Fourteenth Amendment.[20] An originalist could object to this judgment because the legislators who adopted the amendment never considered that it might apply to gay men and lesbians. In fact, both Scalia and Thomas opposed the ruling. In contrast, modernists might argue that discrimination against gays and lesbians is exactly the type of evil that the amendment sought to prevent, even though such an application never occurred to those who wrote it.

**FOR CRITICAL THINKING**

*If the president is able to replace one of the justices on the Supreme Court because of death or retirement, how might the new Court rule on abortion? On affirmative action?*

## 14–6 Assessing the Role of the Federal Courts

The federal courts have often come under attack, particularly in the last decade or so, for many reasons. This should come as no surprise in view of the policymaking power of the courts. After all, a Supreme Court decision can establish national policy on such issues as abortion, racial segregation, and gay rights. Critics, especially on the political right, frequently accuse the judiciary of "legislating from the bench." We discuss these criticisms

**LearningOutcome 14–6**

Identify some of the criticisms of the federal courts and some of the checks on the power of the courts.

in this chapter's *Perception versus Reality* feature on the facing page.

## 14–6a Criticisms of the Federal Courts

Certainly, policymaking by unelected judges and justices in the federal courts has serious implications in a democracy. Some Americans, including many conservatives, contend that making policy from the bench has upset the balance of powers envisioned by the framers of the Constitution. They cite Thomas Jefferson, who once said, "To consider the judges as the ultimate arbiters of all constitutional questions [is] a very dangerous doctrine indeed, and one which would place us under the despotism of an oligarchy."[21] This group believes that we should rein in the power of the federal courts, and particularly judicial activism.

## 14–6b The Case for the Courts

On the other side of the debate over the courts are those who argue in favor of leaving the courts alone. Several federal court judges have sharply criticized congressional efforts to interfere with their authority. They claim that such efforts violate the Constitution's separation of powers. James M. Jeffords, a former independent senator from Vermont, likened the federal court system to a referee: "The first lesson we teach children when they enter competitive sports is to respect the referee, even if we think he [or she] might have made the wrong call. If our children can understand this, why can't our political leaders?"[22]

Others argue that there are already sufficient checks on the courts, some of which we look at next.

**Judicial Traditions and Doctrines** One check on the courts is judicial restraint. Supreme Court justices traditionally have exercised a great deal of self-restraint. Justices sometimes admit to making decisions that fly in the face of their personal values and policy preferences, simply because they feel obligated to do so in view of existing law.

Self-restraint is also mandated by various established judicial traditions and doctrines, including the doctrine of *stare decisis,* which theoretically obligates the Supreme Court to follow its own precedents. Furthermore, the Supreme Court will not hear a meritless appeal just so it can rule on the issue.

Finally, more often than not, the justices narrow their rulings to focus on just one aspect of an issue, even though there may be nothing to stop them from broadening their focus and thus widening the impact of their decisions.

**Other Checks** The judiciary is subject to other checks as well. Courts may make rulings, but they cannot force federal and state legislatures to appropriate the funds necessary to carry out those rulings. For example, if a state supreme court decides that prison conditions must be improved, the state legislature has to find the funds to carry out the ruling or the improvements will not take place.

Additionally, legislatures can revise old laws or pass new ones in an attempt to negate a court's ruling. This may happen when a court interprets a statute in a way that Congress did not intend. Congress may also propose amendments to the Constitution to reverse Supreme Court rulings, and Congress has the authority to limit or otherwise alter the jurisdiction of the lower federal courts. Finally, although it is most unlikely, Congress could even change the number of justices on the Supreme Court, in an attempt to change the ideological balance on the Court. (President Franklin D. Roosevelt proposed such a plan in 1937, without success.)

## The Public's Regard for the Supreme Court

Some have proposed that Congress, not the Supreme Court, be the final arbiter of the Constitution. In debates on this topic, one factor is often overlooked: the American public's high regard for the Supreme Court and the federal courts generally. The Court continues to be respected as a fair arbiter of conflicting interests and the protector of constitutional rights and liberties.

Even when the Court issued its decision to halt the manual recount of votes in Florida following the 2000 elections, which effectively handed the presidency to George W. Bush, Americans respected the Court's decision-making authority—although many disagreed with the Court's decision. Polls continue to show that Americans have much more trust and confidence in the Supreme Court than they do in Congress.

**FOR CRITICAL THINKING**

*Why do you think that Americans trust the Supreme Court much more than they do Congress?*

# Perception versus Reality
## The Supreme Court Legislates from the Bench

Our Constitution gives legislative powers to the Congress exclusively. All executive powers are granted to the president. And all judicial powers are given to the judiciary. The United States Supreme Court is the final arbiter and interpreter of what is and is not constitutional. Because of its power of judicial review, it has the ability to "make law," or so it seems.

## THE PERCEPTION

Using the power of judicial review, the Supreme Court creates new laws. In 1954, the Court determined that racial segregation is illegal, a position that is universally accepted today but was hugely controversial back in the 1950s. The Court has also legalized sexual acts between same-sex adults and, of course, abortion. These decisions, especially the legalization of abortion, remain very divisive today.

Such decisions have had a major impact on the nature of American society. Because citizens elect members of Congress and the president only—and not members of the Supreme Court—it is undemocratic to allow these nine justices to determine laws for our nation.

## THE REALITY

The Supreme Court cannot actually write new laws. It can only eliminate old ones. When the Court threw out laws that criminalized adult sexual activity by gay men and lesbians, it was abolishing laws, not creating them. The Court does not have the power to legislate—to create new laws.

Consider what would happen if the Court decided that some basic level of health care is a constitutional right—a highly unlikely event. Could the Court establish mechanisms by which such a right could be enforced? It could not. It takes members of Congress months of hard work to craft bills that affect our health-care system. Such legislation fills thousands of pages and can be developed only with the assistance of large numbers of experts and lobbyists. The federal courts could not undertake such projects even if they wanted to.

The courts must decide how they will handle the cases that are brought before them. To do so establishes judicial policy. It does not constitute lawmaking. In any event, we have no alternative to judicial review when it comes to determining what is or is not constitutional. Without the Supreme Court, Congress and the president could make all sorts of laws that violate our Constitution and infringe on our rights, and there would be nothing to stop them. As Chief Justice John Roberts said during his confirmation hearings, "Judges are like umpires. Umpires don't make the rules; they apply them."

**BLOG ON** Plenty of bloggers follow the activities of the Supreme Court. You can find some of these blogs by searching on "us supreme court blog." One of the best is SCOTUSblog, sponsored by the law firm Goldstein & Russell. Another is the U.S. Supreme Court Blog, written by Paul M. Rashkind, a Florida lawyer.

# AMERICA AT
# ODDS The Judiciary

A Supreme Court decision can affect the lives of millions of Americans. For example, in 1973 the Supreme Court, in *Roe v. Wade*, held that the constitutional right to privacy included the right to have an abortion. The influence wielded by the Court today is a far cry from the Court's relative obscurity at the founding of this nation. Initially, the Supreme Court was not even included in the plans for government buildings in the national capital. It did not have its own building until 1935. Over time, however, the Court has established a reputation with the public for dispensing justice in a fair and reasonable manner. Still, Americans are at odds over a number of judicial issues:

- Are there terrorist suspects who must be detained indefinitely without trial to protect our safety—or is such an act a violation of our Constitution that does us more damage in the world than a detainee could possibly accomplish if freed?

- Should the United States Supreme Court accept more cases to provide a greater number of definitive rulings—or should it take on relatively few cases so that it can treat each one thoroughly?

- Should senators accept a Supreme Court nomination by a president of the opposing party whenever the nominee appears to have sound judicial temperament—or should senators vote only for those nominees who share their political philosophies?

- Should judges defer to the decisions of legislatures and administrative agencies whenever possible—or should they strictly police the constitutionality of legislative and executive decisions?

- Is it crucial that the Constitution be interpreted in terms of the beliefs of the founders—or should justices take account of modern circumstances that the founders could not have envisioned?

## TAKE ACTION

The founders attempted to insulate the federal judiciary from popular opinion, so it might seem difficult to take action in regard to it. There are points at which the public can exercise leverage, however.

### Lobbying Senators

One way for the public to influence the judiciary is to lobby senators over judicial appointments. Especially if one or more of your senators is of a different political party than the president, that senator is probably of two minds over a presidential nomination to the Supreme Court or any of the lesser courts. Such senators will pay special attention to letters and e-mail from constituents who oppose or support a nomination. If you have voted for the senator or the senator's party in the past, it is helpful to point that out.

### State Judicial Elections

Greater opportunities to take action exist at the state level, especially in states in which judges are either elected or must face the voters after appointment. A characteristic of state judicial elections is that most voters typically know nothing about the candidates. You can have an impact if you gather information and distribute it. Together with a group of your friends, you could research the candidates and pass on what you have learned, perhaps through an opinion piece in the campus newspaper. You may even be able to get academic credit for such an effort. It is very useful to determine the source of a candidate's campaign funds. A candidate who receives large contributions from businesses such as insurance companies that fear lawsuits may handle cases one way. A candidate who receives most of his or her funds from trial lawyers (who do the suing) may handle cases differently.

Family court judge David Guyton looks over documents in his Rock Hill, South Carolina, courtroom.

AP PHOTO/ALLEN BREED

## Ready to study?

- Review what you've read with the quiz below. Check your answers on the Chapter in Review card at the back of the book. For any questions you miss, read the corresponding Learning Outcome section again to prepare for class and your exam.
- Rip out and study the Chapter in Review card.

## ... Or you can go online to CourseMate

**at www.cengagebrain.com for these additional review materials:**

- Practice Quizzes
- Key Term Flashcards or Crossword Puzzles
- Audio Summaries
- Simulations, Animated Learning Modules, and Interactive Timelines
- Videos
- American Government NewsWatch

## Fill-In

1. Primary sources of American law include _____.

2. To bring a case before the Supreme Court, a party may request a _____, which is an order that the Court issues to a lower court requesting that court to send it the record of the case in question.

3. The attorneys involved with a case will present _____ to the Supreme Court, after which the justices discuss the case in conference.

4. A _____ opinion is a statement written by a justice who agrees with the Court's decision, but for reasons different from those outlined in the majority opinion.

5. Because of a practice known as _____, home-state senators of the president's political party may be able to influence the choice of a nominee for the U.S. district court in that state.

6. A restraintist judge or justice generally assumes that the courts should _____.

7. Two important judicial philosophies that describe justices' attitudes toward legal interpretation, both of which are often associated with conservative principles, are _____.

8. Congress can check the power of the courts in several ways, including _____.

## Multiple Choice

9. A precedent is best defined as a
   a. controversy that is not hypothetical or academic but real and substantial.
   b. court decision that furnishes an example or authority for deciding subsequent cases.
   c. ruling that a person has disobeyed a court order.

10. If a federal question is involved, a decision of a state supreme court may be appealed to the U.S.
   a. district courts.
   b. courts of appeals.
   c. Supreme Court.

11. The U.S. courts of appeals
   a. are the courts in which cases involving federal law begin.
   b. hear appeals from the U.S. district courts located within their respective judicial circuits.
   c. hear testimony and evidence before they make decisions in cases.

12. A nominee for the Supreme Court must be confirmed by a
   a. majority vote in the Senate.
   b. two-thirds vote in the Senate.
   c. majority vote in the House Judiciary Committee.

13. The power of the courts to decide on the constitutionality of legislative enactments and of actions taken by the executive branch is called
   a. judicial review.
   b. *stare decisis*.
   c. jurisdiction.

14. Justice _____ typically has held the "swing vote" on the closely divided Roberts Court.
   a. Antonin Scalia
   b. Clarence Thomas
   c. Anthony Kennedy

15. Judicial self-restraint is mandated by various judicial traditions and doctrines, such as _____, which theoretically obligates the Supreme Court to follow its own precedents.
   a. *curiae regis*
   b. *stare decisis*
   c. justiciable controversy

# 15

# Domestic Policy

The **Learning Outcomes** labeled 1 through 4 are designed to help improve your understanding of the chapter. After reading this chapter, you should be able to:

**15–1** Explain what domestic policy is, and summarize the steps in the policymaking process.

**15–2** Discuss the issue of health-care funding and recent legislation on universal health insurance.

**15–3** Summarize the issues of energy independence, global warming, and alternative energy sources.

**15–4** Describe the two major areas of economic policymaking, and discuss the issue of the public debt.

**Remember to visit page 364 for additional Study Tools**

SCOTT OLSON/GETTY IMAGES

# AMERICA AT
# ODDS

## Do We Send Too Many People to Prison?

Currently, there are about 2.3 million U.S. residents in prison or jail. That's roughly one in every one hundred adults. We are setting records—we have thirteen times the share of our population in prison as Japan, nine times more than in Germany, and five times more than in Britain.

Yet, in 1970, the proportion of Americans behind bars—the *incarceration rate*—was only one-fourth of what it is today. Not surprisingly, the number of drug offenders in prison is responsible for much of this increase. Such lockups have multiplied thirteenfold since 1980.

Holding that many prisoners is not cheap. It costs about $50,000 a year to house a convicted criminal in a state prison. Defense attorney Jim Felman of Tampa, Florida, said that America is conducting "an experiment in imprisoning first-time nonviolent offenders for periods of time previously reserved only for those who had killed someone." So, do we send too many Americans to prison?

## Keep Criminals behind Bars—It Works

Supporters of aggressive incarceration policies argue that still more criminals should be behind bars. Putting more people in prison reduces crime rates. After all, incentives matter. If potential criminals know that they will be thrown in jail more readily and stay there longer, they will have less incentive to engage in illegal activities.

Also, the crime rate is strongly determined by the number of criminals at large. When we remove a criminal from the streets and put that person in prison, the prisoner can no longer commit crimes that harm the public. This effect of removal is called *incapacitation*. The evidence shows that during the 1960s, when incarceration rates fell, the crime rate more than doubled. As incarceration rates rose sharply in the 1990s, the crime rate went steadily down. As a comparison, the risk of criminal punishment in England has been falling. In consequence, crime rates have risen in England while they have fallen in the United States.

Tough sentencing is effective. We should not turn career criminals loose on the streets.

## Too Many Laws and Too Many Prisoners

Those who argue against our high rates of incarceration point out that many individuals are convicted of nonviolent crimes. The government should not be spending $50,000 a year or more to keep such people in prison. Too many acts have been criminalized, particularly at the federal level. Many crimes are so vaguely defined that most Americans would not know if they were breaking the law. Granted, hard-core criminals should be behind bars. But what about the casual pot smoker? (In 2010, nearly 800,000 people were arrested for possession of marijuana.) Or someone convicted under a federal statute designed to protect the environment? Lying to a federal official is a felony. Who can say how many people might be imprisoned based on such an act?

Many states have "habitual-offender" laws. In California, for example, almost 4,000 individuals are serving life sentences because they were convicted of a third offense—one that was neither violent nor serious. The cost to society of putting drug users behind bars is much greater than the benefits. Wouldn't that money be better spent on rehabilitation?

## Where do you stand?

1. Could factors other than high incarceration rates be causing our current low crime rates? What might they be?
2. Why do you think federal, state, and local governments arrest so many drug-law violators?

## Explore this issue online

- You can find several articles in the *Economist*, a British magazine, arguing that the United States imprisons too many people. Search on "economist us prison."
- The Criminal Justice Legal Foundation is among the few groups that advocate increased rates of incarceration. See its arguments by entering "cjlf" into a search engine.

# Introduction

Whether we send too many people to prison is just one of the issues that confront our nation's policy-makers today. How are questions of national importance, such as this one, decided? Who are the major participants in the decision-making process?

To learn the answers to these questions, we need to delve into the politics of policymaking. *Policy,* or *public policy,* can be defined as a plan or course of action taken by the government to respond to a political issue or to enhance the social or political well-being of society. Public policy is the end result of the policymaking process, which will be described shortly. **Domestic policy,** in contrast to foreign policy, consists of public policy concerning issues *within* a national unit.

In this chapter, after discussing how policy is made through the policymaking process, we look at several aspects of domestic policy, including health-care policy, energy policy, and economic policy. We focus on these policy areas because they have been the Obama administration's top priorities. An additional priority for the administration is immigration reform. It is an open question, however, as to when this subject can be addressed. We consider immigration reform in this chapter's *Join the Debate* feature on page 346.

Bear in mind that although the focus here is on policy and policymaking at the national level, state and local governments also engage in policymaking and establish policies to achieve goals relating to activities within their boundaries. This is certainly true in relation to the criminal justice issues discussed in this chapter's opening *America at Odds* feature.

**domestic policy** Public policy concerning issues within a national unit, such as national policy concerning health care or the economy.

**policymaking process** The procedures involved in getting an issue on the political agenda; formulating, adopting, and implementing a policy with regard to the issue; and then evaluating the results of the policy.

**agenda setting** Getting an issue on the political agenda to be addressed by Congress; part of the first stage of the policymaking process.

## 15–1 The Policymaking Process

A new law does not appear out of nowhere. First, the problem addressed by the new law has to become part of the political agenda—that is, the problem must be defined as a political issue to be resolved by government action. Furthermore, once the issue gets on the political agenda, proposed solutions to the problem have to be formulated and then adopted. Issue identification and agenda setting, policy formulation, and policy adoption are all parts of the **policymaking process,** which is illustrated in Figure 15–1 on the facing page. The process does not end there, however. Once the law is passed, it has to be implemented and then evaluated.

**Learning Outcome 15–1**
Explain what domestic policy is, and summarize the steps in the policymaking process.

Each phase of the policymaking process involves interactions among various individuals and groups. The president and members of Congress are obviously important participants in the process. Remember from Chapter 6 that interest groups also play a key role. Groups that may be affected adversely by a new policy will try to convince Congress not to adopt the policy. Groups that will benefit from the policy will exert whatever influence they can on Congress to do the opposite. Congressional committees and subcommittees may investigate the problem to be addressed by the policy and, in so doing, solicit input from members of various groups or industries.

The participants in policymaking and the nature of the debates involved depend on the particular policy being proposed, formed, or implemented. Whatever the policy, however, debate over its pros and cons occurs during each stage of the policymaking process. Additionally, making policy decisions inevitably involves *trade-offs,* in which policymakers must sacrifice one goal to achieve another because of budget constraints and other factors.

### 15–1a Issue Identification and Agenda Setting

If no one recognizes a problem, then no matter how important the problem may be, politically it does not yet really exist. Thus, *issue identification* is part of the first stage of the policymaking process. Some group—whether it be the media, the public, politicians, or even foreign commentators—must identify a problem that can be solved politically. The second part of this stage of the policymaking process involves getting the issue on the political agenda to be addressed by Congress. This is called **agenda setting,** or *agenda building.*

FIGURE 15-1

# The Policymaking Process

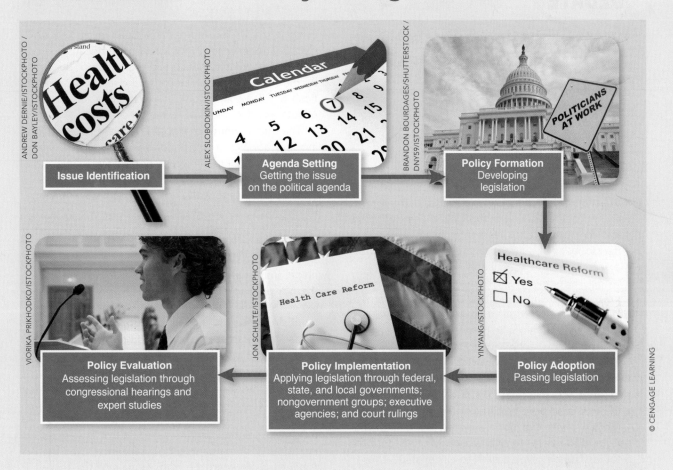

A problem in society may be identified as an issue and included on the political agenda when an event or series of events leads to a call for action. For example, the failure of a major bank may lead to the conclusion that the financial industry is in trouble and that the government should take action to rectify the problem. Dramatic increases in health-care costs may cause the media or other groups to consider health care a priority that should be on the national political agenda. Sometimes, the social or economic effects of a national calamity, such as the Great Depression of the 1930s or the terrorist attacks of September 11, 2001, create a pressing need for government action.

## 15–1b Policy Formulation and Adoption

The second stage in the policymaking process involves the formulation and adoption of specific plans for achieving a particular goal, such as health-care reform. The president, members of Congress, administrative agencies, and interest group leaders typically are the key participants in developing proposed legislation. Remember from Chapter 13 that iron triangles and issue networks work together in forming mutually beneficial policies. To a certain extent, the courts also establish policies when they interpret statutes passed by legislative bodies or make decisions concerning disputes not yet addressed by any law, such as disputes involving new technology.

Note that some issues may become a part of the political agenda but never proceed beyond that stage of the policymaking process. Usually, this happens when it is impossible to achieve a consensus on what policy should be adopted.

## 15–1c Policy Implementation

Because of our federal system, the implementation of national policies necessarily requires the cooperation of the federal government and the various state and local governments. A case in point is the Obama administration's Race to the Top program, which was

## Should Unauthorized Immigrants Be Given a Path to Citizenship?

Apart from Native Americans, all of us are either current immigrants or the descendants of immigrants. Yet immigration remains one of the most divisive issues facing Americans and their elected representatives today.

Congress has reacted in various ways to the issue of illegal immigration. At one time, it established an amnesty program to allow unauthorized immigrants who had been working in the United States for five years to obtain legal residency. More recently, it voted in favor of a large, secure fence on the U.S.–Mexican border to keep illegal immigrants out.

Most recently, the Obama administration initiated, through an executive order, a program to freeze the deportation of young persons brought into the country illegally before they were sixteen years old. Now such individuals can stay in the country and obtain work permits, renewable every two years, if they have graduated from high school or joined the military, are under thirty years old, and have lived here for five continuous years.

Today, there are approximately 11 million illegal immigrants living and working in this country. Should they be given a path to citizenship?

### How Can Any American Be against Immigration?

Some find the "close the door after me" mentality to be very un-American. Just remember, standards of living in the United States have been improving for decades not in spite of immigration but because of it. It's true that an unauthorized immigrant is not playing by the rules. But that is because the rules are so difficult to follow. We should make it easier for current unauthorized immigrants to become legal.

The vast majority of illegal immigrants are working and adding to this nation's well-being. The net taxpayer cost per immigrant is negative. They are normally not eligible to receive welfare benefits. They come here to work, not to receive government handouts.

### A Path to Citizenship Sends the Wrong Signals

Illegal immigrants have broken the law. If we give them a path to citizenship or even to legal status, we are sending the wrong signals to the rest of the world. As a result, we will end up with even more illegal immigrants, all of them hoping to find a path to citizenship one day.

Most unauthorized immigrants have few job skills. Immigrants without high school diplomas now head about a third of immigrant households. Certainly, this country can use more high-skilled immigrants—those with scientific degrees and Ph.D.s. Low-skilled immigrants, in contrast, simply take jobs away from Americans. To send the right signals to the rest of the world, we should also crack down on employers who hire illegal immigrants. These employers are adding to the problem.

**FOR CRITICAL ANALYSIS** How might we rationalize the inconsistency between our being a country of immigrants and wanting to keep out new ones?

---

included in the February 2009 stimulus package. Race to the Top was a competition among state governments to win up to $4.35 billion in federal education grants. The states competed by undertaking reforms to their kindergarten–through–high school educational systems. Reforms included performance-based standards for teachers and promotion of charter schools. All but four states entered the competition.

Successful implementation usually requires the support of groups outside the government. For example, the First Round Race to the Top winners—Delaware and Tennessee—were able to persuade their teachers' unions to support the reforms.

Policy implementation also involves agencies in the executive branch (see Chapter 13). Once Congress establishes a policy by enacting legislation, the executive branch, through its agencies, enforces the new policy. Furthermore, the courts are involved in policy implementation, because the legislation and administrative regulations enunciating the new policy must be interpreted and applied to specific situations by the courts.

## 15–1d Policy Evaluation

The final stage of policy-making involves evaluating the success of a policy during and following its implementation. Groups both inside and outside the government participate in the evaluation process. Congress may hold hearings to obtain feedback from different groups on how a statute or regulation has affected them.

Scholars and scientists may conduct studies to determine whether a particular law, such as an environmental law designed to reduce air pollution, has actually achieved the desired result—less air pollution. Sometimes, feedback obtained in these or other ways indicates that a policy has failed, and a new policymaking process may be undertaken to modify the policy or create a more effective one.

## 15–1e Policymaking and Special Interests

The policymaking steps just discussed seem straightforward, but they are not. Every bill that passes through Congress is a compromise. Every bill that passes through Congress is also an opportunity for individual members of Congress to help constituents, particularly those who were kind enough to contribute financially to the members' reelection campaigns.

KEVORK DJANSEZIAN/GETTY IMAGES

This T-shirt, seen at a demonstration in Los Angeles, opposes the deportation of students. It is based on a famous highway sign near the Mexican border that warns motorists of illegal immigrants attempting to cross the road.

**"THE MORAL TEST OF GOVERNMENT**
is how it treats those who are in the dawn of life, the children; those who are in the twilight of life, the elderly; and those who are in the shadows of life, the sick, the needy, and the handicapped."

~ HUBERT H. HUMPHREY ~
U.S. SENATOR FROM MINNESOTA
1971–1978

Consider the Emergency Economic Stabilization Act of 2008, known as the "bank bailout" bill. This was a $700 billion financial rescue plan that the U.S. Treasury Department urgently demanded on September 19, 2008. After the House defeated the initial "clean" version of the bill, the Senate drafted a second version. This second version was inserted into landmark health-care legislation requiring that insurance companies provide coverage for mental health treatment equivalent to that provided for the treatment of physical illnesses.

The bill also contained almost $14 billion in tax-break extensions for businesses. Special provisions benefited rural schools, film and television producers, makers of toy wooden arrows, victims of the 1989 *Exxon Valdez* oil spill in Alaska, rum distillers in the Virgin Islands and Puerto Rico, auto racetracks, and wool researchers. The second bill passed the House on October 3. Clearly, policymaking, particularly on the economic front, remains a complicated process.

## FOR CRITICAL THINKING

*What role do the media have in the agenda-setting process?*

## 15–2 Health-Care Policy

In March 2010, Congress passed the Patient Protection and Affordable Care Act and a companion bill. The two bills, which President Barack Obama immediately signed, contained health-care

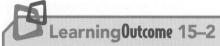

**LearningOutcome 15–2**
Discuss the issue of health-care funding and recent legislation on universal health insurance.

Promoting public health is one of the government's many health-care responsibilities. These students are part of a program to prevent disease through regular handwashing.

Americans—close to 16 percent of the population—still had no health-care insurance as of 2012.

Lack of coverage means that people may put off seeing a physician until it is too late to save their lives or be forced into bankruptcy due to large medical bills. One study has estimated that 20,000 people each year die prematurely because they lack health insurance.[1] (Others dispute these findings.) All other economically advanced nations provide health insurance to everyone, typically through a government program similar to Social Security or Medicare in the United States.

Before discussing the recently passed health-care reforms, let's first look at the programs that are already in place. The most important of these is **Medicare,** which provides health-care insurance to Americans aged sixty-five and over, and **Medicaid,** which funds health-care coverage for low-income persons.

reforms that were among the most consequential government initiatives in many years.

Even before the new legislation was adopted, the federal government was paying the health-care costs of more than 100 million Americans. When President Obama took office, the government was picking up the tab for about 50 percent of the nation's health-care costs. Private insurance was responsible for about a third of all health-care payments, and the rest was met either by patients themselves or by charity. Paying for health-care expenses, in other words, was already a major federal responsibility, and questions about how the government should carry out that function in the future were unavoidable.

Our current system for funding health care suffers from two major problems. One is that health care is expensive. About 17.4 percent of national spending in the United States goes to health care, compared with 11.3 percent in Canada, 10 percent in Sweden, and 8.5 percent in Japan. U.S. health-care costs have been rising for years, as you can see in Figure 15–2 on the facing page. Also, 50 million

## 15–2a Medicaid and Medicare

The federal government pays for health care in a variety of ways. Like many major employers, it buys health-care insurance for its employees. Members of the armed forces, veterans, and Native Americans receive medical services provided directly by the government. Most federal spending on health care, however, is accounted for by Medicare and Medicaid. Both are costly, and each in its own way poses a serious financial problem for the government.

**Medicaid**   A joint federal-state program, Medicaid provides health-care subsidies to low-income persons. The federal government provides about 60 percent of the Medicaid budget, and the states provide the rest. More than 60 million people are in the program. Many Medicaid recipients are elderly residents of nursing homes—the Medicare program does not pay for nursing home expenses.

The cost of Medicaid has doubled in the last decade, and this has put a considerable strain on the budgets of many states. About 17 percent of the average state general fund budget now goes to Medicaid. Recent cost-containment measures have slowed the growth of Medicaid spending, however. Another program, the **Children's Health Insurance Program (CHIP),** covers children in families with incomes that

**Medicare** A federal government program that pays for health-care insurance for Americans aged sixty-five years and over.

**Medicaid** A joint federal-state program that pays for health-care services for low-income persons.

**Children's Health Insurance Program (CHIP)** A joint federal-state program that provides health-care insurance for low-income children.

FIGURE 15-2

# Percentage of Total National
## Income Spent on Health Care in the United States

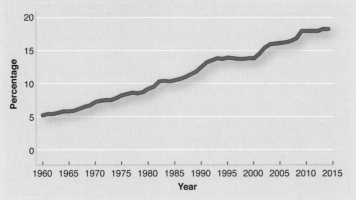

Source: National Health Expenditure Accounts, Centers for Medicare & Medicaid Services.

## 15–2b The Democrats Propose Universal Coverage

As noted earlier, the United States has been the only economically advanced nation that did not provide universal health-insurance coverage to its citizens. Democratic president Bill Clinton (1993–2001) and then-First Lady Hillary Clinton made a serious push for a universal plan during President Clinton's first term, but the project failed to pass Congress.

Many universal health-insurance plans—for example, the systems in Canada and France—involve government monopolies. In these nations, the government is responsible for providing basic health-care insurance to everyone through **national health insurance.** The plan that the United States has adopted, however, provides a larger role for the private sector.

are modest but too high to qualify for Medicaid. By fiscal year 2013, the total cost of Medicaid and CHIP for all levels of government was about $325 billion.

The Great Recession put a considerable strain on the states' ability to pick up their share of Medicaid payments. The Obama administration's February 2009 stimulus package, therefore, included $87 billion to reduce temporarily the Medicaid burden on the states. Congressional Democrats also substantially increased the size of CHIP within weeks of Obama's inauguration.

**Medicare** Medicare is the federal government's health-care program for persons sixty-five years of age and older. Medicare is now the government's second-largest domestic spending program, after Social Security. In 1970, Medicare accounted for only 0.7 percent of total annual U.S. national income (gross domestic product, or GDP). It currently accounts for about 3.3 percent of GDP, and costs are expected to soar as millions of "baby boomers" retire over the next two decades.

By 2030, the sixty-five-and-older population is expected to double. Further, technological developments in health care and the advancement of medical science are driving medical costs up every year. There are simply more actions that medical science can take to keep people alive—and Americans naturally want to take advantage of these services.

**Congress Addresses the Issue** As the legislative process began in 2009, all of the various proposals had common features. All assumed that employer-provided health insurance would continue to be a major part of the system. Large employers who did not offer a plan would be required to pay a penalty. Medicaid would be available to individuals with incomes up to about 1.5 times the federal poverty level. (In 2010, the poverty level for a family of four was $22,050.) A new health-insurance market-place, the Health Insurance Exchange, would allow individuals and small employers to shop for plans. Insurance companies would not be allowed to deny anyone coverage.

Most individuals would be required to obtain coverage or pay an income tax penalty. This requirement is known as the **individual mandate** or the *personal mandate.* Those with low-to-middle incomes would receive help in paying their

**national health insurance** A program, found in many of the world's economically advanced nations, under which the central government provides basic health-care insurance coverage to everyone in the country. Some wealthy nations, such as the Netherlands and Switzerland, provide universal coverage through private insurance companies instead.

**individual mandate** In the context of health-care reform, a requirement that all persons obtain health-care insurance from one source or another. Those failing to do so would pay a penalty.

premiums. Subsidies would be phased out for those earning more than four times the federal poverty level.

House legislation called for a government-sponsored insurance plan known as the *public option*. This plan would compete against private plans in the Health Insurance Exchange. The public option, however, was rejected by the Senate.

The individual mandate was also controversial, because it would require all Americans to have health insurance, whether they wanted it or not. Supporters of reform, however, pointed out that without an individual mandate, reform would not work. Any system that let healthy people avoid buying insurance would face financial collapse.

To fund the program, Congress adopted new tax rates for high-income persons on investments, the Medicare tax, and high-end "Cadillac" health plans.

### Support and Opposition

The Obama administration won considerable support for reform from interest groups that had opposed universal health-care systems in the past. For the first time, the American Medical Association was on board. The greater part of the opposition came not from interest groups but from conservatives.

Opponents were not just hostile to health-care reform. They were upset over what they saw as the growing power of government in general. They believed that health-care reform was only one of several steps toward a federal leviathan that would crush individual freedoms.

> "It helps to think of the government as **an insurance company with an army.**"
>
> ~ MIKE HOLLAND ~
> OFFICE OF SCIENCE AND
> TECHNOLOGY POLICY UNDER
> PRESIDENT GEORGE W. BUSH

### Expected Results

The bills that President Obama signed become effective over a period of several years. One immediate change is that young people can remain covered by their parents' insurance until they turn 26. Another immediate result is subsidies to small employers who obtain insurance plans for their employees.

The most important provisions, however, do not take effect until January 1, 2014. From that day on, subsidies will help citizens purchase health-care insurance if they are not covered by Medicaid or an employer's plan. Individuals and families with incomes up to four times the federal poverty level will be eligible for at least some subsidies. (Currently, the income cutoff would be $88,200 for a family of four, but the exact value will surely change.) About 32 million Americans who do not have health-care insurance will gain coverage.

### The Conservative Reaction

Conservatives argued that the Democrats had ignored the will of the people, who were against the reform legislation. In a typical poll in March 2010, 56 percent of respondents opposed Obamacare. That figure was slightly misleading, however. Only 43 percent opposed the reforms because they were "too liberal." Another 13 percent opposed them because they were "not liberal enough."

One last-ditch method of opposing the reforms was to challenge their constitutionality. Attorney generals in twenty states challenged the measure on the basis that the individual mandate violated the Constitution. (See Chapter 2's *Join the Debate* feature on page 41.)

In the end, the Supreme Court did not accept this argument. It did rule, however, that states could not be required to participate in the Medicaid expansion portion of the reforms. Obamacare addressed the health-insurance needs of the nation's lowest-income families through a substantial expansion in Medicaid eligibility. States that refused to participate would lose all of their Medicaid funding. A majority of the Court found this penalty to be too harsh.[2]

A second method of attack would be to repeal the legislation, and the Republicans made repeal part of their platform for the 2010 and 2012 elections. Republicans had plenty of time to win repeal, because full universal coverage would not go into effect until 2014. Repeal, however, would require specific legislation passed by Congress and signed by the president. To prevent a veto, a Republican president would be necessary. The Republicans would need to keep control of the House, and they would need sixty votes in the Senate to override a Democratic filibuster.[3] In the 2012 elections, the Republicans failed to win control of either the presidency or the Senate.

**FOR CRITICAL THINKING** *Is it reasonable for health care to continue to absorb increasingly larger shares of the nation's budget—or will that interfere too much with our country's ability to purchase other goods and services? Explain your reasoning.*

## 15-3 Energy Policy

**LearningOutcome 15-3**

Summarize the issues of energy independence, global warming, and alternative energy sources.

Energy policy was a second major priority for the Obama administration, but its accomplishments in this area have been relatively modest. The Democrats did move a major energy bill through the House in 2009, but it died in the Senate. Energy policy is important because of two problems: (1) our reliance on imported oil, and (2) the possibility of global warming.

### 15-3a The Problem of Imported Oil

Our nation currently imports 42 percent of its petroleum supply. This figure has fallen substantially in recent years. In 2005, imports were more than 60 percent of consumption. Still, oil imports are a potential problem largely because many of the nations that export oil are not particularly friendly to the United States. Some, such as Iran, are outright adversaries. Other oil exporters that could pose difficulties include Iraq, Libya, Nigeria, Russia, and Venezuela. Even Saudi Arabia, nominally a U.S. friend, is something of a question mark. Most of the terrorists who attacked the United States on 9/11 were Saudis, and many Saudis have anti-Western attitudes. A change of regime in Saudi Arabia could spell big trouble.

Some exporters, including Iraq, Libya, Nigeria, and Venezuela, have recently experienced drops in oil production due to internal disturbances. Fortunately for the United States, the sources of our imported oil are highly diversified, and we are not excessively dependent on any one nation. Canada and Mexico, friendly neighbors, supply 40 percent of our imports. Many of our European and Asian allies, however, are dependent on imports from questionable regimes.

**The Price of Oil**   Until fairly recently, the price of oil was low, and the U.S. government was under little pressure to address our dependence on imports. In 1998, the price per barrel fell below $12. In July 2008, however, on the eve of the collapse of the Lehman Brothers investment bank, the price of oil spiked to more than $125 a barrel, forcing U.S. gasoline prices above $4 per gallon. Thereafter, oil prices fell dramatically when demand collapsed due to the global economic panic. Experts believe, however, that oil prices will rise again. Indeed, even with our current economic troubles, the price of gasoline reached $4 per gallon in some states in 2011 and 2012.

**Fuel Efficiency Standards**   In the 1970s, the federal government responded to an earlier spurt in oil prices by imposing fuel-mileage standards on cars and trucks sold in this country. Under the **Corporate Average Fuel Economy (CAFE) standards,** each vehicle manufacturer had to meet a miles-per-gallon benchmark, which was averaged across all cars and trucks that it sold. Under the rules, trucks were allowed to consume more fuel. One unintended result was that when oil prices dropped in the 1980s, Americans began turning away from automobiles and toward pickups and SUVs, which were considered trucks under the standards.

The steep rise in oil prices in 2007 and 2008, plus the election of a Democratic Congress and president, meant that measures to restrain U.S. fuel consumption were on the agenda again. In 2009, President Obama issued higher fuel efficiency standards for cars and trucks. By 2016, the standards will be 39 miles per gallon for cars and 30 miles per gallon for light trucks. The standards began to take effect in 2010.

In August 2012, the Obama administration issued new rules that raised fuel efficiency standards even higher. By 2025, the nation's combined fleet of new cars and trucks must have an average fuel efficiency of 54.5 miles per gallon.[4]

Because of these government mandates, along with expected high fuel prices, vehicles that are more fuel efficient will almost certainly be part of America's future. Many of the new vehicles will run at least partially on electric power.

> **"NATURE PROVIDES A FREE LUNCH,**
>
> but only if we control our appetites."
>
> ~ WILLIAM DOYLE RUCKELSHAUS ~
> FIRST HEAD OF THE ENVIRONMENTAL
> PROTECTION AGENCY
> 1970–1973

**Corporate Average Fuel Economy (CAFE) standards** A set of federal standards under which each vehicle manufacturer (or the industry as a whole) must meet a miles-per-gallon benchmark averaged across all new cars or trucks.

### 15–3b Global Warming

Observations collected by agencies such as the National Aeronautics and Space Administration (NASA) suggest that during the last half century, average global temperatures increased by about 0.74 degrees Celsius (1.33 degrees Fahrenheit). Figure 15–3 below illustrates this phenomenon. Most climatologists believe that this **global warming** is the result of human activities, especially the release of **greenhouse gases** into the atmosphere.

A United Nations body, the Intergovernmental Panel on Climate Change (IPCC), estimated that during the twenty-first century, global temperatures could rise an additional 1.1 to 6.4 degrees Celsius (2.0 to 11.5 degrees Fahrenheit). Warming may continue in subsequent centuries.

The predicted outcomes of global warming vary, depending on the climate models on which they are based. If the oceans grow warmer, seawater will expand and polar ice will melt. (This last event is already under way.) These two developments will cause sea levels to rise, possibly negatively impacting some coastal areas. Rainfall patterns are expected to change, turning some areas into desert but allowing agriculture to expand elsewhere. Other likely effects could include increases in extreme weather.

**The Global Warming Debate** Some scientists working on climate issues dispute the consensus view of global warming. Those who dispute the consensus argue that any observed warming is due largely to natural causes and may not continue into the future. Although this position is rare among relevant scientists, it is extremely common in the broader community of Americans.

Public opinion polls taken in 2010 revealed that only a third of Americans believed that global warming is the result of human activities. Furthermore, attitudes toward global warming have become highly politicized. Some commentators on the political right contend that global warming is a giant liberal hoax designed to clear the way for increased government control of the economy and society. At the same time, many on the political left believe that the right-wing refusal to accept the existence of global warming threatens the very future of the human race.

Members of Congress are influenced by these attitudes even if they do not necessarily share them, and

**global warming** An increase in the average temperature of the Earth's surface over the last half century and its projected continuation.

**greenhouse gas** A gas that, when released into the atmosphere, traps the sun's heat and slows its release into outer space. Carbon dioxide ($CO_2$) is a major example.

---

## FIGURE 15-3

# Global Warming

This map shows the changes in average temperature around the world between two periods of time. The first period is the years from 1951 to 1980. The second is 2000 to 2010. Temperatures are in degrees Celsius (°C).

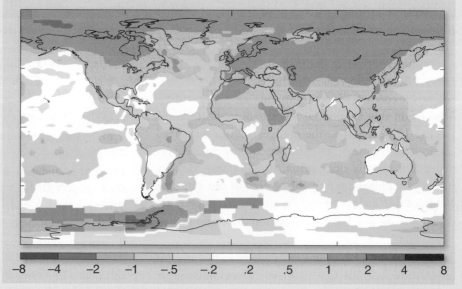

Source: NASA/GISS (Goddard Institute for Space Studies).

as a result, congressional Republicans and Democrats have almost no common ground on questions of how potential global warming might be reduced or its effects mitigated.

By 2012, belief that human activities were responsible for global warming had risen from one-third to about half of all respondents. Hot summers and widespread drought in 2012 may have contributed to these results.

## 15–3c New Energy Sources

The issues of U.S. energy security and potential global warming both raise the question of whether we can develop new energy sources. Energy security means finding energy sources that are produced either in this country or by friendly neighbors such as Canada. A reduction in global warming means deploying energy sources that do not release $CO_2$ and other greenhouse gases into the atmosphere. As explained next, however, new energy sources may be accompanied by problems.

### Expanded Supplies of Oil and Natural Gas

By 2012, many Americans began to realize that they were entering a new era of energy production based on dramatic technological improvements. U.S. oil production, which declined rapidly after 1985, began to grow again in 2009. As noted earlier, crude oil imports are at 42 percent of consumption, down from more than 60 percent. Strikingly, in 2011, U.S. exports of petroleum *products*—refined goods such as gasoline—exceeded imports for the first time since 1949.

Production from oil sands in Alberta, Canada, was not profitable given earlier, lower prices for petroleum. With gasoline prices approaching $4 per gallon, however, extraction is quite feasible. In the United States itself, novel extraction techniques have allowed oil companies to open new oilfields.

**THE NATURAL GAS BOOM.** An even more dramatic development is the increase in supplies of natural gas. Only a few years ago, experts believed that the United States would soon need to import natural gas. Because gas cannot be transported by ship efficiently unless it is converted to *liquefied natural gas* (LNG), imports would be costly.

By 2012, however, gas producers were planning to export LNG from terminals built to import it. The nation was running out of facilities to store all the new gas, some of which was simply flamed off into the atmosphere. Low natural gas prices plus new

air-pollution regulations made coal uncompetitive as a source of electricity. As a result, about one hundred coal-based power plants were closed or scheduled for retirement, and construction of new coal-based plants was at a standstill. Coal-producing regions such as eastern Kentucky and West Virginia faced serious economic difficulties.

An unexpected consequence of the boom in natural gas production was its environmental impact. Burning natural gas does release some $CO_2$ into the atmosphere, but less than half as much as coal. By 2011, U.S. emissions of $CO_2$ were actually down from 2008. The main cause was electricity generation using natural gas instead of coal. A more fuel-efficient national vehicle fleet added to the reduction.

**THE FRACKING REVOLUTION.** Why was it possible for the United States to ramp up oil and natural gas production so greatly during the last several years? The answer is an extraction technique known as hydraulic fracturing, or **fracking.** This method involves pumping a high-pressure mixture of water, sand, and chemicals into oil- or gas-bearing underground rock, usually shale. The water opens up seams containing oil or gas. The sand holds the seams open, and the chemicals make it easier for the oil or gas to flow out. Fracking is not actually a new technique. High prices of oil and gas combined with improvements in the process, however, have made fracking cost-effective.

New oilfields in Texas and North Dakota are based on fracking. Twenty states now produce natural gas through fracking, with some of the largest operations in Pennsylvania and Texas. A growing concern, though, is that the technology could lead to the contamination of underground water sources. Accordingly, various state governments are developing regulations aimed at preventing such contamination.

### Offshore Drilling
One method of reducing our reliance on foreign oil is

**fracking** Technique for extracting oil or natural gas from underground rock by the high-power injection of a mixture of water, sand, and chemicals.

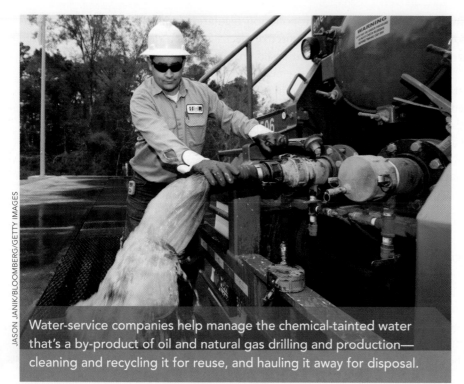

Water-service companies help manage the chemical-tainted water that's a by-product of oil and natural gas drilling and production—cleaning and recycling it for reuse, and hauling it away for disposal.

additional exploration and drilling for oil and natural gas in waters off the American coastline. For twenty years, however, the federal government prohibited offshore drilling in much of the ocean. The concern was that oil spills could severely damage the environment.

During the 2008 elections, Republicans demanded that vast new areas be made available for drilling. Barack Obama also endorsed additional drilling, but in fewer areas. In March 2010, Obama proposed opening up the Atlantic seaboard from Delaware to northern Florida, portions of the eastern Gulf of Mexico, and waters off the northern coast of Alaska.

In April 2010, three weeks after Obama's announcement, an offshore drilling platform in the Gulf of Mexico exploded and sank. Eleven workers died, and a torrent of oil and natural gas began flowing into the Gulf. The drilling platform was leased to BP, formerly known as British Petroleum. BP was unable to stop the leak until July. The well was permanently plugged in September. By that time, 4.9 million barrels of oil had spilled into the Gulf—the largest oil spill in American history.

In reaction to the disaster, President Obama placed a six-month moratorium on new deepwater-drilling projects. In the end, however, the impact of the BP oil spill on new drilling projects may prove to be temporary.

## Nuclear Energy

One energy source that cannot contribute to global warming is nuclear power—nuclear reactors do not release greenhouse gases. Still, due to concern over possible dangers and the difficulty of storing spent nuclear fuel, no new nuclear power plants have been built in the United States in more than thirty years. Because nuclear power appears to solve both the problems of energy security and greenhouse gas emissions, it recently attracted renewed interest. As of 2010, the construction of new plants was supported by most Republicans and some Democrats, including President Obama.

**PROBLEMS WITH COST-EFFECTIVENESS.** Only one new nuclear power plant is currently under construction, however. For a short period of time, the high price of other energy sources made nuclear power appear cost-effective. But uranium, which is used to power these plants, must compete on price with natural gas as a fuel for new power plants. Nuclear energy simply could not compete.

**NUCLEAR CRISIS IN JAPAN.** Nuclear power also suffered a severe blow in 2011 as a result of a series of linked disasters in Japan. In March, an earthquake of magnitude 9.0 shook the Pacific off the northeast coast of Japan. The quake generated a tsunami, a powerful sea wave at least 33 feet high and reaching 97 feet in one location. The coast was devastated, and more than 25,000 people died. Four reactors located on the coast were flooded so badly that three of them experienced "meltdowns," and radioactive material was released into the air. Experts believe that it will take years, even decades, to clean up the area. Following the disaster, support for new nuclear plants in the United States fell from 57 percent to 43 percent in opinion polls.

## Renewable Energy

Not all methods of supplying energy come with potentially hazardous by-products, such as greenhouse gases or nuclear waste. For example, hydroelectric energy, generated by water flowing through dams, is a widely used technology that employs no coal, natural gas, oil, or other fossil fuels.

Energy from such technologies is referred to as **renewable energy,** because it does not rely on extracting resources that can run out, such as oil, coal, or uranium ore. Obviously, renewable energy can reduce potential global warming. The problem is that most existing renewable technologies, such as solar power cells, are expensive. Hydropower is an exception, but the number of feasible locations for new dams in the United States is small, and dams create their own environmental problems.

One renewable technology that is almost as economical as conventional power sources is wind energy, and both the Bush and the Obama administrations have subsidized wind power. Windmills are now under construction in many locations. Of course, even if the price is right, wind power suffers from an obvious problem: the wind does not always blow, so wind cannot provide more than a modest share of the nation's electrical needs. Still, Obama's February 2009 stimulus package set aside billions of dollars for high-tension lines to transport electricity from rural wind farms to major cities.

Federal Reserve chair Ben Bernanke (right) sits with U.S. Treasury secretary Tim Geithner at a meeting of twenty leading nations (the so-called G-20). Since the financial crisis of 2008, the Fed and the U.S. Treasury have worked together much more closely than in the past.

**FOR CRITICAL THINKING** One possible way to reduce greenhouse-gas emissions would be to tax them by imposing a "carbon tax" on fuels that contain carbon. *Why hasn't Congress considered such a solution?*

## 15–4 Economic Policy

**LearningOutcome 15–4**

Describe the two major areas of economic policymaking, and discuss the issue of the public debt.

Under our current troubled economic conditions, policies that affect the economy are more important than any other set of activities the government undertakes. **Economic policy** consists of all actions taken by the government to address the ups and downs in the nation's level of business activity. National economic policy is solely the responsibility of the national government.

### 15–4a The Goals of Economic Policy

Everyone understands that the nation's economy passes through periods of "boom and bust," and that we recently experienced a major bust. Even in times when the economy has been less turbulent, however, the nation has alternated between periods of strong economic growth and periods of weak or no growth. This rhythm seems to be inherent in the capitalist system, and it is called the *business cycle.* A period in which the economy stops growing altogether and undergoes a contraction is called a **recession.** The most recent recession began in December 2007 and officially ended in June 2009. We say "officially," because even though economic growth resumed in 2009, the nation's economy is still operating well below its potential.

**Unemployment** The most important sign that the economy was still troubled was the high rate of **unemployment.** The rate of unemployment is measured by a government survey. People are defined as unemployed if they are

**renewable energy** Energy from technologies that do not rely on extracted resources, such as oil and coal, that can run out.

**economic policy** All actions taken by the national government to address the ups and downs in the nation's level of business activity.

**recession** A period in which the level of economic activity falls; usually defined as two or more quarters of economic decline.

**unemployment** The state of not having a job even when actively seeking one.

without a job and are actively looking for one. An unemployment rate of 8 percent—common throughout 2012—means that there are eight people looking for work for every ninety-two people who have a job. If "discouraged workers," who have given up looking for work, are also counted, the unemployment rate is substantially higher.

Even in the best of times, there is always a degree of unemployment, because some people are between jobs. Unemployment rates of 8 or 9 percent, however, are clear signs of economic and social distress. Few experiences are more psychologically damaging than extended unemployment. Reducing unemployment is a major policy objective.

**Inflation**   Unemployment and recession go hand in hand. A second economic problem that the government must occasionally address is associated with economic booms. That problem is **inflation**, a sustained rise in average prices. A rise in prices is equivalent to a decline in the value of the dollar. High rates of inflation were a serious problem in the 1970s, but rates have fallen since. Even though the rate of inflation is now relatively low, many people are fearful that high rates could return at some point in the future.

The government has two main tools to smooth the business cycle and to reduce unemployment and inflation. These tools are monetary policy and fiscal policy, and we describe them in the following sections.

## 15–4b Monetary Policy

One of the tools used in managing the economy is **monetary policy**, which involves changing the amount of money in circulation so as to affect interest rates, credit markets, the rate of inflation, the rate of economic growth, and the rate of unemployment. Monetary policy is under the control of the Federal Reserve System, an independent regulatory agency.

The Federal Reserve System (the Fed) was established by Congress as the nation's central banking system in 1913. The Fed is governed by a board of seven governors, including the very powerful chairperson. The president appoints the members of the board of governors, and the Senate must approve the nominations. Members of the board serve for fourteen-year terms. In addition to controlling the money supply, the Fed has a number of responsibilities in supervising and regulating the nation's banking system.

Although the Fed's board of governors acts independently, the Fed has, on occasion, yielded to presidential pressure, and the Fed's chairperson must follow a congressional resolution requiring him or her to report monetary targets over each six-month period. Nevertheless, the Fed has remained one of the more independent sources of economic power in the government.

**Easy Money, Tight Money**   The Fed and its **Federal Open Market Committee (FOMC)** make decisions about monetary policy several times each year. In theory, monetary policy is relatively straightforward. In periods of recession and high unemployment, we should pursue an **easy-money policy** to stimulate the economy by expanding the rate of growth of the money supply. An easy-money policy supposedly will lead to lower interest rates and induce consumers to spend more and producers to invest more.

In periods of rising inflation, the Fed does the reverse: it reduces the rate of growth in the amount of money in circulation. This policy should cause interest rates to rise, thus inducing consumers to spend less and businesses to invest less.

**"Pushing on a String"**   In theory, an easy-money policy sounds quite simple. The reality, however, is not simple at all. To give one example, if times are hard enough, people and businesses may not want to borrow even if interest rates go down to zero. The government cannot force anyone to borrow, after all.

This state of affairs is not hypothetical—it has characterized the economy since 2008. The Fed has managed to keep the interest rate for short-term federal obligations almost at zero, but rates of borrowing remain depressed. Instead of percolating into the

**inflation** A sustained rise in average prices; equivalent to a decline in the value of the dollar.

**monetary policy** Actions taken by the Federal Reserve Board to change the amount of money in circulation so as to affect interest rates, credit markets, the rate of inflation, the rate of economic growth, and the rate of unemployment.

**Federal Open Market Committee (FOMC)** The most important body within the Federal Reserve System. The FOMC decides how monetary policy should be carried out by the Federal Reserve.

**easy-money policy** A monetary policy that involves stimulating the economy by expanding the rate of growth of the money supply. An easy-money policy supposedly will lead to lower interest rates and induce consumers to spend more and producers to invest more.

actual economy, much of the extra money created by the Fed has piled up in excess bank reserves. With some reason, the failure of easy-money policy to spur the economy has been described as "pushing on a string."

The Fed has responded to the failure of its easy-money policy by adopting some unorthodox tactics. Ordinarily, the Fed expands the money supply by using the newly created money to purchase short-term federal government debt. In 2010 and 2011, however, it undertook a program of buying long-term federal debt in the hope that long-term purchases would be more effective than short-term ones.

**The Conservative Reaction**  The Fed's recent policies have alarmed many conservatives. A number of economists fear that at some point in the future the extra money created by the Fed—which is currently just sitting there—could pass into the real economy with explosive speed. The result would be increased inflation. In 2011, the Republican leadership in Congress sent a joint letter to the Fed demanding that it halt its activist policies. Texas governor Rick Perry, a candidate for president, went so far as to call the Fed's actions "treasonous."

A second response to the Fed's actions has been the growth in the philosophy of "hard money" among radical conservatives. Led by Representative Ron Paul of Texas, hard-money advocates believe that the government should not be in the business of creating money at all, but should tie the value of the dollar to commodities such as gold. Yet mainstream economists, both liberal and conservative, believe that such a policy would lead to a dramatic contraction in the money supply and a recession of unprecedented severity.

## 15–4c Fiscal Policy

Prior to the onset of the Great Recession, mainstream economists agreed on one point: under ordinary circumstances, monetary policy would be sufficient to steer the economy. If monetary policy proved to be inadequate, however, many economists also recommended use of a second tool—fiscal policy.

The principle underlying **fiscal policy,** like the one that underlies monetary policy, is relatively simple: when unemployment is rising and the economy is going into a recession, fiscal policy should stimulate economic activity by increasing government spending, decreasing taxes, or both. When unemployment is decreasing and prices are rising (that is, when we have inflation), fiscal policy should curb economic activity

by reducing government spending, increasing taxes, or both.

In the past, fiscal policy meant raising or lowering rates of taxation. Such changes could be accomplished quickly and would not trigger disputes about government spending. The severity of the Great Recession, however, led some economists to recommend increases in government spending as well.

> **fiscal policy** The use of changes in government expenditures and taxes to alter national economic variables.
>
> **Keynesian economics** An economic theory proposed by British economist John Maynard Keynes that is typically associated with the use of fiscal policy to alter national economic variables.

U.S. fiscal policy is associated with the economic theories of the British economist John Maynard Keynes (1883–1946). Keynes's theories, which we address next, were the result of his study of the Great Depression of the 1930s.

**Keynes and the Great Depression**  According to **Keynesian economics,** the nation cannot automatically recover from a disaster such as the Great Depression—or for that matter, the Great Recession. In both cases, the shock that initiated the crisis frightened consumers and businesses so much that they, in great numbers, began to reduce their borrowing and spending.

Unfortunately, if everyone in the economy tries to cut spending at the same time, demand for goods and services drops sharply. That, in turn, reduces the

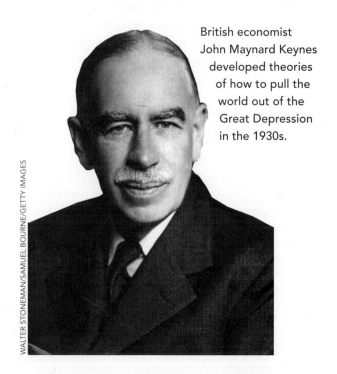

British economist John Maynard Keynes developed theories of how to pull the world out of the Great Depression in the 1930s.

WALTER STONEMAN/SAMUEL BOURNE/GETTY IMAGES

income of everyone selling these goods and services. People become even more reluctant to borrow and spend. The cycle feeds on itself.

The Keynesian solution to this type of impasse is for the government to provide the demand by a huge, if temporary, spending program. The spending has to be financed by borrowing. The government, in other words, begins borrowing when the private sector stops. Some economists believe that just such a spending program broke the back of the Great Depression—that is, the "spending program" known as World War II (1939–1945).

**Keynes and Obama**   If it took World War II to eliminate unemployment in the 1940s, Keynesian economics faces a problem today. The increase in the federal budget deficit necessary to end a great economic crisis could be very large. Some Keynesians outside the Obama administration calculated that, to have a real impact, a stimulus measure would have to be three times the $800 billion that was actually implemented.[5] Most of the larger program would have to involve spending, not tax-rate cuts.

That type of program, however, was politically impossible. Keynesianism was popular in the years after World War II when it meant relatively small changes to rates of taxation. In 2009, Americans, steeped as they are in small-government sentiment, would not accept new government spending programs amounting to trillions of dollars. By the time of his State of the Union address in 2010, Obama himself was employing rhetoric that was substantially anti-Keynesian.

We examine anti-Keynesian economic arguments in this chapter's *Our Challenging Times* feature on the facing page and also look at some Keynesian counterarguments.

## 15–4d  The Federal Tax System

The government raises money to pay its expenses in two ways: through taxes levied on business and personal income and through borrowing.

The American income tax system is progressive—meaning that as you earn more income, you pay a higher tax rate on the additional income earned.

The 2012 tax rates are shown in Table 15–1 on the right. More than 40 percent of American families earn so little that they have no income tax liability at all, and this figure temporarily hit 47 percent at the height of the recession. (For a discussion of the amount of taxes paid by the rich versus other groups in American society, see this chapter's *Perception versus Reality* feature on page 360.)

**The Action-Reaction Syndrome**   The Internal Revenue Code consists of thousands of pages, thousands of sections, and thousands of subsections. In other words, our tax system is not simple. Part of the reason for this complexity is that tax policy has always been plagued by the **action-reaction syndrome,** a term describing the following phenomenon: *for every government action, there will be a reaction by the public.*

Eventually, the government will react with another action, and the public will follow with further reaction. The ongoing action-reaction cycle is clearly operative in policymaking on taxes.

**Tax Loopholes**   Generally, the action-reaction syndrome means that the higher the tax rate—the action on the part of the government—the greater the public's reaction to that tax rate. Individuals and corporations facing high tax rates will react by making concerted attempts to get Congress to add various loopholes to the tax law that will allow them to reduce their taxable incomes.

Years ago, when Congress imposed very high tax rates on high incomes, it also provided for more loopholes. These loopholes enabled many wealthy individuals to decrease their tax bills significantly.

For example, special tax provisions allowed investors in oil and gas wells to reduce their taxable

**action-reaction syndrome** For every government action, there will be a reaction by the public. The government then takes a further action to counter the public's reaction—and the cycle begins again.

### TABLE 15–1

### Tax Rates for Single Persons and Married Couples: Tax Year 2011, Filed in April 2012

| Single Persons | | Married Filing Jointly | |
|---|---|---|---|
| Tax Bracket ($) | Marginal Tax Rate (%) | Tax Bracket ($) | Marginal Tax Rate (%) |
| 0–8,700 | 10 | 0–17,400 | 10 |
| 8,700–35,350 | 15 | 17,400–70,700 | 15 |
| 35,350–85,650 | 25 | 70,700–142,700 | 25 |
| 85,650–178,650 | 28 | 142,700–217,450 | 28 |
| 178,650–388,350 | 33 | 217,450–388,350 | 33 |
| Over 388,350 | 35 | Over 388,350 | 35 |

Source: Internal Revenue Service.

# OUR **CHALLENGING** TIMES

## Keynesian versus Anti-Keynesian Economics

Until recently, support for Keynesianism was relatively bipartisan. Republican president Richard Nixon once said, "I am now a Keynesian." Even President George W. Bush justified his tax cuts with Keynesian rhetoric. During the Obama administration, however, congressional Republicans strongly rejected Keynesianism. What alternative viewpoints were available?

### ANTI-KEYNESIAN ECONOMICS

For several decades, economists at a number of major universities have developed new schools of economic thought radically opposed to Keynesianism. By 2009, these ideas had gained a clear influence on conservative politicians. They included the following:

- *Even in a recession,* government cannot create net demand. Every dollar spent by the government comes out of the rest of the economy. Every dollar borrowed is a dollar that cannot be invested in productive private enterprise.

- Much of our current unemployment is *structural*—that is, it exists because of a mismatch between workers' skills and the available jobs. We don't need many construction workers anymore, and these people will not find work until they learn to do something else.

- Economic activity is also depressed because investors and businesspeople lack *confidence* about the future. They are unsure about how future regulations might interfere with their businesses. Above all, they are spooked by the size of the federal budget deficit and the future high taxes that they may have to pay to bring it under control.

It follows that the government should reduce regulation. Most importantly, it must spend less and cut the deficit. Fiscal austerity will build confidence and eventually heal the economy.

### THE KEYNESIAN RESPONSE

Keynesians have responses for each of these points. Briefly,

- The government can indeed create new demand if resources exist that are currently not in use. That is the case during periods of high unemployment.

- When unemployment is structural, some industries are short of labor. But unemployment currently afflicts all sectors. That is a sign of inadequate demand for goods and services.

- Keynesians agree that confidence is key, but they argue that it is the depressed economy itself that destroys confidence, by curbing demand. The impact of other factors is minor. Businesses aren't failing to hire because they are afraid of the deficit—but because they don't have enough customers.

### THE PEOPLE DECIDE

In the end, though, it doesn't matter whether Keynesians or anti-Keynesians win the argument on the scientific merits. If Keynesians propose policies that voters find unacceptable, then Keynesians lose the argument politically. Clearly, many voters believe it is the anti-Keynesian recommendations that make sense.

**YOU BE THE JUDGE** If the government did engage in large new spending programs, how hard would it be to halt these programs when unemployment returned to normal? Why?

income. Additional loopholes permitted individuals to shift income from one year to the next—which meant that they could postpone the payment of their taxes for one year. Still more loopholes let U.S. citizens form corporations outside the United States in order to avoid some taxes completely. We discussed tax loopholes in the *Join the Debate* feature in Chapter 6 on page 130.

# Perception versus Reality

## Tax-Rate Cuts Allow the Rich to Pay Lower Taxes

As the saying goes, only two things are certain—death and taxes. In recent years, though, different presidents have instituted a number of tax-rate cuts. A major reduction occurred in 2003 under the administration of George W. Bush.

### THE PERCEPTION

You often hear or read that the Bush tax-rate cuts favored the rich. After all, it's the rich who received the lion's share of the benefits from these tax-rate cuts.

### THE REALITY

First, we must distinguish between tax rates and taxes paid. It is true that the Bush tax cuts lowered the top marginal income tax rate from 39.6 percent to 35 percent and that the long-term capital gains tax rate dropped from 20 percent to 15 percent. Also, the rate applied to dividends fell. Therefore, the tax rates on the highest-income individuals did indeed fall after the tax cuts of 2003 were enacted.

At the same time, though, the percentage of taxes paid by the rich went up, not down. Indeed, the share of individual income taxes paid by the top 1 percent of income earners rose steadily from about 1981 to 2000, dropped off a bit from 2000 to 2003, and has risen ever since.

According to the nonpartisan Congressional Budget Office, the top 40 percent of income earners in the United States pay 99.1 percent of all income taxes. The top 10 percent pay more than 70 percent of all income taxes. At the bottom end of the scale, more than 40 percent of this nation's households pay no income taxes at all (though they do pay Social Security and Medicare contributions). Finally, it is true that the rich have been getting richer in the United States. Nevertheless, their individual tax liabilities have gone up more quickly than their share of income.

These data give us some indication of what may happen if Congress fails to extend the Bush tax cuts on the upper tax brackets. If these cuts expire, capital gains taxes will rise from 15 percent to 20 percent. The income tax rate for those making more than $250,000 per year will go up from 35 percent to 39.6 percent. Wealthy individuals, however, are likely to respond to these higher tax rates by adjusting their finances. The higher rates could actually result in the rich paying less in taxes, not more.

## BLOG ON

Scott Adams, creator of the *Dilbert* comic strip, makes hilarious and fresh observations about all sorts of things on his blog. Taxing the rich is just one of his topics—try searching on "dilbert blog tax 2007."

---

**Will We Ever Have a Truly Simple Tax System?** The Tax Reform Act of 1986 was intended to lower taxes and simplify the tax code—and it did just that for most taxpayers. A few years later, however, large federal deficits forced Congress to choose between cutting spending and raising taxes, and Congress opted to do the latter. Tax increases occurred under the administrations of both George H. W. Bush (1989–1993) and Bill Clinton (1993–2001). In fact, the tax rate for the highest income bracket rose from 28 percent in 1986 to 39.6 percent in 1993. Thus, the effective highest marginal tax rate increased significantly.

In response to this sharp increase in taxes, those who were affected lobbied Congress to legislate special exceptions and loopholes so that the full impact of the rate increase would not be felt by the wealthiest Americans. As a result, the tax code is more complicated than it was before the 1986 Tax Reform Act.

While in principle everyone is for a simpler tax code, in practice Congress rarely is able to pass tax-reform legislation. Why? The reason is that those who

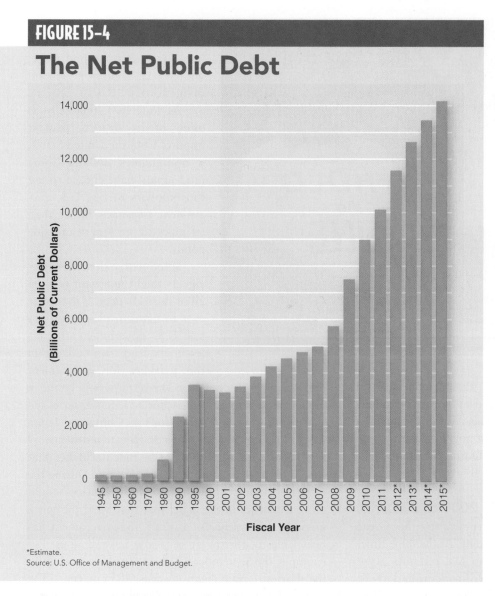

## FIGURE 15-4

# The Net Public Debt

**Net Public Debt (Billions of Current Dollars)** — *vertical axis: 0, 2,000, 4,000, 6,000, 8,000, 10,000, 12,000, 14,000*

**Fiscal Year** — *horizontal axis: 1945, 1950, 1960, 1970, 1980, 1990, 1995, 2000, 2001, 2002, 2003, 2004, 2005, 2006, 2007, 2008, 2009, 2010, 2011, 2012\*, 2013\*, 2014\*, 2015\**

\*Estimate.
Source: U.S. Office of Management and Budget.

The sale of these obligations to corporations, private individuals, pension plans, foreign governments, foreign companies, and foreign individuals is big business. After all, except for a few years in the late 1990s and early 2000s, federal government expenditures have always exceeded federal government revenues.

Every time there is a federal government deficit, there is an increase in the total accumulated **public debt** (also called the *national debt*), which is defined as the total value of all outstanding federal government borrowing. If the existing public debt is $5 trillion and the government runs a deficit of $100 billion, then at the end of the year the public debt is $5.1 trillion. Figure 15–4 on the left shows what has happened to the *net* public debt over time. (The net public debt doesn't count sums that the government owes to itself, although it does include funds held by the Fed.)

now benefit from our complicated tax code will not give up their tax breaks without a fight.

These groups include homeowners who deduct interest on their mortgages (and therefore the home-building industry as well), charities that receive tax-deductible contributions, and businesses that get tax breaks for research and development. Two other groups also benefit greatly from the current complicated tax code: tax accountants and tax lawyers.

## 15–4e The Public Debt

When the government spends more than it receives, it has to finance this shortfall. Typically, it borrows. The U.S. Treasury sells IOUs on behalf of the U.S. government. They are called U.S. Treasury bills, notes, or bonds, depending on how long the funds are borrowed. All are commonly called *treasuries*.

**The Burden of the Public Debt**  We often hear about the burden of the public debt. Some even maintain that the government will eventually go bankrupt. As long as the government can collect taxes to pay interest on its public debt, however, that will never happen. What happens instead is that when treasuries come due, they are simply "rolled over," or refinanced. That is, if a $1 million Treasury bond comes due today and is cashed in, the U.S. Treasury pays it off with the money it gets from selling another $1 million bond.

The interest on treasuries is paid by federal taxes. Even though much of the interest is being paid to American citizens, the more the federal

**public debt** The total amount of money that the national government owes as a result of borrowing; also called the *national debt*.

Every time Congress must raise the national debt ceiling, there are protesters who want the federal government to "Hold the Line."

government borrows to meet these payments, the greater the percentage of its budget that is committed to making interest payments. This reduces the government's ability to supply funds for anything else, including transportation, education, housing programs, and the military.

### Public Debt Explosion in 2009 to 2012

A response of the federal government to the Great Recession was to increase spending. At the same time, the economy was shrinking, so tax revenues were shrinking, too. Between increased spending and lower revenues, the federal budget deficit shot up. The deficit for 2011 was $1.3 trillion. That was about 8.6 percent of the entire economy. (The estimated deficit for 2012 was down to about $1.1 trillion.) If we look at all levels of government together, for every five dollars of spending, three were backed up by tax receipts. The other two were borrowed.

### Debt Held by Foreigners

An additional problem with a growing federal debt involves how much non-Americans own. Today, about half of the U.S. net public debt is owned by foreign individuals, foreign businesses, and foreign central banks. The largest debt holder is the People's Republic of China. The federal government owes China about $1.16 trillion. Japan is in second place, with $1.12 trillion in federal obligations.

As long as China sells us more of its exports than it imports from the United States, it accumulates dollars. China (and Japan) have chosen to use those dollars to buy U.S. government treasuries rather than to import more American-made goods.

Some worry that these foreigners might not want to keep all of this U.S. debt. If that were ever to happen, their efforts to sell U.S. government treasuries might lead to a collapse in the markets for government obligations in this country. The result would be much higher interest rates. If the value of U.S. treasuries fell sharply, however, countries such as China and Japan would lose tremendous sums on their investments.

There does not appear to be much evidence that such a disaster will happen anytime soon. During the recent economic crises, frightened investors bought more treasuries in the belief that they were the safest possible investment. As a result, the government has been able to borrow at very low interest rates. For example, the September 2012 rate for four-week bills, the shortest-term obligations, was 0.055 percent. (The rate for five-year notes was 0.625 percent, and the rate for thirty-year bonds was 2.75 percent.)

## FOR CRITICAL THINKING

*Why would anyone make an almost no-interest loan to the U.S. federal government?*

# ODDS Domestic Policy

The Preamble to the U.S. Constitution states that one of the goals of the new government was to "promote the general Welfare." Domestic policy is certainly the main way in which our government seeks to promote the general welfare. But how should this be done? Americans are at odds over many domestic issues. A few of them are listed here:

- Do we send too many people to prison—or do our current incarceration policies protect the public?

- Should unauthorized immigrants be given the opportunity to regularize their position—or would such a measure merely increase the number of illegal immigrants in the future?

- Should health-care insurance be a right of all citizens—or does such a program sap individual initiative and lead to an over-mighty government?

- Is global warming a serious problem that must be addressed now—or are the risks overblown and the proposed solutions a danger to our economy?

- Is new offshore drilling essential to our energy independence—or is it an unacceptable threat to the environment?

- Is a budgetary stimulus a necessary tool to fight recessions—or does it simply worsen the long-term budget deficit?

## TAKE ACTION

Consider taking action on the issue of *entitlement reform*. Entitlements are government programs that pay out to citizens who meet specified requirements. Social Security is an example. The government issues Social Security checks based on a recipient's age at retirement and past wage or salary income. Other entitlement programs include Medicare, Medicaid, and unemployment compensation. Entitlements lie at the heart of the political differences between liberals and conservatives. For liberals, entitlements are an essential part of the social compact that binds us together. For conservatives, entitlements breed a dangerous dependency on the government.

Entitlements are also an issue because they are expensive. They constitute almost half of all federal spending. And the sums involved are increasing. One reason is that the elderly are a growing share of the nation's population. Another is that the cost of health care is rising faster than the costs of other goods and services. In the future, will we pay higher tax rates to provide for entitlements, or preserve existing tax rates by cutting benefits?

Americans distrust "big government," but they also value the services that big government can provide. In 2012, a belief that Republicans were too enthusiastic about benefit cuts appears to have damaged the Romney presidential campaign.

These demonstrators in Boston, Massachusetts, are protesting proposed cuts to Social Security, Medicare, and Medicaid.

JOHN TLUMACKI/THE BOSTON GLOBE/GETTY IMAGES

Before taking action on entitlement reform, you can learn more by visiting the Web sites of organizations that take stands on the issues. The Heritage Foundation is a conservative think tank that favors cost containment. See its plans by searching on "saving the dream." The National Committee to Preserve Social Security and Medicare is everything that its name suggests. Find it by searching on "ncpssm."

# STUDY TOOLS

## Ready to study?

- Review what you've read with the quiz below. Check your answers on the Chapter in Review card at the back of the book. For any questions you miss, read the corresponding Learning Outcome section again to prepare for class and your exam.
- Rip out and study the Chapter in Review card.

## . . . Or you can go online to CourseMate

at www.cengagebrain.com **for these additional review materials:**

- Practice Quizzes
- Key Term Flashcards or Crossword Puzzles
- Audio Summaries
- Simulations, Animated Learning Modules, and Interactive Timelines
- Videos
- American Government NewsWatch

## Fill-In

1. The stages of the policymaking process are _____.

2. _____ is now the federal government's second-largest domestic spending program, after Social Security.

3. The individual mandate in the 2010 health-care reform legislation is a requirement that _____.

4. The nations of _____ supply 40 percent of our oil imports.

5. The predicted outcomes of global warming include _____.

6. Renewable energy technologies include _____.

7. A period in which the economy stops growing altogether and undergoes a contraction is called a _____.

8. Monetary policy is under the control of the _____, an independent regulatory agency.

9. Today, about half of the U.S. net public debt is owned by foreign individuals, foreign businesses, and foreign central banks. The largest debt holder is _____.

## Multiple Choice

10. A discussion in the media about a problem that might have a political solution is an example of
    a. policy adoption.
    b. policy implementation.
    c. issue identification.

11. About ____ percent of national spending in the United States goes to health care.
    a. 4
    b. 17.4
    c. 29.5

12. One immediate change brought about by the health-care reform bills that passed in 2010 was that young people can remain covered by their parents' insurance until they turn
    a. 26.
    b. 21.
    c. 18.

13. The CAFE standards
    a. regulate offshore drilling.
    b. measure the effect of greenhouse gases.
    c. set a miles-per-gallon benchmark that each vehicle manufacturer (or the industry as a whole) must meet, averaged across all new cars or trucks.

14. _____ policy uses changes in government expenditures and taxes to alter national economic variables.
    a. Monetary
    b. Fiscal
    c. Domestic

15. According to the nonpartisan Congressional Budget Office, more than ____ percent of this nation's households pay no income taxes at all.
    a. 10
    b. 23
    c. 40

# Foreign Policy

MARK WILSON/GETTY IMAGES

The **Learning Outcomes** labeled 1 through 6 are designed to help improve your understanding of the chapter. After reading this chapter, you should be able to:

**16–1** Discuss how foreign policy is made, and identify the key players in this process.

**16–2** Summarize the history of American foreign policy through the years.

**16–3** Identify the foreign policy challenges presented by terrorism.

**16–4** Explain the principal issues dividing the Israelis and the Palestinians and the solutions proposed by the international community.

**16–5** Outline some of the actions taken by the United States to curb the threat of nuclear weapons.

**16–6** Describe China's emerging role as a world power.

**Remember to visit page 387 for additional Study Tools**

# AMERICA AT
# ODDS
## Do Russia's Ambitions Mean Trouble?

ASTAPKOVICH VLADIMIR/ITAR-TASS/LANDOV

In August 2008, the Russian army invaded the small neighboring country of Georgia. The invasion was Russia's first use of troops outside its own borders since the dissolution of the Soviet Union in 1991. Many people around the world drew the obvious conclusion: the "Russian bear" was back—and it posed a threat to world peace.

During the years of the Cold War, from the late 1940s until the end of the 1980s, the Russian-dominated Soviet Union clearly was a threat to peace. The Soviets had occupied Eastern Europe. By the 1960s, even the Chinese were worried that the Soviets might attack them. Soviet nuclear weapons were at least equal to those of the United States. In 1985, the Soviet Union also had a population of 278 million, compared with 238 million in the United States.

The impact of the Soviet breakup on Russian power was almost beyond belief. With the loss of the fourteen other Soviet republics, Russia's population fell to 149 million. Its economy was in a state of collapse. Its inventory of main battle tanks had fallen from 51,000 to 19,500.[1] Russia was unable to prevent its former "satellite states" in Eastern Europe from joining NATO, the American-led alliance originally established to defend the West against the Soviets.

Russia today is nowhere near as formidable as the Soviet Union was—but how much of a threat is it, really? Americans who take an interest in foreign affairs are at odds over this issue.

## A Stronger Russia Is Bad News

Those who believe that Russia poses a threat to world peace point to its attack on Georgia, threats made against Ukraine, and the cyberwar it launched against the tiny nation of Estonia. Russia is regaining the economic power needed to support a large military. Its economy experienced a substantial recovery during the first two terms of President Vladimir Putin (2000–2008). Putin was popular, and his popularity was not damaged by the way he undermined Russia's democratic institutions. Putin reclaimed the presidency in 2012.

Russia is the world's largest exporter of natural gas and the second-largest oil exporter. It currently provides 33 percent of Europe's oil imports and 34 percent of its natural gas. Russia has repeatedly used its energy exports for political purposes. It has temporarily cut off gas supplies to Belarus, the Czech Republic, Georgia, Lithuania, and Ukraine.

## Russia's Future Looks Grim

Those who are less worried about the return of the Russian bear point out several factors that may undermine its future as a world power. In many countries, oil wealth has led to gross corruption and inefficiency, and this has happened in Russia. The greatest threat to Russia's future, however, is its collapsing population. Russia's population is now down to 143 million, and the United Nations estimates that it may fall to 126 million by 2050.

Several developed nations expect to lose people in forthcoming years. No nation, however, is experiencing losses that come close to what is predicted for Russia. If Russia is no longer one of the world's most populous countries, it will not be able to maintain its position as a great power. Russia has not only a low birth rate, but a very high death rate. The life expectancy of a Russian male is only about sixty-four years. Experts attribute this in part to extremely high rates of alcoholism among men.

## Where do you stand?

1. What factors might cause Russia to take a belligerent stand toward neighboring countries?
2. In 2009, President Barack Obama and Secretary of State Hillary Clinton stated that they would "push the reset button" in relations with Russia in an attempt to move beyond the negative feelings that had developed during the Bush administration. Was this attempt successful? Why or why not?

## Explore this issue online

- Entering "russia" into a search engine will provide background information from a variety of sources, including Wikipedia, the Central Intelligence Agency, the U.S. State Department, and the *New York Times*. Searching on "russia demographic" yields stories on Russia's decreasing population—and some arguments that the decline is overestimated.

# Introduction

What we call **foreign policy** is a systematic and general plan that guides a country's attitudes and actions toward the rest of the world. Foreign policy includes all of the economic, military, commercial, and diplomatic positions and actions that a nation takes in its relationships with other countries. Although foreign policy may seem quite removed from the concerns of everyday life, it can and does have a significant impact on the day-to-day lives of Americans.

American foreign policy has been shaped by two principles that are often seen as contradicting each other. One is **moral idealism,** the belief that the most important goal in foreign policy is to do what is right. Moral idealists think that it is possible for nations to relate to each other as part of a rule-based community. Moral idealism appeals to the often-held American belief that our nation is special and should provide an example to the rest of the world.

A contrasting view is **political realism,** the belief that nations are inevitably selfish. Foreign countries, therefore, are by definition dangerous. Foreign policy must be based on protecting our national security, regardless of moral arguments. Although there have been times when one or the other of these two principles has dominated, U.S. foreign policy has usually been a mixture of both.

## 16-1 Who Makes U.S. Foreign Policy?

### LearningOutcome 16–1

Discuss how foreign policy is made, and identify the key players in this process.

The framers of the Constitution envisioned that the president and Congress would cooperate in developing American foreign policy. The Constitution did not spell out exactly how this was to be done, though. As commander in chief, the president has assumed much of the decision-making power in the area of foreign policy. Nonetheless, members of Congress, a number of officials, and a vast national security bureaucracy help to shape the president's decisions and to limit the president's powers.

### 16–1a The President's Role

Article II, Section 2, of the Constitution names the president commander in chief of the armed forces. As commander in chief, the president oversees the military and guides defense policies. Presidents have interpreted this role broadly, sending American troops, ships, and weapons to trouble spots at home and around the world.

The Constitution authorizes the president to make treaties, which must be approved by two-thirds of the Senate. In addition, the president is empowered to form executive agreements—pacts between the president and the heads of other nations. These executive agreements do not require Senate approval.

The president's foreign policy responsibilities have special significance in that the president has ultimate control over the use of nuclear weapons. The president also influences foreign policymaking in the role of head of state. As the symbolic head of our government, the president represents the United States to the rest of the world. When a serious foreign policy issue or international question arises, the nation expects the president to make a formal statement on the matter.

### 16–1b The Cabinet

Many members of the president's cabinet concern themselves with international problems and recommend policies to deal with them. As U.S. power in the world has grown and as economic factors have become increasingly important, the departments of Commerce, Agriculture, Treasury, and Energy have become more involved in foreign policy decisions. The secretary of state and the secretary of defense, however, are the only cabinet members who concern themselves with foreign policy matters on a full-time basis.

**The Department of State** The Department of State is, in principle, the government agency most directly involved in foreign policy. The department is responsible for diplomatic relations with nearly two hundred independent nations around

**foreign policy** A systematic and general plan that guides a country's attitudes and actions toward the rest of the world. Foreign policy includes all of the economic, military, commercial, and diplomatic positions and actions that a nation takes in its relationships with other countries.

**moral idealism** In foreign policy, the belief that the most important goal is to do what is right. Moral idealists think that it is possible for nations to cooperate as part of a rule-based community.

**political realism** In foreign policy, the belief that nations are inevitably selfish, and that we should seek to protect our national security, regardless of moral arguments.

the globe, as well as with the United Nations and other multilateral organizations, such as the Organization of American States. Most U.S. relations with other countries are maintained through embassies, consulates, and other U.S. offices around the world.

As the head of the State Department, the secretary of state has traditionally played a key role in foreign policy-making, and many presidents have relied heavily on the advice of their secretaries of state. Since the end of World War II, though, the preeminence of the State Department in foreign policy has declined dramatically.

### The Department of Defense

The Department of Defense is the principal executive department that establishes and carries out defense policy and protects our national security. The secretary of defense advises the president on all aspects of U.S. military and defense policy, supervises all of the military activities of the U.S. government, and works to see that the decisions of the president as commander in chief are carried out. The secretary advises and informs the president on the nation's military forces, weapons, and bases and works closely with the U.S. military, especially the Joint Chiefs of Staff, in gathering and studying defense information.

The Joint Chiefs of Staff include the chief of staff of the Army, the chief of staff of the Air Force, the chief of naval operations, and the commandant of the Marine Corps. The chairperson of the Joint Chiefs of Staff is appointed by the president for a four-year term.

The joint chiefs regularly serve as the key military advisers to the president, the secretary of defense, and the National Security Council (described next). They are responsible for handing down the president's orders to the nation's military units, preparing strategic plans, and recommending military actions. They also propose military budgets, new weapons systems, and military regulations.

### 16-c Other Agencies

Several other government agencies are also involved in the foreign relations of the United States. Two key agencies in the area of foreign policy are the National Security Council and the Central Intelligence Agency.

> ## "TO BE PREPARED FOR WAR
>
> is one of the most effectual means of preserving peace."
>
> ~ GEORGE WASHINGTON ~
> COMMANDER OF THE CONTINENTAL ARMY
> AND FIRST PRESIDENT OF THE
> UNITED STATES
> 1789–1797

**The National Security Council**  The National Security Council (NSC) was established by the National Security Act of 1947. The formal members of the NSC include the president, the vice president, the secretary of state, and the secretary of defense, but meetings are often attended by the chairperson of the Joint Chiefs of Staff, the director of the Central Intelligence Agency, and representatives from other departments.

The national security adviser, who is a member of the president's White House staff, is the director of the NSC. The adviser informs the president, coordinates advice and information on foreign policy, and serves as a liaison with other officials.

The NSC and its members can be as important and powerful as the president wants them to be. Some presidents have made frequent use of the NSC, whereas others have convened it infrequently. Similarly, the importance of the role played by the national security adviser in shaping foreign policy can vary significantly, depending on the administration and the adviser's identity.

**The Central Intelligence Agency**  The Central Intelligence Agency (CIA) was created after World War II to coordinate American intelligence

SPENCER PLATT/GETTY IMAGES

Former Central Intelligence Agency director David Petraeus.

activities abroad. The CIA provides the president and his or her advisers with up-to-date information about the political, military, and economic activities of foreign governments.

The CIA gathers much of its intelligence from overt sources, such as foreign radio broadcasts and newspapers, people who travel abroad, the Internet, and satellite photographs. Other information is gathered from covert activities, such as the CIA's own secret investigations into the economic or political affairs of other nations.

These covert operations of the CIA may involve secretly supplying weapons to a force rebelling against an unfriendly government, or seizing suspected terrorists in a clandestine operation and holding them for questioning.

The CIA has tended to operate autonomously, and the details of its work, methods, and operating funds are kept secret. Intelligence reform passed by Congress in 2004, however, makes the CIA accountable to a national intelligence director. The CIA is now required to cooperate more with other U.S. intelligence agencies and has lost a degree of the autonomy it once enjoyed.

## 16–1d Powers of Congress

Although the executive branch takes the lead in foreign policy matters, Congress also has some power over foreign policy. Remember that Congress alone has the power to declare war. It also has the power to appropriate funds to build new weapons systems, equip the U.S. armed forces, and provide for foreign aid. The Senate has the power to approve or reject the implementation of treaties and the appointment of ambassadors.

In 1973, Congress passed the War Powers Resolution, which limits the president's use of troops in military action without congressional approval. Presidents since then, however, have not interpreted the resolution to mean that Congress must be consulted before military action is taken. On several occasions, presidents have ordered military action and then informed Congress after the fact.

A few congressional committees are directly concerned with foreign affairs. The most important are the Armed Services Committee and the Committee on Foreign Affairs in the House, and the Armed Services Committee and the Foreign Relations Committee in the Senate. Other congressional committees deal with matters that indirectly influence foreign policy, such as oil, agriculture, and imports.

## 16–2 A Short History of American Foreign Policy

Many U.S. foreign policy initiatives have been rooted in moral idealism. A primary consideration in U.S. foreign policy, though, has always been *national security*—the protection of the independence and political integrity of the nation.

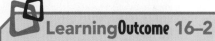

**LearningOutcome 16–2**

Summarize the history of American foreign policy through the years.

Over the years, the United States has attempted to preserve its national security in many ways. These ways have changed over time and are not always internally consistent. This inconsistency is because foreign policymaking, like domestic policymaking, reflects the influence of various political groups in the United States. These groups—including the voting public, interest groups, Congress, and the president and relevant agencies of the executive branch—are often at odds over what the U.S. position should be on particular foreign policy issues.

## 16–2a Isolationism

The nation's founders and the early presidents believed that avoiding political involvement with other nations—**isolationism**—was the best way to protect American interests. The colonies were certainly not yet strong enough to directly influence European developments. As president of the new nation, George Washington did little in terms of foreign policy. Indeed, in his Farewell Address in 1797, he urged Americans to "steer clear of permanent alliances with any portion of the

**isolationism** A political policy of noninvolvement in world affairs.

President James Monroe (1817–1825) said that the United States would not accept foreign intervention in the Western Hemisphere.

STOCK MONTAGE/GETTY IMAGES

true step toward interventionism occurred with the Spanish-American War of 1898. The United States fought this war to free Cuba from Spanish rule. Spain lost and subsequently ceded control of several of its possessions, including Guam, Puerto Rico, and the Philippines, to the United States. The United States thus acquired a **colonial empire** and was acknowledged as a world power.

The growth of the United States as an industrial economy also confirmed the nation's position as a world power. For example, in the early 1900s, President Theodore Roosevelt proposed that the United States could invade Latin American countries when it was necessary to guarantee political or economic stability.

### 16–2c The World Wars

When World War I broke out in 1914, President Woodrow Wilson initially proclaimed a policy of **neutrality**—the United States would not take sides in the conflict. The United States did not enter the war until 1917, after U.S. ships in international waters were attacked by German submarines that were blockading Britain.

Wilson called the war a way to "make the world safe for democracy." In his eyes, Germany was not merely dangerous but evil. Wilson, in short, was our most famous presidential advocate of *moral idealism*.

After World War I ended in 1918, the United States returned to a policy of isolationism. Consequently, we refused to join the League of Nations, an international body intended to resolve peacefully any future conflicts between nations.

But the U.S. policy of isolationism ended when the Japanese attacked Pearl Harbor in 1941. We joined the Allies—Australia, Britain, Canada, China, France, and the Soviet Union—to fight the Axis nations of Germany, Italy, and Japan. One of the most significant foreign policy actions during World War II was the dropping of atomic bombs on the Japanese cities of Hiroshima and Nagasaki in August 1945 in a successful attempt to force Japan to surrender.

### 16–2d The Cold War

After World War II ended in 1945, the wartime alliance between the United States and the Soviet Union began to deteriorate quickly. The Soviet Union opposed America's political and economic systems. Many Americans considered Soviet attempts to spread Communist systems to other countries a major

foreign world." During the 1700s and 1800s, the United States generally attempted to avoid conflicts and political engagements elsewhere.

In accordance with this isolationist philosophy, President James Monroe in 1823 proclaimed what became known as the **Monroe Doctrine**. In his message to Congress in December 1823, Monroe stated that the United States would not tolerate foreign intervention in the Western Hemisphere. In return, promised Monroe, the United States would stay out of European affairs. The Monroe Doctrine buttressed the policy of isolationism toward Europe.

### 16–2b The Beginning of Interventionism

Isolationism gradually gave way to **interventionism** (direct involvement in foreign affairs). The first

**Monroe Doctrine** A U.S. policy, announced in 1823 by President James Monroe, that the United States would not tolerate foreign intervention in the Western Hemisphere, and in return, the United States would stay out of European affairs.

**interventionism** Direct involvement by one country in another country's affairs.

**colonial empire** A group of dependent nations that are under the rule of a single imperial power.

**neutrality** A position of not being aligned with either side in a dispute or conflict, such as a war.

The United States entered World War II after the surprise Japanese attack on Pearl Harbor, Hawaii, on December 7, 1941.

known as the *Truman Doctrine*. It would be "the policy of the United States to support free peoples who are resisting attempted subjugation by armed minorities or by outside pressures."[2]

The Truman administration also instituted a policy of economic assistance to war-torn Europe, called the **Marshall Plan** after George Marshall, who was then the U.S. secretary of state. During the next five years, Congress appropriated $17 billion (about $165 billion in 2013 dollars) for aid to sixteen European countries. By 1952, the nations of Western Europe, with U.S. help, had recovered and were again prospering.

**THE CONTAINMENT POLICY AND NATO.** These actions marked the beginning of a policy of **containment** designed to contain (prevent) the spread of communism by offering threatened nations U.S. military and economic aid.[3] To make the policy of containment effective, the United States initiated a program of collective security involving the formation of mutual defense alliances with other nations.

In 1949, through the North Atlantic Treaty, the United States, Canada, and ten European nations formed a military alliance—the North Atlantic Treaty Organization (NATO)—and declared that an attack on any member of the alliance would be considered an attack against all members.

### The Cold War Begins

Thus, by 1949, almost all illusions of friendship between the Soviet Union and the Western allies had disappeared. The United States became the leader

threat to democracy. After the war ended, countries in Eastern Europe—Bulgaria, Czechoslovakia, East Germany, Hungary, Poland, and Romania—fell under Soviet domination, forming what became known as the **Soviet bloc.**

### The Iron Curtain

Britain's wartime prime minister, Winston Churchill, established the tone for a new relationship between the Soviet Union and the Western allies in a famous speech in 1946:

> An iron curtain has descended across the Continent. Behind that line all are subject in one form or another, not only to Soviet influence but to a very high . . . measure of control from Moscow.

The reference to an **iron curtain** described the political boundaries between the democratic countries in Western Europe and the Soviet-controlled Communist countries in Eastern Europe.

### The Marshall Plan and the Policy of Containment

In 1947, when it appeared that local Communists, backed by the Soviets, would take over Greece and Turkey, President Harry Truman took action. He convinced Congress to appropriate $400 million ($4.2 billion in 2013 dollars) in aid for those countries to prevent the spread of communism.

**THE TRUMAN DOCTRINE AND THE MARSHALL PLAN.** The president also proclaimed what became

**Soviet bloc** The group of Eastern European nations that fell under the control of the Soviet Union following World War II.

**iron curtain** A phrase coined by Winston Churchill to describe the political boundaries between the democratic countries in Western Europe and the Soviet-controlled Communist countries in Eastern Europe.

**Marshall Plan** A plan providing for U.S. economic assistance to European nations following World War II to help those nations recover from the war; the plan was named after George C. Marshall, secretary of state from 1947 to 1949.

**containment** A U.S. policy designed to contain the spread of communism by offering military and economic aid to threatened nations.

of a bloc of democratic nations in Western Europe, the Pacific, and elsewhere.

The tensions between the Soviet Union and the United States became known as the **Cold War**—a war of words, warnings, and ideologies that lasted from the late 1940s through the late 1980s. The term *iron curtain*, from Churchill's speech in 1946, became even more appropriate in 1961, when Soviet-dominated East Germany constructed the Berlin Wall, which separated East Berlin from West Berlin.

Although the Cold War was mainly a war of words and belief systems, "hot" wars in Korea (1950–1953) and Vietnam (1965–1975) grew out of the efforts to contain communism.

### The Arms Race and Deterrence

The tensions induced by the Cold War led both the Soviet Union and the United States to try to surpass each other militarily. They began competing for more and better weapons, particularly nuclear weapons, with greater destructive power.

This phenomenon, known as the *arms race*, was supported by a policy of **deterrence**—of rendering ourselves and our allies so strong militarily that our very strength would deter (stop or discourage) any attack on us. Out of deterrence came the theory of **mutually assured destruction (MAD)**, which held that if the forces of both nations were equally

Britain's Winston Churchill was a valuable ally of the United States during World War II.

capable of destroying each other, neither nation would take a chance on war.

### The Cuban Missile Crisis

In 1962, the United States and the Soviet Union came close to a nuclear confrontation in what became known as the **Cuban missile crisis.** The United States learned that the Soviet Union had placed nuclear weapons on the island of Cuba, ninety miles from the coast of Florida.

The crisis was defused diplomatically: a U.S. naval blockade of Cuba convinced the Soviet Union to agree to remove the missiles. The United States also agreed to remove some of its missiles near the Soviet border in Turkey. Both sides recognized that a nuclear war between the two superpowers was unthinkable.

### Détente and Arms Control

In 1969, the United States and the Soviet Union began negotiations on a treaty to limit the number of antiballistic missiles (ABMs) and offensive missiles that each country could develop and deploy. In 1972, both sides signed the Strategic Arms Limitation Treaty (SALT I). This event marked the beginning of a period of **détente**, a French word that means a "relaxation of tensions."

In 1983, President Ronald Reagan (1981–1989) nearly reignited the arms race by proposing a missile defense system known as the strategic defense initiative (SDI, or "Star Wars"). Nonetheless, Reagan and Soviet leader Mikhail Gorbachev pursued arms control agreements, as did Reagan's successor, President George H. W. Bush (1989–1993).

---

**Cold War** The war of words, warnings, and ideologies between the Soviet Union and the United States that lasted from the late 1940s through the late 1980s.

**deterrence** A policy of building up military strength for the purpose of discouraging (deterring) military attacks by other nations; the policy that supported the arms race between the United States and the Soviet Union during the Cold War.

**mutually assured destruction (MAD)** A phrase referring to the assumption that if the forces of two nations are equally capable of destroying each other, neither nation will take a chance on war.

**Cuban missile crisis** A nuclear standoff that occurred in 1962 when the United States learned that the Soviet Union had placed nuclear warheads in Cuba, ninety miles off the U.S. coast. The crisis was defused diplomatically, but it is generally considered the closest the two Cold War superpowers ever came to a nuclear confrontation.

**détente** French word meaning a "relaxation of tensions." Détente characterized the relationship between the United States and the Soviet Union in the 1970s, as the two Cold War rivals attempted to pursue cooperative dealings and arms control.

**The Dissolution of the Soviet Union** In the late 1980s, the political situation inside the Soviet Union began to change rapidly. Mikhail Gorbachev had initiated an effort to democratize the Soviet political system and decentralize the economy. The reforms quickly spread to other countries in the Soviet bloc. In 1989, the Berlin Wall, constructed nearly thirty years earlier, was torn down, and East Germany and West Germany were soon reunited in 1990.

In August 1991, a number of disgruntled Communist Party leaders who wanted to reverse the reforms briefly seized control of the Soviet central government. Russian citizens rose up in revolt and defied those leaders. The democratically elected president of the Russian republic (the largest republic in the Soviet Union), Boris Yeltsin, confronted troops in Moscow that were under the control of the conspirators. The attempted coup collapsed after three days. The Communist Party in the Soviet Union lost virtually all of its power.

The fifteen republics constituting the Soviet Union—including the Russian republic—declared their independence, and by the end of the year, the Union of Soviet Socialist Republics (USSR) no longer existed.

## 16–2e Post–Cold War Foreign Policy

The demise of the Soviet Union altered the framework and goals of U.S. foreign policy. During the Cold War, the moral underpinnings of American foreign policy were clear to all—the United States was the defender of the "free world" against the Soviet aggressor.

When the Cold War ended, U.S. foreign policymakers were forced, for the first time in decades, to rethink the nation's foreign policy goals and adapt them to a world arena in which, at least for a time, the United States was the only superpower.

Some have argued that the European Union, an economic and political organization of twenty-seven European states, could in time rival the United States. Others are skeptical, as you'll see in the *Our Challenging Times* feature on the following page.

U.S. foreign policymakers have struggled since the end of the Cold War to determine the degree of intervention that is appropriate and prudent for the U.S. military. Should we intervene in a humanitarian crisis,

"Soviet Union foreign policy is a puzzle, inside **a riddle wrapped in an enigma."**

~ WINSTON CHURCHILL ~
BRITISH PRIME MINISTER
DURING WORLD WAR II
1874–1965

such as a famine? Should the U.S. military participate in peacekeeping missions, such as those instituted after civil or ethnic strife in other countries? Americans have faced these questions in Bosnia, Kosovo, Rwanda, Somalia, and Sudan.

Yet no overriding framework emerged in U.S. foreign policy until September 11, 2001. Since that date, our goal has been to capture and punish the terrorists who planned and perpetrated the events of that day and to prevent future terrorist attacks against Americans. Sometimes, that goal has even involved "regime change," one of the objectives of the second Gulf War against Iraq in 2003.

**FOR CRITICAL THINKING**

The Cold War between the United States and the Soviet Union never turned into a shooting war. *Why not?*

## 16–3 The War on Terrorism

One of the most difficult challenges faced by governments around the world is how to control terrorism. Terrorism is defined as the use of staged violence, often against civilians, to achieve political goals. International terrorism has occurred in virtually every region of the world.

**Learning Outcome 16–3**

Identify the foreign policy challenges presented by terrorism.

The most devastating terrorist attack in U.S. history occurred on September 11, 2001, when radical Islamist terrorists used hijacked airliners as missiles to bring down the World Trade Center towers in New York City and to destroy part of the Pentagon building in Washington, D.C. A fourth airplane crashed in a Pennsylvania field after passengers fought back against the hijackers. In all, almost three thousand

## Dark Days in Europe

One of the most serious problems facing our troubled economy is not domestic in origin. Rather, it comes from Europe. In 2010, investors grew afraid that nations such as Greece, Ireland, Portugal, and Spain would be unable to repay their debts. They refused to buy bonds issued by the governments of these countries, precipitating a series of crises. By late 2011, some nations were in danger of financial collapse. Europe's troubles were a drag on our growth as well.

### A FISTFUL OF EUROS

Decades ago, European leaders had a dream of forging a common European union of nations so that world war could never happen again. To that end, they created the Common Market and later the European Union (EU). In 2000, sixteen of the EU's twenty-seven members adopted a common currency, the euro. This step may have been a major mistake.

Adoption of the euro meant that less-developed nations on the periphery of Europe could borrow as cheaply as core nations such as France and Germany. Investors in the core nations poured enormous sums into the periphery, much of it spent on new houses.

When the recession struck, it became clear that people in Greece, Ireland, Portugal, and Spain had borrowed too many euros and would have trouble paying them back. The problem was especially bad in Greece, where the government also had borrowed irresponsibly.

### PAYBACK TIME

Core "Eurozone" countries, such as France and especially Germany, were extremely reluctant to help out the Greeks. Germans did not see the Greeks as fellow Europeans, but rather as foreigners. Greece's problems, however, threatened to spread to other countries. The EU was forced to come up with large bailout packages to defend Greece, Portugal, and other troubled nations. Led by Germany, the EU then demanded that these nations enact austerity measures, slashing government spending and raising tax rates.

By late 2011, it was obvious that the bailouts were not large enough to resolve the issue. Greece, in particular, would probably never be able to repay all its debts. Some believe that the austerity measures demanded by the EU threw the euro periphery countries into severe recessions, reducing their ability to raise the funds needed to pay their creditors.

Unlike the members of the Eurozone, the governments of Britain, Japan, and the United States can never actually run out of money because their central banks can always "print" more of it. Unfortunately for the periphery nations, the European Central Bank (ECB) is prohibited by treaty from lending money directly to governments. In 2012, however, the ECB indicated that it would address the crisis. If necessary, it would buy government bonds on the open market, not directly from the governments themselves.

**YOU BE THE JUDGE** In the United States, no state-government crisis could possibly threaten the dollar. Why?

innocent civilians were killed as a result of these terrorist acts.

Other examples of terrorist acts include the Palestinian attacks on Israeli Olympic athletes in Munich in 1972; the Libyan suitcase bombing of an American airliner over Lockerbie, Scotland, in 1988; the bombing of two U.S. embassies in Africa in 1998; the bombing of the Navy ship USS *Cole* in a Yemeni port in 2000; and coordinated bomb attacks on London's transportation system in 2005.

## 16–3a Varieties of Terrorism

Terrorists are willing to destroy others' lives and property, and often sacrifice their own lives, for a variety of reasons. Terrorist acts generally fall into one of the three broad categories discussed next.

### Local or Regional Terrorism

Some terrorist acts have been committed by extremists who are motivated by the desire to obtain freedom from a nation or government that they regard as an oppressor.

Another motivation for terrorism is to disrupt peace talks. In Israel, for example, numerous suicide bombings by Palestinians against Israeli civilians have served to stall efforts to forge a lasting peace between Israel and the Palestinians.

The Irish Republican Army, which sought to unite British-governed Northern Ireland with the independent Republic of Ireland, conducted bombings and other terrorist acts in Northern Ireland and England over a period of many years. The attacks came to an end in 1997 as part of a peace process that lasted from 1995 until 2005.

Basque separatists in Spain have engaged in terrorism for decades. The separatists were initially—and incorrectly—blamed for bombing a commuter train in Madrid, Spain, on March 11, 2004. That terrorist attack, actually perpetrated by Islamic radicals, killed 191 people and injured hundreds of others.

The United States has also been the victim of homegrown terrorists. The bombing of the Oklahoma City federal building in 1995 was the act of vengeful extremists in the United States who claimed to fear an oppressive federal government. Although Timothy McVeigh and Terry Nichols, who were convicted of the crime, were not directly connected to a particular political group, they expressed views characteristic of the extreme right-wing militia movement in the United States.

### State-Sponsored Terrorism

Some terrorist attacks have been planned and sponsored by governments. For example, the bombing of Pan Am Flight 103, which exploded over Lockerbie, Scotland, in 1988, killing all 259 people on board and 11 on the ground, was later proved to be the work of an intelligence officer working for Libya.

The United Nations imposed economic sanctions against Libya in an effort to force Libyan dictator Moammer Gadhafi to extradite those who were suspected of being responsible for the bombing. More than a decade after the bombing, Libya agreed to hand the men over for trial.

The case of Pan Am Flight 103 illustrates the difficulty in punishing the perpetrators of state-sponsored terrorism. The victim country must first prove who the terrorists are and for whom they were working. Then it must decide what type of retribution is warranted.

### Foreign Terrorist Networks

A relatively new phenomenon in the late 1990s and early 2000s was the emergence of nonstate terrorist networks, such as al Qaeda. Al Qaeda is the nongovernmental terrorist organization that planned and carried out the terrorist

Smoke pours from the twin towers of the World Trade Center after they were hit by two hijacked airliners in a terrorist attack on September 11, 2001, in New York City.

ROBERT GIROUX/GETTY IMAGES

attacks of September 11, 2001. Its leader until his death in 2011 was the Saudi dissident Osama bin Laden.

Throughout the 1990s, al Qaeda conducted training camps in the mountains of Afghanistan, which was ruled by an ultraconservative Islamic faction known as the Taliban. After their training, al Qaeda operatives dispersed into small units across the globe, connected by e-mail and the Internet.

Before September 11, the U.S. government had monitored the activities and movements of al Qaeda operatives and had connected the terrorist attacks on two U.S. embassies in Africa and the bombing of the USS *Cole* to al Qaeda. In 1998, President Bill Clinton (1993–2001) ordered the bombing of terrorist camps in Afghanistan in retaliation for the embassy bombings, but with little effect. Al Qaeda cells continued to operate largely unimpeded until the terrorist attacks of September 11.

## 16–3b The U.S. Response to 9/11— The War in Afghanistan

Immediately after the 9/11 terrorist attacks, Congress passed a joint resolution authorizing President George W. Bush to use "all necessary and appropriate force" against nations, organizations, or individuals that the president determined had "planned, authorized, committed, or aided the terrorist attacks."

In late 2001, supported by a **coalition** of allies, the U.S. military attacked al Qaeda camps in Afghanistan and the ruling Taliban regime that harbored those terrorists. Once the Taliban had been ousted, the United States helped to establish a government in Afghanistan that did not support terrorism. Instead of continuing the hunt for al Qaeda members in Afghanistan,

> ## "FIGHTING TERRORISM IS LIKE BEING A GOALKEEPER.
> You can make a hundred brilliant saves but the only shot that people remember is the one that gets past you."
>
> ~ PAUL WILKINSON ~
> BRITISH TERRORISM EXPERT
> B. 1937

**coalition** An alliance of nations formed to undertake a foreign policy action, particularly a military action. A coalition is often a temporary alliance that dissolves after the action is concluded.

**weapons of mass destruction** Chemical, biological, or nuclear weapons that can inflict massive casualties.

however, the Bush administration increasingly looked to Iraq as a threat to U.S. security.

## 16–3c The Focus on Iraq

On March 20, 2003, U.S. and British forces attacked the nation of Iraq. Iraqi military units crumbled quickly. Saddam Hussein, Iraq's dictator, was captured in December and executed in 2006.

**The First Gulf War** The Iraq War was in fact the second U.S. conflict with that country. In 1990, Hussein attacked and occupied Kuwait, a small neighboring country. This unprovoked aggression was perhaps the most flagrant violation of international law since World War II. U.S. President George H. W. Bush (George W. Bush's father) organized an international coalition to free Kuwait. The coalition forces did not advance into Iraq to unseat Hussein, however.

**Reasons for the Second War** The ceasefire that ended the conflict required Iraq to submit to inspections for chemical, biological, and nuclear weapons—**weapons of mass destruction.** In 1998, however, Hussein ceased to cooperate with the inspections. The George W. Bush administration believed that Hussein was developing an atomic bomb and that the Iraqi regime was in some way responsible for the 9/11 terrorist attacks. (Both beliefs later proved to be incorrect.) Bush sought United Nations support for the use of military force, but China, France, and Russia blocked the move. In March 2003, Bush told Hussein to leave Iraq or face war. Hussein was defiant, and war followed.

**Rise and Fall of the Insurgency** Iraq is divided into three main ethnic or religious groups. Kurdish-speaking people live in the north. Arabs of the Sunni branch of Islam were Hussein's strongest supporters. A majority of the population, however, are Arabs who follow Shiite Islam. Sunni rebels soon launched an insurrection against the occupation forces. The insurgents used terrorist tactics to kill occupation forces and Iraqis cooperating with the Americans.

In 2005, Iraqi voters chose a new government in the first free elections in half a century. Shiite Muslims

JOHN CANTLIE/GETTY IMAGES

U.S. soldiers discuss with a village elder in Afghanistan what will happen after the draw-down of NATO forces.

In 2004, Hamid Karzai became the first democratically elected president of Afghanistan, and in 2005, Afghans elected a parliament. By 2006, however, the Taliban had regrouped and were waging a war of insurgency against the new government. The United States and its NATO allies were now the new government's principal military defenders.

**The Afghan-Pakistani Border** A problem for the coalition forces was that the Taliban were able to take shelter on the far side of the Afghan-Pakistani border, in Pakistan's Federally Administered Tribal Areas. These districts are largely free from central government control. For several years, the United States complained that the government of Pakistan was not doing enough to keep the Taliban out of the Tribal Areas.

In 2009, Taliban forces began to take complete control of districts in the Tribal Areas and in adjacent districts of the Northwest Frontier Province. Facing a direct challenge to Pakistan's sovereignty, the Pakistani military began to engage the Taliban forces in what soon became a major struggle.

dominated the new regime. Sunni insurgents, including the newly organized al Qaeda in Iraq, attacked not only U.S. and Iraqi government forces but also Shiite civilians. Shiite radicals responded with attacks on Sunnis, and Iraq appeared to be drifting toward interethnic civil war. American voters began to turn against the war, and in the 2006 elections they handed Congress to the Democrats.

Instead of withdrawing U.S. troops, however, the Bush administration increased troop levels in 2007. The "surge," as it was called, was surprisingly successful. Many Sunnis, who also had been terrorized by al Qaeda, turned against the insurgency and allied with the Americans.

With the insurgency fatally undermined, the United States planned its withdrawal. President Barack Obama announced that U.S. combat forces would leave Iraq by the end of August 2010, and the rest of the troops would be out by the end of 2011. In fact, U.S. forces departed slightly ahead of schedule.

> "**The risk** that the leaders of a rogue state will use nuclear, chemical, or biological weapons against us or our allies **is the greatest security threat we face.**"
>
> ~ MADELEINE ALBRIGHT ~
> U.S. SECRETARY OF STATE
> 1997–2001

**U.S. Troop Buildup** In February 2009, President Obama ordered 17,000 additional troops into Afghanistan. In October, Obama ordered an additional 30,000 troops to Afghanistan but pledged to start withdrawing U.S. forces by July 2011. A small number of troops were withdrawn in that month.

**U.S. Attacks in Pakistan** Under the George W. Bush administration, the CIA began operating remote-controlled aircraft known as Predators over Pakistan. Predators are equipped with small missiles, which were used to kill a number of

## 16–3d Again, Afghanistan

The war in Iraq tended to draw the Bush administration's attention away from Afghanistan, which was never completely at peace even after the Taliban were ousted from Kabul, the capital.

**Palestine Liberation Organization (PLO)** An organization formed in 1964 to represent the Palestinian people. The PLO has a long history of terrorism but for some years has functioned primarily as a political party.

Taliban and al Qaeda leaders. President Obama ramped up the Predator program significantly.

One result was increasing tensions with Pakistan, which could not openly support the Predator campaign. Pakistan's role in Afghanistan, in fact, has been quite complicated. The nation has been nominally allied with the United States. At the same time, Pakistan's intelligence agency, Inter-Services Intelligence (ISI), has funded a variety of Islamist militant groups, including units that have engaged in terrorist attacks on the government of Afghanistan and U.S. forces in that country.

**The Death of Bin Laden**   During the winter of 2010–2011, U.S. intelligence agencies learned that al Qaeda leader Osama bin Laden might be hiding in the Pakistani city of Abbottabad. On May 1, 2011, U.S. Navy Seals entered bin Laden's residential compound and killed him.

The reaction in America was one of relief and satisfaction. The reaction in Pakistan was quite different. Many Pakistanis considered the incident a violation of their country's sovereignty. American commentators speculated that bin Laden could not have hidden in Abbottabad without support from elements of the military, as that city is home to the Pakistan Military Academy.

**FOR CRITICAL THINKING**

Sometimes, it is possible to negotiate with certain terrorist groups, such as the Irish Republican Army, and "bring them in from the cold." *Why is such a strategy impossible with al Qaeda?*

# 16–4  The Israeli-Palestinian Conflict

The long-running conflict between Israel and its Arab neighbors has poisoned the atmosphere in the Middle East for more than half a century. Some experts have argued that resolving this conflict is key to solving additional problems, such as terrorism. Others doubt that a resolution would really have that effect. Regardless, the conflict has caused enough bloodshed and heartbreak over the years to deserve attention on its own merits. American presidents dating back at least to Richard Nixon (1969–1974) have attempted to persuade the parties to reach a settlement. Barack Obama is only the latest American leader to address the problem.

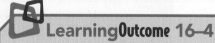

**Learning Outcome 16–4**

Explain the principal issues dividing the Israelis and the Palestinians and the solutions proposed by the international community.

## 16–4a  The Arab-Israeli Wars

For many years after Israel was founded in 1948, the neighboring Arab states did not accept its legitimacy as a nation. The result was a series of wars between Israel and neighboring states, including Egypt, Jordan, and Syria, waged in 1948, 1956, 1967, and 1973. Following the 1948 Arab-Israeli War, a large number of Palestinians—Arab residents of the area, known as Palestine until 1948—were forced into exile, adding to Arab grievances.

The failure of the Arab states in the 1967 war led to additional Palestinian refugees and the rise of the **Palestine Liberation Organization (PLO)**, a nonstate body committed to armed struggle against Israel. In the late 1960s and early 1970s, Palestinian groups launched a wave of terrorist attacks against Israeli targets around the world.

Following the 1973 Yom Kippur War, Egyptian president Anwar el-Sadat launched a major peace initiative. He traveled to Israel in 1977 and addressed the Israeli parliament, a major turning point. U.S. president Jimmy Carter (1977–1981) then sponsored intensive negotiations.

Egypt and Israel signed a peace treaty in 1979 that marked the end to an era of major wars between Israel and other states. Lower-level conflicts continued, however. On several occasions, Israel launched attacks against nonstate militias in Lebanon in response to incursions across the Israeli-Lebanon border. Israel and Jordan eventually signed a peace treaty in 1994, but no peace treaty between Israel and Syria has yet been negotiated, and the conflict between Israel and the Palestinians has remained.

## 16–4b The Israeli-Palestinian Dispute

Resolving the Israeli-Palestinian dispute has always presented more difficulties than achieving peace between Israel and neighbors such as Egypt. One problem is that the hostilities between the two parties run deeper. On the Palestinian side, not only had many families lost their homes after the 1948 war, but after the 1967 war, the West Bank of the Jordan River and the Gaza Strip fell under Israeli control. The Palestinians living in these areas became an occupied people.

On the Israeli side, the sheer viciousness of the Palestinian terrorist attacks—which frequently resulted in the deaths of civilians, including children—made negotiations with those responsible hard to imagine. A further complication was the series of Israeli settlements on the West Bank and the Gaza Strip, which the Palestinians considered their own. Settlers living on the West Bank had an obvious interest in opposing any peace deal that required them to move.

Despite the difficulties, the international community, including the United States, was in agreement on several principles for settling the conflict. Lands seized by Israel in the 1967 war should be granted to the Palestinians, who could organize their own independent nation-state there. In turn, the Palestinians would have to not only recognize Israel's right to exist, but also take concrete steps to guarantee Israel's security.

The international consensus did not address some important issues. These include what compensation, if any, should go to Palestinians who lost homes in what is now Israel. A second issue is whether Israel could adjust its pre-1967 borders to incorporate some of the Israeli settlement areas, plus part or all of eastern Jerusalem, which was under Arab control before 1967.

## 16–4c Negotiations

In 1993, Israel and the PLO met officially for the first time in Oslo, Norway. The resulting **Oslo Accords** were signed in Washington under the watchful eye of President Bill Clinton. A major result was the establishment of a Palestinian Authority, under Israeli control, on the West Bank and the Gaza Strip.

**Negotiations Collapse** Further attempts to reach a settlement in 2000 collapsed in acrimony. After the failure of these talks, an uprising by Palestinian militants led to Israeli military incursions into the West Bank and the almost complete collapse of the Palestinian Authority. Israeli prime minister Ariel Sharon, concluding that he had no credible peace partner, carried out a plan to unilaterally withdraw from the Gaza Strip in 2005 and also to build an enormous security fence between Israel and the West Bank. The fence came under strong international criticism because it incorporated parts of the West Bank into Israel.

**A Divided Palestine** In 2007, Gaza was taken over by Hamas, a radical Islamist party that refuses to recognize Israel. After the imposition of an Israeli blockade, Hamas launched missile attacks on Israel, which in turn briefly occupied the strip in December 2008. The West Bank remained under the control of the PLO-led Palestinian Authority, and so the Palestinians, now politically divided, were in an even worse bargaining position than before.

Developments in 2010 included an attempt in May by Turkish activists to "run" an Israeli blockade of Gaza with a flotilla of six ships. Israeli commandos seized the ships, but resistance by activists led to the death of nine passengers. The incident drew international attention to the blockade and criticisms of the Israeli ban on many ordinary consumer items. In June, Israel substantially eased the terms of the blockade.

On the West Bank, the Palestinian Authority succeeded in reestablishing itself as an effective government, and the territory

> "THE PURPOSE OF FOREIGN POLICY is not to provide an outlet for our own sentiments of hope or indignation; IT IS TO SHAPE REAL EVENTS IN A REAL WORLD."
> ~ JOHN F. KENNEDY ~
> THIRTY-FIFTH PRESIDENT
> OF THE UNITED STATES
> 1961–1963

**Oslo Accords** The first agreement signed between Israel and the PLO; led to the establishment of the Palestinian Authority in the occupied territories.

ALEX WONG/GETTY IMAGES

Secretary of State Hillary Clinton succeeded in getting Israeli Prime Minister Benjamin Netanyahu on the left, to shake hands with Palestinian Authority President Mahmoud Abbas.

Speaking at the UN, Obama opposed the Palestinian measures with some of the strongest pro-Israeli language by an American leader in years. The speech sharply improved Obama's approval ratings among the Israeli public. It sorely disappointed Arabs everywhere. It also revealed that the United States was no longer in the business of restarting Israeli-Palestinian negotiations. Obama was now running for reelection, and any serious U.S. participation in negotiations was off the table until after the 2012 elections.

entered a period of relative stability and economic growth.

**Obama and Netanyahu** On taking office, President Obama sought to restart the Israeli-Palestinian peace talks. The administration's attempts, however, met with failure. Obama initially believed that it was not enough to pressure only the Palestinians. America should also seek to persuade Israel to stop building new settlements on the West Bank. U.S. policy had always opposed the settlements, but the Bush administration had never pressed the issue.

In March 2009, however, Israel chose Benjamin Netanyahu as its new prime minister. Netanyahu's political coalition was unusually conservative, and he proved to be more reluctant to negotiate than previous Israeli prime ministers. A chill soon descended on U.S.–Israeli relations. One factor that made Netanyahu resistant to negotiations was uncertainty due to the "Arab Spring" that swept through the Arab world in 2011. We discuss the prospects of that movement in this chapter's *Perception versus Reality* feature on the facing page.

**The Palestinians and the United Nations** In September 2011, Mahmoud Abbas, president of the Palestinian Authority, appealed to the United Nations (UN) to recognize the West Bank and Gaza as an independent Palestinian state. This step had been planned for some time. It was vehemently opposed by Israel.

*Why do you think that Americans support Israel so strongly?*

## 16–5 Weapons Proliferation in an Unstable World

Although foreign policy in recent years has focused most visibly on Iraq and Afghanistan, the U.S. government has also had to deal with other threats to U.S. and

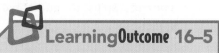

**LearningOutcome 16–5**

Outline some of the actions taken by the United States to curb the threat of nuclear weapons.

global security. The Cold War may be over, but the threat of nuclear warfare—which formed the backdrop of foreign policy during the Cold War—has by no means disappeared. The existence of nuclear weapons in Russia and in other countries around the world continues to challenge U.S. foreign policymakers.

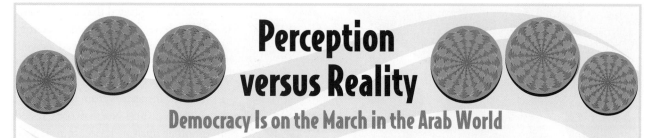

# Perception versus Reality

## Democracy Is on the March in the Arab World

Democracy has been rare in the Arab world. Absolute monarchs and ruthless dictators have ruled almost everywhere. Throughout 2011, however, a series of rebellions called the "Arab Spring" shook almost every Arabic-speaking country. Demonstrators overthrew dictators in Tunisia and Egypt. In Libya, the dictator Moammer Gadhafi was ousted and killed after a seven-month civil war. Elections were held in all three countries. In Syria, an uprising against the dictator Bashar al Assad continued through 2012 and led to thousands of deaths.

### THE PERCEPTION

In 2009, President Obama stated in Cairo, Egypt, that self-government and freedom "are not just American ideas, they are human rights." The rebellions of the Arab Spring demonstrate the truth of this assertion. In the end, democracy will triumph everywhere.

### THE REALITY

Even if democracy eventually prevails in the Arabic-speaking nations, no one should underestimate the difficulties in its path. The people of Egypt, Libya, and other countries have little experience with democratic practices, and there are powerful forces throughout the Arab world that will resist any movement toward popular self-government.

As journalist Fareed Zakaria has argued, freedom is more than elections.[4] It requires the protection of civil liberties and minority rights. It also requires widespread acceptance of election results, even if you disagree with the outcome. Consider Afghanistan, Iraq, and Pakistan (all Muslim, although only Iraq is Arab). In all three countries, the government is elected, but a huge share of the population still considers it illegitimate.

Consider Egypt, the largest Arab nation, with more than 83 million people. The young liberals who brought down dictator Hosni Mubarak are a small minority of the population. Overall, Egypt's people are among the most culturally conservative in the Arab world. Elections in 2011 and 2012 were won by the Muslim Brotherhood, the main Islamist movement.

In Libya, a militia group linked to al Qaeda attacked the U.S. consulate in Benghazi in September 2012, killing the ambassador and three other U.S. diplomats. Most Libyans were appalled, and local citizens sacked the militia's headquarters. Still, the incident proved that the new Libyan government was not fully in control of the country.

**BLOG ON** Entering "arab spring" into a search engine will provide ample background information on these movements, including articles claiming that the revolts will do more harm than good.

---

Concerns about nuclear proliferation mounted in 1998 when India and Pakistan detonated nuclear devices within a few weeks of each other—events that took U.S. intelligence agencies by surprise. Increasingly, American officials have focused on the threat of an attack by a rogue nation or a terrorist group that possesses weapons of mass destruction. Of most concern today are recent developments in North Korea and Iran.

## 16–5a North Korea's Nuclear Program

North Korea signed the Treaty on the Non-Proliferation of Nuclear Weapons in 1985 and submitted to weapons inspections by the International Atomic Energy Agency (IAEA) in 1992. Throughout the 1990s, however, there were discrepancies between North Korean declarations and IAEA inspection findings. In 2002, North Korea expelled the IAEA inspectors.

BULENT KILIC/AFP/GETTY IMAGES

These rebels in Syria continued to fight the existing dictatorial regime through 2012.

**Opening Negotiations** The administration of George W. Bush had been reluctant to engage in diplomatic relations with North Korea. Bush insisted that any talks with North Korea must also include all of North Korea's neighbors—China, Japan, Russia, and South Korea. In 2003, North Korea finally agreed to such talks.

Since that time, it has proved quite difficult to keep North Korea at the bargaining table—its representatives have stormed out of the talks repeatedly, for the most trivial reasons. China is the one power with substantial economic leverage over North Korea, and typically, Chinese leaders have been the ones to lead the North Koreans back to the table.

Tensions heightened in October 2006, when North Korea conducted its first nuclear test. Nevertheless, the Bush administration continued to participate with North Korea's neighbors in multilateral negotiations. In the spring of 2007, North Korea agreed that it would begin to dismantle its nuclear facilities and would allow UN inspectors into the country.

In return, the other nations agreed to provide various kinds of aid, and the United States would begin to discuss normalization of relations with North Korea. By mid-2007, North Korea had shut down one of its nuclear reactors and had admitted a permanent UN inspection team into the country.

**The Collapse of Negotiations** In April 2009, North Korea tested a long-range missile under the guise of attempting to launch a satellite. The UN Security Council voted to unanimously condemn the test. This vote demonstrated that the Chinese, who have a permanent Security Council seat, were annoyed as well. North Korea then pulled out of the six-party talks and expelled all nuclear inspectors from the country. In May 2009, North Korea tested another nuclear device, to universal disapproval.

In March 2010, tensions rose again after the sinking of a South Korean naval ship, the *Cheonan*, with the loss of forty-six lives. An investigation revealed in May that the sinking was due to a North Korean torpedo. In November, North Korea fired a series of artillery rounds at a South Korean island, killing four.

North Korea's aggressive behavior may have been linked to a succession crisis. In 2011, the dictator Kim Jong Il died, and was succeeded by his youngest son, Kim Jong Un. Kim Jong Il himself was the son of North Korea's first Communist dictator. North Korea, therefore, is unique in that it is effectively a Communist monarchy.

## 16–5b Iran: An Emerging Nuclear Threat?

In November 1979, militant students in Tehran, Iran, seized the U.S. embassy and took fifty-two American citizens hostage. The crisis lasted 444 days. Ever since, Iran and the United States have been at odds with each other.

In the years that followed, the rest of the world discovered that Iran was engaged in a covert nuclear program. Investigators for the International Atomic Energy Agency reported that Iran was enriching uranium that could be used in the fabrication of a nuclear bomb.

In spite of numerous UN resolutions, Iran is still producing uranium, and at a faster speed. The existence of a second uranium enrichment plant was made public in the fall of 2009. Simultaneously, Iran has been developing missiles that eventually could be capable of carrying a nuclear payload.

Iranian leaders have publicly stated that they have no intention of using their nuclear program for destructive purposes. They claim that they are seeking only to develop nuclear energy plants.

**Iran as a Security Threat** Like North Korea, Iran has been openly hostile to the United States. Iran has implemented an extensive terrorism campaign in

The current dictator in North Korea is Kim Jong Un, shown here with his wife.

**The Potential for War** With increasing urgency, the government of Israel under conservative prime minister Netanyahu has called for air strikes to destroy Iran's nuclear program. At the United Nations in September 2012, Netanyahu stated that Iran's capability to enrich uranium must be halted before the early summer of 2013.

During 2010, a sophisticated computer "worm" nicknamed "Stuxnet" attacked centrifuges used in Iran's uranium enrichment program. Stuxnet apparently took down about 1,000 of Iran's 5,000 centrifuges, destroying many of them completely. In June 2012, a *New York Times* reporter claimed that Stuxnet was a U.S. project developed with Israeli assistance. The reporter's sources allegedly came from within the White House, where the program was supervised personally by President Obama. A major justification for Stuxnet was to provide an alternative to an Israeli air strike on Iranian facilities.

## FOR CRITICAL THINKING

*If the United States were to bomb Iran's uranium enrichment sites, what might be the consequences?*

hopes of undermining U.S. influence in the Middle East. Many analysts have also tied Iran to Iraqi insurgency efforts against American occupation forces.

The president of Iran, Mahmoud Ahmadinejad, has repeatedly called for the complete destruction of Israel. It is no surprise, therefore, that Israel considers Iranian nuclear weapons to be a threat to its existence. What is more surprising is how much of a threat a potential Iranian bomb is to Iran's Arab neighbors. Leaked U.S. diplomatic cables have revealed Arab leaders urging the United States to take out the Iranian nuclear program by force.

**Diplomatic Efforts** The George W. Bush administration refused to negotiate directly with the Iranians. Therefore, Britain, France, and Germany took the lead in diplomatic efforts to encourage Iran to abandon its nuclear program and engaged in talks with that country. The United Nations has imposed sanctions on Iran in an attempt to curb its nuclear ambitions. The United States has imposed its own sanctions to isolate Iran from the community of nations. Past attempts to strengthen UN sanctions, however, have been frustrated by the opposition of China and Russia.

The Obama administration was open to negotiations with Iran, and so when talks resumed in 2009, the United States was also at the table, as was Russia. The talks have gone nowhere, however.

## 16–6 China—The Next Superpower?

Following former president Richard Nixon's historic visit to China in 1972, American diplomatic and economic relations

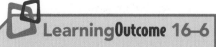

**Learning Outcome 16–6**

Describe China's emerging role as a world power.

with the Chinese gradually improved. Diplomacy with China focused on cultivating a more pro-Western disposition in the formerly isolationist nation. Relations with China are important in part because that nation has enjoyed economic growth averaging almost 10 percent a year for more than thirty years in a row. Such growth has turned China into a great power.

### 16–6a Chinese-American Trade Relations

The rapid growth of the Chinese economy and increasingly close trade ties between the United States and China have helped bring about a policy of diplomatic

This worker monitors the loading of containers in Qingdoa Harbor, located in China's Shandong province.

outreach. Many Americans protested, however, when the U.S. government extended **normal trade relations (NTR) status** to China on a year-to-year basis. Labor groups objected because they feared that American workers would lose jobs that could be performed at lower wages in Chinese factories. Human rights organizations denounced the Chinese government's well-documented mistreatment of its people.

Despite this heavy opposition, Congress granted China permanent NTR status in 2000 and endorsed China's application to the World Trade Organization in 2001.

### 16–6b A Future Challenger to American Dominance

**normal trade relations (NTR) status** A trade status granted through an international treaty by which each member nation must treat other members at least as well as it treats the country that receives its most favorable treatment. This status was formerly known as *most-favored-nation status.*

Many U.S. observers have warned that China is destined to challenge American global supremacy. With one of the fastest-growing economies in the world, along with a population of 1.3 billion, China's gross domestic product (GDP) is expected to surpass that of the United States by 2020. China's GDP is nearly *one hundred times* what it was

in 1978, when China implemented reforms to make the economy more market oriented. Never in the history of the world have so many people been lifted out of poverty so quickly.

The United States already runs a multibillion-dollar trade deficit with China and could be vulnerable if Chinese economic growth continues at its present pace. How much of a problem do China's cheap exports really pose for the United States? We look at that question in this chapter's *Join the Debate* feature on the facing page.

Diplomatic relations between China and the United States have been uneven. China offered its full support of the U.S. war on terrorism following the September 11 attacks, even providing intelligence about terrorist activities. But the Chinese did not support the American invasion of Iraq in 2003. Also, recent attempts by Chinese hackers to steal U.S. intellectual property have raised questions about China's attitudes toward the West.

Although China has not demonstrated any ambition to acquire more territory in general or to become militarily aggressive, it has expressed a desire to take control of the island of Taiwan. China considers Taiwan, a former Chinese province, to be a legal part of China. In practice, however, since 1949 the island has functioned as an independent nation. The United States has historically supported a free and separate Taiwan and has reiterated that any reunion of China and Taiwan must come about by peaceful means.

Relations between China and several Western nations have become strained lately due to criticisms by these nations of Chinese behavior in Tibet. While supposedly autonomous, Tibet is under tight Chinese control.

**FOR CRITICAL THINKING**

*If we have strong trade relations with a country, does that make it less likely that we would ever go to war with that country? Why or why not?*

## JOIN THE DEBATE

### Should We Restrict Chinese Imports?

Some politicians argue that China is flooding the U.S. market with its goods and thereby preventing the U.S. economy from enjoying a vigorous recovery from the Great Recession. During the 2012 presidential debates, Barack Obama and Mitt Romney both made such claims. Others believe that we benefit from our economic relations with China.

### China Hurts Us by Not Playing Fair

American consumers are buying much more from China than China is buying from the United States. As Chinese goods pile up in America, U.S. dollars pile up in China in the form of treasuries held by the Chinese central bank. Today, China is our number-one source for cheap goods.

Why are Chinese goods so inexpensive? One obvious reason is that Chinese workers earn much less than American workers. Another important reason, though, is that the Chinese government maintains a fixed exchange rate between our dollar and the Chinese currency. When China deliberately keeps the value of its currency low relative to the dollar, its exports become cheaper and its imports more expensive.

Many people believe that imports from China are taking jobs away from American workers. These excessive imports need to be stopped. The government should treat China's currency manipulation as an anticompetitive trade practice.

### We Benefit from the China Trade

Another viewpoint is that our trade deficit helps us a great deal more than it helps China. What do we get? Clothing, computers, entertainment gadgets, furniture, shoes, toys—you name it. What does China get? Pieces of U.S. government paper that pay almost no interest. True, under current circumstances, all those imports reduce demand for U.S. goods and services, which makes our economic problems worse. If the U.S. government followed policies that increased our domestic demand, however, the China trade deficit would not matter. Americans who used to make shoes and toys could find jobs doing something else.

The U.S. Congress does have a weapon if it really wants to reduce China's trade with the United States. It can impose taxes, called *tariffs*, on anything that we buy from China. Picking fights using tariffs can be very expensive, though. The last time the world saw a major trade war of this type was during the Great Depression, and trade restrictions made that economic collapse much worse than it already was.

**FOR CRITICAL ANALYSIS** Entering "china trade" into a search engine yields plenty of background information on the topic. To locate opinion pieces, try typing in "china trade politics blog."

# AMERICA AT
# ODDS Foreign Policy

In 1947, Republican senator Arthur Vandenberg of Michigan announced, "Politics stops at the water's edge." By this, Vandenberg, formerly a fierce isolationist, meant that Republicans and Democrats should cooperate in dealing with such foreign policy issues as the Cold War with the Soviet Union.

Bipartisanship was never complete even in Vandenberg's day, however, and it is much less common today. True, the two major parties are more likely to cooperate over a foreign policy issue than over domestic policy. Nevertheless, Americans are at odds over many foreign policy issues, as reflected in Congress. The following are a few of these issues:

- In foreign policy, is it best to ally with other nations whenever possible—or should America carefully guard its ability to act alone?

- Should the president take complete charge of the foreign policy process, including the use of armed force—or should the president collaborate closely with Congress?

- Should the war on terrorism be the central focus of U.S. foreign policy—or should we devote equal energy to managing our relations with rising powers such as China?

- Was President Obama's plan to withdraw forces from Afghanistan in 2011 and 2012 a wise method of putting pressure on the Afghan government—or a recipe for failure in that country?

- In attempting to promote peace between Israelis and Palestinians, should the United States put most of its pressure on the Palestinians—or should it also pressure the Israelis to, for example, suspend the construction of new Jewish settlements on the West Bank?

# TAKE ACTION

Many Americans of all political persuasions are taking action to help "support the troops" now fighting in Afghanistan. For example, a number of groups are working to help improve the lives of soldiers who have returned from the war. For ideas on what you can do to help, you can contact a veterans' group in your area or visit the Web sites of veterans' groups. For ideas, type "support troops" into a search engine. You'll see a wide range of options on how to support our soldiers. One is Support Our Troops, an index of U.S. military–support Web sites. The USO, formerly the United Service Organizations, has another interesting site. Founded during World War II, the USO is among the oldest organizations that support members of our armed forces.

AP PHOTO/KEITH SRAKOCIC

# STUDY TOOLS

## Ready to study?

- Review what you've read with the quiz below. Check your answers on the Chapter in Review card at the back of the book. For any questions you miss, read the corresponding Learning Outcome section again to prepare for class and your exam.
- Rip out and study the Chapter in Review card.

## ... Or you can go online to CourseMate

at www.cengagebrain.com for these additional review materials:

- Practice Quizzes
- Key Term Flashcards or Crossword Puzzles
- Audio Summaries
- Simulations, Animated Learning Modules, and Interactive Timelines
- Videos
- American Government NewsWatch

## Fill-In

1. The executive departments and other government agencies that are most directly involved in foreign policy include the _____.

2. The nation's founders and the early presidents believed that a policy of _____ was the best way to protect American interests.

3. The _____ was a war of words, warnings, and ideologies between the Soviet Union and the United States that lasted from the late 1940s through the late 1980s.

4. In 2001, supported by a coalition of allies, the U.S. military attacked al Qaeda camps in _____ and the ruling Taliban regime that harbored those terrorists.

5. In 2011, U.S. Navy Seals killed Osama bin Laden in Abbottabad, a city in _____.

6. The 1993 Oslo Accords led to the establishment of the _____ in the occupied territories.

7. With respect to the prospects of nuclear proliferation, American officials are most concerned about recent developments in the countries of _____.

8. The Chinese government maintains a fixed exchange rate between our dollar and the Chinese currency. Many Americans believe that the United States should treat this action, known as _____, as an anticompetitive trade practice.

## Multiple Choice

9. The power to declare war belongs to
   a. the president.
   b. Congress.
   c. the Joint Chiefs of Staff.

10. Direct involvement by one country in another country's affairs best defines
    a. political realism.
    b. collective security.
    c. interventionism.

11. Actions taken under the Truman Doctrine and the Marshall Plan marked the beginning of a policy of
    a. containment.
    b. deterrence.
    c. mutually assured destruction.

12. The phrase *weapons of mass destruction* refers to
    a. landmines and cluster munitions.
    b. Improvised Explosive Devices (IEDs).
    c. chemical, biological, or nuclear weapons.

13. For many years after Israel was founded in 1948,
    a. the neighboring Arab states did not accept its legitimacy as a nation.
    b. the only peace treaty that it was able to negotiate was one with Syria.
    c. it lived in peace with its neighbors in the Middle East.

14. During 2010, a sophisticated computer "worm" nicknamed "Stuxnet" attacked centrifuges used in _____ uranium enrichment program.
    a. North Korea's
    b. Iran's
    c. Israel's

15. The U.S. government granted China permanent _____ (NTR) status in 2000.
    a. normal trade relations
    b. national trade reservation
    c. no tariff records

# USE THE TOOLS.

- Rip out the Review Cards in the back of your book to study.

**Or Visit CourseMate to:**

- Read, search, highlight, and take notes in the Interactive eBook
- Review Flashcards (Print or Online) to master key terms
- Test yourself with Auto-Graded Quizzes
- Bring concepts to life with Games, Videos, and Animations!

Go to CourseMate for **GOVT5** to begin using these tools.
Access at **www.cengagebrain.com**

Complete the Speak Up
survey in CourseMate at
**www.cengagebrain.com**

Follow us at
**www.facebook.com/4ltrpress**

©iStockphoto.com/A-Digit | © Cengage Learning 2011

# NOTES

## Chapter 1

1. Harold Lasswell, *Politics: Who Gets What, When, and How* (New York: McGraw-Hill, 1936).
2. Charles Lewis, *The Buying of Congress* (New York: Avon Books, 1998), p. 346.
3. As quoted in Paul M. Angle and Earl Schenck Miers, *The Living Lincoln* (New York: Barnes & Noble, 1992), p. 155.
4. Martin J. Wade and William F. Russell, *The Short Constitution* (Iowa City: American Citizen Publishing, 1920), p. 38.

## Chapter 2

1. The first *European* settlement in today's United States was St. Augustine, Florida (a city that still exists), which was founded on September 8, 1565, by the Spaniard Pedro Menéndez de Ávilés.
2. Archaeologists recently discovered the remains of a colony at Popham Beach, on the southern coast of what is now Maine, that was established at the same time as the colony at Jamestown. The Popham colony disbanded after thirteen months, however, when the leader, after learning that he had inherited property back home, returned—with the other colonists—to England.
3. John Camp, *Out of the Wilderness: The Emergence of an American Identity in Colonial New England* (Middleton, Conn.: Wesleyan University Press, 1990).
4. Jon Butler, *Becoming America: The Revolution before 1776* (Cambridge, Mass.: Harvard University Press, 2000).
5. Ironically, the colonists were in fact protesting a tax reduction. The British government believed that if tea were cheaper, Americans would be more willing to drink it, even though it was still taxed. The Americans viewed the tax reduction as an attempt to trick them into accepting the principle of taxation. If the tea had been expensive, it would have been easy to organize a boycott. Because the tea was cheap, the protesters destroyed it so that no one would be tempted to buy it. (Also, many of the protesters were in the business of smuggling tea, and they would have been put out of business by the cheap competition.)
6. Much of the colonists' fury over British policies was directed personally at King George III, who had ascended the British throne in 1760 at the age of twenty-two, rather than at Britain or British rule *per se*. If you look at the Declaration of Independence in Appendix A, you will note that much of that document focuses on what "He" (George III) has or has not done. George III's lack of political experience, his personality, and his temperament all combined to lend instability to the British government at this crucial point in history.
7. *The Political Writings of Thomas Paine*, Vol. 1 (Boston: J. P. Mendum Investigator Office, 1870), p. 46.
8. The equivalent in today's publishing world would be a book that sells between 9 million and 11 million copies in its first year of publication.
9. As quoted in Winthrop D. Jordan *et al.*, *The United States*, 6th ed. (Englewood Cliffs, N.J.: Prentice Hall, 1987).
10. Some scholars feel that Locke's influence on the colonists, including Thomas Jefferson, has been exaggerated. For example, Jay Fliegelman states that Jefferson's fascination with the ideas of Homer, Ossian, and Patrick Henry "is of greater significance than his indebtedness to Locke." Jay Fliegelman, *Declaring Independence: Jefferson, Natural Language, and the Culture of Performance* (Stanford, Calif.: Stanford University Press, 1993).
11. Well before the Articles were ratified, many of them had, in fact, already been implemented. The Second Continental Congress and the thirteen states conducted American military, economic, and political affairs according to the standards and form specified later in the Articles of Confederation. See Robert W. Hoffert, *A Politics of Tensions: The Articles of Confederation and American Political Ideas* (Niwot, Colo.: University Press of Colorado, 1992).
12. Shays' Rebellion was not merely a small group of poor farmers. The participants and their supporters represented whole communities, including some of the wealthiest and most influential families of Massachusetts. Leonard L. Richards, *Shays' Rebellion: The American Revolution's Final Battle* (Philadelphia: University of Pennsylvania Press, 2003).
13. Madison, however, was much more "republican" in his views—that is, less of a centralist—than Hamilton. See Lance Banning, *The Sacred Fire of Liberty: James Madison and the Founding of the Federal Republic* (Ithaca, N.Y.: Cornell University Press, 1995).
14. The State House was later named Independence Hall. The East Room was the same room in which the Declaration of Independence had been signed eleven years earlier.
15. Charles A. Beard, *An Economic Interpretation of the Constitution of the United States* (New York: Macmillan, 1913; New York: Free Press, 1986).
16. Morris was partly of French descent, which is why his first name may seem unusual. Note, however, that naming one's child *Gouverneur* was not common at the time in any language, including French.

17. Quoted in J. J. Spengler, "Malthusianism in Late Eighteenth-Century America," *American Economic Review* 25 (1935), p. 705.
18. For further detail on Wood's depiction of the founders' views, see Gordon S. Wood, *Revolutionary Characters: What Made the Founders Different* (New York: Penguin Press, 2006).
19. Some scholarship suggests that the *Federalist Papers* did not play a significant role in bringing about the ratification of the Constitution. Nonetheless, the papers have lasting value as an authoritative explanation of the Constitution.
20. The papers written by the Anti-Federalists are online. (Locate them by entering "wepin" into a search engine.) For essays on the positions, arranged in topical order, of both the Federalists and the Anti-Federalists in the ratification debate, see John P. Kaminski and Richard Leffler, *Federalists and Antifederalists: The Debate over the Ratification of the Constitution*, 2d ed. (Madison, Wis.: Madison House, 1998).
21. The concept of the separation of powers generally is credited to the French political philosopher Montesquieu (1689–1755), who included it in his monumental two-volume work entitled *The Spirit of the Laws*, published in 1748.
22. The Constitution does not explicitly mention the power of judicial review, but the delegates at the Constitutional Convention probably assumed that the courts would have this power. Indeed, Alexander Hamilton, in *Federalist Paper* No. 78, explicitly outlined the concept of judicial review. In any event, whether the founders intended for the courts to exercise this power is a moot point, because in an 1803 decision, *Marbury v. Madison*, the Supreme Court successfully claimed this power for the courts—see Chapter 14.
23. Eventually, Supreme Court decisions led to legislative reforms relating to apportionment. The amendment concerning compensation of members of Congress became the Twenty-seventh Amendment to the Constitution when it was ratified 203 years later, in 1992.
24. The Twenty-first Amendment repealed the Eighteenth Amendment, which had prohibited the manufacture or sale of alcoholic beverages nationwide (Prohibition). Special conventions were necessary because prohibitionist forces controlled too many state legislatures for the standard ratification method to work.

## Chapter 3

1. The federal models used by the German and Canadian governments provide interesting comparisons with the U.S. system. See Arthur B. Gunlicks, *Laender and German Federalism* (Manchester, England: Manchester University Press, 2003); and Jennifer Smith, *Federalism* (Vancouver: University of British Columbia Press, 2004).
2. Text of an address by the president to the National Conference of State Legislatures, Atlanta, Georgia (Washington, D.C.: The White House, Office of the Press Secretary, July 30, 1981).
3. An excellent illustration of this principle was President Dwight Eisenhower's disciplining of Arkansas governor Orval Faubus when Faubus refused to allow a Little Rock high school to be desegregated in 1957. Eisenhower federalized the National Guard to enforce the court-ordered desegregation of the school.
4. 5 U.S. 137 (1803).
5. 17 U.S. 316 (1819).
6. 22 U.S. 1 (1824).
7. *Hammer v. Dagenhart*, 247 U.S. 251 (1918). This decision was overruled in *United States v. Darby*, 312 U.S. 100 (1941).
8. *Wickard v. Filburn*, 317 U.S. 111 (1942).
9. *McLain v. Real Estate Board of New Orleans, Inc.*, 444 U.S. 232 (1980).
10. 514 U.S. 549 (1995).
11. *Printz v. United States*, 521 U.S. 898 (1997).
12. *United States v. Morrison*, 529 U.S. 598 (2000).
13. 549 U.S. 497 (2007).
14. *Arizona v. United States*, 567 U.S. ___ (2012).
15. *National Federation of Independent Business v. Sebelius*, 567 U.S. ___ (2012).

## Chapter 4

1. 32 U.S. 243 (1833).
2. 330 U.S. 1 (1947).
3. 370 U.S. 421 (1962).
4. 449 U.S. 39 (1980).
5. *Wallace v. Jaffree*, 472 U.S. 38 (1985).
6. See, for example, *Brown v. Gwinnett County School District*, 112 F.3d 1464 (1997).
7. *Santa Fe Independent School District v. Doe*, 530 U.S. 290 (2000).
8. 393 U.S. 97 (1968).

9. *Edwards v. Aguillard*, 482 U.S. 578 (1987).
10. *Kitzmiller v. Dover Area School District*, 400 F.Supp.2d 707 (M.D.Pa. 2005).
11. 403 U.S. 602 (1971).
12. *Zelman v. Simmons-Harris*, 536 U.S. 639 (2002).
13. *Holmes v. Bush* (Fla.Cir.Ct. 2002). For details about this case, see David Royse, "Judge Rules School Voucher Law Violates Florida Constitution," *USA Today*, August 6, 2002, p. 7D.
14. 98 U.S. 145 (1878).
15. *Police v. City of Newark*, 170 F.3d 359 (3d Cir. 1999).
16. *Schenck v. United States*, 249 U.S. 47 (1919).
17. Ibid.
18. *Gitlow v. New York*, 268 U.S. 652 (1925).
19. 341 U.S. 494 (1951).
20. *Brandenburg v. Ohio*, 395 U.S. 444 (1969).
21. *Liquormart v. Rhode Island*, 517 U.S. 484 (1996).
22. 413 U.S. 15 (1973).
23. *Reno v. American Civil Liberties Union*, 521 U.S. 844 (1997).
24. *Ashcroft v. American Civil Liberties Union*, 542 U.S. 656 (2004). The district court, located in Philadelphia, made its second ruling on the case in 2007. On July 22, 2008, the U.S. Court of Appeals for the Third Circuit upheld the decision in *American Civil Liberties Union v. Mukasey*, 534 F.3d 181 (3d Cir. 2008).
25. *United States v. American Library Association*, 539 U.S. 194 (2003).
26. *Morse v. Frederick*, 551 U.S. 393 (2007).
27. See, for example, *Doe v. University of Michigan*, 721 F.Supp. 852 (1989).
28. 484 U.S. 260 (1988).
29. Brandeis made this statement in a dissenting opinion in *Olmstead v. United States*, 277 U.S. 438 (1928).
30. 381 U.S. 479 (1965).
31. The state of South Carolina challenged the constitutionality of this act, claiming that the law violated states' rights under the Tenth Amendment. The Supreme Court, however, held that Congress had the authority, under its commerce power, to pass the act because drivers' personal information had become an article of interstate commerce. *Reno v. Condon*, 528 U.S. 141 (2000).
32. *Sorrell v. IMS Health*, 131 S.Ct. 857 (2011).
33. 410 U.S. 113 (1973). Jane Roe was not the real name of the woman in this case. It is a common legal pseudonym used to protect a party's privacy.
34. See, for example, the Supreme Court's decision in *Lambert v. Wicklund*, 520 U.S. 1169 (1997). The Court held that a Montana law requiring a minor to notify one of her parents before getting an abortion was constitutional.
35. *Schenck v. ProChoice Network*, 519 U.S. 357 (1997); and *Hill v. Colorado*, 530 U.S. 703 (2000).
36. *Stenberg v. Carhart*, 530 U.S. 914 (2000).
37. *Gonzales v. Carhart*, 550 U.S. 124 (2007).
38. *Washington v. Glucksberg*, 521 U.S. 702 (1997).
39. *Gonzales v. Oregon*, 546 U.S. 243 (2006).
40. 372 U.S. 335 (1963).
41. *Mapp v. Ohio*, 367 U.S. 643 (1961).
42. 384 U.S. 436 (1966). In 1968, Congress passed legislation including a provision that reinstated the previous rule that statements made by defendants can be used against them as long as the statements were made voluntarily. This provision was never enforced, however, and only in 1999 did a court try to enforce it. The case ultimately came before the Supreme Court, which held that the *Miranda* rights were based on the Constitution and thus could not be overruled by legislative act. See *Dickerson v. United States*, 530 U.S. 428 (2000).
43. *Moran v. Burbine*, 475 U.S. 412 (1986).
44. *Arizona v. Fulminante*, 499 U.S. 279 (1991).
45. *Davis v. United States*, 512 U.S. 452 (1994).
46. *Berghuis v. Thompkins*, 130 S.Ct. 2250 (2010).
47. *J.D.B. v. North Carolina*, 564 U.S. ___ (2011).
48. Thomas P. Sullivan, *Police Experiences with Recording Custodial Interrogations* (Chicago: Northwestern University School of Law Center on Wrongful Convictions, Summer 2004), p. 4.
49. This example is drawn from Brenda Koehler, "Respond Locally to National Issues," in *50 Ways to Love Your Country* (Maui, Hawaii: Inner Ocean Publishing, 2004), pp. 110–111.

## Chapter 5

1. *Arizona v. United States*, 567 U.S. ___ (2012).
2. *Michael M. v. Superior Court*, 450 U.S. 464 (1981).
3. See, for example, *Craig v. Boren*, 429 U.S. 190 (1976).
4. *Orr v. Orr*, 440 U.S. 268 (1979).
5. *Mississippi University for Women v. Hogan*, 458 U.S. 718 (1982).
6. 518 U.S. 515 (1996).
7. 163 U.S. 537 (1896).
8. 347 U.S. 483 (1954).
9. 349 U.S. 294 (1955).
10. *Swann v. Charlotte-Mecklenburg Board of Education*, 402 U.S. 1 (1971).
11. *Keyes v. School District No. 1*, 413 U.S. 189 (1973).
12. *Milliken v. Bradley*, 418 U.S. 717 (1974).
13. *Riddick v. School Board of City of Norfolk*, 627 F.Supp. 814 (E.D.Va. 1984).
14. Emily Bazelon, "The Next Kind of Integration," *The New York Times Magazine*, July 20, 2008.
15. *Oncale v. Sundowner Offshore Services*, 523 U.S. 75 (1998).

16. *Faragher v. City of Boca Raton*, 524 U.S. 775 (1998).
17. The Supreme Court upheld these actions in *Hirabayashi v. United States*, 320 U.S. 81 (1943); and *Korematsu v. United States*, 323 U.S. 214 (1944).
18. Historians in the early and mid-twentieth century gave much smaller figures for the pre-Columbian population—as low as 14 million people for the entire New World. Today, 40 million is considered a conservative estimate, and an estimate of 100 million has much support among demographers. If 100 million is correct, the epidemics that followed the arrival of the Europeans killed one out of every five people alive in the world at that time. See Charles C. Mann, *1491* (New York: Vintage, 2006).
19. The 1890 siege was the subject of Dee Brown's best-selling book *Bury My Heart at Wounded Knee* (New York: Holt, Rinehart & Winston, 1971).
20. *County of Oneida, New York v. Oneida Indian Nation*, 470 U.S. 226 (1985).
21. *Sutton v. United Airlines*, 527 U.S. 471 (1999); and *Toyota v. Williams*, 534 U.S. 184 (2002).
22. *Board of Trustees of the University of Alabama v. Garrett*, 531 U.S. 356 (2001).
23. 539 U.S. 558 (2003).
24. 517 U.S. 620 (1996).
25. *Perry v. Brown*, 671 F.3d 1052 (2012).
26. *Massachusetts v. U.S. Department of Health and Human Services*, 698 F.Supp.2nd 234 (2012); and *Gill v. Office of Personnel Management*, 682 F.3d 1 (1st Cir. 2012). Similar cases were decided by courts in Connecticut and New York.
27. *Log Cabin Republicans v. United States*, 716 F.Supp.2d 884 (C.D.Cal. 2010).
28. 438 U.S. 265 (1978).
29. 515 U.S. 200 (1995).
30. 84 F.3d 720 (5th Cir. 1996).
31. 539 U.S. 244 (2003).
32. 539 U.S. 306 (2003).
33. 551 U.S. 701 (2007).
34. *Fisher v. University of Texas*, 631 F.3d 213 (5th Cir. 2011).
35. *Coalition to Defend Affirmative Action v. Regents of the University of Michigan*, ___ F.3d ___ (2011). In September 2011, the Sixth Circuit Court of Appeals voted to rehear *Coalition to Defend Affirmative Action v. Regents of the University of Michigan*, so the decision of July 2011 has been vacated. The court is expected to issue a new decision by the end of 2012.

## Chapter 6

1. David Bicknell Truman, *The Governmental Process: Political Interests and Public Opinion*, 2d rev. ed. (New York: Alfred A. Knopf, 1971). This work is a political science classic.
2. Robert H. Salisbury, *Interests and Institutions: Substance and Structure in American Politics* (Pittsburgh: University of Pittsburgh Press, 1992).
3. *Democracy in America*, Vol. 1, ed. Phillip Bradley (New York: Knopf, 1980), p. 191.
4. Mancur Olson, *The Logic of Collective Action: Public Goods and the Theory of Groups*, rev. ed. (Cambridge, Mass.: Harvard University Press, 1971).
5. Pronounced ah-*mee*-kus *kure*-ee-eye.
6. Fred McChesney, *Money for Nothing: Politicians, Rent Extraction and Political Extortion* (Cambridge, Mass.: Harvard University Press, 1997).
7. The Agricultural Adjustment Act of 1933 (declared unconstitutional) was replaced by the 1937 Agricultural Adjustment Act, which later was changed and amended several times.
8. 558 U.S. 50 (2010).
9. 545 U.S. 913 (2005).
10. *United States v. Harriss*, 347 U.S. 612 (1954).

## Chapter 7

1. Letter to Francis Hopkinson written from Paris while Jefferson was ambassador to France, as cited in John P. Foley, ed., *The Jeffersonian Cyclopedia* (New York: Russell & Russell, 1967), p. 677.
2. The U.S. Senate presents the text of the address at **www.access.gpo.gov/ congress/senate/farewell/sd106-21.pdf**.
3. The association of red with the Republicans and blue with the Democrats is barely a decade old. The terms *red* and *blue* are derived from the colors used by the major television networks to show the states carried by the Republican and Democratic presidential candidates. This use of colors deliberately reverses a traditional pattern. In most European countries, the right-of-center party uses blue, while the left-of-center party employs red. The use of red originated in the socialist movement, from which most European left-of-center parties descend. From time to time, Republicans have accused Democrats of socialism. U.S. television networks thus assigned red to the Republicans precisely so that the networks would not appear to be endorsing that accusation.
4. For an interesting discussion of the pros and cons of patronage from a constitutional perspective, see the majority opinion versus the dissent in the Supreme Court case *Board of County Commissioners v. Umbehr*, 518 U.S. 668 (1996).
5. The term *third party*, although inaccurate (because sometimes there has been a fourth party, a fifth party, and even more), is commonly used to refer to a minor party.

6. Thomas Nast, the cartoonist who drew these images, was a Republican. "Copperhead" was a derisive term for northern Democrats who sympathized with the South during the Civil War, and in the first cartoon Nash condemned Democratic newspapers for abusing Edwin Stanton, Lincoln's secretary of war, following Stanton's death. The elephant in the second cartoon referred to the large size of the Republican vote in the North. Nash depicted the elephant as stampeded into a pit by a jackass dressed in a lion skin. This referred to the *New York Herald*, a Democratic newspaper, which made accusations against Republican president Ulysses S. Grant that caused Republicans to panic.
7. Today, twelve states have multimember districts for their state houses, and a handful also have multimember districts for their state senates.

# Chapter 8

1. The elections that Gallup predicted incorrectly were usually close ones. In 2004, Gallup reported a statistical tie—49 percent each—between Republican George W. Bush and Democrat John Kerry. In 1976, Gallup falsely predicted that Republican incumbent Gerald Ford would prevail over Democrat Jimmy Carter. In 1948, Gallup wrongly predicted that Republican Thomas Dewey would defeat Democratic incumbent Harry Truman. The 2012 elections, however, may have been Gallup's biggest embarrassment to date. Assuming very low Democratic voter turnout, Gallup had Romney well in the lead throughout October. It corrected its last poll to reflect greater turnout, but it still predicted a Romney victory.
2. John M. Benson, "When Is an Opinion Really an Opinion?" *Public Perspective*, September/October 2001, pp. 40–41.
3. As quoted in Karl G. Feld, "When Push Comes to Shove: A Polling Industry Call to Arms," *Public Perspective*, September/October 2001, p. 38.
4. Doris A. Graber, *Mass Media and American Politics*, 8th ed. (Washington, D.C.: CQ Press, 2009).
5. Jimmy Carter, *Palestine: Peace Not Apartheid* (New York: Simon & Schuster, 2007).
6. As quoted in Owen Ullman, "Why Voter Apathy Will Make a Strong Showing," *BusinessWeek*, November 4, 1996.
7. Pew Research Center for the People and the Press, survey conducted September 21–October 4, 2006, and reported in "Who Votes, Who Doesn't, and Why," released October 28, 2006.
8. *Guinn v. United States*, 238 U.S. 347 (1915).
9. *Smith v. Allwright*, 321 U.S. 649 (1944).
10. For more information on voting systems, see the Web site of **verifiedvoting.org**.
11. The argument about the vote-eligible population was first made by Michael P. McDonald and Samuel L. Popkin, "The Myth of the Vanishing Voter," *American Political Science Review*, Vol. 95, No. 4 (December 2001), p. 963.
12. Thomas E. Mann and Norman J. Ornstein, *The Broken Branch: How Congress Is Failing America and How to Get It Back on Track* (New York: Oxford University Press, 2006), p. 277.

# Chapter 9

1. Today, there are 100 senators in the Senate and 435 members of the House of Representatives. In addition, the District of Columbia has three electoral votes, as provided for by the Twenty-third Amendment to the Constitution.
2. This group includes those who support the National Popular Vote movement, a proposed interstate compact that would cast the electoral votes of each participating state for the candidate who won the national popular vote. The compact would go into effect if participating states controlled a majority of the votes in the electoral college.
3. These states award one electoral vote to the candidate who wins the popular vote in a congressional district and an additional two electoral votes to the winner of the statewide popular vote. Other states have considered similar plans.
4. The word *caucus* apparently was first used in the name of a men's club, the Caucus Club of colonial Boston, sometime between 1755 and 1765. (Many early political and government meetings took place in pubs.) We have no certain knowledge of the origin of the word, but it may be from an Algonquin term meaning "elder" or from the Latin name of a drinking vessel.
5. Today, the Democratic and Republican caucuses in the House and Senate (the Republicans now use the term *conference* instead of *caucus*) choose each party's congressional leadership and sometimes discuss legislation and legislative strategy.
6. Due to the customs of the time, none of the candidates could admit that he had made a personal decision to run. All claimed to have entered the race in response to popular demand.
7. Parties cannot use their freedom-of-association rights to practice racial discrimination in state-sponsored elections: *Smith v. Allwright*, 321 U.S. 649 (1944). When racial discrimination is not involved, the parties have regularly won freedom-of-association suits against state governments. Examples are *Tashjian v. Republican Party of Connecticut*, 479 U.S. 208 (1986), and *California Democratic Party v. Jones*, 530 U.S. 567 (2000).
8. In Washington, the state government holds presidential primaries for both parties. The Democratic Party, however, ignores the Democratic primary and chooses its national convention delegates through a caucus/convention system. In 1984, following a dispute with the state of Michigan over primary

rules, the state Democratic Party organized a presidential primary election that was run completely by party volunteers. In 2008, after a similar dispute with its state, the Virginia Republican Party chose its candidate for the U.S. Senate at its state party convention instead of through the Virginia primary elections.
9. The case was *California Democratic Party v. Jones*, cited in footnote 7.
10. *Washington State Grange v. Washington State Republican Party et al.*, 552 U.S. 442 (2008).
11. Christopher Rhoads, "Candidates Try New Web Tactics in Battle to Tap Fresh Supporters," *The Wall Street Journal*, October 30, 2008, p. 16.
12. This act is sometimes referred to as the Federal Election Campaign Act of 1972 because it became effective in that year. The official date of the act, however, is 1971.
13. *Buckley v. Valeo*, 424 U.S. 1 (1976).
14. This figure is from the Center for Responsive Politics.
15. *Colorado Republican Federal Campaign Committee v. Federal Election Commission*, 518 U.S. 604 (1996).
16. Quoted in George Will, "The First Amendment on Trial," *The Washington Post*, December 1, 2002, p. B7.
17. 540 U.S. 93 (2003).
18. 551 U.S. 449 (2007).
19. 558 U.S. 50 (2010).
20. *Speechnow v. FEC*, 599 F.3d 686 (D.C.Cir. 2010).

# Chapter 10

1. *Mutual Film Corporation v. Industrial Commission of Ohio*, 236 U.S. 230 (1915).
2. *Joseph Burstyn, Inc. v. Wilson*, 343 U.S. 495 (1952).
3. *Reno v. American Civil Liberties Union*, 521 U.S. 844 (1997).
4. *United States v. Playboy Entertainment Group*, 529 U.S. 803 (2000).
5. Bernard Cohen, *The Press and Foreign Policy* (Princeton, N.J.: Princeton University Press, 1963), p. 81.
6. Interestingly, in the 2000 campaigns, a Texas group supporting George W. Bush's candidacy paid for a remake of the "daisy" commercial, but the target in the new ad was Al Gore.
7. As quoted in Michael Grunwald, "The Year of Playing Dirtier," *The Washington Post*, October 27, 2006, p. A1.
8. John G. Geer, *In Defense of Negativity: Attack Ads in Presidential Campaigns* (Chicago: University of Chicago Press, 2006).
9. The commission's action was upheld by a federal court. See *Perot v. Federal Election Commission*, 97 F.3d 553 (D.C.Cir. 1996).
10. For more details on how political candidates manage news coverage, see Doris A. Graber, *Mass Media and American Politics*, 7th ed. (Washington, D.C.: CQ Press, 2005).
11. For suggestions on how to dissect spin and detect when language is steering one toward a conclusion, see Brooks Jackson and Kathleen Hall Jamieson, *unSpun: Finding Facts in a World of Disinformation* (New York: Random House, 2007).
12. *Red Lion Broadcasting Co. v. FCC*, 395 U.S. 367 (1969).
13. Kathleen Hall Jamieson, *Everything You Think You Know about Politics . . . and Why You're Wrong* (New York: Basic Books, 2000), pp. 187–195.
14. Debra Reddin van Tuyll and Hubert P. van Tuyll, "Political Partisanship," in William David Sloan and Jenn Burleson Mackay, eds., *Media Bias: Finding It, Fixing It* (Jefferson, N.C.: McFarland, 2007), pp. 35–49.
15. Jamieson, *Everything You Think You Know about Politics*, pp. xiii–xiv.
16. Pew Research Center for the People and the Press and the Project for Excellence in Journalism, *The State of the News Media 2007: An Annual Report on American Journalism*.
17. The term *podcasting* is used for this type of information delivery because initially podcasts were downloaded onto Apple's iPods.

# Chapter 11

1. These states are Alaska, Delaware, Montana, North Dakota, South Dakota, Vermont, and Wyoming.
2. 369 U.S. 186 (1962).
3. 376 U.S. 1 (1964).
4. See, for example, *Davis v. Bandemer*, 478 U.S. 109 (1986).
5. The plan was controversial because it was not implemented in response to the 2000 census. Rather, it was a "midterm" redistricting—held between censuses—that overturned what had been the postcensus redistricting plan in Texas.
6. *Amicus curiae* brief filed by the American Civil Liberties Union (ACLU) in support of the appellants in *Easley v. Cromartie*, 532 U.S. 234 (2001).
7. See, for example, *Shaw v. Reno*, 509 U.S. 630 (1993); *Miller v. Johnson*, 515 U.S. 900 (1995); *Shaw v. Hunt*, 517 U.S. 899 (1996); and *Bush v. Vera*, 517 U.S. 952 (1996).
8. *Easley v. Cromartie*, 532 U.S. 234 (2001).
9. *Powell v. McCormack*, 395 U.S. 486 (1969).
10. Some observers maintain that another reason Congress stays in session longer is the invention of air-conditioning. Until the advent of air-conditioning, no member of Congress wanted to stay in session during the hot and sticky late spring, summer, and early fall months in Washington, D.C.

11. *U.S. Term Limits, Inc. v. Thornton,* 514 U.S. 779 (1995).
12. A term used by Woodrow Wilson in *Congressional Government* (New York: Meridian Books, 1956 [first published in 1885]).

# Chapter 12

1. Lyndon B. Johnson, *The Vantage Point: Perspectives of the Presidency, 1963–1969* (New York: Henry Holt & Co., 1971).
2. *Ex parte Grossman,* 267 U.S. 87 (1925).
3. *Clinton v. City of New York,* 524 U.S. 417 (1998).
4. As cited in Lewis D. Eigen and Jonathan P. Siegel, *The Macmillan Dictionary of Political Quotations* (New York: Macmillan, 1993), p. 565.
5. The Constitution does not grant the president explicit power to remove from office officials who are not performing satisfactorily or who do not agree with the president. In 1926, however, the Supreme Court prevented Congress from interfering with the president's ability to fire those executive-branch officials whom he had appointed with Senate approval. See *Myers v. United States,* 272 U.S. 52 (1926).
6. Ironically, Lincoln believed that the actions of the president ought to be strictly limited when war powers were not concerned. He therefore left most domestic issues that did not involve the war entirely to Congress. In doing so, Lincoln was true to the ideas of his former party, the Whigs. That party advocated a limited role for the presidency in reaction to the sweeping assumption of authority by President Andrew Jackson, their great opponent. See David Donald's classic essay "Abraham Lincoln: Whig in the White House," in *Lincoln Reconsidered: Essays on the Civil War Era,* 3d ed. (New York: Vintage, 2001), pp. 133–147.
7. Richard E. Neustadt, *Presidential Power: The Politics of Leadership* (New York: John Wiley, 1960), p. 10.
8. As quoted in Richard M. Pious, *The American Presidency* (New York: Basic Books, 1979), pp. 51–52.
9. A phrase coined by Samuel Kernell in *Going Public: New Strategies of Presidential Leadership,* 2d ed. (Washington, D.C.: Congressional Quarterly Press, 1992).
10. Congress used its power to declare war in the War of 1812, the Mexican War (1846–1848), the Spanish-American War (1898), and World War I (U.S. involvement lasted from 1916 until 1918) and on six different occasions during World War II (U.S. involvement lasted from 1941 until 1945).
11. Actually, the Republicans had some difficulty controlling the Senate during Bush's first term. After the 2000 elections, the Senate was split 50–50, and the Republicans gained control only when Vice President Dick Cheney cast a tie-breaking vote. Four months later, Senator Jim Jeffords of Vermont left the Republicans to caucus with the Democrats, granting that party control of the chamber. In the 2002 elections, however, the Republicans picked up two net seats and regained control of the Senate, 51–49.
12. As quoted in Thomas E. Cronin, *The State of the Presidency,* 2d ed. (Boston: Little, Brown, 1980), p. 11.

# Chapter 13

1. This definition follows the classic model of bureaucracy put forth by German sociologist Max Weber. See Max Weber, *Theory of Social and Economic Organization,* ed. Talcott Parsons (New York: Oxford University Press, 1974).
2. It should be noted that although the president is technically the head of the bureaucracy, the president cannot always control the bureaucracy—as you will read later in this chapter.
3. Alicia Munnell, Jean-Pierre Aubry, Josh Hurwitz, and Laura Quinby, *Comparing Compensation: State-Local Versus Private Sector Workers,* Center for Retirement Research at Boston College, September 2011 (slge .org/publications/comparing-compensation-state-local-versus-private-sector-workers). Also, Maury Gittleman and Brooks Pierce, "Compensation for State and Local Government Workers," *Journal of Economic Perspectives,* Vol. 26, No. 1, Winter 2012, pp. 217–242 (www.aeaweb.org/articles .php?doi=10.1257/jep.26.1.217).
4. Dennis Cauchon, "Federal Workers Earning Double Their Private Counterparts," *USA Today,* August 13, 2010. According to FactCheck.org, however, the total wage figure from which the $123,049 estimate was derived includes approximately $10,000 per current employee that was actually paid to other employees who retired earlier. Thus, the true average is closer to $113,000. Also, Congressional Budget Office, "Comparing the Compensation of Federal and Private-Sector Employees," January 30, 2012 (www.cbo.gov/publication/42921).
5. For an insightful analysis of the policymaking process in Washington, D.C., and the role played by various groups in the process, see Morton H. Halperin and Priscilla A. Clapp, with Arnold Kanter, *Bureaucratic Politics and Foreign Policy,* 2d ed. (Washington, D.C.: The Brookings Institution, 2006). Although the focus of the book is on foreign policy, the analysis applies in many ways to the general policymaking process.

# Chapter 14

1. 347 U.S. 483 (1954).
2. See *Plessy v. Ferguson,* 163 U.S. 537 (1896).
3. 130 S.Ct. 876 (2010).
4. 494 U.S. 652 (1990).
5. 540 U.S. 93 (2003).
6. Although a state's highest court is often referred to as the state supreme court, there are exceptions. In the New York court system, for example, the supreme court is a trial court, and the highest court is called the New York Court of Appeals.
7. Between 1790 and 1891, Congress allowed the Supreme Court almost no discretion over which cases to decide. After 1925, in almost 95 percent of appealed cases the Court could choose whether to hear arguments and issue an opinion. Beginning in October 1988, mandatory review was virtually eliminated.
8. *United States v. Jones,* 565 U.S. ___ (2012).
9. *Hosanna-Tabor Evangelical Lutheran Church and School v. EEOC,* 565 U.S. ___ (2012).
10. *Arizona v. United States,* 567 U.S. ___ (2012).
11. *National Federation of Independent Business v. Sebelius,* 567 U.S. ___ (2012).
12. 347 U.S. 483 (1954).
13. 84 F.3d 720 (5th Cir., 1996).
14. *Grutter v. Bollinger,* 539 U.S. 306 (2003); and *Gratz v. Bollinger,* 539 U.S. 244 (2003).
15. *Parents Involved in Community Schools v. Seattle School District No. 1,* 551 U.S. 701 (2007).
16. 5 U.S. 137 (1803). The Supreme Court had considered the constitutionality of an act of Congress in *Hylton v. United States,* 3 U.S. 171 (1796), in which Congress's power to levy certain taxes was challenged. That particular act was ruled constitutional, rather than unconstitutional, however, so this first federal exercise of judicial review was not clearly recognized as such. Also, during the decade before the adoption of the federal Constitution, courts in at least eight states had exercised the power of judicial review.
17. For an analysis of the Roberts Court's first term by a Georgetown University law professor, see Jonathan Turley, "The Roberts Court: Seeing Is Believing," *USA Today,* July 6, 2006, p. 11A.
18. *Snyder v. Phelps,* 561 U.S. 3025 (2011).
19. Antonin Scalia, *A Matter of Interpretation: Federal Courts and the Law* (Princeton, N.J.: Princeton University Press, 1997).
20. *Lawrence v. Texas,* 539 U.S. 558 (2003).
21. Letter by Thomas Jefferson to William C. Jarvis, 1820, in Andrew A. Lipscomb and Albert Ellery Bergh, *The Writings of Thomas Jefferson,* Memorial Edition (Washington, D.C.: Thomas Jefferson Memorial Association of the United States, 1904).
22. As quoted in Carl Hulse and David D. Kirkpatrick, "DeLay Says Federal Judiciary Has 'Run Amok,' Adding Congress Is Partly to Blame," *The New York Times,* April 8, 2005, p. 5.

# Chapter 15

1. Stan Dorn, *Uninsured and Dying because of It: Updating the Institute of Medicine Analysis on the Impact of Uninsurance on Mortality* (Washington, D.C.: Urban Institute, 2008).
2. *National Federation of Independent Business v. Sebelius,* 567 U.S. ___ (2012).
3. An alternative possibility would be to change the Senate rules so that sixty votes would no longer be necessary to pass legislation. Changing the rules, however, could easily prove more difficult than assembling sixty votes.
4. The CAFE standards that go into effect fully in 2025 are designed differently from the ones first imposed in the 1970s. At first, the benchmarks were imposed on a manufacturer-by-manufacturer basis. The new standards will be based on vehicle type, with no benchmarks for individual manufacturers. A company that manufactures only luxury vehicles, such as Mercedes Benz, will therefore face lower mile-per-gallon standards than a company that specializes in small cars. The figure of 54.5 miles per gallon is only an estimate based on the predicted mix of vehicles sold in 2025. Example standards follow:

| | | | | | |
|---|---|---|---|---|---|
| Small car | 61.1 | Small SUV | 47.5 | Minivan | 39.2 |
| Midsize car | 54.9 | Midsize SUV | 43.4 | Large pickup | 33.0 |
| Large car | 48.0 | | | | |

5. Paul Krugman, "Romer and Bernstein on Stimulus," in the blog Conscience of a Liberal, *The New York Times,* January 10, 2009.

# Chapter 16

1. David L. Rousseau, *Identifying Threats and Threatening Identities: The Social Construction of Realism and Liberalism* (Palo Alto, Calif.: Stanford University Press, 2006), p. 154.
2. *Public Papers of the Presidents of the United States: Harry S. Truman, 1947* (Washington, D.C.: U.S. Government Printing Office, 1963), pp. 176–180.
3. The containment policy was outlined by George F. Kennan, the chief of the policy-planning staff for the Department of State at that time, in an article that appeared in *Foreign Affairs,* July 1947, p. 575. The author's name was given as "X."
4. Fareed Zakaria, *The Future of Freedom: Illiberal Democracy at Home and Abroad,* paperback with new Afterword (New York: W.W. Norton & Co., 2007).

# THE DECLARATION OF INDEPENDENCE

## IN CONGRESS, JULY 4, 1776

*A Declaration by the Representatives of the United States of America, in General Congress assembled.* When in the Course of human Events, it becomes necessary for one People to dissolve the Political Bands which have connected them with another, and to assume among the Powers of the Earth, the separate and equal Station to which the Laws of Nature and of Nature's God entitle them, a decent Respect to the Opinions of Mankind requires that they should declare the causes which impel them to the Separation.

We hold these Truths to be self-evident, that all Men are created equal, that they are endowed by their Creator with certain unalienable Rights, that among these are Life, Liberty, and the Pursuit of Happiness— That to secure these Rights, Governments are instituted among Men, deriving their just Powers from the Consent of the Governed, that whenever any Form of Government becomes destructive of these Ends, it is the Right of the People to alter or to abolish it, and to institute new Government, laying its Foundation on such Principles, and organizing its Powers in such Forms, as to them shall seem most likely to effect their Safety and Happiness. Prudence, indeed, will dictate that Governments long established should not be changed for light and transient Causes; and accordingly all Experience hath shewn, that Mankind are more disposed to suffer, while Evils are sufferable, than to right themselves by abolishing the Forms to which they are accustomed. But when a long Train of Abuses and Usurpations, pursuing invariably the same Object, evinces a Design to reduce them under absolute Despotism, it is their Right, it is their Duty, to throw off such Government, and to provide new Guards for their future Security. Such has been the patient Sufferance of these Colonies; and such is now the Necessity which constrains them to alter their former Systems of Government. The History of the present King of Great-Britain is a History of repeated Injuries and Usurpations, all having in direct Object the Establishment of an absolute Tyranny over these States. To prove this, let Facts be submitted to a candid World.

He has refused his Assent to Laws, the most wholesome and necessary for the public Good.

He has forbidden his Governors to pass Laws of immediate and pressing Importance, unless suspended in their Operation till his Assent should be obtained; and when so suspended, he has utterly neglected to attend to them.

He has refused to pass other Laws for the Accommodation of large Districts of People, unless those People would relinquish the Right of Representation in the Legislature, a Right inestimable to them, and formidable to Tyrants only.

He has called together Legislative Bodies at Places unusual, uncomfortable, and distant from the Depository of their Public Records, for the sole Purpose of fatiguing them into Compliance with his Measures.

He has dissolved Representative Houses repeatedly, for opposing with manly Firmness his Invasions on the Rights of the People.

He has refused for a long Time, after such Dissolutions, to cause others to be elected; whereby the Legislative Powers, incapable of Annihilation, have returned to the People at large for their exercise; the State remaining in the mean time exposed to all the Dangers of Invasion from without, and Convulsions within.

He has endeavoured to prevent the Population of these States; for that Purpose obstructing the Laws for Naturalization of Foreigners; refusing to pass others to encourage their Migrations hither, and raising the Conditions of new Appropriations of Lands.

He has obstructed the Administration of Justice, by refusing his Assent to Laws for establishing Judiciary Powers.

He has made Judges dependent on his Will alone, for the Tenure of their offices, and the Amount and payment of their Salaries.

He has erected a Multitude of new Offices, and sent hither Swarms of Officers to harrass our People, and eat out their Substance.

He has kept among us, in Times of Peace, Standing Armies, without the consent of our Legislatures.

He has affected to render the Military independent of, and superior to the Civil Power.

He has combined with others to subject us to a Jurisdiction foreign to our Constitution, and unacknowledged by our Laws; giving his Assent to their Acts of pretended Legislation:

For quartering large Bodies of Armed Troops among us:

For protecting them, by a mock Trial, from Punishment for any Murders which they should commit on the Inhabitants of these States:

For cutting off our Trade with all Parts of the World:

For imposing Taxes on us without our Consent:

For depriving us, in many cases, of the Benefits of Trial by Jury:

For transporting us beyond Seas to be tried for pretended Offences:

For abolishing the free System of English Laws in a neighbouring Province, establishing therein an arbitrary Government, and enlarging its Boundaries, so as to render it at once an Example and fit Instrument for introducing the same absolute Rule into these Colonies:

For taking away our Charters, abolishing our most valuable Laws, and altering fundamentally the Forms of our Governments:

For suspending our own Legislatures, and declaring themselves invested with Power to legislate for us in all Cases whatsoever.

He has abdicated Government here, by declaring us out of his Protection and waging War against us.

He has plundered our Seas, ravaged our Coasts, burnt our towns, and destroyed the Lives of our People.

He is, at this Time, transporting large Armies of foreign Mercenaries to compleat the works of Death, Desolation, and Tyranny, already begun with circumstances of Cruelty and Perfidy, scarcely paralleled in the most barbarous Ages, and totally unworthy the Head of a civilized Nation.

He has constrained our fellow Citizens taken Captive on the high Seas to bear Arms against their Country, to become the Executioners of their Friends and Brethren, or to fall themselves by their Hands.

He has excited domestic Insurrections amongst us, and has endeavoured to bring on the Inhabitants of our Frontiers, the merciless Indian Savages, whose known Rule of Warfare, is an undistinguished Destruction, of all Ages, Sexes and Conditions.

In every state of these Oppressions we have Petitioned for Redress in the most humble Terms: Our repeated Petitions have been answered only by repeated Injury. A Prince, whose Character is thus marked by every act which may define a Tyrant, is unfit to be the Ruler of a free People.

Nor have we been wanting in Attentions to our British Brethren. We have warned them from Time to Time of Attempts by their Legislature to extend an unwarrantable Jurisdiction over us. We have reminded them of the Circumstances of our Emigration and Settlement here. We have appealed to their native Justice and Magnanimity, and we have conjured them by the Ties of our common Kindred to disavow these Usurpations, which, would inevitably interrupt our Connections and Correspondence. They too have been deaf to the Voice of Justice and of Consanguinity. We must, therefore, acquiesce in the Necessity, which denounces our Separation, and hold them, as we hold the rest of Mankind, Enemies in War, in Peace, Friends.

We, therefore, the Representatives of the UNITED STATES OF AMERICA, in General Congress Assembled, appealing to the Supreme Judge of the World for the Rectitude of our Intentions, do, in the Name, and by the Authority of the good People of these Colonies, solemnly Publish and Declare, That these United Colonies are, and of Right ought to be, Free and Independent States; that they are absolved from all Allegiance to the British Crown, and that all political Connection between them and the State of Great-Britain, is and ought to be totally dissolved; and that as Free and Independent States, they have full Power to levy War, conclude Peace, contract Alliances, establish Commerce, and to do all other Acts and Things which Independent States may of right do. And for the support of this declaration, with a firm Reliance on the Protection of divine Providence, we mutually pledge to each other our lives, our Fortunes, and our sacred Honor.

# THE CONSTITUTION OF THE UNITED STATES

## PREAMBLE

We the People of the United States, in Order to form a more perfect Union, establish Justice, insure domestic Tranquility, provide for the common defence, promote the general Welfare, and secure the Blessings of Liberty to ourselves and our Posterity, do ordain and establish this Constitution for the United States of America.

## ARTICLE I

**Section 1.** All legislative Powers herein granted shall be vested in a Congress of the United States, which shall consist of a Senate and House of Representatives.

**Section 2.** The House of Representatives shall be composed of Members chosen every second Year by the People of the several States, and the Electors in each State shall have the Qualifications requisite for Electors of the most numerous Branch of the State Legislature.

No Person shall be a Representative who shall not have attained to the Age of twenty five Years, and been seven Years a Citizen of the United States, and who shall not, when elected, be an Inhabitant of that State in which he shall be chosen.

Representatives and direct Taxes shall be apportioned among the several States which may be included within this Union, according to their respective Numbers, which shall be determined by adding to the whole Number of free Persons, including those bound to Service for a Term of Years, and excluding Indians not taxed, three fifths of all other Persons. The actual Enumeration shall be made within three Years after the first Meeting of the Congress of the United States, and within every subsequent Term of ten Years, in such Manner as they shall by Law direct. The Number of Representatives shall not exceed one for every thirty Thousand, but each State shall have at Least one Representative; and until such enumeration shall be made, the State of New Hampshire shall be entitled to chuse three, Massachusetts eight, Rhode Island and Providence Plantations one, Connecticut five, New York six, New Jersey four, Pennsylvania eight, Delaware one, Maryland six, Virginia ten, North Carolina five, South Carolina five, and Georgia three.

When vacancies happen in the Representation from any State, the Executive Authority thereof shall issue Writs of Election to fill such Vacancies.

The House of Representatives shall chuse their Speaker and other Officers; and shall have the sole Power of Impeachment.

**Section 3.** The Senate of the United States shall be composed of two Senators from each State, chosen by the Legislature thereof, for six Years; and each Senator shall have one Vote.

Immediately after they shall be assembled in Consequence of the first Election, they shall be divided as equally as may be into three Classes. The Seats of the Senators of the first Class shall be vacated at the Expiration of the second Year, of the second Class at the Expiration of the fourth Year, and of the third Class at the Expiration of the sixth Year, so that one third may be chosen every second Year; and if Vacancies happen by Resignation, or otherwise, during the Recess of the Legislature of any State, the Executive thereof may make temporary Appointments until the next Meeting of the Legislature, which shall then fill such Vacancies.

No Person shall be a Senator who shall not have attained to the Age of thirty Years, and been nine Years a Citizen of the United States, and who shall not, when elected, be an Inhabitant of that State for which he shall be chosen.

The Vice President of the United States shall be President of the Senate, but shall have no Vote, unless they be equally divided.

The Senate shall chuse their other Officers, and also a President pro tempore, in the Absence of the Vice President, or when he shall exercise the Office of President of the United States.

The Senate shall have the sole Power to try all Impeachments. When sitting for that Purpose, they shall be on Oath or Affirmation. When the President of the United States is tried, the Chief Justice shall preside: And no Person shall be convicted without the Concurrence of two thirds of the Members present.

Judgment in Cases of Impeachment shall not extend further than to removal from Office, and disqualification to hold and enjoy any Office of honor, Trust, or Profit under the United States: but the Party convicted shall nevertheless be liable and subject to Indictment, Trial, Judgment, and Punishment, according to Law.

**Section 4.** The Times, Places and Manner of holding Elections for Senators and Representatives, shall be prescribed in each State by the Legislature thereof; but the Congress may at any time by Law make or alter such Regulations, except as to the Places of chusing Senators.

The Congress shall assemble at least once in every Year, and such Meeting shall be on the first Monday in December, unless they shall by Law appoint a different Day.

**Section 5.** Each House shall be the Judge of the Elections, Returns, and Qualifications of its own Members, and a Majority of each shall constitute a Quorum to do Business; but a smaller Number may adjourn from day to day, and may be authorized to compel the Attendance of absent Members, in such Manner, and under such Penalties as each House may provide.

Each House may determine the Rules of its Proceedings, punish its Members for disorderly Behavior, and, with the Concurrence of two thirds, expel a Member.

Each House shall keep a Journal of its Proceedings, and from time to time publish the same, excepting such Parts as may in their Judgment require Secrecy; and the Yeas and Nays of the Members of either House on any question shall, at the Desire of one fifth of those Present, be entered on the Journal.

Neither House, during the Session of Congress, shall, without the Consent of the other, adjourn for more than three days, nor to any other Place than that in which the two Houses shall be sitting.

**Section 6.** The Senators and Representatives shall receive a Compensation for their Services, to be ascertained by Law, and paid out of the Treasury of the United States. They shall in all Cases, except Treason, Felony and Breach of the Peace, be privileged from Arrest during their Attendance at the Session of their respective Houses, and in going to and returning from the same; and for any Speech or Debate in either House, they shall not be questioned in any other Place.

No Senator or Representative shall, during the Time for which he was elected, be appointed to any civil Office under the Authority of the United States, which shall have been created, or the Emoluments whereof shall have been increased during such time; and no Person holding any Office under the United States, shall be a Member of either House during his Continuance in Office.

**Section 7.** All Bills for raising Revenue shall originate in the House of Representatives; but the Senate may propose or concur with Amendments as on other Bills.

Every Bill which shall have passed the House of Representatives and the Senate, shall, before it become a Law, be presented to the President of the United States; If he approve he shall sign it, but if not he shall return it, with his Objections to the House in which it shall have originated, who shall enter the Objections at large on their Journal, and proceed to reconsider it. If after such Reconsideration two thirds of that House shall agree to pass the Bill, it shall be sent together with the Objections, to the other House, by which it shall likewise be reconsidered, and if approved by two thirds of that House, it shall become a Law. But in all such Cases the Votes of both Houses shall be determined by Yeas and Nays, and the Names of the Persons voting for and against the Bill shall be entered on the Journal of each House respectively. If any Bill shall not be returned by the President within ten Days (Sundays excepted) after it shall have been presented to him, the Same shall be a Law, in like Manner as if he had signed it, unless the Congress by their Adjournment prevent its Return in which Case it shall not be a Law.

Every Order, Resolution, or Vote, to which the Concurrence of the Senate and House of Representatives may be necessary (except on a question of Adjournment) shall be presented to the President of the United States; and before the Same shall take Effect, shall be approved by him, or being disapproved by him, shall be repassed by two thirds of the Senate and House of Representatives, according to the Rules and Limitations prescribed in the Case of a Bill.

**Section 8.** The Congress shall have Power To lay and collect Taxes, Duties, Imposts and Excises, to pay the Debts and provide for the common Defence and general Welfare of the United States; but all Duties, Imposts and Excises shall be uniform throughout the United States;

To borrow Money on the credit of the United States;

To regulate Commerce with foreign Nations, and among the several States, and with the Indian Tribes;

To establish an uniform Rule of Naturalization, and uniform Laws on the subject of Bankruptcies throughout the United States;

To coin Money, regulate the Value thereof, and of foreign Coin, and fix the Standard of Weights and Measures;

To provide for the Punishment of counterfeiting the Securities and current Coin of the United States;

To establish Post Offices and post Roads;

To promote the Progress of Science and useful Arts, by securing for limited Times to Authors and Inventors the exclusive Right to their respective Writings and Discoveries;

To constitute Tribunals inferior to the supreme Court;

To define and punish Piracies and Felonies committed on the high Seas, and Offenses against the Law of Nations;

To declare War, grant Letters of Marque and Reprisal, and make Rules concerning Captures on Land and Water;

To raise and support Armies, but no Appropriation of Money to that Use shall be for a longer Term than two Years;

To provide and maintain a Navy;

To make Rules for the Government and Regulation of the land and naval Forces;

To provide for calling forth the Militia to execute the Laws of the Union, suppress Insurrections and repel Invasions;

To provide for organizing, arming, and disciplining, the Militia, and for governing such Part of them as may be employed in the Service of the United States, reserving to the States respectively, the Appointment of the Officers, and the Authority of training the Militia according to the discipline prescribed by Congress;

To exercise exclusive Legislation in all Cases whatsoever, over such District (not exceeding ten Miles square) as may, by Cession of particular States, and the Acceptance of Congress, become the Seat of the Government of the United States, and to exercise like Authority over all Places purchased by the Consent of the Legislature of the State in which the Same shall be, for the Erection of Forts, Magazines, Arsenals, dock-Yards, and other needful Buildings;—And

To make all Laws which shall be necessary and proper for carrying into Execution the foregoing Powers, and all other Powers vested by this Constitution in the Government of the United States, or in any Department or Officer thereof.

**Section 9.** The Migration or Importation of such Persons as any of the States now existing shall think proper to admit, shall not be prohibited by the Congress prior to the Year one thousand eight hundred and eight, but a Tax or duty may be imposed on such Importation, not exceeding ten dollars for each Person.

The privilege of the Writ of Habeas Corpus shall not be suspended, unless when in Cases of Rebellion or Invasion the public Safety may require it.

No Bill of Attainder or ex post facto Law shall be passed.

No Capitation, or other direct, Tax shall be laid, unless in Proportion to the Census or Enumeration herein before directed to be taken.

No Tax or Duty shall be laid on Articles exported from any State.

No Preference shall be given by any Regulation of Commerce or Revenue to the Ports of one State over those of another: nor shall Vessels bound to, or from, one State be obliged to enter, clear, or pay Duties in another.

No Money shall be drawn from the Treasury, but in Consequence of Appropriations made by Law; and a regular Statement and Account of the Receipts and Expenditures of all public Money shall be published from time to time.

No Title of Nobility shall be granted by the United States: And no Person holding any Office of Profit or Trust under them, shall, without the Consent of the Congress, accept of any present, Emolument, Office, or Title, of any kind whatever, from any King, Prince, or foreign State.

**Section 10.** No State shall enter into any Treaty, Alliance, or Confederation; grant Letters of Marque and Reprisal; coin Money; emit Bills of Credit; make any Thing but gold and silver Coin a Tender in Payment of Debts; pass any Bill of Attainder, ex post facto Law, or Law impairing the Obligation of Contracts, or grant any Title of Nobility.

No State shall, without the Consent of the Congress, lay any Imposts or Duties on Imports or Exports, except what may be absolutely necessary for executing its inspection Laws: and the net Produce of all Duties and Imposts, laid by any State on Imports or Exports, shall be for the Use of the Treasury of the United States; and all such Laws shall be subject to the Revision and Controul of the Congress.

No State shall, without the Consent of Congress, lay any Duty of Tonnage, keep Troops, or Ships of War in time of Peace, enter into any Agreement or Compact with another State, or with a foreign Power, or engage in War, unless actually invaded, or in such imminent Danger as will not admit of delay.

# ARTICLE II

**Section 1.** The executive Power shall be vested in a President of the United States of America. He shall hold his Office during the Term of four Years, and, together with the Vice President, chosen for the same Term, be elected, as follows:

Each State shall appoint, in such Manner as the Legislature thereof may direct, a Number of Electors, equal to the whole Number of Senators and Representatives to which the State may be entitled in the Congress; but no Senator or Representative, or Person holding an Office of Trust or Profit under the United States, shall be appointed an Elector.

The Electors shall meet in their respective States, and vote by Ballot for two Persons, of whom one at least shall not be an Inhabitant of the same State with themselves. And they shall make a List of all the Persons voted for, and of the Number of Votes for each; which List they shall sign and certify, and transmit sealed to the Seat of the Government of the United States, directed to the President of the Senate. The President of the Senate shall, in the Presence of the Senate and House of Representatives, open all the Certificates, and the Votes shall then be counted. The Person having the greatest Number of Votes shall be the President, if such Number be a Majority of the whole Number of Electors appointed; and if there be more than one who have such Majority, and have an equal Number of Votes, then the House of Representatives shall immediately chuse by Ballot one of them for President; and if no Person have a Majority, then from the five highest on the List the said House shall in like Manner chuse the President. But in chusing the President, the Votes shall be taken by States, the Representation from each State having one Vote; A quorum for this Purpose shall consist of a Member or Members from two thirds of the States, and a Majority of all the States shall be necessary to a Choice. In every Case, after the Choice of the President, the Person having the greater Number of Votes of the Electors shall be the Vice President. But if there should remain two or more who have equal Votes, the Senate shall chuse from them by Ballot the Vice President.

The Congress may determine the Time of chusing the Electors, and the Day on which they shall give their Votes; which Day shall be the same throughout the United States.

No person except a natural born Citizen, or a Citizen of the United States, at the time of the Adoption of this Constitution, shall be eligible to the Office of President; neither shall any Person be eligible to that Office who shall not have attained to the Age of thirty five Years, and been fourteen Years a Resident within the United States.

In Case of the Removal of the President from Office, or of his Death, Resignation or Inability to discharge the Powers and Duties of the said Office, the same shall devolve on the Vice President, and the Congress may by Law provide for the Case of Removal, Death, Resignation or Inability, both of the President and Vice President, declaring what Officer shall then act as President, and such Officer shall act accordingly, until the Disability be removed, or a President shall be elected.

The President shall, at stated Times, receive for his Services, a Compensation, which shall neither be increased nor diminished during the Period for which he shall have been elected, and he shall not receive within that Period any other Emolument from the United States, or any of them.

Before he enter on the Execution of his Office, he shall take the following Oath or Affirmation: "I do solemnly swear (or affirm) that I will faithfully execute the Office of President of the United States, and will to the best of my Ability, preserve, protect and defend the Constitution of the United States."

**Section 2.** The President shall be Commander in Chief of the Army and Navy of the United States, and of the Militia of the several States, when called into the actual Service of the United States; he may require the Opinion, in writing, of the principal Officer in each of the executive Departments, upon any Subject relating to the Duties of their respective Offices, and he shall have Power to grant Reprieves and Pardons for Offenses against the United States, except in Cases of Impeachment.

He shall have Power, by and with the Advice and Consent of the Senate to make Treaties, provided two thirds of the Senators present concur; and he shall nominate, and by and with the Advice and Consent of the Senate, shall appoint Ambassadors, other public Ministers and Consuls, Judges of the supreme Court, and all other Officers of the United States, whose Appointments are not herein otherwise provided for, and which shall be established by Law; but the Congress may by Law vest the Appointment of such inferior Officers, as they think proper, in the President alone, in the Courts of Law, or in the Heads of Departments.

The President shall have Power to fill up all Vacancies that may happen during the Recess of the Senate, by granting Commissions which shall expire at the End of their next Session.

**Section 3.** He shall from time to time give to the Congress Information of the State of the Union, and recommend to their Consideration such Measures as he shall judge necessary and expedient; he may, on extraordinary Occasions, convene both Houses, or either of them, and in Case of Disagreement between them, with Respect to the Time of Adjournment, he may adjourn them to such Time as he shall think proper; he shall receive Ambassadors and other public Ministers; he shall take Care that the Laws be faithfully executed, and shall Commission all the Officers of the United States.

**Section 4.** The President, Vice President and all civil Officers of the United States, shall be removed from Office on Impeachment for, and Conviction of, Treason, Bribery, or other high Crimes and Misdemeanors.

# ARTICLE III

**Section 1.** The judicial Power of the United States, shall be vested in one supreme Court, and in such inferior Courts as the Congress may from time to time ordain and establish. The Judges, both of the supreme and inferior Courts, shall hold their Offices during good Behaviour, and shall, at stated Times, receive for their Services a Compensation, which shall not be diminished during their Continuance in Office.

**Section 2.** The judicial Power shall extend to all Cases, in Law and Equity, arising under this Constitution, the Laws of the United States, and Treaties made, or which shall be made, under their Authority;—to all Cases affecting Ambassadors, other public Ministers and Consuls;—to all Cases of admiralty and maritime Jurisdiction;—to Controversies to which the United States shall be a Party;—to Controversies between two or more States;—between a State and Citizens of another State;—between Citizens of different States;—between Citizens of the same State claiming Lands under Grants of different States, and between a State, or the Citizens thereof, and foreign States, Citizens or Subjects.

In all Cases affecting Ambassadors, other public Ministers and Consuls, and those in which a State shall be a Party, the supreme Court shall have original Jurisdiction. In all the other Cases before mentioned, the supreme Court shall have appellate Jurisdiction, both as to Law and Fact, with such Exceptions, and under such Regulations as the Congress shall make.

The Trial of all Crimes, except in Cases of Impeachment, shall be by Jury; and such Trial shall be held in the State where the said Crimes shall have been committed; but when not committed within any State, the Trial shall be at such Place or Places as the Congress may by Law have directed.

**Section 3.** Treason against the United States, shall consist only in levying War against them, or, in adhering to their Enemies, giving them Aid and Comfort. No Person shall be convicted of Treason unless on the Testimony of two Witnesses to the same overt Act, or on Confession in open Court.

The Congress shall have Power to declare the Punishment of Treason, but no Attainder of Treason shall work Corruption of Blood, or Forfeiture except during the Life of the Person attainted.

# ARTICLE IV

**Section 1.** Full Faith and Credit shall be given in each State to the public Acts, Records, and judicial Proceedings of every other State. And the Congress may by general Laws prescribe the Manner in which such Acts, Records and Proceedings shall be proved, and the Effect thereof.

**Section 2.** The Citizens of each State shall be entitled to all Privileges and Immunities of Citizens in the several States.

A Person charged in any State with Treason, Felony, or other Crime, who shall flee from Justice, and be found in another State, shall on Demand of the executive Authority of the State from which he fled, be delivered up, to be removed to the State having Jurisdiction of the Crime.

No Person held to Service or Labour in one State, under the Laws thereof, escaping into another, shall, in Consequence of any Law or Regulation therein, be discharged from such Service or Labour, but shall be delivered up on Claim of the Party to whom such Service or Labour may be due.

**Section 3.** New States may be admitted by the Congress into this Union; but no new State shall be formed or erected within the Jurisdiction of any other

State; nor any State be formed by the Junction of two or more States, or Parts of States, without the Consent of the Legislatures of the States concerned as well as of the Congress.

The Congress shall have Power to dispose of and make all needful Rules and Regulations respecting the Territory or other Property belonging to the United States; and nothing in this Constitution shall be so construed as to Prejudice any Claims of the United States, or of any particular State.

**Section 4.** The United States shall guarantee to every State in this Union a Republican Form of Government, and shall protect each of them against Invasion; and on Application of the Legislature, or of the Executive (when the Legislature cannot be convened) against domestic Violence.

# ARTICLE V

The Congress, whenever two thirds of both Houses shall deem it necessary, shall propose Amendments to this Constitution, or, on the Application of the Legislatures of two thirds of the several States, shall call a Convention for proposing Amendments, which, in either Case, shall be valid to all Intents and Purposes, as part of this Constitution, when ratified by the Legislatures of three fourths of the several States, or by Conventions in three fourths thereof, as the one or the other Mode of Ratification may be proposed by the Congress; Provided that no Amendment which may be made prior to the Year One thousand eight hundred and eight shall in any Manner affect the first and fourth Clauses in the Ninth Section of the first Article; and that no State, without its Consent, shall be deprived of its equal Suffrage in the Senate.

# ARTICLE VI

All Debts contracted and Engagements entered into, before the Adoption of this Constitution shall be as valid against the United States under this Constitution, as under the Confederation.

This Constitution, and the Laws of the United States which shall be made in Pursuance thereof; and all Treaties made, or which shall be made, under the Authority of the United States, shall be the supreme Law of the Land; and the Judges in every State shall be bound thereby, any Thing in the Constitution or Laws of any State to the Contrary notwithstanding.

The Senators and Representatives before mentioned, and the Members of the several State Legislatures, and all executive and judicial Officers, both of the United States and of the several States, shall be bound by Oath or Affirmation, to support this Constitution; but no religious Test shall ever be required as a Qualification to any Office or public Trust under the United States.

# ARTICLE VII

The Ratification of the Conventions of nine States shall be sufficient for the Establishment of this Constitution between the States so ratifying the Same.

# AMENDMENT I [1791]

Congress shall make no law respecting an establishment of religion, or prohibiting the free exercise thereof; or abridging the freedom of speech, or of the press; or the right of the people peaceably to assemble, and to petition the Government for a redress of grievances.

# AMENDMENT II [1791]

A well regulated Militia, being necessary to the security of a free State, the right of the people to keep and bear Arms, shall not be infringed.

# AMENDMENT III [1791]

No Soldier shall, in time of peace be quartered in any house, without the consent of the Owner, nor in time of war, but in a manner to be prescribed by law.

# AMENDMENT IV [1791]

The right of the people to be secure in their persons, houses, papers, and effects, against unreasonable searches and seizures, shall not be violated, and no Warrants shall issue, but upon probable cause, supported by Oath or affirmation, and particularly describing the place to be searched, and the persons or things to be seized.

# AMENDMENT V [1791]

No person shall be held to answer for a capital, or otherwise infamous crime, unless on a presentment or indictment of a Grand Jury, except in cases arising in the land or naval forces, or in the Militia, when in actual service in time of War or public danger; nor shall any person be subject for the same offense to be twice put in jeopardy of life or limb; nor shall be compelled in any criminal case to be a witness against himself, nor be deprived of life, liberty, or property, without due process of law; nor shall private property be taken for public use, without just compensation.

# AMENDMENT VI [1791]

In all criminal prosecutions, the accused shall enjoy the right to a speedy and public trial, by an impartial jury of the State and district wherein the crime shall have been committed, which district shall have been previously ascertained by law, and to be informed of the nature and cause of the accusation; to be confronted with the witnesses against him; to have compulsory process for obtaining witnesses in his favor, and to have the Assistance of Counsel for his defence.

# AMENDMENT VII [1791]

In Suits at common law, where the value in controversy shall exceed twenty dollars, the right of trial by jury shall be preserved, and no fact tried by a jury, shall be otherwise re-examined in any Court of the United States, than according to the rules of the common law.

# AMENDMENT VIII [1791]

Excessive bail shall not be required, nor excessive fines imposed, nor cruel and unusual punishments inflicted.

# AMENDMENT IX [1791]

The enumeration in the Constitution, of certain rights, shall not be construed to deny or disparage others retained by the people.

# AMENDMENT X [1791]

The powers not delegated to the United States by the Constitution, nor prohibited by it to the States, are reserved to the States respectively, or to the people.

# AMENDMENT XI [1798]

The Judicial power of the United States shall not be construed to extend to any suit in law or equity, commenced or prosecuted against one of the United States by Citizens of another State, or by Citizens or Subjects of any Foreign State.

# AMENDMENT XII [1804]

The Electors shall meet in their respective states, and vote by ballot for President and Vice-President, one of whom, at least, shall not be an inhabitant of the same state with themselves; they shall name in their ballots the person voted for as President, and in distinct ballots the person voted for as Vice-President, and they shall make distinct lists of all persons voted for as President, and of all persons voted for as Vice-President, and of the number of votes for each, which lists they shall sign and certify, and transmit sealed to the seat of the government of the United States, directed to the President of the Senate;—The President of the Senate shall, in the presence of the Senate and House of Representatives, open all the certificates and the votes shall then be counted;—The person having the greatest number of votes for President, shall be the President, if such number be a majority of the whole number of Electors appointed; and if no person have such majority, then from the persons having the highest numbers not exceeding three on the list of those voted for as President, the House of Representatives shall choose immediately, by ballot, the President. But in choosing the President, the votes shall be taken by states, the representation from each state having one vote; a quorum for this purpose shall consist of a member or members from two-thirds of the states, and a majority of all states shall be necessary to a choice. And if the House of Representatives shall not choose a President whenever the right of choice shall devolve upon them, before the fourth day of March next following, then the Vice-President shall act as President, as in the case of the death or other constitutional disability of the President.—The person having the greatest number of votes as Vice-President, shall be the Vice-President, if such number be a majority of the whole number of Electors appointed, and if no person have a majority, then from the two highest numbers on the list, the Senate shall choose the Vice-President; a quorum for the purpose shall consist of two-thirds of the whole number of Senators, and a majority of the whole number shall be necessary to a choice. But no person constitutionally ineligible to the office of President shall be eligible to that of Vice-President of the United States.

# AMENDMENT XIII [1865]

**Section 1.** Neither slavery nor involuntary servitude, except as a punishment for crime whereof the party shall have been duly convicted, shall exist within the United States, or any place subject to their jurisdiction.

**Section 2.** Congress shall have power to enforce this article by appropriate legislation.

# AMENDMENT XIV [1868]

**Section 1.** All persons born or naturalized in the United States, and subject to the jurisdiction thereof, are citizens of the United States and of the State wherein they reside. No State shall make or enforce any law which shall abridge the privileges or immunities of citizens of the United States; nor shall any State deprive any person of life, liberty, or property, without due process of law; nor deny to any person within its jurisdiction the equal protection of the laws.

**Section 2.** Representatives shall be apportioned among the several States according to their respective numbers, counting the whole number of persons in each State, excluding Indians not taxed. But when the right to vote at any election for the choice of electors for President and Vice President of the United States, Representatives in Congress, the Executive and Judicial officers of a State, or the members of the Legislature thereof, is denied to any of the male inhabitants of such State, being twenty-one years of age, and citizens of the United States, or in any way abridged, except for participation in rebellion, or other crime, the basis of representation therein shall be reduced in the proportion which the number of such male citizens shall bear to the whole number  of male citizens twenty-one years of age in such State.

**Section 3.** No person shall be a Senator or Representative in Congress, or elector of President and Vice President, or hold any office, civil or military, under the United States, or under any State, who having previously taken an oath, as a member of Congress, or as an officer of the United States, or as a member of any State legislature, or as an executive or judicial officer of any State, to support the Constitution of the United States, shall have engaged in insurrection or rebellion against the same, or given aid or comfort to the enemies thereof. But Congress may by a vote of two-thirds of each House, remove such disability.

**Section 4.** The validity of the public debt of the United States, authorized by law, including debts incurred for payment of pensions and bounties for services in suppressing insurrection or rebellion, shall not be questioned. But neither the United States nor any State shall assume or pay any debt or obligation incurred in aid of insurrection or rebellion against the United States, or any claim for the loss or emancipation of any slave; but all such debts, obligations and claims shall be held illegal and void.

**Section 5.** The Congress shall have power to enforce, by appropriate legislation, the provisions of this article.

# AMENDMENT XV [1870]

**Section 1.** The right of citizens of the United States to vote shall not be denied or abridged by the United States or by any State on account of race, color, or previous condition of servitude.

**Section 2.** The Congress shall have power to enforce this article by appropriate legislation.

# AMENDMENT XVI [1913]

The Congress shall have power to lay and collect taxes on incomes, from whatever source derived, without apportionment among the several States, and without regard to any census or enumeration.

# AMENDMENT XVII [1913]

**Section 1.** The Senate of the United States shall be composed of two Senators from each State, elected by the people thereof, for six years; and each Senator shall have one vote. The electors in each State shall have the qualifications requisite for electors of the most numerous branch of the State legislatures.

**Section 2.** When vacancies happen in the representation of any State in the Senate, the executive authority of such State shall issue writs of election to fill such vacancies: Provided, That the legislature of any State may empower the executive thereof to make temporary appointments until the people fill the vacancies by election as the legislature may direct.

**Section 3.** This amendment shall not be so construed as to affect the election or term of any Senator chosen before it becomes valid as part of the Constitution.

# AMENDMENT XVIII [1919]

**Section 1.** After one year from the ratification of this article the manufacture, sale, or transportation of intoxicating liquors within, the importation thereof into, or the exportation thereof from the United States and all territory subject to the jurisdiction thereof for beverage purposes is hereby prohibited.

**Section 2.** The Congress and the several States shall have concurrent power to enforce this article by appropriate legislation.

**Section 3.** This article shall be inoperative unless it shall have been ratified as an amendment to the Constitution by the legislatures of the several States, as provided in the Constitution, within seven years from the date of the submission hereof to the States by the Congress.

# AMENDMENT XIX [1920]

**Section 1.** The right of citizens of the United States to vote shall not be denied or abridged by the United States or by any State on account of sex.

**Section 2.** Congress shall have power to enforce this article by appropriate legislation.

# AMENDMENT XX [1933]

**Section 1.** The terms of the President and Vice President shall end at noon on the 20th day of January, and the terms of Senators and Representatives at noon on the 3d day of January, of the years in which such terms would have ended if this article had not been ratified; and the terms of their successors shall then begin.

**Section 2.** The Congress shall assemble at least once in every year, and such meeting shall begin at noon on the 3d day of January, unless they shall by law appoint a different day.

**Section 3.** If, at the time fixed for the beginning of the term of the President, the President elect shall have died, the Vice President elect shall become President. If the President shall not have been chosen before the time fixed for the beginning of his term, or if the President elect shall have failed to qualify, then the Vice President elect shall act as President until a President shall have qualified; and the Congress may by law provide for the case wherein neither a President elect nor a Vice President elect shall have qualified, declaring who shall then act as President, or the manner in which one who is to act shall be selected, and such person shall act accordingly until a President or Vice President shall have qualified.

**Section 4.** The Congress may by law provide for the case of the death of any of the persons from whom the House of Representatives may choose a President whenever the right of choice shall have devolved upon them, and for the case of the death of any of the persons from whom the Senate may choose a Vice President whenever the right of choice shall have devolved upon them.

**Section 5.** Sections 1 and 2 shall take effect on the 15th day of October following the ratification of this article.

**Section 6.** This article shall be inoperative unless it shall have been ratified as an amendment to the Constitution by the legislatures of three-fourths of the several States within seven years from the date of its submission.

# AMENDMENT XXI [1933]

**Section 1.** The eighteenth article of amendment to the Constitution of the United States is hereby repealed.

**Section 2.** The transportation or importation into any State, Territory, or possession of the United States for delivery or use therein of intoxicating liquors, in violation of the laws thereof, is hereby prohibited.

**Section 3.** This article shall be inoperative unless it shall have been ratified as an amendment to the Constitution by conventions in the several States, as provided in the Constitution, within seven years from the date of the submission hereof to the States by the Congress.

# AMENDMENT XXII [1951]

**Section 1.** No person shall be elected to the office of the President more than twice, and no person who has held the office of President, or acted as President, for more than two years of a term to which some other person was elected President shall be elected to the office of President more than once. But this Article shall not apply to any person holding the office of President when this Article was proposed by the Congress, and shall not prevent any person who may be holding the office of President, or acting as President, during the term within which this Article becomes operative from holding the office of President or acting as President during the remainder of such term.

**Section 2.** This article shall be inoperative unless it shall have been ratified as an amendment to the Constitution by the legislatures of three-fourths of the several States within seven years from the date of its submission to the States by the Congress.

# AMENDMENT XXIII [1961]

**Section 1.** The District constituting the seat of Government of the United States shall appoint in such manner as the Congress may direct:

A number of electors of President and Vice President equal to the whole number of Senators and Representatives in Congress to which the District would be entitled if it were a State, but in no event more than the least populous state; they shall be in addition to those appointed by the states, but they shall be considered, for the purposes of the election of President and Vice President, to be electors appointed by a state; and they shall meet in the District and perform such duties as provided by the twelfth article of amendment.

**Section 2.** The Congress shall have power to enforce this article by appropriate legislation.

# AMENDMENT XXIV [1964]

**Section 1.** The right of citizens of the United States to vote in any primary or other election for President or Vice President, for electors for President or Vice President, or for Senator or Representative in Congress, shall not be denied or abridged by the United States, or any State by reason of failure to pay any poll tax or other tax.

**Section 2.** The Congress shall have power to enforce this article by appropriate legislation.

# AMENDMENT XXV [1967]

**Section 1.** In case of the removal of the President from office or of his death or resignation, the Vice President shall become President.

**Section 2.** Whenever there is a vacancy in the office of the Vice President, the President shall nominate a Vice President who shall take office upon confirmation by a majority vote of both Houses of Congress.

**Section 3.** Whenever the President transmits to the President pro tempore of the Senate and the Speaker of the House of Representatives his written declaration that he is unable to discharge the powers and duties of his office, and until he transmits to them a written declaration to the contrary, such powers and duties shall be discharged by the Vice President as Acting President.

**Section 4.** Whenever the Vice President and a majority of either the principal officers of the executive departments or of such other body as Congress may by law provide, transmit to the President pro tempore of the Senate and the Speaker of the House of Representatives their written declaration that the President is unable to discharge the powers and duties of his office, the Vice President shall immediately assume the powers and duties of the office as Acting President.

Thereafter, when the President transmits to the President pro tempore of the Senate and the Speaker of the House of Representatives his written declaration that no inability exists, he shall resume the powers and duties of his office unless the Vice President and a majority of either the principal officers of the executive department or of such other body as Congress may by law provide, transmit within four days to the President pro tempore of the Senate and the Speaker of the House of Representatives their written declaration that the President is unable to discharge the powers and duties of his office. Thereupon Congress shall decide the issue, assembling within forty-eight hours for that purpose if not in session. If the Congress, within twenty-one days after receipt of the latter written declaration, or, if Congress is not in session, within twenty-one days after Congress is required to assemble, determines by two-thirds vote of both Houses that the President is unable to discharge the powers and duties of his office, the Vice President shall continue to discharge the same as Acting President; otherwise, the President shall resume the powers and duties of his office.

# AMENDMENT XXVI [1971]

**Section 1.** The right of citizens of the United States, who are eighteen years of age or older, to vote shall not be denied or abridged by the United States or by any State on account of age.

**Section 2.** The Congress shall have power to enforce this article by appropriate legislation.

# AMENDMENT XXVII [1992]

No law, varying the compensation for the services of the Senators and Representatives, shall take effect, until an election of Representatives shall have intervened.

# SUPREME COURT JUSTICES SINCE 1900

## Chief Justices

| Name | Years of Service | State App'd from | Appointing President | Age App'd | Political Affiliation | Educational Background* |
|---|---|---|---|---|---|---|
| Fuller, Melville Weston | 1888–1910 | Illinois | Cleveland | 55 | Democrat | Bowdoin College; studied at Harvard Law School |
| White, Edward Douglass | 1910–1921 | Louisiana | Taft | 65 | Democrat | Mount St. Mary's College; Georgetown College (now University) |
| Taft, William Howard | 1921–1930 | Connecticut | Harding | 64 | Republican | Yale; Cincinnati Law School |
| Hughes, Charles Evans | 1930–1941 | New York | Hoover | 68 | Republican | Colgate University; Brown; Columbia Law School |
| Stone, Harlan Fiske | 1941–1946 | New York | Roosevelt, F. | 69 | Republican | Amherst College; Columbia |
| Vinson, Frederick Moore | 1946–1953 | Kentucky | Truman | 56 | Democrat | Centre College |
| Warren, Earl | 1953–1969 | California | Eisenhower | 62 | Republican | University of California, Berkeley |
| Burger, Warren Earl | 1969–1986 | Virginia | Nixon | 62 | Republican | University of Minnesota; St. Paul College of Law (Mitchell College) |
| Rehnquist, William Hubbs | 1986–2005 | Virginia | Reagan | 62 | Republican | Stanford; Harvard; Stanford University Law School |
| Roberts, John G., Jr. | 2005–present | District of Columbia | G. W. Bush | 50 | Republican | Harvard; Harvard Law School |

*Source: Educational background information derived from Elder Witt, *Guide to the U.S. Supreme Court*, 2d ed. (Washington, D.C.: Congressional Quarterly Press, Inc., 1990). Reprinted with the permission of the publisher.

## Associate Justices

| Name | Years of Service | State App'd from | Appointing President | Age App'd | Political Affiliation | Educational Background* |
|---|---|---|---|---|---|---|
| Harlan, John Marshall | 1877–1911 | Kentucky | Hayes | 61 | Republican | Centre College; studied law at Transylvania University |
| Gray, Horace | 1882–1902 | Massachusetts | Arthur | 54 | Republican | Harvard College; Harvard Law School |
| Brewer, David Josiah | 1890–1910 | Kansas | Harrison | 53 | Republican | Wesleyan University; Yale; Albany Law School |
| Brown, Henry Billings | 1891–1906 | Michigan | Harrison | 55 | Republican | Yale; studied at Yale Law School and Harvard Law School |
| Shiras, George, Jr. | 1892–1903 | Pennsylvania | Harrison | 61 | Republican | Ohio University; Yale; studied law at Yale and privately |
| White, Edward Douglass | 1894–1910 | Louisiana | Cleveland | 49 | Democrat | Mount St. Mary's College; Georgetown College (now University) |
| Peckham, Rufus Wheeler | 1896–1909 | New York | Cleveland | 58 | Democrat | Read law in father's firm |

| Name | Years of Service | State App'd from | Appointing President | Age App'd | Political Affiliation | Educational Background* |
|---|---|---|---|---|---|---|
| McKenna, Joseph | 1898–1925 | California | McKinley | 55 | Republican | Benicia Collegiate Institute, Law Dept. |
| Holmes, Oliver Wendell, Jr. | 1902–1932 | Massachusetts | Roosevelt, T. | 61 | Republican | Harvard College; studied law at Harvard Law School |
| Day, William Rufus | 1903–1922 | Ohio | Roosevelt, T. | 54 | Republican | University of Michigan; University of Michigan Law School |
| Moody, William Henry | 1906–1910 | Massachusetts | Roosevelt, T. | 53 | Republican | Harvard; Harvard Law School |
| Lurton, Horace Harmon | 1910–1914 | Tennessee | Taft | 66 | Democrat | University of Chicago; Cumberland Law School |
| Hughes, Charles Evans | 1910–1916 | New York | Taft | 48 | Republican | Colgate University; Brown University; Columbia Law School |
| Van Devanter, Willis | 1911–1937 | Wyoming | Taft | 52 | Republican | Indiana Asbury University; University of Cincinnati Law School |
| Lamar, Joseph Rucker | 1911–1916 | Georgia | Taft | 54 | Democrat | University of Georgia; Bethany College; Washington and Lee University |
| Pitney, Mahlon | 1912–1922 | New Jersey | Taft | 54 | Republican | College of New Jersey (Princeton); read law under father |
| McReynolds, James Clark | 1914–1941 | Tennessee | Wilson | 52 | Democrat | Vanderbilt University; University of Virginia |
| Brandeis, Louis Dembitz | 1916–1939 | Massachusetts | Wilson | 60 | Democrat | Harvard Law School |
| Clarke, John Hessin | 1916–1922 | Ohio | Wilson | 59 | Democrat | Western Reserve University; read law under father |
| Sutherland, George | 1922–1938 | Utah | Harding | 60 | Republican | Brigham Young Academy; one year at University of Michigan Law School |
| Butler, Pierce | 1923–1939 | Minnesota | Harding | 57 | Democrat | Carleton College |
| Sanford, Edward Terry | 1923–1930 | Tennessee | Harding | 58 | Republican | University of Tennessee; Harvard; Harvard Law School |
| Stone, Harlan Fiske | 1925–1941 | New York | Coolidge | 53 | Republican | Amherst College; Columbia University Law School |
| Roberts, Owen Josephus | 1930–1945 | Pennsylvania | Hoover | 55 | Republican | University of Pennsylvania; University of Pennsylvania Law School |
| Cardozo, Benjamin Nathan | 1932–1938 | New York | Hoover | 62 | Democrat | Columbia University; two years at Columbia Law School |
| Black, Hugo Lafayette | 1937–1971 | Alabama | Roosevelt, F. | 51 | Democrat | Birmingham Medical College; University of Alabama Law School |
| Reed, Stanley Forman | 1938–1957 | Kentucky | Roosevelt, F. | 54 | Democrat | Kentucky Wesleyan University; Foreman Yale; Columbia University |
| Frankfurter, Felix | 1939–1962 | Massachusetts | Roosevelt, F. | 57 | Independent | College of the City of New York; Harvard Law School |
| Douglas, William Orville | 1939–1975 | Connecticut | Roosevelt, F. | 41 | Democrat | Whitman College; Columbia University Law School |
| Murphy, Frank | 1940–1949 | Michigan | Roosevelt, F. | 50 | Democrat | University of Michigan; Lincoln's Inn, London; Trinity College |
| Byrnes, James Francis | 1941–1942 | South Carolina | Roosevelt, F. | 62 | Democrat | Read law privately |

| Name | Years of Service | State App'd from | Appointing President | Age App'd | Political Affiliation | Educational Background* |
|---|---|---|---|---|---|---|
| Jackson, Robert Houghwout | 1941–1954 | New York | Roosevelt, F. | 49 | Democrat | Albany Law School |
| Rutledge, Wiley Blount | 1943–1949 | Iowa | Roosevelt, F. | 49 | Democrat | University of Wisconsin; University of Colorado |
| Burton, Harold Hitz | 1945–1958 | Ohio | Truman | 57 | Republican | Bowdoin College; Harvard University Law School |
| Clark, Thomas Campbell | 1949–1967 | Texas | Truman | 50 | Democrat | University of Texas |
| Minton, Sherman | 1949–1956 | Indiana | Truman | 59 | Democrat | Indiana University College of Law; Yale Law School |
| Harlan, John Marshall | 1955–1971 | New York | Eisenhower | 56 | Republican | Princeton; Oxford University; New York Law School |
| Brennan, William J., Jr. | 1956–1990 | New Jersey | Eisenhower | 50 | Democrat | University of Pennsylvania; Harvard Law School |
| Whittaker, Charles Evans | 1957–1962 | Missouri | Eisenhower | 56 | Republican | University of Kansas City Law School |
| Stewart, Potter | 1958–1981 | Ohio | Eisenhower | 43 | Republican | Yale; Yale Law School |
| White, Byron Raymond | 1962–1993 | Colorado | Kennedy | 45 | Democrat | University of Colorado; Oxford University; Yale Law School |
| Goldberg, Arthur Joseph | 1962–1965 | Illinois | Kennedy | 54 | Democrat | Northwestern University |
| Fortas, Abe | 1965–1969 | Tennessee | Johnson, L. | 55 | Democrat | Southwestern College; Yale Law School |
| Marshall, Thurgood | 1967–1991 | New York | Johnson, L. | 59 | Democrat | Lincoln University; Howard University Law School |
| Blackmun, Harry A. | 1970–1994 | Minnesota | Nixon | 62 | Republican | Harvard; Harvard Law School |
| Powell, Lewis F., Jr. | 1972–1987 | Virginia | Nixon | 65 | Democrat | Washington and Lee University; Harvard Law School |
| Rehnquist, William H. | 1972–1986 | Arizona | Nixon | 48 | Republican | Stanford; Harvard; Stanford University Law School |
| Stevens, John Paul | 1975–present | Illinois | Ford | 55 | Republican | University of Colorado; Northwestern University Law School |
| O'Connor, Sandra Day | 1981–2006 | Arizona | Reagan | 51 | Republican | Stanford; Stanford University Law School |
| Scalia, Antonin | 1986–present | Virginia | Reagan | 50 | Republican | Georgetown University; Harvard Law School |
| Kennedy, Anthony M. | 1988–present | California | Reagan | 52 | Republican | Stanford; London School of Economics; Harvard Law School |
| Souter, David Hackett | 1990–2009 | New Hampshire | Bush, G. H. W. | 51 | Republican | Harvard; Oxford University |
| Thomas, Clarence | 1991–present | District of Columbia | Bush, G. H. W. | 43 | Republican | Holy Cross College; Yale Law School |
| Ginsburg, Ruth Bader | 1993–present | District of Columbia | Clinton | 60 | Democrat | Cornell University; Columbia Law School |
| Breyer, Stephen G. | 1994–present | Massachusetts | Clinton | 55 | Democrat | Stanford; Oxford University; Harvard Law School |
| Alito, Samuel Anthony, Jr. | 2006–present | New Jersey | G. W. Bush | 55 | Republican | Princeton University; Yale Law School |
| Sotomayor, Sonia | 2009–present | New York | Obama | 55 | Democrat | Princeton University; Yale Law School |
| Kagan, Elena | 2010–present | District of Columbia | Obama | 50 | Democrat | Princeton and Oxford Universities; Harvard Law School |

# PARTY CONTROL OF CONGRESS SINCE 1900

| Congress | Years | President | Majority Party in House | Majority Party in Senate |
|---|---|---|---|---|
| 57th | 1901–1903 | T. Roosevelt | Republican | Republican |
| 58th | 1903–1905 | T. Roosevelt | Republican | Republican |
| 59th | 1905–1907 | T. Roosevelt | Republican | Republican |
| 60th | 1907–1909 | T. Roosevelt | Republican | Republican |
| 61st | 1909–1911 | Taft | Republican | Republican |
| 62d | 1911–1913 | Taft | Democratic | Republican |
| 63d | 1913–1915 | Wilson | Democratic | Democratic |
| 64th | 1915–1917 | Wilson | Democratic | Democratic |
| 65th | 1917–1919 | Wilson | Democratic | Democratic |
| 66th | 1919–1921 | Wilson | Republican | Republican |
| 67th | 1921–1923 | Harding | Republican | Republican |
| 68th | 1923–1925 | Coolidge | Republican | Republican |
| 69th | 1925–1927 | Coolidge | Republican | Republican |
| 70th | 1927–1929 | Coolidge | Republican | Republican |
| 71st | 1929–1931 | Hoover | Republican | Republican |
| 72d | 1931–1933 | Hoover | Democratic | Republican |
| 73d | 1933–1935 | F. Roosevelt | Democratic | Democratic |
| 74th | 1935–1937 | F. Roosevelt | Democratic | Democratic |
| 75th | 1937–1939 | F. Roosevelt | Democratic | Democratic |
| 76th | 1939–1941 | F. Roosevelt | Democratic | Democratic |
| 77th | 1941–1943 | F. Roosevelt | Democratic | Democratic |
| 78th | 1943–1945 | F. Roosevelt | Democratic | Democratic |
| 79th | 1945–1947 | Truman | Democratic | Democratic |
| 80th | 1947–1949 | Truman | Republican | Democratic |
| 81st | 1949–1951 | Truman | Democratic | Democratic |
| 82d | 1951–1953 | Truman | Democratic | Democratic |
| 83d | 1953–1955 | Eisenhower | Republican | Republican |
| 84th | 1955–1957 | Eisenhower | Democratic | Democratic |
| 85th | 1957–1959 | Eisenhower | Democratic | Democratic |
| 86th | 1959–1961 | Eisenhower | Democratic | Democratic |
| 87th | 1961–1963 | Kennedy | Democratic | Democratic |
| 88th | 1963–1965 | Kennedy/Johnson | Democratic | Democratic |
| 89th | 1965–1967 | Johnson | Democratic | Democratic |
| 90th | 1967–1969 | Johnson | Democratic | Democratic |
| 91st | 1969–1971 | Nixon | Democratic | Democratic |
| 92d | 1971–1973 | Nixon | Democratic | Democratic |
| 93d | 1973–1975 | Nixon/Ford | Democratic | Democratic |
| 94th | 1975–1977 | Ford | Democratic | Democratic |
| 95th | 1977–1979 | Carter | Democratic | Democratic |
| 96th | 1979–1981 | Carter | Democratic | Democratic |
| 97th | 1981–1983 | Reagan | Democratic | Republican |
| 98th | 1983–1985 | Reagan | Democratic | Republican |
| 99th | 1985–1987 | Reagan | Democratic | Republican |
| 100th | 1987–1989 | Reagan | Democratic | Democratic |
| 101st | 1989–1991 | G. H. W. Bush | Democratic | Democratic |
| 102d | 1991–1993 | G. H. W. Bush | Democratic | Democratic |
| 103d | 1993–1995 | Clinton | Democratic | Democratic |
| 104th | 1995–1997 | Clinton | Republican | Republican |
| 105th | 1997–1999 | Clinton | Republican | Republican |
| 106th | 1999–2001 | Clinton | Republican | Republican |
| 107th | 2001–2003 | G. W. Bush | Republican | Democratic |
| 108th | 2003–2005 | G. W. Bush | Republican | Republican |
| 109th | 2005–2007 | G. W. Bush | Republican | Republican |
| 110th | 2007–2009 | G. W. Bush | Democratic | Democratic |
| 111th | 2009–2011 | Obama | Democratic | Democratic |
| 112th | 2011–2013 | Obama | Republican | Democratic |
| 113th | 2013–2015 | Obama | Republican | Democratic |

# INFORMATION ON U.S. PRESIDENTS

| | Term of Service | Age at Inauguration | Party Affiliation | College or University | Occupation or Profession |
|---|---|---|---|---|---|
| 1. George Washington | 1789–1797 | 57 | None | | Planter |
| 2. John Adams | 1797–1801 | 61 | Federalist | Harvard | Lawyer |
| 3. Thomas Jefferson | 1801–1809 | 57 | Democratic-Republican | William and Mary | Planter, Lawyer |
| 4. James Madison | 1809–1817 | 57 | Democratic-Republican | Princeton | Lawyer |
| 5. James Monroe | 1817–1825 | 58 | Democratic-Republican | William and Mary | Lawyer |
| 6. John Quincy Adams | 1825–1829 | 57 | Democratic-Republican | Harvard | Lawyer |
| 7. Andrew Jackson | 1829–1837 | 61 | Democrat | | Lawyer |
| 8. Martin Van Buren | 1837–1841 | 54 | Democrat | | Lawyer |
| 9. William H. Harrison | 1841 | 68 | Whig | Hampden-Sydney | Soldier |
| 10. John Tyler | 1841–1845 | 51 | Whig | William and Mary | Lawyer |
| 11. James K. Polk | 1845–1849 | 49 | Democrat | U. of N. Carolina | Lawyer |
| 12. Zachary Taylor | 1849–1850 | 64 | Whig | | Soldier |
| 13. Millard Fillmore | 1850–1853 | 50 | Whig | | Lawyer |
| 14. Franklin Pierce | 1853–1857 | 48 | Democrat | Bowdoin | Lawyer |
| 15. James Buchanan | 1857–1861 | 65 | Democrat | Dickinson | Lawyer |
| 16. Abraham Lincoln | 1861–1865 | 52 | Republican | | Lawyer |
| 17. Andrew Johnson | 1865–1869 | 56 | National Union[†] | | Tailor |
| 18. Ulysses S. Grant | 1869–1877 | 46 | Republican | U.S. Mil. Academy | Soldier |
| 19. Rutherford B. Hayes | 1877–1881 | 54 | Republican | Kenyon | Lawyer |
| 20. James A. Garfield | 1881 | 49 | Republican | Williams | Lawyer |
| 21. Chester A. Arthur | 1881–1885 | 51 | Republican | Union | Lawyer |
| 22. Grover Cleveland | 1885–1889 | 47 | Democrat | | Lawyer |
| 23. Benjamin Harrison | 1889–1893 | 55 | Republican | Miami | Lawyer |
| 24. Grover Cleveland | 1893–1897 | 55 | Democrat | | Lawyer |
| 25. William McKinley | 1897–1901 | 54 | Republican | Allegheny College | Lawyer |
| 26. Theodore Roosevelt | 1901–1909 | 42 | Republican | Harvard | Author |
| 27. William H. Taft | 1909–1913 | 51 | Republican | Yale | Lawyer |
| 28. Woodrow Wilson | 1913–1921 | 56 | Democrat | Princeton | Educator |
| 29. Warren G. Harding | 1921–1923 | 55 | Republican | | Editor |
| 30. Calvin Coolidge | 1923–1929 | 51 | Republican | Amherst | Lawyer |
| 31. Herbert C. Hoover | 1929–1933 | 54 | Republican | Stanford | Engineer |
| 32. Franklin D. Roosevelt | 1933–1945 | 51 | Democrat | Harvard | Lawyer |
| 33. Harry S Truman | 1945–1953 | 60 | Democrat | | Businessman |
| 34. Dwight D. Eisenhower | 1953–1961 | 62 | Republican | U.S. Mil. Academy | Soldier |
| 35. John F. Kennedy | 1961–1963 | 43 | Democrat | Harvard | Author |
| 36. Lyndon B. Johnson | 1963–1969 | 55 | Democrat | Southwest Texas State | Teacher |
| 37. Richard M. Nixon | 1969–1974 | 56 | Republican | Whittier | Lawyer |
| 38. Gerald R. Ford[‡] | 1974–1977 | 61 | Republican | Michigan | Lawyer |
| 39. James E. Carter, Jr. | 1977–1981 | 52 | Democrat | U.S. Naval Academy | Businessman |
| 40. Ronald W. Reagan | 1981–1989 | 69 | Republican | Eureka College | Actor |
| 41. George H. W. Bush | 1989–1993 | 64 | Republican | Yale | Businessman |
| 42. William J. Clinton | 1993–2001 | 46 | Democrat | Georgetown | Lawyer |
| 43. George W. Bush | 2001–2009 | 54 | Republican | Yale | Businessman |
| 44. Barack Obama | 2009– | 47 | Democrat | Columbia | Lawyer |

*Church preference; never joined any church.
†The National Union Party consisted of Republicans and War Democrats. Johnson was a Democrat.
**Inaugurated Dec. 6, 1973, to replace Agnew, who resigned Oct. 10, 1973.
‡Inaugurated Aug. 9, 1974, to replace Nixon, who resigned that same day.
§Inaugurated Dec. 19, 1974, to replace Ford, who became president Aug. 9, 1974.

| Religion | Born | Died | Age at Death | Vice President | |
|---|---|---|---|---|---|
| 1. Episcopalian | Feb. 22, 1732 | Dec. 14, 1799 | 67 | John Adams | (1789–1797) |
| 2. Unitarian | Oct. 30, 1735 | July 4, 1826 | 90 | Thomas Jefferson | (1797–1801) |
| 3. Unitarian* | Apr. 13, 1743 | July 4, 1826 | 83 | Aaron Burr | (1801–1805) |
| | | | | George Clinton | (1805–1809) |
| 4. Episcopalian | Mar. 16, 1751 | June 28, 1836 | 85 | George Clinton | (1809–1812) |
| | | | | Elbridge Gerry | (1813–1814) |
| 5. Episcopalian | Apr. 28, 1758 | July 4, 1831 | 73 | Daniel D. Tompkins | (1817–1825) |
| 6. Unitarian | July 11, 1767 | Feb. 23, 1848 | 80 | John C. Calhoun | (1825–1829) |
| 7. Presbyterian | Mar. 15, 1767 | June 8, 1845 | 78 | John C. Calhoun | (1829–1832) |
| | | | | Martin Van Buren | (1833–1837) |
| 8. Dutch Reformed | Dec. 5, 1782 | July 24, 1862 | 79 | Richard M. Johnson | (1837–1841) |
| 9. Episcopalian | Feb. 9, 1773 | Apr. 4, 1841 | 68 | John Tyler | (1841) |
| 10. Episcopalian | Mar. 29, 1790 | Jan. 18, 1862 | 71 | | |
| 11. Methodist | Nov. 2, 1795 | June 15, 1849 | 53 | George M. Dallas | (1845–1849) |
| 12. Episcopalian | Nov. 24, 1784 | July 9, 1850 | 65 | Millard Fillmore | (1849–1850) |
| 13. Unitarian | Jan. 7, 1800 | Mar. 8, 1874 | 74 | | |
| 14. Episcopalian | Nov. 23, 1804 | Oct. 8, 1869 | 64 | William R. King | (1853) |
| 15. Presbyterian | Apr. 23, 1791 | June 1, 1868 | 77 | John C. Breckinridge | (1857–1861) |
| 16. Presbyterian* | Feb. 12, 1809 | Apr. 15, 1865 | 56 | Hannibal Hamlin | (1861–1865) |
| | | | | Andrew Johnson | (1865) |
| 17. Methodist* | Dec. 29, 1808 | July 31, 1875 | 66 | | |
| 18. Methodist | Apr. 27, 1822 | July 23, 1885 | 63 | Schuyler Colfax | (1869–1873) |
| | | | | Henry Wilson | (1873–1875) |
| 19. Methodist* | Oct. 4, 1822 | Jan. 17, 1893 | 70 | William A. Wheeler | (1877–1881) |
| 20. Disciples of Christ | Nov. 19, 1831 | Sept. 19, 1881 | 49 | Chester A. Arthur | (1881) |
| 21. Episcopalian | Oct. 5, 1829 | Nov. 18, 1886 | 57 | | |
| 22. Presbyterian | Mar. 18, 1837 | June 24, 1908 | 71 | Thomas A. Hendricks | (1885) |
| 23. Presbyterian | Aug. 20, 1833 | Mar. 13, 1901 | 67 | Levi P. Morton | (1889–1893) |
| 24. Presbyterian | Mar. 18, 1837 | June 24, 1908 | 71 | Adlai E. Stevenson | (1893–1897) |
| 25. Methodist | Jan. 29, 1843 | Sept. 14, 1901 | 58 | Garret A. Hobart | (1897–1899) |
| | | | | Theodore Roosevelt | (1901) |
| 26. Dutch Reformed | Oct. 27, 1858 | Jan. 6, 1919 | 60 | Charles W. Fairbanks | (1905–1909) |
| 27. Unitarian | Sept. 15, 1857 | Mar. 8, 1930 | 72 | James S. Sherman | (1909–1912) |
| 28. Presbyterian | Dec. 29, 1856 | Feb. 3, 1924 | 67 | Thomas R. Marshall | (1913–1921) |
| 29. Baptist | Nov. 2, 1865 | Aug. 2, 1923 | 57 | Calvin Coolidge | (1921–1923) |
| 30. Congregationalist | July 4, 1872 | Jan. 5, 1933 | 60 | Charles G. Dawes | (1925–1929) |
| 31. Friend (Quaker) | Aug. 10, 1874 | Oct. 20, 1964 | 90 | Charles Curtis | (1929–1933) |
| 32. Episcopalian | Jan. 30, 1882 | Apr. 12, 1945 | 63 | John N. Garner | (1933–1941) |
| | | | | Henry A. Wallace | (1941–1945) |
| | | | | Harry S Truman | (1945) |
| 33. Baptist | May 8, 1884 | Dec. 26, 1972 | 88 | Alben W. Barkley | (1949–1953) |
| 34. Presbyterian | Oct. 14, 1890 | Mar. 28, 1969 | 78 | Richard M. Nixon | (1953–1961) |
| 35. Roman Catholic | May 29, 1917 | Nov. 22, 1963 | 46 | Lyndon B. Johnson | (1961–1963) |
| 36. Disciples of Christ | Aug. 27, 1908 | Jan. 22, 1973 | 64 | Hubert H. Humphrey | (1965–1969) |
| 37. Friend (Quaker) | Jan. 9, 1913 | Apr. 22, 1994 | 81 | Spiro T. Agnew | (1969–1973) |
| | | | | Gerald R. Ford** | (1973–1974) |
| 38. Episcopalian | July 14, 1913 | Dec. 26, 2006 | 93 | Nelson A. Rockefeller§ | (1974–1977) |
| 39. Baptist | Oct. 1, 1924 | | | Walter F. Mondale | (1977–1981) |
| 40. Disciples of Christ | Feb. 6, 1911 | June 5, 2004 | 93 | George H. W. Bush | (1981–1989) |
| 41. Episcopalian | June 12, 1924 | | | J. Danforth Quayle | (1989–1993) |
| 42. Baptist | Aug. 19, 1946 | | | Albert A. Gore | (1993–2001) |
| 43. Methodist | July 6, 1946 | | | Dick Cheney | (2001–2009) |
| 44. United Church of Christ | August 4, 1961 | | | Joe Biden | (2009–   ) |

# FEDERALIST PAPERS NO. 10 AND NO. 51

*The founders completed drafting the U.S. Constitution in 1787. It was then submitted to the thirteen states for ratification, and a major debate ensued. As you read in Chapter 2, on the one side of this debate were the Federalists, who urged that the new Constitution be adopted. On the other side of the debate were the Anti-Federalists, who argued against ratification.*

*During the course of this debate, three men well known for their Federalist views—Alexander Hamilton, James Madison, and John Jay—wrote a series of essays in which they argued for immediate ratifcation of the Constitution. The essays appeared in the New York City* Independent Journal *in October 1787, just a little over a month after the Constitutional Convention adjourned. Later, Hamilton arranged to have the essays collected and published in book form. The articles filled two volumes, both of which were published by May 1788. The essays are often referred to collectively as the* Federalist Papers.

*Scholars disagree as to whether the* Federalist Papers *had a significant impact on the decision of the states to ratify the Constitution. Nonetheless, many of the essays are masterpieces of political reasoning and have left a lasting imprint on American politics and government. Above all, the* Federalist Papers *shed an important light on what the founders intended when they drafted various constitutional provisions.*

*Here we present just two of these essays,* Federalist Paper No. 10 *and* Federalist Paper No. 51. *Each essay was written by James Madison, who referred to himself as "Publius." We have annotated each document to clarify the meaning of particular passages. The annotations are set in italics to distinguish them from the original text of the documents.*

## #10

*Federalist Paper No. 10 is a classic document that is often referred to by teachers of American government. Authored by James Madison, it sets forth Madison's views on factions in politics. The essay was written, in large part, to counter the arguments put forth by the Anti-Federalists that small factions might take control of the government, thus destroying the representative nature of the republican form of government established by the Constitution. The essay opens with a discussion of the "dangerous vice" of factions and the importance of devising a form of government in which this vice will be controlled.*

Among the numerous advantages promised by a well-constructed Union, none deserves to be more accurately developed than its tendency to break and control the violence of faction. The friend of popular governments never finds himself so much alarmed for their character and fate as when he contemplates their propensity to this dangerous vice. He will not fail, therefore, to set a due value on any plan which, without violating the principles to which he is attached, provides a proper cure for it. The instability, injustice, and confusion introduced into the public councils have, in truth, been the mortal diseases under which popular governments have everywhere perished, as they continue to be the favorite and fruitful topics from which the adversaries to liberty derive their most specious declamations. The valuable improvements made by the American constitutions on the popular models, both ancient and modern, cannot certainly be too much admired; but it would be an unwarrantable partiality to contend that they have as effectually obviated the danger on this side, as was wished and expected. Complaints are everywhere heard from our most considerate and virtuous citizens, equally the friends of public and private faith and of public and personal liberty, that our governments are too unstable, that the public good is disregarded in the conflicts of rival parties, and that measures are too often decided, not according to the rules of justice and the rights of the minor party, but by the superior force of an interested and overbearing majority. However anxiously we may wish that these complaints had no foundation, the evidence of known facts will not permit us to deny that they are in some degree true. It will be found, indeed, on a candid review of our situation, that some of the distresses under which we labor have been erroneously charged on the operation of our governments; but it will be found, at the same time, that other causes will not alone account for many of our heaviest misfortunes; and, particularly, for that prevailing and increasing distrust of public engagements and alarm for private rights which are echoed from one end of the continent to the other. These must be chiefly, if not wholly, effects of the unsteadiness and injustice with which a factious spirit has tainted our public administration.

*In the following paragraph, Madison clarifies for his readers his understanding of what the term faction means.*

By a faction I understand a number of citizens, whether amounting to a majority or minority of the whole, who are united and actuated by some common impulse of passion, or of interest, adverse to the rights of other citizens, or the permanent and aggregate interests of the community.

*In the following passages, Madison looks at the two methods of curing the "mischiefs of factions." One of these methods is removing the causes of faction. The other is to control the effects of factions.*

There are two methods of curing the mischiefs of faction: the one, by removing its causes; the other, by controlling its effects.

There are again two methods of removing the causes of faction: the one, by destroying the liberty which is essential to its existence; the other, by giving to every citizen the same opinions, the same passions, and the same interests.

It could never be more truly said than of the first remedy that it was worse than the disease. Liberty is to faction what air is to fire, an aliment without which it instantly expires. But it could not be a less folly to abolish liberty, which is essential to political life, because it nourishes faction than it would be to wish the annihilation of air, which is essential to animal life, because it imparts to fire its destructive agency.

The second expedient is as impracticable as the first would be unwise. As long as the reason of man continues fallible, and his is at liberty to exercise it, different opinions will be formed. As long as the connection subsists between his reason and his self-love, his opinions and his passions will have a reciprocal influence on each other; and the former will be objects to which the latter will attach themselves. The diversity in the faculties of men, from which the rights of property originate, is not less an insuperable obstacle to a uniformity of interests. The protection of these faculties is the first object of government. From the protection of different and unequal faculties of acquiring property, the possession of different degrees and kinds of property immediately results; and from the influence of these on the sentiments and views of the respective proprietors ensues a division of the society into different interests and parties.

The latent causes of faction are thus sown in the nature of man; and we see them everywhere brought into different degrees of activity, according to the different circumstances of civil society. A zeal for different opinions concerning religion, concerning government, and many other points, as well of speculation as of practice; an attachment to different leaders ambitiously contending for pre-eminence and power; or to persons of other descriptions whose fortunes have been interesting to the human passions, have, in turn, divided mankind into parties, inflamed them with mutual animosity, and rendered them much more disposed to vex and oppress each other than to co-operate for their common good. So strong is this propensity of mankind to fall into mutual animosities that where no substantial occasion presents itself the most frivolous and fanciful distinctions have been sufficient to kindle their unfriendly passions and excite their most violent conflicts. But the most common and durable source of factions has been the various and unequal distribution of property. Those who hold and those who are without property have ever formed distinct interests in society. Those who are creditors, and those who are debtors, fall under a like discrimination. A landed interest, a manufacturing interest, a mercantile interest, a moneyed interest, with many lesser interests, grow up of necessity in civilized nations, and divide them into different classes, actuated by different sentiments and views. The regulation of these various and interfering interests forms the principal task of modern legislation and involves the spirit of party and faction in the necessary and ordinary operations of government.

No man is allowed to be a judge in his own cause, because his interest would certainly bias his judgment, and, not improbably, corrupt his integrity. With equal, nay with greater reason, a body of men are unfit to be both judges and parties at the same time; yet what are many of the most important acts of legislation but so many judicial determinations, not indeed concerning the rights of single persons, but concerning the rights of large bodies of citizens? And what are the different classes of legislators but advocates and parties to the causes which they determine? Is a law proposed concerning private debts? It is a question to which the creditors are parties on one side and the debtors on the other. Justice ought to hold the balance between them. Yet the parties are, and must be, themselves the judges; and the most numerous party, or in other words, the most powerful faction must be expected to prevail. Shall domestic manufacturers be encouraged, and in what degree, by restrictions on foreign manufacturers? Are questions which would be differently decided by the landed and the manufacturing classes, and probably by neither with a sole regard to justice and the public good. The apportionment of taxes on the various descriptions of property is an act which seems to require the most exact impartiality; yet there is, perhaps, no legislative act in which greater opportunity and temptation are given to a predominant party to trample on the rules of justice. Every shilling with which they overburden the inferior number is a shilling saved to their own pockets.

It is in vain to say that enlightened statesmen will be able to adjust these clashing interests and render them all subservient to the public good. Enlightened statesmen will not always be at the helm. Nor, in many cases, can such an adjustment be made at all without taking into view indirect and remote considerations, which will rarely prevail over the immediate interest which one party may find in disregarding the rights of another or the good of the whole.

The inference to which we are brought is that the causes of faction cannot be removed and that relief is only to be sought in the means of controlling its effects.

*In the preceding passages, Madison has explored the causes of factions and has concluded that they cannot "be removed" without removing liberty itself, which is one of the causes, or altering human nature. He now turns to a discussion of how the effects of factions might be controlled.*

If a faction consists of less than a majority, relief is supplied by the republican principle, which enables the majority to defeat its sinister views by regular vote. It may clog the administration, it may convulse the society; but it will be unable to execute and mask its violence under the forms of the Constitution. When a majority is included in a faction, the form of popular government, on the other hand, enables it to sacrifice to its ruling passion or interest both the public good and the rights of other citizens. To secure the public good and private rights against the danger of such a faction, and at the same time to preserve the spirit and the form of popular government, is then the great object to which our inquiries are directed. Let me add that it is the great desideratum by which alone this form of government can be rescued from the opprobrium under which it has so long labored and be recommended to the esteem and adoption of mankind.

*According to Madison, one way of controlling the effects of factions is to make sure that the majority is not able to act in "concert," or jointly, to "carry into effect schemes of oppression."*

By what means is this object attainable? Evidently by one of two only. Either the existence of the same passion or interest in a majority at the same time must be prevented, or the majority, having such coexistent passion or interest, must be rendered, by their number and local situation, unable to concert and carry into effect schemes of oppression. If the impulse and the opportunity be suffered to coincide, we well know that neither moral nor religious motives can be relied on as an adequate control. They are not found to be such on the injustice and violence of individuals, and lose their efficacy in proportion to the number combined together, that is, in proportion as their efficacy becomes needful.

From this view of the subject it may be concluded that a pure democracy, by which I mean a society consisting of a small number of citizens, who assemble and administer the government in person, can admit of no cure for the mischiefs of faction. A common passion or interest will, in almost every case, be felt by a majority of the whole; a communication and concert results from the form of government itself; and there is nothing to check the inducements to sacrifice the weaker party or an obnoxious individual. Hence it is that such democracies have ever been spectacles of turbulence and contention; have ever been found incompatible with personal security or the rights of property; and have in general been as short in their lives as they have been violent in their deaths. Theoretic politicians, who have patronized this species of government, have erroneously supposed that by reducing mankind to a perfect equality in their political rights, they would at the same time be perfectly equalized and assimilated in their possessions, their opinions, and their passions.

*In the following six paragraphs, Madison sets forth some of the reasons why a republican form of government promises a "cure" for the mischiefs of factions. He begins by clarifying the difference between a republic and a democracy. He then describes how in a large republic, the elected representatives of the people will be large enough in number to guard against factions—the "cabals," or concerted actions, of "a few." On the one hand, representatives will not be so removed from their local districts as to be unacquainted with their constituents' needs. On the other hand, they will not be "unduly attached" to local interests and unfit to understand "great and national objects." Madison concludes that the Constitution "forms a happy combination in this respect."*

A republic, by which I mean a government in which the scheme of representation takes place, opens a different prospect and promises the cure for which we are seeking. Let us examine the points in which it varies from pure democracy, and we shall comprehend both the nature of the cure and the efficacy which it must derive from the Union.

The two great points of difference between a democracy and a republic are: first, the delegation of the government, in the latter, to a small number of citizens elected by the rest; secondly, the greater number of citizens and greater sphere of country over which the latter may be extended.

The effect of the first difference is, on the one hand, to refine and enlarge the public views by passing them through the medium of a chosen body of citizens, whose wisdom may best discern the true interest of their country and whose patriotism and love of justice will be least likely to sacrifice it to temporary or partial considerations. Under such a regulation it may well happen that the public voice, pronounced by the representatives of the people, will be more consonant to the public good than if pronounced by the people themselves, convened for the purpose. On the other hand, the effect may be inverted. Men of factious tempers, of local prejudices, or of sinister designs, may, by intrigue, by corruption, or by other means, first obtain the suffrages, and then betray the interests of the people. The question resulting is, whether small or extensive republics are most favorable to the election of proper guardians of the public weal; and it is clearly decided in favor of the latter by two obvious considerations.

In the first place it is to be remarked that however small the republic may be the representatives must be raised to a certain number in order to guard against the cabals of a few; and that however large it may be they must be limited to a certain number in order to guard against the confusion of a multitude. Hence, the number of representatives in the two cases not being in proportion to that of the constituents, and being proportionally greatest in the small republic, it follows that if the proportion of fit characters be not less in the large than in the small republic, the former will present a greater option, and consequently a greater probability of a fit choice.

In the next place, as each representative will be chosen by a greater number of citizens in the large than in the small republic, it will be more difficult for unworthy candidates to practice with success the vicious arts by which elections are too often carried; and the suffrages of the people being more free, will be more likely to center on men who possess the most attractive merit and the most diffusive and established characters.

It must be confessed that in this, as in most other cases, there is a mean, on both sides of which inconveniencies will be found to lie. By enlarging too much the number of electors, you render the representative too little acquainted with all their local circumstances and lesser interests; as by reducing it too much, you render him unduly attached to these, and too little fit to comprehend and pursue great and national objects. The federal Constitution forms a happy combination in this respect; the great and aggregate interests being referred to the national, the local and particular to the State legislatures.

*In the remaining passages of this essay, Madison looks at another "point of difference" between a republic and a democracy. Specifically, a republic can encompass a larger territory and a greater number of citizens than a democracy can. This fact, too, argues Madison, will help to control the influence of factions because the interests that draw people together to act in concert are typically at the local level and would be unlikely to affect or dominate the national government. As Madison states, "The influence of factious leaders may kindle a flame within their particular States but will be unable to spread a general conflagration through the other States." Generally, in a large republic, there will be numerous factions, and no particular faction will be able to "pervade the whole body of the Union."*

The other point of difference is the greater number of citizens and extent of territory which may be brought within the compass of republican than of democratic government; and it is this circumstance principally which renders factious combinations less to be dreaded in the former than in the latter. The smaller the society, the fewer probably will be the distinct parties and interests composing it; the fewer the distinct parties and interests, the more frequently will a majority be found of the same party; and the smaller the number of individuals composing a majority, and the smaller the compass within which they are placed, the more easily will they concert and execute their plans of oppression. Extend the sphere and you take in a greater variety of parties and interests; you make it less probable that a majority of the whole will have a common motive to invade the rights of other citizens; or if such a common motive exists, it will be more difficult for all who feel it to discover their own strength and to act in unison with each other. Besides other impediments, it may be remarked that, where there is a consciousness of unjust or dishonorable purposes, communication is always checked by distrust in proportion to the number whose concurrence is necessary.

Hence, it clearly appears that the same advantage which a republic has over a democracy in controlling the effects of faction is enjoyed by a large over a small republic—is enjoyed by the Union over the States composing it. Does this advantage consist in the substitution of representatives whose enlightened views and virtuous sentiments render them superior to local prejudices and to schemes of injustice? It will not be denied that the representation of the Union will be most likely to possess these requisite endowments. Does it consist in the greater security afforded by a greater variety of parties, against the event of any one party being able to outnumber and oppress the rest? In an equal degree does the increased variety of parties comprised within the Union increase this security. Does it, in fine, consist in the greater obstacles opposed to the concert and accomplishment of the secret wishes of an unjust and interested majority? Here again the extent of the Union gives it the most palpable advantage.

The influence of factious leaders may kindle a flame within their particular States but will be unable to spread a general conflagration through the other States. A religious sect may degenerate into a political faction in a part of the Confederacy; but the variety of sects dispersed over the entire face of it must secure the national councils against any danger from that source. A rage for paper money, for an abolition of debts, for an equal division of property, or for any other improper or wicked project, will be less apt to pervade the whole body of the Union than a particular member of it, in the same proportion as such a malady is more likely to taint a particular county or district than an entire State.

In the extent and proper structure of the Union, therefore, we behold a republican remedy for the diseases most incident to republican government. And according to the degree of pleasure and pride we feel in being republicans ought to be our zeal in cherishing the spirit and supporting the character of federalists.

Publius
(James Madison)

# #51

Federalist Paper *No. 51, which was also authored by James Madison, is one of the classics in American*

*political theory. Recall from Chapter 2 that a major concern of the founders was to create a relatively strong national government but one that would not be capable of tyrannizing over the populace. In the following essay, Madison sets forth the theory of "checks and balances." He explains that the new Constitution, by dividing the national government into three branches (executive, legislative, and judicial), offers protection against tyranny.*

To what expedient, then, shall we finally resort, for maintaining in practice the necessary partition of power among the several departments as laid down in the Constitution? The only answer that can be given is that as all these exterior provisions are found to be inadequate the defect must be supplied, by so contriving the interior structure of the government as that its several constituent parts may, by their mutual relations, be the means of keeping each other in their proper places. Without presuming to undertake a full development of this important idea I will hazard a few general observations which may perhaps place it in a clearer light, and enable us to form a more correct judgment of the principles and structure of the government planned by the convention.

*In the following two paragraphs, Madison explains that to ensure that the powers of government are genuinely separated, it is important that each of the three branches of government (executive, legislative, and judicial) should have a "will of its own." Among other things, this means that persons in one branch should not depend on persons in another branch for the "emoluments annexed to their offices" (pay, perks, and privileges). If they did, then the branches would not be truly independent of one another.*

In order to lay a due foundation for that separate and distinct exercise of the different powers of government, which to a certain extent is admitted on all hands to be essential to the preservation of liberty, it is evident that each department should have a will of its own; and consequently should be so constituted that the members of each should have as little agency as possible in the appointment of the members of the others. Were this principle rigorously adhered to, it would require that all the appointments for the supreme executive, legislative, and judiciary magistracies should be drawn from the same fountain of authority, the people, through channels having no communication whatever with one another. Perhaps such a plan of constructing the several departments would be less difficult in practice than it may in contemplation appear. Some difficulties, however, and some additional expense would attend the execution of it. Some deviations, therefore, from the principle must be admitted. In the constitution of the judiciary department in particular, it might be inexpedient to insist rigorously on the principle: first, because peculiar qualifications being essential in the members, the primary consideration ought to be to select that mode of choice which best secures these qualifications; second, because the permanent tenure by which the appointments are held in that department must soon destroy all sense of dependence on the authority conferring them.

It is equally evident that the members of each department should be as little dependent as possible on those of the others for the emoluments annexed to their offices. Were the executive magistrate, or the judges, not independent of the legislature in this particular, their independence in every other would be merely nominal.

*One of the striking qualities of the theory of checks and balances as posited by Madison is that it assumes that persons are not angels but driven by personal interests and motives. In the following two paragraphs, which are among the most widely quoted of Madison's writings, he stresses that the division of the government into three branches helps to check personal ambitions. Personal ambitions will naturally arise, but they will be linked to the constitutional powers of each branch. In effect, they will help to keep the three branches separate and thus serve the public interest.*

But the great security against a gradual concentration of the several powers in the same department consists in giving to those who administer each department the necessary constitutional means and personal motives to resist encroachments of the others. The provision for defense must in this, as in all other cases, be made commensurate to the danger of attack. Ambition must be made to counteract ambition. The interest of the man must be connected with the constitutional rights of the place. It may be a reflection on human nature that such devices should be necessary to control the abuses of government. But what is government itself but the greatest of all reflections on human nature? If men were angels, no government would be necessary. If angels were to govern men, neither external nor internal controls on government would be necessary. In framing a government which is to be administered by men over men, the great difficulty lies in this: you must first enable the government to control the governed; and in the next place oblige it to control itself. A dependence on the people is, no doubt, the primary control on the government; but experience has taught mankind the necessity of auxiliary precautions.

This policy of supplying, by opposite and rival interests, the defect of better motives, might be traced through the whole system of human affairs, private as well as public. We see it particularly displayed in all the subordinate distributions of power, where the constant aim is to divide and arrange the several offices in such a manner as that each may be a check on the other—that the private interest of every individual may be a sentinel over the public rights. These inventions of prudence cannot be less requisite in the distribution of the supreme powers of the State.

*In the next two paragraphs, Madison first points out that the "legislative authority necessarily predominates" in a republican form of government. The "remedy" for this lack of balance with the other branches of government is to divide the legislative branch into two chambers with "different modes of election and different principles of action."*

But it is not possible to give to each department an equal power of self-defense. In republican government, the legislative authority necessarily predominates. The remedy for this inconveniency is to divide the legislature into different branches; and to render them, by different modes of election and different principles of action, as little connected with each other as the nature of their common functions and their common dependence on the society will admit. It may even be necessary to guard against dangerous encroachments by still further precautions. As the weight of the legislative authority requires that it should be thus divided, the weakness of the executive may require, on the other hand, that it should be fortified. An absolute negative on the legislature appears, at first view, to be the natural defense with which the executive magistrate should be armed. But perhaps it would be neither altogether safe nor alone sufficient. On ordinary occasions it might not be exerted with the requisite firmness, and on extraordinary occasions it might be perfidiously abused. May not this defect of an absolute negative be supplied by some qualified connection between this weaker department and the weaker branch of the stronger department, by which the latter may be led to support the constitutional rights of the former, without being too much detached from the rights of its own department?

If the principles on which these observations are founded be just, as I persuade myself they are, and they be applied as a criterion to the several State constitutions, and to the federal Constitution, it will be found that if the latter does not perfectly correspond with them, the former are infinitely less able to bear such a test.

*In the remaining passages of this essay, Madison discusses the importance of the division of government powers between the states and the national government. This division of powers, by providing additional checks and balances, offers a "double security" against tyranny.*

There are, moreover, two considerations particularly applicable to the federal system of America, which place that system in a very interesting point of view.

*First.* In a single republic, all the power surrendered by the people is submitted to the administration of a single government; and the usurpations are guarded against by a division of the government into distinct and separate departments. In the compound republic of America, the power surrendered by the people is first divided between two distinct governments, and then the portion allotted to each subdivided among distinct and separate departments. Hence a double security arises to the rights of the people. The different governments will control each other, at the same time that each will be controlled by itself.

*Second.* It is of great importance in a republic not only to guard the society against the oppression of its rulers, but to guard one part of the society against the injustice of the other part. Different interests necessarily exist in different classes of citizens. If a majority be united by a common interest, the rights of the minority will be insecure. There are but two methods of providing against this evil: the one by creating a will in the community independent of the majority—that is, of the society itself; the other, by comprehending in the society so many separate descriptions of citizens as will render an unjust combination of a majority of the whole very improbable, if not impracticable. The first method prevails in all governments possessing an hereditary or self-appointed authority. This, at best, is but a precarious security; because a power independent of the society may as well espouse the unjust views of the major as the rightful interests of the minor party, and may possibly be turned against both parties. The second method will be exemplified in the federal republic of the United States. Whilst all authority in it will be derived from and dependent on the society, the society itself will be broken into so many parts, interests and classes of citizens, that the rights of individuals, or of the minority, will be in little danger from interested combinations of the majority. In a free government the security for civil rights must be the same as that for religious rights. It consists in the one case in the multiplicity of interests, and in the other in the multiplicity of sects. The degree of security in both cases will depend on the number of interests and sects; and this may be presumed to depend on the extent of country and number of people comprehended under the same government. This view of the subject must particularly recommend a proper federal system to all the sincere and considerate friends of republican government, since it shows that in exact proportion as the territory of the Union may be formed into more circumscribed Confederacies, or States, oppressive combinations of a majority will be facilitated; the best security, under the republican forms, for the rights of every class of citizen, will be diminished; and consequently the stability and independence of some member of the government, the only other security, must be proportionally increased. Justice is the end of government. It is the end of civil society. It ever has been and ever will be pursued until it be obtained, or until liberty be lost in the pursuit. In a society under the forms of which the stronger faction can readily unite and oppress the weaker, anarchy may as truly be said to reign as in a state of nature, where the weaker individual is not secured against the violence of the stronger; and as, in the latter state, even the stronger individuals are prompted, by the uncertainty of their condition, to submit to a government which may protect the weak as well as themselves; so, in the former state, will the more powerful factions or parties be gradually induced, by a like motive, to wish for a government which will protect all parties, the weaker as well as the more powerful. It can be little doubted that if the State of Rhode Island was separated from the Confederacy and left to itself, the insecurity of rights under the popular form of government within such narrow limits would be displayed by such reiterated oppressions of factious majorities that some power altogether independent of the people would soon be called for by the voice of the very factions whose misrule had proved the necessity of it. In the extended republic of the United States, and among the great variety of interests, parties, and sects which it embraces, a coalition of a majority of the whole society could seldom take place on any other principles than those of justice and the general good; whilst there being thus less danger to a minor from the will of a major party, there must be less pretext, also, to provide for the security of the former, by introducing into the government a will not dependent on the latter, or, in other words, a will independent of the society itself. It is no less certain than it is important, notwithstanding the contrary opinions which have been entertained, that the larger the society, provided it lie within a practicable sphere, the more duly capable it will be of self-government. And happily for the *republican cause*, the practicable sphere may be carried to a very great extent by a judicious modification and mixture of the *federal principle.*

Publius
(James Madison)

# HOW TO READ CASE CITATIONS AND FIND COURT DECISIONS

Many important court cases are discussed in references in endnotes throughout this book. Court decisions are recorded and published. When a court case is mentioned, the notation that is used to refer to, or to cite, the case denotes where the published decision can be found.

State courts of appeals decisions are usually published in two places, the state reports of that particular state and the more widely used *National Reporter System* published by West Group. Some states no longer publish their own reports. The *National Reporter System* divides the states into the following geographic areas: Atlantic (A. or A.2d, where 2d refers to *Second Series*), South Eastern (S.E. or S.E.2d), South Western (S.W., S.W.2d, or S.W.3d), North Western (N.W. or N.W.2d), North Eastern (N.E. or N.E.2d), Southern (So. or So.2d), and Pacific (P., P.2d, or P.3d).

Federal trial court decisions are published unofficially in West's *Federal Supplement* (F.Supp. or F.Supp.2d), and opinions from the circuit courts of appeals are reported unofficially in West's *Federal Reporter* (F., F.2d, or F.3d). Opinions from the United States Supreme Court are reported in the *United States Reports* (U.S.), the *Lawyers' Edition of the Supreme Court Reports* (L.Ed.), West's *Supreme Court Reporter* (S.Ct.), and other publications. The *United States Reports* is the official publication of United States Supreme Court decisions. It is published by the federal government. Many early decisions are missing from these volumes. The citations of the early volumes of the *U.S. Reports* include the names of the

actual reporters, such as Dallas, Cranch, or Wheaton. *McCulloch v. Maryland,* for example, is cited as 17 U.S. (4 Wheat.) 316. Only after 1874 did the present citation system, in which cases are cited based solely on their volume and page numbers in the *United States Reports,* come into being. The *Lawyers' Edition of the Supreme Court Reports* is an unofficial and more complete edition of Supreme Court decisions. West's *Supreme Court Reporter* is an unofficial edition of decisions dating from October 1882. These volumes contain headnotes and numerous brief editorial statements of the law involved in the case.

State courts of appeals decisions are cited by giving the name of the case; the volume, name, and page number of the state's official report (if the state publishes its own reports); the volume, unit, and page number of the *National Reporter;* and the volume, name, and page number of any other selected reporter. Federal court citations are also listed by giving the name of the case and the volume, name, and page number of the reports. In addition to the citation, this textbook lists the year of the decision in parentheses. Consider, for example, the case *United States v. Curtiss-Wright Export Co.,* 299 U.S. 304 (1936). The Supreme Court's decision of this case may be found in volume 299 of the *United States Reports* on page 304. The case was decided in 1936.

Today, many courts, including the United States Supreme Court, publish their opinions online. This makes it much easier for students to find and read cases, or summaries of cases, that have significant consequences for American government and politics.

# GLOSSARY

## A

**action-reaction syndrome** For every government action, there will be a reaction by the public. The government then takes a further action to counter the public's reaction—and the cycle begins again.

**adjudicate** To render a judicial decision. In administrative law, it is the process in which an administrative law judge hears and decides issues that arise when an agency charges a person or firm with violating a law or regulation enforced by the agency.

**administrative law** The body of law created by administrative agencies (in the form of rules, regulations, orders, and decisions) in order to carry out their duties and responsibilities.

**affirmative action** A policy that gives special consideration, in jobs and college admissions, to members of groups that have been discriminated against in the past.

**agenda setting** Getting an issue on the political agenda to be addressed by Congress; part of the first stage of the policymaking process. Also, the media's ability to determine which issues are considered to be important by the public and by politicians.

**agents of political socialization** People and institutions that influence the political views of others.

**Anti-Federalists** A political group that opposed the adoption of the Constitution because of the document's centralist tendencies and because it did not include a bill of rights.

**appellate court** A court having appellate jurisdiction. An appellate court normally does not hear evidence or testimony but reviews the transcript of the trial court's proceedings, other records relating to the case, and attorneys' arguments as to why the trial court's decision should or should not stand.

**apportionment** The distribution of House seats among the states on the basis of their respective populations.

**appropriation** A part of the congressional budgeting process—the determination of how many dollars will be spent in a given year on a particular government activity.

**Articles of Confederation** The nation's first national constitution, which established a national form of government following the American Revolution. The Articles provided for a confederal form of government in which the central government had few powers.

**Australian ballot** A secret ballot that is prepared, distributed, and counted by government officials at public expense; used by all states in the United States since 1888.

**authority** The ability to legitimately exercise power, such as the power to make and enforce laws.

**authorization** A part of the congressional budgeting process—the creation of the legal basis for government programs.

**autocracy** A form of government in which the power and authority of the government are in the hands of a single person.

## B

**biased sample** A poll sample that does not accurately represent the population.

**bicameral legislature** A legislature made up of two chambers, or parts. The United States has a bicameral legislature, composed of the House of Representatives and the Senate.

**bill of attainder** A legislative act that inflicts punishment on particular persons or groups without granting them the right to a trial.

**Bill of Rights** The first ten amendments to the U.S. Constitution. They list the freedoms—such as the freedoms of speech, press, and religion—that a citizen enjoys and that cannot be infringed on by the government.

**block grant** A federal grant given to a state for a broad area, such as criminal justice or mental-health programs.

**bureaucracy** A large, complex, hierarchically structured administrative organization that carries out specific functions.

**bureaucrat** An individual who works in a bureaucracy. As generally used, the term refers to a government employee.

**busing** The transportation of public school students by bus to schools physically outside their neighborhoods to eliminate school segregation based on residential patterns.

## C

**cabinet** An advisory group selected by the president to assist with decision making. Traditionally, the cabinet has consisted of the heads of the executive departments and other officers whom the president may choose to appoint.

**campaign strategy** The comprehensive plan developed by a candidate and his or her advisers for winning an election. The strategy includes the candidate's position on issues, slogan, advertising plan, press events, and personal appearances, and other aspects of the campaign.

**capitalism** An economic system based on the private ownership of wealth-producing property, free markets, and freedom of contract. The privately owned corporation is the preeminent capitalist institution.

**case law** The rules of law announced in court decisions. Case law includes the aggregate of reported cases that interpret judicial precedents, statutes, regulations, and constitutional provisions.

**categorical grant** A federal grant targeted for a specific purpose as defined by federal law.

**caucus** A meeting held to choose political candidates or delegates.

**checks and balances** A major principle of American government in which each of the three branches is given the means to check (to restrain or balance) the actions of the others.

**chief diplomat** The role of the president of the United States in recognizing and interacting with foreign governments.

**chief executive** The head of the executive branch of government; in the United States, the president.

**chief of staff** The person who directs the operations of the White House Office and who advises the president on important matters.

**Children's Health Insurance Program (CHIP)** A joint federal-state program that provides health-care insurance for low-income children.

**citizen journalism** The collection, analysis, and dissemination of information online by independent journalists, scholars, politicians, and the general citizenry.

**civil disobedience** The deliberate and public act of refusing to obey laws thought to be unjust.

**civil law** The branch of law that spells out the duties that individuals in society owe to other persons or to their governments, excluding the duty not to commit crimes.

**civil liberties** Individual rights protected by the Constitution against the powers of the government.

**civil rights** The rights of all Americans to equal treatment under the law, as provided for by the Fourteenth Amendment to the Constitution.

**civil rights movement** The movement in the 1950s and 1960s, by minorities and concerned whites, to end racial segregation.

**civil service** Nonmilitary government employees.

**closed primary** A primary in which only party members can vote to choose that party's candidates.

**cloture** A procedure for ending filibusters in the Senate and bringing the matter under consideration to a vote.

**coalition** An alliance of individuals or groups with a variety of interests and opinions who join together to support all or part of a political party's platform. Also, an alliance of nations formed to undertake a foreign policy action, particularly a military action. A coalition is often a temporary alliance that dissolves after the action is concluded.

**Cold War** The war of words, warnings, and ideologies between the Soviet Union and the United States that lasted from the late 1940s through the early 1980s.

**colonial empire** A group of dependent nations that are under the rule of a single imperial power.

**commander in chief** The supreme commander of a nation's military force.

**commerce clause** The clause in Article I, Section 8, of the Constitution that gives Congress the power to regulate interstate commerce (commerce involving more than one state).

**commercial speech** Advertising statements that describe products. Commercial speech receives less protection under the First Amendment than ordinary speech.

**common law** The body of law developed from judicial decisions in English and U.S. courts, not attributable to a legislature.

**competitive federalism** A model of federalism, devised by Thomas R. Dye, in which state and local governments compete for businesses and citizens, who in effect vote with their feet by moving to jurisdictions that offer a competitive advantage.

**concurrent powers** Powers held by both the federal and the state governments in a federal system.

**concurring opinion** A statement written by a judge or justice who agrees (concurs) with the court's decision, but for reasons different from those in the majority opinion.

**confederal system** A league of independent sovereign states, joined together by a central government that has only limited powers over them.

**confederation** A league of independent states that are united only for the purpose of achieving common goals.

**conference** In regard to the Supreme Court, a private meeting of the justices in which they present their arguments concerning a case under consideration.

**conference committee** A temporary committee that is formed when the two chambers of Congress pass differing versions of the same bill. The conference committee consists of members from both the House and the Senate who work out a compromise bill.

**conference report** A report submitted by a congressional conference committee after it has drafted a single version of a bill.

**congressional district** The geographic area that is served by one member in the House of Representatives.

**conservatism** A set of beliefs that include a limited role for the national government in helping individuals and in the economic affairs of the nation, and support for traditional values and lifestyles.

**conservative movement** A strongly ideological movement that arose in the 1950s and 1960s and continues to shape conservative beliefs.

**Constitutional Convention** The convention (meeting) of delegates from the states that was held in Philadelphia in 1787 for the purpose of amending the Articles of Confederation. In fact, the delegates wrote a new constitution (the U.S. Constitution) that established a federal form of government to replace the governmental system that had been created by the Articles of Confederation.

**constitutional law** Law based on the U.S. Constitution and the constitutions of the various states.

**containment** A U.S. policy designed to contain the spread of communism by offering military and economic aid to threatened nations.

**contempt of court** A ruling that a person has disobeyed a court order or has shown disrespect to the court or to a judicial proceeding.

**continuing resolution** A temporary resolution passed by Congress that enables executive agencies to continue work with the same funding that they had in the previous fiscal year.

**cooperative federalism** A model of federalism in which the states and the federal government should cooperate in solving problems.

**Corporate Average Fuel Economy (CAFE) standards** A set of federal standards under which each vehicle manufacturer (or the industry as a whole) must meet a miles-per-gallon benchmark averaged across all cars or trucks.

**Credentials Committee** A committee of each national political party that evaluates the claims of national party convention delegates to be the legitimate representatives of their states.

**criminal law** The branch of law that defines and governs actions that constitute crimes. Generally, criminal law has to do with wrongful actions committed against society for which society demands redress.

**Cuban missile crisis** A nuclear standoff that occurred in 1962 when the United States learned that the Soviet Union had placed nuclear warheads in Cuba, ninety miles off the U.S. coast. The crisis was defused diplomatically, but it is generally considered the closest the two Cold War superpowers came to a nuclear confrontation.

# D

**dealignment** Among voters, a growing detachment from both major political parties.

*de facto* **segregation** Racial segregation that occurs not as a result of deliberate intentions but because of social and economic conditions and residential patterns.

*de jure* **segregation** Racial segregation that occurs because of laws or decisions by government agencies.

**delegate** A person selected to represent the people of one geographic area at a party convention.

**democracy** A system of government in which the people have ultimate political authority. The word is derived from the Greek *demos* ("the people") and *kratia* ("rule").

**détente** French word meaning a "relaxation of tensions." Détente characterized the relationship between the United States and the Soviet Union in the 1970s, as the two Cold War rivals attempted to pursue cooperative dealings and arms control.

**deterrence** A policy of building up military strength for the purpose of discouraging (deterring) military attacks by other nations; the policy of that supported the arms race between the United States and the Soviet Union during the Cold War.

**devolution** The surrender or transfer of powers to local authorities by a central government.

**dictatorship** A form of government in which absolute power is exercised by an individual or group whose power is not supported by tradition.

**diplomat** A person who represents one country in dealing with representatives of another country.

**direct democracy** A system of government in which political decisions are made by the people themselves rather than by elected representatives. This form of government was practiced in some areas of ancient Greece.

**direct primary** An election held within each of the two major parties—Democratic and Republican— to choose the party's candidates for the general election. Voters choose the candidate directly, rather than through delegates.

**direct technique** Any method used by an interest group to interact with government officials directly to further the group's goals.

**dissenting opinion** A statement written by a judge or justice who disagrees with the majority opinion.

**diversity of citizenship** A basis for federal court jurisdiction over a lawsuit that arises when (1) the parties in the lawsuit live in different states or when one of the parties is a foreign government or a foreign citizen, and (2) the amount in controversy is more than $75,000.

**divine right theory** The theory that a monarch's right to rule was derived directly from God rather than from the consent of the people.

**division of powers** A basic principle of federalism established by the U.S. Constitution, by which powers are divided between the national and state governments.

**domestic policy** Public policy concerning issues within a national unit, such as national policy concerning health care or the economy.

**double jeopardy** The prosecution of a person twice for the same criminal offense; prohibited by the Fifth Amendment in all but a few circumstances.

**dual federalism** A system of government in which the federal and the state governments maintain diverse but sovereign powers.

**due process clause** The constitutional guarantee, set out in the Fifth and Fourteenth Amendments, that the government will not illegally or arbitrarily deprive a person of life, liberty, or property.

**due process of law** The requirement that the government use fair, reasonable, and standard procedures whenever it takes any legal action against an individual; required by the Fifth and Fourteenth Amendments.

# E

**easy-money policy** A monetary policy that involves stimulating the economy by expanding the rate of growth of the money supply. An easy-money policy supposedly will lead to lower interest rates and induce consumers to spend more and producers to invest more.

**economic policy** All actions taken by the national government to address the ups and downs in the nation's level of business activity.

**electoral college** The group of electors who are selected by the voters in each state to elect officially the president and vice president. The number of electors in each state is equal to the number of that state's representatives in both chambers of Congress.

**elector** A member of the electoral college.

**electorate** All of the citizens eligible to vote in a given election.

**electronic media** Communication channels that involve electronic transmissions, such as radio, television, and the Internet.

**enabling legislation** A law enacted by a legislature to establish an administrative agency. Enabling legislation normally specifies the name, purpose, composition, and powers of the agency being created.

**entitlement program** A government program (such as Social Security) that allows, or entitles, a certain class of people (such as elderly persons) to receive special benefits. Entitlement programs operate under open-ended budget authorizations that, in effect, place no limits on how much can be spent.

**equality** A concept that holds, at a minimum, that all people are entitled to equal protection under the law.

**equal protection clause** Section 1 of the Fourteenth Amendment, which states that no state shall "deny to any person within its jurisdiction the equal protection of the laws."

**establishment clause** The section of the First Amendment that prohibits Congress from passing laws "respecting an establishment of religion." Issues concerning the establishment clause often center on prayer in public schools, the teaching of fundamentalist theories of creation, and government aid to parochial schools.

**exclusionary rule** A criminal procedural rule requiring that illegally obtained evidence not be admissible in court.

**executive agreement** A binding international agreement, or pact, that is made between the president and another head of state and that does not require Senate approval.

**Executive Office of the President (EOP)** A group of staff agencies that assist the president in carrying out major duties. Franklin D. Roosevelt established the EOP in 1939 to cope with the increased responsibilities brought on by the Great Depression.

**executive order** A presidential order to carry out a policy or policies described in a law passed by Congress.

**executive privilege** An inherent executive power claimed by presidents to withhold information from, or to refuse to appear before, Congress or the courts. The president can also accord the privilege to other executive officials.

**ex post facto law** A criminal law that punishes individuals for committing an act that was legal when the act was committed.

**expressed powers** Constitutional or statutory powers that are expressly provided for by the U.S. Constitution; also called *enumerated powers*.

# F

**faction** A group of persons forming a cohesive minority.

**federalism** A system of shared sovereignty between two levels of government—one national and one subnational—occupying the same geographic region.

**Federalists** A political group, led by Alexander Hamilton and John Adams, that supported the adoption of the Constitution and the creation of a federal form of government.

**federal mandate** A requirement in federal legislation that forces states and municipalities to comply with certain rules. If the federal government does not provide funds to the states to cover the costs of compliance, the mandate is referred to as an *unfunded* mandate.

**Federal Open Market Committee (FOMC)** The most important body within the Federal Reserve System. The FOMC decides how monetary policy should be carried out by the Federal Reserve.

**federal question** A question that pertains to the U.S. Constitution, acts of Congress, or treaties. A federal question provides a basis for federal court jurisdiction.

**federal system** A form of government that provides for a division of powers between a central government and several regional governments. In the United States, the division of powers between the national government and the states is established by the Constitution.

**feminism** The doctrine advocating full political, economic, and social equality for women.

**filibustering** The Senate tradition of unlimited debate undertaken for the purpose of preventing action on a bill.

**first budget resolution** A budget resolution, which is supposed to be passed in May, that sets overall revenue goals and spending targets for the next fiscal year, beginning on October 1.

**First Continental Congress** A gathering of delegates from twelve of the thirteen colonies, held in 1774 to protest the Coercive Acts.

**fiscal federalism** The allocation of taxes collected by one level of government (typically the national government) to another level (typically state or local governments).

**fiscal policy** The use of changes in government expenditures and taxes to alter national economic variables.

**fiscal year** A twelve-month period that is established for bookkeeping or accounting purposes. The government's fiscal year runs from October 1 through September 30.

**foreign policy** A systematic and general plan that guides a country's attitudes and actions toward the rest of the world. Foreign policy includes all of the economic, military, commercial, and diplomatic positions and actions that a nation takes in its relationships with other countries.

**fracking** Technique for extracting oil or natural gas from underground rock by the high-power injection of a mixture of water, sand, and chemicals.

**framing** An agenda-setting technique that establishes the context of a media report. Framing can mean fitting events into a familiar story or filtering information through preconceived ideas.

**free exercise clause** The provision of the First Amendment stating that the government cannot pass laws "prohibiting the free exercise" of religion. Free exercise issues often concern religious practices that conflict with established laws.

**free rider problem** The difficulty that exists when individuals can enjoy the outcome of an interest group's efforts without having to contribute, such as by becoming members of the group.

**fundamental right** A basic right of all Americans, such as First Amendment rights. Any law or action that prevents some group of persons from exercising a fundamental right is subject to the "strict-scrutiny" standard, under which the law or action must be necessary to promote a compelling state interest and must be narrowly tailored to meet that interest.

# G

**gender gap** The difference between the percentage of votes cast for a particular candidate by women and the percentage of votes cast for the same candidate by men.

**general election** A regularly scheduled election to choose the U.S. president, vice president, and senators and representatives in Congress. General elections are held in even-numbered years on the Tuesday after the first Monday in November.

**gerrymandering** The drawing of a legislative district's boundaries in such a way as to maximize the influence of a certain group or political party.

**glass ceiling** An invisible but real discriminatory barrier that prevents women and minorities from rising to top positions of power or responsibility.

**global warming** An increase in the average temperature of the Earth's surface over the last half century and its projected continuation.

**government** The individuals and institutions that make society's rules and also possess the power and authority to enforce those rules.

**government corporation** An agency of the government that is run as a business enterprise. Such agencies engage in primarily commercial activities, produce revenues, and require greater flexibility than most government agencies receive.

**grandfather clause** A clause in a state law that had the effect of restricting the franchise (voting rights) to those whose ancestors had voted before the 1860. It was one of the techniques used in the South to prevent African Americans from exercising their right to vote.

**Great Compromise** A plan for a bicameral legislature in which one chamber would be based on population and the other chamber would represent each state equally. The plan, also known as the Connecticut Compromise, resolved the small-state/large-state controversy.

**greenhouse gas** A gas that, when released into the atmosphere, traps the sun's heat and slows its release into outer space. Carbon dioxide ($CO_2$) is a major example.

# H

**head of state** The person who serves as the ceremonial head of a country's government and represents that country to the rest of the world.

# I

**ideology** Generally, a system of political ideas that are rooted in religious or philosophical beliefs concerning human nature, society, and government.

**imminent lawless action test** The current Supreme Court doctrine for assessing the constitutionality of subversive speech. To be illegal, speech must be "directed to inciting . . . imminent lawless action."

**implied powers** The powers of the federal government that are implied by the expressed powers in the Constitution, particularly in Article I, Section 8.

**independent executive agency** A federal agency that is not located within a cabinet department.

**independent expenditure** An expenditure for activities that are independent from (not coordinated with) those of a political candidate or a political party.

**independent regulatory agency** A federal organization that is responsible for creating and implementing rules that regulate private activity and protect the public interest in a particular sector of the economy.

**indirect technique** Any method used by interest groups to influence government officials through third parties, such as voters.

**individual mandate** In the context of health-care reform, a requirement that all persons obtain health-care insurance from one source or another. Those failing to do so would pay a penalty.

**inflation** A sustained rise in average prices; equivalent to a decline in the value of the dollar.

**inherent powers** The powers of the national government that, although not always expressly granted by the Constitution, are necessary to ensure the nation's integrity and survival as a political unit. Inherent powers include the power to make treaties and the power to wage war or make peace.

**institution** An ongoing organization that performs certain functions for society.

**instructed delegate** A representative who deliberately mirrors the views of the majority of his or her constituents.

**interest group** An organized group of individuals sharing common objectives who actively attempt to influence policymakers.

**interstate commerce** Trade that involves more than one state.

**interventionism** Direct involvement by one country in another country's affairs.

**iron curtain** A phrase coined by Winston Churchill to describe the political boundaries between the democratic countries in Western Europe and the Soviet-controlled Communist countries in Eastern Europe.

**iron triangle** A three-way alliance among legislators, bureaucrats, and interest groups to make or preserve policies that benefit their respective interests.

**isolationism** A political policy of noninvolvement in world affairs.

**issue ad** A political advertisement that focuses on a particular issue. Issue ads can be used to support or attack a candidate's position or credibility.

**issue networks** Groups of individuals or organizations—which consist of legislators and legislative staff members, interest group leaders, bureaucrats, the media, scholars, and other experts—that support particular policy positions on a given issue.

# J

**judicial review** The power of the courts to decide on the constitutionality of legislative enactments and of actions taken by the executive branch.

**judiciary** The courts; one of the three branches of government in the United States.

**jurisdiction** The authority of a court to hear and decide a particular case.

**justiciable controversy** A controversy that is not hypothetical or academic but real and substantial; a requirement that must be satisfied before a court will hear a case. *Justiciable* is pronounced jus-*tish*-a-bul.

# K

**Keynesian economics** An economic theory proposed by British economist John Maynard Keynes that is typically associated with the use of fiscal policy to alter national economic variables.

**kitchen cabinet** The name given to a president's unofficial advisers. The term was coined during Andrew Jackson's presidency.

# L

**labor force** All of the people over the age of sixteen who are working or actively looking for jobs.

**legislative rule** An administrative agency rule that carries the same weight as a statute enacted by a legislature.

***Lemon* test** A three-part test enunciated by the Supreme Court in the 1971 case of *Lemon v. Kurtzman* to determine whether government aid to parochial schools is constitutional. To be constitutional, the aid must (1) be for a clearly secular purpose; (2) neither advance nor inhibit religion in its primary effect, and (3) avoid an "excessive government entanglement with religion." The *Lemon* test has also been used in other types of cases involving the establishment clause.

**libel** A published report of a falsehood that tends to injure a person's reputation or character.

**liberalism** A set of political beliefs that include the advocacy of active government, including government intervention to improve the welfare of individuals and to protect civil rights.

**libertarianism** The belief that government should do as little as possible, not only in the economic sphere, but also in regulating morality and personal behavior.

**liberty** The freedom of individuals to believe, act, and express themselves as they choose so long as doing so does not infringe on the rights of other individuals in the society.

**limited government** A form of government based on the principle that the powers of government should be clearly limited either through a written document or through wide public understanding. It is characterized by institutional checks to ensure that government serves public rather than private interests.

**literacy test** A test given to voters to ensure that they could read and write and thus evaluate political information. This technique was used in many southern states to restrict African American participation in elections.

**lobbying** All of the attempts by organizations or by individuals to influence the passage, defeat, or contents of legislation or to influence the administrative decisions of government.

**lobbyist** An individual who handles a particular interest group's lobbying efforts.

# M

**Madisonian Model** The model of government devised by James Madison, in which the powers of the government are separated into three branches: executive, legislative, and judicial.

**majority leader** The party leader elected by the majority party in the House or in the Senate.

**majority party** The political party that has more members in the legislature than the opposing party.

**malapportionment** A condition in which the voting power of citizens in one district is greater than the voting power of citizens in another district.

**managed news coverage** News coverage that is manipulated (managed) by a campaign manager or political consultant to gain media exposure for a political candidate.

**markup session** A meeting held by a congressional committee or subcommittee to approve, amend, or redraft a bill.

**Marshall Plan** A plan providing for U.S. economic assistance to European nations following World War II to help those nations recover from the war; the plan was named after George C. Marshall, secretary of state from 1947 to 1949.

**mass media** Communication channels, such as newspapers and radio and television broadcasts, through which people can communicate to large audiences.

**material incentive** A reason to join an interest group—practical benefits such as discounts, subscriptions, or group insurance

**Mayflower Compact** A document drawn up by Pilgrim leaders in 1620 on the ship *Mayflower*. The document stated that laws were to be made for the general good of the people.

**media** Newspapers, magazines, television, radio, the Internet, and any other printed or electronic means of communication.

**Medicaid** A joint federal-state program that provides health-care services for low-income persons.

**Medicare** A federal government program that pays for health-care insurance for Americans aged sixty-five years or over.

**minority leader** The party leader elected by the minority party in the House or in the Senate.

**minority-majority district** A district in which minority groups make up a majority of the population.

**minority party** The political party that has fewer members in the legislature than the opposing party.

*Miranda* **warnings** A series of statements informing criminal suspects, on their arrest, of their constitutional rights, such as the right to remain silent and the right to counsel; required by the Supreme Court's 1966 decision in *Miranda v. Arizona*.

**moderate** Persons whose views fall in the middle of the political spectrum.

**monarchy** A form of autocracy in which a king, queen, emperor, empress, tsar, or tsarina is the highest authority in the government. Monarchs usually obtain their power through inheritance.

**monetary policy** Actions taken by the Federal Reserve Board to change the amount of money in circulation so as to affect interest rates, credit markets, the rate of inflation, the rate of economic growth, and the rate of unemployment.

**Monroe Doctrine** A U.S. policy, announced in 1823 by President James Monroe, that the United States would not tolerate foreign intervention in the Western Hemisphere, and in return, the United States would stay out of European affairs.

**moral idealism** In foreign policy, the belief that the most important goal is to do what is right. Moral idealists think that it is possible for nations to cooperate as part of a rule-based community.

**mutually assured destruction (MAD)** A phrase referring to the assumption that if the forces of two nations are equally capable of destroying each other, neither nation will take a chance on war.

# N

**national convention** The meeting held by each major party every four years to select presidential and vice-presidential candidates, write a party platform, and conduct other party business.

**national health insurance** A program, found in many of the world's economically advanced nations, under which the central government provides basic health-care insurance coverage to everyone in the country. Some wealthy nations, such as the Netherlands and Switzerland, provide universal coverage through private insurance companies instead.

**national party chairperson** An individual who serves as a political party's administrative head at the national level and directs the work of the party's national committee.

**national party committee** The political party leaders who direct party business during the four years between the national party conventions, organize the next national convention, and plan how to obtain a party victory in the next presidential elections.

**National Security Council (NSC)** A council that advises the president on domestic and foreign matters concerning the safety and defense of the nation; established in 1947.

**natural rights** Rights that are not bestowed by governments but are inherent within every man, woman, and child by virtue of the fact that he or she is a human being.

**necessary and proper clause** Article I, Section 8, Clause 18, of the Constitution, which gives Congress the power to make all laws "necessary and proper" for the federal government to carry out its responsibilities; also called the *elastic clause.*

**negative political advertising** Political advertising undertaken for the purpose of discrediting an opposing candidate in the eyes of the voters. Attack ads are one form of negative political advertising.

**neutral competency** The application of technical skills to jobs without regard to political issues.

**neutrality** A position of not being aligned with either side in a dispute or conflict, such as a war.

**New Deal** The policies ushered in by the Roosevelt administration in 1933 in an attempt to bring the United States out of the Great Depression. The New Deal included many government-spending and public-assistance programs, in addition to thousands of regulations governing economic activity.

**new federalism** A plan to limit the federal government's role in regulating state governments and to give the states increased power in deciding how they should spend government revenues.

**nominating convention** An official meeting of a political party to choose its candidates. Nominating conventions at the state and local levels also select delegates to represent the citizens of their geographic areas at a higher-level party convention.

**normal trade relations (NTR) status** A trade status granted through an international treaty by which each member nation must treat other members at least as well as it treats the country that receives its most favorable treatment. This status was formerly known as *most-favored-nation status.*

# O

**obscenity** Indecency or offensiveness in speech, expression, behavior, or appearance. Whether specific expressions or acts constitute obscenity is normally determined by community standards.

**Office of Management and Budget (OMB)** An agency in the Executive Office of the President that has the primary duty of assisting the president in preparing and supervising the administration of the federal budget.

**"one person, one vote" rule** A rule, or principle, requiring that congressional districts have equal populations so that one person's vote counts as much as another's vote.

**open primary** A primary in which voters can vote for a party's candidates regardless of whether they belong to the party.

**opinion** A written statement by a court expressing the reasons for its decision in a case.

**opposition research** The attempt to learn damaging information about an opponent in a political campaign.

**oral argument** A spoken argument presented to a judge in person by an attorney on behalf of her or his client.

**Oslo Accords** The first agreement signed between Israel and the PLO; led to the establishment of the Palestinian Authority in the occupied territories.

# P

**Palestine Liberation Organization (PLO)** An organization formed in 1964 to represent the Palestinian people. The PLO has a long history of terrorism but for some years has functioned primarily as a political party.

**parliament** The name of the national legislative body in countries governed by a parliamentary system, such as Britain and Canada.

**partisan politics** Political actions or decisions that benefit a particular party.

**party activist** A party member who helps to organize and oversee party functions and planning during and between campaigns and may even become a candidate for office.

**party identifier** A person who identifies himself or herself as being a supporter of a particular political party.

**party platform** The document drawn up by each party at its national convention that outlines the policies and positions of the party.

**party ticket** A list of a political party's candidates for various offices. In national elections, the party ticket consists of the presidential and vice-presidential candidates.

**patronage** The practice by which elected officials give government jobs to individuals who helped them gain office.

**peer group** Associates, often close in age to one another; may include friends, classmates, co-workers, club members, or religious group members. Peer group influence is a significant factor in the political socialization process.

**personal attack ad** A negative political advertisement that attacks the character of an opposing candidate.

**picket-fence federalism** A model of federalism in which specific policies and programs are administered by all levels of government—national, state, and local.

**pluralist theory** A theory that views politics as a contest among various interest groups—at all levels of government—to gain benefits for their members.

**pocket veto** A special type of veto power used by the chief executive after the legislature has adjourned. Bills that are not signed die after a specified period of time.

**podcasting** The distribution of audio or video files to a personal computer or a mobile device such as smartphones.

**police powers** The powers of a government body that enable it to create laws for the protection of the health, safety, welfare, and morals of the people. In the United States, most police powers are reserved to the states.

**policymaking process** The procedures involved in getting an issue on the political agenda; formulating, adopting, and implementing a policy with regard to the issue; and then evaluating the results of the policy.

**political action committee (PAC)** A committee that is established by a corporation, labor union, or special interest group to raise funds and make contributions on the establishing organization's behalf.

**political advertising** Advertising undertaken by or on behalf of a political candidate to familiarize voters with the candidate and his or her views on campaign issues; also advertising for or against policy issues.

**political consultant** A professional political adviser who, for a fee, works on an area of a candidate's campaign. Political consultants include campaign managers, pollsters, media advisers, and "get out the vote" organizers.

**political culture** The set of ideas, values, and attitudes about government and the political process held by a community or a nation.

**political party** A group of individuals who organize to win elections, operate the government, and determine policy.

**political realism** In foreign policy, the belief that nations are inevitably selfish, and that we should seek to protect our national, security regardless of moral arguments.

**political socialization** The learning process through which most people acquire their political attitudes, opinions, beliefs, and knowledge.

**politics** The process of resolving conflicts over how society should use its scarce resources and who should receive various benefits, such as public health care and public higher education.

**poll tax** A fee of several dollars that had to be paid before a person could vote. This device was used in some southern states to prevent African Americans and low-income whites from voting.

**poll watcher** A representative from one of the political parties who is allowed to monitor a polling place to make sure that the election is run fairly and that fraud doesn't occur.

**power** The ability to influence the behavior of others, usually through the use of force, persuasion, or rewards.

**precedent** A court decision that furnishes an example or authority for deciding subsequent cases involving identical or similar facts and legal issues.

**precinct** A political district within a city, such as a block or a neighborhood, or a rural portion of a county; the smallest voting district at the local level.

**preemption** A doctrine rooted in the supremacy clause of the Constitution that provides that national laws or regulations governing a certain area take precedence over conflicting state laws or regulations governing that same area.

**press secretary** A member of the White House staff who holds news conferences for reporters and makes public statements for the president.

**primary** A preliminary election held for the purpose of choosing a party's final candidate.

**primary election** An election in which voters choose the candidates of their party, who will then run in the general election.

**primary source of law** A source of law that establishes the law. Primary sources of law include constitutions, statutes, administrative agency rules and regulations, and decisions rendered by the courts.

**priming** An agenda-setting technique in which a media outlet promotes specific facts or ideas that may affect the public's thinking on related topics.

**print media** Communication channels that consist of printed materials, such as newspapers and magazines.

**privatization** The transfer of the task of providing services traditionally provided by government to the private sector.

**probable cause** Cause for believing that there is a substantial likelihood that a person has committed or is about to commit a crime.

**progressivism** An alternative, more popular term for the set of political beliefs also known as liberalism.

**public debt** The total amount of money that the national government owes as a result of borrowing; also called the *national debt*.

**public-interest group** An interest group formed for the purpose of working for the "public good." Examples of public-interest groups are the American Civil Liberties Union and Common Cause.

**public opinion** The views of the citizenry about politics, public issues, and public policies; a complex collection of opinions held by many people on issues in the public arena.

**public opinion poll** A survey of the public's opinion on a particular topic at a particular moment.

**public services** Essential services that individuals cannot provide for themselves, such as building and maintaining roads, establishing welfare programs, operating public schools, and preserving national parks.

**purposive incentive** A reason to join an interest group—satisfaction resulting from working for a cause in which one believes.

**push poll** A campaign tactic used to feed false or misleading information to potential voters, under the guise of taking an opinion poll, with the intent to "push" voters away from one candidate and toward another.

# Q

**quota system** A policy under which a specific number of jobs, promotions, or other types of placements, such as university admissions, are given to members of selected groups.

# R

**random sample** In the context of opinion polling, a sample in which each person within the entire population being polled has an equal chance of being chosen.

**rating system** A system by which a particular interest group evaluates (rates) the performance of legislators based on how often the legislators have voted with the group's position on particular issues.

**rational basis test** A test (also known as the "ordinary-scrutiny" standard) used by the Supreme Court to decide whether a discriminatory law violates the equal protection clause of the Constitution. It is used only when there is no classification—such as race or gender—that would require a higher level of scrutiny. Few laws evaluated under this test are found invalid.

**realignment** A process in which the popular support for and relative strength of the parties shift and the parties are reestablished with different coalitions of supporters.

**recession** A period in which the level of economic activity falls; usually defined as two or more quarters of economic decline.

**renewable energy** Energy from technologies that do not rely on extracted resources, such as oil and coal, that can run out.

**representative democracy** A form of democracy in which the will of the majority is expressed through groups of individuals elected by the people to act as their representatives.

**republic** Essentially, a representative democracy in which there is no king or queen and the people are sovereign.

**reverse discrimination** Discrimination against those who have no minority status.

**right-to-work laws** Laws that ban unions from collecting dues or other fees from workers that they represent but who have not actually joined the union.

**rulemaking** The process undertaken by an administrative agency when formally proposing, evaluating, and adopting a new regulation.

**rule of law** A basic principle of government that requires those who govern to act in accordance with established law.

**Rules Committee** A standing committee in the House of Representatives that provides special rules governing how particular bills will be considered and debated by the House. The Rules Committee normally proposes time limits on debate for any bill.

# S

**sample** In the context of opinion polling, a group of people selected to represent the population being studied.

**sampling error** In the context of opinion polling, the difference between what the sample results show and what the true results would have been had everybody in the relevant population been interviewed.

**school voucher** An educational certificate, provided by the government, that allows a student to use public funds to pay for a private or a public school chosen by the student or his or her parents.

**secession** The act of formally withdrawing from membership in an alliance; the withdrawal of a state from the federal Union.

**second budget resolution** A budget resolution, which is supposed to be passed in September, that sets "binding" limits on taxes and spending for the next fiscal year.

**Second Continental Congress** The congress of the colonies that met in 1775 to assume the powers of a central government and to establish an army.

**seditious speech** Speech that urges resistance to lawful authority or that advocates the overthrowing of a government.

**self-incrimination** Providing damaging information or testimony against oneself in court.

**senatorial courtesy** A practice that allows a senator of the president's party to veto the president's nominee to a federal court judgeship within the senator's state.

**separate-but-equal doctrine** A Supreme Court doctrine holding that the equal protection clause of the Fourteenth Amendment did not forbid racial segregation as long as the facilities for blacks were equal to those for whites. The doctrine was overturned in the *Brown v. Board of Education of Topeka* decision of 1954.

**separation of powers** The principle of dividing governmental powers among the legislative, the executive, and the judicial branches of government.

**sexual harassment** Unwanted physical contact, verbal conduct, or abuse of a sexual nature that interferes with a recipient's job performance, creates a hostile environment, or carries with it an implicit or explicit threat of adverse employment consequences.

**Shays' Rebellion** A rebellion of angry farmers in western Massachusetts in 1786, led by former Revolutionary War captain Daniel Shays. This rebellion and other similar uprisings in the New England states emphasized the need for a true national government.

**signing statement** A written statement, appended to a bill at the time the president signs it into law, indicating how the president interprets that legislation.

**sit-in** A tactic of nonviolent civil disobedience. Demonstrators enter a business, college building, or other public place and remain seated until they are forcibly removed or until their demands are met. The tactic was used successfully in the civil rights movement and in other protest movements in the United States.

**slander** The public utterance (speaking) of a statement that holds a person up for contempt, ridicule, or hatred.

**social conflict** Disagreements among people in a society over what the society's priorities should be.

**social contract** A voluntary agreement among individuals to create a government and to give that government adequate power to secure the mutual protection and welfare of all individuals.

**socialism** A political ideology that lies to the left of liberalism on the traditional political spectrum. Socialists are scarce in the United States but common in many other countries.

**soft money** Campaign contributions not regulated by federal law, such as some contributions that are made to political parties instead of to particular candidates.

**solidarity** Mutual agreement among the members of a particular group.

**solidary incentive** A reason to join an interest group— pleasure in associating with like-minded individuals.

**Solid South** A term used to describe the tendency of the southern states to vote Democratic after the Civil War.

**sound bite** A televised comment, lasting for only a few seconds, that captures a thought or a perspective and has an immediate impact on the viewers.

**Soviet bloc** The group of Eastern European nations that fell under the control of the Soviet Union following World War II.

**Speaker of the House** The presiding officer in the House of Representatives. The Speaker has traditionally been a longtime member of the majority party and is often the most powerful and influential member of the House.

**special election** An election that is held at the state or local level when the voters must decide an issue before the next general election or when vacancies occur by reason of death or resignation.

**spin** A reporter's slant on, or interpretation of, a particular event or action.

**spin doctor** A political candidate's press adviser who tries to convince reporters to give a story or event concerning the candidate a particular "spin" (interpretation, or slant).

**standing committee** A permanent committee in Congress that deals with legislation concerning a particular area, such as agriculture or foreign relations.

**standing to sue** The requirement that an individual must have a sufficient stake in a controversy before he or she can bring a lawsuit. The party bringing the suit must demonstrate that he or she has either been harmed or been threatened with a harm.

**stare decisis** A common law doctrine under which judges normally are obligated to follow the precedents established by prior court decisions. Pronounced *ster*-ay dih-*si*-sis.

**statutory law** The body of law enacted by legislatures (as opposed to constitutional law, administrative law, or case law).

**straw poll** A nonscientific poll; a poll in which there is no way to ensure that the opinions expressed are representative of the larger population.

**subcommittee** A division of a larger committee that deals with a particular part of the committee's policy area. Most standing committees have several subcommittees.

**suffrage** The right to vote; the franchise.

**supremacy clause** Article VI, Clause 2, of the Constitution, which makes the Constitution and federal laws superior to all conflicting state and local laws.

**suspect classification** A classification, such as race, that provides the basis for a discriminatory law. Any law based on a suspect classification is subject to strict scrutiny by the courts, meaning that the law must be justified by a compelling state interest.

**symbolic speech** The expression of beliefs, opinions, or ideas through forms other than verbal speech or print; speech involving actions and other nonverbal expressions

# T

**Tea Party movement** A grassroots conservative movement that arose in 2009 after Barack Obama became president. The movement opposes big government and current levels of taxation, and also rejects political compromise.

**third party** In the United States, any party other than one of the two major parties (Republican and Democratic).

**three-fifths compromise** A compromise reached during the Constitutional Convention by which three-fifths of all slaves were to be counted for purposes of representation in the House of Representatives.

**trade organization** An association formed by members of a particular industry, such as the oil industry or the trucking industry, to develop common standards and goals for the industry. Trade organizations, as interest groups, lobby government for legislation or regulations that specifically benefit their groups.

**treaty** A formal agreement between the governments of two or more countries.

**trial court** A court in which trials are held and testimony taken.

**trustee** A representative who tries to serve the broad interests of the entire society and not just the narrow interests of his or her constituents.

**two-party system** A political system in which two strong and established parties compete for political offices.

**tyranny** The arbitrary or unrestrained exercise of power by an oppressive individual or government.

# U

**unemployment** The state of not having a job even when actively seeking one.

**unicameral legislature** A legislature with only one chamber.

**unitary system** A centralized governmental system in which local or subdivisional governments exercise only those powers given to them by the central government.

# V

**veto** A Latin word meaning "I forbid"; the refusal by an official, such as the president of the United States or a state governor, to sign a bill into law.

**veto power** A constitutional power that enables the chief executive (president or governor) to reject legislation and return it to the legislature with reasons for the rejection. This prevents or at least delays the bill from becoming law.

**vital center** The center of the political spectrum; those who hold moderate political views. The center is vital because without it, it may be difficult, if not impossible, to reach the compromises that are necessary to a political system's continuity.

**vote-eligible population** The number of people who are actually eligible to vote in an American election.

**voting-age population** The number of people residing in the United States who are at least eighteen years old.

# W

**ward** A local unit of a political party's organization, consisting of a division or district within a city.

**Watergate scandal** A scandal involving an illegal break-in at the Democratic National Committee offices in 1972 by members of President Nixons reelection campaign staff. Before Congress could vote to impeach Nixon for his participation in covering up the break-in, Nixon resigned from the presidency.

**weapons of mass destruction** Chemical, biological, or nuclear weapons that can inflict massive casualties.

**whip** A member of Congress who assists the majority or minority leader in the House or in the Senate in managing the party's legislative program.

**whistleblower** In the context of government employment, someone who "blows the whistle" (reports to authorities or the press) on gross governmental inefficiency, illegal action, or other wrongdoing.

**White House Office** The personal office of the president. White House Office personnel handle the president's political needs and manage the media, among other duties.

**white primary** A primary election in which African Americans were prohibited from voting. The practice was banned by the Supreme Court in 1944.

**winner-take-all system** A system in which the candidate who receives the most votes wins. In contrast, proportional systems allocate votes to multiple winners.

**writ of *certiorari*** An order from a higher court asking a lower court for the record of a case. *Certiorari* is pronounced sur-shee-uh-*rah*-ree.

**writ of *habeas corpus*** An order that requires an official to bring a specified prisoner into court and explain to the judge why the person is being held in prison.

# INDEX

executive privilege claimed by, 287
expansion of presidential power under, 279
federalism and, 65
fundraising, 275
gay rights, 117
Guantánamo prisoners and rights of, 319
Hispanic vote for, 110
Honest Leadership and Open Government Act, 144
International Criminal Court treaty, 326
Iran and, 383
Iraq War and, 284, 376–377
Keynesian rhetoric, 359
legislative success of, 282
lobbying reform, 144
No Child Left Behind Act, 65
North Korea and talks with, 382
as opinion leader, 181
oversight of, by Congress, 261
Pakistan, 377
Partial Birth Abortion Ban Act, 89
response to 9/11, 376
September 11, 2001 terrorist attacks and, 286
signing statements and, 283
Supreme Court appointments, 120, 331
tax cuts for rich, 158, 360
veto power exercised by, 277–278
war on terrorism, 91, 284, 376–377
wind energy, 355
Business cycle, 355
Business interest groups, 131–132
Busing, 102
Butler, Jon, 26
Byrd, Robert, 251

## C

Cabinet, 287–288
attorney general and, 303
defined, 287
executive departments, 287, 288, 299–300
foreign policymaking and, 367
kitchen, 288
Obama's czars, 288
use of, 287–288
Cain, Herman, 205, 208
Campaign(s)
campaign strategy, 207
cost of, 210–216
direct-mail campaigns, 208–209
financing, 210–216
Internet and, 238–240
candidates' 24/7 exposure, 239
controlling netroots, 239
fundraising on, 208–209
online fundraising, 238
rise of Internet campaign, 238–239
support for local organizing, 209–210
targeting supporters, 209
nominating candidates, 198–206
opposition research, 208
political parties role in running, 160
professional campaign organization, 206–207
responsibilities of campaign staff, 206
typical organization for presidential, 207
Campaign financing, 210–216
Bipartisan Campaign Reform Act, 213

bundled campaign contributions, 144
by business interest groups, 132
*Citizens* decision, 139, 211, 213–214, 215, 336
corporate funding, 213–214, 215
direct-mail campaigns, 208–209
favoring two-party system, 164
Federal Election Campaign Act, 211–213
501(c)4 and 527s, 215
527s, 140
incumbent and, 249–250
independent expenditures, 212–213
Internet fundraising, 208–209
issue campaigns, 213
lobbying regulation and reform, 143–144
moneybomb technique, 209
Obama's fundraising success, 238
online fundraising, 238
political action committees (PACs) and, 212
savings and loan scandal and, 142
skirting campaign-financing rules, 212–213
soft money, 140, 212
super PAC's, 139, 211, 214–215
Campaign for Tobacco-Free Kids, 144
Campaign strategy, 207
Camp David, 270
Canada, 51
Canadian vs. American federalism, 54
health care spending, 348
North Atlantic Treaty Organization (NATO), 371
as oil exporter, 351, 353
powers of provinces, 54
two languages and, 54
World War II and, 370
Candidates
incumbent, power of, 249–251
insurgent candidates, 202
nomination process, 198–206
perception of, and voting behavior, 182
policy choice and voting behavior, 182–183
presidential, 203–206
selecting, 157
television and
debates, 229
news coverage, 230
political advertising, 227–229
popular television, 230
use of Internet, 238–240
write-in, 199
Cantor, Eric, 252
*Cantwell v. Connecticut,* 77
Capitalism, 12–13
Carpenters & Joiners Union, 133
Carter, Jimmy, 270, 277
amnesty for draft resisters, 277
attorney general for, 303
election of 1980
presidential debate and, 229
public opinion polls, 176–177
legislative success of, 282
Middle East peace efforts and, 378
Mondale as vice president, 290
public opinion of, 181
Case law, 322
Castle, Mike, 182
Castro, Fidel, 110
Categorical grants, 67–68
Catholics, 176
insurance for birth control, 83

voting behavior, 183, 185
Catt, Carrie Chapman, 106
Caucuses
defined, 200
historical perspective on, 200
presidential, 203
Cell phones, public opinion polls and, 174
Censorship, 88
of Internet, in China, 221
Central Intelligence Agency (CIA)
creation of, 368
foreign policymaking and, 368–369
formation of, 304
function of, 369
principle duties of, 304
Chamber of Commerce, 131
overview of, 131–132
Change to Win federation, 132
Charitable contribution tax break, 130
Chase, Samuel, 261
Checks and balances
Congress and, 244, 285
defined, 42
judicial review, 333–334
media and, 221
of president, 42
as principle of Constitution, 42
Cheney, Dick, 91
power of, as vice president, 291
*Cheonan,* 382
Chief diplomat, 274
Chief executive role of president, 271–273
Chief of staff, 289
Child labor, 62
Child Online Protection Act, 86
Children, media and opinion formation, 180–181
Children's Health Insurance Program (CHIP), 348–349
Children's Internet Protection Act (CIPA), 86
Chile, 197
China
American trade relations with, 383–384
Communist Party of, and dictatorial power, 7
as debt holder of U.S. public debt, 362
diplomatic relations with U.S., 384
environmental movement in, 142
foreign countries opinion of, 173
as future challenger to American dominance, 384
government-paid bloggers, 236
gross domestic product, 384
Internet censorship and, 221
negotiations with North Korea nuclear cooperation treaty, 382
normal trade relations status, 384
opinion of own national economic condition, 173
political party affiliation in, 161
religious intolerance, 79
restricting imports from, 385
Taiwan and, 384
Tibet and, 5
World War II, 370
WTO membership, 384
Chinese Americans, 111
Chinese Exclusion Act, 111
*Christian Science Monitor,* 223
Chrysler, 155
Churchill, Winston, 371, 372
executive agreement with Roosevelt, 283
*Cincinnati Post,* 223

Cyberspace. *See* Internet
Czechoslovakia, Soviet bloc, 371

# D

Daily Kos, 179
*Daily Show with Jon Stewart, The,* 230
Dealignment, 156
Death penalty, as cruel and unusual
  punishment, 43
Debates
  Republican presidential primary
    debates of 2012, 204–205
  television, 229
Debt, public debt, 361–362
Declaration of Independence
  equality and, 12
  political culture and, 11
  pursuit of happiness, 12
  significance of, 29–30
  slavery and, 37, 38
Declaration of Sentiments, 105
*De facto* segregation, 102
Defense, Department of, 288
  foreign policymaking and, 368
  principle duties of, 301
Defense of Marriage Act (DOMA), 58
*De Jonge v. Oregon,* 77
*De jure* segregation, 102
DeLay, Tom, 247
Delegates
  defined, 200
  national convention, 205–206
  to nominating convention, 200
  unpledged, 201
Democracy. *See also* American democracy
  American, 9–15
  defined, 7
  direct, 7–8
  parliamentary democracy, 9
  presidential democracy, 9
  representative, 8–9
Democratic Party
  African American support for, 16, 153,
    185
  beginning of, 151
  business interest groups and, 132
  civil rights movement and, 16
  Civil rights plank of platform in 1948
    election, 153
  control of Congress, 153, 155, 243,
    261, 285–286
  current condition of, 153–157
  dealignment, 156
  global warming and, 353
  Great Depression and, 152, 181
  growing partisanship, 155–156
  health care proposal, 349–350
  Hispanics identification with, 110
  historical perspective of political
    parties, 149–153
  liberals identify with, 16
  national committees, 163
  national conventions, 163
  online fundraising, 209
  partisan politics and legislative
    gridlock, 156
  Populist movement and, 152
  raising taxes to reduce federal deficit, 2
  realignment elections, 153
  red state vs. blue state, 153–155
  shifting political fortunes, 154–156
  socioeconomic factors
    age, 183

educational attainment, 183
gender and, 183
geographic region and, 185
income and, 154
moderates, 186
occupation and income level, 183
religion and ethnicity, 183, 185
Solid South, 185
symbol of, 165
taxmageddon and budget deficit, 158
tipping, 156–157
trouble for, 155
voter fraud claims, 190
Democratic Republicans, 150
Demonstration techniques, of interest
  groups, 141
Dennis, Eugene, 84
*Dennis v. United States,* 84
Depression. *See* Great Depression
Détente, 372
Deterrence, 372
Devolution, 64, 65
Dictatorship, 7
Die, right to, 89
Diplomat, 273
  role of president as chief, 273–274
Direct democracy
  Athenian model of, 7–8
  defined, 8
Direct-mail campaigns, 208–209
Direct payments, 125
Direct primary, 201
Direct techniques of interest groups,
  136–139
Disabilities, persons with
  civil rights of, 114–115
  reasonable accommodations, 332
Disability payments, federal budget spent
  on, 299
Discouraged workers, 356
Discrimination. *See also* Civil rights
  affirmative action, 118–121
  of African Americans, 101–105
  of Asian Americans, 111, 112
  equal employment opportunity, 118
  equal protection clause and, 99–101
  of gays and lesbians, 115–118
  of Native Americans, 111–114
  reverse, 119
  of women, 105–109
Dissenting opinions, 329
District, 162
District courts, 325, 327
District of Columbia, 244
Disturbance theory, 127
Diversity of citizenship, 324
Divided government
  Bush and, 285–286
  Obama and, 286
  parliamentary system and, 44
Divine right theory, 7
Division of powers, 55–59
Divorce, state power and, 56
Dixiecrat Party, 167
Domestic partnerships, 117–118
Domestic policy, 343–363
  defined, 344
  health care, 347–350
  policymaking process, 344–347
Donkey vote, 197
"Don't ask, don't tell" policy, 118
Double jeopardy, 76, 77, 92
Drinking age debate, 49, 68
Driver's Privacy Protection Act, 88
Drug Enforcement Administration, 299

Dual federalism, 61–62
Due process, 75, 76, 92
  of law, 75
  procedural, 75, 77
  sodomy laws and, 116
  substantive, 77
Dukakis, Michael, 271
Dye, Thomas R., 69

# E

Earmarks, 263
Earned-Income Tax Credit, 137
East Germany
  Berlin Wall, 372, 373
  Soviet bloc, 371
Easy-money policy, 356
Economic policy, 355–362
  easy-money policy, 356
  Emergency Economic Stabilization Act,
    347
  federal tax system, 358–361
  fiscal policy, 357–358
  goals of, 355–356
  inflation and, 356
  Keynesian economics, 357–358
  monetary policy, 356–357
  public debt, 361–362
  pushing on a string, 356–357
  unemployment and, 355–356
*Economic Report of the President,* 280
Economic status, formation of political
  opinion and, 181–182
Economy. *See also* Great Recession
  foreign countries opinion of each other
    and, 173
  as issue in 2008, 2010, 2012 elections,
    182
  president's power to influence, 280, 281
Ecuador, 197
Education. *See also* Schools
  affirmative action at colleges, 118–121
  African American challenges, 105
  aid to parochial schools, 81–82
  Asian Americans, 111, 112
  *Brown* decision and school integration,
    102
  busing, 102
  cyberbullying, 87
  evolution vs. creationism, 81
  federal budget spent on, 298
  formation of political opinion and, 180
  free speech for students, 86–87
  intelligent design, 81
  land-grant colleges, 67
  persons with disabilities and, 114–115
  prayer in schools, 80–81
  race-blind admissions, 121
  Race to the Top, 345–346
  school voucher programs, 82
  socioeconomic class and, 105
  voter turnout and educational
    attainment, 191
  voting behavior and attainment of, 183
Education, Department of, 288, 302
E-fraud, 315
Egypt, 226
  Arab Spring and, 381
  religious intolerance, 79
  Yom Kippur War and, 378
Eighth Amendment
  bails and fines, 92
  death penalty and, 93
  text of, 76

Harlan, John Marshall, 100
Harris Poll, 174
Haskins, Ron, 137
*Hazelwood School District v. Kuhlmeier,* 88
Head of state, 273
Head Start, 62, 63
Health and Human Services, Department of, 288, 301
Health care/health care reform, 347–350
    Clinton and, 275, 349
    conservative reaction, 350
    constitutionality of, 41, 327–328, 336, 350
    current system of funding, 348, 349
    Democrats proposal, 349–350
    employer-provided health-insurance tax break, 130
    expected results, 350
    Health Insurance Exchange, 349, 350
    individual mandate, 41, 66, 327–328, 336, 349–350
    lack of coverage, 348
    Medicaid expansion, 66–67
    Medicare and Medicaid overview, 348–349
    national health insurance, 349
    Obama and content of legislation, 275
    Patient Protection and Affordable Care Act, 347–348
    as percent of national spending, 348, 349
    popularity of Democrats and, 155
    public option, 350
    regulation of, 295
    states' rights and, 66–67
    support and opposition to, 350
Health Insurance Exchange, 349, 350
Help America Vote Act, 189
Henry, Patrick, 34
    as Anti-Federalist, 39
    on slavery, 38
Hill, Anita, 331
Hiroshima, 284, 370
Hispanics
    civil rights of, 109–111
    Latino/Latina term, 110
    party identification, 110
    percent of population, 109
    place of origin, 110
    political participation, 110–111
    poverty, 109, 110
    project racial and ethnic distribution of U.S., 14
    voter turnout, 110, 191
    voting behavior, 185
Hitler, Adolf, 7
Hollande, Francois, 274
Holmes, Oliver Wendell, 83, 84
Homeland Security, Department of, 288
    creation of, 299
    principle duties of, 302
Homeland Security Act, Operation TIPS and, 89
Honest Leadership and Open Government Act, 144
*Hopwood v. State of Texas,* 119, 332–333
Horizontal federalism, 58
Hostile-environment harassment, 108–109
House effect, 175
House Judiciary Committee, 261–262
House of Commons, 44
House of Representatives, United States. *See also* Congress

African Americans in, 105
apportionment of house seats, 244, 245
budgeting process, 262–264
campaign costs for, 210
checks and balances and, 42, 43
committees in, 254–255
debate in, and rules for, 255
differences between House and Senate, 255–256
foreign policymaking and, 369
global warming and, 352–353
Great Compromise, 35
Hispanic Americans in, 111
impeachment power, 37, 261
investigative function, 260–261
leadership in, 252–254
    majority leader, 253
    minority leader, 253
    Speaker of the House, 252–253
    whips, 253–254
legislative process, 256–260
minority leader of, 107
number of citizens represented by, 245, 246
112th Congress, 250
representation function of, 247–249
Republican control of, 14
requirements for, 249
Rules Committee, 255, 259
salary of, 249
size of house, 245, 246
structure of, 244–247
term limits, 251–252
terms of office for, 42, 251–252
three-fifths compromise, 35–36
women in, 106–107
Housing
    low-income programs and federal budget spent on, 299
    mortgage interest tax break, 130
Housing and Urban Development, Department of, 288, 301
Human Rights Campaign, 136
Hungary, Soviet bloc, 371
Hussein, Saddam, 376
Hydroelectric energy, 354–355
Hyperlocalism, 234

# I

Identity interest groups, 135
Ideological interest groups, 135–136
Ideological parties, 166–167
Ideology
    conservatism, 15–16
    defined, 15
    liberalism, 16–17
    traditional political spectrum, 17–19
    voting behavior and, 186
Immigrants/immigration
    Arizona law and, 327
    Asian Americans, 111
    federalism, 66
    national authority over, 66
    path to citizenship for illegal, 346
    state vs. national policy for, 98
    voter turnout and, 191
Imminent lawless action test, 84–85
Impeachment, power of, under Constitution, 37, 261
Implied powers, 55, 60
Incapacitation, 343
Incarceration rate, 343
Income

African Americans, 105
Asian Americans, 111, 112
voter turnout, 191
voting behavior and, 154, 183
women and wage discrimination, 108
Income tax, 55
Incumbents, power of, 249–251
Independent executive agencies, 301, 303–304
Independent expenditures, 140, 212–213
    top groups in 2012, 215
Independent regulatory agencies. *See also* Regulation/regulatory agencies
    defined, 304
    list of selected, 305
Independents, 18
    dealignment and, 156
    increasing number of, 156
India, 51
    detonating nuclear device, 381
    House of the People, 246
Indian Gaming Regulatory Act, 114, 115
Indirect primary, 201
Indirect techniques of interest groups, 139–141
Individual freedom, 11
Individual mandate, 349–350
Individuals with Disabilities Education Act, 114
Inflation
    economic policy and, 356
    fear of, 356
Infotainment, 225
Inherent powers, 55–56, 275–276
    of president, 278
*In re Oliver,* 77
Institution, 3
Instructed delegate, 248
Insurance Institute for Highway Safety, 49
Insurgent candidates, 202
Intelligent design, 81
Interest groups
    campaign financing, 213
    constitutional right to petition government and, 126
    criticism of, 142–144
    defined, 126
    direct techniques of
        election support, 138–139
        lobbying, 136–139
    formation of, 126–129
        defending group's interest, 127
        disturbance theory, 127
        entrepreneurial theory, 127
        free rider problem, 128–129
        importance of leaders, 127
        incentives to join group, 127–128
        increase in government and, 127
    free rider problem, 128–129
    functions of, 129
    incentives to join, 127–128
    indirect techniques of
        demonstrations, 141
        going to court, 140–141
        issues ads and 527s, 140
        mobilizing constituents, 140
        rating systems, 139–140
        shaping public opinion, 139
    influence on policy, 136–141
    iron triangle, 310–311
    issue campaigns, 213
    percentage of Americans belonging to, 127
    pluralist theory and, 129

King's court, 320
Kitchen cabinet, 288
*Klopfer v. North Carolina,* 77
Koch, Charles, 214
Koch, David, 214
Koran, Islamic government and, 9
Korean War, 284, 372
Kosovo, 373
Kucinich, Dennis, 250
Kurds, 376–377
Kuwait, invaded by Iraq, 376

# L

Labor, Department of, 288, 301
Laborers Union, 133
Labor force, 133
Labor interest groups, 132–134
Labor unions. *See* Unions
Land-grant colleges, 67
Landon, Alfred, 173
Landslide election, 198, 199
Langevin, Jim, 114
Lasswell, Harold, 3
Latham, Thomas, 250
Latino, 110
*Law & Order,* 230
*Lawrence v. Texas,* 116, 337
Laws
    administrative, 322
    case, 322
    civil, 322
    common law tradition, 320–321
    constitutional, 321
    criminal, 322–323
    due process of, 75
    election laws favoring two-party
        system, 164
    equal protection of, 11
    *ex post facto* law, 74
    Jim Crow, 100
    legislative process, 256–260
    primary sources of, 321
    rule of law, 40
    rule of precedent, 320–321
    sodomy, 116
    sources of, 321–323325–326
    statutory, 322
    steps in bill becoming a law, 256–260
    sunshine, 314–315
League of Nations, 370
Lebanon, 378
Lee, Richard Henry, 29
Legislation
    enabling, 307
    supermajority to pass important
        legislation, 243
    by Supreme Court, 336, 339
Legislative branch
    checks and balances and, 42, 43
    separation of powers, 42
Legislative process, 256–260
Legislative rules, 307
Legislature
    bicameral, 35
    success of various presidents, 282
    unicameral, 30
Lemon test, 82
*Lemon v. Kurtzman,* 82
Lesbians
    changing attitude toward, 116–117
    changing legal landscape, 116
    civil rights of, 115–118
    "Don't ask, don't tell" policy, 118

in military, 118
    same-sex marriage, 8, 23, 46, 58, 65,
        117–118, 337
Lewinsky, Monica, 287
Lexington, Battle of, 28
Libel, 85
Liberalism/liberals
    bias in media, 233
    big government and, 16
    civil rights movement, 16
    defined, 15
    online fundraising, 209
    progressives and, 17
    roots of, 16
    Supreme Court and, 335
    in traditional political spectrum, 17–19
    Vietnam War and, 16–17
    voting behavior, 186
Libertarianism, 19
Libertarian organizations, online
    fundraising, 209
Libertarian Party, 166–167
Liberty
    civil liberties, 11
    defined, 12
    as political value, 11–12
Liberty for All association, 135
Libya, 226, 351
    Pan Am Flight 103 bombing, 374, 375
    US consulate attack in Benghazi, 381
    US forces sent to aid rebels in, 268
Life events, major, formation of political
    opinion and, 181
Limbaugh, Rush, 222, 231, 232
Limited government
    American democracy and, 10
    defined, 10
    vs. effective, 42
    Magna Carta and, 10
    popular sovereignty, 40
    principle of Constitution, 39–40
Lincoln, Abraham, 288
    election of 1860, 152
    powers of president under, 279
    role of government, 5, 9
Line-item veto, 278
Liquefied natural gas (LNG), 353
Literacy test, 189
*Literary Digest,* 173
Little legislatures, 255
Livingston, Robert, 60
Lobbying Disclosure Act, 143–144
Lobbying/lobbyists. *See also* Interest
    groups
    astroturf lobbying, 140
    defined, 136–137
    direct techniques of, 136–138
    former members of Congress, 138
    Obama administration and, 144
    professional, 142
    reform efforts, 143–144
    regulation of, 143–144
    revolving door syndrome, 142
    state-level, 138
    types of, 138
Local government
    number of, in U.S., 52
    privatization, 314
    public employees and pension plans, 53
    size of bureaucracy, 297–298
    state government and powers of, 51
Local party organization, 162
Locke, John, 10, 25
    Declaration of Independence and, 30
    natural rights, 11

Lockerbie, Scotland Pan Am Flight 103
    bombing, 374, 375
*Logic of Collective Action, The* (Olson),
    128
Louisiana Science Education Act, 81

# M

Maddow, Rachel, 234
Madison, James, 3, 99, 150, 151, 243, 244,
    292
    Bill of Rights, 42
    at Constitutional Convention, 33, 34
    as Federalist, 38, 39
    Madisonian Model, 41–42
    ratification of Constitution and, 37–38
Madisonian Model, 41–42
Magazines, use of, by consumers, 225
Magna Carta, 10
Majority leader
    of the House, 253
    in Senate, 254
Majority party, 159
Majority rule and minority rights, 11
Major League Baseball Players Association,
    132
Malapportionment, 246
Malaysia, 51
Malcolm X, 104
*Malloy v. Hogan,* 77
Managed competition, 314
Managed news coverage, 230
*Mapp v. Ohio,* 77
*Marbury v. Madison,* 60, 333, 334
March on Washington for Jobs and
    Freedom, 103
Marijuana, medical, 136
Marine Corps., 368
Markup session, 258
Marriage
    same-sex, 8, 23, 46, 58, 65, 117–118,
        337
    state power and, 58
Marriage penalty, 158
Marshall, George, 371
Marshall, John, 60, 61, 63, 333, 334
Marshall Plan, 371
Mason, George, 34
Mason-Dixon, 179
Massachusetts Bay Colony, 25
Massachusetts Body of Liberties, 25
*Massachusetts v. Environmental Protection
    Agency,* 64
Mass media, 221
Material incentive, 128
Mayflower Compact, 25
McCain, John
    Bipartisan Campaign Reform Act, 213
    campaign finance reform, 142
    election of 2000, push poll and, 178
    election of 2008
        choice of Palin as running mate, 290
        primaries, 204
        use of Internet, 210
        voter fraud claim, 190
    savings and loan scandal, 142
McCain-Feingold Act, 213
McChesney, Fred, 132
McConnell, Mitch, 253
*McConnell v. Federal Election
    Commission,* 213, 321
McCulloch, James, 60
*McCulloch v. Maryland,* 41, 60, 63
*McDonald v. Chicago,* 77

McKinley, William, 271
McVeigh, Timothy, 375
Media
    bias in, 233–235
        attitudes of journalists, 233
        against losers, 233
        partisan bias, 233
        selection bias, 234–235
    changing news culture, 234–235
    checks and balances, 221
    decline of old media, 221–222
    defined, 180, 221
    electronic, 221
    First Amendment and, 222
    formation of political opinion and,
        180–181
    framing, 224
    freedom of press and, 221, 222
    increased bottom-line pressure, 234
    Internet
        blogs, 237
        censorship of, in China, 221
        citizen journalism, 237
        news organizations online, 235–237
        podcasting news, 236–237
        political campaigns, 238–240
    issue advertising, 213
    managed news coverage, 230
    mass, 221
    medium affect on message, 224–226
    misuse of polls, 177–178
    Murdoch empire, 226–227
    older voters and, 222
    ownership of, 225–226
    presidential elections and effective use
        of, 207
    priming, 224
    print, 221
    role of
        agenda-setting function, 223–224
        fact-checking, 222
        new media and old, 221–222
    sound bites, 225
    talk radio, 231–232
    television
        debates, 229
        impact of, 224–225
        news coverage, 230
        political advertising, 227–229
        popular television, 230
    usage of, by consumer, 225
    usage of, by consumers, 221–222
Medicaid, 62
    cost of, 348
    establishment of, 16
    federal budget spent on, 298
    federal funding to states for, 68
    Great Recession and spending on, 349
    health care reform and, 350
    Obama care and Supreme Court, 66–67
    overview, 348–349
    presidential elections of 2012, 186
    Republican proposed cuts to, 14
    size of government and, 2
    spending on, 349
Medical-marijuana initiative, 65
Medicare, 62
    cost of, 348
    establishment of, 16
    federal budget spent on, 298
    health care reform and, 350
    overview of, 349
    presidential elections of 2012, 186
    Republican proposed cuts to, 14
    size of government and, 2

    spending on, 348
Meetup.com, 209–210
Members of Parliament (MPs), 44
Men, voting behavior and, 183
Merit Systems Protection Board (MSPB),
    307
*Metro-Goldwyn-Mayer Studios, Inc. v.
    Grokster, Ltd.,* 141
Mexican Americans, 110
Mexico, 51
    as oil exporter, 351
Meyerson, Harold, 190
Microtargeting, 209
Mid-term elections, of 2010
    economy as number one issue, 182
    ideology and voter behavior, 186
    perception of candidates and, 182
Military
    ban on torture, 283
    Congressional power to declare war,
        283–284
    demonstrations at funerals of service
        members, 336
    "Don't ask, don't tell" policy, 118
    dropping atomic bomb, 284–285
    federal budget spent on, 299
    gays and lesbians in, 118, 179
    presidential powers in military action,
        268, 283–284
    president of commander in chief, 273
    War Powers Resolution, 284
*Military Times,* 179
*Miller v. California,* 85
Minority government, 44
Minority groups. *See also specific groups*
    distribution of US population by, 14–15
    voter turnout, 191
Minority leader
    of the House, 107, 253
    of Senate, 254
Minority-majority district, 247
Minority party, 159
Minority rights, majority rule and, 11
Minutemen, 28
*Miranda v. Arizona,* 93
Miranda warning, 92–94
Mitchell, John, 303
Mitterrand, Francois, 274
Moderates, 17–18
    voting behavior and, 186
Modernism, original intent vs., 337
Moments of silence, 80–81
Monarchy, 7
Mondale, Walter, 290
Monetary policy, 356–357
    conservative reaction, 357
    hard-money, 357
    president's control over, 281
    pushing on a string, 356–357
Money
    coining of, 55
    monetary policy, 356–357
Moneybomb technique, 209
Monroe, James, 151, 282, 370
Monroe Doctrine, 370
Moral idealism, 367, 370
Mormons, 83
Morris, Gouverneur, 37
Morris, Robert, 34
Mothers Against Drunk Driving (MADD),
    49, 136, 144
Motor Voter Law, 189
Mott, Lucretia, 105
MoveOn.org, 135
MSNBC, 232, 233

Mubarek, Hosni, 381
Mueller, Robert, 90
Multiculturalism, 14
Municipalities, number of, in U.S., 52
Murdoch, Rupert, 226
Muslim Americans, 83
    voting behavior, 185
Muslim Brotherhood, 381
Mutually assured destruction (MAD), 372
MySpace, 210

# N

Nader, Ralph, 167
Nagasaki, 284, 370
NARAL Pro-Choice America, 136
Narrowcasting, 234–235
National Aeronautics and Space
    Administration (NASA), 304, 352
National American Woman Suffrage
    Association, 106
National Assembly, 246, 274
National Association for the Advancement
    of Colored People (NAACP), 102, 135
National Association of Broadcasters, 141
National Association of Manufacturers
    (NAM), 132
National Association of Realtors, 131, 132
National Association of Social Workers, 134
National Automobile Dealers Association,
    132
National Basketball Association, 141
National Beer Wholesalers Association,
    132
National conventions
    Credentials Committee, 206
    defined, 163
    function of, 163
    historical perspective of, 205–206
National Council of La Raza, 144
National Council on Public Polls, 178
National debt, 361
    federal budget spent on, 299
National defense
    as discretionary spending, 262
    government's role in, 5
    as public good, 128
National Education Association (NEA),
    132, 133
National Farmers Union, 134
*National Federation of Independent
    Business v. Sebelius,* 66, 328
National Football League, 141
National government. *See also* Federalism
    authority of, and shifting boundary
        with state authority, 64–67
    commerce clause, 40
    devolution, 64
    division of powers, 55–56
    federalism, 40–41
    federal lands, 56, 57
    interstate relations, 57–58
    Native American tribal governments
        and, 55
    necessary and proper clause, 55
    new federalism, 64
    organization of, 299–306
    powers of, 40, 51
        concurrent powers, 58
        expressed, 55
        implied, 55
        inherent, 55–56
        prohibited, 56
    separation of powers, 41–42

Guantánamo prison, 319
health care reform, 275, 347–348, 349–350
  constitutionality of, 41
  insurance for birth control, 83
Hispanic vote for, 110–111
illegal immigrants, 346
International Criminal Court treaty, 326
Iran and, 383
Iraq War and, 377
Keynesian economics and, 358
legislation under, 275, 279–280, 281, 282
lobbying and, 144
Middle East peace talks and, 380
New Strategic Arms Reduction Treaty (New START), 277
offshore oil drilling, 354
online government, 315
Pakistan, 377–378
public employees and pension plans, 53
Race to the Top, 345–346
refusing federal funding for campaign, 212
renewable energy and, 355
sending troops to Libya, 268
stimulus package, 66, 281
Supreme court appointments, 331–332
talk radio and fairness doctrine, 232
vetoes by, 278
whistleblowers and, 312
withdrawal from Iraq, 377
Obama, Michelle, 289
Obamacare, 41, 66–67, 327–328
Obscenity, 85–86
  in cyberspace, 86
  defined, 85–86
Occupation
  formation of political opinion and, 181–182
  voting behavior and, 183
Occupational Safety and Health Act, 309
Occupational Safety and Health Administration (OSHA), 309
Occupy Wall Street, 141
O'Connor, Sandra Day, 89, 108, 120, 331, 335
O'Donnell, Christine, 182
Office of Management and Budget (OMB), 263, 290, 295
Office of Personnel Management (OPM), 306–307
Office of Special Counsel, 312
Offshore drilling, 353–354
Ogden, Aaron, 60
Oil industry
  expanded supplies of oil and natural gas, 353
  fracking, 353
  offshore drilling and BP oil spill, 353–354
  problem of imported oil, 351
Oklahoma City bombing, 375
Olson, Mancur, 128
Oman, 226
One person, one vote rule, 246
Online piracy, 13
Open primary, 202
Operation TIPS, 89
Opinion leaders, 181
Opinions. *See also* Public opinion
  concurring, 328–329
  defined, 328
  dissenting, 329
  Supreme Court, 328–329

Opposition research, 208
Oral argument, 328
Ordinances, 322
Ordinary-scrutiny standard, 100–101
O'Reilly, Bill, 232, 234
Organization of American States, 368
Original intent, modernism vs., 337
Oslo Accords, 379
Otis, James, Jr., 27
Oversight function of Congress, 260–262

# P

Paine, Thomas, 28–29
Pakistan, 51
  Bin Laden's death and, 378
  detonating nuclear device, 381
  Predator campaign, 377–378
  religious intolerance, 79
  Taliban and al Qaeda in, 377, 378
  war on terrorism and, 377
Palestine/Palestinians, 375
  conflict with Israel, 378–380
  Israel Olympic athletes in Munich attacked by, 374
  United Nations and, 380
Palestinian Authority, 379, 380
Palestinian Liberation Organization (PLO), 378, 379
Palin, Sarah, 290
Pan Am Flight 103 bombing, 374, 375
Pardon, 277
*Parents Involved in Community Schools v. Seattle School District No. 1*, 120–121
*Parker v. Gladden*, 77
Parks, Rosa, 103
Parliament
  defined, 10
  English, 10
Parliamentary democracy, 9
Parliamentary system, 42, 164
  divided government and, 44
  in Great Britain, 44
Parochial schools, aid to, 81–82
Partial Birth Abortion Ban Act, 89
Participatory journalism, 237
Parti Québécois, 54
Partisan politics, 303–304
Partisanship
  growing, 155–156
  independent executive agencies and, 303–304
  legislative gridlock and, 156
  making the other party look weak, 155–156
  Supreme Court justice nomination process and, 329–330
  taxmageddon and budget deficit, 158
  Tea Party movement and, 156
Party activists, 160–161
Party identification, voting behavior and, 182
Party identifiers, 161
Party platforms, 163
Party ticket, 163
Paterson, William, 35
Patient Protection and Affordable Care Act, 347–348
Patriot Act, 90
Patronage, 161, 275
Paul, Ron, 18, 209, 214
  hard-money, 357
Pay-for-performance plans, 313–314
Pearl Harbor, 370
Peer groups

defined, 181
formation of political opinion and, 181
Pelosi, Nancy, 107, 252
Pennsylvania Charter of Privileges, 25
Pennsylvania Frame of Government, 25
Pentagon, terrorist attacks on, 373–374
People journalism, 237
People's Republic of China. *See* China
Perkins, Frances, 107
Perot, H. Ross, 167, 229
Perry, Rick, 205, 214
  Fed and, 357
Personal attack ads, 227–228
Personality party, 167
Personal mandate, 349–350
Petition, freedom of, 76
Petraeus, David, 368
Pew Research Center for the People and the Press, 187, 231, 233, 234, 235
Philippines
  Spanish-American War and, 370
  as unitary system, 51
Physician-assisted suicide, 65
Picket-fence federalism, 63
Piebus, Reince, 162
Pilgrims, 25
Piracy, online, 13
Plessy, Homer, 100
*Plessy v. Ferguson*, 100, 102
Plum Book, 306
Pluralist theory, 129
Plutocracy, 9
Plymouth Company, 25
Pocket veto, 260, 277
Podcasting, 236–237
Poland, Soviet bloc, 371
Police powers, 56–57
Policy. *See also* Domestic policy; Foreign policy
  candidates' position on, voting behavior and, 182–183
  economic, 355–362
  evaluation, 347
  fiscal policy, 357–358
  formulation and adoption, 345
  implementation, 345–346
  interest groups influence on, 136–141
  monetary, 356–357
*Policy and Supporting Positions* (Plum Book), 306
Policymaking
  coordinating, by political parties, 159
  courts and, 332–334
  iron triangle and, 310–311, 345
  issue identification and agenda setting, 344–345
  policy evaluation, 347
  policy formulation and adoption, 345
  policy implementation, 345–346
  policymaking vs. special interest, 347
  process of, 344–347
  trade-offs and, 344
Political action committees (PACs)
  campaign financing and, 212
  *Citizens United* decision, 139
  defined, 138
  money spent by, 138
  number of, 138
  super PACs, 138–139
Political advertising
  attack ads, 227–228
  defined, 227
  democracy and negative advertising, 228–229
  issue ads, 140, 228

military actions, 283–284
nuclear weapons, 284–285
to persuade, 280
proposal and ratification of treaties, 276–277
signing statements, 282–284
veto, 259–260, 277–278
war on terror, 284
War Powers Resolution, 284
presidential succession, 291
relationship with congress, 285–287
requirements of office, 269–271
roles of, 271–275
chief diplomat, 273–274
chief executive, 271–273
chief legislator, 274–275
commander in chief, 273
head of state, 273
overview of, 272
political party leader, 275
Supreme Court appointments and presidential legacy, 330–332
veto power of, 42
President pro tempore, 254
Press, freedom of, 74, 76, 77, 87–88
bad tendency rule, 84
clear and present danger test, 84
cyberbullying, 87
imminent lawless action test, 84–85
importance of, 221
media and, 221, 222
preferred-position doctrine, 87–88
prior restraint, 88
Press secretary, 289
Primary elections (Primaries), 200–202
blanket, 202
candidates running right or left for, 157
closed primary, 202
defined, 157, 201
direct, 201
front-loading, 204
indirect, 201
insurgent candidates, 202
loss of party control, 200–202
open, 202
presidential, 203–206
role of states in, 201
rush to be the first, 204
semiclosed, 202
semiopen, 202
Super-Super Tuesday, 204
Super Tuesday, 204
top two primary, 202
voter turnout, 201
white primary, 189
Primary sources of law, 321
Prime minister, 44
Priming, 224
Print media, 221
Prior restraint, 88
Prisons
cost of, 343
incarceration rate, 343
Privacy, right to, 88–90
abortion, 88–89
national security and, 89–90
Operation TIPS, 89
right to die, 89
Supreme Court and, 332
Privacy Act, 88
Private goods, 128
Privatization, 314
Probable cause, 92
Procedural due process, 75, 77

Professional interest groups, 134
Progressive Party (Bull Moose), 167
Progressive Party (Henry Wallace), 167
Progressives, 17
Progressive taxation, 358
Prohibition Party, 165
Project for Excellence in Journalism, 234, 235
Property
as political value, 12–13
pursuit of happiness, 12
Proposition 8, 23
Protestants, voting behavior, 183, 185
Public Citizen, 135
Public debt, 361–362
burden of, 361–362
expansion of in 2009 and 2010, 362
held by foreigners, 362
Public employees
how bureaucrats get jobs, 306–307
salary for, 308
Public goods, 128
Public-interest groups, 131
Public opinion, 171–192
defined, 172
forming
economic status and occupation, 181–182
family, 180
major life events, 181
media, 180–181
opinion leaders, 181
peer groups, 181
peer groups and, 181
schools and educational attainment, 180
global warming, 352, 353
going public strategy and, 280
interest groups shaping, 139
measuring, 172–178
media agenda setting function and, 223–224
of Supreme Court, 338
Vietnam War and media, 224
Public opinion polls, 172–178
biased samples, 172–173
bias in framing questions, 175–176
checklist for evaluating, 178
defined, 172
early efforts, 172–173
exit polls, 177
Gallup Organization, 173
misuse of, 177–178
pollster-introduced error, 179
push poll, 178
random sampling and, 174
reliability of, 179
Roper Center, 173
samples for, 172–173
sampling error, 175
statistical modeling and house effect, 175
straw poll, 172–173
telephone polls, 174
timing of, 176–177
today, 173–178
types of polls, 174
Public option, for health care, 350
Public sector unions, 134
Public service
defined, 4
government providing, 4–5
Puerto Ricans, 110
Puerto Rico, 244
Spanish-American War and, 370

Punishment, cruel and unusual punishment, 76, 92
Purposive incentive, 128
Pushing on a string, 356–357
Push poll, 178
Putin, Vladimir, 366

# Q

Qaddafi, Muammar, 375
Qatar, 226
Quartering of soldiers, 76, 77
Quota system, 119

# R

Race
distribution of US population by, 14–15
gerrymandering, 247
voter turnout and, 191
Race to the Top, 345–346
Racial gerrymandering, 247
Radio, talk, 231–232
First Amendment and, 222
older voters and, 222
Randolph, Edmund, 34
Random samples, 174
Rating systems, 139–140
Rational basis test, 100–101
Raytheon, 144
Reagan, Ronald, 16, 270, 271
age and voting behavior, 183
attorney general for, 303
election of 1980
presidential debate and, 229
public opinion polls, 176–177
on federalist system, 54
government employment and, 297–298
legislative success of, 282
rolling realignment, 153
signing statements by, 282
strategic defense initiative, 372
Supreme Court appointments, 108, 330, 335
troops sent to Lebanon and Grenada, 284
Realignment, 152
defined, 150
first, 150
hope for, in 2000 and 2006, 156
rolling realignment after 1968, 153
Reasonable accommodations, 332
Recession, 355. See also Great Recession
Reconciliation rule, 243
Redcoats, 28
Redwood National Park, 50
Reform Party, 167
*Regents of the University of California v. Bakke*, 118
Regents' Prayer case, 80
Regulation/regulatory agencies
adjudication, 307–308
administrative law, 322
agency creation, 307–309
cost of, 295
financial crisis of 2008 and, 295
as fourth branch of government, 307–311
golden age of, 307
of health care, 295
independent regulatory agencies, 304, 305

Contract from America, 46
election of senators, 46
as interest group, 135
libertarianism, 19
mid-term elections of 2010, 182, 186
political polarization and, 156
Republican Party and, 148
Technorati, Inc., 235
Telephone polls, 174
Television
  as big business, 225
  candidates and
    debates, 229
    news coverage, 230
    political advertising, 227–229
    popular television, 230
  compared to newspaper coverage, 224–225
  First Amendment and, 222
  impact of, 224–225
  infotainment, 225
  issue advertising, 213
  as main news source, 224–225
  narrowcasting, 234–235
  newspaper circulation decline and, 221
  older voters and, 222
  shaping public opinion, 180–181
  sound bites, 225
  time constraints, 225
  usage of, by consumers, 221–222, 225
  as visual aspect of, 225
  wild west migrates to, 232
Temporary Assistance for Needy Families (TANF), federal budget spent on, 298
Ten Commandments, 80
Tennessee Valley Authority, 306
Tenth Amendment
  constitutional law, 321
  federal grants as bridging, 68
  police powers, 56–57
  residual powers of states, 49, 54, 56–57
  text of, 76
Term limits, 251–252
Terrorism. *See also* September 11, 2001
  terrorist attacks; War on terrorism
  al Qaeda, 375–378
  defined, 373
  focus on Iraq, 376–377
  foreign terrorist networks, 375–376
  government's role in defending against, 5
  local or regional, 375
  state-sponsored, 375
  types of, 375–376
  U.S. consulate attack in Benghazi, 381
  U.S. response to 9/11, 376
Theocracy, 9
Third Amendment
  right to privacy, 88
  text of, 76
Third parties, 165–168
  bringing issues to public attention by, 167
  categories of, 165–167
  defined, 164
  effects of, 167–168
  election laws favoring two-party system and, 164
  ideological parties, 166–167
  issue-oriented parties, 165–166
  nominating conventions, 201
  splinter or personality parties, 167
  as spoiler, 167
  as voice for dissatisfied Americans, 167–168

vote affected by, 167
Thirteenth Amendment, 100
Thomas, Clarence, 330–331, 336, 337
Three-fifths compromise, 35–36
Tibet, 5, 384
Time Warner, 225
Tipping, 156–157
Tocqueville, Alexis de, 127, 128
Top two primary, 202
Torture, George W. Bush and, 283
Totalitarian, 7
Townships, number of, in U.S., 52
Trade-off, policymaking, 344
Trade organizations, 132
Transportation, Department of, 288, 301
Transportation, federal budget spent on, 298
Treasury, Department of, 288
  foreign policymaking and, 367
  original size of, 297
  principle duties of, 301
Treasury bills, 361
Treasury bonds, 361
Treaty, proposal and ratification of, 276–277
Treaty of Paris (1783), 32
Treaty on the Non-Proliferation of Nuclear Weapons, 381
Trial courts, 323
  federal, 325, 327
Trials
  jury
    common law tradition, 320–321
    right to, 76
  right to, 77
  Sixth Amendment and, 92
Truman, David B., 127
Truman, Harry, 269, 270
  armed forces ordered, to Korea, 284
  bombs dropped on Hiroshima and Nagasaki, 284–285
  Marshall Plan, 371
  on presidential power, 280
Truman Doctrine, 371
Trustee, 248
*Tucson Citizen*, 223
Tumblr, 222
Tunisia, 226, 381
Turkey
  communist threat to, 371
  Cuban missile crisis, 372
  opinion of own national economic condition, 173
Twenty-fifth Amendment, 291
Twenty-fourth Amendment, 188
Twenty-second Amendment, 251
Twenty-sixth Amendment, 189
Twenty-third Amendment, 188
Twitter, 222, 236
Two-party system
  defined, 164
  election laws favoring, 164
  institutional barriers to multiparty system, 164–165
  self-perpetuation of, 164–165
*Two Treatises* (Locke), 25
Tyranny, 39

## U

Unemployment
  current rate of, 356
  discouraged workers, 356
  economic policy and, 355–356

federal budget spent on unemployment compensation, 298
  during Great Recession, 5, 6
  number of jobs created and, 6
  political impact of, 6
  structural, 359
  young people and, 6
Unicameral legislature, 30
Unions
  decline of membership, 133–134
  goals of, 132–133
  public employees and pension plans, 53
  public sector unions, 134
  right-to-work laws and, 133–134
Unitary system
  compared to federal system, 51
  defined, 51
United Electrical Workers (UE), 132
United Kingdom. *See also* Great Britain
  constitutional monarchy in, 7
United Nations, 368
  military force in Iraq, not authorized by, 376
  North Korea nuclear missile test and, 382
  Palestine, 380
  sanctions by, 375, 383
United Parcel Service, 132
United States
  Canadian vs. American federalism, 54
  federal system of, 50–54
  foreign countries opinion of, 173
  governmental units in, 52
  racial and ethnic distribution of, 14–15
*United States v. Lopez*, 64
*United States v. Virginia*, 100
Unlawful enemy combatants, 319
Unpledged delegates, 201
Unprotected speech, 85–86
Unreasonable search and seizure, 91
USA Patriot Act, 90
*U.S. Code Congressional and Administrative News*, 282
U.S. district courts, 325, 327
U.S. Postal Service (USPS)
  Economic Value Added program, 314
  facing losses, 305
  as government corporation, 305, 306
USS *Cole*, terrorist attack on, 374, 376

## V

Vandenberg, Arthur, 386
van Tuyll, Debra, 233
van Tuyll, Hubert, 233
Vargas, José Antonio, 140
Venezuela, 351
Ventura, Jesse, 167
Veterans Affairs, Department of, 288, 302
Veterans benefits, federal budget spent on, 298
Veto
  defined, 277
  line-item veto, 278
  overriding, 260
  pocket, 260
  pocket veto, 277
  president's power of, 277–278
Veto power, 42
Vice president
  presidential succession, 291
  as president of Senate, 254
  role of, 290–291

# 1 America in the Twenty-First Century

## KEY TERMS

**authority** The ability to legitimately exercise power, such as the power to make and enforce laws. **4**

**autocracy** A form of government in which the power and authority of the government are in the hands of a single person. **7**

**capitalism** An economic system based on the private ownership of wealth-producing property, free markets, and freedom of contract. The privately owned corporation is the preeminent capitalist institution. **12**

**conservatism** A set of political beliefs that include a limited role for the national government in helping individuals and in the economic affairs of the nation, and support for traditional values and lifestyles. **15**

**conservative movement** A strongly ideological movement that arose in the 1950s and 1960s and continues to shape conservative beliefs. **15**

**democracy** A system of government in which the people have ultimate political authority. The word is derived from the Greek *demos* ("the people") and *kratia* ("rule"). **7**

**dictatorship** A form of government in which absolute power is exercised by an individual or group whose power is not supported by tradition. **7**

**direct democracy** A system of government in which political decisions are made by the people themselves rather than by elected representatives. This form of government was practiced in some parts of ancient Greece. **8**

**divine right theory** A theory that a monarch's right to rule was derived directly from God rather than from the consent of the people. **7**

**equality** A concept that holds, at a minimum, that all people are entitled to equal protection under the law. **12**

**government** The individuals and institutions that make society's rules and also possess the power and authority to enforce those rules. **3**

**ideology** Generally, a system of political ideas that are rooted in religious or philosophical beliefs concerning human nature, society, and government. **15**

**institution** An ongoing organization that performs certain functions for society. **3**

**liberalism** A set of political beliefs that include the advocacy of active government, including government intervention

## SUMMARY

**LearningOutcome 1–1** Explain what is meant by the terms *politics* and *government*. **1** Resolving conflicts over how the society should use its scarce resources and who should receive various benefits is the essence of **politics**. **2** Government—the individuals and institutions that make society's rules and that also possess the **power** and **authority** to enforce those rules—resolves **social conflicts**, provides **public services**, and defends the nation and its culture against attacks by other nations.

**LearningOutcome 1–2** Identify the various types of government systems. **3** Authoritarian rule by an individual is called **autocracy**. **Monarchs** are hereditary autocrats. A **dictatorship** is authoritarian rule by an individual or group unsupported by tradition. **4** Democracy is a system of government in which the people have ultimate political authority. In a **representative democracy,** the will of the people is expressed through groups of individuals elected by the people to act as their representatives. **5** Other forms of government include aristocracy and plutocracy. In a theocracy, the government rules according to religious precepts.

**LearningOutcome 1–3** Summarize some of the basic principles of American democracy and basic American political values. **6** In writing the U.S. Constitution, the framers incorporated two basic principles of government that had evolved in England: **limited government** and representative government. Our democracy resulted from a type of **social contract** among early Americans to create and abide by a set of governing rules. **7** American democracy is based on the principles of equality in voting, individual freedom, equal protection of the law, majority rule and minority rights, and collective voluntary consent to be governed. **8** The rights to **liberty, equality,** and property are fundamental political values shared by most Americans.

**LearningOutcome 1–4** Define common American ideological positions, such as "conservatism" and "liberalism." **9** Often, assumptions as to what the government's role should be in promoting basic values help shape a person's **ideology.** The emergence of the **conservative movement** in the 1950s and 1960s was essential to the development of modern American **conservatism.** Conservatives believe that individuals and families should take responsibility for their own economic circumstances, and they place a high value on the principle of order, on family values, and on patriotism. Religious conservatives believe that government should reflect traditional religious values. While tracing its roots to the New Deal programs of Franklin D. Roosevelt, American **liberalism** took its modern form in the 1960s. Liberals, or **progressives,** argue that big government is a necessary tool for promoting the common welfare. Liberals also strongly favor the separation of church and state. Liberals identify with the Democratic Party, and conservatives identify themselves as Republicans. People whose views fall in the middle are generally called **moderates.** **10** Many Americans have mixed opinions that do not fit neatly under the liberal or conservative label. Some Americans, for example, are both economic progressives and social conservatives. To the left of liberalism on the ideological spectrum is **socialism. Libertarians,** on the right, oppose almost all forms of government regulation, not just the economic activities opposed by the conservative **Tea Party movement.**

to improve the welfare of individuals and to protect civil rights. **16**

**libertarianism** The belief that government should do as little as possible, not only in the economic sphere, but also in regulating morality and personal behavior. **19**

**liberty** The freedom of individuals to believe, act, and express themselves as they choose so long as doing so does not infringe on the rights of other individuals in the society. **12**

**limited government** A form of government based on the principle that the powers of government should be clearly limited either through a written document or through wide public understanding. It is characterized by institutional checks to ensure that government serves public rather than private interests. **10**

**moderates** Persons whose views fall in the middle of the political spectrum. **17**

**monarchy** A form of autocracy in which a king, queen, emperor, empress, tsar, or tsarina is the highest authority in the government. Monarchs usually obtain their power through inheritance. **7**

**natural rights** Rights that are not bestowed by governments but are inherent within every man, woman, and child by virtue of the fact that he or she is a human being. **11**

**parliament** The name of the national legislative body in countries governed by a parliamentary system, such as Britain and Canada. **10**

**political culture** The set of ideas, values, and attitudes about government and the political process held by a community or a nation. **11**

**politics** The process of resolving conflicts over how society should use its scarce resources and who should receive various benefits, such as public health care and public higher education. **3**

**power** The ability to influence the behavior of others, usually through the use of force, persuasion, or rewards. **4**

**progressivism** An alternative, more popular term for the set of political beliefs also known as liberalism. **17**

**public services** Essential services that individuals cannot provide for themselves, such as building and maintaining roads, establishing welfare programs, operating public schools, and preserving national parks. **4**

**representative democracy** A form of democracy in which the will of the majority is expressed through groups of individuals elected by the people to act as their representatives. **8**

**republic** Essentially, a representative democracy in which there is no king or queen and the people are sovereign. **8**

**social conflict** Disagreements among people in a society over what the society's priorities should be. **3**

**social contract** A voluntary agreement among individuals to create a government and to give that government adequate power to secure the mutual protection and welfare of all individuals. **10**

**socialism** A political ideology that lies to the left of liberalism on the traditional political spectrum. Socialists are scarce in the United States, but common in many other countries. **18**

**Tea Party movement** A grassroots conservative movement that arose in 2009 after Barack Obama became president. The movement opposes big government and current levels of taxation, and also rejects political compromise. **19**

# ANSWERS TO STUDY TOOLS QUIZ

## Fill-In

1. Government (LearningOutcome 1–1)
2. it resolves conflicts, provides public services, and defends the nation and its culture against attacks by other nations (LearningOutcome 1–1)
3. autocracy (LearningOutcome 1–2)
4. representative democracy (LearningOutcome 1–2)
5. life, liberty, and property (LearningOutcome 1–3)
6. equality in voting, individual freedom, equal protection of the law, majority rule and minority rights, and voluntary consent to be governed (LearningOutcome 1–3)
7. conservatives and liberals (LearningOutcome 1–4)
8. moderates (LearningOutcome 1–4)
9. Libertarians (LearningOutcome 1–4)

## Multiple Choice

10. c. (LearningOutcome 1–1)
11. b. (LearningOutcome 1–2)
12. c. (LearningOutcome 1–2)
13. b. (LearningOutcome 1–3)
14. a. (LearningOutcome 1–3)
15. a. (LearningOutcome 1–4)

# 2 The Constitution

## KEY TERMS

**Anti-Federalists** A political group that opposed the adoption of the Constitution because of the document's centralist tendencies and because it did not include a bill of rights. **37**

**Articles of Confederation** The nation's first national constitution, which established a national form of government following the American Revolution. The Articles provided for a confederal form of government in which the central government had few powers. **30**

**bicameral legislature** A legislature made up of two chambers, or parts. The United States has a bicameral legislature composed of the House of Representatives and the Senate. **35**

**Bill of Rights** The first ten amendments to the U.S. Constitution. They list the freedoms—such as the freedoms of speech, press, and religion—that a citizen enjoys and that cannot be infringed on by the government. **25**

**checks and balances** A major principle of American government in which each of the three branches is given the means to check (to restrain or balance) the actions of the others. **42**

**commerce clause** The clause in Article I, Section 8, of the Constitution that gives Congress the power to regulate interstate commerce (commerce involving more than one state). **40**

**confederation** A league of independent states that are united only for the purpose of achieving common goals. **30**

**Constitutional Convention** The convention (meeting) of delegates from the states that was held in Philadelphia in 1787 for the purpose of amending the Articles of Confederation. In fact, the delegates wrote a new constitution (the U.S. Constitution) that established a federal form of government to replace the governmental system that had been created by the Articles of Confederation. **33**

**faction** A group of persons forming a cohesive minority. **38**

**Federalists** A political group, led by Alexander Hamilton and John Adams, that supported the adoption of the Constitution and the creation of a federal form of government. **37**

**federal system** A form of government that provides for a division of powers between a central government and several regional governments. In the United

## SUMMARY

**LearningOutcome 2–1 Point out some of the influences on the American political tradition in the colonial years. 1** American politics owes much to the English political tradition, but the colonists derived most of their understanding about limited government and representative government from their own experiences. In 1620, the Pilgrims drew up the **Mayflower Compact,** in which they set up a government and promised to obey its laws. Other colonies, in turn, established fundamental governing rules and principles that were later expressed in the U.S. Constitution and **Bill of Rights. 2** Colonial leaders became familiar with the practical problems of governing. They learned how to build coalitions among groups with diverse interests and how to make compromises.

**LearningOutcome 2–2 Explain why the American colonies rebelled against Britain. 3** After the Seven Years' War (1756–1763), the British Parliament sought to pay its war debts and to finance the defense of its North American empire by imposing taxes on the colonists. **4** The colonists protested, and Britain responded with even more repressive measures. The colonists established the **First Continental Congress** and petitioned King George III to explain their grievances. The congress called for a continued boycott of British goods and required each colony to establish an army. **5** Soon after British soldiers fought colonial citizen soldiers in the first battles of the American Revolution in 1775, delegates gathered for the **Second Continental Congress,** which assumed the powers of a central government. The congress adopted the Declaration of Independence on July 4, 1776.

**LearningOutcome 2–3 Describe the structure of government established by the Articles of Confederation and some of the strengths and weaknesses of the Articles. 6** The **Articles of Confederation** established the Congress of the Confederation as the central governing body. It was a unicameral assembly in which each state had one vote. Congress had several powers, including the power to declare war, to enter into treaties, and to settle disputes among the states under certain circumstances. Nevertheless, the central government created by the Articles was weak. Congress could not force the states to meet military quotas. It could not regulate commerce between the states or with other nations. There was no national judicial system and no executive branch. **7** Disruptions such as **Shays' Rebellion** persuaded American leaders that a true national government had to be created. Congress called on the states to send delegates to a meeting in Philadelphia in 1787 that became the **Constitutional Convention.**

**LearningOutcome 2–4 List some of the major compromises made by the delegates at the Constitutional Convention, and discuss the Federalist and Anti-Federalist positions on ratifying the Constitution. 8** Delegates resolved the small-state/large-state controversy over representation in Congress with the **Great Compromise,** which established a **bicameral legislature.** The **three-fifths compromise** settled a deadlock on how slaves would be counted to determine representation in the House of Representatives. The delegates also agreed that Congress could prohibit the importation of slaves beginning in 1808. The South agreed to let Congress have the power to regulate both **interstate commerce** and commerce with other nations in exchange for a ban on export taxes. **9 Federalists** favored a strong central government and the new Constitution. **Anti-Federalists** argued that the Constitution would lead to aristocratic **tyranny** or an overly powerful central government that would limit personal freedom. To gain support for ratification, the Federalists promised to add a bill of rights to the Constitution.

**LearningOutcome 2–5 Summarize the Constitution's major principles of government, and describe how the Constitution can be amended. 10** The Constitution incorporated the principles of limited government, popular sovereignty, and **rule of law.** A **federal system,** in which the national government shares powers with the state governments, was established. **Separation of powers** and a system of **checks and balances** ensure that no one branch—legislative, executive, or judicial—can exercise exclusive control. **11** An amendment to the Constitution can be proposed either by a two-thirds vote in each chamber of Congress or by a national convention called at the request of two-thirds of the state legislatures. Ratification of an amendment requires either approval by three-fourths of the state legislatures or by three-fourths of the states in special conventions.

# ANSWERS TO STUDY TOOLS QUIZ

## Fill-In

1. Mayflower Compact (LearningOutcome 2–1)
2. imposing taxes on the American colonists and exercising more direct control over colonial trade (LearningOutcome 2–2)
3. Sugar Act, the Stamp Act, and taxes on glass, paint, and lead (LearningOutcome 2–2)
4. Congress of the Confederation (LearningOutcome 2–3)
5. Shays' Rebellion (LearningOutcome 2–3)
6. House of Representatives and the Senate (LearningOutcome 2–4)
7. "Treason, Bribery, or other high Crimes and Misdemeanors" (LearningOutcome 2–4)
8. bill of rights (LearningOutcome 2–4)
9. separation of powers (LearningOutcome 2–5)
10. president's veto power, the power of judicial review, and staggered terms of office (LearningOutcome 2–5)

## Multiple Choice

11. c. (LearningOutcome 2–1)
12. b. (LearningOutcome 2–2)
13. b. (LearningOutcome 2–3)
14. a. (LearningOutcome 2–4)
15. a. (LearningOutcome 2–5)

States, the division of powers between the national government and the states is established by the Constitution. **40**

**First Continental Congress** A gathering of delegates from twelve of the thirteen colonies, held in 1774 to protest the Coercive Acts. **28**

**Great Compromise** A plan for a bicameral legislature in which one chamber would be based on population and the other chamber would represent each state equally. The plan, also known as the Connecticut Compromise, resolved the small-state/large-state controversy. **35**

**interstate commerce** Trade that involves more than one state. **36**

**Madisonian Model** The model of government devised by James Madison, in which the powers of the government are separated into three branches: legislative, executive, and judicial. **41**

**Mayflower Compact** A document drawn up by Pilgrim leaders in 1620 on the ship *Mayflower*. The document stated that laws were to be made for the general good of the people. **25**

**rule of law** A basic principle of government that requires those who govern to act in accordance with established law. **40**

**Second Continental Congress** The congress of the colonies that met in 1775 to assume the powers of a central government and to establish an army. **28**

**separation of powers** The principle of dividing governmental powers among the legislative, the executive, and the judicial branches of government. **42**

**Shays' Rebellion** A rebellion of angry farmers in western Massachusetts in 1786, led by former Revolutionary War captain Daniel Shays. This rebellion and other similar uprisings in the New England states emphasized the need for a true national government. **32**

**three-fifths compromise** A compromise reached during the Constitutional Convention by which three-fifths of all slaves were to be counted for purposes of representation in the House of Representatives. **35**

**tyranny** The arbitrary or unrestrained exercise of power by an oppressive individual or government. **39**

**unicameral legislature** A legislature with only one chamber. **30**

**veto power** A constitutional power that enables the chief executive (president or governor) to reject legislation and return it to the legislature with reasons for the rejection. This prevents or at least delays the bill from becoming law. **42**

# 3 Federalism

## KEY TERMS

**block grant** A federal grant given to a state for a broad area, such as criminal justice or mental-health programs. **68**

**categorical grant** A federal grant targeted for a specific purpose as defined by federal law. **67**

**competitive federalism** A model of federalism, devised by Thomas R. Dye, in which state and local governments compete for businesses and citizens, who in effect "vote with their feet" by moving to jurisdictions that offer a competitive advantage. **69**

**concurrent powers** Powers held by both the federal and the state governments in a federal system. **58**

**confederal system** A league of independent sovereign states, joined together by a central government that has only limited powers over them. **51**

**cooperative federalism** A model of federalism in which the states and the federal government cooperate in solving problems. **62**

**devolution** The surrender or transfer of powers to local authorities by a central government. **64**

**division of powers** A basic principle of federalism established by the U.S. Constitution, by which powers are divided between the national and state governments. **55**

**dual federalism** A system of government in which the federal and the state governments maintain diverse but sovereign powers. **61**

**expressed powers** Constitutional or statutory powers that are expressly provided for by the Constitution; also called *enumerated powers*. **55**

**federalism** A system of shared sovereignty between two levels of government—one national and one subnational—occupying the same geographic region. **50**

**federal mandate** A requirement in federal legislation that forces states and municipalities to comply with certain rules. If the federal government does not provide funds to the states to cover the costs of compliance, the mandate is referred to as an *unfunded* mandate. **64**

**fiscal federalism** The allocation of taxes collected by one level of government (typically the national government) to another level (typically state or local governments). **67**

## SUMMARY

**LearningOutcome 3–1** Explain what federalism means, how federalism differs from other systems of government, and why it exists in the United States. **1** Government powers in a federal system are divided between a national government and subnational governments. The powers of both levels of government are specified and limited. Alternatives to **federalism** include a **unitary system,** in which subnational governments exercise only those powers given to them by the national government, and a **confederal system,** in which the national government exists and operates only at the direction of the subnational governments. **2** The Articles of Confederation failed because they did not allow for a sufficiently strong central government, but the framers of the Constitution were fearful of a too-powerful central government. The appeal of federalism was that it retained state powers and local traditions while establishing a strong national government capable of handling common problems.

**LearningOutcome 3–2** Indicate how the Constitution divides governing powers in our federal system. **3** The national government possesses three types of powers: **expressed, implied,** and **inherent.** The Constitution expressly enumerates twenty-seven powers that Congress may exercise, while the **"necessary and proper" clause** is the basis for implied powers. The national government also enjoys certain inherent powers—powers that governments must have simply to ensure the nation's integrity and survival. In addition, the Constitution expressly prohibits the national government from undertaking certain actions. **4** The Tenth Amendment states that powers that are not delegated to the national government by the Constitution, or prohibited to the states, are "reserved" to the states or to the people. In principle, each state has **police powers**—the ability to regulate its internal affairs and to enact whatever laws are necessary to protect the health, safety, welfare, and morals of its people. **5** The Constitution also contains provisions, such as the full faith and credit clause, relating to interstate relations. **Concurrent powers** can be exercised by both the state governments and the federal government. The **supremacy clause** asserts that national government power takes precedence over any conflicting state action.

**LearningOutcome 3–3** Summarize the evolution of federal–state relationships in the United States over time. **6** The Supreme Court, in *McCulloch v. Maryland* (1819) and *Gibbons v. Ogden* (1824), played a key role in establishing the constitutional foundations for the supremacy of the national government. An increase in the political power of the national government was also a result of the Civil War. **7** The relationship between the states and the national government has evolved through several stages since the Civil War. The model of **dual federalism,** which prevailed until the 1930s, assumes that the states and the national government are more or less equals, with each level of government having separate and distinct functions and responsibilities. The model of **cooperative federalism,** which views the national and state governments as complementary parts of a single governmental mechanism, grew out of the need to solve the pressing national problems caused by the Great Depression. The 1960s and 1970s saw an even greater expansion of the national government's role in domestic policy, but the massive social programs undertaken during this period also precipitated greater involvement by state and local governments. The model in which every level of government is involved in implementing a policy is sometimes referred to as **picket-fence federalism.**

**LearningOutcome 3–4** Describe developments in federalism in recent years. **8** Starting in the 1970s, several administrations favored a shift from nation-centered federalism to state-centered federalism. One of the goals of the **"new federalism"** was to return to the states certain powers that had been exercised by the national government since the 1930s. **9** The federal government and the states now seem to be in a constant tug-of-war over federal regulations, federal programs, and federal demands on the states. Decisions made about welfare reform, educational funding, and same-sex marriages have involved the politics of federalism, as have recent rulings by the Supreme Court in cases involving a state immigration law and national health-care reform.

**LearningOutcome 3–5** **Explain what is meant by the term fiscal federalism. 10** To help the states pay for the costs associated with implementing national policies, the national government gives back some of the tax dollars it collects to the states—in the form of **categorical** and **block grants.** The states have come to depend on grants as an important source of revenue. By giving or withholding federal grant dollars, the federal government has been able to exercise control over matters that traditionally have been under the control of state governments. **11** Sometimes state and local governments engage in **competitive federalism** by offering lower taxes or more services.

# ANSWERS TO STUDY TOOLS QUIZ

## Fill-In

1. the ability to experiment with innovative polices at the state or local level, and the opportunity for the political and cultural interests of regional groups to be reflected in the laws governing those groups (LearningOutcome 3–1)
2. necessary and proper (LearningOutcome 3–2)
3. full faith and credit (LearningOutcome 3–2)
4. implied powers and national supremacy (LearningOutcome 3–3)
5. the Great Depression (LearningOutcome 3–3)
6. picket-fence (LearningOutcome 3–3)
7. federal mandate (LearningOutcome 3–4)
8. threatening to withhold federal highway funds from states that did not comply (LearningOutcome 3–5)

## Multiple Choice

9. a. (LearningOutcome 3–1)
10. c. (LearningOutcome 3–1)
11. b. (LearningOutcome 3–2)
12. c. (LearningOutcome 3–2)
13. a. (LearningOutcome 3–3)
14. c. (LearningOutcome 3–4)
15. b. (LearningOutcome 3–5)

**implied powers** The powers of the federal government that are implied by the expressed powers in the Constitution, particularly in Article I, Section 8. **55**

**inherent powers** The powers of the national government that, although not always expressly granted by the Constitution, are necessary to ensure the nation's integrity and survival as a political unit. Inherent powers include the power to make treaties and the power to wage war or make peace. **55**

**necessary and proper clause** Article I, Section 8, Clause 18, of the Constitution, which gives Congress the power to make all laws "necessary and proper" for the federal government to carry out its responsibilities; also called the *elastic clause.* **55**

**New Deal** A program ushered in by the Roosevelt administration in 1933 to bring the United States out of the Great Depression. The New Deal included many government-spending and public-assistance programs, in addition to thousands of regulations governing economic activity. **62**

**new federalism** A plan to limit the federal government's role in regulating state governments and to give the states increased power in deciding how they should spend government revenues. **64**

**picket-fence federalism** A model of federalism in which specific policies and programs are administered by all levels of government—national, state, and local. **63**

**police powers** The powers of a government body that enable it to create laws for the protection of the health, safety, welfare, and morals of the people. In the United States, most police powers are reserved to the states. **56**

**preemption** A doctrine rooted in the supremacy clause of the Constitution that provides that national laws or regulations governing a certain area take precedence over conflicting state laws or regulations governing that same area. **63**

**secession** The act of formally withdrawing from membership in an alliance; the withdrawal of a state from the federal Union. **61**

**supremacy clause** Article VI, Clause 2, of the Constitution, which makes the Constitution and federal laws superior to all conflicting state and local laws. **58**

**unitary system** A centralized governmental system in which local or subdivisional governments exercise only those powers given to them by the central government. **51**

# 4 Civil Liberties

## KEY TERMS

**bill of attainder** A legislative act that inflicts punishment on particular persons or groups without granting them the right to a trial. **74**

**civil liberties** Individual rights protected by the Constitution against the powers of the government. **74**

**commercial speech** Advertising statements that describe products. Commercial speech receives less protection under the First Amendment than ordinary speech. **85**

**double jeopardy** The prosecution of a person twice for the same criminal offense; prohibited by the Fifth Amendment in all but a few circumstances. **92**

**due process clause** The constitutional guarantee, set out in the Fifth and Fourteenth Amendments, that the government will not illegally or arbitrarily deprive a person of life, liberty, or property. **75**

**due process of law** The requirement that the government use fair, reasonable, and standard procedures whenever it takes any legal action against an individual; required by the Fifth and Fourteenth Amendments. **75**

**establishment clause** The section of the First Amendment that prohibits Congress from passing laws "respecting an establishment of religion." Issues concerning the establishment clause often center on prayer in public schools, the teaching of fundamentalist theories of creation, and government aid to parochial schools. **78**

**exclusionary rule** A criminal procedural rule requiring that any illegally obtained evidence not be admissible in court. **92**

***ex post facto* law** A criminal law that punishes individuals for committing an act that was legal when the act was committed. **74**

**free exercise clause** The provision of the First Amendment stating that the government cannot pass laws "prohibiting the free exercise" of religion. Free exercise issues often concern religious practices that conflict with established laws. **78**

**imminent lawless action test** The current Supreme Court doctrine for assessing the constitutionality of subversive speech. To be illegal, speech must be "directed to inciting . . . imminent lawless action." **84**

## SUMMARY

**LearningOutcome 4–1** Define the term *civil liberties*, explain how civil liberties differ from civil rights, and state the constitutional basis for our civil liberties. **1** Civil liberties are legal and constitutional rights that protect citizens from government actions. Civil rights specify what the government *must* do. Civil liberties set forth what the government *cannot* do. **2** Many of our liberties were added by the Bill of Rights. The United States Supreme Court has used the **due process clause** to incorporate most of the protections guaranteed by the Bill of Rights into the liberties protected from state government actions under the Fourteenth Amendment.

**LearningOutcome 4–2** List and describe the freedoms guaranteed by the First Amendment and explain how the courts have interpreted and applied these freedoms. **3** The First Amendment prohibits government from passing laws "respecting an establishment of religion, or prohibiting the free exercise thereof." Issues involving the **establishment clause** include prayer in the public schools, the teaching of evolution versus creationism or intelligent design, and government aid to parochial schools. The Supreme Court has ruled that public schools cannot sponsor religious activities and has held unconstitutional state laws forbidding the teaching of evolution in the schools. Some aid to parochial schools has been held to violate the establishment clause, while other forms of aid have been held permissible. **4** The Court has ruled consistently that the right to hold any religious belief is absolute, but the right to practice one's beliefs may have some limits. **5** Although the Supreme Court has zealously safeguarded the right to free speech under the First Amendment, at times it has imposed limits on speech in the interests of protecting other rights. These rights include security against harm to one's person or reputation, the need for public order, and the need to preserve the government. **6** The First Amendment freedom of the press generally protects the right to publish a wide range of opinions and information. Over the years, the Court has developed various guidelines and doctrines to use in deciding whether freedom of expression can be restrained.

**LearningOutcome 4–3** Discuss why Americans are increasingly concerned about privacy rights. **7** The Supreme Court has held that a right to privacy is implied by other constitutional rights guaranteed in the Bill of Rights. Congress has also passed laws ensuring the privacy rights of individuals. The nature and scope of this right, however, are not always clear. **8** In 1973, the Court held that the right to privacy is broad enough to encompass a woman's decision to terminate a pregnancy, though the right is not absolute throughout pregnancy. Since that decision, the Court has upheld restrictive state laws requiring certain actions prior to abortions. **9** Privacy issues have also been raised in the context of physician-assisted suicide. **10** Since the terrorist attacks of 9/11, Americans have debated how the United States can address the need to strengthen national security while still protecting civil liberties, particularly the right to privacy. Many civil libertarians argue that when we abandon our civil liberties, we weaken our country rather than defend it. Other Americans believe that those who have nothing to hide should not be concerned about government surveillance or other privacy intrusions undertaken by the government to make our nation more secure against terrorist attacks.

**LearningOutcome 4–4** Summarize how the Constitution and the Bill of Rights protect the rights of accused persons. **11** Constitutional safeguards include the Fourth Amendment protection from unreasonable searches and seizures and the requirement that no warrant for a search or an arrest be issued without **probable cause;** the Fifth Amendment prohibition against **double jeopardy** and the protection against **self-incrimination;** the Sixth Amendment guarantees of a speedy trial, a trial by jury, a public trial, the right to confront witnesses, and the right to counsel at various stages in some criminal proceedings; and the Eighth Amendment prohibitions against excessive bail and fines and against cruel and unusual punishments. The Constitution also provides for the **writ of** *habeas corpus*—an order requiring that an official bring a specified prisoner into court and show the judge why the prisoner is being held in jail.

# ANSWERS TO STUDY TOOLS QUIZ

## Fill-In

1. due process (LearningOutcome 4–1)
2. (1) be for a clearly secular purpose; (2) neither advance nor inhibit religion in its primary effect; and (3) avoid an "excessive government entanglement with religion" (LearningOutcome 4–2)
3. subversive speech (LearningOutcome 4–2)
4. Libel (LearningOutcome 4–2)
5. preferred-position (LearningOutcome 4–2)
6. "National Security Letters" (LearningOutcome 4–3)
7. *Roe v. Wade* (1973) (LearningOutcome 4–3)
8. Fourth (LearningOutcome 4–4)
9. excessive bail and fines, as well as cruel and unusual punishments (LearningOutcome 4–4)

## Multiple Choice

10. b. (Learning Outcome 4–1)
11. c. (Learning Outcome 4–2)
12. a. (Learning Outcome 4–2)
13. b. (Learning Outcome 4–3)
14. a. (Learning Outcome 4–4)
15. b. (Learning Outcome 4–4)

*Lemon* **test** A three-part test enunciated by the Supreme Court in the 1971 case of *Lemon v. Kurtzman* to determine whether government aid to parochial schools is constitutional. To be constitutional, the aid must (1) be for a clearly secular purpose, (2) neither advance nor inhibit religion in its primary effect, and (3) avoid an "excessive government entanglement with religion." The *Lemon* test has also been used in other types of cases involving the establishment clause. **82**

**libel** A published report of a falsehood that tends to injure a person's reputation or character. **85**

*Miranda* **warnings** A series of statements informing criminal suspects, on their arrest, of their constitutional rights, such as the right to remain silent and the right to counsel; required by the Supreme Court's 1966 decision in *Miranda v. Arizona.* **93**

**obscenity** Indecency or offensiveness in speech, expression, behavior, or appearance. Whether specific expressions or acts constitute obscenity is normally determined by community standards. **85**

**probable cause** Cause for believing that there is a substantial likelihood that a person has committed or is about to commit a crime. **92**

**school voucher** An educational certificate, provided by the government, that allows a student to use public funds to pay for a private or a public school chosen by the student or his or her parents. **82**

**seditious speech** Speech that urges resistance to lawful authority or that advocates the overthrowing of a government. **84**

**self-incrimination** Providing damaging information or testimony against oneself in court. **92**

**slander** The public utterance (speaking) of a statement that holds a person up for contempt, ridicule, or hatred. **85**

**symbolic speech** The expression of beliefs, opinions, or ideas through forms other than verbal speech or print; speech involving actions and other nonverbal expressions. **83**

**writ of** *habeas corpus* An order that requires an official to bring a specified prisoner into court and explain to the judge why the person is being held in jail. **74**

# 5 Civil Rights

## KEY TERMS

**affirmative action** A policy that gives special consideration, in jobs and college admissions, to members of groups that have been discriminated against in the past. **118**

**busing** The transportation of public school students by bus to schools physically outside their neighborhoods to eliminate school segregation based on residential patterns. **102**

**civil disobedience** The deliberate and public act of refusing to obey laws thought to be unjust. **103**

**civil rights** The rights of all Americans to equal treatment under the law, as provided by the Fourteenth Amendment to the Constitution. **99**

**civil rights movement** The movement in the 1950s and 1960s, by minorities and concerned whites, to end racial segregation. **103**

*de facto* **segregation** Racial segregation that occurs not as a result of deliberate intentions but because of social and economic conditions and residential patterns. **102**

*de jure* **segregation** Racial segregation that occurs because of laws or decisions by government agencies. **102**

**equal protection clause** Section 1 of the Fourteenth Amendment, which states that no state shall "deny to any person within its jurisdiction the equal protection of the laws." **99**

**feminism** The doctrine advocating full political, economic, and social equality for women. **106**

**fundamental right** A basic right of all Americans, such as First Amendment rights. Any law or action that prevents some group of persons from exercising a fundamental right is subject to the "strict-scrutiny" standard, under which the law or action must be necessary to promote a compelling state interest and must be narrowly tailored to meet that interest. **99**

**glass ceiling** An invisible but real discriminatory barrier that prevents women and minorities from rising to top positions of power or responsibility. **108**

**quota system** A policy under which a specific number of jobs, promotions, or other types of placements, such as university admissions, are given to members of selected groups. **119**

## SUMMARY

**LearningOutcome 5–1** **Explain the constitutional basis for our civil rights and for laws prohibiting discrimination.** 1 Civil rights are the rights of all Americans to equal treatment under the law. The **equal protection clause** of the Fourteenth Amendment has been interpreted by the courts to mean that states may not discriminate unreasonably against a particular group or class of individuals. The amendment also provides a legal basis for civil rights legislation. The United States Supreme Court has developed various standards for determining whether the equal protection clause has been violated.

**LearningOutcome 5–2** **Discuss the reasons for the civil rights movement and the changes it caused in American politics and government.** 2 The equal protection clause was originally intended to protect the newly freed slaves from discrimination after the Civil War. By the late 1880s, however, southern states had begun to pass a series of segregation laws. In 1896, the Supreme Court established the **separate-but-equal doctrine,** which justified segregation for nearly sixty years. 3 In 1954, the Court held that segregation by race in public education was unconstitutional. One year later, the arrest of Rosa Parks for violating local segregation laws spurred a boycott of the bus system in Montgomery, Alabama. The protest was led by the Reverend Dr. Martin Luther King, Jr. In 1956, a federal court prohibited the segregation of buses in Montgomery, marking the beginning of the **civil rights movement.** 4 Civil rights protesters in the 1960s applied the tactic of nonviolent **civil disobedience** in actions throughout the South. As the civil rights movement demonstrated its strength, Congress passed a series of civil rights laws, including the Civil Rights Act of 1964, the Voting Rights Act of 1965, and the Civil Rights Act of 1968. 5 Today, the percentages of voting-age blacks and whites registered to vote are nearly equal. Political participation by African Americans has increased, as has the number of African American elected officials. African Americans continue to struggle for income and educational parity with whites.

**LearningOutcome 5–3** **Describe the political and economic achievements of women in this country over time and identify some obstacles to equality that women continue to face.** 6 The struggle of women for equal treatment initially focused on **suffrage.** In 1920, the Nineteenth Amendment was ratified, granting voting rights to women. **Feminism** shaped a new movement that began in the 1960s. Although women remain underrepresented in politics, increasingly women have gained power as public officials. 7 In spite of federal legislation to promote equal treatment of women in the workplace, women continue to face various forms of discrimination, including a lingering bias that has been described as the **glass ceiling.** 8 The prohibition of gender discrimination has been extended to prohibit **sexual harassment.**

**LearningOutcome 5–4** **Summarize the struggles for equality that other groups in America have experienced.** 9 Latinos constitute the largest ethnic minority in the United States. Economically, Latino households are often members of this country's working poor. 10 Asian Americans suffered from discriminatory treatment in the late 1800s and early 1900s, and again during World War II. Today, Asian Americans lead other minority groups in median income and median education. 11 Native Americans had no civil rights under U.S. laws until 1924. Beginning in the 1960s, some Native Americans formed organizations to strike back at the U.S. government and to reclaim their heritage, including their lands. 12 Persons with disabilities first became a political force in the 1970s. The Americans with Disabilities Act (ADA) of 1990 is the most significant legislation protecting the rights of this group of Americans. 13 In the decades following the 1969 Stonewall Inn incident, laws and court decisions protecting the rights of gay men and lesbians have reflected changing social attitudes. Same-sex marriage is legal in several states.

**LearningOutcome 5–5** Explain what affirmative action is and why it has been so controversial. **14** **Affirmative action** gives special consideration, in jobs and college admissions, to members of groups that have been discriminated against in the past. It has been tested in court cases involving claims of **reverse discrimination.** Some states have banned affirmative action or replaced it with alternative policies.

# ANSWERS TO STUDY TOOLS QUIZ

## Fill-In

1. strict (LearningOutcome 5–1)
2. separate-but-equal (LearningOutcome 5–2)
3. race, color, religion, gender, and national origin (LearningOutcome 5–2)
4. full political, economic, and social equality (LearningOutcome 5–3)
5. 80 cents (LearningOutcome 5–3)
6. Latinos (LearningOutcome 5–4)
7. Japanese (LearningOutcome 5–4)
8. that gives special consideration, in jobs and college admissions, to members of groups that have been discriminated against in the past (LearningOutcome 5–5)
9. strict (LearningOutcome 5–5)

## Multiple Choice

10. b. (LearningOutcome 5–1)
11. a. (LearningOutcome 5–2)
12. c. (LearningOutcome 5–2)
13. a. (LearningOutcome 5–3)
14. c. (LearningOutcome 5–4)
15. a. (LearningOutcome 5–5)

**rational basis test** A test (also known as the "ordinary scrutiny" standard) used by the Supreme Court to decide whether a discriminatory law violates the equal protection clause of the Constitution. It is only used when there is no classification—such as race or gender—that would require a higher level of scrutiny. Few laws evaluated under this test are found invalid. **100**

**reverse discrimination** Discrimination against those who have no minority status. **119**

**separate-but-equal doctrine** A Supreme Court doctrine holding that the equal protection clause of the Fourteenth Amendment did not forbid racial segregation as long as the facilities for blacks were equal to those for whites. The doctrine was overturned in the *Brown v. Board of Education of Topeka* decision of 1954. **101**

**sexual harassment** Unwanted physical contact, verbal conduct, or abuse of a sexual nature that interferes with a recipient's job performance, creates a hostile environment, or carries with it an implicit or explicit threat of adverse employment consequences. **108**

**sit-in** A tactic of nonviolent civil disobedience. Demonstrators enter a business, college building, or other public place and remain seated until they are forcibly removed or until their demands are met. The tactic was used successfully in the civil rights movement and in other protest movements in the United States. **103**

**suffrage** The right to vote; the franchise. **106**

**suspect classification** A classification, such as race, that provides the basis for a discriminatory law. Any law based on a suspect classification is subject to strict scrutiny by the courts—meaning that the law must be justified by a compelling state interest. **100**

# 6 Interest Groups

## KEY TERMS

**direct technique** Any method used by an interest group to interact with government officials directly to further the group's goals. **136**

**free rider problem** The difficulty that exists when individuals can enjoy the outcome of an interest group's efforts without having to contribute, such as by becoming members of the group. **128**

**independent expenditure** An expenditure for activities that are independent from (not coordinated with) those of a political candidate or a political party. **140**

**indirect technique** Any method used by interest groups to influence government officials through third parties, such as voters. **139**

**interest group** An organized group of individuals sharing common objectives who actively attempt to influence policymakers. **126**

**labor force** All of the people over the age of sixteen who are working or actively looking for jobs. **133**

**lobbying** All of the attempts by organizations or by individuals to influence the passage, defeat, or contents of legislation or to influence the administrative decisions of government. **136**

**lobbyist** An individual who handles a particular interest group's lobbying efforts. **137**

**material incentive** A reason to join an interest group—practical benefits such as discounts, subscriptions, or group insurance. **128**

**pluralist theory** A theory that views politics as a contest among various interest groups—at all levels of government—to gain benefits for their members. **129**

**political action committee (PAC)** A committee that is established by a corporation, labor union, or special interest group to raise funds and make campaign contributions on the establishing organization's behalf. **138**

**public-interest group** An interest group formed for the purpose of working for the "public good." Examples of public-interest groups are the American Civil Liberties Union and Common Cause. **131**

**purposive incentive** A reason to join an interest group—satisfaction resulting from working for a cause in which one believes. **128**

## SUMMARY

**LearningOutcome 6–1** Explain what an interest group is, why interest groups form, and how interest groups function in American politics. **1** An **interest group** is an organized group of people sharing common objectives who actively attempt to influence government policymakers through direct and indirect methods. The right to form interest groups and to lobby the government is protected by the First Amendment. Interest groups may form—and existing groups may become more politically active—when the government expands its scope of activities. Interest groups also come into existence in response to a perceived threat to a group's interests, or they can form in reaction to the creation of other groups. **Purposive incentives, solidary incentives,** and **material incentives** are among the reasons people join interest groups. **2** Interest groups (a) help bridge the gap between citizens and government; (b) help raise public awareness and inspire action on various issues; (c) provide public officials with specialized information that may be useful in making policy choices; and (d) serve as another check on public officials. The **pluralist theory** of American democracy views politics as a contest among various interest groups to gain benefits for their members. **3** Although interest groups and political parties are both groups of people joined together for political purposes, they differ in several ways.

**LearningOutcome 6–2** Identify the various types of interest groups. **4** The most common interest groups are those that promote private interests. **Public-interest groups** are formed with the broader goal of working for the "public good," though in reality, all lobbying groups represent special interests. **5** Business has long been well organized for effective action. Hundreds of business groups operate at all levels of government, and there are also umbrella organizations, including the U.S. Chamber of Commerce, that represent business interests. **Trade organizations** support policies that benefit specific industries. Interest groups representing labor have been some of the most influential groups in the nation's history, though the strength and political power of labor unions have waned in the last several decades. Public employee unions, however, have grown in both numbers and political clout in recent years. **6** Most professions that require advanced education or specialized training have organizations to protect and promote their interests. There are many groups working for general agricultural interests at all levels of government, and producers of various specific farm commodities have formed their own organizations. Groups organized for the protection of consumer rights were very active in the 1960s and 1970s, and some are still active today. **7** Americans who share the same race, ethnicity, gender, or other characteristic often have important common interests and form identity interest groups. Some interest groups, including environmental and religious groups, are organized to promote a shared political perspective or ideology. **8** Numerous interest groups focus on a single issue. Efforts by state and local governments to lobby the federal government have escalated in recent years.

**LearningOutcome 6–3** Discuss how the activities of interest groups help to shape government policymaking. **9** Interest groups operate at all levels of government and use a variety of strategies to steer policies in ways beneficial to their interests. Sometimes they attempt to influence policymakers directly, but at other times they try to exert indirect influence on policymakers by shaping public opinion. **10 Lobbying** and providing election support are two important **direct techniques** used by interest groups. Groups also try to influence public policy through third parties or the general public. Indirect techniques include advertising, **rating systems,** issue advocacy through **independent expenditures,** mobilizing constituents, going to court, and organizing demonstrations.

**LearningOutcome 6–4 Describe how interest groups are regulated by government.**
**11** The Lobbying Disclosure Act of 1995 reformed a 1946 law in several ways, particularly by creating stricter definitions of who is a lobbyist. In the wake of lobbying scandals in the early 2000s, additional lobbying reform efforts were undertaken. The Honest Leadership and Open Government Act of 2007 increased lobbying disclosure and placed further restrictions on the receipt of gifts and travel by members of Congress paid for by lobbyists and the organizations they represent. In spite of legislation designed to reduce the "revolving door" syndrome, it remains common for those who leave positions with the federal government to become lobbyists or consultants for the interest groups they helped to regulate.

# ANSWERS TO STUDY TOOLS QUIZ

## Fill-In

### LearningOutcome 6–1

1. First (LearningOutcome 6–1)
2. Disturbance (LearningOutcome 6–1)
3. 11.9 (LearningOutcome 6–2)
4. Right-to-work (LearningOutcome 6–2)
5. all of the attempts by organizations or by individuals to influence the passage, defeat, or contents of legislation or to influence the administrative decisions of government (LearningOutcome 6–3)
6. *amicus curiae* briefs (LearningOutcome 6–3)
7. revolving door (LearningOutcome 6–4)

## Multiple Choice

8. b. (LearningOutcome 6–1)
9. c. (LearningOutcome 6–1)
10. a. (LearningOutcome 6–2)
11. c. (LearningOutcome 6–2)
12. b. (LearningOutcome 6–3)
13. a. (LearningOutcome 6–3)
14. c. (LearningOutcome 6–3)
15. c. (LearningOutcome 6–4)

**rating system** A system by which a particular interest group evaluates (rates) the performance of legislators based on how often the legislators have voted with the group's position on particular issues. **139**

**right-to-work laws** Laws that ban unions from collecting dues or other fees from workers whom they represent but who have not actually joined the union. **133**

**solidary incentive** A reason to join an interest group—pleasure in associating with like-minded individuals. **128**

**trade organization** An association formed by members of a particular industry, such as the oil industry or the trucking industry, to develop common standards and goals for the industry. Trade organizations, as interest groups, lobby government for legislation or regulations that specifically benefit their groups. **132**

# 7 Political Parties

## KEY TERMS

**coalition** An alliance of individuals and groups with a variety of interests and opinions who join together to support all or part of a political party's platform. **159**

**dealignment** Among voters, a growing detachment from both major political parties. **156**

**electorate** All of the citizens eligible to vote in a given election. **160**

**majority party** The political party that has more members in the legislature than the opposing party. **159**

**minority party** The political party that has fewer members in the legislature than the opposing party. **159**

**national convention** The meeting held by each major party every four years to nominate presidential and vice-presidential candidates, write a party platform, and conduct other party business. **163**

**national party chairperson** An individual who serves as a political party's administrative head at the national level and directs the work of the party's national committee. **163**

**national party committee** The political party leaders who direct party business during the four years between the national party conventions, organize the next national convention, and plan how to obtain a party victory in the next presidential election. **163**

**party activist** A party member who helps to organize and oversee party functions and planning during and between campaigns, and may even become a candidate for office. **161**

**party identifier** A person who identifies himself or herself as being a supporter of a particular political party. **160**

**party platform** The document drawn up by each party at its national convention that outlines the policies and positions of the party. **163**

**party ticket** A list of a political party's candidates for various offices. In national elections, the party ticket consists of the presidential and vice-presidential candidates. **163**

**patronage** A system of rewarding the party faithful and workers with government jobs or contracts. **161**

**political party** A group of individuals who organize to win elections, operate the government, and determine policy. **149**

## SUMMARY

**LearningOutcome 7–1** Summarize the origins and development of the two-party system in the United States. 1 After the Constitution was ratified, those who wanted a strong central government supported the Federalist Party. Their opponents, the Jeffersonian Republicans, favored a more limited role for government. In the early 1800s, the Federalists went out of existence, resulting in a **realignment** of the party system. In the mid-1820s, the Republicans split into two groups—the Democrats and the National Republicans (later the Whig Party). As the Democrats and Whigs competed for the presidency during the 1840s and 1850s, the **two-party system** as we know it today emerged. 2 By the mid-1850s, most northern Whigs were absorbed into the new Republican Party, which opposed the extension of slavery. After the Civil War, the Republicans and Democrats were roughly even in strength, although the Republicans were more successful in presidential contests. After the realigning election of 1896, many Americans viewed the Republicans as the party that knew how to manage the nation's economy, and they remained dominant in national politics until the Great Depression. 3 The election of 1932 brought Franklin D. Roosevelt to the presidency and the Democrats back to power at the national level. From the 1960s through the 1980s, however, conservative Democrats in Congress sided with the Republicans on most issues. In time, these conservative Democrats were replaced by conservative Republicans. The result of this "rolling realignment" was that the two major parties were fairly evenly matched.

**LearningOutcome 7–2** Describe the current status of the two major parties. 4 By 2006, the Republican Party had lost points in popularity relative to the Democrats, but within one year of President Barack Obama's inauguration, the Democratic advantage had vanished. In the midterm elections in 2010, many relatively conservative Democrats lost their seats in Congress, and Republicans regained control of the House of Representatives. 5 A key characteristic of recent politics has been the extreme partisanship of party activists and members. Political polarization grew even more severe after the 2010 elections. Many of the new Republican members of Congress were pledged to the Tea Party philosophy of no-compromise conservatism. Also significant is the number of independent voters, reflecting a **dealignment** in the party system.

**LearningOutcome 7–3** Explain how political parties function in our democratic system. 6 Political parties link the people's policy preferences to actual government policies. They select candidates for political office and help educate the public about important current political issues. Parties coordinate policy among the various branches and levels of government, and balance the competing interests of those who support the party. Parties coordinate campaigns and take care of a large number of tasks that are essential to the smooth functioning of the electoral process. In government, the minority party checks the actions of the party in power.

**LearningOutcome 7–4** Discuss the structure of American political parties. 7 The party in the **electorate** consists of **party identifiers** and **party activists**. Each party's organization is decentralized, with national, state, and local offices. Delegates to the **national convention** nominate the party's presidential and vice-presidential candidates, and they adopt the **party platform.** The national party organization includes a **national party committee,** a **national party chairperson,** and congressional campaign committees. The party in government consists of all of the party's candidates who have won elections and now hold public office. The party in government helps to organize the government's agenda by convincing its own party members to vote for its policies.

13

**LearningOutcome 7–5** Describe the different types of third parties and how they function in the American political system. **8** The United States has a two-party system in which the Democrats and the Republicans dominate national politics. American election laws and the rules governing campaign financing tend to favor the major parties. There are also institutional barriers that prevent third parties from enjoying electoral success. Because third parties normally do not win elections, Americans tend not to vote for them. **9** There are different kinds of third parties. An issue-oriented party is formed to promote a particular cause or timely issue. An ideological party supports a particular political doctrine or a set of beliefs. A splinter party develops out of a split within a major party, which may be part of an attempt to elect a specific person. **10** Third parties have brought many issues to the public's attention and can influence election outcomes. Third parties also provide a voice for voters who are frustrated with the Republican and Democratic parties.

# ANSWERS TO STUDY TOOLS QUIZ

## Fill-In

1. Federalists and the Jeffersonian Republicans (LearningOutcome 7–1)
2. Republican (LearningOutcome 7–1)
3. a growing detachment from both major political parties (LearningOutcome 7–2)
4. selecting candidates, informing the public, coordinating policymaking, checking the power of the governing party, balancing competing interests, and running campaigns (LearningOutcome 7–3)
5. primary (LearningOutcome 7–3)
6. national convention (LearningOutcome 7–4)
7. the document drawn up by each party at its national convention that outlines the policies and positions of the party (LearningOutcome 7–4)
8. bringing issues to the public's attention, affecting the vote, and providing a voice for voters who are frustrated with the Republican and Democratic parties (LearningOutcome 7–5)

## Multiple Choice

9. a. (LearningOutcome 7–1)
10. b. (LearningOutcome 7–1)
11. b. (LearningOutcome 7–2)
12. c. (LearningOutcome 7–2)
13. b. (LearningOutcome 7–3)
14. c. (LearningOutcome 7–4)
15. b. (LearningOutcome 7–5)

**precinct** A political district within a city, such as a block or a neighborhood, or a rural portion of a county; the smallest voting district at the local level. **162**

**primary** A preliminary election held for the purpose of choosing a party's final candidate. **157**

**realignment** A process in which the popular support for and relative strength of the parties shift and the parties are reestablished with different coalitions of supporters. **150**

**solidarity** Mutual agreement among the members of a particular group. **161**

**third party** In the United States, any party other than one of the two major parties (Republican and Democratic). **164**

**two-party system** A political system in which two strong and established parties compete for political offices. **164**

**ward** A local unit of a political party's organization, consisting of a division or district within a city. **162**

# 8 Public Opinion and Voting

## KEY TERMS

**agents of political socialization** People and institutions that influence the political views of others. **180**

**biased sample** A poll sample that does not accurately represent the population. **172**

**gender gap** The difference between the percentage of votes cast for a particular candidate by women and the percentage of votes cast for the same candidate by men. **183**

**grandfather clause** A clause in a state law that had the effect of restricting the franchise (voting rights) to those whose ancestors had voted before the 1860s. It was one of the techniques used in the South to prevent African Americans from exercising their right to vote. **189**

**literacy test** A test given to voters to ensure that they could read and write and thus evaluate political information. This technique was used in many southern states to restrict African American participation in elections. **189**

**media** Newspapers, magazines, television, radio, the Internet, and any other printed or electronic means of communication. **180**

**peer group** Associates, often close in age to one another; may include friends, classmates, co-workers, club members, or religious group members. Peer group influence is a significant factor in the political socialization process. **181**

**political socialization** The learning process through which most people acquire their political attitudes, opinions, beliefs, and knowledge. **179**

**poll tax** A fee of several dollars that had to be paid before a person could vote. This device was used in some southern states to discourage African Americans and low-income whites from voting. **189**

**public opinion** The views of the citizenry about politics, public issues, and public policies; a complex collection of opinions held by many people on issues in the public arena. **172**

**public opinion poll** A survey of the public's opinion on a particular topic at a particular moment. **172**

**push poll** A campaign tactic used to feed false or misleading information to potential voters, under the guise of conducting an opinion poll, with the intent to "push" voters away from one candidate and toward another. **178**

## SUMMARY

**LearningOutcome 8–1** **Explain how public opinion polls are conducted, problems with polls, and how they are used in the political process. 1** A **public opinion poll** is a survey of the public's opinion on a particular topic at a particular moment, as measured through the use of **samples. 2** Early polling efforts often relied on **straw polls.** The opinions expressed in straw polls, however, usually represent an atypical subgroup of the population, or a **biased sample.** Over time, more scientific polling techniques were developed. Today, polling organizations frequently conduct polls through telephone interviews, while some pollsters use prerecorded messages that solicit responses. Others specialize in Internet surveys. **3** To achieve the most accurate results possible, pollsters use **random samples,** in which each person within the entire population being polled has an equal chance of being chosen. If the sample is properly selected, the opinions of those in the sample will be representative of the opinions held by the population as a whole. However, public opinion polls are fundamentally statistical. The true result of a poll is not a single figure, but a range of probabilities. Any opinion poll contains a **sampling error. 4** How a question is phrased can significantly affect how people answer it. Polling questions also sometimes reduce complex issues to questions that simply call for "yes" or "no" answers. It is also the case that opinion polls of voter preferences cannot reflect rapid shifts in public opinion unless they are taken frequently. **5** Many journalists base their political coverage during campaigns almost exclusively on poll findings. Media companies often report only the polls conducted by their affiliated pollsters. News organizations use exit polls to give an early indication of the outcome of elections. One tactic in political campaigns is to use **push polls,** which ask "fake" polling questions that are actually designed to "push" voters toward one candidate or another.

**LearningOutcome 8–2** **Describe the political socialization process. 6** Most people acquire their political attitudes, opinions, beliefs, and knowledge through a complex learning process called **political socialization.** Most political socialization is informal. The strong early influence of the family later gives way to the multiple influences of schools, churches, the **media,** opinion leaders, major life events, **peer groups,** and economic status and occupation. People and institutions that influence the political views of others are called **agents of political socialization.**

**LearningOutcome 8–3** **Discuss the different factors that affect voter choices. 7** For established voters, party identification is one of the most important and lasting predictors of how a person will vote. Voters' choices often depend on the perceived character of the candidates rather than on their qualifications or policy positions. When people vote for candidates who share their positions on particular issues, they are engaging in policy voting. Historically, economic issues have had the strongest influence on voters' choices. **8** Socioeconomic factors, including educational attainment, occupation and income, age, gender, religion and ethnicity, and geographic location, also influence how people vote. Ideology is another indicator of voting behavior.

**LearningOutcome 8–4** **Indicate some of the factors that affect voter turnout, and discuss what has been done to improve voter turnout and voting procedures. 9** The Fifteenth Amendment to the Constitution (1870) guaranteed suffrage to African American males. Yet, for many decades, African Americans were effectively denied the ability to exercise their voting rights. Today, devices used to restrict voting rights, such as the **poll tax, literacy tests,** the **grandfather clause,** and **white primaries,** are explicitly prohibited by constitutional amendments, by the Voting Rights Act of 1965, or by court decisions. The Nineteenth Amendment (1920) gave women the right to vote, and the Twenty-sixth Amendment (1971) reduced the minimum voting age to eighteen. **10** Some restrictions on voting rights, such as registration, residency, and citizenship requirements, still exist. Most states also do not permit prison inmates or felons to vote. Attempts to improve voter turnout and voting procedures include simplifying the voter-registration process, conducting voting by mail, updating voting equipment, and allowing early voting. Voter turnout is affected by several factors, including educational attainment, income level, age, and minority status.

# ANSWERS TO STUDY TOOLS QUIZ

## Fill-In

1. each person within the entire population being polled has an equal chance of being chosen (LearningOutcome 8–1)
2. house effect (LearningOutcome 8–1)
3. push poll (LearningOutcome 8–1)
4. family, schools, churches, the media, opinion leaders, and peer groups (LearningOutcome 8–2)
5. party identification (LearningOutcome 8–3)
6. policy voting (LearningOutcome 8–3)
7. educational attainment, occupation and income, age, gender, religion and ethnic background, and geographic region (LearningOutcome 8–3)
8. literacy tests, poll taxes, the grandfather clause, and white primaries (LearningOutcome 8–4)

## Multiple Choice

9. a. (LearningOutcome 8–1)
10. c. (LearningOutcome 8–2)
11. b. (LearningOutcome 8–2)
12. c. (LearningOutcome 8–3)
13. a. (LearningOutcome 8–3)
14. b. (LearningOutcome 8–4)
15. a. (LearningOutcome 8–4)

**random sample** In the context of opinion polling, a sample in which each person within the entire population being polled has an equal chance of being chosen. **174**

**sample** In the context of opinion polling, a group of people selected to represent the population being studied. **172**

**sampling error** In the context of opinion polling, the difference between what the sample results show and what the true results would have been had everybody in the relevant population been interviewed. **175**

**Solid South** A term used to describe the tendency of the southern states to vote Democratic after the Civil War. **185**

**straw poll** A nonscientific poll in which there is no way to ensure that the opinions expressed are representative of the larger population. **172**

**vital center** The center of the political spectrum; those who hold moderate political views. The center is vital because without it, it may be difficult, if not impossible, to reach the compromises that are necessary to a political system's continuity. **186**

**vote-eligible population** The number of people who are actually eligible to vote in an American election. **192**

**voting-age population** The number of people residing in the United States who are at least eighteen years old. **191**

**white primary** A primary election in which African Americans were prohibited from voting. The practice was banned by the Supreme Court in 1944. **189**

# 9 Campaigns and Elections

## KEY TERMS

**Australian ballot** A secret ballot that is prepared, distributed, and counted by government officials at public expense; used by all states in the United States since 1888. **196**

**campaign strategy** The comprehensive plan developed by a candidate and his or her advisers for winning an election. The strategy includes the candidate's position on issues, slogan, advertising plan, press events, and personal appearances, as well as other aspects of the campaign. **207**

**caucus** A meeting held to choose political candidates or delegates. **200**

**closed primary** A primary in which only party members can vote to choose that party's candidates. **202**

**Credentials Committee** A committee of each national political party that evaluates the claims of national party convention delegates to be the legitimate representatives of their states. **206**

**delegate** A person selected to represent the people of one geographic area at a party convention. **200**

**direct primary** An election held within each of the two major parties—Democratic and Republican—to choose the party's candidates for the general election. Voters choose the candidate directly, rather than through delegates. **201**

**elector** A member of the electoral college. **196**

**electoral college** The group of electors who are selected by the voters in each state to elect officially the president and vice president. The number of electors in each state is equal to the number of that state's representatives in both chambers of Congress. **196**

**general election** A regularly scheduled election to choose the U.S. president, vice president, and senators and representatives in Congress. General elections are held in even-numbered years on the Tuesday after the first Monday in November. **196**

**independent expenditure** An expenditure for activities that are independent from (not coordinated with) those of a political candidate or a political party. **212**

**nominating convention** An official meeting of a political party to choose its candidates. Nominating conventions at the state and local levels also select

## SUMMARY

**LearningOutcome 9–1** Explain how elections are held and how the electoral college functions in presidential elections. **1** During **general elections,** regularly scheduled elections held in even-numbered years in November, voters decide who will be the U.S. president, vice president, and members of Congress. **2** An election board supervises the voting process in each precinct. **Poll watchers** from each of the two major parties typically monitor the polling place as well. **3** Citizens do not vote directly for the president and vice president. Instead, they vote for **electors** who will cast their ballots in the **electoral college.** Each state has as many electoral votes as it has U.S. senators and representatives, and there are also three electors from the District of Columbia. **4** The electoral college system is primarily a **winner-take-all system** because, in nearly all states, the candidate who receives the most popular votes in the state is credited with all that state's electoral votes. To be elected through this system, a candidate must win at least 270 electoral votes, a majority of the 538 electoral votes available.

**LearningOutcome 9–2** Discuss how candidates are nominated. **5** The methods used by political parties to nominate candidates have changed over time and have included **caucuses** and **nominating conventions.** Today, candidates who win **primary elections** go on to compete against the candidates from other parties in the general election. In a **direct primary,** which can be either **closed** or **open,** voters cast their ballots directly for candidates. **6** Most of the states hold presidential primaries, which are indirect primaries used to choose **delegates** to the national nominating conventions. In some states, delegates are chosen through a caucus/convention system. Each political party holds a national convention where delegates adopt the official party platform and nominate the party's presidential and vice-presidential candidates.

**LearningOutcome 9–3** Indicate what is involved in launching a political campaign today, and describe the structure and functions of a campaign organization. **7** To run a successful campaign, the candidate's campaign staff must be able to raise funds, get media coverage, produce and pay for political ads, schedule the candidate's time effectively with constituent groups and potential supporters, convey the candidate's position on the issues, conduct **opposition research,** and persuade the voters to go to the polls. Political party organizations are no longer as important as they once were, as campaigns have become more candidate-centered. Professional **political consultants** now manage nearly all aspects of a presidential candidate's campaign. Most candidates have a campaign manager who coordinates and plans the **campaign strategy.**

**LearningOutcome 9–4** Describe how the Internet has transformed political campaigns. **8** Today, the ability to make effective use of social media and the Internet is essential to a candidate. Barack Obama took Internet fund-raising to a new level during his 2008 presidential bid. The Obama campaign attempted to recruit as many supporters as possible to act as fund-raisers who would solicit contributions from their friends and neighbors. **9** Microtargeting, a technique that involves collecting as much information as possible about voters in a database and then filtering out various groups for special attention, was pioneered by the George W. Bush campaign in 2004. **10** In his 2008 presidential campaign, Obama also took Web-based organizing to a new level, using existing sites such as Facebook in addition to his own Web site. In 2012, Obama had seven times as many Facebook supporters as Mitt Romney.

**LearningOutcome 9–5** Summarize the current laws that regulate campaign financing and the role of money in modern political campaigns. **11** Campaign-financing laws enacted in the 1970s provide public funding for presidential primaries and general elections, limit presidential campaign spending of candidates accepting federal funds, require candidates to file periodic reports with the Federal Election Commission, and limit individual and group contributions. **12** The Bipartisan Campaign Reform Act of 2002 addressed the issues of **soft money** and **independent expenditures** to a certain extent. Several court decisions, however, have altered the rules of campaign financing, especially with respect to independent expenditures. The most notable consequence of these rulings has been the rise of super PACS and the huge amounts of money poured into them by wealthy individuals. **13** Total presidential campaign spending, including by candidates who lost in the primaries and through independent expenditures, reached $2.5 billion in the 2011–2012 election cycle.

# ANSWERS TO STUDY TOOLS QUIZ

## Fill-In

1. who receives the largest popular vote in a state is credited with all that state's electoral votes (LearningOutcome 9–1)
2. 270 (LearningOutcome 9–1)
3. direct (LearningOutcome 9–2)
4. the states moving their primaries to earlier in the year in an effort to make their primaries more prominent in the media and influential in the political process (LearningOutcome 9–2)
5. opposition (LearningOutcome 9–3)
6. collecting as much information as possible about voters in a database and then filtering out various groups for special attention (LearningOutcome 9–4)
7. federal income tax returns (LearningOutcome 9–5)
8. super PACs (LearningOutcome 9–5)

## Multiple Choice

9. a. (LearningOutcome 9–1)
10. b. (LearningOutcome 9–1)
11. a. (LearningOutcome 9–2)
12. b. (LearningOutcome 9–2)
13. c. (LearningOutcome 9–3)
14. c. (LearningOutcome 9–4)
15. b. (LearningOutcome 9–5)

delegates to represent the citizens of their geographic areas at a higher-level party convention. **200**

**open primary** A primary in which voters can vote for a party's candidates regardless of whether they belong to the party. **202**

**opposition research** The attempt to learn damaging information about an opponent in a political campaign. **208**

**political consultant** A professional political adviser who, for a fee, works on an area of a candidate's campaign. Political consultants include campaign managers, pollsters, media advisers, and "get out the vote" organizers. **206**

**poll watcher** A representative from one of the political parties who is allowed to monitor a polling place to make sure that the election is run fairly and that fraud doesn't occur. **196**

**primary election** An election in which voters choose the candidates of their party, who will then run in the general election. **201**

**soft money** Campaign contributions not regulated by federal law, such as some contributions that are made to political parties instead of to particular candidates. **212**

**special election** An election that is held at the state or local level when the voters must decide an issue before the next general election or when vacancies occur by reason of death or resignation. **196**

**winner-take-all system** A system in which the candidate who receives the most votes wins. In contrast, proportional systems allocate votes to multiple winners. **197**

# 10 Politics and the Media

## KEY TERMS

**agenda setting** The media's ability to determine which issues are considered to be important by the public and by politicians. **224**

**citizen journalism** The collection, analysis, and dissemination of information online by independent journalists, scholars, politicians, and the general citizenry. **237**

**electronic media** Communication channels that involve electronic transmissions, such as radio, television, and the Internet. **221**

**framing** An agenda-setting technique that establishes the context of a media report. Framing can mean fitting events into a familiar story or filtering information through preconceived ideas. **224**

**issue ad** A political advertisement that focuses on a particular issue. Issue ads can be used to support or attack a candidate's position or credibility. **228**

**managed news coverage** News coverage that is manipulated (managed) by a campaign manager or political consultant to gain media exposure for a political candidate. **230**

**mass media** Communication channels, such as newspapers and radio and television broadcasts, through which people can communicate to large audiences. **221**

**negative political advertising** Political advertising undertaken for the purpose of discrediting an opposing candidate in the eyes of the voters. Attack ads are one form of negative political advertising. **227**

**personal attack ad** A negative political advertisement that attacks the character of an opposing candidate. **227**

**podcasting** The distribution of audio or video files to personal computers or mobile devices such as smartphones. **237**

**political advertising** Advertising undertaken by or on behalf of a political candidate to familiarize voters with the candidate and his or her views on campaign issues; also advertising for or against policy issues. **227**

**priming** An agenda-setting technique in which a media outlet promotes specific facts or ideas that may affect the public's thinking on related topics. **224**

**print media** Communication channels that consist of printed materials, such as newspapers and magazines. **221**

## SUMMARY

**LearningOutcome 10–1 Explain the role of the media in a democracy. 1** What the media say and do has an impact on what Americans think about political issues, but the media also reflect what Americans think about politics. While the new media based on the Internet are becoming increasingly important, the traditional media—radio, television, and print—still remain important to American politics. **2** By helping to determine what people talk and think about, the media help set the political agenda. Of all the media, television still has the greatest impact on most Americans, but the medium of television imposes constraints on how political issues are presented.

**LearningOutcome 10–2 Summarize how television influences the conduct of political campaigns. 3** Candidates for political office spend a great deal of time and money obtaining a TV presence through political ads, debates, and general news coverage. Televised **political advertising** consumes at least half of the total budget for a major political campaign. **Personal attack ads** and **issue ads** frequently appear on TV. Televised debates are a routine feature of presidential campaigns. They provide an opportunity for voters to find out how candidates differ on issues and allow candidates to capitalize on the power of television to improve their images or point out the failings of their opponents. **4** Candidates' campaign managers have become increasingly sophisticated in **managing news coverage**, while press advisers try to convince reporters to give a story or event a **spin** that is favorable to the candidate.

**LearningOutcome 10–3 Explain why talk radio has been described as the Wild West of the media. 5** Talk-show hosts do not attempt to hide their political biases—if anything, they exaggerate them for effect. Sometimes, hosts appear to care more about the entertainment value of their statements than whether they are, strictly speaking, true. No journalistic conventions are observed. **6** Those who think that talk radio is good for the country argue that talk shows, taken together, provide a great populist forum. Others fear that talk shows empower fringe groups, perhaps magnifying their rage.

**LearningOutcome 10–4 Describe types of media bias and explain how such bias affects the political process. 7** The majority of Americans think that the media reflect a bias in either a liberal or a conservative direction. Rather than an ideological or partisan bias, a media bias against losers may play a role in shaping presidential campaigns and elections. The media use the winner-loser framework to describe events throughout the campaigns. **8** The expansion of the media universe to include cable channels and the Internet has increased the competition among news sources. News directors select programming they believe will attract the largest audiences and garner the highest advertising revenues. Many journalists believe that economic pressure is making significant inroads on independent editorial decision making. News organizations are redefining their purpose and looking for special niches in which to build their audiences.

**LearningOutcome 10–5 Indicate the extent to which the Internet is reshaping news and political campaigns. 9** The Internet is a major source of information for many people. Almost every major news organization, both print and broadcast, delivers news online. In addition, there has been a virtual explosion of **citizen journalism** in recent years. Blogs are offered by independent journalists, scholars, political activists, and the citizenry at large. **Podcasting** is another nontraditional form of news distribution. **10** The Internet is an inexpensive way for candidates to contact, recruit, and mobilize supporters, as well as disseminate information about their positions on issues. Candidates hire Web managers to create a well-designed Web site to attract viewers, manage their e-mails, and track their credit-card contributions. The Web manager also hires bloggers to promote the candidate's views, arranges for podcasting of campaign information, and hires staff to monitor the Web for news about the candidates and to track the online publications of netroots groups. **11** Citizen videos have also changed the traditional campaign. A candidate can never know when a comment that he or she makes may be caught on camera by someone with a cell phone or digital camera and published on the Internet for all to see.

**sound bite** A brief televised comment, lasting for only a few seconds, that captures a thought or a perspective and has an immediate impact on the viewers. **225**

**spin** A reporter's slant on, or interpretation of, a particular event or action. **230**

**spin doctor** A political candidate's press adviser who tries to convince reporters to give a story or event concerning the candidate a particular "spin" (interpretation, or slant). **230**

# ANSWERS TO STUDY TOOLS QUIZ

## Fill-In

1. Priming (LearningOutcome 10–1)
2. television (LearningOutcome 10–1)
3. a televised comment, lasting for only a few seconds, that captures a thought or a perspective and has an immediate impact on the viewers (LearningOutcome 10–1)
4. Al Jazeera (LearningOutcome 10–1)
5. John F. Kennedy and Richard Nixon (LearningOutcome 10–2)
6. political candidates' press advisers, who try to convince reporters to give a story or event concerning a candidate a particular interpretation or slant (LearningOutcome 10–2)
7. male, middle-aged, and conservative (LearningOutcome 10–3)
8. talk-show hosts often exaggerate their political biases for effect. Hosts sometimes appear to care more about the entertainment value of their statements than whether they are, strictly speaking, true. No journalistic conventions are observed (LearningOutcome 10–3)
9. losers (LearningOutcome 10–4)
10. the collection, analysis, and dissemination of information online by independent journalists, scholars, political activists, and the general citizenry (LearningOutcome 10–5)

## Multiple Choice

11. a. (LearningOutcome 10–1)
12. c. (LearningOutcome 10–2)
13. c. (LearningOutcome 10–3)
14. c. (LearningOutcome 10–4)
15. b. (LearningOutcome 10–5)

# 11 Congress

## KEY TERMS

**apportionment** The distribution of House seats among the states on the basis of their respective populations. **244**

**appropriation** A part of the congressional budgeting process—the determination of how many dollars will be spent in a given year on a particular government activity. **262**

**authorization** A part of the congressional budgeting process—the creation of the legal basis for government programs. **262**

**cloture** A procedure for ending filibusters in the Senate and bringing the matter under consideration to a vote. **255**

**conference committee** A temporary committee that is formed when the two chambers of Congress pass differing versions of the same bill. The conference committee consists of members from the House and the Senate who work out a compromise bill. **259**

**conference report** A report submitted by a conference committee after it has drafted a single version of a bill. **259**

**congressional district** The geographic area that is served by one member in the House of Representatives. **244**

**continuing resolution** A temporary resolution passed by Congress that enables executive agencies to continue work with the same funding that they had in the previous fiscal year. **264**

**entitlement program** A government program (such as Social Security) that allows, or entitles, a certain class of people (such as elderly persons) to receive special benefits. Entitlement programs operate under open-ended budget authorizations that, in effect, place no limits on how much can be spent. **262**

**filibustering** The Senate tradition of unlimited debate undertaken for the purpose of preventing action on a bill. **255**

**first budget resolution** A budget resolution, which is supposed to be passed in May, that sets overall revenue goals and spending targets for the next fiscal year, beginning on October 1. **264**

**fiscal year** A twelve-month period that is established for bookkeeping or accounting purposes. The government's fiscal year runs from October 1 through September 30. **262**

**gerrymandering** The drawing of a legislative district's boundaries in such a way as to maximize the influence of a certain group or political party. **246**

## SUMMARY

**LearningOutcome 11–1** Explain how seats in the House of Representatives are apportioned among the states. **1** The Constitution provides for the **apportionment** of House seats among the states on the basis of their respective populations, though each state is guaranteed at least one seat. Every ten years, the 435 House seats are reapportioned based on the outcome of the census. **2** Each representative to the House is elected by voters in a **congressional district.** Within each state, districts must contain, as nearly as possible, equal numbers of people. This principle is known as the **"one person, one vote" rule.** Gerrymandering occurs when a district's boundaries are drawn to maximize the influence of a certain group or political party.

**LearningOutcome 11–2** Describe the power of incumbency. **3** If incumbent legislators choose to run for reelection, they enjoy several advantages over their opponents, including name recognition, access to the media, congressional franking privileges, and lawmaking power. Members of Congress also have administrative staffs in Washington, D.C., and in their home districts. A key advantage is their fundraising ability. Most incumbents in Congress are reelected.

**LearningOutcome 11–3** Identify the key leadership positions in Congress, describe the committee system, and indicate some important differences between the House of Representatives and the Senate. **4** The Constitution provides for the presiding officers of both the House and the Senate, and each chamber has added other leadership positions. The majority party in each chamber chooses the major officers of that chamber, selects committee chairpersons, and has a majority on all committees. **5** Chief among the leaders in the House of Representatives is the **Speaker of the House,** who has a great deal of power. Other leaders include the **majority and minority leaders,** and the **whips.** The vice president of the United States is the president of the Senate, and senators elect the president pro tempore ("pro tem"). The real power in the Senate is held by the majority and minority leaders, and their whips. **6** Most of the work of legislating is performed by the **standing committees** and their **subcommittees** in the House and the Senate. **7** With its larger size, the House needs more rules and more formality than the Senate. The House **Rules Committee** proposes time limits on debate for most bills. The Senate normally permits extended debate. The use of unlimited debate to obstruct legislation is called **filibustering,** which may be ended by invoking **cloture.** There are other important differences between the House and the Senate as well.

**LearningOutcome 11–4** Summarize the specific steps in the lawmaking process. **8** After a bill is introduced, it is sent to a standing committee. A committee chairperson will typically send the bill on to a subcommittee, where public hearings might be held. After a **markup session,** the bill goes to the full committee for further action. **9** After a bill is reported to the chamber, it is scheduled for floor debate. After debate, votes are taken on the legislation. When the House and the Senate pass differing versions of the same bill, a **conference committee** is formed to produce a compromise bill. The **conference report** is sent to each chamber for a vote. If the bill is approved by both chambers, it is ready for action by the president.

**LearningOutcome 11–5** Identify Congress's oversight functions and explain how Congress fulfills them. **10** Congress oversees the departments and agencies of the executive branch, and can rein in the power of the bureaucracy by refusing to fund government programs. Congress has the authority to investigate the actions of the executive branch, the need for certain legislation, and even the actions of its own members. It has the power to impeach and remove from office federal officials. The Senate confirms the president's nominees to the federal judiciary and members of the cabinet.

**LearningOutcome 11–6** Indicate what is involved in the congressional budgeting process. **11** The budgeting process, which involves **authorization** and **appropriation**, begins when the president submits a proposed federal budget for the next **fiscal year**. In the **first budget resolution**, Congress sets overall revenue goals and spending targets. The **second budget resolution** sets "binding" limits on taxes and spending. When Congress is unable to pass a complete budget by the start of the fiscal year, it usually passes **continuing resolutions**, which enable executive agencies to keep on doing whatever they were doing the previous year with the same amount of funding.

# ANSWERS TO STUDY TOOLS QUIZ

## Fill-In

1. ten (LearningOutcome 11–1)
2. serve the broad interests of the entire society and act according to his or her perception of national needs (LearningOutcome 11–1)
3. fund-raising ability, franking privileges, professional staffs, lawmaking power, access to the media, and name recognition (LearningOutcome 11–2)
4. preside over sessions of the House, vote in the event of a tie, put questions to a vote, participate in making important committee assignments, and schedule bills for action (LearningOutcome 11–3)
5. cloture (LearningOutcome 11–3)
6. a meeting held by a congressional committee or subcommittee to approve, amend, or redraft a bill (LearningOutcome 11–4)
7. Rules (LearningOutcome 11–4)
8. the federal judiciary and to the cabinet (LearningOutcome 11–5)
9. authorization and appropriation (LearningOutcome 11–6)

## Multiple Choice

10. c. (LearningOutcome 11–1)
11. a. (LearningOutcome 11–2)
12. b. (LearningOutcome 11–3)
13. b. (LearningOutcome 11–4)
14. c. (LearningOutcome 11–5)
15. a. (LearningOutcome 11–6)

**instructed delegate** A representative who deliberately mirrors the views of the majority of his or her constituents. **248**

**majority leader** The party leader elected by the majority party in the House or in the Senate. **253**

**malapportionment** A condition in which the voting power of citizens in one district is greater than the voting power of citizens in another district. **246**

**markup session** A meeting held by a congressional committee or subcommittee to approve, amend, or redraft a bill. **258**

**minority leader** The party leader elected by the minority party in the House or in the Senate. **253**

**minority-majority district** A district in which minority groups make up a majority of the population. **247**

**"one person, one vote" rule** A rule, or principle, requiring that congressional districts have equal populations so that one person's vote counts as much as another's vote. **246**

**pocket veto** A special type of veto power used by the chief executive after the legislature has adjourned. Bills that are not signed die after a specified period of time. **260**

**Rules Committee** A standing committee in the House of Representatives that provides special rules governing how particular bills will be considered and debated by the House. The Rules Committee normally proposes time limits on debate for any bill. **255**

**second budget resolution** A budget resolution, which is supposed to be passed in September, that sets "binding" limits on taxes and spending for the next fiscal year. **264**

**Speaker of the House** The presiding officer in the House of Representatives. The Speaker has traditionally been a longtime member of the majority party and is often the most powerful and influential member of the House. **252**

**standing committee** A permanent committee in Congress that deals with legislation concerning a particular area, such as agriculture or foreign relations. **254**

**subcommittee** A division of a larger committee that deals with a particular part of the committee's policy area. Most standing committees have several subcommittees. **254**

**trustee** A representative who tries to serve the broad interests of the entire society, and not just the narrow interests of his or her constituents. **248**

**whip** A member of Congress who assists the majority or minority leader in the House or in the Senate in managing the party's legislative program. **253**

# 12 The Presidency

## KEY TERMS

**cabinet** An advisory group selected by the president to assist with decision making. Traditionally, the cabinet has consisted of the heads of the executive departments and other officers whom the president may choose to appoint. **287**

**chief diplomat** The role of the president in recognizing and interacting with foreign governments. **274**

**chief executive** The head of the executive branch of government, in the United States, the president. **272**

**chief of staff** The person who directs the operations of the White House Office and who advises the president on important matters. **289**

**commander in chief** The supreme commander of a nation's military force. **273**

**diplomat** A person who represents one country in dealing with representatives of another country. **273**

**executive agreement** A binding international agreement, or pact, that is made between the president and another head of state and that does not require Senate approval. **283**

**Executive Office of the President (EOP)** A group of staff agencies that assist the president in carrying out major duties. Franklin D. Roosevelt established the EOP in 1939 to cope with the increased responsibilities brought on by the Great Depression. **288**

**executive order** A presidential order to carry out a policy or policies described in a law passed by Congress. **282**

**executive privilege** An inherent executive power claimed by presidents to withhold information from, or to refuse to appear before, Congress or the courts. The president can also accord the privilege to other executive officials. **287**

**head of state** The person who serves as the ceremonial head of a country's government and represents that country to the rest of the world. **273**

**kitchen cabinet** The name given to a president's unofficial advisers. The term was coined during Andrew Jackson's presidency. **288**

**National Security Council (NSC)** A council that advises the president on domestic and foreign matters concerning the safety and defense of the nation; established in 1947. **290**

## SUMMARY

**LearningOutcome 12–1** **List the constitutional requirements for becoming president.** 1 Article II of the Constitution sets forth relatively few requirements for becoming president. A person must be a natural born citizen, at least thirty-five years of age, and a resident within the United States for at least fourteen years.

**LearningOutcome 12–2** **Explain the roles that a president adopts while in office.** 2 In the course of exercising his or her powers, the president performs a variety of roles. The president is the nation's **chief executive**—the head of the executive branch—and enforces laws and federal court decisions. The president leads the nation's armed forces as **commander in chief.** As **head of state,** the president performs ceremonial activities as a personal symbol of the nation. As **chief diplomat,** the president directs U.S. foreign policy and is the nation's most important representative in dealing with foreign governments. The president has become the chief legislator, informing Congress about the condition of the country and recommending legislative measures. As political party leader, the president chooses the chairperson of his or her party's national committee, attends party fund-raisers, and exerts influence within the party by using presidential appointment powers.

**LearningOutcome 12–3** **Indicate the scope of presidential powers.** 3 The Constitution gives the president specific powers, such as the power to negotiate **treaties,** to grant reprieves and pardons, and to **veto** bills passed by Congress. The president also has inherent powers—powers that are necessary to carry out the constitutional duties of the presidency. 4 Several presidents have greatly expanded presidential powers. The president, for example, is now expected to develop a legislative program. The president's political skills, the ability to persuade others, and the strategy of "going public" all play a role in determining legislative success. 5 The president's executive authority has been expanded by the use of **executive orders** and **signing statements,** and the ability to make **executive agreements** has enhanced presidential power in foreign affairs. As commander in chief, the president can respond quickly to a military threat without waiting for congressional action, and since 1945, the president has been responsible for deciding if and when to use nuclear weapons.

**LearningOutcome 12–4** **Describe advantages enjoyed by Congress and by the president in their institutional relationship.** 6 Congress has the advantage over the president in the areas of legislative authorization, the regulation of foreign and interstate commerce, and some budgetary matters. The president has the advantage over Congress in dealing with a national crisis, in setting foreign policy, and in influencing public opinion. 7 The relationship between Congress and the president is affected by their different constituencies and election cycles, and the fact that the president is limited to two terms in office. Their relationship is also affected when government is divided, with at least one house of Congress controlled by a different party than the White House.

**LearningOutcome 12–5** **Discuss the organization of the executive branch and the role of cabinet members in presidential administrations.** 8 The heads of the fifteen executive departments are members of the president's **cabinet.** The president may add other officials to the cabinet as well. In general, presidents usually don't rely on the advice of the formal cabinet. Department heads are often more responsive to the wishes of their own staffs, to their own political ambitions, or to obtaining resources for their departments. 9 Since 1939, top advisers and assistants in the **Executive Office of the President (EOP)** have helped the president carry out major duties. Some of the most important staff agencies in the EOP are the **White House**

Office, the **Office of Management and Budget,** and the **National Security Council.** In recent years, the responsibilities of the vice president have grown immensely, and the vice president has become one of the most important of the president's advisers.

# ANSWERS TO STUDY TOOLS QUIZ

## Fill-In

1. the legal profession (LearningOutcome 12–1)
2. commander in chief (LearningOutcome 12–2)
3. chief legislator (LearningOutcome 12–2)
4. presidential orders to carry out policies described in laws passed by Congress (LearningOutcome 12–3)
5. War Powers Resolution (LearningOutcome 12–3)
6. an inherent executive power claimed by presidents to withhold information from, or to refuse to appear before, Congress or the courts (LearningOutcome 12–4)
7. the heads of the executive departments and other officials whom the president may choose to appoint (LearningOutcome 12–5)
8. White House Office, the Office of Management and Budget, and the National Security Council (LearningOutcome 12–5)

## Multiple Choice

9. c. (LearningOutcome 12–1)
10. c. (LearningOutcome 12–2)
11. a. (LearningOutcome 12–2)
12. a. (LearningOutcome 12–3)
13. a. (LearningOutcome 12–3)
14. b. (LearningOutcome 12–4)
15. c. (LearningOutcome 12–5)

**Office of Management and Budget (OMB)** An agency in the Executive Office of the President that has the primary duty of assisting the president in preparing and supervising the administration of the federal budget. **290**

**patronage** The practice by which elected officials give government jobs to individuals who helped them gain office. **275**

**press secretary** A member of the White House staff who holds news conferences for reporters and makes public statements for the president. **289**

**signing statement** A written statement, appended to a bill at the time the president signs it into law, indicating how the president interprets that legislation. **282**

**treaty** A formal agreement between the governments of two or more countries. **276**

**veto** A Latin word meaning "I forbid"; the refusal by an official, such as the president of the United States or a state governor, to sign a bill into law. **277**

**Watergate scandal** A scandal involving an illegal break-in at the Democratic National Committee offices in 1972 by members of President Nixon's reelection campaign staff. Before Congress could vote to impeach Nixon for his participation in covering up the break-in, Nixon resigned from the presidency. **287**

**White House Office** The personal office of the president. White House Office personnel handle the president's political needs and manage the media, among other duties. **288**

# 13 The Bureaucracy

## KEY TERMS

**adjudicate** To render a judicial decision. In administrative law, the process in which an administrative law judge hears and decides issues that arise when an agency charges a person or firm with violating a law or regulation enforced by the agency. **308**

**bureaucracy** A large, complex, hierarchically structured administrative organization that carries out specific functions. **296**

**bureaucrat** An individual who works in a bureaucracy. As generally used, the term refers to a government employee. **296**

**civil service** Nonmilitary government employment. **306**

**enabling legislation** A law enacted by a legislature to establish an administrative agency. Enabling legislation normally specifies the name, purpose, composition, and powers of the agency being created. **307**

**government corporation** An agency of the government that is run as a business enterprise. Such agencies engage primarily in commercial activities, produce revenues, and require greater flexibility than most government agencies receive. **304**

**independent executive agency** A federal agency that is not located within a cabinet department. **301**

**independent regulatory agency** A federal organization that is responsible for creating and implementing rules that regulate private activity and protect the public interest in a particular sector of the economy. **304**

**iron triangle** A three-way alliance among legislators, bureaucrats, and interest groups to make or preserve policies that benefit their respective interests. **310**

**issue networks** Groups of individuals or organizations—which consist of legislators and legislative staff members, interest group leaders, bureaucrats, the media, scholars, and other experts—that support particular policy positions on a given issue. **311**

**legislative rule** An administrative agency rule that carries the same weight as a statute enacted by a legislature. **307**

**neutral competency** The application of technical skills to jobs without regard to political issues. **309**

## SUMMARY

**LearningOutcome 13–1** Describe the size and functions of the U.S. bureaucracy and the major components of federal spending. **1** In the federal government, the head of the **bureaucracy** is the president of the United States, and the bureaucracy is part of the executive branch. The federal bureaucracy exists because Congress, over time, has delegated certain tasks to specialists. The three levels of government employ about 16 percent of the civilian labor force. **2** Over half of the federal budget consists of various social programs, such as Social Security, Medicare, and Medicaid. With veterans' benefits, defense spending is almost 25 percent of total federal spending. Other categories of spending include military and economic foreign aid, as well as interest on the national debt.

**LearningOutcome 13–2** Discuss the structure and basic components of the federal bureaucracy. **3** The fifteen executive departments are the major service organizations of the federal government. Each department was created by Congress as the perceived need for it arose, and each manages a specific policy area. Department heads are appointed by the president and confirmed by the Senate. Each department includes several subagencies. **4 Independent executive agencies** have a single function. Sometimes agencies are kept independent because of the sensitive nature of their functions, but at other times, Congress creates independent agencies to protect them from **partisan politics. Independent regulatory agencies** are responsible for a specific type of policy. Their function is to create and implement rules that regulate private activity and protect the public interest in a particular sector of the economy. **5 Government corporations** are businesses owned by the government. They provide a service that could be handled by the private sector, and they charge for their services. A number of intermediate forms of organization exist that fall between a government corporation and a private one.

**LearningOutcome 13–3** Describe how the federal civil service was established and how bureaucrats get their jobs. **6** Federal bureaucrats holding top-level positions are appointed by the president and confirmed by the Senate. The list of positions that are filled by appointments is published after each presidential election in a book that summarizes about eight thousand jobs. The rank-and-file bureaucrats—the rest of the federal bureaucracy—are part of the **civil service.** They obtain their jobs through the Office of Personnel Management (OPM). The OPM recruits, interviews, and tests potential government workers and makes recommendations to agencies as to which persons meet relevant standards. The Civil Service Reform Act of 1883 established the principle of government employment on the basis of merit through open, competitive examinations.

**LearningOutcome 13–4** Explain how regulatory agencies make rules and how issue networks affect policymaking in government. **7** Regulatory agencies are sometimes regarded as the fourth branch of government. They make **legislative rules** that are as legally binding as laws passed by Congress. When they are engaging in **rulemaking,** agencies must follow certain procedural requirements. Bureaucrats are expected to exhibit **neutral competency,** which means that they are supposed to apply their technical skills to their jobs without regard to political issues. **8 Iron triangles** (alliances among legislators, bureaucrats, and interest groups to make or preserve policies that benefit their respective interests) are well established in almost every part of the bureaucracy. In some policy areas, there are less structured relationships among experts who have strong opinions and interests regarding the direction of policy. These **issue networks** are able to exert a great deal of influence on legislators and bureaucratic agencies.

**LearningOutcome 13–5** Identify some of the ways in which the government has attempted to curb waste and improve efficiency in the bureaucracy. **9** To encourage government employees to report waste and wrongdoing that they observe, Congress has passed laws to protect **whistleblowers** and to make cash awards to them. To improve efficiency, virtually every federal agency has had to describe its goals and methods for evaluating how well those goals are met. President Obama created the position of a chief performance officer who works with other economic officials in an attempt to increase efficiency and eliminate waste in government. Other ideas for reforming government bureaucracies include **privatization** and allowing citizens to file forms and apply for services online.

**partisan politics** Political actions or decisions that benefit a particular party. **303**

**privatization** The transfer of the task of providing services traditionally provided by government to the private sector. **314**

**rulemaking** The process undertaken by an administrative agency when formally proposing, evaluating, and adopting a new regulation. **309**

**whistleblower** In the context of government employment, someone who "blows the whistle" (reports to authorities or the press) on gross governmental inefficiency, illegal activities, or other wrongdoing. **311**

# ANSWERS TO STUDY TOOLS QUIZ

## Fill-In

1. 16 (LearningOutcome 13–1)
2. secretary (LearningOutcome 13–2)
3. Commerce (LearningOutcome 13–2)
4. president; Senate (LearningOutcome 13–3)
5. merit through open, competitive examinations (LearningOutcome 13–3)
6. enabling legislation (LearningOutcome 13–4)
7. a three-way alliance among legislators, bureaucrats, and interest groups to make or preserve policies that benefit their respective interests (LearningOutcome 13–4)
8. reports on gross governmental inefficiency, illegal action, or other wrongdoing (LearningOutcome 13–5)

## Multiple Choice

9. b. (LearningOutcome 13–1)
10. a. (LearningOutcome 13–2)
11. c. (LearningOutcome 13–2)
12. b. (LearningOutcome 13–2)
13. c. (LearningOutcome 13–3)
14. b. (LearningOutcome 13–4)
15. a. (LearningOutcome 13–5)

# 14 The Judiciary

## KEY TERMS

**administrative law** The body of law created by administrative agencies (in the form of rules, regulations, orders, and decisions) in order to carry out their duties and responsibilities. **322**

**appellate court** A court having appellate jurisdiction. An appellate court normally does not hear evidence or testimony but reviews the transcript of the trial court's proceedings, other records relating to the case, and attorneys' arguments as to why the trial court's decision should or should not stand. **325**

**case law** The rules of law announced in court decisions. Case law includes the aggregate of reported cases that interpret judicial precedents, statutes, regulations, and constitutional provisions. **322**

**civil law** The branch of law that spells out the duties that individuals in society owe to other persons or to their governments, excluding the duty not to commit crimes. **322**

**common law** The body of law developed from judicial decisions in English and U.S. courts, not attributable to a legislature. **320**

**concurring opinion** A statement written by a judge or justice who agrees (concurs) with the court's decision, but for reasons different from those in the majority opinion. **328**

**conference** In regard to the Supreme Court, a private meeting of the justices in which they present their arguments concerning a case under consideration. **328**

**constitutional law** Law based on the U.S. Constitution and the constitutions of the various states. **321**

**contempt of court** A ruling that a person has disobeyed a court order or has shown disrespect to the court or to a judicial proceeding. **324**

**criminal law** The branch of law that defines and governs actions that constitute crimes. Generally, criminal law has to do with wrongful actions committed against society for which society demands redress. **322**

**dissenting opinion** A statement written by a judge or justice who disagrees with the majority opinion. **329**

## SUMMARY

**LearningOutcome 14–1** **Summarize the origins of the American legal system and the basic sources of American law.** 1 The American legal system evolved from the **common law** tradition that developed in England. The practice of deciding new cases with reference to **precedents** *(stare decisis)* became a cornerstone of the American judicial system. 2 Various **primary sources of law** provide the basis for **constitutional law, statutory law, administrative law,** and **case law.** 3 **Civil law** spells out the duties that individuals in society owe to other persons or to their governments. **Criminal law** has to do with wrongs committed against the public as a whole. 4 A court must have **jurisdiction** to hear and decide a particular case. Any lawsuit involving a **federal question** can originate in federal court. Federal courts can also hear **diversity of citizenship** cases. To bring a lawsuit before a court, a person must have **standing to sue,** and the issue must be a **justiciable controversy.** The courts have also established procedural rules that apply in all cases.

**LearningOutcome 14–2** **Delineate the structure of the federal court system.** 5 The U.S. district courts are trial courts—the courts in which cases involving federal laws begin. There is at least one federal district court in every state, and there is one in the District of Columbia. The U.S. courts of appeals are **appellate courts** that hear cases on review from the U.S. district courts located within their respective judicial circuits. Decisions made by federal agencies may be reviewed by a district court or a court of appeals, depending on the agency. The Court of Appeals for the Federal Circuit has national jurisdiction over certain types of cases. The U.S. Supreme Court has some original jurisdiction, but most of the Court's work is as an appellate court. The Supreme Court may take appeals of decisions made by the U.S. courts of appeals as well as appeals of cases decided in the state courts when federal questions are at issue. 6 To bring a case before the Supreme Court, a party may request that the Court issue a **writ of** *certiorari.* If the Court grants cert., it will typically hear **oral arguments,** after which the justices discuss the case in **conference.** When the Court has reached a decision, the justices explain their reasoning in written **opinions.**

**LearningOutcome 14–3** **Say how federal judges are appointed.** 7 Federal judges are appointed by the president and confirmed by the Senate, they receive lifetime appointments. The Senate Judiciary Committee holds hearings on judicial nominees and makes its recommendation to the Senate, where it takes a majority vote to confirm a nomination. **Senatorial courtesy** gives home-state senators of the president's party influence over the president's choice of nominees for district courts (and, to a lesser extent, the U.S. courts of appeals). The process of nominating and confirming federal judges often involves political debate and controversy.

**LearningOutcome 14–4** **Explain how the federal courts make policy.** 8 Federal judges can decide on the constitutionality of laws or actions undertaken by the other branches of government through the power of **judicial review.** And it is unavoidable that courts influence or even establish policy when they interpret and apply the law. 9 Generally, activist judges believe that the courts should actively use their powers to check the other two branches of government to ensure that they do not exceed their authority. Restraintist judges generally assume that the courts should defer to the decisions of the other branches.

**LearningOutcome 14–5** **Describe the role of ideology and judicial philosophies in judicial decision making.** 10 There are numerous examples of ideology or policy preferences affecting Supreme Court decisions. Judicial decision making, however, can be complex. How much weight is given to the factors that may be taken into account depends, in part, on the approaches justices take toward the interpretation of laws and the Constitution. Important judicial philosophies include originalism, textualism, and modernism.

**LearningOutcome 14–6** Identify some of the criticisms of the federal courts and some of the checks on the power of the courts. 11 Policymaking by unelected judges has important implications in a democracy. Critics, especially on the political right, frequently accuse the judiciary of "legislating from the bench." There are several checks on the courts, however, including judicial traditions and doctrines, the judiciary's lack of enforcement powers, and potential congressional actions in response to court decisions. The American public continues to have a fairly high regard for the federal judiciary.

# ANSWERS TO STUDY TOOLS QUIZ

## Fill-In

1. constitutions, statutes, administrative agency rules and regulations, and decisions by courts (LearningOutcome 14–1)
2. writ of *certiorari* (LearningOutcome 14–2)
3. oral arguments (LearningOutcome 14–2)
4. concurring (LearningOutcome 14–2)
5. senatorial courtesy (LearningOutcome 14–3)
6. defer to the decisions of the legislative and executive branches (LearningOutcome 14–4)
7. strict construction and originalism (LearningOutcome 14–5)
8. rewriting a statute to negate a court's ruling, proposing constitutional amendments to reverse Supreme Court decisions, or limiting the jurisdiction of the federal courts (LearningOutcome 14–6)

## Multiple Choice

9. b. (LearningOutcome 14–1)
10. c. (LearningOutcome 14–2)
11. b. (LearningOutcome 14–2)
12. a. (LearningOutcome 14–3)
13. a. (LearningOutcome 14–4)
14. c. (LearningOutcome 14–5)
15. b. (LearningOutcome 14–6)

**diversity of citizenship** A basis for federal court jurisdiction over a lawsuit that arises when (1) the parties in the lawsuit live in different states or when one of the parties is a foreign government or a foreign citizen, and (2) the amount in controversy is more than $75,000. **324**

**federal question** A question that pertains to the U.S. Constitution, acts of Congress, or treaties. A federal question provides a basis for federal court jurisdiction. **323**

**judicial review** The power of the courts to decide on the constitutionality of legislative enactments and of actions taken by the executive branch. **333**

**judiciary** The courts; one of the three branches of government in the United States. **320**

**jurisdiction** The authority of a court to hear and decide a particular case. **323**

**justiciable controversy** A controversy that is not hypothetical or academic but real and substantial; a requirement that must be satisfied before a court will hear a case. *Justiciable* is pronounced jus-*tish*-a-bul. **324**

**opinion** A written statement by a court expressing the reasons for its decision in a case. **328**

**oral argument** A spoken argument presented to a judge in person by an attorney on behalf of her or his client. **328**

**precedent** A court decision that furnishes an example or authority for deciding subsequent cases involving identical or similar facts and legal issues. **320**

**primary source of law** A source of law that establishes the law. Primary sources of law include constitutions, statutes, administrative agency rules and regulations, and decisions rendered by the courts. **321**

**senatorial courtesy** A practice that allows a senator of the president's party to veto the president's nominee to a federal court judgeship within the senator's state. **329**

**standing to sue** The requirement that an individual must have a sufficient stake in a controversy before he or she can bring a lawsuit. The party bringing the suit must demonstrate that he or she has either been harmed or been threatened with a harm. **324**

**stare decisis** A common law doctrine under which judges normally are obligated to follow the precedents established by prior court decisions. Pronounced *ster*-ay dih-*si*-sis. **320**

**statutory law** The body of law enacted by legislatures (as opposed to constitutional law, administrative law, or case law). **322**

**trial court** A court in which trials are held and testimony is taken. **323**

**writ of *certiorari*** An order from a higher court asking a lower court for the record of a case. *Certiorari* is pronounced sur-shee-uh-*rah*-ree. **326**

# 15 Domestic Policy

## KEY TERMS

**action-reaction syndrome** For every government action, there will be a reaction by the public. The government then takes a further action to counter the public's reaction—and the cycle begins again. **358**

**agenda setting** Getting an issue on the political agenda to be addressed by Congress; part of the first stage of the policymaking process. **344**

**Children's Health Insurance Program (CHIP)** A joint federal-state program that provides health-care insurance for low-income children. **348**

**Corporate Average Fuel Economy (CAFE) standards** A set of federal standards under which each vehicle manufacturer (or the industry as a whole) must meet a miles-per-gallon benchmark averaged across all new cars or trucks. **351**

**domestic policy** Public policy concerning issues within a national unit, such as national policy concerning health care or the economy. **344**

**easy-money policy** A monetary policy that involves stimulating the economy by expanding the rate of growth of the money supply. An easy-money policy supposedly will lead to lower interest rates and induce consumers to spend more and producers to invest more. **356**

**economic policy** All actions taken by the national government to address the ups and downs in the nation's level of business activity. **355**

**Federal Open Market Committee (FOMC)** The most important body within the Federal Reserve System. The FOMC decides how monetary policy should be carried out by the Federal Reserve. **356**

**fiscal policy** The use of changes in government expenditures and taxes to alter national economic variables. **357**

**fracking** Technique for extracting oil or natural gas from underground rock by the high-power injection of a mixture of water, sand, and chemicals. **353**

**global warming** An increase in the average temperature of the Earth's surface over the last half century and its projected continuation. **352**

**greenhouse gas** A gas that, when released into the atmosphere, traps the sun's heat and slows its release into outer space. Carbon dioxide ($CO_2$) is a major example. **352**

## SUMMARY

**LearningOutcome 15–1** **Explain what domestic policy is, and summarize the steps in the policymaking process. 1** Domestic policy consists of public policy concerning issues within a national unit. **2** The **policymaking process** involves several phases. Issue identification and **agenda setting** begin the process, followed by the formulation and adoption of specific plans for achieving a particular goal. The final stages of the process focus on policy implementation and evaluation. Each phase of the policymaking process involves interactions among various individuals and groups.

**LearningOutcome 15–2** **Discuss the issue of health-care funding and recent legislation on universal health insurance. 3** Most federal spending on health care is accounted for by **Medicare** and **Medicaid.** Medicare is now the government's second-largest domestic spending program, while the annual total cost of Medicaid and the **Children's Health Insurance Program (CHIP)** for all levels of government is about $325 billion. **4** In many countries, the government is responsible for providing basic health-care insurance to everyone through **national health insurance.** Major health-care reform legislation adopted in the United States in 2010, however, provides a larger role for the private sector. Employer-provided health insurance will continue, as will Medicaid. The legislation also includes an **individual mandate**—most individuals would be required to obtain coverage or pay an income tax penalty. **5** One immediate change brought about by the health-care bills is that young people can remain covered by their parents' insurance until they turn 26, but the most important provisions go into effect in 2014, when subsidies will help eligible citizens purchase health-care insurance if they are not covered by Medicaid or an employer's plan. **6** Conservatives were opposed to the Patient Protection and Affordable Care Act, and Republicans made repeal of it part of their platform for the 2010 and 2012 elections.

**LearningOutcome 15–3** **Summarize the issues of energy independence, global warming, and alternative energy sources. 7** Our nation currently imports 42 percent of its petroleum supply. Many of the nations that export oil are not particularly friendly to the United States, though Canada and Mexico supply 40 percent of our imports. In response to a steep rise in oil prices before he took office, President Obama issued higher fuel efficiency standards for cars and trucks that began to take effect in 2010. In 2012, the administration announced new rules that raised fuel efficiency standards even higher. By 2025, the nation's combined fleet of new cars and trucks must have an average fuel efficiency of 54.5 miles per gallon. **8** Most climatologists believe that **global warming** is the result of human activities, especially the release of **greenhouse gases** into the atmosphere. A rise in global temperatures could cause sea levels to rise, rainfall patterns to change, and increases in extreme weather. **9** The issues of U.S. energy security and potential global warming both raise the question of whether we can develop new energy sources. By 2012, dramatic technological improvements led to an increase in U.S. oil production and supplies of natural gas. A recent crisis involving nuclear power in Japan weakened support for new nuclear plants in the United States, and new deepwater-drilling projects were at least temporarily halted as a result of the BP oil spill into the Gulf of Mexico in 2010. Some **renewable energy** technologies, such as solar power cells, are expensive. Hydropower and wind energy also present some difficulties.

**LearningOutcome 15–4** **Describe the two major areas of economic policymaking, and discuss the issue of the public debt. 10** The national government has two main tools to smooth the business cycle and to reduce **unemployment** and **inflation.** **11 Monetary policy** is under the control of the Federal Reserve System (the Fed), an independent regulatory agency. The Fed and its **Federal Open Market Committee**

make decisions about monetary policy several times each year. In theory, monetary policy is relatively straightforward—in periods of recession and high unemployment, an **easy-money** policy should be pursued. Since 2008, however, this policy has failed to spur the economy. **12** A second tool is **fiscal policy,** which usually involves raising or lowering taxes. The severity of the Great Recession led some economists to recommend increases in government spending as well. However, there is now strong political opposition to this aspect of **Keynesian economics. 13** The government raises money to pay its expenses through taxes levied on business and personal income and through borrowing. Tax policy is plagued by the **action-reaction syndrome,** resulting in a complicated tax system that is politically difficult to reform. When the government spends more than it receives, it borrows to finance the shortfall. Every time there is a federal government deficit, there is an increase in the total accumulated **public debt.** In the aftermath of the Great Recession, the federal budget deficit shot up. In 2012 it was about $1.1 trillion, while the net public debt was estimated to be about $11.5 trillion. Today, about half of the U.S. net public debt is held by foreign individuals, foreign businesses, and foreign central banks.

# ANSWERS TO STUDY TOOLS QUIZ

## Fill-In

1. issue identification and agenda setting, policy formulation and adoption, and policy implementation and evaluation (Learning Outcome 15–1)
2. Medicare (Learning Outcome 15–2)
3. all persons obtain health-care insurance from one source or another, or pay a penalty (LearningOutcome 15–2)
4. Canada and Mexico (LearningOutcome 15–3)
5. a rise in sea levels, changes in rainfall patterns, and increases in extreme weather (LearningOutcome 15–3)
6. solar power, hydro-power, and wind power (LearningOutcome 15–3)
7. recession (LearningOutcome 15–4)
8. Federal Reserve System (LearningOutcome 15–4)
9. the People's Republic of China (LearningOutcome 15–4)

## Multiple Choice

10. c. (LearningOutcome 15–1)
11. b. (LearningOutcome 15–2)
12. a. (LearningOutcome 15–2)
13. c. (LearningOutcome 15–3)
14. b. (LearningOutcome 15–4)
15. c. (LearningOutcome 15–4)

**individual mandate** In the context of health-care reform, a requirement that all persons obtain health-care insurance from one source or another. Those failing to do so would pay a penalty. **349**

**inflation** A sustained rise in average prices; equivalent to a decline in the value of the dollar. **356**

**Keynesian economics** An economic theory proposed by British economist John Maynard Keynes that is typically associated with the use of fiscal policy to alter national economic variables. **357**

**Medicaid** A joint federal-state program that provides health-care services to low-income persons. **348**

**Medicare** A federal government program that pays for health-care insurance for Americans aged sixty-five years and over. **348**

**monetary policy** Actions taken by the Federal Reserve Board to change the amount of money in circulation so as to affect interest rates, credit markets, the rate of inflation, the rate of economic growth, and the rate of unemployment. **356**

**national health insurance** A program, found in many of the world's economically advanced nations, under which the central government provides basic health-care insurance coverage to everyone in the country. Some wealthy nations, such as the Netherlands and Switzerland, provide universal coverage through private insurance companies instead. **349**

**policymaking process** The procedures involved in getting an issue on the political agenda; formulating, adopting, and implementing a policy with regard to the issue; and then evaluating the results of the policy. **344**

**public debt** The total amount of money that the national government owes as a result of borrowing; also called the *national debt.* **361**

**recession** A period in which the level of economic activity falls; usually defined as two or more quarters of economic decline. **355**

**renewable energy** Energy from technologies that do not rely on extracted resources, such as oil and coal, that can run out. **355**

**unemployment** The state of not having a job even when actively seeking one. **355**

# 16 Foreign Policy

## KEY TERMS

**coalition** An alliance of nations formed to undertake a foreign policy action, particularly a military action. A coalition is often a temporary alliance that dissolves after the action is concluded. **376**

**Cold War** The war of words, warnings, and ideologies between the Soviet Union and the United States that lasted from the late 1940s through the late 1980s. **372**

**colonial empire** A group of dependent nations that are under the rule of a single imperial power. **370**

**containment** A U.S. policy designed to contain the spread of communism by offering military and economic aid to threatened nations. **371**

**Cuban missile crisis** A nuclear standoff that occurred in 1962 when the United States learned that the Soviet Union had placed nuclear warheads in Cuba, ninety miles off the U.S. coast. The crisis was defused diplomatically, but it is generally considered the closest the two Cold War superpowers ever came to a nuclear confrontation. **372**

**détente** French word meaning a "relaxation of tensions." Détente characterized the relationship between the United States and the Soviet Union in the 1970s, as the two Cold War rivals attempted to pursue cooperative dealings and arms control. **372**

**deterrence** A policy of building up military strength for the purpose of discouraging (deterring) military attacks by other nations; the policy that supported the arms race between the United States and the Soviet Union during the Cold War. **372**

**foreign policy** A systematic and general plan that guides a country's attitudes and actions toward the rest of the world. Foreign policy includes all of the economic, military, commercial, and diplomatic positions and actions that a nation takes in its relationships with other countries. **367**

**interventionism** Direct involvement by one country in another country's affairs. **370**

**iron curtain** A phrase coined by Winston Churchill to describe the political boundaries between the democratic countries in Western Europe and the Soviet-controlled Communist countries in Eastern Europe. **371**

## SUMMARY

**LearningOutcome 16–1** **Discuss how foreign policy is made, and identify the key players in this process. 1** The president oversees the military, guides defense policies, and represents the United States to the rest of the world. The Department of State is responsible for diplomatic relations with other nations and with multilateral organizations. The Department of Defense establishes and carries out defense policy and protects our national security. Two key agencies in the area of foreign policy are the National Security Council and the Central Intelligence Agency. Congress has the power to declare war and the power to appropriate funds to equip the armed forces and provide for foreign aid. The Senate has the power to ratify treaties. A few congressional committees are directly concerned with foreign affairs.

**LearningOutcome 16–2** **Summarize the history of American foreign policy through the years. 2** Early leaders sought to protect American interests through **isolationism.** The Spanish-American War of 1898 marked the first step toward **interventionism. 3** In World War I, the United States initially adopted a policy of **neutrality,** and after the war, returned to a policy of isolationism. That policy ended with the attack on Pearl Harbor in 1941. After World War II, the alliance between the United States and the Soviet Union deteriorated. The Truman Doctrine and the **Marshall Plan** marked the beginning of a policy of **containment** of communism. **4** During the **Cold War,** the United States and the Soviet Union engaged in an arms race supported by a policy of **deterrence,** which led to the theory of **mutually assured destruction (MAD).** In 1962, the two countries came close to a nuclear confrontation during the **Cuban missile crisis.** The fall of the Berlin Wall in 1989 and the demise of the Soviet Union in 1991 altered the framework and goals of U.S. foreign policy.

**LearningOutcome 16–3** **Identify the foreign policy challenges presented by terrorism. 5** Terrorism is defined as the use of staged violence, often against civilians, to achieve political goals. Governments around the world face the challenges of dealing with local or regional terrorism, state-sponsored terrorism, and foreign terrorist networks. After the terrorist attacks on September 11, 2001, the U.S. military, supported by a **coalition** of allies, attacked al Qaeda camps in Afghanistan and the ruling Taliban regime that harbored those terrorists. **6** In 2003, U.S. and British forces attacked the nation of Iraq, believing (though incorrectly) that Iraq's dictator was developing **weapons of mass destruction** and that the Iraqi regime was in some way responsible for the 9/11 terrorist attacks. Following free elections in 2005, Sunni insurgents, including the newly organized al Qaeda in Iraq, attacked U.S. and Iraqi government forces and Shiite civilians. Eventually, the insurgency was fatally undermined. U.S. forces left Iraq in 2011. **7** By 2006, the Taliban had regrouped and were waging a war of insurgency against the new government in Afghanistan. In 2009, President Obama ordered additional troops into that country, but pledged to start withdrawing U.S. forces in 2011. During the winter of 2010–2011, U.S. intelligence agencies learned that al Qaeda leader Osama bin Laden might be hiding in a Pakistani city. In 2011, U.S. Navy Seals killed him in his residential compound.

**LearningOutcome 16–4** **Explain the principal issues dividing the Israelis and the Palestinians and the solutions proposed by the international community. 8** Following the 1967 war, the West Bank of the Jordan River and the Gaza Strip fell under Israeli control, and the Palestinians living in these areas became an occupied people. Palestinian terrorist attacks on Israel have impeded efforts toward peace. **9** The international community agrees that lands seized in the 1967 war should be returned to the Palestinians, who could organize their own independent nation-state there. In turn, the Palestinians would have to recognize Israel's right to exist and take concrete steps to guarantee Israel's security. In 1993, Israel and the **Palestine Liberation**

Organization (PLO) met officially for the first time. A major result of the **Oslo Accords** was the establishment of a Palestinian Authority, under Israeli control, on the West Bank and Gaza Strip. Further attempts to reach a settlement have stalled.

**LearningOutcome 16–5** **Outline some of the actions taken by the United States to curb the threat of nuclear weapons. 10** The pursuit of nuclear technology in North Korea and Iran is of major concern to the United States. Neither weapons inspections nor negotiations have resolved the issue of North Korea's nuclear ambitions. It conducted nuclear tests in 2006 and 2009. **11** Iran has been engaged in a covert nuclear program and, like North Korea, has been openly hostile to the United States. The United Nations and the United States have imposed sanctions on Iran in an attempt to curb its nuclear ambitions and to isolate it from the community of nations. In 2009, a round of talks involving Britain, France, Germany, Iran, Russia, and the United States was begun to discuss Iran's nuclear program, but the talks have gone nowhere. With increasing urgency, the government of Israel has called for air strikes to destroy Iran's nuclear program.

**LearningOutcome 16–6** **Describe China's emerging role as a world power. 12** China has one of the fastest-growing economies in the world and a population of 1.3 billion. Diplomatic relations between China and the United States have been uneven. Congress has granted China **normal trade relations status,** but many Americans are concerned that low-cost imports from China are taking jobs away from American workers. Some argue that the U.S. government should treat China's currency manipulation as an anticompetitive trade practice. Recent attempts by Chinese hackers to steal U.S. intellectual property have also raised questions about China's attitude toward the West.

# ANSWERS TO STUDY TOOLS QUIZ

## Fill-In

1. departments of state and defense, and the National Security Council and the Central Intelligence Agency (LearningOutcome 16–1)
2. isolationism (LearningOutcome 16–2)
3. Cold War (LearningOutcome 16–2)
4. Afghanistan (LearningOutcome 16–3)
5. Pakistan (LearningOutcome 16–3)
6. Palestinian Authority (LearningOutcome 16–4)
7. North Korea and Iran (LearningOutcome 16–5)
8. currency manipulation (LearningOutcome 16–6)

## Multiple Choice

9. b. (LearningOutcome 16–1)
10. c. (LearningOutcome 16–2)
11. a. (LearningOutcome 16–2)
12. c. (LearningOutcome 16–3)
13. a. (LearningOutcome 16–4)
14. b. (LearningOutcome 16–5)
15. a. (LearningOutcome 16–6)

**isolationism** A political policy of non-involvement in world affairs. **369**

**Marshall Plan** A plan providing for U.S. economic assistance to European nations following World War II to help those nations recover from the war; the plan was named after George C. Marshall, secretary of state from 1947 to 1949. **371**

**Monroe Doctrine** A U.S. policy, announced in 1823 by President James Monroe, that the United States would not tolerate foreign intervention in the Western Hemisphere and in return, the United States would stay out of European affairs. **370**

**moral idealism** In foreign policy, the belief that the most important goal is to do what is right. Moral idealists think that it is possible for nations to cooperate as part of a rule-based community. **367**

**mutually assured destruction (MAD)** A phrase referring to the assumption that if the forces of two nations are equally capable of destroying each other, neither nation will take a chance on war. **372**

**neutrality** A position of not being aligned with either side in a dispute or conflict, such as a war. **370**

**normal trade relations (NTR) status** A trade status granted through an international treaty by which each member nation must treat other members at least as well as it treats the country that receives its most favorable treatment. This status was formerly known as *most-favored-nation status*. **384**

**Oslo Accords** The first agreement signed between Israel and the PLO; led to the establishment of the Palestinian Authority in the occupied territories. **379**

**Palestine Liberation Organization (PLO)** An organization formed in 1964 to represent the Palestinian people. The PLO has a long history of terrorism but for some years has functioned primarily as a political party. **378**

**political realism** In foreign policy, the belief that nations are inevitably selfish, and that we should seek to protect our national security, regardless of moral arguments. **367**

**Soviet bloc** The group of Eastern European nations that fell under the control of the Soviet Union following World War II. **371**

**weapons of mass destruction** Chemical, biological, or nuclear weapons that can inflict massive casualties. **376**

✳

# California Politics & Government

*To the futures of Adam and Jodi, Lee, and Rachel Gerston
and the memories of Anna and Teter Christensen and Tillie and Chester Welliever*

# Contents

# Preface

Ask someone to describe California and it's amazing what answers you will hear. Some view California as a land of endless opportunity; others cast the state as the political equivalent of one huge congested freeway mired in hopeless gridlock. Both characterizations have merit along with so many others.

California reminds us of a powerful, rich symphony adorned with a full complement of instruments played by the most talented artists. Yet, when the conductor brings down his baton, the brilliant sounds don't quite mesh. And while it is a state with seemingly limitless horizons for some, it can discourage so many others just trying to get by. Few states possess as many conflicting forces as California. Given its multifaceted composition, we marvel that anything ever moves anywhere but sideways.

Yet its complexity is what makes California so deceptively alluring, if frustrating. Just when you think you have it figured out, you realize that there's yet another layer to examine along with the rest, another facet that marginalizes any conclusions reached to that point. California is a political conundrum, to say the least, which is why we are so fascinated with the state, its people, and its politics.

This edition, our twelfth, proceeds two years after the previous edition, identical to the interims between all of our other editions. Some have asked us why we keep to such a tight writing schedule. You know the answer if you watch California—too many things happen too fast. For that reason, this edition is no different in chronicling the immense changes that have occurred over the past two years.

Since our last post, California has once again revealed its fickleness. On the one hand, we have witnessed new directions. The impact of the 2012 election, brand new legislative and congressional districts courtesy of the Citizens Independent Redistricting Commission, the "top two" primary system, bankrupt local governments, social media breakthroughs, and new state/federal arrangements are among the many changes that have appeared in this short period of time, all of which are discussed along with many others in this volume.

On the other hand, California remains just as plagued by lingering problems today as in the past. It continues to be a state with a terrible imbalance between revenue and spending, a stubbornly weak economy, a society that reveals a huge chasm between those who have and those who don't, an infrastructure in tatters, the growing tension among various racial and ethnic groups, and a political system as disjointed today as any time in the past. These all bear additional discussion because of their seeming permanence, if for no other reason.

There is so much to write about this once-Golden State yet, as with our previous editions, we remain committed to fulfilling our mandate with brevity and as much clarity as possible. We don't linger on themes as much as we try to introduce and connect them in the "nuts and bolts" fashion that has guided our previous efforts. For those who want to know more, we offer additional source materials at the end of each chapter through books and various websites.

Meanwhile, as you explore this book, we hope that you will share our excitement about a state unequalled by any other. Whatever California's future, it surely will be influenced by its rich past and present.

Many have assisted us in our effort to provide the best assessment possible on California. Our friends in politics, the media, and elected office, as well as fellow academics, have provided valuable counsel, information, and insights at various junctures. We would especially like to thank the following reviewers whose comments helped mold this edition: Stephanie Burkhalter, Humboldt State; Traci Fahimi, Irvine Valley College; and John Roche, Palomar College. Most of all, we continue to benefit from our students who, with their penetrating questions and thoughtful observations, push us to explore and report on topics that we might not have considered otherwise. Some have gone on to political careers in local, state, and federal offices, helping us to believe that the next generation is prepared and willing to take ownership of the state and its potential.

Finally, we are indebted to the attentive production staff at Cengage, who artfully managed an incredibly tight schedule to facilitate production within weeks of the November 6, 2012, election. They include Carolyn Merrill, Executive Political Science Editor; Anita Devine, Political Science Acquisitions Editor; Patrick Roach; Assistant Political Science Editor; and Lydia LeStar, Brand Manager, who patiently and efficiently worked with us from manuscript to page proofs. All these people and many others assisted this project to the best of our abilities. Of course, in the end responsibility for the product is ours.

# About the Authors

**Larry N. Gerston,** Professor Emeritus of Political Science at San Jose State University, interacts with the political process as both an author and an observer. As an author, he has written ten academic books in addition to *California Politics and Government: A Practical Approach, including Making Public Policy: From Conflict to Resolution (1983), Politics in the Golden State* (with Terry Christensen, 1984), *The Deregulated Society* (with Cynthia Fraleigh and Robert Schwab, 1988), *American Government: Politics, Process, and Policies* (1993), *Public Policy: Process and Principles* (1987), *Public Policymaking in a Democratic Society: A Guide to Civic Engagement* (2002), *Recall! California's Political Earthquake* (with Christensen, 2004), *American Federalism: A Concise Introduction* (2007), *Confronting Reality: Ten Issues Threatening to Implode American Society and How We Can Fix It* (2009), and *Not So Golden After All: The Rise and Fall of California* (2012). As an observer, Gerston serves as the political analyst for NBC11, a San Francisco Bay Area television station, where he appears on a regular basis. He has written more than a hundred op-ed pieces for newspapers throughout the nation and speaks often on issues such as civic engagement and personal political empowerment.

**Terry Christensen** is a San Jose State University Professor Emeritus of Political Science. Among his other awards for scholarship and service to the university, he was named Outstanding Professor in 1998. He is the author or co-author of nine books and frequent newspaper op-ed pieces. Local and national media regularly call on him for analysis of politics in California and Silicon Valley. In addition to other books co-authored with Larry Gerston, his works include *Projecting Politics: Political Messages in American Films* (2005), co-authored by Peter Haas, and *Local Politics: A Practical Guide to Governing at the Grassroots* (2006), co-authored by Tom Hogen-Esch. Christensen is experienced in practical politics at the local level as an advocate of policy proposals, an adviser to grassroots groups, and an adviser and mentor to candidates for local office—many of whom are his former students. He has served on numerous civic committees and commissions. He was the founding executive director of CommUniverCity San Jose (www.communivercitysanjose.org), a partnership between the City of San Jose, San Jose State University, and adjacent neighborhoods. Through CommUniverCity, hundreds of students are learning about life and politics in their community through service projects selected by neighborhood residents and supported by the city.

## SUPPLEMENTS FOR INSTRUCTORS

**Instructor's Manual with Test Bank Online for Gerston/Christensen**
*California Politics and Government: A Practical Approach*, **12e**

- IBSN-13: 9781133591382

- This password-protected Instructor's Manual and Test Bank are accessible by logging into your account at www.cengage.com/login.

# 1

# California's People, Economy, and Politics: Yesterday, Today, and Tomorrow

## CHAPTER CONTENTS

Colonization, Rebellion, and
Statehood

Railroads, Machines, and
Reform

The Workingmen's Party

The Progressives

The Great Depression
and World War II

Growth, Change, and Political Turmoil

California Today

California's People, Economy,
and Politics

Thanks to the Gold Rush, the Golden Gate Bridge, and over a century of booming growth, California has long been known as "the Golden State," but today some say the Golden State no longer glitters. Googling "California as a failed state" (like Somalia or Greece) produces over 70 million hits. California's economy has been mired in recession since 2007 and the state has suffered over a decade of budget deficits while politics in the state capital seems stuck in gridlock. To many, California politics seems turbulent and unpredictable. Political leaders rise and fall precipitately. Wealthy candidates and special interests are accused of "buying" elections. While state government stalls in gridlock, issues are referred to the voters, who are often confused by complex and sometimes obscure ballot measures. Some say this is democracy gone mad; others have concluded that California is ungovernable.

But however volatile or dysfunctional California politics may seem, it is serious business that affects us all, and it can be understood by examining the history and present characteristics of our state—especially its changing population and economy. Wave after wave of immigrants have made California a diverse, multicultural society, while new technologies repeatedly transform the state's economy. The resulting disparate demographic and economic interests compete for the benefits and protections conferred by government and thus shape the state's politics. To understand California today—and tomorrow—we need to know a little about its past and about the development of the competing interests within the state.

## COLONIZATION, REBELLION, AND STATEHOOD

The first Californians probably were immigrants like the rest of us. Archaeologists believe that the ancestors of American Indians crossed an ice or land bridge or traveled by sea from Asia to Alaska thousands of years ago and then headed south. Europeans began exploring the California coast in the early 1500s, but colonization didn't start until 1769, when the Spanish established a string of missions and military outposts. About 300,000 Native Americans were living here then, mostly near the coast.

These native Californians were brought to the missions as Catholic converts and workers, but European diseases and the destruction of the native culture reduced their numbers to about 100,000 by 1849. Entire tribes were wiped out and the Indian population continued to diminish throughout the nineteenth century. Today, less than 1 percent of California's population is Native American, and many feel alienated from a society that has overwhelmed their peoples, cultures, and traditions. Chronic poverty, however, has been alleviated for some by the development of casinos on native lands, a phenomenon that has also made some tribes major players in state politics.

Apart from building missions, the Spaniards did little to develop their faraway possession. Not much changed when Mexico (including California) declared its independence from Spain in 1822. A few thousand Mexicans quietly raised cattle on vast ranches and built small towns around their central plazas.

Meanwhile, advocates of expansion in the United States coveted California's rich lands and access to the Pacific Ocean. When Mexico and the United States went to war over Texas in 1846, Yankee immigrants to California seized the moment and declared independence from Mexico. After the U.S. victory, Mexico surrendered its claim to lands extending from Texas to California. By this time, foreigners already outnumbered Californians of Spanish ancestry 9,000 to 7,500.

Gold was discovered in 1848, and the '49ers who started arriving in hordes the next year brought the nonnative population to 264,000 by 1852. Many immigrants came directly from Europe. The first Chinese people also arrived to work in the mines, which yielded more than a billion dollars' worth of gold in five years.

The surge in population and commerce moved the new Californians to political action. A constitutional convention consisting of forty-eight delegates (only seven of whom were native Californians) assembled the Constitution of 1849 by cutting and pasting from the constitutions of existing states; the convention requested statehood, which the U.S. Congress quickly granted. The constitutional structure of the new state approximated what we have today, with a two-house legislature; a supreme court; and an executive branch consisting of a governor, lieutenant governor, controller, attorney general, and superintendent of public instruction. The constitution also included a bill of rights, but only white males were allowed to vote. California's Chinese, African American, and Native American residents were soon prohibited by law from owning land, testifying in court, or attending public schools.

The voters approved the constitution, and San Jose became the first state capital. With housing in short supply, many newly elected legislators had to lodge in tents, and the primitive living conditions were exacerbated by heavy rain and flooding. The state capital soon moved on to Vallejo and Benicia, finally settling in 1854 in Sacramento—closer to the gold fields.

As the Gold Rush ended, a land rush began. Small homesteads were common in other states because of federal ownership and allocation of land, but California had been divided into huge tracts by Spanish and Mexican land grants. As early as 1870, a few hundred men owned most of the farmland. Their ranches were the forerunners of the agribusiness corporations of today, and as the mainstay of the state's economy, they exercised even more clout than their modern successors.

In less than fifty years, California had belonged to three different nations. During the same period, its economy and population had changed dramatically as hundreds of thousands of immigrants from all over the world came to claim their share of the "Golden State." The pattern of a rapidly evolving, multicultural polity was set.

## RAILROADS, MACHINES, AND REFORM

Technology wrought the next transformation in the form of railroads. In 1861 Sacramento merchants led by Leland Stanford founded the railroad that would become the **Southern Pacific Railroad**. They persuaded Congress to provide millions of dollars in land grants and loan subsidies for a railroad linking California with the eastern United States, thus greatly expanding the market for California's products. Stanford became governor and used his influence to provide state assistance. Cities and counties also contributed—under the threat of being bypassed by the railroad. To obtain workers at cheap rates, the railroad builders imported 15,000 Chinese laborers.

When the transcontinental track was completed in 1869, the Southern Pacific expanded its system throughout the state by building new lines and buying up existing ones. The railroad crushed competitors by cutting shipping charges, and by the 1880s it had become the state's dominant transportation company, as well as its largest private landowner with 11 percent of the entire state. With its business agents doubling as political representatives in almost every

California city and county, the Southern Pacific soon developed a formidable political machine. "The Octopus," as novelist Frank Norris called the railroad, placed allies in state and local offices through its control of both the Republican and Democratic parties. Once there, these officials protected the interests of the Southern Pacific if they wanted to continue in office. County tax assessors who were supported by the political machine set favorable tax rates for the railroad and its allies, while the machine-controlled legislature ensured a hands-off policy by state government.

## THE WORKINGMEN'S PARTY

People in small towns and rural areas who were unwilling to support the machine lost jobs, businesses, and other benefits. Some moved to cities, especially San Francisco, where manufacturing jobs were available. Chinese workers who had been brought to California to build the railroad also sought work in the cities when it was completed. But when a depression in the 1870s made jobs scarce, these newcomers faced hostile treatment from earlier immigrants. Led by Denis Kearney, Irish immigrants became the core of the **Workingmen's Party**, a political organization that blamed economic difficulties on the railroad and the Chinese.

Small farmers who opposed the railroad united through the Grange movement. In 1879 the Grangers and the Workingmen's Party called California's second constitutional convention in hopes of breaking the railroad's hold on the state. The **Constitution of 1879** mandated regulation of railroads, utilities, banks, and corporations. An elected State Board of Equalization was set up to ensure the fairness of local tax assessments on railroads and their friends, as well as their enemies. The new constitution also prohibited the Chinese from owning land, voting, or working for state or local government.

The railroad soon reclaimed power, however, by taking control of the agencies that were created to regulate it. Nonetheless, efforts to regulate big business and control racial relations became recurring themes in California life and politics, and much of the Constitution of 1879 remains intact today.

## THE PROGRESSIVES

The growth fostered by the railroad eventually produced a new middle class of merchants, doctors, lawyers, teachers, and skilled workers who were not dependent on the railroad. They objected to the corrupt practices and favoritism of the railroad's political machine, which they thought was restraining economic development in their communities. This new middle class demanded honesty and competence, which they called "good government." In 1907 some of these crusaders established the Lincoln-Roosevelt League, a reform group within the Republican Party, and became part of the national Progressive movement. Their leader, Hiram Johnson, was elected governor in 1910; they also captured control of the state legislature.

To break the power of the machine, the **Progressives** introduced a wave of reforms that shape California politics to this day. Predictably, they created a new regulatory agency for the railroads and utilities, the Public Utilities Commission (PUC). Most of their reforms, however, aimed at weakening the political parties as tools of bosses and machines. Instead of party bosses handpicking candidates at party conventions, the voters now were given the power to select their party's nominees for office in primary elections. Cross-filing further diluted party power by allowing candidates to file for and win the nominations of more than one political party. The Progressives made city and county elections "nonpartisan" by removing party labels from local ballots altogether. They also created a civil service system to select state employees on the basis of their qualifications rather than their political connections.

Finally, the Progressives introduced direct democracy, which allowed the voters to amend the constitution and create laws through initiatives, repeal laws through referenda and to recall, or remove, elected officials before their terms expired. Supporters of an initiative, referendum, or recall must circulate petitions and collect a specified number of signatures of registered voters before it goes to the voters.

Like the Workingmen's Party before them, the Progressives were concerned about immigration. Antagonism toward recent Japanese immigrants (who numbered 72,000 by 1910) resulted in Progressive support for a ban on land ownership by aliens and the National Immigration Act of 1924, which effectively halted Asian immigration. Other, more positive changes by the Progressives included giving women the right to vote, passing child labor and workers' compensation laws, and implementing conservation programs to protect natural resources.

Thanks to the Progressive reforms, the railroad's political machine eventually died, although California's increasingly diverse economy also weakened the machine, as the emerging oil, automobile, and trucking industries gave the state alternative means of transportation and shipping. These and other growing industries ultimately restructured economic and political power in California.

The reform movement waned in the 1920s, but the Progressive legacy of weak political parties and direct democracy opened up California's politics to its citizens, as well as to powerful interest groups and individual candidates with strong personalities. A long and detailed constitution is also part of the legacy. The Progressives instituted their reforms by amending (and thus lengthening) the Constitution of 1879 rather than calling for a new constitutional convention. Direct democracy subsequently enabled voters and interest groups to amend the constitution, constantly adding to its length.

## THE GREAT DEPRESSION AND WORLD WAR II

California's population grew by more than 2 million in the 1920s (see Table 1.1). Many newcomers headed for Los Angeles, where employment opportunities in shipping, filmmaking, and manufacturing (of clothing, automobiles, and aircraft) abounded. Then came the Great Depression of the 1930s, which saw the unemployment rate soar from 3 percent in 1925 to 33 percent by 1933. Even so, more

**TABLE 1.1  California's Population Growth, 1850–2010**

| Year | Population | Percentage of U.S. Population |
|------|-----------|-------------------------------|
| 1850 | 93,000 | 0.4 |
| 1900 | 1,485,000 | 2.0 |
| 1950 | 10,643,000 | 7.0 |
| 1970 | 20,039,000 | 9.8 |
| 1990 | 29,733,000 | 11.7 |
| 2010 | 37,253,956 | 12.0 |

SOURCE: U.S. Census.

than a million people came to California, including thousands of poor white immigrants from the "dust bowl" of the drought-impacted Midwest. Many wandered through California's great Central Valley in search of work, displacing Mexicans—who earlier had supplanted the Chinese and Japanese—as farm workers. Racial antagonism ran high, and many Mexicans were arbitrarily sent back to Mexico. Labor unrest reached a crescendo in the early 1930s, as workers on farms, in canneries, and on the docks of San Francisco and Los Angeles fought for higher wages and an eight-hour workday.

The immigrants and union activists of the 1920s and 1930s also changed California politics. Many registered as Democrats, thus challenging the dominant Republicans. The Depression and President Franklin Roosevelt's popular New Deal helped the Democrats become California's majority party in registration, although winning elections proved more difficult. The Democrats finally gained the governorship in 1938, but their candidate, Culbert Olson, was the only Democratic winner between 1894 and 1958.

World War II revived the economic boom, but even in the 1930s, the state and federal governments were investing in California's future, building the Golden Gate Bridge and the Central Valley Project whose dams and canals brought water to the desert and reaffirmed agriculture as a mainstay of California's economy. Then between 1940 and 1946, the federal government spent $35 billion in California, creating 500,000 defense industry jobs. California's radio, electronics, and aircraft industries grew at phenomenal rates. The jobs brought new immigrants, including many African Americans, whose proportion of the state's population quadrupled during the 1940s.

Meanwhile, California's Japanese and Mexican American residents became victims of racial conflict. During the war, 120,000 Japanese Americans, suspected of loyalty to their ancestral homeland, were sent to prison camps (officially called internment centers). Antagonism toward Mexican Americans resulted in the Zoot Suit Riots in Los Angeles in 1943, when Anglo sailors and police attacked Mexican Americans wearing distinctive suits featuring long jackets with wide lapels, padded shoulders, and high-waisted, pegged pants.

Although the voters chose a Democratic governor during the Great Depression, they returned to the Republican fold as the economy revived. Earl Warren, one of a new breed of moderate Republicans, was elected governor in 1942, 1946, and 1950, becoming the only individual to win the office three times until Jerry Brown was elected in 2010. Warren used cross-filing to win the nominations of both parties and staked out a relationship with the voters that he claimed was above party politics. A classic example of California's personality-oriented politics, Warren left the state in 1953 to become chief justice of the U.S. Supreme Court.

## GROWTH, CHANGE, AND POLITICAL TURMOIL

With the Republican Party in disarray due to infighting, Californians elected a Democratic governor, Edmund G. "Pat" Brown, and a Democratic majority in the state legislature in 1958. To prevent Republicans like Warren from taking advantage of cross-filing again, the state's new leaders immediately outlawed that electoral device.

In control of both the governor's office and the legislature for the first time in the twentieth century, Democrats moved aggressively to develop the state's infrastructure. Completion of the massive California Water Project, construction of the state highway network, and creation of an unparalleled higher education system helped accommodate the growing population and stimulated the economy. Meanwhile, in the 1960s, California's black and Latino minorities became more assertive, pushing for civil rights, desegregation of schools, access to higher education, and improved treatment for California's predominantly Latino farm workers.

The demands of minority groups alienated some white voters, however, and the Democratic programs were expensive. After opening their purse strings during the eight-year tenure of Pat Brown, Californians became more cautious about the state's direction. Race riots precipitated by police brutality in Los Angeles, along with student unrest over the Vietnam War, also turned the voters against liberal Democrats such as Brown.

In 1966 Republican Ronald Reagan was elected governor; he moved the state in a more conservative direction before going on to serve as president. His successor as governor, Democrat Edmund G. "Jerry" Brown, Jr., was the son of the earlier governor Brown and a liberal on social issues. Like Reagan, however, the younger Brown led California away from spending on growth-inducing infrastructure, such as highways and schools. In 1978 the voters solidified this change with the watershed tax-cutting initiative, Proposition 13 (see Chapter 8). Although Democrats still outnumbered Republicans among California's registered voters, two Republicans succeeded Brown as governor.

In 1998 California elected Gray Davis, its first Democratic governor in sixteen years. He was reelected in 2002 despite voter concerns about an energy crisis, a recession, and a growing budget deficit. As a consequence of these crises and what some perceived as an arrogant attitude, Davis faced an unprecedented recall election in October 2003. The voters removed him from office and replaced him with Republican Arnold Schwarzenegger. Then in 2010, former governor Jerry Brown was elected governor in a dramatic comeback, making history as California's youngest and oldest governor.

Democrats have had more consistent success in the state legislature and the congressional delegation, where they have dominated since 1960. California voters have also opted for Democrats in every presidential election since 1988.

But recurring conflicts between a Democratic legislature and Republican chief executives have made governing California challenging, a situation that, until 2010, was exacerbated by the constitutional requirement for a supermajority to enact the state budget. Meanwhile, the voters have become increasingly involved in policymaking by initiative and referendum (see Chapter 2). Amendments to California's constitution, which require voter approval, appear on almost every state ballot. As a consequence, California's Constitution of 1879 has been amended over five hundred times; the U.S. Constitution includes just twenty-seven amendments.

Throughout these changes the state's population continued to grow, outpacing most other states so much that the California delegation to the U.S. House of Representatives now numbers fifty-three—more than twenty-one other states combined. Much of this growth was the result of a new wave of immigration facilitated by more flexible national immigration laws during the 1960s and 1970s. Immigration from Asia—especially from Southeast Asia after the Vietnam War—increased greatly. A national amnesty for undocumented residents also enabled many Mexicans to gain citizenship and bring their families from Mexico. In all, 85 percent of the 6 million newcomers and births in California in the 1980s were Asian, Latino, or black. Growth slowed in the 1990s, as 2 million more people left the state than came to it from other states, but California's population continued to increase as a result of births and immigration from abroad. In 1990 whites made up 57 percent of the state's population; by 2010 they were 40 percent.

Constantly increasing diversity enlivened California's culture and provided a steady flow of new workers, but it also increased tensions. Some affluent Californians retreated to gated communities; others fled the state. Racial conflict broke out between gangs on the streets and in prisons. As in difficult economic times throughout California's history, a recession during the early 1990s led many Californians to blame immigrants, especially those who were in California illegally. A series of ballot measures raised divisive race-related issues such as illegal immigration, bilingualism, and affirmative action. The issue of immigration enflames California politics to this day, although the increasing electoral clout of minorities has provided some balance.

## CALIFORNIA TODAY

If California were an independent nation, its economy would rank ninth in the world, with an annual gross national product of nearly $2 trillion. Much of the state's strength stems from its economic diversity (see Table 1.2). The elements of this diversity also constitute powerful political interests in state politics.

Half of California—mostly desert and mountains—is owned by the state and federal governments. In rural areas, a few big corporations control much of the state's rich farmlands. These enormous agribusinesses make California the

**TABLE 1.2 California's Economy**

| Industrial Sector | Employees | Amount (in millions) |
| --- | --- | --- |
| Professional and business services | 2,218,900 | $ 272,248 |
| Education and health services | 1,881,300 | 149,884 |
| Leisure and hospitality services | 1,575,800 | 81,094 |
| Other services | 484,000 | 47,617 |
| Information | 451,700 | 136,046 |
| Government | 2,378,300 | 224,720 |
| Trade, transportation, and utilities | 2,715,200 | 300,789 |
| Manufacturing | 1,242,700 | 229,862 |
| Finance, insurance, and real estate | 775,100 | 405,260 |
| Construction | 574,500 | 58,959 |
| Mining and natural resources | 29,200 | 52,425 |
| Agriculture | 376,700 | 37,500 |
| Total, all sectors | 14,703,400 | $1,996,404 |

SOURCE: California Employment Development Department, www.labormarketinfo.edd.ca.gov (accessed July 2012); and U.S. Department of Commerce, Bureau of Economic Analysis, *Survey of Current Business*, June 2012, http://www.bea.gov /scb/pdf/2012 (accessed July 2012).

nation's leading farm state, producing more than four hundred different food-stuffs, including nearly half of the vegetables, fruits, and nuts and 21 percent of the dairy products consumed nationally. Grapes and wine are also top products, with thousands of growers and 3,364 wineries.

State politics affects this huge economic force in many ways, but most notably in labor relations, environmental regulation, and water supply. Farmers and their employees have battled for decades over issues ranging from wages to safety. Beginning in the 1960s, under the leadership of Cesar Chavez and the United Farm Workers union, laborers organized. Supported by public boycotts of certain farm products, they achieved some improvements in working conditions, but the struggle continues today. California's agricultural industry is also caught up in environmental issues, including the pesticide use and water pollution. In addition, booming growth in the Central Valley has urbanized some farmland, bringing "city" problems such as traffic and crowded schools to once-rural areas. The biggest issue, however, is always water. Most of California's cities and farms must import water from other parts of the state. Thanks to government subsidies, farmers claim 80 percent of the state's water supply at prices so low that they have little reason to improve inefficient irrigation systems. Meanwhile, the growth of urban areas is limited by water supplies. Today, agriculture—and water—is in the thick of California politics as the state strives to balance an essential and powerful industry with the interests of its other citizens.

Agriculture is big business, but many more Californians work in manufacturing, especially in the aerospace, defense, and high-tech industries. Employment in manufacturing, however, has declined in California in recent years, especially after the federal government reduced military and defense spending in the 1990s when the collapse of communism in the Soviet Union brought an end to the Cold War. Jobs in California shifted to postindustrial occupations such as retail sales, tourism, and services, although jobs in these sectors often pay low wages. Government policies on growth, the environment, and taxation affect all of these employment sectors, and all suffer when any one sector goes into a slump.

But the salvation of California's economy is innovation, especially in telecommunications, entertainment, medical equipment, international trade, and high-tech businesses spawned by defense and aerospace companies. In the 1990s, California hosted one-fourth of the nation's high-tech firms, which provided nearly a million jobs. Half of the nation's computer engineers worked in Silicon Valley, named after the silicon chip that revolutionized the computer industry. Running between San Jose and San Francisco, Silicon Valley became a center for innovation in technology from computers to software and Internet-based businesses, including iconic companies like Hewlett-Packard, Intel, Facebook, and Google, which are headquartered there. Biomedical and pharmaceutical companies also proliferated, further contributing to California's transformation.

Computer technology also spurred rapid expansion of the entertainment industry, long a key component of California's economy. This growth particularly benefited the Los Angeles area. Besides film and television production, tourism remains a bastion of the economy, with California regularly ranking first among the states in visitors. Along with agriculture, high-tech, telecommunications, and other industries, these businesses have made California a leader in both international and domestic trade. All these industries are part of a globalized economy, with huge amounts of trade going through the massive port complex of Los Angeles/Long Beach, as well as the San Francisco Bay Port of Oakland.

The California economy has been on a roller coaster for the past few years, though. It has been in and out of recession—first in the early 1990s, and then again after the terrible events of September 11, 2001, when the California-centered Internet boom went bust as thousands of dot-com companies failed to generate projected profits. High tech went into decline, and tens of thousands of workers lost their jobs, some of which were "off-shored" (moved to other countries). At about the same time, an energy crisis hit California; prices for gas and electricity rose and parts of the state experienced shortages of electrical power. All these factors combined to push California into a recession, with unemployment reaching 7 percent statewide and 9 percent in Silicon Valley in 2003 (the national rate was 5.9 percent). As the boom ended, tax revenues declined precipitously, producing a huge state budget deficit. Combined with the energy crisis, the deficit and other issues contributed to the recall of Governor Davis in 2003, but having a new governor didn't solve California's problems.

After a resurgence in 2006–2007, California's economy was hit by the national recession in 2009. Unemployment reached 12.4 percent in 2010 (the U.S. rate was 9.7 percent)—improving to only 10.7 percent in 2012 (U.S. = 8.2 percent). California had lost hundreds of thousands of manufacturing jobs since the 1990s as employers migrated to other states or abroad. The national home finance and foreclosure crisis also hit the California housing market and construction industry hard. Employment in all sectors, even film and television production, declined, with growth only in high tech.

Throughout its history, California has experienced economic ups and downs like these, recovered, reinvented itself, and moved on, thanks to the diversity of its economy and its people and their ability to adapt to change. While some businesses have forsaken California for other states, complaining of burdensome regulation and the high cost of doing business in California, the Public Policy Institute of California reports that the skill and higher productivity of the state's workforce, access to capital, and quality of life compensate for such costs and keep the state attractive to many businesses.[1] Innovation continues to be an economic mainstay as well. Nanotechnology companies, for example, are concentrated in the San Francisco Bay Area, while biotechnology thrives in the San Diego region and green industry (for example, solar power and electric cars) booms throughout California. Access to venture capital investment funds facilitates such innovation in California. In 2012, over half of all venture capital in the United States was invested in California; the Bay Area alone brought in $3.2 billion as compared to New York City's $588 million.[2] Another strength of the California economy is an astounding and ever-growing number of small businesses—many of which are minority-owned. Most other states lack these advantages; some are dependent on a single industry or product, and none can match the energy and optimism brought by California's constant flow of immigrants eager to take jobs in the state's new and old industries.

California's globalized economy consistently attracts more immigrants than any other state; as of 2010, 27.2 percent of the state's population was foreign born, down slightly from previous years. The foreign-born share of the U.S. population was 12.7 percent.[3] Fifty-five percent of California's immigrants are from Latin America (mostly Mexico), and 35 percent are from Asia (especially the Philippines, China, Vietnam, India, and Korea). Significantly for the California economy, 75 percent of the state's immigrant population is of working age (twenty-five to sixty-four).[4] An estimated 2 million immigrants are in California illegally.[5] As a consequence of so much immigration, 43 percent of all Californians over the age of five speak a language other than English at home,[6] resulting in a major challenge for California schools. As in past centuries, immigration and language have been hot-button political issues in California in recent years.

Table 1.3 shows the extent of California's ethnic diversity. Although non-Latino whites remain the single largest group, they are no longer a majority. Overall, the black and white proportions of California's population have

**T A B L E  1.3  California's Racial and Ethnic Diversity**

|  | 1990 | 2000 | 2010 |
|---|---|---|---|
| Non-Latino white | 57.1% | 47.3% | 40.1% |
| Latino | 26.0 | 32.4 | 37.6 |
| Asian/Pacific Islander | 9.2 | 11.4 | 13.1 |
| Black | 7.1 | 6.5 | 5.8 |
| Native American | 0.6 | 0.5 | 0.4 |
| Mixed race | N.A. | 1.9 | 2.6 |

SOURCE: U.S. Census; California Department of Finance, www.dof.ca.gov (accessed July 23, 2012). 2010 figures do not add up to 100% because 0.2% for the new classification "some other race alone" is not included in this table.

decreased, while Asian and Latino numbers have grown rapidly since the 1970s. Currently, over 70 percent of students in California's public schools are nonwhite.[7]

The realization of the California dream is not shared equally among these groups. Although the median household income as of 2010 was $60,883 according to the U.S. Census Bureau, the income of 16 percent of Californians fell below the federal poverty level—slightly above the national average, but the state's rate is considerably higher when the cost of living in California is factored in. Over half the students in California schools qualify for free or reduced-price meals.[8] The gap between rich and poor in California is among the largest in the United States and is still growing. Poverty is worst among Latinos, blacks, and Southeast Asians, who tend to hold low-paying service jobs; other Asians, along with Anglos, predominate in the more comfortable professional classes.

As the poor grow in number, some observers fear that California's middle class is vanishing. Once a majority, many of the middle class have slipped down the economic ladder, and others have simply fled the state. While many people are doing very well at the top of the ladder, more are barely getting by at the bottom, and the middle class is shrinking. The median family income in California fell by over 11 percent between 2007 and 2010; 49.7 percent of Californians were middle class as compared to 60 percent in 1980. Recent growth has concentrated in low- and high-wage jobs, and the income gap continues to widen.[9]

The costs of housing and health care are at the heart of this problem. Home prices dropped during housing crisis of 2008–2011, increasing affordability for some families, but many more suffered losses of equity in their homes, and some lost their homes to foreclosure. With a median home price of $320,540 in 2012 compared with the U.S. median of $189,400,[10] Californians still spent more of their income on housing than the national average, and fewer families were able to afford to own homes, especially in the coastal counties from San Diego to San Francisco. Homes were more affordable in inland California, however. Overall, home ownership in California lags well behind the national average, especially for Latinos and blacks. Health care is also a problem for poor and working Californians. Twenty-two percent (nearly 7 million) have no health insurance.[11]

Geographic divisions complicate California's economic and ethnic diversity. In the past, the most pronounced of these divisions was between the northern and southern portions of the state. The San Francisco Bay Area tended to be diverse, liberal, and in elections, Democratic, while Southern California was staunchly Republican and much less diverse. However, with growth and greater diversity, Los Angeles also began voting Democratic. Today, the greatest division is between the coastal and inland regions of the state (see Figure 2.3). Democrats now outnumber Republicans in San Diego, and even notoriously conservative Orange County has elected a Latina Democrat to Congress.

But even as the differences between northern and southern California fade, the contrast between coastal and inland California has increased. The state's vast Central Valley has led the way in population and job growth, with cities from Sacramento to Fresno to Bakersfield gobbling up farmland. The Inland Empire, from Riverside to San Bernardino, has grown even more rapidly since the late

1990s. Although still sparsely populated, California's northern coast, Sierra Nevada, and southern desert regions are also growing, while retaining their own distinct identities. Water, agriculture, and the environment are major issues in all these areas. Except for Sacramento, inland California is more conservative than the coastal region of the state. Perhaps ironically, the liberal counties of the coast contribute more per capita in state taxes, and the conservative inland counties receive more per capita for social service programs.[12] While coastal California remains politically dominant, the impact of inland areas on California politics increases with every election.

## CALIFORNIA'S PEOPLE, ECONOMY, AND POLITICS

All these elements of California's economic, demographic, and geographic diversity vie with one another for political influence in the context of political structures that were created more than a hundred years ago. Dissatisfaction with this system has resulted in dozens of reforms by ballot measure, a recall election, and even calls for a constitutional convention to rewrite the state constitution entirely. Voter frustration is at a peak. As of 2012, only 30 percent of Californians felt that the state was "going in the right direction" (compared with 55 percent in 2007); only 39 percent approved of the governor's performance (compared with 57 percent in 2007); and 25 percent approved of the performance of the legislature (compared with 41 percent in 2007).[13] Perhaps people see California as a failed state, or maybe they're just frustrated with the current leadership. In the chapters that follow, we'll see how the diverse interests of our state operate in the current political system and gain an understanding of how it all works, why voters and others may feel frustration, and what some are doing to bring about change even as others resist.

## NOTES

1. Public Policy Institute of California, "California 2025, 2012 Update," www.ppic .org (accessed July 27, 2012).

2. *San Jose Mercury News*, August 12, 2012.

3. U.S. Census, http://quickfacts.census.gov/qfd/states/06000.html (accessed July 27, 2012).

4. Hans Johnson, "Just the Facts: Immigrants in California," Public Policy Institute of California, June 2011, www.ppic.org (accessed July 27, 2012).

5. Hans Johnson, "Just the Facts: Illegal Immigrants," Public Policy Institute of California, December 2010, www.ppic.org (accessed July 27, 2012).

6. U.S. Census, op. cit.

7. "A New Diverse Majority," Southern Education Foundation, January 31, 2010, http://www.southerneducation.org/getattachment/73d87cb2-d980-4c05-a1c3-35486c2ed4b2/Publications/A-New-Diverse-Majority-Summary.aspx (accessed July 27, 2012).

8. *Ibid.*

9. Sarah Bohn and Eric Schiff, "The Great Recession and Distribution of Income in California," Public Policy Institute of California, December 2011, www.ppic.org (accessed July 27, 2012).

10. California Association of Realtors, www.car.org, and National Association of Realtors, www.realtor.org/research-and-statistics (accessed July 31, 2012).

11. California Healthcare Foundation, www.chcf.org (accessed July 31, 2012).

12. Report from the Legislative Analyst's Office cited in "California's Unequal Give and Take," *San Jose Mercury News*, June 21, 2010.

13. Public Policy Institute of California, "Statewide Survey Time Trends," www.ppic .org (accessed July 31, 2012).

## LEARN MORE ON THE WEB

The California Constitution:
www.leginfo.ca.gov/const-toc.html

Demographic data:
www.dof.ca.gov/research/demographic
http://quickfacts.census.gov/qfd/states/06000.html

Digitized photographs, documents, newspapers, political cartoons, works of art, diaries, oral histories, advertising, and other cultural artifacts:
www.calisphere.universityofcalifornia.edu

## LEARN MORE AT THE LIBRARY

Sandra Bass and Bruce M. Cain, eds. *Racial and Ethnic Politics in California.* Berkeley: Berkeley Public Policy Press, Institute of Governmental Studies, University of California, 2008.

Larry N. Gerston. *Not So Golden After All: The Rise and Fall of California.* Boca Raton: CRC Press, 2012.

Joe Matthews and Mark Paul. *California Crackup: How Reform Broke the Golden State and How We Can Fix It.* Berkeley: University of California Press, 2010.

Frank Norris. *The Octopus.* New York: Penguin, 1901. A novel of nineteenth-century California.

Kevin Starr. *California: A History.* New York: Modern Library, 2005.

# 2

# California's Political Parties and Direct Democracy

## CHAPTER CONTENTS

**The Progressive Legacy**

**Party Organization—System and Supporters**

*The Official Party System*

*Party Supporters*

**Direct Democracy**

*The Recall*

*The Referendum*

*The Initiative*

*Legislative Initiatives, Constitutional Amendments, and Bonds*

**The Politics of Ballot Propositions**

**Political Parties and Direct Democracy**

Political parties are organizations of like-minded individuals and interest groups that set forth public policies based on their political ideology, put forward candidates for public office, provide the candidates with organizational and financial support, and hold them accountable if they are elected. In some states, parties are strong and do all these things effectively. In California, although party loyalty is strong in the state legislature and among a substantial number of voters, parties are weak as organizations and perform none of these functions effectively. History tells us why: the Progressive reformers intentionally weakened political parties in order to rid California of the railroad-dominated political machine. In doing so, they unintentionally made candidate personalities, media manipulation, and fat campaign war chests as important in elections as political parties—and sometimes more so.

The Progressives also introduced **direct democracy**. Through the initiative, referendum, and recall, California voters gained the power to make law and even to overrule elected officials or remove them between elections. The reformers' intent was to empower citizens, but in practice, interest groups and politicians are more likely to use—and sometimes abuse—direct democracy.

Weak parties and direct democracy are fixtures of the state constitution and modern California politics. Some political observers argue that this combination promotes political disarray, governmental gridlock, and voters who are confused or turned off. Others believe that the system reflects political values that eschew structured authority and maximize opportunities for democratic decision making.

## THE PROGRESSIVE LEGACY

To challenge the dominance of the Southern Pacific Railroad's political machine, Progressive reformers focused on the machine's control of party conventions, where party leaders nominated their candidates for various offices. Republican reformers scored the first breakthrough in 1908, when they succeeded in electing many antirailroad candidates to the state legislature. In 1909 the reform legislators replaced party conventions with **primary elections**, in which the registered voters of each party choose the nominees. Candidates who win their party's primary in these elections face the nominees of other parties in the November **general elections**. By instituting this system, the reformers ended the machine's ability to pick the candidates.

In 1910 Progressives won the office of governor and majorities in the state legislature. They introduced direct democracy to give policymaking authority to the people. They also replaced the party column ballot—which had permitted bloc voting for all the candidates of a single party by making just one mark—with separate balloting for each office. In addition, Progressive reformers introduced **cross-filing**, which permitted candidates of one party to seek the nominations of rival parties. Finally, the Progressives instituted **nonpartisan elections**, which eliminated party labels for candidates in elections for judges, school board members, and local government officials.

These changes reduced the railroad's control of the political parties, but they also sapped the strength of party organizations. By allowing the voters to circumvent an unresponsive legislature, direct democracy paved the way for interest groups to dominate policymaking. Deletion of the party column ballot encouraged voters to cast their ballots for members of different parties for different offices (split-ticket voting), increasing the likelihood of a divided-party government (see Chapter 7). Nonpartisan local elections made it difficult for the parties to groom candidates and build their organizations at the grassroots level.

Party leaders tried to regain control of nominations by settling on favored candidates before the primary elections. Ultimately, however, such **preprimary endorsements** were also outlawed. In 1959, when Democrats gained control of the legislature for the first time in over forty years, they outlawed cross-filing, which had been disproportionately helpful to Republican incumbents. This marked a return to the system in which candidates file for nomination for their own party only.

# PARTY ORGANIZATION—SYSTEM AND SUPPORTERS

Thanks to the Progressive reforms, political parties in California operate under unusual constraints. Although the original reformers have long since departed from the scene, the reform mentality remains very much a part of California's political culture.

## The Official Party System

According to state law, political parties qualify to place candidates on the ballot if a number of voters equal to 1 percent of the state vote in the most recent gubernatorial election sign up for the party when they register to vote; alternatively, parties can submit a petition with signatures amounting to 10 percent of that vote. Once qualified, if a party retains the registration of at least 1 percent of the voters or if at least one of its candidates for any statewide office receives 2 percent of the votes cast, that party remains qualified for the next election. By virtue of their sizes, the Democratic and Republican parties have been fixtures on the ballot almost since statehood.

Minor parties, sometimes called **third parties**, are another story. Some have been on the ballot for decades; others have had brief political lives. In the 2010 general election, the American Independent, Green, Libertarian, and Peace and Freedom parties each secured the minimum 2 percent of the vote for one of their statewide candidates, guaranteeing them positions on the ballot in 2012. The total number of parties qualified for the 2012 California ballot, including Democrats and Republicans, was six.

Nonetheless, breaking the hold of the two major political parties has proved difficult. The Democratic and Republican candidates for governor garnered 95 percent of the vote in 2010—slightly less than the 97.7 percent shared by the Democratic and Republican candidates for president in 2012. Among the smaller parties, the Greens have been the most successful at winning elections. They have earned one seat in the state legislature and elected several city and county officials.

California voters choose their party when they **register to vote**, which must be done fifteen or more days before the election. In 2012, 73.1 percent were registered as either Democrats or Republicans, 6.0 percent signed up with the other parties, and 20.9 percent declared themselves independent (officially known as "decline to state")—see Figure 2.1. The independent percentage has more than doubled since 1986, when it was just 9 percent.

For most of its history, California used **closed primary** elections to select the nominees of each party for state elective office and the U.S. Congress. Voters registered with a political party could cast their ballots in the primary only for that party's nominees for various offices. The winners of each party's primary election faced off in the November general election, when all voters were free to cast their ballots for the candidate of any of the parties.

But in 2010, over the strenuous objections of the political parties (another indication of their weakness), voters approved a **"top-two" primary** system

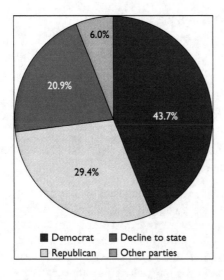

**FIGURE 2.1**  Party Registration in California, 2010. (Courtesy of Terry Christensen)

SOURCE: California Secretary of State.

that went into effect in 2012. In a top-two primary, no matter what their own party, voters may choose their preferred candidate from any party; the top-two vote getters face off in the November election, even if they're from the same party. Advocates of this system hoped that instead of concentrating their appeals on the core of their own parties (liberals for Democrats and conservatives for Republicans), candidates would reach out to independent and moderate voters and that those elected would be more moderate and thus more willing to compromise when they got to Sacramento. In theory, this could break the gridlock in the state capital, but whether it will do so remains to be seen.

The June 2012 election was the first statewide top-two primary. The results were mixed and provided few clues about the long-range impact of the new system, although it appears that these elections became somewhat more competitive, which gives voters more choices.[1] For example, significantly more incumbent office holders were confronted by challengers than in the past and more races were close. Not a single minor party candidate made it to the top two, however, which could mean that these parties will eventually disappear under this system. Five "independents" (stating "no party preference" on the ballot) did advance to the November runoff, however. Perhaps most significantly, the top-two primary resulted in twenty-eight runoffs between candidates of the same party. These are the races that the advocates of the top-two primary hope will result in more moderates in the legislature and better prospects for compromise.

Before the Great Depression, California was steadfastly Republican, but during the 1930s a Democratic majority emerged. Since then, Democrats have dominated in voter registration (see Figure 2.2), although their proportion declined from a peak of 60 percent of registered voters in 1942 to 43.7 percent in 2012. Republican registration has slipped to 29.4 percent, while the independent percentage has more than doubled since 1986, when it was just 9 percent. Despite their advantage in registration, Democrats did not gain a majority in

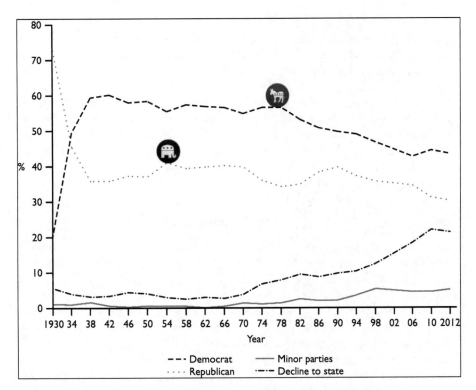

**FIGURE 2.2** Party Registration during Gubernatorial Election Years.
SOURCE: California Secretary of State.

both houses of the state legislature until 1958 and Republican candidates have won eight of the last thirteen gubernatorial elections.

State law dictates registration, voting, and party organization. The main parties have similar structures with the state **central committee** as the highest-ranking body. These committees are comprised of party candidates, office-holders, county chairpersons, and some appointed members. In addition, Democratic voters elect members from each assembly district, and Republican county central committees elect or appoint members. Each party's central committee elects a state chair, who functions as the party spokesperson.

Beneath the state central committee are county central committees. Voters registered with each party choose committee members every two years in primary elections. The party's nominees for state legislature and those who win elections are also members. The state and county party committees draft policy positions for party platforms, although candidates and elected officials often ignore these. Some committees also recruit volunteers and raise money for party candidates. Despite their low public profile, county committees are sometimes sites of intense conflict among activists. Liberals usually dominate Democratic county committees, whereas conservatives rule Republican committees.

California's political parties had an opportunity to strengthen their role in choosing party nominees when the U.S. Supreme Court overturned the state ban on preprimary endorsements in 1990. California Republicans have rarely exercised this power. Democrats have done so more often, although voters don't always pay attention to such endorsements. In 2010, however, the Democratic convention's preprimary endorsement of Assemblyman Dave Jones helped him win the Democratic nomination for state insurance commissioner in an otherwise low-profile race. The influence of such endorsements is limited by the inability of the parties to deliver organizational support to the chosen candidates and by high-spending campaigns and the media, but preprimary endorsements may become more significant with the top-two primary system.

## Party Supporters

Besides the official party organizations, a variety of caucuses and clubs are associated with both major parties. The California Republican Assembly is a staunchly conservative statewide grassroots organization that has dominated the Republican Party, thanks to an activist membership. Republican governor Arnold Schwarzenegger, a moderate, had difficulty with the conservatives in his own party. At the 2007 state party convention, he chastised his fellow California Republicans "for their insularity and narrowness," to which they responded "that they'd rather be ideologically principled than pander to moderates."[2] On the Democratic side, liberals dominate through the California Democratic Council, which comprises hundreds of local Democratic clubs organized by geography, gender, race, ethnicity, or sexual orientation.

Party activists such as these are a tiny percentage of the electorate, however. The remaining support base comes from citizens who designate their party affiliations when they register to vote and usually cast their ballots accordingly. Public opinion polls tell us that voters who prefer the Democratic Party tend to be sympathetic to the poor and immigrants; concerned about health care, education, and the environment; in favor of gay rights, gun control, and abortion rights; and supportive of tax increases to provide public services. Those who prefer the Republican Party are more likely to oppose these views and to worry more about big government and high taxes. Of course, many people mix these positions.[3]

Both major parties enjoy widespread support, but the more liberal Democratic Party fares better with blacks, city dwellers, union members, and residents of coastal California and the Sacramento area (see Figure 2.3). Latino voters also favor Democrats, a tendency that was strengthened by Republican support for several statewide initiatives relating to immigration and affirmative action. Voters among most Asian nationalities also lean Democratic, an inclination that has increased in recent years. As with Latinos, Asian interest in the California Republican Party has been weakened by policies and candidates perceived as anti-immigrant. Thanks in large part to the failure of Republicans to win support from minority voters, California is considered a solidly "blue" (Democratic) state, with Democrats holding every statewide office and majorities in the legislature. Unless the Republican party does more to win over minority group voters, demographic trends suggest that the party may be doomed in California.

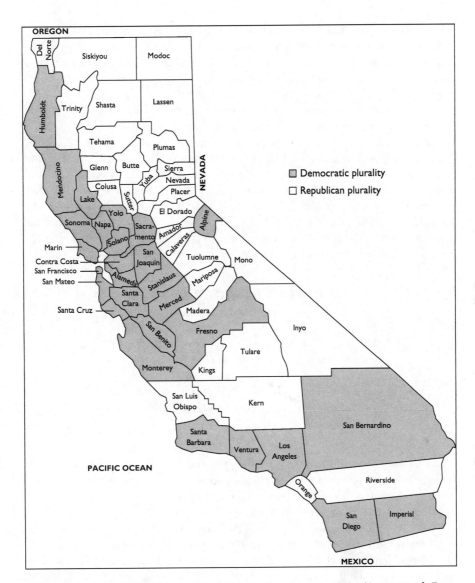

**FIGURE 2.3** California's Partisan Division by County, 2012. (Courtesy of Terry Christensen)

SOURCE: California Secretary of State.

The more conservative Republican Party does better with whites, suburbanites, rural voters, and in Orange County, the Central Valley, and inland California, as well as with older, more affluent voters and with Christian conservatives. These constituencies are more likely to turn out to vote than those that support Democrats, but by 2012, some Republican leaders were worried that the party had declined to such an extent that the advantage in turnout was insufficient. "The California Republican Party has effectively collapsed," declared a prominent Republican political consultant. "It doesn't do any of the things that a political party should do. It doesn't register voters. It doesn't recruit candidates. It doesn't raise money. The Republican Party in the state institutionally has become a small ideological club that is basically in the business of hunting out heretics.… The party is actually shrinking. It's becoming more white. It's becoming older."[4]

In the past, Republican candidates were sometimes successful because they could win the support of Democratic voters thanks to cross-filing (until 1958), charismatic candidates, clever campaigns, and split-ticket voting. But in the 1990s, ticket splitting declined, and instead, voters increasingly voted a straight party-line ticket—either all Democratic or all Republican. This includes decline-to-state voters, who, contrary to common wisdom, are not necessarily independent. Most tilt toward one party or the other, with Democrats enjoying greater support.[5] Some observers assert that the rightward thrust of the Republican Party drove independent voters to the Democrats and was even more important to the Democratic Party's continued success than was winning over minority voters.[6]

## DIRECT DEMOCRACY

Voting for candidates is only one way Californians participate in the political process. To counter the railroad machine's control of state and local governments, the Progressive reformers also guaranteed the people a say through the mechanisms of direct democracy: recall, referendum, and initiative. Referenda and initiatives appear on our ballots as "propositions," with numbers assigned by the secretary of state; local measures are assigned letters by the county clerk.

### The Recall

The least-used form of direct democracy is the **recall**, which empowers voters to remove officeholders at all levels of government between scheduled elections. Advocates circulate a recall petition with a statement of their reasons for wanting a named official to be removed from office. They must collect a specific number of voter signatures within a specific period. The numbers vary with the office in question. At the local level, for example, the number of signatures required varies from 10 to 30 percent of those who voted in the previous local election; these signatures must be collected over periods that vary between 40 and 160 days. A recall petition for a judge or a legislator requires signatures equaling 20 percent of the vote in the last state election, while for state executive officeholders, the figure is 12 percent. In these cases, petitioners have 160 days to collect the signatures. If enough signatures are collected and validated by the secretary of state (for a state officeholder) or by the county clerk (for a local officeholder), an election is held. The ballot is simple: "Shall [name] be removed from the office of [title]?" The recall takes effect if a majority of voters vote yes, and then either an election or an appointment—whichever state or local law requires—fills the vacancy for the office. Elected officials who are recalled cannot be candidates in the replacement election.

Recalling state officeholders is easier in California than in the other seventeen states where recall is possible. Most other states require more signatures, and while any reason suffices in California, other states require corruption or malfeasance by the officeholder. Nevertheless, recalls are rare in California, where the process is most often used in local government, particularly by parents who are angry with school board members. Even so, only a dozen or so recalls are on local ballots in any given year, and only about half of the officials who face recall are removed from office. Only four state legislators have ever been recalled.

Governor Gray Davis is the only statewide official who had ever been recalled. Davis had barely been reelected in November 2002 when opponents launched a recall petition. Thirty-one previous attempts to recall a California governor had failed to make the ballot, and most political observers assumed that the petitioners would be unable to acquire the 897,158 valid signatures required for an election. They underestimated voter discontent, not only with Davis but also with the general condition of California politics. Davis's decline in popularity resulted from his cautious leadership during the state's energy crisis in 2001, a recession, a huge budget deficit, and the inability of the legislature and the governor to agree on solutions to these problems. An aloof personality also contributed to his troubles. His recall opponents discovered a groundswell of support, facilitated by conservative talk radio hosts and the availability of the Internet to circulate petitions.

In July 2003, the secretary of state certified that 1.3 million valid signatures had been gathered—far more than required—and the election was set for October. Ultimately, 135 candidates qualified to run, including actor Arnold Schwarzenegger. His seventy-five-day campaign took the state by storm, gaining far more media and public attention than any other recent election—thanks in part to his status as a movie star. On Election Day, 55.4 percent of the voters said yes to recall, and Schwarzenegger easily outpaced all other replacement candidates with 48.6 percent of the vote. For the first time in California history—and only the second time ever in the United States—a governor had been recalled.

## The Referendum

The **referendum** is another form of direct democracy. A referendum allows the voters to nullify acts of the state government. Referendum advocates have ninety days after the legislature makes a law to collect a number of signatures equal to 5 percent of the votes cast for governor in the previous election (504,760 based on the 2010 vote). Referenda are even rarer than recalls. Of the forty-eight referenda on California ballots since 1912, voters have rejected acts of the government twenty-nine times. A 2004 referendum repealed health-care legislation approved in Governor Davis's last days in office, but in 2012, a referendum that would have repealed a redistricting plan for the state senate failed (see Chapter 5).

## The Initiative

Recalls and referenda are reactions to what elected officials do while initiatives allow citizens to make policy themselves by drafting a new law or a constitutional amendment and then circulating petitions to get it onto the ballot. Qualifying a proposed law requires a number of signatures equal to 5 percent of the votes cast for governor in the last election; constitutional amendments require a number of signatures equal to

8 percent (807,615 based on California's 2010 election). If enough valid signatures are obtained within 150 days, the initiative goes to the voters at the next election or, on rare occasions, in a special election called by the governor. As of 2012, all initiatives are on the November general election ballot only—a move advocated by Democrats because voter turnout is higher in November than in June primary elections. This means that more people participate in these decisions, but it also assures maximum turnout of Democratic voters (see Chapter 3).

The subjects of initiatives vary wildly and are often controversial. In the past, voters have approved limits on bilingual education, banned same-sex marriage, and set standards for the size of chicken cages. Other recent propositions have dealt with tribal gambling (repeatedly), redistricting (repeatedly), DNA sampling, and mental health services. In 2012 voters considered several tax measures, the death penalty, punishment for human (sex) trafficking—and more.

Twenty-three other states provide for the initiative, but few rely on it as heavily as California. Relatively few initiatives appeared on ballots until the 1970s, however (see Table 2.1). Then political consultants, interest groups, and governors rediscovered the initiative, and ballot measures proliferated. The 1988 and 1990 election year ballots witnessed an explosion, with eighteen initiatives on each. In 2012 voters faced a total of twelve initiatives in the primary and general elections.

### Legislative Initiatives, Constitutional Amendments, and Bonds

Propositions can also be placed on the ballot by the state legislature. Such **legislative initiatives** can include new laws that the legislature prefers to put before the voters rather than enact on its own, or proposed **constitutional amendments**, for which voter approval is compulsory. The 2010 top-two primary measure, for example, was

**T A B L E  2.1  The Track Record of State Initiatives**

| Time Period | Number | Number | |
|---|---|---|---|
| | | Adopted | Rejected |
| 1912–1919 | 31 | 8 | 23 |
| 1920–1929 | 34 | 10 | 24 |
| 1930–1939 | 37 | 10 | 27 |
| 1940–1949 | 20 | 7 | 13 |
| 1950–1959 | 11 | 1 | 10 |
| 1960–1969 | 10 | 3 | 7 |
| 1970–1979 | 24 | 7 | 17 |
| 1980–1989 | 52 | 25 | 27 |
| 1990–1999 | 50 | 20 | 30 |
| 2000–2009 | 65 | 20 | 45 |
| 2010–2012 | 23 | 9 | 14 |
| Total | 357 | 120 (33.6%) | 237 (66.4%) |

SOURCE: California Secretary of State.

put on the ballot by the legislature as part of a deal to win the vote of a Republican senator for the proposed budget.

Voter approval is also required when the governor or the legislature seeks to issue **bonds** (borrowing money) to finance parks, schools, transportation, or other infrastructure projects. Few of these proposals are controversial, and more than 60 percent pass with minimal campaigning or spending. In the 2006 and 2008 elections, voters approved $29 billion in bonds for projects ranging from high-speed trains to aid for veterans.

## THE POLITICS OF BALLOT PROPOSITIONS

The proliferation of ballot propositions is hardly the result of a sudden surge in citizen action. Rather, it stems largely from the opportunism of special interests, individual politicians, and public relations firms. Hundreds of millions of dollars have been spent on ballot measures regulating casinos on Native American lands, the most recent of which appeared on the ballot in 2008. In 2010, Pacific Gas and Electric and Mercury Insurance single-handedly funded separate initiatives that were clearly in their self-interest. They were defeated, but Mercury Insurance came back with another initiative in 2012.

Although intended as mechanisms for citizens to shape policy, even the most grassroots-driven initiatives cost half a million dollars to qualify and millions more to mount a successful campaign. "If you pay enough," declared Ronald George, then chief justice of the California Supreme Court, "you can get anything on the ballot. You pay a little bit more and you get it passed."[7] The campaigns for and against the 2008 proposition banning same-sex marriage spent a total of $83 million—much of it coming from out of state, because California is often seen as setting precedents for campaigns elsewhere. Pacific Gas and Electric spent $43 million on its losing 2010 initiative, while tobacco companies spent $66 million in 2006 and $47 million in 2012 defeating initiatives that would have increased tobacco taxes. Total spending for campaigns for or against propositions in any given election year now averages nearly $300 million. Much of it comes from corporations and unions. According to the California Fair Political Practices Commission, "The conclusion is inescapable: A handful of special interests have a disproportionate amount of influence on California elections and public policy."[8]

Besides wealthy individuals such as business magnate Charles Munger (advocating redistricting reform) and high-tech executive Tim Draper (a supporter of school vouchers), politicians also use initiatives to further their own careers or shape public policy. In 1994, Republican governor Pete Wilson sponsored a successful measure on illegal immigration that helped him win re-election. Movie star Arnold Schwarzenegger sponsored a 2002 initiative to fund after-school programs that launched his political career. As governor, he tried to use ballot measures to further his agenda when thwarted by the Democratic majority in the legislature, but his efforts at political and budget reform were rejected by the voters. In 2012, however, Governor Jerry Brown sponsored an initiative to increase state revenues and won voter approval.

Others also take advantage of direct democracy. Public relations firms and **political consultants**, virtual "guns for hire," have developed lucrative careers managing initiative and referenda campaigns; they offer expertise in public opinion polling, computer-targeted mailing, and television advertising—the staples of modern campaigns. Some firms generate initiatives themselves by conducting test mailings and preliminary polls in hopes of snagging big contracts from proposition sponsors. With millions of dollars in campaign spending hanging in the balance, big economic interests gain an advantage over grassroots efforts—surely not what the Progressives intended.

Nevertheless, direct democracy offers hope to those out of power by enabling them to take their case to the public. Stymied by Democratic dominance of the state legislature for so long, conservatives and business interests have often resorted to the initiative process to pursue their agendas, especially regarding taxes (see Chapter 8). Grassroots groups have also won initiative battles in recent years, including funding mental health programs by increasing taxes on the rich and regulating the treatment of farm animals, despite the strong opposition of agribusiness. In 2012 consumers and organic farmers got a proposition requiring labeling genetically engineered foods on the ballot but were defeated by big-spending opponents. Almost every California ballot includes initiatives generated by grassroots groups. Although these measures are often defeated by well-funded corporate interests, at least direct democracy provides such groups an opportunity to make their cases.

Unfortunately, direct democracy does not necessarily result in good laws. Because self-interested sponsors draft initiatives and media masters run campaigns, careful and rational deliberation is rare. Flaws or contradictions in successful initiatives may take years to resolve. This may be done in the process of implementation or through the legislative process. Sometimes the issue goes back to the voters with successor initiatives. Increasingly, however, disputes about initiatives are resolved in state and federal courts, which must rule on whether the initiatives are consistent with other laws and with the state and federal constitutions. In recent years, courts have overturned all or parts of initiatives dealing with illegal immigration, campaign finance, and same-sex marriage (see Chapter 6). Although such rulings seem to deny the will of the voters, the electorate cannot make laws that contradict the state or federal constitutions.

The increased use of direct democracy has also had an impact on the power of our elected representatives. Although we expect them to make policy, their ability to do so has been constrained by initiatives in recent decades. This is particularly the case with the state budget, much of which is dictated by past ballot measures rather than the legislature or the governor.

The proliferation of initiatives, expensive and deceptive campaigns, flawed laws, and court interventions have annoyed voters and policymakers alike. Perhaps as a consequence, two-thirds of all initiatives are rejected (see Table 2.1). Although Californians express anger and frustration with volume of initiatives they face and the expensive and often confusing campaigns, opinion polls report a solid majority in support of direct democracy in concept.[9]

## POLITICAL PARTIES AND DIRECT DEMOCRACY

Authors Mark Baldassare and Cheryl Katz argue that California has evolved into a unique "hybrid democracy," with power divided between elected representatives and the public.[10] Partisan gridlock in Sacramento, voter distrust, and powerful interest groups (see Chapter 4) have resulted in the increased reliance on direct democracy to resolve issues, albeit often imperfectly. California's political parties can't break the gridlock or even control the choice of their own candidates in an electoral system in which money seems to trump party organization. Once elected, our officials seem unable to resolve the issues that confront us. Direct democracy provides an alternative—for political leaders, moneyed interests, and citizens—yet the proliferation of propositions further confounds voters. Does California have too much democracy? Sometimes it seems so. Some voters feel overwhelmed and turned off, but most manage to sift through complex initiatives and seductive campaigns to find the candidates and policies that suit their preferences.

## NOTES

1. Public Policy Institute of California, "California's New Electoral Reforms: How Did They Work?" *Just the Facts*, June 2012, www.ppic.org (accessed August 3, 2012).

2. Peter Schrag, "On Race and Gender, the GOP's Tent Is Teeny," *Sacramento Bee*, September 19, 2007.

3. See Public Policy Institute of California, "California Voter and Party Profiles," *Just the Facts*, August 2011, www.ppic.org (accessed August 3, 2012).

4. Adam Nagourney, "In California, G.O.P. Fights Steep Decline," *New York Times*, July 23, 2012.

5. Edward L. Lascher, Jr., and John L. Korey, "The Myth of the Independent Voter, California Style," *California Journal of Politics and Public Policy* 3, no. 1, 2011.

6. Morris P. Fiorina and Samuel J. Abrams, "Is California Really a Blue State?" in *The New Political Geography of California*, ed. Frederick Douzet, Thad Kousser, and Kenneth P. Miller (Berkeley: Berkeley Public Policy Press, Institute of Governmental Studies, University of California, 2008).

7. Ronald George, "Promoting Judicial Independence," *Commonwealth*, February 2006, p. 9.

8. California Fair Political Practices Commission, *Big Money Talks*, March 2010, www.fppc.ca.gov/reports/Report38104.pdf (accessed August 6, 2012).

9. The Field Poll #2394, October 13, 2011.

10. Mark Baldassare and Cheryl Katz, *The Coming Age of Direct Democracy* (New York: Rowman & Littlefield, 2008).

## LEARN MORE ON THE WEB

Polling data, including archives:
    www.field.com/fieldpoll or "Statewide Survey," www.ppic.org

California's political parties:
    American Independent Party: www.aipca.org
    California Democratic Party: www.cadem.org
    California Republican Party: www.cagop.org
    Green Party of California: www.cagreens.org
    Libertarian Party of California: www.ca.lp.org
    Peace and Freedom Party: www.peaceandfreedom.org

Elections and ballot measures:
    Ballotpedia: www.ballotpedia.org/
    California Voter Foundation: www.calvoter.org
    California Secretary of State: www.sos.ca.gov/elections/elections_j.htm
    League of Women Voters: www.smartvoter.org and www.easyvoterguide
    .org/

## LEARN MORE AT THE LIBRARY

John Allswang. *The Initiative and Referendum in California, 1897–1998*. Stanford, Calif:
    Stanford University Press, 2000.

Center for Government Studies. *Democracy by Initiative*. 2d ed. 2008. www.cgs.org
    (accessed August 6, 2012).

Larry N. Gerston and Terry Christensen, *Recall! California's Political Earthquake*. Armonk,
    N.Y.: M. E. Sharpe, 2004.

## GET INVOLVED

Volunteer or intern for a political party. Contact your local county party offices.

# 3

# California Elections, Campaigns, and the Media

## CHAPTER CONTENTS

**The Voters**

**The Candidates**

**The Money**

**Campaigning California Style**

**The News Media and California Politics**

*Paper Politics*

*Television Politics*

*New Media*

**Elections, Campaigns, and the Media**

A typical California ballot requires voters to make decisions about more than twenty elective positions and propositions. Even the best-informed citizens sometimes find it difficult to choose among candidates for offices they know little about and to decide on obscure and complicated propositions. Political party labels provide some guidance, but candidates, campaigns, and the media are also crucial in the California elections.

Campaigns and the media are especially important because of the mobility that characterizes California society. More than half of all Californians were born elsewhere, and many voters in every California state election are participating for the first time. Residents also move frequently within the state, reducing the political influence of families, friends, and peer groups and boosting that of campaigns and the media.

## THE VOTERS

California citizens who are eighteen years or older are eligible to vote unless they are convicted felons or in mental institutions. Those eligible must **register to vote** at least fifteen days before an election by completing a form available at post offices, fire stations, libraries, and public places where party activists solicit new voters. Registration forms are also available with applications for driver's licenses and at social service agencies or online at www.sos.ca.gov/elections/elections_vr.htm.

Altogether, nearly 23.7 million Californians are eligible to vote. Only 17.1 million (72.3 percent) were registered in 2012, however, and many of those who are registered don't vote. In the gubernatorial election of 2010, only 59 percent of registered voters participated. Turnout is higher in presidential elections. In 2008, 79.4 percent of the state's registered voters participated, although turnout slipped to just 71.3 percent in 2012 election. Far fewer voters participate in June primary elections, however—only 33.3 percent in the 2010 gubernatorial primary and 31 percent in the 2012 presidential primary.

Traditionally, voters go to designated polling places to cast their ballots, but today about half **vote by mail**, having signed up to do so when they register to vote so that ballots are automatically sent to them for every election.

Most of these people simply prefer the convenience of voting by mail given their busy lives; many prefer to deal with the complex ballots at their leisure; and still others vote absentee because campaigns push identified supporters to vote by mail to ensure their participation. With so many more people voting by mail— up to three weeks before Election Day—campaigns have had to change tactics. Rather than a big push in the last few days before the election, they must spread their resources over a longer period.

Voting by mail may have increased participation slightly, but even with this convenience, many Californians choose not to vote. Some don't get around to registering. Millions more who are registered still don't vote. Some are apathetic, some are unaware, and others feel uninformed. Still others believe that voting is a charade because politics "is controlled by special interests." Some people say election information is "too hard to understand," and others are bewildered by all the messages that bombard them during a typical California election. But the reason that people most frequently give for not voting is that they are too busy.[1]

Yet political campaigns are designed to motivate voters to support candidates and causes. This task is complicated, though, because those who vote are not a representative cross-section of the actual population. Non-Latino whites, for example, make up 40 percent of California's population but 66 percent of likely voters. Although Latinos, African Americans, and Asians constitute 60 percent of the state's population, they are only 34 percent of the voters in general elections.[2] This disparity in turnout means that California's voting electorate is not representative of the state's population. The lower participation rate among Latinos and Asians is partly explained by the relative youth of these populations (about one-third of Latinos, for example, are too young to vote) and by the fact that many are not yet citizens.

Language, culture, and socioeconomic status may also be barriers to registration and voting among minority groups. This situation is changing, however;

Latinos were just 8 percent of the state's registered voters in 1978 but are over 20 percent today, and the number continues to rise. Still, voter registration lags among Latino citizens, who comprise an astounding 59 percent of all unregistered voters in California.[3]

Differences in the levels of voter participation do not end with ethnicity. The people most likely to vote are suburban homeowners and Republicans, who tend to be richer, better educated, and older. Lower levels of participation are usually found among poorer, less educated, and younger inner-city residents and Democrats.

According to recent reports, 44 percent of likely voters in California are over the age of fifty-five although this group is 29 percent of the state population, while adults aged eighteen to thirty-four are 33 percent of the population and only 18 percent of likely voters.[4] All this adds up to a voting electorate that is more conservative than the population as a whole, which explains how Republicans sometimes win statewide elections despite the Democratic edge in registration and why liberal ballot measures often fail.

Of course, voting is only one form of political participation. Many people sign petitions, attend public meetings, write letters or e-mails to officials, and contribute money to campaigns. But as we see in Figure 3.1, the number participating diminishes with each form of engagement, and differences among ethnic groups

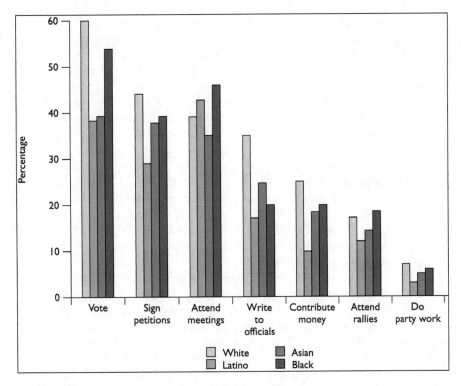

**F I G U R E  3.1**  Political Participation by Ethnic Groups.

SOURCE: From Public Policy Institute of California, "The Ties That Bind," 2004. Reprinted with permission.

persist. As with voting, those who participate most are white, older, more affluent, homeowners, and more highly educated. Does the differential in voting and other forms of participation matter? It seems self-evident that elected officials pay more attention to the concerns of those who participate than those who do not.

## THE CANDIDATES

When we vote, we choose among candidates, but where do candidates come from? Some are encouraged to run by political parties or interest groups seeking to advance their causes. Political leaders looking for allies recruit others, although weak political parties make such overtures less common in California than elsewhere. Most California candidates are self starters with an interest in politics who just decide to run and then seek support. The rising cost and increasing negativity of campaigns have discouraged some people from running, although wealthy individuals who can fund their own campaigns have frequently appeared as candidates in recent years. Most candidates start at the bottom of the political ladder, running for school board or city council, and work their way up, building support as they go. Others gain experience as staff members for elected officials, eventually running for their boss's job. Wealthy candidates sometimes skip such apprenticeships and run directly for higher office, but the voters are often skeptical about their lack of political experience.

Historically, candidates in California have been even less representative of the population than the electorate. Most have been educated white males of above-average financial means. The 1990s brought change, however. Underrepresented groups such as women, racial and ethnic minorities, and gay men and lesbians grew in strength and organization, and structural changes facilitated their candidacies. **Term limits** restricting the number of times legislators could be re-elected were introduced, thus ensuring greater turnover in the state legislature. In addition, **redistricting** after the censuses of 1990 and 2000 resulted in redrawn legislative and congressional districts that gave minority candidates new opportunities at both levels. The redistricting that followed the 2010 census continued that trend.

Latinos have gained the most from these changes, electing a significant number of state legislators and members of Congress. Latinos have also gained representation at the local level, electing more than 1,300 of California's county supervisors, city council members, mayors, and school board members.[5] Most Latino officeholders are Democrats.

Although a smaller minority, African Americans gained a foothold in state politics earlier, including the statewide positions of lieutenant governor and superintendent of public instruction. California Attorney General Kamala Harris is African American, Asian, and Native American. Black representation in the state legislature has shrunk, however, as that of other minorities has increased and California's African American population has not grown proportionately.

Asian Americans remain the most underrepresented of California's racial minorities. In the past, Asian Americans have won election to statewide offices, including U.S. senator, secretary of state, and state treasurer. John Chiang, a

Democrat of Chinese descent, was elected state controller in 2006 and re-elected in 2010. Electing candidates has been difficult for Asian Americans, however, because many are recent immigrants who are not yet rooted in the state's political system and because there are cultural and political differences among the Chinese, Japanese, Vietnamese, Koreans, Indo-Americans, and others. But these groups have generated more candidates in every recent election. Many Asians now serve on city councils and school boards, and ten are members of the state legislature.

Women candidates have been more successful. Both of California's U.S. senators as well as its secretary of state and attorney general are women and San Francisco's Nancy Pelosi is the minority leader of the U.S. Congress. A substantial number of women are state legislators and many of California's city council members, mayors, and county supervisors also are women.

Lesbians and gay men achieved elected office later than any of these groups. Greater bias may be a factor, and in the past, the closeted status of homosexual candidates and elected officials weakened organizing efforts and made gay and lesbian elective successes invisible. Nevertheless, over one hundred openly gay and lesbian individuals have won election to local offices (including twenty judges),[6] and seven serve in the state legislature. John Perez, a gay legislator from Los Angeles, holds the powerful position of Speaker of the Assembly.

Racism and sexism partly explain the underrepresentation of all these groups, but other factors contribute as well. Many members of these groups are economically disadvantaged, which makes it hard to participate in politics, let alone to take on the demands of a candidacy. Women, minorities, and gay men and lesbians are usually not plugged in to the network of lobbyists, interest groups, and big donors that provide funds for California's expensive campaigns. Minorities also have difficulty winning support outside their own groups and may alienate their natural constituencies in the process. The fact that minorities are less likely to vote than whites further reduces their candidates' potential. Nevertheless, organizations within each of these constituencies work to recruit, train, and support candidates, and the diversity of California candidates and elected officials increases with each election.

## THE MONEY

The introduction of primary elections in 1909 shifted the focus of campaigns from political parties to individual candidates. Political aspirants must raise money, recruit workers, research issues, and plot strategy on their own or with the help of expensive consultants rather than with that of political parties, which contribute little in the way of money or staff.

Weak parties mean that candidates must promote themselves, so the cost of running for state assembly or senate often exceeds $1 million. Spending on races for the legislature totaled over $100 million in the 2009–2010 election cycle. Campaigns for statewide offices are even more expensive. Over $254 million was spent on the race for governor in 2010.[7]

Interest groups, businesses, and wealthy individuals provide the money. Much campaign financing is provided by **political action committees (PACs)**, which interest groups use to direct money to preferred campaigns. Legislative leaders such as the speaker of the assembly and the president pro tem of the senate raise huge sums from such sources and channel the money to their allies; individual candidates raise money by asking potential contributors for donations directly and by organizing special fund-raising events, which range from barbecues to banquets and concerts. They also solicit contributions through targeted mailings and the Internet.

Some wealthy candidates finance their own campaigns. Arnold Schwarzenegger provided more than $10 million for his campaigns in 2003 and 2006, but Republican Meg Whitman broke state and national records by spending $142 million of her own money on her campaign for governor in 2010. Voters are skeptical about wealthy candidates who self-finance their campaigns, however, and in the past, most such candidates, including Whitman, have lost.

Concerned about the influence of money and turned off by campaign advertising, Californians have approved a series of initiatives aimed at regulating campaign finance. The **Political Reform Act of 1974** required public disclosure of all donors and expenditures through the **Fair Political Practices Commission (FPPC)**. In 2000, voters approved **Proposition 34**, a legislative initiative setting contribution limits for individuals and committees (see Table 3.1).

Proposition 34 also set voluntary spending limits for candidates (see Table 3.2). Those who accept the limits have their photo and candidate statements published in the official ballot booklets that go to all voters; candidates who decline the limits are excluded 'from the booklet. Most candidates for the

**T A B L E  3.1  Proposition 34 Limits on Contributions to State Candidates, 2011–2012**

| Contributor | Legislature | Statewide except Governor | Governor |
|---|---|---|---|
| Person | $3,900 | $ 6,500 | $26,000 |
| Small contributor committee | $7,800 | $13,000 | $26,000 |
| Political party | No limit | No limit | No limit |

SOURCE: California Fair Political Practices Commission, www.fppc.ca.gov.

**T A B L E  3.2  Voluntary Expenditure Ceilings for Candidates for State Offices, 2011–2012**

| Office | Primary | General Election |
|---|---|---|
| Assembly | $520,000 | $909,000 |
| Senate | 780,000 | 1,169,000 |
| Governor | 7,795,000 | 12,992,000 |
| Other statewide offices | 5,179,000 | 7,795,000 |

SOURCE: California Fair Political Practices Commission, www.fppc.ca.gov.

legislature and statewide offices other than governor comply with the spending limits; those who do not lose the moral high ground to those who do, which may influence voters. There is no limit, however, on how much a candidate can contribute to his or her own campaign, which enables candidates such as Whitman to substantially fund their campaigns.

Like most reforms, Proposition 34 has had unintended consequences. Money is given to political parties to spend on behalf of candidates rather than to the candidates themselves. More significantly, the new spending limits have been subverted by **independent expenditures** by PACs or groups specially organized by political consultants in support of candidates. Independent spending topped $82 million in California's 2010 elections, including over $45 million for the candidates for governor. Jerry Brown, the victor, was the primary beneficiary. Top independent expenditure groups include the Chamber of Commerce, the California Teachers Association, and other union groups.[8] In some campaigns, independent expenditures exceed those of the candidates. Such spending increased exponentially after the U.S. Supreme Court ruled that the First Amendment prohibited government limits on independent expenditures by unions and corporations in 2010. The only restriction on independent expenditures is that they cannot be coordinated with the campaigns of the candidates they support. Because they are not directly associated with the candidates, "independent" mailings and television ads often feature the most vicious attacks on opponents.

Between independent expenditures, PACs with names that cloak their real purpose and backers (the "Senior Advocates League" was funded by business interests rather than senior groups), and PACs that contribute to other PACs to obscure the individuals and interests who are actually funding campaigns, tracking this information—to "follow the money"—has become ever more complex and difficult. Proposition 34 regulations have been condemned as "ineffective" and even cynically deceptive "reforms."[9] Meanwhile, groups like Common Cause continue to seek ways to limit the role of money in politics.

## CAMPAIGNING CALIFORNIA STYLE

Campaign contributors hope to elect allies who will support their interests and expect their money to buy ready access and long-term influence. Candidates deny making specific deals, however, insisting that they and their contributors merely share views on key issues. Millions of dollars flow into candidates' coffers through this murky relationship. In the 2010 election, for example, labor unions generously supported Democrat Jerry Brown, while business interests gave to Meg Whitman.

So much money is needed because California campaigns, whether local or statewide, are highly professionalized. Unable to count on the political parties for funds and support, candidates hire political consultants to recruit workers, raise money, conduct public opinion polls, design advertising, and perform virtually all other campaign activities. These specialists understand the behavior of California voters and use their knowledge to a candidate's benefit.

Television has made campaign management firms indispensable, allowing candidates instant entry into voters' homes. It also enables candidates to put their message across at the exact moment of their choosing—on broadcast or cable TV, between wrestling bouts, during the local news or *Oprah*, or just after *American Idol*, depending on the targeted audience. The efficacy of the medium is proved repeatedly when relatively unknown candidates spend big money on television commercials and become major contenders, as eBay billionaire Meg Whitman did when she saturated the airwaves beginning in late 2009 in the 2010 race for governor. A statewide advertising buy on television may cost $1 million—and one round of ads is never enough.

More than in smaller, more compact states where people are more connected, Californians rely heavily on television for political information. As a consequence, television advertising accounts for a majority of all spending for statewide races in California. In such a big state, it is the only way to reach the mass of voters. At the height of the gubernatorial campaigns, candidates run hundreds of ads a day in California's major media markets. Well-funded initiative campaigns also rely almost exclusively on television advertising, sometimes very effectively. In 2012, an initiative increasing the tax on cigarettes was overwhelmingly supported by the public until the tobacco industry poured $50 million into a confusing and deceptive television ad campaign against the tax and the measure narrowly failed.

Television is too costly for most candidates for legislative and local offices, however. A thirty-second prime-time spot can cost over $20,000 in Los Angeles, and because most television stations broadcast to audiences much larger than a legislative district, the message is wasted on many viewers. Advertising during the day or on cable is cheaper, however, and many legislative candidates have turned to these alternatives. Most, however, have found a more efficient way to spend their money: **direct mail**. Computers have revolutionized political mail by enabling campaign strategists to target selected voters with personal messages.

Direct-mail experts develop lists of voters and their characteristics and then send special mailings to people who share particular qualities. In addition to listing voters by party registration and residence, these experts compile data banks that identify various groups, including liberals and conservatives, ethnic voters, retired people, homeowners and renters, union members, women, gay men and lesbians, and those most likely to vote. Campaigns even do data mining on consumer interests that might predict the political or policy concerns of voters so their mailing can be microtargeted. Once the targets have been identified, campaign strategists can develop just the right message to send to them. Conservatives may be told of the candidate's opposition to gay marriage; liberals may be promised action on the environment. For the price of a single thirty-second television spot, local or legislative candidates can send multiple mailings to their selected audiences.

Television and direct mail dominate California campaigns because they reach the most voters, but the use of these media is not without problems. Because television and direct mail are expensive, campaign costs have risen, as has the influence of major donors. Candidates who are unable to raise vast sums of money are usually left at the starting gate. Incumbent officeholders, who are masters at fund-raising and are well connected to major contributors, become invincible. Furthermore, these media are criticized for oversimplifying issues and emphasizing the negative. Television commercials for ballot measures reduce complicated issues to emotional thirty-second spots aimed at uninformed voters. Candidates' ads and mailings indulge in the same oversimplification, often in the form of attacks on opponents. When the candidates portray each other negatively, voters may feel that they must choose the lesser evil rather than make a decision on the policies and positive traits of the candidates. Voters have grown skeptical of such attacks, yet they are hard to resist and campaign consultants, who are usually blamed for the phenomenon, are certain that the public pays more attention to negative messages than to positive ones.

Candidates also take their campaigns to the Internet, with Web sites and e-mail lists to communicate with the media and with supporters. Campaigns have targeted e-mails to particular constituencies, such as Christian conservatives, and used the Internet to recruit volunteers and solicit donations. The political impact of Internet campaigning is unclear, however. Whereas television and mail enable candidates to reach us whether we're interested or not, the voters themselves must usually initiate contact on the Internet, which limits the audience to those who are already engaged. Campaigns are mining data on Internet users, however, and developing ways to identify potential supporters and get messages and even ads to them online. Interest groups also use e-mail to send campaign messages and mobilize their members.

Overall, California's media-oriented campaigns reinforce both the emphasis on candidates' personalities and voter cynicism. Some people blame such campaigns for declining voter turnout. Contemporary campaigns may also depress voter turnout by aiming all their efforts at regular voters and ignoring those who are less likely to vote—particularly minority or young voters. Although this is a sensible way to use campaign resources, it is not a way to stimulate democracy.

Some candidates try to revive old-fashioned door-to-door or telephone campaigns and get-out-the-vote drives on Election Day. Labor union volunteers have become a force in elections in Los Angeles and San Jose, for example, and the Democratic and Republican parties rely on volunteers to turn out voters for their candidates. Grassroots campaigns have a long and honorable tradition in California, but even in small-scale, local races, they are often up against not only big-money opponents but also the California lifestyle: few people are at home to be contacted, and those who are may let calls go to voice mail or be mistrustful of strangers at their door. For good or ill, candidates need money for their campaigns; those with the most money don't always win, but those with too little rarely even become contenders.

## THE NEWS MEDIA AND CALIFORNIA POLITICS

From candidates and campaigns to public policy, almost everything Californians know about politics—which is not necessarily very much—comes from the news media. They have a profound impact on ideas, issues, and leaders. Until the

1950s, a few family-owned newspapers dominated the media. Then television gave the newspapers some competition while expanding the cumulative clout of the mass media. Today, new media like the Internet and a plethora of ethnic publications also play a role.

## Paper Politics

California's great newspapers were founded in the nineteenth century by ambitious men such as Harrison Gray Otis of the *Los Angeles Times*, William Randolph Hearst of the *San Francisco Examiner*, and James McClatchy of the *Sacramento Bee*. These print-media moguls used their newspapers to boost their communities, their political candidates, and their favored causes. Most were like Otis, an ardent conservative who fought labor unions and pushed for growth while making a fortune in land investments. In the heyday of bosses and machines, his *Los Angeles Times* supported the Southern Pacific Railroad's political machine and condemned Progressive leader Hiram Johnson as a demagogue, as did many other newspapers in the state. Other journalists, however, helped found the Lincoln-Roosevelt League and led the campaign for reform.

After the Progressives triumphed over the machine, newspapers continued to play a crucial role in California politics. In Los Angeles, San Francisco, Oakland, San Jose, and San Diego, Republican publishers used the power of the press—on editorial and news pages—to promote their favorite candidates and causes. They were instrumental in keeping Republicans in office long after the Democrats gained a majority of registered voters.

Change came in the 1970s, when most of California's family-owned newspapers became part of corporate chains. The new managers brought in more professional editors and reporters. News coverage became more objective, and opinion was more consistently confined to the editorial pages, which became distinctly less conservative. The main newspaper in San Diego, the *U-T*, is an exception to this change. Under the ownership of a local businessman who often uses the newspaper to advocate his own interests, the *U-T* is conservative and pro-business on both its news and editorial pages, like the newspapers of half a century ago.[10]

All these newspapers are extremely influential in California politics through the way they cover the news and through editorials expressing the opinion of the publisher or, more commonly, an editorial board made up of journalists. Voters often follow editorial recommendations on candidates and issues for lack of alternative sources of advice, especially on lower-profile races and ballot measures. Nevertheless, today's editorial pages are less influential than they once were as the number of newspapers and their circulation have declined.

At one time, there were hundreds of newspapers in California, with several competing with one another in most large cities. Today, less than a hundred survive, and most cities have just one. But that's not the only change. As a result of the loss of readers and advertisers to other media, the surviving newspapers have shrunk in both news coverage and staffing. The *Los Angeles Times*, for example, now employs less than half as many journalists as it did in 1998.[11]

As a consequence of these changes, newspaper coverage of California politics is less extensive than it once was. Newspapers now share reporters or rely on the Associated Press or the *Los Angeles Times*, which still maintains the largest and most respected Sacramento bureau. Other media, including television and the Internet, have become more important to many people.

## Television Politics

Public opinion surveys report that 37 percent of Californians say they get most of their news and information about politics from television, with 15 percent citing newspapers, 10 percent radio, and 24 percent the Internet.[12] But television coverage of California politics leaves a lot to be desired.

Before Arnold Schwarzenegger was elected governor, not one of California's television stations, other than those based in Sacramento, operated a news bureau in the state capital. Television news editors avoided state political coverage because they believed that viewers wanted big national stories or local features. The minimal television coverage of state politics—a tiny percentage of newscast time, according to various studies—was mainly drawn from newspaper articles, wire service stories, or events staged by politicians, who struggled to gain any coverage at all. Even candidates for governor had a hard time making local news broadcasts, and most television stations declined to broadcast live candidate debates out of fear of low ratings. Cynics pointed out that if television doesn't provide news coverage, candidates are forced to buy advertising time—on television. As a consequence, candidate ads take up more time than news coverage of campaigns during the nightly news on California television stations—and provide a major source of revenue for the stations.

Nevertheless, television coverage of state politics has improved somewhat in the twenty-first century. A movie star governor and his carefully staged media events brought the cameras back to Sacramento. Coverage also increased with the advent of transmission by satellite vans, which made it easier for television stations to send reporters to cover breaking news and major events "live from the Capitol!" without the necessity of investing in permanent Sacramento bureaus. Ongoing conflict between the Republican governor and Democratic majorities in the legislature added drama, as did the state's persistent budget crisis.

Californians who prefer their politics raw—without reporters or commentary—can watch their government in action on the California Channel, now available on 114 cable systems.

## New Media

The traditional print and broadcast media still dominate, but in recent years more alternative sources of news and information have become available to Californians. Nearly seven hundred ethnic broadcasting outlets and publications now serve Californians in Spanish, Vietnamese, Mandarin, and many other languages.[13] Latino newspapers and television and radio stations reach major audiences, especially in Southern California. Many of these ethnic media are virtually obsessed with politics as their communities generate candidates or factional conflict.

Talk radio has also become a political fixture, especially in a state where people spend so much time in their cars. Politics is a hot topic on talk radio, which played a crucial role in stirring up the recall of Governor Gray Davis in 2003.

But the medium with the most spectacular recent impact on politics is the Internet. Access to news and information on the Internet has given audiences exponentially more information and sources and diverted audiences and advertisers from more traditional media, especially newspapers. Thousands of Web sites focus on state or local politics and give citizens direct access to their governments. Blogs by political junkies offer news and opinion and often break stories. Listservs and social networking keep members of traditional interest groups in touch with one another and create whole new communities. Seventy-two percent of Californians have a broadband connection at home and 84 percent regularly use the Internet; 44 percent of Californians cite the Internet as a primary source of political news. Latinos, elders, and lower-income residents are less likely to have access to computers or use the Internet, however, so access is not equally distributed.[14]

## ELECTIONS, CAMPAIGNS, AND THE MEDIA

The influence of money and the media is greater in California politics than in most other states. Candidates must organize their own campaigns, raise vast sums of money, and then take their cases to the people by mail and television. Such campaigns are inevitably personality oriented, with substantive issues taking a back seat to puff pieces or attacks on opponents. The media provide a check of sorts, but declining coverage limits its impact.

All of this takes us back to the issue of declining voter turnout. Presidential elections increase turnout, but only momentarily. Turnout in primaries and non-presidential elections is much lower. Could stronger parties, more news coverage, and more substantive, issue-oriented campaigns revive voter participation? Maybe, but campaign consultants and the media say that they are already giving the public what it wants.

## NOTES

1. California Voter Foundation, "California Voter Participation Survey," March 2005, www.calvoter.org (accessed August 8, 2012).

2. Public Policy Institute of California, "California's Likely Voters," *Just the Facts*, August 2012, www.ppic.org (accessed August 30, 2012).

3. *Ibid.*

4. *Ibid.*

5. National Association of Latino Elected Officials, "2012 Primary Election: California," www.naleo.org (accessed August 9, 2012).

6. Gay and Lesbian Victory Institute, www.victoryinstitute.org/out_officials/ (accessed August 9, 2012).

7. National Institute on Money in Politics, "California 2010," www.followthemoney .org (accessed August 9, 2012).

8. *Ibid.*

9. Dan Walters, "Proposition 34 Only Gave the Appearance of Reform," *San Jose Mercury News*, June 6, 2010.

10. David Carr, "Newspaper as Business Pulpit," *New York Times*, June 10, 2012.

11. "As Cities Downsize from Two Newspapers to Just One, Some Talk of Zero," *New York Times*, March 12, 2009.

12. Public Policy Institute of California, "Californians' News and Information Sources," *Just the Facts*, November 2010, www.ppic.org (accessed August 10, 2012).

13. Marcelo Ballve et al., *Profiles of Ethnic Media: California's New Civic Communicators* (San Francisco: New California Media, 2002).

14. Public Policy Institute of California, "California's Digital Divide," *Just the Facts*, June 2011, www.ppic.org and The Field Poll, Release #2382, June 27, 2011, www.field.com/fieldpollonline/subscribers/ (both accessed August 10, 2012).

## LEARN MORE ON THE WEB

Public opinion polls:
　　Public Policy Institute of California: www.ppic.org
　　The Field Poll: http://field.com/fieldpollonline/subscribers/

Elections, political reform, and campaign finance:
　　California Secretary of State: www.sos.ca.gov
　　California Fair Political Practices Commission: www.fppc.ca.gov
　　California Voter Foundation: www.calvoter.org
　　League of Women Voters: www.ca.lwv.org
　　Smart Voter: www.smartvoter.org
　　National Institute on Money in State Politics: www.followthemoney.org

News on state politics, campaigns, and elections:
　　*California Watch:* www.californiawatch.org
　　*Capitol Weekly:* www.capitolweekly.net
　　*California Report* (radio): www.californiareport.org
　　Rough & Tumble (links to news articles on California politics): www .rtumble.com

Listings of publications and broadcast media in California:
　　ABYZ News Links: www.abyznewslinks.com/uniteca.htm

Blogs—for lively opinion and information on California politics:
　　www.calbuzz.com
　　www.calitics.com (progressive)
　　www.flashreport.org (conservative)

## LEARN MORE AT THE LIBRARY

Sandra Bass and Bruce E. Cain, eds., *Racial and Ethnic Politics in California*, (Berkeley: Berkeley Public Policy Press, Institute of Governmental Studies, University of California, 2008).

Greg Mitchell, *The Campaign of the Century: Upton Sinclair's Race for Governor of California and the Birth of Media Politics*. New York: Random House, 1992.

Ethan Rarick, ed. *California Votes: The 2010 Governor's Race*. Berkeley: Berkeley Public Policy Press, Institute of Governmental Studies, University of California, 2012.

## GET INVOLVED

Volunteer or intern for a campaign. Search for candidates in your district online with www.aroundthecapitol.com or http://votesmart.org/

Register to vote online at http://www.sos.ca.gov/elections/elections_vr.htm.

# 4

# Interest Groups: The Power behind the Dome

## CHAPTER CONTENTS

**The Evolution of Group Power in California**

**Types of Groups**

*Economic Groups*

*Professional Associations and Unions*

*Demographic Groups*

*Single-Issue Groups*

*Public Interest Groups*

**Techniques and Targets: Interest Groups at Work**

*Lobbying*

*Campaign Support*

*Litigation*

*Direct Democracy*

**Regulating Groups**

**Measuring Group Clout: Money, Numbers, and Credibility**

Many people belong to one or more **interest groups**,—organizations formed to protect and promote the shared political objectives of their members. Existing in all shapes and sizes, interest groups range from labor unions, ethnic organizations, and business associations to student unions, environmental entities, and automobile clubs. Whatever their differences, interest groups seek to influence the actions of public policymakers. Sometimes, they are referred to as "special interests" for the special attention they seek and sometimes receive from public officials.

In California, interest groups have prospered and proliferated, and in some ways become more important than political parties. That's because weak political parties and the state's election system provide a fertile political environment for

43

organized groups to exercise influence. Weak political parties leave candidates dependent on groups for campaign contributions, while direct democracy often enables groups to take their issues directly to the voters, circumventing the legislature and other elected policymakers.

Besides exercising their influence through campaign assistance and direct democracy, interest groups also influence legislators in the lobbies beneath the capitol dome. Some observers view these efforts as assisting the legislative process; others see them as manipulating that process.

## THE EVOLUTION OF GROUP POWER
## IN CALIFORNIA

Interest group influence is found throughout California's lengthy constitution. In other states, groups gain advantages such as tax exemptions through acts of the legislature, which can be changed at any time. In California, such protections are often written into the constitution, making alteration difficult because constitutional amendments require the approval of the electorate.

Different interests have benefited throughout California's colorful history. In the early days, the mining industry and ranchers dominated the state's public policy environment. From about 1870 to 1910, the Southern Pacific Railroad monopolized California's economy and politics, with incredible control over both of California's major political parties in the state legislature. Land development, shipping, and horse racing interests next dominated the political landscape through the mid-twentieth century, followed by the automobile and defense industries. Agricultural interests have remained strong through all these periods.

These days, banking and service businesses tower over manufacturing, while high-tech industries have surpassed defense and aerospace. Insurance companies, teachers' associations, physicians' and attorneys' groups, and other vocation-related associations also routinely lobby state government. Agribusiness also remains influential, particularly with respect to water policy and land use. Organized labor and business interests—almost always at odds—continue to battle for preeminence with the legislature and voters. They have been joined by the California Nations Indian Gaming Association, the largest contributor to several ballot propositions that have asked the voters to ratify gaming agreements between the tribes and the state. Narrow social issue groups, such as Gun Owners of California and Mothers Against Drunk Driving (MADD), have entered the fray, along with evangelical, pro-choice, right-to-life, minority, feminist, and gay and lesbian groups. Public interest groups, such as the League of Women Voters, Common Cause, and The Utility Reform Network (TURN), are also part of the ever-growing interest group mix. Pressured by these many organizations and their financial contributions, California politicians often find themselves responding to the demands of interest groups rather than governing them.

## TYPES OF GROUPS

Interest groups vary in size, resources, and goals. At one extreme, groups with narrow and targeted economic benefits tend to have relatively small memberships but substantial financial resources. At the other end of the spectrum, public interest groups with large memberships tend to have little money. A few, such as the Consumer Attorneys of California (CAC), whose membership consists of 3,000 trial lawyers, have the dual advantage of being both large and well funded. Others, such as the Consumers for Auto Reliability and Safety (CARS), operate on a shoestring. Still others, such as the California Teachers Association and California Chamber of Commerce, have more members paying dues than the state Democratic and Republican parties.

### Economic Groups

**Economic groups** that seek various financial gains or hope to prevent losses dominate the state's interest group environment. Every major corporation in the state, from Southern California Edison to the California Northern Railroad, is represented in Sacramento either by its own lobbyists or by lobbying firms hired to present the corporation's cases to policymakers. Often, individual corporations or businesses with similar goals form broad-based associations to further their general objectives. These umbrella organizations include the California Manufacturers and Technology Association, the California Business Alliance (for small enterprises), the California Bankers Association, and the California Council for Environmental and Economic Balance (for utilities and oil companies). The California Chamber of Commerce alone boasts 16,000 member companies with one-fourth of the state's private sector workforce. Each year the Chamber publishes a list of "job killer" bills under consideration and then produces a report on the final outcome which shows defeat of most of the list either by the legislature or governor's veto. In 2011, the Chamber was successful on eleven of twelve bills it opposed.

Agribusiness is particularly active, because farming depends on the government on issues such as water availability and the regulation of pesticides. The giant farming operations maintain their own lobbyists, but various producer groups also form associations. Most of the state's winemakers, for example, are represented by the 1,000-member Wine Institute. The California Cotton Ginners Association has only forty-two members, yet produces 700 million bales of cotton annually. Broader organizations, such as the California Farm Bureau Federation, one of the state's most powerful lobby groups, speak for agribusiness in general by representing 85,000 members with crops in excess of $40 billion in value.

Recently, high-tech industries have asserted their interests on issues ranging from Internet taxation and H-1B visas for foreign workers to transportation and public education. Organizations such as TechNet, the Silicon Valley Leadership Group, and the American Electronics Association have lobbied for regulatory changes, tax relief, research and development tax credits, "green" incentives in new areas such as solar energy, and other changes. The tech-heavy Silicon Valley

Leadership Group alone represents 375 companies that provide $3 trillion worth of services and products in the global economy, exceeding the entire gross domestic product of France.

## Professional Associations and Unions

Professional associations such as the California Medical Association (CMA), the California Association of Realtors (CAR), and the Consumer Attorneys of California (CAOC) are among the state's most active groups, and they are regularly among the largest campaign contributors. Other professionals, such as chiropractors, dentists, and general contractors, also maintain active associations. Because all these professionals serve the public, many promote their concerns as broader than self-interest. Their credibility is further enhanced by expertise they possess in their respective fields.

Teachers' associations and other public employee organizations fall somewhere between business associations and labor unions. Their members view themselves as professionals but in recent years have increasingly resorted to traditional labor union tactics, among them collective bargaining, strikes, and political campaign donations. Other public workers, including the highway patrol and state university professors, have their own organizations.

Unions have done well in California, which ranks sixth (tied with Oregon) among the fifty states in per capita union membership. Unions here represent 17 percent of the workforce, compared with 12 percent nationwide. Traditional labor unions represent nurses, machinists, carpenters, public utility employees, and dozens of other occupations. In the past few years, they have persuaded the legislature to enact the nation's first paid family leave program, allowing workers to take leave from their jobs for up to six weeks, and provide paid paternity leave, which also was the first program of its kind in the nation. The laws drew the wrath of the California Chamber of Commerce, which predicted that they would create hardship for businesses, yet only a fraction of those eligible to participate actually do so.[1]

Perhaps the most controversial union in state politics is the California Correctional Peace Officers Association (CCPOA), which contributed more than $600,000 to the reelection campaign of Governor Gray Davis in 2002, just before the governor signed a three-year pay increase of 35 percent in the midst of a huge state budget deficit. The agreement added fuel to the recall accusation that Davis was little more than a tool of major contributors. In 2004 Governor Arnold Schwarzenegger renegotiated the contract and won a slight modification in the pay raises. Still, the CCPOA has persevered its own interests. In 2008 the union funneled $1.8 million into a campaign to help defeat a ballot proposition which would have provided drug treatment and rehabilitation programs for many nonviolent drug offenders who otherwise would be sent to prison.

## Demographic Groups

Groups that depend more on membership numbers than on money can be described as **demographic groups**. Based on characteristics that distinguish their members from other segments of the population, such as their ethnicity, gender, or age, such groups usually have an interest in overcoming discrimination. Most racial and ethnic organizations fall into this category.

Virtually all of California's minorities have organizations that represent their voice. One of the earliest was the Colored Convention, which fought for the rights of African Americans in California in the nineteenth century. Today, several such groups advocate for African Americans, Asian Americans, and Native Americans. The United Farm Workers (UFW), GI Forum, Mexican American Legal Defense Fund (MALDEF), and Mexican American Political Association (MAPA) represent Latinos.

The National Organization for Women (NOW), EMILY's List (Early Money Is Like Yeast), and National Women's Political Caucus (NWPC) actively support women candidates and feminist causes. Unlike some of the other statewide organizations, these groups are better organized at the local level than at the state level, however.

Several organizations have become prominent over the definition of sexual equality. Gay rights groups have increased in numbers and voice in recent years, particularly over the issue of gay marriage. Equality California, the largest, has worked to elect gay legislators, obtain passage of equal rights legislation, and pursue gay marriage through both the courts and the legislative process. They have been opposed by groups like Campaign for California Families, which define marriage as a union only between a man and woman.

With California's aging population heavily dependent on public services, this demographic also plays a role in state politics. Organizations such as AARP (formerly the American Association of Retired Persons), with 3 million members in California, have achieved a high profile in state politics, particularly on health-care issues.

## Single-Issue Groups

The groups discussed so far tend to have broad bases and deal with a wide range of issues. Another type of interest group operates with a broad base of support for the resolution of narrow issues. **Single-issue groups** push for a specific question to be decided on specific terms. They support only candidates who agree with their particular position on an issue. The California Abortion Rights Action League (CARAL), for example, endorses only candidates who support a woman's right to choose (pro-choice), whereas antiabortion (or pro-life) groups such as the ProLife Council work only for candidates on the opposite side. Likewise, the Howard Jarvis Taxpayers Association evaluates candidates and ballot propositions solely in terms of whether they meet the association's objective of no unnecessary taxes and no wasteful government spending. Antitax groups have been very effective, especially with Republican legislators.

A single-interest group's potential ability to deliver a solid bloc of voters on a controversial issue can affect the outcome of an election and thus enhance its clout, at least on a temporary basis. That's what happened in 1994 when then Republican Governor Pete Wilson sailed to reelection on the tail wind of "Save Our State," an anti-immigrant proposition supported by the California

Coalition for Immigration Reform. An exception occurred in 2008, when anti-gay groups qualified and campaigned heavily for **Proposition 8**, a proposed constitutional amendment designed to overturn a state supreme court decision that had legalized same-sex marriage.[2] Advocates urged voters to use presidential candidate positions on the proposition as a guide to their presidential election votes. Barack Obama opposed the measure, yet he won California handily as the initiative squeaked by.

## Public Interest Groups

Although virtually all organized interest groups claim to speak for the broader public interest, some groups clearly seek no private gain and thus more correctly can claim to be **public interest groups**. These groups are distinguished from other organizations by the fact that they pursue goals to benefit society, not just their members.

Some public interest groups, such as California OneCare, have been instrumental in the fight for health-care reform. Others, such as The Utility Reform Network (TURN), monitor rate requests by the utilities before the state Public Utilities Commission. In 2010, TURN led a coalition of consumer groups against a PG&E-sponsored ballot proposition that would have made it very difficult for municipalities to purchase renewable power.

Environmental organizations such as the Sierra Club and Friends of the Earth have been very active in California on water management, offshore oil drilling, air pollution, transportation, and pesticide use. Another important concern of these groups is land use, both for private development in sensitive areas and for public lands, which make up half the state. Surveys have reported that one in nine Californians claims membership in an environmental group.[3] The Sierra Club alone has more than 1.4 million members.

Other public interest groups, such as California Public Interest Research Group (CALPIRG), the California Budget Project, Common Cause, and the League of Women Voters, focus on governmental reform, campaign finance, and voter participation.

A final type of public interest group isn't really a group at all: local governments. Cities, school districts, special districts, and counties all lobby the state government—on whose funds they depend heavily—through the League of California Cities, the California School Boards Association (CSBA), and the California State Association of Counties (CSAC). Dozens of cities and counties employ their own lobbyists in Sacramento, as do other governmental agencies. One study found that local governments collectively spend more on lobbying than do organized labor, oil companies, or businesses.[4] They also endorse ballot measures that affect their interests and, on rare occasions, even sponsor initiatives.

Unlike other groups, cities and counties cannot make campaign contributions, but they can speak out. In 2010, local governments banded together to promote **Proposition 22, the Local Taxpayers, Public Safety and Transportation Act**, an initiative to keep the state government from borrowing or raiding funds that voters have dedicated to public safety.

## TECHNIQUES AND TARGETS:
## INTEREST GROUPS AT WORK

Interest groups seek to influence public policy. To do this, they must persuade policymakers. The legislature, the executive branch, the courts, the bureaucracy, and sometimes the people are thus the targets of the various techniques these groups may use. Their primary weapons include lobbying, campaign support, litigation, and direct democracy.

### Lobbying

The term **lobbying** refers to the activity that once went on in the foyers adjacent to the legislative chambers. Advocates for various causes or issues would buttonhole legislators on their way in or out of the chambers and make their cases. This still goes on in the lobbies and hallways of the capitol, as well as in nearby bars and restaurants and wherever else policymakers congregate. Lobbyists are so integral to the legislative process that they are commonly referred to as members of the "third house," alongside the assembly and senate.

Until the 1950s, lobbying was a crude and completely unregulated activity. Lobbyists lavished food, drink, gifts, and money on legislators in exchange for favorable votes. Today's lobbyists, however, are experts on the legislative process. Many have served as legislators or staff for legislators. Often, they focus on legislative committees and leaders, lobbying the full legislature only as a last resort.

Unlike old-time lobbyists, today's advocates must be well informed to be persuasive. When inexperienced legislators are unable to grasp major issues, lobbyists fill the void, often by actually writing proposed legislation and assembling the coalitions of legislators necessary to pass it. One study during the 2007–2008 legislative session found that 60 percent of the bills that became laws had been introduced by legislators on behalf of lobbyists.[5] Today's lobbyists still use money, but less cavalierly than in the past, instead strategically contributing to campaigns. Legislators and lobbyists alike assert that contributions buy access, not votes, but the tie between money and access can be powerful in its own right. "The bottom line," one strategist states, is that "the system favors the moneyed—and there's been no sign of political reform."[6] All of this makes lobbying not only a highly specialized profession but also an expensive activity. As an example, during the 2011 session, lobby firms spent about $286 million just to influence the legislature alone—up from $151 million in 2009. That averages $2.4 million per legislator.[7]

Although most lobbying activity is focused on the legislature, knowledgeable professionals also target the executive branch, from the governor down to the bureaucracy. The governor not only proposes the budget but also must respond to thousands of bills that await his or her approval or rejection. In the process, the governor frequently meets with lobbyists in an effort to find common ground on proposed legislation.[8]

Bureaucrats also are targets of astute interest groups. The bureaucracy must interpret new laws and make future recommendations to the governor and legislature. Moreover, on questions ranging from tax exemptions to coastal access to energy regulations, bureaucrats often have the final say on how laws will work. One study on the implementation of AB 32, the Global Warming Solutions Act of 2006, found energy interests lobbying the California Air Resources Board more than the governor or legislature to gain favorable regulations. In the words of one lobbyist, "I'm not going to say we love the thing (AB 32), but if that's the way the state wants to go … we want to make sure that we write regulations that we can comply with and are feasible to do."[9] Sometimes lobbyists will go so far as to offer "talking points" to help bureaucrats justify their decisions on public matters. "It's called 'spoon feeding,'" a lobbyist recently explained to a California coastal commissioner regarding a matter before the commission, "but we're happy to do it."[10]

Lately, the public has become a target of lobbying, too. In media-addicted California, groups have begun making their cases through newspaper and television advertising between elections. Health care, education, energy, Indian gaming, and other issues have been subjects of costly media campaigns with the intent to motivate voters to communicate with state leaders.

**Professional Lobbyists.** Between 1977 and 2011, the number of registered lobbyists in Sacramento nearly doubled, from 582 to about 1,200, including about fifty former legislators. That's about ten lobbyists per legislator. State law prevents former legislators from lobbying for one year after they leave office, but as one legislator has noted, "I would certainly be available to give people political advice."[11] Even at that, legislators often wait out the transition year by serving as "consultants"—one more example of the blurry connection between those in and out of elected office.

Most lobbyists represent a particular business, union, organization, or group. Others are **contract lobbyists**, advocates who work for several clients simultaneously. Whether contract or specialized, more and more lobbyists make a career of their professions, accruing vast knowledge and experience. These long-term professionals became even more powerful when term limits eliminated senior legislators with countervailing knowledge, although some lobbyists complain that term limits mean they must constantly reestablish their credibility with new decision makers. One prominent lobbyist, however, explains his lack of concern about term limits or other reforms: "Whatever your rules are, I'm going to win."[12]

**Nonprofessional Lobbyists.** Some groups can't afford to hire a lobbyist, so they rely on their members instead. Even groups with professional help use their members on occasion to show elected officials the breadth of their support. Typically, this sort of lobbying is conducted by individuals who live in the districts of targeted legislators, although groups sometimes lobby en masse, busing members to the capitol for demonstrations or concurrent lobbying of many elected officials.

Such grassroots efforts by nonprofessionals have special credibility with legislators, but well-financed groups have learned to mimic grassroots efforts by forming front groups or "Astroturf" organizations that conceal their real interests. In 2009, for example, representatives of pornography filmmakers flooded the capitol for hearings on a bill that would have hiked taxes on the industry from 8 percent to 25 percent, adding $665 million to the beleaguered state coffers. Bill opponents included spokespersons from the Free Speech Coalition (FSC), an adult industry-funded group purportedly concerned with government efforts to limit free speech, regardless of the topic or issue. In this case, the FSC representatives argued that the tax would discriminate against those with different opinions. Through this vehicle, the porn industry appeared less self-serving and provided the logic for legislators to defeat the bill.

## Campaign Support

Most groups also try to further their cause by helping sympathetic candidates win election and reelection, commonly through financial contributions to their campaigns. Groups with limited financial resources do so by providing volunteers to go door-to-door or to serve as phone-bank callers for candidates. Labor unions typically fall into this category, along with public education interests. Business groups, however, tend to be the most successful in having their way through generous financial support.

Take the issue of consumer protection from cell phone companies. In general, the telecommunications industry has thwarted efforts to make fees transparent, eliminate monthly charges for unlisted numbers, and ease consumer ability to reject phone books according to a recent study.[13] Much of that success is due to the campaign support from AT&T. State records show that between 2004 and 2011, AT&T spent $36.8 million attempting to influence lawmakers three times as much as the next closest company. In 2011 alone, every single member of the legislature received a campaign contribution from the telecommunications giant.[14] Table 4.1 shows the largest campaign contributor groups for 2010.

**T A B L E 4.1   Top Ten Campaign Contributor Groups, 2010**

| Category | Money |
| --- | --- |
| Electric utilities | $50,954,029 |
| Public-sector unions | 45,763,576 |
| General trade unions | 28,928,580 |
| Party committees | 25,135,721 |
| Insurance | 24,653,667 |
| Candidate committees | 22,544,852 |
| Securities & investment | 19,885,802 |
| Pro-environmental policy | 18,903,579 |
| Oil & gas | 18,766,717 |
| Lawyers & lobbyists | 14,343,096 |

SOURCE: Institute on Money in State Politics, www.followthemoney.org.

Campaign contributors claim that their money merely buys them access to decision makers. The press and the public often suspect a more conspiratorial arrangement, however, and evidence of money-for-vote trades has emerged in recent years. In 1994, fourteen people, including five state legislators, were convicted of providing favors in exchange for campaign contributions. In another instance Chuck Quackenbush, California's elected insurance commissioner, was forced to resign in 2000 after he let insurance companies accused of wrongdoing avoid big fines by contributing to foundations that spent the money on ads and other activities featuring the commissioner. And in 2005, Secretary of State Kevin Shelley resigned from his office after several allegations of illegal activities, including campaign contributions from a company that was awarded a major grant from his office.

As a result of these scandals, politicians and contributors probably exercise greater caution. The high cost of campaigning in California, though, means that candidates continue to ask and lobbyists and interest groups continue to give. Of significance, however, is that the campaign funds come from a variety of interest groups, as well as other sources.

## Litigation

**Litigation** is an option when a group questions the legality of legislation, and in recent years many groups have turned to the courts for a final interpretation of the law. Groups have challenged state laws, regulations, and actions by the executive branch in court. In 2010, for example, the California Nurses Association successfully sued to force Governor Arnold Schwarzenegger to comply with a new state law that reduced the nurse-to-patient ratio. Although the governor lost that battle, he won another when he fended off a court challenge by the powerful California Teachers Association because he rescinded an earlier promise to return $2 billion he had denied the schools the previous year.

Over the years, interest groups have also raised legal challenges to several successful ballot measures—including measures on immigration, affirmative action, campaign finance, bilingual education, and same-sex marriage—hoping that the initiatives would be declared unconstitutional. Even if a group loses its case, it may be able to delay the implementation of a new law or at least establish a principle for debate in the future. In 2001 MALDEF challenged the legislature's redistricting plan, claiming under representation of Latinos. Although the legislature's plan prevailed, MALDEF's tactic kept the issue on the public agenda throughout the decade, helping to set the stage for more favorable redistricting consideration in 2011.

## Direct Democracy

In his 1911 inaugural address, Governor Hiram Johnson championed direct democracy to "place in the hands of the people the means by which they may protect themselves." He and his fellow Progressives envisioned the public as the ultimate custodian of the legislative process. A century later, however, only broad-based or well-financed groups have the resources to collect the necessary signatures or to pay for expensive campaigns. **Direct democracy** gives interest groups the opportunity to promote their policy proposals through initiatives and referenda.

Sometimes interest groups mobilize to gain passage of a ballot proposition; other times they work to defeat one. In 1998, for example, tribal supporters of gambling on Indian lands spent $10 million qualifying an initiative for the ballot in just thirty days—the most expensive petition drive in history. The subsequent campaign on the proposition itself also broke records, with the two sides spending a total of $96 million. The voters ultimately approved the initiative. Since then, the costs have gone up. In 2008 the voters were asked to ratify four agreements allowing for 17,000 more slot machines in Indian casinos in addition to the 62,000 already in place, providing the state with $450 million in new revenues. The pro-gaming interests spent more than $150 million on campaign activities—far exceeding the "no" side, which spent less than $40 million. The ballot propositions sailed through.

Big money was spent against another initiative in 2012 when the tobacco industry marshaled nearly $50 million against Proposition 29, which sought to increase tobacco taxes by $1.00 per cigarette package. Health and environmental interests were able to raise only $12 million in a losing battle.

But the largest campaign war chests don't always win. For example, utility giant PG&E spent more than $3 million in 2010 gathering signatures for Proposition 16, the so-called Taxpayers Right to Vote Act. The proposal was actually a thinly veiled effort to change the state constitution to require any municipal power company to get a two-thirds vote of the people before buying renewable energy. PG&E poured more than $46 million into the effort against about $90,000 spent by the "no" side. The proposal was defeated, even though the opponents were outspent by a margin of 19,565 to 1.

The recall is also sometimes used by interest groups, usually to remove local elected officials. Teachers' unions, conservative Christians, and minority groups have conducted recall campaigns against school trustees, for example. These efforts, however, pale in comparison with the recall effort against Governor Gray Davis. The People's Advocate, a conservative antitax group, was among the leading forces early in that recall effort. During the campaign, groups ranging from the Howard Jarvis Taxpayers Association to the League of Conservation Voters weighed in on the issue.

## REGULATING GROUPS

Free spending by interest groups and allegations of corruption led to the Political Reform Act of 1974 (introduced in Chapter 3), an initiative sponsored by Common Cause. Overwhelmingly approved by the voters, the law requires politicians to report their assets, disclose contributions, and declare how they spend campaign funds. Other provisions compel lobbyists to register with the secretary of state, file quarterly reports on their campaign-related activities, and reveal the beneficiaries of their donations. The measure also established the **Fair Political Practices Commission (FPPC)**, an independent regulatory body, to monitor these activities. When the commission finds incomplete or inaccurate reporting, it may fine the violator. Of greater concern than the financial penalty, however, is the bad press for those who incur the commission's reprimand.

The voters approved new constraints in 1996, when they enacted strict limits on interest groups' practice of rewarding supportive legislators with travel and generous fees for speeches. However, this legislation was soon challenged, creating an atmosphere of uncertainty. In 2000 voters approved yet another initiative which placed new constraints on political action committees and attempted to limit contributions to political campaigns. Yet between self-financed campaigns and the vigorous activities of groups engaged in independent expenditures, any thoughts of reduced spending quickly vanished.

## MEASURING GROUP CLOUT: MONEY, NUMBERS, AND CREDIBILITY

Campaign regulations are generally intended to reduce the disproportionate influence of moneyed interests in state politics, but economic groups still have the advantage. Their stable of resources gives them the staying power to outlast the enthusiasm and energy of grassroots groups.

Public interest groups and demographic groups, however, gain strength from numbers, credibility, and motives other than self-interest. Occasionally they prevail, such as in 1998, when children's groups and health groups overcame a financial disadvantage to pass Proposition 10, a cigarette tax dedicated to children's health programs, and in 2010, when financially impotent public interest groups won the Proposition 16 battle against PG&E. More commonly, interest groups affected by potentially harmful new costs rise to the occasion, as was the case in 2006, when the oil and tobacco industries spent nearly $200 million and reversed public opinion—and the votes—on measures to tax oil and increase tobacco taxes.

How powerful are interest groups and their lobbyists? It's hard to tell, but one informal survey of twelve first-time legislators reported that lobbyists wrote 70 percent of the bills they proposed,[20] perhaps reflecting the extent that new legislators are most vulnerable to interest group activity.

Whatever the balance among groups, they are central to California politics. In a political environment characterized by weak political parties and direct democracy, California's myriad interests have plenty of opportunity to thrive.

## NOTES

1. *California Business Issues, 2004* (Sacramento: California Chamber of Commerce, 2004), p. 77; also see "Few Take State's Family Leave," *San Jose Mercury News*, July 4, 2006, pp. 1C, 9C.

2. The ruling was *In re Marriage Cases*, S147999.

3. Public Policy Institute of California, *Statewide Survey*, June 2000, www.ppic.org.

4. "Cities, Counties, Pay Price for Capitol Clout," *Los Angeles Times*, September 10, 2007, pp. B1, B4.

5. "How Our Laws Are Really Made," *San Jose Mercury News*, July 11, 2010, pp. A1, A6, A7.

6. "Special Interests: How They Get around Voter-Approved Limits on Campaign Contributions," *San Francisco Chronicle*, February 11, 2008, pp. A1, A6.

7. "Lobbying of Legislators Sets Record," *Los Angeles Times*, March 6, 2012, pp. AA1, AA4.

8. See "A Lobbyist by Any Other Name?" *San Jose Mercury News*, May 20, 2005, pp, 1A, 17A.

9. "Lobbyists Heat Up over Climate Law," *Sacramento Bee*, July 12, 2010, pp. A1, A10.

10. "E-mails Put California Coastal Commissioner in an Awkward Spot," *Los Angeles Times*, July 10, 2010, p. AA3.

11. "Elective Office Improves a Resume," *Los Angeles Times*, November 24, 2006, pp. B1, B11.

12. Douglas Foster, "The Lame Duck State," *Harper's*, February 1994.

13. "Business Interests Have an Edge in Lobbying," *San Francisco Chronicle*, December 26, 2011, pp. A1, A11.

14. "AT&T Is Dialed In to Sacramento," *Los Angeles Times*, April 22, 2012, pp. A1, A17.

15. Foster, *op. cit.*

## LEARN MORE ON THE WEB

California Association of Realtors (CAR):
 www.car.org

California Chamber of Commerce:
 www.calchamber.com

California Labor Federation:
 www.calaborfed.org

Common Cause:
 www.commoncause.org

Howard Jarvis Taxpayers Association:
 www.hjta.org

Latino Issues Forum:
    www.lif.org
League of Women Voters of California:
    www.ca.lwv.org
Sierra Club:
    www.sierraclub.org/ca

## LEARN MORE AT THE LIBRARY

Mark Arax and Rick Wartzman. *The King of California.* New York: Public Affairs Press, 2003.

Derek Cressman. *The Recall's Broken Promise: How Big Money Still Runs California Politics.* Sacramento, CA: The Poplar Institute, 2007.

Frank Norris. *The Octopus.* New York: Doubleday and Company, 1901.

Stephanie S. Pincetl. *Transforming California: A Political History of Land Use and Development.* Baltimore, MD: The Johns Hopkins University Press, 1999.

Arthur H. Samish and Bob Thomas. The Secret Boss of California. New York: Crown Books, 1971.

Dan Walters and Jay Michael. *The Third House.* Berkeley: Berkeley Public Policy Press, Institute of Governmental Studies, University of California, 2002.

## GET INVOLVED

Volunteer or intern for an interest group in your community—just search on the Internet for the one that interests you.

# 5

# The Legislature: The Perils of Policymaking

## CHAPTER CONTENTS

Thousands of bills are passed in the California legislature every year. Some are narrow in focus, such as a law that bans children under eighteen from using tanning beds (passed in 2011). Others are sweeping in impact, like the first-of-its kind Homeowners Bill of Rights (passed in 2012). Some of these laws may seem trivial to the casual observer, but the bottom line is that the legislature is responsible for tackling the state's problems, big and small.

Of course, the legislature does not act in a policymaking vacuum; rather, it must share power with the other branches of government, particularly the executive branch. In addition, the legislature has internal problems to manage, due to political—and philosophical—battles not only between Democrats and Republicans, but also internally between assembly Democrats and senate Democrats and assembly Republicans and senate Republicans. As one beleaguered assembly

57

member once said, "More times than not, it seems that we have four political parties in the legislature alone!" Partisanship and ideological schisms fracture the legislative process in California, and these stark divisions often leave the body tied in political knots.

Then there's the question of public policy priorities. Some observers have wondered in recent years how the legislature could immerse itself in issues such as regulations on imported kangaroo leather and banning shark fins, yet seemingly avoid questions about tax reform, water policy, underfunded public education, and a frayed infrastructure. It's no wonder that a 2012 public opinion survey found a whopping 71 percent of likely voters critical of the state legislature—a disapproval rating nearly twice as high as that for Governor Jerry Brown.[1] Still, the legislature was established as the state institution most directly linking the people with their government. The question is, does it still do its job in the twenty-first century?

## THE MAKING AND UNMAKING OF A MODEL LEGISLATURE

Structurally and numerically, much of today's state legislature parallels its original design and intent. But a series of circumstances in the state's political environment have left the legislative branch considerably different than its national counterpart.

### A Little History

California's first constitution, in 1849, provided a **bicameral (two-house) legislature** similar to the U.S. Congress. When the constitution was revised thirty years later, the senate was fixed at forty members serving four-year terms (with half the body elected every two years); the assembly was set at eighty members serving two-year terms. Those numbers and terms of office continue to this day. Throughout the first century of governance, legislators met on a part-time basis, with budgets crafted in two-year increments—characteristics that would change over time.

Beginning in 1926, the organization of the legislature paralleled that of the U.S. Congress. Assembly members, like their counterparts in the House of Representatives, were elected on the basis of population, and senators were elected by county in the same way that each state has two U.S. senators.[2] The large number of lightly populated counties north of the Tehachapi Mountains enabled the rural north to dominate the state senate despite Southern California's growth. By 1965, twenty-one of the forty state senators in California represented only 10 percent of the population; Los Angeles County, then home to 35 percent of the state's residents, had but a single state senator.

### The Shift toward Professionalism

Then came change. The U.S. Supreme Court's **Reynolds v. Sims** decision in 1964 ordered all states to organize their upper houses by population rather than by county or territory. In California, urban and southern representation increased dramatically, with rural and northern areas experiencing a corresponding decline. The new legislators were younger, better educated, more ideological, and with more varied ethnic and gender backgrounds. The transition to modernity was completed in 1966, when the voters created a full-time legislature with full-time salaries.

These days, the legislature meets an average of more than two hundred days per year, with full-time salaries to match. As of 2013, the legislators' base salary is $90,526, the highest among the fifty states. Perks push annual incomes close to $120,000.[3] Only nine other states have full-time legislatures.[4]

## Redistricting: Keeping and Losing Control

By law, every ten years after the national census, the state realigns congressional and state legislative districts to have approximately the same populations. This process is known as **redistricting**. Until 2011, redistricting had been carried out by the legislature, as in most states. Consequently, the partisan composition of the legislature remained almost identical throughout the decade because the districts contained artificially high numbers of Democrats or Republicans, reflecting the parties of the incumbents. For example, after the 2001 redistricting process, one senate district was two hundred miles in length, while others appeared almost as a Rorschach inkblot personality test. To many the process appeared to be little more than an "incumbency protection plan."[5] As one legislator complained, "What happened to drawing lines for the people of the state rather than ourselves?"[6] During the entire decade between 2001 and 2010, only 1 of the 173 seats (120 in the state legislature and 53 in Congress) changed party hands.

In 2008, Governor Arnold Schwarzenegger joined with Common Cause, the League of Women Voters, and other reform groups to craft **Proposition 11, the Voters FIRST Initiative**. The ballot proposal placed redistricting in the hands of a fourteen-member independent commission composed of five Democrats, five Republicans, and four members not affiliated with either major party. Similar proposals had been defeated by the voters on seven previous occasions. This time, the voters approved the measure.

As of January 1, 2010, California's population was estimated at 38,600,000. So, during 2011, the state's new **Citizens Redistricting Commission** realigned legislative districts to be equal in size once again—482,500 for each assembly district and 965,000 in each senate district. Unlike the legislature's previous efforts, however, the Commission considered community geography and neighborhood compositions over political advantages associated with incumbency. Figures 5.1 and 5.2 show the same area of Southern California after the legislature's redistricting in 2001 and after the commission's work in 2011. Most new districts are much more compact than their predecessors.

With a new redistricting system in place, it remains to be seen whether the legislature will become less partisan and more effective. Table 5.1 displays the partisan breakdown of the legislature since 1985.

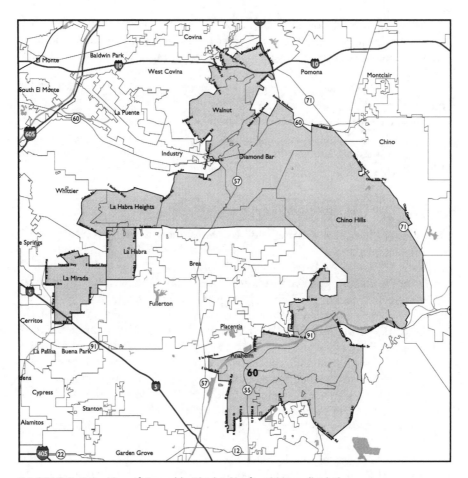

**FIGURE 5.1**   Map of Assembly District 60 after 2001 redistricting.

## Term Limits

For some time, the public has been critical of the legislature's inability to solve thorny issues and pass on-time budgets. In 1990, the voters passed **Proposition 140**, an initiative that limited elected executive branch officers and state senators to two 4-year terms and assembly members to three 2-year terms, while reducing the legislature's operating budget (and thus its staff) by 38 percent.

Term-limits advocates envisioned a "turnstile" type of legislature, with members in office for relatively short periods. The system was designed to guarantee new faces, reduce the influence of money, and prevent incumbents from becoming entrenched in excess. Of the fifteen states currently with term limits, California has one of the most severe conditions in the nation. Unlike most other states with term limits, once state legislators in California complete their terms of service, they may never run for the legislature again.

Some objectives associated with **term limits** have been met, while others show no sign of coming to pass. New faces have certainly appeared—particularly women and minorities in much larger numbers than in the past—but in many

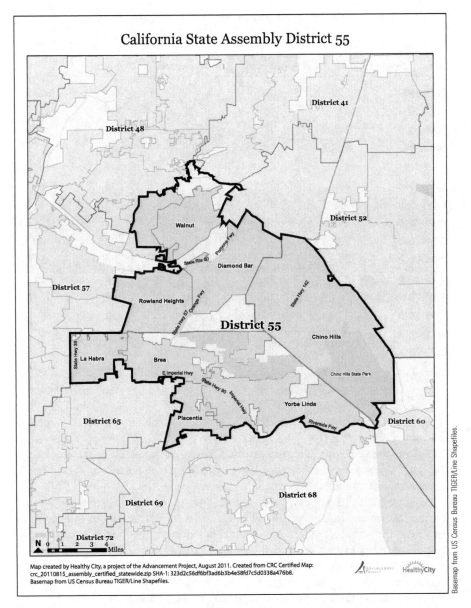

California State Assembly District 55

District 41

District 48

District 52

Walnut

Pomona Fwy

State Rte 60

Diamond Bar

District 57

State Hwy 142

Rowland Heights

State Hwy 57 Orange Fwy

**District 55**

Chino Hills

State Hwy 39

La Habra     Brea

Chino Hills State Park

E Imperial Hwy

State Hwy 90  Imperial Hwy

Yorba Linda

District 65     Placentia

Riverside Fwy

District 60

District 69

District 68

District 72

N    0  1  2  3  4
Miles

Map created by Healthy City, a project of the Advancement Project, August 2011. Created from CRC Certified Map:
crc_20110815_assembly_certified_statewide.zip SHA-1: 323d2c56df6bf3ad6b3b4e58fd7c5d0338a476b8.
Basemap from US Census Bureau TIGER/Line Shapefiles.

ADVANCEMENT
Project     HealthyCity

Basemap from US Census Bureau TIGER/Line Shapefiles.

**FIGURE 5.2**  Map of Assembly District 55 after 2011 redistricting.

cases legislators have simply jumped from one house to the other. Nevertheless, those from relatively affluent backgrounds continue to be disproportionately elected to the legislature. In this sense, little has changed.

There also have been increasing instances of political cannibalism. Some **termed-out** assembly members have challenged senators from their own political party who are eligible to serve another term. In other cases, senators who have time left in the assembly have attempted to return to that house. In other instances still, termed-out legislators have returned home to run for county

**TABLE 5.1  Political Parties in the State Legislature, 1985–2014**

| Legislative Session | Senate | | | Assembly | |
|---|---|---|---|---|---|
| | Democrats | Republicans | Independents | Democrats | Republicans |
| 1985–1986 | 25 | 15 | | 47 | 33 |
| 1987–1988 | 24 | 15 | 1 | 44 | 36 |
| 1989–1990 | 24 | 15 | 1 | 47 | 33 |
| 1991–1992 | 27 | 12 | 2 | 47 | 33 |
| 1993–1994 | 23 | 15 | 2 | 49 | 31 |
| 1995–1996 | 21 | 17 | 2 | 39 | 41 |
| 1997–1998 | 22 | 17 | 1 | 42 | 38 |
| 1999–2000 | 25 | 15 | | 48 | 32 |
| 2001–2002 | 26 | 14 | | 50 | 30 |
| 2003–2004 | 25 | 15 | | 48 | 32 |
| 2005–2006 | 25 | 15 | | 48 | 32 |
| 2007–2008 | 25 | 15 | | 48 | 32 |
| 2009–2010 | 25 | 15 | | 50 | 30 |
| 2011–2012 | 25 | 13 | | 52 | 28 |
| 2013–2014 | 29 | 11 | | 55 | 25 |

SOURCE: California Secretary of State.

supervisor. The term-limits concept in California has spawned the state's version of "musical chairs."

Meanwhile, the overall costs of campaigning continue to set new records. Research also reveals that another significant impact of term limits has been a considerable decline in the quality of legislation since its adoption.[7]

Another criticism of term limits centers on the loss of legislative knowledge because of the rapid turnover. Because legislators have little opportunity to gain expertise, they tend to rely more on the governor and lobbyists,[8] the former because of policy experts who work as aids in the governor's office, and the latter because of the permanence of the lobbyists in the state capital. Legislators may be termed out, but lobbyists are not.

As a result of term limits, leadership positions in the legislature no longer carry the clout that once made that branch an effective counterweight to the executive branch. Current Assembly Speaker John Perez was elected to the assembly's highest post in 2010 with only a year of experience under his belt. Clearly, problems can develop with erratic leadership changes and inexperienced leaders.

Some of the leadership problems may have been addressed with the passage of **Proposition 28** in 2012. Effective 2014, legislators may serve all of their time in one house or the other, but with a limit of twelve years instead of fourteen. Proponents of this proposition believe that the ability to stay in one house for a longer time will allow legislators to develop more expertise.

Nationwide, the term limits movement seems to be abating. Four states with term limits have rejected the concept since 1999—Mississippi, Idaho, Oregon, and Utah. But in California, the voters continue to favor term limits. A public opinion poll in 2012 found that a resounding 62 percent of Californians supported the constraint, compared with only 12 percent who rejected it.[9]

## New Rules, New Players

Redisricting, the change from part-time to full-time legislators, and term limits transformed the legislature, albeit unevenly. To be sure, the new framework attracted better-educated and more professional individuals and also made election to office more feasible for women and minorities. Thus, in 2013, the assembly included 21 women, 15 Latinos, 7 African Americans, 7 Asian Americans, and 5 openly gay members; the senate included 9 women, 8 Latinos, 3 African Americans, 2 Asian Americans, and 2 openly gay members (see Figure 5.3).

Despite greater diversity, the legislature has narrowed in terms of vocational backgrounds. During the 1980s, legislative aspirants from the business world were flanked by large numbers of lawyers, local activists, educators, and former legislative aides. But increasingly, the "business candidate" has emerged as the dominant category of self-description. During the 1990s, about half of all legislative candidates on the ballot listed some form of business as their occupation. Beginning in the late 1990s, large numbers of people from city- and county-elected posts also took seats in the legislature.[10] These patterns continue today.[11]

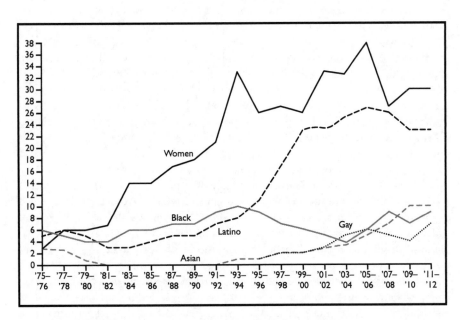

**F I G U R E  5.3**  Women and Minorities in the California Legislature.

## LEADERS AND STAFF MEMBERS

Although the two houses share lawmaking responsibilities, they function differently. Because the assembly is larger, it is more hierarchical in organization. The **speaker of the assembly** is clearly in charge of that body and wields considerable power. The speaker controls the flow of legislation, designation of committee chairs and assignments, and distribution of vast campaign funds to the members of his or her political party. The number of standing, or topical, committees varies each term with the speaker's term in office. For example, there were thirty such committees in the assembly during 2011–2012, the same as in the previous session. Some committees are far more important than others, so the speaker's friendship is of great value to a legislator. The speaker also may carry favor with the governor, especially if the two work well together.

By tradition, the party with a majority in the assembly chooses the speaker in a closed meeting, or caucus. A vote is then taken by the full assembly, with the choice already known to all. The minority party selects its leader in a similar fashion. Majority and minority floor leaders, as well as their whips (assistants), provide further support for the legislative officers. With solid majorities for most of the past half-century, the Democrats have controlled the speakership for all but four years during the period.

Before the term-limits era, speakers often held their posts for ten years or more. However, these days the tenures of speakers have been limited to between one and three years. The current speaker, John Perez, may stretch that life span a bit. He was elected to his post in 2009 and may serve through 2014, assuming he is reelected. His successor may fare even better in the post-Proposition 29 era if he or she elects to serve all or most of his or her twelve years in the assembly.

Prior to the court-ordered redistricting in 1966, the senate emphasized collegiality and cooperation over strong leadership, strict rules, and tight organization. But since then, the senate has been almost as partisan as the assembly. The most powerful member is the **president pro tem**, who, like the speaker, is elected by the majority party after each general election. The minority party also elects its leader at that time. The key to senate power lies with the five-member **Rules Committee**, which is chaired by the president pro tem and controls all other committee assignments and the flow of legislation. In 2011–2012 the senate had twenty-three standing committees, the same number as the previous session.

When Democrat John Burton presided as the pro tem, he used the office to raise and dispense large sums of money to grateful fellow Democrats. Burton was president pro tem for six years (1998–2004). More significantly, he had been an assembly member for nearly twenty years, mostly before the term limits era. Because of his experience, Burton became the legislature's lightning rod against Governor Arnold Schwarzenegger. Many observers viewed him as the legislature's most formidable leader, despite the assembly speaker's traditionally dominant role.

The current president pro tem, Democrat Darrell Steinberg, was elected to the position in 2008. He will not be termed out until 2014. Like most others in leadership positions, Steinberg assumed his post with relatively little senate experience, but his previous six years in the state assembly gave him a level of knowledge and influence exceeding that of his assembly counterpart, John Perez.

Although Democrats hold leadership positions in both houses, in recent years they have had trouble dealing with one another. Some of this difficulty may be due to the differing leadership styles of Senate President Pro Tem Steinberg and Assembly Speaker Perez. Steinberg has a record of crossing party lines to forge necessary, if distasteful, compromises. Perez has a reputation for being unwilling to part with core values.[12] Their internal gridlock has taken considerable pressure off the minority Republicans, who have watched internal struggles within the majority party with some glee. Nowhere has this been more evident than in the struggle to balance annual state budgets facing huge deficits. As the legislature grappled with its responsibilities in 2010, interest groups loyal to both sides actually began letter-writing campaigns and purchased television ads—all of which points to the lack of cohesion within the political parties.[13]

## STAFFING THE PROFESSIONAL LEGISLATURE

The evolution of the legislature into a full-time body was accompanied by a major expansion of its support staff. These days about 2,200 staff assistants (commonly called "staffers") work for the members and committees—a far cry from the 485 employed by the last part-time legislature in 1966. Those in the capital usually concentrate on pending legislation and research, whereas staffers in the legislators' home district offices spend much of their time responding to constituents' problems.

Legislators spend much of their time in committees, the heart of the legislative process. Most committees cover specialized policy areas such as education or natural resources. A few, such as the senate and assembly rules committees, deal with procedures and internal organization. Each committee employs staff consultants who are experts on the committee's subject area and who are politically astute individuals in general—important attributes because they serve at the pleasure of the committee chair. Besides the traditional or standing committees, staffers assist more than sixty select committees that address narrow issues and nine joint committees that coordinate two-house policy efforts.

Another staff group is even more political. Employed by the Democratic and Republican caucuses in the senate and assembly, these assistants are supposed to deal with possible legislation. However, their real activities usually center on advancing the interests of their political party.

In addition to personal, committee, and leadership staffers, legislators have created neutral support agencies. With a staff of fifty-six, the **legislative analyst** (a position created in 1941) provides fiscal expertise, reviewing the annual budget and assessing programs that affect the state's coffers. The **legislative counsel** (created in 1913) employs about eighty attorneys to draft bills for legislators and determine their potential impact on existing legislation. The **state auditor** (created in 1955) assists the legislature by periodically reviewing and evaluating ongoing programs.

Historically, staffing has enhanced the legislature's professionalism. Yet some staffers, especially those who work for the legislative leaders, clearly spend more time on partisan politics than on legislation. Many have used their positions as apprenticeships to gain knowledge, skills, and contacts for their own campaign efforts or future employment as lobbyists. All this, critics point out, is funded by the taxpayers. Defenders of the system counter that this staffing arrangement helps compensate for weak party organizations and the information gaps associated with rapid legislative turnover.

## HOW A BILL BECOMES A LAW

The legislature passes laws. It also proposes constitutional amendments, which are submitted for voter approval after they receive absolute two-thirds majority votes in both houses (the votes of two-thirds of the full membership—that is, twenty-seven votes in the senate and fifty-four in the assembly). The same absolute two-thirds majority votes are required for the legislature to offer bond measures—money borrowed for long-term, expensive state projects. Proposed constitutional amendments and bond measures must then obtain majority votes at the next election before becoming law.

Most of the legislature's energy, however, is spent on lawmaking. Absolute majorities—twenty-one votes in the senate and forty-one votes in the assembly—are required to pass the annual budget and basic laws intended to take effect the following January, but absolute two-thirds votes in both houses are required for urgency measures (those that become law immediately upon the governor's signature), and overrides of the governor's veto. The process, however, is far from simple.

### The Formal Process

The legislative process begins when the assembly member or senator sponsoring a bill gives the clerk of the chamber a copy, which is recorded and numbered (see Figure 5.4). The process is known as moving the bill "across the desk" (of the receiving clerk), signifying that the proposed measure is now officially under consideration. The bill then undergoes three readings and several hearings before it is sent to the other house, where the process is repeated. The first reading simply acknowledges the bill's submission.

Depending upon the house of origin, either the senate Rules Committee or the assembly Rules Committee decides on the route of the bill. The chairs of these important committees can affect a bill's fate by sending it to "friendly" or "hostile" committees and by assigning it a favorable or unfavorable route. Typically, a bill is assigned to two or three committees for careful scrutiny by members who are experts in that bill's subject area. More than half of all bills die in committee, either through a formal vote or because the chair decides not to call for a vote.

Typically, between five thousand and six thousand bills are introduced during each two-year session, with assembly members limited to fifty proposals and senators limited to sixty-five. Given such volume, the **legislative committees** are essential to getting laws passed. They hold hearings, debate, and may eventually vote on each bill delegated to them. Most committees deal in narrow areas, but a few—such as the senate Budget and Fiscal Review Committee and the assembly Committee on Appropriations—focus on the collection and distribution of funds and thus enjoy clout that goes beyond any one policy area.

At the conclusion of its hearings, a committee can kill a bill, release it without recommendation, or approve it with a "do pass" proposal. It may also recommend approval contingent on certain changes or amendments, which can be substantial or minor and technical. Only when a bill receives a positive recommendation from all of the committees to which it was assigned is it likely to get a second reading by the full legislative body. At this stage, the house considers additional amendments. After all proposed revisions have been discussed, the bill is printed in its final form and presented to the full house for a third reading. After further debate on the entire bill, a vote is taken.

Sometimes, the bill changes so dramatically that the original author abandons sponsorship in disgust; the bill then dies unless another legislator assumes sponsorship. On other occasions, a bill is introduced about a topic of little significance or with little more than a number. Then, later in the term, when the deadline for introductions has passed, the author may strip the bill of its original language and offer replacement language to deal with a pressing topic new to the legislative agenda. This strategy, known as **gut-and-amend**, isn't pretty but gives a legislator flexibility he or she would not have otherwise. It also circumvents the normal legislative process of committee hearings and due deliberation, sometimes to the chagrin of some lobbyists and interest groups.

If a bill is approved by the members of one house, it goes to the other house, where the process starts anew. Again, the bill may die anywhere along the perilous legislative path. If the two houses pass different versions of the same bill, the versions must be reconciled by a **conference committee**. Senate members are appointed by the Rules Committee; assembly members are chosen by the speaker, yet another sign of the power that comes with that position. If the conference committee agrees on a single version and if both houses approve it by the required margins, the bill goes to the governor for his or her approval. Otherwise, the proposed legislation is dead.

Usually, a bill becomes law if the governor signs it or takes no action within twelve days. However, if it is passed immediately before a session's end, the governor has thirty days to act. If the governor vetoes a bill, an absolute two-thirds majority must be attained in both houses for it to become law. Attaining such a lopsided vote is next to impossible, so vetoed bills generally fall by the wayside.

## The Informal Process

Politics permeates the formal, "textbook" process by which a bill becomes law. This means that every piece of legislation is considered not only on its merits but also on the basis of a variety of factors, including political support, interest group pressure, public opinion, and personal power.

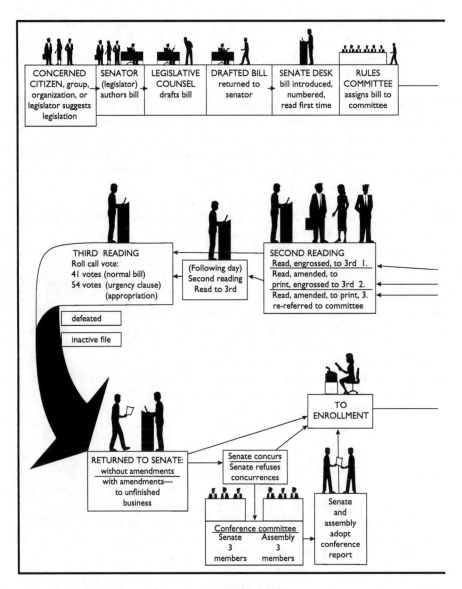

**FIGURE 5.4** How a Bill Becomes a Law (Continued).

Members of the majority party chair most, if not all, of the committees in any given year. With Democrats in control for most of the last five decades, they have reaped the benefits of the committee chairs (extra staff, procedural advantages, and so forth), secured the best committee assignments, and been assigned the best offices. Likewise, when assembly Republicans briefly held a bare majority in 1996, they assumed control of twenty-five of the twenty-six committees, and the benefits were reversed.

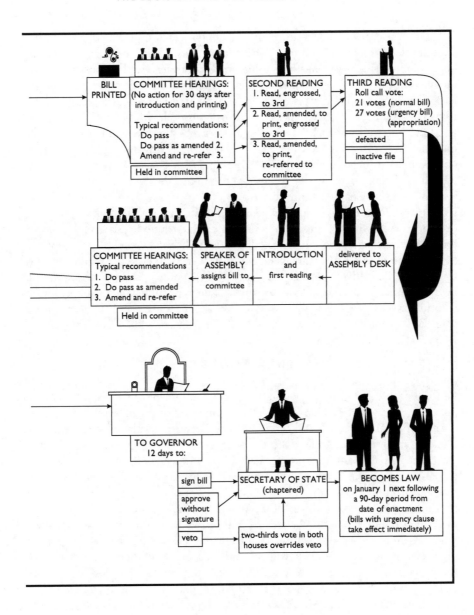

Political support within the legislature is essential to numerous decisions. So many bills flow through the process that members often vote on measures they haven't even read, relying on staff, committee, or leadership recommendations. Sometimes, a bill's fate rests with key legislative leaders, who can use their positions to stifle or speed up a proposal at various points in the legislative process. In the assembly, the speaker may actually appoint extra members to a committee temporarily to move a bill along. Outcomes are also affected by **logrolling**, a give-and-take bargaining process where legislators agree to support each other's bills. More often than not, legislators give away their votes on matters of little concern to them in hopes of mollifying opponents or pleasing powerful leaders. And on occasion, some members of the assembly have been known to cast the votes of other members by clicking their electronic devices. This illegal activity, called **ghost voting**,[14] can't take place in the senate, where members cast votes by a show of hands.

Public opinion also affects legislation, sometimes dramatically. Recent statutes on children's safety and health, cellphone use while driving, higher education opportunities for illegal immigrants, environmental quality, and homeowners' rights have been enacted in direct response to public concern.

As noted in Chapter 4, pressure from interest groups permeates the legislative process. The relationship between the private and public policy arenas has only intensified with the growth of a full-time, year-round legislature. The combined cost of legislative campaigns has soared from $7 million in 1966 to $101 million in 2010. With an average of just over $1 million per legislative seat, California's legislative elections are the most expensive state contests in the nation.[15] And given the millions of dollars spent by independent expenditure committees that were not tied officially to any candidate, the total spent on legislative campaigns in the state in all likelihood exceeded $150 million.

## OTHER FACTORS

Personal power within the legislature remains a component of the political process, especially in cases of conflict. One such example occurred in 2008, when then senate president pro tem Don Perata and the Democratic majority of the senate Rules Committee blocked four Schwarzenegger nominees to the twelve-member California Parole Board. For months, Perata had complained about California's low parole rate, implying that the problem rested with the parole board. This action sent a clear message to both the board and the governor.[16]

Sometimes the mere threat of an initiative spurs legislative action. In 2012, medical marijuana advocates abandoned an initiative effort for statewide regulation when Assemblyman Tom Ammiano introduced a bill with many of the same objectives. Ammiano secured passage from the assembly but then had to withdraw the proposal after senate resistance. Conversely, the legislature's work on climate change was nearly undone in November 2010 by a business-sponsored initiative to delay implementation of AB 32. On this occasion, the voters elected to let the controversial law remain in place.

## UNFINISHED BUSINESS

Today's legislature faces myriad issues, ranging from a poorly working public education system to a deteriorating infrastructure. Faced with revolving participants, the legislature operates with little stability and less tradition. Term limits, decimated state budgets (see Chapter 8), and recession for most of the last decade have added to the woes of this policymaking body. Until 2011, the absolute two-thirds vote requirement for the annual budget often delayed badly needed services for months at the beginning of each fiscal year. In 2010, the voters attempted to ease budget gridlock by passing **Proposition 25**, a ballot measure which reduced the required budget vote to a simple majority. And in 2012, Democrats won absolute two-thirds majorities in both houses, allowing them to pass controversial policies–including tax increases–without Republican obstruction. Whether this success hails a new era of party unity remains to be seen.

With all these pressures, legislators often seem to react to problems rather than to anticipate or solve them. As a consequence, public policies are made increasingly by initiative, the governor, or the courts. Nevertheless, the legislature continues to grapple with the leading issues of the day, and at least sometimes, lawmakers manage to overcome assorted obstacles in a fractured political environment to enact policies of substance.

## NOTES

1.  *Californians and Their Government*, Public Policy Institute of California Statewide Survey (San Francisco: PPIC, May 2012).

2.  In general, the plan provided one senator per county. In a few cases, two low-populated counties shared a senator, and in one case, three low-populated counties—Alpine, Inyo, and Mono—shared a senator.

3.  Legislators receive monthly allowances for cars (including gasoline and maintenance); life, health, dental, vision, and disability insurance; and a daily housing allowance when they are in session in Sacramento. On average these benefits amount to about $30,000 annually, almost all of which is nontaxable.

4.  The other full-time legislatures are Alaska, Florida, Massachusetts, Michigan, New Jersey, New York, Ohio, Pennsylvania, and Wisconsin.

5.  "Plan to Redraw Districts Passes," *Los Angeles Times*, September 14, 2001, p. B8.

6.  *Ibid.*

7.  Rene Bukovichik Van Vechten, "Taking the Politics Out of Politics? State Legislative Politics and Institutional Reform in Twentieth Century California" (Ph.D. diss., University of California, Irvine 2002), 203–213, p. 21.

8.  "Report Chronicles Downside of Term Limits," Stateline.org, August 16, 2006, www.stateline.org/live/details/story?contentId=134247.

9.  "Drop in Support for Cigarette Tax, Most Support Term Limits Change,"Public Policy Institute of California (San Francisco: PPIC, May 23, 2012).

10.  Kathleen Les, "Mr. Mayor Goes to the Capitol," *California Journal* 30, no. 10 (October 1999): 36–38.

11.  See Bruce E. Cain and That Kousser, *Adapting to Term Limits: Recent Experiences and New Directions* (San Francisco: Public Policy Institute of California, 2004), p. 15.

12.  "Choosing Sides in State Budget Fiasco," *Los Angeles Times*, June 26, 2010, pp. A1, A14.

13.  *Ibid.*

14.  See "Ghost Voting: A Long History," *San Francisco Chronicle*, June 10, 2008, pp. A1, A16.

15.  Institute for State Government and Politics, http://maplight.org/california /contributions.

16.  "Dems Reject Two of Schwarzenegger's Parole Appointees," *Sacramento Bee*, June 26, 2008, p. A3.

## LEARN MORE ON THE WEB

California State Assembly:
www.assembly.ca.gov

California State Senate:
www.senate.ca.gov

Campaign finance:
www.followthemoney.org

Daily politics and policy-related news:
www.rtumble.com

Legislative Analyst's Office:
www.lao.ca.gov

Legislative histories and bill analyses:
www.leginfo.ca.gov/bilinfo.html

National Conference of State Legislatures:
www.ncsl.org

Search for your legislator:
www.legislature.ca.gov/legislators_and_districts/districts/districts.html

Watch or listen to the legislature in session:
www.legislature.ca.gov/the_state_legislature/calendar_and_schedules
/audio_tv.html

## LEARN MORE AT THE LIBRARY

Bill Boyarsky. *Big Daddy: Jesse Unruh and the Art of Power Politics*. Berkeley: University of California Press, 2008.

Willie L. Brown, Jr., and P. J. Corkery. *Basic Brown: My Life and Our Times*. New York: Simon & Schuster, 2008.

Gerald C. Lubenow, ed. *Governing California*, 2d ed. Berkeley, Calif.: Institute of Governmental Studies Press, 2006.

Gary F. Moncrief, Peverill Squire, and Malcolm Jewel. *Who Runs for the Legislature?* Upper Saddle River, N.J.: Prentice Hall, 2001.

Peter Schrag. *California: America's High Stakes* Experiment. Berkeley: University of California Press, 2006.

## GET INVOLVED

Contact your state senator or assembly member to volunteer or apply for an internship in his or her district office. To find your representatives, go to: www.legislature.ca.gov/legislators_and_districts/districts/districts.html.

# 6

# California Law: Politics
# and the Courts

## CHAPTER CONTENTS

Courts are very much a part of the political process. Judges and politicians have always known this, but the public has been slower to understand the political nature of the judiciary. When governors—or presidents—make controversial appointments to the courts, however, judicial politics becomes a very public matter. Court decisions overturning popular initiatives have also made judicial politics apparent.

What makes the courts political? It's not just controversial judicial decisions or even the involvement of party politicians. Courts are political because their judgments are choices between public policy alternatives. When judges consider cases, they evaluate the issues before them both in terms of existing legislation and in the context of the U.S. and California constitutions. Rulings based on differing judicial interpretations of these documents help some people and hurt others. This is why the courts, like members of the executive and legislative branches, are subject to the attentions and pressures of California's competing interests, and this is why the courts are political.

## THE CALIFORNIA COURT SYSTEM

The California court system is the largest in the nation, with more than two thousand judicial officers and twenty-one thousand court employees. The three levels within the system are linked, but each has its own responsibilities. Most cases begin and end at the lowest level. Only a few move up the state's judicial ladder through the appeals process (see Figure 6.1), and even fewer end up in the U.S. Supreme Court.

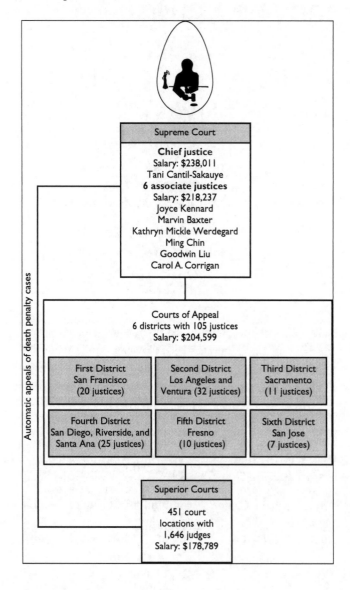

**FIGURE 6.1** The California Court System.

SOURCE: California Judicial Council.

## The Judicial Ladder

The vast majority of cases begin and end in trial courts, the bottom rung of the judicial ladder. In California, **superior courts** in each county are the trial courts, handling misdemeanor cases (minor crimes, including most traffic offenses), felonies (serious crimes subject to sentences of one year or more in state prison), civil suits (noncriminal disputes), divorces, and juvenile cases. Superior courts also operate small claims courts, where individuals can take cases with damage claims up to $10,000 before a judge without attorneys—sort of like television's *Judge Judy*.

Losers in trial courts may ask the court on the next rung of the judicial ladder to review the decision. Most cases aren't appealed, but when major crimes and penalties or big money are involved, the losers in the cases sometimes request a review by one of California's six district **courts of appeal**. As appellate bodies, these courts do not hold trials like the ones we see on television. Lawyers make arguments and submit briefs to panels of three justices, who try to determine whether the original trial was conducted fairly. These justices consider only possible legal errors, not the verdict in the case. If they find errors, they can send the case back for another trial or even dismiss the charges.

Ultimately, parties to the cases may petition for review by the seven-member state **supreme court**, the top of California's judicial ladder. Few cases reach this level because most are resolved in the lower courts and the high court declines most of the petitions. When the California Supreme Court hears a case, its decision is final unless issues of federal law or the U.S. Constitution arise; the U.S. Court may consider such cases.

If a higher court refuses an appeal, the lower court's decision stands. Even when a case is accepted, the justices of the higher court have agreed only to consider the issues. They may or may not overturn the decision of the lower court.

## Judicial Election and Selection

Although the tiered structure of the California courts is similar to that of the federal courts, the selection of judges is not. Federal judges and members of the U.S. Supreme Court are appointed by the president subject to confirmation by the U.S. Senate. Once appointed, they serve for life. California judges and justices, however, gain office through a more complicated process and regularly face the voters. This periodic scrutiny by the public, the media, and interest groups helps keep judges and their decisions in the news.

Formal qualifications to become a judge are few: candidates must have been admitted to practice law in California for at least ten years. Technically, superior court judges are elected, but most actually gain office through appointment by the governor when a sitting judge dies, retires, or is promoted between elections, or sometimes when the legislature creates new judgeships. A governor who is elected to two terms of office may appoint as many as half of the state's sitting judges, significantly affecting judicial practices. Governors generally appoint judges who are members of their own political parties, although Republican Governor Arnold Schwarzenegger was more willing than any of his predecessors to appoint judges who were not members of his own political party. Prior service as a district attorney (prosecutor) has been common for successful appointees—a fact leading to complaints that judges are biased against defendants and defense attorneys. Governor Jerry Brown, however, has appointed several judges who have had experience as defense attorneys.

Appointed judges must run for office when their terms expire, but running as incumbents—often unopposed—they almost always win. Superior court judges can also gain office simply by declaring their candidacy for a specific judicial office—usually when there is a vacancy—and then running. If no candidate wins a majority in the primary election, the two candidates with the most votes face each other in a **runoff election** in November. Superior court judges serve six-year terms and then may run for reelection, usually without opposition. Judges have no term limits.

### Appointments and the Higher Courts

Unlike lower court judges, members of the district courts of appeal and the state supreme court attain office only by gubernatorial appointment. The governor's possible nominees are first screened by the state's legal community through its Commission on Judicial Nominees Evaluation. Then the nominees must be approved by the **Commission on Judicial Appointments**, consisting of the attorney general, the chief justice of the state supreme court, and the senior presiding justice of the courts of appeal. The commission may reject a nominee, but it has done so only twice since its creation in 1934.

Once approved by the Commission on Judicial Appointments, the new justices take office, but they must go before the voters at the next gubernatorial election. No opponents or political party labels appear on the ballot; the voters simply check yes or no on the retention of the justices in question. If approved, they serve the remainder of the twelve-year term of the person they have replaced, at which time they can seek voter confirmation for a standard twelve-year term and additional terms after that.

Eleven other states select their supreme court justices in a similar fashion, but twenty-six rely solely on elections. The governor or legislature appoints justices in the remaining states.

### Firing Judges

Almost all judges easily win election and reelection, mostly without opposition. Those who designed the system probably intended it to be this way. They wanted to distance judges somewhat from politics and to ensure their independence by giving them relatively long terms, thus also ensuring relatively consistent interpretation of the law. Avoiding costly election campaigns that depend on financial contributors also promotes independence. The framers of the U.S. Constitution put such a high value on judicial continuity and independence that they provided for selection by appointment rather than by election and allowed judges to serve for life. For most of California's history, these values also seemed well entrenched in the political culture, and the state's judges functioned without much criticism or interference. Nevertheless, California's constitution provides several mechanisms of judicial accountability. Judges can be removed through elections, but they can also be reprimanded or removed by the judicial system itself.

Incumbent justices of the California Supreme Court routinely win reelection without serious challenge. In the 1970s and 1980s, however, both high court justices and superior court judges faced challenges from critics of decisions that supported racial integration or were seen as lenient toward criminals. Some superior court judges were defeated and in 1986 Supreme Court Chief Justice Rose Bird and two other liberal justices appointed by Jerry Brown during his first term as governor were swept out of office—the only justices removed by the voters in California history. Since then, the anticourt fervor has subsided. Today, sitting judges are rarely challenged.

Judges also can be removed by the **Commission on Judicial Performance**, which investigates charges of misconduct or incompetence. Its members include three judges (appointed by the supreme court), two lawyers (appointed by the governor), and six public members (two each appointed by the governor, the senate Rules Committee, and the speaker of the assembly). Few investigations result in any action, but if the charges are confirmed, the commission may impose censure, removal from office, or forced retirement.

In 2011, the 1,168 complaints against judges were filed with the commission and 172 were investigated.[1] In the rare cases in which the commission finds a judge to be at fault, it issues a warning or reprimand. Even more rarely, the commission may remove a judge from the bench. In recent years, judges have been removed for lying about campaign funds, threatening a district attorney, inappropriate interventions in trials, and in one case, excessive delays and neglect of court orders. Actual removals from the bench are rare, however, because those whose conduct is questionable usually resign before the commission's investigation is completed.

## THE COURTS AT WORK

In 2010–2011, 10,074,941 cases were filed in California's trial courts. Traffic infractions made up 58 percent of these cases. Felony and misdemeanor (criminal) cases numbered 1,571,494 (16 percent), and the balance were civil suits (such as liability or contract disputes) divorce, juvenile, or family law cases.[2]

California's constitution guarantees the right to a jury trial for both criminal and civil cases; if both parties agree, however, a judge alone hears the case. In jury trials, prospective jurors are drawn from lists of licensed drivers, voters, and property owners, but finding a twelve-member jury is often difficult. Many people avoid jury duty because it takes time away from work and pays only a few dollars a day. Homemakers and retired people are most readily available, but they alone cannot make up a balanced jury. Poor people and minorities tend to be underrepresented because they are less likely to be on the lists from which jurors are drawn and because some avoid participation in a system that they distrust.

The parties in civil cases provide their own lawyers, although legal aid societies sometimes help those who can't afford counsel. In criminal cases, the **district attorney**, an elected county official, carries out the prosecution. Defendants hire their own attorney or are provided with a court-appointed attorney if they cannot afford one. California's larger counties employ a **public defender** to provide such assistance. Well over half of all felony defendants require court-appointed help.

Most cases never go to trial, though. Over 97 percent of all criminal cases are settled out of court, mostly when the defendant pleads guilty and **plea bargaining** produces a pretrial agreement on a plea and a penalty. Plea bargaining reduces the heavy workload of the courts and guarantees some punishment or restitution, but it also allows those charged with a crime to serve shorter sentences than they might have received if convicted of all charges. Most civil suits are also settled without a trial because the parties to the cases reach an agreement to avoid the high costs and long delays of a trial. Only about 0.1 percent of all cases are tried before a jury (11,047 in 2009–2010); a judge alone hears the others that go to trial.[3]

It is important to note that the judicial system as a whole—including judges, prosecutors, public defenders, lawyers, and juries—does not reflect the diversity of California's people. About 72 percent of California's 175,617 active attorneys are non-Hispanic whites, even though minority group members make up 60 percent of the population. About one-third of the state's attorneys are women, however—a number that is quickly rising. Ethnic representation among California's judges is similar: 79 percent are male, and 72 percent are white.[4] These numbers lead critics to express concern about the fact that a predominantly white judicial system metes out justice to defendants who are, in the majority, nonwhite and that punishment is less severe for whites than for minorities convicted of the same crime.[5] African Americans, and to a lesser extent other minorities, perceive this situation and express deep mistrust of the system. Minority participation as attorneys and court officials has increased over time (Table 6.1 shows increasing diversity in judicial appointments), but considerable disparities remain.

## Appeals

When a dispute arises over a trial proceeding or its outcome, the losing party may appeal to a higher court to review the case. Most appeals are refused, but the higher courts may agree to hear a case because of previous procedural problems (for instance, if the defendant was not read his or her rights) or because it raises untested legal issues. Appellate courts do not retry the case or review the facts in evidence; their job is to determine whether the original trial was fair and the law was applied appropriately. In addition to traditional appellate cases, the state supreme court automatically reviews all death penalty decisions. Although few in number (twenty-nine in 2009–2010), these cases take up a substantial

**T A B L E  6.1  Judicial Appointments by California Governors, 1959–2011**

|  | Male | Female | White | Black | Hispanic | Asian |
|---|---|---|---|---|---|---|
| Ronald Reagan (R), 1967–1975 | 97.4% (478) | 2.6% (13) | 93.1% (457) | 2.6% (13) | 3.3% (16) | 1.0% (5) |
| Jerry Brown (D), 1975–1983 | 84.0 (691) | 16.0 (132) | 75.5 (621) | 10.9 (90) | 9.4 (77) | 4.3 (35) |
| George Deukmejian (R), 1983–1991 | 84.8 (821) | 15.2 (147) | 87.7 (849) | 3.6 (35) | 5.0 (49) | 3.6 (35) |
| Pete Wilson (R), 1991–1998 | 74.6 (517) | 25.4 (176) | 84.4 (585) | 5.2 (36) | 4.9 (34) | 5.5 (38) |
| Gray Davis (D), 1999–2003 | 65.8 (237) | 34.2 (123) | 70.8 (255) | 9.25 (33) | 12.8 (46) | 7.2 (26) |
| Arnold Schwarzenegger (R), 2003–2010 | 65.0 (370) | 35.0 (199) | 73.7 (419) | 7.6 (43) | 10.7 (61) | 8.0 (46) |
| Jerry Brown (D), 2011–2012 | 62.9 (22) | 37.1 (13) | 51.5 (18) | 17.1 (6) | 20.0 (7) | 11.4 (4) |

SOURCE: Governor's Office.

amount of the supreme court's time. Neither the courts of appeal nor the state supreme court can initiate cases. No matter how eager they are to intervene in an issue, they have to wait for someone else to bring the case to them.

Every year, about 10,000 petitions are filed with the California Supreme Court, mostly requesting reviews of cases decided by the courts of appeal. Each year the members of the court, meeting "in conference," choose about two hundred petitions for consideration, a task that consumes an estimated 40 percent of the court's time. By refusing to hear a case, the court allows the preceding decision to stand. When the court grants a hearing, one of the justices (or a staff member) writes a "calendar memo" analyzing the case. Attorneys representing the two sides present written briefs and then oral arguments, during which they face rigorous questioning by the justices.

After hearing the oral arguments, the justices discuss the case "in conference" and vote in order of seniority; the chief justice casts the final, and sometimes decisive, vote. If the chief justice agrees with the majority, he or she can assign a justice to write the official court opinion; usually this is the same justice who wrote the initial calendar memo. A draft of the opinion then circulates among the justices, each of whom may concur, suggest changes, or write a dissenting opinion. Finally, after many months, the court's decision is made public. The court issued ninety-six opinions in 2009–2010—about 1 percent of all the petitions filed.

This time-consuming process allows plenty of room for politicking among the justices and depends on a high degree of cooperation and deferential behavior among them—what judges call **collegiality**—as a way of building consensus on issues under consideration. With seven independent minds on the court, ongoing negotiations are needed to reach a majority and a decision.

### Managing the Courts

Besides leading the court through its decision making, the chief justice is responsible for managing the entire California court system and serves as chair of the **Judicial Council**, an appointed body of judges, attorneys, and legislators. The Judicial Council makes the rules for court procedures, collects data on the operations and workload of the courts, and oversees the Administrative Office of the Courts with 844 employees. The budget for the courts is set through the political process by the governor and the legislature and, like other state agencies, the courts have suffered budget cuts in recent years, despite an increased workload and complaints from the chief justice and other leaders of the judiciary. Reduced funding has resulted in political battles within the court system over whether to cut administrative or trial court costs.

## THE HIGH COURT AS A POLITICAL BATTLEGROUND

The courts are especially important and powerful in California because of the nature of California government and politics. The state constitution has been amended more than five hundred times since it was written in 1879, making it both long and elaborately specific, with components addressing all sorts of matters, both major and mundane—and its density is constantly increased by initiatives. The length, detail, and continually changing complexity of California's constitution enhance the power of the state courts because they have the job of determining whether laws and public policy are consistent with the constitution. One scholar called the courts a "shadow government"[6] because of their importance in shaping public policy, but others view this as the courts' appropriate constitutional role.

The state supreme court is the ultimate interpreter of the state constitution (unless issues arise under the U.S. Constitution). The court's power makes it a center of political interest: governors strive to appoint justices who share their values and choose their appointees carefully. As governors have changed, so have the sorts of justices they appoint. And as its membership has changed, the California Supreme Court has moved across the spectrum from liberal to conservative.

Regardless of its collective political values, the court has not backed away from tackling controversial issues, including occasionally overturning decisions of the legislature or the people (as expressed in initiatives). This willingness is less because of interventionist attitudes on the part of the justices than because of a long, complex, and frequently amended constitution and poorly written laws and initiatives.

### Governors, Voters, and the Courts

Long dominated by liberals, California's supreme court took a distinct turn toward the right in 1986, after the voters rejected the reelections of three liberal justices, including Rose Bird, the controversial chief justice at the time.

Appointed in 1977 by then-Governor Jerry Brown, Bird and her colleagues waded into controversy with unpopular rulings on busing for school desegregation and Proposition 13 (the popular property tax reduction initiative), as well as consistently reversing death sentences even as public concern about crime increased. When Bird and two other liberal justices were on the ballot in 1986, conservative Republican Governor George Deukmejian led a successful campaign to defeat them. With three new openings, Deukmejian transformed the court with conservative appointees, including a new chief justice.

Subsequent appointees have maintained the court's conservative majority. Today's court includes Marvin Baxter and Joyce Kennard (both Deukmejian appointees); Kathryn Werdegar and Ming Chin (appointed by Republican Governor Pete Wilson) and Carol A. Corrigan and Chief Justice Tani Cantil-Sakauye (both appointed by Governor Arnold Schwarzenegger). The newest member of the court—and its only Democrat—is Gordon Liu, appointed by Governor Jerry Brown in 2011. Minority members of the court include Cantil-Sakauye (who is Filipina), Liu and Chin (who are Chinese), and Kennard (who is Dutch-Indonesian). Four of the court's seven members are women. All of the current justices have won voter approval, with 65 to 76 percent voting for their retention. Cantil-Sakauye was confirmed for a twelve-year term by the voters in 2010 and Justice Liu will be up for confirmation in 2014.

With a majority of the justices appointed by Republican governors and solidly confirmed by the voters, California's supreme court today is moderately conservative and less controversial than in the past. The court's conservatism is reflected in its tendency to be pro-prosecution in criminal cases and pro-business in economic cases. The court also disappointed local governments seeking new taxes with rulings that rigidly applied a requirement for two-thirds voter approval, a strict interpretation of 1978's Proposition 13 (see Chapter 8) and when they upheld the right of the state to dissolve local redevelopment agencies (see Chapter 9).

Overall, the supreme court avoids **judicial activism** (making policy through court decisions rather than through the legislative or electoral process), but even the current conservative court sometimes asserts its independence, wading into political controversy and significantly affecting state politics. For example, it has followed the Bird court's precedent of approving state-funded abortions and the court rejected plans by the Governor Schwarzenegger and state legislature to solve their own budget problems by taking transportation and redevelopment funds from local governments. In 2011, the Republican-dominated court rejected an appeal by the state Republican Party to overturn the legislative districts by the voter-created Citizens Redistricting Commission (see Chapter 5), upholding the work of the commission.

Most controversially, the courts sometimes overrule decisions of the voters, as they did when they struck down portions of voter-approved initiatives that required tougher sentences for criminals because the proposals shifted discretion from judges to prosecutors. Probably the highest-profile and most controversial action taken by the California Supreme Court, however, was its 2008 ruling on same-sex marriage. When the city and county of San Francisco licensed such marriages in 2004, the supreme court ruled the marriages illegal on the basis of state law, as approved by the voters in 2002. But the constitutionality of that law was challenged in 2008, and on a four-to-three vote, the court ruled that "the California Constitution properly must be interpreted to guarantee this basic civil right to all Californians, whether gay or heterosexual, and to same-sex couples as well as to opposite-sex couples."[7] Opponents quickly qualified **Proposition 8**, an initiative constitutional amendment to restrict marriage to opposite-sex couples. Voters approved the measure, thus overruling the court. That initiative was subsequently challenged in court, but the California Supreme Court accepted it as a legitimate amendment to the state constitution. Then Chief Justice George wrote that the court's decision was not based on whether Proposition 8 "is wise or sound as a matter of policy," but rather "concerns the right of the people … to change or alter the state constitution itself…. Regardless of our views as individuals on this question of policy, we recognize as judges and as a court our responsibility to confine our consideration to a determination of the constitutional validity and legal effect of the measure in question."[8]

This decision did not put the issue to rest, however. The federal courts are sometimes drawn into battles over California initiatives, too. Since the 1990s, federal courts have overturned initiatives on campaign finance, open primary elections, and limits on public services for immigrants as violations of the U.S. Constitution, which trumps any state law or state constitution. In 2010, proponents of same-sex marriage took their case to a federal district court, arguing that Proposition 8 constituted a denial of equal rights under the U.S. Constitution. The judge in that case ruled in favor of the plaintiffs, thus overriding both the voters of the state of California and the state supreme court. The federal court ruling is being appealed, and the final decision will rest with the U.S. Supreme Court—or the voters of California when the issue comes back to them in yet another initiative.

Judicial rulings against voter-approved laws may appear undemocratic, but the courts are doing their duty by interpreting these controversial propositions not only for their content but also for their consistency with the California and U.S. constitutions. When the courts find an act of another branch of government or of the voters to be contrary to existing law or to the state or federal constitution, it is their responsibility to overturn that law, even if their decision is unpopular. "When we invalidate one of these initiatives," former chief justice George argued, "what we are doing is not thwarting the public's will. We are adhering to the ultimate expression of the popular will: the Constitution of the United States, or the Constitution of the State of California, which has been adopted by the people and which imposes limits on the initiative process and on lawmaking by legislatures and by the executive."[9]

As controversial as the California Supreme Court's decisions sometimes are, the court's influence goes well beyond this state. A study of court decisions throughout the country found that courts in other states followed precedents set in California more than precedents set in the courts of any other state.[10] This suggests that the California court is well within the mainstream of jurisprudence in the United States. It's also one reason why the court battle over same-sex marriages was so hard fought.

## COURTS AND THE POLITICS OF CRIME

Crime topped the list of voter concerns in California and the nation during much of the 1980s and 1990s. Murder, rape, burglary, gang wars, and random violence seemed all too common. Republicans were elected governor at least partly because they were seen as law-and-order candidates.

Capital punishment was a key issue in the 1980s, when a liberal supreme court overturned the vast majority of the death penalty cases it reviewed. Since 1986, when the voters rejected these liberals, the supreme court has affirmed most death sentences. The issue has not gone away, however. Law-and-order advocates condemn the lengthy and costly delays that plague death penalty appeals—up to ten years for the state courts and another ten years for the federal courts—but experts say that much of the delay is caused by the inability of the courts to find legal counsel for the condemned or handle the workload. Meanwhile, forensic methods such as DNA testing have revealed wrongful convictions in death penalty cases and the federal courts have suspended executions in California due to concerns about the drugs used for lethal injections and the conditions of outdated prison facilities for executions.

Over seven hundred condemned murderers are on death row and none has been executed since 2006. The system has been called "broken" and "dysfunctional" and Chief Justice Cantil-Sakauye has said the death penalty is "not effective."[11] Arguing that capital punishment constitutes "cruel and unusual punishment" and that it actually costs more than life imprisonment, reformers put a proposition banning the death penalty on the 2012 ballot, but with polls showing continued strong voter support for capital punishment, the measure was defeated.

The law-and-order movement of the 1980s and 1990s also produced a series of propositions that strengthened penalties for many crimes, including the "three-strikes" initiative in 1994. Reflecting the view that liberal judges who were "soft on crime" were letting criminals off with light sentences, "**three strikes**" required anyone convicted of three felonies to serve a sentence of twenty-five years to life: "three strikes and you're out."

The three-strikes law quickly increased the state's prison population, as well as spending on prisons (see Chapter 8). With many of the state's worst criminals incarcerated for life, three-strikes prosecutions declined, and so did California's crime rate. Violent crime in California peaked in 1992 (two years before the three-strikes law) and has declined since then. In 2010 the number of violent crimes was lower than in 1979, even with 15 million more people living in the state.[12] Conservatives attribute this decline to tougher judges and penalties, but many experts argue that the declining crime rate was due to economic prosperity and demographics, with fewer people in the age group most commonly associated with criminal activity. Even in the recent recession, crime rates continue to decline. With crime less of a worry and concerns that the three-strikes law was too tough when the third strike was a minor crime, voters approved a 2012 ballot measure restricting third-strike penalties to serious, violent crimes.

Meanwhile, the prison population in California is huge, which means the cost of incarcerating all these men and women is also huge. But despite a massive investment of tax funds, California's prisons are overcrowded and beset by violence and disease. A system built for 84,271 inmates housed 173,479 in 2006 (a historic high).[13] Conditions in the prison health-care system were so bad that a class action suit was brought to a federal court, which intervened on grounds that these conditions constituted "cruel and unusual punishment" under the U.S. Constitution. In 2005 a federal judge put the prison health system in the hands of a court-appointed monitor. In 2009, seeing minimal progress, federal judges ordered the state to come up with a plan to reduce the prison population. The state of California appealed to the U.S. Supreme Court but in 2011, the court ruled against the state and ordered a substantial reduction in prison population within two years on grounds that overcrowding and health concerns violated the U.S. Constitution. Governor Brown responded by transferring lesser, nonviolent offenders from prisons to county jails. Designated "**realignment**," this system reduced the prison population as well as the cost of incarceration, since jails are cheaper to operate, but it also imposed new responsibilities and costs on local governments (see Chapter 9).

## CALIFORNIA LAW

Crime and other issues discussed in this chapter remind us that the courts play a central role in the politics of our state. Controversies about judicial appointments and decisions make the political nature of the courts apparent, especially when the rulings of the court conflict with the will of the electorate as expressed in initiatives. Yet the courts can never be free of politics. They make policy and interpret the law, and their judgments vary with the values of those who make them.

## NOTES

1. State of California Commission on Judicial Performance, 2011 Annual Report, http://cjp.ca.gov (accessed August 15, 2012).

2. Judicial Council of California, *2011 Court Statistics Report*, www.courts.ca.gov (accessed August 17, 2012).

3. *Ibid.*

4. "Governor Brown Releases 2011 Judicial Appointment Data," Office of the Governor, March 1, 2012, http://gov.ca.gov/news.php?id=17437 (accessed August 16, 2012).

5. Elsa Y. Chen, "Cumulative Disadvantage and Racial and Ethnic Disparities in California Federal Sentencing," in *Racial and Ethnic Politics in California*, ed. Sandra Bass and Bruce M. Cain (Berkeley: Public Policy Press, Institute of Governmental Studies, University of California, 2008).

6. Charles Price, "Shadow Government," *California Journal*, October 1997, p. 38.

7. *In re Marriage Cases*, S147999.

8.  *Strauss v. Horton*, S168047; *Tyler v. State of California*, S168066; and *City and County of San Francisco v. Horton*, S168078, www.courtinfo.ca.gov/courts/supreme.

9.  Ronald George, "Promoting Judicial Independence," *Commonwealth*, February 2006, p. 10.

10. Jake Dear and Edward W. Jesson, "Followed Rates and Leading Cases, 1940–2005," *University of California, Davis, Law Review* 41 (April 2007): 683.

11. California Commission on the Fair Administration of Justice, "Fair Administration of the Death Penalty," June 30, 2008, www.ccfaj.org (accessed August 17, 2012) and 12/24/2011, "Top Judge Casts Doubt on Capital Punishment," *Los Angeles Times*, December 24, 2011.

12. "California Crime Rates, 1960–2010," www.disastercenter.com/crime/cacrime.htm (accessed August 17, 2012).

13. Department of Corrections, "Population Reports," www.cdcr.ca.gov (accessed August 17, 2012).

## LEARN MORE ON THE WEB

California's court system:
www.courts.ca.gov

Justice Corps (service learning):
www.courts.ca.gov/programs-justicecorps.htm

For more on the courts:
www.judgepedia.org

State Bar of California:
www.calbar.org

Ratings of attorneys:
www.avvo.com

## LEARN MORE AT THE LIBRARY

Rodney F. Kingsnorth, "Change How We Appoint Judges," in *Remaking California*, ed. R. Jeffrey Lustig (Berkeley: Heyday Books, 2010).

Preble Stolz, Gerald F. Uelmen, and Susan Rasky, "The California Supreme Court," in *Governing California*, 2d ed., edited by Gerald C. Lubenow. Berkeley: Berkeley Public Policy Press, Institute of Governmental Studies, University of California, 2006.

## GET INVOLVED

You can learn about law and the courts through the Justice Corps, an Americorps service learning program with some compensation: www.courts.ca .gov/programs-justicecorps.htm.

# 7

# The Executive Branch: Coping with Fragmented Authority

## CHAPTER CONTENTS

**The Governor: First among Equals**

*Formal Powers*

*Informal Powers*

*Ever-Changing Relationships*

**The Supporting Cast**

*The Lieutenant Governor*

*The Attorney General*

*The Secretary of State*

*The Superintendent of Public Instruction*

*The Money Officers*

*The Insurance Commissioner*

*The Supporting Cast—Snow White's Seven Dwarfs?*

**The Bureaucracy**

**Making the Pieces Fit**

I f California's executive branch were composed solely of the governor, appointed department heads, and the civil service system, it would parallel the federal executive branch. But the state's executive branch also includes a lieutenant governor, an attorney general, a secretary of state, a controller, a treasurer, an insurance commissioner, a superintendent of public instruction, and a five-member Board of Equalization. All are elected at the same time and serve four-year terms. Unlike the president and vice president, though, who are elected on the same political party ticket, each of these officeholders runs independently. The result is a cluttered branch of state government with competing sources of power.

Endless schisms between officeholders in the executive branch contribute to the state's jurisdictional fragmentation. Occasionally, these executives clash over the use of authority, leading to political stalemate or conflicts in the courts, and most of all confusion among the electorate. Thus, the executive branch is anything but a unified body.

## THE GOVERNOR: FIRST AMONG EQUALS

The **governor** is California's most powerful public official. He or she shapes the state budget, appoints key policymakers in the executive and judicial branches, and both responds to and shapes public opinion by taking positions on controversial issues. The governor also is the state's chief administrator; the unofficial leader of his or her political party; and liaison to other states, the U.S. government, and other nations. On occasion, the governor's powers extend even to international issues such as immigration or global warming.

The current governor of California, Democrat Edmund J. ("Jerry") Brown, Jr., was elected in 2010. Brown succeeded Arnold Schwarzenegger, who had been elected after the recall of Gray Davis from office (see Table 7.1). With an annual salary of $165,288, the office ranks tenth among the highest-paid chief executives of the fifty states. The pay was $212,179 as recently as 2009, but hard times have led the state Salary Compensation Commission to cut the governor's salary along with those of other elected state officials three years in a row. In fact, the governor's salary is well below the incomes earned by many other government employees in California, particularly in large cities and counties, as well as the heads of University of California and California State University campuses. Even among state employees, prison wardens, retirement program coordinators, and physicians earn considerably more than the governor.

**T A B L E  7.1  California Governors and Their Parties, 1943–2015**

| Name | Party | Dates in Office |
|---|---|---|
| Earl Warren | Republican* | 1943–1953 |
| Goodwin J. Knight | Republican | 1953–1959 |
| Edmund G. Brown, Sr. | Democrat | 1959–1967 |
| Ronald Reagan | Republican | 1967–1975 |
| Jerry Brown | Democrat | 1975–1983 |
| George Deukmejian | Republican | 1983–1991 |
| Pete Wilson | Republican | 1991–1999 |
| Gray Davis | Democrat | 1999–November 2003 |
| Arnold Schwarzenegger | Republican | 2003–2011 |
| Jerry Brown | Democrat | 2011–2015 |

*Warren cross-filed as both a Republican and a Democrat in 1946 and 1950.
SOURCE: California Secretary of State.

Jerry Brown's election to the governor's office is the latest example of California's bizarre politics. A political fixture in the state since his first election to the Los Angeles Community College District Board of Trustees in 1969 (that's not a typo!), Brown was elected governor in 1974 and 1978 after serving as the secretary of state. His father, Edmund G. (Pat) Brown also was elected governor in 1958 and 1962. Because his governorship occurred before California adopted term limits in 1990, Jerry Brown was eligible to run again. With his third term Brown is in rare company. Only Earl Warren was elected to three terms in the pre-term limit era.

Brown's election is significant in another way: he was outspent by a margin of more than 6-to-1, courtesy of opponent Meg Whitman's largely self-funded campaign in which the Republican donated $175 million to her ill-fated cause. Indeed, a key theme of Brown's campaign accused Whitman of trying to buy the governorship. Apparently there was no sale.

## Formal Powers

Much of the governor's authority comes from formal powers written into the state's constitution and its laws. These responsibilities guide his or her relationships with the legislative and judicial branches, as well as with the other office-holders in the executive branch.

**Submission of an Annual Budget.**    No formal power is more important than the governor's budgetary responsibilities. The state constitution requires the governor to recommend a balanced budget to the legislature within the first ten days of each calendar year. The budget outlines the sources of state revenues and the recipients of state funds. Budget work is virtually a year-round task, consuming more of the governor's time than just about any other activity except emergencies such as earthquakes or fires. The governor is assisted in this effort by an appointed **director of finance**, who crafts the budget document after gathering data and funding requests from the dozens of departments and agencies within the state's bureaucracy. Initial preparations begin on July 1—the start of the fiscal year—and culminate with the governor's submission of a proposal to the legislature the following January (see Chapter 8). Officially, the process ends with the signing of the budget by the governor before the end of the fiscal year on June 30, so that the next year can begin with a budget in place.

**Vetoes.**    Under most circumstances, the governor has twelve days to act after the legislature passes a bill. On the hundreds of bills enacted by the legislature at a session's end, however, the governor has thirty days to act. Only a veto can keep a bill from becoming law. After the governor's time limit has passed, any unsigned or unvetoed bill becomes law the following January, unless the bill is an urgency measure, in which case it takes effect immediately upon signature. Governors use the **general veto**, which rejects a bill in its entirety. This exercise of power can be overturned only by an absolute two-thirds vote in each house, which rarely occurs.

The governor has special powers on spending bills passed by the legislature, many of which are associated with passage of the annual state budget. With spending bills, the governor cannot add money, but he or she can reduce or eliminate expenditures through use of the **item veto** before signing the budget into law. As with the general veto, an absolute two-thirds vote from each house of the legislature is necessary to overturn item vetoes. Because of that high threshold, legislators often attempt to head off vetoes by negotiating with the governor in advance.

Between 1982 and 2012, five successive governors exercised general and item vetoes without any repercussions from the legislature, and they did so with increasing frequency (see Table 7.2). More than any governor in history, Arnold Schwarzenegger turned the veto into a potent legislative weapon by rejecting more than one-fourth of the bills that reached his desk. The current governor, Jerry Brown, has used the veto more prudently. Ironically, the last time the legislature overturned a governor's veto was in 1979 when Jerry Brown was governor.

**Special Session.**    If the governor believes that the legislature has not addressed an important issue, he or she can take the dramatic step of calling a **special session**. At that time, the lawmakers must discuss only the specific business proposed by the governor. Special sessions often are called to respond to specific crises, as when Governor Schwarzenegger called on the legislature in 2006 to correct a prison system so overcrowded that a federal judge assumed oversight responsibilities. He also called special sessions on health-care reform, water policy, public education, and repeatedly on state budget deficits. Schwarzenegger called sixteen special sessions during his years in office—the most of any governor in state history—leading some to believe that he had diluted the significance of the concept.[1]

**Executive Order.**    On occasion, the governor can make policy by signing an **executive order**, an action that looks similar to legislation. Governors must

**TABLE 7.2  Vetoes and Overrides, 1967–2012**

| Governor | Bills Vetoed (%) | Vetoes Overridden |
| --- | --- | --- |
| Ronald Reagan (1967–1975) | 7.3 | 1 |
| Jerry Brown (1975–1983) | 6.3 | 13 |
| George Deukmejian (1983–1991) | 15.1 | 0 |
| Pete Wilson (1991–1999) | 16.6 | 0 |
| Gray Davis (1999–November 2003) | 17.6 | 0 |
| Arnold Schwarzenegger (November 2003–2011) | 26.4 | 0 |
| Jerry Brown (2011–2012) | 13.1 | 0 |

SOURCE: Clerk, California State Senate.

exercise this power carefully because such moves often lead to lawsuits over the breadth of their powers. Shortly after taking office in 2011, Jerry Brown signed several orders designed to curb state spending in the face of the state's huge budget deficit. They included a state hiring freeze, drastic cutbacks on the purchase of state automobiles, and even the return of 48,000 cell phones used by state employees. Said Brown, "In the face of a multibillion-dollar budget deficit, a cellphone might not seem like a big expense, but spending $20 million, and perhaps far more than that, on cell phones can't be justified."[2]

**Appointment Powers.** Before the Progressive reforms, California governors used patronage, or the "spoils" system, to hire friends and political allies. Today, 99 percent of all state employees are not appointed by the governor but rather are selected through a civil service system based on merit. Still, the governor fills about 2,500 key positions in the executive departments and cabinet agencies, except for the Departments of Justice and Education, whose heads are elected by the public. Together, these appointees direct the state bureaucracy (see Figure 7.1).

The state senate must approve most of the governor's appointees. Generally, senate confirmation is routine, but occasionally the governor's choice for a key post is rejected for reasons other than qualifications. In instances of an opening in the executive branch, both houses must weigh in with positive majorities. In early 2010, Governor Schwarzenegger nominated Republican State Senator Abel Maldonado to fill the lieutenant governor vacancy resulting from Lieutenant Governor John Garamendi's election to a vacated congressional seat. After several months of fits and starts, Maldonado was confirmed, only to lose in the November 2010 general election to Democrat Gavin Newsom.

The governor also appoints people to more than three hundred state boards and commissions. Membership on some boards—such as the Arts Council and the Commission on Aging, which have only advisory authority—is largely ceremonial and without pay. Other boards, however, such as the California Energy Commission (CEC), the Public Utilities Commission (PUC), the California Coastal Commission (CCC), and the California Air Resources Board (CARB) make important policies free from direct gubernatorial control. Nevertheless, the governor affects key "independent" boards through his or her appointments and manipulation of the budget.

Perhaps the most enduring of all gubernatorial appointments are judgeships. The governor fills both vacancies and new judgeships that are periodically created by the legislature. Most judges continue to serve long after those who appointed them have gone. However, the governor's power is checked here to a degree, too, by various judicial commissions and by the voters in future elections. During his tenure as governor, Arnold Schwarzenegger was much less partisan with his judicial appointments than his predecessors (see Chapter 6). Current Governor Jerry Brown has acknowledged the state's diversity by appointing high numbers of people of color and women to judicial posts.

In addition to the major areas of formal authority discussed earlier, the governor has a wide range of other formal powers. He or she is commander in chief

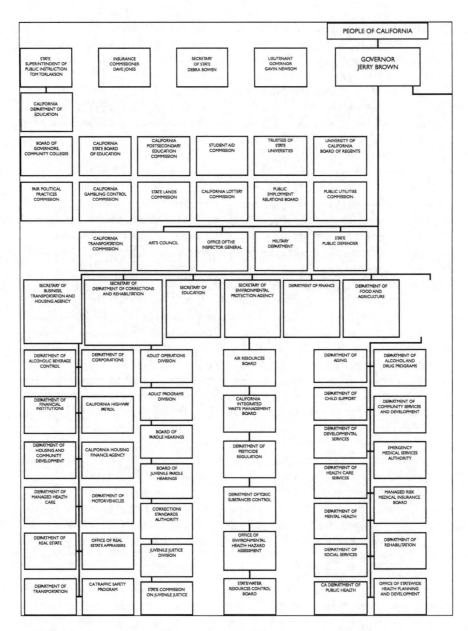

**FIGURE 7.1** State Departments and Agencies.

of the California National Guard, which on occasion is sent to help manage local crises in the state on a short-term basis. The governor also has the power to grant pardons, reprieves, or sentence commutations, although such authority is rarely exercised. Finally, the governor is the ceremonial head of state for greeting dignitaries from other countries. Along with the other major functions, these powers keep the governor very active and in the public eye.

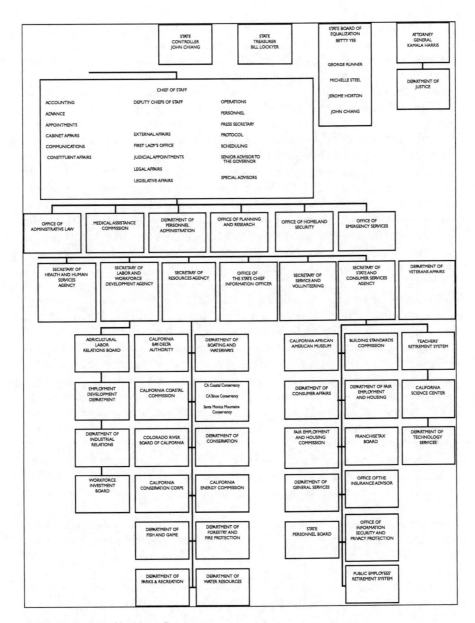

**FIGURE 7.1** (Continued)

## Informal Powers

Formal constraints on the governor can be offset to some extent by a power that is not written into the constitution at all, yet effective nonetheless: the governor's popularity. When the governor is in good stead with other legislators and/or the public, he or she is often able to overcome political opponents.

Historically, California's governors have used the prestige of their office to push their own agendas. Republican Governor Pete Wilson touted **Proposition 187**, an attempt to reduce government benefits to illegal immigrants that was ultimately rejected by the federal courts. In 1996 Wilson championed **Proposition 209**, titled the California Civil Rights Initiative, to eliminate affirmative action. And in 1998 he promoted **Proposition 227**, an initiative restricting bilingual education. These initiatives benefitted Wilson initially but have since hurt the Republican party's reputation with the state's increasingly diverse racial and ethnic diversity—a stigma that remains to this day.

Democratic Governor Gray Davis operated with a personality that left little room for disagreement. He attacked the other branches of state government, claiming that state legislators were supposed to implement his vision[3] and that judicial appointees should reflect his views.[4] His obsession with constant fund-raising from individuals and organizations in search of state business added to his image problems. When Davis was reelected in 2002, the state suffered a perfect storm with exorbitant energy costs, a lengthy recession, and huge budget shortfalls. As the state's condition worsened, the voters lost patience with Davis. In a July 2003 Field poll, 61 percent of the respondents blamed Davis for the state's problems.[5] Thus, as an unprecedented recall effort moved along during 2003, Davis first lost his public support and informal power, and soon after that, his job.[6]

Arnold Schwarzenegger used his informal power to circumvent the legislature whose members he called "girlie men" for not adopting his budgets.[7] Repeatedly, he cut deals directly with organizations and institutions from local governments to universities, prison guards, and Indian gaming interests. In 2010, Schwarzenegger negotiated pension reforms with several state employee unions that mandated higher employee contributions—something the legislature had not dared to even tackle.[8]

Schwarzenegger had mixed results with the voters. In March 2004 he successfully barnstormed the state for a ballot measure, described as a $15 billion "recovery" bond that temporarily balanced the state budget. But in 2005 Schwarzenegger suffered a stinging defeat, when voters rejected his ballot measures on teacher tenure, union campaign contributions, strict state budget controls, and legislative redistricting. His standing in public opinion polls plummeted from 64 percent to 35 percent in ten short months,[9] and he never fully recovered.

Still, Schwarzenegger used his personality even in defeat to reconnect with the public. Immediately after the 2005 election, he reflected, "I should have listened to my wife [prominent Democrat Maria Shriver], who said don't do this."[10] That self-effacing approach helped gain Schwarzenegger reelection in 2006. But his ballot box success was short-lived. In 2009, Schwarzenegger asked voter support for a series of five budget-related initiatives; all were rejected.

Schwarzenegger's vision often exceeded his ability to deliver. In successive years, he declared the "year" of political reform, which ended with the defeat of four Schwarzenegger-tailored ballot measures; the "year" of health-care reform, which fizzled in the legislature; and the "year" of education reform, which sputtered out after he cut public funding several years in a row to leave

California near the bottom of the fifty states in per capita spending. More times than not, Schwarzenegger's performance failed to match his bravado.

Jerry Brown has approached his current occupancy of the governorship much differently than his first go-around thirty-six years earlier. With his election in 2010 at the age of seventy-two, Brown became the oldest person to be elected to the position; coincidentally, when he was elected in 1974 at the age of thirty-six, he was the state's youngest in history, a record that stands to this day. During his first two terms, Brown had a contentious relationship with the legislature. He was nick-named "Governor Moonbeam" for a variety of futuristic, and sometimes whimsical proposals thought by many to be couched in anything but reality.

That was then. Between stints in the governor's office, Brown was chair of the state Democratic party, served as mayor of Oakland, and elected state attorney general. And he married. The totality of these experiences and more helped facilitate the transformation of Jerry Brown.

In his first two years of the current term, Brown has shown a blend of patience and quiet urgency with the legislature about solving the state's issues. He has assiduously courted Democrats and Republicans, liberals and conservatives. His efforts notwithstanding, Brown has not been able to suture the differences within the legislature. As he recently lamented, "There's not a thread of common purpose" between the two sides.[11]

Still, Brown has persevered. He has battled with the legislature on the budget, going so far as to veto the entire document in 2011 before accepting a modified version (see Chapter 8 for budget issues). Elsewhere, in 2011 he convinced the legislature to pass his **"realignment"** plan to move nonviolent prisoners from state facilities to less expensive county jails. In 2012, he persuaded the legislature to spend most of a $10 billion bond on the first leg of the state's proposed high-speed rail system, despite skittish public opinion and uncertain future funds. In the same year, he helped narrow future state budget deficits by securing agreements from public employee unions on wage cuts of almost 5 percent and convinced the legislature to pass pension reforms. Jerry Brown hasn't won all his battles, but he has enjoyed support in public opinion polls at levels far greater than support for the legislature.

### Ever-Changing Relationships

The powers of the governor's office remain basically the same year after year and administration after administration. But how those powers are managed depends on the issues, the times, the political environment, and the personality of the occupant. Yet one fact remains indisputable: the governor is clearly first among equals in the executive branch.

## THE SUPPORTING CAST

Most states provide for the election of a lieutenant governor, a secretary of state, a treasurer, and an attorney general, but few elect an education officer, a controller, a Board of Equalization, and an insurance regulator. Moreover, most states require the governor and the lieutenant governor (and others, in some cases) to run on the same party ticket, thus providing some cohesion. Not so in California, where each elected member of the executive branch is elected independently of the others.

The consequences can be quite serious. For example, when Governor Schwarzenegger unilaterally withheld $3.1 billion from the public schools in 2005 in defiance of what many believed were state guarantees, Superintendent of Public Instruction Jack O'Connell sued. Ultimately, O'Connell dropped the suit after the governor and public school officials found agreement. On another occasion, then-state Republican Insurance Commissioner Steve Poizner sued to stop the sale of the state-run workers' compensation insurance fund, proposed by fellow Republican Governor Arnold Schwarzenegger. The issue was dropped after Schwarzenegger and Poizner left office. These examples show the extent to which very public fights can occur between two independently operating office-holders in the executive branch.

## The Lieutenant Governor

The **lieutenant governor** is basically an executive-in-waiting with few formal responsibilities. If the governor becomes disabled or is out of the state, the lieutenant governor fills in as acting governor. If the governor leaves office, the lieutenant governor takes over. This has happened seven times in the state's history; most recently in 1953, when Goodwin Knight replaced Earl Warren, who became chief justice of the U.S. Supreme Court. The current lieutenant governor, Democrat and former San Francisco mayor Gavin Newsom, was elected in 2010, displacing Abel Maldonado, who had been appointed to the office earlier in the year.

The lieutenant governor heads some units, such as the State Lands Commission and the Commission on Economic Development, and is an ex officio member of the University of California Board of Regents and California State University Board of Trustees. He or she also serves as president of the state senate, but this job, too, is long on title and short on substance. As senate president, the lieutenant governor may vote to break 20-20 ties, an event that last occurred in 1976. So minimal are the responsibilities of the lieutenant governor; one occupant once quipped his biggest daily task was to wake up, check the morning newspaper to see whether the governor had died, and then return to bed![12] That description may stretch the point a bit, but not by much. As current Lieutenant Governor Newsom recently said about the office, "it's just so dull."[13]

## The Attorney General

Despite the lieutenant governor's higher rank, the **attorney general** is usually considered the second-most powerful member of the executive branch. As head of the Department of Justice, the attorney general oversees law enforcement activities, acts as legal counsel to state agencies, represents the state in important cases, and renders opinions on (interprets) proposed and existing laws. In the 2010 contest for attorney general, former San Francisco district attorney Kamala Harris narrowly defeated Los Angeles County District Attorney Steve Cooley for the position. She succeeded Jerry Brown, who served between 2006 and 2010. Harris is also the first female and person of color to hold the post.

Substantial authority and independent election allow the attorney general to chart a course separate from the governor on important state questions. During his tenure as attorney general, for example, Jerry Brown sued insurance companies for misleading ads, prosecuted companies for not paying at least the minimum wage, and petitioned the federal government to regulate greenhouse gases.

Harris has made her own mark. In 2011, she resisted going along with a $20 billion settlement of a suit accepted by forty-eight other states against five major banks for abusive practices. But Harris held out, arguing that Californians would be short-changed. A few months later, the banks agreed to settle at $32 billion, enabling California to gain a much larger share of the disbursement.[14]

## The Secretary of State

Unlike the U.S. cabinet official who bears the same title, the **secretary of state** of California is basically a records keeper and elections supervisor. The job entails certifying the number and validity of signatures obtained for initiatives, referenda, and recall petitions; producing sample ballots and ballot arguments for the voters; publishing official election results; and keeping candidate campaign finance records. The current secretary of state, Democrat Debra Bowen, was first elected in 2006. She has brought order to an office that was rocked by scandal in 2005, when then secretary of state Kevin Shelley resigned because of receiving illegal campaign contributions.

Recently, the secretary of state has had responsibility for converting California's election system from paper ballots to electronic voting machines. Bowen, a skeptic about electronic voting, has been in no great hurry. In 2007 she announced a ban on almost all electronic voting machines in thirty-nine counties until it could be demonstrated that the machines are not prone to any viruses or manipulation. This policy has required counties to either invest in new state-certified machines that include paper verification or resort to paper ballots.

## The Superintendent of Public Instruction

The **superintendent of public instruction** heads the Department of Education. He or she is the only elected official in the executive branch chosen by nonpartisan ballot. Unless one candidate wins a majority in the June primary, the top two candidates face each other in the November general election. The superintendent's powers are severely limited. Funding is determined largely by the governor's budgetary decisions, and policies are closely watched by the governor-appointed state board of education and the education committees of the legislature.

In general, the electorate knows little about the office, but teachers' unions, education administrators, and other affected groups take great interest in the choice of superintendent because this official is the advocate for California's massive public education system. The current superintendent of public instruction, former state senator and assemblyman Tom Torlakson, was elected in 2010 with strong support from the California Teachers' Association, the most powerful education organization in the state.

## The Money Officers

Perhaps the most fractured part of the executive branch of California government is the group of elected officials who manage the state's money. Courtesy of the Progressive reformers who feared a concentration of power, the controller, the treasurer, and the Board of Equalization have separate but overlapping responsibilities in this area. The **controller** supervises all state and local tax collection and writes checks for the state, including those to state employees. The controller is also an *ex officio* (automatic, by virtue of the office) member of several agencies, including the Board of Equalization, the Franchise Tax Board, and the State Lands Commission. Of all the "money officers," the controller is the most powerful, and thus the most prominent. The current controller, Democrat and former Board of Equalization member John Chiang, was elected in 2006 in his first run for statewide office and reelected in 2010. He has been an outspoken critic of California's ongoing budget crisis.

The **treasurer** invests state funds raised through taxes and other means until they are needed for expenditures. The treasurer also borrows money for the state by issuing bonds approved by the voters. Typically amounting to several billion dollars, the bonds are sold in financial markets to permit development of long-term projects such as highways, water projects, or other infrastructure needs. The state then "redeems" the bonds over time through interest payments. Democrat Bill Lockyer, former state attorney general, was elected to this office in 2006 and reelected in 2010. He has gained some notoriety by publishing periodic reports that reflect on the state's financial status with lending institutions that purchase California bonds.

The **Board of Equalization**, also part of California's fiscal system, oversees the collection of excise taxes on sales, gasoline, and liquor. The board also reviews county property assessment practices to ensure uniform calculation methods and practices. The board has five members—four of whom are elected in districts of equal population, plus the controller. Historically, the board has attracted little attention, but in 2007 the members voted to tax "alcopops"—sweet alcohol drinks often consumed by underage drinkers—at the same rate as hard liquor instead of beer. The change would have raised the tax from 20 cents per gallon to $3.30 per gallon, increasing the cost of alcopop drinks by about 25 percent. But manufacturers avoided the tax by lowering the alcohol content.

## The Insurance Commissioner

The office of **insurance commissioner** exemplifies the persistent reform mentality of California voters. Until 1988, the office was part of the state's Business, Housing, and Transportation Agency. However, with soaring insurance rates, voters approved an initiative that called for 20 percent across-the-board reductions in automobile insurance premiums and created the elected position of insurance commissioner. Consumer Watchdog, the public interest group behind the proposition, claims that the law saved California drivers more than $60 billion during its first twenty years of existence.

Democrat Dave Jones, a termed-out member of the state assembly, was elected to the office in 2010, succeeding Steve Poizner, who unsuccessfully sought the Republican nomination for governor. Jones campaigned with the promise to hold health insurance companies accountable for any rate increases, an authority not held by the commissioner. However, with the passage of the Affordable Care Act by Congress, most observers expect the legislature to give this responsibility to Jones, as is the case in thirty other states.

### The Supporting Cast—Snow White's Seven Dwarfs?

Combined, the seven other elected members of the executive branch (plus the Board of Equalization) present an appearance of tremendous political activity. Still, their efforts often center on narrow policy areas and frequently are in opposition to one another, as well as to the much more powerful governor.

## THE BUREAUCRACY

Elected officials are just the most observable part of the state's administrative machinery. Backing them up, implementing their programs, and dealing with citizens on a daily basis are about 341,000 state workers—the **bureaucracy**. Only about 5,000 of these workers are appointed by the governor or by other executive officers. The remainder are hired and fired through the state's **civil service system** on the basis of their examination results, performance, and job qualifications. The Progressives designed this system to insulate government workers from political influences and to make them more professional than those who might be hired out of friendship.

The task of the bureaucracy is to carry out the programs established by the policymaking institutions: the executive branch, the legislature, and the judiciary, along with a handful of regulatory agencies. However, because bureaucrats are permanent, full-time professionals, they sometimes influence the content of programs and policies, chiefly by advising public officials or by exercising the discretion built into the laws that define bureaucratic tasks. The bureaucracy can also influence policy through the lobbying efforts of its employee organizations (see Chapter 4).

State bureaucrats work for various departments and agencies (see Figure 7.1), each run by an administrator who is appointed by the governor and confirmed by the senate. Sometimes, political appointees and civil servants clash over the best ways to carry out state policy. If the bureaucracy becomes too independent, the governor can always use his or her budgetary powers to bring it back into line or, in some cases, dismiss appointees.

In recent years, California's bureaucrats have been particularly ambitious on climate change. The California Energy Commission (CEC) has instituted energy efficiency standards for televisions and other electrical appliances. Also, the

California Air Resources Board (CARB) has led the way in regulating greenhouse gas levels. These efforts have kept California's energy consumption flat during the past three decades, compared with a 40 percent increase in energy consumption nationwide. They have also established California as a trendsetting state on the issues of global warming and energy use.

Some observers have criticized California's bureaucracy as unnecessarily inflated and unresponsive, even though the size of the state's system ranks forty-eighth of the fifty states on a per capita basis.[15] Still, there is no denying that slim or not, the state's bureaucracy grew under the Schwarzenegger administration to about 350,000, despite his promise to "blow up the boxes" of the bureaucracy shortly after taking office. Under Governor Jerry Brown, the size of the state bureaucracy has actually declined by nearly 10,000 employees, as he and the legislature have struggled to find ways to reduce the cost of state government. Brown has also successfully promoted pension reform, which reduces the state's obligations to state government retirees.

## MAKING THE PIECES FIT

The executive branch is a hodgepodge of independently elected authorities who serve in overlapping and conflicting institutional positions. Nobody, not even the governor, is really in charge. Each official simply attempts to carry out his or her mission with the hope that passable policy will result. Occasionally, reformers have suggested streamlining the system by consolidating functions and reducing the number of elective offices, but the only relative recent change has been the addition of yet another office, that of insurance commissioner.

Despite these obstacles, the officeholders—most notably governors—have been active policymakers. Pete Wilson waged war against illegal immigrants, affirmative action, and welfare while trumpeting "law and order." Gray Davis responded to the state's power shortage crisis. Arnold Schwarzenegger was instrumental in environmental reform. And Jerry Brown has championed "efficiency," perhaps more out of necessity than desire.

Still, the governor does not operate in a vacuum. He or she must contend with other members of the executive branch, a fractured and suspicious legislature, independent courts, a professional bureaucracy, and most of all, an electorate with a highly erratic collective pulse. Whether these conditions are challenges or impediments, they make the executive branch a fascinating element of California government.

## NOTES

1. "Special Sessions Define Schwarzenegger," *Sign on San Diego*, October 22, 2009, http://signonsandiego.printthis.clickability.com/pt/cpt?action=cpt&tit.
2. "Gov. Jerry Brown Orders California Workers to Turn in 48,000 Cellphones," *Los Angeles Times*, January 12, 2011, http://articles.latimes.com/print/2011/jan/12/local/la-me-cell-phones-20110112.

3. "Tensions Flare between Davis and His Democrats," *Los Angeles Times*, July 22, 1999, pp. A1, A28.

4. "Davis Comments Draw Fire," *San Jose Mercury News*, March 1, 2000, p. 14A.

5. *The Field Poll*, Release #2074, July 15, 2003.

6. For an account of how Davis fell from power, see Larry N. Gerston and Terry Christensen, *Recall! California's Political Earthquake* (Armonk, N.Y.: M. E. Sharpe, 2004).

7. "Gov. Criticizes Legislators as 'Girlie Men,'" *Los Angeles Times*, July 18, 2004, pp. B1, B18.

8. "Governor Slashes Workers' Pay," *San Francisco Chronicle*, July 2, 2010, pp. C1, C6.

9. "Schwarzenegger's Popularity Slide," *Los Angeles Times*, October 28, 2005, p. B2.

10. "Schwarzenegger Says the Fault Is His," *New York Times*, November 11, 2006, p. A14.

11. "Policymaking on Hold as Brown Nurses His Wounds," *Los Angeles Times*, August 17, 2011, pp. AA1, AA4.

12. "The Most Invisible Job in Sacramento," *Los Angeles Times*, May 10, 1998, pp. A1, A20.

13. "Uh, Gavin…," *San Francisco Chronicle*, May 31, 2012, p. A15.

14. "Rising Star Mixes Idealism, Political Savvy," *San Francisco Chronicle,* April 29, 2012, pp. A1, A12.

15. "Looking for Waste," *Economist*, May 1, 2010, p. 33.

## LEARN MORE ON THE WEB

Office of the Attorney General:
www.caag.state.ca.us

Office of the Governor:
www.gov.ca.gov

Office of the Secretary of State:
www.ss.ca.gov

Office of the State Board of Equalization:
www.boe.ca.gov

Office of the State Controller:
www.sco.ca.gov

Office of the State Insurance Commissioner:
www.insurance.ca.gov

Office of the State Treasurer:
www.treasurer.ca.gov

Office of the State Superintendent of Public Instruction:
www.cde.ca.gov/eo

Salaries of state employees:
www.capitolweekly.net/salaries/index.php?_c=yzbexjathf9ge0

## LEARN MORE AT THE LIBRARY

John C. Bollens and G. Robert Williams. *Jerry Brown in a Plain Brown Wrapper*. Pacific Palisades, Calif.: Palisades Publishers, 1978.

Larry N. Gerston and Terry Christensen. *Recall! California's Political Earthquake*. Armonk, N.Y.: M. E. Sharpe, 2004.

Gary G. Hamilton and Nicole Woolsey Biggert. *Governor Reagan, Governor Brown: A Sociology of Executive Power*. New York: Columbia University Press, 1984.

Joe Mathews. *The People's Machine*. New York: Public Affairs Press, 2006.

# 8

# Taxing and Spending: Budgetary Politics and Policies

## CHAPTER CONTENTS

No issue is more critical to Californians than taxation, and no resource is more important to state policymakers than the revenues generated from taxation. Those dollars become the foundation of the annual state budget, which determines where and how state funds will be spent.

The connection between taxing and spending can be difficult. Even though most people may agree on taxes in principle, they often disagree on how much should be collected and from whom, as well as the recipients of those funds. When policymakers seem to stray from general public values on budgetary issues, the voters are not shy about using direct democracy to reorder the state's fiscal priorities—and with so many more policy areas of need than dollars available, much is at stake.

## CALIFORNIA'S BUDGET ENVIRONMENT

Unlike the national government, which usually operates with a deficit, state constitutions require balanced budgets. This has been difficult in California, where a steady flow of immigrants, a burgeoning school-aged population, massive attention to crime, and deteriorating infrastructure combine for a challenging budget environment. Since a recession in 2002, the state has struggled with one projected state revenue deficit after another regardless of who has been in power.

A deficit of more than $20 billion helped seal the fate of Governor Gray Davis in the unprecedented 2003 recall election. His replacement, Arnold Schwarzenegger promised fiscal soundness, and found himself victimized by California's unpredictable fiscal climate. In fact, his first budget was $8 billion out of balance immediately upon signature. A temporary economic upswing in 2006 facilitated a balanced, on-time budget for the first time in years. But the joy was short-lived.

By 2008, the state faced a revenue shortfall in excess of $15 billion, once again forcing drastic cuts. Twice in 2009, the governor and legislature grappled with the deficit. First, they sutured a massive $42 billion hole in March through a combination of new taxes, program cuts, and transfers. Three months later, state leaders had to overcome a new $24 billion gap, this time in program and services cuts only. The state's economic malaise persisted into the 2010–2011 fiscal year, when the weary governor and legislature faced a new $21 billion hole. Again they cut.

On his return to the state's office in 2011, Jerry Brown found himself haunted by the same environment that had plagued his predecessors. This time, the state faced a $26 billion deficit for the coming fiscal year, leading to more cuts in almost every program area except prisons. By 2012, an exasperated Governor Brown and the legislature plugged half of a $16 billion hole for the 2012–2013 fiscal year. But Brown warned there would be three fewer weeks in the school year if the voters did not pass a November initiative producing temporary tax increases of about $8 billion annually for seven years to generate the rest. They did. Even so, California's state budget has shrunk from about $105 billion in 2005–2006 to $91 billion in 2012–2013, as the state's population has grown from 36 million to 38.6 million.

The voters haven't helped with this ongoing dilemma. Repeatedly, the public has rejected new taxes while embracing new programs and services. When two Field polls in March 2010 asked the best way to balance the state budget, respondents who favored spending cuts outnumbered those who favored tax increases by a margin of nearly 4 to 1.[1] Yet when survey respondents were asked where the cuts should be made, majorities could be found in only two of fourteen major public policy areas—prisons and parks.[2] Moreover, over the past quarter century, voters have passed a series of ballot propositions directing the state to spend money on various programs ranging from longer prison sentences to more comprehensive public education without providing the funds. This is the political environment in which elected officials must make tough decisions.

## THE BUDGETARY PROCESS

Budget making is a complicated and lengthy activity in California. Participants include the governor and various executive-branch departments, the legislature and its support agencies, the public (via initiative and referendum), and increasingly, the courts when judges uphold or overturn commitments made by the other policymakers.

### The Governor and Other Executive Officers

Preparation of the annual budget is the governor's most important formal power. Other policymakers participate in the budgetary process, but no other individual has as much clout. The governor frames the document before it goes to the legislature and then has additional say afterward through use of the item veto. Given this unique power position, legislative leaders often negotiate with the chief executive over what he or she will accept long before the budget lands on the governor's desk.

During the summer and fall, the governor's director of finance works closely with the heads of state agencies. Supported by a staff of fiscal experts and researchers, the director of finance gathers and assesses information about the anticipated needs of each department and submits a "first draft" budget to the governor in late fall. The governor presents a refined version of this draft to the legislature the following January. The state constitution gives the legislature until June 15 to respond.

### Legislative Participants

Upon receiving the budget in January, the legislature's leaders do little more than refer the document to the legislative analyst. Over the next two months, the legislative analyst and his or her staff scrutinize each part of the budget, considering needs, costs, and other factors. Often, the analyst's findings clash with those of the governor, providing the legislature with an independent source of data and evaluation.

Meanwhile, two key legislative units in each house—the appropriations committees and the budget committees—shepherd the budget proposal through the legislative process. After the staffs of these committees spend about two months scrutinizing the entire document, each house assigns portions to various other committees and their staffs. During this time, lobbyists, individual citizens, government officials, and other legislators testify on the proposed budget before committees and subcommittees. By mid-April, the committees conclude their hearings, combine their portions into a single document, and bring the budget bill to their respective full house for a vote.

As June nears and the two houses hone their versions, a select group of leaders enter into informal negotiations over the document. Known as the **Big Five**, the governor, the speaker of the assembly, the president pro tem of the senate, and the minority party leaders of each house become the nucleus of the final budgetary decisions. In recent years, the Big Five have cast long shadows over just about all of the other players. Should the two houses differ on specifics, the bill goes to a two-house conference committee for reconciliation, after which both houses vote again. With passage of **Proposition 25** in 2010, it now takes a simple majority to pass the budget, a change from the previous long-standing two-thirds requirement. However, inasmuch as a two-thirds vote is still required for revenue increases, the significance of this change is questionable.

## The Courts

Sometimes, the courts weigh in on key budget issues to address some of the "quick fixes" to complex budget issues enacted by public policymakers or the voters. Governor Schwarzenegger was humbled in 2005 when a state superior court judge ruled that he was obligated to enforce a new law that reduced the ratio of patients to nurses from 6–1 to 5–1. In 2008, a decision by the U.S. District Court forced the state to spend billions of dollars on improved prison conditions, adding still more to a budget already billions in the red. In 2009 a federal court rejected $500 million in social service cuts as incompatible with federal law, a decision that added to the budget crisis of that year. And even as California attempted to comply with a federal court order to reduce the inmate population of its overcrowded state prisons, a court-appointed receiver rejected the state's effort to reduce costs as excessive. Clearly, the courts have found reason to shape state budgets.

Even the will of the voters has been subject to judicial review on matters relating to the state budget. Particularly significant have been the many cases arising from Proposition 13. Also, decisions on the death penalty and the famous "three strikes and you're out" initiative (see Chapter 6) have added greatly to state incarceration costs.

## The Public

On occasion, the public shapes the budget through initiatives or referenda. The voters relied on ballot propositions to approve the sales tax (1933) and repeal the inheritance tax (1982).

In 1993 the voters passed a proposition that increased the state sales tax by 0.5 percent, with new revenues exclusively earmarked for public safety provided by local governments. In 2004 the voters enacted an initiative that created an additional 1 percent tax bracket for people with taxable incomes of $1 million or more, with the funds designated for mental health programs. And in 2012, the voters passed **Proposition 30**, which temporarily increased sales and income taxes for individuals with annual incomes over $250,000 to offset declining state revenues.

The public doesn't always agree to increases, however. The voters soundly rejected a 2006 initiative that would have added an additional tax bracket of 1.7 percent beyond the highest level for individuals with taxable incomes of $400,000 or more, with the revenues earmarked for a statewide preschool program.

In 2009, the governor and legislature strung together five ballot proposals that would simultaneously cap spending and temporarily increase sales taxes (0.25 percent), income taxes (1 percent), and motor vehicle fees (0.50 percent). The public said no to all five propositions.

Perhaps the most dramatic tax-altering event came in 1978 with the passage of **Proposition 13**, an initiative that reduced local property taxes by 57 percent. Since then, property owners have saved more than $528 billion in taxes,[3] while local governments have become increasingly dependent on the state for relief. As a result, the state has become the major funder for local services such as public education, although support has varied with the health of the economy. This uncertainty has brought endless criticism from local government officials.

The bottom line is that there are many more players in the budget process than meet the eye. This complexity both slows down the process and requires near unanimity among the various parties before any major decisions are made.

## REVENUE SOURCES

Like most states, California relies on several forms of taxation for its general fund budget (that is, the budget exclusive of federal funds). The largest sources of revenue are personal income tax, sales tax, and bank and corporation taxes. Smaller revenue supplies come from motor vehicle, fuel, insurance, tobacco, and alcohol taxes. The state's major revenue sources and expenditures for fiscal year 2012–2013 are shown in Figure 8.1.

Other taxes are levied by local governments. Chief among these is the property tax, although its use was reduced considerably by Proposition 13. This tax is collected by counties rather than by the state, but the state allocates it among the different levels of local government, and it still is a part—directly or indirectly—of the tax burden of all Californians.

All too aware of the state's antitax mood, policymakers have refused to add taxes to cope with burgeoning needs. As a result, the state's commitments to most services have decreased considerably over the past three decades. Individual recipients, school districts, and local governments have been thrown into turmoil. Infrastructure projects, such as highway maintenance programs and Sacramento delta levee repairs, have been stretched out. Placement of a new earthquake-resistant Oakland–San Francisco Bay bridge will not be complete until 2013, twenty-four years after the earthquake that caused its damage. And

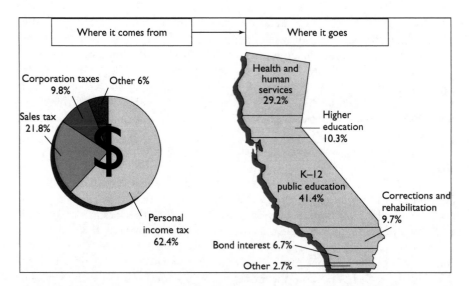

**FIGURE 8.1**   California's Revenue Sources and Expenditures, 2012–2013.
SOURCE: Legislative Analyst's Office

a recent study finds two-thirds of the state's roads in disrepair and 30 percent of the state's bridges "structurally deficient or fundamentally obsolete."[4]

## The Sales Tax

Until the Great Depression of 1929, a relatively small state government garnered funds by relying on minor taxes on businesses and utilities. After the economic crash, however, the state was forced to develop new tax sources to cope with hard times. The first of these, a 2.5 percent **sales tax** on certain goods and products except food, was adopted to provide permanent funding for schools and local governments. Today, the statewide sales tax is 7.50 percent, courtesy of the one quarter addition that was part of Proposition 30. Of that amount, cities and counties get 2 percent to help meet health and public safety needs. The state keeps the rest. In addition, as much as 1.5 percent is tacked on by cities and counties engaged in state-approved projects, most of which are transportation related. Today, the sales tax accounts for about 21.8 percent of the state's tax revenues.

## The Personal Income Tax

A second major revenue source, the personal income tax, was modeled after its federal counterpart to collect greater amounts of money from those residents with greater earnings. Today, the personal income tax varies between 1.0 and 12.3 percent, depending on one's income. The 11.3 percent and 12.3 percent brackets, however, have seven-year life spans for individuals earning between $350,000 and $500,000 and more than $500,000, as a result of Proposition 30.

The personal income tax is now the fastest-growing component of state revenue (see Figure 8.2)—a significant fact because Californians ranked eleventh

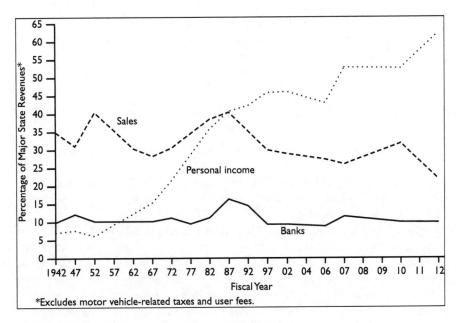

**FIGURE 8.2** California's Tax Burden, 1942–2012.

SOURCE: Department of Finance

among the fifty states in per capita income in 2011. As of 2012, the personal income tax accounted for 62.4 percent of the state tax bite.

## Corporation Taxes

Corporation income taxes contribute much less to California's budget than do sales and personal income taxes. Taxes on corporate incomes did not exceed 5.5 percent until 1959, when the legislature enacted the first of a series of rate hikes. Since 1996, the corporate tax rate has remained at 8.84 percent. Corporation taxes now account for about 9.8 percent of state revenues.

Aside from Proposition 13 and the reliance on **user taxes**, such as those levied on gasoline and cigarettes, California's revenue collection system has undergone gradual adjustments over the past sixty years. Figure 8.2 shows the changing weight of the sales, personal income, and corporation taxes from 1942 to the present. Along with a steady drift toward increased dependence on the personal income tax, the state has experienced decreased dependence on sales and corporation taxes.

## Bonds

From time to time, state leaders have asked voters to approve bonds, thus obligating the electorate to long-term commitments. These projects, sometimes lasting as long as forty years, finance major infrastructure commitments such as school classroom, transportation, and water projects.

The state has turned to bonds with increasing frequency. In 1991, California ranked thirty-second among the fifty states in indebtedness on a per capita basis. By 2010, the state's bond debt increased to more than $140 billion, $70 billion of which had been enacted during the Schwarzenegger administration alone. That represents a per capita indebtedness of $2,362, second only to New York.

### Taxes in Perspective

Viewed in a comparative context, the overall tax burden for California ranks ninth in the nation on a per capita basis, remarkably close to its per capita income ranking. Nevertheless, there have been changes in the state tax blend, with the state becoming increasingly dependent on the personal income tax as its primary source of income.

On a per capita basis, the state ranks third in personal income taxes, ninth in corporation taxes, twelfth in sales taxes, and twenty-ninth in property taxes.[5] In other areas, California taxes are near the bottom, due largely to the influence of powerful interest groups. For example, the state ranks forty-ninth in both fuel taxes and alcoholic beverage taxes. Reformers attempted to establish oil production taxes of $400 million over ten years via initiative in 2006, but the measure was soundly defeated at the polls. As a result, California is the only one of fourteen major oil-producing states that does not tax oil. With respect to tobacco taxes, California ranks thirty-third in the nation.[6] Had the voters approved a ballot proposition in 2012 increasing the tobacco tax by $1.00 per pack, the state would be collecting an additional $1 billion for children's health care, but that measure, too, was defeated. In these and other cases, interest groups have carried great sway with the legislature and public.

## SPENDING

The annual state budget addresses thousands of financial commitments, both large and small. Major areas include public education (grades K through 12), health and welfare, higher education, and prisons. Outlays in these four areas account for nearly 90 percent of the general fund. The remainder of the budget (the difference between total expenditures and the general fund) goes to designated long-term projects such as transportation, parks, and veterans' programs, many of which have been authorized by public ballot or include federal funds.

Since 1979, several voter-passed ballot propositions have created a budget system that is largely formula-driven. K-12 public education, transportation programs, and mental health are among the many program areas where either percentages of the budget or specific revenues are directed for specific areas. Thus, public education receives at least 40 percent of the general fund unless two-thirds of the legislature grants a waiver because of a fiscal emergency. Likewise motor vehicle fees are directed exclusively for transportation-related services and projects. Some critics have characterized the formula approach as a political "straitjacket" that is unresponsive to changing times and needs. Defenders of "formula government" argue that it is the only way to keep state leaders from operating with a blank check.

## Public Education: Grades K through 12

The state constitution gives public education a "superior right" to state funds; as such, public schools get the largest share of the state budget. Local school districts periodically add relatively small amounts to education through voter-approved bonds and parcel taxes, but the preponderance of support comes from the state legislature through its annual allocations.

Funding for public education in California has an uneven history. The state ranked among the top-funded states throughout the 1950s and 1960s. Then the pattern changed. During the 1970s and 1980s, the state consistently reduced its per capita support for K through 12 public education, shrinking it to 37 percent of the general fund in 1988. That same year, amid growing concerns about weak funding and poor classroom performance, education reformers secured voter approval of **Proposition 98**, a measure that established 40 percent as a minimum funding threshold except in times of fiscal emergency. With this mandate, the state poured money into reducing class sizes in grades K through 3 and lengthened the school year from 180 to 190 days. But the upward direction was short-lived.

State aid for public education has dropped precipitously with declining state revenues. Between 2008 and 2012 alone, support fell from $50.3 billion to $37.8 billion. At $9,908 per student (2011–2012 figures), California expenditures remain about $2,800 below the national average,[7] and thousands more below comparable industrialized states. According to former state superintendent of public instruction Jack O'Connell, California ranks forty-sixth of the fifty states in per capita expenditures, despite having one of the highest per capita incomes in the nation (see Figure 8.3).[8] Meanwhile, the school year minimum has fallen to 175 days, three full weeks less classroom instruction than fifteen years ago. Only four states require less attendance from their students.

California ranks fiftieth among the states in its student-teacher ratio, a commonly used criterion for assessing education effectiveness. The state also ranks forty-seventh in the number of computers per classroom. All this has produced a sorry, if not unexpected, outcome in terms of high school graduation, where the state ranks forty-eighth.[9] According to studies by the National Assessment of Educational Progress, a well-known nonprofit group, California hovers near the bottom of almost every assessment category. Table 8.1 shows the most recent data available.

With Latino and Asian American students accounting for 51 percent and 12 percent of the school population, respectively, language-related issues have emerged. In 1998 the passage of **Proposition 227**, a measure limiting bilingual education for non-English-speaking students to one year, added to the debate over how to "mainstream" the diverse California student community. All of this has occurred in a state where one-fourth of all public school students are "English learners" (English is not the first language), compared with 9 percent nationally.

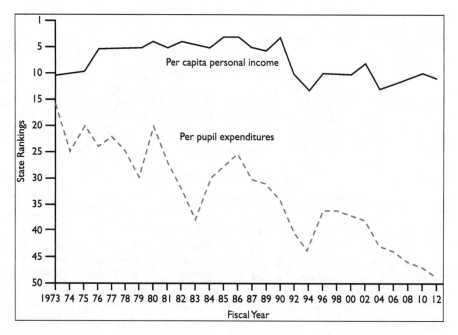

**FIGURE 8.3**  Personal Income and Public School Spending in California, 1973–2012.

**TABLE 8.1  California Rankings in Key Education Categories**

| Category | Rank | Year |
| --- | --- | --- |
| Reading, 4th grade | 47th | 2011 |
| Reading, 8th grade | 48th | 2011 |
| Math, 4th grade | 44th | 2011 |
| Math, 8th grade | 46th | 2011 |
| Science, 8th grade | 48th | 2011 |

SOURCE: National Assessment of Education Progress, 2012.

There are chilling consequences from these policies. For starters, California has a high school dropout rate of 24 percent, or about 125,000 students annually.[10] With few skills, their futures are very limited. At the other end of the spectrum, large numbers of those who do graduate high school are unprepared for college. A California State University study found that 55 percent of the incoming freshman class needed remedial instruction in either English or math.[11] Neither of these statistics points to educational excellence.

Nevertheless, the debate goes on. Some reformers have turned to "charter schools"—independent, community-controlled alternatives to what many describe as a broken system. As of 2012, there were about nine hundred charter schools in California, still a small number compared with the state's 9,700 traditional public schools, although up from six hundred in 2008. Other reformers have promoted vouchers—cash payments for parents to use in selecting an educational institution—but the voters have rejected such measures twice in recent years.

The process of fixing California's K-12 public education problems will be neither quick nor cheap. In 2007 a 1,700-page report commissioned by Governor Arnold Schwarzenegger declared that it would cost a staggering $1.5 trillion more each year to make all students academically proficient in traditional core knowledge areas such as reading, math, and science.[12] With current state, local, and federal expenditures for public education in the neighborhood of $75 billion, even the first step in such a leap would seem highly unlikely.

## Higher Education: Colleges and Universities

California's budget woes have cut deeply into support for higher education. Once viewed as the role model for public universities,[13] the higher education system has suffered for a lack of funding and greatly reduced admission slots.

Three components share responsibility for higher education in the state. The state's 112 two-year community colleges enroll about 2.6 million students. Historically, community colleges have been viewed as the entry institutions for students who otherwise did not qualify for, or who could not afford to attend, California's four-year public universities. They also provide valuable training programs. Funding for community colleges is connected to the formula for primary and secondary public schools; to that extent, they have benefited from Proposition 98. Still, reduced budget allocations from the state have forced the community colleges to pare back instruction offerings. Between 2009 and 2012, state support dropped by 13 percent, while the number of course offerings fell by 10 percent. Meanwhile, student fees increased to $36 per unit from $26 per unit. As a result, community college enrollments have dropped by 300,000.[14]

With 222,000 students, the University of California (UC) educates both undergraduate and graduate students at ten campuses throughout the state. Designated as the state's primary research university, UC is the only public institution permitted to award professional degrees (such as medical and law degrees) and doctorates. The California State University (CSU) system, with 417,000 students at twenty-three campuses, concentrates on undergraduate instruction, awarding master's degrees most commonly in such fields as education, engineering, and business.

State support for public universities was fairly constant until the 1990s, holding at about 11 percent of the general fund budget, and it peaked at 12.7 percent during the 2002–2003 fiscal year. Support has eroded considerably since those heady days. For fiscal year 2012–2013, only 10.3 percent of the general fund was dedicated to the public universities. More significantly, the state's share of the cost of education has decreased dramatically. For example, whereas California provided 90 percent of UC's education costs in 1969–1970, support dropped less than half by 2010. And at CSU, the 90 percent paid by the state in 1969–1970 fell to 54 percent in 2011–2012. Students have been forced to make up the shortfall. At both UC and CSU, student fees have more than tripled between 2003–2004 and 2011–2012. Meanwhile, CSU has cut back new enrollments by 40,000; UC has reduced enrollments by 1,500. Between tuition increases and the lack of room, the college participation rate of nineteen-year-olds has fallen precipitously—from 22 percent to 18 percent between 2007 and 2012 alone, dropping California from seventeenth to forty-sixth place among the fifty states.[15]

## Health and Human Services

Health and human services programs receive the second-largest share of the state budget. The programs accounting for the most significant state commitment include California Work Opportunity and Responsibility to Kids (CalWORKS), Medi-Cal, and the Supplemental Security Income (SSI) program. Medi-Cal provides health-care benefits for the poor, and SSI offers state assistance to the elderly and the disabled. But no program is as politically charged as CalWORKS, the primary welfare program.

California has sizable welfare costs. With about 12 percent of the nation's population, the state is home to 25 percent of all welfare recipients. In 1990, in contrast, California had 10.5 percent of the nation's population and 12 percent of all welfare recipients.

As welfare numbers have increased, per capita spending has gone down. Changes in state policy began in 1997 after Congress passed the Welfare Reform Act, limiting welfare payments to no more than five years. Shortly thereafter, the legislature passed its CalWORKS legislation, which provides cash grants and welfare-to-work services for needy families with children ten years of age or younger and requires all adults to work at least thirty-two hours per week. The eligibility period was reduced to four years under the Schwarzenegger administration. As of 2011, about 1.1 million Californians were CalWORKS recipients, two-thirds of whom were children.

In 2012, health and human services programs accounted for about 29.2 percent of the general fund. Average monthly welfare payments were $460 for the typical family of three, down by one-fourth from a decade earlier. Still, with the state scrambling to close a $16 billion budget hole for the coming fiscal year, Governor Brown and the legislature cut the eligibility period for CalWORKS recipients to two years, saving $880 million.

## Prisons

Of the major state allocation categories, the budgets for prisons and corrections have grown the most in recent years. As with education, the public has played a role in this policy area. Several initiatives have established mandatory prison terms for various crimes and extended the terms for many other crimes. The most sweeping changes occurred in 1994, when the legislature (and later the voters, through an initiative) enacted a new "**three strikes**" law for repeat felons. As of 2012, about 9,000 of the state's 130,000 prisoners were incarcerated under the three-strikes classification.

As a result of the three-strikes law and other policy changes, California's prison population swelled beyond belief. In 1994 the total prison population was 125,000. It had jumped to 168,000 by 2009, with the cost for incarceration averaging $49,000 per convict per year. The demographics are equally interesting: 37 percent Latino, 27 percent African American, and 27 percent white. Phenomenal incarceration growth has forced the construction of new prisons. Still, with a soaring inmate population, in 2006 Governor Schwarzenegger asked the legislature to build at least two more state prisons at a cost of $500 million each.

Between 1994 and 2012, corrections and rehabilitation was the fast growing area of state spending, ultimately reaching 10 percent of the annual budget. But prisoner lawsuits on overcrowding and medical conditions resulted in the federal courts ordering the state to reduce the number of inmates by at least 40,000 inmates to better match the prison population with prison capacity. Governor Jerry Brown responded to the order by creating a program to move 30,000 of the state's least violent offenders to county jails with the promise of state funds to accompany the shift. Under his plan known as **realignment**, sentencing and parole protocols were altered to permit more inmates either in county jails or out under local supervision. Also in 2012, the voters passed **Proposition 36**, which made it easier for about 3,000 nonviolent offenders to request reduced sentences. The new policy reduced state spending on incarceration to 9.7 percent of the state budget by 2012–2013, with an anticipated reduction to 7.5 percent by 2015–2016. Still, local officials remained skeptical of its success, given their new responsibilities.[16]

## Other Budget Obligations

California's budget crisis has many sources, some obvious and others not. Clearly, a prolonged recession has contributed mightily to the state's revenue grief. On the expenditure side of the budget ledger, out-of-control prison spending and welfare costs have been of great concern. Two other less known, yet fast-growing state expenditure categories are payment of bond debt and pension payouts. Together, they now consume close to 10 percent of the state general fund and show little sign of slowing down.

**Bonds.**   While voter-approved borrowing through bonds represents an "easy" way to fund major projects over time, cumulatively these bonds are taking a toll on the state. California now ranks tenth among the states in per capita bond debt, up from thirty-second in 1991. Our propensity to rely upon bonds has generated the lowest credit rating of any state, which adds to the interest costs to retire the bonds. About 6.7 percent of the state budget now goes to paying interest on the debt. Moreover, State Treasurer Bill Lockyer estimated in 2009 that at present rates, 10 percent or more of the state budget will be dedicated to debt payment by the middle of this decade.[17] The state's propensity for financing through bonds has left it with the lowest bond rating of any state, which means the highest interest payments.

**Retirement Pensions.**    California's massive public employee pension program, the California Public Employees' Retirement System (CalPERS), covers more than 1.6 million employees, retirees, and their families, or about 4 percent of the state's population. Just over 500,000 are retirees who have worked for various state government agencies. Employees contribute a small portion of their salary to the program, with the state providing the rest as part of the salary compensation package. For years CalPERS gushed with surpluses, thanks to a robust financial market that contained most of the fund's investments. Since the onslaught of the recession in 2008, CalPERS payments have exceeded revenues. By law, the state must make up for any shortfall, and that money comes out of the state budget. In fiscal year 2011–2012, the state was required pay out $2 billion of the general fund into CalPERS—double the amount paid in 2006. Because of spiraling costs, Governor Jerry Brown and the legislature enacted new cost control legislation in 2012, requiring higher employee contributions and extending retirement ages.

## CALIFORNIA'S BUDGET: TOO LITTLE, TOO MUCH, OR JUST RIGHT?

Have you ever met anyone who claims that he or she should pay more taxes? Neither have we. Almost everybody dislikes paying taxes, and almost everybody thinks that the money collected is spent incorrectly or unwisely. That seems to be a perennial dilemma in California. However, although most people oppose increased taxes, they also oppose program cuts. It's a modern-day dilemma for state policymakers and the public alike.

Like their counterparts elsewhere, California policymakers have struggled to find a fair system of taxation to pay for needed programs. Given the involvement of so many public and private interests, however, it's difficult to determine what is fair. Moreover, during the last few decades, taxation and budget decisions have been subject to radical change. Somehow, the state's infrastructure has survived, although critics have been less than thrilled with the fiscal uncertainty that has become commonplace in California government.

## NOTES

1.  Field Poll, Release No. 2329, March 2, 2010.
2.  Field Poll, Release No. 2335, March 24, 2010.
3.  Howard Jarvis Taxpayers Association, 2009, www.hjta.org/index.php.
4.  Tax Foundation, "Tax Data: California, March 3, 2011, http://www.taxfoundation .org/taxdata/show/228.html; "National and State Corporate Income Tax Rates, U.S. States and OECD Countries 2011," http://taxfoundation.org/article /national-and-state-corporate-income-tax-rates-us-states-and-oecd-countries-2011;

"Ranking State and Local Taxes," September 22, 2011, http://taxfoundation.org/article/ranking-state-and-local-sales-taxes-1, "Finance," in *Governing: State and Local Government Sourcebook* (Washington, D.C.: Congressional Quarterly, 2006), pp. 32–36.

5. "A Decade of Disinvestment: California Education Spending Nears the Bottom," California Budget Project, Sacramento, Calif., October 2011, p. 1.

6. "State Cigarette Excise Tax Rates and Rankings, 2012," www.tobaccofreekids.org.

7. Testimony before Assembly Budget Subcommittee No. 2, March 11, 2008.

8. *See Just the Facts* (Albany: Public Policy Institute of New York State, 2007).

9. "More Kids Staying in School," *San Francisco Chronicle*, June 28, 2012, pp. C1, C5.

10. "CSU Freshmen Face Challenges," *Los Angeles Times*, March 15, 2006, p. B9.

11. "No Quick, Cheap Fix for State's Schools," *Los Angeles Times*, March 15, 2007, pp. B1, B10.

12. See James Richardson, "What Price Glory?" *UCLA Magazine*, February 1997, p. 30; also see "A Crown Jewel of Education Struggles with Cuts in California," *New York Times*, November 20, 2009, pp. A1, A25.

13. "Colleges' Chancellor to Step Down," *Los Angeles Times*, March 7, 2012, p. AA3.

14. See Hans Johnson, "Defending Higher Education," Public Policy Institute of California, San Francisco, Calif., May 2012, pp. 7–8, and Christopher Neufeld and Stanton Glantz, "Ending the California Dream," op-ed in *San Francisco Chronicle*, July 14, 2009, p. A11.

15. "Counties Brace for Stream of State Prisoners," *San Francisco Chronicle*, October 2, 2011, pp. A1, A14.

16. "Rising Debt a Threat to State General Fund," *San Francisco Chronicle*, November 24, 2009, p. C3.

17. "California Bond Rating Now Lowest of Any State," *Los Angeles Times*, February 4, 2009, pp. A1, A11.

## LEARN MORE ON THE WEB

California Budget Project:
www.cbp.org

California state budget—Department of Finance:
www.dof.ca.gov

California state budget—Legislature:
www.lao.ca.gov

California Tax Reform Association:
www.caltaxreform.org

California Taxpayers' Association:
www.caltax.org

National Center for Education Statistics:
www.nces.ed.gov

National Governors Association:
www.nga.org

## LEARN MORE AT THE LIBRARY

Jack Citrin and Isaac William Martin, eds. *After the Revolt: California's Proposition 13.* Berkeley, Calif.: Berkeley Public Policy Press, 2009.

John Decker. *California in the Balance: Why Budgets Matter.* Berkeley, Calif.: Berkeley Public Policy Press, 2009.

Larry N. Gerston, *Not So Golden After All: The Rise and Fall of California.* New York, Taylor & Francis, 2012.

Alvin Rabushka and Pauline Ryan. *The Tax Revolt.* Stanford, Calif.: Hoover Institution Press, 1982.

Peter Schrag. *California: America's High-Stakes Experiment.* Berkeley: University of California Press, 2006.

# 9

# California's Local Governments: Politics at the Grassroots

## CHAPTER CONTENTS

News media tend to focus on state and national politics, but the activities of local governments often have a greater impact on our daily lives. Our city governments make decisions about traffic on our streets; safety in our neighborhoods; and access to parks, libraries, and affordable housing. Our county governments manage transit systems and provide important social services to those most in need, including people who are homeless, mentally ill, and impoverished. Our school districts decide what sorts of teachers are in our classrooms and what our children are taught.

Yet local governments are created by the state, which assigns them their rights and duties, mandating some responsibilities and prohibiting others. The state also allocates taxing powers and shares revenues with local governments. But the state can change the rights and powers granted to local governments, expanding or reducing their tasks, funding, and independence. Cities and counties are infuriated when the state tells them to do things they don't think they can afford or takes away previously committed funds to balance the state budget. School districts depend on the state for funding but are exasperated by burdensome state rules, regulations, and testing requirements.

Yet local government is also where we have the greatest influence over our lives, simply because we are closer to it than to Sacramento or Washington, D.C. We can participate directly in local politics precisely because it's local. We can volunteer for candidates, whom we can actually meet and get to know or even run for office ourselves. We can lobby elected officials without relying on paid professionals. We can attend city council meetings and testify in person. We can find allies and form interest groups like those described in Chapter 4 (and all those types exist in communities). Local government is the most democratic of all levels of government, and thousands of people participate constantly—go to your own city hall and see for yourself.

## COUNTIES AND CITIES

California's 58 counties and 482 cities were created in slightly different ways and perform distinctly different tasks.

### Counties

California is divided into counties (see the map inside the front cover) ranging in size from San Francisco's 47 square miles to San Bernardino County's 20,164, and ranging in population from Alpine County's 1,102 residents to Los Angeles County's 9,889,056. **Counties** function both as local governments and as administrative units of the state. As local governments, counties provide police and fire protection, maintain roads, and perform other services for rural and unincorporated areas (those that are not part of any city). They also run jails; operate transit systems; protect health and sanitation; and keep records on property, marriages, and deaths. As agencies of the state, counties oversee elections, operate the courts, administer the state's welfare system, and collect some taxes. The responsibilities of counties were expanded in 2012, when Governor Jerry Brown's **realignment** program assigned incarceration of nonviolent felons from prisons to county jails, a cost saving for the state even with reimbursement of the cost to counties. Some counties complained, however, that their reimbursements don't cover the costs of realignment and others fear they'll be in the same situation in the future.

State law prescribes the organization of county government. A county's central governing body is a five-member **board of supervisors**, whom voters elect by districts to staggered four-year terms. The board sets county policies and oversees the budget and usually hires a chief administrator, or **county executive**, to carry out its programs. Besides the members of the board of supervisors, voters

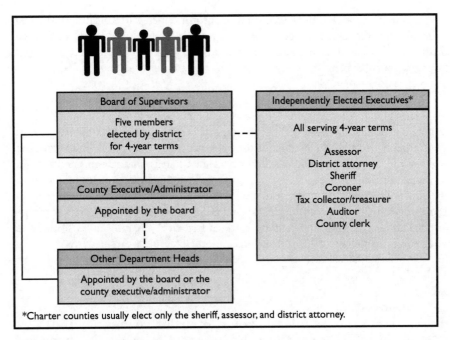

**FIGURE 9.1** County Government: An Organizational Chart for California's Forty-four General Law Counties

elect the sheriff, district attorney, tax assessor, and sometimes other department heads (see Figure 9.1). Conflicts often occur as the elected board tries to manage the budget and the elected executives attempt to deliver services. Unlike most of their state counterparts, these local officials are chosen in nonpartisan elections, a Progressive legacy that keeps party labels off the ballot; all serve four-year terms. As of 2010, California's 296 elected county supervisors were overwhelmingly white and male; only 23.5 percent were female, 9.5 percent were Latino, 3.4 percent were Asian, and 1.7 percent were African American.

Although most counties operate under this general-law system, fourteen have used a state-provided option to organize their own governmental structures through documents called **charters**. Most of these charter counties, including Los Angeles, Sacramento, San Diego, and Santa Clara, are highly urbanized. County voters must approve the charter and any proposed amendments. Generally, a "home rule" or **charter county** uses its local option to replace elected executives with appointees of the board of supervisors or to strengthen the powers of the appointed county executive.

San Francisco is unique among California's local governments because it operates as both a city and a county. Most counties have several cities within their boundaries, but the separate city and county governments of San Francisco were consolidated in 1911. San Francisco thus has a board of supervisors with eleven members rather than a city council, but unlike any other county, it has a mayor.

No new county has been formed in California since 1907, although in some large counties such as Los Angeles, San Bernardino, and Santa Barbara, rural areas frustrated by urban domination have tried unsuccessfully to break away and form their own jurisdictions.

## Cities

Whereas counties are created by the state, **cities** are established at the request of their citizens through the process of **incorporation**. Starting with just 8 cities in 1850, California has 482 today. As unincorporated areas urbanize, residents begin to demand more services than their county government can provide. These may include police and fire protection, street maintenance, water, or other services. Residents may also wish to form a city to preserve the identity of their community or to avoid being annexed by some other city. Wealthy areas sometimes incorporate to protect their tax resources or their ethnic homogeneity from the impact of an adjacent big city and its economic and racial problems. Jurupa Valley in Riverside County, incorporated in 2011 with a population of 95,004, is California's newest city.

The process of incorporation starts with a petition from citizens who live in the area. Then the county's **local agency formation commission (LAFCO)** determines whether the area has a sufficient tax base to support city services and makes sense as an independent entity. If LAFCO approves, the county's board of supervisors holds a hearing, and then the voters of the proposed city approve or reject the incorporation.

Once formed, cities can grow by annexing unincorporated (county) territory. Sometimes, small cities that can't provide adequate services disband themselves by consolidating with an adjacent city. More rarely, residents of an existing city seek to de-annex, or secede. The San Fernando Valley and other parts of the city of Los Angeles have felt ignored by their city government and attempted to secede in 2002, but voters in the city as a whole, who must agree to any secession, rejected the plan.

Like California counties, most California cities operate under the state's general law, which prescribes their governmental structure. **General law cities** typically have a five-member **city council**, with members elected in nonpartisan elections for four-year terms. The council appoints a **city manager** to supervise daily operations; the manager, in turn, appoints department heads such as the police and fire chiefs (see Figure 9.2).

Cities with populations exceeding 3,500 may choose to write their own charters. A hundred and twenty-one California cities have done so. A **charter city** has more discretion in choosing the structure of its government than a general law city does, as well as somewhat greater fiscal flexibility and the freedom to set policies, provided that no state law supersedes them. All of California's largest cities have their own charters.

Even after incorporation, the county provides for courts, jails, social services, elections, tax collection, public health, and public transit, but once incorporated, a city takes on extensive responsibilities, including police and fire protection,

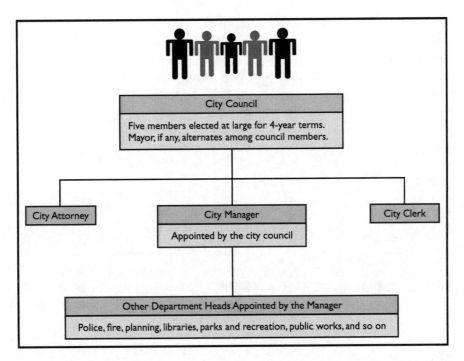

**F I G U R E 9.2** City Government: An Organizational Chart for California's 361 General Law Cities

sewage treatment, garbage disposal, parks and recreational services, streets and traffic management, library operation, and land use planning. The latter is arguably the greatest power given to cities. By zoning land for particular uses—housing, offices, shopping centers, or industry—city governments determine the nature of their communities as well as their financial resources, since some land uses generate more income than others.

## POWER IN THE CITY: COUNCIL MEMBERS, MANAGERS, AND MAYORS

Most of California's cities have five-member city councils with appointed city managers as executives, as set forth by state law. Some cities, particularly older and larger communities, have developed municipal government structures uniquely suited to their own needs and preferences. City councils, for example, may be chosen in different ways or expanded in size to allow for more representation, particularly in larger cities. Los Angeles has fifteen council members, San Jose ten, and San Diego eight. San Francisco's board of supervisors has eleven members. The executive office also varies among these cities; some opt for a stronger mayor rather than the manager prescribed by the state for general law cities.

## Elections

In most California cities, each council member is chosen by the whole city in **at-large elections**. This system was created by the Progressives to replace **district elections**, in which each council member represents only part of the city. At-large elections were intended to reduce the parochial influence of machine-organized ethnic neighborhoods on the city as a whole. The strategy worked, but as a result, ethnic minority candidates, unable to secure enough votes from the city as a whole to win at large, were rarely elected.

As cities grew, citywide campaigns also became extremely costly. The Progressives added to the difficulties of minority candidates and further raised the costs of campaigns by making local elections nonpartisan. This weakened the old party machines, but voters lost the modest cue provided by the listing of parties on the ballot.

To increase minority representation and cut campaign costs, some cities have returned to district elections. Los Angeles has used district elections since 1924; Sacramento converted in 1971, followed by San Jose, Oakland, Fresno, San Diego, and San Francisco. Thirty-eight California cities use some form of district elections. Most are large cities, and most have reverted to district elections through voter-approved charter amendments.

District elections increased opportunities for minority candidates in some cities, but minorities remain substantially underrepresented among California's local elected officials. Women and minority candidates, as well as gay and lesbian candidates, have been more successful in local elections than in state elections; they are still held back, however, by discrimination, low participation, at-large elections, and the cost of campaigns.

In most California cities, especially smaller cities that elect their councils at large, candidates who get the most votes win election even if they don't get a majority. In larger cities and cities that elect their council members by district, if no candidate wins a majority in the primary election, the top two compete in a **runoff election**, ensuring that the winner is elected with a majority. Critics object to the high cost of such elections—both to taxpayers and in campaign spending. In 2004 San Francisco responded to such criticism with **instant runoff voting**, in which voters rank their top three choices of candidates in order of preference. Oakland followed with the same system in 2010. If no candidate wins a majority, the candidate with the fewest votes is eliminated and those votes are assigned to the voters' second choice—and so on until one candidate attains a majority. In the 2010 mayoral election in Oakland, Don Perata, the candidate who won the most votes fell short of a majority and when the second and third choices votes were recorded Jean Quan was elected mayor—much to the chagrin of some voters. Supporters of this system hope that it saves time and money, but voters and candidates have experienced considerable confusion in its implementation.

Whatever the system, voter participation varies considerably from city to city. Turnout is generally higher in cities with elected mayors and district elections, but the key factor related to turnout is when the elections are held. About one-third of California's cities hold their elections separate from state and national elections.

Median turnout in these elections is less than 30 percent.[1] Los Angeles, for example, holds its elections separately, and turnout in that city's 2009 city council and mayoral contests was 18 percent, while turnout in San Francisco's 2011 mayoral election was only 39 percent. Lower turnout significantly affects outcomes because the composition of the electorate changes along with the number of voters; older, more affluent voters predominate, giving an advantage to more conservative candidates. Researchers report that in cities with low voter turnout, less money is spent on programs that might help the poor and more goes to downtown development and other projects that aid business. In short, local governments spend their revenues on those who vote.[2] Turnout in cities that hold their elections concurrently with state and national elections is nearly twice as high.[3] The Silicon Valley city of Santa Clara started holding local elections at the same time as state and national elections in 1988, and voter turnout went from 23–24 percent to 74 percent. Unlike cities, California counties hold their elections at the same time as the state and national elections. Voting for local officials may still be lower, however, due to "drop-off," with some voters declining to cast ballots because of lack of interest or information.

As with state-level campaigns, local reformers have been concerned about the costs of city and county races and the influence of money on politics. Spending on local campaigns has risen steadily since the 1980s, when professional campaign consultants and their techniques (see Chapter 3) became common in local races. One hundred and fifty-one California cities and counties have enacted local campaign-finance laws requiring disclosure of contributors and expenditures and sometimes limit contributions. In most cases, the data are available to the public online. Los Angeles and a few other cities restrict spending and provide limited public financing for campaigns. Even in these communities, however, candidates and interest groups raise and spend substantial sums on campaigns, often through independent expenditures.

## Executive Power

Most people assume that mayors lead cities and have substantial power, but that's not usually the case in California communities. Because mayors were once connected with political machines, the Progressive reformers shifted executive authority to council-appointed city managers who were intended to be neutral, professional administrators. Most California cities use this **council-manager system**. While the manager administers the city's programs, appoints department heads, and proposes the budget, the council members alternate as mayor—a ceremonial post that involves chairing meetings and cutting ribbons.

San Francisco, however, uses a strong-mayor form of government, in which the mayor is elected directly by the people to a four-year term and holds powers similar to those of the president in the national system, including the veto, budget control, and appointment of department heads. High-profile mayors with these powers include Ediwn Lee of San Francisco and Jean Quan of Oakland, both of whom are of Chinese ancestry. Voters in Los Angeles gave their mayor enhanced authority, including the power to appoint forty-four department heads, when they approved a new charter in 1999. Mayor Antonio Villaraigosa thus exercises more authority than any of his predecessors. Fresno (in 1997), Oakland (in 1998), and San Diego (in 2005) have also switched to a strong-mayor form of government. Sacramento mayor Kevin Johnson has pushed for such a change in his city, but the city council has declined putting a charter amendment to the voters.

Many California cities have moved away from the pure council–manager system of government, however. While retaining their city managers, 149 California cities have revised the system so that the mayor is directly elected and serves a four-year term. Some have also increased the powers of their mayors, although they continue to sit as council members. Even without much authority, being a directly elected mayor brings visibility and influence. Mayors of San Jose, for example, exercise substantial clout despite their limited official power.

California mayors will probably continue to grow stronger, partly because of media attention but also due to the need for leadership in the tempest of city politics. Elected officials and community groups often complain about the inherent lack of direct accountability in the city manager form where the executive is somewhat insulated from the voters. Giving more authority to mayors and council members makes accountability more direct, but it may also decrease the professionalism of local government.

## MORE GOVERNMENTS

In addition to cities and counties, California has thousands of other, less visible local governments (see Table 9.1). Created by the state or by citizens, they provide designated services and have taxing powers, mostly collecting their revenues as small portions of the property taxes paid by homeowners and businesses or by charging for their services. Yet except for school districts, most of us are unaware of their existence.

### School Districts and Special Districts

In California, 1,050 local governments called school districts provide education. They are created and overseen by the state and governed by elected boards,

**T A B L E  9.1  California's Local Governments, 2012**

| Type | Number |
|------|-------:|
| Counties | 58 |
| Cities | 482 |
| School districts | 1,050 |
| Special districts | 4,792 |
| TOTAL | 6,382 |

SOURCE: California State Controller, www.sco.ca.gov, and Ed-Data, www.ed-data.ca.us.

which appoint professional educators as superintendents to oversee day-to-day operations. Except for parents and teachers, whose involvement is intense, voter participation in school elections and politics is low. One challenge for the schools is that while the majority of students are Latino, Asian, or African American, a majority of those who vote in school elections and most school board members are non-Hispanic whites.

Funding is another problem with revenues for schools down nearly 10 percent since the 2007–2008 budget year. Of the $56.7 billion in school spending in 2010–2011, the state supplied 58 percent, the federal government provided 14 percent, and 28 percent came from local property taxes and other local sources.[4] The decline in funding has not been without costs; California has ranked low among the states in per-pupil spending for years.[5] While the $56.7 billion goes to salaries and operating expenses, money for building repairs and construction of new schools comes mostly from **bonds** (borrowed money paid by local taxes), which require a supermajority of voters (55 percent) to approve—and usually get it.

**Special districts** are an even more common form of local government, with no fewer than 4,792 in California. Unlike cities and counties, which are "general-purpose" governments, special districts provide a single service. California law provides for fifty-three different types of special districts, ranging from water and waste disposal districts to hospital and cemetery districts. They are created when citizens or governments want a particular function performed but have no appropriate agency to provide the service or prefer not to delegate it to a city or county. Sometimes special districts are formed when small communities share responsibilities for fire protection, sewage treatment, or other services that can be more efficiently provided on a larger scale. When Proposition 13 passed in 1978, the number of special districts increased because that initiative imposed tax constraints on general-purpose local governments (cities and counties) and local leaders discovered that it was easier to fund some services through special districts. Depending on the nature of the special district, funding usually comes from property taxes or charges for the service it provides. Altogether, California's special districts spend over $40 billion a year, while California's cities spend $53 billion and its counties spend $57 billion.

A city council or a county board of supervisors governs some special districts, but most are overseen by a commission or board of directors that may be elected or appointed by other officials. Like a school board, this body usually appoints a professional administrator to manage its business. Accountability to the voters and taxpayers is a problem, however, because most of us aren't even aware of these officials.

## Coping with So Many Governments

The existence of so many sorts of local governments means that many operate in every urban region of California. The vast urban areas between Los Angeles and San Diego or between San Francisco and San Jose, for example, consist of many cities, counties, and special districts, with no single authority in charge of the whole area. Los Angeles County alone hosts eighty-eight cities and two hundred special districts. This fragmentation creates small-scale governments that are accessible to citizens, but that are sometimes too small to provide services efficiently. In addition, problems such as transportation and air pollution go far beyond the boundaries of any one entity.

Many California cities deal with this situation by **contracting for services** from counties, larger cities, or private businesses. Cities in Los Angeles County, for example, may pay the county to provide any of fifty-eight services, from dog catching to tree planting. Small cities commonly contract with the county sheriff for police protection rather than fund their own forces. Contracting allows such communities to provide needed services while retaining local control, although some see the system as unfair because wealthy communities can afford more than poor ones.

Another solution to urban fragmentation is **consolidation**, or the merger of existing governmental entities. With voter approval, small school districts, special districts, or even cities can unite to provide services more efficiently. In the past, consolidation has occurred mostly with school districts, but proposals for consolidations have become more common lately due to California's prolonged budget crisis.[6]

Special districts are yet another way to address fragmentation and regional problems—particularly problems, such as air pollution and transportation, that extend beyond the boundaries of existing cities or counties. For example, California has forty-seven transit districts that run bus and rail systems. Most are countywide, but some, including the Bay Area Rapid Transit (BART) system, cover several counties.

As regional problems have grown and competition among cities has increased, the need for regional planning has also grown. The state has asserted its authority over local governments to require the implementation of regional plans through **councils of government (COGs)**, such as the Southern California Association of Governments (SCAG) and the nine-county Association of Bay Area Governments (ABAG) in Northern California, in which all of the cities and counties in the region are represented. Other state-created agencies, such as the Metropolitan Water District and the South Coast Air Quality Management Board in Southern California, also exercise great power.

## DIRECT DEMOCRACY IN LOCAL POLITICS

Direct democracy is used even more locally than statewide. Between 1995 and 2011 an average of 402 local ballot measures were voted on by Californians each year.[7] Voters must approve all charter amendments—such as increasing the powers of the mayor or introducing district council elections. Proposals for local governments to introduce or raise taxes or to borrow money by issuing bonds must also win voter approval. Charter changes require a simple majority, but most tax increases require a two-thirds super majority. These requirements have severely restricted the ability of local governments to raise money, because voters are usually reluctant to increase taxes.

Most local measures are placed on the ballot by a city council, county board of supervisors, or school board. Besides tax measures and charter amendments, the most common measures have to do with schools (usually seeking additional funding). Citizens also put proposals to the voters through the initiative process, although initiatives constitute only a tiny percentage of local measures. Most often, the initiatives are attempts to control growth or amend charters. Some are frivolous, like the 2008 San Francisco initiative that proposed renaming the city sanitation facility the "George W. Bush Sewage Plant," but most are more serious. District elections, for example, were introduced in some cities by initiative, as were **term limits** (usually restricting elected officials to two 4-year terms). Several California counties and over forty cities now limit the terms of elected officials. As a last resort, voters may express their dissatisfaction with elected officials through recall elections. Recalls of local officials are rare, however, averaging fewer than a dozen a year.

A more frequent use of direct democracy in California communities has been by citizens seeking to control growth. Local government decisions about land use affect us all. If a local government encourages growth in the form of housing, industry, or shopping centers, for example, the economy may boom, but streets may become clogged, schools overcrowded, sewage treatment plants strained, and police and fire protection stretched too thin. Frustrated residents may demand controls on growth. If the city or county leaders are unresponsive, discontented groups may take their case to the voters through an initiative. Most California communities have enacted some form of growth control, with grassroots groups with little money battling big-spending developers and builders. This issue lost salience in recent years, however, when the recession halted growth in most places.

## LOCAL BUDGETS

The way local governments raise and spend money reveals a great deal, not only about what they do but also about the limits they face in doing it.

The biggest single source of money for California's local governments was once the **property tax**, an annual assessment based on the value of land and buildings. Then, in 1978, taxpayers revolted with **Proposition 13**, a statewide initiative that cut property tax revenues by 57 percent. Cities adjusted by cutting jobs and services to save money. Many introduced or increased **charges for services** such as sewage treatment, trash collection, building permits, and the use of recreational facilities. Such charges are now the largest source of income for most cities (see Figure 9.3). Local governments also came to rely more on the state's 7.5 percent sales tax, 2 percent of which goes to the city or county where the sale occurs. Some cities and counties add to the base sales tax to fund transportation or other services. Some have also added taxes on hotel rooms, utilities, or other things such as Oakland's tax on the sale of medical marijuana.

The shift from property taxes to other sources of revenue also affects local land use decisions. When a new development is proposed, most cities now prefer retail businesses to housing or industry because of the sales taxes that such businesses generate. This trend has been labeled the **fiscalization of land use** because instead of choosing the best use for the land, cities opt for the one that produces the most revenue. Housing, especially affordable housing, never falls into this category.

With more legal constraints on their taxing powers, counties had an even rougher time after Proposition 13. State aid to counties increased slightly, but with no alternative local taxes readily available after the passage of Proposition 13, most counties cut spending deeply. Years later, they are still struggling to provide essential services. Like cities, most counties increased charges and fees for services.

Over half of county revenues come from the state and federal governments (33.3 percent and 22 percent, respectively), but this money must be spent on required programs such as social services, health care, and the courts. Even so, state and federal aid does not cover the cost of these mandatory services, leaving counties with little money to spend as they choose.

Just as the revenue sources of cities and counties differ, so do their spending patterns, largely because the state assigns them different responsibilities (see Figure 9.3). Public safety is the biggest expenditure for California cities, whereas welfare is the biggest county expenditure.

## Budget Woes

Although Proposition 13 is much loved by homeowners for reducing property tax bills, the initiative caused serious fiscal problems for local governments by cutting property tax revenues and making approval of new taxes or tax increases more difficult. That combination necessitated severe budget cuts for cities and counties. Beyond that, Proposition 13 gave the state the responsibility to allocate property taxes among local governments even as Proposition 98 (see Chapter 8) mandated allocation of a fixed percentage of the state budget to education. As a consequence, a portion of property taxes that had previously gone to cities and counties was shifted to schools—putting even further pressure on city and county budgets and resulting in further cuts in services. Moreover, cities and counties, which previously had some control of their own revenues, became dependent on the state for property and sales tax revenues, a significant loss of local control.[8]

These problems have been compounded by recessions in the early 1990s and again in 2001–2003 and 2009–2010 followed by a very slow recovery. Parts of the state were hit hard by foreclosures on home loans, property values fell across the state, and property tax revenues for local governments fell—along with sales tax revenues. Other factors exacerbated the crisis for local governments.

In 2004 Governor Arnold Schwarzenegger exacerbated circumstances for local governments by drastically reducing vehicle license fees, which had previously been a significant source of local revenues. In 2009, facing a continued deficit, the state resorted—not for the first time—to a massive "take-back" of local property tax revenues, diverting nearly $4 billion in local property taxes from schools, cities, counties, and redevelopment agencies. Then in 2011,

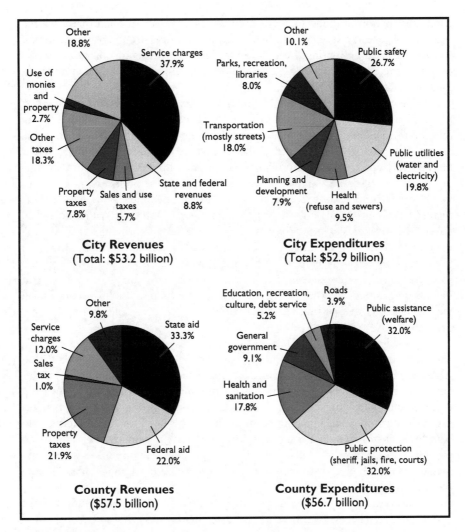

**FIGURE 9.3** Revenues and Expenditures of California Cities (2009–2010) and Counties (2010–2011)

SOURCE: California State Controller, 2012, http://www.sco.ca.gov.

Governor Brown abolished local redevelopment agencies—governmental entities created by cities to fund new development in declining areas—and transferred most of their $5 billion in annual revenues to schools and other state services.

Frustrated by all this, cities and counties pushed back with ballot measures to prevent state take-backs and transfers and guarantee future revenues. Voters approved propositions designed to do this in 2004 and 2010, and the state is now somewhat more constrained. Take-backs can still occur, but the state must eventually repay the funds. Nevertheless, in the short term the take-backs only worsened the fiscal problems of local governments. Cities also challenged the state's elimination of redevelopment agencies, but the courts ruled that since the state had created the agencies, the state had the authority to do away with them. Meanwhile, counties worried the state would not provide adequate compensation for the costs of moving nonviolent felons from prisons to county jails (Governor Brown's "realignment").

All of this has driven many California cities and counties to the fiscal brink. Oakland and other cities have laid off hundreds of police officers, despite rising crime rates. Los Angeles mayor Antonio Villaraigoso, usually an ally of public employees, proposed layoffs and demanded salary concessions from the city's unions. Maywood, in Southern California, laid off all its city employees, including police officers, and contracted with other cities for some services and with Los Angeles County for police protection. "We will become 100 percent a contracted city," said Maywood's interim city manager.[9] Other cities also considered contracting for services. San Jose has "outsourced" graffiti abatement and some maintenance work. Redding, in Northern California, and Santa Clarita, in Southern California, have contracted with a private company to provide library services. Still other cities considered merging police or fire departments with neighboring cities. In some areas, reformers called for consolidation of small school districts, special districts, and cities as a partial solution to budget problems.

Many cities and other local agencies also face fiscal strain due to the pensions and other benefits they offered their employees when their budgets were flush with cash. Now unable to meet these commitments but bound by contracts, local governments have sought to renegotiate contracts to win concessions from current employees or to move to a two-tier pension system, preserving benefits for current workers but reducing them for future hires. Voters in Modesto, Palo Alto, San Diego, San Francisco, and San Jose have overwhelmingly approved pension reform, but the problem persists and pensions take up an ever-growing portion of local budgets—money that might otherwise fund police, libraries, and other local services.

More drastically, some cities, including Vallejo (near San Francisco) in 2008 and Mammoth Lakes, San Bernardino, and Stockton in 2012, have declared bankruptcy. Unable to pay employee salaries or repay bonded indebtedness, bankruptcy allowed these cities to legally suspend payments and renegotiate contracts while a bankruptcy judge determines which creditors should be paid. In all cases, city services, including public safety, were cut drastically. Unique circumstances in each of these cities contributed to their dire straits, but some observers worried that bankruptcies would spread to other California cities.

## LOCAL GOVERNMENT IN PERSPECTIVE

Despite their fiscal trials, local governments remain a major component of the California economy, with nearly 1.5 million employees (half are in education) and combined budgets totaling over $207 billion. Local governments cost a lot, but they also do a lot.

Yet, as demonstrated by Proposition 13, realignment, and ongoing budget battles, the state limits what local governments can do. Some may dispute such interventions, but the state's authority remains supreme. Nevertheless, opinion polls consistently report that Californians view local government more favorably than state government. Whatever its limitations, California's political system gives residents many opportunities to decide what sort of communities they want, and many Californians take advantage of these opportunities by engaging in local politics.

## NOTES

1. Zoltan L. Hajnal, Paul G. Lewis, and Hugh Louch, "Municipal Elections in California: Turnout, Timing, and Competition," Public Policy Institute of California, March 2002.

2. Jessica Trounstine and Zoltan Hajnal, "Low Voter Turnout Does Matter: Spending Priorities in Local Politics" (paper presented at the annual meeting of the Midwest Political Science Association, Chicago, April 2004).

3. Hajnal, Lewis, and Louch, *op. cit.*

4. EdSource, www.edsource.org (accessed August 21, 2012).

5. *Ibid.* (accessed August 22, 2012) or see California Budget Project, "School Finance Facts," October 2011, www.cbp.org (accessed August 22, 2012).

6. For more on regional fragmentation and special districts, see Brian, P. Janiskee, "The Problem of Local Government in California," in *California Republic*, ed. Brian P. Janiskee and Ken Masugi (Lanham, Md.: Rowman and Littlefield, 2004).

7. California Elections Data Archive, Institute for Social Research, California State University, Sacramento, www.csus.edu/isr (accessed August 22, 2012).

8. For further discussion of these effects of Proposition 13, see John Decker, *California in the Balance* (Berkeley, Calif.: Berkeley Public Policy Press, 2009), pp. xi, 116, 137–138.

9. "Maywood to Lay Off All City Employees, Dismantle Police Department," June 22, 2010, www.latimesblogs.latimes.com/lanow/2010/06.

## LEARN MORE ON THE WEB

ABZY News Links (listing state and local media and online news sources):
www.abyznewslinks.com/uniteca.htm

California Elections Data Archive (CEDA) (information on local elections):
www.csus.edu/isr/reports/california_elections/index.html

California State Association of Counties:
www.csac.counties.org

California State Controller (data on cities, counties, schools, and special districts):
www.sco.ca.gov

On instant runoff voting (IRV):
www.instantrunoff.com

League of California Cities:
www.cacities.org

Public Policy Institute of California (studies on local government):
www.ppic.org

## LEARN MORE AT THE LIBRARY

Terry Christensen and Tom Hogen-Esch. *Local Politics: A Practical Guide to Governing at the Grassroots.* Armonk, N.Y.: M. E. Sharpe, 2006.

Jack Citrin and Isaac William Martin, eds. *After the Tax Revolt: California's Proposition 13 Turns 30.* Berkeley: Institute of Government Studies, 2009.

Paul G. Lewis. *Deep Roots: Local Government Structure in California.* San Francisco: Public Policy Institute of California, 1998.

## GET INVOLVED

Contact your city's mayor or a member of your city council or county board of supervisors to volunteer or to apply for an internship. Go to your city or county's Web site to find the elected officials. You can also intern with a community group—just search for one that interests you on the Internet.

# 10

# State-Federal Relations: Conflict, Cooperation, and Chaos

## CHAPTER CONTENTS

California's Clout with the President

California's Clout with Congress

   *Divisiveness*

   *Controversy over the Proposed Auburn Dam—Case in Point*

High-Speed Rail

Immigration

Climate Change

Water

Shared Resources

California Today: Golden State or Fool's Gold?

California's uniqueness stems in part from its position as the nation's most populated state; it also emanates from the state's vast resources, size, diversity, and engagement in thorny issues. We see problems and their outcomes on a scale here unequaled elsewhere. And so it is with the state's relationship with the federal government, which can be described as wary, uneven, and often fraught with controversy.

Sometimes state and national leaders differ over California's management. Public education reform is one such policy area, with the federal government and state legislature at odds over the definition of *reform*. On other issues, such as water policy, however, the two governments have worked well together. There are also instances where California has acted with its own response to national issues, with the federal government eventually moving into line; nowhere is this more obvious than with environmental protection. Deciding the best responses to problems that affect both the nation and state can be a challenge because, like its forty-nine counterparts, California is both a self-governing entity and a member of the larger national government.

Matters become even more complicated when determining financial responsibility for costly issues such as massive transportation projects, immigration control, or health-care policy, to name a few. Because the state is so large and complex, federal assistance almost always seems inadequate. When federal aid or programs are cut, California seems to suffer disproportionately compared with other states.

Nevertheless, when the state confronts a complex issue, its struggle is often the precursor of similar concerns likely to affect the rest of the nation. The women's right-to-choose movement, gun control, the tax revolt, medical marijuana, stem cell research, and same-sex marriage all had early beginnings, and in some cases, origins—in California.

In this chapter we review California's impact on national policymaking and policy actors. We also explore some of the critical policy areas that test California's relationship with the federal government: immigration, greenhouse gas emissions, and the distribution of federal resources to the state of California. Each topic touches on the delicate balance between state autonomy and national objectives—perspectives in federalism that are not always viewed the same ways by state and federal government leaders.

## CALIFORNIA'S CLOUT WITH THE PRESIDENT

Despite its size and huge bloc of Electoral College votes, California hasn't figured prominently in presidential elections in recent years, largely because the state has been predictably secure for Democratic candidates on every occasion since 1992. As a consequence, we don't see the candidates as much as voters do in other states. Republican presidential candidates do not invest significant resources on California because they don't see much return, and Democrats stay away because of their need to pursue electoral votes in more competitive states. But California is important to both national political parties in one major respect, namely, as the top state for campaign contributions. That alone keeps candidates coming to places such as Orange County, Silicon Valley, and Hollywood.

California has had an uneven relationship with the nation's presidents. For example, Republican President George W. Bush was not particularly helpful to the state largely due to his general hands-off attitude on domestic policy issues. When then-Governor Gray Davis demanded federal prosecution of big power companies for a price-fixing scheme that caused an energy crisis in 2001, the Bush administration refused, although the courts eventually found otherwise. Other areas of disinterest on the president's part included agriculture, border patrol assistance, and terrorism funding. Given the clash of cultural and political values between most Californians and the conservative Republican president, it's easy to see why the distance between the state and the president was more than a matter of miles.

President Barack Obama has been somewhat more responsive to California's issues, particularly on questions relating to government support for "green" technology research and production. The Obama administration has also embraced California's strict rules on automobile exhaust emissions, a departure from the approach of George W. Bush. On transportation, Obama has funneled federal funds for the state's massive high-speed rail project, although California's recent budget problems have led many to question the wisdom of the $69 billion effort, even with federal dollars. Still, not everything has gone California's way. The Obama administration compensated California for only a fraction of the hundreds of millions of dollars spent by the state on incarcerate of illegal immigrants awaiting deportation to their home countries. And California has wrested very little of Obama's "Race to the Top" education improvement funds at a time when public education has been gasping for support. Still, on balance, California has had more success with President Obama than his predecessor.

## CALIFORNIA'S CLOUT WITH CONGRESS

As the nation's most populated state, California has fifty-three members in the House of Representatives, dwarfing the delegations of every other state. Texas and New York are second and third, with thirty-two and twenty-nine members, respectively. The majority party in each house of Congress chooses committee chairs who, in turn, control the flow of national legislation.

The twenty-first century began with Republicans enjoying control of both houses. In 2006 growing discontent with the war in Iraq, an uneven national economy, and political corruption in Congress led the nation's voters to elect a Democratic majority to the House of Representatives. San Francisco's Nancy Pelosi, elected in 2002 to the post of minority leader, was elected Speaker. With that elevation, she assumed the highest national leadership post ever held in the United States by a woman. As a result of the election outcome, several prominent California Democrats assumed key committee chairmanships by virtue of their years of seniority in the House.

Political party fortunes turned in 2010 when the Republicans captured control of the House, resulting in four committee chairmanships for California Republicans: Oversight and Governmental Reform (Darrell Issa); Armed Services (Howard "Buck" McKeon; House Administration (Dan Lungren); and Rules (David Dreier). In addition, Kevin McCarthy was elected majority whip, the third highest party post after Speaker and majority leader. Republicans retained control of the House after the 2012 election.

The political winds also have shifted in the U.S. Senate, but not as much as in the House. Although the upper house is a bit less partisan than the lower house, the majority party still controls all committee chairmanships, and therefore the flow of legislation. In 2006 the off-year revolution produced a slim 51-to-49 Democratic majority, thanks to two independents who promised their loyalty to the Democratic side of the aisle. Suddenly, Senators Dianne Feinstein and Barbara Boxer, both first elected in 1992, emerged as key players on issues dealing with the environment, foreign relations, and the judiciary. By 2009 the Democratic majority hit 60, a number large enough to cut off filibusters. Since then, the Democratic majority has narrowed considerably. Still, California Democrats retain clout. Boxer, reelected in 2010, chairs the Environment and Public Works Committee and the Senate Select Committee on Ethics. Feinstein, reelected in 2012, chairs the Senate Select Committee on Intelligence.

Democrats in California enjoy a comfortable margin of 38–15 over Republicans in the House of Representatives. In other respects California's congressional makeup is as diverse as the rest of the state. As of 2013, the delegation includes 9 Latinos, 3 African-Americans, 5 Asian-Americans, 18 women and 1 gay member. Both of California's U.S. senators are women as well.

## Divisiveness

One other fact must be added to the discussion of Californians in Washington: historically, California's **congressional delegation** has been notoriously fractured on key public policy issues affecting California. Much of the conflict stems from the state's complexity. North/south, urban/suburban/rural, and coastal/valley/mountain divisions separate the state geographically. Other differences exist, too, in terms of wealth, ethnicity, and basic liberal/conservative distinctions. To be sure, no congressional district is completely homogeneous, yet most members of Congress tend to protect their districts' interests more than those of the state as a whole. Thus, on issues ranging from desert protection to immigration reform, California's representatives have often canceled each other's votes, leaving states such as Texas far more powerful because of their relatively unified stances. Even on foreign trade, members from California often have worked at cross-purposes, depending on the industries, interest groups, and demographic characteristics of their districts.

Only on the question of offshore oil drilling have most members of the state's delegation voted the same way. In 2008, with gasoline prices hitting record levels, President George W. Bush called for an end to the twenty-seven–year federal moratorium on offshore drilling. Almost the entire California delegation opposed the proposal, and the damaging Gulf of Mexico offshore oil blowout in 2010 silenced any further discussion.

## Controversy over the Proposed Auburn Dam—Case in Point

The struggle over the proposed Auburn Dam in Northern California is a current case in point. California hungers for more water, but the real debate has been over the best ways to get it and at what cost. The massive $9.6 billion proposal has been considered in Congress since 1960. Federal agencies have spent $325 million just on feasibility studies. Yet California lawmakers in Washington have remained paralyzed over the issue, largely due to the conflicting objectives of environmentalists and farmers. The various sides struck a compromise in 2003 by upgrading another dam downstream. But concerns over California's weakened levee system led House Republican Dan Lungren to pursue the idea yet again in 2007 after the release of a 152-page report by the U.S. Department of the Interior.[1] Meanwhile, Democrats Pete Stark and George Miller have used their clout to thwart consideration of the project as an environmentally unsound proposal. Ironically, both Stark and Lungren lost their seats in the 2012 election. The issue of whether the project is a boondoggle or a vital flood-control program is not as significant as the fact that it has polarized the California congressional delegation. Meanwhile, as Californians have fussed among themselves over this vexing question, representatives from other states have worked in bipartisan ways to garner federal dollars for their projects.

## HIGH-SPEED RAIL

In 2008, California voters passed **Proposition 1A**, which committed the state $9.95 billion in bonds to partially fund an 800-mile long high-speed rail program. Officially known as the Safe, Reliable High-Speed Passenger Train Bond Act for the 21st Century, the ballot proposition was the down payment of a transportation system projected to cost $43 billion. Proponents touted the rail network as an environmentally friendly enterprise equivalent to the addition of twelve polluting highway lanes up and down the length of the state.

The new Obama administration gushed over the transportation network as a twenty-first century infrastructure gem and immediately made available $3.3 billion in matching federal funds for the first segment of construction, which federal transportation officials required on the 130-mile stretch between Chowchilla and Bakersfield. The money would be available as long as the state committed to the project no later than September 2012. In July 2012, the legislature voted to spend $2.7 billion of the 2008 bond for the first leg of construction.

Meanwhile, critics began to question the legitimacy of the high-speed rail project. The Great Recession hit California even harder than most states, causing state budget revenues to tank. Every year between 2008 and 2012, state leaders had to find ways to overcome annual deficits of $20 billion or more. Technically, the state budget was separate from the High-Speed Rail Bonds, but few Californians made that distinction. In addition, the transportation project suffered a double-whammy through a new estimated cost of $99 billion and projections of fewer riders.[2] At the same time, leaders in the now Republican-led House of Representatives balked at providing federal funds. Ironically, the opposition effort was led by two Californians, Central Valley-based Jeff Denham, who voted for the project earlier as a state legislator, and Kevin McCarthy, the House majority whip from Bakersfield.[3]

In 2012, the High-Speed Rail Commission, the project's governing authority, produced a revised plan which cut the cost of the transportation system to $68 billion over about 520 miles of track. But that did little to assuage the growing number of opponents. The nonpartisan Legislative Analyst's Office urged lawmakers to end the project. Public opinion polls found the voters now wanting to vote again on the idea, with sizable numbers against it. Still, Governor Jerry Brown remained supportive of the project "without any hesitation."[4] Proponents added that new state funds would come from the state's cap-and-trade pollution revenues beginning in 2014, with the continued implementation of California's AB32, the state's Global Warming Solutions Act.

Countless questions remain about the High-Speed Rail program. Will the federal government continue to provide funding in a tie of great austerity? Will the state generate enough funds to pay for the railroad? If constructed, will the new transportation network fulfill expectations? For the moment, the outcome of this story remains a mystery.

## IMMIGRATION

California has long been a magnet for those in search of opportunity. And they have come—first the Spanish; then Yankee, Irish, and Chinese immigrants during the nineteenth century; followed by Japanese, Eastern European, African American, and Vietnamese immigrants beginning in the 1970s, Asian Indians in the 1990s, and more Latinos throughout the last half century (see Table 10.1). But over the past two decades, several factors have converged to influence the moods of the state's residents and would-be residents. Lack of opportunity in other nations has led millions to choose California as an alternative; meanwhile, an overburdened and underfunded infrastructure has led many of those already here to oppose further immigration. Much of the antipathy has been directed at

**T A B L E  10.1   California's Immigrants: Leading Countries of Origin, 2009**

| Country | Number |
|---|---|
| Mexico | 4,308,000 |
| Philippines | 783,000 |
| China (incl. Taiwan) | 681,000 |
| Vietnam | 457,000 |
| El Salvador | 413,000 |
| India | 319,000 |
| Korea | 307,000 |
| Guatemala | 261,000 |
| Iran | 214,000 |
| Canada | 132,000 |
| United Kingdom | 125,000 |
| Japan | 105,000 |

SOURCE: U.S. Decennial Census, 2009.

Latinos—particularly those from Mexico—but anger has also been aimed at Asians.

The numbers are substantial. Whereas 15.1 percent of California's population were foreign born in 1980, 27.2 percent fell within that category in 2010, with projections showing that percentage remaining in place through 2030.[5] During the same period, the percentage of foreign-born residents of the United States as a whole nearly doubled to 12.1 percent from 6.2 percent (see Figure 10.1). Between 1990 and 2005, more than 40 percent of California's population growth came from foreign immigration. In 2010 the Pew Hispanic Center estimated that there were between 11.4 million and 12.4 million illegal immigrants nationwide, with between 2.5 million and 2.85 million of them in California.[6] Still, the percentage of illegal immigrants living in California dropped from 42 percent to 22 percent, indicating greater movement elsewhere.[7]

With these dramatic events reshaping California, experts have argued about whether the immigrants help or harm the state's economy. One recent study finds that only about one-third of recent immigrants have health insurance, suggesting a financial burden for public health institutions and services.[8] Yet other studies show that immigrants, legal and illegal combined, are very similar in economic makeup to the rest of America.[9] Moreover, illegal immigrants are critical to some industries such as California farming, where they make up as much

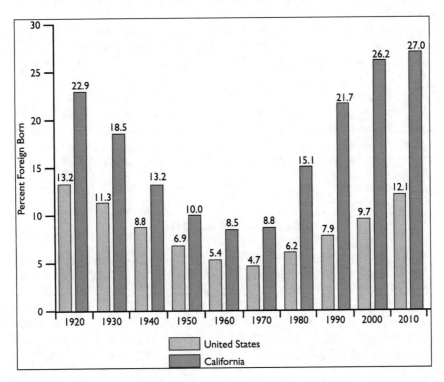

**FIGURE 10.1** Population of Foreign-Born Residents, California and United States Comparison

as 90 percent of the harvest workforce. To the extent that these workers are excluded from the fields, California's $40 billion agriculture industry could suffer irreparable damage.[10] All these findings suggest a growing ambivalence toward the illegal immigration issue in California.

None of this has stopped the federal government from moving on immigration, although not always with consistency. In 2008 the Bush administration increased surveillance of U.S. companies with illegal immigrant employees, leading to fines for employers, deportation for undocumented workers, and workforce shortages. Between a more vigilant border protection system and a declining U.S. economy, the number of attempted border crossings by illegal immigrants declined. That, and a weak American economy, led more than 1 million illegal immigrants to return to their home countries by 2010.[11]

The largest issue related to immigration is determining which level of government should assume responsibility for its costs. While the federal government has long established the criteria for immigration and the conditions for enforcement, it leaves the states responsible for meeting the needs of immigrants. Nowhere does this contradiction ring louder than in California. Among unauthorized immigrants alone, recent estimates cite health-care costs of $1.5 billion, education costs for 923,000 of their children at $4 billion, and incarceration costs for 19,000 illegal immigrants at $970 million.[12] Few of these costs have been completely absorbed by the federal government, yet their day-to-day impact is a reality.

Controversy continues over the illegal immigration issue. Since his election, President Obama repeatedly has pushed Congress for immigration reform that would allow citizenship after a multi-year period of residence, assuming law-abiding behavior by illegal immigrants. The Republican-led majority in the House of Representatives has resisted the proposal, leaving individual states to wrestle with the issue. Clearly, the role of each government in managing the immigration question remains a tough issue to sort out. President Obama added to the drama in 2012 when he signed an executive order allowing as many as 800,000 young illegal immigrants to remain in the United States under specific conditions.[13]

## CLIMATE CHANGE

California and the federal government have had a rocky relationship with respect to climate change. At times, the state has fought national objectives; at others, California has taken the lead. So it is with the issue of air quality. According to the U.S. **Environmental Protection Agency (EPA)**, the ten smoggiest counties in the nation are found in California. Metropolitan Los Angeles, an area that extends east to Riverside and south to Long Beach, tops the list as the smoggiest area in the nation. Actually, the number of "unhealthful" days in the L.A. basin declined from an average of 189.6 during the 1996–1998 period to 141.8 between 2006 and 2008, according to the American Lung Association, although progress has slowed since 2004.[14] Statewide, the costs have been great. One recent study finds that annual losses in California from unhealthy air amount to $28 billion in the form of premature deaths, illness, and lost productivity in the workplace.[15]

Congress and the EPA have been unhappy with the inability of the state to move forward on clean air. But given the state's dependence on manufacturing, particularly in the vast Los Angeles basin, it has been difficult to meet national standards without choking off the local economy. In 1992 state regulators established the Regional Clean Air Incentives Market Program (RECLAIM) in Southern California, a program in which manufacturers buy and sell emissions permits as a means of encouraging emissions reduction. The program has led to substantial reductions in environmental decay, although the region remains far from healthy.

Automobile exhaust is another story, however. California has led the nation in reducing auto emissions which account for 28 percent of the state's greenhouse gases. Since the passage of the federal Clean Air Act of 1970, state environmental regulators have asked for and received forty-four waivers from the EPA to establish standards beyond federal requirements. That's what happened routinely until 2007, when the Bush administration's EPA rejected the claim that auto emissions contained greenhouse gases, to the amazement of most scientists in the United States and worldwide.[16] Since the agency gave no scientific explanation for its ruling, California and sixteen other states sued the EPA for not carrying out its mandate. The United States Supreme Court agreed.

The political environment regarding auto emissions changed dramatically with the election of Barack Obama to the presidency in 2008. Early in 2009 he asked his new EPA administrator to review previous decisions on California's waiver petitions. In June 2009 the agency approved California's proposal and announced a new national policy on higher gasoline mileage and lower emissions by 2017, based on California's standards. On this occasion, at least, California set the trend for the rest of the nation.

## WATER

Not all of California's jurisdictional disputes have occurred with the federal government. On the issue of water, California repeatedly has tangled with other states. Simply put, the state doesn't have enough. Three-quarters of California's water comes from north of Sacramento, while 80 percent is consumed south of Sacramento. Most of the imbalance is corrected through two giant transfer systems. The federal Central Valley Project, which dates from 1937, supplies the farmers of the southern Central Valley. The State Water Project, begun in 1960, largely supplies southern urban areas. Both systems intercept freshwater near the Sacramento–San Joaquin Delta before it can flow out to the ocean. Still, California gasps for more water, which has led to confrontations with other states.

The linchpin of the water frenzy among western states is the Colorado River, the freshwater source that begins in Colorado and empties into the Gulf of California. Under a 1922 multistate agreement, California is entitled to 4.4 million acre-feet, or 59 percent, of the lower basin river annually. Yet according to some critics, California exceeded its share by as much as 800,000 acre-feet per year, enough to provide for the annual water needs of 1.6 million households in rapidly growing Arizona and Nevada.[17]

Fearing a bruising battle that would spill into Congress, officials from seven states held talks for eighteen months to resolve the problem. In 2000 they agreed to a formula that would allow California to gradually reduce its consumption of the excess over a fifteen-year period. But the end date for that agreement is fast approaching, and it remains to be seen what, if any new arrangement will follow. At least for the time being, the seven western states have solved a troublesome issue without federal participation.

Meanwhile, the federal government's Department of the Interior and the state of California quieted the ongoing three-way battle among agribusiness (which consumes 80 percent of the state's water), environmentalists seeking to preserve rivers and deltas, and urban areas in need of water to grow. The two governments developed a plan in 2000 to expand existing federal reservoirs in California, improve drinking water quality, and develop a creative water recycling program. Most of the $8.5 billion price tag has been shouldered by the federal government, with Californians providing $825 million. In 2004 Congress committed another $10 billion over thirty years to improve the quality of water flowing into the Sacramento Delta and San Francisco Bay.

Uncertainties remain, however. In 2002 the U.S. Department of the Interior modified a plan previously favored by environmentalists by directing more water from the Central Valley Project to farmers, rather than using it for ecosystem restoration. Still, water can be distributed to customers only if it is available, and recent droughts in California and the West have left the region thirsty. For example, in 2007, a record-low snowpack in the Sierra Nevada Mountains and concern for endangered species led a federal court judge to reduce deliveries of Northern California water to Southern California by 25 percent, imperiling agriculture and construction projects alike.[18]

In 2012, Governor Jerry Brown laid out plans to divert additional water from the Sacramento Delta in an effort to meet the state's growing needs. No sooner than the governor delivered his announcement, several members of the California congressional delegation registered concerns with U.S. Secretary of the Interior Ken Salazar about southern California interests "who would steal our water."[19] So the struggle over water continues, both between California and the federal government and also between farmers, environmentalists, and developers.

## SHARED RESOURCES

"Federalism" refers to the multifaceted political relationship that binds the state and national governments. One aspect centers on financial assistance that wends its way from federal coffers to state and local treasuries, and that amounted to about $567 billion in fiscal year 2013, down from $625 billion in fiscal year 2011. Most of this assistance comes in the form of **grants-in-aid**, amounting to about 20 percent of all state and local government revenues. The money flows through more than six hundred federal programs covering areas from agricultural development to high-tech research.

For decades, California received more than its fair share of grants-in-aid from the federal government. That has changed. In 1983 California had 10 percent of the national population but received 22 percent of the national government's expenditures, thanks largely to defense- and space-related research. Then came the slide. With a pared defense budget, cutbacks in infrastructure work, and the push for a balanced budget, federal contributions have shrunk considerably over the past two decades. As of 2010 California had 11.9 percent of the nation's population but received 10.8 percent of the nation's federal funds. The state now ranks forty-fourth in the distribution of federal spending on a per capita basis-down sharply from twentieth in 1990.[20]

There is another way to appreciate the changing relationship between the federal government and California. Because of the state's massive growth, California had a long history of getting more dollars from the federal government than it contributed. Beginning in 1986, however, California became a "donor" state. Ever since, California has contributed more money to the national treasury than it has received, and the disparity is increasing every year. In 1992, for every dollar California sent to Washington, D.C., the state received 93 cents in federal goods and services. By 2005, for every dollar California sent to Washington, only 78 cents came back in goods and services (see Table 10.2). Even when California and the rest of the states received a larger federal commitment from the Economic Stimulus Act in 2009 and 2010, the state's share ranked in the bottom half of the per capita federal expenditures. No matter how you slice it, California is getting less of the federal "pie" today than in the past.

**T A B L E  10.2  Federal Expenditures per Dollar of Taxes, Fiscal Years 1992 and 2010—California and Selected States**

|  | Expenditures per Dollar of Taxes | | Ranking | |
|---|---|---|---|---|
|  | FY1992 | FY2010 | FY1992 | FY2010 |
| **New Mexico** | $2.08 | $2.05 | 11 | 4 |
| **California** | $.93 | $1.09 | 38 | 27 (t)* |
| **Kansas** | $1.05 | $1.04 | 27 | 29 |
| **Texas** | $.93 | $.91 | 37 | 41 (t)* |
| **Maryland** | $1.27 | $.86 | 15 | 44 |
| **Massachusetts** | $1.01 | $.83 | 31 | 46 |
| **New Jersey** | $.66 | $.77 | 50 | 48 |

*t means tied with another state.

SOURCES: Tax Foundation, Bureau of Economic Analysis, Internal Revenue Service.

But there is more to the story than just dollars in and dollars out; it's what the dollars buy that makes a huge difference, and in California the high cost of living makes national numbers meaningless. Data compiled in 2011 by California Watch, an independent research organization, found that a family of four in this state needs about $63,000 per year to cover basic needs; that's nearly triple the federal level.[21] And when we consider that the state's immigrant population is more than twice the national average on a per capita basis, it becomes clear that the state's needs fare particularly poorly when it comes to federal funding.

California fared slightly better with the distribution of funds from the American Recovery and Reinvestment Act in 2009 and 2010, when Congress passed an $831 billion bill to help pull the nation out of the worst recession since the Great Depression. On a per capita basis, California ranked twenty-ninth in federal payments. However, at the same time, the state's unemployment was the third highest in the nation.[22] It's important to remember that although the state gained a larger share of federal funds because of the economic crisis, those dollars stopped coming in 2011.

The data presented here counter the political posturing that has emerged from both Congress and the presidency in recent years. They reveal a state that has given much more to the federal government in taxes than it has received in programs and services. They also reflect the fragmentation that has haunted the state's congressional delegation. As a result, California's "Golden State" nickname has a different meaning in Washington than in California—namely, sizable economic resources that have landed disproportionately in the federal treasury.

## CALIFORNIA TODAY: GOLDEN STATE
## OR FOOL'S GOLD?

Is today's California still the state with unlimited potential or the state with too many burdens to survive? When it comes to relations with the federal government, perhaps the answer is a little of both. California is king when it comes to campaign contributions for national candidates, research and development, the center of agriculture, and auto emissions standards. At the same time, California is a pauper in matters of dealing with a perpetual state budget deficit, a dilapidated infrastructure, and a frayed social safety net. Once upon a time, the state would have looked to the federal government for rescue, and the federal government might have provided some relief. That relationship has been replaced by one in which the two governments are often at odds.

As noted at the beginning of this chapter, some of the shift has been because of the ebb and flow of national politics. Thus, during the Clinton years, the state benefited from extra federal attention on research and development tax credits, H1-B visas for skilled workers, and even some defense contracts. During the Bush years, California didn't fare so well, as attested by the administration's disregard for the state's immigration issues, water management, and exorbitant electricity bills.

Under President Obama, California has received support for continuation of the research and development tax credit, high-speed rail, and assistance for

California homeowners dealing with foreclosure issues. At the same time, federal dollars for public education and recovery from the Great Recession have been relatively sparse. Whether Obama's second term provides more financial support for California remains to be seen.

If nothing else, California operates with more financial autonomy from the federal government today than in the times of heavy government defense spending. To this extent the state has experienced a reduced federal reliance, although the state's woefully unbalanced annual budget surely would benefit from more federal support. Accordingly, California's growing fiscal self-reliance may be the hallmark of the state's direction in the coming years. Whatever the future, it will be an interesting experiment.

## NOTES

1. U.S. Department of Interior, "Reclamation: Managing Water in the West, Auburn-Folsom South Unit Special Report," December 2006.

2. "Forecast Dire for Riders, Revenue," *San Jose Mercury News*, October 11, 2011, pp. A1, A8.

3. "Bullet Train Funds in GOP Sights," *Los Angeles Times*, October 23, 2011, pp. AA1, AA4.

4. "Jerry Brown Defends High-Speed Rail," *San Francisco Chronicle*, January 19, 2012, p. A1.

5. U.S. Census Bureau, http//quickfacts.census.gov/qfd/states/06000.html (accessed July 27, 2012).

6. Jeffrey Passel and D'Vera Cohn, "Unauthorized Immigrant Population: National and State Trends, 2010," Pew Hispanic Center, 2011, www.pewhispanic.org (accessed August 31, 2012).

7. "Illegal Immigrants Become Subject of Coverage Debate," *San Francisco Chronicle*, September 11, 2009, pp. A1, A18.

8. *The Size and Characteristics of the Unauthorized Migrant Population in the U.S.* (Washington, D.C.: Pew Hispanic Center, 2006), pp. A1, A18.

9. "Immigrants in the Work Force: Study Belies Image," *The New York Times*, April 10, 2010, pp. A1, A3.

10. "Farmers Oppose G.O.P. Bill to Require Verification of Workers' Immigration Status," *The New York Times*, July 31, 2011, pp. A12, A16.

11. "Number of Illegal Immigrants from Mexico Drops," http://www.azcentral.com /news/politics/articles/2012/04/23/20120423illegal-immgrant-population-study -mexico-united-states.html, April 23, 3012.

12. "Illegal Immigrants Are a Factor in the Budget Map Gap," *Los Angeles Times*, February 2, 2009, http://articles.latimes.com/2009/feb/02/local/me-cap2.

13. According to The *New York Times*, the U.S. government "will no longer initiate the deportation of illegal immigrants who came to the United States before age 16, have lived here for at least five years, and are in school, are high school graduates or are military veterans in good standing. The immigrants must also be not more than

30 years old and have clean criminal records." "Obama to Permit Young Migrants to Remain in the United States," *The New York Times*, http://www.nytimes.com /2012/06/16/us/us-to-stop-deporting-some-illegal-immigrants.html?pagewanted=all.

14. "Smog in L.A. Still Tops in Nation," *Los Angeles Times*, April 28, 2010, pp. AA1, AA6.

15. Daniel A. Mazmanian, "Achieving Air Quality: The Los Angeles Experience" (unpublished paper,) University of Southern California, March 2006, p. 28.

16. "E.P.A. Says 17 States Can't Set Greenhouse Gas Rules for Cars," The *New York Times*, December 20, 2007, pp. A1, A30.

17. "California Water Users Miss Deadline for Pact Sharing," The *New York Times*, January 1, 2003. The six states in addition to California are Arizona, Colorado, Nevada, New Mexico, Utah, and Wyoming.

18. "Enforcing Recent Water Laws May Throttle State's Growth," *Los Angeles Times*, January 14, 2008, pp. B1, B8.

19. "California Members of Congress Demand That the Bay Delta Conservation Plan Be Fair and Equitable," YubaNet.com, http://yubanet.com/california/California-Members-of-Congress-Demand-that-the-Bay-Delta-Conservation-Plan-Be-Fair-and-Equitable_printer.php, (accessed May 17, 2012).

20. U.S. Census, Consolidated Federal Funds Report for Fiscal Year 2010, September 2011, http//www.census.gov/prod/2011pubs/effr-10pdf (accessed August 31, 2012).

21. "Federal Poverty Level Doesn't Meet Basic Needs, Data Shows," *California Watch*, October 11, 2011, http//californiawatch.org/print/12903 (accessed August 31, 2012).

22. "Stimulus Benefits and Unemployment," *USA Today*, August 4, 2010, p. 5A.

## LEARN MORE ON THE WEB

California and federal taxes:
  www.taxfoundation.org

Californi Institute for Federal Policy Research:
  www.calinst.org

Environmental Protection Agency:
  www.epa.gov

Immigration:
  www.irps.ucsd.edu

Office of Management and Budget:
  www.whitehouse.gov/omb

U.S. House of Representatives:
  www.house.gov

U.S. Senate:
  www.senate.gov

## LEARN MORE AT THE LIBRARY

Larry N. Gerston. *American Federalism: A Concise Introduction*. Armonk, N.Y.: M. E. Sharpe, 2007.

Laurence J. O'Toole. *American Intergovernmental Relations: Foundations, Perspectives, and Issues*. 4th ed. Washington, D.C.: CQ Press, 2007.

David Brian Robertson, *Federalism and the Making of America*. New York, Routledge, 2012.

G. Ross Stephens and Nelson Wikstrom. *American Intergovernmental Relations: A Fragmented Federal Polity*. New York: Oxford University Press, 2007.

## GET INVOLVED

Contact your congress member to volunteer or apply for an internship in his or her district office. To find your representative, go to: www.house.gov /representatives/find/.

# Glossary

**at-large elections** City council elections in which all candidates are elected by the community as a whole rather than by districts.

**attorney general** The elected top law enforcement officer and legal counsel; the second most powerful member of the executive branch.

**bank and corporation tax** A tax on the profits of lending institutions and businesses; the third most important source of state revenue.

**bicameral legislature** Organization of the state legislature into two houses: the forty-member senate (elected for four-year terms) and the eighty-member assembly (elected for two-year terms).

**Big Five** The governor, assembly speaker, assembly minority leader, senate president pro tem, and senate minority leader, who gather together informally to thrash out decisions on the annual budget and other major policy issues.

**Board of Equalization** The five-member state board that maintains uniform property tax assessments and oversees the collection of sales, gasoline, and liquor taxes; members are elected by district; part of the executive branch.

**board of supervisors** The five-member governing body of counties; elected by district to four-year terms.

**bonds** Subject to voter approval, state and local governments can borrow money by issuing bonds, which are repaid (with interest) from the general fund budget or from special taxes or fees.

**bureaucracy** State or local government workers employed through the civil service system rather than appointed by the governor or other elected officials.

**central committees** Political party organizations at county and state levels; weakly linked to one another.

**charges for services** Local government fees for services such as sewage treatment, trash collection, building permits, and the use of recreational facilities; a major source of income for cities and counties since the passage of Proposition 13 in 1978.

**charter** The equivalent of a constitution for a local government; includes government structures, election systems, powers of officeholders, conditions for employing local government workers, and often much more.

**charter city or county** A local government that drafts its own structures and organization through a document like a local constitution (also known as a "home-rule" charter), subject to voter approval.

**cities**  Local governments in urban areas, run by city councils and mayors or city managers; principal responsibilities include police and fire protection, land use planning, street maintenance and construction, sanitation, libraries, and parks.

**Citizens Redistricting Commission**  Enacted by the voters in Proposition 11 (2008), this commission is responsible for determining the boundaries of congressional and state legislative districts and Board of Equalization districts.

**city council**  The governing body of a city; members are elected at large or by district to four-year terms.

**city manager**  The top administrative officer in most California cities; appointed by the city council.

**civil service system**  A system for hiring and retaining public employees on the basis of their qualifications or merit; replaced the political machine's patronage, or spoils, system; encompasses 98 percent of state workers.

**closed primary**  An election of party nominees in which only registered party members may participate.

**collegiality**  Deferential behavior among justices as a way of building consensus on issues before the court.

**Commission on Judicial Appointments**  A commission to review and make recommendations on the governor's nominees for appellate and supreme courts; consists of the attorney general, the chief justice of the state supreme court, and the senior presiding judge of the courts of appeal.

**Commission on Judicial Performance**  The state board empowered to investigate charges of judicial misconduct or incompetence.

**conference committee**  A committee of senate and assembly members that meets to reconcile different versions of the same bill.

**congressional delegation**  Members of the House of Representatives and Senate representing a particular state.

**consolidation**  The merger of cities, school districts, or special districts; usually requires voter approval.

**Constitution of 1849**  California's first constitution, which was copied from constitutions of other states and featured a two-house legislature, a supreme court, and an executive branch including a governor, lieutenant governor, controller, attorney general, and superintendent of public instruction, as well as a bill of rights. Only white males were allowed to vote.

**Constitution of 1879**  California's second constitution, which retained the basic structures of the Constitution of 1849 but added institutions to regulate railroads and public utilities and to ensure fair tax assessments. Chinese individuals were denied the right to vote, own land, or work for the government.

**constitutional amendments**  May be placed on the ballot by a two-thirds vote of the legislature or through the initiative process; must be approved by a simple majority of the voters.

**constitutional convention**  An occasion for extensive revision or reform of the state constitution. A two-thirds vote of the state legislature is required to put a proposal for a convention on the ballot. If voters approve, delegates are elected by district.

**contract lobbyist**  An individual or company that represents the interests of clients before the legislature and other policymaking entities.

**contracting for services**  Smaller cities contract with counties, special districts, other cities, or private companies to provide services they cannot efficiently provide themselves.

**controller**  An independently elected state executive who oversees taxing and spending.

**council–manager system** A form of government in which an elected council appoints a professional manager to administer daily operations; used by most California cities.

**councils of government (COGs)** Regional planning organizations with representation for cities and counties.

**counties** Local governments and administrative agencies of the state, run by elected boards of supervisors; principal responsibilities include welfare, jails, courts, roads, and elections.

**county executive** The top administrative officer in most California counties; appointed by the board of supervisors.

**courts of appeal** Three-justice panels that hear appeals from lower courts.

**cross-filing** An election system that allowed candidates to win the nomination of more than one political party; eliminated in 1959.

**demographic groups** Interest groups based on race, ethnicity, gender, or age; usually concerned with overcoming discrimination.

**direct democracy** Progressive reforms giving citizens the power to make and repeal laws (initiative and referendum) and to remove elected officials from office (recall).

**direct mail** A campaign technique by which candidates communicate selected messages to selected voters by mail.

**director of finance** The state officer primarily responsible for preparation of the budget; appointed by the governor.

**district attorney** The chief prosecuting officer elected in each county; represents the people against the accused in criminal cases.

**district elections** Elections in which candidates are chosen by only one part of the city, county, or state.

**economic groups** Interest groups with sizable financial stakes in the political process who seek to influence legislators and other public policymakers.

**Environmental Protection Agency (EPA)** The federal government body charged with carrying out national environmental policy objectives.

**executive order** The power of the governor to make rules that have the effect of laws; may be overturned by the legislature.

**Fair Political Practices Commission (FPPC)** Established by the Political Reform Act of 1974, this independent regulatory commission monitors candidates' campaign finance reports and lobbyists.

**federalism** The distribution of power, resources, and responsibilities among the national, state, and local governments.

**fiscalization of land use** Cities and counties, when making land use decisions, opt for the alternative that produces the most revenue.

**general elections** Statewide elections held on the first Tuesday after the first Monday of November in even-numbered years. Voter turnout is higher than in primary elections and highest during presidential elections.

**general-law city or county** A city or county whose organization and structure of government are derived from state law.

**general veto** The gubernatorial power to reject an entire bill or budget; overruled only by an absolute two-thirds vote of both houses of the state legislature.

**ghost voting** When legislators cast electronic votes in place of assembly members who are not at their posts; this practice is against the law.

**governor** California's highest-ranking executive officeholder; elected every four years.

**grants-in-aid** Payments from the national government to states to assist in fulfilling public policy objectives.

**gut-and-amend** The process of removing the original provisions from a bill and inserting new, unrelated content, usually at the last minute.

**incorporation** The process by which residents of an urbanized area form a city.

**independent expenditures** Campaign spending by interest groups and political action committees on behalf of candidates.

**initiative** A Progressive device by which people may put laws and constitutional amendments on the ballot after securing the required number of voters' signatures.

**instant runoff voting** Voters rank candidates in order of preference. If no candidate wins a majority, the candidate with the fewest votes is eliminated, and those votes are assigned to the voters' second choice—and so on until one candidate attains a majority.

**insurance commissioner** An elected state executive who regulates the insurance industry; created by a 1988 initiative.

**interest group** An organized group of individuals sharing common political objectives who actively attempt to influence policymakers.

**item veto** The power of the governor to delete or reduce the budget within a bill without rejecting the entire bill or budget; an absolute two-thirds vote of both houses of the state legislature is required to override.

**judicial activism** Making policy through court decisions rather than through the legislative or electoral process.

**Judicial Council** Chaired by the chief justice of the state supreme court and composed of twenty-one judges and attorneys; makes the rules for court procedures, collects data on the courts' operations and workload, and gives seminars for judges.

**legislative analyst** An assistant to the legislature who studies the annual budget and proposed programs.

**legislative committees** Small groups of senators or assembly members who consider and make legislation in specialized areas such as agriculture or education.

**legislative counsel** Assists the legislature in preparing bills and assessing their impact on existing legislation.

**legislative initiatives** Propositions placed on the ballot by the legislature rather than by citizen petition.

**lieutenant governor** The chief executive when the governor is absent from the state or disabled; succeeds the governor in case of death or other departure from office; casts a tiebreaking vote in the senate; is independently elected.

**litigation** An interest group tactic of challenging a law or policy in the courts to have it overruled, modified, or delayed.

**lobbying** Interest group efforts to influence political decision makers, often through paid professionals (lobbyists).

**local agency formation commission (LAFCO)** A county agency set up to oversee the creation and expansion of cities.

**logrolling** A give-and-take process in which legislators trade support for each other's bills.

**mayor** The ceremonial leader of a city; usually a position that alternates among council members, but in some large cities the mayor is directly elected and given substantial powers.

**nonpartisan elections** A Progressive reform that removed party labels from ballots for local and judicial offices.

**personal income tax** A graduated tax on individual earnings adopted in 1935; the largest source of state revenues.

**plea bargaining** An agreement between the prosecution and the accused in which the latter pleads guilty to a reduced charge and lesser penalty.

**political action committees (PACs)** Mechanisms by which interest groups direct campaign contributions to preferred candidates.

**political consultants** Expert professionals in political campaigning available for hire; most consultants work exclusively for candidates of one of the major political parties.

**Political Reform Act of 1974** An initiative requiring officials to disclose conflicts of interest, campaign contributions, and spending; also requires lobbyists to register with the Fair Political Practices Commission.

**preprimary endorsement** Political parties' designation of preferred candidates in party primary elections, thus strengthening the role of party organizations in selecting candidates; banned by state law until 1990.

**president pro tem** The legislative leader of the state senate; chairs the Rules Committee; selected by the majority party.

**primary elections** Elections to choose nominees for public office; held in June of even-numbered years. Voter turnout is typically low.

**Progressives** Members of an anti-machine reform movement that reshaped the state's political institutions between 1907 and the 1920s.

**property tax** A tax on land and buildings; until the passage of Proposition 13 in 1978, the primary source of revenues for local governments.

**Proposition 1A** (2008) A $10 billion bond passed by the voters to begin construction of a high-speed rail system; officially called the Safe, Reliable High-Speed Passenger Train Bond Act for the 21st Century.

**Proposition 8** (2008) An initiative that amended the state constitution to restrict marriage to opposite-sex couples.

**Proposition 11, Voters FIRST Initiative** (2008) An initiative that placed legislative redistricting in the hands of a fourteen-member citizens commission instead of the state legislature.

**Proposition 13** (1978) Also known as the Jarvis-Gann initiative; a ballot measure that cut property taxes and significantly reduced revenues for local governments.

**Proposition 22, California Defense of Marriage Act** (2000) A ballot initiative that declared marriage an act between a man and a woman.

**Proposition 22, Local Taxpayers, Public Safety, and Transportation Act** (2010) An initiative that keeps the state government from taking local government funds.

**Proposition 25, Majority Vote for the Legislature to Pass the Budget Act** (2010) An initiative that lowered the votes required for the legislature to pass a budget from two-thirds to a simple majority.

**Proposition 28, California Change Term Limits Initiative** (2012) An initiative which allows state legislators to serve for no more than twelve years in either house of the legislature, with no restrictions on how they divide their time.

**Proposition 30** (2012) Governor Brown's initiative to increase sales taxes for five years and income taxes for affluent Californians for seven years.

**Proposition 36** (2012) An initiative that made it easier for nonviolent "three strikes" convicts to petition for reduced sentences.

**Proposition 98** (1988) An initiative awarding public education a fixed percentage of the state budget.

**Proposition 140** (1990) An initiative limiting assembly members to three 2-year terms and senators and statewide elected officials to two 4-year terms and cutting the legislature's budget.

**Proposition 187** (1994) An initiative reducing government benefits for illegal immigrants; parts of Proposition 187 were declared unconstitutional by federal courts in 1995.

**Proposition 209** (1996) An initiative that eliminated affirmative action in California.

**Proposition 227** (1998) An initiative limiting bilingual education to no more than one year.

**public defender** A county officer representing defendants who cannot afford an attorney; appointed by the county board of supervisors.

**public interest groups** Organizations that purport to represent the general good rather than private interests.

**realignment** The transfer of some state-provided services to counties, most recently observed with the movement of state prisoners to county jails.

**reapportionment** The adjustment of legislative district boundaries to keep all districts equal in population; done every ten years after the national census; done by a citizens commission beginning in 2011.

**recall** A Progressive reform allowing voters to remove elected officials by petition and majority vote.

**redistricting** Another term for reapportionment, the adjustment of legislative districts by population every ten years.

**referendum** A Progressive reform requiring the legislature to place certain measures before the voters, who may also repeal legislation by petitioning for a referendum.

**register to vote** Citizens who are over eighteen years of age and who are not incarcerated or in a mental institution are eligible to sign up to vote by completion of a registration form. Nearly 30 percent of those eligible to register in California do not do so and thus cannot participate in elections.

*Reynolds v. Sims* A 1964 U.S. Supreme Court decision that ordered redistricting of the upper houses of all state legislatures by population instead of land area.

**Rules Committee** *See Senate Rules Committee.*

**runoff election** When no candidate receives more than 50 percent of the vote in a nonpartisan primary for trial court judge or local office, the top two candidates face each other in a runoff.

**sales tax** A statewide tax on most goods and products; adopted in 1933; local governments receive a portion of this tax.

**school districts** Local governments created by states to provide elementary and secondary education; governed by elected school boards.

**secretary of state** An elected state executive who keeps election records and supervises elections.

**Senate Rules Committee** A five-member committee consisting of the senate president pro tem and two other members from each party in the senate; assigns chairs and committee appointments; functions as the gatekeeper of most senate legislation.

**Silicon Valley** The top area for high-tech industries; located between San Jose and San Francisco.

**single-issue groups** Organized groups with narrow policy objectives; not oriented toward compromise.

**Southern Pacific Railroad** A railroad company founded in 1861; developed a political machine that dominated California state politics through the turn of the century.

**Speaker of the assembly** The legislative leader of the assembly; selected by the majority party; controls committee appointments and the legislative process.

**special districts** Local government agencies providing a single service, such as fire protection or sewage disposal.

**special session** A legislative session called by the governor; limited to discussion of topics specified by the governor.

**state auditor** An assistant to the legislature who analyzes ongoing programs.

**superintendent of public instruction** The elected state executive in charge of public education.

**superior courts** Lower courts in which criminal and civil cases are first tried.

**supreme court** California's highest judicial body; hears appeals from lower courts.

**term limits** Limits on the number of terms that officeholders may serve; elected executive branch officers and state senators are limited to two 4-year terms, and assembly members are limited to three 2-year terms. Some local elected officials are limited to two or three 4-year terms.

**termed out** An elected official must leave office when he or she has completed all the terms of office allowed under California's term limits law.

**third parties** Minor political parties that capture a small percentages of the vote in the general election but are viewed as important protest vehicles.

**"three strikes"** A 1994 law and initiative requiring sentences of twenty-five years to life for anyone convicted of three felonies.

**top-two primary** Voters in primary elections may cast their ballots for any listed candidate for an office irrespective of the voters' party affiliation; the top two vote winners proceed to a runoff in the general election; instituted by a 2010 ballot measure; first in effect in 2012.

**treasurer** The elected state executive responsible for managing state funds between collection and spending.

**user taxes** Taxes on select commodities or services "used" by those who benefit directly from them; examples include gasoline taxes and cigarette taxes.

**veto** See *general veto* and *item veto*.

**vote by mail** Voters who prefer not to vote at their polling places or who are unable to vote on Election Day may apply to their county registrar of voters for an absentee ballot and vote by mail or register as permanent absentee voters; over half of those who vote in California elections vote by mail.

**voter turnout** The proportion of eligible and/or registered voters who actually participate in an election. When turnout is high, the electorate is usually more diverse and liberal; when it is low, the electorate is usually older, more affluent, and more conservative.

**Workingmen's Party** Denis Kearney's antirailroad, anti-Chinese organization; instrumental in rewriting California's constitution in 1879.

# Index